Edexcel A-Level

Pure Mathematics

Year 1 & AS-Level

This CGP Student Book is the definitive guide to every Pure topic from Edexcel AS Mathematics and Year 1 of the A-Level course.

It contains clear study notes, advice, examples, hundreds of practice questions and a realistic practice exam — with fully worked answers at the back.

How to access your free Online Edition

Go to **cgpbooks.co.uk/extras** and enter this code:

0074 2272 8210 2524

This code will only work once. If someone has used this book before you, they may have already claimed the Online Edition.

Contents

About this Book iv

1 Modelling and Problem Solving

1.1 Using Mathematical Models 2

1.2 The Problem Solving Cycle 4

2 Proof

2.1 Notation 7

2.2 Proof 8

Review Exercise 10

3 Algebra

3.1 Expanding Brackets 16

3.2 Factorising 19

3.3 Algebraic Fractions 21

3.4 Laws of Indices 25

3.5 The Laws of Surds 28

3.6 Rationalising the Denominator 30

Review Exercise 32

4 Quadratics and Cubics

4.1 Factorising a Quadratic 39

4.2 The Quadratic Formula 43

4.3 Completing the Square 46

4.4 Quadratics Involving Functions of x 49

4.5 The Roots of a Quadratic Function 51

4.6 Using the Discriminant 54

4.7 Sketching Quadratic Graphs 58

4.8 Factorising a Cubic (When x is a Factor) 65

4.9 The Factor Theorem 67

4.10 Factorising a Cubic (When x isn't a Factor) 70

4.11 Algebraic Division 73

Review Exercise 75

5 Inequalities and Simultaneous Equations

5.1 Linear Inequalities 83

5.2 Quadratic Inequalities 86

5.3 Graphing Inequalities 91

5.4 Simultaneous Equations — Both Linear 95

5.5 Simultaneous Equations — if One is not Linear 98

Review Exercise 102

6 Coordinate Geometry, Graphs and Circles

6.1 Equations of the Form $y - y_1 = m(x - x_1)$ 108

6.2 Equations of the Form $y = mx + c$ 108

6.3 Equations of the Form $ax + by + c = 0$ 111

6.4 Parallel Lines 114

6.5 Perpendicular Lines 116

6.6 Direct Proportion 120

6.7 Sketching Cubic and Quartic Graphs 123

6.8 Graphs of Reciprocal Functions and Negative Powers 127

6.9 Translations 129

6.10 Stretches and Reflections 132

6.11 The Equation of a Circle 137

6.12 Rearranging Circle Equations 141

6.13 Using Circle Properties 144

Review Exercise 150

7 The Binomial Expansion

7.1 Binomial Expansions — $(1 + x)^n$ 158

7.2 Binomial Expansions — $(1 + ax)^n$ 163

7.3 Binomial Expansions — $(a + b)^n$ 166

Review Exercise 169

Contents

8 Trigonometry

8.1	Trig Values from Triangles	175
8.2	Trig Values from the Unit Circle	176
8.3	The Sine Rule	177
8.4	The Cosine Rule	180
8.5	More Trig Rules	183
8.6	Trig Identities	186
8.7	Graphs of Trig Functions	189
8.8	Solving Trig Equations by Sketching a Graph	195
8.9	Solving Trig Equations Using a CAST Diagram	198
8.10	Solving Trig Equations by Changing the Interval	201
8.11	Using Trig Identities to Solve Equations	205
	Review Exercise	208

9 Exponentials and Logarithms

9.1	Exponentials	216
9.2	Logarithms	220
9.3	Laws of Logs	224
9.4	Changing the Base of a Log	226
9.5	Solving Equations with Exponentials and Logs	228
9.6	Modelling Exponential Growth and Decay	232
9.7	Logarithmic Graphs in Linear Form	237
	Review Exercise	241

10 Differentiation

10.1	Finding the Gradient of a Curve	248
10.2	Differentiating from First Principles	249
10.3	Differentiating x^n	252
10.4	Differentiating Functions	254
10.5	Finding Tangents and Normals	257
10.6	Finding Second Order Derivatives	261
10.7	Stationary Points	262
10.8	Maximum and Minimum Points	265
10.9	Increasing and Decreasing Functions	268
10.10	Curve Sketching	270
10.11	Speed and Acceleration Problems	274
10.12	Length, Area and Volume Problems	276
	Review Exercise	281

11 Integration

11.1	Integration	289
11.2	Integrating x^n	290
11.3	Integrating Functions	292
11.4	Integrating to Find Equations of Curves	294
11.5	Evaluating Definite Integrals	297
	Review Exercise	303

12 Vectors

12.1	Introducing Vectors	310
12.2	Position Vectors	316
12.3	Calculating with Vectors	320
12.4	Modelling with Vectors	325
	Review Exercise	330

Practice Paper	335
Answers	341
Glossary	508
Index	512
Formula Sheet	514

About this Book

This book has been produced to be a complete resource for your learning and practice. Throughout, we've focused on three core concepts of A-level maths — mathematical methods, problem solving and modelling.

Each chapter starts with a page that includes Learning Objectives and a Prior Knowledge Check.

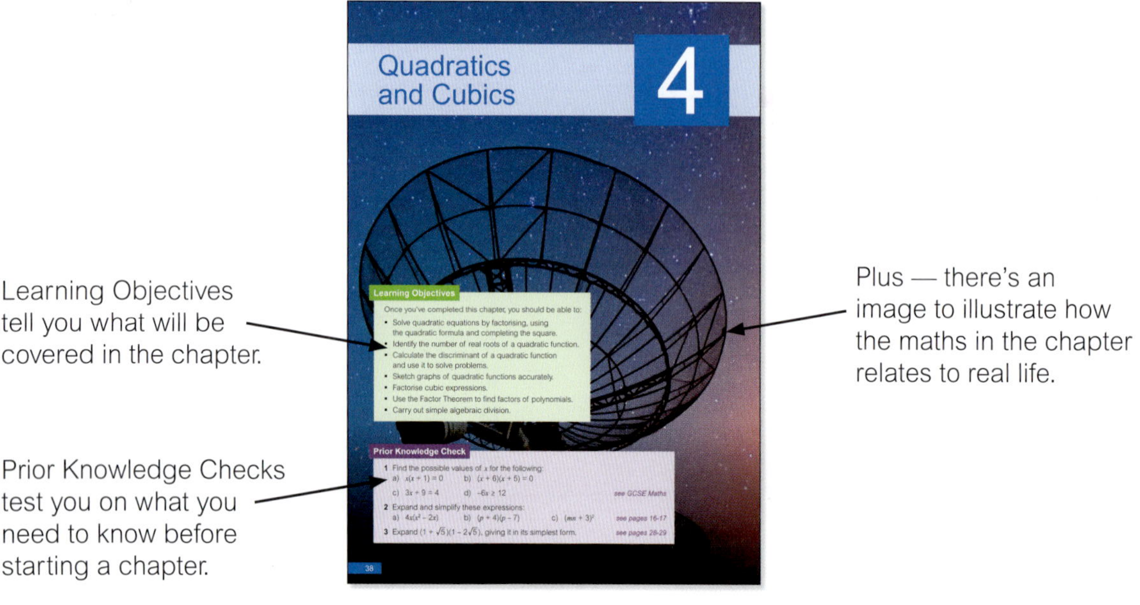

Learning Objectives tell you what will be covered in the chapter.

Prior Knowledge Checks test you on what you need to know before starting a chapter.

Plus — there's an image to illustrate how the maths in the chapter relates to real life.

The main pages have theory, examples and exercises.

Exercises provide lots of practice for every topic, with fully worked answers at the back of the book. Answers to exam-style questions come with a full mark scheme.

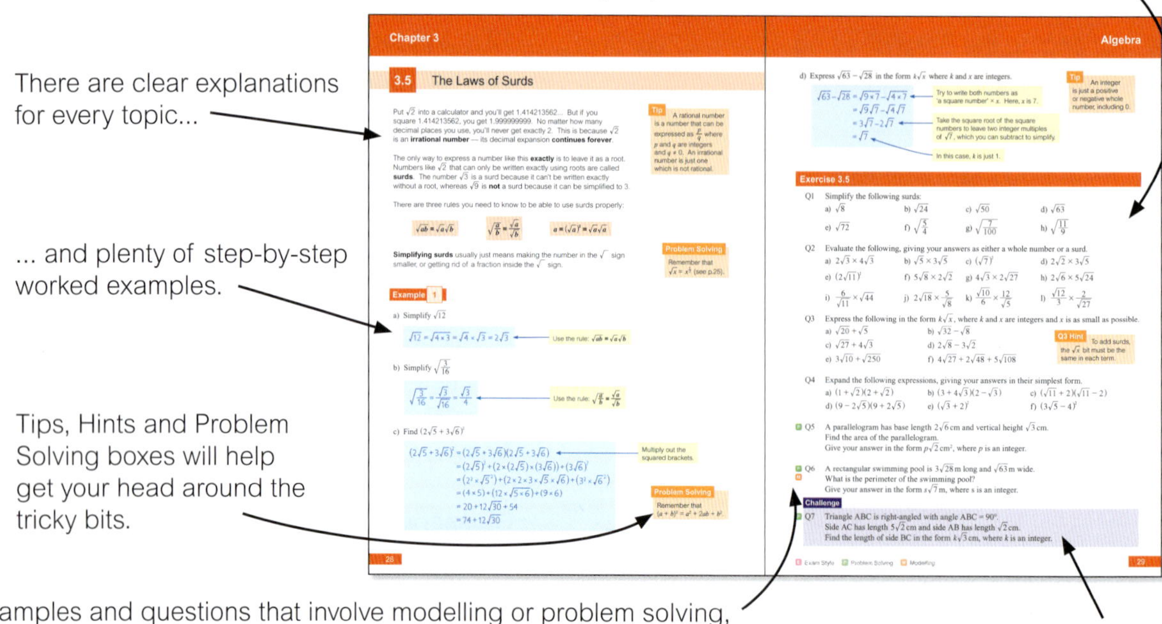

There are clear explanations for every topic...

... and plenty of step-by-step worked examples.

Tips, Hints and Problem Solving boxes will help get your head around the tricky bits.

Examples and questions that involve modelling or problem solving, and questions that are exam style are indicated with stamps:

E Exam Style P Problem Solving M Modelling

The solutions to Problem Solving questions may require knowledge and methods from more than one Chapter of this book.

Challenge Questions at the end of exercises will test your mastery of a topic.

There's a Review Exercise at the end of each chapter and a Practice Paper after the last chapter.

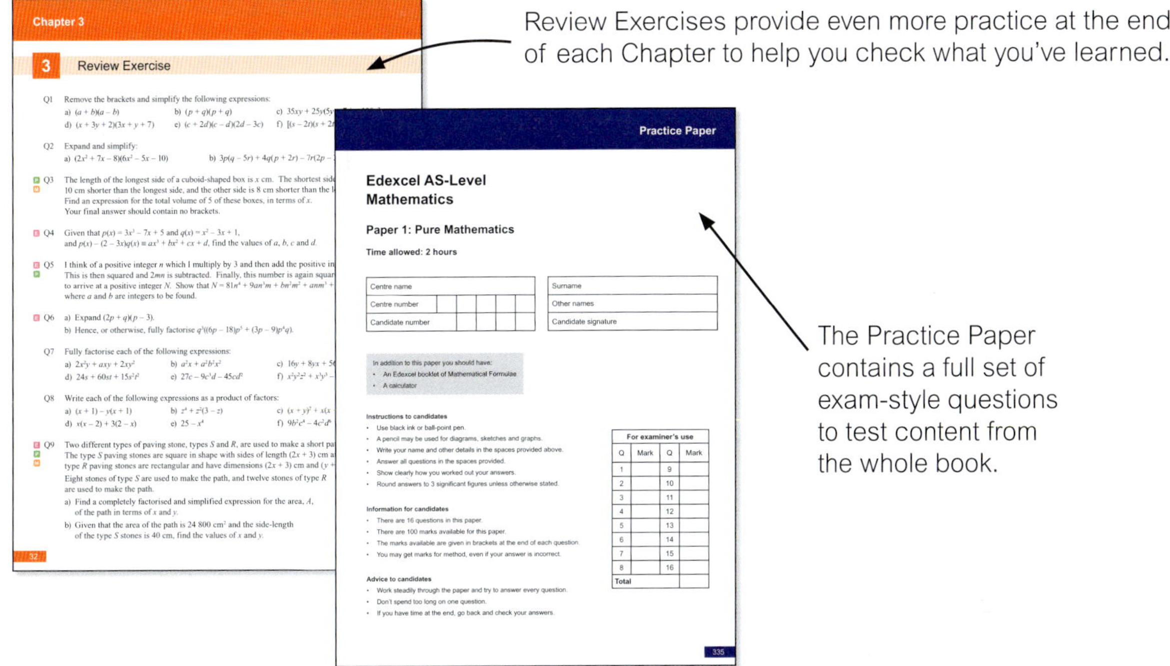

Review Exercises provide even more practice at the end of each Chapter to help you check what you've learned.

The Practice Paper contains a full set of exam-style questions to test content from the whole book.

You can find the Glossary and Formula Sheet at the back of the book.

The Formula Sheet has the relevant formulas you'll get in the exam.

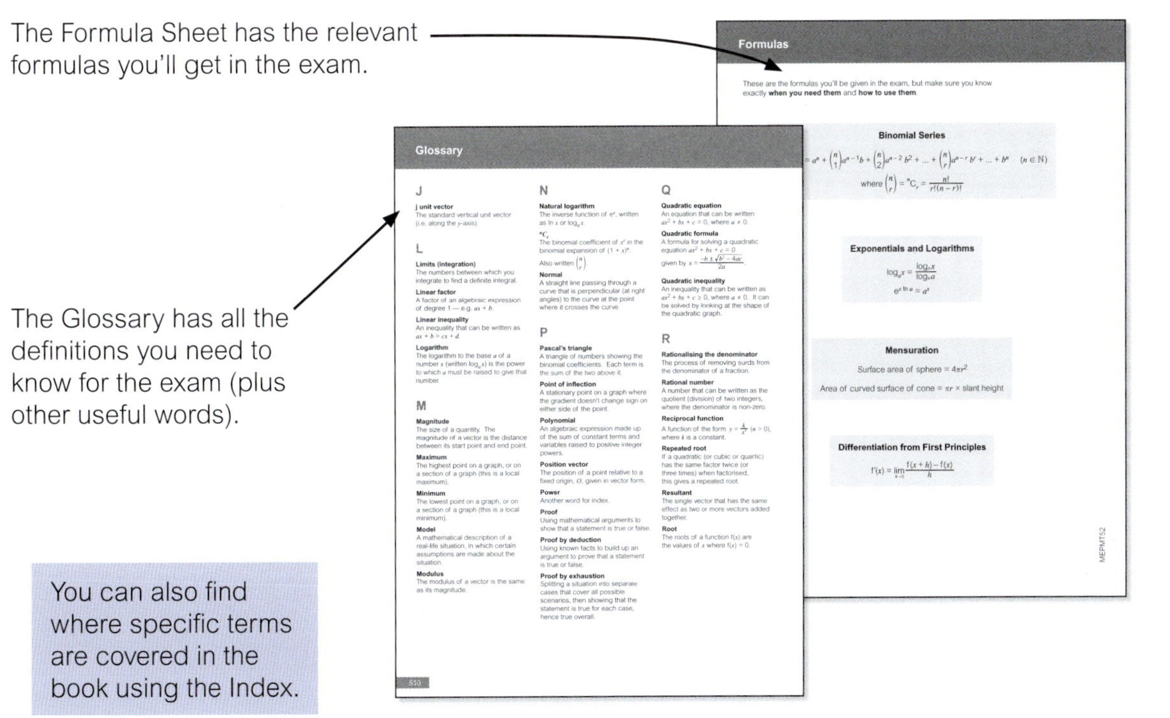

The Glossary has all the definitions you need to know for the exam (plus other useful words).

You can also find where specific terms are covered in the book using the Index.

Published by Coordination Group Publications Ltd
Broughton House, Griffin Street, Broughton-in-Furness, Cumbria, UK, LA20 6HH

www.cgpbooks.co.uk

Design coordination and cover design by Beckie Doyle and Kirsty Goodall.

Editors:
Martha Bozic, Michael Bushell, Liam Dyer, Sammy El-Bahrawy, Sarah George, Ruth Greenhalgh, Shaun Harrogate, Simon Little, Samuel Mann, Sean McParland, Tom Miles, Ali Palin, Rosa Roberts, David Ryan, Ben Train, Michael Weynberg.

Contributors:
Katharine Brown, John Fletcher, Aleksander Goodier, Alan Mason, Rosemary Rogers, Simon Thornhill, Janet West.

Proofreading:
Mona Allen, Rosie Hanson, Lauren McNaughten and Glenn Rogers.

Photo credits:
Cover image © Unicus/Shutterstock.com used under license from Shutterstock.com

Page 1 © R_TYPE/iStock/Getty Images; Page 6 © StudioM1/iStock/Getty Images; Page 15 © James O'Neil/The Image Bank/Getty Images; Page 38 © snvv/iStock/Getty Images; Page 82 © tomluddington/iStock/Getty Images; Page 107 © everste/iStock/Getty Images; Page 157 © Edgar Olvera/iStock/Getty Images; Page 174 © Digital Vision./Photodisc/Getty Images; Page 215 © MR.Cole_Photographer/Moment/Getty Images; Page 247 © smaehl/iStock/Getty Images; Page 288 © correctomundo/iStock/Getty Images; Page 309 © antoniokhr/istock/Getty Images

Clipart from Corel®

With thanks to Lottie Edwards for the copyright research.

Printed by Elanders Ltd, Newcastle upon Tyne.

ISBN: 978 1 78908 839 7

Modelling and Problem Solving

1

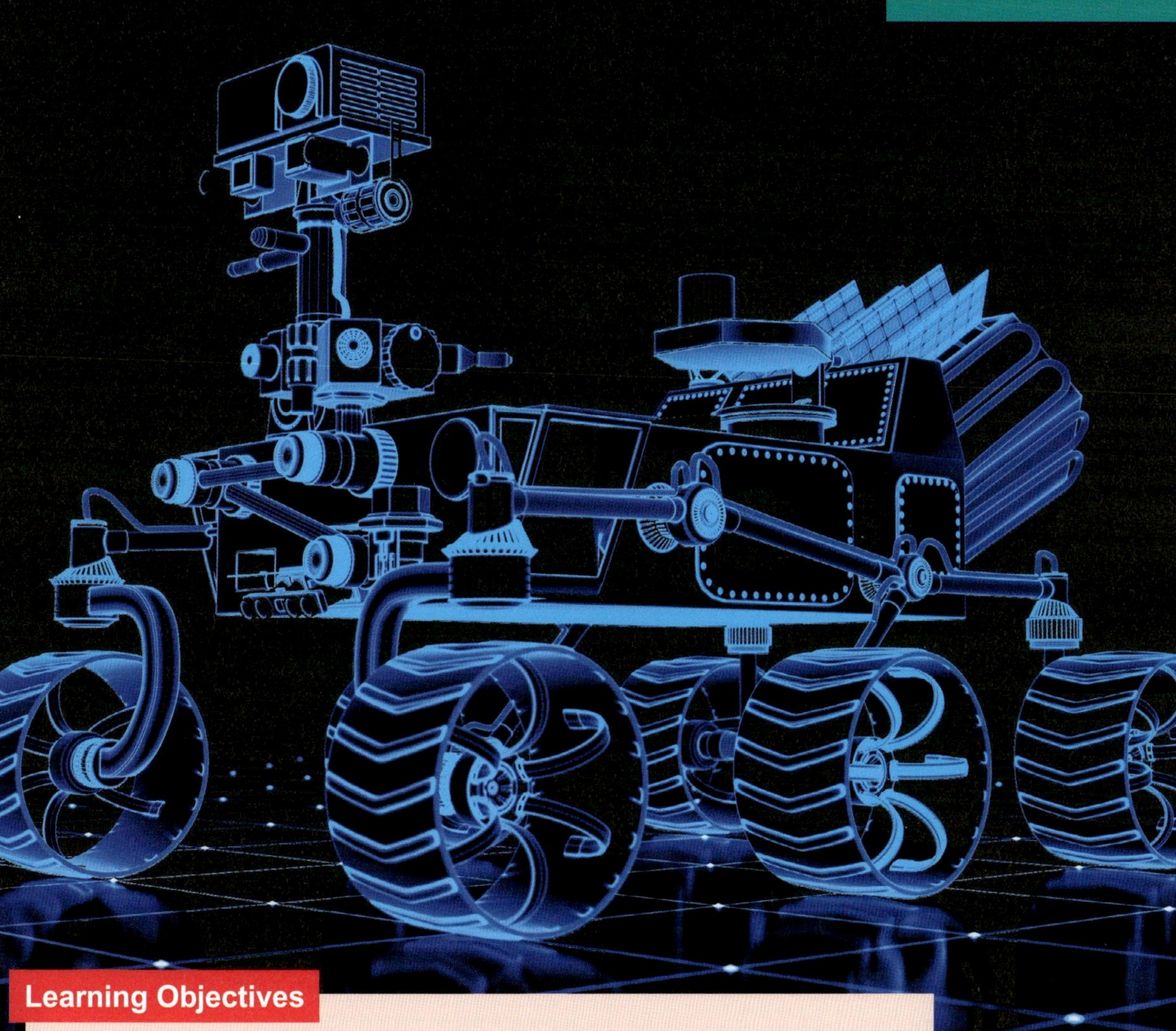

Learning Objectives

Once you've completed this chapter, you should be able to:

- Understand the mathematical modelling process.
- Describe some examples of mathematical modelling.
- Understand the process of refining a mathematical model.
- Understand the problem solving cycle.
- Apply problem solving skills to maths questions.

1.1 Using Mathematical Models

Modelling in maths generally boils down to using an **equation** or a set of equations to **predict** what will happen in real life. You'll meet mathematical models in all areas of this course. For example:

- In algebra, formulas involving exponentials are used to model things like population growth (see pages 232-234).
- In mechanics, equations are used to model how the speed and acceleration of a moving object changes over time.
- In statistics, probability distributions are models which are used to predict the probability of a particular outcome in a trial.

Example 1

A company predicts that its latest product will sell 500 units in its first month on sale, and that sales will gradually increase by an average of 250 units per month.

Write an equation to model the predicted sales, s, of the product during its mth month on sale.

s is the mth term of an arithmetic sequence with first term $a = 500$ and common difference $d = 250$.

So $s = a + (m - 1)d = 500 + 250(m - 1)$
$= 250 + 250m$
$= 250(m + 1)$

The scenario in Example 1 is a model because it's based on a prediction of how the sales will go. The actual sales might end up being much higher or lower if the company has got its predictions wrong.

Modelling assumptions

Models are always **simplifications** of the real-life situation. When you construct a model, you have to make **assumptions** — you **ignore** or **simplify** some factors that affect the real-life outcome to keep the maths simpler. There are many reasons for making assumptions — a factor might only have a small effect or be hard to predict, or you might not have enough data to model it accurately. For example:

- A population growth model might ignore the fact that the population will eventually run out of **food**, because that won't happen in the **time period** you're modelling.
- A model for the speed of a moving object might ignore some of the forces acting upon it (e.g. **air resistance**), because including them would make the maths **more complicated**, or because you might want a **general result** for objects of all shapes and sizes.

Example 2

Leon owns a gooseberry farm. This week, he had 5 workers picking fruit, and they picked a total of 1000 punnets of gooseberries. Leon wants to hire more workers for next week. He predicts that next week, if the number of workers on his farm is w, the farm will produce p punnets of gooseberries, where $p = 200w$. Suggest three assumptions Leon has made in his model.

Leon's model predicts that the mean number of punnets produced per worker next week will be the same as this week. That means he's assumed all the conditions next week will be the same as the conditions this week. For example:

- Leon has assumed all the new workers he employs next week will work at the same speed on average as the ones he employed this week.
- He has assumed that the weather next week will be good enough to allow each worker to work as many hours as this week.
- He has assumed that there will be enough gooseberries to fill 200 punnets per worker, however many workers he employs.

Tip Don't forget to link your answers back to the original context of the question.

Refining models

An important part of the modelling process is **refining** a model. This usually happens after the model has been **tested** by comparing it with real-world outcomes, or if you find out some **extra information** that affects the model.

Refining a model usually means changing some of the **assumptions**. For example:

- You might adjust a population growth model if you found that **larger populations** were more susceptible to **disease**, so grew more slowly.
- You might decide to refine a model for the speed of an object to take into account the **friction** from the surface the object is travelling over.

Tip You could be asked to criticise or evaluate a model — e.g. you might need to assess if any assumptions are unrealistic. There's more on this on page 234.

Example 3

Leon discovers that the weather forecast for next week is bad, and his workers are only likely to be able to pick gooseberries for half the number of hours they did this week. How should he refine his model?

Leon's original model was $p = 200w$, based on all the workers next week picking at the same average weekly rate as this week. If his workers can only pick for half the time, they can only pick half as many gooseberries. So the refined model would be $p = 200w \div 2 \Rightarrow p = 100w$

The model is refined because there's new information. He might also refine his model at the end of next week, e.g. if he found that his new workers were a lot slower or faster than his current ones.

Modelling is one of the **overarching themes** of the AS and A-Level Maths courses. It could come up within any other topic — you might be given a model to use, or be asked to create one yourself.

1.2 The Problem Solving Cycle

Like modelling, problem solving is an overarching theme that will come up throughout the course. Whenever maths is used to solve a real-life problem, the process used can be described using a **problem solving cycle**. The basic cycle looks like this:

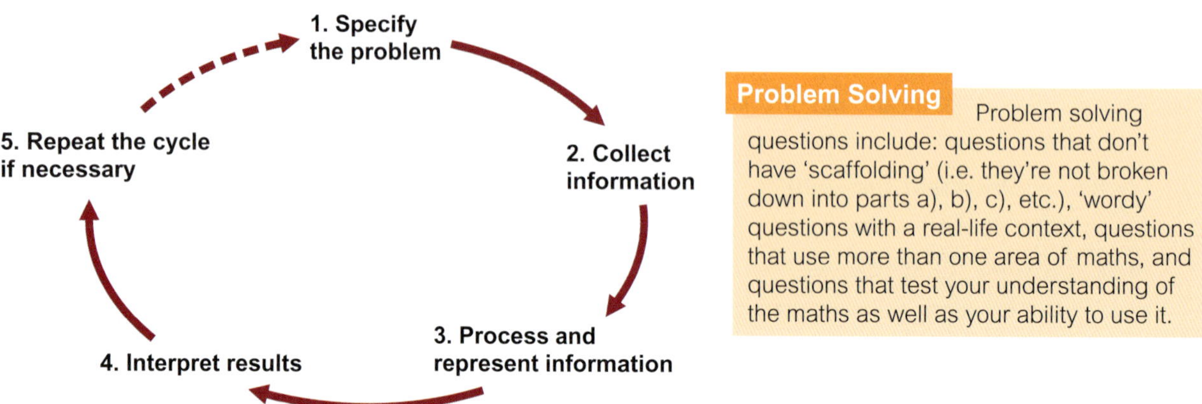

Problem Solving Problem solving questions include: questions that don't have 'scaffolding' (i.e. they're not broken down into parts a), b), c), etc.), 'wordy' questions with a real-life context, questions that use more than one area of maths, and questions that test your understanding of the maths as well as your ability to use it.

These steps apply to pretty much anything you can use maths for.

1) **Specify the problem**
   The **problem** is the actual question you want to answer. It could be anything from "What's the probability I roll a 6 on this dice?" to "How long will it take this ball to fall 10 m?" to "What's the angle of elevation from here to the top of that lighthouse?"
2) **Collect information**
   You'll need some **numbers** to solve the problem. This step might involve taking measurements, carrying out surveys or looking up data.
3) **Process and represent information**
   Once you've got the information you need, you can do the **calculations**. Representing the information might involve drawing a **graph** or **diagram**.
4) **Interpret results**
   Once you've done the calculation, you might need to **interpret** it to work out what the numerical answer means in terms of the original question.
5) **Repeat the cycle if necessary**
   You might decide to **repeat** the process. E.g. if you collected your information via a survey, you might want to repeat it with a larger or more representative sample. If your calculations involved modelling, you might want to **refine** your model (see previous page).

Problem solving in maths questions

You can apply a version of the problem solving cycle to any maths question where it's not immediately obvious what you're supposed to do.

1) Specify the problem
The first thing to do is work out what the question is actually asking. The question might be phrased in an unusual way to try to throw you, or it might be written in a 'wordy' context, where you need to turn the words into maths.

2) Collect information
Write down what you know. All the information you need to answer the question will either be given in the question somewhere, or it'll require facts that you should already know.

3) Process and represent information
When you know what you're trying to find out, and what you already know, you can do the calculation to answer the question.

4) Interpret results
Don't forget to give your answer in terms of the original context. The result of your calculation won't necessarily be the final answer.

Tip When you're doing a maths question, it's unlikely you'll need to repeat the problem solving cycle once you've found the answer — just be aware that it's part of the real-world problem solving process.

Example 1 

Armand cuts out a semicircle of cardboard from a rectangular sheet of cardboard measuring 20 cm by 40 cm and throws the rest away. The cardboard he throws away has an area of 398.08 cm². How long is the straight side of the semicircle? (Use $\pi = 3.14$.)

The length of the straight side of a semicircle is the diameter of the full circle, which is twice the radius. So that's what we're looking for here. ← **Specify the problem.** What are you trying to find?

The total area of the sheet of cardboard is 20 cm × 40 cm. 398.08 cm² was thrown away and the rest is the area of the semicircle. ← **Collect information.** What do you know?

Area of a semicircle $= \frac{1}{2} \times$ area of a circle $= \frac{1}{2}\pi r^2$ ← **Process and represent information.** Do the maths.

Area of semicircle $= 20 \times 40 - 398.08$
$= 800 - 398.08 = 401.92$ cm²

So $401.92 = \frac{1}{2}\pi r^2 = \frac{1}{2} \times 3.14 \times r^2 = 1.57 \times r^2$
$\Rightarrow r^2 = 401.92 \div 1.57 = 256$
$\Rightarrow r = \sqrt{256} = 16$ cm
$\Rightarrow d = 2r = 2 \times 16 = 32$ cm

The length of the straight side of the semicircle is 32 cm. ← **Interpret results.** Give the answer in the context of the question.

Problem Solving You wouldn't normally do so much writing for a problem solving question — it's written out like this here as an example of how the problem solving thought process might work.

Proof

2

Learning Objectives

Once you've completed this chapter, you should be able to:

- Be comfortable with mathematical notation for sets, functions, logical arguments and equivalence.
- Show that sums and products of integers are odd or even.
- Use proof by exhaustion and proof by deduction to show that statements are true.
- Use disproof by counter-example to show that statements are false.

Prior Knowledge Check

1. Write an expression for the product of two consecutive square numbers. *see GCSE Maths*
2. The lengths of a triangle's three sides are consecutive even integers. Write an expression for the perimeter of the triangle. *see GCSE Maths*
3. Given that $x > y$, are there integer values of x and y where $x^2 < y^2$? *see GCSE Maths*

2.1 Notation

Set notation

In maths, a '**set**' is just a **collection** of objects or numbers (called **elements**) — a set is often represented by a capital letter. To show something is a set you put **curly brackets** around it, e.g. A = {0, 1, 2}. You can write out the **complete list** of elements: {1, 3, 5, 7, 9, 11, 13, 15, 17, 19}. Or you can write out the **rule** that connects the elements: {odd numbers between 0 and 20}. The rule can also be written out using numbers and symbols: $\{x: x < 0\}$. In words, this means "the set of values of x such that x is less than 0".

A set containing **no elements** is called the **empty set**, written as: $\varnothing = \{\}$.

If you have more than one set you can talk about their **union** and **intersection**:

The **union** of two sets A and B is the combination of both sets — so it contains **all the elements** of **both sets**. It is written $A \cup B$.

The **intersection** of two sets A and B is a smaller set that contains only the elements present in **both** sets. It is written $A \cap B$.

Tip Have a look at p.83-84 to see how set notation is used to show solutions to inequalities.

So if A = {1, 3, 5, 7, 9} and B = {1, 4, 9, 16}, then $A \cup B$ = {1, 3, 4, 5, 7, 9, 16} and $A \cap B$ = {1, 9}.

Function notation

A **function** of x, written **f(x)**, takes a value of x, does something to it, and then outputs another value — it's just like an **equation** of x, but y is replaced with **f(x)**. E.g. the function $f(x) = x^2 + 1$ takes a value of x, squares it and then adds 1. So if $x = 4$, $f(4) = (4)^2 + 1 = 17$. You'll see function notation used a lot in the chapters on quadratics (Chapter 4) and differentiation (Chapter 10).

Logical notation

The symbols $\Rightarrow$ and $\Leftrightarrow$ crop up all over the place. These are logic symbols — they show when one thing **implies** another.

'$p \Rightarrow q$' means 'p implies q'. You can read it as '**if** p, **then** q' — so **if** p is true, **then** q must also be true — e.g. $x = 2 \Rightarrow x^2 = 4$.

'$p \Leftrightarrow q$' means 'p implies q and q implies p'. This means that p is true **if and only if** (or **iff**) q is true — e.g. $x^2 = 4 \Leftrightarrow x = \pm 2$.

Tip You might also see an arrow like this $\Leftarrow$. It works in the same way as the other implication arrow — it just goes the opposite way. E.g. $p \Leftarrow q$ means 'q implies p'.

Equivalence notation

There are three variations on the equals sign that you also need to know.

$\neq$ means **not equal to** — e.g. $\sin 90° \neq \cos 90°$

$\approx$ means **approximately equal to** — e.g. $1 \div 3 \approx 0.33$.

$\equiv$ is the **identity symbol**. It means that two things are **identically equal** to each other. So $(a + b)(a - b) \equiv a^2 - b^2$ is true for **all values** of a and b (unlike an equation like $a^2 = 9$, which is only true for certain values of a).

Tip Identities crop up again in trigonometry — see Chapter 8.

2.2 Proof

Simple proofs — odd and even numbers

Before you get on to the trickier proofs, there are some nice simple proofs about **odd** and **even** numbers that are really useful. But first you need to know these 'proper' definitions for them:

Any **even** number can be written as $2a$, where a is an integer.

Any **odd** number can be written as $2b + 1$, where b is an integer.

Tip Integers are just whole numbers — they can be positive, negative or 0.

Example 1

a) Prove that the sum of two even numbers is even.

Take 2 even numbers, $2l$ and $2m$, where l and m are integers.

$2l + 2m = 2(l + m) = \text{even}$

It can be written as $2 \times$ an integer, so it's divisible by two, i.e. it's an even number.

b) Prove that the sum of an odd number and an even number is odd.

Take one odd number, $2j + 1$, and one even number, $2l$, where j and l are integers.

$(2j + 1) + (2l) = 2j + 2l + 1 = 2(j + l) + 1 = \text{odd}$

c) Prove that the product of two odd numbers is odd.

Take two odd numbers, $2j + 1$ and $2k + 1$, where j and k are integers.

$(2j + 1)(2k + 1) = 4jk + 2j + 2k + 1 = 2(2jk + j + k) + 1 = \text{odd}$

Problem Solving You can prove that e.g. the product of two even numbers is even in a similar way.

Proof by deduction

A **proof by deduction** is when you use **known facts** to build up your argument and show a statement **must** be true.

Example 2 

A definition of a rational number is 'a number that can be written as a quotient of two integers, where the denominator is non-zero'. Use this definition to prove that the following statement is true:
"The product of two rational numbers is always a rational number."

Problem Solving A quotient is what you get when you divide one number by another.

Let $a = \frac{p}{q}$ and $b = \frac{r}{s}$, for integers p, q, r and s and $q, s \neq 0$.

Define two rational numbers and write them as fractions.

Then the product $ab = \frac{p}{q} \times \frac{r}{s} = \frac{pr}{qs}$.

Multiply them together to find their product.

pr and qs are the products of integers, so they must also be integers, and because q and s are non-zero, qs must also be non-zero.

So ab is a quotient of two integers and has a non-zero denominator, so by definition, ab is rational. Hence the original statement is true.

Now explain why the result is also a rational number.

Proof by exhaustion

In **proof by exhaustion** you break things down into two or more **cases**. You have to make sure that your cases cover **all possible situations**, then prove separately that the statement is true for **each case**.

Example 3 

Prove the following statement: *"For any integer x, the value of* $f(x) = x^3 + x + 1$ *is an odd integer."*

First, let $x = 2n$, where n is an integer, so that x is even:
$f(2n) = (2n)^3 + 2n + 1 = 8n^3 + 2n + 1 = 2(4n^3 + n) + 1$

n is an integer $\Rightarrow$ $(4n^3 + n)$ is an integer
$\Rightarrow$ $2(4n^3 + n)$ is an even integer
$\Rightarrow$ $2(4n^3 + n) + 1$ is an odd integer

So $f(x)$ is odd when x is even.

To prove the statement, split the situation into **two cases** that cover all possible situations: x is **even** and x is **odd**. Start with even x and substitute it into $f(x)$.

$f(x)$ has the form $2k + 1$ where k is an integer, so $f(x)$ is an odd integer when x is even.

Now let $x = 2m + 1$, where m is an integer, so that x is odd:

$$
\begin{aligned}
f(2m + 1) &= (2m + 1)^3 + 2m + 1 + 1 \\
&= (8m^3 + 12m^2 + 6m + 1) + 2m + 1 + 1 \\
&= 8m^3 + 12m^2 + 8m + 3 \\
&= 2(4m^3 + 6m^2 + 4m + 1) + 1
\end{aligned}
$$

Now assume that x **is odd** and substitute it into $f(x)$.

m is an integer $\Rightarrow$ $(4m^3 + 6m^2 + 4m + 1)$ is an integer
$\Rightarrow 2(4m^3 + 6m^2 + 4m + 1)$ is an even integer
$\Rightarrow 2(4m^3 + 6m^2 + 4m + 1) + 1$ is an odd integer

So $f(x)$ is odd when x is odd.

$f(x)$ has the form $2j + 1$ where j is an integer, so $f(x)$ is also an odd integer when x is odd.

$f(x)$ is odd both when x is even and when x is odd, so $f(x)$ is odd for all integer values of x.

As any integer x must be either odd or even, you have shown that $f(x)$ is odd for any integer x, so the statement is true.

Disproof by counter-example

Disproof by **counter-example** is the easiest way to show a mathematical statement is **false**. All you have to do is find **one case** where the statement doesn't hold.

Example 4

Disprove the following statement: *"For any pair of integers x and y, if* $x > y$*, then* $x^2 + x > y^2 + y$.*"*

Let $x = 2$ and $y = -4$.
Then $2 > -4 \Rightarrow x > y$
But $x^2 + x = 2^2 + 2 = 6$ and $y^2 + y = (-4)^2 + (-4) = 12$,
so $x^2 + x < y^2 + y$

So when $x = 2$ and $y = -4$, the first part of the statement holds, but the second part doesn't.
So the statement is not true.

To disprove the statement, it's enough to find just one example of x and y where $x > y$, but $x^2 + x \le y^2 + y$.

You might have to try a few different numbers before you come up with an example that doesn't work.

2 Review Exercise

Q1 a) Prove that the sum of two odd numbers is even.

b) Prove that the product of two even numbers is even.

c) Prove that the product of an odd number and an even number is even.

Q2 Prove that when an odd number is subtracted from an even number, the result is always odd.

E Q3 Prove the following statement:
"For any integer value of x, $f(x) = 2x^2 + 2x + 3$ is odd." *[2 marks]*

E P Q4 Prove that the sum of the squares of two consecutive odd integers is an even number. *[4 marks]*

P Q5 Prove that raising an even number to an odd power gives an even number.

E P Q6 Prove that one more than the product of two consecutive odd numbers is a square number. *[3 marks]*

E P Q7 Prove algebraically that $(4n + 1)^2 - (2n - 1)$ is an even number for every positive integer n. *[3 marks]*

E P Q8 Prove that $5(n + 5)^2 + 3n^2 - 15(2n - 3)$ is an even number for every positive integer n. *[3 marks]*

E P Q9 An isosceles triangle has two identical angles, each measuring $y°$, and another angle measuring $x°$.
Given that y is an odd number, prove algebraically that x is an even number. *[3 marks]*

E Q10 a) Expand and simplify

(i) $(n+1)^3$ *[2 marks]*

(ii) $(n-1)^3$ *[1 mark]*

b) Using the results from part a), or otherwise, prove that the sum of any three consecutive cube numbers is always divisible by 3. *[2 marks]*

Q11 Prove that $a^m \times a^n = a^{m+n}$ for all positive integers m and n.

Q12 Given that $x^2 \geq 0$ for all real numbers x, prove the following statement:

$a^2 + 2ab + b^2 \geq 0$, for any real numbers a and b.

E P Q13 Given that $x < y$, prove that $x < \frac{x+y}{2} < y$. *[3 marks]*

P Q14 Prove that a square number must always have an even number of prime factors (where repeated prime factors are counted separately).

P Q15 Given that n and m are both exactly divisible by k, prove that $pn + qm$ is also divisible by k, where n, m, p, q and k are all positive integers.

P Q16 Prove the following statement:

"$11^n - 1$ is divisible by 10 for all integers $n \geq 1$."

P Q17 Prove that, for any integer x, $(x+5)^2 + 3(x-1)^2$ is always divisible by four.

E P Q18 Prove that the difference between any two rational numbers is also a rational number. *[3 marks]*

P Q19 Prove by exhaustion that the product of any three consecutive integers is even.

E P Q20 Prove by exhaustion that for any integer n, $n^2 - 6$ is never a multiple of 4. *[4 marks]*

P Q21 a) Prove the following statement: "For any integer n, $n^2 - n - 1$ is always odd."

b) Hence prove that $(n^2 - n - 2)^3$ is always even.

P Q22 By finding a counter-example, disprove the following statement:

"If p is a non-zero integer, then $\frac{1}{p^2} < \frac{1}{p}$."

E P Q23 Disprove the following statement: "$x^3 > x$, when $x \neq 0$." *[2 marks]*

P Q24 Disprove the following statement:

"$n^2 - n - 1$ is a prime number for any integer $n > 2$."

E P Q25 Disprove the following statement:

"$ax = bx$ implies that $a = b$ for all rational numbers a, b and x." *[2 marks]*

P Q26 Disprove the following: $\sqrt{x^2 + y^2} < x + y$.

P Q27 Given that x, y and z are integers, disprove the following statement:

"If 4 is a factor of $x + y$ and 4 is a factor of $y + z$, then 4 is a factor of $x + 4y + z$."

E P Q28 Disprove the following statement:

"$n^3 + n^2 + 17$ is prime for all positive integers n." *[2 marks]*

P Q29 Disprove the following statement:

"No integer $N \geq 2$ can be both a square number and a cube number."

E Q30 a) Ananthi says, "If $x \geq y$, then $x^2 + xy + y^2 \geq 3y^2$."
Show by means of a counter-example that Ananthi is wrong. *[2 marks]*

b) Alan says, "For all positive real values of x and y, $x^2 + xy + y^2 \geq 1$."
Show by means of a counter-example that Alan is wrong. *[2 marks]*

Q31 Find a counter-example to disprove the following statement:

"$y^2 + 5y + 4$ is positive for all real numbers y."

E Q32 Disprove the following statement:

"The product of two different irrational numbers is always irrational." *[2 marks]*

P Q33 Disprove the following statement:

"When one rational number is divided by another rational number, the result is always rational."

Challenge

E P Q34 Prove that for all positive real numbers x, $x^2 + \frac{4}{x^2} \geq 4$. *[3 marks]*

E P Q35 a) Prove that if n is an integer that is not a multiple of 3, then $2n^2 + 1$ is a multiple of 3. *[4 marks]*

b) Explain why, if n is an integer, then $1 - 6n^2$ is never divisible by 3. *[1 mark]*

E P Q36 Any two-digit positive integer can be written in the form $(10a + b)$, where a is the digit in the tens position and b is the digit in the units position.

Suppose $(10a + b)$ is a two-digit integer that is exactly divisible by 9.
Prove algebraically that $a + b$ is a multiple of 9. *[3 marks]*

E P Q37 a) Prove that $n^2 + 3n$ is even for all integer values of n. *[3 marks]*

b) Hence, or otherwise, prove that $(n^4 + 3n^2)(n^2 + 3n)$ is a multiple of 8 for all integer values of n. *[5 marks]*

2 Chapter Summary

1 A set is a collection of objects or numbers, shown using curly brackets, e.g. {7, 13, 22}.

2 The objects or numbers in a set are called its elements.

3 The empty set ∅ or {} is the set containing no elements.

4 The union of two sets, A ∪ B, contains all the elements of both sets.

5 The intersection of two sets, A ∩ B, contains only the elements that appear in both sets.

6 A function f(x) takes a value of x, does something to it, and then outputs another value.

7 '$p \Rightarrow q$' means 'p implies q', '$p \Leftarrow q$' means 'q implies p', and '$p \Leftrightarrow q$' means 'p implies q and q implies p'.

8 $\neq$ means 'not equal to', $\approx$ means 'approximately equal to', and $\equiv$ means that two things are identically equal.

9 To prove that an expression is even, you need to show that it can be written in the form $2m$, where m is an integer.

10 To prove that an expression is odd, you need to show that it can be written in the form $2j + 1$, where j is an integer.

11 In proof by deduction, you use known facts to show that a statement must be true.

12 In proof by exhaustion, you split the situation up into different cases (such as odd and even numbers), and prove that the statement is true in each case.

13 To disprove a statement, you only need to find one case for which the statement isn't true. This is known as 'disproof by counter-example'.

Algebra

Learning Objectives

Once you've completed this chapter, you should be able to:

- Use and expand brackets.
- Identify common factors and take them outside the brackets.
- Simplify complicated expressions including algebraic fractions.
- Use the laws of indices to simplify expressions.
- Simplify expressions containing surds.
- Rationalise denominators.

Prior Knowledge Check

1 Expand: a) $4(x-7)$ b) $a(3-2b)$ see GCSE Maths

2 Factorise fully: a) $3x+6y$ b) $9x^2-5x$ see GCSE Maths

3 Write $\frac{x+2}{x}+\frac{3}{x^2}$ as a single fraction in its simplest form. see GCSE Maths

4 Simplify: a) $3^4 \times 3^7$ b) $2^6 \div 2^{12}$ c) $(5^2)^4$ see GCSE Maths

5 Simplify: a) $(\sqrt{8})^2$ b) $\sqrt{3}\times\sqrt{5}$ c) $2\sqrt{7}+3\sqrt{7}$ see GCSE Maths

3.1 Expanding Brackets

Single brackets

When you've got just **one set of brackets** multiplied by a single number or letter, multiply each term in the brackets by the term outside the brackets.

$$a(b + c + d) = ab + ac + ad$$

Double brackets

For **two sets** of brackets multiplied together (where there are **two terms** in each), multiply **each term** in one set of brackets by **each term** in the other. You should **always** get **four terms** from multiplying out double brackets (though sometimes two of the terms will **combine**).

$$(a + b)(c + d) = ac + ad + bc + bd$$

Squared brackets

Squared brackets are just a **special case** of double brackets where both brackets are the **same**. Write them out as two sets of brackets until you're comfortable with it.

$$(a + b)^2 = (a + b)(a + b) = a^2 + ab + ba + b^2 = a^2 + 2ab + b^2$$

A common **mistake** is to write $(a + b)^2 = a^2 + b^2$ — remember that $(a + b)^2$ is actually $(a + b)(a + b)$.

Long brackets

Long brackets are brackets with **many terms**. Just like with double brackets, you need to multiply each term in the first set of brackets by each term in the second — you just do it with more terms.

Write out the expression again with each term from the first set of brackets separately multiplied by the second set of brackets — always use this middle step so you don't get confused by all the terms.

$$(x + y + z)(a + b + c + d) = x(a + b + c + d) + y(a + b + c + d) + z(a + b + c + d)$$

Then multiply out each of these single brackets, **one at a time**.

Many brackets

When you've got **many sets** of brackets multiplied together, multiply them out **two at a time**, treating each set of two as double brackets or long brackets.

Multiply out the first **two** sets of brackets...

$$(a + b)(c + d)(e + f) = (ac + ad + bc + bd)(e + f)$$

...then multiply out the remaining **two sets**.

$$= ac(e + f) + ad(e + f) + bc(e + f) + bd(e + f)$$

Now multiply out each of these single brackets, **one at a time**.

Tip Once you've multiplied out the first pair, the resulting terms may cancel or simplify — making the second step easier.

Example 1

Expand and simplify $3xy(x^2 + 2x - 8)$.

$$(3xy \times x^2) + (3xy \times 2x) + (3xy \times (-8))$$
$$= (3x^3y) + (6x^2y) + (-24xy)$$
$$= 3x^3y + 6x^2y - 24xy$$

Multiply each term inside the brackets by the bit outside — separately.

Example 2

Expand and simplify $(2y^2 + 3x)^2$.

$$(2y^2 + 3x)(2y^2 + 3x)$$
$$= 2y^2 \cdot 2y^2 + 2y^2 \cdot 3x + 3x \cdot 2y^2 + 3x \cdot 3x$$
$$= 4y^4 + 6xy^2 + 6xy^2 + 9x^2$$
$$= 4y^4 + 12xy^2 + 9x^2$$

Either write it as two sets of brackets, multiply it out and collect like terms...

$$(2y^2 + 3x)^2 = (2y^2)^2 + 2(2y^2)(3x) + (3x)^2$$
$$= 4y^4 + 12xy^2 + 9x^2$$

...or do it in one go, using $(a + b)^2 = a^2 + 2ab + b^2$.

Example 3

Expand and simplify $(2x^2 + 3x - 6)(4x^3 + 6x^2 + 3)$.

$$(2x^2 + 3x - 6)(4x^3 + 6x^2 + 3)$$
$$= 2x^2(4x^3 + 6x^2 + 3) + 3x(4x^3 + 6x^2 + 3) + (-6)(4x^3 + 6x^2 + 3)$$
$$= (8x^5 + 12x^4 + 6x^2) + (12x^4 + 18x^3 + 9x) + (-24x^3 - 36x^2 - 18)$$
$$= 8x^5 + 24x^4 - 6x^3 - 30x^2 + 9x - 18$$

Multiply each term in the first set of brackets by the whole second set of brackets.

Now multiply out each of these sets of brackets and simplify it all.

Example 4

Expand and simplify $(2x + 5)(x + 2)(x - 3)$.

$$(2x + 5)(x + 2)(x - 3) = (2x^2 + 4x + 5x + 10)(x - 3)$$
$$= (2x^2 + 9x + 10)(x - 3)$$

Multiply the first two sets of brackets.

$$= 2x^2(x - 3) + 9x(x - 3) + 10(x - 3)$$

Now multiply the long bracket by the final set of brackets.

$$= (2x^3 - 6x^2) + (9x^2 - 27x) + (10x - 30)$$
$$= 2x^3 + 3x^2 - 17x - 30$$

Expand the single brackets and simplify.

Exercise 3.1

Q1 Expand the brackets in these expressions:

a) $5(x + 4)$ b) $a(4 - 2b)$ c) $-2(x^2 + y)$

d) $6mn(m + 1)$ e) $-4ht(t^2 - 2ht - 3h^3)$ f) $7z^2(2 + z)$

g) $4(x + 2) + 3(x - 5)$ h) $p(3p^2 - 2q) + (q + 4p^3)$ i) $7xy(x^2 + z^2)$

Q2 Expand and simplify:

a) $(x + 5)(x - 3)$ b) $(2z + 3)(3z - 2)$ c) $(u + 8)^2$

d) $(ab + cd)(ac + bd)$ e) $(10 + f)(2f^2 - 3g)$ f) $(7 + q)(7 - q)$

g) $(2 - 3w)^2$ h) $(4rs^2 + 3)^2$ i) $(5k^2l - 2kn)^2$

Q3 Expand and simplify the following expressions:

a) $(l + 5)(l^2 + 2l + 3)$ b) $(2 + q)(3 - q + 4q^2)$ c) $(m + 1)(m + 2)(m - 4)$

d) $(r + s)^3$ e) $(3x + 2)(x - 4)(2x + 1)$ f) $(4 + x + y)(1 - x - y)$

g) $(j + 2k - 3)(j^2 + 2j + 1)$ h) $(2c^2 - cd + d)(2d - c - 5c^2)$ i) $(2f^3 - 4f - 1)(f^2 + 3f + 2)$

Q4 Expand and simplify by collecting like terms:

a) $(2x + 1)(3x - 4)(x + 7) - 2(x + 2)(2x - 3)$

b) $(2x - 1)(x^2 + x + 1) + 2(x - 3)((x + 1)(x + 2) + 5)$

E Q5 Expand and simplify $\frac{2}{3}(x + 3)(x^2 + 1) + \frac{1}{4}(x^2 + 4x - 7)$, writing your answer in the form $ax^3 + bx^2 + cx + d$, where a, b, c and d are fractions written in their lowest terms. *[4 marks]*

P M Q6 The volume of a cylinder is given by $\pi r^2 h$, where r is the radius and h is the height. A certain cylinder has a radius of 3 times its height (h cm), minus 2 cm. Find the volume of the cylinder in terms of h. There should be no brackets in your answer.

P M Q7 Carole's garden is a square with sides of length x metres. Mark's garden is a rectangle. One side of the rectangle is 3 metres longer than the side of the square and the other is twice as long as the side of the square, plus an extra metre. Find the difference in area between Mark's garden and Carole's. Give your answer as a simplified expression in x.

E Q8 Given that $(ax + b)(x^2 - 4x - 12) \equiv 2x^3 - 7x^2 + cx - 12$, find the values of a, b and c. *[4 marks]*

E Q9 a) Show that $(a + b)^3 = a^3 + 3a^2b + 3ab^2 + b^3$ *[2 marks]*

b) Using the result from a), expand $(2x + 3y)^3$ *[3 marks]*

Challenge

E Q10 Expand and simplify $(2x + y - 1)^2 + (2 - 4x)(y - 1)$ *[4 marks]*

E P Q11 Determine the coefficient of x^3 if the brackets in the expression $(2x^3 + 5x - 8)(3x^4 - 4x^2 + x + 2)(5 - x^2)$ were to be expanded out. *[3 marks]*

3.2 Factorising

Common Factors

The **factors** of a term are all the bits that **multiply together** to make it up — if something is a factor of a term, the term will be **divisible** by it.

For example, consider the term $12xy^2$ — it has many factors including:

- All the **factors of 12** — 1, 2, 3, 4, 6 and 12.
- The **variables** x and y (and also y^2).
- Any **combinations** of these multiplied together, e.g. $3xy$, $12y^2$, $6x$, etc.

Remember that 1 and the term itself are always factors.

Tip The definition of a term is a collection of numbers, letters and brackets all multiplied or divided together.

Example 1

Find all the factors of $6x$.

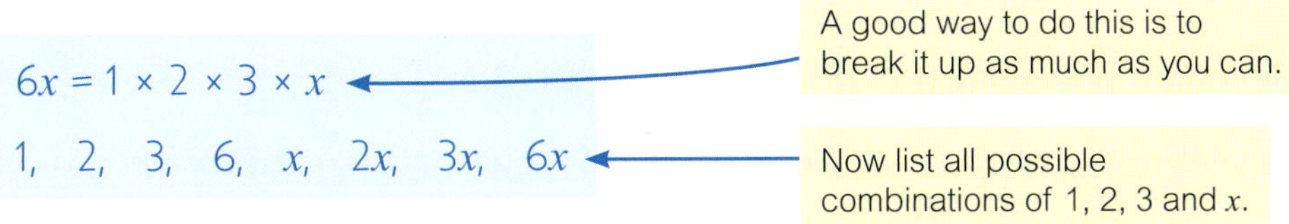

A factor which is in every term of an expression is called a **common factor**. They can be '**taken out**' and put outside brackets — when you've taken out **all** possible factors, an expression is **completely factorised**.

Example 2

Factorise $2x^3z + 4x^2yz + 14x^2y^2z$ completely.

Numbers: There's a common factor of 2 as 2 divides into 2, 4 and 14.

Look for any factors that are in each term.

Variables: There's at least an x^2 and a z in each term.

Tip There is an x^3 in one term but only an x^2 in the other two, so each term has at least an x^2 in it.

So there's a common factor of $2x^2z$ in this expression.

This can be seen more easily if you write each term as $2x^2z \times$ 'something'.

$$2x^3z + 4x^2yz + 14x^2y^2z$$
$$= 2x^2z \cdot x + 2x^2z \cdot 2y + 2x^2z \cdot 7y^2$$
$$= 2x^2z(x + 2y + 7y^2)$$

Write the common factor outside a set of brackets and put what's left of each term inside the brackets. The terms in the brackets have no common factors, so this expression is completely factorised.

You should check that you did the factorisation right by multiplying it out again and comparing the result to the original expression. For example, in the last example, $2x^2z(x + 2y + 7y^2) = 2x^3z + 4x^2yz + 14x^2y^2z$, which is the same as the starting expression.

It's not just numbers and variables that you need to look for — you can sometimes take out **whole sets of brackets** as factors of an expression. You might be asked to write an expression as a **product of factors** — this means write all its factors multiplied together, which is exactly the **same** as **factorising**.

Example 3

Express $(y + a)^2(x - a)^3 + (x - a)^2$ as a product of factors.

$(y + a)^2(x - a)^3 + (x - a)^2$
$= (y + a)^2(x - a)(x - a)^2 + (x - a)^2$
$= (x - a)^2[(y + a)^2(x - a) + 1]$

This can be written to make it easier to see common factors.

$(x - a)^2$ is a common factor — write it outside a set of brackets and put what's left inside the brackets. The two terms in the brackets share no common factors so the expression is completely factorised.

Difference of two squares

If you expand brackets of the form $\boldsymbol{(a - b)(a + b)}$, the '$ab$' terms cancel and you're left with one square minus another:

$(a - b)(a + b) = a^2 + ab - ba - b^2 = a^2 + ab - ab - b^2 = a^2 - b^2$

This result is called the **difference of two squares**: $\boldsymbol{a^2 - b^2 = (a - b)(a + b)}$

Watch out for it when factorising — if you spot that an expression is 'a squared term minus another squared term', you can use this result to rewrite the expression as a pair of brackets.

Example 4

a) Factorise $x^2 - 36y^2$.

This is a difference of two squares.

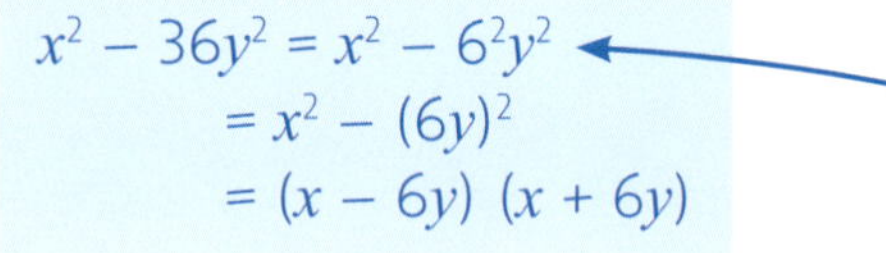

36 is a square number so $36y^2$ can be written as a square.

b) Write $x^2 - 5$ in the form $(x - a)(x + a)$.

$x^2 - 5 = x^2 - (\sqrt{5})^2$
$= (x - \sqrt{5})(x + \sqrt{5})$

5 isn't a square number but you can still write it as a square.

Problem Solving

Any number can be written as the square of its square root (see p.28).

Exercise 3.2

Q1 Factorise the following expressions completely:

a) $9k + 15l$ b) $u^2 - uv$ c) $2x^2y - 12xy^2$ d) $f^2g^2 - fg$
e) $p^3 + 3pq^3 + 2p$ f) $mnp^2 + 7m^2np^3$ g) $2ab^4 + 3a^3b^2 - 4ab$ h) $36xyz - 8x^2z^2 + 20y^2z^2$

Q2 Write the following expressions as products of factors:

a) $x^2 - y^2$ b) $9a^2 - 4b^2$ c) $25x^2 - 49z^2$ d) $a^2c - 16b^2c$
e) $y^2 - 2$ f) $m^2 - 11$ g) $4x^2 - 3$ h) $7p^2 - 13$

Q3 Express the following as the product of factors.

a) $(4 - z)^2(2 - z) + p(2 - z)$ b) $(r - d)^3 + 5(r - d)^2$

c) $(b + c)^5(a + b) - (b + c)^5$ d) $l^2m(a - 2x) + rp^2(2x - a)$

Q3d) Hint

Remember that $(b - a) = -(a - b)$

Q4 Simplify each expression, leaving your answer in its factorised form.

a) $(p + q)^2 + 2q(p + q)$ b) $2(2x - y)^2 - 6x(2x - y)$ c) $(l + w + h)^2 - l(l + w + h)$

E Q5 a) Factorise fully $(2x + 1)(x - 3)(3x - 1) - 2(x - 3)(x + 2)(2x + 1)$. *[3 marks]*

b) Hence, or otherwise, find all solutions to the equation $(2x + 1)(x - 3)(3x - 1) - 2(x - 3)(x + 2)(2x + 1) = 0$. *[1 mark]*

E Q6 Completely factorise the expression $6(5x - 7y)^3 - 4(x + y)(5x - 7y)^2$. *[3 marks]*

E Q7 Factorise $12m^3n^6(1 + 6n^2) + 18m^2n^7(1 - 4mn)$ completely. *[2 marks]*

Challenge

Q8 Simplify these expressions by expanding brackets, factorising or both.

a) $(m + 5)(m^2 - 5m + 25)$ b) $(p - 2q)(p^2 + 2pq + 4q^2)$

c) $(u - v)(u + v) - (u + v)^2$ d) $(c + d)^3 - c(c + d)^2 - d(c + d)^2$

3.3 Algebraic Fractions

The rules for **algebraic fractions** should be familiar from working with numerical fractions.

Adding and subtracting

If you're **adding fractions** together that all have the same **denominator**, you just add the **numerators**.

$$\frac{a}{x} + \frac{b}{x} + \frac{c}{x} \equiv \frac{a + b + c}{x}$$

x is the **common denominator**

Tip

This equals sign with 3 lines $\equiv$ means it's true for all values of a, b, c or x — this is called an identity (see page 7).

If the fractions you want to add don't have a common denominator you can 'find' one — **rewrite** the fractions so that the denominators are the same by multiplying **top** and **bottom** by the same thing.

Example 1

Express $\frac{1}{2x} - \frac{1}{3x} + \frac{1}{5x}$ as a single fraction.

$$\frac{1}{2x} - \frac{1}{3x} + \frac{1}{5x} = \frac{1}{2x} \cdot \frac{15}{15} - \frac{1}{3x} \cdot \frac{10}{10} + \frac{1}{5x} \cdot \frac{6}{6}$$

Find a common denominator. **30** is the lowest number that 2, 3 and 5 all go into and each denominator contains an x, so make the common denominator **30x**.

$$= \frac{15}{30x} - \frac{10}{30x} + \frac{6}{30x}$$

$$= \frac{15 - 10 + 6}{30x} = \frac{11}{30x}$$

Then, just add the numerators.

Example 2

Simplify $\frac{3}{x+2} + \frac{5}{x-3}$.

$$\frac{3(x-3)}{(x+2)(x-3)} + \frac{5(x+2)}{(x+2)(x-3)}$$

Again, find a **common denominator**. You need an expression that both **(x + 2)** and **(x – 3)** divide into — you can get one by multiplying the denominators together to give a common denominator of **(x + 2)(x – 3).**

$$= \frac{3(x-3)+5(x+2)}{(x+2)(x-3)}$$

$$= \frac{3x-9+5x+10}{(x+2)(x-3)}$$

Once the denominators are all the same, you can just add the numerators and simplify.

$$= \frac{8x+1}{(x+2)(x-3)}$$

Trickier algebraic fractions

Sometimes, finding a common denominator can be a bit more difficult. Although you can always **multiply** the denominators together, it often won't result in the **simplest** common denominator.

Find a term which **both** denominators divide into. You must include each different factor at least once in your term — but you may need some **more than once**.

Tip Finding any old common denominator is easy — just multiply all the denominators together. But if you're careful and don't include any bits twice, you'll have a lot less simplifying to do at the end.

Example 3

Simplify $\frac{3}{2x^2} + \frac{6}{5x}$.

$2x^2 = 2 \times x \times x$

$5x = 5 \times x$

Common denominator is $2 \times 5 \times x \times x = 10x^2$

The different factors are 2, 5 and x so you need at least one of each — there are two factors of x in the first denominator so you'll need an x^2, but you don't need another x for the second denominator since this is accounted for by multiplying by the x^2.

$$\frac{3}{2x^2} + \frac{6}{5x} = \frac{3 \times 5}{2x^2 \times 5} + \frac{6 \times 2x}{5x \times 2x}$$

As before, multiply the top and bottom lines of each fraction by whatever makes the bottom line the same as the common denominator.

$$= \frac{15}{10x^2} + \frac{12x}{10x^2}$$

$$= \frac{15+12x}{10x^2} = \frac{3(5+4x)}{10x^2}$$

Then add the numerators and simplify by factorising.

Simplifying

Algebraic fractions can sometimes be simplified by cancelling **factors** that appear in both the numerator and denominator. You can do this in **two ways** — use whichever method you prefer, but make sure you understand the ideas behind both.

Example 4

Simplify $\frac{ax+ay}{az}$

Method 1:

$$\frac{ax+ay}{az}=\frac{a(x+y)}{az}=\frac{\cancel{a}(x+y)}{\cancel{a}z}=\frac{x+y}{z}$$

Factorise the numerator and then cancel the 'a'.

Method 2:

$$\frac{ax+ay}{az}=\frac{ax}{az}+\frac{ay}{az}$$

This is the rule from page 21 for adding fractions, but backwards.

$$=\frac{\cancel{a}x}{\cancel{a}z}+\frac{\cancel{a}y}{\cancel{a}z}=\frac{x}{z}+\frac{y}{z}=\frac{x+y}{z}$$

Split into two fractions, then cancel.

Exercise 3.3

Q1 Express each of these as a single fraction.

a) $\frac{x}{3}+\frac{x}{4}$ b) $\frac{2}{t}+\frac{13}{t^2}$ c) $\frac{1}{2p}-\frac{1}{5q}$

d) $\frac{2}{3h}+\frac{1}{2h}-\frac{3}{4h}$ e) $\frac{ab}{c}+\frac{bc}{a}+\frac{ca}{b}$ f) $\frac{2}{mn}-\frac{3m}{n}+\frac{n^2}{m}$

g) $\frac{2}{ab^3}-\frac{9}{a^3b}$ h) $\frac{1}{x}+\frac{2x}{y}+\frac{4}{x^2}$ i) $2+\frac{a^2}{b}-\frac{2b}{a^2}$

Q2 Express the following as single fractions in their simplest form.

a) $\frac{5}{y-1}+\frac{3}{y-2}$ b) $\frac{7}{r-5}-\frac{4}{r+3}$ c) $\frac{8}{p}-\frac{1}{p-3}$

d) $\frac{w}{2(w-2)}+\frac{3w}{w-7}$ e) $\frac{z+1}{z+2}-\frac{z+3}{z+4}$ f) $\frac{1}{q+1}+\frac{3}{q-2}$

g) $\frac{x}{x+z}+\frac{2z}{x-z}$ h) $\frac{y}{2x+3}-\frac{2y}{3-x}$ i) $\frac{5}{r-4}+\frac{3}{r}-\frac{r}{r+1}$

Q3 Simplify these expressions.

a) $\frac{2x+10}{6}$ b) $\frac{6a-12b-15c}{3}$ c) $\frac{np^2-2n^2p}{np}$

d) $\frac{4st+6s^2t+9s^3t}{2t}$ e) $\frac{10yz^3-40y^3z^3+60y^2z^3}{10z^2}$ f) $\frac{12cd-6c^2d+3c^3d^2}{12c^2de}$

g) $\frac{2x+x^2y-x^2}{x^2+3x}$ h) $\frac{2w^3+14w^2}{w^2-49}$ i) $\frac{4g^2-4h^2}{g^2+gh}$

Q4 Fully simplify:

a) $\frac{x+3}{(2x+1)^2(x-1)} - \frac{1}{(2x+1)(x-1)^2}$

b) $\frac{8}{x} - \left(\frac{5}{2x-1} + \frac{x+4}{x}\right)$

c) $\frac{2x+3}{(x-5)(x+9)} + \frac{x}{(x-3)(x-5)}$

d) $\left(\frac{3}{x+1}\right)^2 - \frac{2}{x+1}$

E Q5 Express the following as a single fraction:

$$\frac{8}{2x+1} - 4\left(\frac{3}{x+4} + \frac{1}{2}\right)$$

[4 marks]

P M Q6 Maya has a ribbon of length 10 cm and Hal has a ribbon of length 15 cm.
Maya cuts her ribbon into x equal pieces. Hal cuts his into three more pieces than Maya.
What is the total length of one of Maya's pieces and one of Hal's pieces laid end to end?
Give your answer as a single fraction involving x.

E Q7 Given that, for $x \neq -4$ and $x \neq 3$:

$$\frac{12}{2(x-3)} - \frac{6}{3(x+4)} \equiv \frac{Ax+B}{(x-3)(x+4)}$$

find the values of A and B. *[3 marks]*

Challenge

E P Q8 a) Show that for constants a and b and for all $x \neq -\frac{1}{2}$ or 3 that:

$$\frac{a}{2x+1} + \frac{b}{x-3} \equiv \frac{(a+2b)x+(b-3a)}{(2x+1)(x-3)}$$

[3 marks]

b) Given that:

$$\frac{a}{2x+1} + \frac{b}{x-3} \equiv \frac{x-17}{(2x+1)(x-3)}$$

find the values of a and b. *[2 marks]*

3.4 Laws of Indices

You should already know that the expression x^n just means n **lots** of x multiplied together. The n is called the **index** or power of x. So when you square a number (e.g. x^2), the index or power is 2.

> **Tip** Index and power mean the same thing — we'll use power for the rest of the section.

- If you multiply two numbers, you **add** their powers: $a^m \times a^n = a^{m+n}$
- If you divide two numbers, you **subtract** their powers: $\frac{a^m}{a^n} = a^{m-n}$
- If you have a power to the power of something else, you **multiply** the powers together: $(a^m)^n = a^{mn}$

There are also laws for manipulating **fractional** and **negative** powers...

$a^{\frac{1}{m}} = \sqrt[m]{a}$

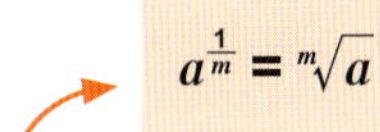

This works because, e.g.:
$a^{\frac{1}{2}} \times a^{\frac{1}{2}} = a^{\frac{1}{2}+\frac{1}{2}} = a^1 \Rightarrow a^{\frac{1}{2}} = \sqrt{a}$

$a^{-m} = \frac{1}{a^m}$

This works because, e.g.:
$a^{-2} = a^1 \div a^3 = \frac{a}{a \times a \times a} = \frac{1}{a^2}$

$a^{\frac{m}{n}} = \sqrt[n]{a^m} = (\sqrt[n]{a})^m$

> **Tip** $\sqrt[m]{a}$ is the mth root of a.

...and one simple law for **zero** powers, which works for any non-zero number or letter.

$a^0 = 1$

Example 1

Simplify the following:

a) (i) a^2a (ii) $x^{-2} \cdot x^5$ (iii) $(a+b)^2(a+b)^5$ (iv) $ab^3 \cdot a^2b$

> **Tip** Note that $x = x^1$.

(i) $a^2a = a^{2+1} = a^3$ ← Use the rule: $a^m \times a^n = a^{m+n}$

(ii) $x^{-2} \cdot x^5 = x^{-2+5} = x^3$

(iii) $(a+b)^2(a+b)^5 = (a+b)^{2+5} = (a+b)^7$

(iv) $ab^3 \cdot a^2b = a^{1+2}b^{3+1} = a^3b^4$ ← Add the powers of a and b separately.

b) (i) $(x^2)^3$ (ii) $\{(a+b)^3\}^4$ (iii) $(ab^2)^4$

(i) $(x^2)^3 = x^6$ ← Use the rule: $(a^m)^n = a^{mn}$

(ii) $\{(a+b)^3\}^4 = (a+b)^{12}$

(iii) $(ab^2)^4 = a^4(b^2)^4 = a^4b^8$ ← This power of 4 applies to both bits inside the brackets.

> **Problem Solving** For part b) (iii), remember that:
> $(ab^2)^4 = (ab^2) \cdot (ab^2) \cdot (ab^2) \cdot (ab^2)$
> $= a \cdot a \cdot a \cdot a \cdot b^2 \cdot b^2 \cdot b^2 \cdot b^2$
> $= a^4 \cdot (b^2)^4 = a^4b^8$

c) (i) $\dfrac{x^{\frac{3}{4}}}{x}$ (ii) $\dfrac{x^3y^2}{xy^3}$

(i) $\dfrac{x^{\frac{3}{4}}}{x} = x^{\frac{3}{4}-1} = x^{-\frac{1}{4}} = \dfrac{1}{x^{\frac{1}{4}}}$ ← Use the rule: $\dfrac{a^m}{a^n} = a^{m-n}$

(ii) $\dfrac{x^3y^2}{xy^3} = x^{3-1}y^{2-3} = x^2y^{-1} = \dfrac{x^2}{y}$ ← Subtract the powers of x and y separately.

Tip For part c) (i), you could simplify further to $\dfrac{1}{\sqrt[4]{x}}$.

d) (i) $4^{\frac{1}{2}}$ (ii) $125^{\frac{1}{3}}$

(i) $4^{\frac{1}{2}} = \sqrt{4} = 2$ ← Use the rule: $a^{\frac{1}{m}} = \sqrt[m]{a}$

(ii) $125^{\frac{1}{3}} = \sqrt[3]{125} = 5$

e) (i) $9^{\frac{3}{2}}$ (ii) $16^{\frac{3}{4}}$

(i) $9^{\frac{3}{2}} = (9^{\frac{1}{2}})^3 = (\sqrt{9})^3 = 3^3 = 27$ ← Use the rule: $a^{\frac{m}{n}} = \sqrt[n]{a^m} = (\sqrt[n]{a})^m$

(ii) $16^{\frac{3}{4}} = (16^{\frac{1}{4}})^3 = (\sqrt[4]{16})^3 = 2^3 = 8$ ← It's often easier to work out the root first, then raise it to the power.

f) (i) 2^{-3} (ii) $(x+1)^{-1}$

(i) $2^{-3} = \dfrac{1}{2^3} = \dfrac{1}{8}$ ← Use the rule: $a^{-m} = \dfrac{1}{a^m}$

(ii) $(x+1)^{-1} = \dfrac{1}{x+1}$

g) (i) 2^0 (ii) $(a+b)^0$

(i) $2^0 = 1$ (ii) $(a+b)^0 = 1$ ← Use the rule: $a^0 = 1$

Example 2

Express $\dfrac{(7^{\frac{1}{3}})^6 \times (7^{-1})^4}{(7^{-4})^{-2}}$ as 7^k, where k is an integer.

$\dfrac{(7^{\frac{1}{3}})^6 \times (7^{-1})^4}{(7^{-4})^{-2}} = \dfrac{7^{\frac{6}{3}} \times 7^{-1\times 4}}{7^{-4\times -2}}$ ← Use the $(a^m)^n = a^{mn}$ rule to get rid of the brackets.

$= \dfrac{7^2 \times 7^{-4}}{7^8} = \dfrac{7^{2-4}}{7^8} = \dfrac{7^{-2}}{7^8}$ ← Combine the powers of 7 on the top of the fraction using the $a^m \times a^n = a^{m+n}$ rule.

$= 7^{-2-8}$ ← Get rid of the fraction using the $\dfrac{a^m}{a^n} = a^{m-n}$ rule.

$= 7^{-10}$

Exercise 3.4

Q1 Simplify the following, leaving your answer as a power:

a) 10×10^4 b) $y^{-1} \times y^{-2} \times y^7$ c) $5^{\frac{1}{2}} \times 5^3 \times 5^{\frac{-3}{2}}$ d) $6^5 \div 6^2$

e) $3^4 \div 3^{-1}$ f) $\frac{6^{11}}{6}$ g) $\frac{r^2}{r^6}$ h) $(3^2)^3$

i) $(k^{-2})^5$ j) $(z^4)^{-\frac{1}{8}}$ k) $(8^{-6})^{-\frac{1}{2}}$ l) $\frac{p^5q^4}{p^4q}$

m) $\frac{c^{-1}d^{-2}}{c^2d^4}$ n) $(ab^2)^2$ o) $\frac{12yz^{-\frac{1}{2}}}{4yz^{\frac{1}{2}}}$ p) $\left(mn^{\frac{1}{2}}\right)^4$

Q2 Evaluate:

a) $4^{\frac{1}{2}} \times 4^{\frac{3}{2}}$ b) $\frac{2^3 \times 2}{2^5}$ c) $\frac{7^5 \times 7^3}{7^6}$ d) $\frac{6^4}{6^{\frac{5}{4}} \times 6^{\frac{3}{4}}}$

e) $(3^2)^5 \div (3^3)^3$ f) $\left(4^{-\frac{1}{2}}\right)^2 \times \left(4^{-3}\right)^{-\frac{1}{3}}$ g) $\frac{(2^{\frac{1}{2}})^6 \times (2^{-2})^{-2}}{(2^{-1})^{-1}}$ h) 1^0

i) $\left(\frac{4}{5}\right)^0$ j) $(-5.726324)^0$ k) 8.374936^1 l) $\frac{(3^3)^2}{(9^{\frac{1}{2}})^4 \times (9^{\frac{1}{4}})^8}$

Q3 Express the following as negative or fractional powers or both:

a) $\frac{1}{p}$ b) $\frac{5}{y^4}$ c) $\sqrt{q}$ d) $\sqrt{r^3}$

e) $\sqrt[4]{s^5}$ f) $\frac{1}{\sqrt[3]{t}}$ g) $\left(\frac{1}{\sqrt[3]{x}}\right)^4$ h) $\frac{\sqrt{z}}{z^3}$

Q4 Evaluate:

a) $9^{\frac{1}{2}}$ b) $8^{\frac{1}{3}}$ c) $4^{\frac{3}{2}}$ d) $27^{-\frac{1}{3}}$

e) $16^{-\frac{3}{4}}$ f) $125^{\frac{2}{3}}$ g) $81^{\frac{1}{4}}$ h) $64^{\frac{1}{2}} \times 64^{-\frac{1}{3}}$

P Q5 Clare thinks of a number, x. She takes the cube root of the number, and then raises the result to the power 6. Finally, she divides by the number she thought of. What number does she have now?

P Q6 If $p = \frac{1}{16}q^2$, write the following expressions in terms of q:

a) $p^{\frac{1}{2}}$ b) $2p^{-1}$ c) $p^{\frac{1}{2}} \div 2p^{-1}$

d) p^2q e) $\frac{4p}{q^3}$ f) $\frac{q^2}{4p^2}$

Challenge

P Q7 $a = 8^{-3}$, $b = 64^3$ and $c = 8^{\frac{1}{2}}$. Write $\frac{a^{-5}}{b^{\frac{1}{2}} \times c^4}$ as a single power of 8.

P Q8 Find the value of x for each of the following:

a) $4^x = \sqrt[3]{16}$ b) $9^x = \frac{1}{3}$ c) $\sqrt{5} \times 5^x = \frac{1}{25}$

d) $(16^x)^2 = \frac{1}{4}$ e) $x^{-3} = -8$ f) $\sqrt{100^x} = 0.001$

3.5 The Laws of Surds

Put $\sqrt{2}$ into a calculator and you'll get 1.414213562... But if you square 1.414213562, you get 1.999999999. No matter how many decimal places you use, you'll never get exactly 2. This is because $\sqrt{2}$ is an **irrational number** — its decimal expansion **continues forever**.

The only way to express a number like this **exactly** is to leave it as a root. Numbers like $\sqrt{2}$ that can only be written exactly using roots are called **surds**. The number $\sqrt{3}$ is a surd because it can't be written exactly without a root, whereas $\sqrt{9}$ is **not** a surd because it can be simplified to 3.

There are three rules you need to know to be able to use surds properly:

$$\sqrt{ab} = \sqrt{a}\sqrt{b} \qquad \sqrt{\frac{a}{b}} = \frac{\sqrt{a}}{\sqrt{b}} \qquad a = (\sqrt{a})^2 = \sqrt{a}\sqrt{a}$$

Simplifying surds usually just means making the number in the $\sqrt{\ }$ sign smaller, or getting rid of a fraction inside the $\sqrt{\ }$ sign.

Tip A rational number is a number that can be expressed as $\frac{p}{q}$ where p and q are integers and $q \neq 0$. An irrational number is just one which is not rational.

Problem Solving Remember that $\sqrt{x} = x^{\frac{1}{2}}$ (see p.25).

Example 1

a) Simplify $\sqrt{12}$

$$\sqrt{12} = \sqrt{4 \times 3} = \sqrt{4} \times \sqrt{3} = 2\sqrt{3}$$

Use the rule: $\sqrt{ab} = \sqrt{a}\sqrt{b}$

b) Simplify $\sqrt{\frac{3}{16}}$

$$\sqrt{\frac{3}{16}} = \frac{\sqrt{3}}{\sqrt{16}} = \frac{\sqrt{3}}{4}$$

Use the rule: $\sqrt{\frac{a}{b}} = \frac{\sqrt{a}}{\sqrt{b}}$

c) Find $(2\sqrt{5} + 3\sqrt{6})^2$

$$\begin{aligned}(2\sqrt{5}+3\sqrt{6})^2 &= (2\sqrt{5}+3\sqrt{6})(2\sqrt{5}+3\sqrt{6}) \\ &= (2\sqrt{5})^2 + (2\times(2\sqrt{5})\times(3\sqrt{6})) + (3\sqrt{6})^2 \\ &= (2^2\times\sqrt{5}^2) + (2\times2\times3\times\sqrt{5}\times\sqrt{6}) + (3^2\times\sqrt{6}^2) \\ &= (4\times5) + (12\times\sqrt{5\times6}) + (9\times6) \\ &= 20 + 12\sqrt{30} + 54 \\ &= 74 + 12\sqrt{30}\end{aligned}$$

Multiply out the squared brackets.

Problem Solving Remember that $(a + b)^2 = a^2 + 2ab + b^2$.

d) Express $\sqrt{63} - \sqrt{28}$ in the form $k\sqrt{x}$ where k and x are integers.

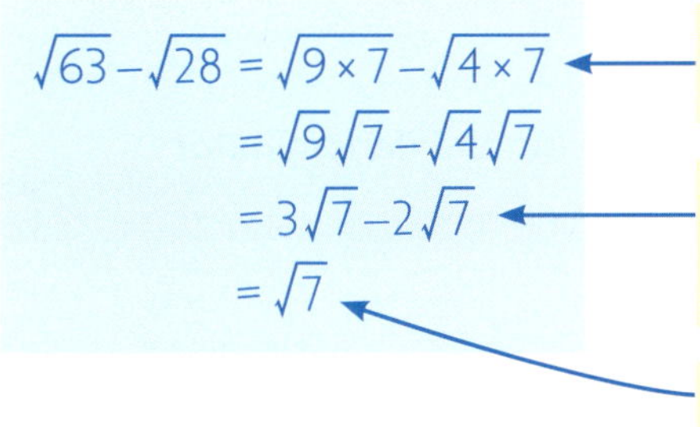

Try to write both numbers as 'a square number' $\times\ x$. Here, x is 7.

Take the square root of the square numbers to leave two integer multiples of $\sqrt{7}$, which you can subtract to simplify.

In this case, k is just 1.

Tip An integer is just a positive or negative whole number, including 0.

Exercise 3.5

Q1 Simplify the following surds:

a) $\sqrt{8}$ b) $\sqrt{24}$ c) $\sqrt{50}$ d) $\sqrt{63}$

e) $\sqrt{72}$ f) $\sqrt{\frac{5}{4}}$ g) $\sqrt{\frac{7}{100}}$ h) $\sqrt{\frac{11}{9}}$

Q2 Evaluate the following, giving your answers as either a whole number or a surd.

a) $2\sqrt{3} \times 4\sqrt{3}$ b) $\sqrt{5} \times 3\sqrt{5}$ c) $(\sqrt{7})^2$ d) $2\sqrt{2} \times 3\sqrt{5}$

e) $(2\sqrt{11})^2$ f) $5\sqrt{8} \times 2\sqrt{2}$ g) $4\sqrt{3} \times 2\sqrt{27}$ h) $2\sqrt{6} \times 5\sqrt{24}$

i) $\frac{6}{\sqrt{11}} \times \sqrt{44}$ j) $2\sqrt{18} \times \frac{5}{\sqrt{8}}$ k) $\frac{\sqrt{10}}{6} \times \frac{12}{\sqrt{5}}$ l) $\frac{\sqrt{12}}{3} \times \frac{2}{\sqrt{27}}$

Q3 Express the following in the form $k\sqrt{x}$, where k and x are integers and x is as small as possible.

a) $\sqrt{20} + \sqrt{5}$ b) $\sqrt{32} - \sqrt{8}$

c) $\sqrt{27} + 4\sqrt{3}$ d) $2\sqrt{8} - 3\sqrt{2}$

e) $3\sqrt{10} + \sqrt{250}$ f) $4\sqrt{27} + 2\sqrt{48} + 5\sqrt{108}$

Q3 Hint To add surds, the $\sqrt{x}$ bit must be the same in each term.

Q4 Expand the following expressions, giving your answers in their simplest form.

a) $(1 + \sqrt{2})(2 + \sqrt{2})$ b) $(3 + 4\sqrt{3})(2 - \sqrt{3})$ c) $(\sqrt{11} + 2)(\sqrt{11} - 2)$

d) $(9 - 2\sqrt{5})(9 + 2\sqrt{5})$ e) $(\sqrt{3} + 2)^2$ f) $(3\sqrt{5} - 4)^2$

P Q5 A parallelogram has base length $2\sqrt{6}$ cm and vertical height $\sqrt{3}$ cm.
Find the area of the parallelogram.
Give your answer in the form $p\sqrt{2}$ cm^2, where p is an integer.

P M Q6 A rectangular swimming pool is $3\sqrt{28}$ m long and $\sqrt{63}$ m wide.
What is the perimeter of the swimming pool?
Give your answer in the form $s\sqrt{7}$ m, where s is an integer.

Challenge

P Q7 Triangle ABC is right-angled with angle ABC = 90°.
Side AC has length $5\sqrt{2}$ cm and side AB has length $\sqrt{2}$ cm.
Find the length of side BC in the form $k\sqrt{3}$ cm, where k is an integer.

3.6 Rationalising the Denominator

You can remove surds from the denominators of fractions by **rationalising the denominator**.

To rationalise the denominator you multiply **top and bottom** of the fraction by an **expression** that will get rid of surds in the denominator. (Multiplying a fraction by the same thing on the top and bottom doesn't change its value.)

Example 1

a) Show that $\frac{9}{\sqrt{3}} = 3\sqrt{3}$.

$$\frac{9}{\sqrt{3}} = \frac{9 \times \sqrt{3}}{\sqrt{3} \times \sqrt{3}}$$

To get rid of the surd, multiply the top and bottom by $\sqrt{3}$.

$$= \frac{9\sqrt{3}}{3} = 3\sqrt{3}$$

You can cancel 3 from the top and bottom.

b) Rationalise the denominator of $\frac{1}{1+\sqrt{2}}$.

$$\frac{1}{1+\sqrt{2}} \times \frac{1-\sqrt{2}}{1-\sqrt{2}} = \frac{1-\sqrt{2}}{(1+\sqrt{2})(1-\sqrt{2})}$$

If the denominator is of the form $a+\sqrt{b}$, multiply top and bottom by $a-\sqrt{b}$. Just change the sign in front of the surd.

$$= \frac{1-\sqrt{2}}{1^2 - \sqrt{2} + \sqrt{2} - \sqrt{2}^2}$$

$$= \frac{1-\sqrt{2}}{1-2}$$

Using the difference of two squares rule (see page 20), the surds in the denominator cancel each other out.

$$= \frac{1-\sqrt{2}}{-1}$$

$$= -1+\sqrt{2}$$

Multiply top and bottom by –1 to give the answer in its simplest form.

c) Rationalise the denominator of $\frac{7+\sqrt{5}}{3+\sqrt{5}}$.

$$\frac{7+\sqrt{5}}{3+\sqrt{5}} \times \frac{3-\sqrt{5}}{3-\sqrt{5}} = \frac{(7+\sqrt{5})(3-\sqrt{5})}{(3+\sqrt{5})(3-\sqrt{5})}$$

Multiply top and bottom by $3-\sqrt{5}$.

$$= \frac{(7 \times 3) - 7\sqrt{5} + 3\sqrt{5} - (\sqrt{5})^2}{3^2 - 3\sqrt{5} + 3\sqrt{5} - (\sqrt{5})^2}$$

Expand the brackets on the top and bottom and simplify. The surds on the bottom cancel each other out.

$$= \frac{21 - 4\sqrt{5} - 5}{9-5}$$

$$= \frac{16 - 4\sqrt{5}}{4}$$

$$= 4 - \sqrt{5}$$

Cancel 4 from the top and bottom of the fraction to give the answer in its simplest form.

Exercise 3.6

Q1 Simplify the following, giving your answers in the form $p\sqrt{q}$, where q is an integer and p is an integer or fraction:

a) $\frac{6}{\sqrt{3}}$ b) $\frac{21}{\sqrt{7}}$ c) $\frac{30}{\sqrt{5}}$

d) $\sqrt{45}+\frac{15}{\sqrt{5}}$ e) $\frac{\sqrt{54}}{3}-\frac{12}{\sqrt{6}}$ f) $\frac{\sqrt{300}}{5}+\frac{30}{\sqrt{12}}$

g) $\frac{1}{\sqrt{18}}-\frac{1}{\sqrt{2}}$ h) $\frac{1}{\sqrt{28}}+\frac{3}{\sqrt{7}}$ i) $\frac{2}{\sqrt{72}}-\frac{5}{\sqrt{8}}$

Q2 Express the following in the form $a+b\sqrt{k}$, where a, b and k are integers:

a) $\frac{4}{1+\sqrt{3}}$ b) $\frac{8}{-1+\sqrt{5}}$ c) $\frac{18}{\sqrt{10}-4}$

d) $\frac{\sqrt{6}}{2-\sqrt{6}}$ e) $\frac{3}{5+2\sqrt{7}}$ f) $\frac{6}{3\sqrt{2}-4}$

Q3 Express the following in the form $p+q\sqrt{r}$, where r is an integer, and p and q are integers or fractions:

a) $\frac{\sqrt{2}+1}{\sqrt{2}-1}$ b) $\frac{\sqrt{5}+3}{\sqrt{5}-2}$ c) $\frac{3-\sqrt{3}}{4+\sqrt{3}}$

d) $\frac{3\sqrt{5}-1}{2\sqrt{5}-3}$ e) $\frac{\sqrt{2}+\sqrt{3}}{3\sqrt{2}-\sqrt{3}}$ f) $\frac{2\sqrt{7}-\sqrt{5}}{\sqrt{7}+2\sqrt{5}}$

g) $\frac{2\sqrt{2}+\sqrt{3}}{\sqrt{3}-\sqrt{12}}$ h) $\frac{6-4\sqrt{2}}{5\sqrt{2}-\sqrt{8}}$ i) $\frac{\sqrt{3}+3}{\sqrt{5}+\sqrt{15}}$

Q4 Express the following in the form $k(\sqrt{x}\pm\sqrt{y})$, where x and y are integers and k is an integer or fraction.

a) $\frac{4}{\sqrt{7}-\sqrt{3}}$ b) $\frac{24}{\sqrt{11}-\sqrt{17}}$ c) $\frac{2}{\sqrt{13}+\sqrt{5}}$

d) $\frac{\sqrt{5}}{\sqrt{6}+\sqrt{3}}$ e) $\frac{\sqrt{3}}{\sqrt{21}-3\sqrt{5}}$ f) $\frac{3\sqrt{2}}{2\sqrt{3}+\sqrt{20}}$

P Q5 Find the reciprocal of $4\sqrt{3}-2\sqrt{5}$. Give your answer in the form $k(\sqrt{x}\pm\sqrt{y})$, where x and y are integers and k is an integer or fraction.

P Q6 Solve the equation $12=\sqrt{3}z$ giving your answer in the form $k\sqrt{3}$ where k is an integer.

P Q7 Solve the equation $8=(\sqrt{5}-1)x$ giving your answer in the form $a+b\sqrt{5}$ where a and b are integers.

Challenge

P Q8 Solve the equation $5+\sqrt{7}=(3-\sqrt{7})y$ giving your answer in the form $p+q\sqrt{7}$ where p and q are integers.

P Q9 A rectangle has an area of $(2+\sqrt{2})$ cm^2 and a width of $(3\sqrt{2}-4)$ cm. Find the length of the rectangle. Give your answer in the form $a+b\sqrt{2}$ where a and b are integers.

3 Review Exercise

Q1 Remove the brackets and simplify the following expressions:

a) $(a + b)(a - b)$ b) $(p + q)(p + q)$ c) $35xy + 25y(5y + 7x) - 100y^2$

d) $(x + 3y + 2)(3x + y + 7)$ e) $(c + 2d)(c - d)(2d - 3c)$ f) $[(s - 2t)(s + 2t)]^2$

Q2 Expand and simplify:

a) $(2x^2 + 7x - 8)(6x^2 - 5x - 10)$ b) $3p(q - 5r) + 4q(p + 2r) - 7r(2p - 3q)$

P M Q3 The length of the longest side of a cuboid-shaped box is x cm. The shortest side of the box is 10 cm shorter than the longest side, and the other side is 8 cm shorter than the longest side. Find an expression for the total volume of 5 of these boxes, in terms of x.
Your final answer should contain no brackets.

E Q4 Given that $p(x) = 3x^3 - 7x + 5$ and $q(x) = x^2 - 3x + 1$,
and $p(x) - (2 - 3x)q(x) \equiv ax^3 + bx^2 + cx + d$, find the values of a, b, c and d. *[3 marks]*

E P Q5 I think of a positive integer n which I multiply by 3 and then add the positive integer m to. This is then squared and $2mn$ is subtracted. Finally, this number is again squared to arrive at a positive integer N. Show that $N = 81n^4 + 9an^3m + bn^2m^2 + anm^3 + m^4$ where a and b are integers to be found. *[3 marks]*

E Q6 a) Expand $(2p + q)(p - 3)$. *[1 mark]*

b) Hence, or otherwise, fully factorise $q^3((6p - 18)p^5 + (3p - 9)p^4q)$. *[3 marks]*

Q7 Fully factorise each of the following expressions:

a) $2x^2y + axy + 2xy^2$ b) $a^2x + a^2b^2x^2$ c) $16y + 8yx + 56x$

d) $24s + 60st + 15s^2t^2$ e) $27c - 9c^3d - 45cd^2$ f) $x^2y^2z^2 + x^3y^3 - x^2yz$

Q8 Write each of the following expressions as a product of factors:

a) $(x + 1) - y(x + 1)$ b) $z^4 + z^2(3 - z)$ c) $(x + y)^2 + x(x + y)$

d) $x(x - 2) + 3(2 - x)$ e) $25 - x^4$ f) $9b^2c^4 - 4c^2d^6$

E P M Q9 Two different types of paving stone, types S and R, are used to make a short path.
The type S paving stones are square in shape with sides of length $(2x + 3)$ cm and the type R paving stones are rectangular and have dimensions $(2x + 3)$ cm and $(y + 2)$ cm.

Eight stones of type S are used to make the path, and twelve stones of type R are used to make the path.

a) Find a completely factorised and simplified expression for the area, A, of the path in terms of x and y. *[3 marks]*

b) Given that the area of the path is 24 800 cm^2 and the side-length of the type S stones is 40 cm, find the values of x and y. *[3 marks]*

Q10 Put the following expressions over a common denominator:

a) $\frac{2x}{3}+\frac{y}{12}+\frac{x}{5}$ b) $\frac{5}{xy^2}-\frac{2}{x^2y}$ c) $\frac{1}{x}+\frac{x}{x+y}+\frac{y}{x-y}$

d) $\frac{a}{b}+\frac{4}{a}-\frac{7}{a^2}$ e) $3x-\frac{4}{3xy}$ f) $\frac{2s}{t^2}+\frac{5}{2t}-\frac{t}{s^2}$

Q11 Simplify these expressions:

a) $\frac{2a}{b}-\frac{a}{2b}$ b) $\frac{2p}{p+q}+\frac{2q}{p-q}$ c) $\frac{c+d}{(c-d)^2}+\frac{1}{c+d}$

d) $\frac{1}{1+x}-\frac{1-x}{2x^2}$ e) $\frac{2k}{k^2-1}+\frac{k^2}{k-1}$ f) $\frac{4}{z+1}+\frac{2}{y+z}-\frac{6}{y-1}$

E Q12 Add the algebraic fractions $\frac{4}{3}+\frac{x+2}{x}+\frac{x-3}{5}$.
Express your answer as a single algebraic fraction, simplified as much as possible. *[3 marks]*

E Q13 Express as a single algebraic fraction $\frac{4}{5}\left(\frac{x+1}{x}\right)-\frac{1}{4}\left(\frac{1-2x}{3x+1}\right)$ *[3 marks]*

E Q14 Express as a single algebraic fraction $\frac{3}{x+1}-\frac{x+2}{(x+1)^2}-\frac{2x+1}{(x+1)^3}$ *[3 marks]*

P M Q15 The diagram on the right shows part of a garden.
The combined area of the lawn and flower bed is $3x^2$ m^2.
The area of the flower bed is x^2 m^2.
Show that y can be expressed as:

$$y=\frac{x^2(2x-15)}{(x+6)(x-3)}$$

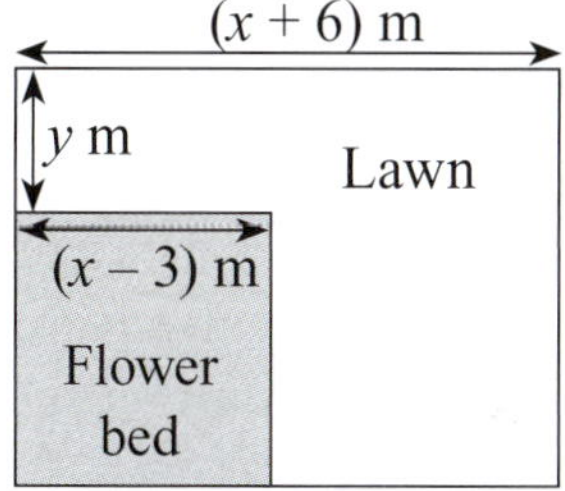

Q16 Simplify:

a) $x^3\times x^5$ b) $a^7\times a^8$ c) $\frac{x^8}{x^2}$

d) $(a^2)^4$ e) $(xy^2)(x^3yz)$ f) $\frac{a^2b^4c^6}{a^3b^2c}$

Q17 Simplify:

a) $g^2\times g^{-5}$ b) $p^4r^2\div p^5r^{-6}$ c) $(k^{\frac{1}{3}})^6$

d) $(mn^8\times m^4n^{-11})^{-2}$ e) $s^4t^3\times\left(\frac{1}{s^2t^5}\right)^{-3}$ f) $\frac{a^2}{b^2c}\times\frac{b^6}{a^4c^{-2}}\div\frac{c^2}{a^3b}$

E Q18 Fully simplify $\frac{(3a^2b^2)^2\times(2a^2b)^2}{(8a^6b^{-3})^{\frac{1}{3}}}$ *[2 marks]*

E P Q19 Find x such that:

a) $9^x=3$ *[1 mark]*

b) $9^{3x}\cdot 81^{2x-1}=27$ *[3 marks]*

Q20 Work out the following:

a) $16^{\frac{1}{2}}$ b) $8^{\frac{1}{3}}$ c) $81^{\frac{3}{4}}$

d) x^0 e) $49^{-\frac{1}{2}}$ f) $\frac{1}{27^{-\frac{2}{3}}}$

E P Q21 Show that $6^{\frac{1}{3}} + 6^{\frac{1}{3}} + 6^{\frac{1}{3}} = 2^p 3^q$, where p and q are constants to be found. *[2 marks]*

E Q22 Write the following expression in the form $a^p b^q$, where p and q are linear algebraic expressions:

$$\frac{(ab^5)^x}{a^y \sqrt{b^{3-2x}}}$$

[4 marks]

E P Q23 Given that x and y have prime factorisations $x = 2^{10} \times 3^6 \times 5^7 \times 11$ and $y = 2^8 \times 5^5 \times 7^{12} \times 11^8$, find the prime factorisation of $\sqrt[3]{xy}$. *[3 marks]*

Q24 Simplify:

a) $\sqrt{28}$ b) $\sqrt{\frac{5}{36}}$ c) $\sqrt{18}$ d) $\sqrt{\frac{9}{16}}$

Q25 Simplify the following expressions by writing them in the form $k\sqrt{x}$, where k and x are integers and x is as small as possible.

a) $\sqrt{3} - \sqrt{12}$ b) $3\sqrt{5} + \sqrt{45}$ c) $\sqrt{7} + \sqrt{448}$

d) $\sqrt{52} + \sqrt{117}$ e) $4\sqrt{150} + \sqrt{54} - \sqrt{5}\sqrt{120}$

P M Q26 The diagram on the right shows a shape which has been made by cutting a small square from one corner of a larger square. The area of the larger square was 1920 cm². The area of the smaller square was 1080 cm². Find the value of a. Give your answer in the form $k\sqrt{x}$, where k and x are integers and x is as small as possible.

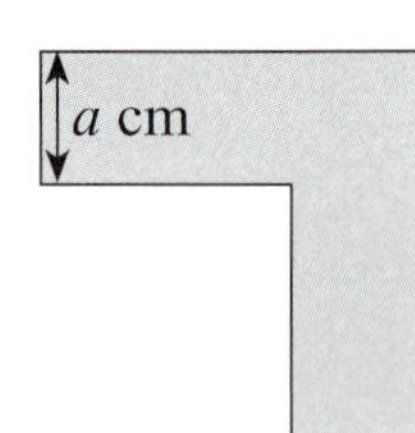

E P Q27 Three numbers are given as $5 - 2\sqrt{m}$, $10 + 9\sqrt{m}$ and $n\sqrt{m}$, where m and n are positive constants.

a) The mean of the three numbers is $5 + 4\sqrt{m}$. What is the value of n? *[2 marks]*

b) The range of the three numbers is $5 + 11\sqrt{m}$. What range of values can m take? *[5 marks]*

E P M Q28 A circular pond has circumference 10π m.
A circular path of width x m is going to be built around the pond.
There is 20π m² of surfacing material available for the path.

Find the maximum possible value of x, giving x in the form $a\sqrt{b} \pm c$, where a, b and c are integers to be found. *[6 marks]*

Q29 Find $(6\sqrt{3} + 2\sqrt{7})^2$.

E Q30 Express $(3\sqrt{5} - 5\sqrt{3})^2$ in the form $a(b + \sqrt{c})$ where a, b and c are integers. *[3 marks]*

Q31 Show that: a) $\frac{8}{\sqrt{2}} = 4\sqrt{2}$ b) $\frac{\sqrt{2}}{2} = \frac{1}{\sqrt{2}}$

Q32 Rationalise the denominator of $\frac{2}{3 + \sqrt{7}}$.

E Q33 a) Write $(2\sqrt{2} + \sqrt{3})^2$ in the form $a + b\sqrt{6}$ where a and b are integers. *[2 marks]*

b) Hence, or otherwise, rationalise the denominator of this expression:

$$\frac{1}{(2\sqrt{2} + \sqrt{3})^2}$$ *[2 marks]*

Q34 Write the following in the form $p + q\sqrt{r}$, where r is an integer, and p and q are integers or fractions:

a) $\frac{11 + \sqrt{13}}{5 - \sqrt{13}}$ b) $\frac{2\sqrt{7} + 9}{3 - \sqrt{7}}$ c) $\frac{3\sqrt{5} + \sqrt{15}}{\sqrt{60} - \sqrt{20}}$

E Q35 Fully simplify the number given by this expression:

$$\frac{(\sqrt{32} + \sqrt{128})^2}{\sqrt{5} + \sqrt{3}}$$ *[3 marks]*

E Q36 a) Show that $(a + b + c)(a - b - c) \equiv a^2 - b^2 - c^2 - 2bc$. *[2 marks]*

b) Hence, or otherwise, rationalise the denominator of:

$$\frac{1}{(\sqrt{11} + \sqrt{3} + \sqrt{2})(\sqrt{11} - \sqrt{3} - \sqrt{2})}$$

Give your answer in the form $\frac{p + \sqrt{q}}{q}$, where p and q are integers. *[3 marks]*

E Q37 a) Show that, for $x \neq \pm 1$:

$$\frac{1}{2(x - 1)} - \frac{1}{2(x + 1)} \equiv \frac{1}{x^2 - 1}$$ *[2 marks]*

b) Hence, or otherwise, find the exact value of $\frac{1}{\sqrt{32} - 2} - \frac{1}{\sqrt{32} + 2}$. *[2 marks]*

E Q38 Factorise the expression below. Write your answer in the form $p(x)q(x)$, where $p(x)$ and $q(x)$ are both quadratic expressions.

$$(2x^2 + 3x - 1)^2 - (x^2 + x + 3)^2$$ *[3 marks]*

E Q39 Simplify: $\frac{\sqrt{x}}{\sqrt{x} + \sqrt{y}} + \frac{\sqrt{y}}{\sqrt{x} - \sqrt{y}}$ *[3 marks]*

Challenge

E P Q40 Given $x, y > 0$ are integers such that $x \neq y$, and x, y and xy are **not** square numbers, find the value of k for which $(\sqrt{x}-\sqrt{y})(3\sqrt{x}+7\sqrt{y})+k\sqrt{x}(2\sqrt{y}+\sqrt{x})$ is rational. *[3 marks]*

E P Q41 Find the solution to the equation: $\left(\frac{5}{6}\right)^{x+3}=\left(\frac{125}{216}\right)^{x-4}$ *[4 marks]*

E Q42 Write the number given by the following expression as a fraction in its simplest terms:

$$\left(\frac{125}{64}\right)^{-\frac{1}{3}} \div \left(\frac{64}{49}\right)^{-\frac{1}{2}}$$

[4 marks]

E Q43 Solve the simultaneous equations:

$$3x+2y=23+5\sqrt{5}$$

$$\sqrt{5}x+y=12+4\sqrt{5}$$

[7 marks]

E P Q44 Given that $\frac{(\sqrt{2})^{4x}}{64^y}=2\left(\frac{1}{4}\right)^y \times 2^{7x}$,

a) show that $kx+(k-1)y+1=0$ for some integer k. *[3 marks]*

b) Hence, or otherwise, solve the simultaneous equations:

$$\frac{(\sqrt{2})^{4x}}{64^y}=2\left(\frac{1}{4}\right)^y \times 2^{7x}$$

$$2x+y=8$$

[3 marks]

E P Q45 Write the following in the form $a+b\sqrt{5}$, where a and b are rational numbers:

$$\sqrt{\frac{3-\sqrt{5}}{3+\sqrt{5}}}$$

[3 marks]

E P Q46 a) Express the following in the form $a+b\sqrt{3}$, where a and b are integers:

$$\frac{1-\sqrt{3}}{1+\sqrt{3}}$$

[2 marks]

b) Hence, or otherwise, show that $x=\frac{1-\sqrt{3}}{1+\sqrt{3}}$

is a solution to the quadratic equation $x^2+4x+1=0$. *[2 marks]*

c) Without further calculation, state the exact value of the second solution of the equation. *[1 mark]*

3 Chapter Summary

1 Expand double brackets by using the FOIL method: **F**irst **O**utside **I**nside **L**ast

2 Split squared brackets into double brackets and then expand: $(x + y)^2 = (x + y)(x + y)$

3 Expand long brackets by multiplying each term in the first set of brackets by each term in the second set.

4 When there are many brackets, expand them two at a time using the methods above.

5 A factor of a term is something that divides the term exactly — 1 and the term itself are always factors. A common factor of an expression is a factor that is in every term of the expression.

6 Factorise an expression by dividing each term by a common factor and writing the common factor outside of a set of brackets.

7 Watch out for the difference of two squares when factorising: $x^2 - y^2 = (x + y)(x - y)$

8 To add or subtract algebraic fractions, put them over a common denominator.

9 For any a, m and n: $a^m \times a^n = a^{m+n}$, $\frac{a^m}{a^n} = a^{m-n}$, $(a^m)^n = a^{mn}$, $a^0 = 1$

10 Indices can be negative and fractional: $a^{\frac{1}{m}} = \sqrt[m]{a}$, $a^{-m} = \frac{1}{a^m}$, $a^{\frac{m}{n}} = \sqrt[n]{a^m} = (\sqrt[n]{a})^m$

11 For any a and b: $\sqrt{ab} = \sqrt{a}\sqrt{b}$, $\sqrt{\frac{a}{b}} = \frac{\sqrt{a}}{\sqrt{b}}$, $a = (\sqrt{a})^2 = \sqrt{a}\sqrt{a}$

12 To rationalise the denominator of $\frac{1}{(a + \sqrt{b})}$, multiply the top and bottom by $a - \sqrt{b}$.

Quadratics and Cubics

4

Learning Objectives

Once you've completed this chapter, you should be able to:

- Solve quadratic equations by factorising, using the quadratic formula and completing the square.
- Identify the number of real roots of a quadratic function.
- Calculate the discriminant of a quadratic function and use it to solve problems.
- Sketch graphs of quadratic functions accurately.
- Factorise cubic expressions.
- Use the Factor Theorem to find factors of polynomials.
- Carry out simple algebraic division.

Prior Knowledge Check

1 Find the possible values of x for the following:

a) $x(x + 1) = 0$ b) $(x + 6)(x + 5) = 0$

c) $3x + 9 = 4$ d) $-6x \geq 12$ *see GCSE Maths*

2 Expand and simplify these expressions:

a) $4x(x^2 - 2x)$ b) $(p + 4)(p - 7)$ c) $(mn + 3)^2$ *see pages 16-17*

3 Expand $(1 + \sqrt{5})(1 - 2\sqrt{5})$, giving it in its simplest form. *see pages 28-29*

4.1 Factorising a Quadratic

Quadratic equations are equations of the general form: where a, b and c are constants (i.e. numbers) and $a \neq 0$.

$$ax^2 + bx + c = 0$$

Factorising a quadratic means putting it into two brackets called **factors** — the **solutions** to the equation can be easily worked out from these factors. There are **two cases** that you need to know: when $a = 1$, and when $a \neq 1$.

Factorising when $a = 1$

Fortunately, there's a step-by-step method you can follow when factorising this sort of quadratic:

To factorise a quadratic with $a = 1$:

1. Rearrange into the standard $ax^2 + bx + c$ form.
2. Write down the two **brackets**: $(x \quad)(x \quad)$
3. Find two numbers that **multiply** to give 'c' and **add/subtract** to give 'b' (ignoring signs).
4. Put the numbers in the brackets and choose their **signs**.

Tip All quadratics can be rearranged into this standard form — but not all will factorise. Methods of solving quadratics that don't factorise are covered later in this chapter.

This will all make more sense once you've seen a worked example...

Tip Be careful with the values of b and c — don't let the minus signs catch you out.

Example 1

Solve $x^2 - 8 = 2x$ by factorising.

$x^2 - 2x - 8 = 0$ — Subtract $2x$ from both sides to rearrange into standard $ax^2 + bx + c = 0$ form. So $a = 1$, $b = -2$, $c = -8$.

$x^2 - 2x - 8 = (x \quad)(x \quad)$ — Write down the two brackets with x's in. Since $a = 1$, you know that there will be an x in each bracket, which will multiply together to give x^2.

1 and 8 multiply to give 8 — and add / subtract to give 9 and 7.
2 and 4 multiply to give **8** — and add / subtract to give 6 and **2**.

Find two numbers that multiply together to make c but which also add or subtract to give b. You can ignore any minus signs for now.

These are the values for c and b you're after — so this is the right combination: 2 and 4.

$x^2 - 2x - 8 = (x \quad 2)(x \quad 4)$

$2 \times (-4) = -8$
$2 + (-4) = 2 - 4 = -2$

Now all you have to do is put in the plus or minus signs. It must be +2 and –4 because they multiply and add to give you the right values for c and b.

$x^2 - 2x - 8 = (x + 2)(x - 4)$

continued on the next page...

$(x + 2)(x - 4) = 0$ ← Now that you've factorised using the step-by-step method, you can use the factors to solve the equation.

$\Rightarrow x + 2 = 0$ or $x - 4 = 0$ ← The factors (brackets) multiply to give 0, so one of them **must** be 0.

$\Rightarrow x = -2$ or $x = 4$ ← Don't forget this last step. The factors aren't the answer.

Example 2

Solve $x^2 + 4x - 21 = 0$ by factorising.

$x^2 + 4x - 21 = (x \quad)(x \quad)$ ← It's already in the standard form, so start by writing down the brackets:

1 and 21 multiply to give 21
— and add / subtract to give 22 and 20.
3 and 7 multiply to give **21**
— and add / subtract to give 10 and **4**.

← These are the values you need, so 3 and 7 are the right numbers.

$x^2 + 4x - 21 = (x \quad 3)(x \quad 7)$

$7 + (-3) = 4$
$7 \times (-3) = -21$

$x^2 + 4x - 21 = (x - 3)(x + 7)$

← c is negative so we need opposite signs. The signs must be –3 and +7 because $7 - 3 = 4$ and $7 \times (-3) = -21$

$(x - 3)(x + 7) = 0$

$\Rightarrow x = 3$ or $x = -7$

← Solve the equation to find x. If two things multiply together to give 0, one of them must be equal to 0.

Factorising when $a \neq 1$

The basic method's the same as before — but it can be a bit more awkward.

To factorise a quadratic with $a \neq 1$:

1. Rearrange into the standard $ax^2 + bx + c$ form.
2. Write down the two **brackets**, but instead of just having x in each, you need two things that will multiply to **give** ax^2:
   $(nx \quad)(mx \quad)$
   where n and m are two numbers that **multiply** to give a.
3. Find two numbers that **multiply** to give 'c' but which will give you bx when you **multiply** them by nx and mx, and then **add / subtract** them.
4. Put the numbers in the brackets and choose their **signs**.

Problem Solving

In practice, this third step involves working through all possible cases until you get it right.

Again, a worked example will help.

Example 3

Solve $3x^2 + 4x - 15 = 0$.

$3x^2 + 4x - 15 = (3x \quad)(x \quad)$

This quadratic's already in the standard form so you don't need to rearrange it.

As before, write down two brackets — but instead of just having x in each, you need two things that will multiply to give $3x^2$.

$(3x \quad 1)(x \quad 15) \Rightarrow x$ and $45x$
which then add or subtract to give $46x$ and $44x$.

$(3x \quad 15)(x \quad 1) \Rightarrow 15x$ and $3x$
which then add or subtract to give $18x$ and $12x$.

$(3x \quad 3)(x \quad 5) \Rightarrow 3x$ and $15x$
which then add or subtract to give $18x$ and $12x$.

$(3x \quad 5)(x \quad 3) \Rightarrow 5x$ and $9x$
which then add or subtract to give $14x$ and $\mathbf{4x}$.

You need to find two numbers that multiply together to make 15 — but which will give you $4x$ when you multiply them by x and $3x$, and then add / subtract them.

It's a good idea to write out the brackets for each possible number combination — it makes it easier to see if you've got the right numbers.

This is the value you're after — so this is the right combination.

$(3x \quad 5)(x \quad 3) = 3x^2 + 4x - 15$

$9x - 5x = 4x$
$-5 \times 3 = -15$

'c' is negative — that means the signs in the brackets are opposite. You've only got two choices for the signs of the numbers, –5 and 3 or 5 and –3. If you're unsure which it is, just multiply each case out to see which is right.

$(3x - 5)(x + 3) = 3x^2 + 4x - 15$

$(3x - 5)(x + 3) = 0 \Rightarrow x = \frac{5}{3}$ or $x = -3$

Solve the equation to find x.

Exercise 4.1

Q1 Factorise the following expressions.

a) $x^2 - 6x + 5$ b) $x^2 - 3x - 18$
c) $x^2 + 22x + 121$ d) $x^2 - 12x$
e) $y^2 - 13y + 42$ f) $x^2 + 51x + 144$
g) $x^2 - 121$ h) $x^2 - 35x + 66$

Q1 Hint

If b or c is zero, use the factorising methods from Chapter 3. For d), you can't just divide by x — you would miss the solution $x = 0$ when solving.

Q2 Solve the following equations.

a) $x^2 - 3x - 10 = 0$ b) $2x^2 + 2x - 40 = 0$
c) $p^2 + 21p + 38 = 0$ d) $x^2 - 15x + 54 = 0$
e) $x^2 + 18x = -65$ f) $x^2 - x = 42$
g) $x^2 + 1100x + 100\,000 = 0$ h) $3x^2 - 3x - 6 = 0$

Problem Solving

Look out for questions where the equation can be simplified before factorising — for example by dividing through by a number.

Q3 Factorise the following expressions.

a) $4x^2 - 4x - 3$ b) $2x^2 + 23x + 11$ c) $7x^2 - 19x - 6$ d) $-x^2 - 5x + 36$
e) $6x^2 - 7x - 3$ f) $2x^2 - 2$ g) $3x^2 - 3$ h) $-x^2 + 9x - 14$

Q4 Solve the following equations.

a) $-5x^2 - 22x + 15 = 0$ b) $32x^2 + 60x + 13 = 0$ c) $5a^2 + 12a = 9$

d) $8x^2 + 22x + 15 = 0$ e) $4q^2 + 6 = 11q$ f) $24y^2 + 23y - 12 = 0$

Q5 Solve $(x - 1)(x - 2) = 37 - x$.

E Q6 a) Factorise the quadratic expression $2x^2 - x - 15$. *[1 mark]*

b) Hence, or otherwise, solve the equation $2x^2 - x - 15 = (x + 7)(x - 3)$. *[3 marks]*

P Q7 $f(x) = -x^2 + 7x + 30$.
Find the x-coordinates of the point or points at which the graph of $f(x)$ meets the x-axis.

P Q8 $f(x) = (x - 8)(x + 10)$ and $g(x) = (3x + 2)(x - 11)$.
Find the x-coordinates of the points of intersection of the two functions.

Problem Solving
Solve for x where $f(x) = g(x)$.

E P Q9 A rectangle has a length of $(3x + 1)$ m and a width of $(2x - 3)$ m.
Given that the area of the rectangle is 2 m^2,
find the exact length and width of the rectangle. *[4 marks]*

M Q10 In a scientific experiment, the temperature, T °C, is modelled by the equation $T = -2h^2 + 13h - 20$, where h is the time in hours from the start of the experiment.
Find both times at which the temperature is 0 °C.

P Q11 Factorise $x^2 + 6xy + 8y^2$.

P Q12 The perimeter of a square is $(2z + 5)$ cm.
Find the possible values of z if the area of the square is $\frac{9z}{2}$ cm^2.

Challenge

P Q13 The area of the triangle shown on the right is $(9x + 3)$ m^2.

By solving a quadratic equation to find x, find the exact length of the hypotenuse.

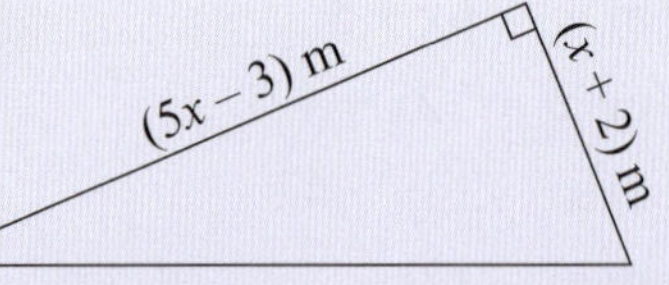

E P Q14 a) The quadratic $p(x) = 18x^2 + 39x - 70$ has roots a and b, where $b < a$.
Find the values of a and b. *[2 marks]*

A second expression $q(x) = 9x^2 + rx + s$ has roots $2a - 2$ and $b + 4$.

b) Express $q(x)$ in a factorised form. *[2 marks]*

Q15 a) Factorise the quadratic $10x^2 - 7\sqrt{15}x - 12$.

b) Hence, find the exact solutions of the equation $10x^2 - 7\sqrt{15}x - 12 = 0$, giving your answers as single fractions with rational denominators.

4.2 The Quadratic Formula

You should now be comfortable with solving quadratics by factorising.
But there are two important points to bear in mind:

- The expression **won't** always factorise.
- Sometimes factorising is so messy that it's **easier** to just use other methods.

So if the question doesn't tell you to factorise, **don't assume** it will factorise.

Example 1

Solve $6x^2 + 87x - 144 = 0$.

$(6x \quad)(x \quad)$ or $(3x \quad)(2x \quad)$

For each of these, there are 8 possible ways of making 144 to try.

This will actually factorise, but there are 2 possible bracket forms to try.

If you tried to factorise this example, you'd be going all day. Luckily, there's a formula which will work out the **solutions** of a quadratic equation, even when you can't factorise — it's known as **the quadratic formula**.

If $ax^2 + bx + c = 0$ then:

$$x = \frac{-b \pm \sqrt{b^2 - 4ac}}{2a}$$

Example 2

Solve the quadratic equation $3x^2 - 4x = 8$, leaving your answer in surd form.

$3x^2 - 4x = 8$

$\Rightarrow 3x^2 - 4x - 8 = 0$

$a = 3 \quad b = -4 \quad c = -8$

$$x = \frac{-b \pm \sqrt{b^2 - 4ac}}{2a}$$

$$x = \frac{-(-4) \pm \sqrt{(-4)^2 - 4 \times 3 \times (-8)}}{2 \times 3}$$

$$x = \frac{4 \pm \sqrt{16 + 96}}{6}$$

continued on the next page...

The mention of surds in the question suggests that the quadratic will be too hard to factorise, so we'll use the quadratic formula instead.

Get the equation in the standard $ax^2 + bx + c = 0$ form.

Write down the coefficients a, b and c — making sure you don't forget minus signs.

Very carefully, plug these numbers into the formula.

It's best to write down each stage of the simplification as you do it.

Problem Solving

If the question asks you to give your answer in surd form or as a decimal, that's a big hint to use the quadratic formula instead of trying to factorise.

Tip

If any of the coefficients in your quadratic equation are negative, be especially careful. There are a couple of minus signs in the formula which can catch you out if you're not paying attention.

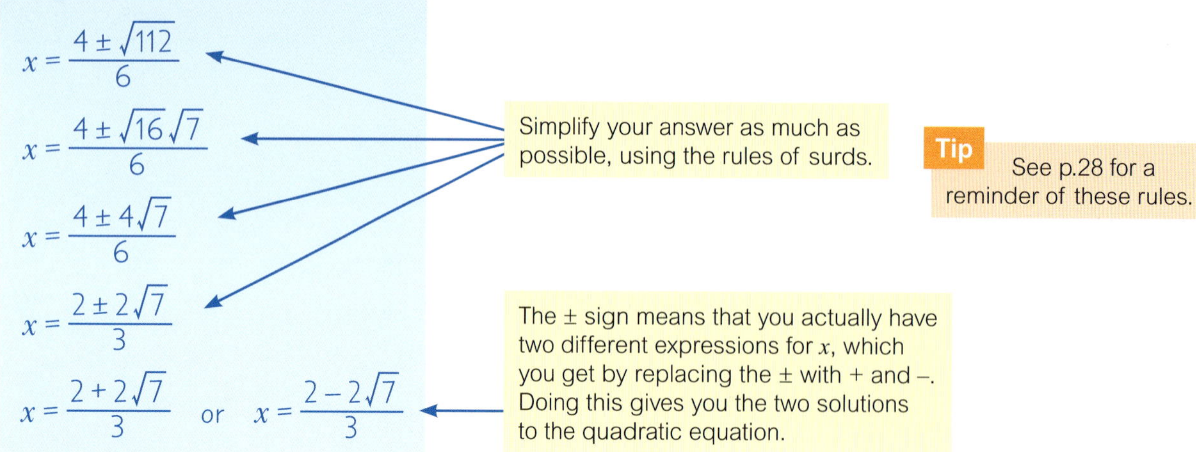

Tip See p.28 for a reminder of these rules.

Example 3

Solve the quadratic equation $2x^2 = 4x + 3$, leaving your answer in the form $p \pm q\sqrt{r}$ where p, q and r are whole numbers or fractions.

$2x^2 = 4x + 3$

$\Rightarrow 2x^2 - 4x - 3 = 0$

Get the equation in the standard $ax^2 + bx + c = 0$ form.

$a = 2 \quad b = -4 \quad c = -3$

$$x = \frac{-b \pm \sqrt{b^2 - 4ac}}{2a}$$

$$x = \frac{-(-4) \pm \sqrt{(-4)^2 - 4 \times 2 \times (-3)}}{2 \times 2}$$

Plug the values of a, b and c into the quadratic formula.

$$x = \frac{4 \pm \sqrt{16 + 24}}{4} = \frac{4 \pm \sqrt{40}}{4} = \frac{4 \pm 2\sqrt{10}}{4}$$

$$x = \frac{2 \pm \sqrt{10}}{2} = \frac{2}{2} \pm \frac{1}{2}\sqrt{10} = 1 \pm \frac{1}{2}\sqrt{10}$$

Using a calculator

You can also use a **graphical calculator** to solve quadratic equations. There are two different ways to do this:

- Use the calculator to **plot** the graph of the quadratic, then work out where it crosses the x-axis — these values of x are the solutions to $f(x) = 0$ (there's more about this on pages 54-59).
- Some calculators will allow you to **solve** quadratic equations directly — enter the values for a, b and c, and it'll give you the solutions.

Tip Different calculators work in different ways — make sure you know how to do this on your calculator.

In each case, you'll have to make sure your equation is in the **standard form** ($ax^2 + bx + c$). Be careful though — sometimes your calculator will only give you one solution (even if there are two), and it won't usually give answers in surd form.

Exercise 4.2

Q1 Solve the following equations using the quadratic formula, giving your answers in surd form where necessary.

a) $x^2 - 4x = -2$
b) $x^2 - 2x - 44 = 0$
c) $x^2 + 3x = 12$
d) $x^2 - 14x + 42 = 0$
e) $4x^2 + 4x - 1 = 0$
f) $-x^2 + 4x - 3 = 0$
g) $x^2 - \frac{5}{6}x + \frac{1}{6} = 0$
h) $x^2 - 2\sqrt{11}x + 11 = 0$

Q1 Hint Have a go at solving these equations using a calculator too.

Q2 a) Multiply out $(x - 2 + \sqrt{5})(x - 2 - \sqrt{5})$.
b) Solve the equation $x^2 - 4x - 1 = 0$ using the quadratic formula.
c) How does your answer to b) relate to the expression given in a)?

Q3 The roots of the equation $x^2 + 8x + 13 = 0$ can be written in the form $x = \text{A} \pm \sqrt{\text{B}}$ where A and B are integers. Find A and B.

Q4 Solve the following equations, giving your answers in surd form where necessary.

a) $x^2 + x + \frac{1}{4} = 0$
b) $x^2 - \frac{7}{4}x + \frac{2}{3} = 0$
c) $25x^2 - 30x + 7 = 0$
d) $60x - 5 = -100x^2 - 3$
e) $2x(x - 4) = 7 - 3x$
f) $(3x - 5)(x + 2) = 3x - 2$

Q5 a) Show that the solutions to the equation $\frac{3x-5}{x-1} = \frac{x+3}{x+2}$ also satisfy the equation $2x^2 - x - 7 = 0$.
b) Hence, solve $\frac{3x-5}{x-1} = \frac{x+3}{x+2}$, giving your answers in surd form.

E Q6 Find the exact solutions to the equation $\frac{x}{3x-2} = \frac{4}{x-3} + 1$. *[4 marks]*

E P M Q7 The height, h metres, of a ball above a level playing field is given by the equation $h = 10t - 5t^2$, where t is the time in seconds after the ball is kicked.
a) Find the time of the first bounce of the ball. *[2 marks]*
b) Find the length of time, to the nearest tenth of a second, that the ball is at least 3 metres above the ground before its first bounce. *[3 marks]*

Challenge

P Q8 One of the roots of the equation $kx^2 + 4x - 2 = 0$ is $x = \frac{\sqrt{14}}{5} - \frac{2}{5}$.
Find k, and state the exact value of the other root.

P M Q9 A shopper leaves a supermarket at 2 pm and walks home, which is 1 km away. The walk can be modelled by the equation $d = 2t^2 - 5t + 1$, where d is their distance from home in km, and t is the time taken in hours. At what time, to the nearest minute, will they arrive home?

E P Q10 The surface area of a closed cylinder is 200 cm^2. The height of the cylinder is 14 cm. Find the radius of the cylinder to the nearest tenth of a centimetre. *[4 marks]*

4.3 Completing the Square

You could be asked to **solve** a quadratic equation by **completing the square** so you need to know this method just as well as the others.

And what's more — it gives you loads of **useful information** about the quadratic, which will come in really handy when you're asked to sketch the graph of the quadratic (see p.51-53, 59-60).

Completing the square just means writing a quadratic expression $ax^2 + bx + c$ in the form: $a(x + p)^2 + q$

- Basically, the '**square**' is this bit: $a(x + p)^2$
- p is chosen so that it will produce the correct x^2 and x terms when the square is multiplied out. $p = \frac{b}{2a}$
- But this square won't always give the right constant term — so you need to '**complete**' it by adding another number, q. $q = c - \frac{b^2}{4a}$
- The completed square expression is the **same** as the original quadratic. $a(x + \frac{b}{2a})^2 + \left(c - \frac{b^2}{4a}\right)$

Tip You don't need to memorise the completed square form of a general quadratic. It's often easier to just work it out when you know the numbers.

The method can seem complicated at first, but is actually very simple when you get it. As always, working through examples is the best way to learn it.

When a = 1

We'll start with the slightly easier case of $a = 1$ — it's easier because p always equals $\frac{b}{2}$.

Example 1

Rewrite $x^2 + 6x + 3$ by completing the square.

$(x + 3)^2$ ← First, write down a square of the form $(x + p)^2$. Choose p so that when you multiply the square out you get the correct x^2 and x terms — 3 is just half the coefficient of x, i.e. $\frac{b}{2}$.

$(x + 3)^2 = x^2 + 6x + 9$ ← The square multiplies out to give $x^2 + 6x + 9$ but we need the constant term to be +3.

$x^2 + 6x + 3 = (x + 3)^2 - 6$ ← Subtract 6 from the square to match the original quadratic.

It's a good idea to always check that your answer multiplies out to give the expression that you started with. For the example above:

$(x + 3)^2 - 6 = x^2 + 3x + 3x + 9 - 6 = x^2 + 6x + 3$ ✔

Example 2

Rewrite $x^2 - 5x - 1$ by completing the square.

$\left(x - \frac{5}{2}\right)^2$ ← Again, start by writing down the square. This example has a negative coefficient of x — so make sure you have a minus sign in the brackets. Remember, the number in the brackets is just $\frac{b}{2}$.

$\left(x - \frac{5}{2}\right)^2 = x^2 - 5x + \frac{25}{4}$ ← The square multiplies out to give $x^2 - 5x + \frac{25}{4}$ but we need the constant term to be –1, so subtract the $\frac{25}{4}$ and then 'add' –1.

$\left(x - \frac{5}{2}\right)^2 - \frac{25}{4} - 1$

$x^2 - 5x - 1 = \left(x - \frac{5}{2}\right)^2 - \frac{29}{4}$ ← Simplify the number.

Tip You can always find the number that completes the square by subtracting off the number term you get from multiplying out the bracket and adding on the number term from the original quadratic.

You can check your answer by multiplying out the brackets:

$$\left(x - \frac{5}{2}\right)^2 - \frac{29}{4} = x^2 - \frac{5}{2}x - \frac{5}{2}x + \frac{25}{4} - \frac{29}{4} = x^2 - 5x - 1 \checkmark$$

When $a \neq 1$

In cases where a is not 1, you have to put a outside of the squared bracket, and allow for this when choosing the number to go inside the bracket — this means that $p = \frac{b}{2a}$.

Example 3

Rewrite $2x^2 + 3x - 5$ by completing the square.

$2\left(x + \frac{3}{4}\right)^2$ ← Start by writing the square. $a = 2$ so it will be of the form $2(x + p)^2$. The number p is always the coefficient of x divided by $2a$, i.e. $\frac{b}{2a}$.

$2\left(x + \frac{3}{4}\right)^2 = 2x^2 + 3x + \frac{9}{8}$ ← The square multiplies out to give $2x^2 + 3x + \frac{9}{8}$, but we need the constant term to be –5, so subtract the $\frac{9}{8}$ and then 'add on' –5.

$2\left(x + \frac{3}{4}\right)^2 - \frac{9}{8} - 5$

$2x^2 + 3x - 5 = 2\left(x + \frac{3}{4}\right)^2 - \frac{49}{8}$ ← Simplify the number. (If the constant terms are fractions, don't forget to put them over a common denominator before you try to add / subtract them.)

Multiply out the brackets to check your answer:

$$2\left(x + \frac{3}{4}\right)^2 - \frac{49}{8} = 2\left(x^2 + \frac{3}{2}x + \frac{9}{16}\right) - \frac{49}{8} = 2x^2 + 3x + \frac{9}{8} - \frac{49}{8} = 2x^2 + 3x - 5 \checkmark$$

Example 4

> **Problem Solving** If it helps, rewrite the expression in the standard form $ax^2 + bx + c$.

Rewrite $3 - 4x - x^2$ by completing the square.

$-(x + 2)^2$ — Again, start by writing the square. Here $a = -1$. The number in the brackets is just $\frac{b}{2a}$ again.

$-(x + 2)^2 = -x^2 - 4x - 4$

$3 - 4x - x^2 = -(x + 2)^2 + 7$ — The square multiplies out to give $-x^2 - 4x - 4$ but we want the constant to be +3, so add 7 to the square to make it match the original quadratic.

Now you can check your answer:

$-(x + 2)^2 + 7 = -(x^2 + 4x + 4) + 7 = -x^2 - 4x - 4 + 7 = -x^2 - 4x + 3$ $(= 3 - 4x - x^2)$ ✔

Once you've completed the square, a quadratic equation becomes very easy to **solve**:

- Take the **constant term** to the other side of the equals sign.
- Take the square root of both sides — don't forget the **negative** square root.
- **Rearrange** to find the solutions.

> **Tip** When you take the square root of something, you need to put a ± sign in front of the $\sqrt{\ }$ sign.

Example 5

Solve $3 - 4x - x^2 = 0$ by completing the square.

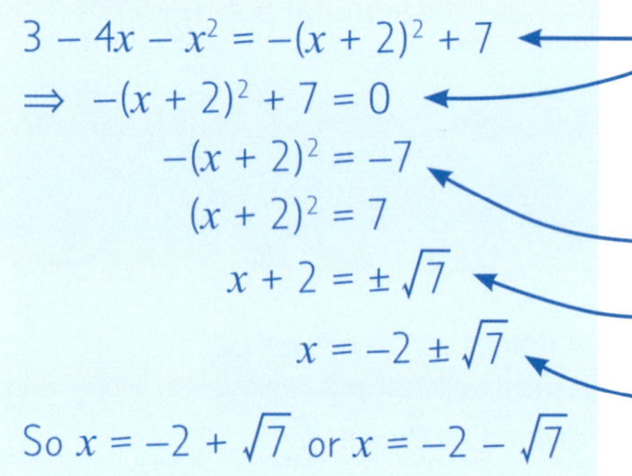

From Example 4, you can write $3 - 4x - x^2$ as $-(x + 2)^2 + 7$ by completing the square. So now all you need to do is set this equal to zero and rearrange.

Take the constant to the other side.

Take a square root — don't forget the ± sign.

Subtract 2 from both sides.

Exercise 4.3

Q1 Solve the following equations, leaving your answer in surd form where appropriate:

a) $(x + 4)^2 = 25$ b) $(2x + 5)^2 = 9$ c) $(5x - 3)^2 = 21$

> **Q1 Hint** In these questions you don't need to complete the square — they'll just give you practice at the 'solving' bit.

Q2 Rewrite the following expressions in the form $p(x + q)^2 + r$:

a) $x^2 + 6x + 8$ b) $x^2 + 8x - 10$ c) $x^2 - 3x - 10$

d) $x^2 - 20x + 15$ e) $x^2 - 2mx + n$ f) $x^2 + 6tx + s$

g) $3x^2 - 12x + 7$ h) $2x^2 - 4x - 3$ i) $6x^2 + 30x - 20$

j) $-x^2 - 9x + 9$ k) $4x^2 - 22x + 5$ l) $-3x^2 + 9x + 1$

Q3 Solve the following equations by completing the square:

a) $x^2 - 6x - 16 = 0$ b) $p^2 - 10p = 200$ c) $x^2 + 2x + k = 0$

d) $x^2 + 4x - 8 = 0$ e) $4x^2 + 24x - 13 = 0$ f) $9x^2 + 18x = 16$

g) $2x^2 - 12x + 9 = 0$ h) $2x^2 - 12x - 54 = 0$ i) $5x^2 + 10x = 1$

j) $-3x^2 - 18x + 2 = 0$ k) $3x^2 + 2x = \frac{7}{6}$ l) $5x^2 - 3x + \frac{2}{5} = 0$

P Q4 By completing the square, show that the expression $3x^2 - 12x + 14$ is positive for all x.

Challenge

P Q5 By completing the square, show that the solutions to $ax^2 + bx + c = 0$ are $x = \frac{-b \pm \sqrt{b^2 - 4ac}}{2a}$.

4.4 Quadratics Involving Functions of x

Sometimes you'll be asked to solve an equation that doesn't look like a quadratic — it might involve different powers of x, or functions like sin x or e^x. However, as long as it's in the form **a(something)^2 + b(something) + c**, you can solve it like a normal quadratic. Instead of 'x = ', you'll be left with 'something = ', which you'll then have to solve.

The way to solve these equations is:

- Identify the function of x, and replace it with a different letter, say u.
- Solve the resulting quadratic equation for u.
- Replace u with the original function, and solve it to find x.

This will make more sense with a worked example:

Tip There's more on solving trig equations in Chapter 8, and on solving exponential equations in Chapter 9.

Example 1 

Solve the equation $x^{\frac{2}{3}} + 3x^{\frac{1}{3}} - 40 = 0$.

Take $u = x^{\frac{1}{3}}$, so $u^2 = x^{\frac{2}{3}}$

So the equation can be written as:
$u^2 + 3u - 40 = 0$, where $u = x^{\frac{1}{3}}$.

$u^2 + 3u - 40 = 0 \Rightarrow (u + 8)(u - 5) = 0$
So $u = -8$ or $u = 5$.

Now solve this quadratic — luckily it factorises.

$x^{\frac{1}{3}} = -8$, so $x = (-8)^3 = -512$ or
$x^{\frac{1}{3}} = 5$, so $x = 5^3 = 125$

Finally, substitute $x^{\frac{1}{3}}$ back into the equations and solve for x.

Problem Solving To treat this as a quadratic, you need to find a function of x, $u = f(x)$, that allows you to rewrite the equation in the form $au^2 + bu + c = 0$.

Exercise 4.4

P Q1 Find an expression for u, in terms of x, that allows you to write each equation below in the form $au^2 + bu + c = 0$. You do **not** need to solve the resulting equations.

a) $2x + 4x^{\frac{1}{2}} - 7 = 0$ b) $3^x(3^x - 6) = 8$

c) $5^x + 5^{2x} = 4$ d) $2\cos^2 x + 3 = 5\cos x$

Problem Solving

The tricky part of these questions is choosing a suitable substitution $u = \text{f}(x)$. Most of the time $\text{f}(x)$ will be a function of x that you can see in the original equation.

P Q2 a) Rewrite the equation $x^2 + 6x + 7$ in the form $(x + m)^2 + n$.

b) Hence solve the equation $(2x + 1)^2 + 6(2x + 1) + 7 = 0$. Leave your answers in surd form.

E P Q3 a) Solve the quadratic equation $2x^2 + 3x - 9 = 0$. *[2 marks]*

b) Hence, find all real solutions to the equation $2x^4 + 3x^2 - 9 = 0$. Give your answers in the form $p\sqrt{q}$, where p is a rational number and q is an integer. *[3 marks]*

P Q4 Using a suitable substitution, find the exact solutions to $3(x - 2)^2 - 2(x - 2) - 6 = 0$. Give your answers as single fractions.

P Q5 Find all four solutions to the equation $x^4 - 17x^2 + 16 = 0$.

P Q6 Solve the equations:

a) $\dfrac{3}{(5x+2)^2} + \dfrac{1}{5x+2} = 10$ b) $3x + \sqrt{x} = 14$

E P Q7 a) Show that $(2x^2 + x + 3)(2x^2 - x + 3) \equiv 4x^4 + 11x^2 + 9$. *[2 marks]*

b) Hence, find the exact solutions to the equation $(2x^2 + x + 3)(2x^2 - x + 3) = 12$. *[3 marks]*

E P Q8 a) Show that the substitution $u = 2^x$ transforms the equation $2^{2x+1} - 33(2^x) + 16 = 0$ into the quadratic equation $2u^2 - 33u + 16 = 0$. *[2 marks]*

b) Hence, solve the equation $2^{2x+1} - 33(2^x) + 16 = 0$. *[3 marks]*

E P Q9 Given that $x \geq 0$, find all solutions to the equation $8x^3 - 117x^{\frac{3}{2}} - 125 = 0$. *[3 marks]*

Challenge

P M Q10 An ornithologist predicts the increase in population of a bird species in a coastal area using the equation: $p = 5y^3 - y^6$, where p is the population growth in 1000s of birds, and y is the time from now in 100s of years. Using this model, what is the shortest time it would take, to the nearest year, for there to be 1000 more birds in the area?

E P Q11 Find the solutions to the equation $2x - 9\sqrt{x} + 5 = 0$. Give your answers in the form $a + b\sqrt{41}$, where a and b are rational numbers. *[4 marks]*

4.5 The Roots of a Quadratic Function

Quadratic functions are just functions of the form $f(x) = ax^2 + bx + c$. Their graphs all have the same **general shape**, no matter what the values of a, b and c are. This general shape is called a **parabola**. Parabolas are either '**u**'-shaped or '**n**'-shaped:

Tip You'll see how to draw graphs of quadratic functions later in the chapter.

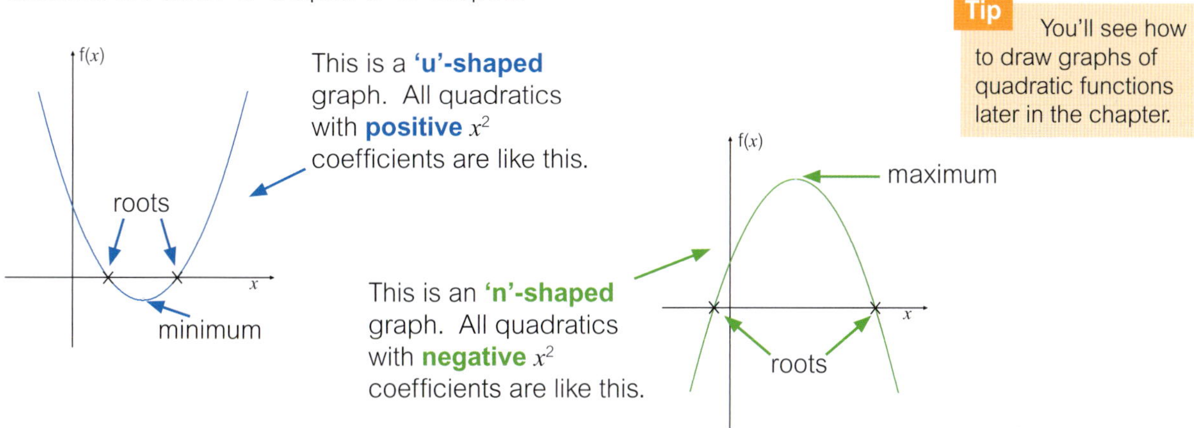

The **roots** of a quadratic function are the values of x where the function $f(x)$ is equal to **zero** — i.e. where the graph **crosses the x-axis**. They are the **solutions** to the quadratic equation $f(x) = 0$. The functions above each have 2 roots because their graphs cross the x-axis twice.

A quadratic function may have **0**, **1** or **2 roots**. You'll see two methods for finding out which it is — **completing the square** and using the **discriminant**.

Using the completed square

If you've already **completed the square**, you can easily work out the number of roots by examining the completed square.

The function will look like this: $\mathbf{f(x) = p(x + q)^2 + r}$

The key to this method is remembering that anything squared is ≥ 0.

So, let's assume for now that p is positive:

- Since p is **positive**, the graph will be **u-shaped** and have a minimum.
- The smallest value that $f(x)$ can take will occur when the bracket is 0 (since the square is ≥ 0). At that point $f(x)$ is just r, and x must be $-q$.
- So the minimum is $\mathbf{(-q, r)}$. This also tells you that the graph of $f(x)$ has a **line of symmetry** at $\mathbf{x = -q}$.

Now the **value of r** tells us the number of roots — the number of times the graph crosses the x-axis depends on whether the minimum is above, below or on the axis.

- If $r < 0$, the minimum is below the x-axis, so the graph must cross the axis twice — meaning there are **two roots**. (Picture the u-shaped graph.)
- If $r > 0$, the graph is always above the x-axis — so there are **no roots**.
- If $r = 0$, the minimum point is on the x-axis, so there's **one root**.

Next, we'll see what happens when p is negative:

$f(x) = p(x + q)^2 + r$

- Since p is **negative**, the graph will be **n-shaped** and have a **maximum**.
- And also because p is negative, the highest value of $p(x + q)^2$ will be when the bracket is 0. At that point $f(x)$ is just r, and x is $-q$.
- So the maximum is $(-q, r)$. Again, this tells you that the graph has a **line of symmetry** at $x = -q$.

Tip The coordinates of the maximum are actually just the same as those we found for the minimum: $(-q, r)$.

Look at the **value of r** to work out the number of roots.

- If $r < 0$, the graph is always below the x-axis — so there are **no roots**.
- If $r > 0$, the maximum is above the x-axis, so the graph must cross the axis twice, meaning there are **two roots**.
- If $r = 0$, the maximum point is on the x-axis, so there's **one root**.

Let's see what this all means for a few functions.

Two real roots

$y = x^2 - 6x + 8$

- The completed square is $(x - 3)^2 - 1$.
- The minimum is $(3, -1)$, which is below the x-axis.
- So there are two roots ($x = 2$ and $x = 4$).

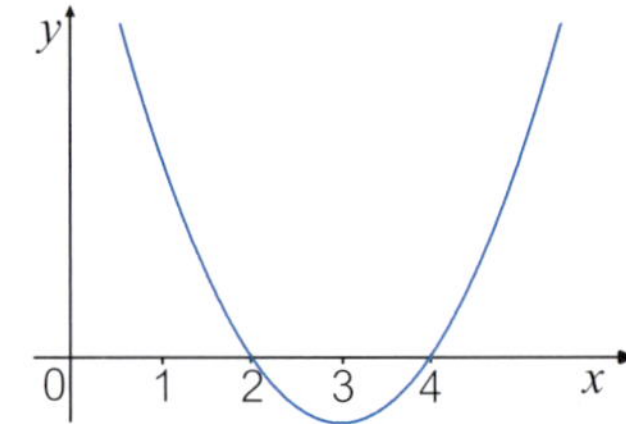

Tip Remember, real numbers are just all the rational and irrational numbers. Look at p.54 for an explanation of what is meant by 'real' roots.

One real root

$y = x^2 - 6x + 9$

- The completed square is $(x - 3)^2$.
- The minimum is $(3, 0)$, so the graph just touches the x-axis.
- $x = 3$ is the only root.

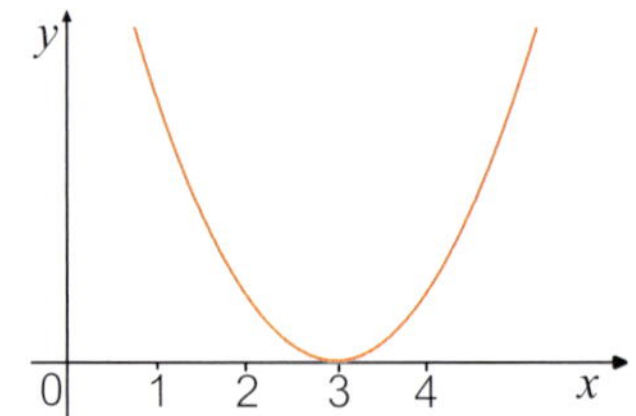

Tip When you're factorising a quadratic equation, if both factors come out the same, in this case $(x - 3)(x - 3)$, the function has one root. We call this one **repeated** root.

No real roots

$y = x^2 - 6x + 10$

- The completed square is $(x - 3)^2 + 1$.
- The minimum is $(3, 1)$, which is above the x-axis.
- So the graph never touches the x-axis, and there are no roots.

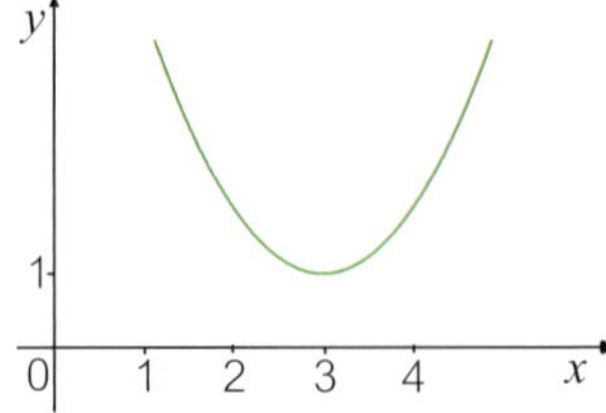

All the different cases we've covered can actually be summarised in these three simple rules:

For a quadratic function of the form $f(x) = p(x + q)^2 + r$:
- If p and r have **different signs**, the function has **two** real roots.
- If $r = 0$ then the function has **one** real root.
- If p and r have the **same sign**, the function has **no** real roots.

Example 1

How many real roots does the quadratic function $f(x) = x^2 + 4x + 7$ have?

$f(x) = p(x + q)^2 + r = (x + 2)^2 + 3$ ← Completing the square, you can rewrite the function in the form $f(x) = p(x + q)^2 + r$:

$p = 1$ and $r = 3$ are of the same sign, so the function has no real roots. ← You can see why this works using the following argument:
The smallest $(x + 2)^2$ can be is zero (at $x = -2$).
The number added on (3) is positive.

If a quadratic function has no real roots, then:

a) The graph of $f(x)$ never crosses the x-axis, so

b) $f(x)$ is either always negative or always positive.

Exercise 4.5

Q1 How many real roots does each quadratic function have?

a) 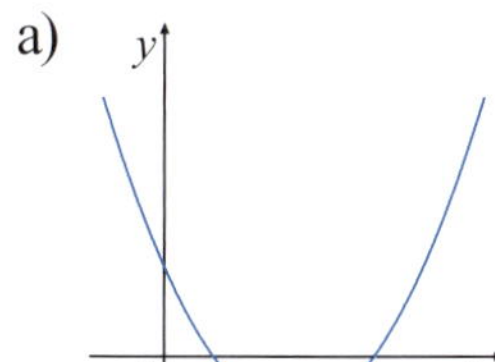

b) 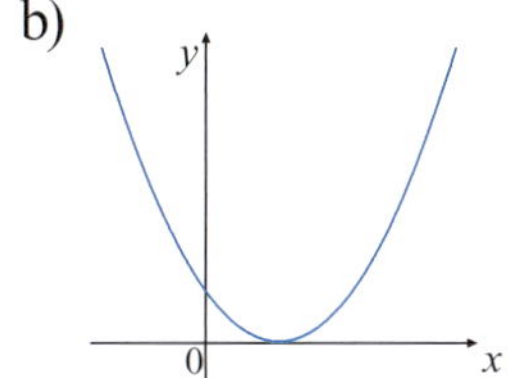

c) 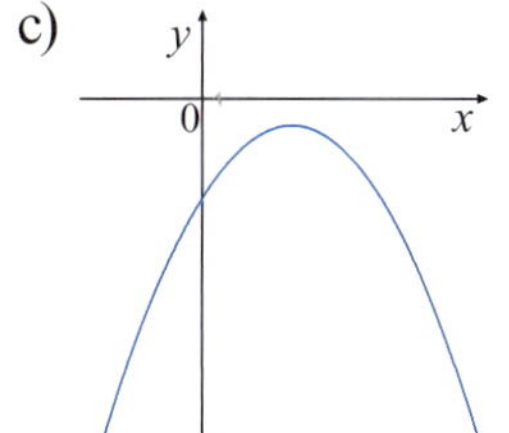

d) 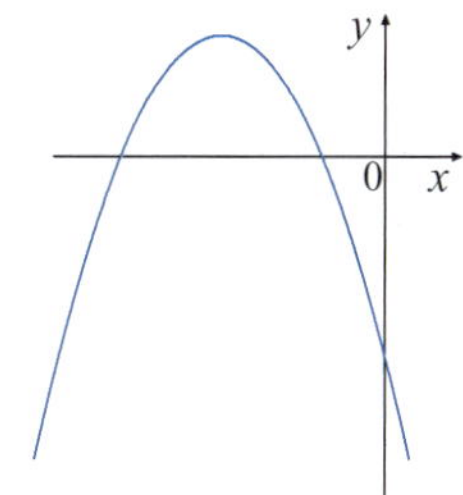

Q2 Express $f(x) = x^2 + 6x + 10$ in the form $f(x) = (x + q)^2 + r$, where q and r are positive or negative constants. Using your answer, state whether $f(x)$ has any real roots and give the equations of any lines of symmetry of the graph of $f(x)$.

Q3 The function $f(x) = -x^2 - 7x - 6$ can be expressed in the form $f(x) = -\left(x + \frac{7}{2}\right)^2 + \frac{25}{4}$. Does this function have any real roots? Explain your answer.

Q4 Express the function $g(x) = 4x^2 - 3x - 5$ in the form $g(x) = p(x + q)^2 + r$, where p, q and r are positive or negative constants. Use your answer to find the number of real roots $g(x)$ has, and give the coordinates of the turning point of the graph of $g(x)$.

E Q5 $p(x) = -2x^2 + 7x - 10$.

a) Complete the square on $p(x)$. *[2 marks]*

b) Hence, determine the coordinates of the turning point of the graph with equation $y = p(x)$. *[1 mark]*

c) Using your answers to parts a) and b), explain why the graph of $y = p(x)$ must lie entirely below the x-axis. *[2 marks]*

Challenge

P Q6 The function $f(x) = -2x^2 + 3x + k$ has one real root.

a) Find the value of k.

b) Give the equation of the line of symmetry of the graph of $f(x)$.

c) State the coordinates of the turning point of the graph of $f(x)$ and whether it is a maximum or a minimum.

E P Q7 By completing the square, show that the quadratic $f(x) = x^2 + 6kx + 5k^2$ has real roots, where k is a real number. *[4 marks]*

E P Q8 a) Complete the square on the quadratic expression $x^2 + 2(3k + 1)x + 3(k + 7)$. *[2 marks]*

b) Hence, determine the possible values of k for which the equation $x^2 + 2(3k + 1)x + 3(k + 7) = 0$ has real solutions. *[3 marks]*

c) Using your answers to parts a) and b), determine whether the equation $3x^2 - 5x + 14 = 7x - 40$ has any real solutions. Do not attempt to calculate any solutions to the equation. *[3 marks]*

4.6 Using the Discriminant

Remember the **quadratic formula** for solving an equation of the form $ax^2 + bx + c = 0$:

$$x = \frac{-b \pm \sqrt{b^2 - 4ac}}{2a}$$

The $b^2 - 4ac$ bit is called the **discriminant**.

- If the discriminant is **positive**, the formula will give you **two** different values for x — when you **add** and **subtract** the $\sqrt{b^2 - 4ac}$ bit.
- If it's **zero**, you'll only get **one** value for x, since adding and subtracting zero gets the same value.
- If it's **negative**, you don't get any (real) values for x because you can't take the square root of a negative number.

Tip In some areas of maths, you can actually take the square root of negative numbers and get 'imaginary' numbers. That's why we say no 'real' roots.

To picture what this means, recall the examples from page 52:

Two real roots

$b^2 - 4ac > 0$

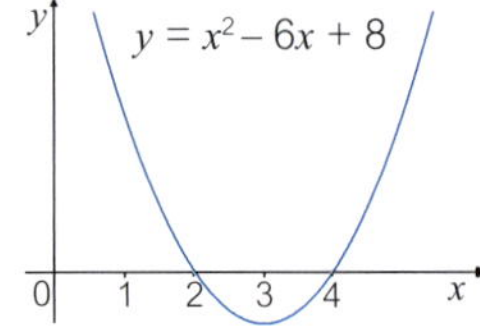

One real root

$b^2 - 4ac = 0$

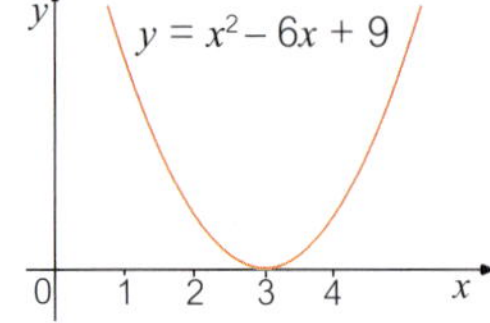

No real roots

$b^2 - 4ac < 0$

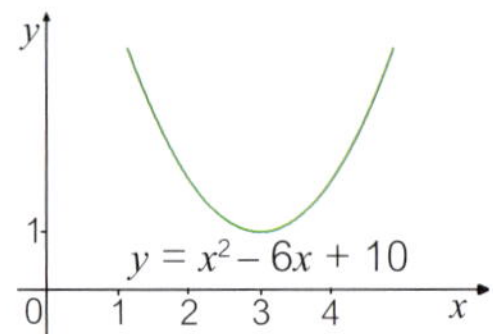

When working out the **discriminant**, the first thing to do is work out what $\boldsymbol{a}$, $\boldsymbol{b}$ and $\boldsymbol{c}$ are. Make sure you get them the right way round — it's easy to get mixed up if the quadratic's in a different order.

Example 1

Find the discriminant of $15 - x - 2x^2$.
How many real roots does the function $f(x) = 15 - x - 2x^2$ have?

$15 - x - 2x^2 = -2x^2 - x + 15$

$a = -2$, $b = -1$ and $c = 15$

First, identify a, b and c by rewriting as $-2x^2 - x + 15$. (Don't make the mistake of writing $a = 15$, $b = -1$ and $c = -2$.

$b^2 - 4ac = (-1)^2 - (4 \times -2 \times 15)$
$= 1 + 120 = 121$

Then put these values into the formula for the discriminant.

The discriminant is > 0,
so $15 - x - 2x^2$ has two distinct real roots.

You may need to work with a quadratic where one or more of a, b and c are given in terms of an **unknown**. This means that you'll end up with an equation or inequality for the discriminant in terms of the unknown — you might have to solve it to find the **value** or **range of values** of the unknown.

Example 2

Find the range of values of k for which the function $f(x) = 3x^2 + 2x + k$:
a) has 2 distinct roots, b) has 1 root, c) has no real roots.

$a = 3$, $b = 2$, $c = k$

First, decide what a, b and c are.

$b^2 - 4ac = 2^2 - 4 \times 3 \times k$
$= 4 - 12k$

Then work out what the discriminant is.

a) Two distinct roots means $b^2 - 4ac > 0$.

$\Rightarrow 4 - 12k > 0$
$\Rightarrow 4 > 12k$
$\Rightarrow k < \frac{1}{3}$

Solve to find k for the different values of the discriminant.

b) One root means $b^2 - 4ac = 0$.

$\Rightarrow 4 - 12k = 0$
$\Rightarrow 4 = 12k$
$\Rightarrow k = \frac{1}{3}$

c) No roots means $b^2 - 4ac < 0$.

$\Rightarrow 4 - 12k < 0$
$\Rightarrow 4 < 12k$
$\Rightarrow k > \frac{1}{3}$

The working is exactly the same in all three cases. The only difference is the equality / inequality symbol.

Problem Solving

The discriminant often comes up in exam questions — but sometimes they'll be sneaky and not actually tell you that's what you have to find. Any question that mentions **roots** of a quadratic will probably mean that you need to find the **discriminant**.

Example 3 

The equation $kx^2 + 12x + 9k = 0$ has two distinct roots.
Find the range of possible values for k.

$a = k,\ b = 12,\ c = 9k$ ← First, decide what a, b and c are.

$b^2 - 4ac = 12^2 - 4 \times k \times 9k$
$= 144 - 36k^2$ ← Then work out what the discriminant is.

$b^2 - 4ac > 0$ ← Two distinct roots means $b^2 - 4ac > 0$.
$\Rightarrow 144 - 36k^2 > 0$
$\Rightarrow 36k^2 < 144$
$\Rightarrow k^2 < 4$

$\Rightarrow -2 < k < 2$

Tip You'll learn more about quadratic inequalities in Chapter 5 — but here you just need to notice that if $k^2 < 4$, then k must be between –2 and 2.

Exercise 4.6

Q1 Find the discriminant, and hence the number of real roots, for each of the following:

a) $x^2 + 8x + 15$
b) $x^2 + 2\sqrt{3}x + 3$
c) $(2x + 1)(5x - 3)$
d) $-3x^2 - \frac{11}{5}x - \frac{2}{5}$
e) $9x^2 + 20x$
f) $\frac{19}{16}x^2 - 4$

Problem Solving Make sure the equation is written in the form $ax^2 + bx + c$ before trying to calculate the discriminant.

P Q2 The discriminant of the equation $15x^2 + bx = 2$ is 169, where b is a positive number. Find all possible values of b.

P Q3 The equation $0 = ax^2 + 7x + \frac{1}{4}$ has one real root. Find a.

Q4 Determine the number of real roots of the following equations, without solving them:

a) $13x^2 + 8x + 2 = 0$
b) $\frac{x^2}{3} + \frac{5}{2}x + 3 = 0$
c) $4 - \frac{x}{3} - \frac{x^2}{2} = 0$

P Q5 Find the range of values of p for which $x^2 - 12x + 27 + p = 0$ has two distinct real roots.

P Q6 Find the range of values of q for which $10x^2 - 10x + \frac{q}{2} = 0$ has two distinct real roots.

P Q7 The equation $2x^2 + (10p + 1)x + 5 = 0$ has no real roots.
Show that p satisfies: $p(5p + 1) < \frac{39}{20}$

P Q8 Find the range of values of k for which $-2x^2 - 2x + k = 0$ has:

a) two distinct roots.
b) one real root.
c) no roots.

P Q9 The equation $x^2 + (k + 5)x + \frac{k^2}{4} = 0$, where k is a constant, has no real roots.

a) Show that k satisfies $10k + 25 < 0$.
b) Find the range of possible values of k.

P Q10 a) Find the discriminant of $\left(k - \frac{6}{5}\right)x^2 + \sqrt{k}\,x + \frac{5}{4}$.

b) For what values of k would the equation $\left(k - \frac{6}{5}\right)x^2 + \sqrt{k}\,x + \frac{5}{4} = 0$ have:

(i) one real root? (ii) no real roots? (iii) two distinct real roots?

P Q11 For what values of m would the equation $\left(\frac{m}{\sqrt{3}} + 1\right)x + \frac{m}{2}x^2 + \frac{m}{6} = 0$ have:

a) one real root? b) no real roots? c) two distinct real roots?

E P Q12 a) Show that the discriminant of $\text{p}(x) = (k-1)x^2 + (k^2 - 5)x + \frac{1}{2}(k+1)$ is given by the expression $k^4 - 12k^2 + 27$. *[2 marks]*

b) Hence find the values of k for which the quadratic $\text{p}(x)$ has a repeated root. *[4 marks]*

P M Q13 A primary school teacher marks out a rectangular space in the playground with a single rope. The rectangle's length is twice its width, w metres.
She then reduces the length by 5 m and increases the width by 5 m.

a) Write an expression for the area of the new rectangle in terms of w.

b) The new rectangle has an area of 25 m^2.

(i) By evaluating the discriminant, show that there are two real solutions for the value of w.

(ii) Explain why there might not be two possible values for w in practice.

E P Q14 The graph of the curve with equation $y = 2x^2 + 4x - 5$ passes through two points, P and Q. For both points, the x-coordinate is equal to the y-coordinate.

a) Find the exact coordinates of P and Q. *[4 marks]*

$\text{p}(x) = ax^2 + bx + c$, where a, b and c are constants with $a \neq 0$. The graph of $y = \text{p}(x)$ passes through at least one point at which the x-coordinate is equal to the y-coordinate.

b) Show that $(b-1)^2 - 4ac \geq 0$. *[2 marks]*

Challenge

E P Q15 Find the set of values of k for which the simultaneous equations $y = kx + 1$ and $y = x^2 - 3x + 3$ have exactly two distinct solutions. *[5 marks]*

E P Q16 a) Given that k is a real number, show that the discriminant of the quadratic $\text{p}(x) = \frac{1}{2\sqrt{2}}x^2 - (k+1)x - \frac{1}{\sqrt{2}}k^2$ is given by the expression $2k^2 + 2k + 1$. *[2 marks]*

b) Hence, explain why $\text{p}(x) = 0$ has two distinct real solutions when k is a real number. *[3 marks]*

P Q17 a) Line l has equation $y = kx + 9$ and circle C has equation $(x-4)^2 + (y-5)^2 = 9$.
Find the values of k for which line l is a tangent to the circle.
Leave your answers in an exact form.

b) Without further calculation, give the range of possible values of k for which l does not intersect the circle.

4.7 Sketching Quadratic Graphs

There are two pieces of information you **always need** to know about a quadratic function before you can sketch it.

- The **shape** — u-shaped or n-shaped.
- The coordinates of the **points of intersection** with the x- and y-axes.

Sometimes, there will be two **different** graphs which have the same points of intersection and shape — in this case you'll need to work out the location of the **vertex point** (maximum or minimum) to decide which graph is right.

Tip The vertex of a quadratic graph is just the point where the graph changes direction. It is either a maximum point or a minimum point depending on the shape of the graph.

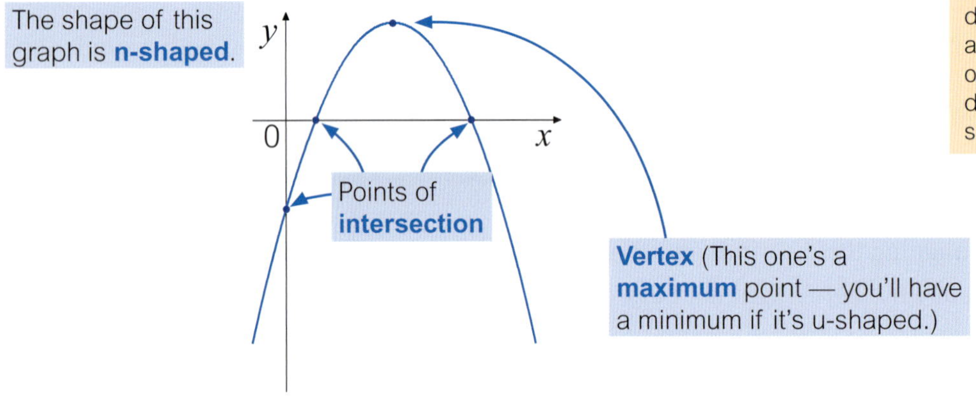

The shape of this graph is **n-shaped**.

Points of **intersection**

Vertex (This one's a **maximum** point — you'll have a minimum if it's u-shaped.)

Shape

The first thing you need to decide is the **shape** of the graph — look at the coefficient of the x^2 term.

- If the coefficient of x^2 is **positive** — the graph will be **u-shaped**.
- If the coefficient of x^2 is **negative** — the graph will be **n-shaped**.

Intercepts

The next bit of information you need is where the graph **intersects the axes** — set x or y equal to zero and work out the other coordinate. If you're sketching the function $y = ax^2 + bx + c$:

- To find the **y-intercept** — let $x = 0$ and calculate the value of y.
- To find the **x-intercepts** — let $y = 0$ and solve the equation $0 = ax^2 + bx + c$ to find the value or values of x.

Don't forget the x-intercepts correspond to the roots of the quadratic function — bear in mind that there may be only **one** root, or **no** roots.

Problem Solving

Use one of the methods of solving quadratics from earlier in the chapter to work out the x-intercepts — they're just the solutions of the equation.

Example 1

Sketch the graph of the quadratic function $f(x) = x^2 - 4x + 3$, including any points of intersection with the axes.

The coefficient of x^2 is positive, so the graph is u-shaped.

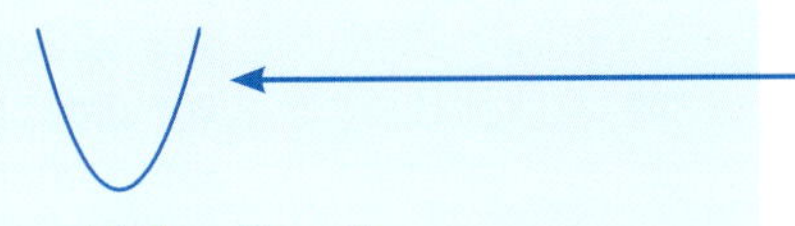

Look at the coefficient of x^2 to decide on the shape.

When $x = 0$, $f(x) = f(0) = (0)^2 - 4(0) + 3 = 3$, so the y-intercept is at 3.

Substitute $x = 0$ into the function to find the y-intercept.

When $f(x) = 0$, $x^2 - 4x + 3 = 0$
$\Rightarrow$ $(x - 3)(x - 1) = 0$
$\Rightarrow$ $x - 3 = 0$ or $x - 1 = 0$
$\Rightarrow$ $x = 3$ or $x = 1$
So the x-intercepts are at 1 and 3.

Set $f(x)$ equal to 0 to find the x-intercepts. You can factorise this equation to solve it.

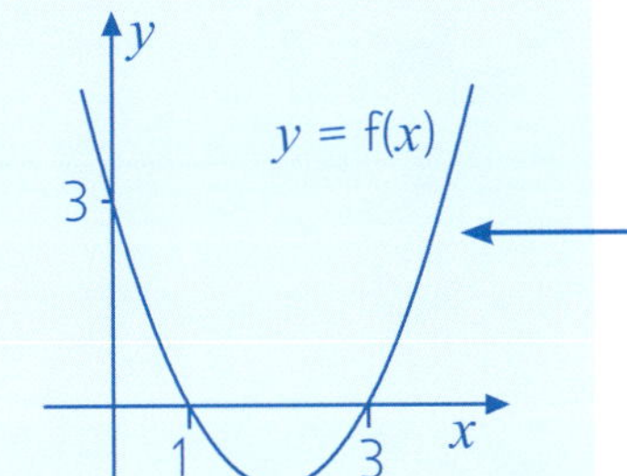

Put all this information together to sketch the graph.

Vertex points

You'll sometimes need to find the minimum or maximum of the graph — which one it is depends on whether your graph is u-shaped or n-shaped. One way to find the vertex is to **complete the square** and then interpret this. You did this back on pages 46-47 — have a look back at those pages to remind yourself of the method. But here's the key result you need...

A graph with an equation of the form $\boldsymbol{y = p(x + q)^2 + r}$ has a vertex at $\boldsymbol{(-q, r)}$.

If $p > 0$, the graph is u-shaped, so the vertex is a minimum.

If $p < 0$, the graph is n-shaped, so the vertex is a maximum.

This comes from the fact that a square is always positive or 0 and so can never be less than 0.

Example 2

a) Find the vertex of the graph of $y = f(x)$, where $f(x) = 3x^2 - 6x - 7$, stating whether it is a maximum or minimum.

The coefficient of x^2 is positive, so the graph is u-shaped. So the vertex must be a minimum.

You can tell whether the vertex is a maximum or minimum by looking at the coefficient of x^2.

$f(x) = 3x^2 - 6x - 7 = 3(x - 1)^2 - 10.$

$(x - 1)^2$ is never negative, so $f(x)$ reaches its minimum value when $(x - 1)^2 = 0$, i.e. when $x = 1$.

Complete the square, then set the squared part equal to 0 to find the x-coordinate of the vertex.

When $x = 1$, $f(x) = f(1) = 3(0)^2 - 10 = -10$

Plug this x-value into the completed-square form of $f(x)$ to find the y-coordinate.

So the vertex is $(1, -10)$, which is a minimum.

b) Find where the graph of $y = f(x)$ crosses the axes and hence sketch the graph.

When $x = 0$, $y = f(0) = 3(0)^2 - 6(0) - 7 = -7$
So the y-intercept is at -7.

Plug $x = 0$ into the function to find where $f(x)$ crosses the y-axis.

$3x^2 - 6x - 7 = 0$
$\Rightarrow 3(x - 1)^2 - 10 = 0$
$\Rightarrow (x - 1)^2 = \frac{10}{3}$
$\Rightarrow x - 1 = \pm\sqrt{\frac{10}{3}}$
$\Rightarrow x = 1 \pm\sqrt{\frac{10}{3}}$

Set $f(x)$ equal to 0 to find the x-intercepts, and solve the equation using the completed square form you found in part a).

So the x-intercepts are at
$x = 1 + \sqrt{\frac{10}{3}}$ and $x = 1 - \sqrt{\frac{10}{3}}$

Tip You could also solve this equation using the quadratic formula:

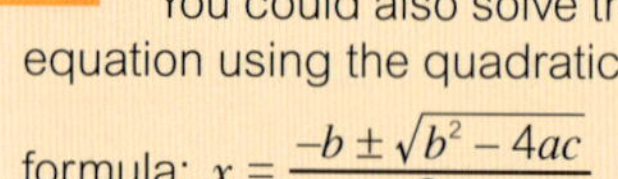

$x = \frac{-b \pm \sqrt{b^2 - 4ac}}{2a}$
$= \frac{-(-6) \pm \sqrt{(-6)^2 - 4(3)(-7)}}{2(3)}$
$= \frac{6 \pm \sqrt{120}}{6} = 1 \pm \sqrt{\frac{10}{3}}$

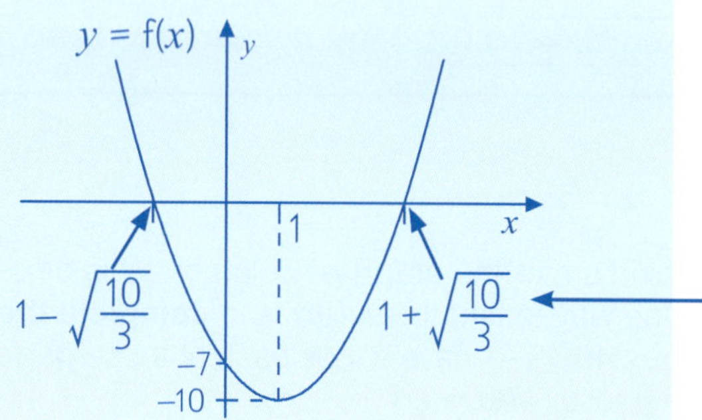

Now use all this information to sketch the graph — label the values of the x- and y-intercepts and the vertex.

If a function has **no real roots**, the shape and the axis intercepts won't be **enough** to draw the graph. You'll **have** to find the coordinates of the **vertex point**, even if the question doesn't ask you to.

Example 3

Sketch the graph of the function $y = 2x^2 - 4x + 3$, showing any intersection points with the axes.

The coefficient of x^2 is positive, so the graph is u-shaped.

Look at the coefficient of x^2 to decide on the shape.

$y = 2x^2 - 4x + 3$
When $x = 0$, $y = (2 \times 0)^2 - (4 \times 0) + 3 = 3$
so the y-intercept is at 3.

Substitute $x = 0$ into the function to find where the graph crosses the y-axis.

continued on the next page...

Let $2x^2 - 4x + 3 = 0$

Discriminant $= b^2 - 4ac$
$= (-4)^2 - 4 \times 2 \times 3$
$= 16 - 24$
$= -8 < 0$

Now set $y = 0$ to see if the graph meets the x-axis. Use the discriminant $b^2 - 4ac$ to find if there are any real roots.

Tip You could use the quadratic formula to try to solve the equation. If you did, you'd see there are no solutions in the same way when you got to the $b^2 - 4ac$ part.

The discriminant is negative, so the function has no real roots, and doesn't cross the x-axis.

So the graph looks like one of these options:

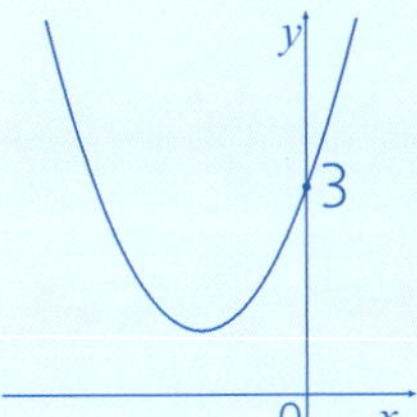

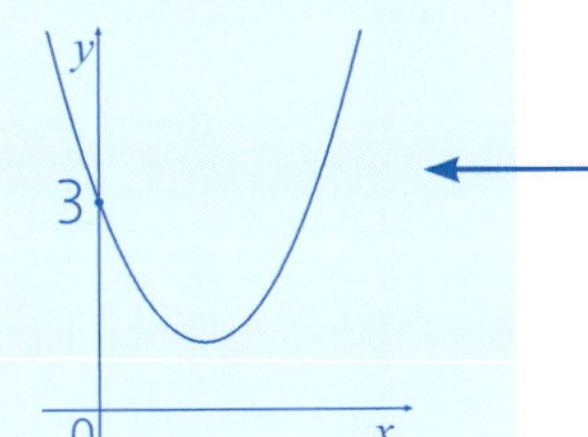

The information we have so far isn't enough to say exactly what the graph will look like.

Find the coordinates of the vertex:
$y = 2x^2 - 4x + 3 = 2(x - 1)^2 + 1$

To find which graph option is correct, work out the coordinates of the minimum of the graph by completing the square.

y reaches its minimum value when $(x - 1)^2 = 0$, i.e. when $x = 1$.

When $x = 1$, $y = 2(0)^2 + 1 = 1$, so the vertex is at $(1, 1)$.

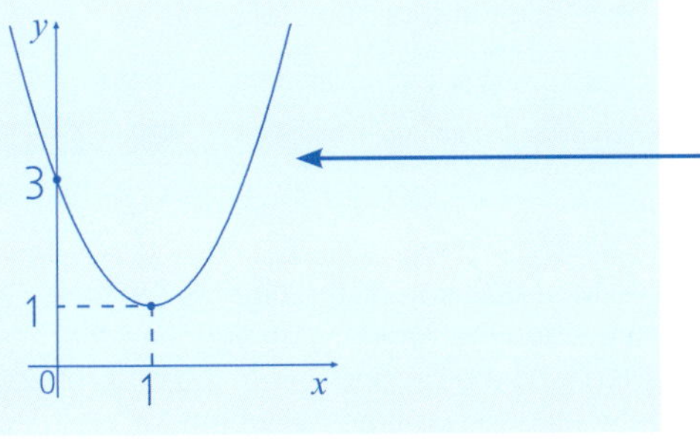

Put all this information together to draw the sketch. Label the y-intercept and the vertex.

So we've seen a couple of examples of finding the vertex by completing the square. But if you've already worked out the roots, and found that there are **one** or **two** real roots, you can work out the vertex more easily like this:

<u>If the function has **two distinct roots** — use symmetry of quadratic graphs</u>

The graph of a quadratic function is **symmetrical**, so the x-coordinate of the vertex is **halfway** between the roots of the function.

Work out the x-value halfway between the two roots and put it into the function to find the corresponding y-value of the vertex.

<u>If the function has **one root** — the vertex is at the root</u>

If a function has one root, then its graph just **touches** the x-axis at the root — this point will always be the vertex.

You can also find the vertex of a quadratic function using differentiation — see p.262-3.

Example 4 M

A rocket is launched from the ground. Its height, h m, is modelled by the equation $h = 30t - 5t^2$, where t is the time in seconds. Sketch a graph to show the rocket's flight, and hence find its maximum height above the ground and the total duration of its flight.

Problem Solving Don't let the different letters put you off — y has been replaced by h, and x has been replaced by t.

The coefficient of t^2 is negative so the graph is n-shaped.

Look at the coefficient of t^2 to find the shape of the graph.

Putting $t = 0$ gives $h = 0$ as the h-intercept.

Putting $h = 0$ gives:

$30t - 5t^2 = 0 \Rightarrow 5t(6 - t) = 0$

$\Rightarrow t = 0$ and $t = 6$ as the t-intercepts

Now find the places where the graph crosses the axes.

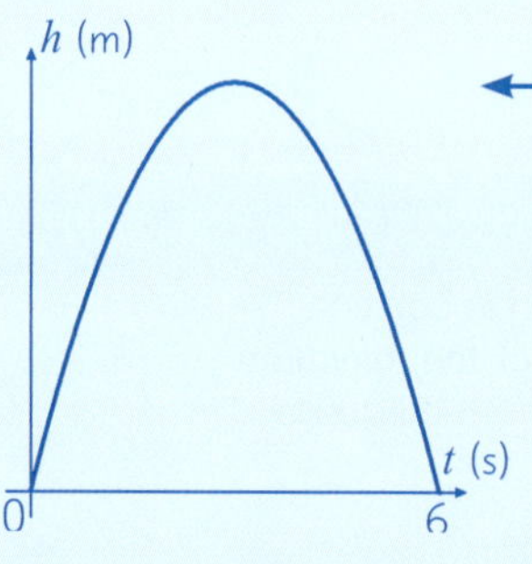

Put all this together to draw the sketch.

Tip Just ignore the parts of the graph where t and h are less than 0 — time and height can't be negative in this example.

Find the rocket's maximum height:

The t-value of the maximum point is halfway between 0 and 6, so it is at $t = 3$.

$t = 3$ gives $h = 30(3) - 5(3)^2$

$= 90 - 45 = 45$ m.

So the rocket's maximum height is 45 m.

Now use your graph to answer the questions. First, use the symmetry of the graph to find its vertex. The h-value at this point tells you the maximum height.

Find the total duration of the flight:

$h = 0$ when $t = 0$ and $t = 6$,

so the flight lasted for $6 - 0 = 6$ s.

The total duration of the flight is the time from when the rocket was launched to when it hit the ground — i.e. the difference between the two times at which $h = 0$.

Exercise 4.7

Q1 Sketch the following graphs on the same set of axes, indicating the x-intercepts of each.

a) $y = x^2 - 1$ b) $y = x^2 - 9$

Q2 a) Factorise the expression $f(x) = x^2 - 10x + 9$.

b) Use your answer to a) to sketch the graph of $f(x)$, showing the points where it crosses both axes.

c) Sketch the graph of $-f(x)$ on the same axes.

Tip Remember that the graph of $y = -f(x)$ is just $y = f(x)$ reflected in the x-axis (see page 132 for more on this).

Q3 For each of the following quadratic functions:

(i) Describe its shape.

(ii) Find the y-intercept.

(iii) Find the number of real roots.

(iv) Find the values of x at which the graph intersects the x-axis — if it does.

(v) Find the coordinates of the vertex.

(vi) Sketch the graph of the function, marking on all the information you've found.

a) $y = -x^2 + 2x + 1$ b) $y = x^2 - 7x + 15$ c) $y = 2x^2 + 4x - 9$ d) $y = -x^2 + 4x - 7$

Q4 The graph on the right shows the quadratic function $y = f(x)$.

a) $f(x)$ can be written in the form $f(x) = (x + q)^2 + r$, where q and r are integers. Use the graph to find the values of q and r.

b) Copy the sketch, and on the same axes, sketch the function $g(x) = (x + 4)^2$.

c) How many real roots does each function have?

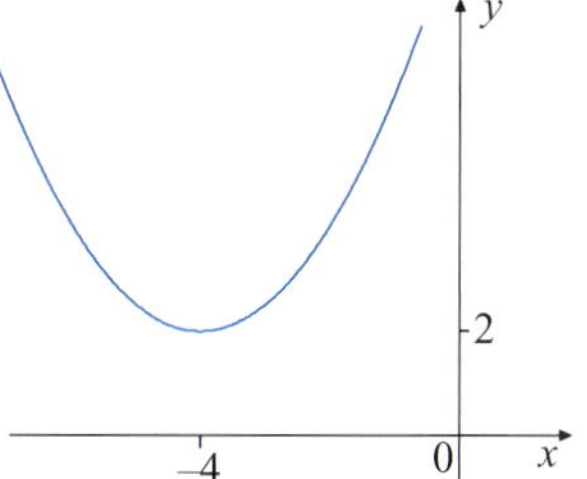

Q5 a) Complete the square of the expression $x^2 - 6x + 5$.

b) Use part a) to solve the equation $x^2 - 6x + 5 = 0$

c) Draw a graph of $y = x^2 - 6x + 5$ showing any intersections with the axes and marking the vertex.

Q6 Sketch the following graphs, showing any intersections with the axes:

a) $y = x^2 - 2x + 1$ b) $y = x^2 + x - 1$ c) $y = x^2 - 8x + 18$

d) $y = -x^2 + 3$ e) $y = 2x^2 + 5x + 2$ f) $y = 2x^2 - 5x - 1$

Q7 Sketch the graph of $y = f(x)$, where $f(x) = (x + 3)^2$, showing the coordinates of the vertex and any intersection points with the axes.

Q8 Sketch the graph of $y = g(x)$, where $g(x) = x^2 - 2x - 15$, showing the coordinates of the vertex and any intersection points with the axes.

E P Q9 a) Find the coordinates of the vertex of $y = p(x)$, where $p(x) = x^2 - 5x + 8$. *[2 marks]*

b) Sketch the graph of $y = p(x)$, clearly labelling the coordinates of the vertex and any intersection points with the axes. *[3 marks]*

c) State the coordinates of the maximum point of $y = -p(x)$. *[1 mark]*

E Q10 a) Solve the quadratic equation $2x^2 + 3x - 6 = 0$, giving your answers in the form $p + q\sqrt{57}$, where p and q are rational numbers. *[2 marks]*

b) Hence, or otherwise, find the coordinates of the vertex of the graph with equation $y = 2x^2 + 3x - 6$. *[2 marks]*

c) Sketch the graph of $y = 2x^2 + 3x - 6$, clearly labelling the coordinates of the vertex and any intersection points with the axes. *[3 marks]*

P Q11 a) What are the roots of the quadratic function shown in the graph on the right?

b) The quadratic can be written in the form $y = -x^2 + px + q$ where p and q are integers. Use your answer to part a) to find p and q.

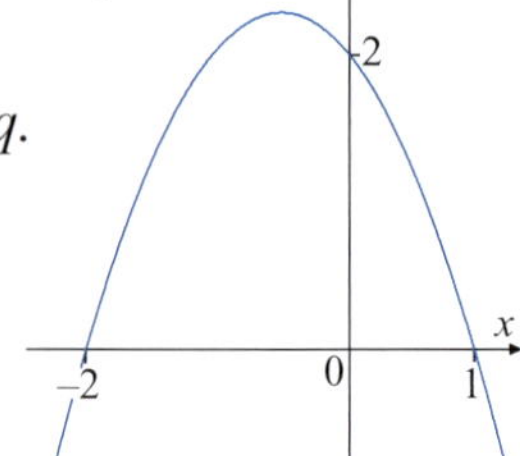

M Q12 A tiddlywink is fired from the ground. Its height, h cm, is modelled by the equation $h = 24t - 16t^2$, where t is the time in seconds.

a) Sketch a graph to show the tiddlywink's flight.

b) Find the maximum height that the tiddlywink reaches.

P M Q13 A theme park is designing a new roller coaster that starts on a raised platform then goes underground. The first 10 seconds of the roller coaster's vertical path are modelled by the equation $h = 0.25t^2 - 2.5t + 4$, where h is the height in metres above the ground and t is the time in seconds.

a) Sketch a graph showing height of the roller coaster during the first 10 seconds of the ride.

b) For the first 10 seconds of the ride, use your graph to find:
(i) the height of the raised platform. (ii) the lowest point of the roller coaster.
(iii) how long the roller coaster is underground for.

P M Q14 The height of an aeroplane stunt, h m, is modelled by the equation $h = 0.5t^2 - 13t + 100$, where t is the time in seconds.
The stunt is completed when the aeroplane returns to the starting height.

a) Sketch a graph of the aeroplane's flight showing the time taken to complete the stunt.

b) Find the minimum height that the aeroplane reaches.

Challenge

E P Q15 $p(x) = 2x^2 + ax + b$, where a and b are constants. The graph with equation $y = p(x)$ has a minimum with coordinates (2, 3), and intersects the y-axis at the point A.

a) Find the coordinates of A. *[4 marks]*

b) Sketch the graph of $y = p(x)$, clearly labelling the coordinates of the minimum point and any intersection points with the axes. *[2 marks]*

E P Q16 C is the graph with equation $y = p(x)$, where $p(x) = 2x^2 - 10x + 8$.

a) By completing the square, find the coordinates of the minimum point of $p(x)$. *[2 marks]*

b) Sketch the graph, C, clearly labelling the coordinates of the minimum point and any intersection points with the axes. *[3 marks]*

C is reflected in the line $x = 1$ to produce the graph C', with equation $y = q(x)$.

c) Using your answer to part a), or otherwise, find the coordinates of the minimum point of the graph C'. *[1 mark]*

d) Find an expression for $q(x)$, giving your answer in the form $ax^2 + bx + c$. *[1 mark]*

4.8 Factorising a Cubic (When x is a Factor)

Factorising a **cubic** means exactly what it meant with a quadratic — writing it as a product of **factors** in **brackets**. Let's start with factorising cubics that have an x in **every term**.

For a cubic of the form $ax^3 + bx^2 + cx$, **take out x** as your first factor as follows:

$$ax^3 + bx^2 + cx = x(ax^2 + bx + c)$$

Now you can just factorise the **quadratic** inside the brackets to get the other factors using the methods given earlier in the chapter. Once you've factorised, you can solve a cubic equation just as you would solve a quadratic.

Tip Cubic equations can have one, two or three real solutions. So unlike quadratics, they always have at least one real root.

Example 1

Factorise and solve the following cubic equations.

a) $x^3 - 2x^2 - 24x = 0$

$x^3 - 2x^2 - 24x = x(x^2 - 2x - 24)$ ← Start by taking out a factor of x.

$= x(x \quad)(x \quad)$ ← Then factorise the quadratic: put in the x's...

$= x(x \quad 6)(x \quad 4)$ ← ... work out the numbers...

$= x(x - 6)(x + 4)$ ← ... then choose the signs.

$\Rightarrow x(x - 6)(x + 4) = 0$

So either $x = 0$, $x - 6 = 0$ or $x + 4 = 0$ ← Set each factor equal to 0 to find the solutions.

$\Rightarrow x = 0$, $x = 6$ or $x = -4$

Tip You can't just divide by x at the start — you would miss the solution $x = 0$.

b) $-x^3 - 2x^2 + 3x = 0$

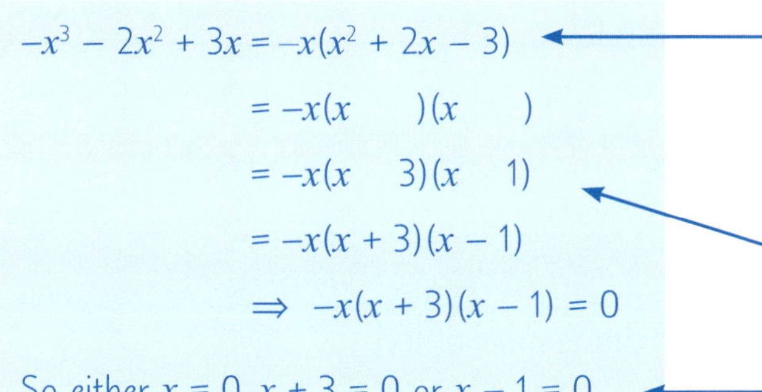

$-x^3 - 2x^2 + 3x = -x(x^2 + 2x - 3)$ ← If the x^3 coefficient is negative, it makes things easier if you take out a factor of $-x$.

$= -x(x \quad)(x \quad)$

$= -x(x \quad 3)(x \quad 1)$ ← Factorise the quadratic using the normal method.

$= -x(x + 3)(x - 1)$

$\Rightarrow -x(x + 3)(x - 1) = 0$

So either $x = 0$, $x + 3 = 0$ or $x - 1 = 0$ ← The factors are all different, so the cubic equation has three real solutions.

$\Rightarrow x = 0$, $x = -3$ or $x = 1$

Tip Remember to change the sign of each term in the bracket when you take out a minus sign.

Example 2

Solve the cubic equation $-4x^3 - 4x^2 + x = 0$.

$$-4x^3 - 4x^2 + x = 0$$
$$\Rightarrow -x(4x^2 + 4x - 1) = 0$$

The first thing you need to do is factorise. The x^3 coefficient is negative, so take out a factor of $-x$.

So $x = 0$ or $4x^2 + 4x - 1 = 0$

$x = 0$ is one solution and solving the quadratic equation will give the other two.

Solve the quadratic:

$$x = \frac{-b \pm \sqrt{b^2 - 4ac}}{2a} = \frac{-4 \pm \sqrt{4^2 - 4 \times 4 \times (-1)}}{2 \times 4}$$
$$= \frac{-4 \pm \sqrt{32}}{8} = \frac{-4 \pm 4\sqrt{2}}{8}$$
$$= -\frac{1}{2} \pm \frac{1}{2}\sqrt{2}$$

This quadratic won't factorise, so use the quadratic formula.

So the solutions are $x = 0$, $x = -\frac{1}{2} + \frac{1}{2}\sqrt{2}$ and $x = -\frac{1}{2} - \frac{1}{2}\sqrt{2}$.

Make sure you list all the solutions — don't forget about $x = 0$.

Exercise 4.8

Q1 Factorise the following cubic expressions:

a) $x^3 + 5x^2 + 6x$ b) $x^3 + 6x^2 - 7x$ c) $x^3 - 18x^2 + 81x$

d) $x^3 + 7x^2 + 10x$ e) $-x^3 + 4x^2 - 3x$ f) $x^3 + 4x^2 + 3x$

g) $x^3 + 2x^2 - 35x$ h) $x^3 - 6x^2 - 16x$ i) $-x^3 - 3x^2 + 4x$

j) $2x^3 + 15x^2 + 25x$ k) $2x^3 - 7x^2 + 6x$ l) $4x^3 + 13x^2 - 12x$

m) $x^3 - \frac{4}{25}x$ n) $x^3 - 49x$ o) $x^3 - \frac{9}{4}x$

Q2 Solve the following cubic equations:

a) $-x^3 + 2x^2 + 24x = 0$ b) $x^3 - \frac{7}{9}x^2 + \frac{10}{81}x = 0$

c) $2x^3 + 9x^2 + 4x = 0$ d) $3x^3 - 3x^2 + 4x = 0$

e) $4x - x^3 = 0$ f) $5x^3 + 7x^2 - 3x = 0$

g) $3x^3 + 26x^2 - 9x = 0$ h) $x^3 + \frac{2}{3}x^2 - \frac{8}{9}x = 0$

i) $x^2(4x + 3) = x$ j) $2x^3 + 8x^2 = -3x$

Q2 Hint Some of the quadratics may not factorise — use the quadratic formula to get the remaining solutions.

Q3 a) Factorise the expression $f(x) = -x^3 + 36x$

b) Use your answer to part a) to write down all of the roots of $f(x)$.

P Q4 Show that the equation $2x^3 + 3x = x^2$ has only one real solution.

4.9 The Factor Theorem

When x **isn't** a factor of the cubic, factorising it becomes a lot trickier. First, you'll need to **find a linear factor** (i.e. of the form $(ax + b)$), and then you need to **divide** the cubic by that factor (there are a couple of ways of doing this, which are covered later in this section).

Before you can do that, you'll need to learn the **Factor Theorem**. The Factor Theorem gives you a quick way of finding a **factor** of a polynomial, **without** having to do the division.

The **Factor Theorem** states:

> If **f(*x*)** is a polynomial, and **f(*a*) = 0**, then **(*x* – *a*)** is a factor of **f(*x*)**.

This also works the other way round — if $(x - a)$ is a factor of $f(x)$, then $\mathbf{f(a) = 0}$.

Remember, a root is just a value of x that makes $f(x) = 0$. So if you know the roots of $f(x)$, you also know the factors of $f(x)$ — and vice versa.

Tip A polynomial is an algebraic expression made up of the sum of constant terms and variables raised to positive integer powers, such as quadratics and cubics.

Example 1

Use the Factor Theorem to show that $(x - 2)$ is a factor of $(x^3 - 5x^2 + x + 10)$.

$f(2) = 2^3 - (5 \times 2^2) + 2 + 10 = 8 - 20 + 2 + 10 = 0$ ← Here $a = 2$, so work out f(2).

$f(2) = 0$, so $(x - 2)$ must be a factor of $x^3 - 5x^2 + x + 10$. ← By the Factor Theorem, $(x - 2)$ divides into $x^3 - 5x^2 + x + 10$ exactly.

If you're given factors of a polynomial, you can also use the Factor Theorem to find any **unknown coefficients** in the original polynomial.

Example 2 P

$(x + 1)$ and $(x - 3)$ are factors of $f(x) = x^3 + bx + c$.
Use the Factor Theorem to find the values of b and c.

$f(-1) = 0 \Rightarrow (-1)^3 + b(-1) + c = 0$ ← $(x + 1)$ and $(x - 3)$ are factors, so using the Factor Theorem, $f(-1) = 0$ and $f(3) = 0$.

$\Rightarrow -1 - b + c = 0$

Rearranging gives $c = 1 + b$ (equation 1) ← Use the fact that $f(-1) = 0$ to form an equation in b and c.

$f(3) = 0 \Rightarrow (3)^3 + b(3) + c = 0$

$\Rightarrow 27 + 3b + c = 0$

Rearranging gives $c = -27 - 3b$ (equation 2) ← Use the fact that $f(3) = 0$ to form another equation in b and c.

Equating equations 1 and 2: $1 + b = -27 - 3b$

$\Rightarrow 4b = -28 \Rightarrow b = -7$

Sub b into equation 1: $c = 1 - 7 = -6$ ← Solve the two equations in b and c simultaneously.

So $f(x) = x^3 - 7x - 6$

If you have a polynomial with a factor in the form of $(ax - b)$ you can use this extension of the Factor Theorem:

If $\mathbf{f(x)}$ is a polynomial, and $\mathbf{f\left(\frac{b}{a}\right) = 0}$, then $(ax - b)$ is a factor of $\mathbf{f(x)}$.

This also means that if $(ax - b)$ is a factor of $f(x)$, then $f\left(\frac{b}{a}\right) = 0$.

Tip $\frac{b}{a}$ is just the value of x that would make the bracket 0. If a divides b exactly, you can write $(ax - b)$ as $a(x - \frac{b}{a})$ in a full factorisation.

Example 3

Show that $(2x + 1)$ is a factor of $f(x) = 2x^3 - 3x^2 + 4x + 3$.

$f\left(\frac{b}{a}\right) = f\left(-\frac{1}{2}\right) = 2\left(-\frac{1}{8}\right) - 3\left(\frac{1}{4}\right) + 4\left(-\frac{1}{2}\right) + 3$ ← Show that $f\left(\frac{b}{a}\right) = 0$, where $a = 2$ and $b = -1$.

$= -\frac{1}{4} - \frac{3}{4} - 2 + 3 = 0$

$f\left(-\frac{1}{2}\right) = 0$, so $(2x + 1)$ is a factor of $f(x)$. ← If $f\left(\frac{b}{a}\right) = 0$, $(ax - b)$ is a factor of $f(x)$.

You can see why this is true using the original Factor Theorem (from the previous page):

We saw above that $f\left(-\frac{1}{2}\right) = 0$.

So, by the Factor Theorem, $\left(x + \frac{1}{2}\right)$ is a factor of $f(x)$. ← If $f\left(-\frac{1}{2}\right) = 0$, then the Factor Theorem says that $\left(x - \left(-\frac{1}{2}\right)\right) = \left(x + \frac{1}{2}\right)$ is a factor.

So $2\left(x + \frac{1}{2}\right) = (2x + 1)$ is also a factor. ← A multiple of any factor is also a factor.

Just one more useful thing to mention about polynomials and factors:

If the **coefficients** in a polynomial **add up to 0**, then $(x - 1)$ is a **factor**.

This works for all polynomials — there are no exceptions.
For example, $(x - 1)$ is a factor of $4x^3 + 2x^2 - 5x - 1$, as $4 + 2 - 5 - 1 = 0$.

Tip If you put $x = 1$ into a polynomial $f(x)$, x^2, x^3 etc. are all just 1, so $f(1)$ is the sum of the coefficients.

Example 4

Factorise the polynomial $f(x) = 6x^2 - 7x + 1$.

Try adding the coefficients: $6 + (-7) + 1 = 0$. ← The coefficients add up to 0, which means $f(1) = 0$, and so $(x - 1)$ is a factor.

So $(x - 1)$ is a factor of $f(x)$.

$f(x) = 6x^2 - 7x + 1 = (6x - 1)(x - 1)$ ← Complete the factorisation of the quadratic.

Exercise 4.9

Q1 Use the Factor Theorem to show that:

a) $(x - 1)$ is a factor of $x^3 - x^2 - 3x + 3$

b) $(x + 1)$ is a factor of $x^3 + 2x^2 + 3x + 2$

c) $(x + 2)$ is a factor of $x^3 + 3x^2 - 10x - 24$

d) $(x - 3)$ is a factor of $x^3 + 2x^2 - 9x - 18$

Q2 Use the Factor Theorem to show that:

a) $(2x - 1)$ is a factor of $2x^3 - x^2 - 8x + 4$ b) $(3x - 2)$ is a factor of $3x^3 - 5x^2 - 16x + 12$

Q3 Use the Factor Theorem to show that:

a) $(5x + 1)$ is a factor of $5x^3 - 44x^2 + 61x + 14$ b) $(1 - 2x)$ is a factor of $-2x^3 + 3x^2 + 11x - 6$

Q4 a) Use the Factor Theorem to show that $(x - 3)$ is a factor of $x^3 - 2x^2 - 5x + 6$.

b) Show, by adding the coefficients, that $(x - 1)$ is also a factor of this cubic.

Q5 $f(x) = 3x^3 - 5x^2 - 58x + 40$.
Use the Factor Theorem to show that the following are factors of $f(x)$:

a) $(x + 4)$ b) $(3x - 2)$ c) $(x - 5)$

P Q6 $(x - 2)$ is a factor of the cubic $2x^3 - 7x^2 + px + 20$. Find the value of p.

P Q7 $(x - 3)$ is a factor of the cubic $qx^3 - 4x^2 - 7qx + 12$. Find the value of q.

E P Q8 Given that $p(x) = bx^3 - (b + 1)x^2 + b^2x + b + 1$, where b is a constant, and that $(x - 2)$ is a factor of $p(x)$, find the possible values of b. *[3 marks]*

P M Q9 A cuboid is made from a number of centimetre cube blocks.
The volume, V cm^3, of the cuboid can be modelled by the function:
$V(x) = 6x^3 + 37x^2 + 37x + 10$, where x is a positive integer number of blocks.

a) Use the Factor Theorem to show that the cuboid has a length, width and height of $(3x + 2)$ blocks, $(2x + 1)$ blocks and $(x + 5)$ blocks.

b) Find the smallest possible volume of the cuboid.

Challenge

P Q10 The polynomial $f(x) = x^3 + cx^2 + dx - 2$ has factors $(x - 1)$ and $(x - 2)$.
Using the Factor Theorem, find the values of c and d.

E P Q11 This diagram shows the graph of $f(x)$. All intersections with the coordinate axes are labelled.

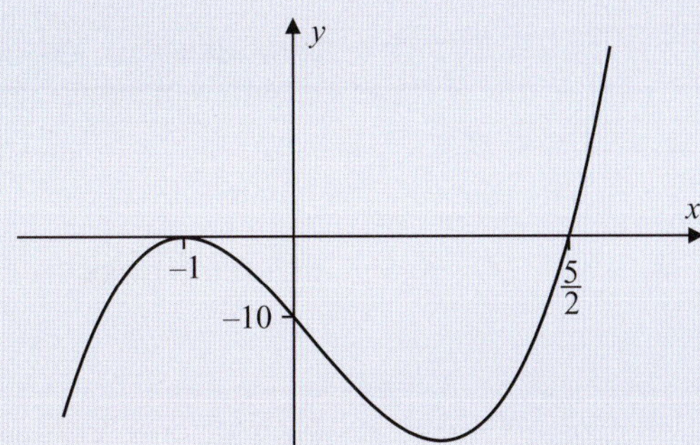

Given that $f(x)$ is a cubic function, find an expression for $f(x)$ in its factorised form. *[3 marks]*

4.10 Factorising a Cubic (When x isn't a Factor)

You can use the **Factor Theorem** to factorise cubics that **don't** have an x in every term. First, you need to use the Factor Theorem (and a bit of trial and error) to find one of the factors of the cubic:

- First, **add up** the **coefficients** to check if $(x - 1)$ is a factor.
- If that doesn't work, keep trying small numbers (find f(–1), f(2), f(–2), f(3), f(–3) and so on) until you find a number that gives you **zero** when you put it in the **cubic**. Call that number k. $(x - k)$ is a **factor of the cubic**.

> **Tip** You only need to try integer values of k that are factors of the constant term (ignoring signs).

Once you've found one of the factors, here's how to **factorise the cubic**:

1. Write down the **factor** you know $(x - k)$, and another set of brackets: $(x - k)(\quad\quad)$.
2. In the brackets, put the x^2 **term** needed to get the right x^3 term.
3. In the brackets, put in the **constant** (that when multiplied by k gives the constant in the cubic).
4. Put in nx as the x **term** and then **multiply** to find the x^2 terms.
5. **Equate the coefficients** of the x^2 terms you've just found with the coefficient of x^2 from the question, then **solve** to find n. Check that it gives you the correct x term as well.
6. **Factorise** the quadratic you've found — if that's possible. If the quadratic can't be factorised, just leave it as it is.

Example 1

> **Tip** To "equate the coefficients" you just compare the terms that have the same power of x. For example, $ax^2 + 2x = 3x^2 + bx \Rightarrow a = 3$ and $2 = b$.

$f(x) = x^3 + 6x^2 + 5x - 12$

Factorise f(x) and find all the solutions of f(x) = 0.

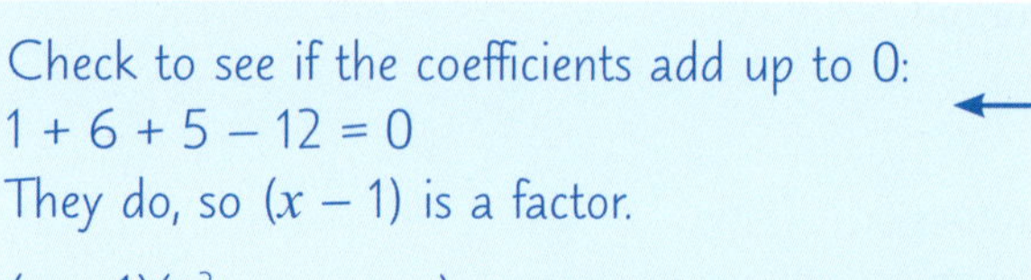

Check to see if the coefficients add up to 0:
$1 + 6 + 5 - 12 = 0$
They do, so $(x - 1)$ is a factor.

Add up the coefficients to see if $(x - 1)$ is a factor.

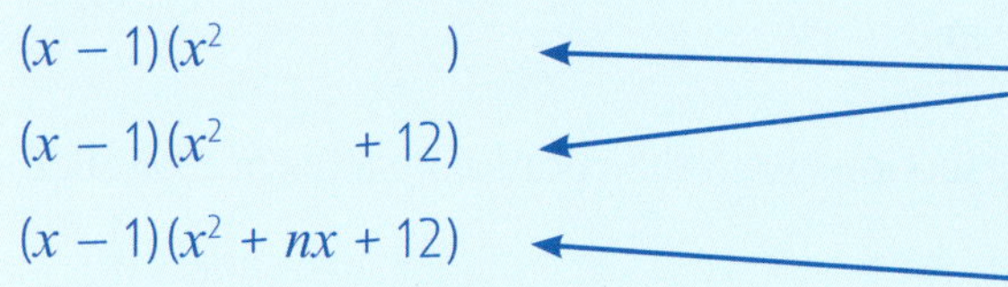

$(x - 1)(x^2 \quad\quad)$

$(x - 1)(x^2 \quad\quad + 12)$

Now find the quadratic factor. First, work out the term that gives x^3 when multiplied by x. Then find the constant term that gives –12 when multiplied by –1.

$(x - 1)(x^2 + nx + 12)$

Equate x^2 coefficients with f(x):
$nx^2 - x^2 = 6x^2 \Rightarrow n - 1 = 6 \Rightarrow n = 7$

Now write in nx, then multiply out and equate the x^2 term with the one in f(x) to find the value of n.

So $f(x) = (x - 1)(x^2 + 7x + 12)$
Check the x coefficients: $12x - 7x = 5x$ ✓

Check this gives the correct x-term too.

So $x^3 + 6x^2 + 5x - 12 = (x - 1)(x^2 + 7x + 12)$

$x^2 + 7x + 12 = (x + 3)(x + 4)$

Then factorise the quadratic factor.

So $x^3 + 6x^2 + 5x - 12 = (x - 1)(x + 3)(x + 4)$

So the solutions to f(x) = 0 are:
$x = 1$, $x = -3$ and $x = -4$

Set each bracket equal to 0 to find the solutions of f(x) = 0.

Example 2

$f(x) = 2x^3 - 3x^2 - 12x + 20$.
Factorise $f(x)$ and find all the solutions of $f(x) = 0$.

Check to see if the coefficients add up to 0:
$f(1) = 2 - 3 - 12 + 20 = 7$
They don't add up to 0, so $(x - 1)$ is not a factor.

First try adding up the coefficients.

$f(-1) = (2 \times -1) - (3 \times 1) - (12 \times -1) + 20 = 27$ ✗
$f(2) = (2 \times 8) - (3 \times 4) - (12 \times 2) + 20 = 0$ ✓
$\Rightarrow$ $(x - 2)$ is a factor

$(x - 1)$ isn't a factor here, so use trial and error for values of x, until you find one that gives you $f(x) = 0$. Then write down the corresponding factor.

$$2x^3 - 3x^2 - 12x + 20 = (x - 2)(2x^2 + x - 10)$$
$$= (x - 2)(x - 2)(2x + 5)$$
$$= (x - 2)^2(2x + 5)$$

Now work out the quadratic factor, then factorise that to complete the factorisation of $f(x)$.

The solutions of $f(x) = 0$ are: $x = 2$ and $x = -\frac{5}{2}$

One of the factors is repeated, so there are only 2 solutions.

Example 3

$f(x) = 4x^3 + 9x^2 - 30x - 8$. Given that $x = -\frac{1}{4}$ is one solution of $f(x) = 0$, fully factorise $f(x)$ and find all the other solutions of $f(x) = 0$.

$-\frac{1}{4}$ is a root, so $\left(x + \frac{1}{4}\right)$ is a factor
$\Rightarrow$ $(4x + 1)$ is a factor.

Find a factor that corresponds to $x = -\frac{1}{4}$.

Tip You could also use $\left(x + \frac{1}{4}\right)$ as the factor, but it's a lot harder to find the quadratic when you have fractions in the expression.

$f(x) = (4x + 1)(x^2 + 2x - 8)$
$f(x) = (4x + 1)(x - 2)(x + 4)$

Then complete the factorisation of the cubic.

$x = -\frac{1}{4}$, $x = 2$ and $x = -4$

Finally, write down the solutions of $f(x) = 0$.

Exercise 4.10

Q1 Factorise the following:

a) $x^3 - 3x^2 + 2x$
b) $2x^3 + 3x^2 - 11x - 6$
c) $x^3 - 3x^2 + 3x - 1$
d) $x^3 - 3x^2 + 4$
e) $x^3 - x^2 - 7x + 7$
f) $x^3 + 2x^2 - 5x - 6$

Q2 Find all solutions to $f(x) = 0$, where:

a) $f(x) = x^3 - 3x^2 - 33x + 35$
b) $f(x) = x^3 - 28x + 48$

Q3 $f(x) = x^3 + 4x^2 - 8$

a) Write f(x) as the product of a linear factor and a quadratic factor.

b) Find the solutions of $f(x) = 0$.
Give your answers in surd form where appropriate.

Q3b) Hint The mention of surds suggests that you'll need to use the quadratic formula.

Q4 Find the roots of the cubic equation $x^3 - 2x^2 - x + 2 = 0$.

Q5 Find the roots of the cubic equation $x^3 - x^2 - 3x + 3 = 0$.

Q6 $f(x) = 6x^3 + 37x^2 + 5x - 6$. Use the fact that $(3x - 1)$ is one factor of f(x) to fully factorise f(x).

P Q7 $f(x) = x^3 - px^2 + 17x - 10$, where $(x - 5)$ is a factor of f(x).

a) Find the value of p. b) Factorise f(x). c) Find the solutions to $f(x) = 0$.

Q8 Factorise the following cubic equations:

a) $3x^3 + 2x^2 - 7x + 2$ b) $5x^3 - 13x^2 + 4x + 4$

Q9 Factorise and solve the cubic equation $4x^3 - 7x = -3$.

P Q10 Show that $x = 2$ is the only real root of the cubic equation $2x^3 - x^2 - 2x - 8 = 0$.

E P Q11 a) Show that $(x - 2)$ is a factor of $p(x) = 3x^3 - 4x^2 - 5x + 2$. *[1 mark]*

b) Hence, find all solutions to the simultaneous equations
$y = 3x^3 - 4x^2 - 8x + 6$ and $y = 4 - 3x$. *[5 marks]*

Challenge

E P Q12 $q(x) = p(x) - k$ for some real constant k, and $p(a) = k$.

a) Show that $(x - a)$ is a factor of q(x). *[2 marks]*

b) Show that $f(-4) = 3$ for $f(x) = x^3 - 6x^2 - 19x + 87$. *[1 mark]*

c) Hence, find all solutions to the equation $f(x) = 3$. *[4 marks]*

E P Q13 $p(x) = 2x^3 - 17x^2 + 40x - 16$ and $q(x) = x^3 - 8x^2 + 22x + k$, where k is a constant.

a) Show that $(x - 4)$ is a factor of p(x). *[1 mark]*

b) Find the value of k if $(x - 4)$ is also a factor of q(x). *[1 mark]*

c) Using the value of k found in part b), find all solutions to the equation
$p(x) = q(x)$, giving your answers in surd form where appropriate. *[4 marks]*

E P Q14 a) Show that $(3x - 1)$ is a factor of the cubic $p(x) = 3x^3 - 7x^2 - 22x + 8$. *[1 mark]*

b) Hence, sketch a graph of $y = p(x)$, clearly labelling
all intersection points with the axes. *[4 marks]*

c) Use your graph to determine the set of values of x such that $p(x) > 0$. *[1 mark]*

4.11 Algebraic Division

Once you've found one linear factor of a cubic, you can use **algebraic long division** to find the quadratic factor.

The best way to explain how this works is with a worked example:

Tip This is an alternative method for factorising cubics — use the method on p.70 if you prefer.

Example 1

$x - 2$ is a factor of the cubic $f(x) = 2x^3 - 5x - 6$. Use algebraic long division to write $f(x)$ as the product of a linear factor and a quadratic factor.

$$x - 2\,\overline{)\,2x^3 + 0x^2 - 5x - 6}$$

Write it out as a long division. If the cubic doesn't contain one of the powers of x, you'll need to add in a term with a coefficient of 0.

Tip Use the factor you already know as the divisor.

$$\begin{array}{r} 2x^2 \qquad\qquad\quad \\ x - 2\,\overline{)\,2x^3 + 0x^2 - 5x - 6} \end{array}$$

Start by dividing the first term in the cubic ($2x^3$) by the first term of the divisor (x): $2x^3 \div x = 2x^2$. Write this answer above the cubic.

$$\begin{array}{r} 2x^2 \qquad\qquad\quad \\ x - 2\,\overline{)\,2x^3 + 0x^2 - 5x - 6} \\ 2x^3 - 4x^2 \qquad\quad \end{array}$$

Multiply the divisor $(x - 2)$ by this answer ($2x^2$) to get $2x^3 - 4x^2$ and write this under the first two terms of the cubic.

$$\begin{array}{r} 2x^2 \qquad\qquad\quad \\ x - 2\,\overline{)\,2x^3 + 0x^2 - 5x - 6} \\ \underline{-(2x^3 - 4x^2)} \qquad\quad \\ 4x^2 - 5x \qquad \end{array}$$

Subtract $2x^3 - 4x^2$ from the main expression to get $4x^2$. Bring down the $-5x$ term just to make things clearer for the next subtraction.

$$\begin{array}{r} 2x^2 + 4x \qquad\quad \\ x - 2\,\overline{)\,2x^3 + 0x^2 - 5x - 6} \\ \underline{-(2x^3 - 4x^2)} \qquad\quad \\ 4x^2 - 5x \qquad \end{array}$$

Now divide the first term of the remaining polynomial ($4x^2$) by the first term of the divisor (x) to get $4x$ (the second term in the answer).

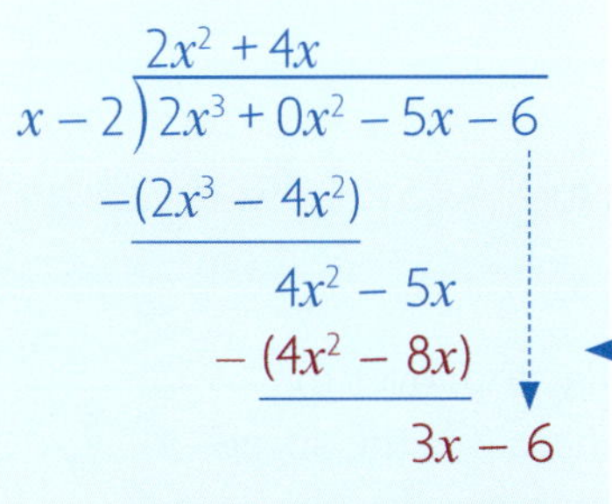

$$\begin{array}{r} 2x^2 + 4x \qquad\quad \\ x - 2\,\overline{)\,2x^3 + 0x^2 - 5x - 6} \\ \underline{-(2x^3 - 4x^2)} \qquad\quad \\ 4x^2 - 5x \qquad \\ \underline{-\,(4x^2 - 8x)} \qquad \\ 3x - 6 \end{array}$$

Multiply $(x - 2)$ by $4x$ to get $4x^2 - 8x$, then subtract again and bring down the -6 term.

Tip There are quite a few steps to algebraic division, so don't stop too soon. You need to keep going until you get either zero or a constant when you subtract — see next page.

continued on next page...

$$\begin{array}{r} 2x^2 + 4x + 3 \\ x - 2 \overline{)\, 2x^3 + 0x^2 - 5x - 6} \\ - \underline{(2x^3 - 4x^2)} \\ 4x^2 - 5x \\ - \underline{(4x^2 - 8x)} \\ 3x - 6 \\ - \underline{(3x - 6)} \\ 0 \end{array}$$

Divide $3x$ by x to get 3 (the third term in the answer). Then multiply $(x - 2)$ by 3 to get $3x - 6$.

After subtracting, you're left with 0 — you know this is right because $(x - 2)$ is a factor.

$f(x) = (x - 2)(2x^2 + 4x + 3)$

Don't forget the final step — writing $f(x)$ as a product of a linear factor and a quadratic factor. This quadratic won't factorise, so $f(x)$ is fully factorised.

Tip

The result of the division (ignoring any remainders) is called the quotient.

Exercise 4.11

Q1 Use algebraic long division and the given factors to fully factorise the following expressions:

a) $x^3 - 2x^2 - 15x + 36$, factor: $(x - 3)$ b) $x^3 - x^2 - 11x - 10$, factor: $(x + 2)$

c) $2x^3 + 11x^2 - 23x - 14$, factor: $(x - 2)$ d) $x^3 + 10x^2 + 31x + 30$, factor: $(x + 5)$

Q2 Write $x^3 - 5x + 4$ as the product of a linear factor and a quadratic factor using long division.

Q2, 4, 5 Hint

Remember to add in any missing terms, giving them a coefficient of 0.

Q3 $f(x) = x^3 + 2x^2 - 7x - 2$. Use algebraic long division to express $f(x)$ in the form $(x - 2)g(x)$, where $g(x)$ is a quadratic.

Q4 $f(x) = x^3 - 7x - 6$ and $f(-2) = 0$.
Use algebraic long division to find all the solutions of $f(x) = 0$.

Q5 Write $x^3 + x^2 - 12$ as the product of a linear factor and a quadratic factor using long division.

P Q6 a) Using algebraic long division, find the remainder when you divide $f(x) = x^3 - 2x^2 + x - 1$ by $(x + 3)$.

b) Write $f(x)$ in the form $(x + 3)g(x)$ + remainder, where $g(x)$ is a quadratic.

Problem Solving

When dividing by something that isn't a factor of the cubic, you'll end up with a non-zero constant as the answer to the final subtraction step. This is the remainder.

P Q7 a) Use algebraic division to find the remainder when $f(x) = x^3 - 8x^2 + 20x - 3$ is divided by $(x - 2)$.

b) Hence find the solutions to $f(x) - 13 = 0$.

P Q8 Use algebraic division to show that $x = 5$ is the only real solution to $x^3 - 15x^2 + 75x = 125$.

Challenge

P M Q9 The speed of a car is recorded as it accelerates and decelerates to a stop, over the time period $0 \leq t \leq T$, and modelled as $S = -t^3 + 2t^2 + 13t + 10$, where S is the speed in miles per hour, t is the time in minutes, and T is the time at which the car stops. Given that $(t + 1)$ is a factor of the function, use algebraic division to find T.

4 Review Exercise

Q1 Factorise the following expressions:

a) $x^2 + 2x + 1$ b) $x^2 - 13x + 30$ c) $x^2 - 4$

d) $3 + 2x - x^2$ e) $2x^2 - 7x - 4$ f) $5x^2 + 7x - 6$

Q2 Solve the following equations:

a) $x^2 - 3x + 2 = 0$ b) $x^2 + x - 12 = 0$ c) $2 + x - x^2 = 0$

d) $x^2 + x - 16 = x$ e) $3x^2 - 15x - 14 = 4x$ f) $4x^2 - 1 = 0$

g) $6x^2 - 11x + 9 = 2x^2 - x + 3$ h) $3x^2 + 10x - 8 = 2 - x - 3x^2$ i) $4 - 9x^2 = 0$

Q3 Solve these quadratic equations, leaving your answers in surd form where necessary.

a) $3x^2 - 7x + 3 = 0$ b) $2x^2 - 6x - 2 = 0$ c) $x^2 + 4x + 6 = 12$

E Q4 a) Find the exact solutions to the equation $x^2 + 4x - 11 = 0$, giving your answers in their simplest forms. *[2 marks]*

b) Hence, express the quadratic $x^2 + 4x - 11$ in the form $(x + a)(x + b)$. *[1 mark]*

P Q5 a) Rewrite the expression $x^2 + 6x + 7$ in the form $(x + m)^2 + n$.

b) Hence solve the equation $(2x + 1)^2 + 6(2x + 1) + 7 = 0$. Leave your answers in surd form.

E M Q6 A car travels along a straight road. The distance of the car, d km, from a fixed point, O, on the road is modelled by $d = \frac{15}{2} + t - \frac{1}{10}t^2$, where $t \geq 0$ is the time in minutes.

a) Find the initial distance of the car from O. *[1 mark]*

b) Find the time taken by the car to reach O. *[3 marks]*

c) By completing the square, show that the furthest distance that the car reaches from O is 10 km. *[2 marks]*

P Q7 Find all four solutions to the equation $x^4 - 17x^2 + 16 = 0$.

E P Q8 a) Factorise and solve the equation $2x^2 - 5x - 3 = 0$. *[2 marks]*

b) Hence, or otherwise, solve the equation $2x - 5\sqrt{x} = 3$. *[3 marks]*

E M Q9 A fox, F, chases a rabbit, R, along a straight path. The distances, in metres, of F and R from a fixed point on the path, O, at time t seconds after the fox starts running are given by $f(t) = t$ and $r(t) = \frac{1}{4}t^2 - 3t + 17$ respectively. The fox attempts to catch the rabbit, and $d(t)$ is the distance, in metres, between F and R at time t.

a) Find an expression for $d(t)$. *[1 mark]*

b) Use the discriminant of $d(t)$ to show that the fox doesn't catch the rabbit. *[2 marks]*

c) By completing the square, find the smallest distance between the fox and rabbit. *[2 marks]*

P Q10 If the quadratic equation $x^2 + kx + 4 = 0$ has two distinct real roots, what are the possible values of k?

E P Q11 The equation $2kx^2 + 5x + k = 0$ has repeated roots.
Find the possible values for k.
Give your answers in simplified surd form. *[5 marks]*

Q12 Rewrite these quadratics by completing the square.
Then state their maximum or minimum value and the value of x where this occurs.
Also, say if and where their graphs cross the x-axis.

a) $x^2 - 4x - 3$ b) $x^2 + 5x + 8$ c) $3 - 3x - x^2$

d) $2x^2 - 4x + 11$ e) $4x^2 - 28x + 48$ f) $14 + 12x - 3x^2$

E P Q13 a) Complete the square on the quadratic $y = \frac{1}{2}x^2 + kx + 25$. *[2 marks]*

b) Using your answer from part a), determine the range of possible values of k such that the graph of $y = \frac{1}{2}x^2 + kx + 25$ crosses the x-axis at exactly two points.
Simplify any surds in your answers. *[3 marks]*

Q14 How many roots do these quadratic equations have?
Sketch the graph of each quadratic function.

a) $x^2 - 2x - 3 = 0$ b) $x^2 - 6x + 9 = 0$ c) $2x^2 + 4x + 3 = 0$

E Q15 Consider the function $f(x) = x^2 - 2x - 14$.

a) (i) Rewrite the function in the form $f(x) = (x + a)^2 + b$, where a and b are integers to be found. *[2 marks]*

(ii) Hence, or otherwise, find the exact solutions to the equation $f(x) = 0$. *[2 marks]*

b) Sketch the graph of $y = f(x)$, labelling all intersections with the axes. *[3 marks]*

E Q16 a) Factorise the quadratic expression $28 - 13x - 6x^2$. *[1 mark]*

b) Using your answer to part a), find the solutions to $28 - 13x - 6x^2 = 0$. *[1 mark]*

c) Hence sketch the graph of the function $y = 28 - 13x - 6x^2$, clearly labelling any intersection points with the axes. *[3 marks]*

E P Q17 a) Show algebraically that the graph of $y = 2x^2 + 12x + 21$ doesn't cross the x-axis. *[2 marks]*

b) Express $2x^2 + 12x + 21$ in the form $a(x + b)^2 + c$, where a, b and c are rational numbers. *[2 marks]*

c) Find the maximum value of the function $y = \frac{10}{2x^2 + 12x + 21}$, and the value of x at which this maximum value occurs. *[3 marks]*

P M **Q18** A car travels through a multistorey car park. It starts above ground level, then goes underground. The first 10 seconds of the car's vertical path are modelled by the equation $h = 0.25t^2 - 2.75t + 6$, where h is the height in metres above the ground and t is the time in seconds.

a) Sketch a graph showing the height of the car during the first 10 seconds.

b) For the first 10 seconds of the car's journey, use your graph to find:

(i) the initial height of the car.

(ii) the lowest point of the car.

(iii) how long the car is underground for.

E **Q19** a) Express $3x^2 + 2x + 1$ in the form $a(x + b)^2 + c$, where a, b and c are rational numbers. *[2 marks]*

b) Hence sketch the graph with equation $y = 3x^2 + 2x + 1$, clearly labelling the coordinates of the vertex and any intersection points with the axes. *[3 marks]*

E P **Q20** The diagram shows part of the graph of the quadratic with equation $y = 2x^2 + bx + c$ where b and c are constants.

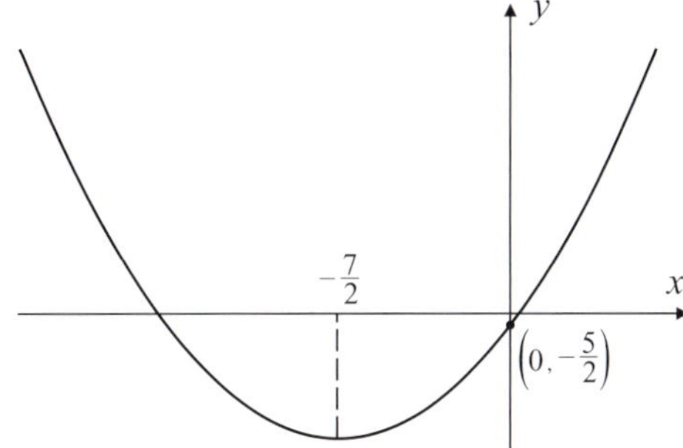

a) Find the values of b and c. *[3 marks]*

b) Using your answer to part a), find the solutions to the equation $2x^2 + bx + c = 0$. *[2 marks]*

Q21 a) Factorise the quadratic expression $\frac{1}{7}x^2 - \frac{62}{21}x - 1$.

b) Using your answer to part a), find the minimum value of the expression $\frac{1}{7}x^2 - \frac{62}{21}x - 1$, and the value of x at which this minimum value occurs.

E P **Q22** The graph of the curve with equation $y = -10 + 7x - x^2$ crosses the x-axis at points A and B, where the x-coordinate of B is greater than the x-coordinate of A. The graph has a vertex at the point C.

a) Find the coordinates of A and B. *[2 marks]*

b) Find the coordinates of C. *[2 marks]*

c) Explain why the triangle ABC is isosceles, and find its area. *[3 marks]*

E Q23 For the function $f(x) = x^3 + x^2$, show that the curve with equation $y = f(x)$ intersects the x-axis more than once.
State the coordinates of the points where $y = f(x)$ intersects the axes. *[3 marks]*

Q24 Solve the following cubic equations:

a) $x^3 - 4x^2 = 0$ b) $x^3 + 5x^2 - 6x = 0$ c) $x^3 - 6x^2 + 9x = 0$

d) $2x^3 + 5x^2 + 15x = x^3 - 3x^2$ e) $2x^3 + 20x^2 + 12x = 9x^3 - 20x^2$ f) $6x^3 - 5x^2 - 4x = 0$

E Q25 Find the exact solutions to the equation $2x^3 + 4x^2 - x + 4 = (x + 2)^2$. *[4 marks]*

P Q26 a) Find the coordinates of the points of intersection of the graphs of $y = f(x)$ and $y = g(x)$, where $f(x) = 5x^3 - 13x^2 + 6x$ and $g(x) = -5x^3 + 7x^2 + 6x$.

b) Express $f(x) = 5x^3 - 13x^2 + 6x$ as the product of three factors.

P Q27 a) Show that the x-coordinates of the points where the curves $y = x(x - 6)^2$ and $y = -x(2x - 31)$ intersect are given by the solutions to the equation $x^3 - 10x^2 + 5x = 0$.

b) Find the x-coordinates of the points where the two curves meet. Where appropriate, express your answers in surd form.

E P Q28 The graph of $y = f(x)$ is shown on the right.

Given that the coefficient of x^3 in $f(x)$ is 1, use the sketch of the curve $f(x)$ to find:

a) the coordinates of the unlabelled x-intercept, *[3 marks]*

b) $f(x)$ in the form $ax^3 + bx^2 + cx + d$. *[2 marks]*

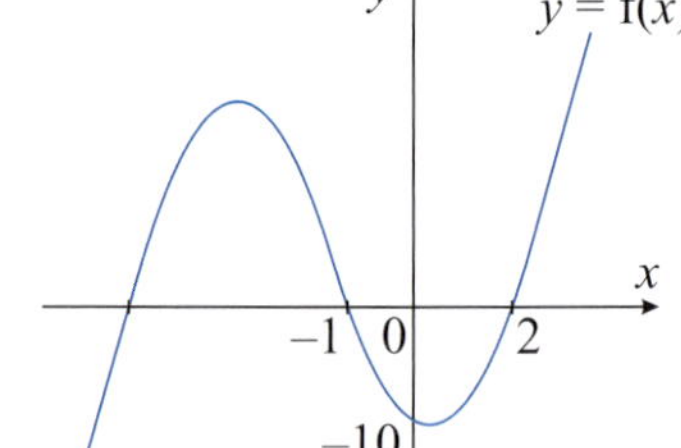

P Q29 Which of the following are factors of $f(x) = x^5 - 4x^4 + 3x^3 + 2x^2 - 2$?

a) $x - 1$ b) $x + 1$ c) $x - 2$ d) $2x - 2$

E Q30 Consider the function $p(x) = 4x^3 + 4x^2 - 5x - 3$.

a) Use the Factor Theorem to show that $(x - 2)$ is not a factor of $p(x)$. *[1 mark]*

b) Use the Factor Theorem to show that $(2x + 3)$ is a factor of $p(x)$. *[1 mark]*

E Q31 a) Use the Factor Theorem to show that $(x^2 - 1)$ is a factor of $f(x) = 2x^3 + 3x^2 - 2x - 3$. *[3 marks]*

b) Sketch the graph of $y = f(x)$, including all intersections with the axes. *[4 marks]*

E Q32 Given that the cubic $p(x) = ax^3 - 9x^2 + 23x + b$ is divisible by $(x - 5)$ and $(x - 3)$, find the values of a and b. *[3 marks]*

E P Q33 a) Show that $p^3 - q^3 \equiv (p - q)(p^2 + pq + q^2)$. *[2 marks]*

b) Hence, or otherwise, prove that the equation $(x - 1)^3 - (3 - 2x)^3 = 0$ has exactly one solution and state its value. *[4 marks]*

P Q34 $f(x) = (x + 5)(x - 2)(x - 1) + k$. If $(x + 2)$ is a factor of $f(x)$, find the value of k.

P Q35 Find the values of c and d so that $2x^4 + 3x^3 + 5x^2 + cx + d$ is exactly divisible by $(x - 2)(x + 3)$.

P Q36 Given that $(x - 3)$ is a factor of the cubic $f(x) = x^3 - 9x^2 + 7x + 33$, find the exact solutions of $f(x) = 0$.

E Q37 a) Use the Factor Theorem to factorise the cubic $p(x) = 2x^3 + 3x^2 - 3x - 2$. *[3 marks]*

b) Hence, or otherwise, find all solutions to the equation $p(x) = 0$. *[2 marks]*

E Q38 $p(x) = -x^3 + 7x^2 + ax + 12$, where a is a constant and $(x - 2)$ is a factor of $p(x)$.

a) Find the value of a. *[2 marks]*

b) Factorise $p(x)$. *[2 marks]*

c) Sketch the graph with equation $y = p(x)$, clearly labelling any intersection points with the axes. *[3 marks]*

P Q39 Find the roots of $f(x) = 0$ where $f(x) = x^3 + 6x^2 + 11x + 6$.

E Q40 For the function $f(x) = 4x^3 - 6x^2 - 3x + 5$, find the x-values such that $f(x) = 0$. *[4 marks]*

E Q41 Consider the function $f(x) = x^3 + 3x^2 - 4x - 12$.

a) (i) Find the value of $f(-2)$. *[2 marks]*

(ii) Hence, or otherwise, fully factorise $f(x)$. *[3 marks]*

b) Sketch the graph of $y = f(x)$, labelling all intersections with the axes. *[4 marks]*

E Q42 Fully factorise $f(x) = 2x^3 - 5x^2 - 4x + 3$ given that $(2x - 1)$ is a factor of $f(x)$. *[3 marks]*

E P Q43 Given that $(3x - 1)$ and $(2x + 1)$ are both factors of the cubic $6x^3 - 29x^2 + Px + Q$, find the values of P and Q. *[4 marks]*

Q44 Use long division to divide the cubics below. In each case state the quotient and remainder.

a) $x^3 - x^2 - 3x + 3$ by $(x + 3)$

b) $x^3 - 3x^2 - 5x + 6$ by $(x - 2)$

c) $x^3 + 2x^2 + 3x + 2$ by $(x + 2)$

Q45 Write the following functions $f(x)$ in the form $f(x) = (x + 2)g(x) +$ remainder, where $g(x)$ is a quadratic:

a) $f(x) = 3x^3 - 4x^2 - 5x - 6$

b) $f(x) = x^3 + 2x^2 - 3x + 4$

c) $f(x) = 2x^3 + 6x - 3$

E Q46 a) Find the quotient when $x^3 + 7x^2 + 15x + 9$ is divided by $(x + 3)$. *[2 marks]*

b) Hence, or otherwise, find all solutions to the equation $x^3 + 7x^2 + 15x + 9$. *[3 marks]*

P Q47 a) Write $f(x) = x^3 - 5x^2 - 2$ in the form $f(x) = (x + 2)g(x) +$ remainder, where $g(x)$ is a quadratic.

b) Hence show that $x = -2$ is the only solution to $f(x) + 30 = 0$.

Challenge

E P Q48 Consider the functions $p(x) = x^2 + 6$ and $q(x) = 6 + 5x - x^2$.

a) Show that the graph of $y = q(x)$ passes through the vertex of $y = p(x)$ and the graph of $y = p(x)$ passes through the vertex of $y = q(x)$. *[4 marks]*

b) Hence, sketch the graphs of both $y = p(x)$ and $y = q(x)$ on the same axes, clearly labelling the coordinates of the points of intersection between the two graphs, and between the graphs and the axes. *[3 marks]*

P Q49 $q(x)$ is a quadratic function, and the graph of $y = q(x)$ crosses the x-axis at the points $x = a$ and $x = a + 5$, where $-5 < a < -2$.

a) State the solutions to the equation $(x - a - 2)q(x) = 0$.

The graph of $y = q(x)$ intersects the y-axis at the point $(0, -3)$.

b) Sketch the graph of $y = (x - a - 2)q(x)$, clearly labelling the points of intersection with the coordinate axes in terms of a. Justify the shape of the graph.

E P Q50 Consider the function $p(n) = 8n^3 + 60n^2 + 142n + 105$.

a) Find the value of $p(10)$. *[1 mark]*

b) Find the quotient when $p(n)$ is divided by $(2n + 5)$. *[2 marks]*

c) Using your answer to part b), show that $p(n)$ is a product of three consecutive odd numbers for all integers $n \geq 0$. *[3 marks]*

d) Hence, or otherwise, find the three consecutive odd numbers whose product is equal to your answer to part a). *[1 mark]*

E P Q51 a) Find the quotient when $p(x) = 3x^3 - 11x^2 + 8x + 4$ is divided by $(x - 2)$. *[2 marks]*

The graph of a straight line, $y = mx + c$, is tangent to the curve $y = f(x)$ at $x = a$, whenever $x = a$ is a repeated solution to the equation $f(x) = mx + c$.

b) Using your answer to part a), show that the graph of the line with equation $y = 3x - 2$ is tangent to the curve with equation $y = 3x^3 - 11x^2 + 11x + 2$ at a point P, and find the coordinates of P. *[4 marks]*

E P Q52 a) Show that $(x - 1)(x^2 - (k - 1)x - (k^2 - 1)) \equiv x^3 - kx^2 + k(1 - k)x + (k^2 - 1)$, where k is a constant. *[2 marks]*

b) Hence find the values of k for which the graph of $y = x^3 - kx^2 + k(1 - k)x + (k^2 - 1)$ intersects the x-axis at a single point that is not a repeated root. *[4 marks]*

4 Chapter Summary

1 Quadratic equations have the general form $ax^2 + bx + c = 0$, where a, b and c are constants and $a \neq 0$.

2 Factorising a quadratic expression means writing it in the form $(nx + k)(mx + j)$. Once you have a quadratic equation in the form $(nx + k)(mx + j) = 0$, you can find the solutions by setting each bracket equal to 0 in turn.

3 If a quadratic $ax^2 + bx + c = 0$ can't be factorised, you can solve it using the quadratic formula: $x = \frac{-b \pm \sqrt{b^2 - 4ac}}{2a}$.

4 Another method for solving quadratic equations is 'completing the square'. Here you write the quadratic in the form $p(x + q)^2 + r$.

5 You can use the methods above to solve any equation of the form $a(\text{something})^2 + b(\text{something}) + c = 0$. The 'something' can be any function of x.

6 The graphs of quadratic functions have the shape of a parabola. The x-coordinates of the points where a quadratic graph $y = f(x)$ crosses the x-axis are called the real roots of the function — a quadratic function can have 0, 1 or 2 real roots. These values are the solutions of the quadratic equation $f(x) = 0$.

7 You can work out how many real roots a quadratic has by completing the square, or by using the discriminant $b^2 - 4ac$. If the discriminant is positive there are two real roots, if it's zero there is one real root, and if it's negative there are no real roots.

8 To sketch a quadratic graph, you need to work out what shape it has — if the coefficient of x^2 is positive then it's 'u'-shaped, and if the coefficient of x^2 is negative then it's 'n'-shaped. You also need to find the coordinates of any points where it crosses the x- and y-axes.

9 You can find the coordinates of the vertex (maximum or minimum point) of a quadratic graph by completing the square. If the graph has equation $y = p(x + q)^2 + r$, the vertex is at $(-q, r)$. You can also use symmetry to find the vertex if you know the roots.

10 If a cubic equation has the form $ax^3 + bx^2 + cx = 0$, you can solve it by taking out a factor of x to get $x(ax^2 + bx + c) = 0$. That gives $x = 0$ as one solution. You can then set the quadratic part equal to 0 and solve to find any other solutions.

11 The Factor Theorem says that for a polynomial $f(x)$, if $f(a) = 0$ then $(x - a)$ is a factor of $f(x)$. An extension of this theorem says that if $f\left(\frac{b}{a}\right) = 0$, then $(ax - b)$ is a factor of $f(x)$.

12 To factorise a cubic which doesn't have x as a factor, use the Factor Theorem to find one linear factor. The quadratic factor can then be found either directly by factorising, or using algebraic long division. Then factorise the quadratic (if you can) to complete the factorisation.

Inequalities and Simultaneous Equations

5

Learning Objectives

Once you've completed this chapter, you should be able to:

- Solve linear and quadratic inequalities.
- Represent inequalities graphically.
- Solve pairs of linear simultaneous equations.
- Solve simultaneous equations where one is linear and one is quadratic.

Prior Knowledge Check

1 If x is an integer in the interval $1 \leq x \leq 10$, list all the elements of:
a) $A = \{x : x \text{ is prime}\}$ b) $B = \{x : x \text{ is even}\}$ c) $C = A \cap B$ d) $D = A \cup B$ *see page 7*

2 Expand the brackets in these expressions:
a) $3(x - 1)$ b) $-8(2x - 5y)$ c) $a(a^2 + b)$ *see page 16*

3 Factorise the following expressions completely:
a) $8c - 36d$ b) $m^3 + 2mn$ c) $6pq^2 + 9p^2q$ *see page 19*

4 Solve the following quadratic equations:
a) $x^2 + 3x - 28 = 0$ b) $2x^2 + 13x + 15 = 0$ c) $5x^2 + 8x - 4 = 0$ *see pages 39-48*

5.1 Linear Inequalities

Solving where the inequality sign doesn't change direction

Solve inequalities like you solve equations — anything you do to one side, you do to the other.

- If you **add** or **subtract** something from both sides of an inequality, the inequality sign **doesn't** change direction.
- Multiplying or dividing both sides of an inequality by a **positive** number **doesn't** affect the direction of the inequality sign.

You might have to give your answers in **set notation** — see page 7 for a reminder of what this means.

> **Tip** You may also have seen interval notation. For example, $1 < x \le 2$ can be written as (1, 2]. The round bracket means 1 is not included and the square bracket means 2 is included.

Example 1

Find the set of values for x which satisfy:

a) $x - 3 < -1 + 2x$

$x - 2 < 2x$ ← Add 1 to both sides of the inequality.

$-2 < x$ ← Subtract x from both sides.

b) $2(4x + 1) \ge 2x + 17$

$8x + 2 \ge 2x + 17$ ← Expand the brackets.

$8x \ge 2x + 15$ ← Subtract 2 from both sides.

$6x \ge 15$ ← Subtract $2x$ from both sides.

$\frac{6x}{6} \ge \frac{15}{6}$ ← Divide both sides by 6.

$x \ge \frac{5}{2}$

> **Tip** The direction of the inequality sign is not affected by any of the steps taken to solve these inequalities.

Solving where the inequality sign does change direction

Multiplying or dividing an inequality by a **negative** number **changes** the direction of the inequality sign.

Example 2

Find the set of values of x for which $4 - 3x \le 16$.

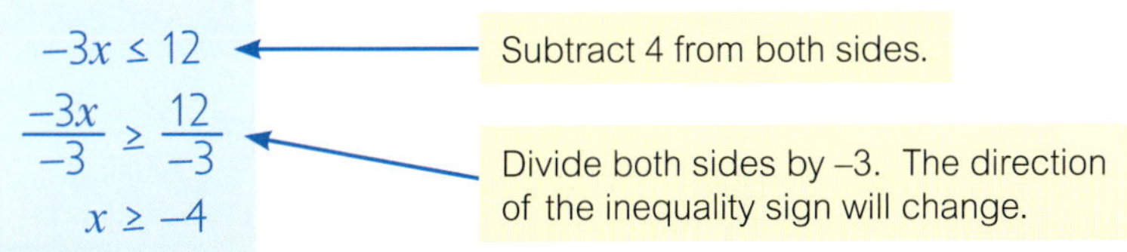

> **Tip** Dividing by –1 is the same as swapping everything from one side to the other. So when you divide by any negative number the sign changes.

Example 3

Find the set of values of x for which $\frac{2-4x}{3} > \frac{5-3x}{4}$. Give your answer in set notation.

$4(2 - 4x) > 3(5 - 3x)$

$8 - 16x > 15 - 9x$

Multiply both sides by 12 to remove the fractions, and expand the brackets.

$-16x > 7 - 9x$

$-7x > 7$

Subtract 8 from both sides, then add $9x$ to both sides.

$x < -1$

Divide both sides by –7 and change the direction of the inequality sign.

$\{x : x < -1\}$

Write the final answer in set notation.

Finding the solution to two inequalities

You may be given two inequalities and be asked to find a solution which satisfies **both** of them.

Example 4

Find the set of values for x which satisfy both the inequalities $x - 5 < -3 + 2x$ and $2x > 4x - 6$.

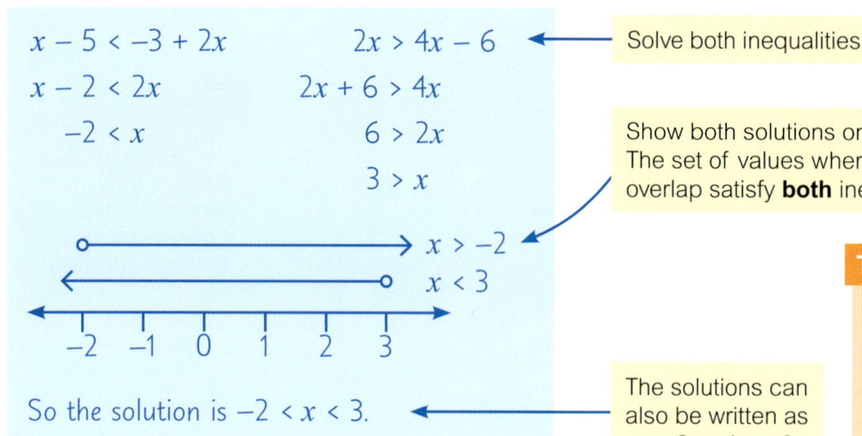

Solve both inequalities separately.

Show both solutions on a number line. The set of values where the two lines overlap satisfy **both** inequalities.

The solutions can also be written as $x > -2$ and $x < 3$.

Tip Each line has an open circle at the end to show that this number isn't a possible value of x. Solutions with a $\leq$ or $\geq$ sign end with a filled-in circle (●►) to show that the number is a possible value of x.

Exercise 5.1

Q1 Find the set of values for x which satisfy:

a) $2x - 1 < x + 4$ b) $4 - 3x \geq 10 - 5x$ c) $5x + 7 > 3x + 1$

d) $3 - 2x \leq 5x - 4$ e) $9 - x \geq 7x + 5$ f) $12x - 9 \leq 4x + 11$

g) $3x - 6 > 6 - 3x$ h) $-4x < 16 - 7x$

Q2 Find the set of values for x which satisfy the inequalities below. Give your answers in set notation.

a) $2(x + 3) > 3(x + 2)$ b) $5(1 + 3x) \leq 7$ c) $12 \geq 2(5 - 2x)$

Q2 Hint Multiply out the brackets first.

Q3 Find the set of values for x which satisfy:

a) $\frac{6-5x}{2} < \frac{4-8x}{3}$ b) $\frac{3x-1}{4} \geq 2x$ c) $\frac{x-2}{2} - \frac{2x+3}{3} < 7$

Q4 Find the set of values for x which satisfy the inequalities below. Give your answers in set notation.

a) $-5 < 2x - 3 < 15$ b) $-5 \leq 4 - 3x < 19$ c) $5 \leq 7 + 6x \leq 11$

Q5 Solve the following inequalities, and represent the solutions on a number line:

a) $2x \geq 3 - x$ b) $5x - 1 < 3x + 5$

c) $2x + 1 \geq 3x + 2$ d) $3(x - 3) \leq 5(x - 1)$

e) $9 - x \leq 3 - 4x$ f) $\frac{2(x-3)}{3} + 1 < \frac{2x-1}{2}$

Q5 Hint Look at the inequality sign to decide the direction of your arrow and whether the line should end with an open or filled-in circle.

Q6 a) Find the set of values of x for which $7 \leq 3x - 2 < 16$.

b) Show your solution to part a) on a number line.

Q7 Find the set of values for x which satisfy both $4 - 2x < 10$ and $3x - 1 < x + 7$. Give your answer in set notation.

Q8 Find the values of x which satisfy both inequalities:

a) $2x \geq 3x - 5$ and $3x - 2 \geq x - 6$ b) $5x + 1 \leq 11$ and $2x - 3 < 5x - 6$

c) $2x - 1 \leq 3x - 5$ and $5x - 6 > x + 22$ d) $3x + 5 < x + 1$ and $6x - 1 \geq 3x + 5$

E P Q9 Find the set of values for x that satisfy both inequalities $4x - 2 > x + 4$ and $4x - 16 < 19 - 3x$. *[3 marks]*

E Q10 $P = \frac{3t+5}{4} + \frac{2t-1}{5}$. Find the set of values of t for which P is greater than 73. *[3 marks]*

E Q11 Solve the inequality $\frac{6x+5}{3} < \frac{3-2x}{5} + 2(x+7)$. Give your answer in set notation. *[3 marks]*

E Q12 Solve the inequality $3 + x\sqrt{7} < 2x - 3$. Give your answer in the form $a\sqrt{7} + b$, where a and b are rational numbers. *[3 marks]*

Challenge

Q13 a) For $a, b > 0$, prove $\frac{1}{a} < \frac{1}{b} \Rightarrow a > b$. *[2 marks]*

b) Using your answer from part a), solve the inequality $\frac{1}{3x+2} < \frac{3}{5x+11}$ for $x > 0$. *[3 marks]*

E P Q14 Find the set of values of x for which the graph of $3x - 2y + 7 = 0$ is above the graph of $5y + 3 = 9x$. *[3 marks]*

E Exam Style P Problem Solving M Modelling

5.2 Quadratic Inequalities

When solving inequalities, it's important that you **don't divide** or **multiply** by **variables** (anything you don't know the value of, e.g. x or y). The variable might be **negative**, so the inequality sign may end up pointing in the wrong direction. Or the variable could be equal to **zero** — you can't divide something by zero.

Problem Solving

If you have an x on the bottom of a fraction (e.g. $\frac{2}{x} < 1$), you have to multiply both sides by x^2 (as this is always positive). So $\frac{2}{x} < 1$ would become $2x < x^2$.

Example 1

Simplify the quadratic inequality $36x < 6x^2$.

$36x < 6x^2 \Rightarrow 6x < x^2$ ← Divide by 6.

$\Rightarrow 0 < x^2 - 6x$, which is $x^2 - 6x > 0$. ← Don't divide by x because x could be negative (or zero). Instead, subtract $6x$ from both sides.

In general, the best way to **solve** a **quadratic inequality** is to do the following:

- **Rewrite the inequality** with zero on one side.
- **Sketch the graph** of the quadratic function.
- Use the graph to **find the solution**.

Example 2

Find the values of x which satisfy $-x^2 + 2x + 4 \geq 1$.

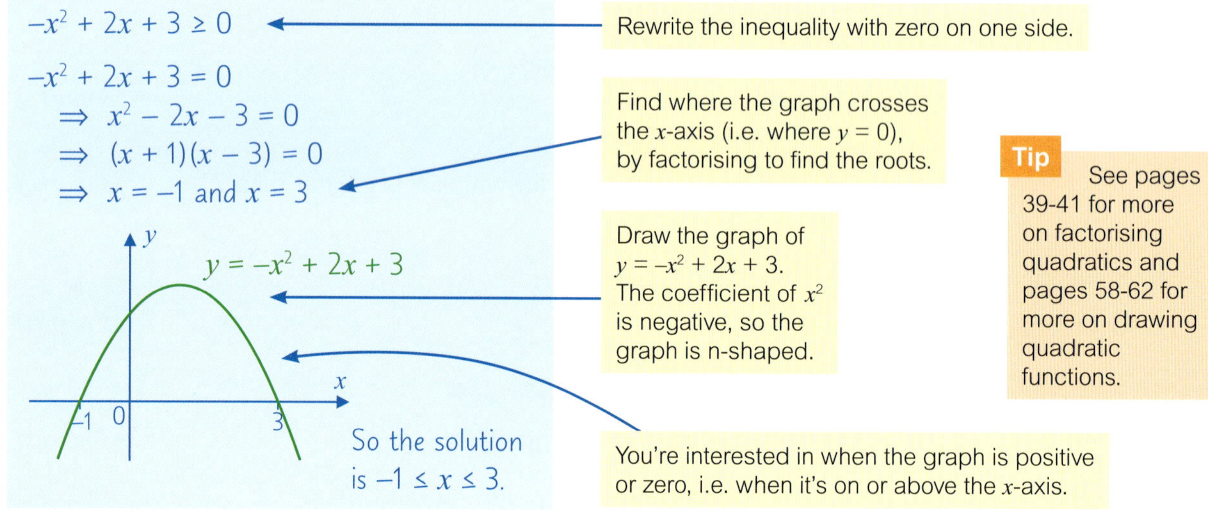

Tip

See pages 39-41 for more on factorising quadratics and pages 58-62 for more on drawing quadratic functions.

Example 3

Find the values of x which satisfy $2x^2 + 2x - 5 > 3x - 2$. Give your answer in set notation.

$2x^2 - x - 3 > 0$ ← Rewrite the inequality with zero on one side.

$2x^2 - x - 3 = 0 \Rightarrow (2x - 3)(x + 1) = 0$ ← Factorise the quadratic equation.

continued on the next page...

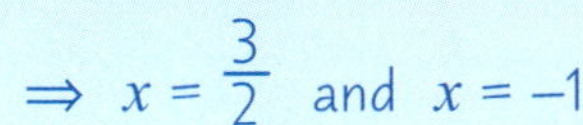

$\Rightarrow x = \frac{3}{2}$ and $x = -1$

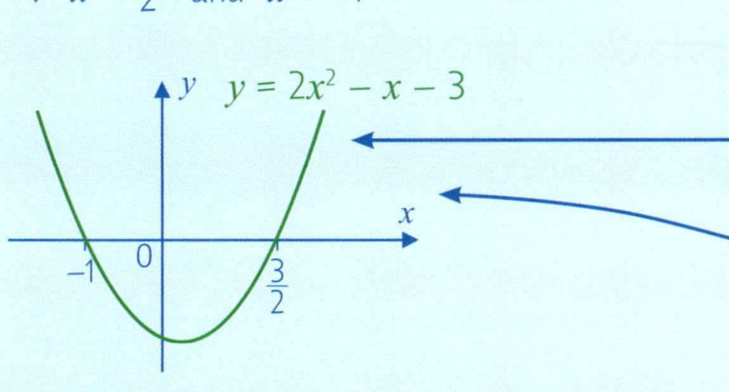

Draw the graph of $y = 2x^2 - x - 3$. The coefficient of x^2 is positive, so the graph is u-shaped.

Look at where the graph is positive — this is when x is less than –1 and when x is greater than $\frac{3}{2}$.

So the solution is: $x < -1$ or $x > \frac{3}{2}$

In set notation, this is: $\{x : x < -1\} \cup \left\{x : x > \frac{3}{2}\right\}$

Example 1 revisited

Find the values of x which satisfy $36x < 6x^2$.

$36x < 6x^2$

$\Rightarrow x^2 - 6x > 0$

Simplify $36x < 6x^2$ (this was done on the last page).

$x^2 - 6x = 0$

$\Rightarrow x(x - 6) = 0$

$\Rightarrow x = 0$ and $x = 6$

Factorise the quadratic equation to find the roots.

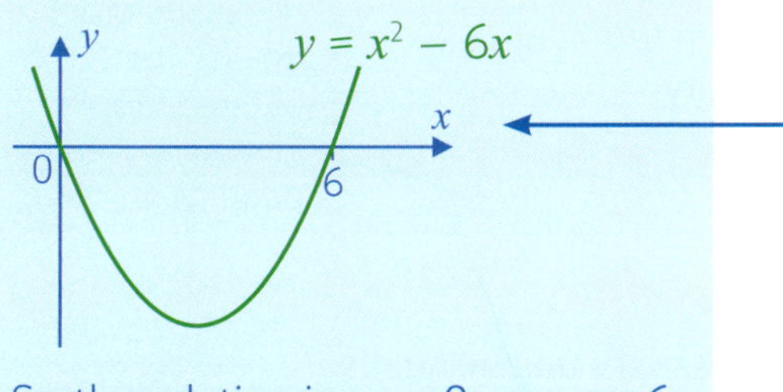

Draw the graph of $y = x^2 - 6x$. Look at where the graph is positive — this is when x is less than 0 and when x is greater than 6.

So the solution is: $x < 0$ or $x > 6$

Problem Solving

If you had divided the inequality $6x < x^2$ by x, you would have missed the $x < 0$ part of the solution.

You may be asked to find the set of values for x which satisfy **both** a quadratic inequality and a linear inequality. To do this, you just work out the solution of each inequality separately and then use a **graph** to help you find the solution that satisfies both.

Example 4

Find the set of values of x which satisfy:

a) $5x - 10 > 4x - 7$

$5x - 10 > 4x - 7 \Rightarrow 5x > 4x + 3 \Rightarrow x > 3$

Solve the linear inequality in the usual way (see page 83 as a reminder).

b) $2x^2 - 11x + 5 < 0$

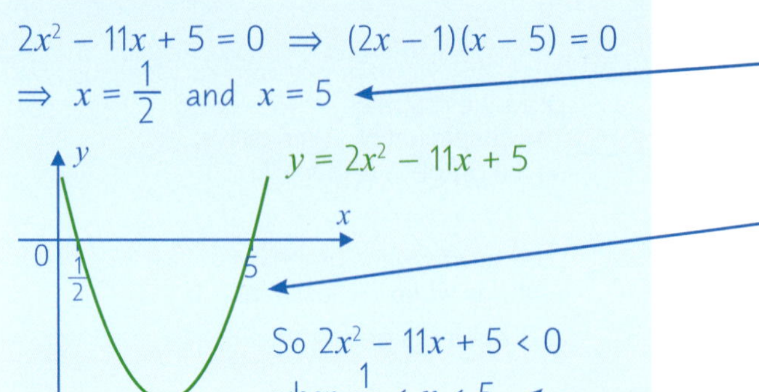

You've already got zero on one side, so just factorise the quadratic to find where the graph crosses the x-axis.

The coefficient of x^2 is positive, so the graph is u-shaped.

You're interested in when this is negative, i.e. when it's below the x-axis. From the graph, this is when x is between $\frac{1}{2}$ and 5.

c) both $5x - 10 > 4x - 7$ and $2x^2 - 11x + 5 < 0$

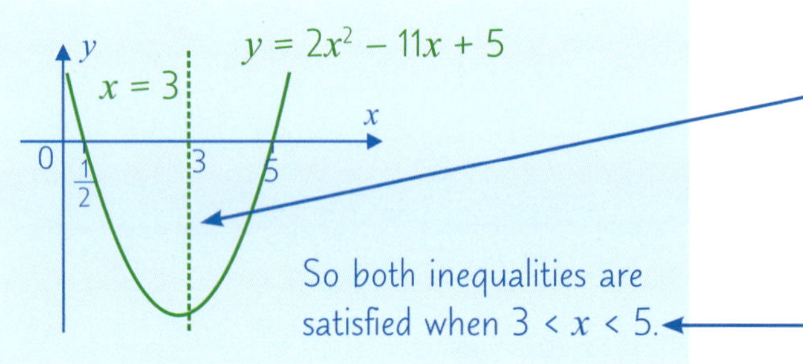

You already know the solutions to both inequalities — and the graph above shows the solution to the quadratic inequality. So add the line $x = 3$ to your graph.

You're now interested in when the curve is negative, and when the x values are greater than 3.

Solving a quadratic inequality to find k

On page 55, you saw a quadratic containing an unknown constant (k) and used the formula for the **discriminant** to form a **linear inequality** in terms of k. The example below is similar, but it results in a **quadratic inequality**.

Tip The discriminant is the $b^2 - 4ac$ bit of the quadratic formula — see page 54 for more.

Example 5 

The equation $kx^2 + (k + 3)x + 4 = 0$ has two distinct real solutions.
Show that $k^2 - 10k + 9 > 0$, and find the set of values of k which satisfy this inequality.

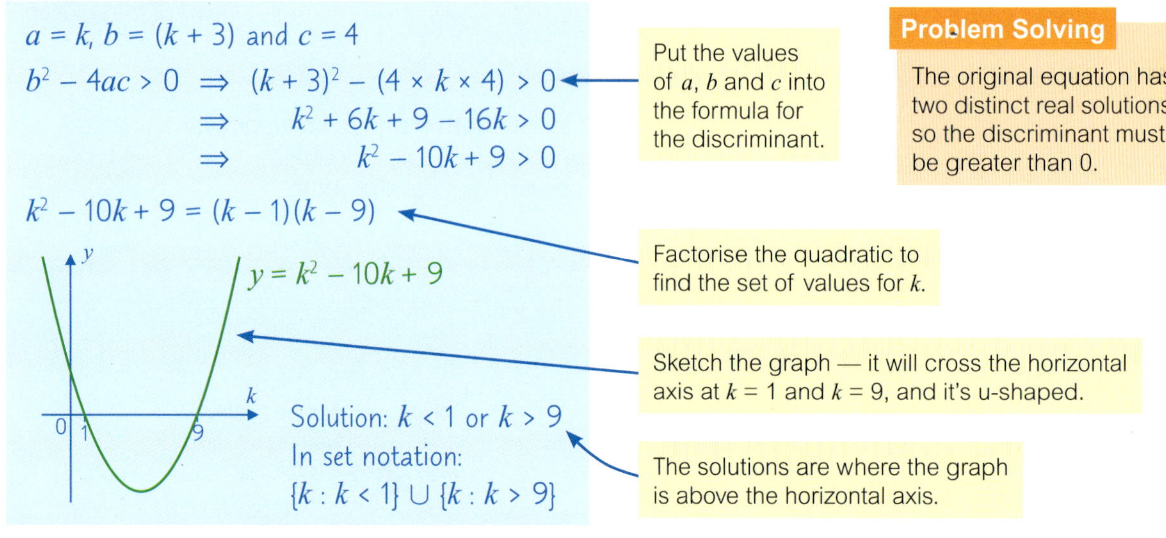

Exercise 5.2

Q1 Use the graphs given to solve the following quadratic inequalities:

a) $x^2 + 2x - 3 < 0$

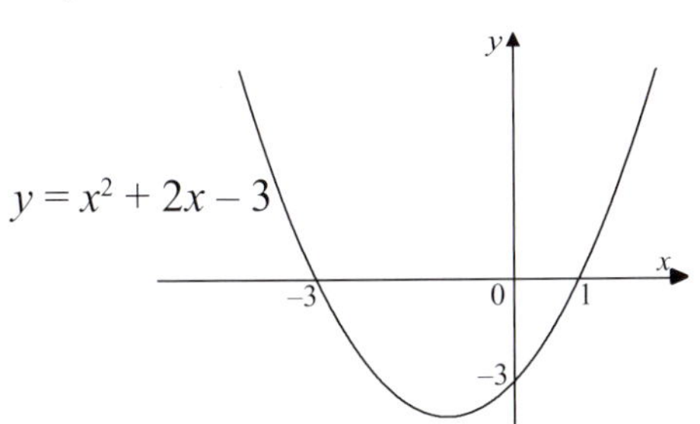

b) $4x - x^2 < 0$

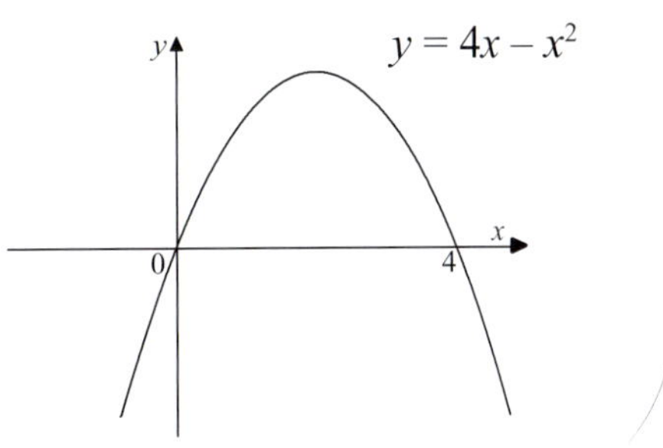

c) $2x^2 \geq 5 - 9x$

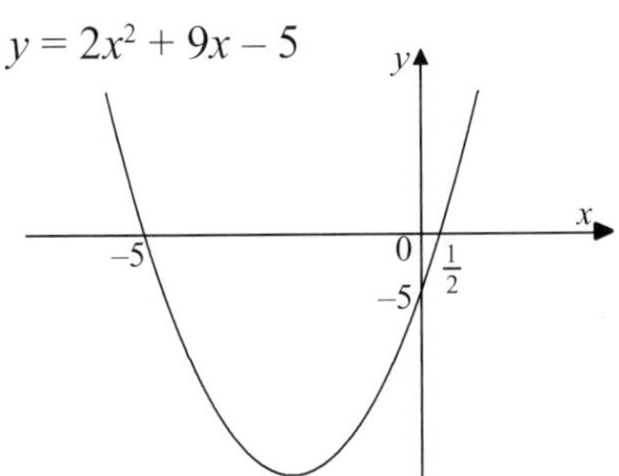

d) $x^2 - 2x - 5 > 0$

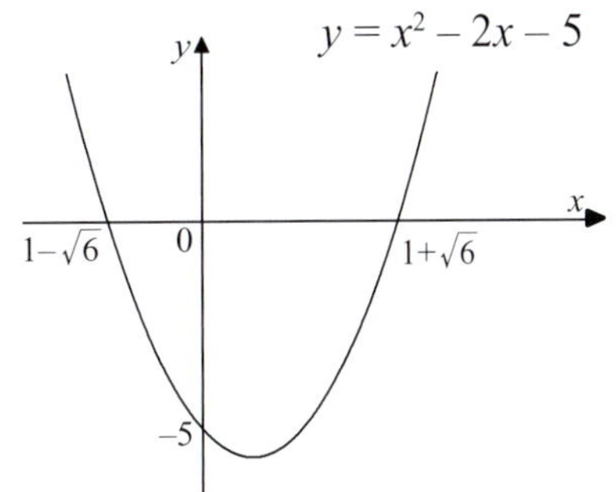

Q2 Use the graphs given to help you solve the quadratic inequalities below. Give your answers in set notation.

a) $x^2 \leq 4$

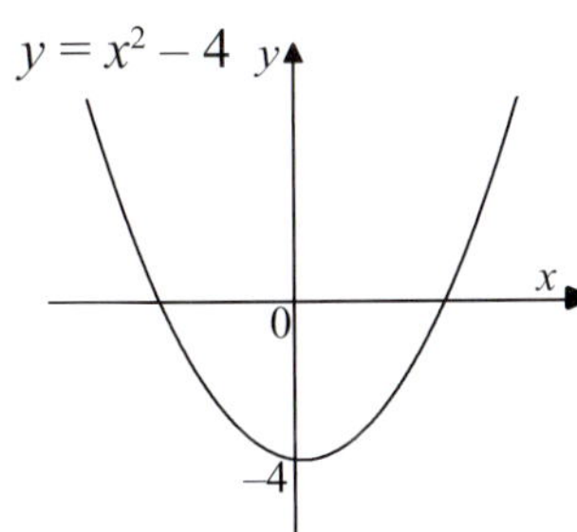

b) $13x < 3x^2 + 4$

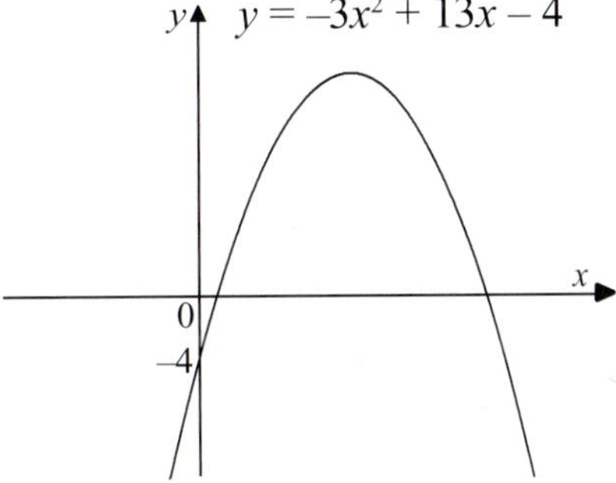

c) $x^2 + 4 < 6x$

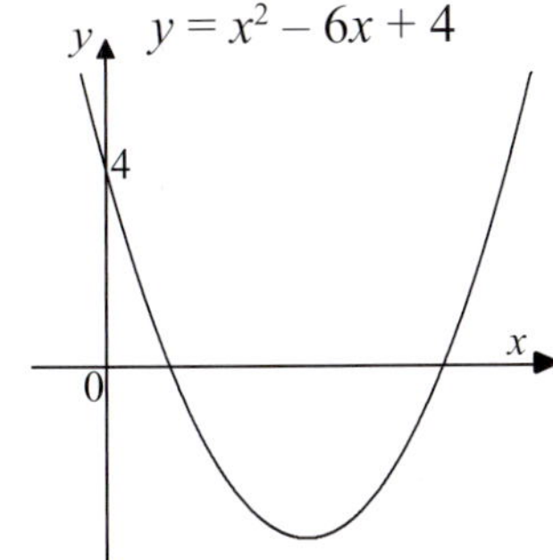

d) $7x > 4 - 2x^2$

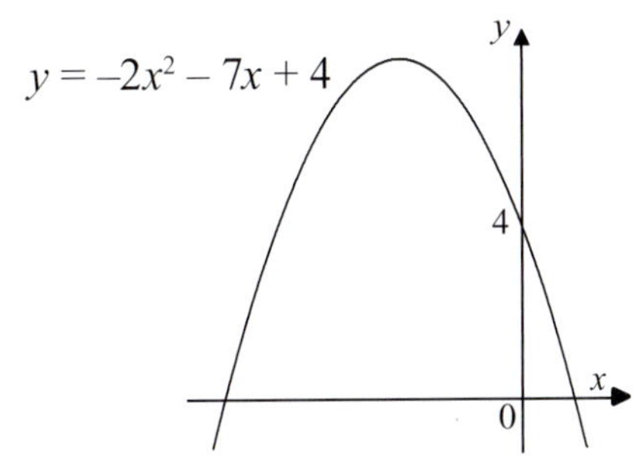

Q3 Find the ranges of values of x which satisfy the following quadratic inequalities. Include a sketch of the graph for each answer.

a) $x^2 + 5x - 6 \geq 0$ b) $x^2 - 3x + 2 < 0$ c) $6 - 5x > 6x^2$

d) $x^2 - 5x + 24 \leq 5x + 3$ e) $36 - 4x^2 \leq 0$ f) $x^2 - 6x + 3 > 0$

g) $x^2 - x + 3 > 0$ h) $6 \geq 5x^2 + 13x$ i) $2x^2 > 3(x + 3)$

j) $(x + 4)^2 \leq 5x$ k) $x^2 + 5x < \frac{1}{2}$ l) $\frac{3}{4}x^2 \geq 1 + \frac{1}{4}x$

Q4 Find the values of x which satisfy the following inequalities, giving your answers in set notation:

a) $\frac{1}{x} > 5$ b) $7 > \frac{3}{x}$

c) $-5 > \frac{2}{x}$ d) $-\frac{6}{x} > 1$

Q4 Hint To recap what to do when x is on the bottom of a fraction, see the Problem Solving tip on p.86.

P Q5 Use the following graphs to find the values of x which satisfy the corresponding inequalities. Give your answers in set notation.

a) $x^2 - 6x - 7 < 0$ and $x \leq 4$

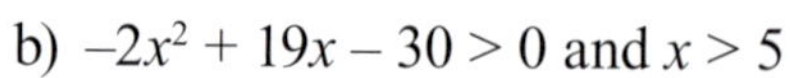

b) $-2x^2 + 19x - 30 > 0$ and $x > 5$

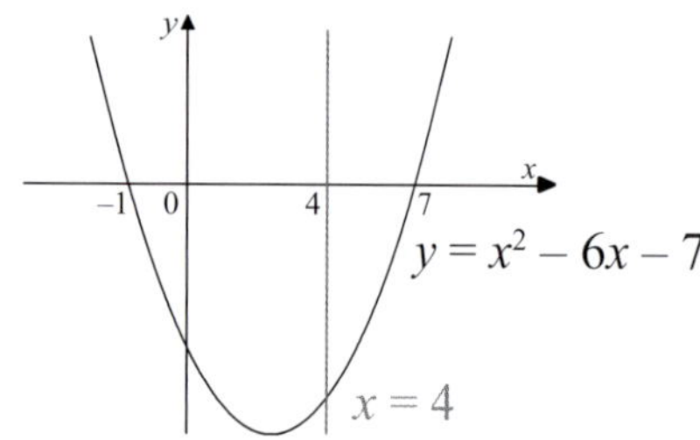

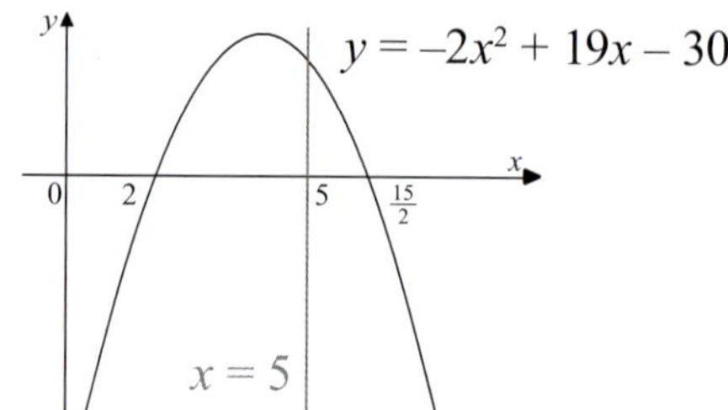

c) $x^2 - x \leq 56$ and $\frac{1}{x} + \frac{1}{x^2} > 0$ d) $4x \leq \frac{x^2}{3}$ and $5x - 2 < 4x + 8$

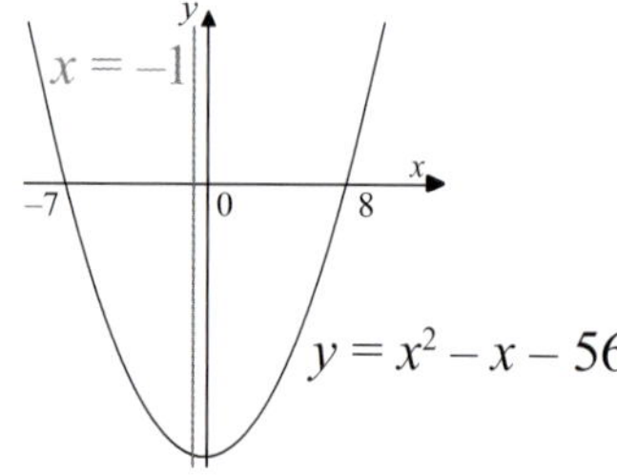

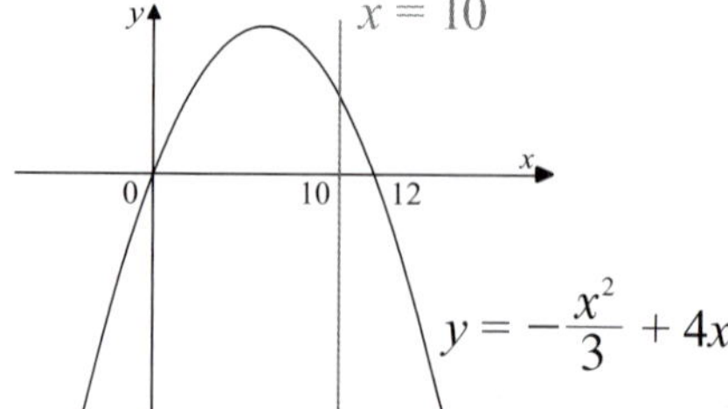

P M Q6 A rectangular office is to be built, measuring $(x - 9)$ metres wide and $(x - 6)$ metres long. Given that at least 28 m^2 of floor space is required, find the set of possible values of x.

P Q7 a) Find the set of values of k for which $kx^2 - 6x + k = 0$ has two distinct real solutions.

b) Find the set of values for k which gives the equation $x^2 - kx + k = 0$ no real roots. Give your answer in set notation.

P Q8 Find the values of x which satisfy both $4(3 - x) \geq 13 - 5x$ and $7x + 6 \geq 3x^2$.

5.3 Graphing Inequalities

You've seen on the last few pages how **graphs** can be used to solve quadratic inequalities. You can also show **regions** on a graph that satisfy **more than one inequality** in **two variables** (x and y) — whether they're linear or quadratic. The method has four steps:

1. Write each inequality as an equation.
Just put = wherever you have an inequality sign, and **rearrange** into the form "$y = ...$". You might have to **split up** any inequalities that are of the form $a < x < b$ into two separate bits — i.e. $a = x$ and $x = b$.

2. Draw the graph for each equation.
If the original inequality was **<** or **>**, draw a **dotted line**, and draw a **solid line** for **≤** or **≥**.

3. Work out which side of each line you want.
Look back at each inequality and **substitute** in the coordinates of a point to see whether or not it **satisfies** the inequality (usually the **origin** is an easy point to use). If it does, you want the side of the line that the point is on, and if not, you want the other side.

Problem Solving If the origin lies on one of the lines, you might have to use a different point — but the method is the same.

4. Label the correct region.
Once you know which side of each line you need, shade the **other side** (the side that does **not** satisfy the inequality). Once you've done this for each inequality, **label** the **unshaded** area. This will be the region that satisfies **all** of the inequalities.
Make sure you read the question **carefully** — you could be asked to shade the region that **satisfies** the inequalities rather than the regions that don't.

Example 1

Draw the following inequalities on a graph and label the region that satisfies all three:

$2x + y > 4 \qquad x - y < 1 \qquad y \leq 3$

$y = 4 - 2x \qquad y = x - 1 \qquad y = 3$

Change the inequalities into equations.

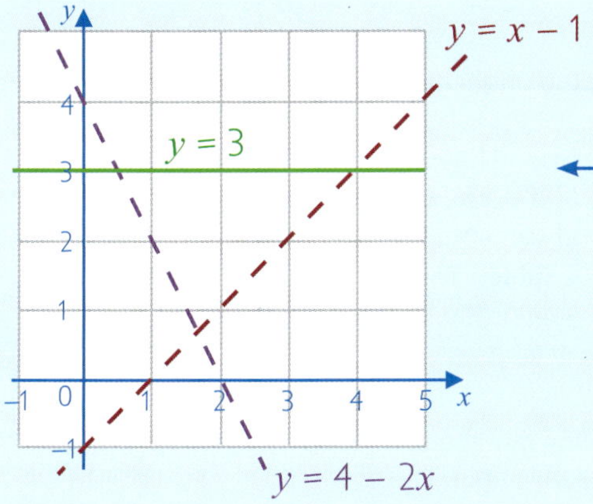

Plot the lines on your graph, using dotted lines for the first two, and a solid line for $y = 3$.

continued on the next page...

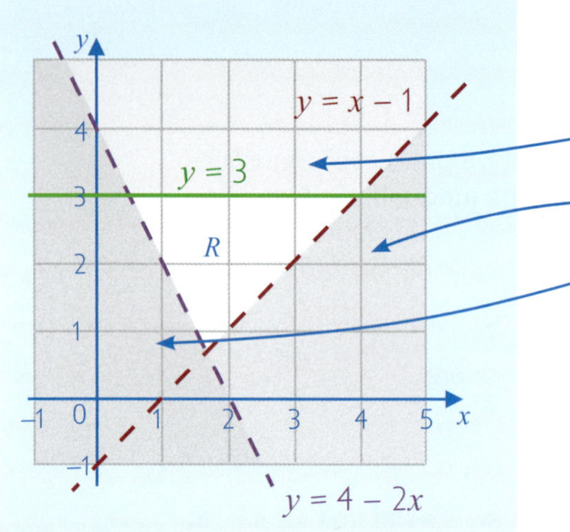

Decide which side of each line you want.
Try the origin (0, 0) in each inequality.

- $y \leq 3 \Rightarrow 0 \leq 3$, which is **true**. The origin is on the **correct** side of the line, so shade the other side.
- $x - y < 1 \Rightarrow 0 - 0 < 1$, which is **true**. The origin is on the **correct** side of the line, so shade the other side.
- $2x + y > 4 \Rightarrow 0 + 0 > 4$, which is **false**. The origin is on the **wrong** side of the line, so shade this side.

The unshaded region is the area you want — it satisfies all three inequalities. Don't forget to label it — this one is labelled R.

Tip You can check your answer by testing a point — for example, the point (2, 2) lies in the unshaded region and satisfies all three inequalities here.

Example 2

Draw and label the region that satisfies the following inequalities: $y > x^2 - x - 2$ $\quad y \geq 4 + 7x - 2x^2$

$y = x^2 - x - 2$
$= (x + 1)(x - 2)$

$y = 4 + 7x - 2x^2$
$= (4 - x)(1 + 2x)$

Write out the inequalities as equations and factorise.

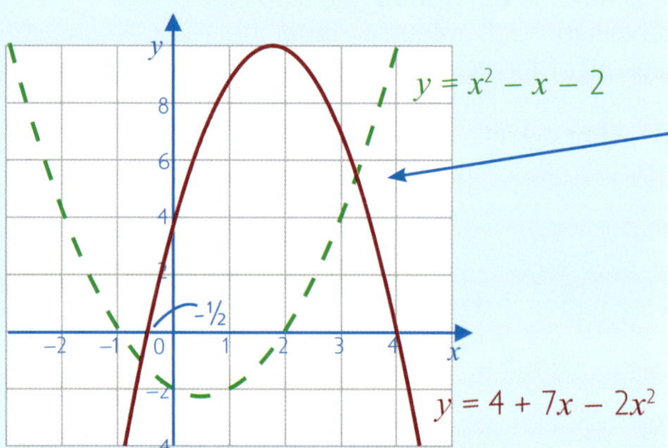

Draw the graphs of these equations, using a **dotted line** for $y = x^2 - x - 2$ and a **solid line** for $y = 4 + 7x - 2x^2$.

Tip Try to sketch the quadratics as accurately as you can (by finding the x- and y-intercepts and vertices — see pages 58-62).

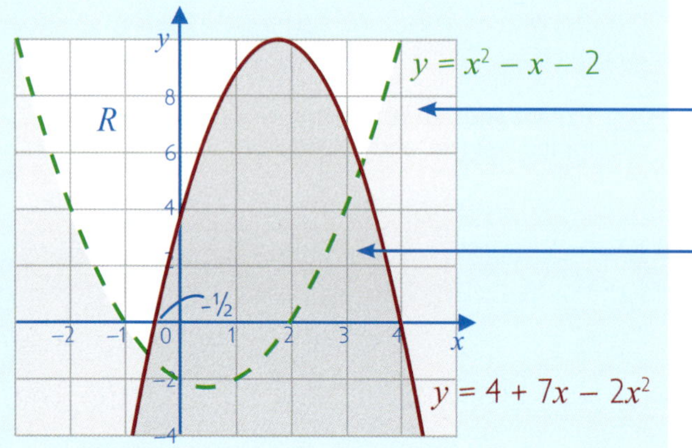

Try the origin in each inequality:

- $y > x^2 - x - 2 \Rightarrow 0 > 0 - 0 - 2$, which is **true**. The origin is on the **correct** side of the line, so shade the other side.
- $y \geq 4 + 7x - 2x^2 \Rightarrow 0 \geq 4 + 0 - 0$, which is **false**. The origin is on the **wrong** side of the line, so shade this side.

Notice that the unshaded region is not enclosed — it continues upwards to infinity.

Exercise 5.3

Q1 Work out whether the following statements are true or false:

a) The point (2, 4) is in the region that satisfies $3y > 8x - 3$.

b) The point (–3, –5) lies outside the region that satisfies $4y + x^2 \leq 3$.

c) The point (8, –4) is in the region that satisfies $y^2 + (x + 6)^2 \geq 68$.

d) The point (1, 3) is in the region that satisfies $x + 2y > 4$ and $3x^2 > 20 - 4y$.

e) The point $\left(\frac{1}{2}, \frac{3}{2}\right)$ lies outside the region that satisfies $y^2 < 10 - 8x^2$ and $3x + 4y \geq 6$.

Q2 Give the inequalities that define the shaded regions on the following graphs.

a)

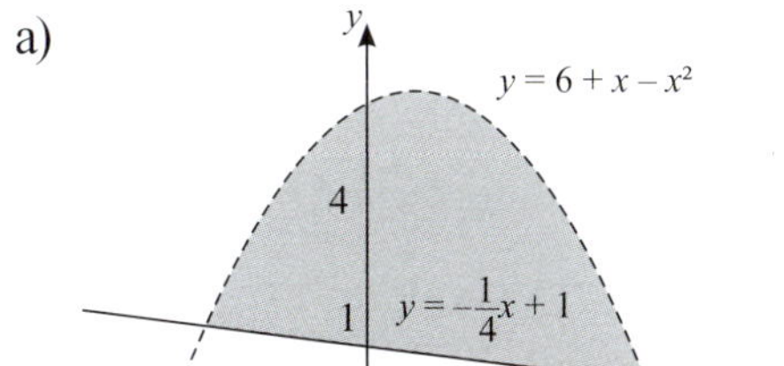

b)

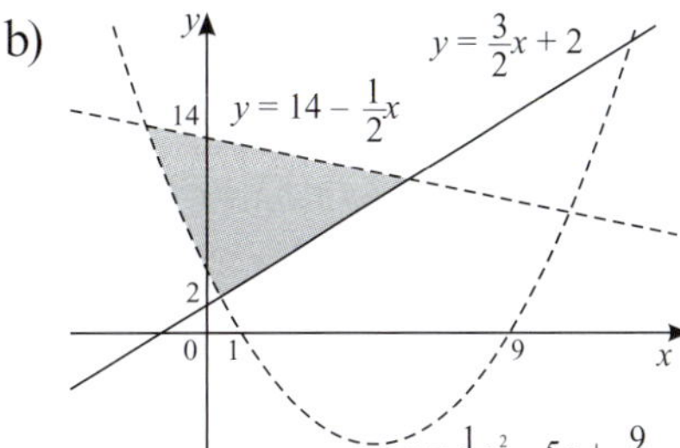

Q3 Draw and shade the regions that satisfy the following sets of inequalities:

a) $x + y < 5, \quad 2x + y \geq 4, \quad x + 2y > 6$

b) $x \leq 4, \quad y \leq 7, \quad x + y > 4$

c) $y > x^2, \quad x - y \geq -3$

d) $y - 2 \leq x^2, \quad 2x^2 - y < 2$

e) $4x^2 > y - 5, \quad 3x + 5y \leq 40$

f) $2y + 4x^2 < 6x + 10, \quad 5y > 2x + 5$

Q3 Hint The question asks you to shade the region that satisfies the inequalities, not the region that doesn't.

E Q4 A region, R, of the plane is determined by the inequalities:

$$y \geq 2x + 2, x + y - 7 > 0 \text{ and } x \leq 5$$

A is the point where the lines with equations $y = 2x + 2$ and $x + y - 7 = 0$ intersect, and B is the point where the lines with equations $y = 2x + 2$ and $x - 5 = 0$ intersect.

a) Determine which, if any, of the points A or B lie in the region R. You must justify your answers. *[2 marks]*

b) Sketch the graphs of the inequalities and shade the region R. *[4 marks]*

E Q5 A region, R, of the plane is determined by the inequalities $y + 2x > 6$ and $y \geq 2x^2 + 5x - 9$.

a) Find the coordinates of the points at which the graph of $y + 2x = 6$ intercepts the coordinate axes. *[1 mark]*

b) Find the coordinates of the y-intercept and turning point of the graph of $y = 2x^2 + 5x - 9$. *[2 marks]*

c) Sketch the graphs of the inequalities and shade the region R. *[3 marks]*

P Q6 Regions A and B are described by the sets of inequalities below:

A: $x + 2y \leq 12$, $2y - 3x \leq 4$, $y \geq 2$ B: $x \geq 3$, $2x \leq y + 9$, $x + 3y \leq 15$

Which region has the greater area?

E Q7 a) Find the coordinates of the turning points of the graphs of the quadratic equations $y = 2x^2 - 10x + \frac{21}{2}$ and $y = \frac{3}{4} + 5x - x^2$. *[3 marks]*

b) Hence, sketch and shade a diagram to show the region, R, determined by the inequalities $y > 2x^2 - 10x + \frac{21}{2}$ and $y < \frac{3}{4} + 5x - x^2$. *[3 marks]*

E P Q8 a) Sketch the graphs of the inequalities $y < x + 3$ and $y \geq 2x^2 - x - 3$, and shade the region R that is satisfied by both. *[3 marks]*

The graphs of $y = x + 3$ and $y = 2x^2 - x - 3$ intersect when $x = \frac{1 - \sqrt{13}}{2}$ and $x = \frac{1 + \sqrt{13}}{2}$.

Region S is the set of points that satisfy the inequalities $x > k$, $y < x + 3$ and $y \geq 2x^2 - x - 3$, where k is a real number.

b) Given that S is not the empty set, determine the range of possible values of k. *[1 mark]*

Challenge

P M Q9 A bakery is running out of ingredients and wants to see how many sponge cakes and baguettes they can make. A cake requires 1 lb of flour and 3 eggs, and a baguette requires 2 lb of flour and 1 egg.

The bakery can make x cakes and y baguettes. They have 24 lb of flour remaining, which can be represented by the inequality $x + 2y \leq 24$.

a) They only have 42 eggs left. Use this information to form another inequality in x and y.

b) On a graph, draw and label the region that satisfies both of these inequalities.

c) A customer requests 8 cakes and 10 baguettes for a fête. Can the bakery meet their order? If not, what ingredient(s) do they not have enough of?

Problem Solving

Note that x and y can't be negative (since they can't make a negative number of cakes/baguettes). So $x \geq 0$ and $y \geq 0$ have to be satisfied as well.

5.4 Simultaneous Equations — Both Linear

Solving by elimination

Simultaneous equations are just a pair of equations containing two unknown quantities, often x and y.

This is how simultaneous equations are often shown: $3x + 5y = -4$
$-2x + 3y = 9$

But they'll look different sometimes, maybe like this: $4 + 5y = -3x$
$-2x = 9 - 3y$

Solutions to a pair of simultaneous equations make both equations true at the same time.
You can solve two linear simultaneous equations in two different ways — by **substitution** (see page 98) and by **elimination**.

Before you can use the elimination method, you need to **rearrange** the equations as '$ax + by = c$'.

$$4 + 5y = -3x \qquad \qquad 3x + 5y = -4$$
$$-2x = 9 - 3y \quad \longrightarrow \quad -2x + 3y = 9$$

The elimination method involves **four** steps:

1. Match the coefficients
Multiply the equations by numbers that will make either the x's or the y's **match** in the two equations (ignoring minus signs).

2. Eliminate to find one variable
If the coefficients are the **same** sign, you'll need to **subtract** one equation from the other. If the coefficients are **different** signs, you need to **add** the equations.

3. Find the other variable (that you eliminated)
When you've found one variable, put its value into one of the **original equations** so you can find the **other** variable.

4. Check your answer
Put the values you found into the **other original equation**.

Tip Multiply each equation by the number that gives the lowest common multiple (LCM) of the coefficients.

Tip You should always check your answer to make sure you've worked out x and y correctly. Then pat yourself on the back if you have. You deserve it.

Example 1

Solve the simultaneous equations $3x + 5y = -4$ and $-2x + 3y = 9$.

① $3x + 5y = -4$
② $-2x + 3y = 9$

Number your equations 1 and 2 so you know which one you're working with.

① × 2: $6x + 10y = -8$ → ③
② × 3: $-6x + 9y = 27$ → ④

Match the coefficients. To get the x's to match, multiply the first equation by 2 and the second by 3.

Number the new equations as 3 and 4.

continued on the next page...

③ + ④: $19y = 19$
$y = 1$

Eliminate to find one variable. Add the new equations together to eliminate the x's.

$y = 1$ in ①: $3x + 5 = -4$
$3x = -9$
$x = -3$

Find the variable you eliminated: $y = 1$, so substitute that value for y into one of the original equations to find x.

So the solution is $x = -3$, $y = 1$.

Check using ②: $-2x + 3y = 9$
$-2 \times (-3) + 3 \times 1 = 6 + 3 = 9$

Put the values $x = -3$ and $y = 1$ into the other equation. If the answer matches the right–hand side, your variables are correct.

If you drew the **graph** of each equation you'd get two straight lines.

- The point where these two lines **intersect** gives the **solution** to the two simultaneous equations.
- For the last example, the graph of the two lines $3x + 5y = -4$ and $-2x + 3y = 9$ would look like this:

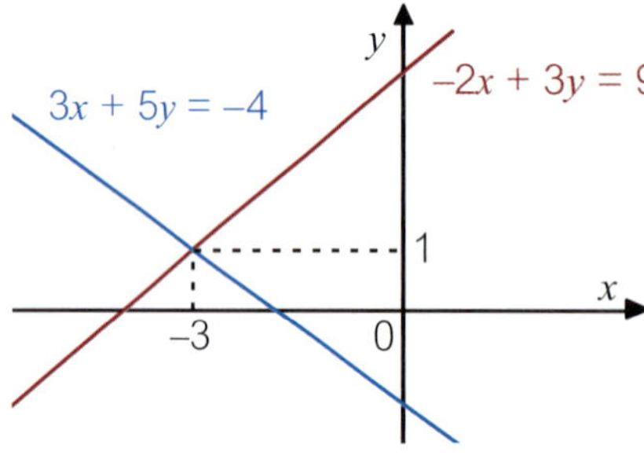

Tip See Chapter 6 for more on straight-line graphs and their equations.

- The two lines intersect at the point (–3, 1), which is the same as the answer worked out above.
- However, **not all** simultaneous equations have solutions that work in both equations — for example, no values of x and y satisfy both $2x + 3y = 5$ and $4x + 6y = 7$. This would be obvious if you **sketched the graphs** — the lines are **parallel** so they never intersect.

If you're asked to find the coordinates of the point of intersection, you need to find them using an **algebraic method**, rather than reading off the graph.

Exercise 5.4

Q1 Solve the following simultaneous equations:

a) $2x - 3y = 3$
$x + 3y = 6$

b) $3x + 2y = 7$
$7x - y = -12$

c) $4x + 3y = -4$
$6x - 4y = 11$

d) $7x - 6y = 4$
$11x + 9y = -6$

e) $6x + 2y - 8 = 0$
$4x + 3 = -3y$

f) $2x + 18y - 21 = 0$
$-14y = 3x + 14$

g) $2x + 16y = 10$
$64y - 5 + 3x = 0$

h) $4x - 3y = 15$
$5y - 12 = 9x$

Q1 Hint Rearrange the equations so they're in the form $ax + by = c$.

Q2 Find the point of intersection of each pair of straight lines.

a) $y = 2x - 3$
$y = \frac{1}{2}x + 3$

b) $y = -\frac{2}{3}x + 7$
$y = \frac{1}{2}x + \frac{21}{2}$

c) $x + 2y + 5 = 0$
$3x - 5y - 7 = 0$

d) $2x - 3y = 7$
$5x - \frac{15}{2}y = 9$

e) $8x = -3y + 10$
$9y = 3 - 6x$

f) $7x - 5y = 15$
$2x - 9 = 3y$

g) $6x + 3y = 10$
$-9 = 8y - 4x$

h) $10y = 3 - x$
$5y = 6x + 5$

i) $\frac{7}{3}x = 2 + \frac{5}{3}y$
$y = \frac{3}{4}x + \frac{1}{3}$

j) $\frac{3}{4}y = \frac{9}{5}x - 10$
$-\frac{3}{5}y + \frac{3}{2}x + 10 = 0$

Q2 Hint Remember, not all simultaneous equations have solutions (see previous page).

P M Q3 Three roads on a map are modelled (in (x, y) coordinates) by the following equations:

A: $5x + 2y = -11$ B: $2x = y + 1$ C: $5y = 13 + x$

Signposts are placed at each intersection of the roads. Find the coordinates of each signpost.

E M Q4 Small wooden blocks have a mass of x kg, and large wooden blocks have a mass of y kg.
5 small blocks and 10 large blocks have a total mass of 36 kg.
10 small blocks and 2 large blocks have a total mass of 18 kg.

a) Write down two equations to represent the masses of the blocks. *[1 mark]*

b) Find the mass of each block. *[3 marks]*

E P M Q5 The prices (c, in £) of two different stocks are modelled by the equations $2c - t = 64$ and $6c - 2t = 291$ respectively, where $t \geq 0$ is time in months, and $t = 0$ on 1st January 2015.

a) (i) In what year will the prices of the two stocks be the same? *[3 marks]*

(ii) What will the price of the stocks be at that time? *[1 mark]*

b) Give a reason why linear models may not be suitable for modelling this situation. *[1 mark]*

Challenge

E P Q6 a) By solving the simultaneous equations $3x + 2y = k$ and $x - y = 3k + 2$, where k is a constant, find expressions for x and y in terms of k. *[3 marks]*

The graphs of the lines $3x + 2y = k$ and $x - y = 3k + 2$ intersect at a point, A, which has equal x- and y-coordinates.

b) Determine the coordinates of A. *[3 marks]*

E P Q7 Solve the simultaneous equations $2x - y = 2$ and $5x - y\sqrt{5} = 3\sqrt{5}$.
Give your answers in the form $a + b\sqrt{5}$ where appropriate. *[4 marks]*

5.5 Simultaneous Equations — if One is not Linear

Solving by substitution

Elimination is great for simple equations, but it won't always work. Sometimes one of the equations has not just x's and y's in it — but bits with x^2 and y^2 as well. When one of the equations has quadratic terms, you can **only** use the **substitution** method. The substitution method involves **four** steps:

1. **Isolate variable in linear equation** — rearrange the linear equation to get x or y on its own.
2. **Substitute into the quadratic equation** — to get a quadratic equation in just one variable.
3. **Solve to get values for one variable** — either by factorising or using the quadratic formula.
4. **Substitute the values in the linear equation** — to find corresponding values for the other variable.

Tip Always check your answer at the end too, by putting the values back into the original equations.

Example 1

Solve the simultaneous equations $-x + 2y = 5$ and $x^2 + y^2 = 25$.

Tip The linear equation is the one with only x's and y's in. The quadratic is the one with x^2 or y^2 terms.

① $-x + 2y = 5$
② $x^2 + y^2 = 25$

Start by labelling the two equations. Here, the linear equation is labelled 1, and the equation with quadratic terms is labelled 2.

① $-x + 2y = 5$
$\Rightarrow x = 2y - 5$

Rearrange the linear equation so that either x or y is on its own on one side of the equals sign.

Sub into ②: $x^2 + y^2 = 25$
$\Rightarrow (2y - 5)^2 + y^2 = 25$

Substitute this expression into the quadratic...

$\Rightarrow (4y^2 - 20y + 25) + y^2 = 25$
$\Rightarrow 5y^2 - 20y = 0$
$\Rightarrow 5y(y - 4) = 0$
$\Rightarrow y = 0$ or $y = 4$

...and then rearrange this into the form $ax^2 + bx + c = 0$, so you can solve it — either by factorising or using the quadratic formula.

When $y = 0$:
① $-x + 2y = 5$
$\Rightarrow x = -5$

When $y = 4$:
① $-x + 2y = 5$
$-x + 8 = 5$
$\Rightarrow x = 3$

Put both these values back into the linear equation to find corresponding values for x.

Solution: $x = -5, y = 0$ and $x = 3, y = 4$

Solving these simultaneous equations has produced a **pair** of solutions. You'll often (but not always) get a pair of solutions if one of the equations is quadratic.

Check:

$x = -5, y = 0$:
$(-5) + 2 \times 0 = 5$ ✓
$(-5)^2 + 0^2 = 25$ ✓

$x = 3, y = 4$:
$-(3) + 2 \times 4 = 5$ ✓
$3^2 + 4^2 = 25$ ✓

Now, **check your answers** by putting each set of values back into the original equations.

If you were to draw the graphs, you would find that the quadratic equation in the last example ($x^2 + y^2 = 25$) is actually a circle about the origin with radius 5, and the linear equation is just a standard straight line.

So by solving the simultaneous equations you're finding the **two points** where the line passes through the circle — the points (–5, 0) and (3, 4).

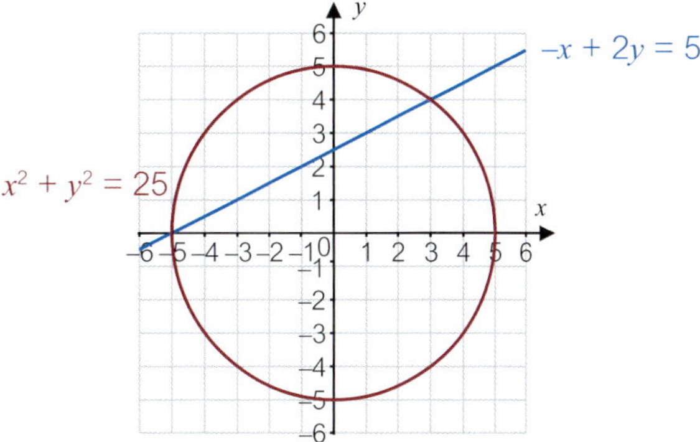

Example 2

Find any points of intersection of the following graphs:

a) $y = x^2 - 4x + 5$ and $y = 2x - 4$

① $y = x^2 - 4x + 5$
② $y = 2x - 4$

Label the two equations.

Substitute ② into ①:

$$2x - 4 = x^2 - 4x + 5$$
$$x^2 - 6x + 9 = 0$$
$$(x - 3)^2 = 0$$
$$x = 3$$

Substitute one equation into the other, rearrange into the form $ax^2 + bx + c = 0$ and solve.

When $x = 3$:

② $y = 2x - 4 = 2 \times 3 - 4 \Rightarrow y = 2$

Substitute the solution for x into the linear equation to find y.

So there's one solution: $x = 3, y = 2$
This means there's one point of intersection: (3, 2)

Tip The quadratic equation in this example has a double root — i.e. you only get one solution from the quadratic equation.

b) $y = x^2 - 4x + 5$ and $y = 2x - 5$

① $y = x^2 - 4x + 5$
② $y = 2x - 5$

Label the two equations.

Substitute ② into ①:

$$2x - 5 = x^2 - 4x + 5$$
$$x^2 - 6x + 10 = 0$$

$$b^2 - 4ac = (-6)^2 - 4 \times 1 \times 10$$
$$= 36 - 40 = -4$$

Substitute, rearrange and try to solve with the quadratic formula (since it won't factorise). Start by finding the discriminant (see p.54).

The simultaneous equations have no solutions and there are no points of intersection.

Since $b^2 - 4ac < 0$, the quadratic has no real roots and the equations cannot be solved. This means the graphs never meet.

If you were to sketch the graphs of the equations from the example, they'd look like this:

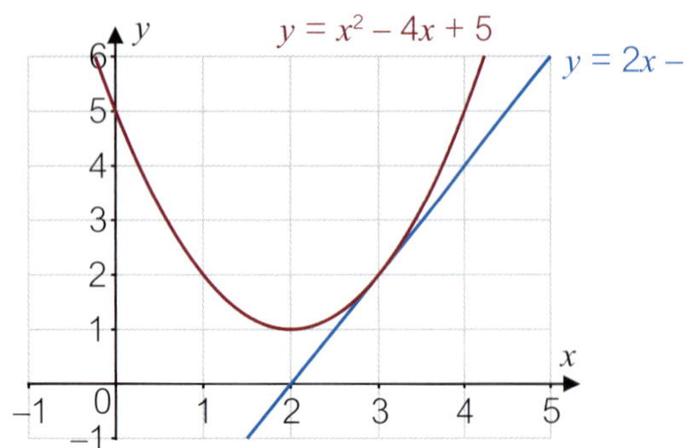

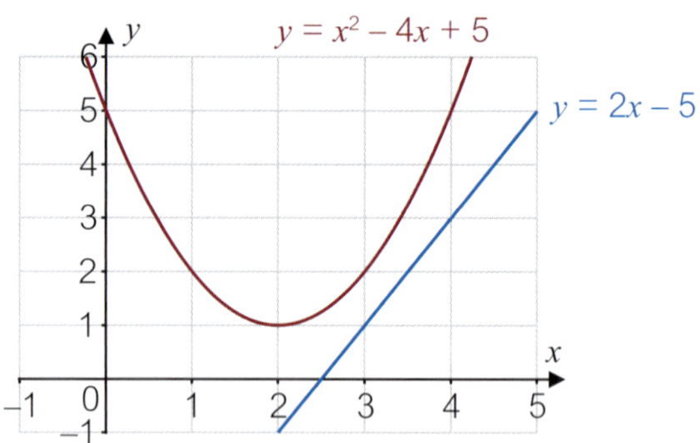

Since the equations from part a) have only one solution and the two graphs only meet at one point, the straight line is actually a **tangent** to the curve. In part b), you can see that the graphs never meet.

Tip A tangent is a straight line that just touches a curve at a single point.

Exercise 5.5

Q1 Solve the following simultaneous equations using substitution:

a) $y = 4x + 3$
$2y - 3x = 1$

b) $5x + 2y = 16$
$2y - x - 4 = 0$

Q2 Solve the following simultaneous equations:

a) $y = 2x + 5$
$y = x^2 - x + 1$

b) $y = 2x^2 - 3$
$y = 3x + 2$

c) $2x^2 - xy = 6$
$y - 3x + 7 = 0$

d) $xy = 6$
$2y - x + 4 = 0$

e) $y = x^2 - 2x - 3$
$y + x + 8 = 0$

f) $y = 2x^2 - 3x + 5$
$5x - y = 3$

g) $2x^2 + 3y^2 + 18x = 347$
$4x + y = 7$

h) $2y = 2x^2 + x + 1$
$y + 2x = 2$

i) $x^2 + 4x = 4y + 40$
$12y + 5x + 30 = 0$

j) $y - x = x + 2$
$\frac{1}{4}y^2 + 25 = 3x^2 + 11x$

Q2 Hint For these sets of equations you'll need to do some rearranging.

E Q3 Find all solutions to the simultaneous equations $x^2 + 2xy = y + 1$ and $2x + 5y - 2 = 0$. *[5 marks]*

Q4 Find the points of intersection between the lines and curves on the graphs below.

a)
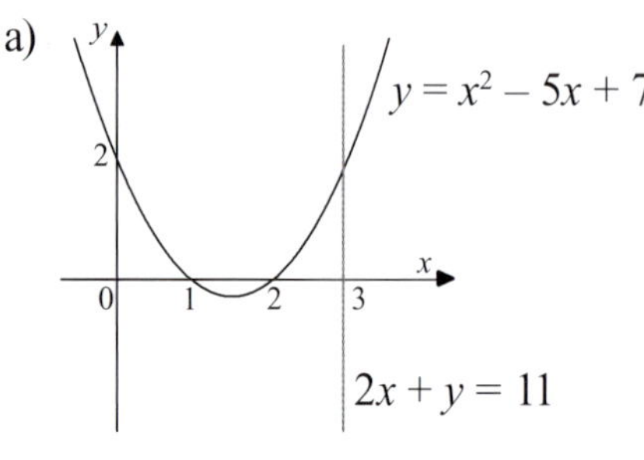

b)
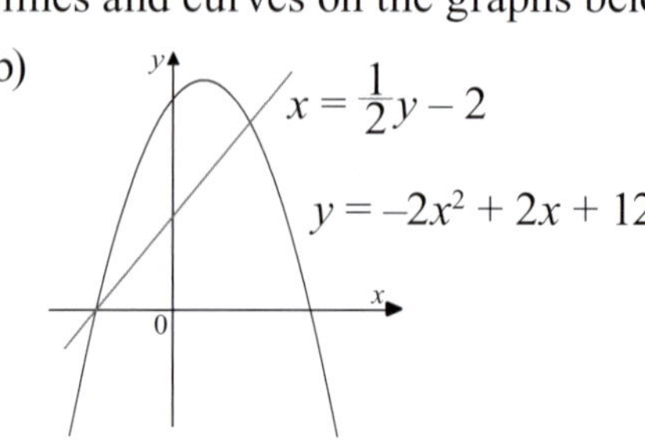

Q5 Find the points of intersection of the following curves and straight lines:

a) $y = \frac{1}{2}x^2 + 4x - 8$
$y = 4 + \frac{3}{2}x$

b) $y = 2x^2 + x - 6$
$5x - y + 10 = 0$

c) $x^2 + y^2 = 50$
$x + 2y = 5$

d) $2x^2 - y + 3x + 1 = 0$
$y - x - 5 = 0$

e) $3x^2 + 9x + 1 = 6y$
$2x + 3y = \frac{11}{2}$

f) $4x - y + 10 = 0$
$2y - 19 = 4x^2 + 8x$

Q6 a) Solve the simultaneous equations $x^2 + y^2 = 10$ and $x - 3y + 10 = 0$.

b) Say what your answer to part a) means geometrically.

Q6b) Hint You don't need to draw a graph, just describe what your answer to part a) means.

P Q7 Without drawing the graphs, determine whether the following curves and lines intersect at one or two points, or do not intersect at all:

a) $y = x^2 + 6x - 7$ and $y = 2x - 3$

b) $3x^2 + 4y^2 + 6x = 9$ and $x + 2y = 3$

c) $xy + 2x - y = 8$ and $x + y = 1$

Challenge

E P Q8 Given that $p - 2q = 4$ and $q = \frac{1}{4}p^2 - 2p + 4$

a) Show that $q = q^2$. *[2 marks]*

b) Hence, or otherwise, solve the simultaneous equations
$p - 2q = 4$ and $q = \frac{1}{4}p^2 - 2p + 4$. *[3 marks]*

E P M Q9 Two water tanks, P and Q, are filled with water.
From 08:00 the temperature (in °C) of the water in tank P is varied and is given by $\text{p}(t) = 20 + t$, where t is measured in hours after 08:00. Exactly two hours later at 10:00 the temperature of Q is varied (independently of P) and the temperature (in °C) is given by $\text{q}(T) = 20 + 8T - T^2$ where T is measured in hours after 10:00.

a) Express T in terms of t. *[1 mark]*

b) Hence find an expression for the temperature of the water in tank Q, t hours after 08:00. State the values of t for which this expression is valid. *[3 marks]*

c) Find the times, to the nearest minute, for which the temperature of the water in both tanks is the same. *[3 marks]*

d) Suggest a possible limitation for this model. *[1 mark]*

5 Review Exercise

Q1 Solve:

a) $7x - 4 > 2x - 42$ b) $12y - 3 \leq 4y + 4$ c) $9y - 4 \geq 17y + 2$

d) $x + 6 < 5x - 4$ e) $4x - 2 > x - 14$ f) $7 - x \leq 4 - 2x$

g) $11x - 4 < 4 - 11x$ h) $1 + 10y \geq 7y - 12$ i) $8y - 6 \leq 6 - 8y$

E Q2 Solve the inequality $3(2x - 5) + 2(4 - x) \geq x + 7$. *[3 marks]*

Q3 Find the set of values for x that satisfy the following inequalities:

a) $3x^2 - 5x - 2 \leq 0$ b) $x^2 + 2x + 7 > 4x + 9$

c) $3x^2 + 7x + 4 \geq 2(x^2 + x - 1)$ d) $x^2 + 3x - 1 \geq x + 2$

e) $2x^2 > x + 1$ f) $3x^2 - 12 < x^2 - 2x$

g) $3x^2 + 6x \leq 2x^2 + 3$ h) $(x + 2)(x - 3) \geq 8 - 3x^2$

E Q4 Solve the inequality $2x^2 - 5x - 3 > 0$, giving your solution in set notation. *[4 marks]*

E P Q5 N is the smallest positive integer that satisfies the inequality $x^2 - 23x - 472 \geq 0$. Find the value of N. *[4 marks]*

Q6 Draw and shade the region which satisfies each of the following sets of inequalities.

a) $8 \leq y - x, \quad y < 12 - x, \quad 9x + 2y < -4$

b) $x + 3y > 15, \quad 3x + y < 12, \quad 4y \leq x + 36$

c) $10y + 10x > x^2, \quad y < -x^2 + 8x - 12$

E Q7 Find the set of values of x for which the graph with equation $y = \frac{1}{2}x^2 + 4x - \frac{5}{2}$ lies below the x-axis. *[2 marks]*

E M Q8 Barry has to stop his car and wait for the engine to cool down when the temperature of the engine is 100 °C or more.

The temperature, T °C, of the engine is modelled by the equation $T = -\frac{1}{18}t^2 + \frac{18}{5}t + 55$, where $t \geq 0$. t is measured in minutes and $t = 0$ is when Barry starts his journey.

a) Based on this model, how long will Barry have to stop his car for during his journey? *[4 marks]*

b) Why will Barry probably have to stop the car for a different amount of time than this in reality? *[1 mark]*

E Q9 The diagram on the right shows a region R.

Determine the inequalities that are satisfied by this region.

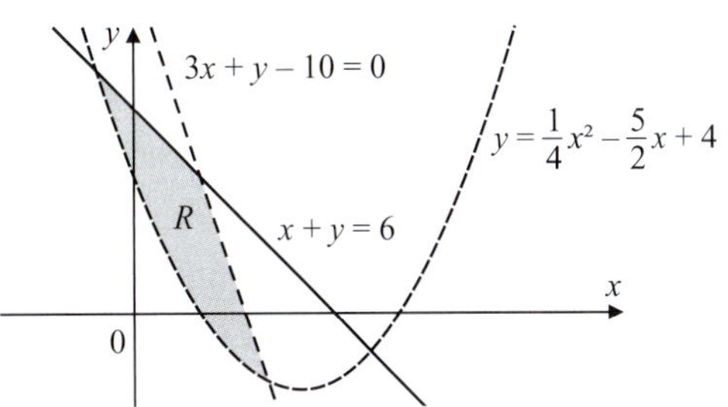

[2 marks]

E Q10 a) On a set of axes, sketch the graph of $y = x^2$, where $-2 \leq x \leq 4$. [1 mark]

b) Sketch the graph of $y = 2x + 3$ on the same set of axes, labelling all axis intercepts. [2 marks]

c) Shade in the region on your sketch that is represented by the set $\{(x, y): y \geq x^2\} \cap \{(x, y): y \leq 2x + 3\}$. [1 mark]

E P M Q11 A machine cuts shapes out of sheets of metal. It is programmed with inequalities to determine a region, R, that defines the shape to be cut.

The machine is programmed with the inequalities $y \geq 0$, $y < 2x$ and $y \leq -\frac{1}{5}x + k$, where k is a real number and can be varied.

a) For $k > 0$, sketch the graphs of the inequalities and shade the region R. [4 marks]

b) The machine produces an error for $k < 0$. Explain why this might be. [1 mark]

c) The area of the shape to be cut is 4 units^2. Find the value of k which corresponds to this shape. [3 marks]

E P Q12 The graph of the quadratic equation $y = 3 + 6x - x^2$ has a turning point at (p, q).

a) Find the values of p and q. [2 marks]

b) Show that when $x = p$, the lines with equations $y = 4x - 5$ and $3y - x = 18$ pass through the same point. [1 mark]

c) Sketch and shade a diagram to show the region, R, determined by the inequalities $y \leq 4x - 5$, $3y \geq x + 18$ and $y < 3 + 6x - x^2$. [3 marks]

Q13 Solve these sets of simultaneous equations:

a) $3x - 4y = 7$ and $-2x + 7y = -22$

b) $2x - 3y = \frac{11}{12}$ and $x + y = -\frac{7}{12}$

c) $2x + 3y = 8$ and $6y = 5 - 4x$

d) $11y = 9x + 4$ and $3x - 2y = 7$

e) $\frac{1}{2}x + \frac{1}{3}y = 50$ and $x + 4y = 25$

f) $x + 4y = \frac{1}{4}$ and $y + 2x = \frac{1}{5}$

Q14 Find where the following lines meet:

a) $y = 3x - 4$ and $y = 7x - 5$

b) $y = 13 - 2x$ and $7x - y - 23 = 0$

c) $2x - 3y + 4 = 0$ and $x - 2y + 1 = 0$

d) $5x - 7y = 22$ and $3y - 4x - 13 = 0$

e) $9 - 8y = \frac{2}{3}x$ and $\frac{1}{3}x + \frac{2}{3}y = 10$

f) $24x + 15y = 2$ and $18x + 36y = 5$

E P M Q15 James and Kimiko are repotting flowers in two different-sized flowerpots. They each have a 40-litre bag of compost to use to fill their pots.

- James completely fills 14 large pots and 18 small pots. He has 0.5 litres of compost left over.
- Kimiko completely fills 12 large pots and 21 small pots. She has 0.85 litres of compost left over.

Determine the volumes of the large and small pots. *[4 marks]*

E P Q16 Consider the equations: $2x + ay = 4$
$3x - 2y = 1$, where a is constant

a) Assuming a solution exists, find x and y as fractions in terms of a. *[4 marks]*

b) Find the value of a for which no solution for the equations exists. Explain your reasoning. *[2 marks]*

c) What is the geometrical significance of the value of a in part b)? *[2 marks]*

E Q17 a) Show that the graphs of the lines with equations $y = 2x - 7$ and $4x + 3y = 7$ intersect and find the coordinates of the point of intersection. *[3 marks]*

b) Show that the graphs of the lines with equations $y = 2x - 7$ and $5y - 10x = 1$ do not intersect. *[2 marks]*

Q18 Find, where possible, the solutions to these sets of simultaneous equations. Interpret your answers geometrically.

a) $y = x^2 - 7x + 4$ and $2x - y - 10 = 0$

b) $y = 30 - 6x + 2x^2$ and $y = 2(x + 11)$

c) $2x^2 + 2y^2 - 3 = 0$ and $y = x + 4$

d) $4y + 3x = 8$ and $2y - 2x^2 - 4x = 7$

e) $\frac{1}{4}x^2 + 3x + 15 = 4y$ and $2y = 3x + 3$

f) $(x - 3)^2 + (y + 4)^2 = 25$ and $x - 7y = 6$

P Q19 Without drawing the graphs, decide whether the curve $y = x^2 - 2x - 3$ and the line $y = 3x + 11$ intersect at one or two points, or do not intersect at all.

E P Q20 a) Show that the x-coordinates of any solutions to the simultaneous equations $2x - y + 3 = 0$ and $y = -x^2 + 3x - 2$ satisfy the quadratic equation $x^2 - x + 5 = 0$. *[2 marks]*

b) Hence show that there are no solutions to the simultaneous equations. *[2 marks]*

E Q21 a) Find the coordinates of the points where the curve $y = 3x^2 + 7x + 15$ and the line $y = 6x + 25$ intersect. *[5 marks]*

b) Hence find the range of values for x where $3x^2 + 7x + 15 > 6x + 25$. *[2 marks]*

E P Q22 Show that the curve C and the line l do not intersect, where:

C: $3x^2 + 5y = 14$ and l: $5x - 10y = -38$ *[4 marks]*

E Q23 The straight line $y = 2x + 7$ intersects the circle $(x - 9)^2 + (y - 5)^2 = 160$ at two points. Find the coordinates of the points of intersection. *[5 marks]*

E P Q24 The line with equation $y = 2x + k$ is a tangent to the curve with equation $y = x^2 - 4x + 6$. Find the value of k and the point on the curve at which the line is a tangent. *[6 marks]*

E Q25 a) Find the solutions to the simultaneous equations $4x + y + 6 = 0$ and $y = 4x^2 + 16x + 15$. *[5 marks]*

b) On the same axes, sketch the graphs of $y = 4x^2 + 16x + 15$ and $y = -4x - 6$. Label the points of intersection of the two graphs. *[3 marks]*

E P M Q26 A cafe owner always buys coffee beans from either supplier A or supplier B. In April, he notices the price of coffee beans has started to change rapidly, and models the price (in £ per kilogram) of coffee beans from each supplier.

He uses the equation $a(t) = 23 + \frac{1}{2}t$ for supplier A and $b(t) = \frac{1}{10}t^2 - 2t + 28$ for supplier B, where $t \geq 0$ is measured in days and $t = 0$ is midnight at the start of 1st April.

a) Which supplier is cheaper initially? Justify your answer. *[1 mark]*

b) Find the price of coffee beans at the first time when the price per kilogram is the same from both suppliers. *[4 marks]*

Challenge

E P Q27 The diagram shows a sketch of the graphs of the straight line $y = 2x + 2$ and the quadratic $y = 2x^2 - 9x + 14$, which intersect at points A and B.

Lines parallel to the y-axis are drawn from A and B and intersect the x-axis at the points D and C respectively.

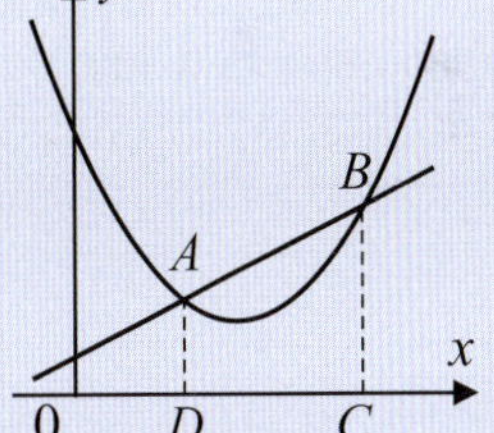

a) Find the coordinates of the points A and B. *[5 marks]*

b) Hence find the area of quadrilateral $ABCD$. *[3 marks]*

E P Q28 Given that $2y - z = -5$ and $2x - y + 3z = 4$,

a) Show that $2x + 5y = -11$. *[2 marks]*

b) Hence solve the three simultaneous equations $2y - z = -5$, $2x - y + 3z = 4$ and $4y + 5x + 2 = 0$. *[4 marks]*

E P Q29 a) Write $\frac{(\sqrt{2})^{3x} \times 9^{2x-y}}{18^{y+\frac{1}{2}x}}$ in the form $2^p \times 3^q$, where p and q are linear algebraic expressions. *[3 marks]*

b) Hence solve $\frac{(\sqrt{2})^{3x} \times 9^{2x-y}}{18^{y+\frac{1}{2}x}} = 6^{10}$. *[4 marks]*

5 Chapter Summary

1 Solve linear inequalities as you would linear equations — but remember to reverse the inequality sign if you multiply or divide by a negative number.

2 To find the solution to two inequalities, solve each one individually, then show them on a number line and look for where the solutions overlap.

3 Solutions to inequalities can be written in set notation.
For instance, the solutions to $x > -3$ and $x \leq 5$ can be written as $\{x : -3 < x \leq 5\}$.

4 To solve inequalities involving quadratics, rearrange the inequality to get 0 on one side, sketch the graph and then use this to identify the solution. Never divide or multiply by the variable.

5 To shade regions that satisfy inequalities, first sketch the graph of each inequality as an equation. Then use a point, e.g. the origin, to identify which side of each graph should be shaded.

6 Often the easiest way to solve a pair of linear simultaneous equations is by using the elimination method, but the substitution method also works.

7 The **only** way to solve a pair of simultaneous equations where one is not linear (e.g. it has quadratic terms) is by using the substitution method.

8 The solutions to a pair of simultaneous equations are the points where the graphs intersect:
- If the graphs of the equations never intersect, there are **no** solutions (i.e. no real roots).
- If the graphs intersect once, there is **one** solution at the point of intersection.
- If the graphs intersect twice, there are **two** solutions — one at each point of intersection.

Coordinate Geometry, Graphs and Circles

Learning Objectives

Once you've completed this chapter, you should be able to:

- Find the equation of a straight line passing through any given points and write them in the forms: $y - y_1 = m(x - x_1)$, $y = mx + c$ and $ax + by + c = 0$.
- Recall and use the conditions for two straight lines to be parallel or perpendicular to each other.
- Interpret direct proportion and convert a statement of proportion into an algebraic equation, including finding the constant of proportionality.
- Sketch graphs of simple cubic and quartic functions, reciprocal functions and those with negative powers.
- Know the effect and sketch the graphs of the transformations of graphs.
- Find the equation of a circle.
- Find the radius and coordinates of the centre of a circle, given the equation of the circle.

Prior Knowledge Check

1 For each of the following, state the gradient and y-intercept, then draw the graph.
a) $y = 2x - 4$ b) $y - 3 = 1 - 3x$ c) $5x - y = 2$ *see GCSE Maths*

2 Write an algebraic equation using x, y and a constant, k, where:
a) y is inversely proportional to x b) x is directly proportional to y *see GCSE Maths*

3 Factorise fully: a) $3x^2 - 11x - 20$ b) $x^3 - 3x^2 - 6x + 8$ *see pages 39 and 65*

4 A straight line goes through the points (3, –2) and (1, 6). Find the exact length and midpoint of the line segment between these points. *see GCSE Maths*

5 For $f(x) = x^2 + 4x - 7$:
a) Find f(2). b) Rewrite f(x) by completing the square. *see pages 7 and 46*

6.1 Equations of the Form $y - y_1 = m(x - x_1)$

Any straight line can be described by an equation made up of an x term, y term and constant term (some of these may be zero). You can arrange straight-line equations in any of three standard forms.

$y - y_1 = m(x - x_1)$ is the first form you need to know. m is the **gradient**, x_1 and y_1 are the **coordinates** of one of the points on the line. If you're told **two points** that a straight line passes through, this is probably the easiest one to use.

You do need to be a little careful using the formula, so here's a method to follow:

1. **LABEL** the points (x_1, y_1) and (x_2, y_2).
2. **GRADIENT** — find this using $m = \frac{y_2 - y_1}{x_2 - x_1}$.
3. **WRITE DOWN THE EQUATION** $y - y_1 = m(x - x_1)$.
4. **SUBSTITUTE** in your values for m, x_1 and y_1. (You could use x_2 and y_2 instead — the equation would look different, but still represent the line.)

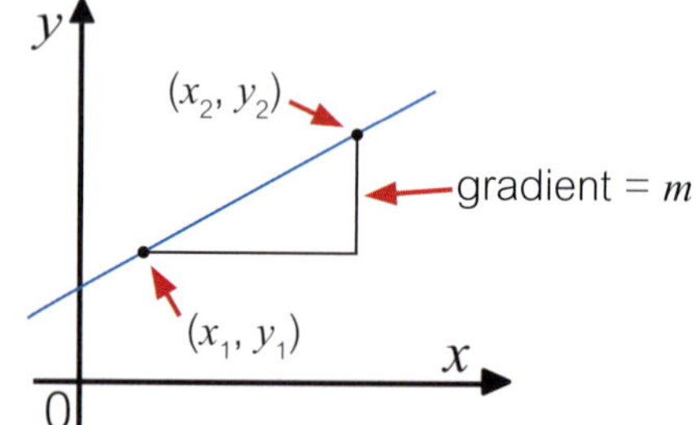

Example 1

Find the equation of the line that passes through the points (–3, 10) and (1, 4), and write it in the form $y - y_1 = m(x - x_1)$.

Point 1 — $(x_1, y_1) = (-3, 10)$
Point 2 — $(x_2, y_2) = (1, 4)$

Label the points.

$$m = \frac{4-10}{1-(-3)} = \frac{-6}{4} = -\frac{3}{2}$$

Find the gradient of the line using $m = \frac{y_2 - y_1}{x_2 - x_1}$.

$y - y_1 = m(x - x_1)$

Write down the equation of the line.

$x_1 = -3$, $y_1 = 10$, $m = -\frac{3}{2}$

$\Rightarrow y - 10 = -\frac{3}{2}(x - (-3))$

Finally, substitute in the values for m, x_1 and y_1.

$\Rightarrow y - 10 = -\frac{3}{2}(x + 3)$

Tip
When finding the gradient, make sure you subtract the same way round on the top and bottom of the fraction.
Don't do this: $\frac{y_2 - y_1}{x_1 - x_2}$

6.2 Equations of the Form $y = mx + c$

This form for the straight-line equation is probably the most popular — it's certainly the easiest form to make sense of. m is the **gradient** of the line, and c is the **y-intercept** (where it crosses the y-axis).

When in $y = mx + c$ form, you can simply read off the values of m and c — and together these give you a fairly good idea of what the graph will look like.

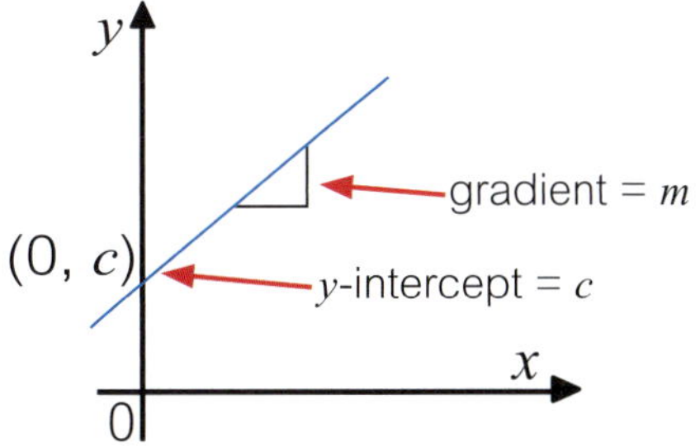

Tip This diagram shows a straight line with positive values for m and c. A negative value for m would make the graph slope downwards.

As well as being easy to interpret, it's fairly easy to find the equation of a line in $y = mx + c$ form. Here are a couple of examples — you're given different information in each case.

Example 1

A straight line has a gradient of –2 and passes through the point (3, 1). Find the equation of the line.

$y = mx + c$

$1 = (-2 \times 3) + c \Rightarrow 7 = c$ — To find c, sub in the values of m, x and y given in the question.

$y = -2x + 7$ — Then put your values of m and c into the equation $y = mx + c$.

Tip Put the x- and y-values of your given point into your final equation to check it's right.

Example 2

Find the equation of the straight line that passes through the points (–18, 16) and (10, 2).

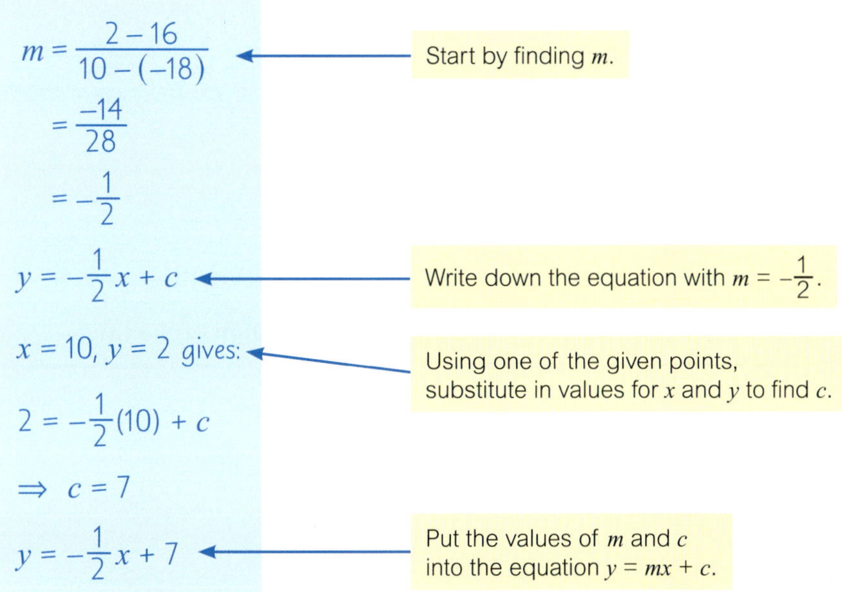

The method in Example 2 is very similar to that on the previous page — find the gradient, then put in the x and y values of one of the points.

Exercise 6.1-6.2

Q1 Give the gradient and y-intercept of the following straight lines:

a) $y = -4x + 11$ b) $y = 4 - x$ c) $y = 1.7x - 2.3$

Q2 Give equations for the following straight lines in the form $y = mx + c$:

a) gradient –3, y-intercept (0, 2) b) gradient 5, y-intercept (0, –3)

c) gradient $\frac{1}{2}$, y-intercept (0, 6) d) gradient 0.8, y-intercept (0, 1.2)

e) gradient –0.4, y-intercept (0, –7) f) gradient $-\frac{5}{3}$, y-intercept $(0, \frac{1}{2})$

Q3 Use the information in the diagrams to the find the equation of each straight line in the form $y = mx + c$.

a)

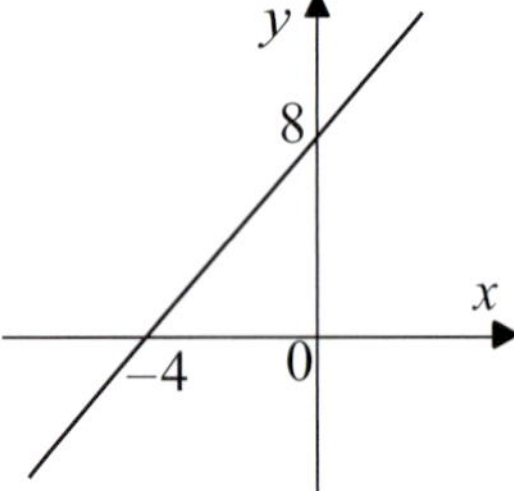

b)

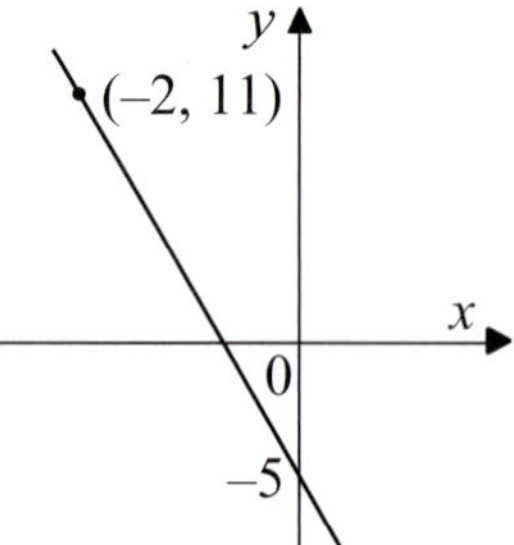

Q4 Find the equations of the lines that pass through the following pairs of points. Give each answer in these forms: (i) $y - y_1 = m(x - x_1)$ (ii) $y = mx + c$.

a) (2, –2), (6, 10) b) (–1, –6), (3, 4) c) (4, 1), (0, –3)

d) (12, –3), (14, 1) e) (5, 7), (–2, 5) f) (–3, 6), (4, –2)

Q5 A straight line l goes through the points (–0.3, 0.65) and (0.2, –1.85).

a) Find the gradient of the line l.

b) Find the equation of l in the form $y = mx + c$.

Q6 Find the equation of the straight line which passes through the point (–4, –3) and has a gradient of $\frac{1}{4}$. Give your answer in the form $y = mx + c$.

Q7 A line with gradient $-\frac{2}{5}$ passes through the point (–8, 2). Find the equation of the line in the form $y - y_1 = m(x - x_1)$ and in the form $y = mx + c$.

P Q8 A straight line has gradient 3 and passes through the point (2, –7). State which of the following coordinates are points on the line.

a) (1, –10) b) (–2, –7) c) (5, 2)

d) (0.5, 2.5) e) (7, 8) f) (0, –12)

P Q9 A straight line passes through the points (6, 6) and (–1, 20). Which of the following coordinates are also on the line?

a) (2, 14) b) (–4, –24) c) (10, –2)

d) (26, –34) e) (–34, 88) f) (2.5, 13)

P M **Q10** The distance travelled by a car is modelled by a straight-line graph. At time $t = 0$ hours, it starts at distance $d = 0$ kilometres, and its speed (the gradient) is a constant 32 km/h throughout the journey.

a) Give the equation of the line in the form $d = mt + c$.

b) How long does it take the car to travel a distance of 9.6 km? Give your answer in minutes.

c) Give one criticism of this model.

Problem Solving

In this question, x and y have been replaced with t and d respectively.

E P M **Q11** Sally's dog eats 650 g of dog food per day. She opens a new bag of dog food at midday on 16th July, and after 6 days she finds that there is 16.1 kg remaining in the bag.
Sally models the amount of dog food in the bag using the equation $W = at + b$, where W is the weight of the remaining dog food, measured in kg, and $t \geq 0$ is time measured in days, with $t = 0$ the time at which the bag was opened.

a) Find the values of a and b, and interpret them in context. *[4 marks]*

b) On which date, according to the model, will Sally have to open a new bag of dog food? *[2 marks]*

c) Suggest a possible limitation of this model. *[1 mark]*

Challenge

E P **Q12** a) Find the equation of the line, l, that passes through the points A and B with coordinates $(-2, 4)$ and $(3, 7)$ respectively. Give your answer in the form $y = mx + c$. *[2 marks]*

The point C lies on l and is a distance of $2\sqrt{34}$ from A. The x-coordinate of C is $x = k$.

b) Find the possible values of k. *[4 marks]*

c) Hence, or otherwise, find the possible coordinates of C. *[2 marks]*

6.3 Equations of the Form $ax + by + c = 0$

This is the last form you need to know for straight-line equations. In this form, a, b and c are **integers**.

This form doesn't involve m, so it's not as easy to work with. If you're asked to give an equation in this form, it's often easiest just to find it in one of the previous two forms, then rearrange it at the end.

It's important to remember that a, b and c are integers, so you must get rid of any fractions.

Example 1

Find the gradient and y-intercept of the line $7x + 3y - 6 = 0$.

$7x + 3y - 6 = 0$

$\Rightarrow 3y = -7x + 6 \Rightarrow y = -\frac{7}{3}x + 2$

The easiest way to answer this question is to rearrange the equation into the form $y = mx + c$.

$m = -\frac{7}{3}$ and $c = 2$

gradient $= -\frac{7}{3}$, y-intercept is $(0, 2)$

Compare the equation with $y = mx + c$. m is the gradient, c is the y-intercept.

Example 2

Find the equation of the line that passes through the point (2, –15) and has gradient $-\frac{3}{2}$, giving your answer in the form $ax + by + c = 0$, where a, b and c are integers.

$m = -\frac{3}{2}$ gives: $y - y_1 = -\frac{3}{2}(x - x_1)$ ← Start by finding the equation in one of the easier forms. We'll use $y - y_1 = m(x - x_1)$, (but $y = mx + c$ would be just as easy).

$y + 15 = -\frac{3}{2}(x - 2)$ ← Now sub in $x_1 = 2$ and $y_1 = -15$.

$y + \frac{3}{2}x + 15 - 3 = 0 \Rightarrow y + \frac{3}{2}x + 12 = 0$

$\Rightarrow 3x + 2y + 24 = 0$ ← Rearrange into $ax + by + c = 0$ form.

Exercise 6.3

Q1 Write the following equations in the form $ax + by + c = 0$, where a, b and c are integers.

a) $y = 5x + 2$ b) $3y = -\frac{1}{2}x + 3$ c) $2(x - 1) = 4y - 1$

d) $7x - 3 = 2y + 6$ e) $\frac{1}{2}(4x + 3) = 3(y - 2)$ f) $3(y - 4) = 4(x - 3)$

Q2 Find the gradient and y-intercept of the following lines:

a) $6x - 2y + 3 = 0$ b) $-9x + 3y - 12 = 0$ c) $-x - 4y - 2 = 0$

d) $7x + 8y + 11 = 0$ e) $2x - 14y + 1 = 0$ f) $-3x + 28y - 16 = 0$

g) $0.1x + 0.2y + 0.3 = 0$ h) $-10x + 0.1y + 11 = 0$ i) $\frac{6}{7}x - 3y + \frac{3}{4} = 0$

Q3 Find the equation of the straight line that passes through the following points. Write your answer in the form $ax + by + c = 0$, where a, b and c are integers.

a) (0, 1), (–1, –1) b) (5, 5), (0, 0.2) c) (5, 2), (3, 4)

d) (9, –1), (7, 2) e) (–6, 1), (4, 0) f) (–12, 3), (5, 7)

Q4 Find the equations of the lines below in the form $ax + by + c = 0$, where a, b and c are integers.

Q4 Hint It's easiest to find the equation in a different form, then convert it at the end.

a)

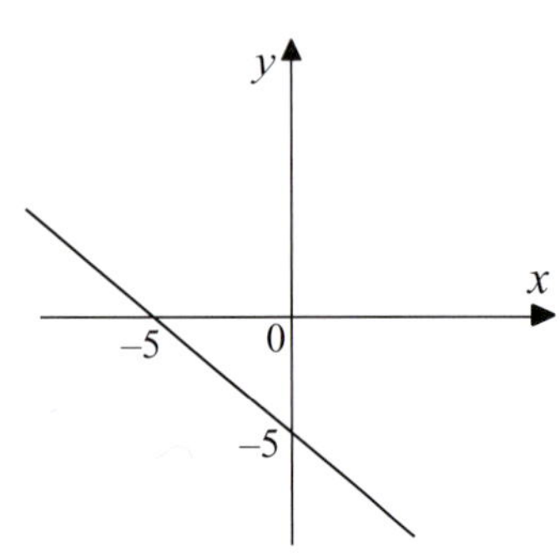

b)

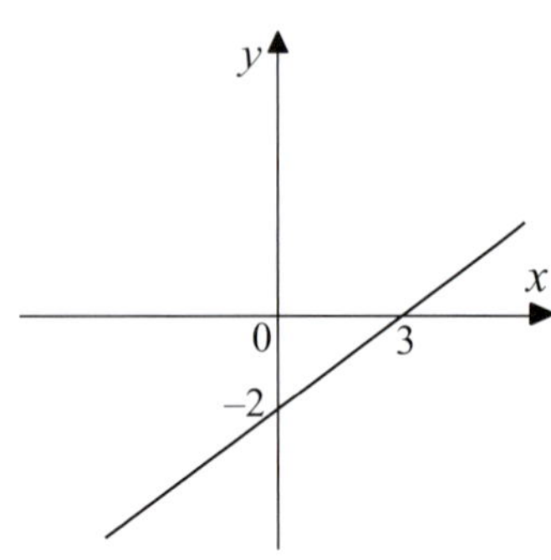

P Q5 A straight line goes through the points (–6, 1) and (–2, 7). Find the equation of the line, giving your answer in the form $ax + by + c = 0$, where a, b and c are integers.

E Q6 The straight line l passes through the points with coordinates (2, 5) and (6, –2).

a) Find the equation of l in the form $ax + by + c = 0$, where a, b and c are constants. *[2 marks]*

b) Find the coordinates of the points where l intersects the coordinate axes. *[2 marks]*

Q7 Match the equations of the straight lines with their correct graphs:

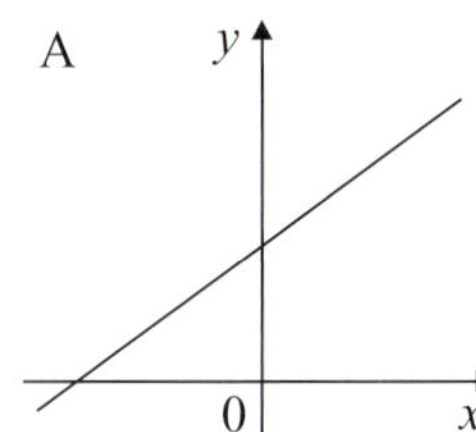

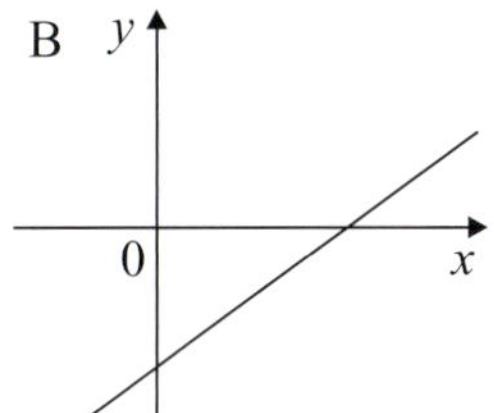

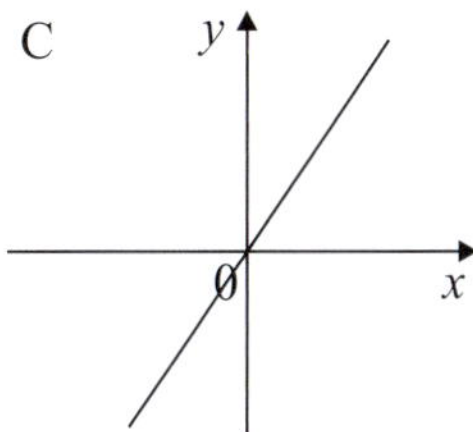

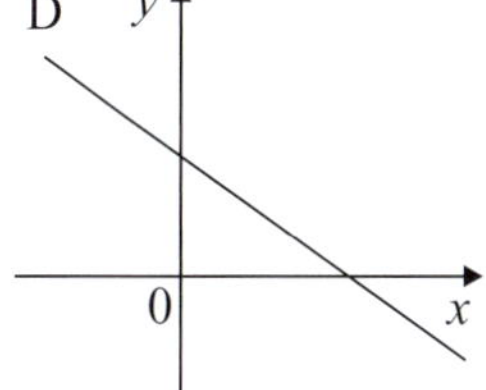

a) $2x - 3y = 6$

b) $3y - 2x - 15 = 0$

c) $3y + 2x - 15 = 0$

d) $y = \frac{3}{2}x$

E Q8 a) Find the equation of the straight line, l, with gradient $\frac{2}{3}$ that passes through the point with coordinates (6, 5). Give your answer in the form $ax + by + c = 0$. *[2 marks]*

b) Given that l also passes through the point with coordinates $\left(\frac{3}{4}, k\right)$, where k is a constant, find the value of k. *[2 marks]*

P Q9 A rectangle ABCD has vertices A(–3, 2), B(–3, 5), C(6, 5) and D(6, 2). Find the equations of the diagonals AC and BD in the form $ax + by + c = 0$.

E P Q10 a) The straight line l passes through the points A $\left(1, -\frac{2}{15}\right)$ and B $\left(\frac{25}{8}, -\frac{11}{6}\right)$. Find the equation of the line, l, in the form $ax + by + c = 0$. *[2 marks]*

The point C has coordinates $\left(\frac{5}{3}, -\frac{1}{3}\right)$.

b) Show that the three points A, B and C do not all lie on the same straight line. *[2 marks]*

P M Q11 At a cafe, a small cup of coffee costs £x and a large cup of coffee costs £y. Maisie buys 3 small cups and 4 large cups for £18.

a) Write this as an equation in the form $ax + by + c = 0$, where a, b and c are all integers.

b) Draw the straight-line graph of this equation.

c) Amani buys 1 small cup and 2 large cups for £8. Write a second equation (in the same form) to represent this and plot the graph on the same set of axes.

d) Write down the cost of a small cup of coffee and the cost of a large cup of coffee.

6.4 Parallel Lines

Parallel lines have **equal gradient**. So when finding the equation of a line parallel to a line with a given equation, you know the gradient will be the same for both.

Tip You could also use the form $y - y_1 = m(x - x_1)$ to find the equations of parallel lines — see p.108.

Example 1

Find the line parallel to $y = \frac{3}{4}x - \frac{7}{4}$ that:

a) has a y-intercept of (0, 4)

$y = \frac{3}{4}x - \frac{7}{4}$ and $y = mx + c$: $m = \frac{3}{4}$ ← Compare $y = \frac{3}{4}x - \frac{7}{4}$ with $y = mx + c$. Remember that parallel lines have the same gradient.

So the gradient of the parallel line is also $\frac{3}{4}$.

$c = 4$ ← You then need to find c — this is just the given y-intercept.

$y = \frac{3}{4}x + 4$ ← Put m and c into the equation $y = mx + c$.

b) passes through the point (3, –1).

$y = \frac{3}{4}x + c$ ← The gradient is $\frac{3}{4}$, so the equation has this form.

$-1 = \frac{3}{4}(3) + c \Rightarrow c = -\frac{13}{4}$ ← You then need to find c. We know that the line passes through point (3, –1), so put $x = 3$ and $y = -1$ into the equation to find c.

$y = \frac{3}{4}x - \frac{13}{4}$ ← This is the equation of the line.

Example 2

Find the line parallel to $2x - 8y + 11 = 0$ that passes through the point (3, –1). Give your equation in the form $ax + by + c = 0$, where a, b and c are integers.

$2x - 8y + 11 = 0 \Rightarrow -8y = -2x - 11$

$\Rightarrow y = \frac{1}{4}x + \frac{11}{8}$ ← First, put the given line in a more useful form, i.e. $y = mx + c$.

When $x = 3$, $y = -1$:

$y = \frac{1}{4}x + c \Rightarrow -1 = \frac{1}{4}(3) + c \Rightarrow c = -\frac{7}{4}$ ← Use the gradient of the given line, $\frac{1}{4}$, and the given point (3, –1) to find the constant c.

$y = \frac{1}{4}x - \frac{7}{4} \Rightarrow x - 4y - 7 = 0$ ← Write the equation in the correct form.

You may be asked whether two lines are parallel — to do this you need to **compare** the gradients. This is easiest when both equations are in the **same form** — so one or both equations may need **rearranging**.

Example 3

Line l_1 is given by the equation $y = \frac{1}{2}x + 6$ and line l_2 is given by the equation $3x + 6y - 1 = 0$. Find out whether the lines are parallel.

$3x + 6y - 1 = 0 \Rightarrow 6y = -3x + 1$

$\Rightarrow y = -\frac{3}{6}x + \frac{1}{6} \Rightarrow y = -\frac{1}{2}x + \frac{1}{6}$

To compare the gradients, you want both lines in the form $y = mx + c$. So rearrange line l_2 into this form.

$y = \frac{1}{2}x + 6$ (Line l_1) $y = -\frac{1}{2}x + \frac{1}{6}$ (Line l_2)

Then compare the two equations.

Line l_1 has a gradient of $\frac{1}{2}$.

Line l_2 has a gradient of $-\frac{1}{2}$.

You're only concerned about the gradient, so look at the bit before the x.

So the lines l_1 and l_2 are NOT parallel.

Exercise 6.4

Q1 State which of the following straight lines are parallel to $y = -3x - 1$.

a) $2y = -6x + 2$ b) $y - 3x - 1 = 0$ c) $6y + 18x = 7$

d) $\frac{1}{3}(y + 1) = x$ e) $-9y - 2 = 27x$ f) $4y = 12x$

Q2 Find the equations of the parallel lines shown as solid lines.
Write them in the form $ax + by + c = 0$, where a, b and c are integers.

a) $y = 4x - 1$, $(3, 2)$

b) $(-4, -5)$, $4x - 2y - 1 = 0$

Q3 State whether the following pairs of lines are parallel.

a) $y = 2x + 1,\ y + \frac{1}{2}x = 1$ b) $2x - 3y + 1 = 0,\ y = \frac{2}{3}x + 2$

c) $-5x + 4y + 3 = 0,\ 8y = 10x$ d) $3x - 4y + 7 = 0,\ 16x + 12y - 3 = 0$

Q4 Line A passes through the point (4, 3) and is parallel to the line $2x - 4y + 3 = 0$.
Find the equation of line A in the form: a) $y = mx + c$, b) $ax + by + c = 0$.

Q5 Find the equations of the lines which are parallel to each of the following lines and pass through the points given. Give your answers in the form $ax + by + c = 0$, where a, b, and c are integers.

a) $y = 2x - 1$, $(2, 1)$ b) $5x + y - 11 = 0$, $(3, -1)$ c) $3y = \frac{1}{3}x + 2$, $(-6, 2)$

d) $x - \frac{1}{4}y + 1 = 0$, $(-6, -5)$ e) $x - y = 13$, $(0, 0)$ f) $100 = y + \frac{1}{5}x$, $(50, 50)$

g) $0.5x + 2.2y - 12 = 0$, $(4, 8)$ h) $3(x + 1) - 2(y - 1) = 4$, $(-2, 2)$ i) $\frac{y - 3x}{2} = \frac{4 + y}{3}$, $(2, 3)$

E Q6 a) Find the equation of the straight line l_1 that passes through the points with coordinates (5, 7) and $\left(\frac{15}{4}, \frac{1}{2}\right)$. *[2 marks]*

b) Show that the straight line l_2 that passes through the points with coordinates $\left(\frac{10}{13}, -15\right)$ and $\left(2, -\frac{43}{5}\right)$ is parallel to the line l_1. *[2 marks]*

c) Show that the straight line l_3 that passes through the points with coordinates $\left(\frac{7}{5}, -12\right)$ and (5, 6) is not parallel to the line l_1. *[2 marks]*

E P Q7 The line l_1 has equation $kx - 7y = 3$, and the line l_2 has equation $(k - 2)^2x + 2y = 5$, where k is a constant. Show that l_2 cannot be parallel to l_1 for any value of k. *[5 marks]*

Challenge

E P Q8 A parallelogram has vertices A, B, C and D. A has coordinates (4, 0) and B has coordinates (6, 7). The side AB is parallel to the side DC, and the side BC is parallel to the side AD. The diagonal of the parallelogram through A and C has equation $4y = 5x - 20$ and the line through A and D has equation $y = \frac{1}{2}x - 2$.

a) Find the coordinates of C. *[4 marks]*

b) Hence find the coordinates of the point D. *[2 marks]*

6.5 Perpendicular Lines

Finding the equations of **perpendicular** lines (or '**normals**') is just as easy as finding the equations of parallel lines — you just need to know one key fact:

The gradients of perpendicular lines **multiply to give –1**.

Which means: Gradient of the perpendicular line = **–1 ÷ the gradient of the other one**.

So if a line has a gradient of m, a line perpendicular to it will have a gradient of $-\frac{1}{m}$.

Example 1

Find the equation of the line perpendicular to $y = \frac{1}{3}x - 1$ that passes through (–2, 4).

Gradient of perpendicular line

$= -1 \div \frac{1}{3} = -3$ — The gradient rule is –1 ÷ gradient of the other one.

So: $y = -3x + c$

$4 = (-3) \times (-2) + c$ — To find c, put the coordinates (–2, 4) into the equation.

$\Rightarrow c = 4 - 6 = -2$

$y = -3x - 2$ — So this is the equation of the line.

Tip Remember, to divide by a fraction, turn it upside down and then multiply by it.

Example 2

Find the equation of the line perpendicular to $7x - 3y + 5 = 0$ that passes through the point $(-3, -11)$.

$7x - 3y + 5 = 0 \Rightarrow -3y = -7x - 5$
$\Rightarrow y = \frac{7}{3}x + \frac{5}{3}$, so the gradient is $\frac{7}{3}$.

Start by converting the equation into a more useful form.

Gradient of perpendicular line $= -1 \div \frac{7}{3} = -\frac{3}{7}$

Now use the gradient rule.

So $y = -\frac{3}{7}x + c$

$-11 = -\frac{3}{7}(-3) + c \Rightarrow c = -11 - \frac{9}{7} = -\frac{86}{7}$

Substitute in $(-3, -11)$ to find c.

$y = -\frac{3}{7}x - \frac{86}{7} \quad \Rightarrow \quad 3x + 7y + 86 = 0$

So the perpendicular line has this equation.

You can use the fact that the gradients of perpendicular lines **multiply** to give **–1** to work out whether two lines are perpendicular.

Example 3 

Show that the line $2x + 5y + 3 = 0$ is perpendicular to $y = \frac{5}{2}x + 5$.

$2x + 5y + 3 = 0$
$\Rightarrow 5y = -2x - 3 \Rightarrow y = -\frac{2}{5}x - \frac{3}{5}$
So the gradient is $-\frac{2}{5}$.

To work out if they are perpendicular, first find the gradient of both lines.

To do this, rearrange $2x + 5y + 3 = 0$ into the form $y = mx + c$.

Comparing $y = \frac{5}{2}x + 5$ to $y = mx + c$,
its gradient is $\frac{5}{2}$.

Compare $y = \frac{5}{2}x + 5$ to $y = mx + c$ to find the gradient of this line.

$-\frac{2}{5} \times \frac{5}{2} = -1$

So the two lines are perpendicular.

The two lines are perpendicular if the gradients of the two lines multiply together to make –1.

Example 4

The points A (2, 5) and B (6, 0) lie on the line l_1.
The line l_2 is perpendicular to l_1 and passes through point A.

a) Find an equation for l_2 in the form $ax + by + c = 0$, where a, b and c are integers.

$(x_1, y_1) = (2, 5)$, $(x_2, y_2) = (6, 0)$

$m = \frac{0 - 5}{6 - 2} = -\frac{5}{4}$

continued on the next page...

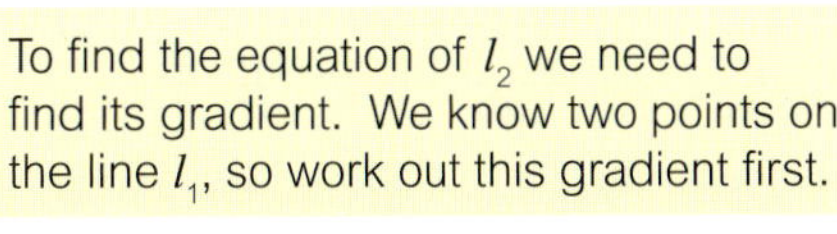
To find the equation of l_2 we need to find its gradient. We know two points on the line l_1, so work out this gradient first.

$m = -1 \div -\frac{5}{4} \Rightarrow m = \frac{4}{5}$ ← The gradient of a perpendicular line is –1 ÷ the other one.

So the equation of l_2 is: $y = \frac{4}{5}x + c$

$5 = \frac{4}{5} \times 2 + c \Rightarrow c = \frac{17}{5}$ ← Put the coordinates of A (2, 5) into the equation to find c.

$y = \frac{4}{5}x + \frac{17}{5} \Rightarrow 4x - 5y + 17 = 0$ ← So this is the equation of the line l_2.

b) Find the coordinates of point C.

$y = \frac{4}{5} \times 0 + \frac{17}{5} = \frac{17}{5}$ ← At C, $x = 0$. So put $x = 0$ into the equation $y = \frac{4}{5}x + \frac{17}{5}$.

So the coordinates of point C are $\left(0, \frac{17}{5}\right)$.

Exercise 6.5

Q1 Find the equations of the dotted lines. Give your answers in the form $y = mx + c$

a)

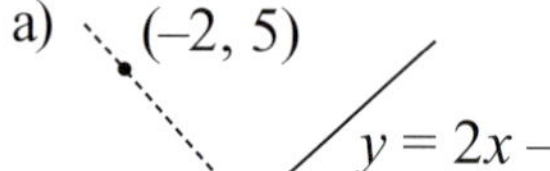

b)

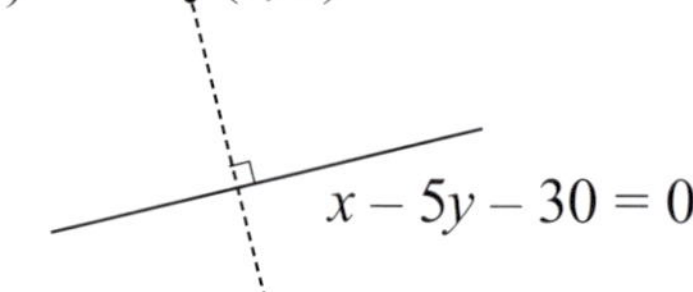

Q2 Find the equations of the lines perpendicular to each of the following that pass through the points given. Give your answers in the form $ax + by + c = 0$, where a, b, and c are integers.

a) $y = \frac{1}{4}x - 1$ (–1, 2)
b) $2x + 3y - 1 = 0$ (–3, –1)
c) $5x - 10y + 1 = 0$ (6, –5)
d) $y = \frac{3}{2}x + 2$ (2, 1)
e) $-4x + 21y = 2$ (0.5, 7)
f) $5(2 - x + 3y) = 2$ (–5, –1)
g) $7y + 1 = \frac{2x - 3}{8}$ (7, 8)
h) $y = 2(2x + 0.1y) + 1$ (3, 4.4)

Q3 Work out which of the following pairs of lines are perpendicular.

a) $y = \frac{4}{3}x - 2$ and $3x + 4y - 1 = 0$
b) $y = \frac{3}{2}x - 1$ and $3x + 2y - 3 = 0$
c) $4x - y + 3 = 0$ and $2x + 8y + 1 = 0$
d) $3x - 5y + 10 = 0$ and $15x + 6y - 4 = 0$

P Q4 Given P = (4, –2) and Q = (–1, 7), find the equation of the line that is perpendicular to PQ and passes through the point (2, 5). Give your answer in the form $ax + by + c = 0$.

P Q5 Triangle ABC has vertices at A (0, 2), B (4, 3) and C (5, –1).

a) Find the equations of the lines AB, BC and AC in the form $y = mx + c$.

b) What type of triangle is ABC? Explain why.

P Q6 A quadrilateral PQRS has vertices at P (1, –1), Q(0, 2), R (3, 3) and S (4, 0).

a) Find the equations of the lines PR and QS in the form $y = mx + c$.

b) Hence, or otherwise, show that PQRS is a square.

P Q7 Line A passes through the point (a, b) and is perpendicular to the line $3x - 2y = 6$. Find an equation of line A in terms of a and b.

P Q8 The perpendicular bisector of a line segment AB is the line that is perpendicular to AB, passing through its midpoint. Find the equation of the perpendicular bisector of the line AB, where A = (1, 4) and B = (5, 2).

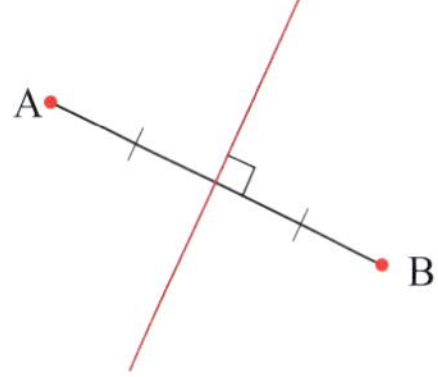

Tip A line segment is just the part of a straight line between two points.

E P Q9 a) The line l_2 passes through the point with coordinates (10, –1) and is parallel to the line l_1 with equation $y = -\frac{1}{2}x$. Find the equation of the line l_2. *[2 marks]*

b) Find the equation of the normal to the line l_1 that passes through the point with coordinates $\left(-\frac{8}{5}, \frac{4}{5}\right)$. *[2 marks]*

c) Hence find the shortest distance between l_1 and l_2. *[3 marks]*

Q9c) Hint The shortest distance between two parallel lines is the perpendicular distance between them.

Challenge

E P Q10 A triangle has vertices A (0, 0), B (4, 10) and C (10, 0). D, E and F are the midpoints of the sides, as shown in the diagram.

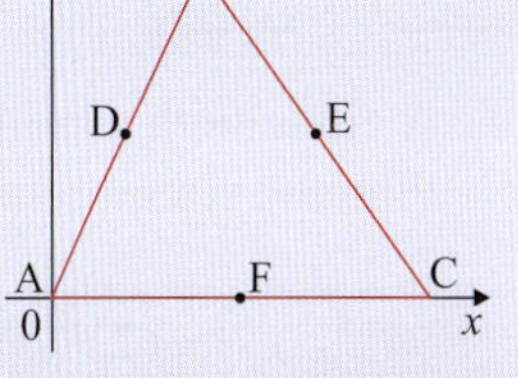

a) Find the equation of the line, l_1, through points A and B. *[1 mark]*

b) Find the equation of the line, l_2, that is perpendicular to l_1 and passes through the point C. *[3 marks]*

c) Find the coordinates of the point G, where lines l_1 and l_2 intersect. *[2 marks]*

d) Show that the line segments FG and DE are equal in length. *[2 marks]*

E P Q11 Find the shortest distance from the point with coordinates (–2, 5) to the line with equation $2y + x = 38$. *[6 marks]*

E P Q12 a) Show that the point P (8, 5) lies on the line, l, with equation $2y + 5x = 50$. *[1 mark]*

b) Find the coordinates of the point Q, at which l passes through the x-axis. *[1 mark]*

c) The lines l_1 and l_2 are both perpendicular to l, and pass through the points P and Q respectively. Find the equations of the lines l_1 and l_2. *[3 marks]*

d) Find the area of the quadrilateral bounded by the lines l, l_1, l_2 and the y-axis. *[3 marks]*

6.6 Direct Proportion

If two variables are in **direct proportion**, it means that changing one variable will change the other by the same scale factor. So doubling one variable will result in the other variable doubling, and the same for tripling, halving, etc. In fact, multiplying or dividing by **any** constant will have the same effect on both.

To say that "y is directly proportional to x", you can write: $\boldsymbol{y \propto x}$

This is equivalent to writing: $\boldsymbol{y = kx}$

where k is a constant. k is sometimes called the **constant of proportionality**.

If you compare this equation to $y = mx + c$, you can see that the graph of two variables in direct proportion is a straight line. The gradient of the line is the constant of proportionality, k, and the y-intercept is 0 — i.e. the line passes through the origin (0, 0). Any time you have two variables in direct proportion, the graph will be a straight line through the origin.

Example 1

The circumference of a circle, C, is directly proportional to its radius, r.

a) What is the constant of proportionality linking C and r?

$C \propto r \Rightarrow C = kr$
Circumference of a circle = $2\pi r$
So $kr = 2\pi r \Rightarrow k = 2\pi$

Compare the proportionality with the formula for circumference.

b) A circle with a radius of p cm has a circumference of 13 cm. Find the circumference of a circle with a radius of $2.5p$ cm.

$C \propto r$, so $C = 2.5 \times 13$
$= 32.5$ cm

You could use the formula to find p, but you don't need to.

As the radius of the second circle is 2.5 times the size of the original, the circumference will be 2.5 times the original as well.

c) Sketch the graph of C against r.

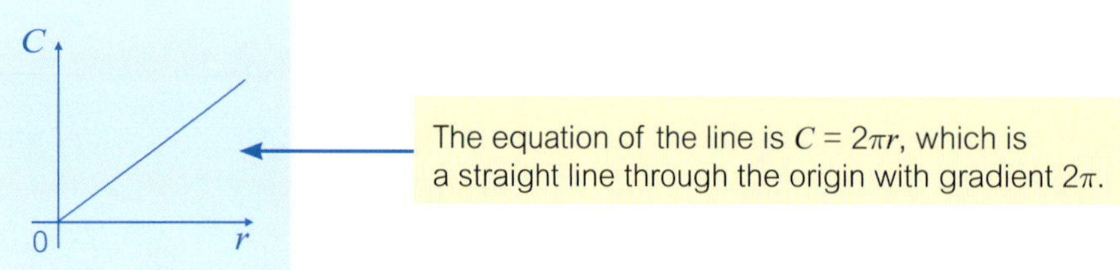

Proportion can also be used for relationships that are **not linear**. These are not 'direct' proportion, but they do work in a similar way. For example:

$$y \propto \frac{1}{x} \Rightarrow y = \frac{k}{x}$$
$$V \propto r^3 \Rightarrow V = kr^3$$
$$\omega \propto \frac{1}{\sqrt{m}} \Rightarrow \omega = \frac{k}{\sqrt{m}}$$

Tip
When $y \propto \frac{1}{x}$, this is known as inverse proportion — when one doubles, the other halves (and so on). Similarly, "y is inversely proportional to x^2" means $y \propto \frac{1}{x^2}$.

You might see these written as e.g. "y is proportional to the cube root of x" instead of $y \propto \sqrt[3]{x}$. In any case, you can always replace the $\propto$ with "$= k \times$" to convert a proportion statement into an equation.

Example 2 M

The average speed that a car travels at is inversely proportional to the time taken for the journey. A car travels from City A to City B at an average speed, s, of 40 mph, which takes a time, t, of 2.5 hours.

a) What is the constant of proportionality linking s and t?

$s \propto \frac{1}{t}$ can be written as $s = \frac{k}{t}$.

$40 = \frac{k}{2.5} \Rightarrow k = 100$ ← Substitute in the values given for s and t to find k.

Tip
In this case, the constant of proportionality is equal to the total distance travelled in miles.

b) Find how long the journey would take if the car travelled at an average speed of 60 mph.

$s = \frac{100}{t} \Rightarrow t = \frac{100}{s}$ ← Rearrange the formula to make t the subject.

$\Rightarrow t = \frac{100}{60}$ ← Substitute in 60 mph.

$= 1.\dot{6} = 1$ hour 40 minutes

Exercise 6.6

Q1 Given that $y \propto x$ in each case, find the value of a if:

a) $y = 24$ when $x = 8$ and $y = a$ when $x = 5$ b) $y = 28$ when $x = 7$ and $y = 96$ when $x = a$

Q2 Find the value of a, given that x and y are inversely proportional:

a) $y = 3$ when $x = 6$ and $y = a$ when $x = 9$

b) $y = 12$ when $x = 12$ and $y = 36$ when $x = a$

P Q3 For each equation below, explain whether $y \propto x$:

a) $y = 7x + 2$ b) $y = ax - bx$ (a and b are constants)

c) $y = 2x + 2x^2 - 2 - x - 2x^2$ d) $y = (x + 3)^2 - (x - 3)^2$

Q4 Given that y is proportional to x^2 ($x > 0$), and that $y = 40$ when $x = 4$:

a) Find the value of y when x is 2. b) Find the exact value of x when y is 45.

P Q5 Prove that if $y \propto x$ and $y \propto z$, then $x \propto z$.

E Q6 Given that y is directly proportional to x, and that $y = 15$ when $x = 3$, draw a graph of y against x for $0 \leq x \leq 6$. *[3 marks]*

P M Q7 Siobhan is modelling the motion of a sliding box. She finds that the frictional force on the box is directly proportional to its mass. If the frictional force, F, is 15 N when its mass, m, is 12 kg, estimate the frictional force when the mass of the box is increased to 18 kg.

E P Q8 x is inversely proportional to y, and x is proportional to the square root of z ($z > 0$).

a) Show that y is inversely proportional to the square root of z. *[4 marks]*

Given that $y = 8$ when $z = 225$:

b) Find the value of y when $z = 72$. *[2 marks]*

c) Find the value of z when $y = 105$. *[2 marks]*

E M Q9 A container of fixed volume is filled with a gas. It is found that the pressure, P pascals, of the gas in the container is directly proportional to the temperature, T kelvins, of the gas. During an experiment, the temperature of the gas in the container is measured to be 400 kelvins and the pressure is measured to be 150 000 pascals.

a) Show that $P = kT$ where k is a constant whose value is to be found (you do not need to state the units of k). *[2 marks]*

b) Find the temperature of the gas in the container when the pressure is 216 000 pascals. *[1 mark]*

c) Interpret the value of k in this context. *[1 mark]*

d) Hence, or otherwise, find the increase in pressure corresponding to an increase in temperature of 112 kelvins. *[1 mark]*

E P M Q10 The diagrams show graphs of I against V, and I against R, where I is the current (in amps), V is the potential difference (in volts) and R is the resistance (in ohms) in an electrical circuit.

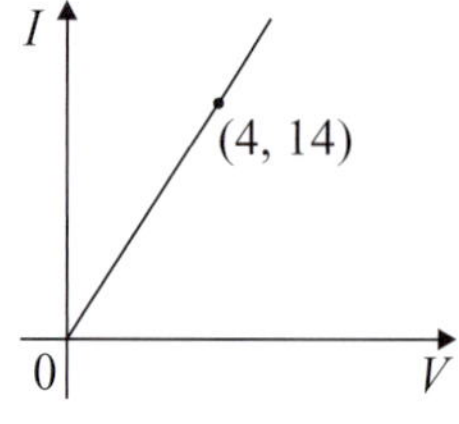

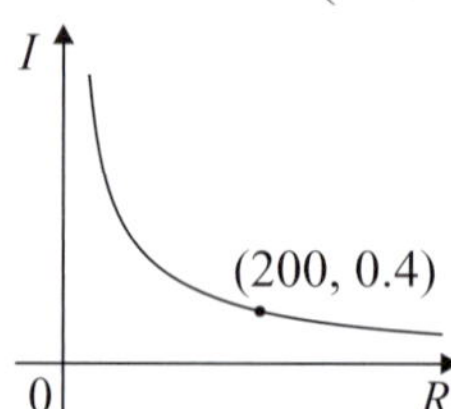

a) Given that I is directly proportional to V, use the information in the diagram to find an expression for I in terms of V. *[2 marks]*

b) Find the value of V when $I = 12$ amps. Give your answer to 2 significant figures. *[1 mark]*

c) Given that I is inversely proportional to R, use the information in the diagram to find an expression for I in terms of R. *[2 marks]*

d) Find the value of I when $R = 500$ ohms. *[1 mark]*

6.7 Sketching Cubic and Quartic Graphs

Cubic functions are **polynomials** that have an x^3 term in them as the highest power of x. Similarly, quartics go up to x^4. Here are the graphs of some cubic and quartic functions:

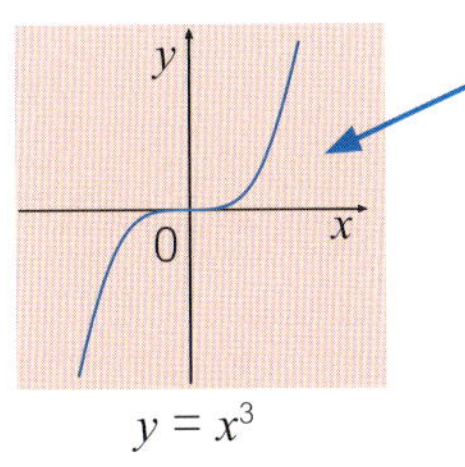

$y = x^3$

For a **cubic**, a **positive** coefficient of x^3 gives a '**bottom-left** to **top-right**' shape.

A **negative** coefficient of x^3 gives a '**top-left** to **bottom-right**' shape.

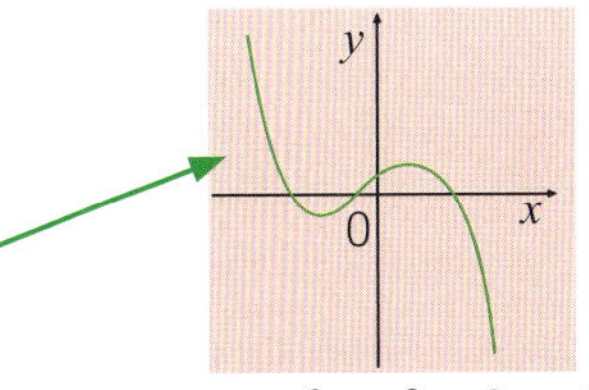

$y = -x^3 + x^2 + 9x - 9$

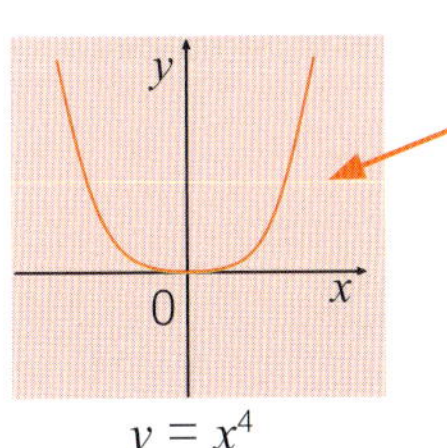

$y = x^4$

For a **quartic**, a **positive** coefficient of x^4 gives a '**top-left** to **top-right**' shape.

A **negative** coefficient of x^4 gives a '**bottom-left** to **bottom-right**' shape.

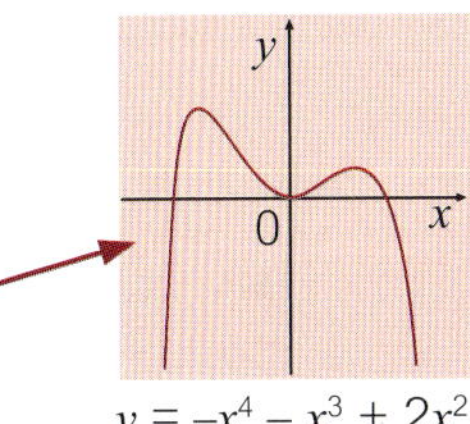

$y = -x^4 - x^3 + 2x^2$

In general, for any graph in the form $y = kx^n$ (when n is positive):

- When **n is EVEN**, you get a u-shape or an n-shape.
- If **k is POSITIVE**, you get a u-shape above the x-axis.
- And if **k is NEGATIVE**, you get an n-shape below the x-axis.

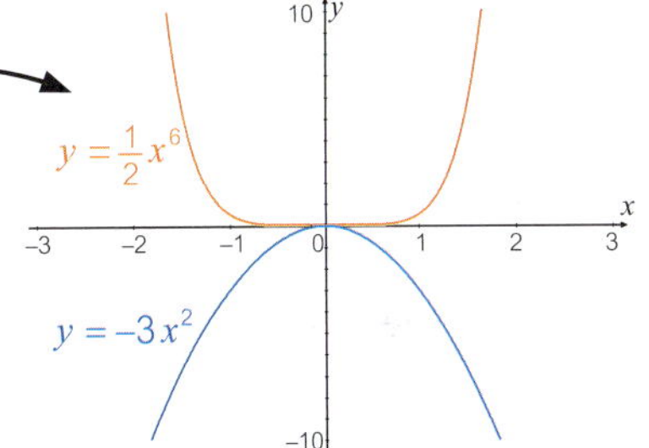

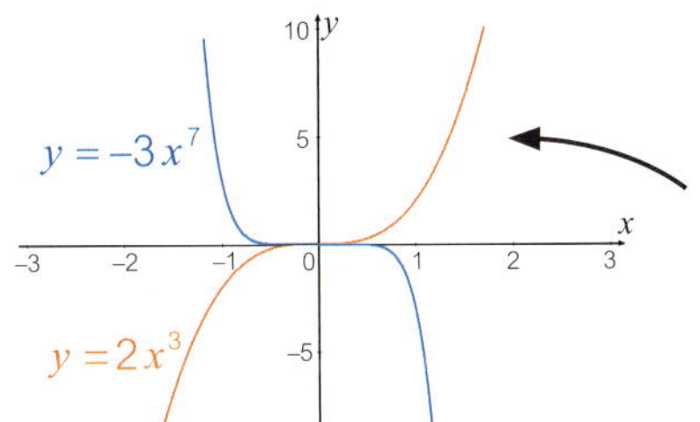

- When **n is ODD**, you get a 'corner-to-corner' shape.
- If **k is POSITIVE**, you get a 'bottom-left to top-right' shape.
- And if **k is NEGATIVE**, you get a 'top-left to bottom-right' shape.

These graphs show the basic shape for $y = kx^n$ — if the polynomial has other terms, the graph may have extra peaks or troughs. A constant term gives the y-intercept, just like in the equation of a straight line.

You may be asked to sketch some simple cubic and quartic graphs. The key to this is finding where the graph **crosses the axes**.

- To find where a graph crosses the y-axis, just set $x = 0$ and find the value of y.
- The easiest way to find where it crosses the x-axis is to **factorise** the polynomial — it crosses the x-axis when **each bracket** is set equal to **0**.

When you're sketching cubics and quartics, watch out for any **repeated roots**.
Repeated roots occur when a **factor** is repeated (i.e. when a bracket is squared, cubed, etc.).

- A **squared** bracket means it's a **double root**, and the graph will only **touch** the x-axis, not cross it, at this point (see part b) of the example below).
- A **cubed** bracket means a **triple root**, which still crosses the x-axis, but **flattens out** as it does so (see part c) on the next page).

Example 1

Sketch the graphs of the following cubic functions.

a) $f(x) = x(x - 1)(2x + 1)$

$f(x) = x(x - 1)(2x + 1) = 2x^3 - x^2 - x$

Expand the brackets to find the highest power of x and its coefficient.

The coefficient of x^3 is positive, so the graph will have a 'bottom-left to top-right' shape.

$f(0) = 0(-1)(1) = 0 \Rightarrow$ y-intercept $= 0$

Find where the graph crosses the y-axis, i.e. where $x = 0$.

$f(x) = x(x - 1)(2x + 1) = 0 \Rightarrow x = 0, 1$ and $-\frac{1}{2}$

Find where the graph crosses the x-axis, i.e. where $f(x) = 0$.

So the curve crosses the x-axis three times and will look like this.

b) $g(x) = (x - 3)^2(x + 1)(x - 1)$

$g(x) = (x - 3)^2(x + 1)(x - 1) = (x^2 - 6x + 9)(x^2 - 1)$
$= x^4 - 6x^3 + 8x^2 + 6x - 9$

Multiply out the brackets.

The coefficient of x^4 is positive, so the graph will have 'top-left to top-right' shape.

$g(0) = (0 - 3)^2 \times (0 + 1) \times (0 - 1) = -9$

So the y-intercept is $(0, -9)$

Find where it meets both axes.

$(x - 3)^2(x + 1)(x - 1) = 0$

$\Rightarrow x = 3, x = 1$ and $x = -1$

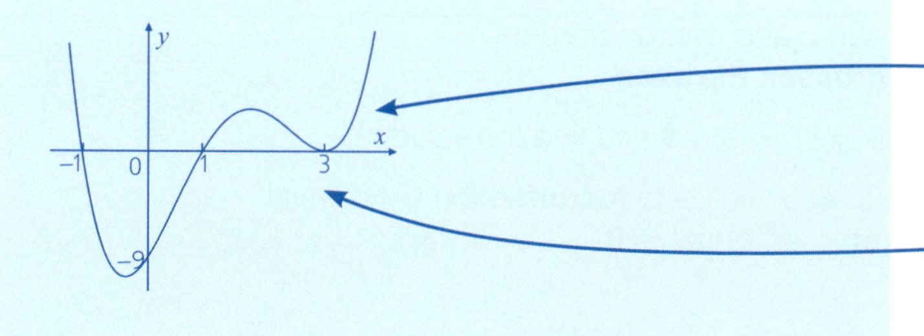

So the graph meets the x-axis three times and looks like this.

The $(x - 3)$ bracket is squared, so the quartic has a double root at $x = 3$ — the graph touches the x-axis here, but doesn't cross it.

c) $h(x) = (2 - x)^3$

$h(x) = 8 - 12x + 6x^2 - x^3$. ← Multiply out the brackets.

The coefficient of x^3 is negative, so the graph will have a 'top-left to bottom-right' shape.

$h(0) = (2 - 0)^3 = 8 \Rightarrow$ y-intercept is $(0, 8)$ ← Find where it crosses both axes.

$(2 - x)^3 = 0 \Rightarrow x = 2$ — this is a triple root as the bracket is cubed.

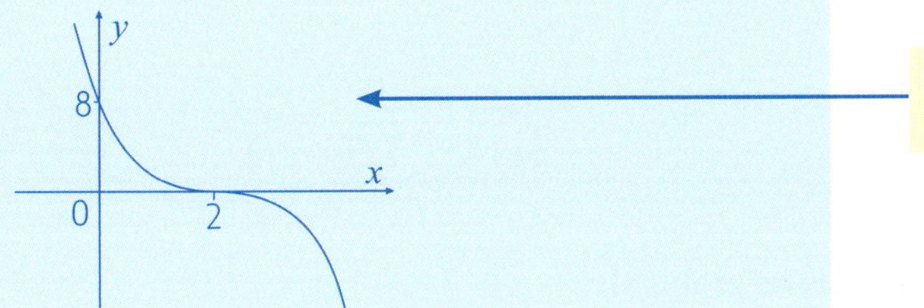

← So the graph looks like this.

Tip This graph is just the graph of $y = -x^3$ shifted 2 to the right — there's more about graph transformations from page 129.

Exercise 6.7

Q1 The diagram shows four graphs A, B, C and D.
State which graph would represent each of the following functions.

a) $y = -1.5x^4$ b) $y = 0.5x^3$ c) $y = 2x^6$ d) $y = -3x^3$

A

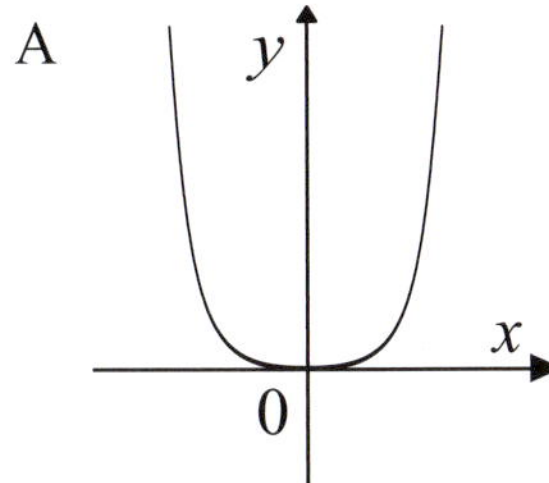

B

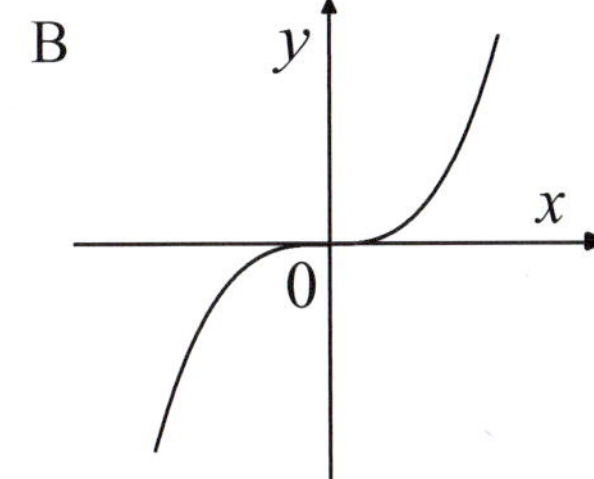

C

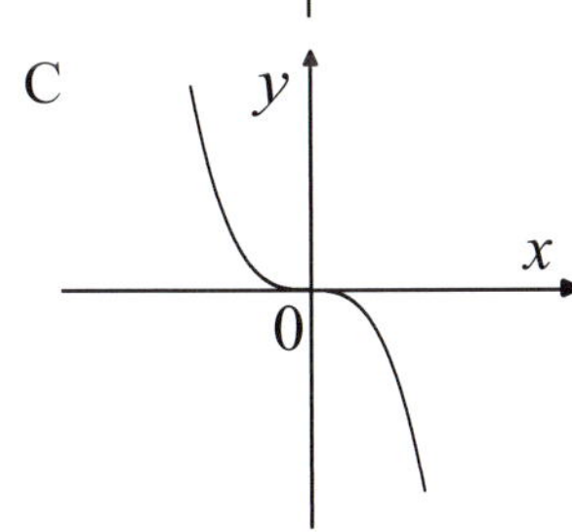

D

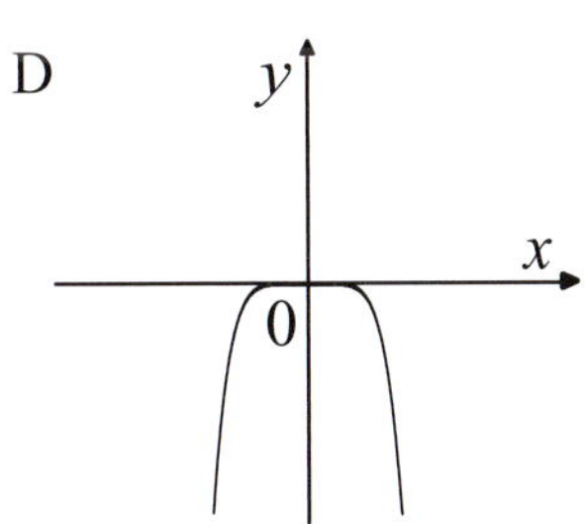

Q1 Hint If you're not sure what the graph will do, stick some values for x into the function — the table function on a calculator is handy for this. Numbers near to the roots are good places to start, or very large positive and negative numbers (to check what happens at the extremes).

For Questions 2-4, sketch the graphs of the functions, showing clearly where they meet the x-axis.

Q2 a) $y = x(x + 2)(x - 3)$ b) $y = (x + 1)(2x - 1)(x - 3)$ c) $y = x(x + 1)(2 - x)$

Q3 a) $y = x^2(2x - 5)$ b) $y = x(5 - x)^2$ c) $y = (1 - x)(2 - x)^2$

Q4 a) $y = -5x^2(3x - 2)$ b) $y = (7 - x)(9 - 2x)(3 - x)$ c) $y = (4 + x)^3$

Q5 Match the following equations with their correct graphs:

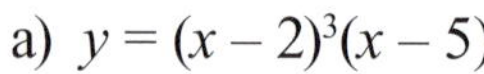

a) $y = (x - 2)^3(x - 5)$

b) $y = (x - 2)(x - 5)^3$

c) $y = (x - 2)^2(x - 5)^2$

d) $y = (x - 2)^3(5 - x)$

A
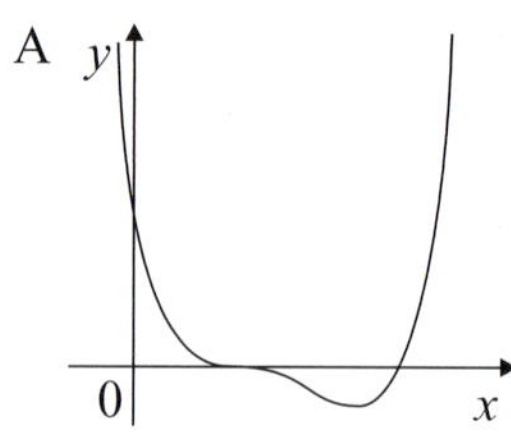

B
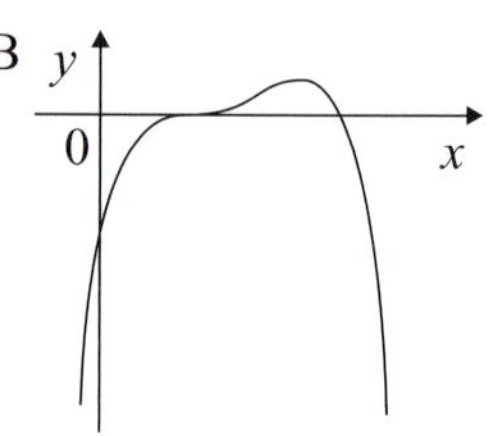

C
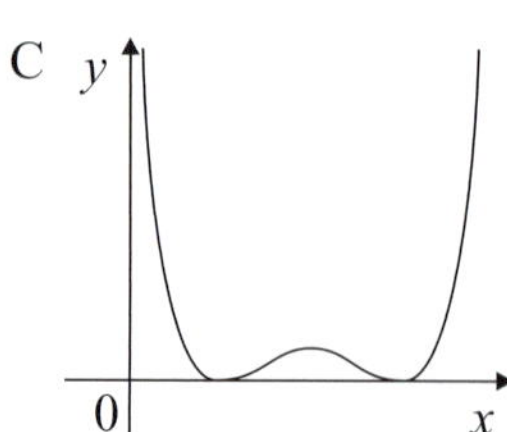

D
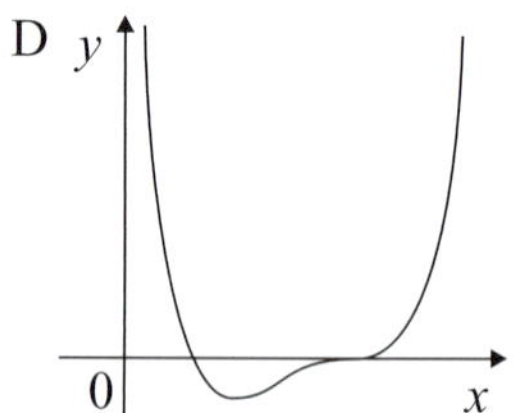

Q6 a) Factorise completely $x^3 - 7x^2 + 12x$.

b) Use your answer to part a) to sketch the graph of $y = x^3 - 7x^2 + 12x$, showing clearly where the graph meets the coordinate axes.

Q7 Sketch the graphs of these functions, showing clearly where the graph meets the coordinate axes.

a) $y = x^3 - 16x$ b) $y = 2x^3 - 12x^2 + 18x$ c) $y = -3x^2 - x^3$

Q8 Sketch the graph of $y = \text{f}(x)$, where:

a) $\text{f}(x) = 3x(x - 4)^2(2x - 1)$ b) $\text{f}(x) = -3x^2(2x - 7)^2$ c) $\text{f}(x) = (4 - x)(x + 2)^3$

E Q9 Sketch the graph of the function $y = (9 - x^2)(x^2 - 40)$. Clearly indicate the coordinates of the points at which the graph intersects the coordinate axes. *[4 marks]*

Q10 Sketch the graphs of the following quartics:

a) $y = x^2(x^2 - 9x + 14)$ b) $y = (x + 1)(2 - 3x)(4x^2 - 9)$ c) $y = (x - 5)(2x^3 + 5x^2 - 3x)$

P Q11 Sketch the graph of $y = 4x^3 + 4x^2 - 5x - 3$, showing where the graph meets the axes.

P Q12 a) Given that $x = 1$ is a root of the equation $y = (x + 1)(2x^3 - 5x^2 + x + 2)$, factorise y fully.

b) Hence, sketch the graph of y, showing the points where the graph meets the x- and y- axes.

Challenge

P Q13 Sketch the graph of $y = (x - 3)(x^3 - 7x^2 + 14x - 8)$, given that its roots are all positive integers.

E P Q14 a) Sketch the graph of the cubic with equation $y = \text{f}(x)$ where $\text{f}(x) = (x - 2)(2x^2 + 5x - 1)$, clearly indicating the coordinates of the points at which the graph intersects the coordinate axes. *[4 marks]*

b) Hence, or otherwise, sketch the graph of the curve with equation $y = x\text{f}(x)$. *[2 marks]*

6.8 Graphs of Reciprocal Functions and Negative Powers

Reciprocal functions are those of the form $y = \frac{k}{x}$, where k is a constant.

The graph of a reciprocal function always has **asymptotes**.

An **asymptote** of a curve is a **line** which the curve gets infinitely close to, but **never** touches.

You need to be able to sketch the graphs of reciprocal functions. Here are some examples:

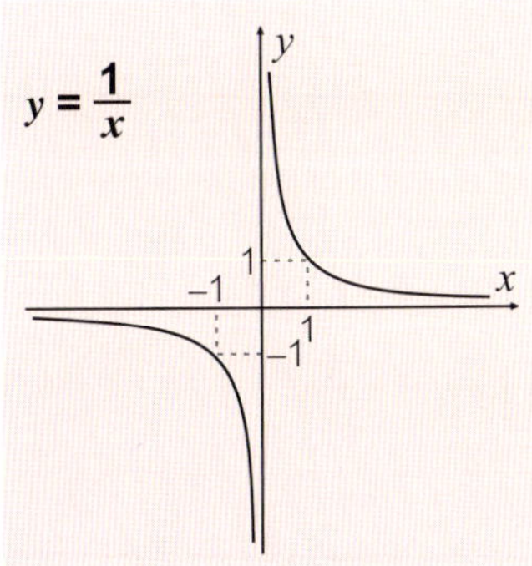

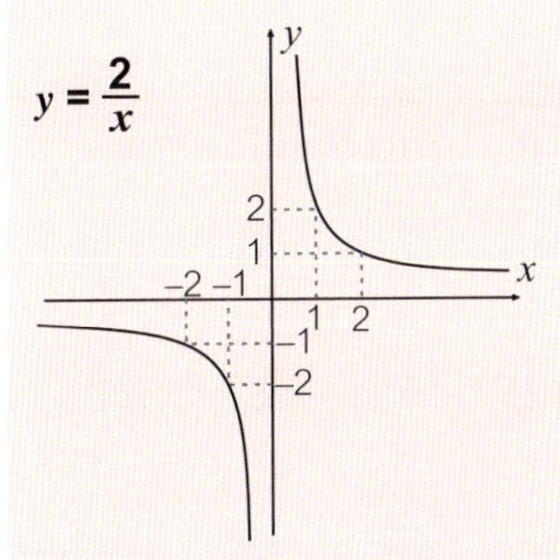

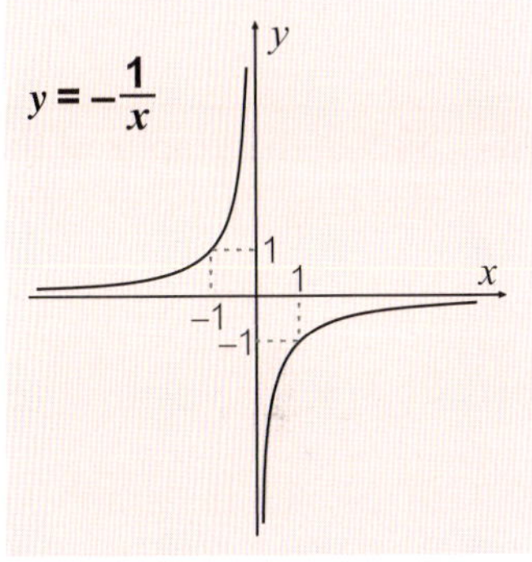

The graph never crosses the x- or y-axes, as you can't divide by zero. So the y-axis is a vertical asymptote ($x = 0$) and the x-axis is a horizontal asymptote ($y = 0$). For reciprocal graphs of the form $y = \frac{1}{x+a} + b$, the asymptotes will be at $y = b$ and $x = -a$ (see Example 2 on page 130).

The function $y = \frac{k}{x}$ can also be written as $y = kx^{-1}$.
In general, **negative powers** of x (i.e. functions of the form $y = kx^{-n}$, such as $y = 2x^{-3}$) can also be written in the form $y = \frac{k}{x^n}$.

Tip You need to be familiar with functions written in either form.

For any graph in the form $\boldsymbol{y = \frac{k}{x^n}}$ or $\boldsymbol{kx^{-n}}$:

- When $\boldsymbol{n}$ **is EVEN**, you get a graph with two bits next to each other.
- If $\boldsymbol{k}$ **is POSITIVE**, both parts of the graph are above the x-axis
- And if $\boldsymbol{k}$ **is NEGATIVE**, the graph is below the x-axis.

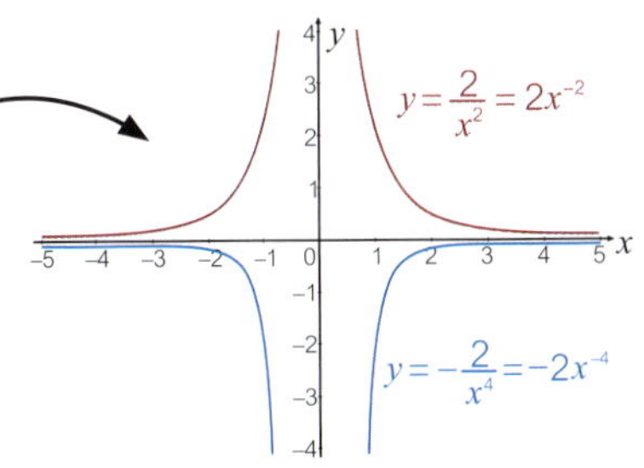

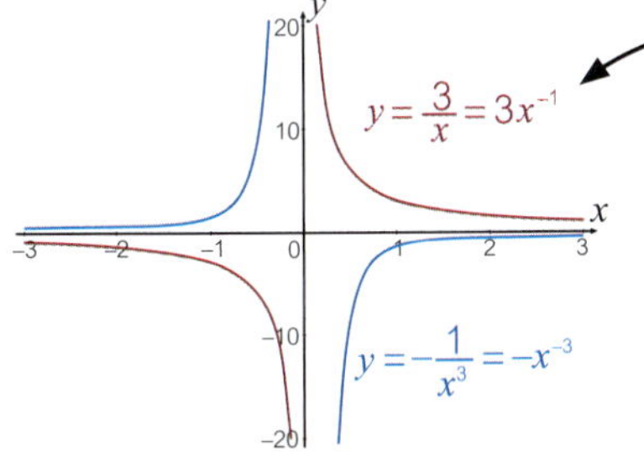

- When $\boldsymbol{n}$ **is ODD**, you get a graph with two bits opposite each other.
- If $\boldsymbol{k}$ **is POSITIVE**, the graph is in the top-right and bottom-left quadrants.
- And if $\boldsymbol{k}$ **is NEGATIVE**, it's in the top-left and the bottom-right.

Exercise 6.8

Q1 The diagram shows four graphs A, B, C and D.
State which graph would represent each of the following functions:

a) $y = x^{-2}$ b) $y = -3x^{-3}$ c) $y = -\frac{3}{x^4}$ d) $y = 2x^{-5}$

A

B

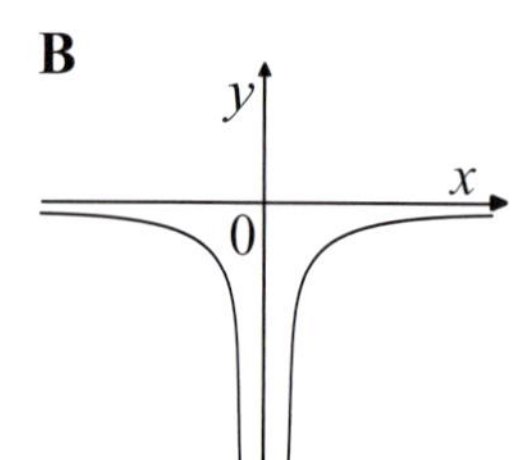

C

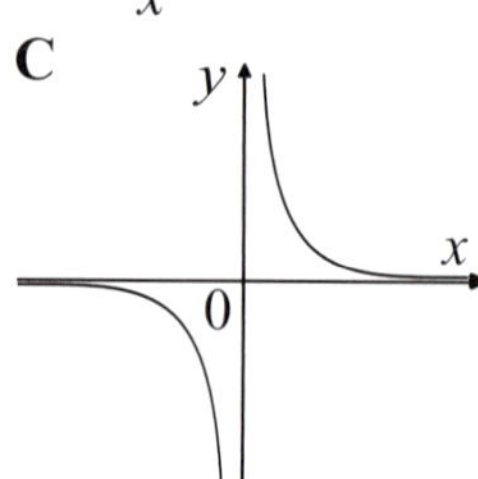

D

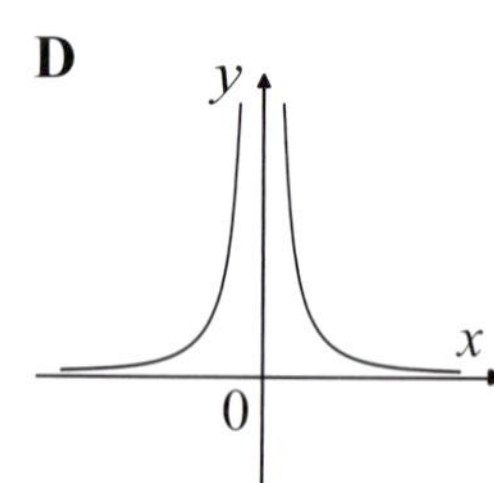

Q2 Sketch the graphs of the following reciprocal functions, showing the points where $x = 1$ and $x = -1$:

a) $y = 1.5x^{-5}$ b) $y = 7x^{-2}$ c) $y = -\frac{6}{x}$ d) $y = -1.2x^{-4}$

e) $y = \frac{3}{x^3}$ f) $y = \frac{1}{2}x^{-6}$ g) $y = \frac{1}{3x^2}$ h) $y = \frac{4}{5x^{11}}$

P Q3 a) Sketch the graphs of $y = 3x^{-2}$ and $y = -x^3 - 2x^2$ on the same axes.

b) Find the number of real roots of $3x^{-2} = -x^3 - 2x^2$.

E P Q4 a) For $x \neq 0$, find the solutions to the equation $\frac{1}{x} = \frac{1}{x^3}$. *[2 marks]*

b) On the same axes, sketch the graphs of $y = \frac{1}{x}$ and $y = \frac{1}{x^3}$, clearly indicating the coordinates of the points of intersection of the two graphs. *[3 marks]*

P Q5 Find the values of the constants a, b, c and d, using the graphs shown below:

$y = \frac{1}{x^a}$

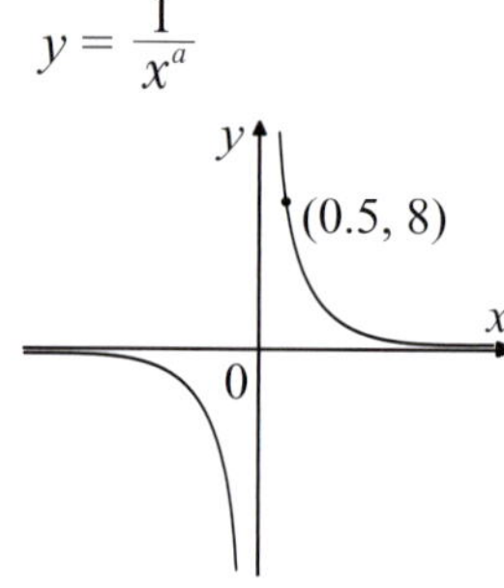

$y = bx^{-2}$

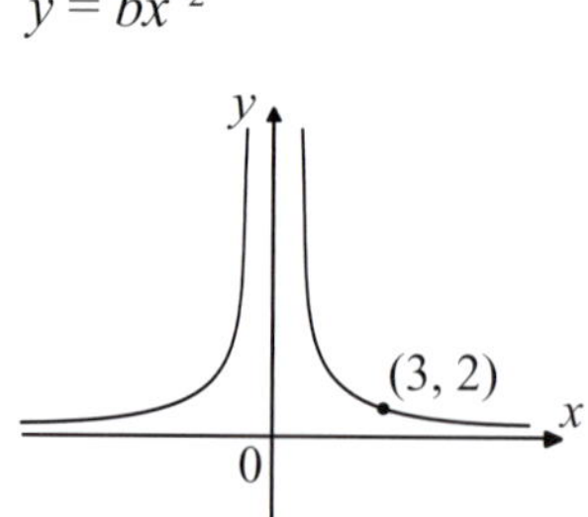

$y = \frac{c}{x^d}$

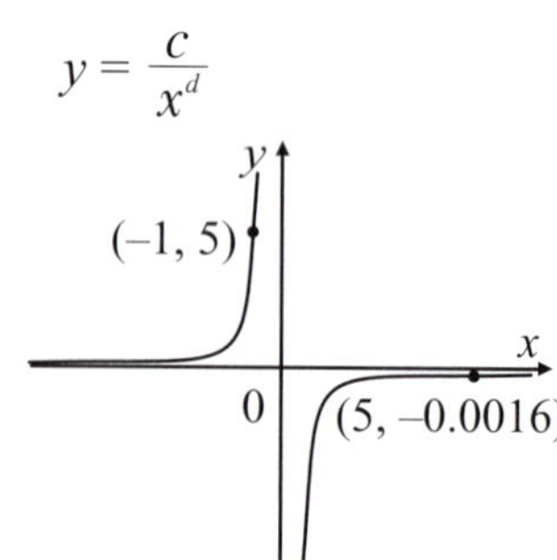

Challenge

P Q6 a) Use graph paper to draw the graphs of $y = -\frac{2}{x}$ and $y = 4 - x^2$ on the same axes for $-3 \leq x \leq 3$. Use a scale of 2 cm for 1 unit.

b) Use your answer to part a) to estimate the solutions to $-\frac{2}{x} = 4 - x^2$.

6.9 Translations

Translating the graph of a function means moving it **horizontally**, **vertically** or **both**. The shape of the graph itself doesn't change, it just moves. There are two types of translation:

$y = f(x) + a$

Adding a number to the **whole function** translates the graph in the **y-direction**.

If $a > 0$, the graph goes **upwards**.

If $a < 0$, the graph goes **downwards**.

This can be described by a **column vector**: $\begin{pmatrix} 0 \\ a \end{pmatrix}$ or $\begin{bmatrix} 0 \\ a \end{bmatrix}$.

$y = f(x + a)$

Writing '$x + a$' instead of 'x' means the graph moves **sideways** ("translated in the **x-direction**").

If $a > 0$, the graph goes to the **left**.

If $a < 0$, the graph goes to the **right**.

As a **column vector**, this would be $\begin{pmatrix} -a \\ 0 \end{pmatrix}$ or $\begin{bmatrix} -a \\ 0 \end{bmatrix}$.

Example 1

Shown to the right is the graph of $y = f(x)$, where $f(x) = x(x + 2)(x - 2)$.

a) Sketch the graph $y = f(x) + 2$.

$y = f(x) + 2$ is a translation by the vector $\begin{pmatrix} 0 \\ 2 \end{pmatrix}$.

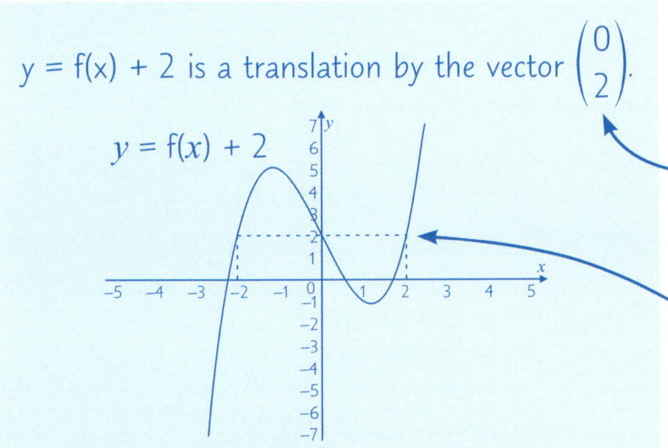

2 is added to the whole function, i.e. $a = 2$. So the graph will be translated 2 units in the y-direction, i.e. shifted upwards by 2.

The point (0, 0) on $f(x)$ has become the point (0, 2).

The other roots of $f(x)$, (–2, 0) and (2, 0) have become (–2, 2) and (2, 2).

Tip When sketching a transformed graph, you need to show what happens to its key points, e.g. where it crosses the axes, max/min points, etc.

b) Sketch the graph $y = f(x - 1)$.

$y = f(x - 1)$ is a translation by the vector $\begin{pmatrix} 1 \\ 0 \end{pmatrix}$.

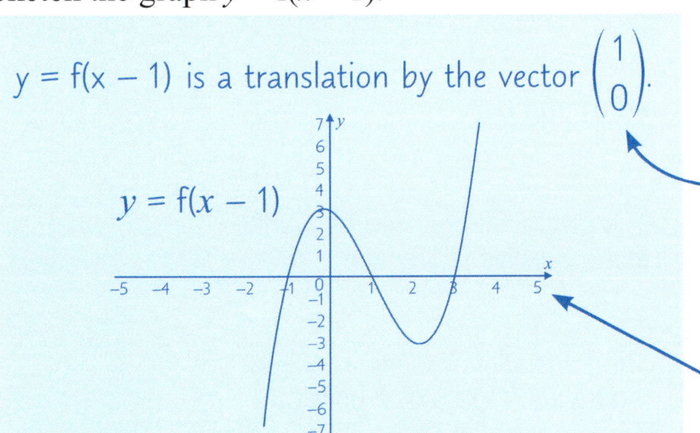

It's the form $y = f(x + a)$ so it's a translation in the x-direction. $a = -1$, which is negative, so it's a translation to the right by 1 unit.

1 is added to the x-coordinate of every point.

E.g. (2, 0) becomes (3, 0).

Example 2

Given that $f(x) = \frac{1}{x}$:

a) Sketch the graph of $y = f(x) + 2$ and state the equations of the asymptotes.

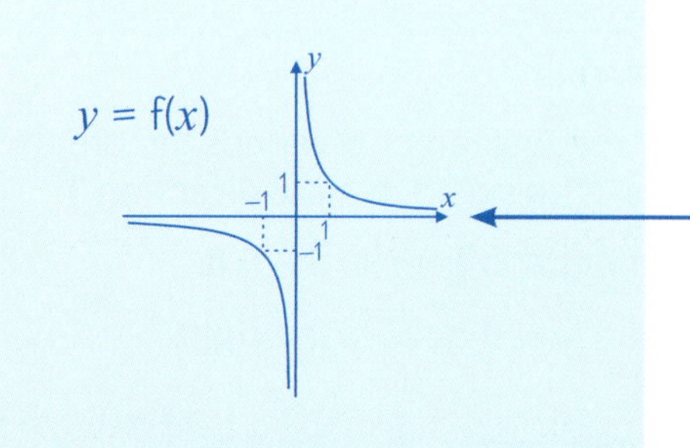

First, sketch the graph of $f(x) = \frac{1}{x}$.

It has asymptotes at $x = 0$ and $y = 0$.

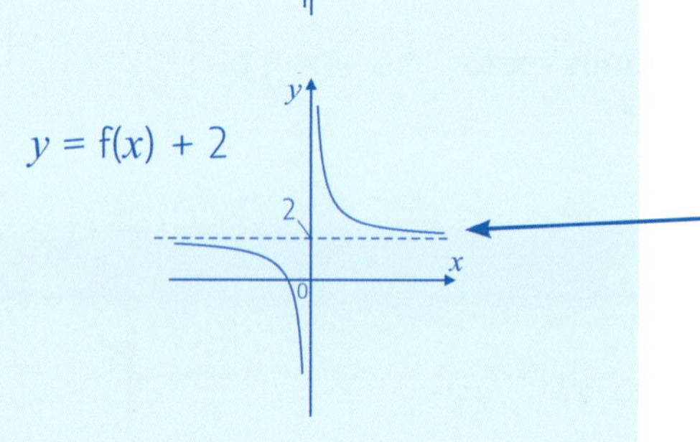

The graph $y = f(x) + 2$ is a translation of the graph upwards by 2, so the asymptotes of $y = f(x)$ are also translated upwards by 2.

It has asymptotes at $x = 0$ and $y = 2$.

The horizontal asymptote at $y = 0$ becomes $y = 2$ but the vertical asymptote is still $x = 0$ because the graph has only moved upwards.

b) Sketch the graph of $y = f(x + 2)$ and state the equations of the asymptotes.

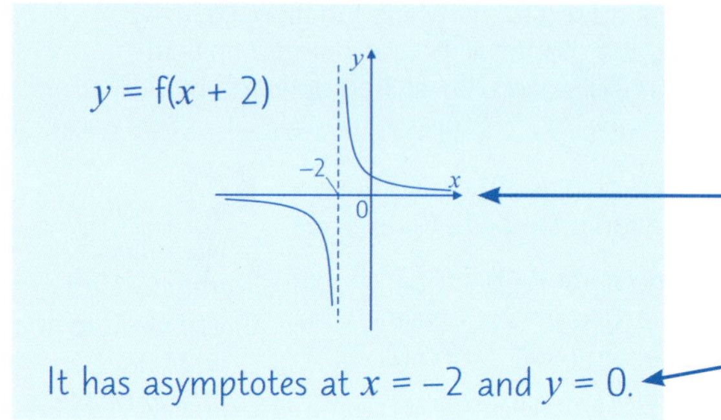

The graph of $f(x + 2)$ is a translation to the left by 2.

It has asymptotes at $x = -2$ and $y = 0$.

This time, the horizontal asymptote remains at $y = 0$ but the vertical asymptote moves to $x = -2$.

c) What column vectors describe the translations in parts a) and b)?

The translation vector in part a) is $\begin{pmatrix} 0 \\ 2 \end{pmatrix}$.

The graph is translated by 2 units in the positive y-direction.

The translation vector in part b) is $\begin{pmatrix} -2 \\ 0 \end{pmatrix}$

The translation is in the negative x-direction (again by 2 units).

Exercise 6.9

Q1 The diagram on the right shows the graph of $y = f(x)$. The curve has a maximum at (2, 4) and meets the x-axis at (0, 0) and (5, 0).

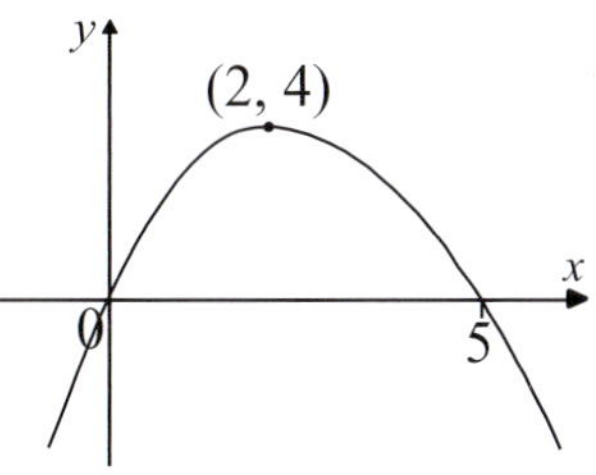

a) Sketch the graph of $y = f(x) + 2$, labelling the coordinates of the maximum and where the curve meets the y-axis.

b) Sketch the graph of $y = f(x + 2)$, labelling the points where the curve meets the x-axis and the maximum.

Q2 If $g(x) = -\frac{2}{x}$, sketch these graphs and write down the equations of the asymptotes for each:

a) $y = g(x)$ b) $y = g(x + 3)$ c) $y = g(x) + 3$

P Q3 Given that $y = x^2(x - 4)$, use a column vector to describe the translation that gives the graph of:

a) $x^2(x - 4) + 1$ b) $y = (x - 2)^2(x - 6)$ c) $y = x(x + 4)^2$

E Q4 The graph of $y = f(x)$ is translated such that the point (5, 8) is mapped to the point $\left(\frac{13}{2}, \frac{7}{3}\right)$.

a) Describe the translation, giving your answer as a column vector. *[2 marks]*

b) Find the coordinates of the point $\left(-2, \frac{5}{7}\right)$ after this translation. *[1 mark]*

P Q5 Explain how the graph of $y = x^3 + 3x + 7$ can be translated to give the graph of $y = x^3 + 3x + 2$. Include a column vector in your answer.

P Q6 The graph of $y = x^2 - 3x + 7$ is translated by the vector $\begin{pmatrix}-1\\0\end{pmatrix}$. Write down the equation of the new graph. Give your answer in as simple a form as possible.

Q7 The diagram shows the graph of $y = f(x)$. The graph has a maximum at (5, 3), crosses the x-axis at (3, 0) and (6, 0) and crosses the y-axis at (0, –1).

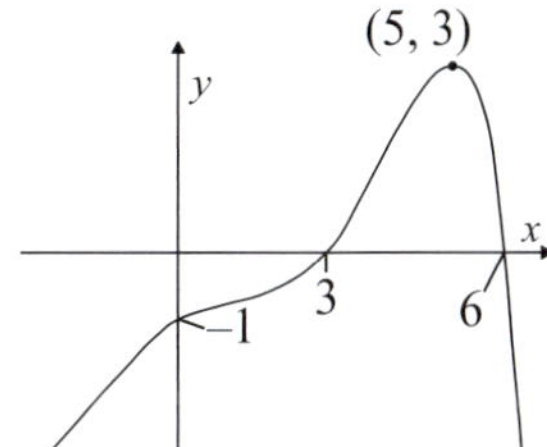

a) Sketch the graph of $y = f(x) - 2$.

b) Label the coordinates of the maximum and the point where the graph meets the y-axis.

P Q8 a) The graph of $f(x) = x^2 + 5$ is translated to the left by 3 to give the graph of $g(x)$. Find the equation of $g(x)$ in its simplest form.

b) The graph of $g(x)$ is then translated downwards by 4 to give the graph of $h(x)$. Find the equation of $h(x)$ in its simplest form.

E Q9 Describe the transformation which maps the graph of the function $y = x^2$ to the graph of the function $y = x^2 - \frac{5}{2}x + 8$. *[2 marks]*

E P Q10 Given that $f(x) = 2x^2 - 11x + 24$:

a) Find the range of values for a for which the graph of $y = f(x) + a$ does not intersect the x-axis. *[3 marks]*

b) Find the range of values for b for which the line of symmetry of $f(x - b)$ is between the lines $x = -2$ and $x = 2$. *[2 marks]*

P Q11 Give the equations of the asymptotes of the following graphs:

a) $y = \frac{1}{x} - 4$ b) $y = \frac{1}{x+3}$ c) $y = \frac{1}{x-1} + 7$

E Q12 a) Give the equations of the asymptotes of the graph of $y = 4 - \frac{5}{3-x}$. *[2 marks]*

b) Find the coordinates of the points of intersection of this graph with the axes. *[2 marks]*

c) Hence sketch the graph of $y = 4 - \frac{5}{3-x}$. *[2 marks]*

Challenge

P Q13 a) Sketch the graph of $y = (x - 1)(2x - 3)(4 - x)$ and label the points where the graph meets the coordinate axes.

b) The graph in part a) is translated by the vector $\begin{pmatrix} 2 \\ 0 \end{pmatrix}$.
Give the equation of the translated graph in its simplest form.

c) On separate axes, sketch the graph of the equation from part b), labelling all the points where the graph meets the x-axis.

E P Q14 The point A (2, 5) lies on the graph of $y = f(x)$, where $f(x) = x^2 + 1$.
The graph of $y = f(x)$ is translated 10 units along the line $y = \frac{4}{3}x$ in the positive x direction, to give the graph of $y = g(x)$.

a) Find the coordinates of A after the translation. *[5 marks]*

b) Find an expression for $g(x)$. *[1 mark]*

6.10 Stretches and Reflections

The graph of a function can be stretched, squashed or reflected by **multiplying** the whole function or the x's in the function by a number. The result you get depends on what you multiply and whether the number is positive or negative.

$y = a\text{f}(x)$

Multiplying the **whole function** by a stretches the graph **vertically** (i.e. parallel to the y-axis) by a scale factor of a.

- If $a > 1$ or $a < -1$, the graph is **stretched**.
- If $-1 < a < 1$, the graph is **squashed**.
- If a is **negative**, the graph is **also reflected** about the **x-axis**.

For every point on the graph, the x-coordinate stays the same and the y-coordinate is multiplied by a.

Tip Don't describe a transformation as a "squash" in the exam — call it a "stretch with a scale factor of...".

Example 1

The diagram shows the graph of a function f(x).

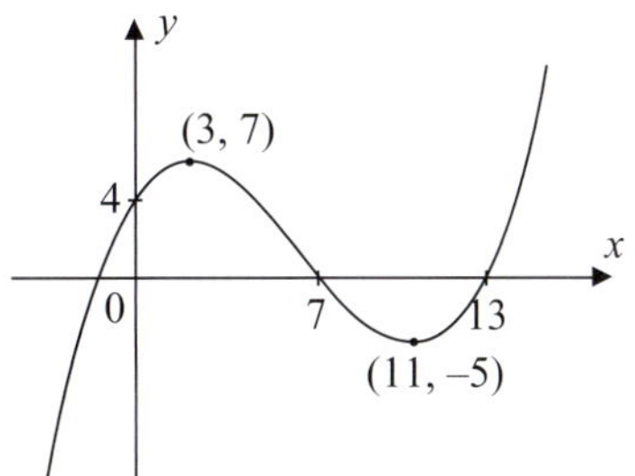

a) Sketch the graph $y = \frac{1}{3}\text{f}(x)$.

The graph will be stretched vertically by a scale factor of $\frac{1}{3}$.

As $\frac{1}{3}$ is less than 1, the 'stretch' will actually be a squash.

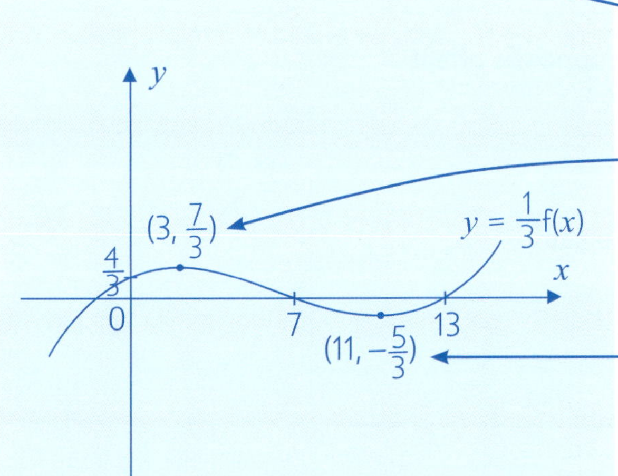

The diagram gives 5 key points on the graph — (0, 4), (3, 7), (7, 0), (11, –5) and (13, 0). You need to show where each of these points has moved to on the transformed graph.

The x-coordinates don't change — just multiply the y-coordinates by a.

Tip The graph still crosses the x-axis at the same points as the original graph — this is true for all $y = a\text{f}(x)$ transformations.

b) Sketch the graph $y = -2\text{f}(x)$.

Here, the whole function has been multiplied by –2.

The graph will be stretched vertically by a factor of 2, but also reflected in the x-axis.

Because –2 is negative, the graph will be reflected vertically (in the x-axis).

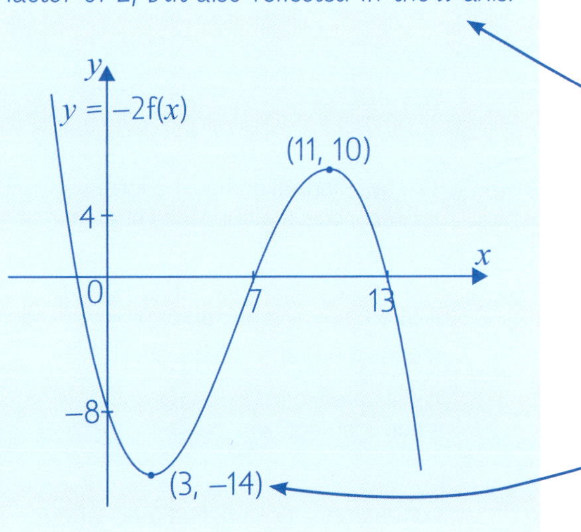

Again, you need to show what has happened to each key point.

So that's vertical stretches covered. Next up are horizontal stretches...

$y = f(ax)$

Writing 'ax' instead of 'x' stretches the graph **horizontally** by a scale factor of $\frac{1}{a}$.

- If $a > 1$ or $a < -1$, the graph is **squashed**.
- If $-1 < a < 1$, the graph is **stretched**.
- Negative values of a reflect the basic shape in the y-axis.

For these transformations, the y-coordinate of each point stays the same and the x-coordinate is multiplied by $\frac{1}{a}$.

Notice that a being bigger or smaller than 1 has the **opposite effect** for horizontal stretches compared to vertical stretches.

Example 2

The diagram to the right shows the graph of $y = f(x)$ again.

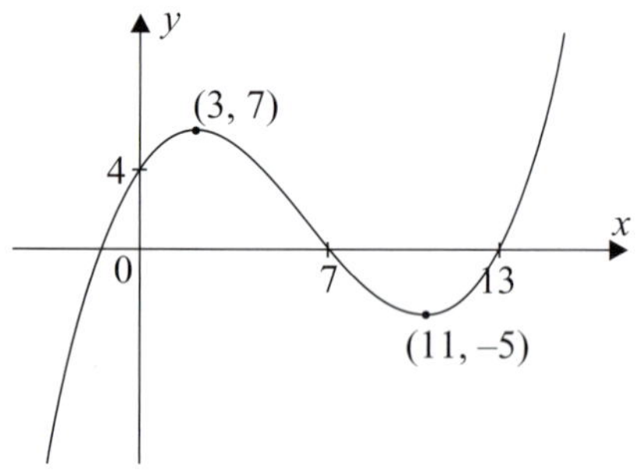

a) Sketch the graph of $y = f\left(\frac{1}{2}x\right)$.

$\frac{1}{2}$ is positive and between –1 and 1, so the graph will be stretched horizontally by a scale factor of 2.

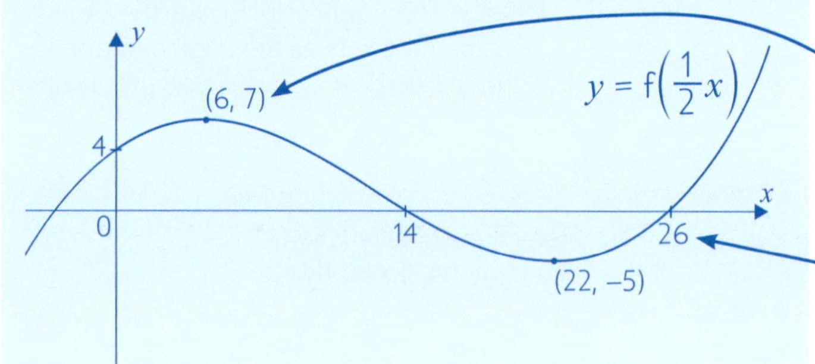

The transformation has the form $y = f(ax)$, so it's a horizontal stretch.

For each point given, the x-coordinate is multiplied by 2 but the y-coordinate doesn't change.

This time, the y-intercept doesn't change, but the two x-intercepts do.

b) Sketch the graph $y = f(-3x)$.

a = –3, so the graph will be 'stretched' by a scale factor of $\frac{1}{3}$, and reflected in the y-axis.

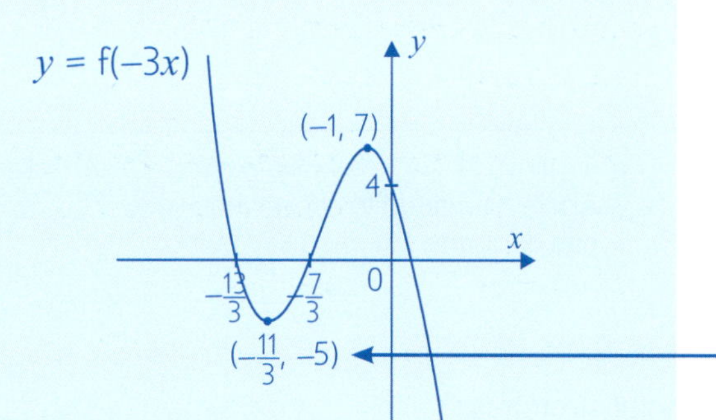

The transformation has the form $y = f(ax)$, so it's a horizontal stretch.

A stretch by a scale factor of $\frac{1}{3}$ means the graph is 'squashed'.

It's also reflected in the y-axis since a is negative.

For each point given, find (and label) the new position by multiplying the x-coordinate by $-\frac{1}{3}$ (and leaving the y-coordinate the same.)

Exercise 6.10

Q1 The diagram below shows the graph of $y = g(x)$. The graph has a minimum at $(-2, -3)$, a maximum at $(2, 3)$ and crosses the x-axis at $(0, 0)$, $(-4, 0)$ and $(4, 0)$.

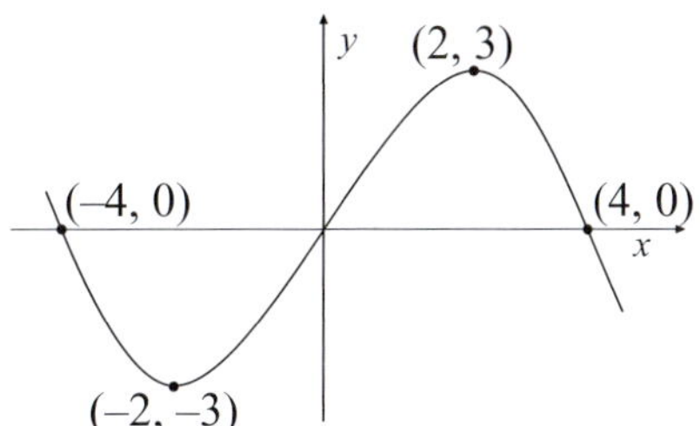

Sketch the graphs of these functions, labelling clearly the coordinates of any maximums, minimums and intersections with the axes:

a) $y = 2g(x)$ b) $y = g(2x)$ c) $y = -2g(x)$ d) $y = g(-2x)$

Q2 The diagram shows the graph of $f(x)$ and Graph A of a function that is a transformation of $f(x)$.

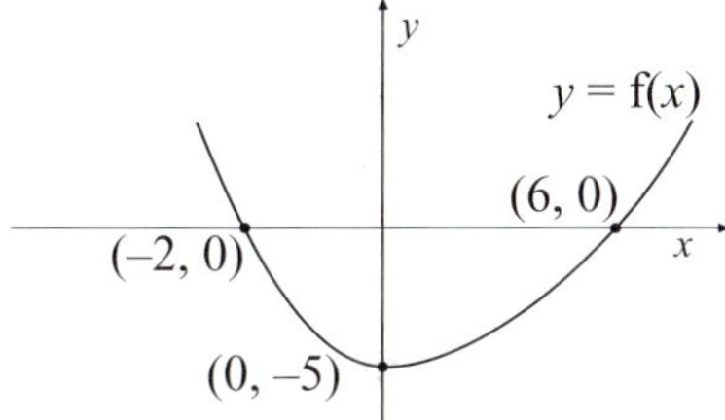

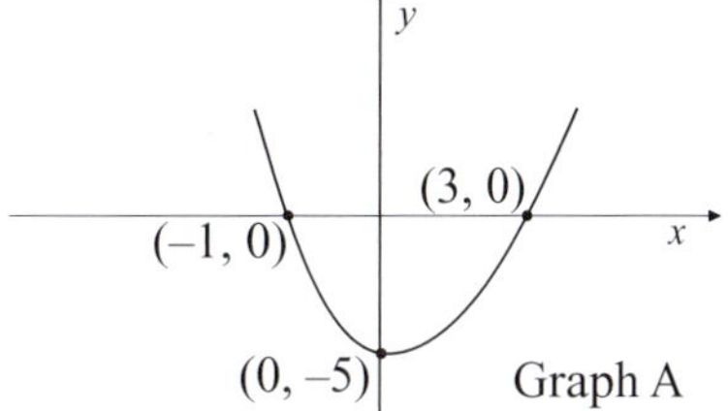

Which of these equations gives the transformed graph?

a) $y = 2f(x)$ b) $y = f(2x)$ c) $y = f(0.5x)$ d) $y = 0.5f(x)$

Q3 The diagram shows the graph of $f(x)$ and Graph A of a function that is a transformation of $f(x)$.

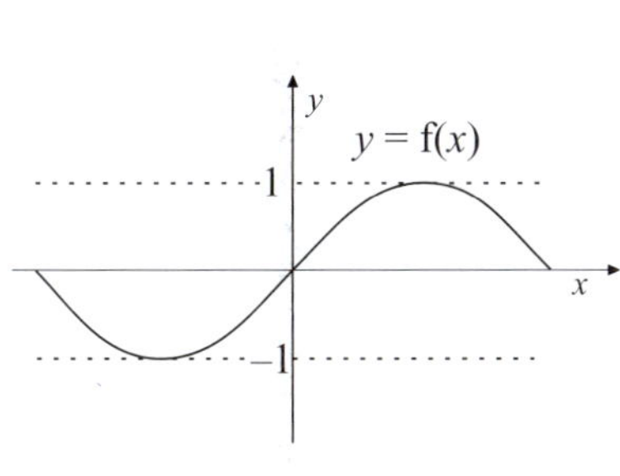

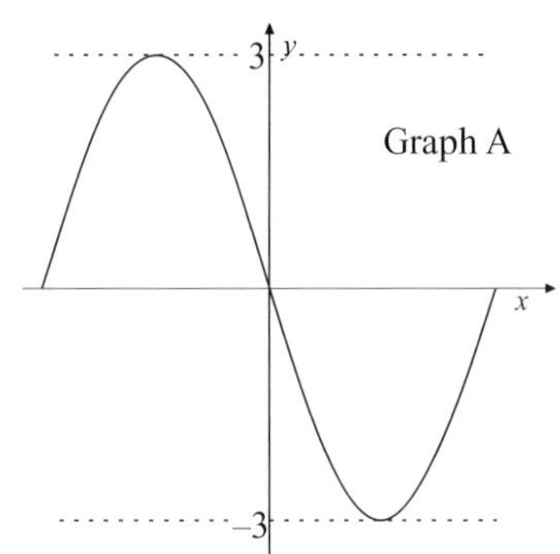

Which of these equations could give the transformed graph?

a) $y = 3f(x)$ b) $y = -3f(x)$ c) $y = f(-3x)$ d) $y = f(3x)$

Q4 Given that $f(x) = x^3 - x$, sketch the graphs of the following functions:

a) $y = f(x) + 2$ b) $y = f(x - 2)$ c) $y = f(-2x)$ d) $y = -2f(x)$

e) $y = f(2x)$ f) $y = -0.2f(x)$ g) $y = f(0.2x)$ h) $y = 0.2f(x)$

P Q5 Describe clearly the transformation that is required to take the graph of $y = x^3 + 2x + 4$ to the graph of $y = 3x^3 + 6x + 12$.

P Q6 Describe clearly the transformation that is required to take the graph of $y = x^2 + x + 4$ to the graph of $y = 4x^2 - 2x + 4$.

Q7 Hint
e is just a constant number — see page 216.

P Q7 The diagram shows the graph of $y = e^x$. Use this to sketch the graphs below, labelling clearly where the transformation takes the point (0, 1) to.

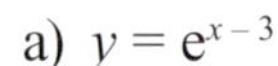

a) $y = e^{x-3}$ b) $y = e^x + 1$

c) $y = 0.1e^x$ d) $y = -4e^x$

e) $y = -\frac{1}{2}e^x$ f) $y = e^{7x}$

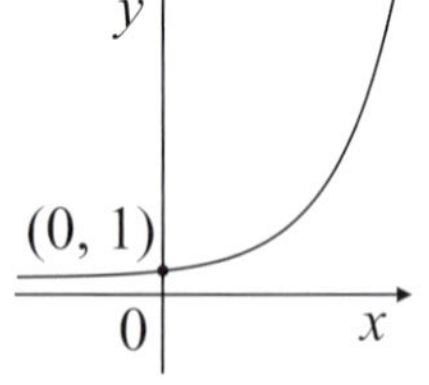

P Q8 The graph of $f(x) = x^2 - 3x + 3$ is transformed to give the graph of $g(x)$. Give the equation of $g(x)$ in its simplest form if the transformation that takes the graph of $f(x)$ to the graph of $g(x)$ is:

a) vertical stretch, scale factor 2 b) translation by $\begin{pmatrix} -3 \\ 0 \end{pmatrix}$

c) horizontal stretch, scale factor 0.25

P Q9 a) Sketch the graph of $f(x) = x^2 - 6x - 7$ showing clearly the coordinates of any maximum or minimum points and where the curve meets the coordinate axes.

b) Write down the equation of the graph obtained by stretching the graph of $f(x)$ vertically with a scale factor of -2.

c) Sketch the graph with equation you found in part b) showing clearly the coordinates of any maximum or minimum points and where the curve meets the coordinate axes.

Problem Solving
Complete the square — see pages 46-48 and 58-59 for a recap.

E Q10 a) Given that $f(x) = 2 + \frac{1}{x+3}$, state the equations of the asymptotes of the graph of $y = f(x)$. *[1 mark]*

b) Hence find the equations of the asymptotes of these transformed graphs:

(i) $y = f(3x)$ *[2 marks]*

(ii) $y = -\frac{5}{3}f(x)$ *[2 marks]*

E **P** Q11 The graph of $y = f(2k - x)$ is obtained by reflecting the graph of $y = f(x)$ in the line $x = k$.

The diagram shows the graph of $y = f(x)$ with the coordinates of the points A, B, C and D labelled. The graph of $y = f(x)$ is reflected in the line $x = a$ to obtain the graph of $y = f(5 - x)$.

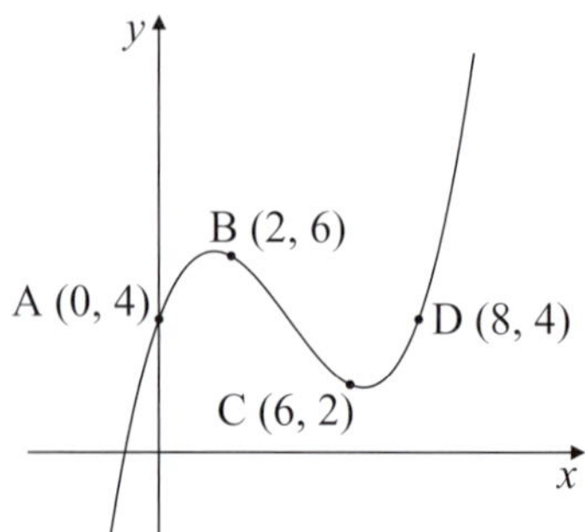

a) Write down the value of a. *[1 mark]*

b) Sketch the graph of $y = f(5 - x)$, clearly indicating the positions and coordinates of the points A, B, C and D after the reflection. *[3 marks]*

6.11 The Equation of a Circle

Circles with centre (0, 0)

The diagram to the right shows a circle centred on the origin (0, 0) and with radius r.

You can describe a circle centred on the origin, with radius r, using the equation: $x^2 + y^2 = r^2$

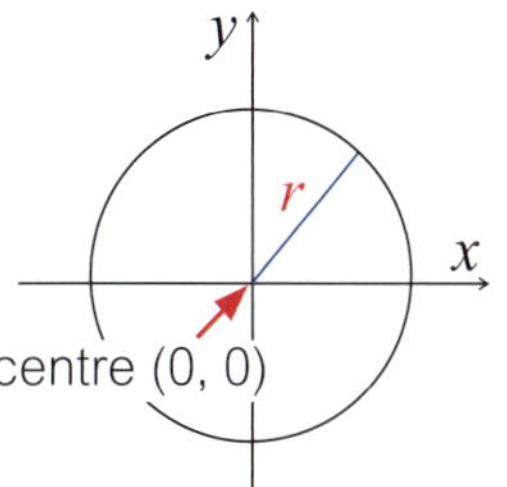

Even though you're dealing with circles, you get the equation above using **Pythagoras' theorem**. Here's how:

- The **centre** of the circle is at the origin, labelled **C**.
- A is any point on the circle, and has the coordinates (x, y).
- B lies on the x-axis and has the same x-coordinate as A.
- So the length of line **CB** $= x$, and **AB** $= y$.

Therefore, using Pythagoras' theorem to find the radius r, we get:

$$CB^2 + AB^2 = r^2$$

Which is... $x^2 + y^2 = r^2$

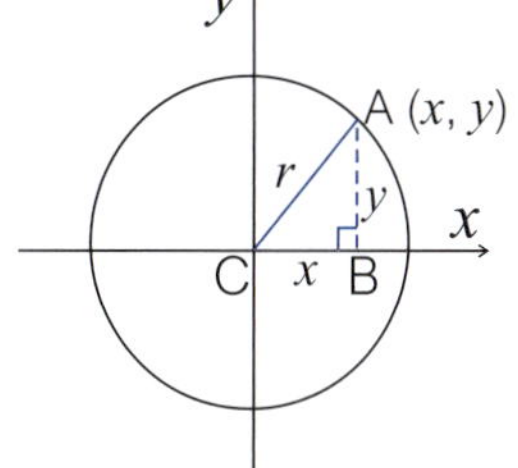

If you're given the equation of a circle in the form $x^2 + y^2 = r^2$, you can work out the radius of the circle by taking the square root of the r^2 part.

Tip A common mistake is to forget to take the square root to find the radius — e.g. $x^2 + y^2 = 5$ has a radius of $\sqrt{5}$, not 5.

Example 1

A circle has the equation $x^2 + y^2 = 4$. Find the radius of the circle.

$r^2 = 4$ ← Compare the equation $x^2 + y^2 = 4$ to $x^2 + y^2 = r^2$.

$\Rightarrow r = 2$ ← Take the positive square root of r^2 to find r. Ignore the negative square root as the radius will be positive.

Circles with centre (a, b)

Unfortunately, circles aren't always centred at the origin. This means we need a general equation for circles that have a centre somewhere else — the point (a, b).

The general equation for circles with **radius r** and **centre (a, b)** is: $(x - a)^2 + (y - b)^2 = r^2$

Notice that if the circle had a centre at (0, 0), then you'd get $a = 0$ and $b = 0$, so you'd just get $x^2 + y^2 = r^2$ (the equation for a circle centred at the origin).

The example below shows how you get the equation of a circle when the coordinates of the centre and the value of the radius are given.

Example 2

Find the equation of the circle with centre (6, 4) and radius 3.

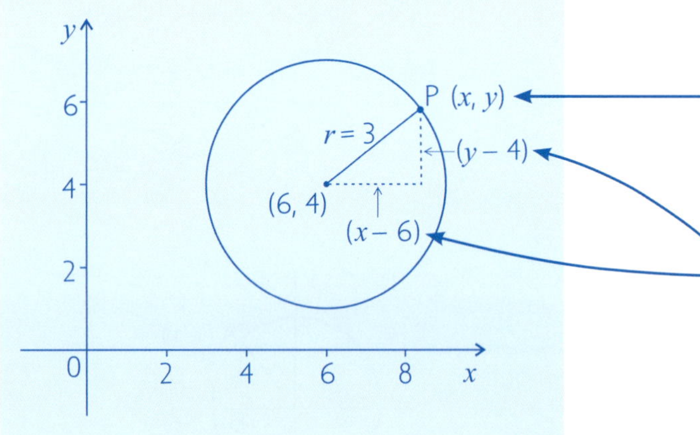

If you draw a point P (x, y) on the circumference of the circle and join it to the centre (6, 4), you can create a right-angled triangle.

The sides of this right-angled triangle are made up of the radius r (the hypotenuse), and sides of length $(x - 6)$ and $(y - 4)$.

$$(x - 6)^2 + (y - 4)^2 = 3^2$$

Now use Pythagoras' theorem.

or: $$(x - 6)^2 + (y - 4)^2 = 9$$

Example 3

What is the centre and radius of the circle with equation $(x - 2)^2 + (y + 3)^2 = 16$?

$$(x - a)^2 + (y - b)^2 = r^2$$

So $a = 2$, $b = -3$ and $r = \sqrt{16} = 4$.

Compare $(x - 2)^2 + (y + 3)^2 = 16$ with the general form.

The centre (a, b) is $(2, -3)$ and the radius (r) is 4.

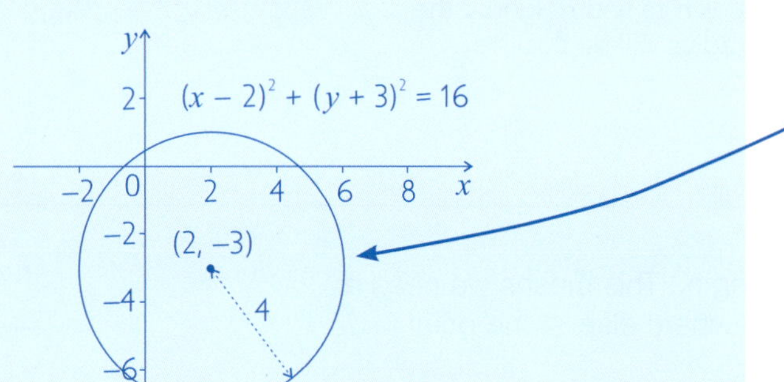

On a set of axes, the circle would look like this.

Tip When you're doing harder circle questions, it'll often help to draw a diagram so you can see what's going on.

If you're given the centre and radius of a circle and you're asked to find the equation of the circle, just put the values of a, b and r into the equation $(x - a)^2 + (y - b)^2 = r^2$.

Example 4

Write down the equation of the circle with centre (–4, 2) and radius 6.

The centre of the circle is (–4, 2), so $a = -4$ and $b = 2$.

Compare to the general equation for a circle $(x - a)^2 + (y - b)^2 = r^2$.

The radius is 6, so $r = 6$.

So the equation of the circle is $(x + 4)^2 + (y - 2)^2 = 36$

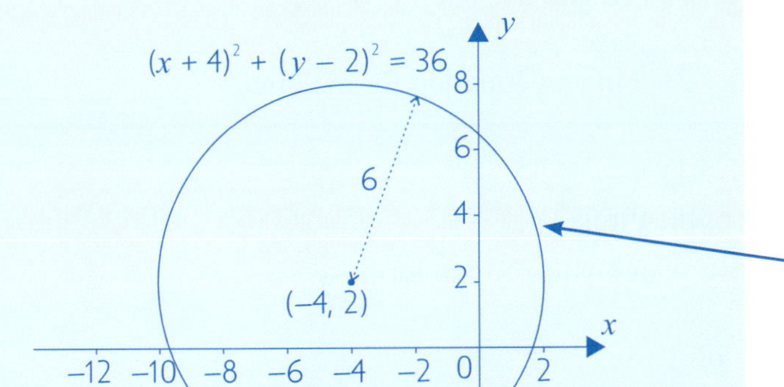

On a set of axes, the circle would look like this.

Tip 'Write down...', means you don't need to do much working.

Exercise 6.11

Q1 Find an equation for a circle with centre (0, 0) and radius:

a) 5 b) 7 c) $\sqrt{23}$ d) $3\sqrt{2}$

Q2 Find the equation for each of the following circles:

a) centre (2, 5), radius 3 b) centre (–3, 2), radius 5 c) centre (–2, –3), radius 7

d) centre (3, 0), radius 4 e) centre (–1, 3), radius 7 f) centre (5, 4), radius $\sqrt{11}$

g) centre (–7, 5), radius $\sqrt{27}$ h) centre (–10, 7), radius 11 i) centre (8, 0), radius $\sqrt{17}$

Q3 Write down the equation of each of the following circles:

a)

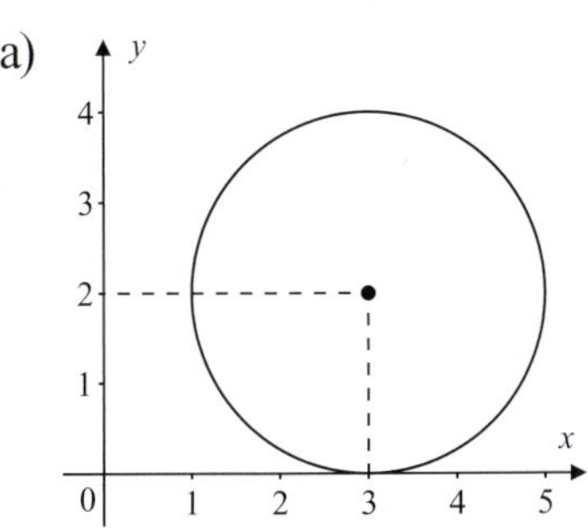

b)

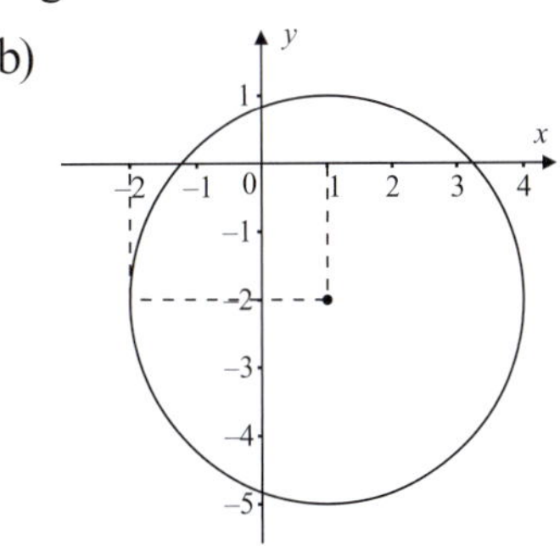

Q4 Find the centre and radius of the circles with the following equations:

a) $(x-1)^2+(y-5)^2=4$
b) $(x-3)^2+(y-5)^2=64$
c) $(x-3)^2+(y+2)^2=25$
d) $(x-6)^2+(y-4)^2=20$
e) $(x+8)^2+(y+1)^2=27$
f) $x^2+(y-12)^2=147$

Q5 A circle has centre (5, 3) and radius 8. Find an equation for the circle.

Q6 A circle has centre (3, 1) and a radius of $\sqrt{31}$. Find an equation for the circle.

Q7 Find the centre and radius of the circle with equation $x^2+(y+3)^2=18$.

Q8 A circle has radius $\sqrt{5}$ and centre (–3, –2). Find an equation for the circle.

Q9 The equation of the circle C is $(x+9)^2+(y-3)^2=45$.

a) Find the coordinates of the centre of the circle.
b) Find the radius of the circle and give your answer in the form $p\sqrt{5}$.

P Q10 A circle has centre (6, 3) and a radius of $4\sqrt{5}$.
Identify which coordinates below give points that lie on this circle.

a) (–2, 7)
b) (10, –3)
c) (14, –1)
d) (2, 5)

P Q11 Circle C has its centre at (3, 5) and passes through the point (10, 4).
Find the exact radius of the circle and hence give the equation of C.

P Q12 A circle has centre (–2, 9) and goes through the point (–11, 7).
Find an equation for the circle.

P Q13 A circle has its centre at point A and passes through the origin.
Find the equation of the circle if:

a) A = (1, 1)
b) A = (–7, 13)
c) A = (8, –6)
d) A = (14, 22)

P Q14 Points A (–3, –10) and B (7, –2) lie on a circle C. The line AB is a diameter of C.

a) Find: (i) the length of the line AB, (ii) the midpoint of the line AB.
b) Hence, or otherwise, write down the equation of circle C.

P Q15 The equation of the circle C is $(x-2)^2+(y+3)^2=17$.

a) Determine whether these points are inside, outside, or on the circumference of the circle:
(i) (–1, –6) (ii) (2, 1) (iii) (–2, –2)

b) For each of the following circles, determine whether they intersect circle C at one point, at two points, or do not intersect at all:
(i) $(x-4)^2+(y-8)^2=17$
(ii) $(x-7)^2+(y+1)^2=17$
(iii) $(x-4)^2+(y+11)^2=17$

Problem Solving

Compare the distance between the centres of the circles to the sum of their radii.

6.12 Rearranging Circle Equations

Sometimes you'll be given an equation for a circle that doesn't look much like $(x-a)^2 + (y-b)^2 = r^2$ — e.g. $x^2 + y^2 + 8x + 6y + 3 = 0$.

The general form of this type of equation is: $\mathbf{x^2 + y^2 + 2fx + 2gy + c = 0}$

In this form, you can't immediately tell what the **radius** is or where the **centre** is.
All you'll need to do is a bit of **rearranging** to get the equation into the form $(x-a)^2 + (y-b)^2 = r^2$.
To do this, you'll normally have to **complete the square**
— this is shown in the examples below.

Example 1

The equation of a circle is $x^2 + y^2 - 6x + 4y + 4 = 0$.
Find the centre of the circle and the radius.

Get the equation $x^2 + y^2 - 6x + 4y + 4 = 0$ into the form $(x-a)^2 + (y-b)^2 = r^2$.

$x^2 - 6x + y^2 + 4y + 4 = 0$ ← To do this, complete the square. First rearrange the equation to group the x's and the y's together.

$(x-3)^2 - 9 + (y+2)^2 - 4 + 4 = 0$ ← Complete the square for the x- and the y-terms.

$(x-3)^2 + (y+2)^2 = 9$ ← Then rearrange to get it into the form $(x-a)^2 + (y-b)^2 = r^2$.

Centre: $(3, -2)$, radius $= \sqrt{9} = 3$ ← Use this equation to find the centre and radius.

Example 2 P

a) Show that the circle with equation $x^2 + y^2 + 2fx + 2gy + c = 0$,
where f, g and c are constants, has its centre at $(-f, -g)$ and a radius of $\sqrt{f^2 + g^2 - c}$.

$x^2 + y^2 + 2fx + 2gy + c = 0$
$\Rightarrow x^2 + 2fx + y^2 + 2gy + c = 0$
$\Rightarrow (x+f)^2 - f^2 + (y+g)^2 - g^2 + c = 0$
$\Rightarrow (x+f)^2 + (y+g)^2 = f^2 + g^2 - c$

Complete the square for the x-terms and y-terms to rearrange $x^2 + y^2 + 2fx + 2gy + c = 0$ into the form $(x-a)^2 + (y-b)^2 = r^2$.

So $a = -f$, $b = -g$ and $r^2 = f^2 + g^2 - c$,
i.e. the circle has its centre at $(-f, -g)$
and its radius is $\sqrt{f^2 + g^2 - c}$.

Now compare this to the general equation of a circle (given above) to find a, b and r.

b) Use this result to find the centre and radius of the circle given by the equation $x^2 + y^2 - 5x - 5y + 10 = 0$.

$$x^2 + y^2 + 2\left(-\frac{5}{2}x\right) + 2\left(-\frac{5}{2}y\right) + 10 = 0$$

Write $x^2 + y^2 - 5x - 5y + 10 = 0$ in the form $x^2 + y^2 + 2fx + 2gy + c = 0$.

So $f = g = -\frac{5}{2}$ and $c = 10$.

Centre of the circle $= (-f, -g) = \left(\frac{5}{2}, \frac{5}{2}\right)$

Use the results from part a) to work out the centre and radius.

Radius $= \sqrt{f^2 + g^2 - c}$

$$= \sqrt{\left(-\frac{5}{2}\right)^2 + \left(-\frac{5}{2}\right)^2 - 10}$$

$$= \sqrt{\frac{25}{4} + \frac{25}{4} - 10} = \sqrt{\frac{50}{4} - \frac{40}{4}}$$

$$= \sqrt{\frac{10}{4}} = \sqrt{\frac{5}{2}} \left(\text{or } \frac{\sqrt{10}}{2}\right)$$

Tip

You could use your calculator to do this working for you, but be careful if the question asks for an 'exact' answer — sometimes your calculator will only give you a decimal.

Exercise 6.12

Q1 A circle has the equation $x^2 + y^2 + 2x - 4y - 3 = 0$.

a) Find the centre of the circle.

b) Find the radius of the circle. Give your answer in the form $k\sqrt{2}$.

Q2 A circle has the equation $x^2 + y^2 - 3x + 1 = 0$.

a) Find the coordinates of the centre of the circle.

b) Find the radius of the circle. Simplify your answer as much as possible.

Q3 For each of the following circles find the radius and the coordinates of the centre.

a) $x^2 + y^2 + 2x - 6y - 6 = 0$

b) $x^2 + y^2 - 2y - 4 = 0$

c) $x^2 + y^2 - 6x - 4y = 12$

d) $x^2 + y^2 - 10x + 6y + 13 = 0$

e) $x^2 + y^2 + 14x - 8y - 1 = 0$

f) $x^2 + y^2 - 4x + y = 3.75$

g) $x^2 + y^2 + 2x + 3y - 1.25 = 0$

h) $(x - 2)^2 + y^2 + 2x + 4y - 12 = 0$

Q4 A circle has centre $(0, -3)$ and radius $\sqrt{10}$. Find the equation of the circle in the form $x^2 + y^2 + 2fx + 2gy + c = 0$ and give the values of f, g and c.

Q5 A circle has centre $(-4, 2)$ and passes through the origin. Find the equation of the circle in the form $x^2 + y^2 + 2fx + 2gy + c = 0$ and give the values of f, g and c.

Q6 Find the equation for each of the circles below in the form $x^2 + y^2 + 2fx + 2gy + c = 0$ and give the values of f, g and c.

a)

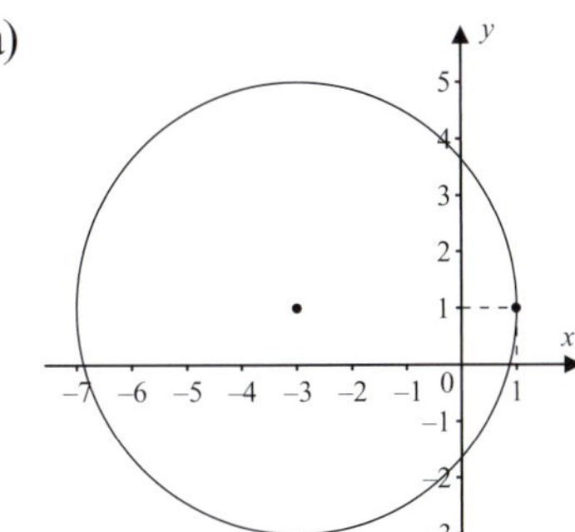

b)

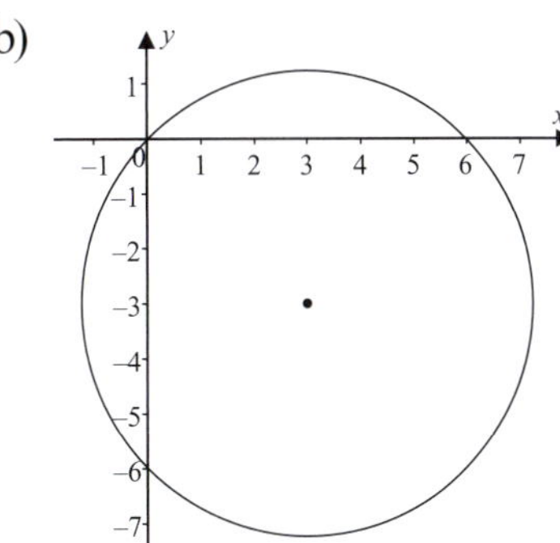

Q7 A circle has the equation $2x^2 + 2y^2 + 16x - 8y = 2$.
Find the coordinates of the centre and the exact radius of the circle.

Q8 Match the equations to the correct graphs.

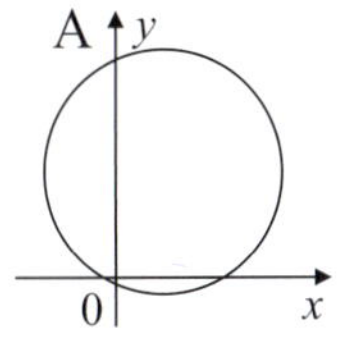

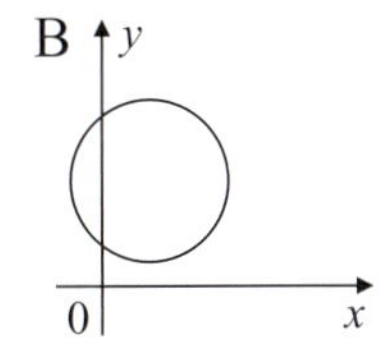

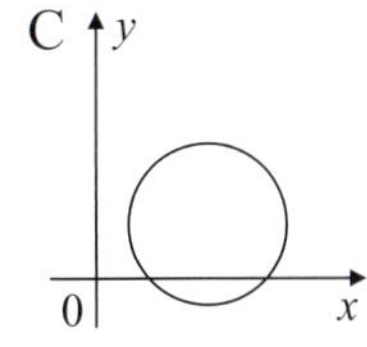

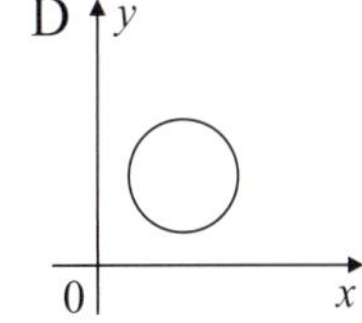

a) $x^2 - 6x + y^2 - 10y + 18 = 0$

b) $x^2 - 6x + y^2 - 10y - 2 = 0$

c) $x^2 - 6x + y^2 - 10y + 30 - 0$

d) $x^2 - 10x + y^2 - 6y + 18 = 0$

P Q9 A circle has the equation $x^2 + y^2 + 6ax - 7y - \frac{3}{4} = 0$, where a is a constant.

a) Find the centre and radius of the circle in terms of a.

b) Given that the point $\left(3, -\frac{1}{2}\right)$ lies on the circle, find the value of a.

E Q10 a) Find the radius and the coordinates of the centre of the circle C, which has equation $x^2 - 18x + y^2 - 6y + 78 = 0$ *[2 marks]*

b) Explain why the circle intersects the x-axis but not the y-axis. *[1 mark]*

c) Hence find the coordinates of the points at which C intersects the x-axis. *[2 marks]*

Challenge

E P Q11 A circle has equation $(x + 4)^2 + (y - 1)^2 = 20$. The line l_1 has equation $y = 2x + 9$.

a) Show that l_1 passes through the centre of the circle. *[1 mark]*

Line l_2 has equation $y = kx - 5$, where k is a constant.

b) Find the coordinates of the point of intersection of l_1 and l_2 in terms of k. *[2 marks]*

D is the distance from the centre of the circle to the point of intersection of l_1 and l_2.

c) Show that $D^2 = \dfrac{20(2k+3)^2}{(k-2)^2}$ *[3 marks]*

d) Hence find the range of values for k for which the lines l_1 and l_2 intersect in the interior of the circle. *[3 marks]*

6.13 Using Circle Properties

Here's a reminder of some of the most useful circle properties. Although it might not be obvious when you first look at a question, these rules could help you answer some tricky-sounding circle questions.

The **triangle** formed from the ends of a **diameter** has a **right angle**.

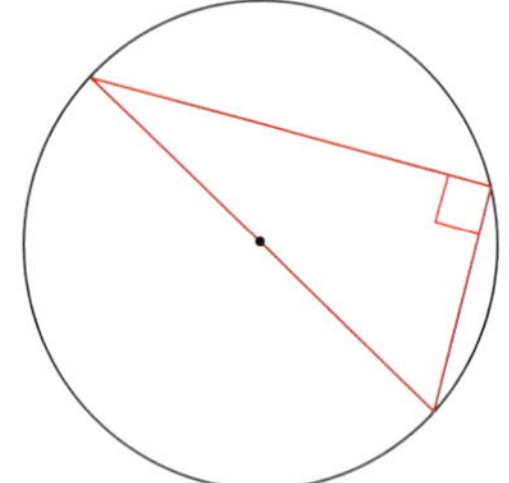

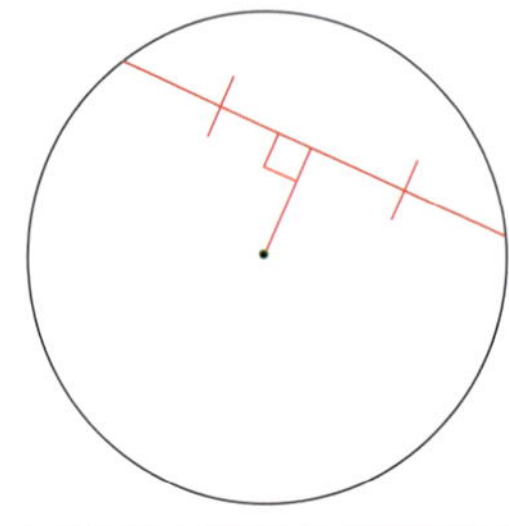

The **perpendicular from** the **centre** to a **chord** **bisects** the **chord**.

A **tangent** to the circle **meets** a **radius** at a **right angle**.

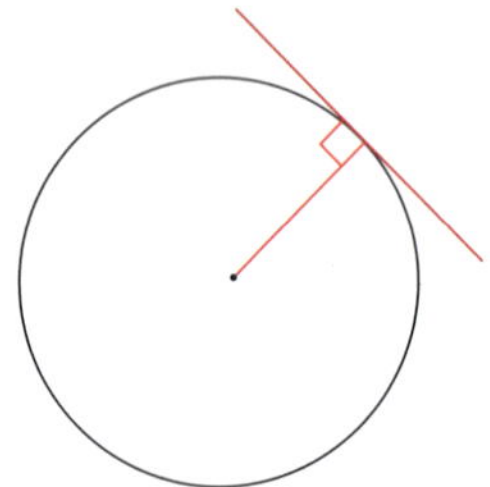

Make sure you're happy with what these terms mean — a chord is a line joining two points which lie on the circumference of a circle, and 'bisecting' just means dividing into two equal parts.

Example 1

The circle shown is centred at C. Points A and B lie on the circle. Point B has coordinates (6, 3). The midpoint, M, of the line AB has coordinates (4, 4). Line l passes through both C and M.

Find an equation for the line l.

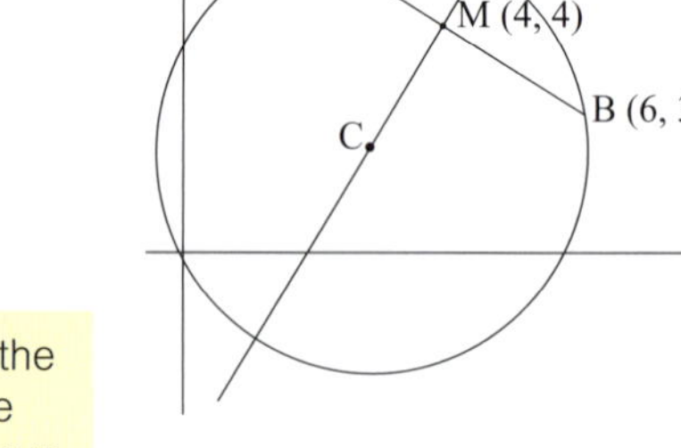

AB is a chord. l goes through the centre of the circle and bisects the chord, so the line l is perpendicular to the chord.

This is from the middle circle property above.

Gradient of AB $= \frac{3-4}{6-4} = -\frac{1}{2}$

You know two points on AB, so you can find its gradient.

Gradient of $l = \frac{-1}{-\frac{1}{2}} = 2$

The gradients of perpendicular lines multiply to give –1 (see page 116), so the gradient of l will be –1 divided by the gradient of the chord.

Equation of l: $y - y_1 = m(x - x_1)$

$\Rightarrow y - 4 = 2(x - 4)$

$\Rightarrow y - 4 = 2x - 8$

$\Rightarrow y = 2x - 4$

Substitute the gradient, 2, and the point on l that you know, (4, 4), into one of the equations for a straight line to work out the equation.

Tip In the exam, after a question like this, they might then give you a bit more info and ask you to work out the equation for the circle.

Example 2

Point A (6, 4) lies on a circle with the equation $x^2 + y^2 - 4x - 2y - 20 = 0$.

a) Find the centre and radius of the circle.

$x^2 - 4x + y^2 - 2y - 20 = 0$ ← First, rearrange so that the x's and y's are together.

$(x - 2)^2 - 4 + (y - 1)^2 - 1 - 20 = 0$
$\Rightarrow (x - 2)^2 + (y - 1)^2 = 25$ ← Complete the square and rearrange to get it into the form $(x - a)^2 + (y - b)^2 = r^2$.

Centre: (2, 1), radius = 5 ← Read off the centre and radius.

b) Find the equation of the tangent to the circle at A.

Tip Drawing a sketch makes it much easier to see where the circle properties can be used.

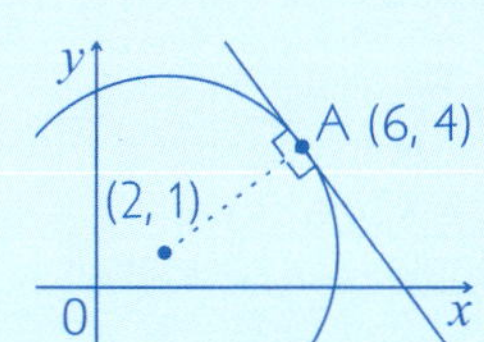

The tangent is at right angles to the radius at (6, 4).

Gradient of radius at (6, 4): $\frac{4-1}{6-2} = \frac{3}{4}$ ← Find the gradient of the line from (2, 1) to (6, 4) — this is a radius of the circle.

So gradient of tangent: $\frac{-1}{\frac{3}{4}} = -\frac{4}{3}$ ← The tangent and the radius are perpendicular, so do –1 divided by the gradient of the radius.

$y - 4 = -\frac{4}{3}(x - 6) \Rightarrow 3y - 12 = -4x + 24$
$\Rightarrow 4x + 3y - 36 = 0$ ← Using $y - y_1 = m(x - x_1)$.

Example 3 

The points A (–2, 4), B (n, –2) and C (5, 5) all lie on the circle shown on the right. AB is a diameter of the circle. Show that $n = 6$.

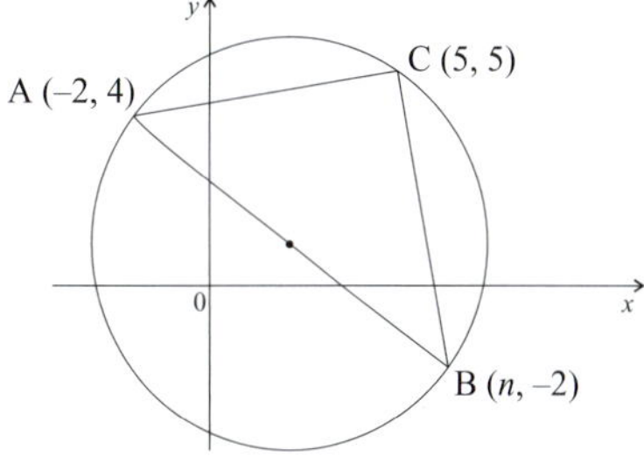

Line AB is a diameter, so angle ACB is an angle in a semicircle and must be a right angle.
So lines AC and BC are perpendicular to each other.
The gradients of two perpendicular lines multiply to give –1.

$m_1 = \frac{5-4}{5-(-2)} = \frac{1}{7}$ ← First, find the gradient of AC.

$m_2 = \frac{-2-5}{n-5} = \frac{-7}{n-5}$ ← Then find the gradient of BC.

$\frac{1}{7}\left(\frac{-7}{n-5}\right) = -1 \Rightarrow \frac{-1}{n-5} = -1$ ← Use the gradient rule that $m_1 \times m_2 = -1$.

$\Rightarrow 1 = n - 5 \Rightarrow n = 6$ as required

A circle that passes through all three vertices of a triangle is called the **circumcircle** of the triangle. Working out the equation of a circumcircle involves using the properties of circles, perpendicular lines and lots of algebra.

Example 4 P

Find the equation of the circumcircle of the triangle ABC where:

A = (3, 9) B = (6, 0) C = (10, 8)

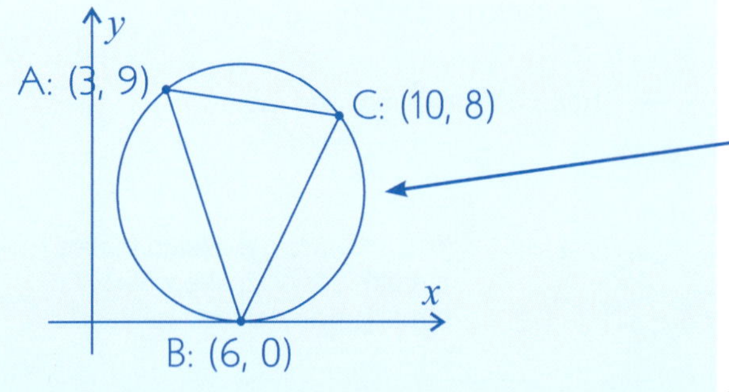

To find the equation of the circle, you need to work out the centre and the radius. The best way to begin is to sketch the triangle and its circumcircle.

AB, BC and AC are chords, so their perpendicular bisectors will all pass through the centre of the circle.

From the circle properties, you know that a line from the centre of the circle that meets one of these chords at right angles also bisects it.

AB: Gradient $= \frac{0-9}{6-3} = \frac{-9}{3} = -3$

Midpoint $= \left(\frac{3+6}{2}, \frac{9+0}{2}\right) = \left(\frac{9}{2}, \frac{9}{2}\right)$

You only need to find where two of the lines meet to find the centre of the circle, so pick any two chords — here we've used AB and BC.

So the perpendicular bisector of AB has a gradient of $\frac{-1}{-3} = \frac{1}{3}$ and passes through the point $\left(\frac{9}{2}, \frac{9}{2}\right)$.

$$y - y_1 = m(x - x_1) \Rightarrow y - \frac{9}{2} = \frac{1}{3}\left(x - \frac{9}{2}\right)$$
$$\Rightarrow y = \frac{1}{3}x - \frac{3}{2} + \frac{9}{2}$$
$$\Rightarrow y = \frac{1}{3}x + 3$$

Now you know the gradient and midpoint of AB, you can use these to find the equation of the perpendicular bisector of AB.

BC: Gradient $= \frac{8-0}{10-6} = \frac{8}{4} = 2$

Now do the same for BC.

Midpoint $= \left(\frac{6+10}{2}, \frac{0+8}{2}\right) = (8, 4)$

Tip Make sure you show clearly in your working exactly what you're working out at each stage — especially in a question like this, where you have to work out multiple gradients, midpoints and straight-line equations.

So the perpendicular bisector of BC has a gradient of $\frac{-1}{2} = -\frac{1}{2}$ and passes through the point (8, 4).

$$y - y_1 = m(x - x_1) \Rightarrow y - 4 = -\frac{1}{2}(x - 8)$$
$$\Rightarrow y = -\frac{1}{2}x + 4 + 4$$
$$\Rightarrow y = -\frac{1}{2}x + 8$$

As before, use one of the equations for a straight line to find the equation of the perpendicular bisector of BC.

continued on the next page...

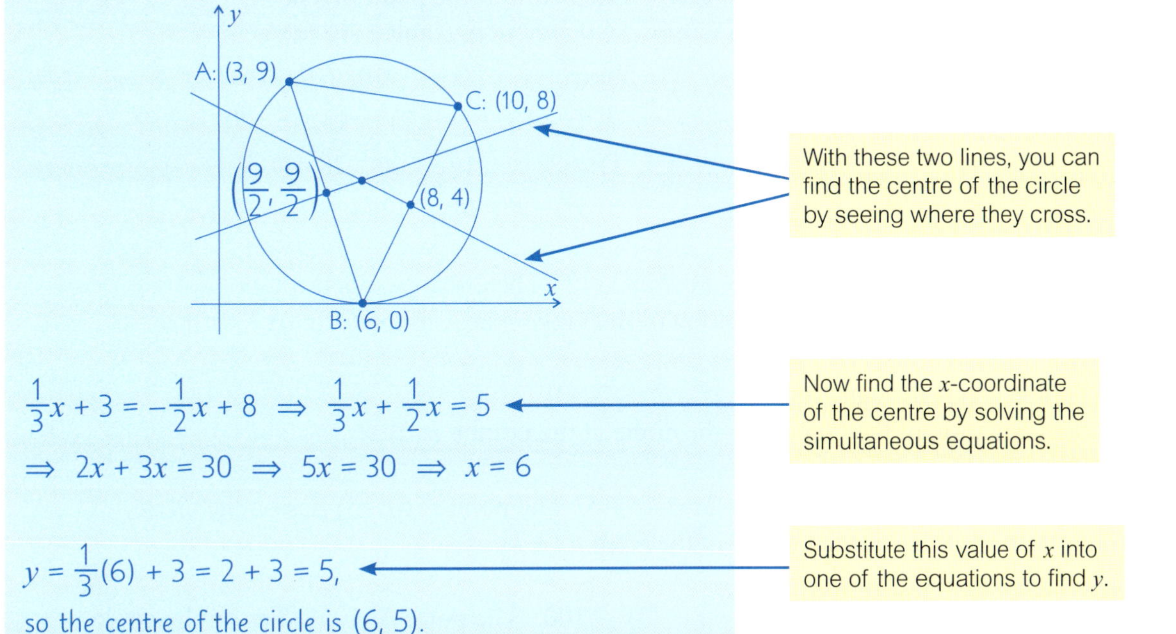

$\frac{1}{3}x + 3 = -\frac{1}{2}x + 8 \Rightarrow \frac{1}{3}x + \frac{1}{2}x = 5$

$\Rightarrow 2x + 3x = 30 \Rightarrow 5x = 30 \Rightarrow x = 6$

Now find the x-coordinate of the centre by solving the simultaneous equations.

$y = \frac{1}{3}(6) + 3 = 2 + 3 = 5$,

so the centre of the circle is (6, 5).

Substitute this value of x into one of the equations to find y.

The distance from the centre (6, 5) to point B (6, 0) is 5, so the radius is 5.

You could use Pythagoras' theorem to find the distance from the centre to A or C, but this is much easier.

So the equation of the circle is: $(x - 6)^2 + (y - 5)^2 = 25$

Exercise 6.13

Q1 The circle shown below has the equation $(x - 3)^2 + (y - 1)^2 = 10$.
The line shown is a tangent to the circle and touches it at point A (4, 4).

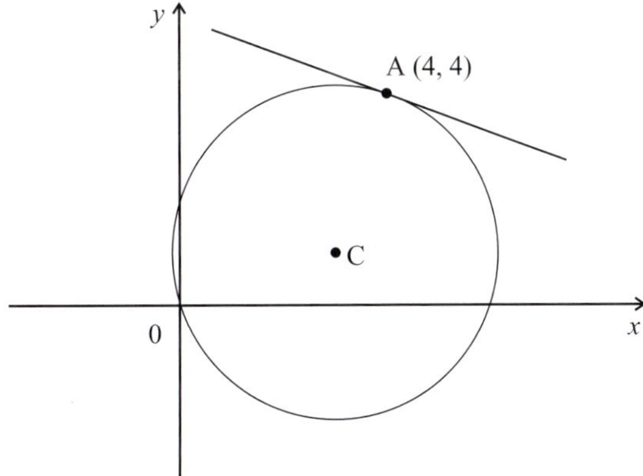

a) Find the centre of the circle, C.

b) Work out the gradient of the radius at (4, 4).

c) Find the equation of the tangent at A in the form $ax + by = c$.

Q2 Find the equation of the tangent to each circle below at the point given. Give your answers in the form $ax + by + c = 0$, where a, b and c are integers.

a) $(x-3)^2 + (y+4)^2 = 37$, $(2, -10)$
b) $x^2 + y^2 + 8x - 9 = 0$, $(-7, 4)$
c) $x^2 + y^2 - 6x + 10y = 7$, $(8, -1)$
d) $(x-8)^2 + (y+2)^2 = 13$, $(6, -5)$
e) $(x-4)^2 + (y+2)^2 = 26$, $(9, -3)$
f) $x^2 + y^2 + 16x - 6y + 28 = 0$, $(-11, 9)$
g) $(x+3)^2 + (y+1)^2 = 13$, $(-5, -4)$
h) $x^2 + y^2 - 14x - 12y = 61$, $(-4, 1)$

Q3 A circle has the equation $(x+1)^2 + (y-2)^2 = 13$. The circle passes through the point A $(-3, -1)$. Find the equation of the tangent at A in the form $ax + by + c = 0$.

Q4 The circle C has the equation $x^2 + y^2 + 2x - 7 = 0$. Find an equation of the tangent to the circle at the point $(-3, 2)$.

Q5 A circle has the equation $x^2 + y^2 + 2x + 4y = 5$. The point A $(0, -5)$ lies on the circle. Find the tangent to the circle at A in the form $ax + by = c$.

Q6 The circle C has equation $(x-2)^2 + (y-1)^2 = 100$. The point A $(10, 7)$ lies on the circle. Find an equation of the tangent at A.

P Q7 A circle with centre $(-2, 4)$ passes through the point A $(n, 1)$. Given that the tangent to the circle at A has a gradient of $\frac{5}{3}$, find the value of n.

P Q8 The circle shown has centre C. Points A and B lie on the circle. Point A has coordinates $(-3, 7)$. The midpoint of the line AB, M, has coordinates $(-1, 1)$. Line l passes through both C and M.

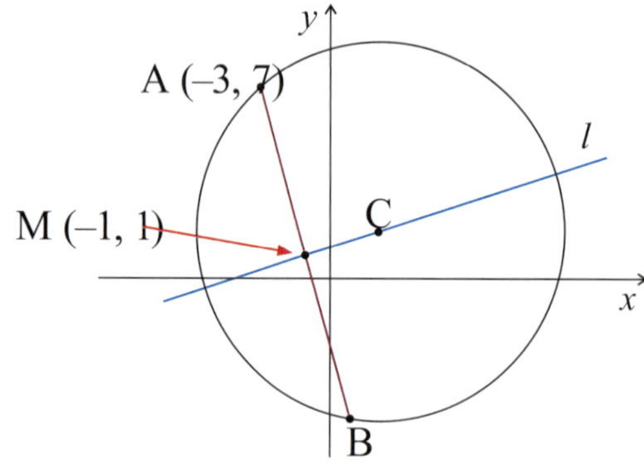

a) Use the information above to find an equation for the line l.

b) The coordinates of C are $(2, 2)$. Find an equation for the circle.

E P Q9 Two points, A and B, are the points of intersection between a circle with centre C $(2, 4)$ and radius 5, and the line $x + 2y = 15$. M is the midpoint of the chord AB.

a) Show that the length CM is $\sqrt{5}$. *[7 marks]*

b) Hence, find the area of the triangle ABC. *[3 marks]*

P Q10 The points A (–2, 12), B (4, 14) and C (8, 2) all lie on the circle shown below.

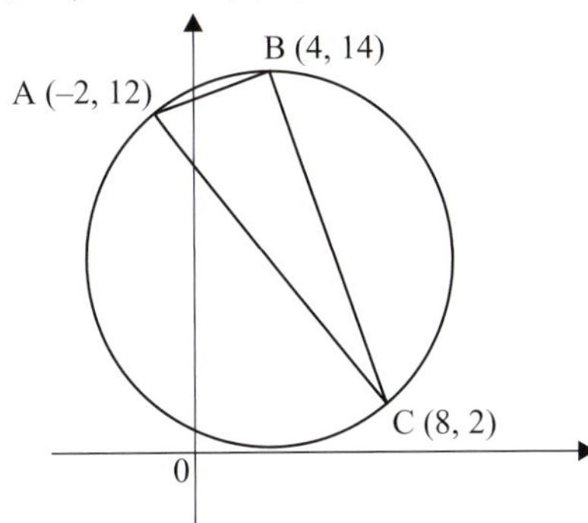

a) Prove that the line AC is a diameter of the circle.

b) Hence find the equation of the circle.

P Q11 Points P and Q lie on a circle as shown on the diagram. P has coordinates (–8, 6) and Q has coordinates (–3, 7). M is the midpoint of PQ and C is the centre of the circle.

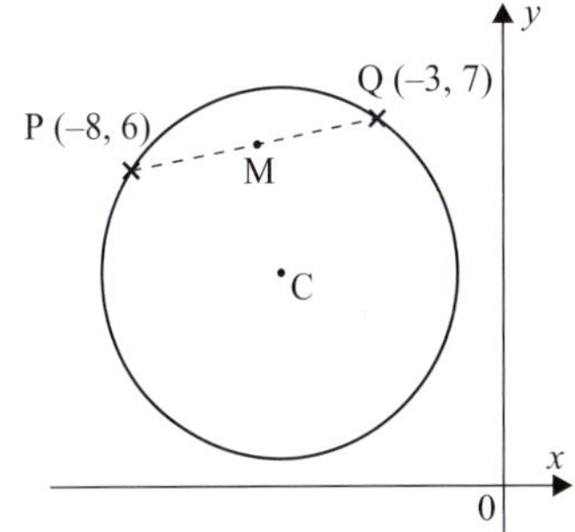

Find the equation, in the form $ax + by + c = 0$, of the line passing through M and C.

E P Q12 A triangle XYZ has vertices with coordinates X (7, 6), Y (–1, –10) and Z (13, –12).

a) Find the equation of the perpendicular bisector of XY. *[2 marks]*

b) Hence, or otherwise, find the equation of the circumcircle of the triangle XYZ. *[6 marks]*

P Q13 Find the equation of the circumcircle of the triangle XYZ where:

a) X = (8, 2), Y = (–4, –4), Z = (2, 8) b) X = (2, 6), Y = (5, 9), Z = (–5, 9)

c) X = (14, 14), Y = (22, 6), Z = (22, 10) d) X = (17, –14), Y = (–7, 10), Z = (–11, –2)

Challenge

P Q14 A circle has centre (3, –1) and goes through the point (4, 3).

a) Find the equation of the circle.

Line l is the tangent to the circle at the point (4, 3).

b) Show that the area of the triangle formed by the line l and the positive x- and y-axes is 32 units^2.

P Q15 A triangle ABC has vertices with coordinates A (2, –2), B (11, 1) and C (10, –6).

a) Find the equation of the circumcircle of the triangle ABC.

A fourth point D (3, –5) also lies on the circumcircle of ABC.

b) Show that BD is a diameter of the circumcircle.

6 Review Exercise

Q1 Find the equations of the straight lines that pass through the following pairs of points. Write each of them in the forms: (i) $y - y_1 = m(x - x_1)$, (ii) $y = mx + c$, (iii) $ax + by + c = 0$, where a, b and c are integers.

a) $(2, -1), (-4, -19)$ b) $\left(0, -\frac{1}{3}\right), \left(5, \frac{2}{3}\right)$ c) $(8, 7), (-7, -2)$

d) $(5, 5), \left(2, \frac{5}{2}\right)$ e) $(1.3, 2), (1.8, 0)$ f) $(4.6, -2.3), (-5.4, -0.3)$

E Q2 Points A and B have coordinates $(-2, 4)$ and $(4, -10)$ respectively.

a) Find the exact length AB. *[2 marks]*

b) Find the gradient of the line segment AB. *[2 marks]*

c) Find the equation of the line that passes through points A and B, giving your answer in the form $ax + by + c = 0$, where a, b and c are integers to be found. *[3 marks]*

E P Q3 A triangle has vertices A, B and C. The coordinates of A and B are $(2, -1)$ and $(10, -1)$ respectively and C is a point on the line, l, with equation $y - 2x + 5 = 0$.

a) Show that A also lies on l. *[1 mark]*

b) Given that the x-coordinate of C is k, find the y-coordinate of C in terms of k. *[1 mark]*

The area of the triangle is 32 units^2.

c) Find the equation of the line through B and C in the form $y = mx + c$. *[3 marks]*

E Q4 Determine whether the following lines are parallel to the line with equation $4x - 6y = 7$. You must give a suitable justification in each case.

a) $8x + 12y = 15$ *[2 marks]*

b) $3y - 2x = 7$ *[2 marks]*

c) $y = \frac{4x + 3}{6}$ *[2 marks]*

E P Q5 The points A (1, 7), B (20, 7) and C (p, q) are the vertices of a triangle ABC, as shown below. The point D (8, 2) is the midpoint of AC.

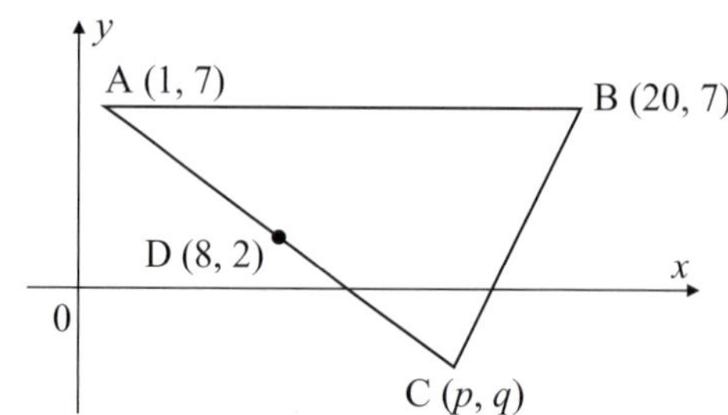

a) Find the value of p and q. *[2 marks]*

The line l, which passes through D and is perpendicular to AC, intersects AB at E.

b) Find an equation for l in the form $ax + by + c = 0$, where a, b and c are integers. *[4 marks]*

c) Find the exact x-coordinate of E. *[2 marks]*

Q6 a) The line l_1 has equation $y = \frac{3}{2}x - \frac{2}{3}$. Find the equation of the line parallel to l_1, passing through the point with coordinates (4, 2).

b) The line l_2 passes through the point (6, 1) and is perpendicular to $2x - y - 7 = 0$. Find the equation of the line l_2.

Q7 The coordinates of points R and S are (1, 9) and (10, 3) respectively. Find the equation of the line perpendicular to RS, passing through the point (1, 9).

E Q8 Points A and B have coordinates (5, 9) and (11, 13) respectively.

a) Find the equation of the perpendicular bisector of the line segment AB. *[3 marks]*

Point P lies on the line that goes through point A and point B, but not on the line segment AB. P is twice as far from point A as it is from point B.

b) Find the equation of the line perpendicular to the line through A and B that passes through point P. *[2 marks]*

Q9 Given that y is directly proportional to x, and that $x = 4.5$ when $y = 3$, find:

a) y when $x = 21$ b) y when $x = -3$ c) x when $y = 58$

E P M Q10 A farmer plants seeds in rows. The total number of seeds planted, N, is proportional to the number of rows of seeds planted, r.

a) Given that there are 1536 seeds in total when 48 rows have been planted, find an expression for N in terms of r. *[2 marks]*

b) Give an interpretation of the constant of proportionality in this context. *[1 mark]*

c) Find the number of rows required to plant 2720 seeds. *[1 mark]*

Q11 Given that s is inversely proportional to t^3, and that $s = 18$ when $t = 6$, find:

a) s when $t = 3$ b) s when $t = 0.5$ c) t when $s = 486$

E M Q12 The size of the gravitational force, F newtons, between two objects is inversely proportional to the square of the distance, r metres, between their centres.

The centres of two spheres, A and B, are a distance of 3 metres apart, and the gravitational force between them is measured to be 3.56×10^{-6} newtons.

a) Show that $F = \frac{k}{r^2}$, where k is a constant to be found. Give the value of k in standard form. *[3 marks]*

A and B are moved such that their centres are now 15 metres apart.

b) Using your answer from part a), find the size of the gravitational force between A and B, giving your answer in standard form. *[2 marks]*

Sphere B is replaced with sphere C. It is found that the gravitational force between A and C is given by the formula $F = \frac{5k}{r^2}$. The centres of spheres A and C are x metres apart and the gravitational force between the two spheres is measured to be 7.11×10^{-9} newtons.

c) Find the distance between the centres of A and C to the nearest metre. *[2 marks]*

Q13 Sketch these cubic graphs:

a) $y = (x - 4)^3$ b) $y = (3 - x)(x + 2)^2$ c) $y = (1 - x)(x^2 - 6x + 8)$

d) $y = (x - 1)(x - 2)(x - 3)$ e) $y = 3x^3 - 6x^2$ f) $y = x^3 - x^2 - 12x$

Q14 Sketch the graphs of the following quartic functions:

a) $y = (x - 4)^4$ b) $y = -(x + 1)^2(x - 1)^2$ c) $y = x^2(x^2 - 16)$

Q15 Draw rough sketches of the following curves:

a) $y = -2x^4$ b) $y = \frac{7}{x^2}$ c) $y = -5x^3$ d) $y = -\frac{2}{x^5}$

e) $y = \frac{2}{3}x^5$ f) $y = -4x^{-4}$ g) $y = \frac{x^2}{2}$ h) $y = \frac{4}{5x^6}$

Q16 Given that $a > 1$, use the graph of f(x) to sketch the graph of:

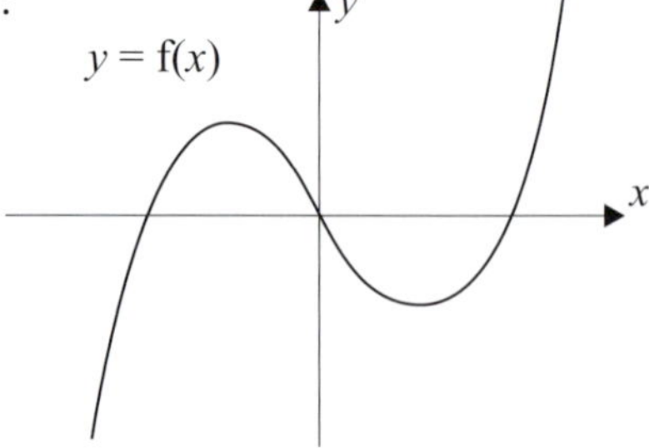

a) $y = f(ax)$ b) $y = f\left(\frac{1}{a}x\right)$

c) $y = af(x)$ d) $y = \frac{1}{a}f(x)$

e) $y = f(x + a)$ f) $y = f(x - a)$

g) $y = f(x) + a$ h) $y = f(x) - a$

P Q17 Describe the transformation that is required to take the graph of f(x) to the graph of g(x), if:

a) $f(x) = 3x - 9x^2 - 6x^3$ and $g(x) = 2x^3 + 3x^2 - x$

b) $f(x) = 2x^2 - 4x + 8$ and $g(x) = \frac{1}{2}x^2 - 2x + 8$

c) $f(x) = (x - 1)(x - 4)$ and $g(x) = (x - 2)(x - 3)$

E P Q18 Describe the transformation that takes the graph of $y = (x + 1)(x + 3)(x + 7)$ to the graph of:

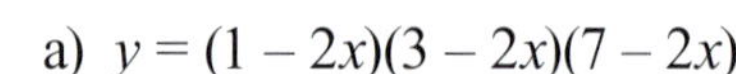

a) $y = (1 - 2x)(3 - 2x)(7 - 2x)$ *[2 marks]*

b) $y = (3x + 3)(2x + 6)(x + 7)$ *[2 marks]*

P Q19 The graph of $f(x) = x^4 - 3x^3 + 4x$ passes through the point (2, 0).

a) Sketch the graph of f(x), marking clearly where the curve meets the coordinate axes.

b) The graph of f(x) is translated by the column vector $\begin{pmatrix} 2 \\ 0 \end{pmatrix}$ to give g(x). Sketch the graph of g(x).

c) Write down an expression for the function g(x) (you do not have to simplify your answer).

Q20 The diagram shows the graph of $y = f(x)$. The curve has a maximum at (–1, 3) and meets the x-axis at (–3, 0) and (1, 0). Sketch the graphs of the following functions, labelling clearly the coordinates of any maxima or minima and where the curve meets the x-axis.

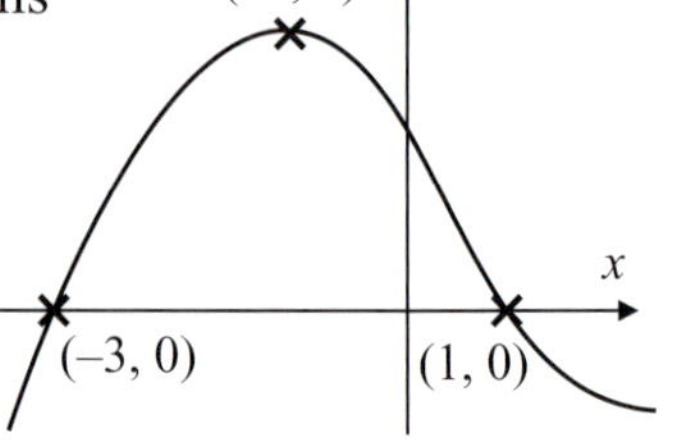

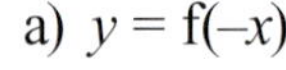

a) $y = f(-x)$ b) $y = -f(x)$

c) $y = 3f(x)$ d) $y = f(3x)$

E Q21 The diagram shows the graph of the function $y = f(x)$.

Given that $f(x) = a + \frac{b}{x+c}$, use the information in the diagram to find the values of a, b and c.

[3 marks]

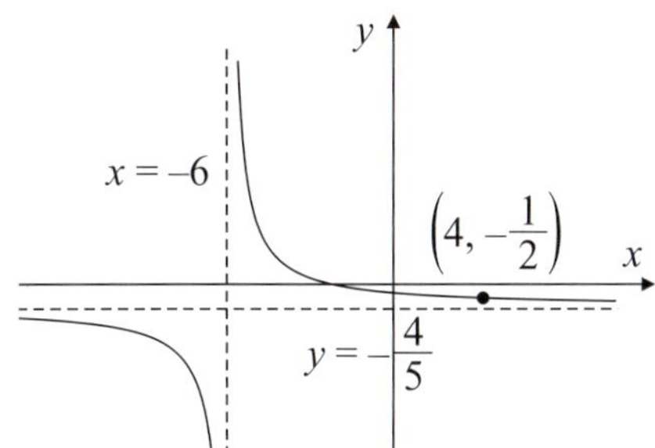

Q22 Give the radius and the coordinates of the centre of the circles with the following equations:

a) $x^2 + y^2 = 9$ b) $(x - 2)^2 + (y + 4)^2 = 4$ c) $x(x + 6) = y(8 - y)$

Q23 Write down the equation for the circle with centre $(0, -3)$ and radius $\sqrt{14}$.

Q24 A circle has the equation $x^2 + y^2 - 4x + 6y - 68 = 0$.
Find the coordinates of the centre of the circle and its radius.

Q25 The circle C has equation $x^2 + y^2 - 12x + 2y + 11 = 0$. The point A $(1, -2)$ lies on the circle. Find an equation of the tangent at A.

E P Q26 A circle has centre $(2, -3)$ and radius r. Its equation is $x^2 + y^2 + ax + by - 4 = 0$.
Find the exact radius of the circle and the values of a and b. *[4 marks]*

E P Q27 Line l_1 has the equation $3x + 2y - 12 = 0$ and line l_2 has the equation $y = -5x - 1$.
Determine whether the lines l_1 and l_2 intersect at a point that lies inside, outside, or on the circumference of the circle with equation $x^2 - 12x + y^2 - 26y + 124 = 0$. *[4 marks]*

E P Q28 Circle C_1 has centre $(-1, 6)$ and radius $\sqrt{13}$.
Circle C_2 has equation $x^2 - 10x + y^2 + 6y + 21 = 0$.
Determine whether C_1 and C_2 intersect at one point, two points, or do not intersect at all. You must justify your answer. *[4 marks]*

P Q29 Points A and B lie on a circle with its centre at C and a radius of 15. Point X lies at the midpoint of the chord AB. Given that the length of AB is 18, find the distance of X from the centre of the circle.

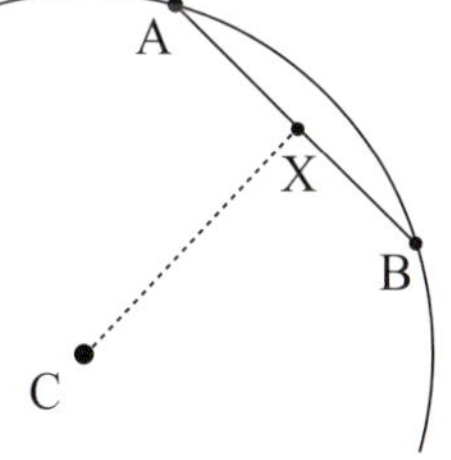

E P Q30 A circle with centre C has equation $x^2 + y^2 - 4x + 12y + 15 = 0$.

a) Find the coordinates of the centre point and the radius of circle C. *[4 marks]*

b) Explain why the circle C lies entirely below the x-axis. *[2 marks]*

c) The point $(-1, k)$ lies on the circle. Find the possible values of k. *[3 marks]*

P Q31 The points A (2, a), B (4, –1) and C (0, 1) lie on a circle, and AB is a diameter of the circle.

a) Find the value of a.

b) Find the equation of the circle.

E P Q32 C is a circle with centre A (25, 15) and radius $5\sqrt{5}$.

a) Show that the point P, with coordinates (20, 25), lies on C. *[1 mark]*

b) Find the equation of the tangent, l_1, to C at point P. *[2 marks]*

l_1 passes through the point B with coordinates (0, 15).

c) Find the equation of a second line, l_2, that passes through B and is tangent to C. Write down the coordinates of Q, the point of intersection between C and l_2. *[2 marks]*

d) Hence find the area of the quadrilateral with vertices A, P, B and Q. *[1 mark]*

P Q33 Find the equation of the circumcircle of the triangle ABC, where A = (4.5, 7.5), B = (2, 5) and C = (4, 5).

P Q34 A triangle PQR has vertices P = (2, 11), Q = (6, 5) and R = (–9, 0). Find the equation of the circumcircle of PQR.

Challenge

E P Q35 A line l has equation $(k - 2)y = (3 - k)x + (k^2 - 6)$ where $k \neq 2$ is a constant.

a) Find the two values of k for which l passes through the point (–4, 7). *[2 marks]*

b) Write, in the form $y = mx + c$, the equations of the lines corresponding to the two values of k found in part a). *[3 marks]*

c) Show that l cannot pass through the point (6, –2) for any real value of k. *[2 marks]*

E P Q36 The diagram below shows the trapezium ABCD, in which sides AB and CD are parallel. The point C has coordinates (6, 6) and the point D has coordinates (–4, 2).

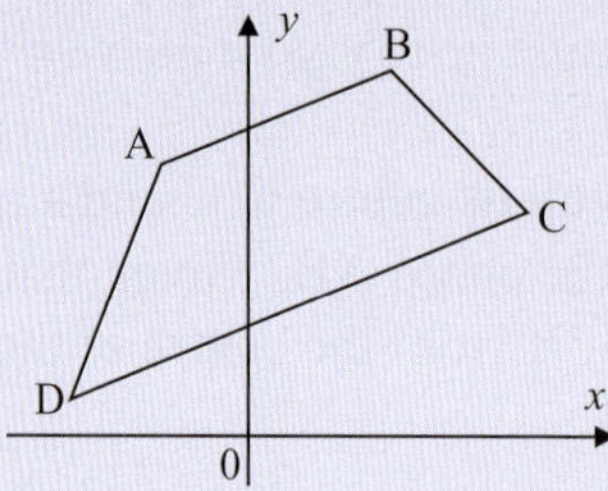

a) Find the equation of the straight line passing through C and D, giving your answer in the form $ax + by + c = 0$, where a, b and c are integers. *[3 marks]*

b) Given that the gradient of BC is –1, find an equation of the line BC. *[2 marks]*

c) Point A has coordinates (–2, 7). Find the coordinates of the point B. *[4 marks]*

d) Show that $\angle DBC = 90°$. *[2 marks]*

E P Q37 A line has equation $4x + 3y = 24$.

a) Find the equation of the line l_1 that is perpendicular to $4x + 3y = 24$ and passes through the point (8, 4). *[3 marks]*

b) Find the coordinates of the point A, where l_1 intersects $4x + 3y = 24$. *[2 marks]*

Two lines, perpendicular to the coordinate axes, are drawn through (8, 4). They intersect the x and y-axes at B and C respectively.

c) Show that A, B and C all lie on the same straight line. *[3 marks]*

E P Q38 Consider $y = af(x) + (3x + b)g(x)$, where a and b are constants, and $f(x) = x^3 + 4x^2 + 7x + 2$ and $g(x) = x^2 + 3x + 6$.

a) Given that y is directly proportional to the square of x, find the values of a and b. *[4 marks]*

b) Find the value of y when g(x) is at its minimum value. *[3 marks]*

E P Q39 a) Show that $\frac{3x-1}{x-2} \equiv a + \frac{b}{x-2}$, $x \neq 2$, where a and b are constants to be found. *[2 marks]*

b) Hence, or otherwise, find the equations of the asymptotes of $y = f(x) = \frac{3x-1}{x-2}$. *[2 marks]*

c) Sketch the graph of $y = f(x)$, clearly indicating the equations of the asymptotes and the coordinates of any points of intersection with the coordinate axes. *[3 marks]*

P Q40 Points X (–2, 4), Y (3, 9) and Z (7, 1) lie on a circle with its centre at point C.

a) Find the exact length, and the coordinates of the midpoint, M, of the line segment XY.

b) Find the equation of the circle.

c) Hence, or otherwise, find the exact area of triangle CXY.

E P Q41 A circle has equation $x^2 + y^2 - 10x - 7 = 0$. The point A (9, p) lies on the circle where $p > 0$.

a) Find the value of p. *[2 marks]*

b) Find the equation of the tangent at the point A, giving your answer in the form $ax + by = c$. *[5 marks]*

c) The tangent at A meets the x-axis at the point Q. Find the area of the triangle OAQ, where O is the origin. *[3 marks]*

E P Q42 The lines l_1 and l_2 are both tangents to the circle C. l_1 has equation $y = -\frac{5}{7}x + 22$. l_2 has equation $5x + 7y = 80$ and touches C at the point with coordinates (9, 5). Find the equation of C. *[7 marks]*

E P Q43 Circle C_1 has centre (5, –2) and touches circle C_2 at a single point, A, with coordinates (7, 6). Line l has equation $y + 4x = 109$, and is tangent to circle C_2. The point of contact, B, between l and C_2 has coordinates (22, 21).

a) Explain why the line through the centre of C_1 and the point A must also pass through the centre of C_2. *[2 marks]*

b) Find the equation of C_2. *[6 marks]*

6 Chapter Summary

1 A straight line can have the form $y - y_1 = m(x - x_1)$, where x_1 and y_1 are coordinates of a point on the line and m is the gradient of the line.

2 For two points (x_1, y_1) and (x_2, y_2) on a straight line, the gradient m of the line is: $m = \frac{y_2 - y_1}{x_2 - x_1}$.

3 Two other forms of a straight line are $y = mx + c$ (where m is the gradient of the line and c is the y-intercept), and $ax + by + c = 0$ (where a, b and c are integers).

4 If two straight lines have the same gradient then they are parallel.

5 If two straight lines are perpendicular then their gradients will multiply to give –1. So: gradient of one perpendicular line = –1 ÷ gradient of the other perpendicular line.

6 If y is directly proportional to x, you can write $y \propto x$. This is the same as writing $y = kx$, where k is a constant.

7 When given a value of y and x, you can work out k: $k = \frac{y}{x}$.
Then use the value of k in the equation $y = kx$ to find new values of y or x.

8 Cubic functions are polynomials that have an x^3 term in them as the highest power.
Quartic functions are polynomials where the x^4 term is the highest power.

9 Reciprocal functions have the form $y = \frac{k}{x}$ and their graphs always have asymptotes which are lines that the curve gets infinitely close to but never touches.

10 For the graph of a function $f(x)$ and a constant a, the graph of:
- $f(x + a)$ is translated horizontally and $f(x) + a$ is translated vertically.
- $af(x)$ is stretched or reflected vertically.
- $f(ax)$ is stretched or reflected horizontally.

11 The general equation of a circle with centre (a, b) and radius r is $(x - a)^2 + (y - b)^2 = r^2$.
Another form of a circle equation is $x^2 + y^2 + 2fx + 2gy + c = 0$.
To change this into the general equation, complete the square for x and y.

12 There are three important circle properties:
- The triangle formed from the ends of a diameter has a right angle.
- The perpendicular from the centre to a chord bisects the chord.
- A tangent to the circle meets a radius at a right angle.

13 The circle that passes through all three vertices of a triangle is called the circumcircle of the triangle.

The Binomial Expansion

7

Learning Objectives

Once you've completed this chapter, you should be able to:

- Use Pascal's triangle to find the coefficients of a binomial expansion.
- Find binomial coefficients using factorials and using the notation $\binom{n}{r}$ or ${}^nC_r$.
- Use the binomial formula to expand binomials of the form $(1 + x)^n$, $(1 + ax)^n$ and $(a + bx)^n$.
- Use the binomial expansion to make approximations.

Prior Knowledge Check

1 Simplify the following: a) $(-5x)^2$ b) $(x + 4)^0$ c) $(-2z)^3$ d) $(z - 2)^1$

see GCSE Maths

2 Expand the brackets in these expressions:

a) $x^2(x - 3)$ b) $(2z - 3)(5z + 4)$ c) $(8 - 2w)^2$ d) $(p - q)^3$

see GCSE Maths

3 Expand and simplify:

a) $(3x + 1)(4x - 1)(5x + 4)$ b) $(2x^2 + 3x - 1)(x^3 - 4x^2 - 6x + 12)$

see pages 16-17

4 Evaluate:

a) $\left(\frac{x}{4}\right)^2$ b) $\left(\frac{-x}{2}\right)^3$ c) $\left(\frac{5x}{3}\right)^4$

see pages 25-26

7.1 Binomial Expansions — $(1 + x)^n$

Pascal's triangle

A **binomial expansion** is what you get when you **multiply out the brackets** of a binomial (a polynomial with only two terms) that is raised to a power, e.g. $(1 + x)^5$ or $(2 - 3x)^8$. It would take ages to multiply out a bracket like this by hand if the power was really big — fortunately, binomial expansions **follow a pattern**:

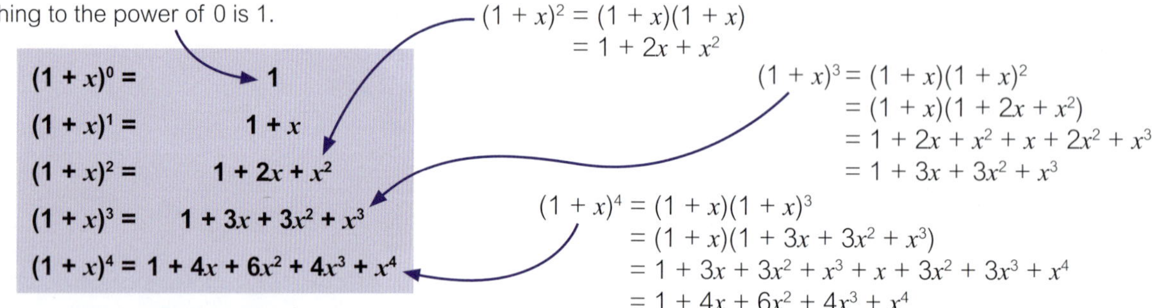

A French man called Blaise Pascal spotted the pattern in the **coefficients** and wrote them down in a **triangle**, so it's known as '**Pascal's triangle**'. Each number is the **sum** of the two above it — and the triangle is symmetrical, so you only need to work out the first half of the coefficients:

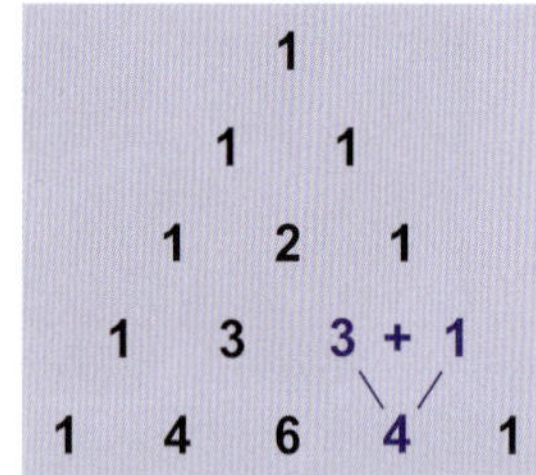

The next line is: **1 5 10 10 5 1**, so $(1 + x)^5 = 1 + 5x + 10x^2 + 10x^3 + 5x^4 + x^5$.

If you're expanding a binomial with a power that's not too huge, writing out a quick **Pascal's triangle** is a good way to **find the coefficients**. Make sure you go down to the **correct row** — you need **one more row** than the **power** you're raising the bracket to. You usually write the expansion in increasing powers of x, from x^0 to x^n.

Example 1

Find the binomial expansion of $(1 + x)^6$.

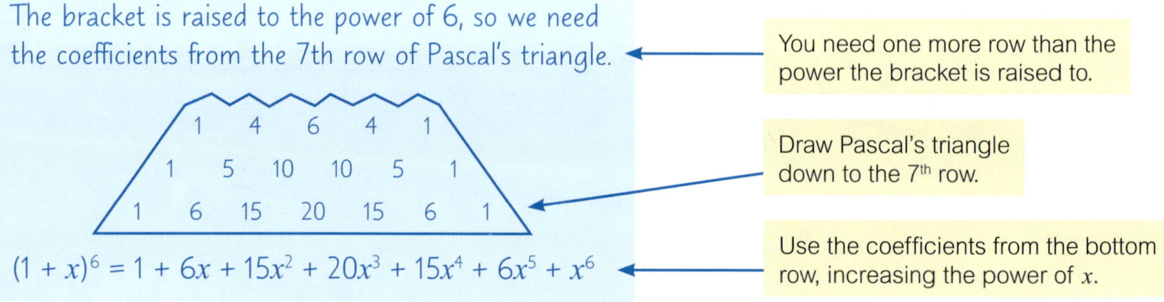

The binomial formula

For expansions with higher powers you don't need to write out Pascal's triangle — use the binomial formula instead:

$$(1+x)^n = 1 + \frac{n}{1}x + \frac{n(n-1)}{1\times 2}x^2 + \frac{n(n-1)(n-2)}{1\times 2\times 3}x^3 + \ldots + x^n$$

At first glance this looks a bit awful, but each term follows a pattern:

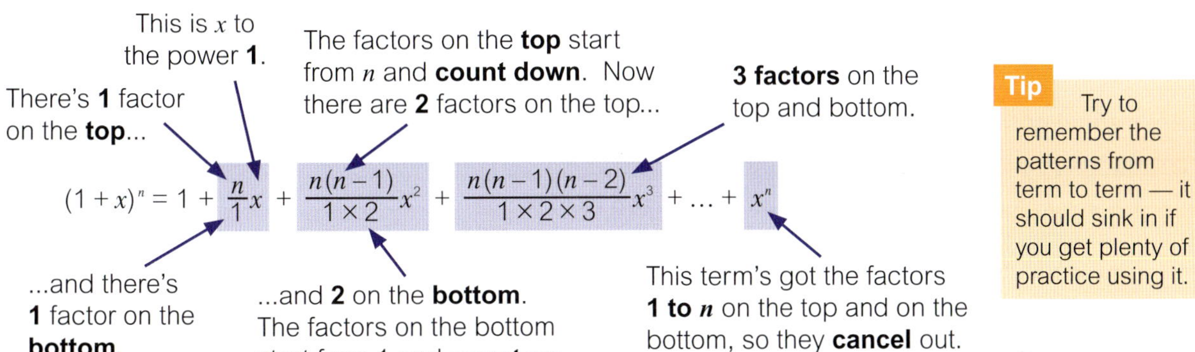

Tip Try to remember the patterns from term to term — it should sink in if you get plenty of practice using it.

Once you get **halfway** along, the **factors** on the top and bottom start to **cancel**, and the coefficients repeat themselves (they're symmetrical):

$$(1+x)^5 = 1 + \frac{5}{1}x + \frac{5\times 4}{1\times 2}x^2 + \frac{5\times 4\times \cancel{3}}{1\times 2\times \cancel{3}}x^3 + \frac{5\times \cancel{4}\times \cancel{3}\times \cancel{2}}{1\times \cancel{2}\times \cancel{3}\times \cancel{4}}x^4 + \frac{\cancel{5}\times \cancel{4}\times \cancel{3}\times \cancel{2}\times \cancel{1}}{\cancel{1}\times \cancel{2}\times \cancel{3}\times \cancel{4}\times \cancel{5}}x^5$$

$$= 1 + \frac{5}{1}x + \frac{5\times 4}{1\times 2}x^2 + \frac{5\times 4}{1\times 2}x^3 + \frac{5}{1}x^4 + x^5$$

$$= 1 + 5x + 10x^2 + 10x^3 + 5x^4 + x^5$$

Example 2

a) Expand $(1+x)^{20}$, giving the first four terms only.

$$(1+x)^n = 1 + \frac{n}{1}x + \frac{n(n-1)}{1\times 2}x^2 + \frac{n(n-1)(n-2)}{1\times 2\times 3}x^3 + \ldots + x^n$$ ← Write down the binomial formula.

$$(1+x)^{20} = 1 + \frac{20}{1}x + \frac{20\times 19}{1\times 2}x^2 + \frac{20\times 19\times 18}{1\times 2\times 3}x^3 + \ldots + x^{20}$$ ← You're looking for $(1+x)^{20}$, so here, $n = 20$.

$$(1+x)^{20} = 1 + \frac{20}{1}x + \frac{\overset{10}{\cancel{20}}\times 19}{1\times \cancel{2}}x^2 + \frac{\overset{10}{\cancel{20}}\times 19\times \overset{6}{\cancel{18}}}{1\times \cancel{2}\times \cancel{3}}x^3 + \ldots$$ ← Cancel as much as you can.

$$= 1 + 20x + (10\times 19)x^2 + (10\times 19\times 6)x^3 + \ldots$$ ← The first four terms only go up to x^3.

So the first four terms of the expansion are:

$(1+x)^{20} = 1 + 20x + 190x^2 + 1140x^3 + \ldots$

b) What is the term in x^7 in this expansion? Give your answer in its simplest form.

$$\text{Term in } x^7 = \frac{20 \times 19 \times 18 \times 17 \times 16 \times 15 \times 14}{1 \times 2 \times 3 \times 4 \times 5 \times 6 \times 7} x^7$$

$$= (19 \times 17 \times 16 \times 15)x^7 = 77\,520x^7$$

The term in x^7 has 7 factors on the top and bottom of the coefficient. Here $n = 20$, so on the top you count down from 20.

Don't forget to simplify.

Factorials

There's some **notation** you need to know that will make writing out the binomial formula a bit easier.

- The product on the **bottom** of each binomial coefficient is **1 × 2 × ... ×** r, where r is the **power** x **is raised to** in that term.

- This product can be written as a **factorial**: $r! = 1 \times 2 \times ... \times r$
E.g. in the binomial expansion of $(1 + x)^{20}$, the coefficient of the term in x^3 is: $\frac{20 \times 19 \times 18}{1 \times 2 \times 3} = \frac{20 \times 19 \times 18}{3!}$

Tip $r! = 1 \times 2 \times ... \times r$ is said 'r factorial'. By convention, $0! = 1$.

- In fact, you can write the whole coefficient using factorials. For example, the coefficient of x^3 in Example 2 above is:

$$\frac{20 \times 19 \times 18}{1 \times 2 \times 3} = \frac{20 \times 19 \times 18 \times 17 \times ... \times 2 \times 1}{1 \times 2 \times 3 \times 1 \times 2 \times ... \times 17} = \frac{20 \times 19 \times ... \times 1}{(1 \times 2 \times 3)(1 \times 2 \times ... \times 17)} = \frac{20!}{3!17!}$$

Tip Here you've multiplied top and bottom by 17! — this is just so you can write the factors on the top as a factorial (you need to multiply all the way down to 1 to do this).

- For a general binomial expansion of $(1 + x)^n$, the coefficient of x^r is:

$$\frac{n \times (n-1) \times ... \times (n-(r-1))}{1 \times 2 \times ... \times r}$$
$$= \frac{n \times (n-1) \times ... \times (n-(r-1)) \times (n-r) \times ... \times 2 \times 1}{1 \times 2 \times ... \times r \times 1 \times 2 \times ... \times (n-r)}$$
$$= \frac{n \times (n-1) \times ... \times 1}{(1 \times 2 \times ... \times r)(1 \times 2 \times ... \times (n-r))}$$
$$= \frac{n!}{r!(n-r)!}$$

Tip The two numbers on the bottom of the factorial fraction always add up to the number on the top.

- So each term in a **binomial expansion** of $(1 + x)^n$ is of the form:

$$\frac{n(n-1)(n-2)...(n-(r-1))}{1 \times 2 \times 3 \times ... \times r} x^r = \frac{n!}{r!(n-r)!} x^r$$

where n is the power you're raising the **bracket** to, and r is the power of x in the **term** the coefficient belongs to.

${}^nC_r$ notation

There are a couple of even **shorter ways** of writing the **binomial coefficients**: $\frac{n!}{r!(n-r)!} = \binom{n}{r} = {}^nC_r$

Tip This is in the formula booklet.

For these coefficients, you would say 'n choose r', e.g. $\binom{3}{2}$ is '3 choose 2'.

Going back to the coefficient of x^3 in the expansion of $(1+x)^{20}$:

$$\frac{20 \times 19 \times 18}{1 \times 2 \times 3}x^3 = \frac{20!}{3!17!}x^3 = \binom{20}{3}x^3 = {}^{20}C_3x^3$$

Tip These coefficients will always come out as a whole number. ${}^nC_r$ is the number of ways to choose r objects from a set of n objects — you'll see lots more about this in Year 1 Statistics.

The binomial formula can be written using any of these notations, and you need to be familiar with all of them.

$$(1+x)^n = 1 + \frac{n!}{1!(n-1)!}x + \frac{n!}{2!(n-2)!}x^2 + \frac{n!}{3!(n-3)!}x^3 + ... + x^n$$

$$(1+x)^n = 1 + \binom{n}{1}x + \binom{n}{2}x^2 + \binom{n}{3}x^3 + ... + x^n$$

$$(1+x)^n = 1 + {}^nC_1x + {}^nC_2x^2 + {}^nC_3x^3 + ... + x^n$$

Tip ${}^nC_0 = {}^nC_n = 1$.

Most **calculators** will have an '**nCr**' button for finding binomial **coefficients**. To use it, put in n, press '**nCr**', then put in r. This is particularly handy if you're just looking for a **specific term** in a **binomial expansion** and you don't want to write the whole thing out. (If you get confused between which number is n and which is r, remember that n is always greater than or equal to r.)

Example 3

Find the x^5 term of the expansion of $(1+x)^8$.

The bracket is raised to the power of 8, so $n = 8$

For the x^5 term, $r = 5$

${}^8C_5 = 56$, so the x^5 term is $56x^5$

Put '8 nCr 5' into your calculator to find the coefficient. The question asks for the whole term, so don't forget to include x^5 in your answer too.

Exercise 7.1

Q1 Use Pascal's triangle to expand $(1+x)^3$.

P Q2 a) Show that $\binom{n}{n-r} = \binom{n}{r}$.

b) Using the result from part a), complete the following rows of Pascal's triangle:

(i) $(1+x)^{10} = 1, 10, 45, 120, 210, 252, \ldots$

(ii) $(1+x)^{13} = 1, 13, 78, 286, 715, 1287, 1716, \ldots$

Q3 Use your calculator to work out the following:

a) ${}^6C_2$ b) $\binom{12}{5}$ c) $\frac{30!}{4!26!}$ d) ${}^8C_8$

Q4 Without using a calculator, work out the following:

a) $\frac{9!}{4!5!}$ b) ${}^{10}C_3$ c) $\frac{15!}{11!4!}$ d) $\binom{8}{6}$

Q5 Find the first 4 terms, in ascending powers of x, of the binomial expansion of $(1 + x)^{10}$. Give each term in its simplest form.

Q6 Find the first 4 terms in the expansion of $(1 + x)^7$.

Q7 Find the first three terms, in ascending powers of x, of the binomial expansion of:

a) $(1 + x)^{11}$ b) $(1 + x)^{12}$ c) $(1 + x)^{15}$ d) $(1 + x)^{30}$

E P Q8 a) Write out the expansion of $(1 + x)^5$. *[2 marks]*

b) How could you use the expansion of $(1 + x)^5$ to find the expansion of $(1 + x)^6$? *[1 mark]*

c) Hence, or otherwise, expand $(1 + x)^6$. *[1 mark]*

P Q9 The coefficient of x^{12} in the expansion of $(1 + x)^{17}$ is a. Find the value of a.

P Q10 For the expansion of $(1 + x)^5 + (2 - 3x)$:

a) Find the term in x. b) Write down the coefficient of x^4.

P Q11 a) Write out the expansions of $(1 + x)^3$ and $(1 + x)^4$ in terms of ${}^nC_r$.

b) By choosing an appropriate value for x, use your answer to part a) to show that:

(i) $\binom{3}{0}+\binom{3}{1}+\binom{3}{2}+\binom{3}{3}=2^3$

(ii) ${}^4C_0 + {}^4C_1 + {}^4C_2 + {}^4C_3 + {}^4C_4 = 2^4$

c) Use a similar approach to that used above to show that, in general:

$$\binom{n}{0}+\binom{n}{1}+\binom{n}{2}+\ldots+\binom{n}{n-1}+\binom{n}{n}=2^n$$

d) Hence, find the sum of the numbers in the row of Pascal's triangle which starts with the numbers 1, 12, ...

Challenge

E P Q12 a) Write out the expansion of $(1 + x)^3$. *[2 marks]*

b) Hence, describe the transformation that could be used to transform the graph of $y = x^3$ into the graph of $y = 6 + 3x + 3x^2 + x^3$. *[2 marks]*

E Q13 a) Write out the expansion of $(1 + x)^4$. *[2 marks]*

b) Hence, or otherwise, express $(1+\sqrt{5})^4$ in the form $a+b\sqrt{5}$. *[2 marks]*

c) Simplify the expression $\sqrt{\frac{56}{25}+\frac{24\sqrt{5}}{25}}$ to the form $c+d\sqrt{5}$. *[3 marks]*

P Q14 a) Solve ${}^nC_2 = 28$, where n is a positive integer.

b) Solve $\binom{m+2}{3} = 120$, where m is a positive integer.

7.2 Binomial Expansions — $(1 + ax)^n$

When the **coefficient of x** in your binomial **isn't 1** (e.g. $(1 + 2x)^6$) you have to substitute the **whole x term** (e.g. $2x$) into the **binomial formula**:

$$(1+ax)^n = 1 + \binom{n}{1}(ax) + \binom{n}{2}(ax)^2 + \binom{n}{3}(ax)^3 + \ldots + (ax)^n$$

When a is **–1** (i.e. $(1 - x)^n$) the formula looks just like the formula for $(1 + x)^n$, but the **signs** of the terms **alternate**:

$$\begin{aligned}(1-x)^n &= (1+(-x))^n \\ &= 1 + \frac{n}{1}(-x) + \frac{n(n-1)}{1\times 2}(-x)^2 + \frac{n(n-1)(n-2)}{1\times 2\times 3}(-x)^3 + \ldots + (-x)^n \\ &= 1 - \frac{n}{1}x + \frac{n(n-1)}{1\times 2}x^2 - \frac{n(n-1)(n-2)}{1\times 2\times 3}x^3 + \ldots \pm x^n\end{aligned}$$

Tip The sign of the last term is plus if n is even and minus if n is odd.

So for $(1 - x)^n$ you just use the usual binomial **coefficients**, but with **alternating signs**:

$$(1-x)^n = 1 - \binom{n}{1}x + \binom{n}{2}x^2 - \binom{n}{3}x^3 + \ldots \pm x^n$$

Example 1 P

a) What is the term in x^5 in the expansion of $(1 - 3x)^{12}$?

$(1 - 3x)^n = (1 + (-3x))^n$

$(1+(-3x))^n = 1 + \frac{n}{1}(-3x) + \frac{n(n-1)}{1\times 2}(-3x)^2 + \frac{n(n-1)(n-2)}{1\times 2\times 3}(-3x)^3 + \ldots + (-3x)^n$ ← Write the formula with $a = -3$.

$(1-3x)^{12} = 1 + \frac{12}{1}(-3x) + \frac{12\times 11}{1\times 2}(-3x)^2 + \frac{12\times 11\times 10}{1\times 2\times 3}(-3x)^3 + \ldots + (-3x)^{12}$

So the term in x^5 is $\frac{12!}{5!7!}(-3x)^5 = \binom{12}{5}(-3)^5x^5 = (792 \times -243)x^5 = -192\ 456x^5$ ← Plug in $n = 12$ and work out the x^5 term.

b) Find the coefficient of x^2 in the expansion of $(1 + 6x)^4(1 - 2x)^6$.

Problem Solving Consider the two binomials separately to start with.

$(1+6x)^4 = 1 + \binom{4}{1}(6x) + \binom{4}{2}(6x)^2 + \ldots = 1 + 24x + 216x^2 + \ldots$

$(1-2x)^6 = 1 + \binom{6}{1}(-2x) + \binom{6}{2}(-2x)^2 + \ldots = 1 - 12x + 60x^2 - \ldots$

← To find the x^2 term in the combined expansion, you need to find all the terms up to x^2 in both expansions.

$$\begin{aligned}(1 + 6x)^4(1 - 2x)^6 &= (1 + 24x + 216x^2 + \ldots)(1 - 12x + 60x^2 - \ldots) \\ &= 1 - 12x + 60x^2 - \ldots \\ &\quad + 24x - 288x^2 + 1440x^3 - \ldots \\ &\quad + 216x^2 - 2592x^3 + 12\ 960x^4 - \ldots \\ &= 1 + 12x - 12x^2 + \text{(higher power terms)} + \ldots\end{aligned}$$

← Multiply the two separate expansions together.

← Simplify the expression and pick out the coefficient of x^2.

So the coefficient of x^2 is –12

Approximations

You can use a binomial expansion to find **approximations** of a number raised to a power.

Approximating usually involves taking a really small value for x so that you can **ignore high powers** of x (because they'll be really, really small).

For example, if you're asked to approximate 1.001^9, then you just substitute $x = 0.001$ into the expansion of $(1 + x)^9$. Because 0.001 is small, 0.001^2 is really small and adding on really small terms won't make much difference, so just the **first few terms** will give a good approximation.

Example 2

a) Expand $(1 + 2x)^7$ to find the first 4 terms in ascending powers of x.

$$(1 + 2x)^7 = 1 + {}^7C_1(2x) + {}^7C_2(2x)^2 + {}^7C_3(2x)^3 + \dots$$
$$= 1 + 7(2x) + 21(4x^2) + 35(8x^3) + \dots$$
$$= 1 + 14x + 84x^2 + 280x^3 + \dots$$

You can find the binomial coefficients using any of the methods from pages 158-161 — just pick whichever one you prefer.

b) When x is small, x^3 and higher powers can be ignored. Hence show that for small x: $(2 - x)(1 + 2x)^7 \approx 2 + 27x + 154x^2$.

$$(2 - x)(1 + 2x)^7 \approx (2 - x)(1 + 14x + 84x^2)$$
$$= 2 + 28x + 168x^2 - x - 14x^2 - 84x^3$$
$$= 2 + 27x + 154x^2 - 84x^3$$
$$\approx 2 + 27x + 154x^2 \text{ as required}$$

Use the expansion of $(1 + 2x)^7$ from the first part of the question, ignoring x^3 and higher powers.

You can ignore the x^3 term as x is small.

Example 3

Problem Solving Think carefully about what value of x will give you the expansion you need.

a) Find the first 3 terms of the expansion of $\left(1 - \frac{x}{4}\right)^9$.

$$\left(1-\frac{x}{4}\right)^9 = 1 + \binom{9}{1}\left(-\frac{x}{4}\right) + \binom{9}{2}\left(-\frac{x}{4}\right)^2 + \dots$$
$$= 1 - 9\left(\frac{x}{4}\right) + 36\left(\frac{x^2}{16}\right) - \dots = 1 - \frac{9}{4}x + \frac{9}{4}x^2 - \dots$$

Use the formula, but replace x with $\left(-\frac{x}{4}\right)$.

b) Use your expansion to estimate $(0.998)^9$.

$$(0.998)^9 = (1 - 0.002)^9 = \left(1 - \frac{x}{4}\right)^9 \text{ when } x = 0.008$$
$$(0.998)^9 = \left(1 - \frac{0.008}{4}\right)^9 \approx 1 - \frac{9}{4}(0.008) + \frac{9}{4}(0.008)^2$$
$$= 1 - 0.018 + 0.000144$$
$$= 0.982144$$

Write $(0.998)^9$ in the same form as the expansion.

Substitute $x = 0.008$ into the expansion — the first three terms are enough as 0.008^3 and higher powers will be very small.

Exercise 7.2

Q1 Find the full expansions of:

a) $(1 + 3x)^4$ b) $(1 - x)^4$ c) $(1 - x)^6$ d) $(1 - 2x)^5$

e) $(1 - 4x)^3$ f) $(1 - 5x)^5$ g) $(1 + 2x)^6$ h) $(1 + x)^9 - (1 - x)^9$

Q2 What is the term in x^4 in the expansion of $(1 - 2x)^{16}$?

Problem Solving

In Q3, go up to x^2 in both expansions, then multiply the expansions together.

P Q3 Find the first 3 terms in the expansion of $(1 + x)^3(1 - x)^4$.

P Q4 Find the coefficient of x^3y^2 in the expansion of $(1 + x)^5(1 + y)^7$.

P Q5 Find the coefficient of x^3 in the expansion of $(1 + 4x)^4(1 - 6x)^3$.

P Q6 a) Find the first 4 terms, in ascending powers of x, of the binomial expansion of $(1 + kx)^8$, where k is a non-zero constant.

b) If the fourth term of the above expansion is $448x^3$, find the value of k.

P Q7 In the expansion of $(1 - kx)^6$, the coefficient of x^2 is 135.
Use this information to find the value of k, given that k is positive.

P Q8 If x is small, so that x^2 and higher powers can be ignored,
show that $(1 + x)(1 - 3x)^6 \approx 1 - 17x$.

E Q9 a) Find, in their simplest form, the first 5 terms in the expansion of $\left(1 + \frac{x}{2}\right)^{12}$, in ascending powers of x. *[3 marks]*

b) Use the expansion to work out the value of 1.005^{12} to 7 d.p. *[2 marks]*

E Q10 a) Find the first 3 terms, in ascending powers of x, in the expansion of $\left(1 + \frac{3}{2}x\right)^{14}$. *[3 marks]*

b) Use your answer to part a) to estimate 1.015^{14} to 5 significant figures. *[2 marks]*

P Q11 Marc finds the expansion of $(1 + x)^{10}$ up to the term in x^3. He wants to substitute $x = 1.6$ into this expression to approximate 2.6^{10}. Explain why this will not be a good approximation.

Challenge

P Q12 In the expansion of $(1 + 7x)^n$, the coefficient of the term in x^2 is 490.

a) Given that n is positive, find the value of n.

b) Find the term in x^3.

E P Q13 a) Find the first 3 terms, in ascending powers of x, in the expansion of $(1 - 4x)^6$. *[3 marks]*

The equation $\frac{1}{100}(1 - 4x)^6 = 3x$ has two solutions, a and b, where $a < b$.

b) Use your answer to a) to find approximations for a and b to 2 s.f. *[3 marks]*

c) The true values of a and b are such that $0.003 < a < 0.004$ and $0.85 < b < 0.9$. Explain why the approximation of a found in b) is very close to the true value, but the approximation of b is a relatively poor approximation. *[2 marks]*

7.3 Binomial Expansions — $(a + b)^n$

When your binomial is of the form $(a + b)^n$ (e.g. $(2 + 3x)^7$, where $a = 2$ and $b = 3x$) you can use a slightly **different formula**:

$$(a+b)^n = a^n + \binom{n}{1}a^{n-1}b + \binom{n}{2}a^{n-2}b^2 + \dots + \binom{n}{n-1}ab^{n-1} + b^n$$

Tip The powers of a decrease (from n to 0) as the powers of b increase (from 0 to n). The sum of the powers of a and b in each term is always n.

This formula is in the **formula booklet** and you don't need to know the proof, but seeing where it comes from might make things a bit clearer. You can find it from the binomial formula you've already seen:

- First rearrange so the binomial is in a form you can work with.

$$(a+b)^n = \left(a\left(1 + \frac{b}{a}\right)\right)^n = a^n\left(1 + \frac{b}{a}\right)^n$$

- You expand this by putting '$\frac{b}{a}$' into the binomial formula for $(1 + x)^n$, just like in the previous section.

$$= a^n\left(1 + \binom{n}{1}\left(\frac{b}{a}\right) + \binom{n}{2}\left(\frac{b}{a}\right)^2 + \dots + \binom{n}{n-1}\left(\frac{b}{a}\right)^{n-1} + \left(\frac{b}{a}\right)^n\right)$$

$$= a^n\left(1 + \binom{n}{1}\frac{b}{a} + \binom{n}{2}\frac{b^2}{a^2} + \dots + \binom{n}{n-1}\frac{b^{n-1}}{a^{n-1}} + \frac{b^n}{a^n}\right)$$

- **Multiply** through by a^n.

$$= a^n + \binom{n}{1}a^{n-1}b + \binom{n}{2}a^{n-2}b^2 + \dots + \binom{n}{n-1}ab^{n-1} + b^n$$

This is a general formula that works for any a and b, including 1 and x. So given **any binomial**, you can pop your values for a, b and n into this formula and you'll get the **expansion**.

You can use any of the methods from pages 158-161 to find the $\binom{n}{r}$ values.

Example 1

Give the first three terms, in ascending powers of x, of the expansion of $(4 - 5x)^7$.

Tip Ascending powers of x just means you write the constant term first, then the x term, then x^2 etc.

Using the binomial formula for $(a + b)^n$ with $a = 4$, $b = -5x$ and $n = 7$:

$(4 - 5x)^7 = (4 + (-5x))^7$

$$= 4^7 + \left(\binom{7}{1} \times 4^6 \times (-5x)\right) + \left(\binom{7}{2} \times 4^5 \times (-5x)^2\right) + \dots$$

$= 16\ 384 + (7 \times 4096 \times -5x) + (21 \times 1024 \times 25x^2) + \dots$

$= 16\ 384 - 143\ 360x + 537\ 600x^2 + \dots$

Plug a, b and n into the formula at the top of the page. Be careful — b comes with a minus sign.

Take care with the minus signs when you're simplifying.

You could instead **factorise** the binomial $(a+b)^n$ so you get $a^n\left(1+\frac{b}{a}\right)^n$, then plug $\frac{b}{a}$ into the **original binomial formula** (as you did with $(1+ax)^n$ expansions in the last section). Be careful, though — this can end up being more complicated than the method on the previous page.

Example 2 **P**

Find the coefficient of x^4 in the expansion of $(2+5x)^7$.

$(2+5x) = 2\left(1+\frac{5}{2}x\right)$, so $(2+5x)^7 = 2^7\left(1+\frac{5}{2}x\right)^7$ ← Factorise the bracket to get it in the form $a^n\left(1+\frac{b}{a}\right)^n$.

The x^4 term in $\left(1+\frac{5}{2}x\right)^7$ is $\binom{7}{4}\times\left(\frac{5}{2}x\right)^4 = \frac{7\times6\times5\times4}{1\times2\times3\times4}\times\frac{5^4}{2^4}x^4$
$= 35\times\frac{5^4}{2^4}x^4 = \frac{21875}{16}x^4$ ← Find the coefficient of x^4 in the expansion of $\left(1+\frac{5}{2}x\right)^7$.

So the coefficient of x^4 in the expansion of $(2+5x)^7$ is
$2^7\times\frac{21875}{16} = 175\,000$ ← Multiply this by 2^7 to get the coefficient of x^4 in the original binomial.

You can find an **unknown** in a binomial expansion if you're given information about the coefficients:

Problem Solving Don't be put off by unknown values in the binomial — you can still use the same expansions.

Example 3 **P**

a) The coefficient of x^5 in the binomial expansion of $(4+kx)^7$ is 81 648. Find k.

${}^7C_5 4^2(kx)^5 = 21\times16\times k^5\times x^5 = 336k^5x^5$ ← Use the $(a+b)^n$ formula to find the term in x^5.

$336k^5 = 81\,648 \Rightarrow k^5 = 243 \Rightarrow k = 3$ ← Solve $336k^5 = 81\,648$ to find k.

b) In the expansion of $(1+x)^n$, the coefficient of x^5 is twice the coefficient of x^4. Find n.

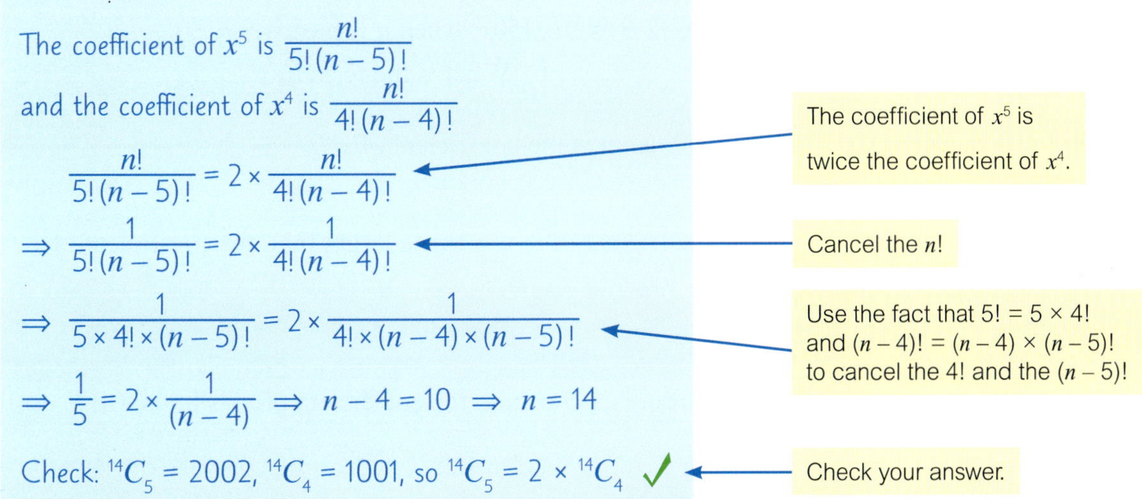
The coefficient of x^5 is $\frac{n!}{5!(n-5)!}$

and the coefficient of x^4 is $\frac{n!}{4!(n-4)!}$

$\frac{n!}{5!(n-5)!} = 2\times\frac{n!}{4!(n-4)!}$ ← The coefficient of x^5 is twice the coefficient of x^4.

$\Rightarrow \frac{1}{5!(n-5)!} = 2\times\frac{1}{4!(n-4)!}$ ← Cancel the $n!$

$\Rightarrow \frac{1}{5\times4!\times(n-5)!} = 2\times\frac{1}{4!\times(n-4)\times(n-5)!}$ ← Use the fact that $5! = 5\times4!$ and $(n-4)! = (n-4)\times(n-5)!$ to cancel the 4! and the $(n-5)!$

$\Rightarrow \frac{1}{5} = 2\times\frac{1}{(n-4)} \Rightarrow n-4 = 10 \Rightarrow n = 14$

Check: ${}^{14}C_5 = 2002$, ${}^{14}C_4 = 1001$, so ${}^{14}C_5 = 2\times{}^{14}C_4$ ✓ ← Check your answer.

Exercise 7.3

Q1 Find the first 4 terms of the binomial expansion of $(3 + x)^6$.

Q2 Find the full expansion of:

a) $(2 + x)^4$ b) $(2 + 2x)^4$ c) $(2 - 2x)^4$ d) $\left(\frac{1}{2} + \frac{1}{2}x\right)^4$

P Q3 In the expansion of $(1 + \lambda x)^8$, the coefficient of x^5 is 57 344.

a) Work out the value of λ. b) Find the first 3 terms of the expansion.

E Q4 a) Find the first 5 terms in the expansion of $(2 + x)^8$. *[3 marks]*

b) Use this expansion to find an approximation for 2.01^8 to 5 d.p. *[2 marks]*

Q5 Find the first 4 terms in the expansion of $(3 + 5x)^7$.

E Q6 a) Expand $(2 + 2x)^5$ in ascending powers of x, up to and including the term in x^3. *[4 marks]*

b) Use your answer to part a) to estimate the value of 2.04^5, giving your answer correct to 3 decimal places. *[2 marks]*

E Q7 a) Find the first 5 terms, in ascending powers of x, of the expansion of $\left(3 + \frac{x}{4}\right)^{11}$. Give each term in its simplest form. *[3 marks]*

b) Use your expansion to find an estimate for the value of $(3.002)^{11}$ to 3 decimal places. *[2 marks]*

P Q8 Find the first 5 terms, in ascending order, of $(1 + x)(3 + 2x)^6$.

E P Q9 Find the coefficient of x^5 in the binomial expansion of $(2 - x + x^2)(2 + 3x)^7$. *[5 marks]*

P Q10 Find the full expansion of:

a) $(1 + 3x)(2 - x)^5$ b) $(1 + 3x)^5(2 - x)$ c) $(1 + 3x)^2(2 - x)^4$ d) $(1 + 3x)^3(2 - x)^3$

P Q11 The term in x^2 for the expansion of $(2 - 5x)^n$ is $150x^2$ when n is positive.

a) What is the value of n? b) What is the term in x^3?

P Q12 In the expansion of $(1 + 2x)^5(3 - x)^4$, what is the coefficient of x^3?

Challenge

P Q13 In the expansion of $(1 + x)^n$, the coefficient of x^3 is 3 times larger than the coefficient of x^2.

a) Calculate the value of n.

b) If the coefficient of x^2 is $a \times$ (the coefficient of x), what is a?

P Q14 In the expansion of $(2 + \mu x)^8$, where μ is a constant, the coefficient of x^2 is 87 808. What are the possible values of μ?

E P Q15 Find the coefficient of x^2 in the expansion of $[(x + 2)^3(x + 3)^2]^2$. *[6 marks]*

7 Review Exercise

E P Q1 Find the value of n, given that $\frac{(n-4)!}{34 \times 35} = 33!$ *[2 marks]*

E P Q2 a) Given that $\binom{37}{33} = \frac{37!}{33!k!}$, write down the value of k. *[1 mark]*

b) In the expansion of $(1-x)^{37}$, the coefficient of x^{33} is p. Find the value of p. *[2 marks]*

Q3 Find the first 3 terms, in ascending powers of x, of the binomial expansion of:

a) $(1+x)^{40}$ b) $(1-x)^{20}$ c) $(1+3x)^{20}$ d) $(2+3x)^{10}$

P Q4 a) Find the first 5 terms, in ascending powers of x, of the expansion of $(1+ax)^8$, where a is a non-zero constant.

b) Given that the coefficient of x^2 in this expansion is double the coefficient of x^3, find the value of a and the coefficient of x.

E P Q5 The coefficient of x^2 in the binomial expansion of $(1-3x)^n$ is 495.
Find the value of n. *[4 marks]*

Q6 a) Find the first 4 terms of the expansion of $\left(1+\frac{x}{3}\right)^9$ in ascending powers of x, giving each term in its simplest form.

b) Use your expansion to estimate the value of $(1.003)^9$ to 6 decimal places.

E P Q7 a) Find the first 3 terms in ascending powers of x in the expansion of $(1+x)^{12}$. *[1 mark]*

b) Hence obtain an approximation, to 5 significant figures, for the value of 1.02^{12}. *[2 marks]*

The percentage error of an approximation can be calculated using this formula:

$$\frac{\text{True value} - \text{Approximate value}}{\text{True Value}} \times 100$$

c) Use a calculator and the given formula to show that the percentage error of the estimate obtained in b) is approximately 0.15%. *[1 mark]*

Q8 Use the terms up to x^3 of the binomial expansion of $(1-3x)^8$ to approximate the value of 0.97^8 to 3 decimal places.

P Q9 a) Find the first 5 terms, in ascending powers of x, of the expansion of $(1+x)^{15}$.

b) Explain why this would not give an accurate estimate of the value of 2.01^{15}.

E P Q10 The coefficient of x^4 in the expansion of $(1+ax)^5$ is equal to the coefficient of x^2 in the expansion of $(1+ax)^9$. Given that $a \neq 0$, find the possible values of a. *[3 marks]*

E Q11 Simplify the expression $(1 + 4x)^2 + (1 - 3x)^4$.
Write your answer in ascending powers of x. *[3 marks]*

E Q12 a) Expand $\left(1 + \frac{3}{4}x\right)^{17}$ in ascending powers of x, up to and including the term in x^3. *[3 marks]*
b) Use your answer to part a) to find an approximation for the value of 1.075^{17}.
Write down all the digits in your answer. *[2 marks]*
c) Explain, with suitable justification, whether your approximation is an underestimate or overestimate of the true value of 1.075^{17}. *[1 mark]*

E P Q13 The coefficient of x^3 in the expansion of $(1 + kx)^8$ is a.
Given that $7 < a < 189$, find the range of possible values of k. *[3 marks]*

E P M Q14 A water tank is leaking at a rate of P% of the remaining volume per minute.
The volume, V m^3, of water in the tank n minutes after the tank starts to leak is modelled by the equation $V = 5\left(1 - \frac{P}{100}\right)^n$.
a) What is the initial volume of water in the tank? *[1 mark]*
b) Find an expression for V corresponding to the time 12 minutes after the leak first appears. Use the terms up to and including P^2 in your expansion. *[2 marks]*
c) Each minute, 1% of the water in the tank leaks out. Use your answer to part b) to find an estimate of the volume of water in the tank after 12 minutes. *[2 marks]*

P Q15 Find the coefficient of x^2 in the following binomial expansions:

a) $(4 + 2x)^5$ b) $(2 - 5x)^8$ c) $2x\left(1 + \frac{1}{2}x\right)^7$ d) $(5 + x)(3x - 1)^9$

Q16 Find the first 3 terms, in ascending powers of x, of the binomial expansion of $(4 - 5x)^7$.
Give each term in its simplest form.

E Q17 Expand $(x - x^{-1})^3$, fully simplifying each term in your answer. *[4 marks]*

Q18 Use the terms up to x^3 of the expansion of $(3 - 2x)^7$ to give an approximate value to 2 d.p. of:
a) 2.998^7 b) 2.8^7 c) 2.94^7 d) 3.002^7

Q19 a) Approximate the value of 2.5^6 using the terms up to x^3 of the following expansions:
(i) $(2 + x)^6$ (ii) $(3 - x)^6$
b) Given that the actual value of 2.5^6 is 244.14 (2 d.p.), which expansion provides the better approximation?

P Q20 In the expansion of $(a + 3x)^8$, the coefficient of x^2 is $\frac{32}{27}$ times bigger than the coefficient of x^5. What is the value of a?

E P **Q21** a) Fully expand $(3x + 4)^3$. *[4 marks]*

b) Hence find the only solution to the equation $27x^3 + 108x^2 + 144x + 56 = 0$. *[3 marks]*

E **Q22** a) Find the first 3 terms in the expansion of $(2 + x)^9$. *[3 marks]*

b) Use your answer to part a) to find an approximation for 2.01^9. Write down all the digits in your answer. *[2 marks]*

c) Explain how you could find a better approximation of 2.01^9 using the expansion of $(2 + x)^9$. *[1 mark]*

E P **Q23** a) Find the full expansion of $(x^2 + 2)^6$. *[4 marks]*

b) Using your answer from part a), find the full expansion of $\left(1 + \frac{2}{x^2}\right)^6$. *[2 marks]*

E P **Q24** a) Find the first 3 terms, in ascending powers of x, of the expansion of $(2 - 5x)^7$. *[4 marks]*

b) Use your answer to part a) with the value $x = 0.01$ to find an approximation for 0.195^7. Write down all the digits in your answer. *[2 marks]*

P **Q25** a) Find the first 4 terms, in ascending powers of x, of the binomial expansion of $\left(\frac{x}{3} - 2\right)^6$.

b) Given that terms in x^3 or higher powers can be ignored, find an approximation of:

(i) $4x\left(\frac{x}{3} - 2\right)^6$ (ii) $(3 - x)\left(\frac{x}{3} - 2\right)^6$ (iii) $\left(\frac{x}{3} - 2\right)^6(x + 1)^{16}$

E P **Q26** a) Find the first 3 terms in the expansion of $(1 - 2x)^{11}$. *[3 marks]*

The expansion of $(2 + x)^{10}$ in ascending powers of x up to the term in x^2 is $1024 + 5120x + 11\,520x^2$.

b) Find the expansion of $(1 - 2x)^{11}(2 + x)^{10}$ up to the term in x^2. *[3 marks]*

c) Use your answer to part b) to estimate the value of $2.001^{10} \times 0.998^{11}$ to 4 d.p. *[2 marks]*

E P **Q27** a) Expand $(2 + 7x)^7$, in ascending powers of x, up to and including the term in x^2. *[3 marks]*

b) Use your answer to part a) to find an approximation for the value of 2.035^7. Write down all the digits in your answer. *[2 marks]*

c) Explain why the expansion from part a) would not be suitable to use to find an approximation for the value of 10.4^7. *[1 mark]*

Challenge

P **Q28** Show that:

a) $(7!)^8 < (8!)^7$

b) ${}^{15}C_5 \times {}^{10}C_4 \times {}^{6}C_3 \times {}^{3}C_2 \times {}^{1}C_1 = \frac{15!}{5! \times 4! \times 3! \times 2! \times 1!}$

c) $\binom{n}{2} + \binom{n-1}{2}$ is a square number for integers $n \geq 2$.

P Q29 a) Without using a calculator, find the values of:

(i) $\binom{10}{7}$ (ii) $^{12}C_3$ (iii) $\frac{8!}{5! \times 3!}$

b) Write $\frac{13!}{9!4!} + \frac{13!}{10!3!} + \frac{14!}{11!3!}$ in the form $\binom{n}{r}$ where n and r are positive integers.

E P Q30 a) Find the first three terms, in ascending powers of x, in the binomial expansion of $\left(1 - \frac{x}{2}\right)^8$. Give each term in its simplest form. *[3 marks]*

The function f is defined by $f(x) = \left(1 - \frac{x}{2}\right)^8 (p + qx)$, where p and q are constants.

b) In the binomial expansion of $f(x)$, the x term has coefficient –26 and the x^2 term has coefficient 50. Find the values of p and q. *[6 marks]*

P Q31 a) Find the first 3 terms, in ascending powers of x, of the binomial expansion of $(2 + kx)^{13}$, where k is a non-zero constant.

b) Given that the coefficient of x in this expansion is $\frac{1}{6}$ of the coefficient of x^2, find the value of k.

P Q32 a) The binomial expansion of $a(bx + c)^3$ is $108x^3 - 216x^2 + 144x - 32$, where a, b and c are integers and $a > 0$. Find the values of a, b and c.

b) Hence or otherwise, completely factorise $108x^3 - 216x^2 + 117x - 14$.

E P Q33 a) Expand $(5 + 2x)^4$ in ascending powers of x. *[4 marks]*

b) Hence or otherwise expand $(5 - 2x)^4$ in ascending powers of x. *[2 marks]*

c) Hence show that $(5 + 2\sqrt{3})^4 + (5 - 2\sqrt{3})^4$ is an integer and state its value. *[3 marks]*

E P Q34 a) Fully expand $\left(2 + \frac{1}{2}x\right)^5$. *[4 marks]*

b) Hence describe the transformation that would transform the graph of $y = \left(2 + \frac{1}{2}x\right)^5$ into the graph of $y = \frac{1}{32}x(1280 + 640x + 160x^2 + 20x^3 + x^4)$. *[2 marks]*

E P Q35 a) Find the expansion of $(2 - 3x)^4$. *[4 marks]*

b) Without further calculation, state the expansion of $(2 + 3x)^4$. *[1 mark]*

c) Use your answers to parts a) and b) to find the value of $\sqrt{(2 + 3\sqrt{2})^4 + (2 - 3\sqrt{2})^4 + 56}$. *[3 marks]*

P Q36 a) Expand $(2 + x)^3$ in ascending powers of x.

b) Hence show that $(2 + \sqrt{3})^3 = a + b\sqrt{3}$, where a and b are integers to be found.

c) Use your answer to part b) to find the exact value of $\left(\frac{702 + 405\sqrt{3}}{125}\right)^{\frac{2}{3}}$, giving your answer in the form $p + q\sqrt{3}$, where p and q are rational numbers.

7 Chapter Summary

1 A binomial expansion is what you get when you multiply out the brackets of a polynomial with two terms, e.g. $(a + b)^n$.

2 The $(n + 1)^{\text{th}}$ row of Pascal's triangle gives the coefficients for the binomial expansion of $(1 + x)^n$. Each number in the triangle is the sum of the two above it.

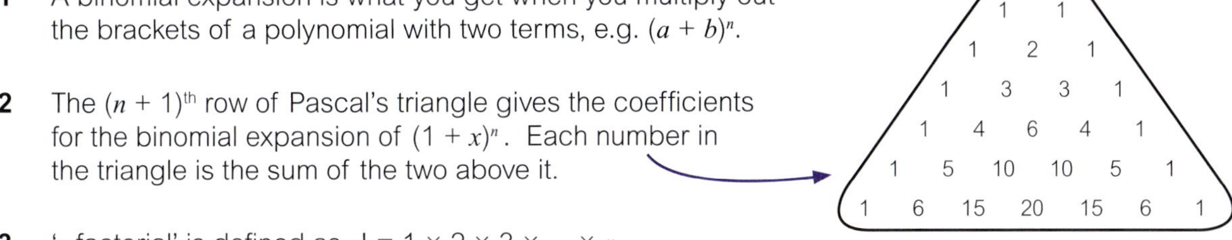

3 'r factorial' is defined as $r! = 1 \times 2 \times 3 \times \ldots \times r$.

4 'n choose r' is defined as ${}^nC_r = \binom{n}{r} = \dfrac{n!}{r!\,(n-r)!}$.

5 The binomial formula for the expansion of $(1 + x)^n$ is:

$$(1+x)^n = 1 + \frac{n}{1}x + \frac{n(n-1)}{1\times 2}x^2 + \frac{n(n-1)(n-2)}{1\times 2\times 3}x^3 + \ldots + x^n = 1 + \binom{n}{1}x + \binom{n}{2}x^2 + \binom{n}{3}x^3 + \ldots + x^n$$

6 When the coefficient of x in the binomial isn't 1, the binomial formula is:

$$(1+ax)^n = 1 + \binom{n}{1}(ax) + \binom{n}{2}(ax)^2 + \binom{n}{3}(ax)^3 + \ldots + (ax)^n$$

7 If the coefficient of x in the binomial is negative, then the signs in the expansion alternate between positive and negative for even and odd powers.

E.g. $(1-x)^n = 1 - \binom{n}{1}x + \binom{n}{2}x^2 - \binom{n}{3}x^3 + \ldots \pm x^n$

8 You can ignore the higher powers in a binomial expansion to approximate a number raised to a power, as long as the value of x used is much smaller than 1.

9 The binomial formula for the expansion of $(a + b)^n$ is:

$$(a+b)^n = a^n + \binom{n}{1}a^{n-1}b + \binom{n}{2}a^{n-2}b^2 + \ldots + \binom{n}{n-1}ab^{n-1} + b^n$$

Trigonometry

8

Learning Objectives

Once you've completed this chapter, you should be able to:

- Know the values of sin, cos and tan of 30°, 60° and 45°
- Use the unit circle to find values of sin and cos.
- Know and use the sine and cosine rules.
- Find the area of a triangle using the formula $\frac{1}{2}ab\sin C$.
- Know and use the trig identities $\tan\theta \equiv \frac{\sin\theta}{\cos\theta}$ and $\sin^2\theta + \cos^2\theta \equiv 1$.
- Sketch the graphs of $\sin x$, $\cos x$ and $\tan x$ and of common transformations.
- Solve trig equations by sketching a graph, using a CAST diagram, or using trigonometric identities.
- Solve trig equations of the form $\sin kx = n$ and $\sin(x + c) = n$.

Prior Knowledge Check

1 Find the values of a, b and c to 3 s.f. in the diagrams below:

a)

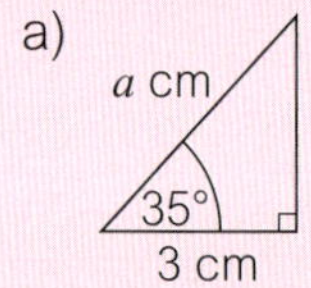

b) 6 cm, 28°, b cm

c) 5 cm, c°, 7 cm

see GCSE Maths

2 State whether or not the following are correct identities:

a) $b + a \equiv a + b$ b) $4y^2 - 2y + 3 \equiv 0$ c) $x^2 - 16 \equiv (x + 4)(x - 4)$ see page 7

3 $f(x) = x^3 + 6x^2 - x - 30$ has roots at $x = -5$, $x = -3$ and $x = 2$.
Use this information to sketch the graph of $y = f(x)$. see page 123

8.1 Trig Values from Triangles

You need to know the values of **sin**, **cos** and **tan** at 30°, 60° and 45°, and there are two **triangles** that can help you remember them. It may seem like a long-winded way of doing it, but once you know how to do it, you'll always be able to work them out — even without a calculator.

The idea is you draw the triangles below, putting in their angles and side lengths. Then you can use them to work out special trig values like **sin 45°** or **cos 60°** with exact values instead of the decimals given by calculators.

First, make sure you can remember SOHCAHTOA:

$$\sin = \frac{\text{opp}}{\text{hyp}} \qquad \cos = \frac{\text{adj}}{\text{hyp}} \qquad \tan = \frac{\text{opp}}{\text{adj}}$$

These are the two triangles that you'll use:

Half an equilateral triangle with sides of length 2:

Splitting the equilateral triangle in half creates a right-angled triangle with angles of **90°**, **60°** and 60° ÷ 2 = **30°**.

You can work out the height using Pythagoras' theorem: height = $\sqrt{2^2 - 1^2} = \sqrt{3}$.

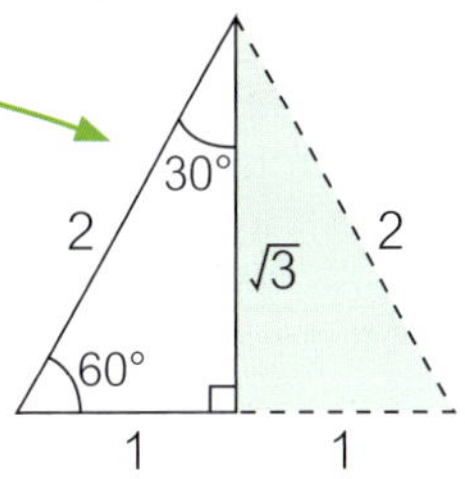

Then you can use the triangle and SOHCAHTOA to work out sin, cos and tan of 30° and 60°.

$$\sin 30° = \frac{1}{2} \qquad \cos 30° = \frac{\sqrt{3}}{2} \qquad \tan 30° = \frac{1}{\sqrt{3}}$$

$$\sin 60° = \frac{\sqrt{3}}{2} \qquad \cos 60° = \frac{1}{2} \qquad \tan 60° = \sqrt{3}$$

Right-angled triangle with two sides of length 1:

The triangle is isosceles so you know the other two angles are (180° – 90°) ÷ 2 = **45°**.

You can work out the hypotenuse using Pythagoras' theorem: hypotenuse = $\sqrt{1^2 + 1^2} = \sqrt{2}$.

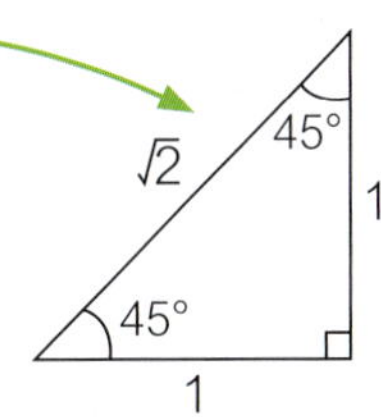

Then you can use the triangle and SOHCAHTOA to work out sin, cos and tan of 45°.

$$\sin 45° = \frac{1}{\sqrt{2}} \qquad \cos 45° = \frac{1}{\sqrt{2}} \qquad \tan 45° = 1$$

8.2 Trig Values from the Unit Circle

You can also find trig values from the **unit circle** — a circle with **radius 1**, centred on the **origin**. Take a point on the unit circle and make a right-angled triangle:

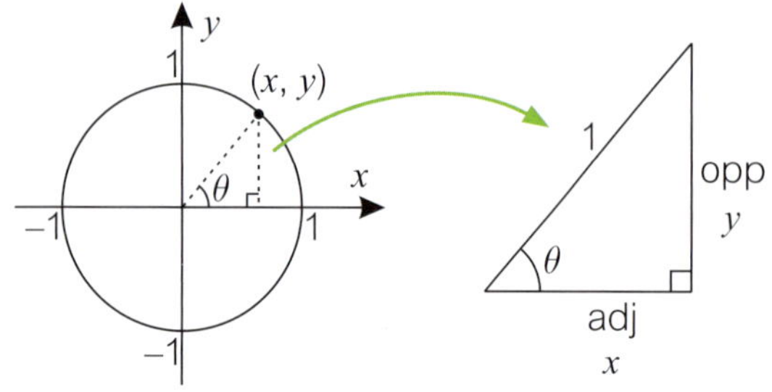

The hypotenuse is always the radius — so it's always 1. From this you know that:

$\sin\theta = \frac{\text{opp}}{1} = \text{opp} = y$

$\cos\theta = \frac{\text{adj}}{1} = \text{adj} = x$

So on the unit circle, the y-coordinate is **sin θ** and the x-coordinate is **cos θ**.

For any point on the unit circle, the coordinates are $(\cos\theta, \sin\theta)$, where θ is the angle measured from the **positive** x-axis in an **anticlockwise** direction.

This is true for **all** values of θ, including values greater than 90°.

You can use the unit circle to easily find sin and cos of **0°** and **90°** — they're just **points** on the **axes**. E.g. at point (0, 1), cos 90° = 0 and sin 90° = 1.

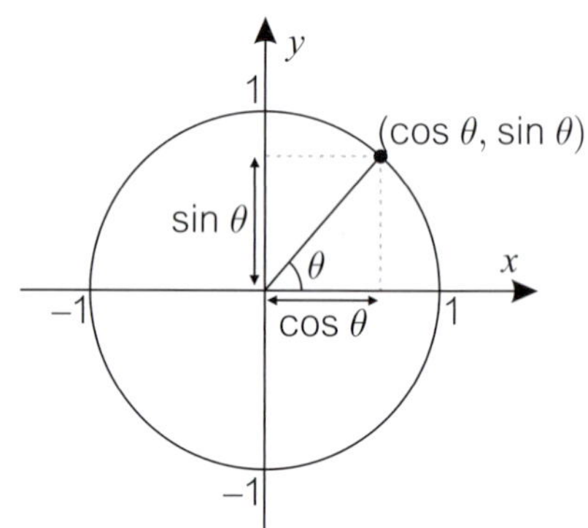

Example 1

The coordinates of a point on the unit circle, given to 3 s.f., are shown on the diagram to the right. Find θ to the nearest degree.

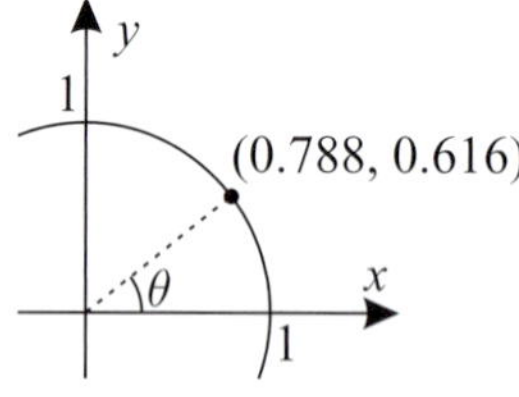

So $\cos\theta = 0.788$ and $\sin\theta = 0.616$ ← The point is on the unit circle, so you know that the coordinates are $(\cos\theta, \sin\theta)$.

$\cos\theta = 0.788$

$\Rightarrow \theta = \cos^{-1}(0.788) = 38°$ (to the nearest degree) ← You only need one of these to find the value of θ.

Example 2

Find the coordinates of the point A on the unit circle, shown on the diagram to the right. Give your answer to 2 d.p.

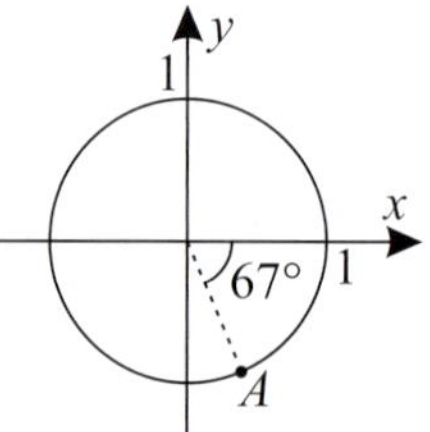

$360° - 67° = 293°$ ← You need the angle from the positive x-axis in an **anticlockwise** direction.

$x = \cos 293° = 0.3907...$,

and $y = \sin 293° = -0.9205...$

So the coordinates of A are $(0.39, -0.92)$ to 2 d.p. ← Work out the x and y-coordinates of A.

8.3 The Sine Rule

There are three useful formulas you need to know for working out information about a triangle. There are **two** for finding the **angles** and **sides** (called the **sine rule** and **cosine rule**) and one for finding the **area**. These rules work on **any** triangle, not just right-angled triangles.

To decide which rule to use, look at what you know about the triangle.

The sine rule is given by the formula: $\frac{a}{\sin A} = \frac{b}{\sin B} = \frac{c}{\sin C}$

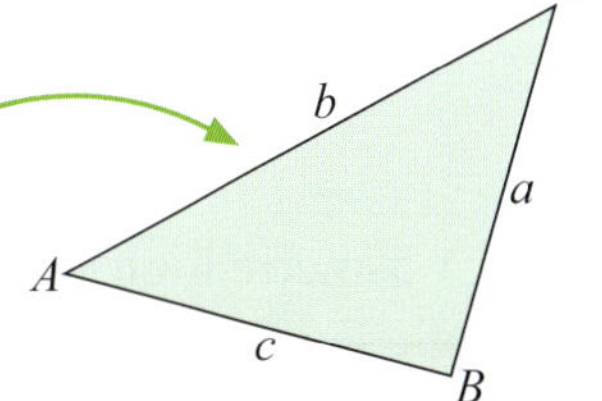

where a, b and c are the lengths of the sides, and A, B and C are the angles opposite the sides with the same letters (so angle C is opposite side c).

You can use any **two** bits of the sine rule to make a **normal equation** with just one '=' sign.

The sine rule also works if you flip all the fractions **upside down**: $\frac{\sin A}{a} = \frac{\sin B}{b} = \frac{\sin C}{c}$

You can use the **sine rule** if:

You know **any two angles** and a **side**.

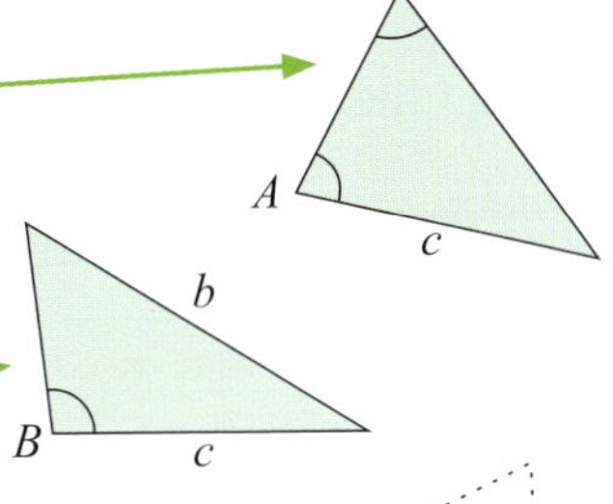

You can **sometimes** use the **sine rule** if:

You know **two sides** and an **angle that isn't between them**.

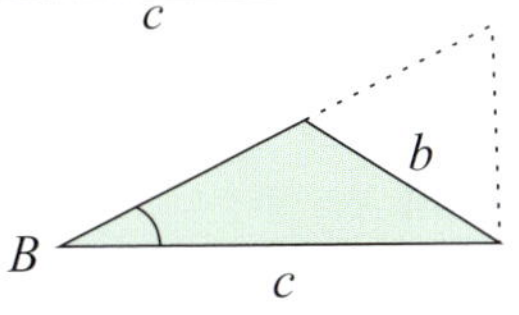

Tip A calculator will give you an acute angle for $\sin^{-1}(\theta)$, but sometimes there's an obtuse angle that also works — see p.195-200 for more on this.

This doesn't always work though — sometimes there are **2 possible** triangles:

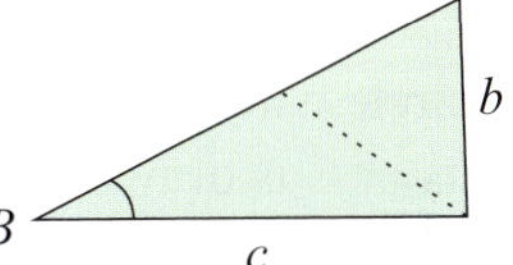

Example 1 P

Find the missing sides and angles for ΔABC, in which $A = 40°$, $a = 27$ m and $B = 73°$.

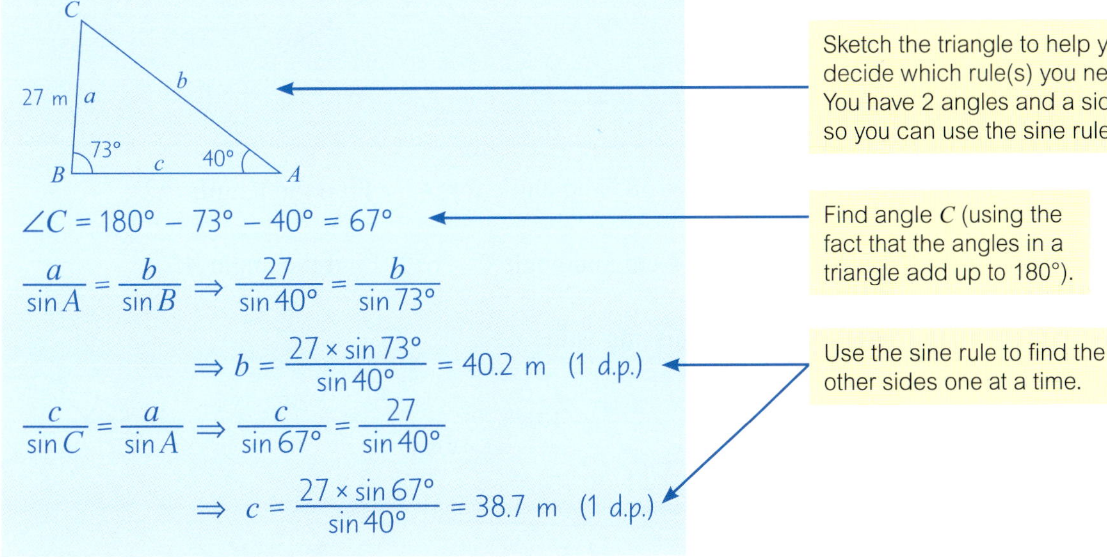

Sketch the triangle to help you decide which rule(s) you need. You have 2 angles and a side, so you can use the sine rule.

$\angle C = 180° - 73° - 40° = 67°$

Find angle C (using the fact that the angles in a triangle add up to 180°).

$\frac{a}{\sin A} = \frac{b}{\sin B} \Rightarrow \frac{27}{\sin 40°} = \frac{b}{\sin 73°}$

$\Rightarrow b = \frac{27 \times \sin 73°}{\sin 40°} = 40.2 \text{ m} \quad (1 \text{ d.p.})$

$\frac{c}{\sin C} = \frac{a}{\sin A} \Rightarrow \frac{c}{\sin 67°} = \frac{27}{\sin 40°}$

$\Rightarrow c = \frac{27 \times \sin 67°}{\sin 40°} = 38.7 \text{ m} \quad (1 \text{ d.p.})$

Use the sine rule to find the other sides one at a time.

Exercise 8.1-8.3

Give all answers to 3 significant figures unless otherwise stated.

Q1 Find the coordinates of points P, Q and R on the unit circle.

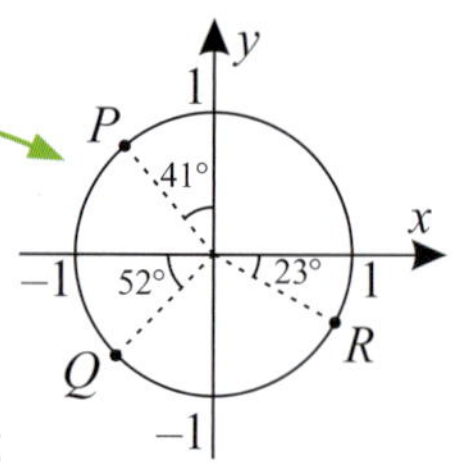

Q2 The sketch on the left shows a point S on the unit circle.
Find the value of θ in degrees when the coordinates of S are:

a) (0.899, 0.438) b) (0.669, 0.743) c) (0.089, 0.996)

E M Q3 A 5-metre high vertical pole, OP, is erected in one corner of a level rectangular playground, $OABC$, with sides of length 15 m and 12 m respectively, as in the diagram.

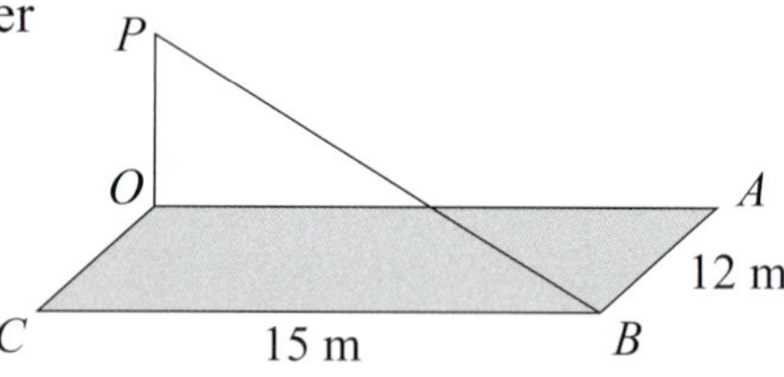

One end of a taut rope is fastened to the top of the pole at P and the other end is fastened to the opposite corner of the playground at B.

Find the size of the angle OPB that the rope makes with the pole. *[3 marks]*

E P Q4 Given that x is an acute angle and $\sin x = \frac{5}{9}$, find the exact values of:

a) $\cos x$ *[2 marks]*

b) $\tan x$ *[1 mark]*

E P Q5 C is a circle with radius 6 and centre O. AB is a chord of the circle C of length 8.5. A radius of C is drawn to the point A.

a) Find the size of angle OAB. *[2 marks]*

b) Find the shortest distance (to 1 d.p.) from the centre of the circle to the chord. *[1 mark]*

Q6 Use the sine rule to find the length TW.

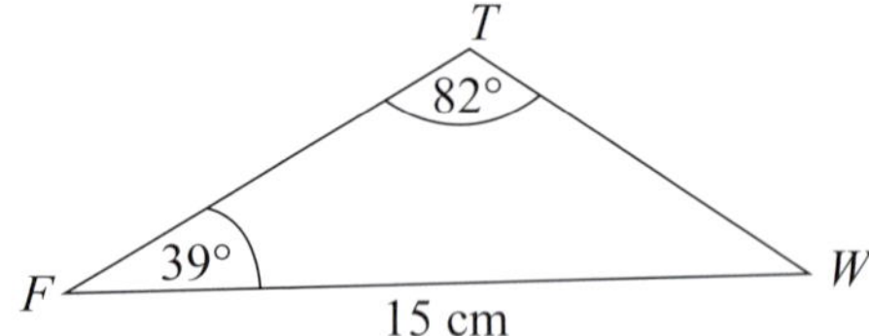

P Q7 In triangle PQR: $PR = 48$ m, angle $P = 38°$ and angle $R = 43°$. Find the length PQ.

P Q8 In triangle ABC: $AB = 17$ cm, $AC = 14$ cm and angle $C = 67°$. Find the angle A.

Q9 For the following triangles, find the missing value x.

a)

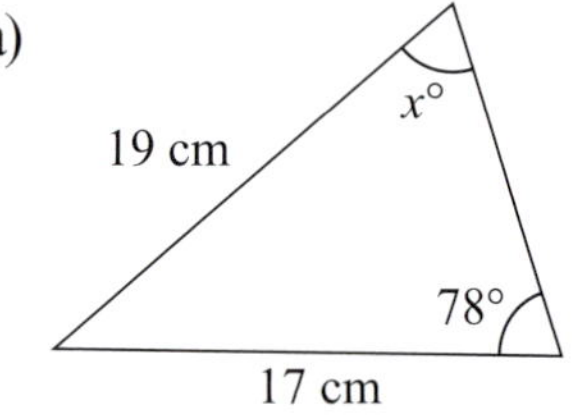

b)

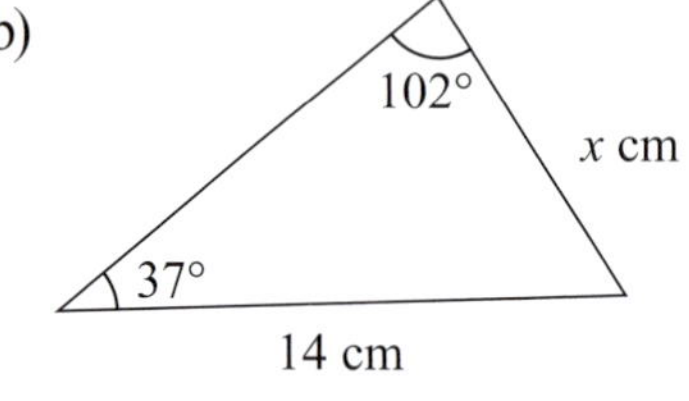

c)

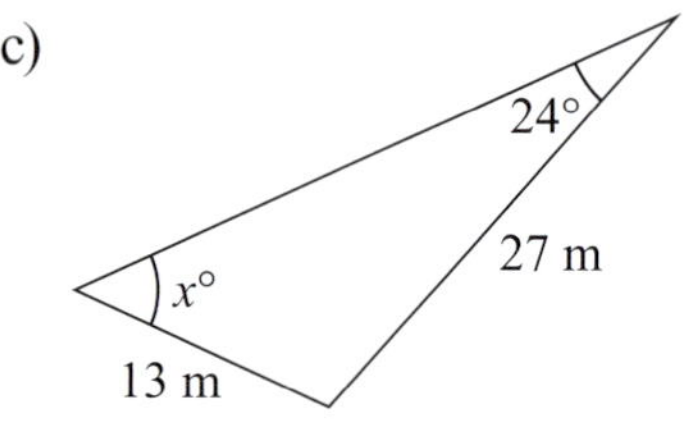

d) 38 m, 22°, x m, 29°

e) 71°, 6 mm, x°, 11 mm

f)

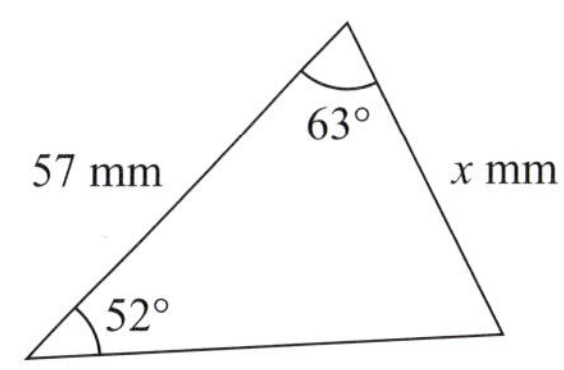

E P Q10 The diagram shows a trapezium $ABCD$ with parallel sides AD of length 6.3 cm and BC of length 11.2 cm. The angle BCD is 42°.

A line is drawn joining the vertices A and C. Find the size of angle ACD.

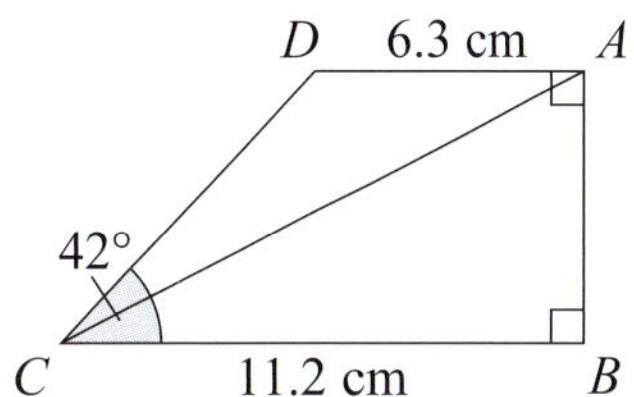

[4 marks]

P M Q11 A building has a wall that slopes inward at an angle of 81° to the horizontal ground. A safety inspector calculates that a ladder leaning against the outside of the wall must be at an angle of 78° to the ground. What distance up the wall would a 5 m ladder safely reach?

P M Q12 Two points, A and B, are both at sea level and on opposite sides of a mountain. The distance between them is 5 km. From A, the angle of elevation of the top of the mountain (M) is 21°, and from B, the angle of elevation is 17°.

a) Find the distance BM. b) Hence find the height of the mountain to the nearest metre.

E P Q13 Solve these simultaneous equations:

$2x \cos 30° + y \tan 45° = 2\sqrt{6}$ and $2x \sin 45° - 4y \sin 60° = 2 - 6\sqrt{2}$ *[4 marks]*

Challenge

E P Q14

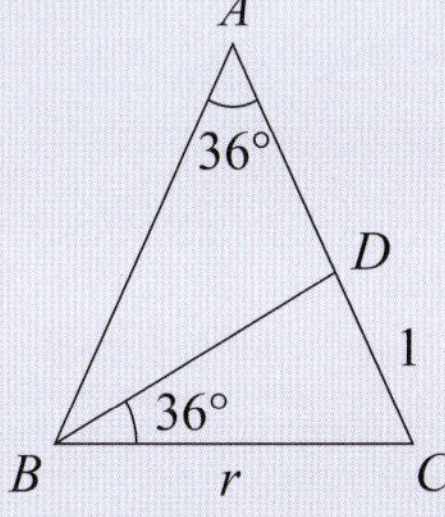

ABC is an isosceles triangle with AB and AC of equal lengths, base BC of length r and vertex angle BAC equal to 36°. A line is drawn through B meeting AC at D such that $\angle DBC = 36°$ and the length of DC is 1, as shown in the diagram.

a) Show that the length of AD is equal to r. *[2 marks]*

b) Show that:

(i) $\sin 18° = \dfrac{r}{2(r+1)}$ (ii) $\sin 18° = \dfrac{1}{2r}$ *[4 marks]*

c) Hence, show that $r^2 - r - 1 = 0$. *[2 marks]*

d) Hence or otherwise find the exact value of sin 18°. *[3 marks]*

E P M Q15 A small plane takes off on a bearing of 135° from an airfield at the point O. After travelling in a straight line the plane reaches the point P and changes direction to fly on a bearing of 020° for 15 km to arrive at a point Q. The distance of Q from O is 23.2 km.

a) Determine the bearing, to 1 decimal place, that the plane must fly along to return to O from Q. *[4 marks]*

b) Find the distance OP. *[2 marks]*

8.4 The Cosine Rule

The cosine rule is given by the formula: $a^2 = b^2 + c^2 - 2bc\cos A$

You can use the **cosine rule** if:

You know **all three** sides...

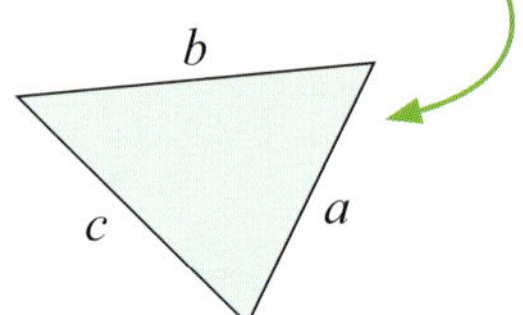

...or you know **two sides** and the **angle** that's **between** them.

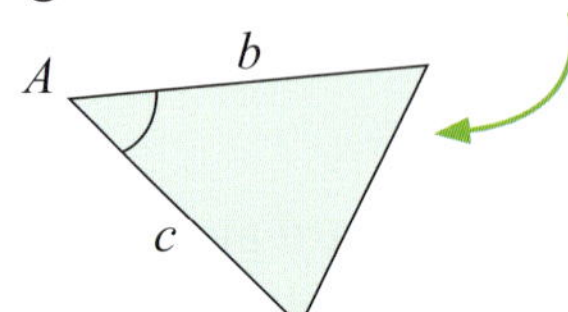

Tip To find the missing side when you're given two sides and the angle between them, substitute the values into the form of the formula at the top of this page and take the positive square root.

You can also find an angle by **rearranging** the cosine rule into the **form**:

$$\cos A = \frac{b^2 + c^2 - a^2}{2bc}$$

When you're given **three sides**, you can find all **three angles**. You don't need to know whether they will be **acute** or **obtuse**, as the **cosine rule** will always give the right answer for this (the **sine rule** will always give you an **acute** angle).

Example 1

Find the values of X, Y and Z in the triangle on the right.

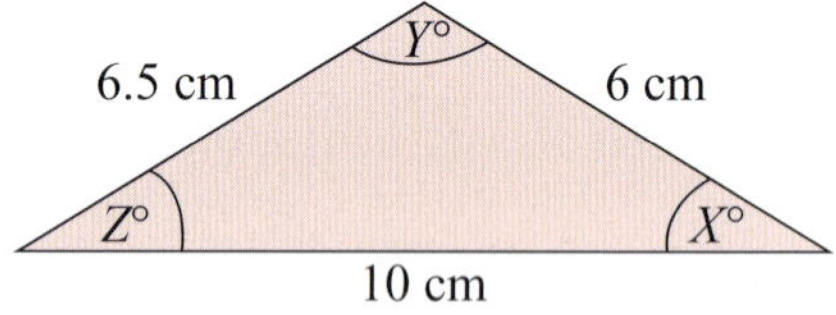

$$a^2 = b^2 + c^2 - 2bc\cos A$$

$$\Rightarrow \cos A = \frac{b^2 + c^2 - a^2}{2bc}$$

You've been given all three sides but none of the angles, so pick one of them to start with. Find it using the rearranged form of the formula.

$$\Rightarrow \cos Y = \frac{6^2 + 6.5^2 - 10^2}{2 \times 6 \times 6.5} = -0.278...$$

$$\Rightarrow Y = 106.191... = 106.2° \text{ (1 d.p.)}$$

$$\cos Z = \frac{10^2 + 6.5^2 - 6^2}{2 \times 10 \times 6.5} = 0.817...$$

Use the cosine rule again to find the value of another angle. It doesn't matter which one you go for next (using Z here).

$$\Rightarrow Z = 35.183...° = 35.2° \text{ (1 d.p.)}$$

$$X = 180° - 106.191...° - 35.183...° = 38.624...° = 38.6° \text{ (1 d.p.)}$$

Now that you have two of the angles, you can find the other by subtracting them from 180°.

Exercise 8.4

Give all answers to 3 significant figures unless otherwise stated.

Q1 Use the cosine rule to find the length QR.

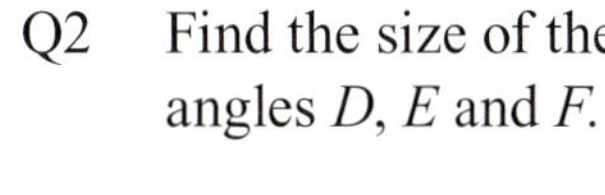

Q2 Find the size of the angles D, E and F.

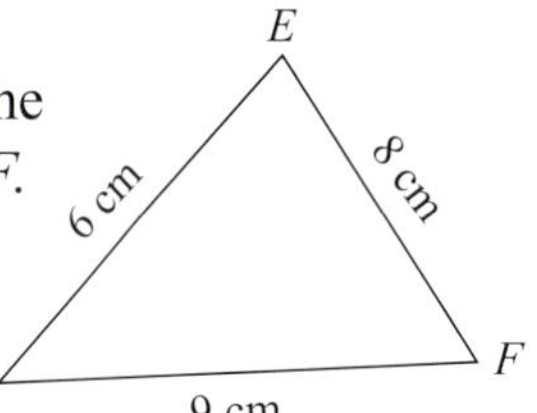

Q3 For the following triangles, find the missing value x.

a)

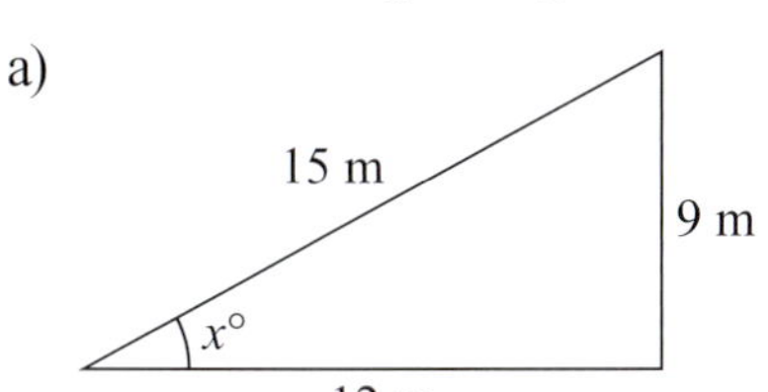

b)

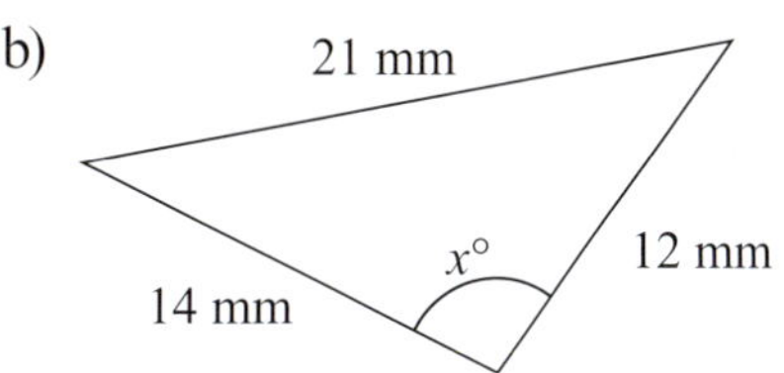

c)

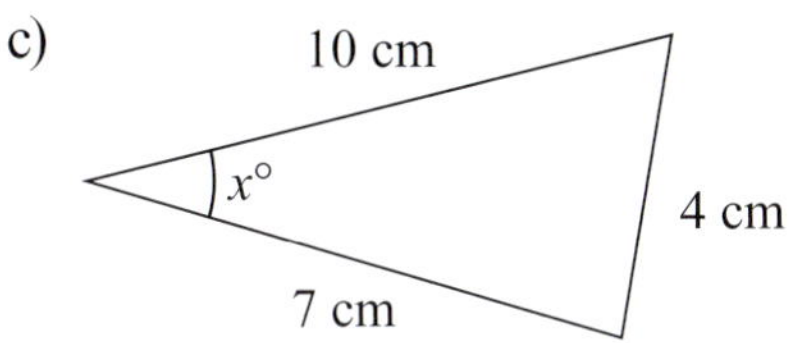

d)

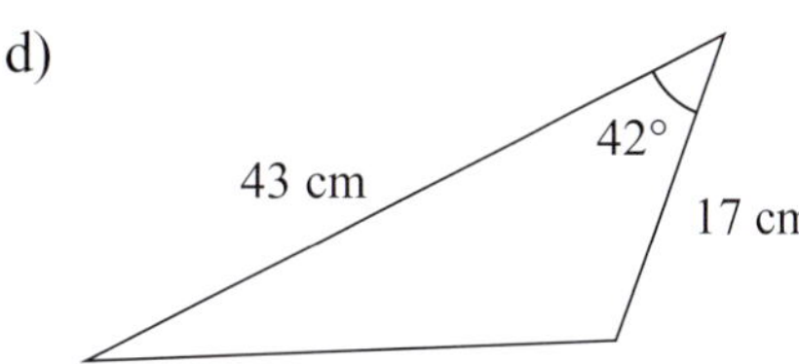

e)

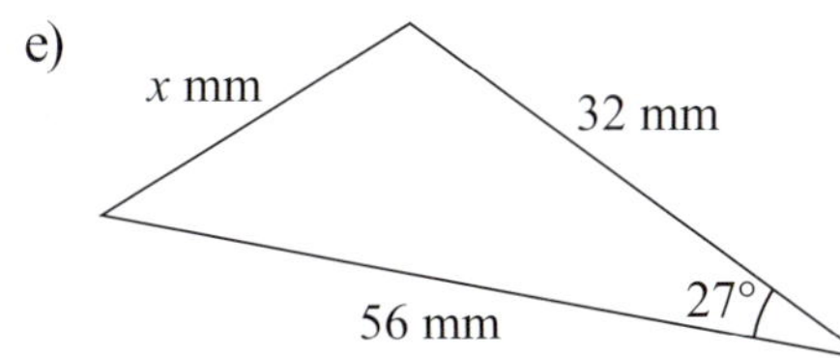

f)

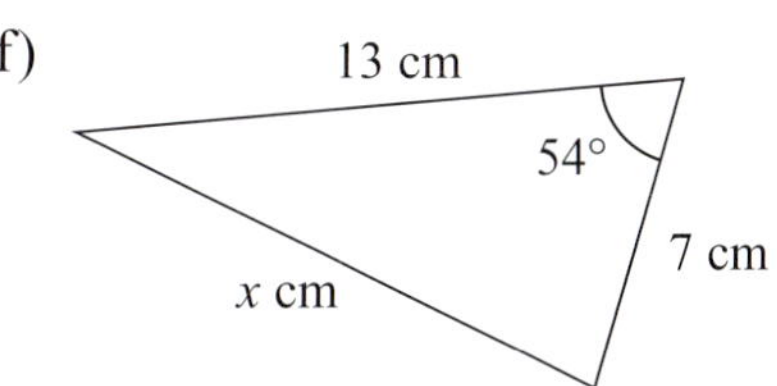

Q4 In triangle JKL: $JL = 24$ cm, $KL = 29$ cm and angle $L = 62°$. Find the length JK.

Q5 In triangle ABC: $AB = 32$ cm, $AC = 28$ cm and angle $A = 48°$. Find the length BC.

P Q6 In triangle DEF:
$DE = 8$ cm, $EF = 11$ cm and $DF = 16$ cm.
Find the smallest angle.

P Q7 In triangle PQR:
$PQ = 7.6$ mm, $QR = 6.8$ mm and $PR = 5.9$ mm.
Find the largest angle.

Q6-7 Problem Solving

Sketching the triangle will make it easier to see which angle you need to find — the smallest angle is opposite the shortest side and the largest angle is opposite the longest side.

E P Q8 A line segment with endpoints A and B has a length of 8.2 cm.
A circle C_1 with radius 5.2 cm is centred at A and a second circle C_2 with radius 4.3 cm is centred at B. The circles intersect at two points, one of which is P.
Find the size of the angle APB to 1 decimal place. *[3 marks]*

P Q9 The vertices of triangle XYZ have coordinates X: (–2, 2), Y: (5, 8) and Z: (3, –2). Find the angle XYZ.

E Q10 A triangle ABC has sides AB and AC of lengths $(2+\sqrt{3})$ m and $(2-\sqrt{3})$ m respectively, and the angle BAC is 60°. Find the exact length of the side BC. Show all of your working. *[3 marks]*

E Q11 $ABCD$ is a parallelogram with AB parallel to DC and BC parallel to AD.
The lengths of AB and BC are 6.3 cm and 14.1 cm respectively.
The length of the diagonal AC is 9.7 cm.
Find the length of the diagonal BD to 1 decimal place. *[4 marks]*

E P M Q12 Two strings, p and q, each have one of their ends attached to the mass M. The other ends of p and q are attached to the points A and B respectively, on the horizontal ceiling of a room, so that the mass, M, is suspended from the ceiling by p and q, and AMB forms a triangle.

The points A and B are 2 m apart and the lengths of p and q are 1.20 m and 1.45 m respectively.

a) Find the angle between the two strings. *[2 marks]*

Some time later it is found that the string q has stretched but the length of p remains unchanged. The angle BAM is found to be 50°

b) Determine the change in the length, in cm, of q. *[2 marks]*

Challenge

P Q13 A triangle ABC has sides $AB = (x - 1)$, $BC = 2x$ and angle $B = 60°$.

a) Given that side $AC = \sqrt{13}$, find the value of x.

b) Find the size of the smallest angle in the triangle ABC.

E P Q14 The diagram below shows a triangle ABC and a point, O, inside the triangle.
Lines are drawn from O to each of the vertices of the triangle.

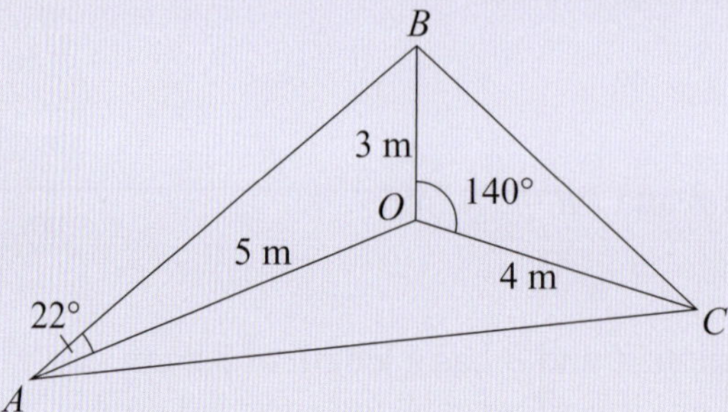

Using the information in the diagram, find the perimeter of the triangle ABC. *[5 marks]*

8.5 More Trig Rules

You can use trigonometry to find the area of any triangle, using the formula: **Area = $\frac{1}{2}ab \sin C$**

Example 1

Find the area of the triangle ABC, where AB = 12 cm, BC = 19 cm and angle B = 59°.

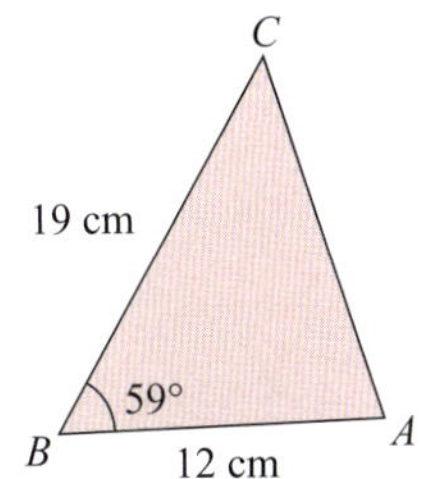

Area of $\Delta ABC = \frac{1}{2}ab \sin C = \frac{1}{2} \times 12 \times 19 \times \sin 59°$ ← Use the formula for area.

$= 97.7 \text{ cm}^2$ (1 d.p.)

You can find the areas of more **complicated** shapes by dividing them into **triangles**, then using the **sine** and **cosine rules** on each individual triangle. You might need to use more than one rule, or use a rule multiple times.

This method can be used for working out angles and sides in real-life problems, such as calculating distances travelled or areas covered. Sometimes you'll see a problem that uses **bearings**.

Example 2  

Rasmus the trawlerman has cast his nets between buoys in the North Sea (shown on the diagram).

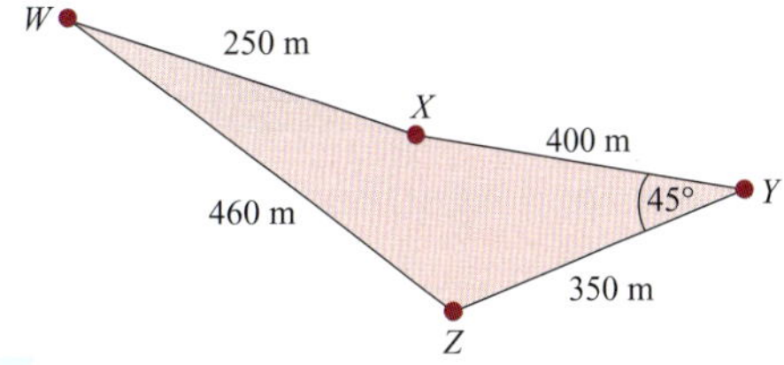

a) Find the area of sea his nets cover to 2 s.f.

$a^2 = b^2 + c^2 - 2bc \cos A$

$\Rightarrow y^2 = 400^2 + 350^2 - 2 \times 400 \times 350 \times \cos 45°$ ← Find the distance between X and Z (let's call it y) — this will split the area into 2 triangles. Do this by treating XYZ as a triangle and using the cosine rule.

$= 84\,510.1...$

$\Rightarrow y = 290.7$ m (1 d.p.)

$\cos A = \frac{b^2 + c^2 - a^2}{2bc}$

$\Rightarrow \cos W = \frac{460^2 + 250^2 - 290.70...^2}{2 \times 460 \times 250} = 0.824...$ ← Now you have all three sides for the left-hand triangle, so you can find an angle (let's say W) using the rearranged form of the cosine rule.

$\Rightarrow W = 34.5°$ (1 d.p.)

WXZ (left): $A = \frac{1}{2}ab \sin C$

$= \frac{1}{2} \times 250 \times 460 \times \sin 34.48...°$ ← You have enough information to find the area of each triangle with the formula above.

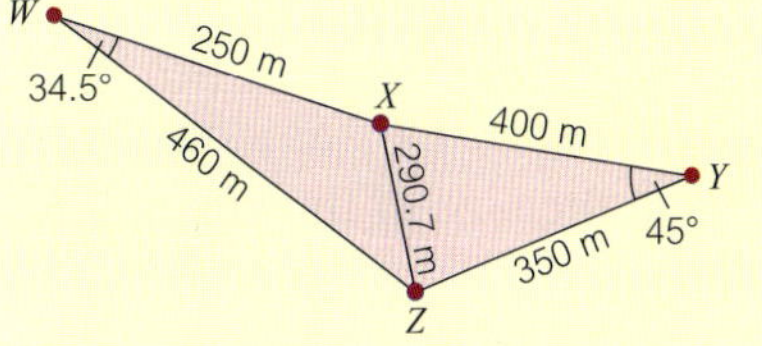

$= 32\,600 \text{ m}^2$ (3 s.f.)

XYZ (right): $A = \frac{1}{2}ab \sin C$

$= \frac{1}{2} \times 400 \times 350 \times \sin 45°$

$= 49\,500 \text{ m}^2$ (3 s.f.)

$32\,600 + 49\,500 = 82\,000 \text{ m}^2$ (2 s.f.) ← Add them to get the total area covered.

b) If X is on a bearing of 100° from W, on what bearing does Rasmus have to sail to get from X to Y (to 3 s.f.)?

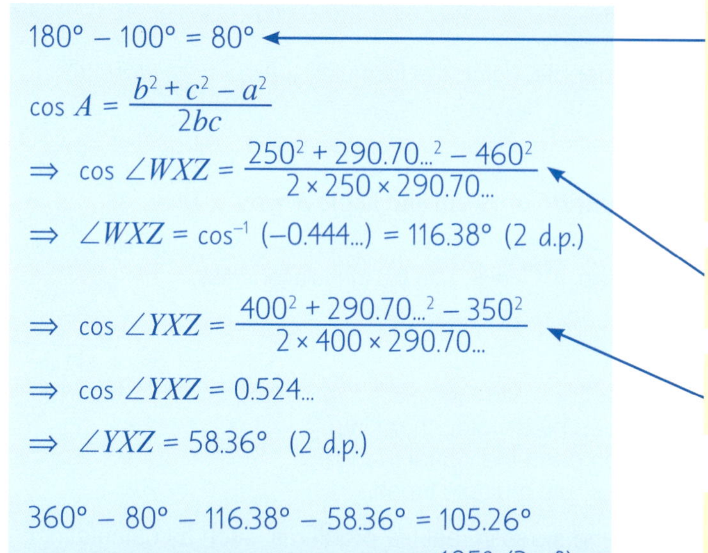

$180° - 100° = 80°$

$$\cos A = \frac{b^2 + c^2 - a^2}{2bc}$$

$$\Rightarrow \cos \angle WXZ = \frac{250^2 + 290.70...^2 - 460^2}{2 \times 250 \times 290.70...}$$

$$\Rightarrow \angle WXZ = \cos^{-1}(-0.444...) = 116.38° \text{ (2 d.p.)}$$

$$\Rightarrow \cos \angle YXZ = \frac{400^2 + 290.70...^2 - 350^2}{2 \times 400 \times 290.70...}$$

$$\Rightarrow \cos \angle YXZ = 0.524...$$

$$\Rightarrow \angle YXZ = 58.36° \text{ (2 d.p.)}$$

$$360° - 80° - 116.38° - 58.36° = 105.26°$$
$$= 105° \text{ (3 s.f.)}$$

Find all the other angles round X.

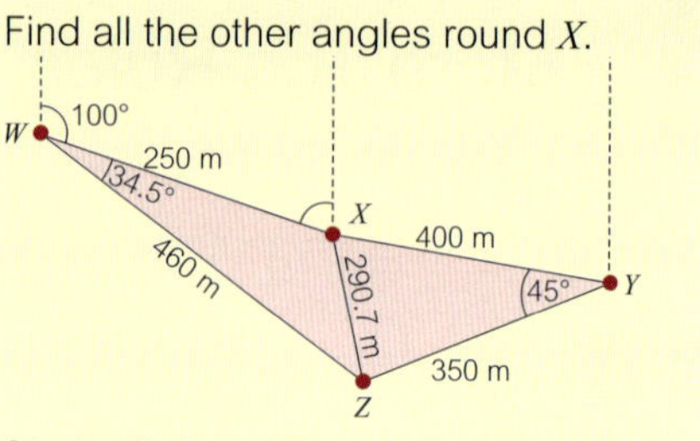

Start with the unknown that is marked.

To find the angle $\angle WXZ$, use the cosine rule on the left-hand triangle.

Then do the same for angle $\angle YXZ$, using the right-hand triangle.

Subtract all the angles from 360° to find the bearing Rasmus should sail on to get from X to Y.

Exercise 8.5

Give all answers to 3 significant figures unless otherwise stated.

Q1 Find the area of the following triangles.

a)

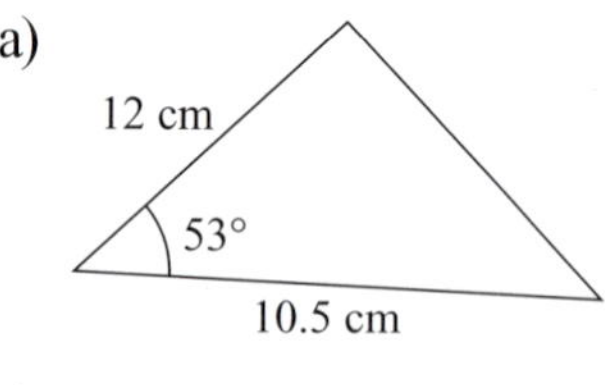

b)

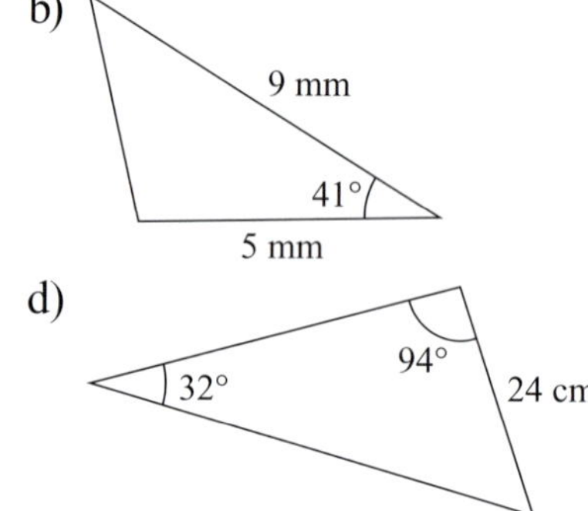

c) 5 cm, 4.2 cm, 7 cm

d) 32°, 94°, 24 cm

Q2 In triangle PQR: $PQ = 4$ cm, $QR = 7$ cm and angle $Q = 49°$. Find the area of triangle PQR.

P M Q3 A gardener places three pieces of rope, with lengths 1.9 m, 2.7 m and 2.9 m, end to end to rope off a triangle of land for a vegetable patch. What is the total area of land roped off?

Q4 A triangle JKL has sides $JL = 12$ cm and $KL = 8$ cm, and an area of 30 cm². Find the size of the angle JLK, giving your answer to 1 decimal place.

P Q5 A triangle ABC has a side $AC = 14$ cm and angles $\angle BAC = 35°$ and $\angle ABC = 52°$. Find the area of the triangle ABC.

P Q6 In ΔDEF: $DE = 7$ mm, $DF = 13$ mm and $EF = 16$ mm. Find the area of ΔDEF.

P M Q7 A ship sails 8 km on a bearing of 070°, and then changes direction to sail 10 km on a bearing of 030°.

a) Draw a diagram to represent the situation.

b) What is the ship's distance from its starting position?

c) On what bearing must it now sail to return to its starting position?

Q7 Hint Bearings are measured clockwise from the vertical (North).

P Q8 Find the area of the quadrilateral $ABCD$ shown on the right.

P Q9 a) Find the length of the line QS in the shape on the right.

b) Given that QST is a straight line, find the total area of the shape.

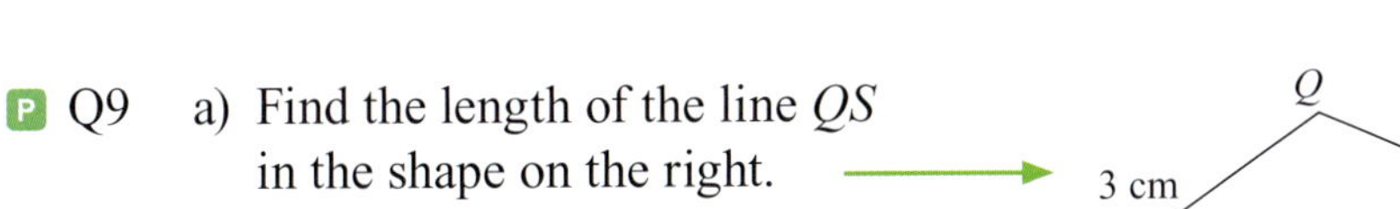

P Q10 Find the areas of the following shapes.

a)

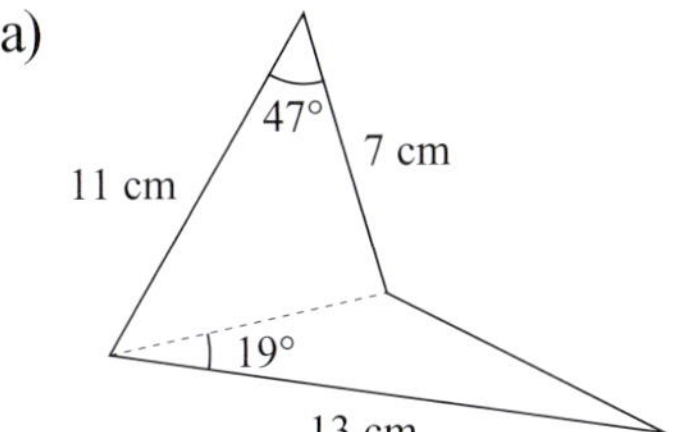

b)

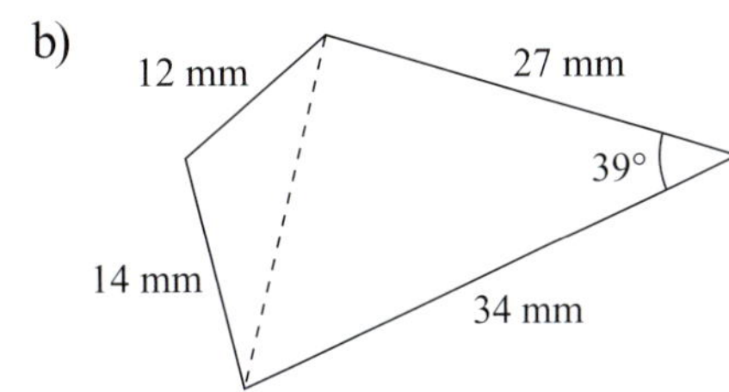

E P M Q11 A hiker starts at point A and walks 3.2 km on a bearing of 110° to point B. From there, they turn and walk p km along a bearing of 067° to point C. Then, they turn again and walk q km on a bearing of 273°, finishing the walk back at point A.

a) Draw a diagram to represent this situation. *[3 marks]*

b) Find the three angles in the triangle formed by this walk. *[3 marks]*

c) Calculate the total length of the walk. *[4 marks]*

Challenge

P Q12 The triangle on the right has an area of 220 cm^2. Find the perimeter of the triangle.

E P Q13 A triangle ABC has sides $AB = 4$ cm, $BC = 6$ cm, $CA = 5$ cm.

a) Use this information to find the exact value of cos $\angle CAB$. *[2 marks]*

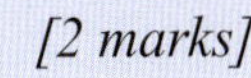

b) Given that $\angle CAB$ is an acute angle, use the result from a) to find the exact value of the area of the triangle. *[3 marks]*

E P Q14 ABC is a triangle with angle $\angle ABC$ equal to 68°. The centre, O, of the circumcircle of ABC lies inside the triangle, and the circumcircle has radius 6 cm.

Given that angle $\angle AOB$ is equal to 118°, find the area of triangle ABC. *[4 marks]*

Q14 Hint A circumcircle is a circle drawn around a polygon that touches all its vertices.

8.6 Trig Identities

There are **two trig identities** you need to know — they're really useful, and also fairly straightforward to find using results you already know.

You know that $\sin\theta = \frac{\text{opp}}{\text{hyp}}$, $\cos\theta = \frac{\text{adj}}{\text{hyp}}$ and $\tan\theta = \frac{\text{opp}}{\text{adj}}$ (see p.175).

So $\sin\theta \div \cos\theta = \frac{\text{opp}}{\text{hyp}} \div \frac{\text{adj}}{\text{hyp}} = \frac{\text{opp}}{\cancel{\text{hyp}}} \times \frac{\cancel{\text{hyp}}}{\text{adj}} = \frac{\text{opp}}{\text{adj}} = \tan\theta$.

So for all values of θ: $\tan\theta \equiv \frac{\sin\theta}{\cos\theta}$

Tip The '≡' means that the relation is true for all values of θ.

On page 176 you saw that the coordinates (x, y) of a point on the **unit circle** can be written as $(\cos\theta, \sin\theta)$ — i.e. $x = \cos\theta$ and $y = \sin\theta$.

The equation of the unit circle is $x^2 + y^2 = 1$ (see p.137).
Substituting in **cos θ** and **sin θ** gives the equation $\mathbf{\cos^2\theta + \sin^2\theta = 1}$.

Tip $\sin^2\theta$ is another way of writing $(\sin\theta)^2$.

This is true for all values of θ, so you can write it as an **identity**:

$$\sin^2\theta + \cos^2\theta \equiv 1$$

This can be rearranged into $\mathbf{\sin^2\theta \equiv 1 - \cos^2\theta}$ or $\mathbf{\cos^2\theta \equiv 1 - \sin^2\theta}$.

You can use these identities to **prove** that two expressions are equivalent, although the substitutions aren't always easy to spot. Look out for things like differences of two squares, or 1's that can be replaced by $\sin^2\theta + \cos^2\theta$.

Example 1

Show that $\frac{\cos^2\theta}{1 + \sin\theta} \equiv 1 - \sin\theta$.

$$\frac{\cos^2\theta}{1+\sin\theta} \equiv \frac{1-\sin^2\theta}{1+\sin\theta}$$

Start with the left-hand side of the identity and use the trig identity for $\cos^2\theta$.

$$\frac{1-\sin^2\theta}{1+\sin\theta} \equiv \frac{(1+\sin\theta)(1-\sin\theta)}{1+\sin\theta}$$

The top of the fraction is a difference of two squares (see p.20).

$$\frac{(1+\sin\theta)(1-\sin\theta)}{1+\sin\theta} \equiv 1 - \sin\theta$$

Now you can just cancel the $1 + \sin\theta$ from the top and bottom of the fraction.

Example 2

Find the exact value of $\sin\theta$ if $\cos\theta = \frac{2}{3}$, given that θ is an acute angle.

$\sin^2\theta + \cos^2\theta \equiv 1$

$\Rightarrow \sin^2\theta \equiv 1 - \cos^2\theta$ ← Rearrange the identity $\sin^2\theta + \cos^2\theta \equiv 1$ to find $\sin\theta$.

$\Rightarrow \sin\theta \equiv \sqrt{1-\cos^2\theta}$

$\sin\theta = \sqrt{1-\left(\frac{2}{3}\right)^2} = \sqrt{\frac{5}{9}} = \frac{\sqrt{5}}{3}$ ← Then put in the value of $\cos\theta$ and simplify.

Tip θ is acute here, which means that $\sin\theta$ is positive, so you can ignore the negative square root.

Exercise 8.6

Q1 Use the identity $\tan\theta \equiv \frac{\sin\theta}{\cos\theta}$ to show that $\frac{\sin\theta}{\tan\theta} - \cos\theta \equiv 0$.

Q2 Use the identity $\sin^2\theta + \cos^2\theta \equiv 1$ to show that $\cos^2\theta \equiv (1 - \sin\theta)(1 + \sin\theta)$.

Q3 Given that x is acute, find the exact value of $\cos x$ if $\sin x = \frac{1}{2}$.

Q4 Given that x is acute, find the exact value of $\tan x$ if $\sin^2 x = \frac{3}{4}$.

Q3-4 Hint You're told that x is acute, so ignore the negative roots.

Q5 Show that $4\sin^2 x - 3\cos x + 1 \equiv 5 - 3\cos x - 4\cos^2 x$.

Q5 Hint If you're not told which identity to use, just play around with the ones you know until something works.

P Q6 Show that $(\tan x + 1)(\tan x - 1) \equiv \frac{1}{\cos^2 x} - 2$.

E P Q7 In a triangle ABC, the lengths of AC and BC are 12 cm and 11 cm respectively. Angle BAC is equal to 60° and angle ABC is equal to θ°.

a) Find the exact value of $\sin\theta$. *[2 marks]*

b) Use the result from a) with appropriate identities to find the exact values of

(i) $\cos^2\theta$ *[2 marks]*

(ii) $\tan^2\theta$ *[2 marks]*

P Q8 A student is asked to solve the equation $\sin\theta = \frac{1}{2}\tan\theta$, where $0° \le \theta \le 90°$. Their working is shown below:

$$\sin\theta = \frac{1}{2}\tan\theta \Rightarrow \sin\theta = \frac{1}{2} \times \frac{\sin\theta}{\cos\theta}$$

$$\Rightarrow \cos\theta\sin\theta = \frac{1}{2}\sin\theta \Rightarrow \cos\theta = \frac{1}{2} \Rightarrow \theta = 60°.$$

Find the error they made and explain how this has resulted in an incomplete solution.

P Q9 Show that $\tan x + \frac{1}{\tan x} \equiv \frac{1}{\sin x \cos x}$.

Q9 Problem Solving Here you'll need to use the reciprocal of the identity linking tan, sin and cos: $\frac{1}{\tan x} \equiv \frac{\cos x}{\sin x}$

Q10 Show that $2\cos^2 x + 5\sin x + 1 \equiv (3 - \sin x)(2\sin x + 1)$.

Q11 Show that $4 + \sin x - 6\cos^2 x \equiv (2\sin x - 1)(3\sin x + 2)$.

P Q12 Show that $\sin^2 x \cos^2 y - \cos^2 x \sin^2 y \equiv \cos^2 y - \cos^2 x$.

E Q13 Write $\frac{1}{2}\left(\frac{\sin x \cos x}{1 - \sin^2 x} + \frac{1 - \cos^2 x}{\sin x \cos x}\right)$ as a single trigonometric function. *[3 marks]*

P Q14 Show that $\frac{\tan^2 x + 1}{\tan^2 x} \equiv \frac{1}{\sin^2 x}$.

P Q15 Show that $\frac{\sin^4 x - \cos^4 x}{\sin^2 x - \cos^2 x} \equiv 1$.

E P Q16 The diagram shows an acute-angled triangle ABC.

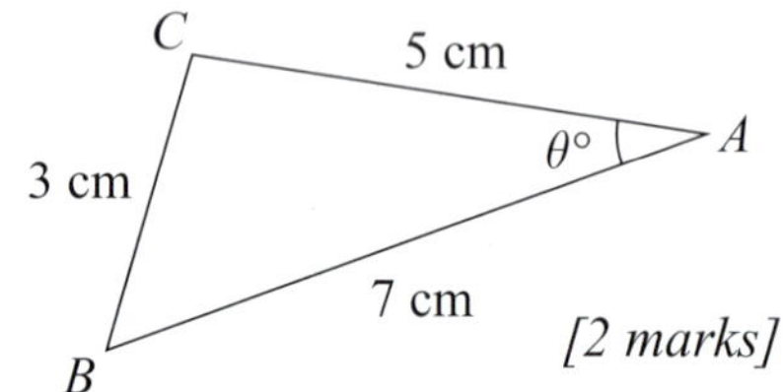

a) Use the triangle to find the exact value of $\cos\theta$. *[2 marks]*

b) Use appropriate trigonometric identities to find the exact values of $\sin\theta$ and $\tan\theta$. *[3 marks]*

Challenge

E P M Q17 A window cleaner uses a ladder to reach the upstairs window of a house.

The ladder makes an angle of $\theta°$ with the horizontal ground at point A, touches the vertical wall at point B, and touches a fixed cuboid storage container at a single point, P, 1.2 m from A.

The ladder is 3 m in length, and the dimensions of the storage container are $2x$ m by $3x$ m, as shown in the diagram.

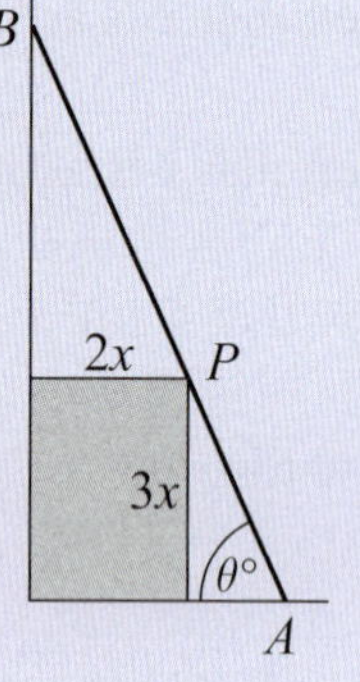

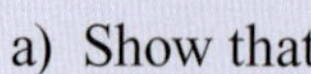

a) Show that

(i) $\cos\theta = \frac{10x}{9}$ *[1 mark]*

(ii) $\sin\theta = \frac{5x}{2}$ *[1 mark]*

The ladder is safe to use only if $70° \le \theta° \le 75°$

b) Use an appropriate trigonometric identity and the result from a) to determine whether the ladder is safe to use. *[3 marks]*

P Q18 Use the identity $\sin^2\theta + \cos^2\theta \equiv 1$ to prove Pythagoras' theorem.

E P Q19 A point B lies in the first quadrant and is a distance c from the point $A(0, 0)$. AB makes an angle $\theta°$ with the positive x-axis, as shown in the diagram.

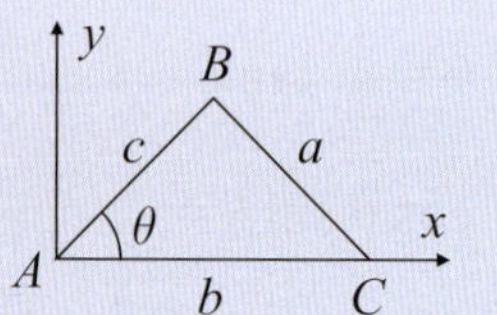

a) Find the coordinates of B in terms of c and θ. *[2 marks]*

The point C lies on the positive x-axis at a distance b from A and the length of BC is a.

b) Use the result from a) and any appropriate trigonometric identities to verify the formula for the cosine rule. *[3 marks]*

8.7 Graphs of Trig Functions

You should be able to draw the graphs of **sin x**, **cos x** and **tan x** without looking them up — including all the important points, like where they cross the **axes** and their **maximum** and **minimum** points.

The graphs of sin x and cos x are the **same shape** but shifted **90°** along the **x-axis**. This makes them easier to remember, but make sure you don't get them mixed up.

sin x

- The graph of $y = \sin x$ is **periodic** — it repeats itself every 360°. So $\sin x = \sin(x + 360°) = \sin(x + 720°) = \sin(x + 360n°)$, where n is an integer.
- It bounces between $y = -1$ and $y = 1$, and it can **never** have a value outside this range.
- It goes through the **origin** (as $\sin 0° = 0$) and then crosses the x-axis every **180°**.
- $\sin(-x) = -\sin x$. The graph has **rotational symmetry** about the origin, so you could rotate it 180° about (0, 0) and it would look the same.
- The graph of $y = \sin x$ looks like this:

Tip You say that sin x has a period of 360°.

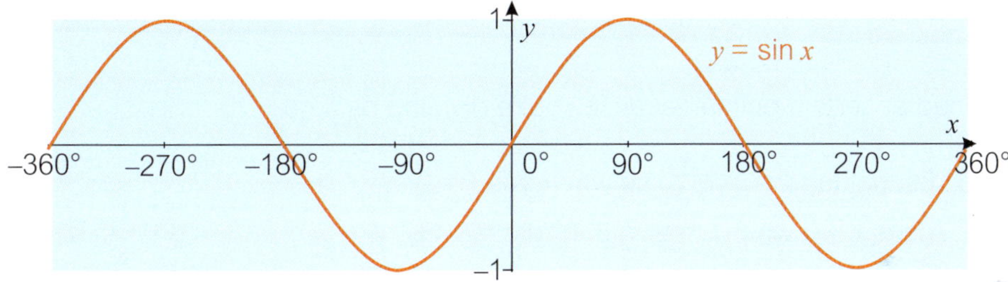

cos x

- The graph of $y = \cos x$ is also **periodic** with period 360°. $\cos x = \cos(x + 360°) = \cos(x + 720°) = \cos(x + 360n°)$, where n is an integer.
- It also bounces between $y = -1$ and $y = 1$, and it can **never** have a value outside this range.
- It crosses the y-axis at **$y = 1$** (as $\cos 0° = 1$) and the x-axis at **±90°**, **±270°** etc.
- $\cos(-x) = \cos x$. The graph is **symmetrical** about the y-axis, so you could reflect it in the **y-axis** and it would look the same.
- The graph of $y = \cos x$ looks like this:

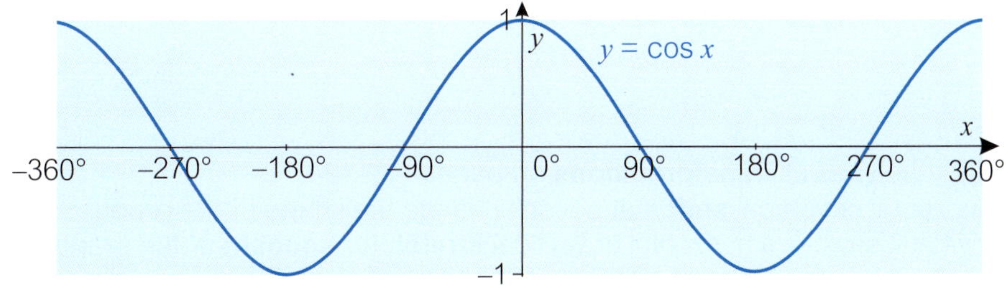

tan x

- The graph of $y = \tan x$ is also **periodic**, but this time it repeats itself every 180°. So $\tan x = \tan (x + 180°) = \tan (x + 360°) = \tan (x + 180n°)$, where n is an integer.
- It takes values between $-\infty$ and ∞ in each **180° interval**.
- It goes through the **origin** (as $\tan 0° = 0$).
- It's **undefined** at ±90°, ±270°, ±450°... — at these points it **jumps** from ∞ to $-\infty$ or vice versa.
- $\tan (-x) = -\tan x$. The graph has **rotational symmetry** about the origin, so you could rotate it 180° about (0, 0) and it would look the same.

The graph of $y = \tan x$ looks like this:

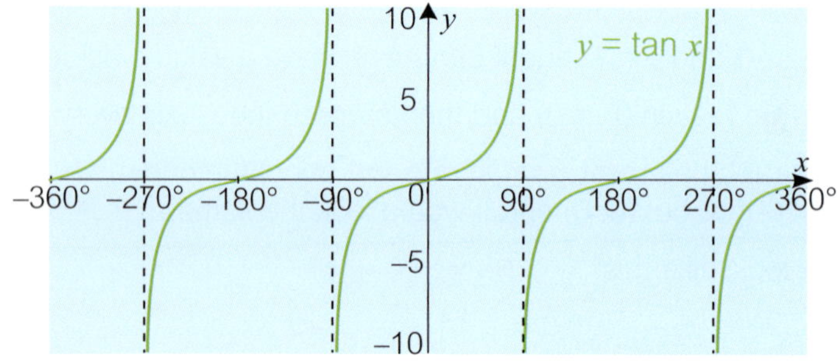

$y = \tan x$ is undefined at certain points because you're dividing by zero.

Remember from p.186 that $\tan x = \frac{\sin x}{\cos x}$, so when $\cos x = 0$, $\tan x$ is undefined — $\cos x = 0$ when $x = 90°$, 270° etc.

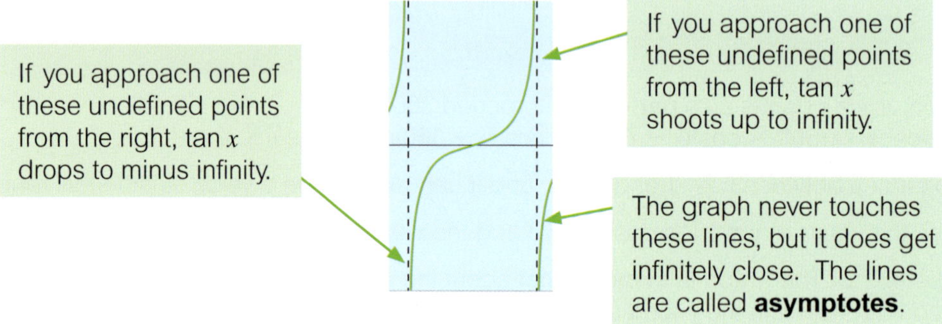

The best way to learn these functions is to **practise sketching them** and marking on the **key points**.

Transformations

You came across different types of **transformations** on pages 129-134.
A **translation** is a horizontal or vertical **shift** that doesn't change the shape of the graph.
A **stretch** is exactly what it says — a horizontal or vertical **stretch** (or **squash**) of the graph.
You need to be able to apply these types of transformation to **trig functions**.

1. A translation along the y-axis: $y = \sin(x) + c$

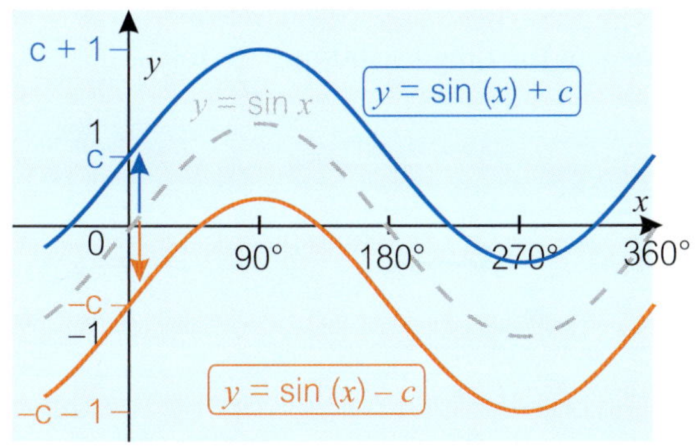

- For $c > 0$, $\sin(x) + c$ is just $\sin x$ **shifted c up**.
- Similarly, $\sin(x) - c$ is just $\sin x$ **shifted c down**.

> **Tip** The same transformations will apply to the graphs of $y = \cos x$ and $y = \tan x$ as well as $y = \sin x$.

2. A translation along the x-axis: $y = \sin(x + c)$

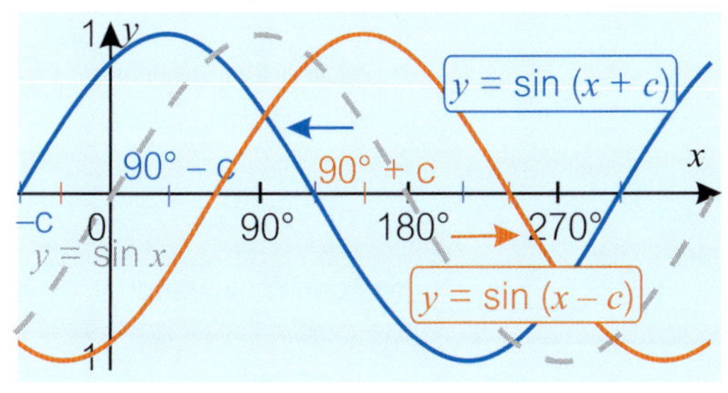

- For $c > 0$, $\sin(x + c)$ is just $\sin x$ **shifted c to the left**.
- Similarly, $\sin(x - c)$ is just $\sin x$ **shifted c to the right**.

3. A vertical stretch: $y = n \sin x$

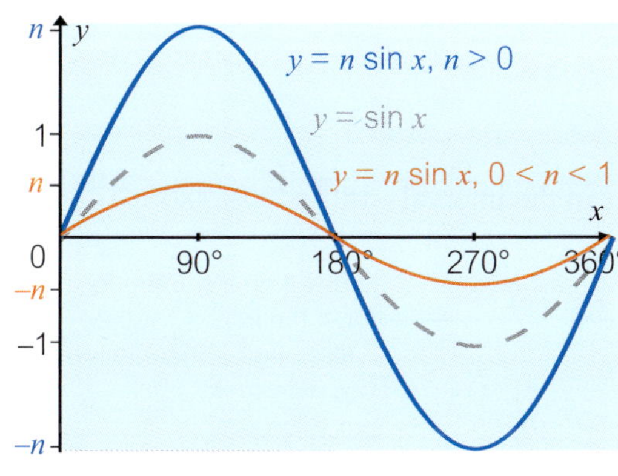

- For $y = n \sin x$, the graph of $y = \sin x$ is **stretched vertically** by a factor of n.
- If $n > 1$, the graph gets taller, and if $0 < n < 1$, the graph gets flatter.
- And if $n < 0$, the graph is also **reflected** in the **x-axis**.

> **Tip** In this case, n is 2 for the blue curve and 0.5 for the orange curve.

> **Tip** When n is between 0 and 1, it looks like a squash but it's still called a stretch.

4. A horizontal stretch: $y = \sin nx$

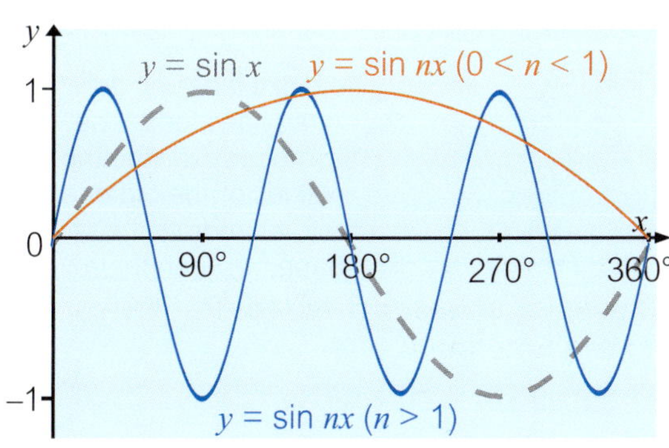

- For $y = \sin nx$, the graph of $y = \sin x$ is **stretched horizontally** by a factor of $\frac{1}{n}$.
- If $0 < n < 1$, the graph of $y = \sin x$ is **stretched horizontally outwards**, and if $n > 1$ the graph of $y = \sin x$ is **squashed inwards**.
- If $n < 0$, the graph is also **reflected** in the **y-axis**.

> **Tip** Make sure you know which way the stretch goes. The larger n is, the more squashed the graph becomes. In the diagram, n is 3 for the blue curve and 0.5 for the orange curve.

Example 1

On the same axes, sketch the graphs of $y = \cos x$ and $y = -2\cos x$ in the range $-360° \leq x \leq 360°$.

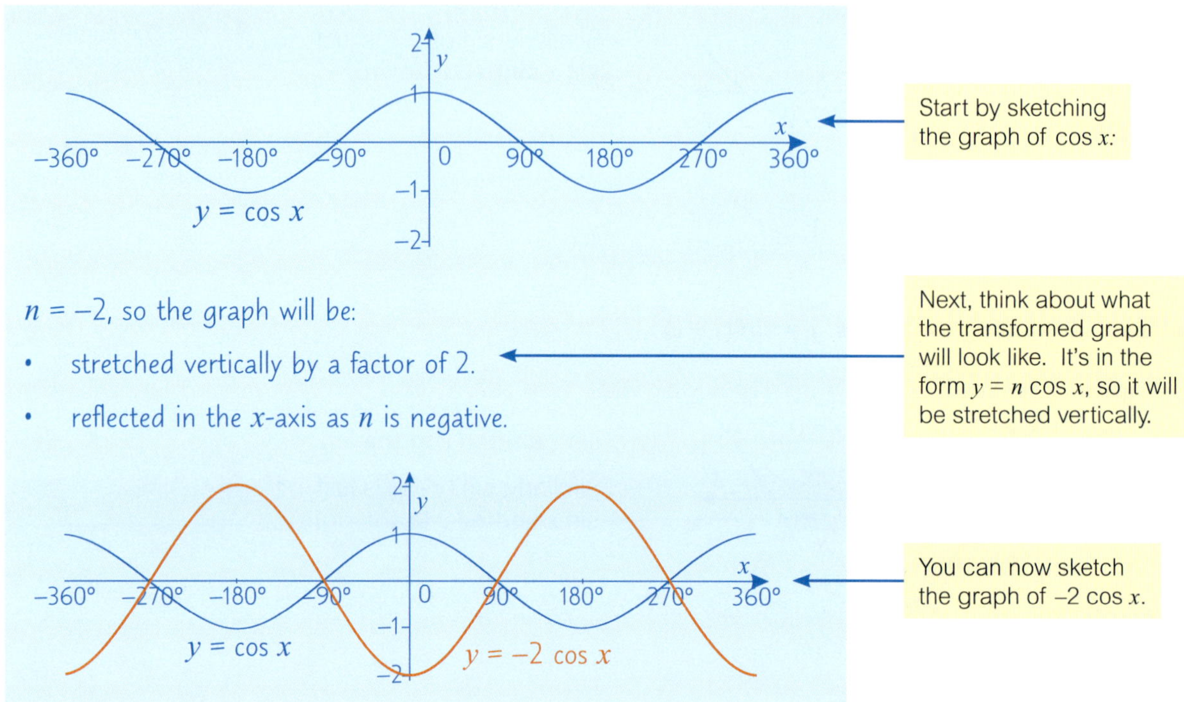

Start by sketching the graph of $\cos x$:

Next, think about what the transformed graph will look like. It's in the form $y = n\cos x$, so it will be stretched vertically.

You can now sketch the graph of $-2\cos x$.

Example 2

On the same axes, sketch the graphs of $y = \tan x$ and $y = \tan 2x$ in the interval $-180° \leq x \leq 180°$.

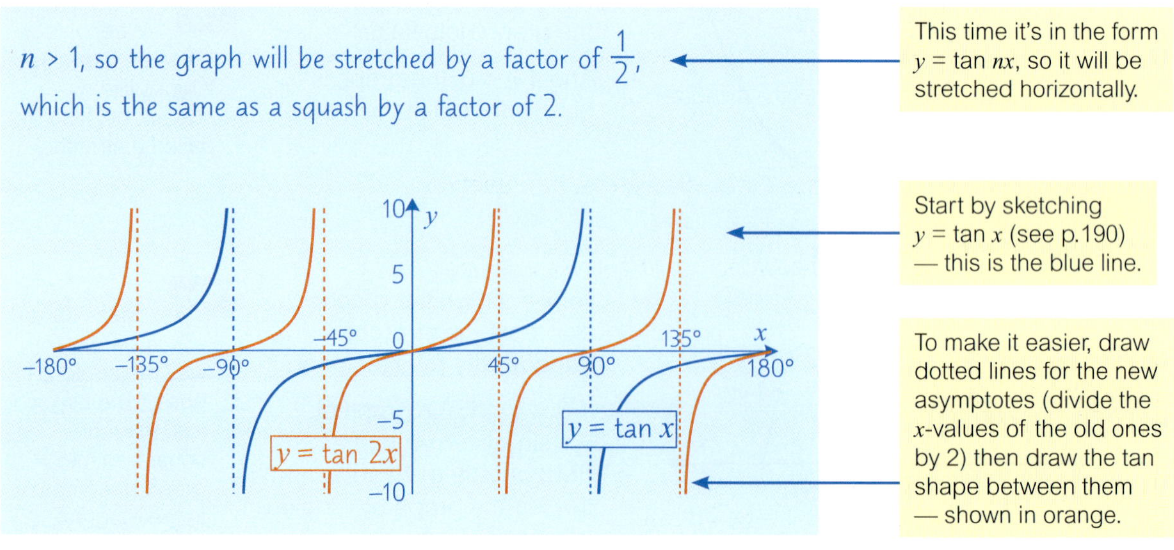

This time it's in the form $y = \tan nx$, so it will be stretched horizontally.

Start by sketching $y = \tan x$ (see p.190) — this is the blue line.

To make it easier, draw dotted lines for the new asymptotes (divide the x-values of the old ones by 2) then draw the tan shape between them — shown in orange.

Exercise 8.7

Q1 On the same set of axes, sketch the graphs of $y = \cos x$ and $y = \cos x + 3$ in the interval $-360° \leq x \leq 360°$.

Q2 On the same set of axes, sketch the graphs of $y = \cos x$ and $y = \cos(x + 90°)$ in the interval $-180° \leq x \leq 180°$.

Q3 On the same set of axes, sketch the graphs of $y = \tan x$ and $y = \tan(x - 45°)$ in the interval $-180° \leq x \leq 360°$.

Q4 On the same set of axes, sketch the graphs of $y = \sin x$ and $y = \frac{1}{3}\sin x$ in the interval $-180° \leq x \leq 180°$.

Q5 On the same set of axes, sketch the graphs of $y = \sin x$ and $y = \sin 3x$ in the interval $0° \leq x \leq 360°$.

Q6 On the same set of axes, sketch the graphs of $y = \cos x$ and $y = -\cos x$ in the interval $0° \leq x \leq 360°$.

Q7 On the same set of axes, sketch the graphs of $y = \tan x$ and $y = \tan(-x)$ in the interval $0° \leq x \leq 360°$

Q8 The graph of $y = \sin x$ is translated up by 4 units. Write down the equation of the transformed graph.

Q9 The graph of $y = \cos x$ is stretched horizontally by a factor of 5. Write down the equation of the transformed graph.

E Q10 The graph of $y = \tan x$ is transformed such that the equation of the transformed graph is $y = \tan 2x$.

a) Find the points where the transformed graph crosses the x-axis in the interval $-180° \leq x \leq 180°$. *[2 marks]*

b) Write down the equations of the asymptotes of the transformed graph in the interval $-180° \leq x \leq 180°$. *[2 marks]*

Q11 a) Sketch the graph of $f(x) = \tan x$ in the interval $-90° \leq x \leq 270°$.

b) Translate this graph 90° to the left and sketch it on the same set of axes as part a).

c) Write down the equation of the transformed graph.

Q11c) Hint Look at what's happened to the graph, then think about which type of transformation is needed to achieve it.

Q12 a) Sketch the graph of $y = \sin x$ in the interval $-360° \leq x \leq 360°$.

b) Stretch the graph horizontally by a factor of 2 and sketch it on the same set of axes as part a).

c) Write down the equation of the transformed graph.

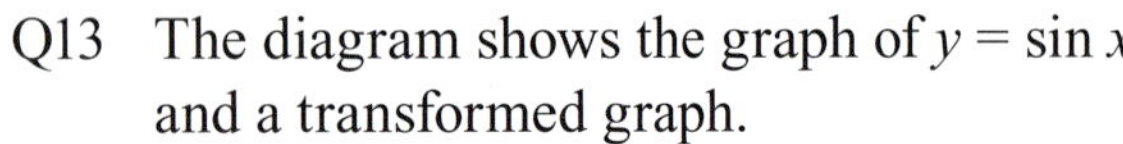

Q13 The diagram shows the graph of $y = \sin x$ and a transformed graph.

a) Describe the transformation.

b) Write down the equation of the transformed graph.

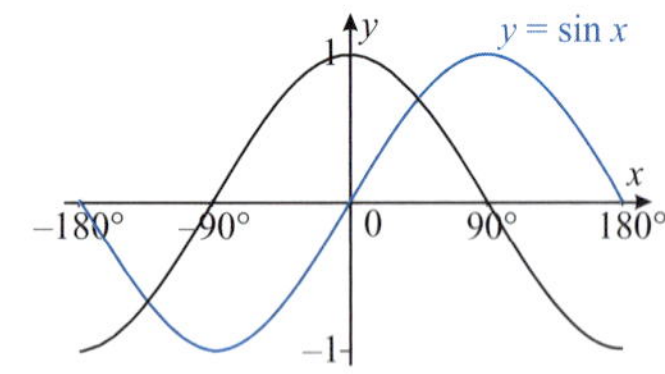

Q14 The diagram shows the graph of $y = \cos x$ and a transformed graph.

a) Describe the transformation.

b) Write down the equation of the transformed graph.

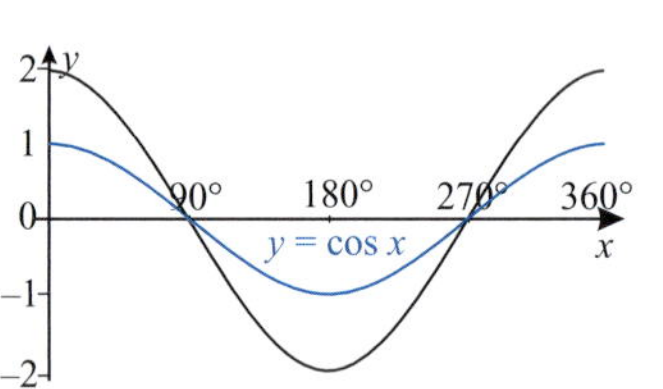

Q15 The diagram shows the graph of $y = \tan x$ and a transformed graph.

a) Describe the transformation.

b) Write down the equation of the transformed graph.

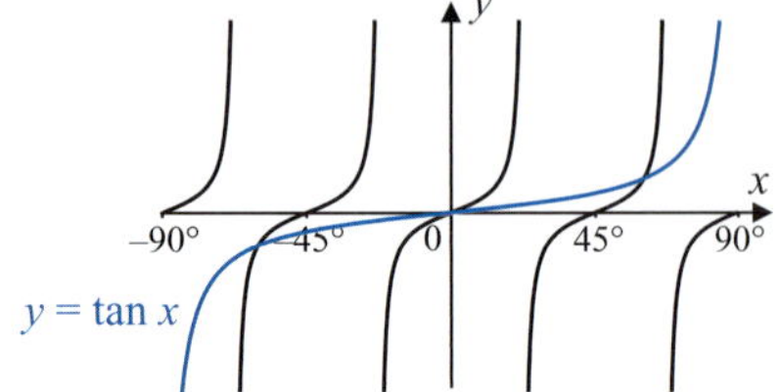

P Q16 A transformed graph has the equation $y = \cos px$. Given that the graph crosses the x-axis at the point (180°, 0), find the smallest possible positive value of p.

P Q17 A transformed graph has the equation $y = \sin (x + q)$.

a) Given that the graph is at a maximum at the point (60°, 1), find a possible value for q.

b) Explain why there is more than one possible value for q.

Challenge

E P Q18 a) On the same axes sketch the graphs of $y = \tan x$ and $y = \cos\left(\frac{1}{2}x\right)$ in the interval for $0° \leq x \leq 360°$. *[3 marks]*

b) Using the diagram sketched in a), determine the number of solutions of the equation $\tan x = \cos\left(\frac{1}{2}x\right)$ in the interval $0° \leq x \leq 360°$. *[1 mark]*

P Q19 The graph of $y = a \sin bx$, where $a < 0$ and $b > 0$ are integers, has a minimum at the point (150°, –5), and exactly one other minimum point for $0° \leq x < 150°$.

a) Find the value of: (i) a (ii) b

b) Use the results from part a) to describe the transformations which would transform the graph of $y = \sin x$ into the graph of $y = a \sin bx$.

c) Sketch the graph of $y = a \sin bx$ for $0° \leq x \leq 180°$.

8.8 Solving Trig Equations by Sketching a Graph

To solve trig equations in a **given interval** you can use one of two methods. The first is drawing a **graph** of the function and reading solutions off the graph. You'll often find that there's **more than one** solution to the equation — in every **360° interval**, there are usually **two** solutions to an equation, and if the interval is bigger (see Example 2 below), there'll be even more solutions.

Example 1

Solve $\cos x = \frac{1}{2}$ for $0° \leq x \leq 360°$.

Tip This is actually one of the common trig angles from page 175.

For $\cos x = \frac{1}{2}$, $x = 60°$

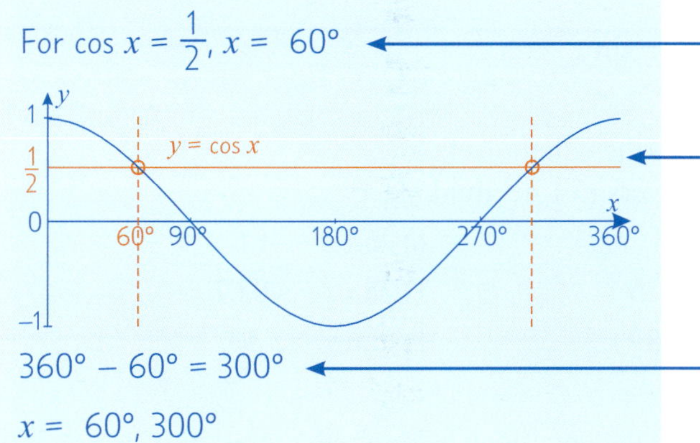

$360° - 60° = 300°$

$x = 60°, 300°$

Use your calculator to work out the first value.

Sketch a graph of $\cos x$ in the interval you're interested in, and draw a horizontal line across for $y = \frac{1}{2}$. The points where the line and curve meet are all the solutions of the equation.

The graph is symmetrical, so the second solution will be the same distance from 360° as the first is from 0°.

If you had an interval that was **larger** than **one repetition** of the graph (i.e. 360° for sin and cos, and 180° for tan), you'd just add or subtract **multiples** of 360° (for sin and cos) or 180° (for tan) onto the solutions you've found until you have **all** the solutions in the **given interval**.

Example 2

Solve $\sin x = -0.3$ for $0° \leq x \leq 720°$. Give your answers to 3 s.f.

For $\sin x = -0.3$, $x = -17.45...°$

$-17.45...° + 360° = 342.54...°$

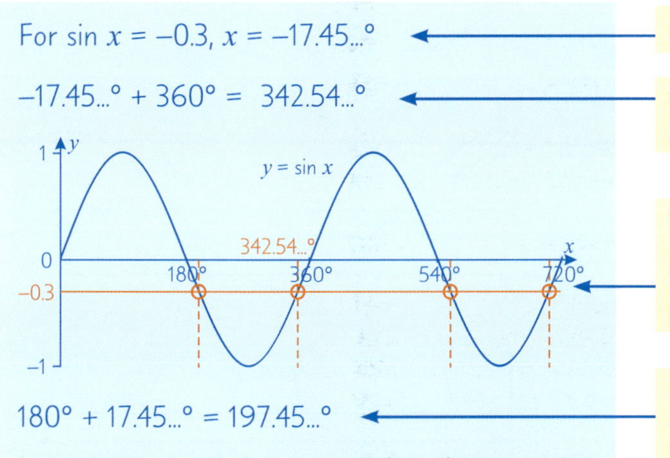

$180° + 17.45...° = 197.45...°$

continued on the next page...

Use your calculator to work out the first value.

This is outside the given interval for x, so add on 360° to find a solution in the interval.

Now sketch a graph of $\sin x$ and draw a horizontal line across at $y = -0.3$. This time, you'll need to draw the graph for the interval between $x = 0°$ and $x = 720°$.

Looking at the graph, the other solution between 0° and 360° will be 17.45...° away from 180°.

197.45...° + 360° = 557.45...°
and 342.54...° + 360° = 702.54...°

So the solutions to $\sin x = -0.3$ for $0° \leq x \leq 720°$ are: $x = 197°, 343°, 557°, 703°$ (all to 3 s.f.)

For the next two solutions (the ones between 360° and 720°), just add 360° onto the values you've already found.

Exercise 8.8

Q1 a) Sketch the graph of $y = \sin x$ for $-180° \leq x \leq 180°$.

b) State the exact values of sin 45° and sin 60°.

c) Hence, find all the solutions to the equations below in the interval $-180° \leq x \leq 180°$.

(i) $\sin x = \frac{1}{\sqrt{2}}$ (ii) $\sin x = -\frac{\sqrt{3}}{2}$

Q2 By sketching a graph, find all the solutions to the equations below in the interval $0° \leq x \leq 360°$. Give your answers to 1 decimal place.

a) $\sin x = 0.75$ b) $\cos x = 0.31$ c) $\tan x = -1.5$

d) $\sin x = -0.42$ e) $\cos x = -0.56$ f) $\tan x = -0.67$

g) $\sin x = 0.32$ h) $\cos x = -0.89$ i) $\tan x = 2.3$

Q3 By sketching a graph, find all the solutions to the equations below in the interval $0° \leq x \leq 360°$.

a) $\cos x = \frac{1}{\sqrt{2}}$ b) $\tan x = \sqrt{3}$ c) $\sin x = \frac{1}{2}$

d) $\tan x = \frac{1}{\sqrt{3}}$ e) $\tan x = 1$ f) $\cos x = \frac{\sqrt{3}}{2}$

Q4 One solution of $\sin x = 0.7$ is 44.43° (2 d.p.). Use the graph to find all the solutions in the interval $-180° \leq x \leq 180°$.

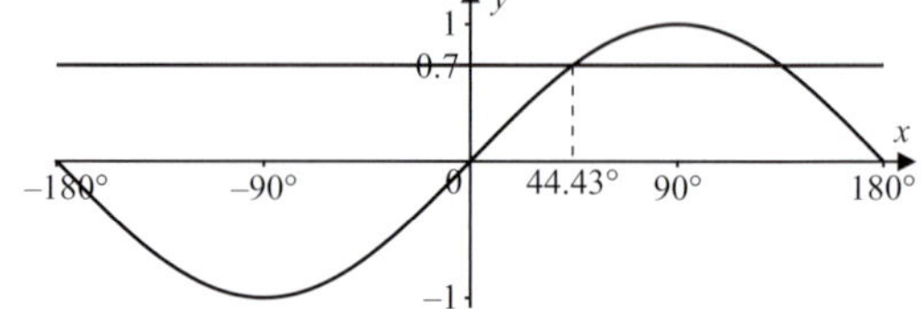

Q5 One solution of $\cos x = -0.8$ is 143.1° (1 d.p.). Use the graph to find all the solutions in the interval $0° \leq x \leq 360°$.

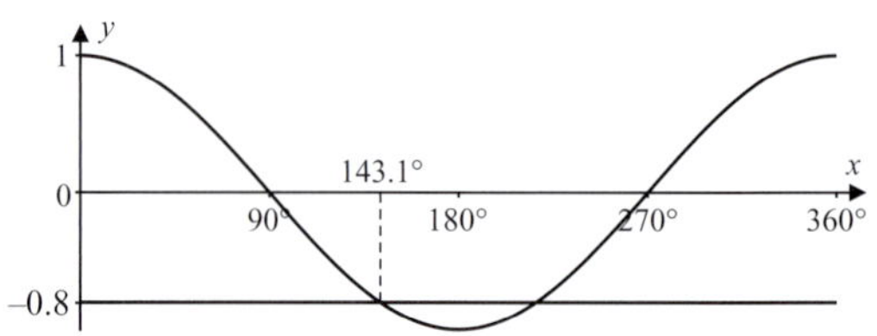

Q6 One solution of $\tan x = 1.9$ is 62.2° (3 s.f.). Use the graph to find all the solutions in the interval $0° \leq x \leq 540°$.

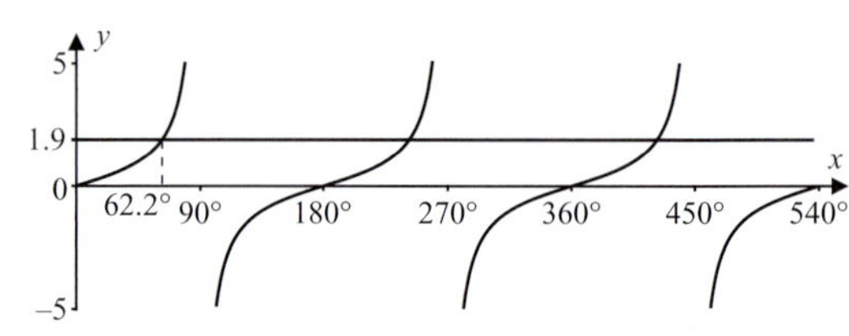

Q7 Find all the solutions of the equation $\tan x = 2.5$ in the interval $0° \leq x \leq 1080°$. Give your answers to 1 decimal place.

Q7-8 Hint Be careful with the intervals here — and remember that tan repeats every 180°.

Q8 Find all the solutions of the equation $\sin x = 0.81$ in the interval $-360° \leq x \leq 360°$. Give your answers to 3 significant figures.

Q9 Find all the solutions to the equation $\sin x = 0.23$ in the interval $-360° \leq x \leq 540°$, giving your answers to 1 decimal place.

Q10 Find all the solutions to the equation $\cos x = -0.96$ in the interval $-360° \leq x \leq 720°$, giving your answers to 3 significant figures.

Q11 Find all the solutions to the equation $\tan x = -1.75$ in the interval $-360° \leq x \leq 720°$, giving your answers to 1 decimal place.

P Q12 Find all the solutions to the equation $5 \sin x - 3 \cos x = 0$ in the interval $0° \leq x \leq 360°$. Give your answers to 3 significant figures.

P Q13 Find all the solutions to the equation $3 \cos x + 8 \sin x = 0$ in the interval $0° \leq x \leq 360°$. Give your answers to 2 decimal places.

Problem Solving In Q12-13, use a trig identity to rearrange the equations so that they're in terms of tan x.

E P Q14 a) Sketch the graph of $y = \tan x$ in the interval $-180° \leq x \leq 180°$. *[2 marks]*

b) Find all solutions, to 1 decimal place, of the equation $4 \cos x = 7 \sin x$ in the interval $-180° \leq x \leq 180°$. Mark the approximate positions of the solutions on the diagram drawn in part a). *[3 marks]*

E P Q15 a) Sketch the graph of $y = \sin x$ for $0° \leq x \leq 720°$. *[2 marks]*

b) Using the graph sketched in a), find all solutions of the equation $5 \sin x - 3 = 0$ in the interval $0° \leq x \leq 720°$. Give your answers to 1 decimal place. *[3 marks]*

c) Find the value of k if the equation $15 \sin x = k$ has the same solutions as the equation in part b). *[1 mark]*

Challenge

E P Q16 a) Sketch the graph of $y = \tan x$ for $-360° \leq x \leq 360°$. *[2 marks]*

b) Using the graph sketched in a), determine the exact solutions to the equation $2(\tan x - \sqrt{3}) = 3 - \sqrt{3} \tan x$ in the range $-360° \leq x \leq 360°$. Mark the approximate positions of the solutions on the diagram in a). *[4 marks]*

E P Q17 Given the simultaneous equations, $2 \sin x - 5 \cos y = \frac{1}{4}$ and $\sin x - \cos y = -\frac{1}{4}$,

a) Show that $\sin x = -\frac{1}{2}$ and $\cos y = -\frac{1}{4}$. *[3 marks]*

b) Hence, find all solutions of the simultaneous equations for $0° \leq x, y \leq 360°$. Give your answers to 1 decimal place. *[3 marks]*

8.9 Solving Trig Equations Using a CAST Diagram

The second way of finding the solutions to a trig equation is by using a **CAST diagram**. CAST stands for Cos, All, Sin, Tan, and it shows you where each of these functions is **positive** by splitting a 360° period into **quadrants**.

Tip CAST diagrams are useful because they summarise the information from the graphs of sin, cos and tan without you actually having to sketch the graphs.

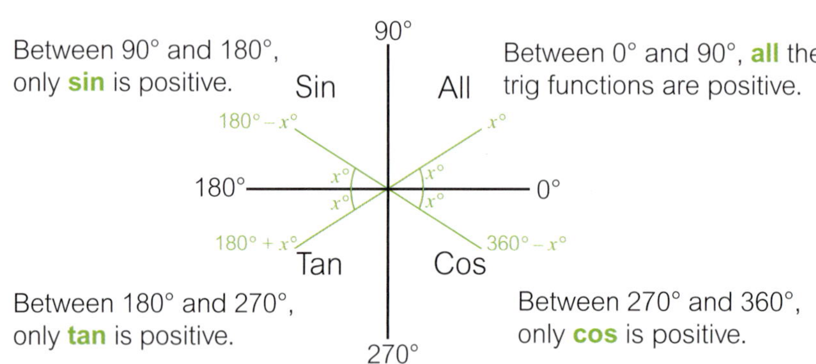

To use a CAST diagram, you need to use your **calculator** to find the first solution of the trig function (or, if it's a common angle, you might just be able to recognise it). The angle you put into the CAST diagram should be **acute** (i.e. between 0° and 90°).

You then make the **same angle** from the **horizontal** in each of the four quadrants (shown in the diagram above), then measure each angle **anticlockwise** from 0°. So if the first solution was 45°, the solution in the 'sin' quadrant would be 135° (180° – 45°) measured anticlockwise from 0°, and so on.

Ignore the ones that give a **negative** result (unless the given value is negative — in which case you want the two quadrants in which the trig function is **negative**).

Example 1

Find all the solutions of $\sin x = \frac{1}{2}$ for $0° \leq x \leq 360°$.

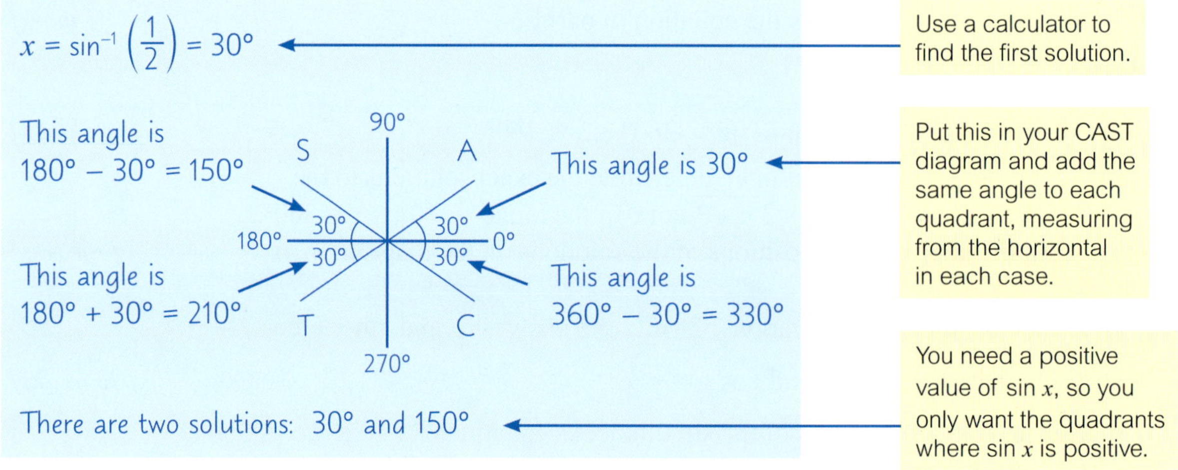

For values **outside** the interval $0° \leq x \leq 360°$, just find solutions between 0° and 360° and then **add** or **subtract multiples of 360°** to find solutions in the correct interval (see the example below).

Example 2

Find all the solutions of $\tan x = -6$ for $0° \leq x \leq 720°$.
Give your answers to 1 d.p.

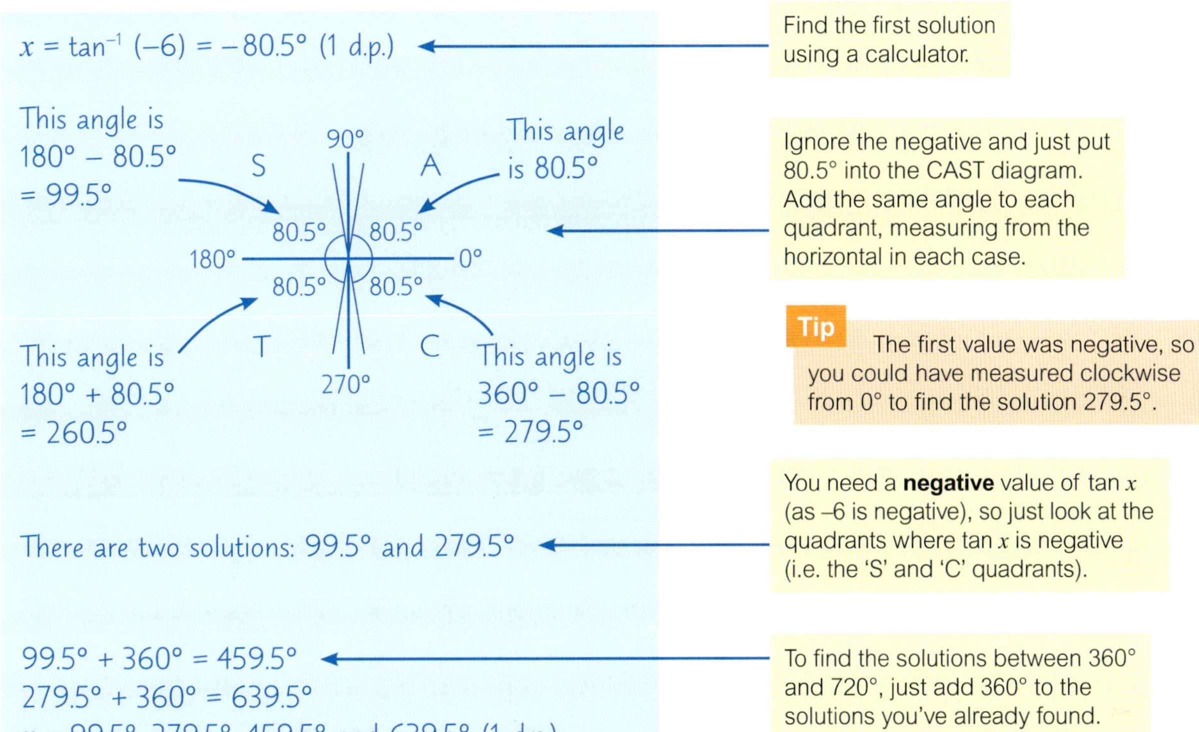

Exercise 8.9

Q1 One solution of $\sin x = 0.45$ is $x = 26.7°$ (1 d.p.).
Use a CAST diagram to find all the solutions in the interval $0° \leq x \leq 360°$.

Q2 The equation $\cos x = 0.68$ has a solution $x = 47.2°$ (1 d.p.).
Use a CAST diagram to find all the solutions in the interval $0° \leq x \leq 360°$.

Q3 Use a CAST diagram to find the solutions of the following equations in the interval $0° \leq x \leq 360°$. Give your answers to 1 d.p.

a) $\cos x = 0.8$
b) $\tan x = 2.7$
c) $\sin x = -0.15$
d) $\tan x = 0.3$
e) $\tan x = -0.6$
f) $\sin x = -0.29$

Q4 One solution of the equation $\sin x = -0.87$ is $x = -60.5°$ (1 d.p.).
Use a CAST diagram to find all the solutions in the interval $-180° \le x \le 360°$.

Q5 Use a CAST diagram to find all the solutions to the following equations in the given interval, giving your answers to 3 s.f.

a) $\tan x = -8.4$ for $0° \le x \le 360°$
b) $\sin x = 0.82$ for $0° \le x \le 720°$
c) $\cos x = 0.72$ for $0° \le x \le 540°$
d) $\tan x = 3.58$ for $-180° \le x \le 180°$

Q6 Use a CAST diagram to find all the solutions to $\sin x = -0.06$ in the interval $0° \le x \le 1080°$. Give your answers to 1 d.p.

Q7 Use a CAST diagram to find all the solutions to $\tan x = 11.8$ in the interval $-360° \le x \le 360°$. Give your answers to 1 d.p.

P Q8 Use a CAST diagram to find all the solutions to $5 \cos x - 2 = 0$ in the interval $0° \le x \le 360°$. Give your answers to 1 d.p.

P Q9 Use a CAST diagram to find all the solutions to $\frac{1}{4} \tan x = 1.4$ in the interval $0° \le x \le 360°$. Give your answers to 3 s.f.

P Q10 Use a CAST diagram to solve the following equations, giving your answers to 1 d.p.

a) $4 \sin x - 3 = 0$ $0° \le x \le 720°$
b) $2 - 3 \cos x = 0$ $-180° \le x \le 180°$
c) $6 \tan x = -11$ $-180° \le x \le 540°$
d) $8 \sin x = -5$ $-360° \le x \le 720°$

E P Q11 Find all solutions to the equation $\tan^2 x = \tan x$ in the interval $0° \le x < 360°$. *[4 marks]*

Challenge

E P Q12 A triangle has base XZ and vertex Y. The angle YXZ is equal to 26° and angle XYZ is equal to $a°$. The length of the side YZ is 10 cm and the perpendicular distance from XZ to Y is 7.5 cm.

a) Explain why $\sin(a + 26°) = \frac{3}{4}$ *[4 marks]*

b) Using the result from a), find the possible values of a to 1 decimal place. *[2 marks]*

E P Q13 Given that $p(x) = 6x^3 + 11x^2 - 3x - 2$:

a) Show that $(2x - 1)$ is a factor of $p(x)$ and hence, obtain a complete factorisation of $p(x)$ *[3 marks]*

b) Use the result from a) to find all solutions to the equation $6 \sin^3 \theta + 11 \sin^2 \theta - 3 \sin \theta - 2 = 0$ in the interval $-180° \le \theta° \le 180°$. Give your answers to 1 decimal place. *[4 marks]*

8.10 Solving Trig Equations by Changing the Interval

Sometimes you'll have to solve equations of the form **sin $kx = n$** or **sin $(x + c) = n$** (where n, k and c are numbers). It's usually easiest to **change the interval** you're solving for, then **solve as normal** for kx or $x + c$. You'll then need to get the final solutions either by **dividing by k** or **subtracting c** at the end.

Solving equations of the form sin $kx = n$

- First, **multiply** the **interval** you're looking for solutions in by k. E.g. for the equation $\sin 2x = n$ in the interval $0° \leq x \leq 360°$, you'd look for solutions in the interval $0° \leq 2x \leq 720°$. Then **solve** the equation over the new interval.
- This gives you solutions for kx — then you need to **divide** each solution by k to find the values of x.

You can either **sketch the graph** over the new interval (this will show you **how many** solutions there are) or you can use the **CAST method** to find solutions between 0° and 360° then add on multiples of 360° until you have all the solutions in the new interval — use whichever method you prefer.

Example 1

Solve $\cos 4x = 0.6$ for $0° \leq x \leq 360°$. Give your answers to 1 d.p.

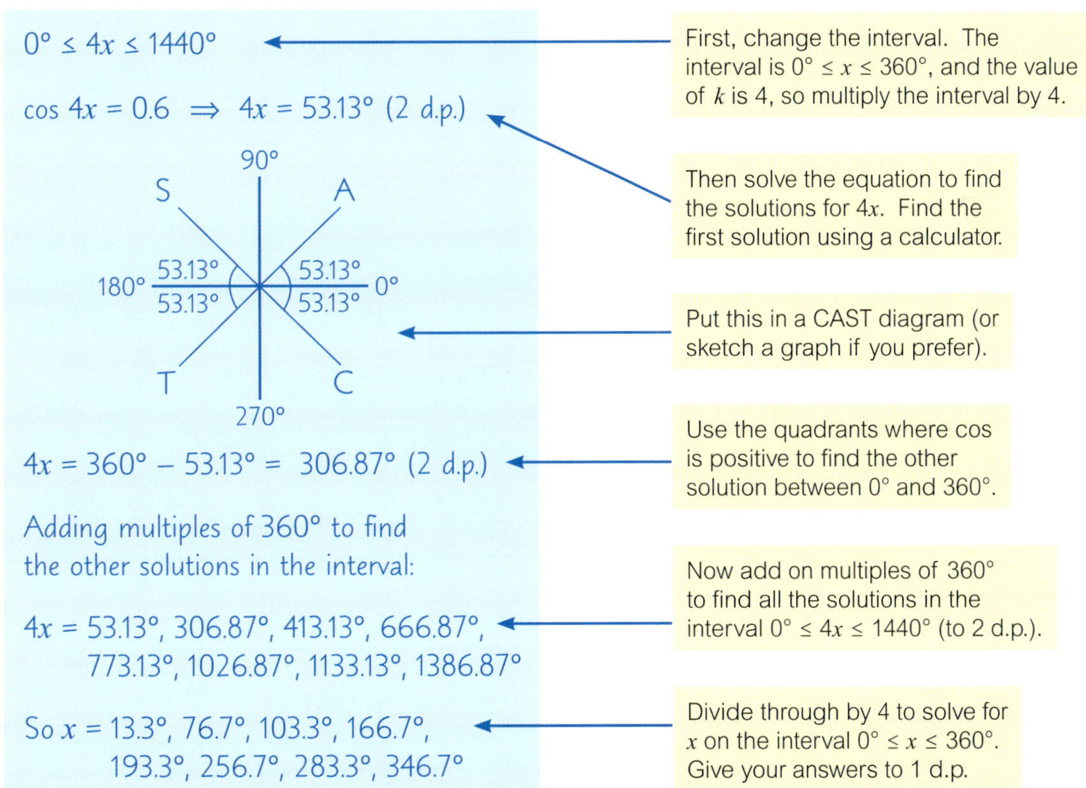

It's a good idea to check your answers — put your values of x into $\cos 4x$ to check if they give you 0.6. Make sure you have the right number of solutions too — there are 2 solutions to $\cos x = 0.6$ in the interval $0° \leq x \leq 360°$, so there are 8 solutions to $\cos 4x = 0.6$ in the same interval.

Example 2

Solve $\sin 3x = -\frac{1}{\sqrt{2}}$ for $0° \leq x \leq 360°$.

$0° \leq 3x \leq 1080°$

You've got $3x$ instead of x, so you need to multiply the interval by 3.

$\sin 3x = -\frac{1}{\sqrt{2}} \Rightarrow 3x = -45°$

Use your calculator to find a solution. This is outside the interval for $3x$, so use the pattern of the graph of $\sin x$ to find solutions in the interval.

The sine curve repeats every 360°, so a solution is: $-45° + 360° = 315°$

Tip This is one of the common angles from p.175 — so you could have found it without a calculator.

The curve is symmetrical in each interval of 180°, so the other solution is: $180° + 45° = 225°$

Use the symmetry of the graph to find the other solution between 0° and 360°.

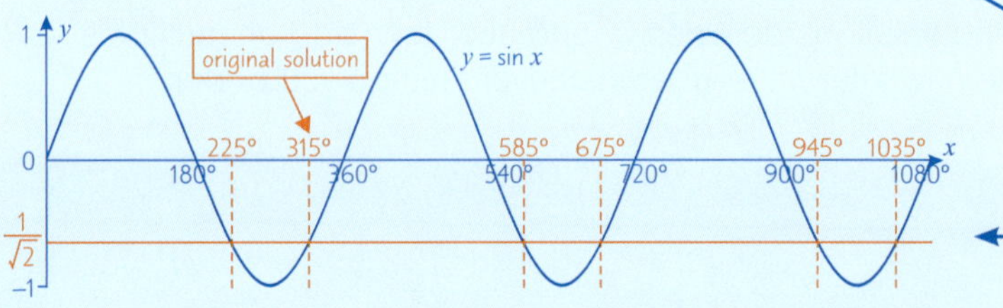

Then add on lots of 360° to the answers you've found to find the other solutions in the interval.

From the graph, $3x = 225°, 315°, 585°, 675°, 945°, 1035°$

So $x = 75°, 105°, 195°, 225°, 315°, 345°$

You have 6 solutions for $3x$. Divide by 3 to get the values of x on the interval $0° \leq x \leq 360°$.

Example 3 P

Find all the solutions of $0.9 + 3 \tan 2x = 5.1$ for $0° \leq x \leq 360°$. Give your answers to 1 d.p.

$0.9 + 3 \tan 2x = 5.1 \Rightarrow 3 \tan 2x = 4.2$

$\Rightarrow \tan 2x = 1.4$

First, rearrange into a more familiar format.

$0° \leq 2x \leq 720°$

It's $2x$, so multiply the interval by 2.

$2x = \tan^{-1}(1.4) = 54.46°$ (2 d.p.)

Use a calculator to work out the first solution.

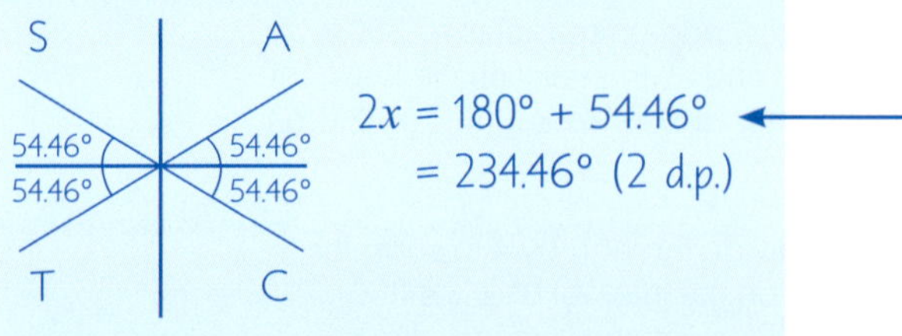

$2x = 180° + 54.46°$
$= 234.46°$ (2 d.p.)

Use a CAST diagram to find the other solution between 0° and 360°. You want the other quadrant where tan is positive (bottom left).

$54.46° + 360° = 414.46°$ (2 d.p.)
$234.46° + 360° = 594.46°$ (2 d.p.)

Add 360° to the solutions you've found to find the solutions between 360° and 720°.

$x = 27.2°, 117.2°, 207.2°, 297.2°$ (1 d.p.)

Finally, to find the solutions for x between 0° and 360°, just divide by 2.

Solving equations of the form sin $(x + c) = n$

The method for solving equations of the form **sin $(x + c) = n$** is similar — but instead of multiplying the interval, you have to add or subtract the value of c.

- **Add** (or **subtract**) the value of c to the **whole interval** — so the interval $0° \le x \le 360°$ becomes $c \le x + c \le 360° + c$ (you add c onto each limit of the interval).
- **Solve** the equation over the **new interval** — you can either sketch a graph or use a CAST diagram.
- Finally, **subtract** c from (or **add** it to) your solutions to give the values for x.

Example 4

Solve $\cos(x + 60°) = \frac{3}{4}$ for $-360° \le x \le 360°$, giving your answers to 1 d.p.

The new interval is: $-300° \le x + 60° \le 420°$

You've got $\cos(x + 60°)$ instead of $\cos x$ — so add 60° to each limit of the interval.

$\cos(x + 60°) = \frac{3}{4} \Rightarrow x + 60° = 41.4°$ (1 d.p.)

Use your calculator to find a solution.

$360° - 41.4° = 318.6°$ (1 d.p.)

Use the symmetry of the graph to find the other solution between 0° and 360°.

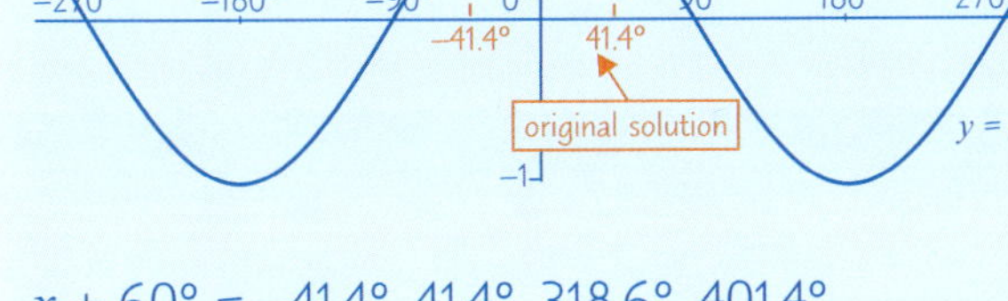

Find the other solutions in the interval by adding or subtracting 360° from the answers you've found.

$x + 60° = -41.4°, 41.4°, 318.6°, 401.4°$

$x = -101.4°, -18.6°, 258.6°$ and $341.4°$

Subtract 60° from each value to find the solutions for x (to 1 d.p.).

Tip Check your answers by putting them back into $\cos(x + 60°)$ and making sure you get $\frac{3}{4}$.

Example 5

Solve $\tan(x - 75°) = 2$ for $0° \le x \le 360°$. Give your answers to 1 d.p.

The new interval is: $-75° \le x - 75° \le 285°$

You've got $\tan(x - 75°)$ instead of $\tan x$ — so subtract 75° from each limit of the interval.

$\tan(x - 75°) = 2 \Rightarrow x - 75° = 63.4°$ (1 d.p.)

Use your calculator to find a solution.

Tan is positive in the first and third quadrants, so the other solution is:
$63.4° + 180° = 243.4°$ (1 d.p.)

S A T C
63.4° 63.4° 63.4° 63.4°

Put 63.4° into a CAST diagram (or use a graph) to find the other solution in the interval.

$x = 138.4°, 318.4°$ (1 d.p.)

Finally, add on 75° to find the solutions in the interval $0° \le x \le 360°$.

Example 6

Solve $2 \sin (x + 50°) + \sqrt{3} = 0$ for $0° \le x \le 720°$.

$2 \sin (x + 50°) + \sqrt{3} = 0$ — First, rearrange the equation.

$\Rightarrow 2 \sin (x + 50°) = -\sqrt{3}$

$\Rightarrow \sin (x + 50°) = -\frac{\sqrt{3}}{2} \Rightarrow x + 50° = -60°$ — $\frac{\sqrt{3}}{2}$ is a common trig value — $\sin 60° = \frac{\sqrt{3}}{2}$.

$50° \le x + 50° \le 770°$ — Add 50° to each limit of the interval.

$x + 50° = 180° + 60°$
$= 240°$
and $x + 50° = 360° - 60°$
$= 300°$

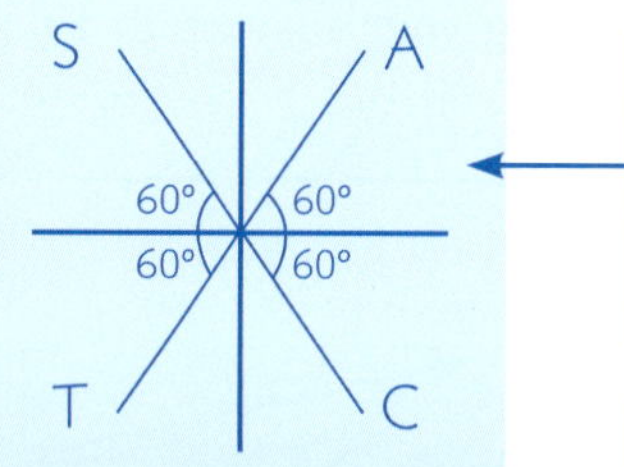

Put 60° into a CAST diagram. You have $-\frac{\sqrt{3}}{2}$, so you want the solutions where sin is **negative** — i.e. the third and fourth quadrants.

$x + 50° = 240°, 300°, 600°, 660°$ — To find the other solutions (between 410° and 770°), add 360° to these solutions.

$x = 190°, 250°, 550°, 610°$ — Finally, subtract 50° from each solution to find the values of x.

Exercise 8.10

In this exercise, give all non-integer answers to 1 d.p.

Q1 Solve the following equations in the interval $0° \le x \le 360°$:

a) $\sin 2x = 0.6$ b) $\tan 4x = 4.6$ c) $\cos 3x = -0.24$

d) $\sin 3x = 0.94$ e) $\cos 5x = 0.5$ f) $\tan 2x = -6.7$

Q2 Solve $\tan \frac{x}{2} = 2.1$ in the interval $0° \le x \le 360°$.

Q2 Hint Don't let the $\frac{x}{2}$ throw you — just like before, you multiply the interval by $\frac{1}{2}$ (i.e. divide by 2).

Q3 Find all the solutions to $\sin \frac{2x}{3} = 0.52$ in the interval $0° \le x \le 270°$.

Q4 Solve $\cos \frac{x}{3} = \frac{\sqrt{3}}{2}$ in the interval $-180° \le x \le 180°$.

Q5 Find all the solutions to $\cos (x - 27°) = 0.64$ in the interval $0° \le x \le 360°$.

Q6 Solve $\tan (x - 140°) = -0.76$ in the interval $0° \le x \le 360°$.

E Q7 Find all the solutions to $\tan (x + 73°) = 1.84$ in the interval $0° \le x \le 360°$. *[3 marks]*

E Q8 Find all the solutions to $\sin (x - 45°) = -0.25$ in the interval $-180° \le x \le 360°$. *[3 marks]*

Q9 Solve $\cos (x + 22.5°) = 0.13$ in the interval $0° \le x \le 360°$.

Q10 Solve $\tan(x - 32°) - 3 = 4.5$ in the interval $-180° \leq x \leq 180°$.

E Q11 Solve $4 \cos 3x = 2.8$ in the interval $0° \leq x \leq 360°$. *[4 marks]*

P Q12 Find all the solutions to $\frac{1}{2} \sin 3x - 0.61 = -0.75$ in the interval $0° \leq x \leq 360°$.

P Q13 Find all the solutions to $\frac{1}{3} \cos(x - 67°) = 0.23$ in the interval $0° \leq x \leq 540°$.

P Q14 Find all the solutions to $2 \sin(x + 19°) + \sqrt{2} = 0$ in the interval $0° \leq x \leq 360°$.

8.11 Using Trig Identities to Solve Equations

Sometimes you'll be asked to find solutions to an equation that has a **tan** term as well as a sin or cos term in it. In these situations you might need to use the **trig identity** for tan x (p.186):

$$\tan x \equiv \frac{\sin x}{\cos x}$$

This will **eliminate** the tan term, and you'll be left with an equation just in terms of sin or cos.

Similarly, if you have a **sin² x** or **cos² x**, you can use the other identity to rewrite one trig function in terms of the other.

$$\sin^2 x + \cos^2 x \equiv 1$$

If you're left with a quadratic equation (e.g. one that contains both $\sin^2 x$ and $\sin x$), you might need to factorise to solve it. To do this, it's usually easiest to make a substitution (e.g. $y = \sin x$ — see p.49).

Example 1 P

Solve $6 \cos^2 x + \cos x \tan x = 5$ for $0° \leq x \leq 360°$.
Give any non-exact answers to 1 d.p.

$6 \cos^2 x + \cos x \tan x = 5$

$\Rightarrow 6 \cos^2 x + \cos x \frac{\sin x}{\cos x} = 5$ — The equation has both cos x and tan x in it, so writing tan x as $\frac{\sin x}{\cos x}$ is a good place to start.

$\Rightarrow 6 \cos^2 x + \sin x = 5$

$\Rightarrow 6(1 - \sin^2 x) + \sin x = 5$ — Now the cos x terms will cancel and the equation has both sin x and cos x in it. So replace the $\cos^2 x$ with $1 - \sin^2 x$.

$\Rightarrow 6 - 6 \sin^2 x + \sin x - 5 = 0$

$\Rightarrow 6 \sin^2 x - \sin x - 1 = 0$ — Multiply out the bracket and rearrange it so that you've got zero on one side — you get a quadratic in sin x.

$\Rightarrow 6y^2 - y - 1 = 0$

$\Rightarrow (2y - 1)(3y + 1) = 0$ — It's easier to factorise the quadratic if you make the substitution $y = \sin x$.

$\Rightarrow (2 \sin x - 1)(3 \sin x + 1) = 0$

continued on the next page...

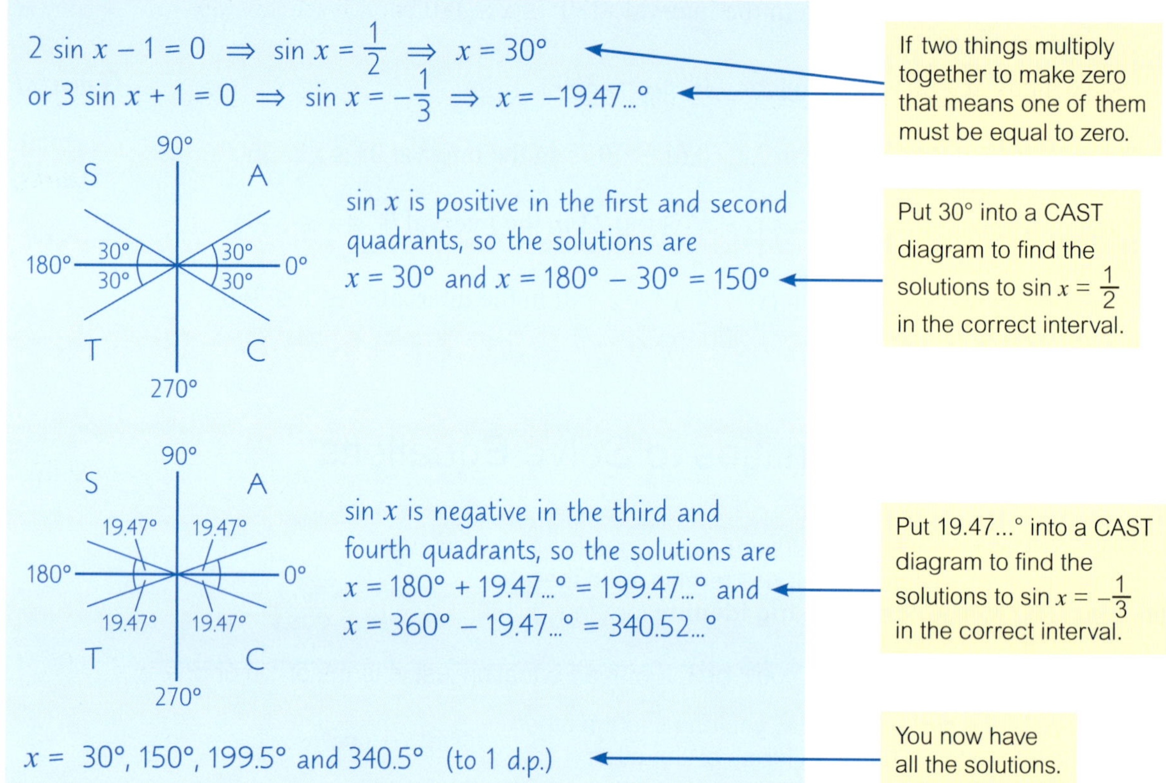

Exercise 8.11

In this exercise, give all non-exact answers to 1 d.p. unless otherwise stated.

P Q1 Solve each of the following equations for values of x in the interval $0° \leq x \leq 360°$:

a) $(\tan x - 5)(3 \sin x - 1) = 0$

b) $5 \sin x \tan x - 4 \tan x = 0$

c) $\tan^2 x = 9$

d) $4 \cos^2 x = 3 \cos x$

e) $3 \sin x = 5 \cos x$

f) $5 \tan^2 x - 2 \tan x = 0$

g) $6 \cos^2 x - \cos x - 2 = 0$

h) $7 \sin x + 3 \cos x = 0$

P Q2 Find the solutions to each of the following equations in the given interval:

a) $\tan x = \sin x \cos x \quad 0° \leq x \leq 360°$

b) $5 \cos^2 x - 9 \sin x = 3 \quad -360° \leq x \leq 720°$

c) $2 \sin^2 x + \sin x - 1 = 0 \quad -360° \leq x \leq 360°$

d) $2 \sin x \tan x = -3 \quad -360° \leq x \leq 360°$

e) $4 - \tan^2 x = 0 \quad -180° \leq x \leq 180°$

P Q3 a) Show that the equation $4 \sin^2 x = 3 - 3 \cos x$ can be written as $4 \cos^2 x - 3 \cos x - 1 = 0$.

b) Hence solve the equation $4 \sin^2 x = 3 - 3 \cos x$ in the interval $0° \leq x \leq 360°$.

P Q4 Solve the equation $3 \cos x - 2 \sin^2 x = 0$ in the interval $0° \leq x \leq 360°$.

P Q5 Solve the equation $2 \sin^2 x + 5 \cos^2 x - 7 \cos x = 0$ in the interval $0° \leq x \leq 360°$.

P Q6 Find all the solutions of the equation $9 \sin^2 2x + 3 \cos 2x = 7$ in the interval $0° \leq x \leq 360°$.

E P Q7 a) Show that $\sin x - \sin x \cos^2 x \equiv \sin^3 x$. *[2 marks]*

b) Hence solve the equation $3 \sin x - 3 \sin x \cos^2 x - 1 = 0$ in the interval $-180° \leq x \leq 180°$. *[3 marks]*

P Q8 Solve the equation $4 \cos \frac{x}{2} - 3 \sin^2 \frac{x}{2} = -1$ in the interval $0° \leq x \leq 720°$.

P Q9 Find all the solutions of the equation $\frac{\cos x}{\tan x} + \sin x = 3$ in the interval $-360° \leq x \leq 360°$. *[4 marks]*

P Q10 Find all the solutions of the equation $\sin^2 x \cos x - \cos x = 0.86$ in the interval $-180° \leq x \leq 180°$.

P Q11 Find all the solutions of the equation $4 \cos^2 x \tan x + \sin x = 0$ in the interval $0° \leq x \leq 360°$.

P Q12 Find all the solutions of the equation $\frac{\cos^2 x}{\sin x - 1} = -0.25$ in the interval $-360° \leq x \leq 360°$.

P Q13 Find the coordinates of all of the points of intersection between the graphs of the functions $f(x) = 2 + 3 \cos^2 x$ and $g(x) = 7 \sin x - 1$ in the interval $0° \leq x \leq 360°$, giving your answers to 3 s.f.

E P Q14 a) Show that the equation $5 \sin x - 2 \tan x = 2 \cos x \sin x$ can be written in the form $2 \cos^2 x - 5 \cos x + 2 = 0$ when $\sin x \neq 0$. *[3 marks]*

b) Hence, find all solutions to $5 \sin x - 2 \tan x = 2 \cos x \sin x$ in the interval $-90° \leq x \leq 90°$. *[4 marks]*

Challenge

E P Q15 a) Show that $4 \sin^4 x + 7 \sin^2 x \cos^2 x - 3 \cos^4 x \equiv 4 - \cos^2 x - 6 \cos^4 x$. *[3 marks]*

b) Using your answer to part a), find all solutions to the equation $4 \sin^4 x + 7 \sin^2 x \cos^2 x - 3 \cos^4 x = 6 - 14 \cos^2 x$ in the interval $-180° \leq x \leq 180°$. *[4 marks]*

E P Q16 Find the possible values of k for which the equation $3 \sin^2 x + (k^2 + 6) \cos x = 3 + 2k^2$ has no solutions. *[4 marks]*

E P Q17 Given the functions $f(x) = 3 \cos^2 x$ and $g(x) = 1 - \sin x$, solve $f(x) = g(x)$ in the interval $0° \leq x \leq 360°$. Give your answers to 1 decimal place. Solutions based only on graphical or numerical methods are not acceptable. *[6 marks]*

8 Review Exercise

Give all answers to 3 significant figures unless otherwise stated.

Q1 Write down the exact values of cos 30°, sin 30°, tan 30°, cos 45°, sin 45°, tan 45°, cos 60°, sin 60° and tan 60°.

Q2 The points below lie on the unit circle. For each point, if a line from the origin to the point makes an angle of θ when measured in an anticlockwise direction from the positive x-axis, find the exact value of θ, where $0° \leq \theta \leq 180°$.

a) $\left(\frac{1}{2}, \frac{\sqrt{3}}{2}\right)$ b) $\left(\frac{\sqrt{3}}{2}, \frac{1}{2}\right)$ c) $(-1, 0)$

E P Q3 Using the information in the diagram, find the following to 1 decimal place:

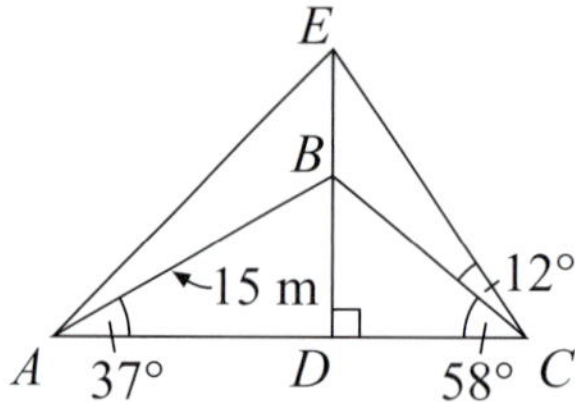

a) the length of AC, [2 marks]

b) the length of EB, [2 marks]

c) the size of angle EAB. [2 marks]

Q4 For triangle ΔABC, in which $A = 30°$, $C = 25°$ and $b = 6$ m:

a) Find all the sides and angles of the triangle.

b) Find the area of the triangle.

E Q5 In an acute-angled triangle, ABC, a line is drawn through the vertex A perpendicular to the side BC and meeting BC at the point D, as shown in the diagram.

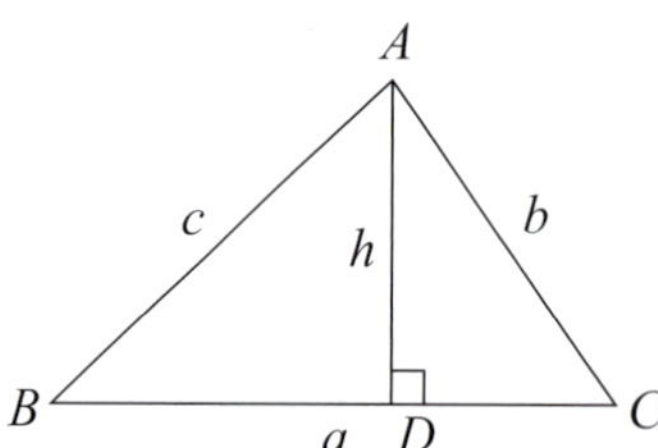

The lengths of the sides of the triangle are a, b and c respectively. The length of AD is h.

a) Verify that the equality $\frac{\sin B}{b} = \frac{\sin C}{c}$ holds. [2 marks]

b) Hence find the size of angle C when $b = 6.4$ cm, $c = 4.3$ cm and $B = 71°$. [2 marks]

Q6 For triangle ΔPQR, in which $p = 13$ km, $q = 23$ km and $R = 20°$:

a) Find all the sides and angles of the triangle.

b) Find the area of the triangle.

Q7 Find all the angles in the triangle on the right. → Give your answers in degrees to 1 d.p.

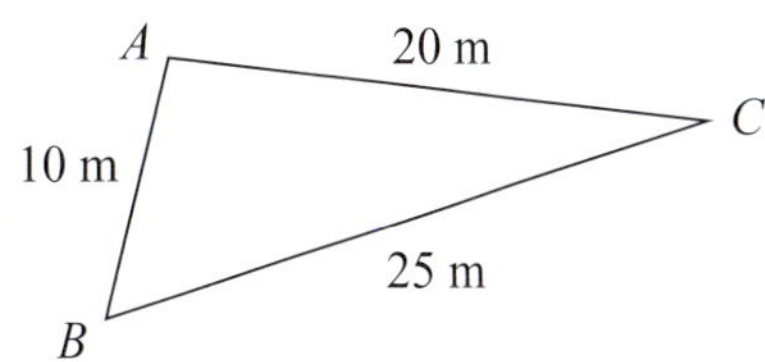

E Q8 The diagram shows a triangle, ABC, with AB of length x m.

a) Use the information in the diagram and the cosine rule to show that $x^2 - 6x + 8 = 0$. *[2 marks]*

b) Hence, or otherwise, find the possible values of x. *[1 mark]*

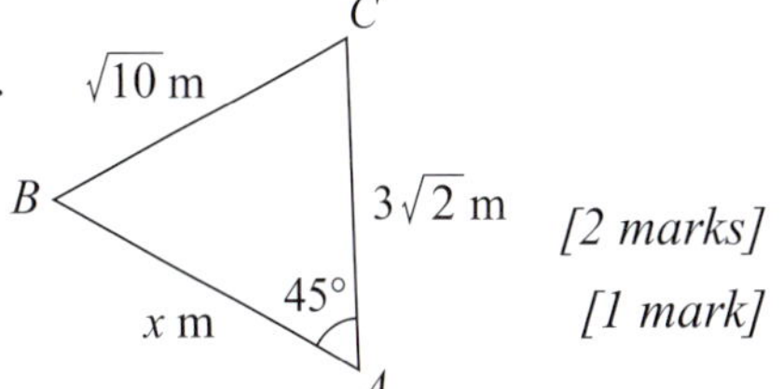

P Q9 Find the missing sides and angles for the 2 possible triangles ΔABC which satisfy $b = 5$, $a = 3$, $A = 35°$.

E P Q10 A triangle has sides of length 4.90 cm, 11.6 cm and 13.2 cm. Find the difference in size between the largest and the smallest angles in the triangle. *[4 marks]*

E P Q11 In the triangle PQR, $PQ = 16$ m, $QR = 12$ m and $\angle RPQ = 37°$. Find the possible areas of the triangle, giving your answers to 3 significant figures. *[6 marks]*

E P Q12 The diagram shows two radii, OA and OB, of a circle C of radius 8 m, centred at point O. Given that angle AOB is equal to 60°, find the exact area of the shaded region. *[4 marks]*

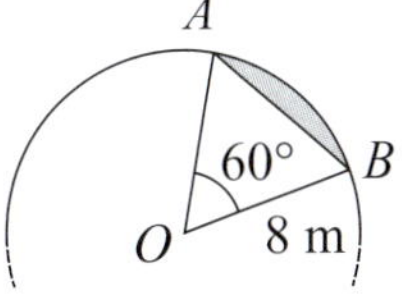

E P Q13 The diagram shows a square-based pyramid with four identical triangular faces. Each of the triangular faces is an isosceles triangle with vertex angle 30° and two sides of length $\sqrt{2}$ m, as shown.

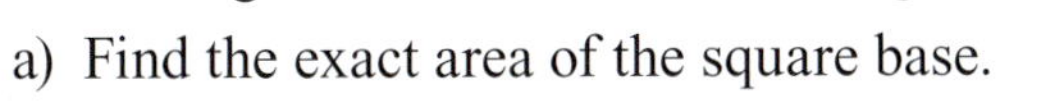

a) Find the exact area of the square base. *[2 marks]*

b) Hence find the exact surface area of the pyramid. *[2 marks]*

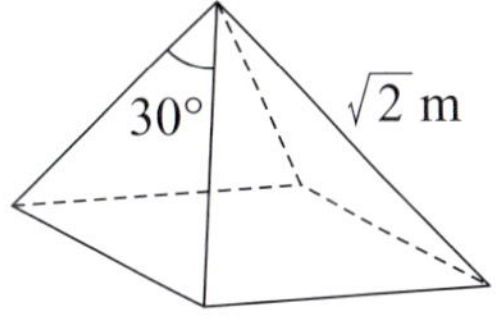

P Q14 Show that $\tan x - \sin x \cos x \equiv \sin^2 x \tan x$.

P Q15 Show that $\tan^2 x - \cos^2 x + 1 \equiv \tan^2 x(1 + \cos^2 x)$.

P Q16 Simplify: $(\sin y + \cos y)^2 + (\cos y - \sin y)^2$.

P Q17 Show that $\dfrac{\sin^4 x + \sin^2 x \cos^2 x}{\cos^2 x - 1} \equiv -1$.

E P Q18 Prove that $\dfrac{\cos x}{\tan x} + \sin x \equiv \dfrac{1}{\sin x}$. *[3 marks]*

Q19 Sketch the following graphs in the interval $-360° \leq x \leq 360°$, making sure you label all of the key points.

a) $y = \cos x$ b) $y = \sin x$ c) $y = \tan x$

Q20 Below is the graph of $y = \cos x$ and a transformation of the graph. What is the equation of the transformed graph?

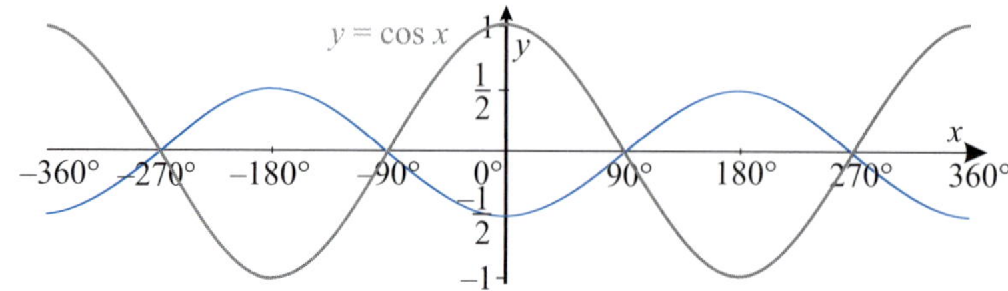

Q21 Below is a graph of $y = \sin x$ and a transformation of the graph. What is the equation of the transformed graph?

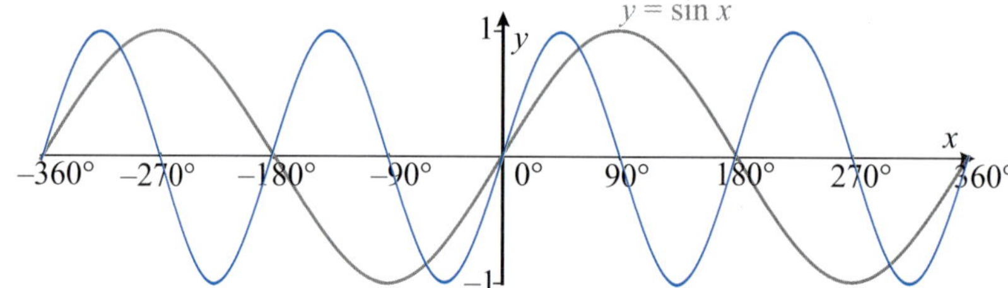

Q22 Sketch the following pairs of graphs on the same axes:

a) $y = \cos x$ and $y = \frac{1}{2} \cos x$ (for $0° \leq x \leq 360°$)

b) $y = \sin x$ and $y = \sin (x + 30°)$ (for $0° \leq x \leq 360°$)

c) $y = \tan x$ and $y = \tan 3x$ (for $0° \leq x \leq 180°$)

E Q23 On separate axes and for $0° \leq x \leq 360°$, sketch the graphs of

a) $y = \sin(-2x)$ *[2 marks]*

b) $y = 1 + \cos(x + 60°)$ *[2 marks]*

E P Q24 The graph below shows the curve with equation $y = p \sin qx$ in the interval $-180° \leq x \leq 180°$.

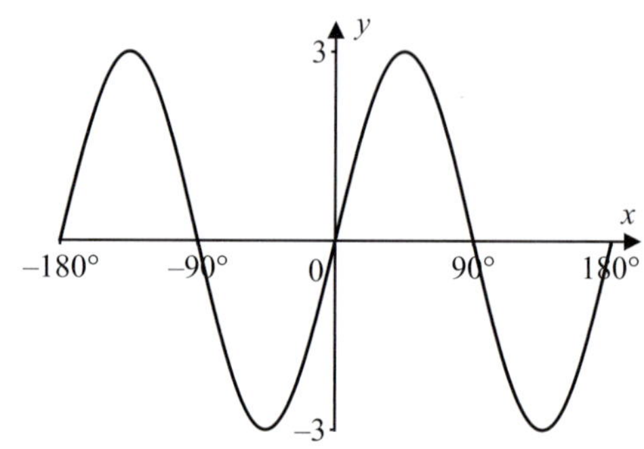

Find the values of p and q. *[3 marks]*

E Q25 The graph below shows the curve $f(x) = \tan x$ in the interval $-360° \leq x \leq 360°$.

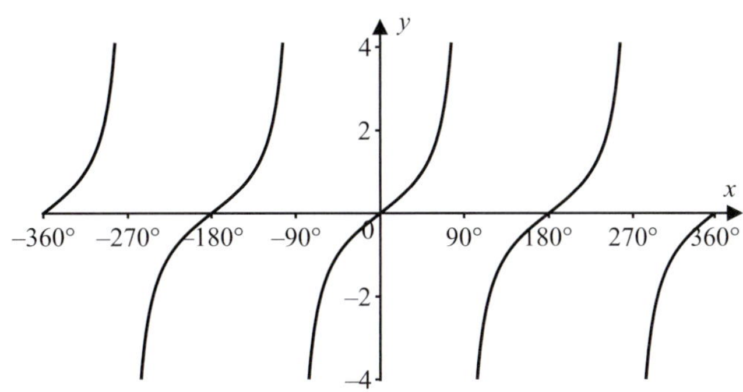

a) (i) Write down the coordinates of any points where the function $g(x) = \tan(x - 30°)$ intersects the x-axis. *[2 marks]*

(ii) Write down the equations of the asymptotes of $g(x)$ in the given interval. *[2 marks]*

b) Explain why the asymptotes exist in the function $f(x)$. *[1 mark]*

c) Given that $\tan(-30°) = -\frac{\sqrt{3}}{3}$, use the graph to determine the value of $\tan 30°$. *[2 marks]*

Q26 a) Solve each of these equations for $0° \leq \theta \leq 360°$:

(i) $\sin\theta = \frac{\sqrt{3}}{2}$ (ii) $\tan\theta = -1$ (iii) $\cos\theta = -\frac{1}{\sqrt{2}}$

b) Solve each of these equations for $-180° \leq \theta \leq 180°$ (giving your answers to 1 d.p.):

(i) $\cos 4\theta = -\frac{2}{3}$ (ii) $\sin(\theta + 35°) = 0.3$ (iii) $\tan\frac{\theta}{2} = 500$

E Q27 Find the solutions of the equation $2\sin(x + 30°) = \frac{1}{4}$ for $-360° \leq x \leq 360°$. Give your answers to 1 decimal place. *[5 marks]*

Q28 a) On the same axes, sketch the graphs of $y = 5 + \cos x$ and $y = 2\sin\left(\frac{1}{2}x\right)$ in the interval $0° \leq x \leq 360°$.

b) Explain with reference to the graphs in a) why the equation $5 + \cos x = 2\sin\left(\frac{1}{2}x\right)$ has no solutions in the same interval.

c) Give the range of possible values of k for which the equation $k + \cos x = 2\sin\left(\frac{1}{2}x\right)$ has at least one solution in the same interval.

E P Q29 a) Sketch the graph of $y = \cos x$ in the range $-360° \leq x \leq 360°$. *[2 marks]*

Given that $x = a$ is the smallest positive solution of the equation $k\cos x + 1 = 0$, where $k > 1$ is a positive integer,

b) Using the graph sketched in a), write expressions, in terms of a, for all solutions to the equation $k\cos 2\theta + 1 = 0$ in the interval $-180° \leq \theta \leq 180°$. *[3 marks]*

E P Q30 a) Sketch the graph of $y = \cos x$ for $-360° \leq x \leq 360°$. *[2 marks]*

Given that $f(x) = \frac{2}{3 + 2\cos x}$,

b) Using the graph from a) where necessary, find all solutions, to 1 decimal place, of the equation $f(x) = \frac{3}{4}$ for $-360° \leq x \leq 360°$. *[3 marks]*

c) Determine the maximum value of f(x) and find the smallest positive value of x at which the maximum occurs. *[2 marks]*

E P Q31 a) Given that $3\sin x - 4\cos x = 0$, show that $\tan x = \frac{4}{3}$. *[2 marks]*

b) Hence, find the values of x in the interval $0° \leq x \leq 360°$ for which $3\sin x - 4\cos x = 0$, giving your answers to 1 decimal place. *[3 marks]*

P Q32 Find all the solutions to $6\sin^2 x = \cos x + 5$ in the interval $0° \leq x \leq 360°$, giving your answers to 1 d.p. where appropriate.

P Q33 Solve $3\tan x + 2\cos x = 0$ for $-90° \leq x \leq 90°$.

P Q34 Find all the solutions of the equation $\tan x - 3\sin x = 0$, in the interval $0° \leq x \leq 720°$. Give your answers to 1 d.p.

P Q35 Find all the solutions of the equation $8\sin^2 x + 2\sin x - 1 = 0$ in the interval $0° \leq x \leq 360°$, giving your answers to 1 d.p. where appropriate.

E P Q36 Using trigonometric identities wherever necessary, find all solutions to the equation $2\cos(\theta - 80°) = 3\tan(\theta - 80°)$ in the range $0° \leq \theta \leq 360°$. *[6 marks]*

E P Q37 a) Prove the trigonometric identity $\cos^4 x - \cos^2 x \equiv \sin^4 x - \sin^2 x$. *[2 marks]*

b) Hence, or otherwise, find all solutions, to 1 decimal place, to the equation $2\sin^4 x - 2\cos^4 x = \cos x - 1$ for $0° \leq x < 360°$. *[4 marks]*

Challenge

E P M Q38 The function $T(t) = 15 + 8\sin(45t)°$ models how the temperature changes in a room over time, where T represents the temperature in °C and t represents time in hours.

a) What is the temperature after three hours? *[2 marks]*

b) Within the model, what are the maximum and minimum possible temperatures? *[2 marks]*

c) How many times will the temperature reach 20 °C during the first 8 hours? Show your working. *[6 marks]*

E P **Q39** Show that:

a) $\frac{1-2\sin\theta\cos\theta}{1+2\sin\theta\cos\theta} \equiv \left(\frac{\sin\theta-\cos\theta}{\sin\theta+\cos\theta}\right)^2$ *[2 marks]*

b) $\frac{\sin x - \sin^2 x}{\cos x + \cos^2 x} \equiv \frac{(1-\sin x)(1-\cos x)}{\sin x \cos x}$ *[3 marks]*

E P M **Q40** The diagram shows a cross-section, $ABCD$, of a cuboid-shaped container inclined at 30° to the horizontal ground OP and resting against a vertical wall OQ.

AD and DC have lengths of 1.75 m and 1 m respectively. Some water is in the container and the area of the cross-section formed by the water is 1.3 m^2. XY is the horizontal level of the water.

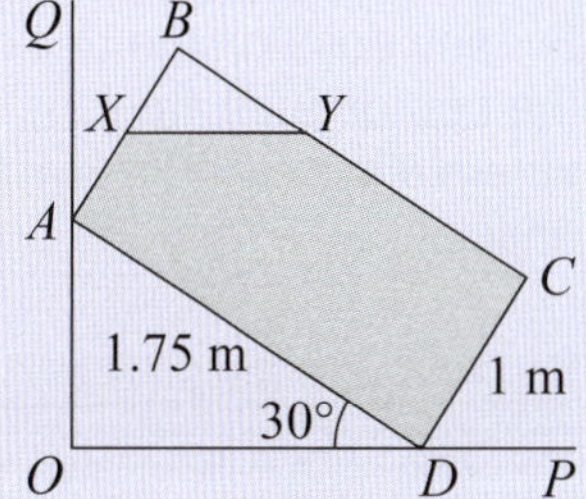

Find the following to 2 decimal places:

a) the height of B above the ground, *[3 marks]*

b) the length BY, *[2 marks]*

c) the height of the surface of the water above the ground. *[2 marks]*

E P **Q41** a) Sketch the graph of $y = \sin x$ in the range $0° \le x \le 360°$ *[2 marks]*

Given that $f(x) = \sin^2 x$ and $0° \le x \le 360°$, using the graph from a) where necessary:

b) State the maximum and minimum values of f(x) and determine the values of x for which the maximum and minimum values occur in the given range. *[2 marks]*

c) Determine the values of x for which $f(x) = \frac{1}{4}$. *[2 marks]*

d) Use the results from a) and b) to sketch the graph of $y = f(x)$ in the range $0° \le x \le 360°$. *[2 marks]*

E P M **Q42** The daily water level in a dock is modelled using the equation $H = 5.5 - \cos(30t)$ where H is the height of the water measured in feet and t is time measured in hours after midnight.

a) What are the highest and lowest water levels in the dock? *[1 mark]*

b) Sketch the graph of H for the values $0 \le t \le 24$. *[2 marks]*

It is only safe to take boats in and out of the dock when the water level is at least 5 feet. Anna wishes to take her boat out of the dock and return the same day.

c) Given that the water is at its lowest level at midnight, find the earliest time that Anna can take her boat out and the latest time that she can return on the same day. *[4 marks]*

E P **Q43** a) Show that the equation $3\cos x \tan x = 10\cos^2 x - 6$ can be written as $10\sin^2 x + 3\sin x - 4 = 0$. *[4 marks]*

b) Hence, find all solutions to $3\cos 2x \tan 2x = 10\cos^2 2x - 6$ in the interval $-45° \le x \le 45°$. *[4 marks]*

8 Chapter Summary

1 The trig values for 30°, 45° and 60° can be derived using the trig formulas (SOHCAHTOA) and the two right-angled triangles shown on the right.

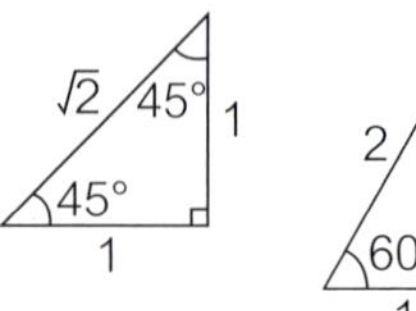

2 For any point on the unit circle, the coordinates are ($\cos\theta$, $\sin\theta$), where θ is the angle taken anticlockwise from the positive x-axis.

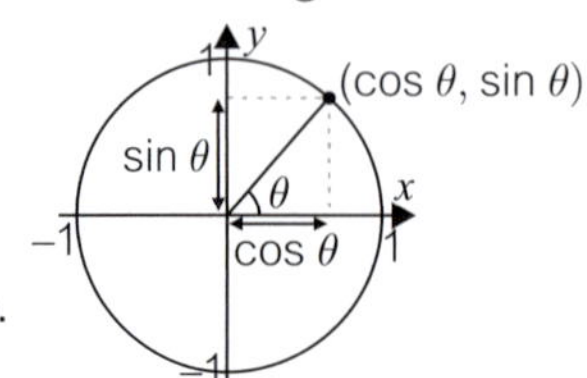

3 You can use the sine and cosine rules to find missing lengths and angles in a triangle:

- The sine rule is given by the formula: $\frac{a}{\sin A} = \frac{b}{\sin B} = \frac{c}{\sin C}$
- The cosine rule is given by the formula: $a^2 = b^2 + c^2 - 2bc\cos A$
- It can be rearranged into the form: $\cos A = \frac{b^2 + c^2 - a^2}{2bc}$

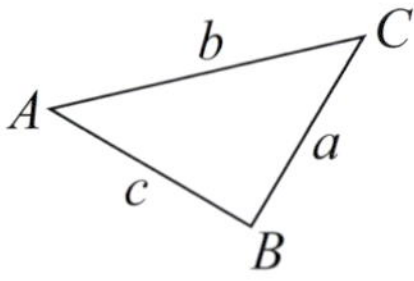

4 To find the area of a triangle, you can use the formula: Area $= \frac{1}{2}ab\sin C$

5 You can use the trig identites $\tan\theta \equiv \frac{\sin\theta}{\cos\theta}$ and $\sin^2\theta + \cos^2\theta \equiv 1$ to prove that two expressions are equivalent.

6 The graphs of $\sin x$ and $\cos x$ repeat every 360°, and $\tan x$ repeats every 180°.

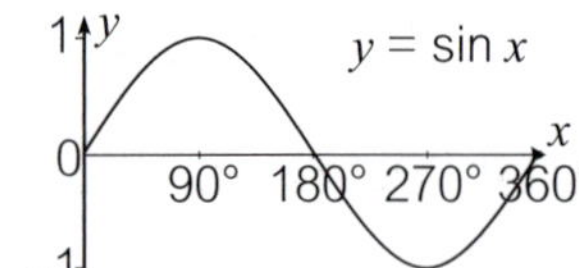

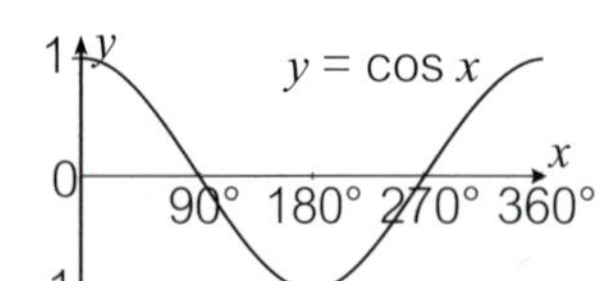

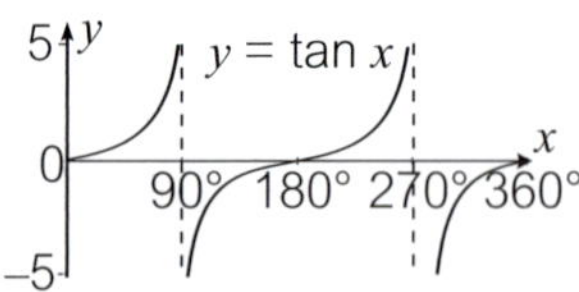

7 Trig graphs can be transformed in the same way as regular graphs, e.g. for $y = \sin x$:

- $y = \sin(x) + c$ represents a translation of $+c$ units along the y-axis.
- $y = \sin(x + c)$ represents a translation of $-c$ units along the x-axis.
- $y = n\sin x$ represents a vertical stretch with scale factor n.
- $y = \sin nx$ represents a horizontal stretch with scale factor $\frac{1}{n}$.

8 You can use the symmetry and periodicity of trig graphs to find all of the solutions to a trig equation in a given interval.

9 A CAST diagram shows where each trig function is positive.

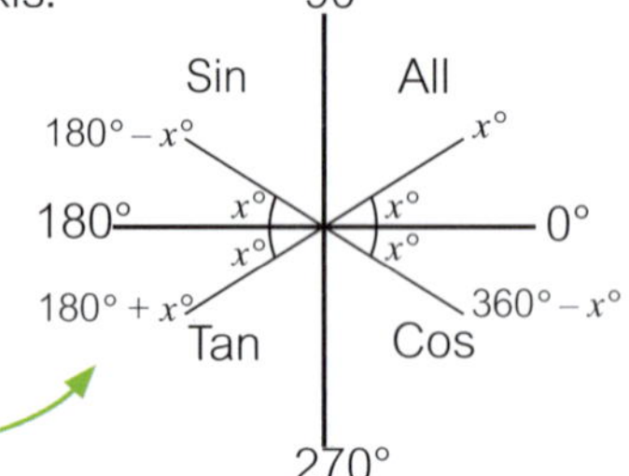

10 Equations of the form $\sin kx = n$ or similar can be solved by multiplying the x interval by k, solving for kx over the new interval and then dividing each solution by k. Similarly equations of the form $\sin(x + c) = n$ can be solved by adding c to the interval, solving for $x + c$ over the new interval and then subtracting c.

11 You can use the trig identities $\tan\theta \equiv \frac{\sin\theta}{\cos\theta}$ and $\sin^2\theta + \cos^2\theta \equiv 1$ to simplify and solve equations that involve more than one trig function.

Exponentials and Logarithms

9

Learning Objectives

Once you've completed this chapter, you should be able to:

- Recognise the graph of the exponential function $y = a^x$ and its transformations.
- Understand the significance of the number e and the function $y = e^x$, and recall that the gradient of Ae^{kx} is kAe^{kx}.
- Convert between index and log notation, and use the natural logarithm, ln.
- Use the laws of logs to solve equations, and use the change of base formula.
- Use exponential functions as models for real-world situations, and understand their limitations.
- Plot equations of the form $y = ax^n$ and $y = kb^x$ as straight-line graphs and use them to estimate values.

Prior Knowledge Check

1 Calculate the simple interest earned on an investment of £1600 for 4 years at an annual rate of 5%. *see GCSE Maths*

2 Write down the gradient and the coordinates of the y-intercept for the graph of $y = 8 - 7x$. *see GCSE Maths*

3 Plot a scatter graph for the data in this table and draw a line of best fit:

x	10	60	100	40	110
y	120	45	50	80	30

see GCSE Maths

4 Evaluate: a) $27^{\frac{1}{3}}$ b) 12^0 c) 9^{-2} d) $16^{\frac{3}{2}}$ *see pages 25-26*

5 a) Rewrite $x - 7x^{\frac{1}{2}} + 6 = 0$ in the form $au^2 + bu + c = 0$.
b) Hence solve $x - 7x^{\frac{1}{2}} + 6 = 0$. *see page 49*

6 The graph of $y = f(x)$ has a minimum point at (4, –6) and a maximum point at (–2, 8). Give the coordinates and natures of the turning points of the graph of $y = f(-x)$. *see pages 132-134*

9.1 Exponentials

Exponentials are functions of the form $y = a^x$ (or $f(x) = a^x$), where $\boldsymbol{a > 0}$. **All** graphs of exponential functions have the **same basic shape**.

$y = a^x$ for $a > 1$

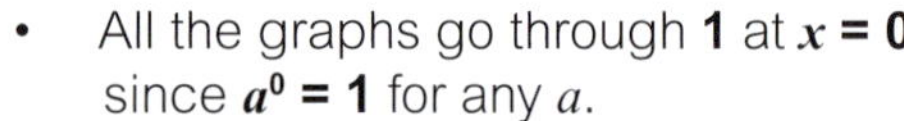

- All the graphs go through **1** at $\boldsymbol{x = 0}$ since $\boldsymbol{a^0 = 1}$ for any a.
- $a > 1$ — so y **increases as** x **increases**.
- The **bigger** a is, the **quicker** the graph increases (so the curve is **steeper**).
- As x **decreases**, y **decreases** at a **smaller and smaller rate** — y approaches zero, but never actually gets there.
- So as $\boldsymbol{x \to \infty, y \to \infty}$ and as $\boldsymbol{x \to -\infty, y \to 0}$.

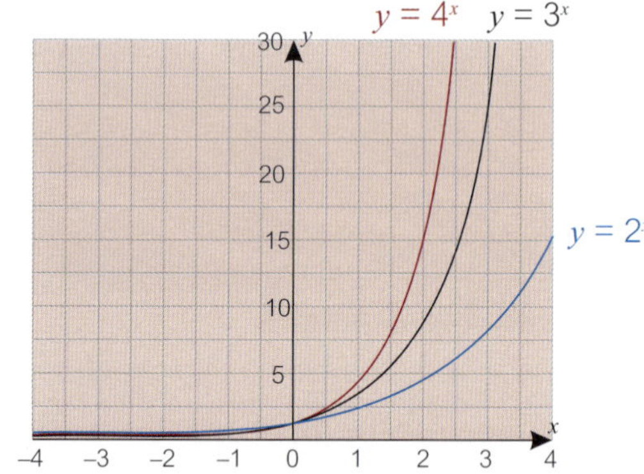

$y = a^x$ for $0 < a < 1$

- All the graphs go through **1** at $\boldsymbol{x = 0}$ since $\boldsymbol{a^0 = 1}$ for any a.
- $0 < a < 1$ — so y **decreases as** x **increases**.
- The **smaller** a is, the **faster** the graphs decrease (so the curve is **steeper**).
- As x **increases**, y **decreases** at a **smaller and smaller rate** — y will approach zero, but never actually get there.
- So as $\boldsymbol{x \to \infty, y \to 0}$ and as $\boldsymbol{x \to -\infty, y \to \infty}$.

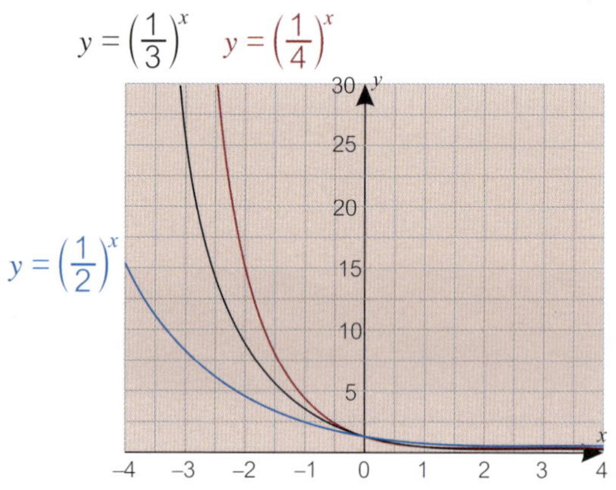

The notation $x \to \infty$ just means 'x tends to infinity' (i.e. x gets bigger and bigger). Similarly $y \to 0$ means 'y tends to 0' (gets smaller and smaller). a^x gets infinitely close to 0 but never reaches it, so $y = 0$ is an asymptote of the graph — see p.127.

The exponential function, e^x

The main feature of **exponential graphs** or functions is that the rate of increase or decrease of the function is **proportional** to the function itself.

You need to know about a value of 'a' for which the **gradient** of $y = a^x$ is **exactly the same** as a^x. That value is known as **e**, an **irrational number** around 2.7183 (it's stored in your calculator just like π). This **special case** of an exponential function, $y = e^x$, is called **'the' exponential function**.

Tip An irrational number is a real number which can't be written as a fraction $\frac{a}{b}$ (where a and b are both integers and $b \neq 0$).

Because e is just a number, the graph of $\boldsymbol{y = e^x}$ has all the properties of $y = a^x$:

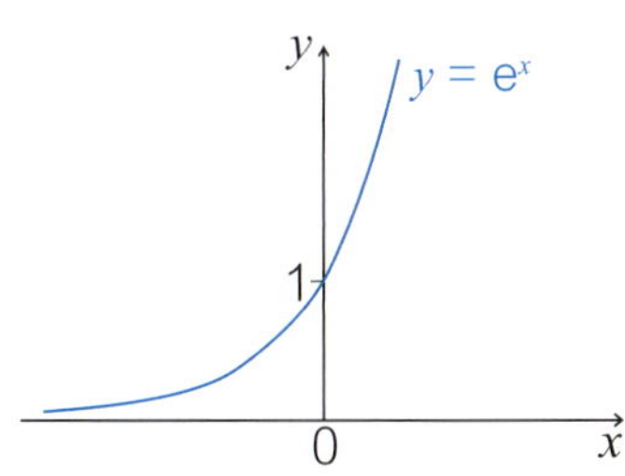

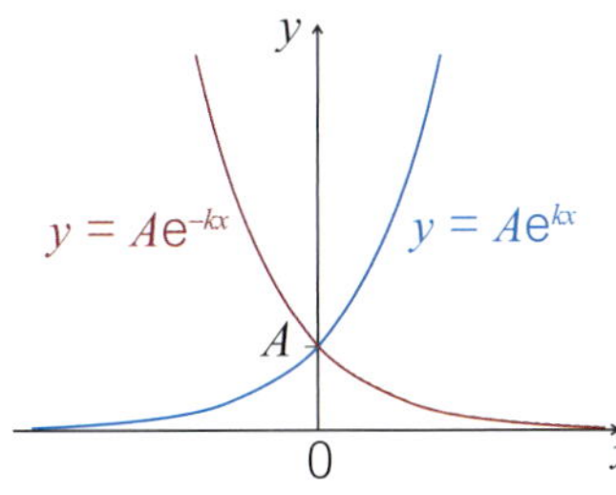

- $y = e^x$ cuts the y-axis at (0, 1).
- As $x \to \infty$, $e^x \to \infty$ and as $x \to -\infty$, $e^x \to 0$.
- $y = e^x$ does not exist for $y \leq 0$ (i.e. $e^x > 0$ — it can't be zero or negative).

For **positive constants** A and k, the graph of Ae^{kx} looks similar to the graph of e^x, except that it cuts the y-axis at **(0, A)**. For the graph of Ae^{-kx}, you just reflect the graph of Ae^{kx} in the y-axis. The graphs of Ae^{kx} and Ae^{-kx} come up a lot in modelling (see p.232-234).

Gradient of $y = Ae^{kx}$

As mentioned above, an interesting property of $y = e^x$ is that its gradient is e^x. This can be generalised:

> For the graph $y = e^{kx}$, where k is a constant, its gradient is ke^{kx}.
> For the graph $y = Ae^{kx}$, where A and k are constants, its gradient is kAe^{kx}.

The gradient of a curve is the same as the gradient of the **tangent** to the curve at a point — for example, on the curve $y = e^x$, the gradient of the tangent to the curve at $x = 2$ is e^2 (so the gradient of the curve is also e^2 at this point). There's more on finding the gradient of a curve on p.248-249.

The gradient shows the **rate of change** of the function. So the rate of change of Ae^{kx} is **directly proportional** to the function itself. This means that an **exponential model** is suitable in situations where the rate of increase/decrease of y is proportional to the value of y.

If the **signs** for A and k are **different** (e.g. $y = -2e^{3x}$ or $y = 4e^{-x}$), then the gradient will be negative — i.e. it's a **decreasing** function (see p.268).

Example 1

Find the gradient of the curve $f(x) = 5e^{8x}$ at the points $x = 0$ and $x = 2$. Leave your answers as exact solutions.

Gradient of $f(x) = kAe^{kx}$
$= 8 \times 5 \times e^{8x} = 40e^{8x}$

The equation is in the form $f(x) = Ae^{kx}$, where $A = 5$ and $k = 8$, so use the formula to find an expression for the gradient.

At $x = 0$, the gradient of $f(x) = 40e^{8 \times 0}$
$= 40e^0 = 40$

At $x = 2$, the gradient of $f(x) = 40e^{8 \times 2}$
$= 40e^{16}$

Evaluate the gradients at the points $x = 0$ and $x = 2$.

Tip
If a question asks for an **exact** answer, leave it in terms of e. You could also be asked for a certain number of decimal places or significant figures, e.g. $40e^{16} = 355\,000\,000$ to 3 s.f.

Example 2 M

The number of geese, g, at a nature reserve after t days is modelled using the formula $g = Ae^{kt}$, where A and k are constants.

After 1 day, there were 80 geese, and the gradient of the curve plotted from the data collected was 241. Find A and k, giving your answers to 1 s.f.

When $t = 1$, $g = 80 \Rightarrow 80 = Ae^k$

At this point, the gradient is 241 $\Rightarrow 241 = kAe^k$

"After 1 day" means $t = 1$.

$241 = kAe^k \Rightarrow 241 = 80k \Rightarrow k = \frac{241}{80} = 3.0125$

So $k = 3$ (1 s.f.)

Solve the two equations in A and k simultaneously by substituting $Ae^k = 80$ into $241 = kAe^k$.

$80 = Ae^k \Rightarrow 80 = Ae^{3.0125} \Rightarrow A = \frac{80}{e^{3.0125}} = 3.933...$

So $A = 4$ (1 s.f.)

Put the unrounded value of k back into one of the original equations to find A. In real-life situations, A is called the initial value — and it's usually positive.

The equation of the curve is $g = 4e^{3t}$

Exercise 9.1

Q1 On the same axes, sketch the graphs of:

a) (i) $y = 2^x$ (ii) $y = 3^{-x}$ (iii) $y = e^x$

b) (i) $y = \left(\frac{3}{4}\right)^x$ (ii) $y = \left(\frac{1}{5}\right)^x$ (iii) $y = 5^x$

E Q2 Sketch the graph of $y = \left(\frac{2}{3}\right)^{x+1}$, showing the coordinates of any intersections with the axes. *[2 marks]*

Q2 Hint Remember that $a^{m+n} = a^m \times a^n$.

Q3 Match each of the following functions to one of the graphs below:

a) $y = 3e^{3x}$

b) $y = 3^x$

c) $y = 3e^{-x}$

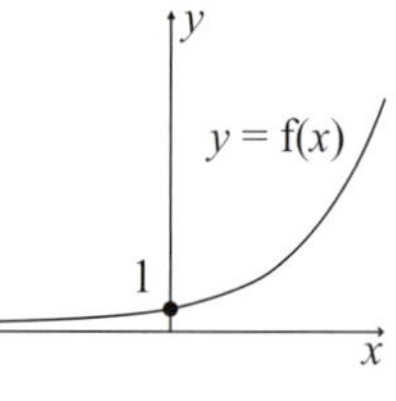

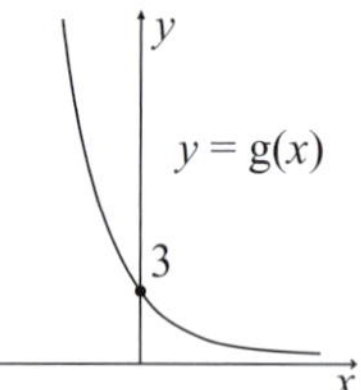

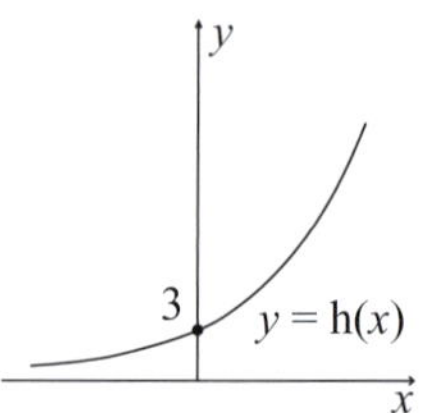

E P Q4 Sketch the graph of $y = e^{x+3}$, showing the coordinates of any intersections with the axes. *[2 marks]*

E P Q5 Consider the functions $f(x) = e^{2x}$ and $g(x) = e^x$. Rewrite each of these transformations of $f(x)$ in terms of $g(x)$.

a) $f(-x)$ *[2 marks]*

b) $f(x - 1)$ *[2 marks]*

Q6 For the function $f(x) = 1.5^x$, match each of the following equations to one of the graphs below:

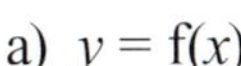

a) $y = f(x)$

b) $y = f(x) + 2$

c) $y = f(-x)$

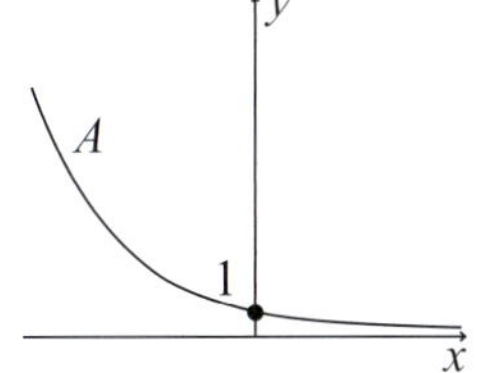

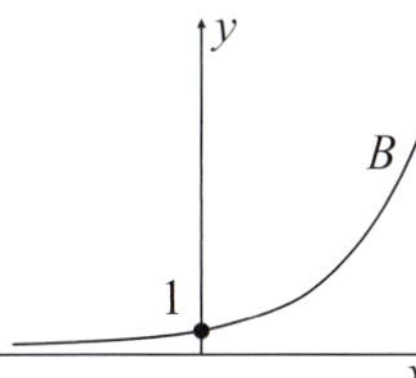

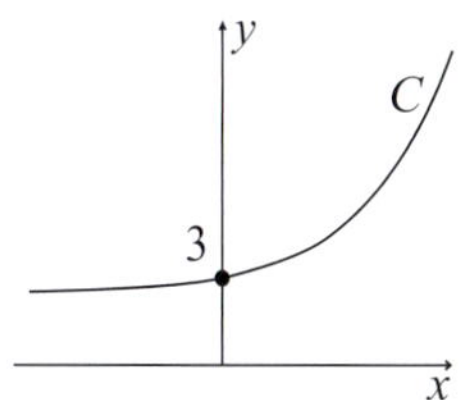

E P Q7 Consider the function $f(x) = e^x$. Sketch the graphs of the following transformations on separate axes. Label the coordinates of any intersections with the axes and the equations of any horizontal or vertical asymptotes.

a) $y = f(x + 1)$ *[3 marks]*

b) $y = f(x) + 1$ *[3 marks]*

Q8 Find the gradient of each curve at the points given. Leave your answers in exact form.

a) $y = e^{3x}$ at the points $x = 0$ and $x = 1$

b) $y = 5e^{0.5x}$ at the points $x = -2$ and $x = 2$

c) $x = 2.5e^{6t}$ at the points $t = \frac{1}{3}$ and $t = 5$

d) $y = 4e^{-2x}$ at the points $x = -5$ and $x = 0.5$

P Q9 The graph of $y = Ae^{kx}$ has gradient $12e^3$ at the point $x = 2$. Find the values of A and k, and hence find the exact y-coordinates when $x = 4$ and $x = 12$.

E P Q10 Consider the curve with equation $y = Ae^{bx}$.

a) Write down the coordinates of the y-intercept in terms of A and b. *[1 mark]*

b) The gradient of the curve at the point $x = 4$ is $2e^2$. Find the values of A and b. *[3 marks]*

E P M Q11 The estimated number of termites living in a termite mound can be modelled by the following function:

$N = 500e^{kt}$, where t is measured in months since the first observation.

The gradient function of the curve is $200e^{kt}$.

a) Find the value of k. *[2 marks]*

b) Hence estimate the number of termites in the mound 1 year after the initial observation. *[1 mark]*

Challenge

P M Q12 The population of rabbits in a wood is modelled using the function $f(t)$, where t is the number of years since the population was first counted. The gradient of the curve of $f(t)$ is always 0.4 times the value of $f(t)$. When first counted, there were 7 rabbits. Find the function $f(t)$ and use it to estimate the number of rabbits in the wood after 5 years.

P Q13 Sketch the graphs of $y = 2^{1-x}$ and $y = 4^x$ on the same pair of axes. On your sketch, label the coordinates of any intersections with the axes and any points where the two graphs intersect.

9.2 Logarithms

A **logarithm** is just the power that a number needs to be **raised to** in order to produce a given value.

Before now, you've used **index notation** to represent powers, but sometimes it's easier to work with **log notation**. In **index notation**, 3^5 means that **5** lots of **3** are multiplied together. **3** is known as the **base**. You now need to be able to **switch** from index notation into **log notation**, and vice versa.

Log notation looks like this: $\log_a b = c$ ... which means the **same** as the **index notation**... $a^c = b$

- The little number 'a' after 'log' is the **base**.
- 'c' is the **power** the base is being **raised to**.
- 'b' is the answer you get when a is raised to the power c.
- Log means '**power**', so the log above really just means: "what is the power you need to raise a to if you want to end up with b?"

Tip If you're struggling with this, try putting in some numbers — e.g. $\log_3 9 = 2$ is the same as $3^2 = 9$.

$\log_a b = c$ is the same as $a^c = b$, so:

$\log_a a = 1$ and $\log_a 1 = 0$

In index notation, this is saying that $a^1 = a$, and $a^0 = 1$.

- The **base** of a log must be a **positive number ≠ 1** (or the log isn't defined for some, or all, values).
- For $a > 1$, if $b > 1$, then c is **positive**. And if $0 < b < 1$, then c is **negative**. For $0 < a < 1$, the **opposite** is true.

Common Bases

There are two bases that are more common than others: the first is **base 10**. The button marked 'log' on your calculator uses base 10.

Index notation: $10^2 = 100$

or

log notation: $\log_{10} 100 = 2$

So the **logarithm** of 100 to the **base 10** is 2, because 10 raised to the **power** of 2 is 100.

The base goes here but it's usually left out if it's 10.

The other common base is **base e** — this is known as the **natural logarithm** and is written 'ln':

Index notation: $e^3 = 20.085...$

or

log notation: $\ln 20.085... = 3$

So the **natural logarithm** of 20.085... is 3, because e raised to the **power** of 3 is 20.085...

You don't need to write the base — 'ln' tells you that it's e.

Example 1

a) Write down the value of $\log_2 8$.

Here the base (a) is 2, and the answer (b) is 8. ← Compare to $\log_a b = c$.

8 is 2 raised to the power of 3, or $2^3 = 8$. ← Think about the power (c) that you'll need to raise 2 to in order to get 8.

This means the value of $\log_2 8$ is 3.

b) Write down the value of $\log_9 3$.

3 is the square root of 9, or $9^{\frac{1}{2}} = 3$, so $\log_9 3 = \frac{1}{2}$ ← Work out the power that 9 needs to be raised to to get 3.

c) Write $3^0 = 1$ using log notation.

0 is the power (c) or logarithm that 3 (a, the base) is raised to to get 1 (b). ← You just need to make sure you get things in the right place.

So $\log_3 1 = 0$ ← Substitute the values into $\log_a b = c$.

Inverse Functions

An **inverse function** does the **opposite** to the function. So if the function was '+ 1', then the inverse would be '– 1'. And if the function was '× 2', the inverse would be '÷ 2'. The inverse for a function f(x) is written $\mathbf{f^{-1}(x)}$.

Tip Not every function has an inverse. You'll learn more about which functions have inverses if you carry on to Year 2 of the A-Level course.

For the function $f(x) = a^x$, its inverse is $f^{-1}(x) = \log_a x$.
And for $g(x) = e^x$, its inverse is $g^{-1}(x) = \ln x$.

Doing an inverse function to the original gets you **back to x** on its own. This gives you the following very useful formulas which will help you to solve equations later in the chapter:

$$a^{\log_a x} = x$$
$$\log_a (a^x) = x$$

$$e^{\ln x} = x$$
$$\ln (e^x) = x$$

(for any positive $a \neq 1$)

Tip $\log_a a = 1$ and $\ln e = 1$.

The graph of an inverse function is a **reflection** in the line $y = x$:

- $y = \ln x$ is the reflection of $y = e^x$ in the line $y = x$.
- It cuts the x-axis at **(1, 0)** (so **ln 1 = 0**).
- As $x \to \infty$, $\ln x \to \infty$, but it happens very slowly.
- As $x \to 0$, $\ln x \to -\infty$.
- $\ln x$ **does not exist** for $x \leq 0$ (i.e. x can't be zero or negative).

The graphs of $y = a^x$ and $y = \log_a x$ look very similar to the graphs for $y = e^x$ and $y = \ln x$ — they'll just have steeper or gentler curves, depending on the value of a.

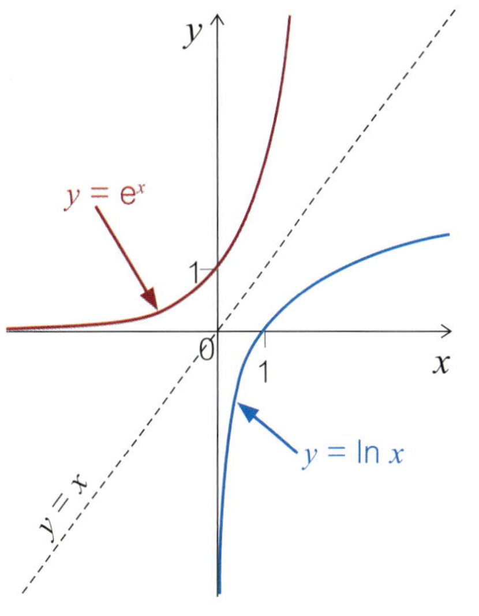

Example 2

Solve the following equations, giving your answers as exact solutions.

a) $e^x = 10$

$e^x = 10$

$\ln e^x = \ln 10$ ← Apply ln to both sides to remove the 'e' function.

$x = \ln 10$ ← Remember, $\ln e^x = x$

b) $\ln x = 2$

$\ln x = 2$

$e^{\ln x} = e^2$ ← Raise e to the power of both sides to remove the ln function.

$x = e^2$ ← Remember, $e^{\ln x} = x$

Exercise 9.2

In this exercise, log means $\log_{10}$.

Q1 Hint Work out a, b and c first, then substitute them into $\log_a b = c$.

Q1 Write the following using log notation:

a) $2^3 = 8$ b) $5^4 = 625$ c) $49^{\frac{1}{2}} = 7$ d) $8^{\frac{2}{3}} = 4$

e) $10^{-2} = \frac{1}{100}$ f) $2^{-3} = 0.125$ g) $4^x = 9$ h) $x^3 = 40$

i) $8^{11} = x$ j) $64^{\frac{3}{2}} = 512$ k) $25^{-\frac{1}{2}} = \frac{1}{5}$ l) $x^{2y} = 4096$

Q2 Write the following using index notation (you don't need to work out any values):

a) $\ln a = 6$ b) $\log_5 t = 0.2$ c) $\log_4 m = 1$ d) $\ln p = 13$

e) $\log k = 5$ f) $\log_x a = m$ g) $\ln k = z$ h) $\log q = r$

Q3 Find the value of the following. Give your answer to 3 d.p. where appropriate.

a) $\log 1000$ b) $\log 0.01$ c) $\log 3$ d) $\log 125$

e) $\ln 2$ f) $\ln 1$ g) $\ln 6$ h) $\ln 20$

Q4 Without using your calculator, find the value of:

a) $\log_2 4$ b) $\log_3 27$ c) $\log_5 0.2$ d) $\log_{0.5} 0.25$

Q5 Find the value of x, where $x \geq 0$, by writing the following in index notation:

a) $\log_x 49 = 2$ b) $\log_x 8 = 3$ c) $\log_x 100\,000 = 5$

d) $\log_x 3125 = 5$ e) $\log_x 3 = \frac{1}{2}$ f) $\log_x 7 = \frac{1}{3}$

g) $\log_x 2 = \frac{1}{5}$ h) $\log_x 9 = \frac{1}{4}$ i) $\log_x 0.5 = 0.8$

Q6 Solve these equations, giving (i) an exact solution, and (ii) a solution correct to 3 s.f.

a) $e^x = 5$ b) $\ln x = 8$ c) $e^{3t} = 11$ d) $\ln 10x = 4$

E Q7 State the values of the following:

a) $2\log_a a$ *[1 mark]*

b) $\frac{1}{3}\log_b 1$, for $b > 1$ *[1 mark]*

P Q8 In each part, use index notation to write y in terms of x, given that:

a) $\log_a x = 2$ and $\log_a y = 4$

b) $\log_a x = 3$ and $\log_{2a} y = 3$

c) $\ln x = 5$ and $\ln y = 20$

E Q9 Find the value of the following, leaving your answers in exact form:

a) $\log_{10} 0.001 \times \log_2 4\sqrt{2}$ *[2 marks]*

b) $\dfrac{\log_4 16^e}{e \ln e^7}$ *[2 marks]*

E Q10 Find the positive value of x such that:

a) $\log_x \frac{81}{16} = 4$ *[1 mark]*

b) $\log_x \frac{3}{4} = \frac{1}{2}$ *[1 mark]*

E Q11 Solve the following, leaving your answers in exact form:

a) $\log_x 2 = \frac{1}{4}$ *[1 mark]*

b) $\log_x 4e^2 = 2$ *[1 mark]*

E P Q12 Rewrite the following as x in terms of y:

a) $y = \frac{1}{2}\log_{10} x$ *[1 mark]*

b) $y = e^{3x}$ *[1 mark]*

c) $y = \ln x^2$ *[1 mark]*

E P Q13 You are given that $\log_{10} b = 2a + 3$.

a) Find the exact value of b when $a = -2$. *[1 mark]*

b) Find an expression for b in the form pq^a, where p and q are integers. *[2 marks]*

Challenge

P Q14 Given that $y = \log_b x + 1$, where x and y are any real numbers greater than 1:

a) Prove that b cannot be equal to 1.

b) Explain why b cannot be negative.

9.3 Laws of Logs

You'll need to be able to **simplify** expressions containing logs in order to answer trickier questions — e.g. to **add** or **subtract** two logs you can combine them into one. To do this, you'll need to use the **laws of logarithms**. These **only work** if the **base** of each log is the **same**:

Tip These laws work exactly the same for the natural log (ln) too.

$\log_a x + \log_a y = \log_a (xy)$ $\log_a x - \log_a y = \log_a \left(\frac{x}{y}\right)$ $\log_a x^k = k \log_a x$

So $\log_a \frac{1}{x} = \log_a (x^{-1}) = -\log_a x$ and $\log_a \sqrt{x} = \log_a \left(x^{\frac{1}{2}}\right) = \frac{1}{2} \log_a x$

Example 1

Simplify the following:

a) $\log_3 4 + \log_3 5$

$\log_3 4 + \log_3 5$ ← Check that the logs you're adding have the same base — both are base 3 so you can combine them.

$= \log_3 (4 \times 5) = \log_3 20$ ← Use the law $\log_a x + \log_a y = \log_a (xy)$.

b) $\log_3 4 - \log_3 5$

$\log_3 4 - \log_3 5 = \log_3 \left(\frac{4}{5}\right)$ ← Use the law $\log_a x - \log_a y = \log_a \left(\frac{x}{y}\right)$.

c) $3 \ln 2 + 2 \ln 5$

$3 \ln 2 = \ln (2^3) = \ln 8$

$2 \ln 5 = \ln (5^2) = \ln 25$

← Use the law $\ln x^k = k \ln x$ to get rid of the 3 and 2 in front of the logs.

$\ln 8 + \ln 25 = \ln (8 \times 25) = \ln 200$

Tip $\ln = \log_e$, so you can use the laws of logs in the same way.

Example 2

Write the expression $2 \log_a 6 - \log_a 9$ in the form $\log_a n$, where n is a number to be found.

$2 \log_a 6 = \log_a 6^2 = \log_a 36$ ← Use $\log_a x^k = k \log_a x$ to simplify $2 \log_a 6$.

$\log_a 36 - \log_a 9 = \log_a (36 \div 9) = \log_a 4$ ← Then use $\log_a x - \log_a y = \log_a \left(\frac{x}{y}\right)$.

Example 3

Write the expression $\ln \frac{(ex)^2}{y^3}$ in terms of $\ln x$ and $\ln y$.

$\ln \frac{(ex)^2}{y^3} = \ln (ex)^2 - \ln y^3$ ← Use $\log_a \left(\frac{x}{y}\right) = \log_a x - \log_a y$.

$= \ln e^2x^2 - \ln y^3$

$= \ln e^2 + \ln x^2 - \ln y^3$ ← Use $\log_a (xy) = \log_a x + \log_a y$ on $\ln e^2x^2$.

$= 2 \ln e + 2 \ln x - 3 \ln y$ ← Use $\log_a x^k = k \log_a x$ on each term.

$= 2 + 2 \ln x - 3 \ln y$ ← Finally, use $\log_a a = 1$ to write $2 \ln e$ as 2.

Exercise 9.3

Q1 Write each of the following in the form $\log_x n$ (or $\ln n$), where n is a number to be found:

a) $\log_a 2 + \log_a 5$ b) $\ln 8 + \ln 7$ c) $\log_b 8 - \log_b 4$

d) $\log_m 15 - \log_m 5$ e) $3 \log_a 4$ f) $2 \ln 7$

g) $\frac{1}{2}\log_b 16$ h) $\frac{2}{3}\log_a 125$ i) $\frac{1}{5}\ln 4^5$

Q2 Write in the form $a \log b$, where b is the smallest possible positive integer:

a) $\log 0.5$ b) $\log \sqrt{3}$ c) $\log 0.25$ d) $\log \sqrt[3]{5}$

Q3 Given that $x > 0$, state the value of the following:

a) $8 \log_x \sqrt[4]{x}$ b) $\log_x (x^2)^3$

Q4 Simplify the following:

a) $\log_{10} x^2 + 2\log_{10} x$ b) $2\log_a x - 5\log_a y$

Q5 Write each of the following expressions as a single log:

a) $2 \log_a 5 + \log_a 4$ b) $3 \log_m 2 - \log_m 4$ c) $3 \ln 4 - 2 \ln 8$

d) $\frac{2}{3} \ln 216 - 2 \ln 3$ e) $1 + \log_a 6$ f) $2 - \log_b 5$

P Q6 If $\log_a 2 = x$, $\log_a 3 = y$ and $\log_a 5 = z$, write in terms of x, y and z:

a) $\log_a 6$ b) $\log_a 16$ c) $\log_a 60$

Problem Solving

In Q6, try rewriting the numbers as products of their prime factors.

E Q7 Rewrite $\log_3 5 - \log_3 \frac{1}{5}$ in the form $\log_3 m$, where m is an integer to be found. *[2 marks]*

Q8 Simplify each of the following as much as possible:

a) $\log_b b^3$ b) $\log_a \sqrt{a}$ c) $\ln 4e - 2 \ln 2$ d) $\ln 9 + \ln \frac{e}{3} - \ln 3$

E Q9 Simplify $\ln\sqrt{e} + 2\ln e^3$. *[2 marks]*

P Q10 It is given that $n = \log_x a$ and $m = \log_x b$.
Rewrite the following logarithmic expressions in terms of n and m:

a) $2\log_x b + \log_x a^3$

b) $2 \log_x \frac{b}{a}$

E P Q11 Rewrite $10 + 2\log_a 3$ in the form $\log_a n$, where n is an expression in terms of a. *[2 marks]*

P Q12 Show that: a) $\log_2 4^x = 2x$ b) $\frac{\ln 54 - \ln 6}{\ln 3} = 2$

Q13 Find the value of $4 + \log_c \frac{1}{c^2} + \log_c \sqrt{c}$.

E P Q14 Given that $2\log_a 6a^2$ can be written in the form $\log_a p + q$, where p and q are integers, find $\log_3\left(\frac{p}{q}\right)$. *[3 marks]*

Challenge

E P Q15 Given that $y = nx^{\frac{1}{m}}$, express $\log_{10} x$ in the form $\log_{10} p - \log_{10} q$, where p and q are given in terms of y, n and m. *[3 marks]*

9.4 Changing the Base of a Log

As well as the three laws on page 224, there is another rule to learn which lets you **change bases**.

- Your calculator should have a button to work out any log for you, but some scientific calculators can only work out $\mathbf{log_{10}}$ or **ln** — this makes it trickier to calculate logs with a **different base**.
- You can **change the base** of any log to **any other base** using this formula:

Change of Base: $\log_a x = \frac{\log_b x}{\log_b a}$

- So $\log_a x = \frac{\log_{10} x}{\log_{10} a}$ or $\log_a x = \frac{\ln x}{\ln a}$.
- Even if your calculator **can** work out any log, you still need to **learn** this — it's quite useful when it comes to solving equations with logs.

Example 1

By converting to $\log_{10}$:

a) Find the value of $\log_7 4$ to 4 d.p.

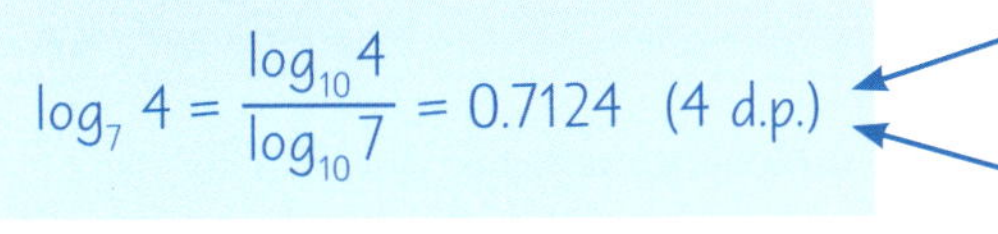

Here, $a = 7$ and $x = 4$. And we want $b = 10$.

Check this on your calculator by doing $7^{0.7124...} = 4$.

Tip You're trying to work out what power you'd need to raise 7 to to get 4.

b) Find the value of $\log_3 2$ to 4 d.p.

$$\log_3 2 = \frac{\log_{10} 2}{\log_{10} 3} = 0.6309 \quad \text{(4 d.p.)}$$

Here, $a = 3$ and $x = 2$. And we want $b = 10$.

Exercise 9.4

Q1 Write the following in terms of $\log_{10}$:

a) $\log_9 2$ b) $\log_4 8$ c) $\log_{17} 16$ d) $\log_{21} 14$

Q2 Find the value of the following logs to 3 s.f.:

a) $\log_6 3$ b) $\log_9 2$ c) $\log_3 13$ d) $\log_5 4$

E Q3 Rewrite $\log_9 5$ in the form $\log_3 m$. *[2 marks]*

P Q4 By changing the base, write each of the following expressions as a single log:

a) $\frac{\log_{10} 19}{\log_{10} 11}$ b) $\frac{\log_6 2}{\log_6 7}$ c) $\log_3 4 \times \log_4 5$ d) $\ln 2 \times \log_2 10$

P Q5 $\log_{10} 3x = \frac{\ln 2}{\ln 10}$. Find the exact value of x without using a calculator.

E P Q6 a) Write $\log_4 10 - \log_4 \frac{1}{10}$ in the form $\log_2 x$. *[3 marks]*

b) Hence, find the value of x for which $\log_8 x = \log_4 10 - \log_4 \frac{1}{10}$. *[3 marks]*

P Q7 Use the change of base method to write each of the following as an integer:

a) $\log_a 5 \times 3\log_5 a$

b) $\frac{1}{2}\log_a 9 \times \log_3 a^2$

Challenge

E P Q8 Write the following in the form $k \ln a$, where a is the smallest possible integer:

$$\left(\frac{\log_3 2}{\log_3 e} + \log_e 3\right) - \left(\log_e 6 + \frac{\log_2 9}{\log_2 e}\right)$$ *[4 marks]*

9.5 Solving Equations with Exponentials and Logs

You saw earlier on page 221 that exponentials and logs are the inverses of each other, and that: $a^{\log_a x} = x = \log_a a^x$

Tip You can also write a^x as $e^{x \ln a}$: $e^{x \ln a} = e^{\ln a^x} = a^x$

You can prove this using the laws of logs: $\log_a a^x = x \log_a a = x$.

So you can use logs to **get rid** of exponentials and vice versa — including using e^x and $\ln x$ to cancel each other out, as you saw on page 221. This is useful for solving equations.

Example 1

Solve $2^{4x} = 3$ to 3 significant figures.

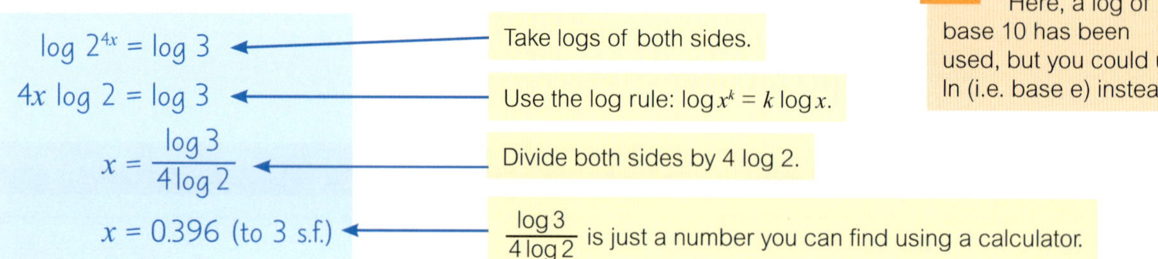

Tip Here, a log of base 10 has been used, but you could use ln (i.e. base e) instead.

Example 2

Solve $7 \log_{10} x = 5$ to 3 significant figures.

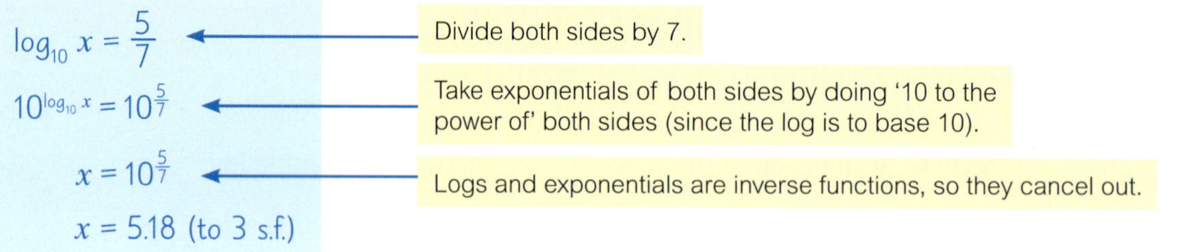

Problems involving exponentials and logs

In an exam, you might be asked to solve an equation where you have to use a **combination** of the methods covered in this chapter. It can be tricky to work out what's needed, but just remember that you're trying to get ***x* on its own** — and think about which laws will help you do that.

If you're asked to give an **exact** solution, leave your answer in exponential or log form (i.e. don't actually calculate the decimal value of it).

Example 3

Solve $\ln(2x - 1) = 2$, giving your answer as an exact solution.

$\ln(2x - 1) = 2$

$e^{\ln(2x-1)} = e^2$ — Apply e to both sides to remove the ln function.

$2x - 1 = e^2$ — Use the rule $e^{\ln y} = y$.

$2x = e^2 + 1 \Rightarrow x = \frac{e^2 + 1}{2}$

Example 4 

Find the two exact solutions of the equation $e^x + 5e^{-x} = 6$.

$$e^x + 5e^{-x} = 6$$

$$e^{2x} + 5 = 6e^x$$

Multiply each part of the equation by e^x to get rid of e^{-x}. Remember basic powers laws: $(e^x)^2 = e^{2x}$ and $e^{-x} \times e^x = e^0 = 1$.

$$e^{2x} - 6e^x + 5 = 0$$

$$y^2 - 6y + 5 = 0$$

Substitute y for e^x to get a quadratic in y.

$$(y - 1)(y - 5) = 0$$

Factorise the equation to find exact solutions.

$$y = 1 \quad \text{and} \quad y = 5$$

$$e^x = 1 \quad \text{and} \quad e^x = 5$$

Put e^x back in and apply the inverse function $\ln x$ to both sides.

$$\ln e^x = \ln 1 \quad \text{and} \quad \ln e^x = \ln 5$$

$$x = \ln 1 = 0 \quad \text{and} \quad x = \ln 5$$

Remember, $\ln e^x = x$.

Problem Solving

A big clue here is that you're asked for more than one solution — think quadratics... (see page 49).

Example 5

Solve $6^{x-2} = 3^x$, giving your answer to 3 s.f.

$$\log 6^{x-2} = \log 3^x$$

Take logs of both sides (you can use any base, so use 10).

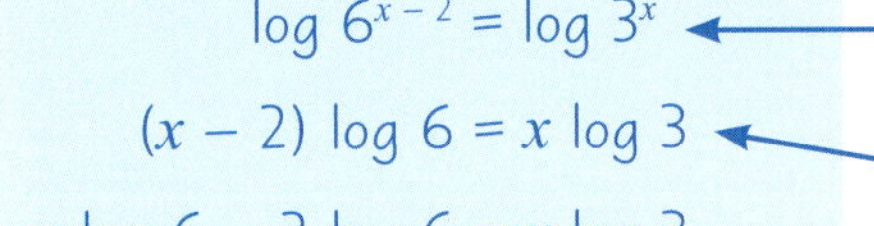

$$(x - 2)\log 6 = x \log 3$$

Now use $\log x^k = k \log x$ on both sides.

$$x \log 6 - 2 \log 6 = x \log 3$$

$$x \log 6 - x \log 3 = 2 \log 6$$

Multiply out the brackets and collect all the x terms on one side.

$$x(\log 6 - \log 3) = 2 \log 6$$

$$x(\log 2) = 2 \log 6$$

Use $\log_a x - \log_a y = \log_a \left(\frac{x}{y}\right)$ on the bracket.

$$\Rightarrow x = \frac{2 \log 6}{\log 2} = 5.17 \text{ (3 s.f.)}$$

Example 6 P

Solve $7^{30x} = 5^{70}$, giving your answer as a single log in the form $a \log_b c$, where a is a number and b and c are integers.

$$\log_7 7^{30x} = \log_7 5^{70}$$

Take logs of both sides. Use base 7 so you can simplify later.

$$30x \log_7 7 = 70 \log_7 5$$

Use $\log_a x^k = k \log_a x$.

$$30x = 70 \log_7 5$$

Use $\log_a a = 1$.

$$x = \frac{7}{3} \log_7 5$$

Problem Solving

By taking logs of base 7, you can replace $\log_7 7$ with 1, which simplifies your working. You could take logs of a different base — but you'd have to use the change of base formula for your final answer.

Exercise 9.5

Q1 Solve each of these equations for x, to 3 s.f.

a) $2^x = 3$ b) $7^x = 2$ c) $1.8^x = 0.4$ d) $0.7^x = 3$

e) $3^{5x} = 890$ f) $0.2^{4x} = 0.016$ g) $2^{3x-1} = 5$ h) $0.4^{5x-4} = 2$

E Q2 Solve the equation $125 \times 5^x = 879$. Give your answer to 3 significant figures. *[2 marks]*

Q3 Solve these equations, giving your answers in the form $a \log_b c$, where a, b and c are integers, and c is as small as possible:

a) $2^{4x} = 3^{100}$ b) $11^{6x} = 10^{90}$ c) $6^{50-x} = 2^{50}$ d) $4^{5+x} = 20^5$

P Q4 Find the smallest integer P such that $1.5^P > 1\,000\,000$.

Q5 Find the value of x for each case:

a) $\log 5x = 3$ b) $\log_2 (x + 3) = 4$ c) $\log_3 (5 - 2x) = 2.5$

Q6 Solve each of these equations for x:

a) $4^{x+1} = 3^{2x}$ b) $2^{5-x} = 4^{x+3}$ c) $3^{2x-1} = 6^{3-x}$

E P Q7 a) Given that $y = 3^x$, find an expression in terms of y for:

(i) 3^{x+1} *[1 mark]*

(ii) 3^{2x-1} *[1 mark]*

b) Hence, or otherwise, solve the equation $3^{x+1} - 6 = 3^{2x-1}$. Give your answers correct to 3 significant figures where appropriate. *[5 marks]*

E P Q8 a) Sketch the graph of $y = 7^x$, showing the coordinates of any intersections with the axes. *[2 marks]*

b) Solve the equation $7^{2x} - 3(7^x) + 2 = 0$, giving your answers to 3 significant figures. *[4 marks]*

E Q9 Given that $4^{2x} = 3(2^{x-1})$, show that $x = \frac{1}{3}(\log_2 3 - 1)$. *[5 marks]*

P Q10 Find the value(s) of x which satisfy each of the following equations:

a) $\log_6 x = 1 - \log_6 (x + 1)$ b) $\log_2 (2x + 1) = 3 + 2 \log_2 x$

E P Q11 Solve $\log_3 (x - 1) = 2 - \log_3 (2x + 1)$. *[5 marks]*

E P Q12 Solve $\log_2 (11 - 6x) = 2\log_2 (x - 1) + 3$. *[5 marks]*

Q13 Solve these equations, giving your answers in terms of ln 3.

a) $e^{3x} = 27$ b) $e^{(6x-1)} = \frac{1}{3}$ c) $\frac{1}{3}e^{(1-x)} - 3 = 0$

Q14 Solve these equations, giving your answers as exact solutions.

a) $5e^{3t} = 11$ b) $e^{(0.5x+3)} = 9$ c) $10 - 3e^{(1-2x)} = 8$

d) $3 \ln (2x) = 7$ e) $\ln (5t - 3) = 4$ f) $6 - \ln (0.5x) = 3$

E Q15 Solve the equation $e^{3x+1} = 10$, giving your answer to 3 significant figures. *[2 marks]*

P Q16 Solve these equations, giving exact answers.

a) $\ln 5 + \ln x = 7$ b) $\ln (2x) + \ln (3x) = 15$

c) $2\ln x - \ln (2x) = 2$ d) $\ln (2x - 7) + \ln 4 = -3$

e) $\ln (x^2 - 4) - \ln (2x) = 0$ f) $3 \ln (x^2) + 5 \ln x = 2$

g) $2e^{2x} + e^x = 3$ h) $e^{8x} - e^{4x} - 6 = 0$

E P Q17 Given that x and y are positive constants, solve the equations $x = 3y$ and $\log_3 x + \log_3 y = 2$ simultaneously. Give your solutions in exact form. *[5 marks]*

P Q18 Solve the equations $9^{x-2} = 3^y$ and $\log_3 2x = 1 + \log_3 y$ simultaneously.

P Q19 Find the exact solutions of $2(10^{2x}) - 7(10^x) + 5 = 0$.

P Q20 Find, where possible, the solutions of the following equations:

a) $2^{2x} - 5(2^x) + 4 = 0$ b) $4^{2x} - 17(4^x) + 16 = 0$ c) $3^{2x+2} - 82(3^x) + 9 = 0$

d) $2^{2x+3} - 9(2^x) + 1 = 0$ e) $e^{4x} + 4e^{2x} + 5 = 0$ f) $3e^{2x} + 10e^x + 3 = 0$

E P Q21 Given $y = 2x^3$:

a) Show that $\log_2 y = 1 + 3 \log_2 x$. *[2 marks]*

b) Hence, or otherwise, solve the equation,

$$1 + 3 \log_2 x = 1 + \log_2(7x^2 - 10x).$$ *[4 marks]*

E P Q22 a) Given that $y = \log_3 x$, find expressions in terms of y for:

(i) $\log_3 x^2$ *[1 mark]*

(ii) $\log_9 x$ *[2 marks]*

b) Hence, or otherwise, solve the equation $\log_3 x^2 - 4 = \log_9 x$. *[3 marks]*

Challenge

E P Q23 Given that $x > 0$, solve the following equation:

$$\log_3(4 + 11x) - 2\log_3 x - 1 = 6\ln (\log_3 3)$$ *[6 marks]*

E P Q24 Use the substitution $y = \log_2 x$ to solve the following equation, giving your answer(s) to 3 significant figures:

$$2 \log_2 \frac{x}{2} + \log_4 \sqrt{x} - 8 = 0$$ *[6 marks]*

9.6 Modelling Exponential Growth and Decay

Logs can be used to solve **real-life** problems involving **exponential growth** and **decay**.

- Exponential **growth** is when the rate of growth **increases** faster as the amount gets bigger.
- Exponential **decay** is just **negative** exponential growth.
  The **rate** of decay gets slower and slower as the amount gets smaller.

Example 1

The exponential growth of a colony of bacteria can be modelled by the equation $B = 60e^{0.03t}$, where B is the number of bacteria and t is the time in hours from the point at which the colony is first monitored ($t \geq 0$). Use the model to:

a) Work out the initial population of bacteria.

$B = 60e^{0.03t}$
$= 60e^{(0.03 \times 0)}$ ← The initial population of bacteria is given by the formula when $t = 0$.
$= 60e^0$
$= 60 \times 1$ ← $e^0 = 1$
$B = 60$

b) Predict the number of bacteria after 4 hours.

$B = 60 \times e^{(0.03 \times 4)}$ ← Substitute $t = 4$ into the equation to find B after 4 hours.
$= 60 \times 1.1274...$
$= 67.6498...$

So $B = 67$ bacteria ← Round down because you want to know the number of whole bacteria.

c) Predict the time taken for the colony to grow to 1000.

$B = 1000$ so:
$1000 = 60e^{0.03t}$ ← You need to find the time, t, when the population is 1000, so substitute in the value of B.
$e^{0.03t} = 1000 \div 60$
$= 16.6666...$
$\ln e^{0.03t} = \ln(16.6666...)$ ← Take 'ln' of both sides.
$0.03t = 2.8134...$
$t = 2.8134... \div 0.03$
$= 93.8$ hours (3 s.f.)

Example 2

£350 is initially paid into a bank account that pays 3% interest per year. No further money is deposited or withdrawn from the account. Create a model to show how much money will be in the account after t years. Use this model to calculate how many whole years it will be before there is over £1000 in the account.

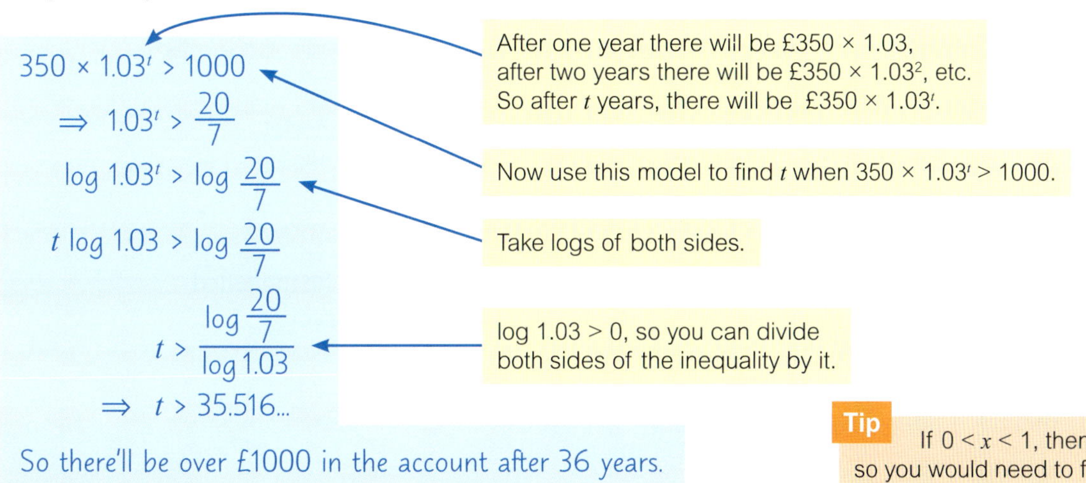

Tip If $0 < x < 1$, then $\log x < 0$, so you would need to flip the inequality sign when dividing.

Example 3

The concentration (C) of a drug in the bloodstream, t hours after taking an initial dose, decreases exponentially according to $C = Ae^{-kt}$, where A and k are constants. If the initial concentration is 0.72, and this halves after 5 hours, find the values of A and k and sketch a graph of C against t.

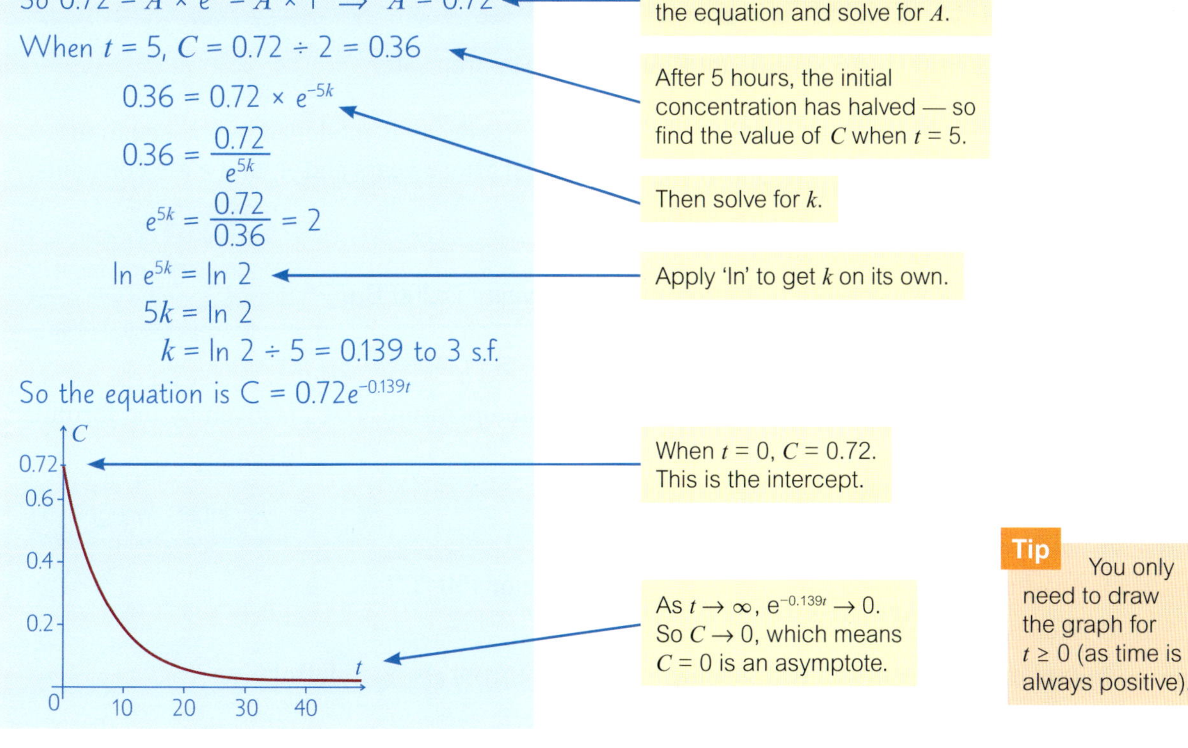

Tip You only need to draw the graph for $t \geq 0$ (as time is always positive).

Limitations of modelling

The real world can't always be simplified to a couple of variables — it's usually much more **complicated** than that. Models **ignore** most factors, leaving only the ones you're interested in. This simplification means that models aren't spot on — they have **drawbacks**:

- Often an exponential model will match the real-world scenario for only a **short amount of time** — beyond that the numbers get too big or too small.
- A model may need tweaking for different values to reflect this — for example, there may be an **upper limit** to stop a value increasing to infinity.

You can only use the model to make predictions within the time frame of the model. If it's outside the time frame, then you're **extrapolating**, which is likely to be much less accurate.

Example 4

The penguin population of a small island is surveyed. The population, P, can be modelled by the formula $P = 5000e^{0.1t}$, where t is the number of years after the initial survey.

a) What does the '5000' in the formula represent?

5000 is the initial number of penguins (when $t = 0$).

b) Explain why this model may not be appropriate for the long term.

After 60 years ($t = 60$), the penguin population is over 2 million. This seems unrealistic — it's much too large a population. The model doesn't take into account other factors (e.g. predators, food supply) and allows the population to grow infinitely.

Exercise 9.6

Give your answers correct to 3 significant figures where appropriate.

M Q1 A radioactive substance has a half-life of 10 years. Its decay is modelled by the equation $A = A_0e^{-kt}$, where A is the activity in Bq (becquerels) after t years and A_0 and k are constants.

a) After how many years will the substance be reduced to a quarter of its original activity?

b) Find the original activity if the activity after 5 years is 200 Bq.

c) Find the activity remaining after 15 years.

Q1 Hint Half-life is the length of time it takes for the activity of the sample to halve.

M Q2 An oven is turned on at 12:00. After t minutes its temperature, T °C, is given by the formula: $T = 225 - 207e^{-\frac{t}{8}}$

a) What was the initial temperature of the oven?

b) What was the temperature after 5 minutes?

c) At what time does the oven reach a temperature of 190 °C?

d) Sketch the graph of T against t.

e) Explain how the model restricts the temperature from rising indefinitely.

Q2d) Hint Make sure you label any significant points, e.g. where the curve meets any axes.

M Q3 The value of a motorbike (£V) varies with age (in t years from new) according to $V = 7500e^{-0.2t}$.

a) What is its value after 10 years (to the nearest £)?

b) After how many years will the motorbike's value have fallen below £500?

c) Sketch a graph showing how the value of the motorbike varies with age, labelling any key points.

E M Q4 A boiler tank is switched on and the temperature of the water inside begins to rise. This temperature is modelled by the equation $T = 95 - 70e^{-0.1t}$, where T is measured in °C and t is measured in minutes.

a) What was the initial temperature of the water? *[1 mark]*

b) Calculate the water temperature after 6 minutes of heating. *[1 mark]*

c) How long will it take for the water to reach 70 °C? *[3 marks]*

d) What is the maximum water temperature the boiler can achieve? *[1 mark]*

E M Q5 A fungus is being grown under controlled conditions in a laboratory. Initially, it covers an area of 4 mm^2. After t hours, its area is F mm^2, where $F = F_0e^{gt}$ (F_0 and g are constants). After 6 hours its area is 10 mm^2.

a) Find the values of F_0 and g. *[4 marks]*

b) Predict the area of the fungus after 12 hours. *[1 mark]*

c) How long will it take for the fungus to grow to 15 mm^2? *[3 marks]*

d) Describe one limitation of the model used. *[1 mark]*

E P M Q6 The half-life of a particular anxiety medication is 2 days. The concentration of the drug in a person's bloodstream can be modelled by the equation $C = C_0e^{-kt}$, where t is measured in days after the last dose of the drug was taken and C is measured in mg/l. A patient is being monitored after being given the medication.

a) Given that the initial concentration of the drug in the patient's bloodstream was 2.5 mg/l, calculate the concentration level after 5 days. *[4 marks]*

The drug is considered to be clear from the bloodstream once the concentration level drops below 0.2 mg/l.

b) Calculate the time it will take for this to happen for the patient. Give your answer to a suitable degree of accuracy. *[3 marks]*

E P M Q7 After a colony of rats was accidentally introduced to a small Pacific island, its population began to grow exponentially. Their numbers can be modelled by the equation $P = P_0e^{bt}$, where t is the number of years since 2015. In 2015 the population was estimated to be 1500. Two years later it had risen to 1800.

a) Using the information above, estimate the population in the year 2020. *[4 marks]*

b) In what year will the population be expected to exceed 3000 rats? *[3 marks]*

E P M Q8 A new fungal infection is threatening oak trees across the country. The number of infected trees is modelled using the equation $N = N_0e^{kt}$, where N is measured in 1000's of trees and t is measured in months since May 2020. In May 2020, the number of trees estimated to have this infection was 1200. Four months later, the number was estimated to be 1800.

a) Estimate the number of infected trees in May 2021. *[4 marks]*

b) In what month and year would the number of infected trees be expected to exceed 5000? *[3 marks]*

P M Q9 A woman is prescribed a medicine, and the concentration of the medicine in her bloodstream is monitored. Initially the concentration in her bloodstream is 3 mg per litre of blood (mg/l). After t hours, the concentration of the drug is N mg/l, where $N = Ae^{-t}$.

a) What is the concentration after 30 minutes?

b) How long does it take for the level to reduce to 0.1 mg/l?

c) Sketch the graph of N against t.

d) What is the gradient of the graph in terms of t?

Problem Solving

In Q9, read the units carefully — in the question t is in hours but here you're asked about minutes, so you need to convert first.

E P M Q10 The area covered by a forest changes due to deforestation. The changes over the last 35 years can be modelled using the equation $P = P_0e^{-kt}$, where P is the percentage of remaining forest coverage compared to the 1985 figure and t is measured in years.
Taking the 1985 figure to be 100%, it has been estimated that by 2020 there has been a 13% reduction in forest coverage. Assuming the model continues to hold, estimate:

a) The percentage of forest remaining by 2030. *[4 marks]*

b) The year in which one quarter of the forest will have been lost to deforestation. *[3 marks]*

Challenge

P M Q11 The value of a car (£V) t years after purchase can be modelled by the formula:

$$V = 1500 + 9000e^{-\frac{t}{3}}$$

a) Explain the significance of the negative coefficient of t.

b) What was its price when new?

c) What was its value after 5 years?

d) After how many whole years will it be worth less than £2500?

e) Sketch the graph of V against t.

P M Q12 A forest fire spreads in such a way that the burnt area (H hectares) after t hours is given by the relation $H = 20e^{bt}$. Assume that the fire burns unchecked.

a) Interpret the value 20 used in the model.

b) If $e^b = 1.8$, find b.

c) Find the area burnt after 3 hours.

d) How long would it take to burn an area of 500 hectares?

e) What constant factor is the burnt area multiplied by every hour? What percentage does the burnt area increase by each hour?

f) Describe one limitation of the model.

9.7 Logarithmic Graphs in Linear Form

Equations of the form $\boldsymbol{y = ax^n}$ or $\boldsymbol{y = kb^x}$ can be a bit awkward to use. Fortunately, you can use the **laws of logs** to rewrite them in the form $\boldsymbol{y = mx + c}$, which is much easier to work with. Graphs of $y = ax^n$ or $y = kb^x$ can get **very steep very quickly**, but linear graphs are much more straightforward — and you can use them to read off values, find the gradient of the line, etc.

Logarithmic graphs for $y = ax^n$

To convert $y = ax^n$ to linear form, just **take logs** of both sides and rearrange:

$$y = ax^n \Rightarrow \log y = \log ax^n$$
$$\Rightarrow \log y = \log a + \log x^n$$
$$\Rightarrow \log y = n \log x + \log a$$

This is in the **straight-line** form $y = mx + c$. n is the gradient and **log** a is the vertical intercept.

When drawing the graph, plot the values of **log** y against **log** x and label the axes accordingly.

If you're given values for x and y, you can plot $\log y$ against $\log x$. The line of best fit will have the equation $\log y = n \log x + \log a$, so from this you can work out the equation for y in terms of x.

Example 1 M

The number of employees, p, working for a company t years after it was founded can be modelled by the equation $p = at^b$. The table below shows the number of employees the company has:

Age of company (t years)	2	5	8	13	25
Number of employees (p)	3	7	10	16	29

Plot a linear graph to represent this data, and use this to find the values a and b.

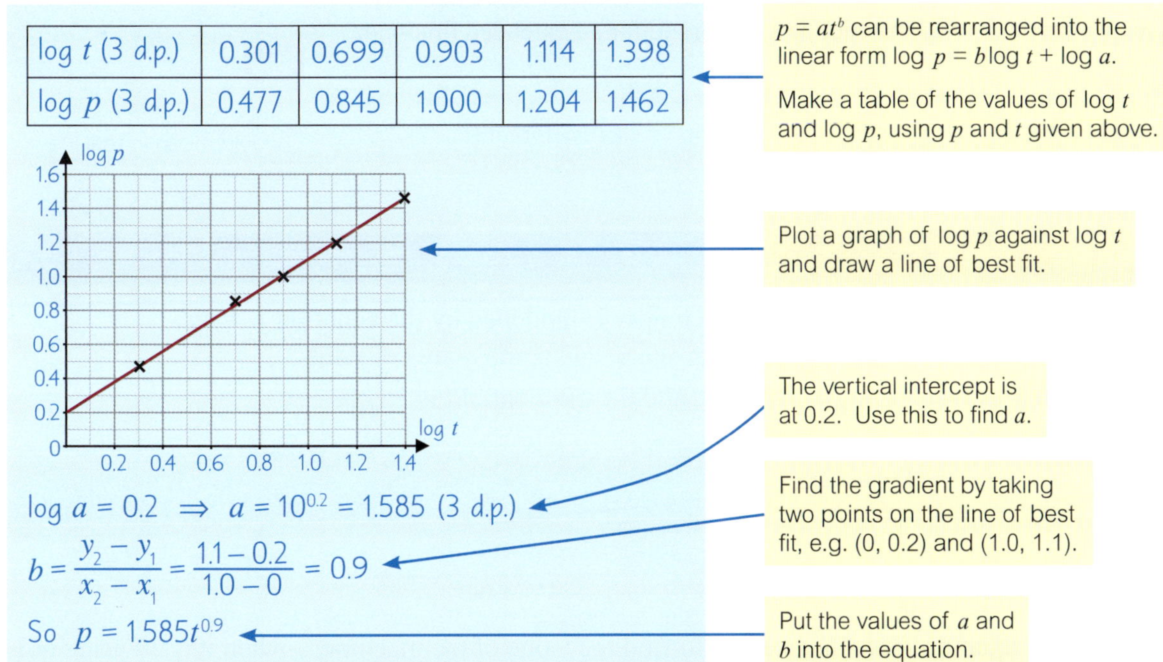

log t (3 d.p.)	0.301	0.699	0.903	1.114	1.398
log p (3 d.p.)	0.477	0.845	1.000	1.204	1.462

$\log a = 0.2 \Rightarrow a = 10^{0.2} = 1.585$ (3 d.p.)

$b = \frac{y_2 - y_1}{x_2 - x_1} = \frac{1.1 - 0.2}{1.0 - 0} = 0.9$

So $p = 1.585t^{0.9}$

$p = at^b$ can be rearranged into the linear form $\log p = b \log t + \log a$.

Make a table of the values of $\log t$ and $\log p$, using p and t given above.

Plot a graph of $\log p$ against $\log t$ and draw a line of best fit.

The vertical intercept is at 0.2. Use this to find a.

Find the gradient by taking two points on the line of best fit, e.g. (0, 0.2) and (1.0, 1.1).

Put the values of a and b into the equation.

Logarithmic graphs for $y = kb^x$

Graphs of the form $y = kb^x$ can also be rearranged to be in linear form, but slightly differently:

$$y = kb^x \Rightarrow \log y = \log kb^x$$
$$\Rightarrow \log y = \log k + \log b^x$$
$$\Rightarrow \log y = x \log b + \log k$$

This is in the straight-line form $y = mx + c$ where $\log b$ is the gradient and $\log k$ is the vertical intercept. This time, plot $\log y$ against x.

Example 2 M

The populations (y) of rabbits and foxes on an island over time (t) are modelled using the graph on the right.

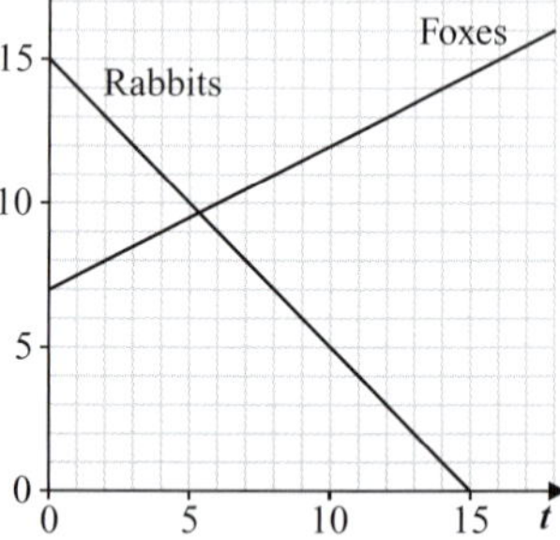

a) Calculate the combined population (to 3 s.f.) when the number of rabbits and foxes are equal.

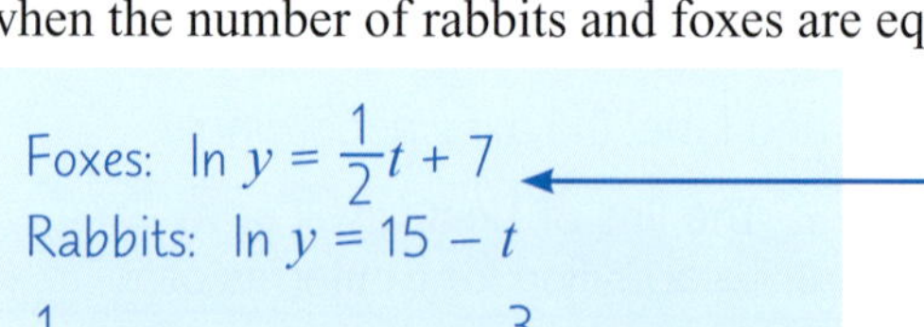

Foxes: $\ln y = \frac{1}{2}t + 7$

Rabbits: $\ln y = 15 - t$

Find the equation for each line. Note the vertical axis is $\ln y$, not y.

$\frac{1}{2}t + 7 = 15 - t \Rightarrow \frac{3}{2}t = 8$

$\Rightarrow t = \frac{16}{3}$

The populations are equal when the lines on the graph cross.

$\ln y = 15 - t$

$\Rightarrow \ln y = 15 - \frac{16}{3} = \frac{29}{3}$

Put this value back into one of the above equations, e.g. rabbits, to find one population.

$\Rightarrow y = e^{\frac{29}{3}} = 15\,782.652...$

$2 \times 15\,782.652... = 31\,600$ (3 s.f.)

This is the same as the fox population, so double it to find the combined population.

b) Explain why this model may not be appropriate for an extended timescale.

After 15 years there'll be less than 1 rabbit, and the fox population will continue to grow exponentially — this is clearly unrealistic.

Tip Think carefully about what the numbers would mean in real life.

Exercise 9.7

P M Q1 The value, £V, of a large piece of machinery is modelled by the equation $V = pq^t$, where t is the age of the machinery in years, and p and q are constants.
The line l below plots $\log V$ against t, and the gradient of l is $-\frac{1}{40}$.

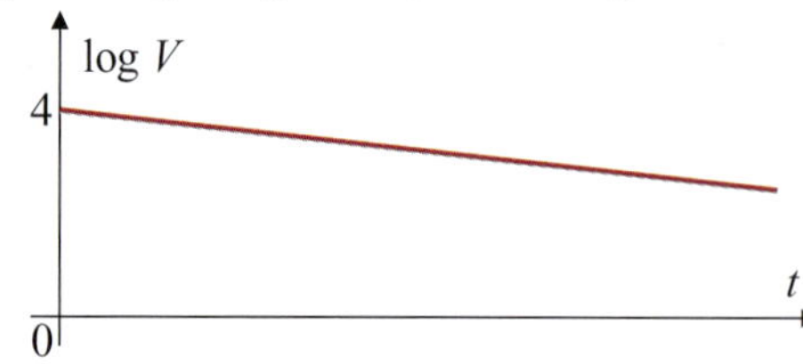

Write an equation for l, and use this to find the value of the machinery when it is 20 years old.

E Q2 The graph of $\log_{10}y$ against x is a straight line, as shown in the diagram below.

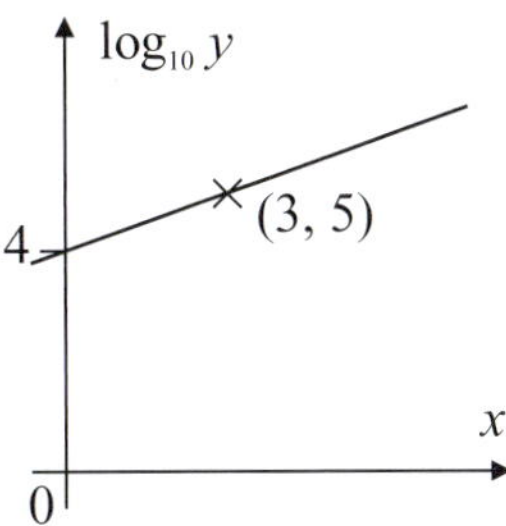

a) Find the equation of the line in terms of $\log_{10} y$ and x. *[2 marks]*

b) Write an equation of the form $y = mA^n$, where m and n are constants and $A = 10^x$. *[2 marks]*

M Q3 A blogger believes that the number of subscribers (y) to her blog over time (t days) can be modelled by the formula $y = at^b$. The number of subscribers is shown in the table below:

t (days)	7	14	21	28
y	224	1000	1585	3981

a) Plot a linear graph to show this data.

b) Find the values of a and b.

c) Use the model to predict how many subscribers the blog had after 10 days.

A rival blog is losing subscribers.
The number of subscribers to the rival blog is modelled by the equation $y = 15t^{-1}$.

d) Write this equation in linear form.

e) Plot the linear graph on the same axes as for part a).

f) Using your graphs or otherwise, find the day on which the two blogs had the same number of subscribers.

g) Explain why these models may not be realistic over a long period of time.

M Q4 A tank is being filled with water. At time $s = 0$, there is 2 mm of water in the tank, and after s secs, the height, h mm, of the water in the tank can be modelled by the equation $h = 2 \times 3^s$.

a) (i) Sketch the graph of h against s.

(ii) Sketch the graph of $\log_3 h$ against s.

(iii) Which is the more useful graph for calculations? Explain your reasoning.

b) Explain why this model is unsuitable for long time periods, and suggest an improvement to the model.

M Q5 The number of bacteria, p, in a petri dish is observed over a period of time, t. The bacteria population can be modelled by the formula $p = at^b$, where a and b are constants. The results from the observations are shown in the table below.

t (days)	1	3	4	6	9
p (1000s)	2	14	22	44	88

Plot a linear graph to represent this data, and use this to find the values of a and b.

E P M Q6 A grain silo is being filled with grain. Initially, the depth of grain is 5 cm. After t seconds the depth (d cm) of grain in the silo can be modelled by $d = 5 \times 2^t$.

a) After how many seconds will the depth be 16 cm? *[2 marks]*

b) (i) Sketch a graph of d against t. *[2 marks]*

(ii) What does the shape of the graph suggest about the shape of the silo? *[1 mark]*

c) (i) Sketch a graph of $\log_2 d$ against t. *[2 marks]*

(ii) Suggest a limitation of this model for the depth of grain in the silo. *[1 mark]*

P M Q7 The activity, x, of a radioactive substance decreases over time, t. The activity follows the formula $x = kb^t$, where k and b are constants. The measurements from an experiment are shown in the table below.

t (days)	5	50	100	200	300
x (Bq)	80.449	32.411	11.803	1.565	0.207

Draw a linear graph of this data, and use a line of best fit to calculate the initial activity of the substance, to the nearest Bq.

E P M Q8 A mug of tea is made and then left to cool over time. The table below shows temperature readings taken at various time intervals after the tea was made.

Time (minutes)	10	15	20	25	30
Temperature (°C)	70	62	52	46	42

It is given that the room temperature was maintained at a constant 20 °C. D is the difference between the observed temperature of the tea and the room temperature at time t minutes.
The relationship between D and t can be modelled as $D = D_0 10^{-kt}$.

a) Show that this equation can be rewritten in the form $\log_{10} D = -kt + \log_{10} D_0$. *[2 marks]*

b) Complete a table of values for $\log_{10} D$ at each time t.
Plot a graph of $\log_{10} D$ against t and draw a line of best fit. *[4 marks]*

c) Use your graph to estimate values for k and D_0 and hence obtain an estimate for the temperature of the tea after 40 minutes. *[4 marks]*

Challenge

P M Q9 The rules of a sport say that the length, l m, and the width, w m, of the rectangular playing field can be any value, as long as the area is 120 m^2. Use logs to model the relationship between l and w as a straight line, and show this graphically.

E P M Q10 The value, V, of a luxury yacht is modelled by the equation $V = at^{-k}$, where t is the age of the yacht in years and a and k are constants. The diagram on the right shows the graph of $\log_{10} V$ against $\log_{10} t$.

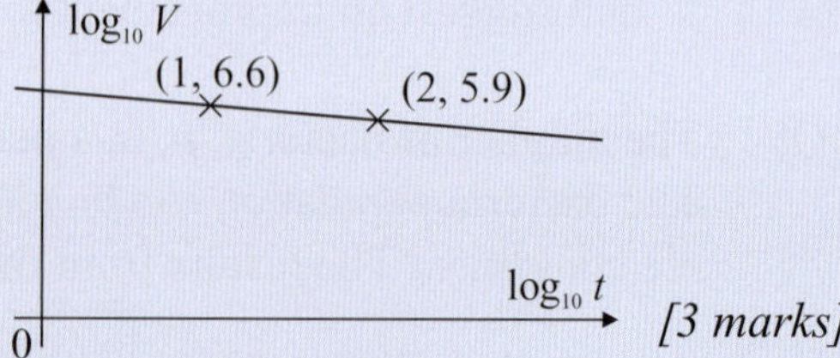

a) Write an equation for $\log_{10} V$ in terms of $\log_{10} t$. *[3 marks]*

b) By first finding the values of a and k, work out how much the value of the yacht drops in the 2nd year. Give your answer to 2 significant figures. *[5 marks]*

c) Identify one limitation of the mathematical model as given. *[1 mark]*

9 Review Exercise

Q1 The graph on the right shows the equation $y = Ae^{kx}$, where A and k are constants.

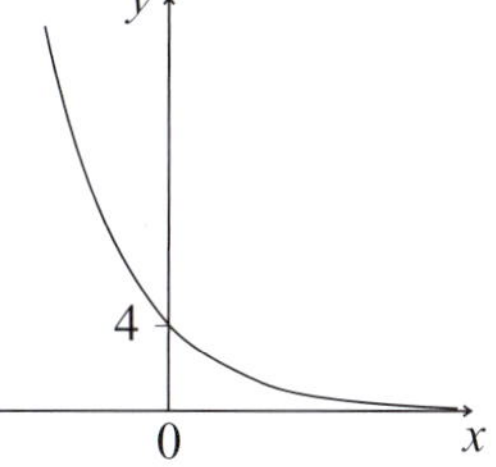

a) Which of the following is the equation of the graph?

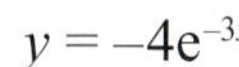

$y = -4e^{-3x}$ $\quad$ $y = 4e^{3x}$ $\quad$ $y = 4e^{-3x}$

b) Use your answer to part a) to find the exact gradient of the graph at the following points:

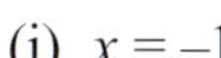

(i) $x = -1$ $\quad$ (ii) $x = 0$ $\quad$ (iii) $x = 4$

E Q2 Sketch the graph of $y = 4 \times 5^{-x}$, showing the coordinates of any intersections with the axes. *[2 marks]*

E Q3 Find the gradient of the curve $y = 2e^{\frac{3}{2}x}$ at the point where $x = \frac{1}{3}$. Leave your answer in exact form. *[2 marks]*

E P Q4 Show that the tangent line to the curve $y = e^{2x}$ at the point with coordinates $\left(\frac{1}{2}, e\right)$ passes through the origin. *[3 marks]*

Q5 Write the following using log notation:

a) $4^2 = 16$ $\quad$ b) $216^{\frac{1}{3}} = 6$ $\quad$ c) $3^{-4} = \frac{1}{81}$

Q6 Write down the values of the following:

a) $\log_3 27$ $\quad$ b) $\log_3 \left(\frac{1}{27}\right)$ $\quad$ c) $\log_3 18 - \log_3 2$

Q7 Write down the exact value for x such that:

a) $\ln x = 3$

b) $e^x = 4$

E P Q8 Explain whether each of the following is true or false:

a) If $\log_{10} a = 3$ and $\log_{10} b = 1$, then $a = b^3$. *[2 marks]*

b) If $\ln a^2 = 8$ and $\ln b = 2$, then $a^2 = b^3$. *[2 marks]*

Q9 Simplify the following:

a) $\log 3 + 2\log 5$ $\quad$ b) $\frac{1}{2}\log 36 - \log 3$ $\quad$ c) $\log 2 - \frac{1}{4}\log 16$

Q10 Express in terms of $\log_a x$:

a) $6\log_a \sqrt{x}$

b) $\log_a x^{\frac{3}{2}} + 2\log_a x$

E Q11 Evaluate $3 - \log_x \frac{1}{x^2} + 2\log_x \sqrt{x}$. *[3 marks]*

P Q12 Simplify $\log_b (x^2 - 1) - \log_b (x - 1)$.

P Q13 Prove that $\frac{2 + \log_a 4}{\log_a 2a} = 2$.

Problem Solving In Q13, try using laws of logs to find a common factor of the numerator and denominator.

Q14 Find the values of the following, giving your answers to 3 s.f.:

a) $\log_7 12$ b) $\log_5 8$ c) $\log_{16} 125$

Q15 Rewrite the following expressions in terms of a single log:

a) $\log_2 3 \times 3\log_3 5$

b) $\ln 4 \times 2\log_2 5$

Q16 a) Copy and complete the table for the function $y = 4^x$:

x	−3	−2	−1	0	1	2	3
y							

b) Plot a graph of $y = 4^x$ for $-3 \leq x \leq 3$.

c) Use the graph to solve the equation $4^x = 20$.

d) Solve the equation $4^x = 20$ algebraically, giving your answer to 3 s.f.

Q17 Solve the following, giving your answers to 3 s.f.:

a) $10^x = 240$ b) $\log_{10} x = 5.3$ c) $10^{2x+1} = 1500$ d) $4^{x-1} = 200$

Q18 Find the value of x, to 4 decimal places, when:

a) $e^{2x} = 6$ b) $3e^{-4x+1} = 5$ c) $\ln (x + 3) = 0.75$ d) $\ln x + \ln 5 = \ln 4$

E P Q19 a) Express $\log_a x^3 + \log_a \frac{1}{x}$ as a multiple of $\log_a x$. *[2 marks]*

b) Given that $\log_{10} B + \log_{10} C = 5$, find B in terms of C. *[2 marks]*

E P Q20 Find all the solutions to the equation below in the form $a \ln b$, where b is the smallest possible integer.

$$e^x - \frac{40}{e^x} = 3$$ *[3 marks]*

E P Q21 Given that $\log_{10} y = 1 + \log_{10} (x + 2)$:

a) Show that $y = 10x + 20$. *[2 marks]*

b) Hence solve the simultaneous equations:
$\log_{10} y = 1 + \log_{10} (x + 2)$ and $10^{15x-y} = 10\,000$ *[3 marks]*

E P Q22 Given that $a^x = b^y$ where $a, b > 1$:

a) Show that $x = y \log_a b$. *[1 mark]*

b) Hence solve the equation $2^{k-2} = 3^{2k-5}$ giving your answer in the form $\frac{p + q\log_2 3}{r + s\log_2 3}$ where p, q, r and s are integers. *[3 marks]*

P M Q23 Scientists are monitoring the population of curly-toed spiders at a secret location. It appears to be dropping at a rate of 25% a year. When the population has dropped below 200, the species will be in danger of extinction. At the moment the population is 2000. In which year will the spiders be in danger of extinction?

E P M Q24 A nature reserve has a population of 20 leopards in 2010. The number of leopards in the nature reserve can be modelled by the formula $L = L_0 e^{\frac{t}{12}}$ where L is the number of leopards in the population, L_0 is the initial population size in 2010 and t is the time in years.

a) How many leopards does the model predict the nature reserve will have after 10 years? *[1 mark]*

b) The reserve has enough space for 60 leopards. How long will it be until the reserve runs out of space? *[3 marks]*

When some of the leopards are released into the wild, the wild population can be modelled by $W = W_0 e^{-\frac{t}{3}}$ where W is the population, t is the time in years and W_0 is the initial population.

c) If the nature reserve releases a population of 15 leopards into the wild, predict how many will be in this population after 5 years in the wild. *[2 marks]*

E P M Q25 The value of a new car begins to depreciate immediately after it is sold. The value of a particular model of car can be modelled over time using the equation $V = 1000 + 8050e^{-kt}$, where V is in pounds (£) and t is measured in years.

a) Calculate the initial sale price of the car. *[1 mark]*

The car was estimated to have dropped in value by 30% after 5 years.

b) Estimate the value of the car after 6 years. *[4 marks]*

c) After how many years will the value have reduced to half the initial sale price? *[3 marks]*

P M Q26 The spread of a zombie apocalypse through a population can be modelled by the formula: $Z = 10 + 20e^t$ where Z is the number of zombies and t is the time in weeks.

a) How many zombies were there initially?

b) Predict how many people will have become zombies after 2 weeks if it spreads according to the model.

c) How many weeks will have passed before there are 60 million zombies?

E P M Q27 A block of ice, initially with mass 100 kg, is exposed to a high temperature and begins to melt. Renata suggests that the mass, M, of the ice t minutes after it begins to melt can be modelled by the equation $M = Ab^t$.

The diagram shows the graph of $\log_{10} M$ against t.

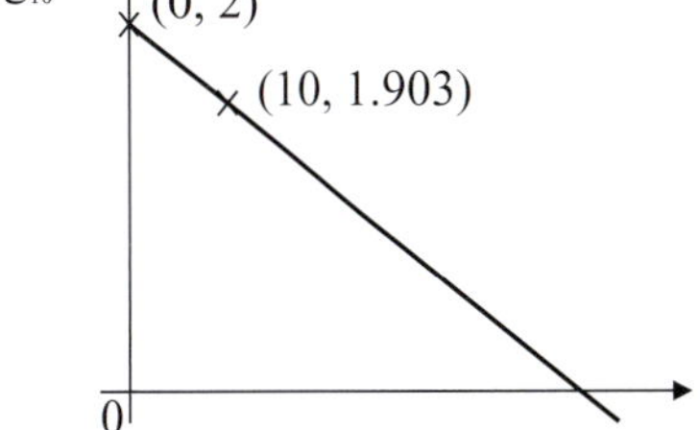

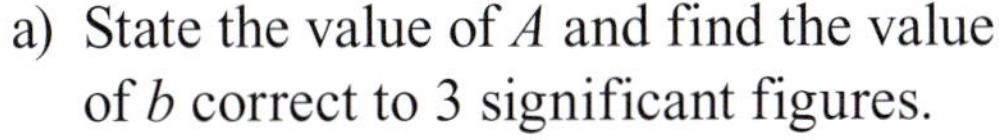

a) State the value of A and find the value of b correct to 3 significant figures. *[4 marks]*

b) Using the values found in a), calculate how long, to the nearest minute, it will take for 60% of the block of ice to melt according to the model. *[2 marks]*

c) Why might Renata's model not be suitable for large values of t? *[1 mark]*

P M **Q28** The populations (y) of red and grey squirrels in a forest over time (t months) are modelled using the graph below right. Grey squirrels were introduced to the forest at time $t = 0$.

a) Find an exponential equation for the population of red squirrels in the forest.

b) Find an exponential equation for the population of grey squirrels in the forest.

c) The population of red squirrels is considered critical when there are fewer than 20 left in the forest. In which month will the population reach a critical level?

d) Explain why this model may not be suitable to predict the number of red and grey squirrels over a long timescale.

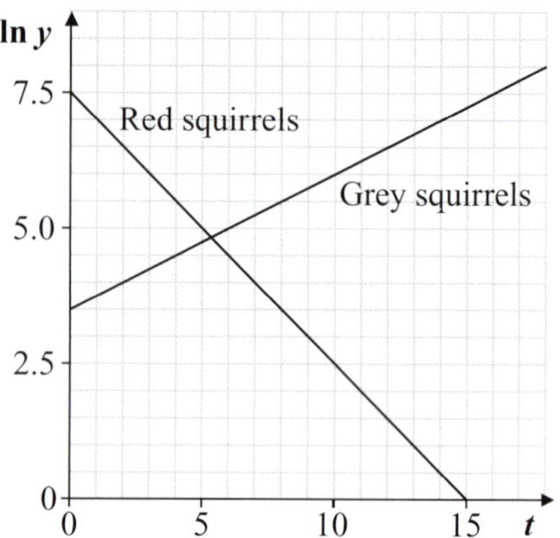

P M **Q29** A group of scientists is investigating how the salt concentration in river water changes as you move upstream. They measured the salt concentration at 6 different points along the length of a river. The data collected is shown in the table below, where x is the distance in km from the river mouth and y is the salt concentration in grams per litre of water.

x (km)	y (g/l)
1	7.6
1.5	6.3
2	5.4
2.5	4.9
3	4.5
3.5	4.2

The level of salt concentration can be modelled by the equation $y = Ax^{-b}$.

a) Show that this equation can be rewritten in the form $\log_{10}y = -b\log_{10}x + \log_{10}A$.

b) (i) Using the data above, make a table of values for $\log_{10}x$ and $\log_{10}y$.

(ii) Plot these values on a graph and draw a line of best fit through the data points.

(iii) Use your line of best fit to estimate values for b and A.

(iv) Hence, estimate the salt concentration in the water at a point 8 km from the mouth of the river.

(v) Suggest a limitation of this model.

Problem Solving

It's easy to get a sign wrong in part b)(iii). By considering the model carefully, you'll know whether to expect the values of A and b to be positive or negative.

E P M Q30 A small population of crown-of-thorns starfish have been causing damage to a coral reef. In an attempt to keep their numbers in check, conservationists introduce some sea snails which are a natural predator of the starfish. The populations of both species are carefully monitored over time to assess the impact of this marine experiment.

a) The graph below shows the populations (y) of sea snails and starfish over time (x). Calculate the combined number of starfish and sea snails when the populations are equal. *[5 marks]*

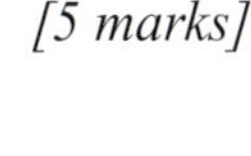

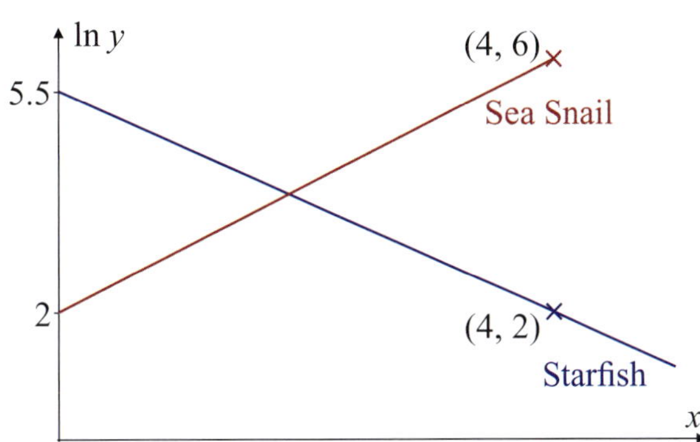

b) Write an equation in the form $y = Ae^{Bx}$ for the number of sea snails, where A and B are constants. *[2 marks]*

c) Explain why the model used to describe the population of sea snails may not be appropriate in the long term. *[1 mark]*

Challenge

E P M Q31 At the start of June 2020, a tree surgeon noticed that a large redwood tree was rotting. She estimated that it had started to rot at the beginning of 2020 and that approximately 7% of the tree had already rotted. The proportion of the tree that has rotted can be modelled by the equation $P = Ae^{-kt}$, where P is the percentage of the tree that is healthy and t is measured in months.

a) The tree needs to be cut down if less than 80% is healthy. Estimate how many months the surgeon has before she needs to cut it down. *[5 marks]*

b) Assuming the tree surgeon doesn't cut the tree down, which would be the first year during which less than 10% of the tree became rotten? *[3 marks]*

c) Identify one limitation of the model. *[1 mark]*

E P M Q32 The rate of change in the population of harbour seals in a river estuary is $e^{0.2t}$, where t is the number of years since the start of 2020.
The rate of change in the population is proportional to the function that models the actual population of harbour seals in the river estuary.

a) Write an expression for the population of seals as a function of t. *[2 marks]*

b) When the harbour seal population reaches 30 it is expected that their population will start to decline at a rate of $-3e^{-0.1t}$. In which year does the model predict that the population will be back at the levels of 2020? *[6 marks]*

9 Chapter Summary

1 Graphs of exponential functions all have the same basic shape.

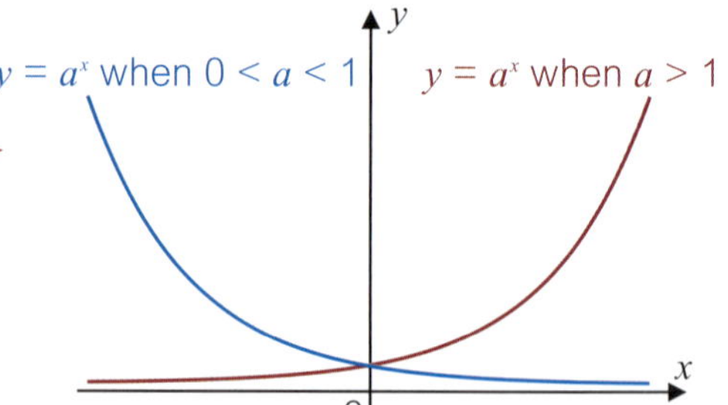

2 For the exponential function $y = e^x$, the gradient is e^x.

3 For the exponential function with constants A and k, the gradient of $y = Ae^{kx}$ is kAe^{kx}.

4 $\log_a b = c$ in log notation is the same as $a^c = b$ in index notation.

5 If $f(x) = a^x$, then the inverse function is $f^{-1}(x) = \log_a x$.
When $f(x) = e^x$, the inverse function is $f^{-1}(x) = \ln x$.

6 The graph of $y = \ln x$ is a reflection of $y = e^x$ in the line $y = x$.

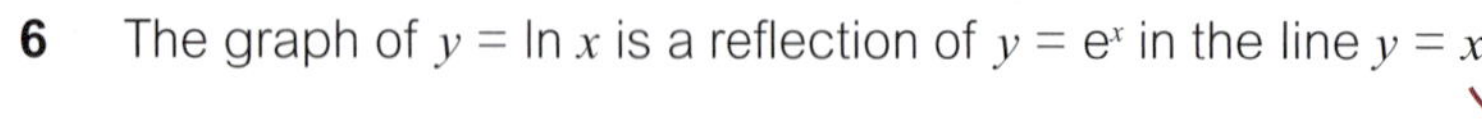

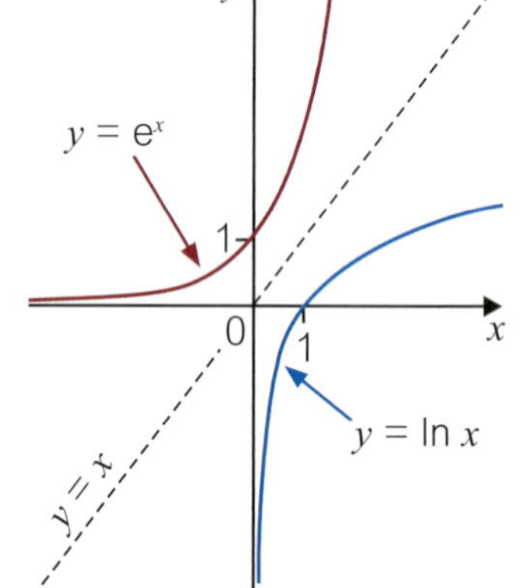

7 Logarithms can be simplified using the rules:

$\log_a x + \log_a y = \log_a (xy)$

$\log_a x - \log_a y = \log_a \left(\frac{x}{y}\right)$

$\log_a x^k = k \log_a x$

8 The formula $\log_a x = \frac{\log_b x}{\log_b a}$ changes the base of a logarithm from a to b.

9 $e^{x \ln a} = e^{\ln a^x} = a^x$ and $a^{\log_a x} = x = \log_a a^x$

10 Exponential growth and decay can be modelled using equations involving Ae^{kx} and Ae^{-kx}, where k and A are constants. However, these models always have limitations.

11 For $y = px^q$, the linear graph is a plot of $\log y$ against $\log x$, with gradient q and vertical intercept $\log p$.

12 For $y = pq^x$, the linear graph is a plot of $\log y$ against x, with gradient $\log q$ and vertical intercept $\log p$.

Differentiation 10

Learning Objectives

Once you've completed this chapter, you should be able to:

- Find the gradient of a curve by differentiating from first principles.
- Differentiate functions containing powers of x to find $f'(x)$.
- Find tangents and normals to a curve.
- Find the second derivative of functions and understand that it represents the rate of change of the gradient.
- Use differentiation to find, and identify the nature of, all the stationary points on a curve.
- Find where a function is increasing or decreasing, and hence sketch the graph of a function.
- Use differentiation to solve real-life problems.

Prior Knowledge Check

1 Find the gradients of the straight lines that pass through the following points:
a) $(-2, 6)$ and $(5, -8)$ b) $(-3, -1)$ and $(1, 5)$ see page 108

2 Solve: a) $x^2 + 5x - 6 = 0$ b) $x^3 - 8x^2 + 12x = 0$ see pages 39 and 65

3 Solve: a) $4x - 1 < 0$ b) $4x \geq 12x^2$ see pages 83-88

4 Find the value of: a) 5^{-2} b) $64^{\frac{1}{2}}$ see page 25

5 Sketch the curves with the following equations:
a) $y = x^3 - 9x$ b) $y = (x - 3)(x + 1)(x + 2)$ see page 123

10.1 Finding the Gradient of a Curve

The **gradient** of a curve is just how **steep** it is.
Unlike a straight line, the steepness of a curve **changes** as you move along it — you can only give an **exact value** for the gradient at a **particular point** on the curve.

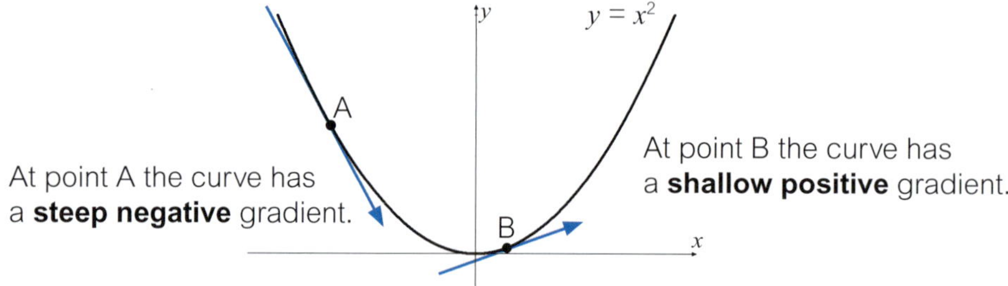

- At a **point**, the gradient of a curve is the same as the gradient of the **tangent line** to the curve at that point.
- The tangent line is a **straight line** which **just touches** the curve at that point, without going through it.
- Sadly, you can't work out the gradient of this tangent using the normal method of picking **two points** and finding the change in y ÷ change in x. This is because you only know **one point** on the line — the point where the tangent **meets the curve**.
- So we need another method to find the gradient of a curve — it's known as **differentiation**.

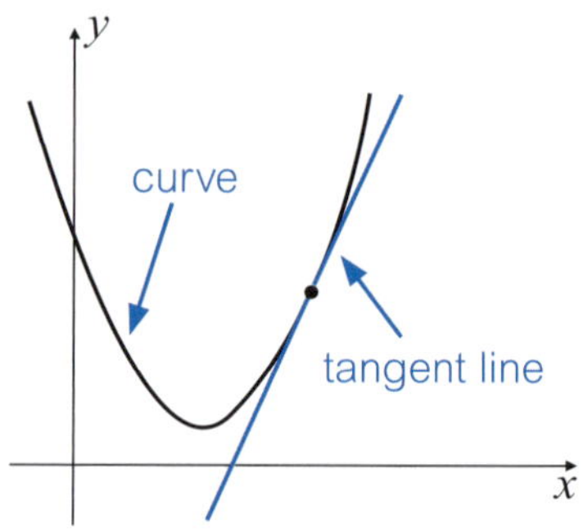

Differentiating produces an **algebraic expression** for the gradient as a **function of x** — its numerical value **changes** as you move along the curve.

Before we get started with differentiation, there's some **notation** to learn:

The function you get from differentiating **y with respect to x** is called the **derivative** of y with respect to x and it's written $\frac{dy}{dx}$.

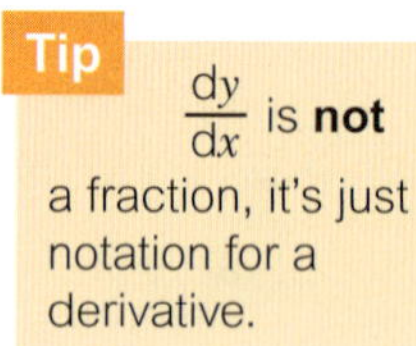

$\frac{dy}{dx}$ represents the **rate of change** of y with x. In other words, it tells you how quickly y is changing for a given value of x. This is the same as the **gradient** of the curve $y = f(x)$.

The notation **f′(x)** means the derivative of $y = f(x)$ with respect to x.
It's sometimes used instead of $\frac{dy}{dx}$.

10.2 Differentiating from First Principles

To find the derivative of a function you need to find its gradient as a function of x.

You can get **close** to the gradient of the tangent (and so the curve) at a point $(x, f(x))$, by finding the gradient of the line joining $(x, f(x))$ and another point **close to** it on the curve.

- On the diagram, the point $(x + h, f(x + h))$ is a small distance further along the curve from $(x, f(x))$.
- As h gets smaller, the distance between the two points gets smaller.
- The closer the points, the **closer** the line joining them will be **to the tangent line**.

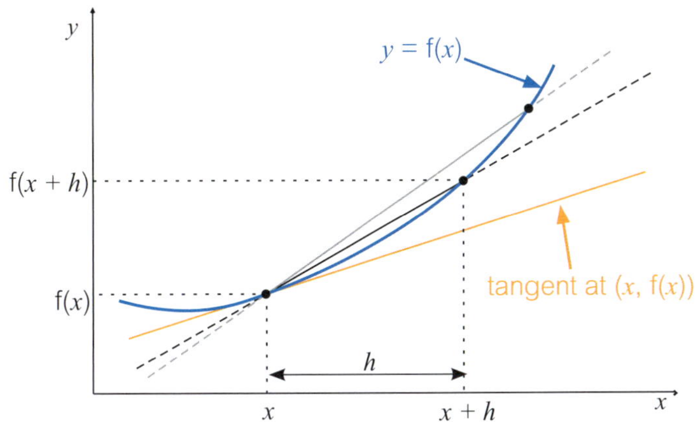

Now you can write an expression for the gradient of the **straight line** joining the two points $(x, f(x))$ and $(x + h, f(x + h))$ like this:

$$\frac{f(x+h)-f(x)}{(x+h)-x}$$

Tip Remember, the gradient of a line passing through points (x_1, y_1) and (x_2, y_2) is given by: $\frac{y_2 - y_1}{x_2 - x_1}$.

As h gets **smaller**, the gradient of the straight line gets **closer and closer** to the gradient of the **curve** at $(x, f(x))$. So you can write an expression for the gradient of the curve $\boldsymbol{y = f(x)}$ like this:

$$f'(x) = \lim_{h \to 0}\left[\frac{f(x+h)-f(x)}{(x+h)-x}\right]$$

'$(x + h) - x$' simplifies to 'h'

$\lim_{h \to 0}$ just means 'what the function goes towards as h goes towards zero'.

This method of differentiation is known as differentiating from **first principles** and the formula can be used to find the gradient of a curve as a function of x.

Tip You might also see these expressions with 'δx' instead of 'h' — this just means a small change in x.

Example 1

Find an expression for the gradient of the function $f(x) = x^2$ by differentiating from first principles.

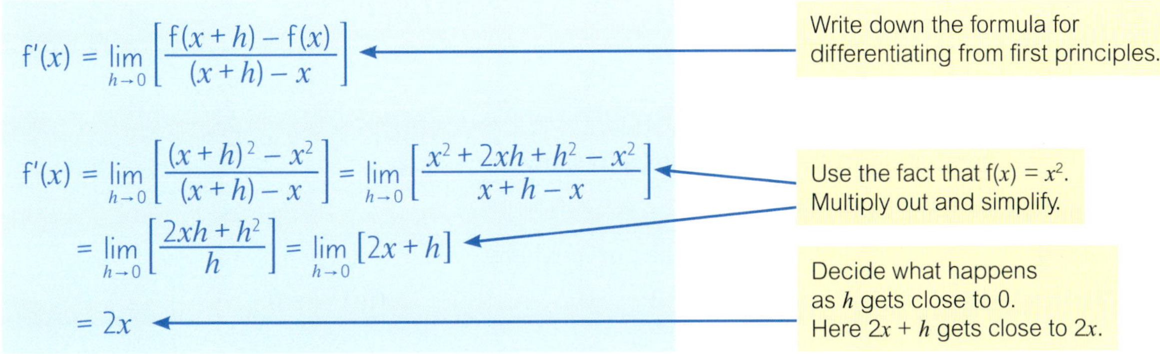

$$f'(x) = \lim_{h \to 0}\left[\frac{f(x+h)-f(x)}{(x+h)-x}\right]$$

Write down the formula for differentiating from first principles.

$$f'(x) = \lim_{h \to 0}\left[\frac{(x+h)^2-x^2}{(x+h)-x}\right] = \lim_{h \to 0}\left[\frac{x^2+2xh+h^2-x^2}{x+h-x}\right]$$

$$= \lim_{h \to 0}\left[\frac{2xh+h^2}{h}\right] = \lim_{h \to 0}[2x+h]$$

Use the fact that $f(x) = x^2$. Multiply out and simplify.

$$= 2x$$

Decide what happens as h gets close to 0. Here $2x + h$ gets close to $2x$.

Example 2

Find the gradient of the curve $y = 0.5x$ by differentiating from first principles.

$$\frac{dy}{dx} = \lim_{h \to 0}\left[\frac{f(x+h) - f(x)}{(x+h) - x}\right]$$

$$= \lim_{h \to 0}\left[\frac{0.5(x+h) - 0.5x}{(x+h) - x}\right] = \lim_{h \to 0}\left[\frac{0.5h}{h}\right]$$

Substitute in $f(x) = 0.5x$ and simplify.

$$= \lim_{h \to 0}[0.5] = 0.5$$

There are no h's so the limit is just 0.5.

Tip A straight line will always have a constant gradient.

Exercise 10.1-10.2

Q1 The curve C is given by $y = f(x)$ where $f(x) = x^3$.

a) Find the gradient of the straight line joining the point on the curve where $x = 1$ and the point on the curve where:

(i) $x = 2$ (ii) $x = 1.5$ (iii) $x = 1.1$

b) The gradient of the curve at the point (1, 1) is 3. What do you notice about the gradient of the straight lines in part a) as the value of x moves closer to 1?

Q2 Derive from first principles expressions for the gradients of the following curves:

a) $y = x$ b) $f(x) = x^3$ c) $f(x) = 2x$

d) $f(x) = 2x^2$ e) $f(x) = x - 7$ f) $f(x) = -x^3$

Q3 For the following, find the derivative of y with respect to x by differentiating from first principles.

a) $y = 5x^2 + 1$ b) $y = x - x^2$ c) $y = 3x^3$

d) $y = 2x^3 + 3x$ e) $y = x^3 + x$ f) $y = (2 - x)^2$

E Q4 a) Show that, for any real number p, the point $(p, 2p^2)$ lies on the curve $y = 2x^2$. *[1 mark]*

b) Using differentiation from first principles, find the gradient of the curve $y = 2x^2$ at the point $(p, 2p^2)$. *[4 marks]*

c) Given that the gradient of the curve $y = 2x^2$ at the point $(p, 2p^2)$ is –8, find the value of p. *[1 mark]*

P Q5 The curve C is given by $y = x^3 + 2x^2 + 3x$.

a) Use differentiation from first principles to show that the gradient of the curve is $\frac{dy}{dx} = 3x^2 + 4x + 3$.

b) Find the gradient of the tangent to the curve where:

(i) $x = -1$ (ii) $x = 2$ (iii) $x = 0$

E P Q6 Points A (–1, –1) and $B\left(-1+h, \frac{1}{-1+h}\right)$ lie on the curve $y = \frac{1}{x}$.

a) Find the gradient of the chord AB in terms of h. *[3 marks]*

b) By taking a suitable limit, show that the gradient of the curve $y = \frac{1}{x}$ at the point A is –1. *[2 marks]*

E Q7 a) Use differentiation from first principles to find an expression for the gradient of the curve $y = f(x)$, when $f(x) = x(2x + 1)$. *[4 marks]*

b) Find the coordinates of the points of intersection between the curve $y = f(x)$ and the line $y = 15$. *[2 marks]*

c) Find the gradients of the tangents to the curve $y = f(x)$ at the points where $y = 15$. *[2 marks]*

P Q8 a) Use differentiation from first principles to prove that, for any real constant a, the derivative of $af(x)$ is equal to $af'(x)$.

b) Use differentiation from first principles to prove that, for any real constants a and b, the derivative of $af(x) + bg(x)$ is equal to $af'(x) + bg'(x)$.

E Q9 The curve C has equation $y = 3x^2 + 2x$. The point P (1, 5) lies on C. Using differentiation from first principles, find the gradient of C at P. *[5 marks]*

E P Q10 For a function f(x), $\lim_{h \to 0} \frac{f(h+1) - f(1)}{h} = 5$.

a) State the gradient of the curve $y = f(x)$ at the point where $x = 1$. *[1 mark]*

b) Given also that $f(x) = kx^2$, where k is a constant, find the value of k. *[6 marks]*

Challenge

P Q11 The points P, Q and R lie on the curve $y = x^2 + ax + b$. The x-coordinate of P is 1. The gradient of the chord PQ is 5.001 and the gradient of the chord PR is 5.01.

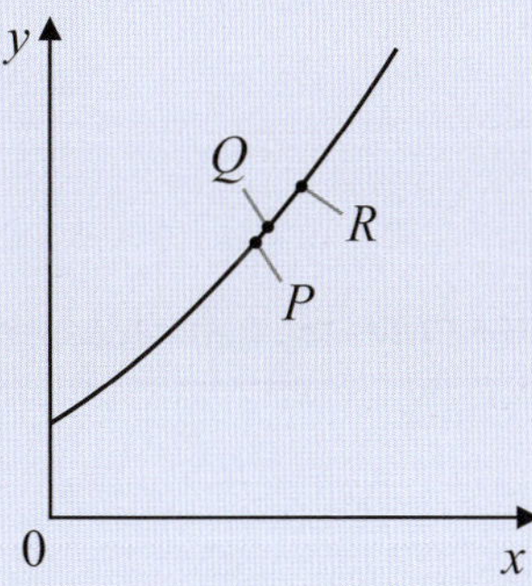

a) What do these results suggest about the gradient of the curve at the point P?

b) Approximate the value of a.

E P Q12 a) Show that, if a and b are non-zero real numbers, then $\sqrt{a} - \sqrt{b} = \frac{a-b}{\sqrt{a}+\sqrt{b}}$. *[2 marks]*

b) Hence, use differentiation from first principles to find the derivative of $f(x) = \sqrt{x}$. *[4 marks]*

10.3 Differentiating x^n

Expressions are much easier to **differentiate** when they're written using **powers of x** — like writing $\sqrt{x}$ as $x^{\frac{1}{2}}$ or $\frac{3}{x^2}$ as $3x^{-2}$.

When you've done this, you can use this **formula** to differentiate:

$$\text{If } y = x^n\text{, then } \frac{dy}{dx} = nx^{n-1}$$

The formula comes from differentiating x^n from **first principles**.

Tip Here, 'differentiate' actually means 'differentiate with respect to x' as it's a function of x you're differentiating.

Example 1

Differentiate each of the following using the formula for powers of x.

a) $y = x^2$

$$\frac{dy}{dx} = nx^{n-1} = 2x^1 = 2x$$

Use the formula with $n = 2$.

b) $y = \sqrt{x}$

$$y = x^{\frac{1}{2}} \quad \left(n = \frac{1}{2}\right)$$

First write the square root as a fractional power of x.

$$\frac{dy}{dx} = nx^{n-1} = \frac{1}{2}x^{\left(-\frac{1}{2}\right)} = \frac{1}{2\sqrt{x}}$$

Then put n into the formula and simplify.

c) $y = \frac{1}{x^2}$

$$y = x^{-2} \quad (n = -2)$$

Write the fraction as a negative power of x.

$$\frac{dy}{dx} = nx^{n-1} = -2x^{-3} = -\frac{2}{x^3}$$

d) $y = 4x^3$

$$y = 4x^3$$

$$\frac{dy}{dx} = 4(nx^{n-1}) = 4(3x^2) = 12x^2$$

If there's a number in front of the x^n term, multiply the derivative by it. If $y = ax^n$, $\frac{dy}{dx} = anx^{n-1}$.

Example 2

Differentiate $y = 5$ using the formula for powers of x.

$y = 5x^0, \quad n = 0$

$\frac{dy}{dx} = 5(nx^{n-1}) = 5(0x^{-1}) = 0$

There are no powers of x in this expression for y, so multiply by $x^0 = 1$.

Tip Differentiating $y = a$ where a is just a constant gives zero, because the line has a gradient of 0 (it's horizontal).

You could be asked to **use** your gradient function to work out the **numerical value** of the gradient at a **particular point** on the curve.

Example 3

Find the gradient of the curve $y = x^2$ at $x = 1$ and $x = -2$.

$y = x^2 \Rightarrow \frac{dy}{dx} = 2x$

When $x = 1$, $\frac{dy}{dx} = 2$. Gradient at $x = 1$ is 2.

When $x = -2$, $\frac{dy}{dx} = -4$. Gradient at $x = -2$ is -4.

You need the gradient of the graph, so differentiate the function.

Use $\frac{dy}{dx} = 2x$ to find the gradient for each x-value.

Exercise 10.3

Q1 Differentiate to find $\frac{dy}{dx}$ for:

a) $y = x$ b) $y = x^6$ c) $y = x^3$ d) $y = 15x^2$

e) $y = x^{-2}$ f) $y = 3x^2$ g) $y = 7x$ h) $y = \frac{1}{2}x^4$

i) $y = 3$ j) $y = 3\sqrt{x}$ k) $y = 2x^{-1}$ l) $y = \frac{1}{x^3}$

Q2 Differentiate to find $f'(x)$ for:

a) $f(x) = x^5$ b) $f(x) = x^7$ c) $f(x) = x^{-4}$ d) $f(x) = 4x^3$

e) $f(x) = 2x^{-3}$ f) $f(x) = 8\sqrt{x}$ g) $f(x) = 3\sqrt[3]{x}$ h) $f(x) = -7$

i) $f(x) = 4x^{-2}$ j) $f(x) = -3x^3$ k) $f(x) = -5x^{-4}$ l) $f(x) = \frac{4}{x^3}$

Q3 Find the gradient of each of the following functions:

a) $y = 2x^2$ when $x = 4$ b) $y = x^{-1}$ when $x = 2$

c) $y = -4x^5$ when $x = 1$ d) $y = \frac{2}{x}$ when $x = 10$

e) $f(x) = 2\sqrt{x}$ at the point (9, 6) f) $f(x) = x^4$ at the point (–2, 16)

g) $f(x) = -2x^3$ when $f(x) = -250$ h) $f(x) = -3x^{-2}$ when $f(x) = -\frac{3}{4}$

P Q4 The line $y = 5x$ and the curves $y = 5x^2$ and $y = 5x^3$ all pass through the point $P(1, 5)$. Show which of these has the steepest gradient at point P.

10.4 Differentiating Functions

If there are **loads** of terms in the expression, just differentiate each term **separately** and this will give you the derivative of the **whole expression**.

Formally, this means: $$\frac{d}{dx}(x^m + x^n) = \frac{d}{dx}(x^m) + \frac{d}{dx}(x^n)$$

Tip If there's a number in front of the function, multiply the derivative by the same number.

Example 1

a) Differentiate $f(x) = x^4 + 3x^2 - 2$.

$$f(x) = x^4 + 3x^2 - 2$$
$$f'(x) = 4x^3 + 3(2x) - 0$$
$$= 4x^3 + 6x$$

Differentiate each term separately.

b) Find $\frac{d}{dx}\left(6x^2 + \frac{4}{\sqrt[3]{x}} - \frac{2}{x^2} + 1\right)$.

Tip The notation $\frac{d}{dx}(...)$ just means the derivative with respect to x of whatever is in the brackets.

$$6x^2 + \frac{4}{\sqrt[3]{x}} - \frac{2}{x^2} + 1 = 6x^2 + 4x^{-\frac{1}{3}} - 2x^{-2} + 1$$

Rewrite the function first to get powers of x.

$$6x^2 + 4x^{-\frac{1}{3}} - 2x^{-2} + 1$$
$$6(2x) + 4\left(-\frac{1}{3}x^{-\frac{4}{3}}\right) - 2(-2x^{-3}) + 0$$

Then differentiate each term separately.

$$\frac{d}{dx}\left(6x^2 + \frac{4}{\sqrt[3]{x}} - \frac{2}{x^2} + 1\right) = 12x - \frac{4}{3\sqrt[3]{x^4}} + \frac{4}{x^3}$$

Simplify the expression, being careful with the signs.

You'll often need to **simplify** a function before you can differentiate it by multiplying out **brackets** or simplifying **fractions**. If you have a fraction to simplify, check first whether the denominator is a **factor** of the numerator, otherwise you'll need to **split it up** into terms.

Example 2

For the function $f(x) = (x + 2)^2(x - 10)$:

a) Find $f'(x)$.

$$f(x) = (x + 2)^2(x - 10) = (x^2 + 4x + 4)(x - 10)$$
$$= x^3 - 10x^2 + 4x^2 - 40x + 4x - 40$$

Multiply out the brackets and simplify.

$$= x^3 - 6x^2 - 36x - 40$$

Differentiate term by term.

$$f'(x) = 3x^2 - 12x - 36 - 0$$
$$= 3x^2 - 12x - 36$$

b) Sketch the graph of $y = f'(x)$.

The coefficient of x^2 in $f'(x)$ is positive, so the graph is u-shaped.

When $x = 0$, $f'(0) = 3(0)^2 - 12(0) - 36 = -36$

When $y = 0$, $f'(x) = 3x^2 - 12x - 36 = 0$

$\Rightarrow x^2 - 4x - 12 = 0$

$\Rightarrow (x + 2)(x - 6) = 0$

$\Rightarrow x = -2$ or $x = 6$

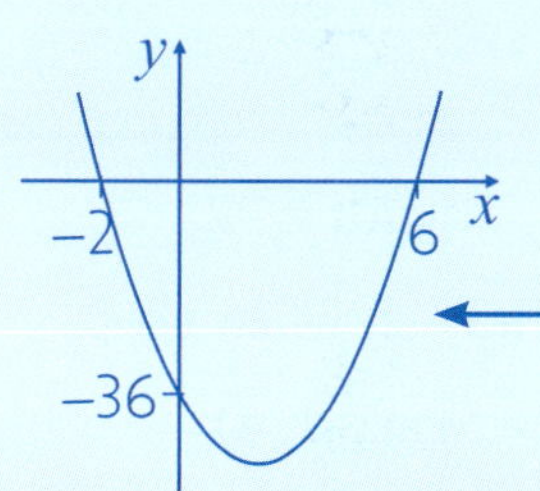

Decide if the graph is u- or n-shaped.

Set $x = 0$ to find the y-intercept, and then set $y = 0$ to find the x-intercepts.

Put all this together to draw the sketch.

Example 3

Problem Solving If the denominator is an expression instead of just one term, chances are it will cancel with a factor of the numerator.

a) Differentiate $y = \frac{x^3 - 5x^2 + 6x}{x - 2}$.

$$y = \frac{x^3 - 5x^2 + 6x}{x - 2} = \frac{x(x^2 - 5x + 6)}{x - 2} = \frac{x(x - 3)(x - 2)}{x - 2}$$

Factorise the numerator.

$$= x(x - 3) = x^2 - 3x$$

Cancel $(x - 2)$ to simplify the fraction and expand the remaining brackets.

$$\frac{dy}{dx} = 2x - 3$$

Differentiate term by term.

b) Differentiate the function $f(x) = \frac{x^3 + 4x + 1}{2x^2}$.

$$f(x) = \frac{x^3 + 4x + 1}{2x^2} = \frac{x^3}{2x^2} + \frac{4x}{2x^2} + \frac{1}{2x^2} = \frac{x}{2} + \frac{2}{x} + \frac{1}{2x^2}$$

This numerator won't factorise. Instead, split the fraction up into three fractional terms.

$$= \frac{1}{2}x + 2x^{-1} + \frac{1}{2}x^{-2}$$

Write each term as a power of x.

$$f'(x) = \frac{1}{2} + 2(-x^{-2}) + \frac{1}{2}(-2x^{-3})$$

Differentiate term by term.

$$= \frac{1}{2} - 2x^{-2} - x^{-3} = \frac{1}{2} - \frac{2}{x^2} - \frac{1}{x^3}$$

Exercise 10.4

Q1 Differentiate these functions:

a) $y = 4x^3 - x^2$ b) $y = x + \dfrac{1}{x}$ c) $y = 3x^2 + \sqrt{x} - 5$

d) $f(x) = -2x^5 + 4x - \dfrac{1}{x^2}$ e) $f(x) = \sqrt{x^3} - x$ f) $f(x) = 5x - \dfrac{2}{x^3} + \sqrt[3]{x}$

Q2 Find:

a) $\dfrac{d}{dx}(x(x^6 - 1))$ b) $\dfrac{d}{dx}((x - 3)(x + 4))$ c) $\dfrac{d}{dx}(x(x - 1)(x - 2))$

d) $\dfrac{d}{dx}((x - 3)(x + 4)(x - 1))$ e) $\dfrac{d}{dx}(x^2(x - 4)(3 - x^3))$ f) $\dfrac{d}{dx}((x - 3)^2(x^2 - 2))$

Q3 Find the gradient of each of the following curves:

a) $y = x^4 - x^2 + 2$ when $x = 3$ b) $y = 2x^5 + \dfrac{1}{x}$ when $x = -2$

c) $y = x(x - 1)(x - 2)$ when $x = -3$ d) $y = 5(x^2 - 1)(3 - x)$ when $x = 0$

e) $y = \sqrt{x}(x - 1)$ at (4, 6) f) $f(x) = x^3(x^2 - 5)$ at (–1, 4)

g) $f(x) = \dfrac{1}{x^2}(x^3 - x)$ at $x = 5$ h) $f(x) = \dfrac{3x^3 + 18x^2 + 24x}{x + 4}$ at (–2, 0)

E Q4 Given that $y = \dfrac{3}{x} - 4$:

a) Find $\dfrac{dy}{dx}$. *[1 mark]*

b) Find the coordinates of the points on the curve $y = \dfrac{3}{x} - 4$ with gradient –2. *[3 marks]*

Q5 For the following graphs, sketch the graph of $f'(x)$ for $0 \le x \le 10$:

a) 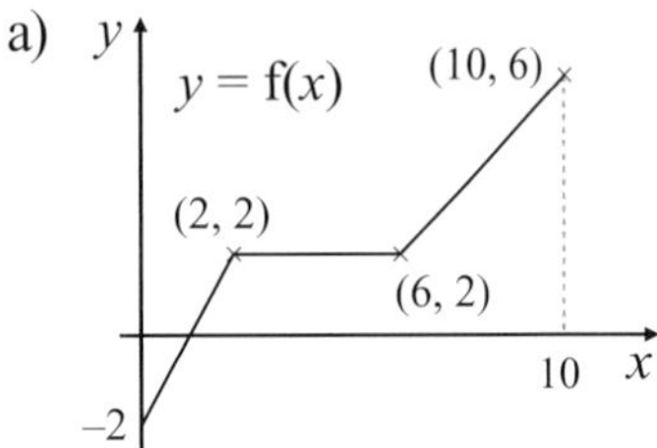

b) 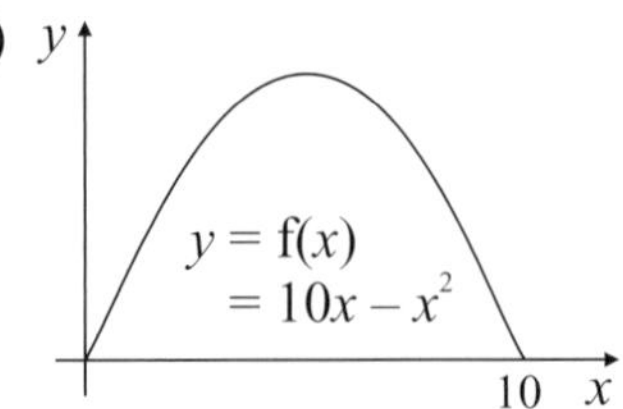

c) 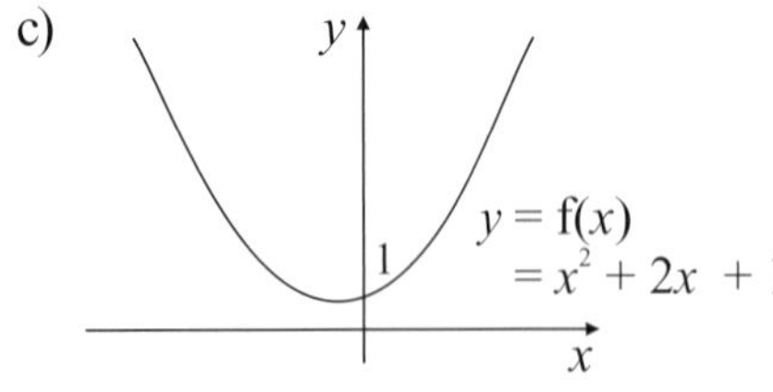

d) 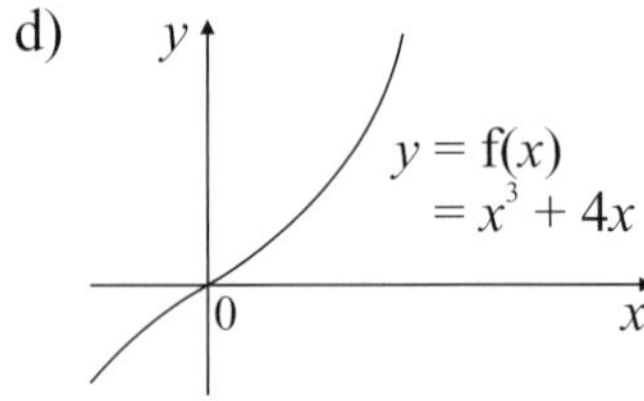

Q6 For each of the following curves, sketch the graph of $y = f'(x)$.

a) $f(x) = (x + 3)(x + 4)$ b) $f(x) = \dfrac{x^3 - 3x^2 + 2x}{x - 1}$

c) $f(x) = x^4 - 4x^3 + 4x^2 - 9$ d) $f(x) = (x - 1)^2(x + 5)$

P Q7 For each of the following functions, find the coordinates of the point or points where the gradient is 0:

a) $y = x^2 - 2x$ b) $y = 3x^2 + 4x$ c) $y = 5x^2 - 3x$

d) $y = 9x - 3x^3$ e) $y = 2x^3 - x^2$ f) $y = 2x^3 + 3x^2 - 12x$

P Q8 Differentiate these functions:

a) $y = \frac{x^2 - 3x - 4}{x + 1}$ b) $f(x) = \frac{x^4 - 9}{x^2 + 3}$ c) $f(x) = \frac{x^5 - 16x^3}{x + 4}$

d) $y = \frac{1}{x}(x - 3)(x - 4)$ e) $y = \sqrt{x}(x^3 - \sqrt{x})$ f) $f(x) = \frac{3 - \sqrt{x}}{\sqrt{x}}$

g) $f(x) = \frac{x + 5\sqrt{x}}{\sqrt{x}}$ h) $f(x) = \frac{x - 3\sqrt{x} + 2}{\sqrt{x} - 1}$ i) $y = \frac{4 - x}{2 + \sqrt{x}}$

E Q9 a) Fully expand $(2 + x)^4$ in ascending powers of x. *[4 marks]*

b) Given that $y = (2 + x)^4$, use your answer to part a) to find $\frac{dy}{dx}$. *[3 marks]*

c) Find the gradient of the curve $y = (2 + x)^4$ at the point (1, 81). *[2 marks]*

E Q10 Consider the function $f(x) = x^3 - 3x^2 + 2$.

a) Write down $f(2x)$. *[1 mark]*

b) Hence, find $f'(2x)$. *[2 marks]*

Challenge

E **P** Q11 A function is defined as $f(x) = \sqrt{3kx} + \sqrt{k} + 2x$, where k is a constant. When $x = 3$, the gradient of the curve $y = f(x)$ is 3. Find the value of k. *[4 marks]*

10.5 Finding Tangents and Normals

Differentiation can be used to find the gradient at a point on a curve.
This makes it easy to find the equation for the **tangent** or **normal** at that point.

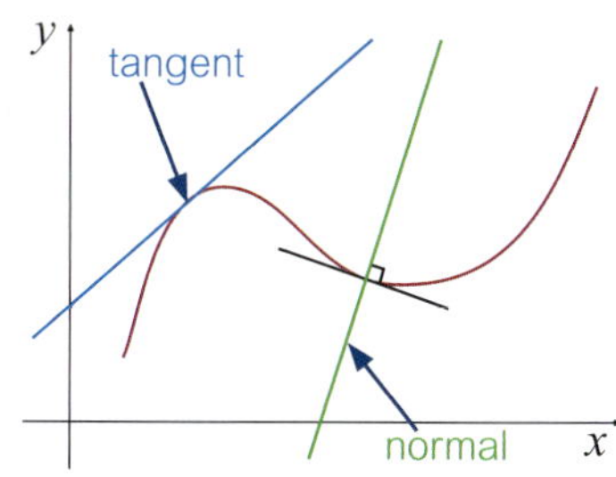

You already know that a **tangent** is a straight line that just **touches** the curve and has the **same gradient** as the curve at that point.

A **normal** is a straight line that is **perpendicular** (at right angles) to the curve at a particular point.

Now, there's one key fact to remember for normals — tangents and normals are perpendicular, and as a result, their **gradients multiply to give –1**:

gradient of tangent × gradient of normal = –1

$$\text{gradient of normal} = \frac{-1}{\text{gradient of tangent}}$$

Armed with this rule, we can write down a step-by-step method for finding the equation of a tangent or normal to a curve — see next page.

To find the equation of the tangent or normal to a curve at a point:

- **Differentiate** the function.
- Find the **gradient** of the curve at that point.
- Use this to deduce the gradient, m, of the tangent or normal:

  gradient of the **tangent** = gradient of the curve

  gradient of the **normal** = $\dfrac{-1}{\text{gradient of the curve}}$

- Write the **equation** of the tangent or normal in the form $y = mx + c$.
- Work out the **constant value** c in the equation by using the coordinates of the point (which you know lies on the tangent/normal).

Tip The tangent and normal are always straight lines, so their equations can be written $y = mx + c$. They can also be written in the form $y - y_1 = m(x - x_1)$ or $ax + by + c = 0$ if you prefer.

Example 1

Find the equation of the tangent to the curve $y = (4 - x)(x + 2)$ at the point (2, 8), giving your answer in the form $ax + by + c = 0$, where a, b and c are integers.

$y = (4 - x)(x + 2) = 4x + 8 - x^2 - 2x = 8 + 2x - x^2$

$\frac{dy}{dx} = 0 + 2 - 2x = 2 - 2x$

Expand the brackets, then differentiate term by term.

$x = 2 \Rightarrow \frac{dy}{dx} = 2 - (2 \times 2) = 2 - 4 = -2$

Work out the gradient of the curve at (2, 8) to find the gradient of the tangent.

Gradient of curve at (2, 8) = –2, so using $y = mx + c$,

$m = -2$ and equation of tangent is $y = -2x + c$.

$x = 2, y = 8 \Rightarrow 8 = -4 + c \Rightarrow c = 12$

Use the point (2, 8) to work out the value of c.

$y = -2x + 12 \Rightarrow 2x + y - 12 = 0$

Write the equation of the tangent and rearrange into the form $ax + by + c = 0$.

Example 2

Find the equation of the normal to the curve $y = x(x - 3)(x + 2)$ at the point (2, –8) in the form $y = mx + c$.

$y = x(x - 3)(x + 2) = x^3 - x^2 - 6x$

$\frac{dy}{dx} = 3x^2 - 2x - 6$

Simplify and differentiate.

$x = 2 \Rightarrow \frac{dy}{dx} = 3(2^2) - 2(2) - 6 = 2$

Find the gradient of the curve at (2, –8).

Gradient of normal, $m = \dfrac{-1}{\text{gradient of curve at } (2, -8)} = -\frac{1}{2}$.

Find the gradient of the normal at (2, –8).

So using $y = mx + c$, equation of normal is $y = -\frac{1}{2}x + c$.

$x = 2, y = -8 \Rightarrow -8 = -1 + c \Rightarrow c = -7$

Use the point (2, –8) to work out the value of c.

$y = -\frac{1}{2}x - 7$

Write the equation of the normal.

Example 3

Find the equation of the normal to the curve $y = \frac{(x+2)(x+4)}{6\sqrt{x}}$ at the point (4, 4), giving your answer in the form $ax + by + c = 0$, where a, b and c are integers.

$y = \frac{(x+2)(x+4)}{6\sqrt{x}} = \frac{x^2+6x+8}{6x^{\frac{1}{2}}} = \frac{x^2}{6x^{\frac{1}{2}}} + \frac{6x}{6x^{\frac{1}{2}}} + \frac{8}{6x^{\frac{1}{2}}}$ ← Simplify the equation — the denominator is one term so it'll probably need splitting up.

$= \frac{1}{6}x^{\frac{3}{2}} + x^{\frac{1}{2}} + \frac{4}{3}x^{-\frac{1}{2}}$

$\frac{dy}{dx} = \frac{1}{6}\left(\frac{3}{2}x^{\frac{1}{2}}\right) + \frac{1}{2}x^{-\frac{1}{2}} + \frac{4}{3}\left(-\frac{1}{2}x^{-\frac{3}{2}}\right) = \frac{1}{4}\sqrt{x} + \frac{1}{2\sqrt{x}} - \frac{2}{3\sqrt{x^3}}$ ← Differentiate term by term.

$x = 4 \Rightarrow \frac{dy}{dx} = \frac{1}{4}\sqrt{4} + \frac{1}{2\sqrt{4}} - \frac{2}{3\sqrt{4^3}} = \frac{1}{2} + \frac{1}{4} - \frac{1}{12} = \frac{2}{3}$ ← Find the gradient of the curve at (4, 4).

Gradient of normal, $m = \frac{-1}{\text{gradient of curve at (4, 4)}} = -\frac{3}{2}$ ← Find the gradient of the normal at (4, 4).

So using $y = mx + c$, equation of normal is $y = -\frac{3}{2}x + c$

$x = 4, y = 4 \Rightarrow 4 = -\frac{3}{2}(4) + c \Rightarrow c = 10$ ← Use the point (4, 4) to work out c.

$y = -\frac{3}{2}x + 10 \Rightarrow 3x + 2y - 20 = 0$ ← Write the equation of the normal in the form $ax + by + c = 0$.

Exercise 10.5

Q1 Find the equation of the tangent to each of these curves at the given point. Give your answer in the form $y = mx + c$.

a) $y = 9x - 2x^2$, (1, 7)
b) $y = x^3 - 2x + 3$, (2, 7)
c) $y = (x + 2)(2x - 3)$, (2, 4)
d) $y = x(x - 1)^2$, (–1, –4)
e) $y = x^2(x + 3) - 10$, (2, 10)
f) $y = x(2x + 4)(x - 3)$, (–1, 8)

Q2 Find the tangent to each of these curves at the given point, giving your answer in the form $ax + by + c = 0$, where a, b and c are integers.

a) $y = \frac{1}{x} + x + 3$, $\left(2, 5\frac{1}{2}\right)$
b) $y = 4x^2 - 3\sqrt{x}$, (1, 1)
c) $y = \frac{3}{x} + 2\sqrt{x}$, $\left(4, 4\frac{3}{4}\right)$
d) $y = \frac{1}{x} + \frac{4}{x^2}$, $\left(2, 1\frac{1}{2}\right)$
e) $y = \frac{1}{3}x^2 - 4\sqrt{x} - \frac{1}{3}$, (4, –3)
f) $y = x - \frac{2}{x} + \frac{3}{x^2}$, (–3, –2)

E P Q3 The curve $xy + 2y - x^3 - 2x^2 = 0$ is defined for $x > 0$.
Find the equation of the tangent to the curve at the point (2, 4). *[5 marks]*

Q4 Find the normal to each of these curves at the given point, giving your answer in the form $ax + by + c = 0$, where a, b and c are integers.

a) $y = 3x^2 - 4x + 2$, (2, 6)

b) $y = x^2(x + 4) - 5x$, (–1, 8)

c) $y = x(x - 1)(x - 2)$, (3, 6)

d) $y = x(x - 3)(x + 4) - 10$, (–2, 10)

e) $y = \dfrac{x^3 - 5x^2 - 14x}{x + 2}$, (5, –10)

f) $y = \dfrac{2x^3 - 32x}{x + 4}$, (3, –6)

Q5 Find the normal to each of these curves at the given point, giving your answer in an appropriate form.

a) $y = \dfrac{2x^5 - 2x^4}{3x^3}$, (–2, 4)

b) $y = \dfrac{5x^2 - 2x + 3}{x^2}$, $\left(2, 4\frac{3}{4}\right)$

c) $y = \dfrac{3x - x^2}{\sqrt{x}}$, (4, –2)

d) $y = \dfrac{1}{x} - \dfrac{3}{x^2} - \dfrac{4}{x^3} + \dfrac{7}{4}$, (–2, 1)

e) $y = \dfrac{x^3 - 5x^2 - 4x}{x\sqrt{x}}$, (4, –4)

f) $y = \dfrac{4x^4 - 2x^2 + 3\sqrt{x}}{\sqrt{x^5}}$, (1, 5)

P Q6 Consider the curve with equation $y = f(x)$ where $f(x) = x^3 - 3x^2 + 3$.

a) Find the coordinates of the point where $f'(x) = 9$ and $x > 0$.

b) Find the equation of the tangent to the curve at this point, giving your answer in the form $y = mx + c$.

c) Find the equation of the normal to the curve at this point, giving your answer in the form $ax + by + c = 0$, where a, b and c are integers.

P Q7 a) Show that the curve $y = \dfrac{x^3 + x^2 + x + 5}{x^2}$ passes through the point $\left(-2, -\frac{1}{4}\right)$.

b) Find the equation of the tangent to the curve at this point, giving your answer in the form $ax + by + c = 0$, where a, b and c are integers.

c) Find the equation of the normal to the curve at this point, giving your answer in the form $ax + by + c = 0$, where a, b and c are integers.

E P Q8 Given that $f(x) = \dfrac{x - \sqrt{x} - 2}{1 + \sqrt{x}}$, $x > 0$,

a) Find $f'(x)$. *[3 marks]*

b) Find the equation of the normal to the curve $y = f(x)$ at the point where $x = 1$. Give your answer in the form $y = mx + c$. *[4 marks]*

c) The normal to the curve crosses the x-axis at A and the y-axis at B. Find the exact area of the triangle OAB, where O is the origin. *[3 marks]*

E Q9 a) Expand $(1 - x)^3$. *[2 marks]*

b) Given that $y = (1 - x)^3$, find $\dfrac{dy}{dx}$. *[2 marks]*

c) Find the equation of the tangent to the curve $y = (1 - x)^3$ at the point where the curve crosses the y-axis. *[2 marks]*

10.6 Finding Second Order Derivatives

If you differentiate y with respect to x, you get the derivative $\frac{dy}{dx}$.

If you then differentiate $\frac{dy}{dx}$ with respect to x, you get the **second order derivative**, denoted $\frac{d^2y}{dx^2}$.

The **second derivative** gives the **rate of change** of the **gradient** of the curve with respect to x. In other words, it tells you how quickly the **gradient** of $y = f(x)$ is changing for any given value of x. In function notation, the **second derivative** is written **f″(x)**.

Example 1

For the function $f(x) = 2x^3 + 4x^2 + x$, find $f'(x)$ and $f''(x)$.

$f(x) = 2x^3 + 4x^2 + x$

$f'(x) = 2(3x^2) + 4(2x) + 1 = 6x^2 + 8x + 1$ ← Differentiate f(x) term by term for f′(x).

$f''(x) = 6(2x) + 8 = 12x + 8$ ← Differentiate f′(x) to get the second derivative, f″(x).

Exercise 10.6

Q1 Find $\frac{dy}{dx}$ and $\frac{d^2y}{dx^2}$ for each of these functions:

a) $y = x^3$ b) $y = x^5$ c) $y = x^4$ d) $y = x$

e) $y = 2x^2$ f) $y = 4x^3$ g) $y = \frac{1}{2}x^4$ h) $y = 3x^{-2}$

i) $y = \frac{1}{x}$ j) $y = \sqrt{x}$ k) $y = \frac{1}{x^2}$ l) $y = x\sqrt{x}$

Q2 Find the second order derivatives of the following functions:

a) $y = x^2 + x^4$ b) $f(x) = x^3 - x$ c) $y = 2x^6 + 3x^2$

d) $f(x) = -2x^{-2} + 5x$ e) $y = 4x^4 + \sqrt{x}$ f) $f(x) = -x^5 - 4\sqrt{x}$

Q3 Find $f'(x)$ and $f''(x)$ for each of these functions:

a) $f(x) = x(4x^2 - x)$ b) $f(x) = (x^2 - 3)(x - 4)$ c) $f(x) = x^2(3x - x^2)$

d) $f(x) = (x^{-1} + 5)(x^{-1} - 5)$ e) $f(x) = \frac{x^3 + 8}{x}$ f) $f(x) = 3\sqrt{x} + x\sqrt{x}$

g) $f(x) = \frac{4x^5 + 12x^3 - 40x}{4(x^2 + 5)}$ h) $f(x) = \frac{1}{x}(3x^4 - 2x^3)$ i) $f(x) = \frac{x^2 - x\sqrt{x} + 7x}{\sqrt{x}}$

Q4 Find the value of the second derivative at the given value for x.

a) $f(x) = 15x^3,\ x = \frac{1}{3}$

b) $y = \frac{x^4 - 2x^3}{12},\ x = 4$

c) $f(x) = x^3 - x^2,\ x = 3$

d) $y = x\sqrt{x} - \frac{1}{x},\ x = 4$

e) $f(x) = x^2(x - 5)(x^2 + x),\ x = -1$

f) $y = \frac{x^5 + 4x^4 - 12x^3}{x + 6},\ x = 5$

g) $f(x) = \frac{9x^2 + 3x}{3\sqrt{x}},\ x = 1$

h) $y = \left(\frac{1}{x^2} + \frac{1}{x}\right)(5 - x),\ x = -3$

P Q5 Find the coordinates of the point(s) with the given value for the second derivative.

a) $y = x^3 + 3x^2,\ \frac{d^2y}{dx^2} = 18$

b) $f(x) = \frac{4}{15}x^{\frac{5}{2}}$ (where $f(x) \geq 0$), $f''(x) = 2$

c) $y = (2x^2 + 4)(2x^2 - 4),\ \frac{d^2y}{dx^2} = 768$

d) $y = \frac{1}{4}x^4 - \frac{5}{3}x^3 + 2x^2 - 20x,\ \frac{d^2y}{dx^2} = 12$

P Q6 For the function $f(x) = (x - 3)^3$, find, in a fully factorised form:

a) $f'(x)$

b) $f''(x)$

Challenge

E P Q7 Given that $f(x) = \frac{(x^2 - \sqrt{x} + 1)}{x}$, show that $4x^2f''(x) + 2xf'(x) - 2f(x) = \frac{a}{x}$, where a is a constant to be found. *[6 marks]*

10.7 Stationary Points

Stationary points occur when the **gradient** of a graph is **zero**. There are three types of stationary point:

Maximum
When the gradient changes from positive to negative.

Minimum
When the gradient changes from negative to positive.

Point of inflection
When the gradient doesn't change sign either side of the stationary point.

Some stationary points are called **local** maximum or minimum points because the function takes on higher or lower values in other parts of the graph. The ones shown above are both local.

Because stationary points occur when the gradient is zero, you can use **differentiation** to find them:

1. Differentiate $f(x)$.
2. Set $f'(x) = 0$.
3. Solve $f'(x) = 0$ to find the x-values.
4. Put the x-values back into the original equation to find the y-values.

Tip Don't forget this last step — once you've found x you also need to find y to give the coordinates of each point.

Example 1

Find the stationary points on the curve $y = 2x^3 - 3x^2 - 12x + 5$.

$y = 2x^3 - 3x^2 - 12x + 5 \Rightarrow \frac{dy}{dx} = 6x^2 - 6x - 12$

You need to find where $\frac{dy}{dx} = 0$, so start by differentiating the function.

At stationary points, $6x^2 - 6x - 12 = 0$

Then set the derivative equal to zero.

$\Rightarrow x^2 - x - 2 = 0$
$\Rightarrow (x + 1)(x - 2) = 0$
$\Rightarrow x = -1$ and $x = 2$

Now solve this equation — it's just a normal quadratic.

$x = -1 \Rightarrow y = 2(-1)^3 - 3(-1)^2 - 12(-1) + 5 = 12$
$x = 2 \Rightarrow y = 2(2)^3 - 3(2)^2 - 12(2) + 5 = -15$

This gives the coordinates $(-1, 12)$ and $(2, -15)$.

You've found the x-values of the stationary points. To find the y-values, put these x-values into the original equation.

Example 2 P

The sketch to the right is of the graph $y = x^3(x^2 + x - 3)$.
One stationary point occurs at $(-1.8, 9.1)$.
Show that the other two occur when $x = 0$ and when $x = 1$, and find their coordinates.

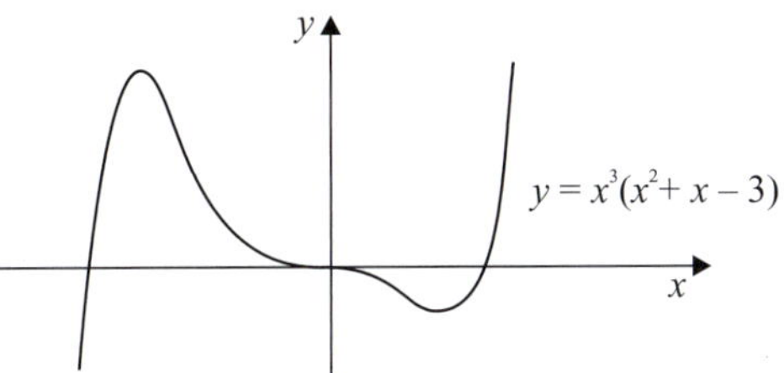

$y = x^3(x^2 + x - 3) = x^5 + x^4 - 3x^3$

$\frac{dy}{dx} = 5x^4 + 4x^3 - 9x^2$

Multiply out the brackets, then differentiate.

$5x^4 + 4x^3 - 9x^2 = 0$
$\Rightarrow x^2(5x^2 + 4x - 9) = 0$
$\Rightarrow x^2(5x + 9)(x - 1) = 0$
$\Rightarrow x = 0, x = -\frac{9}{5} = -1.8$ (given above) and $x = 1$

Stationary points occur when the gradient is equal to zero, so set $\frac{dy}{dx}$ equal to zero and solve for x.

So the other two stationary points occur at $x = 0$ and $x = 1$.

$x = 0 \Rightarrow y = x^3(x^2 + x - 3)$
$= 0^3(0^2 + 0 - 3) = 0(-3) = 0$

$x = 1 \Rightarrow y = x^3(x^2 + x - 3)$
$= 1^3(1^2 + 1 - 3) = 1(-1) = -1$

To find the coordinates of these points, put the x-values into the original equation.

So coordinates of the stationary points are $(0, 0)$ and $(1, -1)$.

Exercise 10.7

Q1 Without doing any calculations, say how many stationary points the graphs below have in the intervals shown.

a) 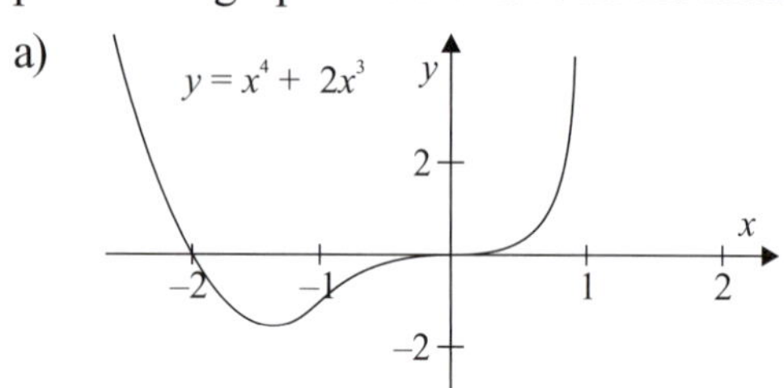

b) 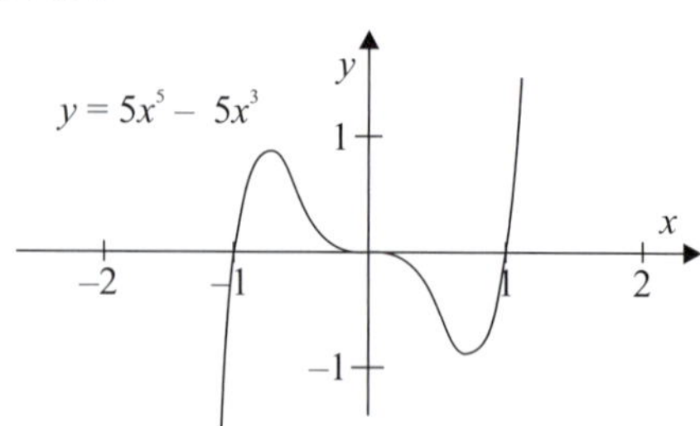

Q2 Find the x-coordinates of the stationary points of the curves with the following equations:

a) $y = x^2 + 3x + 2$ b) $y = (3 - x)(4 + 2x)$

c) $y = x^3 + 4x^2 - 3x$ d) $y = x^4 - 12x^3$

Q3 Find the coordinates of the stationary points of the curves with the following equations:

a) $y = 2x^2 - 5x + 2$ b) $y = -x^2 + 3x - 4$

c) $y = 7 - 6x - 3x^2$ d) $y = (x - 1)(2x + 3)$

Q4 Find the coordinates of the stationary points of the curves with the following equations:

a) $y = x^3 - 3x + 2$ b) $y = 4x^3 + 5$

c) $y = 3x^3 + 6x^2$ d) $4x^3 + 12x^2 + 8$

Q5 Find the coordinates of the stationary points of the graph of $y = x^3 - 6x^2 - 63x + 21$.

P Q6 Show that the graph of the function given by $f(x) = x^5 + 3x + 2$ has no stationary points.

Problem Solving

If there are no stationary points, there are no values of x for which $f'(x) = 0$.

Q7 a) Differentiate $y = x^3 - 7x^2 - 5x + 2$.

b) Hence find the coordinates of the stationary points of the curve with equation $y = x^3 - 7x^2 - 5x + 2$.

P Q8 A graph is given by the function $f(x) = x^3 + kx$, where k is a constant. Given that the graph has no stationary points, find the range of possible values for k.

E P Q9 The curve C, with equation $y = x + k\sqrt{x}$, where k is a constant, has one stationary point at the point P.

a) Find $\frac{dy}{dx}$, giving your answer in terms of k. *[2 marks]*

b) Given that the x-coordinate of P is $\frac{9}{4}$, find:

(i) the value of k, *[2 marks]*

(ii) the y-coordinate of P, *[1 mark]*

10.8 Maximum and Minimum Points

Once you've found where the stationary points are, you might be asked to decide if each one is a **maximum** or **minimum**. Maximum and minimum points are also known as **turning points**.

To decide whether a stationary point is a maximum or minimum, **differentiate again** to find $\frac{d^2y}{dx^2}$ or $f''(x)$ (see page 261).

Tip When a question asks you to "determine the nature of the turning points" it means you need to work out whether each point is a maximum or minimum.

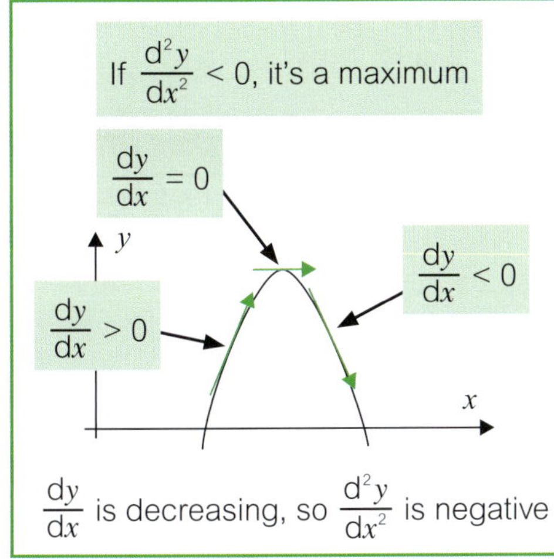

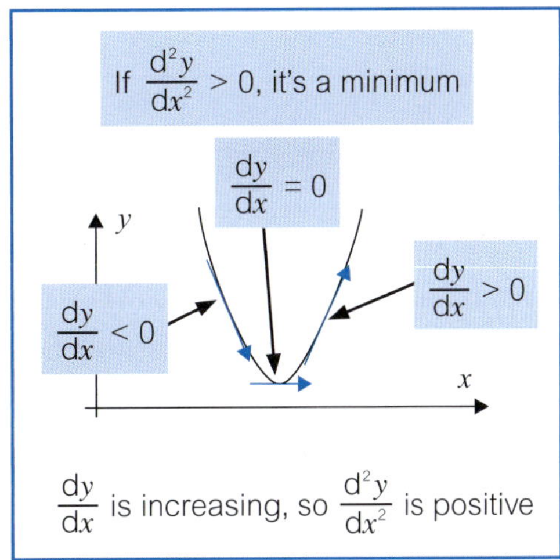

If the second derivative is **equal to zero**, you **can't** tell what type of stationary point it is.

Example 1

Determine the nature of the stationary points in Example 1 on p.263 ($y = 2x^3 - 3x^2 - 12x + 5$).

$\frac{dy}{dx} = 6x^2 - 6x - 12$ ← The first derivative has been found already.

$\Rightarrow \frac{d^2y}{dx^2} = 12x - 6$ ← To determine the nature of the stationary points, differentiate again.

$x = -1$, $\frac{d^2y}{dx^2} = -18$ $x = 2$, $\frac{d^2y}{dx^2} = 18$ ← Then just put in the x-values of the coordinates of the stationary points (you found these on page 263).

$\frac{d^2y}{dx^2} < 0$ at $(-1, 12)$ so it's a maximum

$\frac{d^2y}{dx^2} > 0$ at $(2, -15)$ so it's a minimum

← Use $\frac{d^2y}{dx^2}$ to determine the nature of the points.

← Since you know the turning points and the fact that it's a cubic with a positive coefficient of x^3, you can now sketch the graph.

Exercise 10.8

Q1 The diagram on the right shows a sketch of the graph of $y = \mathrm{f}(x)$. For each turning point, say whether $\mathrm{f}''(x)$ would be positive or negative.

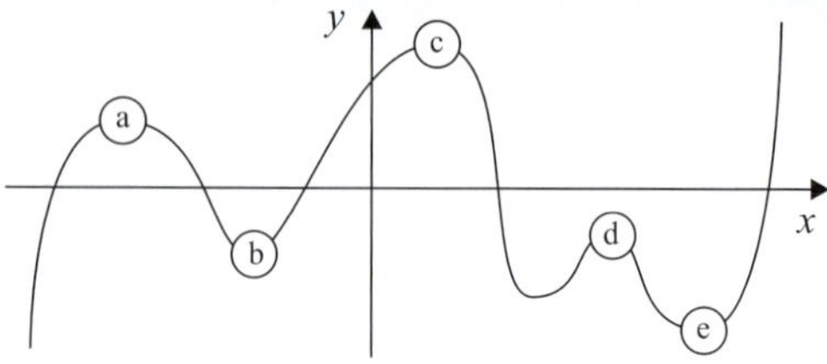

Q2 For each of the following, find the second derivative of the function and say whether the given point is a maximum or a minimum:

a) $y = x^2 + 14x - 3$ at $(-7, -52)$.
b) $y = x^3 - 12x + 4$ at $(2, -12)$.
c) $y = 2x^3 - x^2$ at $\left(\frac{1}{3}, -\frac{1}{27}\right)$.
d) $y = 2x^4 - 16x^3 + 900$ at $(6, 36)$.
e) $y = 4x^5 + 15x^4 - 250$ at $(-3, -7)$.
f) $y = x^5 - 5x^4 + 5x^2 - 40x + 400$ at $(4, 64)$.

P Q3 A function $y = \mathrm{f}(x)$ is such that $\mathrm{f}(1) = 3$, $\mathrm{f}'(1) = 0$ and $\mathrm{f}''(1) = 7$.

a) Give the coordinates of one of the turning points of $\mathrm{f}(x)$.
b) Determine the nature of this turning point, explaining your answer.

Q4 Find the stationary points on the graphs of the following functions and if possible say whether they're maximum or minimum turning points:

a) $y = 5 - x^2$
b) $y = \frac{1}{2}x^2 + 21x + 12$
c) $y = 2x^3 - 6x + 2$
d) $y = x^3 - 3x^2 - 24x + 15$
e) $y = \frac{1}{12}x^4 + \frac{2}{9}x^3$
f) $y = x^4 + 4x^3 + 4x^2 - 10$

Q5 Find the stationary points on the graphs of the following functions and say whether they're maximum or minimum turning points:

a) $\mathrm{f}(x) = 8x^3 + 16x^2 + 8x + 1$
b) $\mathrm{f}(x) = \frac{1}{3}x^3 - 6x^2 - 45x$
c) $\mathrm{f}(x) = \frac{1}{4}x^4 + 2x^3 - 8x^2 + 1$
d) $\mathrm{f}(x) = \frac{27}{x^3} + x$

Q6 a) Given that $\mathrm{f}(x) = x^3 - 3x^2 + 4$, find $\mathrm{f}'(x)$ and $\mathrm{f}''(x)$.

b) Hence find the coordinates of any stationary points on the graph $\mathrm{f}(x)$ and say whether they're maximum or minimum turning points.

Q7 A function is given by $y = x^2 + \frac{2000}{x}$.

a) Find the value of x at which y is stationary.
b) Is this a minimum or maximum point?

P Q8 A curve is given by $\mathrm{f}(x) = 2x^3 + 4x^2 + c$, where c is an integer.
Find the value of c, given that the y-coordinate of the maximum point is $-\frac{260}{27}$.

E Q9 The curve $y = 5x - 1 + \frac{2}{x}$ has a minimum at point A and a maximum at point B. Use calculus to find the coordinates of A and B. *[7 marks]*

P Q10 The curve given by $f(x) = x^3 + ax^2 + bx + c$ has a stationary point with coordinates (3, 10). If $f''(1) = 0$ at (3, 10), find a, b and c.

E P Q11 The functions f and g are defined as $f(x) = x^3 - 2x^2 + x + 2$ and $g(x) = \frac{1}{x^3 - 2x^2 + x + 2}$.

a) (i) Use calculus to find the x-values at the stationary points of $f(x)$. *[4 marks]*

(ii) Determine the nature of the stationary points of $f(x)$. *[3 marks]*

b) Hence, or otherwise, find the coordinates of the stationary points of $g(x)$, and determine their natures. *[4 marks]*

E Q12 A curve has equation $y = \frac{3}{5}x^{\frac{5}{3}} + \frac{3}{4}x^{\frac{4}{3}} - 2x - 1$.

a) Show that $\frac{dy}{dx} = x^{\frac{2}{3}} + x^{\frac{1}{3}} - 2$. *[2 marks]*

b) Find the coordinates of the stationary points on the curve. *[4 marks]*

c) Determine the nature of each stationary point on the curve. *[3 marks]*

P Q13 a) Given that a curve with the equation $y = x^4 + kx^3 + x^2 + 17$ has only one stationary point, show that $k^2 < \frac{32}{9}$.

b) Find the coordinates of the stationary point and say whether it's a maximum or a minimum point.

Challenge

E P Q14 The diagram below shows a sketch of the curve $y = \frac{1}{x^2}$.

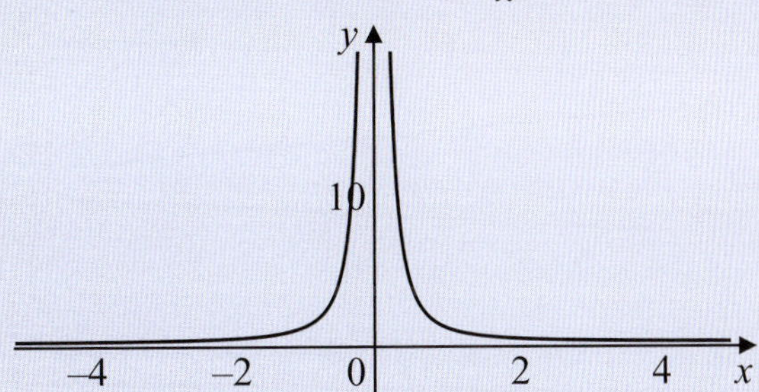

a) Show that the square of the distance from the origin, O, to a point $P(x, y)$ on the curve is given by $OP^2 = x^2 + \frac{1}{x^4}$. *[3 marks]*

b) Let $f(x) = x^2 + \frac{1}{x^4}$. Find $f'(x)$. *[2 marks]*

c) Find the values of x for which $f'(x) = 0$. *[2 marks]*

d) For each of the values found in part c), use calculus to determine whether it corresponds to a maximum or minimum point of $f(x)$. *[3 marks]*

e) Hence find the minimum distance from the origin O to the curve $y = \frac{1}{x^2}$. *[2 marks]*

10.9 Increasing and Decreasing Functions

As differentiation is about finding the gradients of curves, you can use it to find if a function is **increasing** or **decreasing** at a given point. This can help you to sketch and determine the nature of turning points.

A function is **increasing** when the gradient is **positive**.

y gets bigger... ...as x gets bigger — $\frac{dy}{dx} > 0$

A function is **decreasing** when the gradient is **negative**.

y gets smaller... ...as x gets bigger — $\frac{dy}{dx} < 0$

You can also tell how **quickly** a function is increasing or decreasing by looking at the size of the gradient — the **bigger** the gradient (positive or negative), the **faster** the function is increasing or decreasing.

A large increase in x and a small increase in y means a **small positive** gradient.

A small increase in x and a big increase in y means a **large positive** gradient.

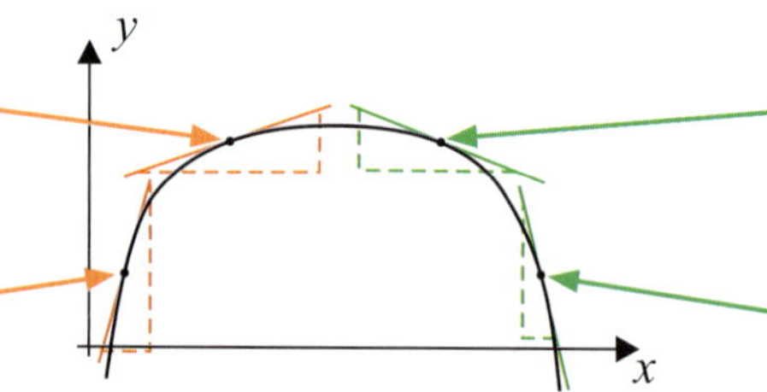

A large increase in x and a small decrease in y means a **small negative** gradient.

A small increase in x and a big decrease in y means a **large negative** gradient.

Example 1

Find the values of x for which the function $y = x^3 - 6x^2 + 9x + 3$, $x > 0$ is increasing.

Method 1: $y = x^3 - 6x^2 + 9x + 3 \Rightarrow \frac{dy}{dx} = 3x^2 - 12x + 9$

You want to know when y is increasing — so differentiate.

$\frac{dy}{dx} > 0 \Rightarrow 3x^2 - 12x + 9 > 0$

$\Rightarrow x^2 - 4x + 3 > 0 \Rightarrow (x - 3)(x - 1) > 0$

It's increasing when the derivative is greater than zero, so write an inequality and solve it.

$x - 1 > 0$ and $x - 3 > 0$

$\Rightarrow x > 1$ and $x > 3 \Rightarrow x > 3$

or $x - 1 < 0$ and $x - 3 < 0$

$\Rightarrow x < 1$ and $x < 3 \Rightarrow x < 1$

For the inequality to be true, either both brackets must be positive or both brackets must be negative.

From the question $x > 0$, so $0 < x < 1$ or $x > 3$.

Or, in set notation, $\{x : 0 < x < 1\} \cup \{x : x > 3\}$

Method 2: Find stationary points using $\frac{dy}{dx} = 0$.

From above, $(x - 3)(x - 1) = 0 \Rightarrow x = 1$ and $x = 3$.

$\frac{dy}{dx} = 3x^2 - 12x + 9 \Rightarrow \frac{d^2y}{dx^2} = 6x - 12$

$x = 1$, $\frac{d^2y}{dx^2} = -6$, so it's a maximum

$x = 3$, $\frac{d^2y}{dx^2} = 6$, so it's a minimum

You could also look at the nature of the stationary points — this tells you where the function goes from increasing to decreasing and vice versa.

So the function is increasing when $0 < x < 1$ or $x > 3$.

The function is increasing as it approaches $x = 1$, is decreasing between $x = 1$ and $x = 3$ and starts increasing after $x = 3$.

Exercise 10.9

Q1 For each of these functions, calculate the first derivative and use this to find the range of values for which the function is increasing.

a) $y = x^2 + 7x + 5$ b) $y = 5x^2 + 3x - 2$ c) $y = \frac{1}{4}x^2 - 6x + 32$

d) $y = 2 - 9x^2$ e) $y = -3x^2 - 4x + 15$ f) $y = -\left(\frac{3x^2 - 8x + 10}{5}\right)$

Q2 For each of these functions, find $f'(x)$ and find the range of values of x for which $f(x)$ is decreasing.

a) $f(x) = 16 - 3x - 2x^2$ b) $f(x) = (x + 3)(x - 2)$ c) $f(x) = (2x - 1)(x - 7)$

d) $f(x) = (6 - 3x)(6 + 3x)$ e) $f(x) = (1 - 2x)(7 - 3x)$ f) $f(x) = (5x - 2)(2 - 5x)$

Q3 Calculate $\frac{dy}{dx}$ for each of these functions and state the range of values for which the function is increasing.

a) $y = x^3 - 6x^2 - 15x + 25$ b) $y = x^3 + 6x^2 + 12x + 5$

c) $y = x(x^2 - 4x - 16)$ d) $y = \frac{x^3 - 3x^2 - 9x - 1}{9}$

Q4 Find the first derivative of each function and state the range of values for which the function is decreasing.

a) $f(x) = x^3 - 3x^2 - 9x + 1$ b) $f(x) = x^3 - 4x^2 + 4x + 7$

c) $f(x) = 3x^3 + \frac{3}{2}x^2 - 72x + 4$ d) $f(x) = \frac{2x^3 - x^2 - 8x + 3}{4}$

Q5 Use differentiation to explain why $f(x) = x^3 + x$ is an increasing function for all real values of x.

Q5 Hint An increasing function is one where $f'(x) > 0$ for all values of x.

Q6 Is the function $f(x) = 3 - 3x - x^3$ an increasing or decreasing function? Explain your answer.

Q7 Use differentiation to find the range of values of x for which each of these functions is decreasing:

a) $y = 2x^4 + x$ b) $y = x^4 - 18x^2 + 7$

c) $y = x^4 - 2x^3 - 5x^2 + 6$ d) $y = 2x^4 + \frac{4}{3}x^3 - 2x^2 + 14$

Q8 Differentiate these functions and find the range of values for which each function is increasing.

a) $y = x^2 + \sqrt{x}, x > 0$ b) $y = x^{-1} + 16x, x > 0$

c) $y = 4x^2 + \frac{1}{x}, x \neq 0$ d) $y = -\left(\frac{3x^{-2} + 18x}{2}\right), x \neq 0$

P Q9 The function $y = 5 - 3x - ax^5$ is a decreasing function for all real values of x. Find the range of possible values for a.

P Q10 The function $y = x^k + x$, where k is a positive integer, is an increasing function for all real values of x. Find all possible values of k.

E P Q11 a) Given that $x^3 + kx$ is an increasing function when $x = 3$, find the range of possible values of k. *[3 marks]*

b) Given that $3 + mx - x^2$ is a decreasing function when $x = 1$, find the range of possible values of m. *[3 marks]*

E Q12 The curve C has the equation $y = x^4 + 4x^3 + 6x^2 + 4x - 2$.

a) Find $\frac{dy}{dx}$. *[2 marks]*

b) Show that $\frac{dy}{dx}$ is an increasing function for all real values of $x \neq -1$. *[2 marks]*

c) Hence show that no points on the curve C have the same gradient. *[1 mark]*

Challenge

E P Q13 A curve has the equation $y = \sqrt{x} + \frac{3}{x\sqrt{x}}$, where $x > 0$.

a) Find $\frac{dy}{dx}$. *[3 marks]*

b) Find the set of values for which y is a decreasing function. *[3 marks]*

10.10 Curve Sketching

You covered some curve sketching in Chapter 6, so you should know the basic shapes of different types of graph. Now you'll see how differentiation can be used to find out more about the **shape** of the graph and to work out some **key points** like the turning points. Use the following **step-by-step** method to get all the information you need to draw an accurate sketch:

1. **Find where the curve crosses the axes.**

   To find where it crosses the **y-axis**, just put $x = 0$ into the function and find the value of y.

   To find where it crosses the **x-axis**, set the function equal to zero and solve for x (you'll probably have to **factorise** and find the **roots**).

2. **Decide on the shape of the graph.**

   Look at the **highest power** of x and its **coefficient** — this determines the overall **shape** of the graph (have a look back at pages 123-127). The most common ones are **quadratics**, **cubics** and **reciprocals**.

   A **quadratic** with a **positive** coefficient of x^2 will be **u-shaped**, and if the coefficient is **negative**, it'll be **n-shaped**.

   A **cubic** will go from **bottom left** to **top right** if the coefficient of x^3 is **positive**, and **top left** to **bottom right** if the coefficient is **negative**.

   Reciprocals (e.g. $\frac{1}{x}$) and other **negative powers** have **two separate curves** in **opposite quadrants**, each with **asymptotes**.

3. **Differentiate to find the stationary points.**

   Find the **stationary points** by **differentiating** and setting $f'(x) = 0$.

   Then **differentiate again** to decide whether these points are **maximums** or **minimums**.

Example 1

Sketch the curve of the equation $y = \mathrm{f}(x)$, where $\mathrm{f}(x) = x^3 - 4x^2 + 4x$.

When $x = 0$, $y = 0$, so the curve goes through the origin.

> Start by finding where the curve crosses the y-axis.

$x^3 - 4x^2 + 4x = 0 \Rightarrow x(x^2 - 4x + 4) = 0$

$\Rightarrow x(x - 2)(x - 2) = 0$

$\Rightarrow x = 0$ and $x = 2$

> Find where it crosses the x-axis by solving the equation $\mathrm{f}(x) = 0$.

$\mathrm{f}(x) = x^3 - 4x^2 + 4x \Rightarrow \mathrm{f}'(x) = 3x^2 - 8x + 4$

> Find $\mathrm{f}'(x)$ by differentiating.

$\mathrm{f}'(x) = 0 \Rightarrow 3x^2 - 8x + 4 = 0$

$\Rightarrow (3x - 2)(x - 2) = 0$

$\Rightarrow x = 2$ and $x = \frac{2}{3}$

> Solve $\mathrm{f}'(x) = 0$ to find the x-values at the stationary points.

$y = (2)^3 - 4(2)^2 + 4(2) = 0$ and

$y = \left(\frac{2}{3}\right)^3 - 4\left(\frac{2}{3}\right)^2 + 4\left(\frac{2}{3}\right) = \frac{32}{27}$

> Put the x-values back into the original equation to find the y-values of the stationary points.

$\mathrm{f}''(x) = 6x - 8$

At $x = 2$, $\mathrm{f}''(x) = 4$, so this is a minimum.

At $x = \frac{2}{3}$, $\mathrm{f}''(x) = -4$, so this is a maximum.

> Differentiate again to find out if the stationary points are maximums or minimums.

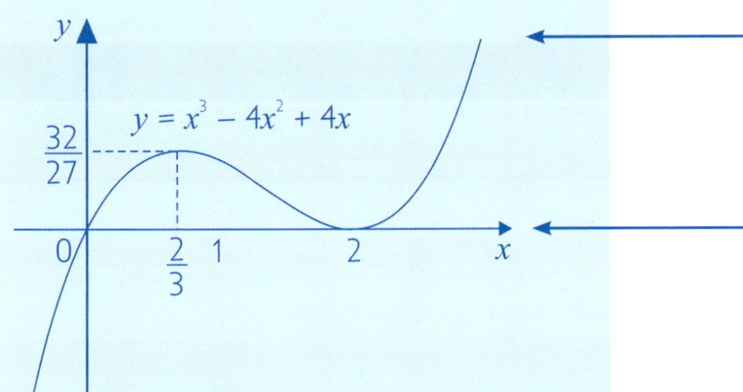

> Now you have all the information you need to sketch the graph. It's a cubic equation with a positive coefficient of x^3, so the graph will go from bottom left to top right.

> Notice that the x-intercept $x = 2$ is also the minimum.

Example 2

Sketch the graph of $f(x) = -8x^3 + 2x$.

When $x = 0$, $f(x) = 0$ so the curve goes through the origin.

Set $x = 0$ to find where the curve crosses the y-axis.

$-8x^3 + 2x = 0 \Rightarrow 2x(-4x^2 + 1) = 0$

So $x = 0$ or $-4x^2 + 1 = 0 \Rightarrow x^2 = \frac{1}{4} \Rightarrow x = \pm\frac{1}{2}$

Solve $f(x) = 0$ to find where the curve crosses the x-axis.

$f(x) = -8x^3 + 2x \Rightarrow f'(x) = -24x^2 + 2$

$f'(x) = 0 \Rightarrow -24x^2 + 2 = 0$

$\Rightarrow x^2 = \frac{1}{12} \Rightarrow x = \pm\sqrt{\frac{1}{12}} = \pm\frac{1}{2\sqrt{3}}$

Next differentiate the function to find the stationary point(s).

$x = \frac{1}{2\sqrt{3}} \Rightarrow f(x) = \frac{2}{3\sqrt{3}}$ and $x = -\frac{1}{2\sqrt{3}} \Rightarrow f(x) = -\frac{2}{3\sqrt{3}}$

$f''(x) = -48x$

Differentiate again to see if these points are maximums or minimums.

At $x = \frac{1}{2\sqrt{3}}$, $f''(x) = -\frac{24}{\sqrt{3}} < 0$ so it's a maximum.

At $x = -\frac{1}{2\sqrt{3}}$, $f''(x) = \frac{24}{\sqrt{3}} > 0$ so it's a minimum.

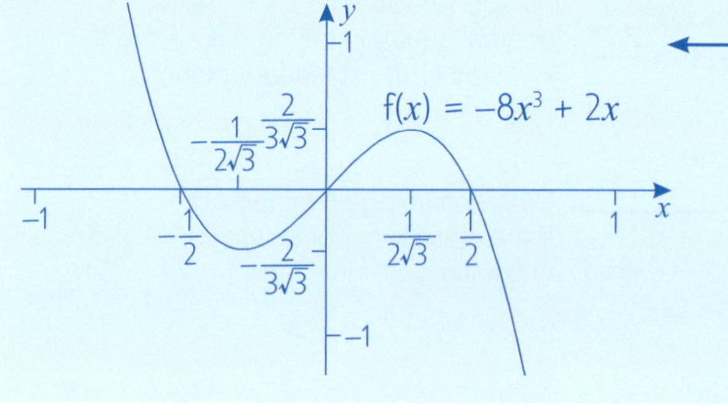

Now you have all the information you need to sketch the graph. The highest power is 3, so it's a cubic. It has a negative coefficient, so the graph will go from top left to bottom right.

Exercise 10.10

Q1 For the graph $y = x^3 - 2x^2$:

a) Find the coordinates of the points at which it crosses each axis.

b) Find $\frac{dy}{dx}$ and hence the coordinates of the points where $\frac{dy}{dx} = 0$.

c) Identify whether the stationary points are maximums or minimums.

d) Sketch the graph of $y = x^3 - 2x^2$.

Q2 a) Solve the equation $x^3 + x^2 = 0$.

b) Find the stationary points of the graph of $f(x) = x^3 + x^2$ and say whether they're maximum or minimum points.

c) Use your answers to parts a) and b) to sketch the graph of $f(x) = x^3 + x^2$, labelling the coordinates of the stationary points and places where the curve meets the axes.

Q3 a) Find the first and second derivatives of the function $f(x) = x^4 - x^3$.

b) Write down the ranges of values of x for which $f(x)$ is increasing and decreasing.

c) Sketch the graph of $y = f(x)$, labelling the coordinates of all stationary points and the points where the curve crosses the axes.

Q4 Sketch the graphs of the equations below, labelling the coordinates of any stationary points and the points where the curves cross the axes.

a) $y = 3x^3 + 3x^2$ b) $y = -x^3 + 9x$

c) $y = x^4 - x^2$ d) $y = x^4 + x^2$

Q5 Given that $x^3 - x^2 - x + 1 = (x + 1)(x - 1)^2$, sketch the graph of $y = x^3 - x^2 - x + 1$, labelling the coordinates of all the stationary points and the points where the curve crosses the axes.

Q6 a) Show that $x^3 - 4x = 0$ when $x = -2$, 0 and 2.

b) Use first and second derivatives to show that the graph of $y = x^3 - 4x$ has a minimum at (1.2, –3.1) and a maximum at (–1.2, 3.1), where all coordinates are given to 1 d.p.

c) Use your answers to parts a) and b) to sketch the graph of $y = x^3 - 4x$, labelling the coordinates of the stationary points and the points at which the curve crosses the axes.

P Q7 a) Show that the graph of $f(x) = x + \frac{1}{x}$, $x \neq 0$ has 2 stationary points.

b) Calculate the coordinates of these stationary points and say whether they're maximum or minimum points.

c) Describe what happens to $f(x)$ as $x \to 0$ from both sides.

d) Describe what happens to $f(x)$ as $x \to \infty$ and $x \to -\infty$.

e) Hence sketch the graph of the function $x + \frac{1}{x}$.

Problem Solving

The '→' symbol means 'tends to' or 'approaches' — you need to say what happens as x gets close to zero and to $\pm\infty$.

P Q8 a) Show that for the graph of $y = x^4 + \frac{8}{\sqrt{x}}$, $x > 0$, $\frac{dy}{dx} = 0$ when $x = 1$.

b) Sketch the graph of $y = x^4 + \frac{8}{\sqrt{x}}$, $x > 0$, labelling the coordinates of the stationary point.

E P Q9 The curve C has equation $y = f(x)$, where $f(x) = x^3 + 2x^2 + 1$.

a) Given that the only point at which C cuts the x-axis is (–2.21, 0), sketch the curve C, labelling the coordinates of any stationary points. *[8 marks]*

b) Sketch $y = f'(x)$, labelling the coordinates of any turning points and points of intersection with the coordinate axes. *[4 marks]*

Challenge

E P Q10 A curve has the equation $y = (x - 1)(x - 2)(x + 3)$.

a) Use calculus to find the coordinates of the turning points, giving your answers correct to 3 significant figures. *[4 marks]*

b) Sketch the curve, labelling the coordinates of any turning points and points of intersection with the coordinate axes. *[3 marks]*

c) Find the equation of the tangent to the curve that is parallel to the tangent at (–3, 0). *[5 marks]*

10.11 Speed and Acceleration Problems

M

Until now, all the examples have been about differentiating functions of x to find gradients of curves. But **real-life** examples often involve a function of time, t, and you'll need to differentiate to find the **rate of change** over time. The maths is the **same**, the **letters** are just different.

The next example looks at the **distance** a car has travelled as a function of **time**.

Example 1

A car pulls away from a junction and travels x metres in t seconds.
For the first 10 seconds, its journey is modelled by the equation $x = 2t^2$.

a) Find the speed of the car after 8 seconds.

$x = 2t^2$

$\frac{dx}{dt} = 4t$

When $t = 8$, $\frac{dx}{dt} = 32$

So after 8 seconds the car is travelling at 32 ms^{-1}.

Speed is the rate of change of distance with respect to time. To work out the speed as a function of t, differentiate x to find $\frac{dx}{dt}$.

You've got speed as a function of t, so put $t = 8$ seconds into the expression.

b) Find the car's acceleration during this period.

$\frac{dx}{dt} = 4t$

$\frac{d^2x}{dt^2} = 4$

So the car's acceleration during this period is 4 ms^{-2}.

Acceleration is the rate of change of speed with respect to time — so differentiate the speed with respect to time to get the second derivative $\frac{d^2x}{dt^2}$.

Exercise 10.11

M Q1 A particle moves along a path described by the equation $x = 3t^2 - 7t$, where t is the time in seconds and x is the distance in metres.

a) Find the speed, $\frac{dx}{dt}$, of the particle as a function of t.

b) What is the speed of the particle in ms^{-1} at: (i) $t = 2$ seconds? (ii) $t = 5$ seconds?

c) Find the value of t when the speed is 17 ms^{-1}.

d) Find the acceleration $\frac{d^2x}{dt^2}$ of the particle as a function of t.

M Q2 A particle moves along a path described by the equation $x = 2t^3 - 4t^2$, $t > 0$, where t is the time in seconds and x is the distance in metres.

a) Find the speed of the particle after t seconds.

b) Find x and t when the speed is 30 ms^{-1}.

c) Find the acceleration of the particle after t seconds.

d) Find the acceleration at $t = 5$ seconds in ms^{-2}.

e) Find the speed when the acceleration is 16 ms^{-2}.

Q2 Hint For part e), use the information you've been given to work out the value of t and then put the t value into the expression for speed.

M Q3 A train moving away from a station travels x metres in t seconds.
For the first minute, the train's journey is modelled by the equation $x = \frac{t^2}{4}$.

a) Find the speed of the train after t seconds.

b) Find the acceleration of the train during this period.

c) Find the train's speed at $t = 45$ seconds.

d) How far will the train have travelled when its speed reaches 25 ms^{-1}?

E M Q4 The displacement-time graph below shows the distance of a particle from its starting point, x metres, against time, t seconds.

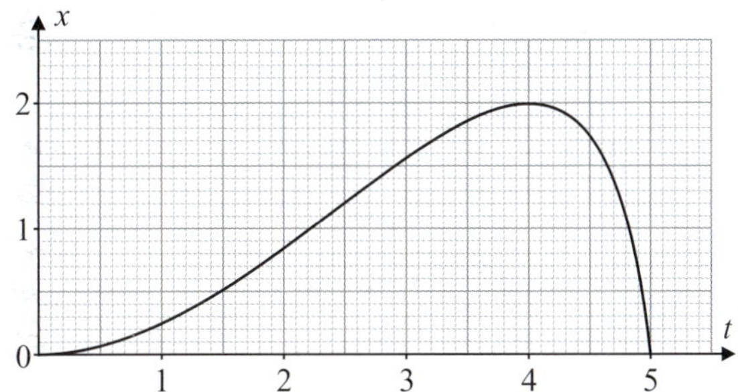

a) Sketch the corresponding velocity-time graph for $0 \leq t \leq 5$. *[3 marks]*

b) On the graph, mark the point A at which the acceleration of the particle is zero. *[1 mark]*

E M Q5 A particle moves with velocity $v = 5t + 2$ ms^{-1} when $0 \leq t \leq 2$, and $v = \frac{5}{4}t^2 + 7$ ms^{-1} when $2 < t \leq 4$, where t is time in seconds.

a) Find the acceleration of the particle when $t = 1$. *[1 mark]*

b) Find the acceleration of the particle when $t = 3$. *[2 marks]*

E P M Q6 A remote-control car travels along a straight track.
The position of the car at time t is given by $x = \frac{1}{4}t^3(t-4)^2$ for $0 \leq t \leq 4$, where t is time in seconds and x is the distance travelled by the car in metres.

a) Find the velocity of the car after t seconds. *[4 marks]*

b) Find the acceleration of the car after t seconds. *[2 marks]*

c) Find the greatest distance that the car reaches from its starting position. Give your answer to 3 significant figures. *[4 marks]*

10.12 Length, Area and Volume Problems

M

Because differentiation can be used to find the maximum value of a function, it can be used in **real-life problems** to maximise a quantity subject to certain factors, e.g. maximising the volume of a box that can be made with a set amount of cardboard.

To find the maximum value of something, all you need is an equation **in terms of only one variable** (e.g. x) — then just **differentiate as normal**. Often there'll be too many variables in the question, so you've got to know how to manipulate the information to get rid of the unwanted variables.

Example 1 

A farmer wants to build a rectangular sheep pen with length x m and width y m. She has 20 m of fencing in total, and wants the area inside the pen to be as large as possible. How long should each side of the pen be, and what will the area inside the pen be?

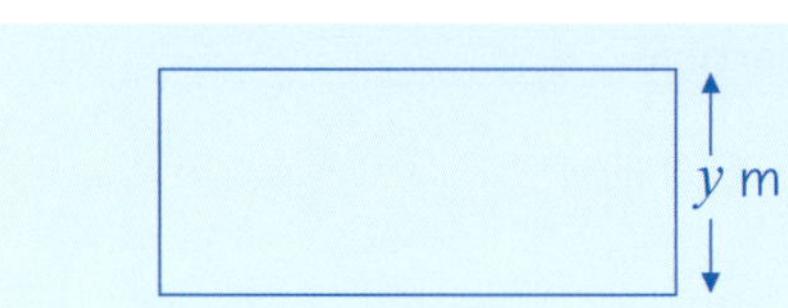

Area = length × width = xy m^2 ← Start by writing down an expression for the area of the pen.

Perimeter = 20 m = $2x$ m + $2y$ m ← Use what you know about the total amount of fencing available to find an expression for y in terms of x.

$\Rightarrow y = \frac{20 - 2x}{2} = 10 - x$

$A = xy = x(10 - x) = 10x - x^2$ ← Now you can substitute this into the expression you wrote down for the area and use differentiation to maximise it.

So $\frac{dA}{dx} = 10 - 2x$

$\frac{dA}{dx} = 0 \Rightarrow 10 - 2x = 0$ ← Now find when $\frac{dA}{dx} = 0$.

So $x = 5 \Rightarrow y = 10 - x = 5$

$\frac{d^2A}{dx^2} = -2$, which is negative, ← To check that this value of x gives a maximum for A, differentiate again.

so this will give a maximum for A.

So the pen should have length 5 m and width 5 m, and the area will be 5 m × 5 m = 25 m^2 ← Finally, find the value of the maximum area.

Example 2 

A cuboid jewellery box with a lid has dimensions $3x$ cm by x cm by y cm. It is made using a total of 450 cm^2 of wood.

Show that the volume of the box can be expressed as $V = \dfrac{675x - 9x^3}{4}$, and use calculus to find the maximum volume.

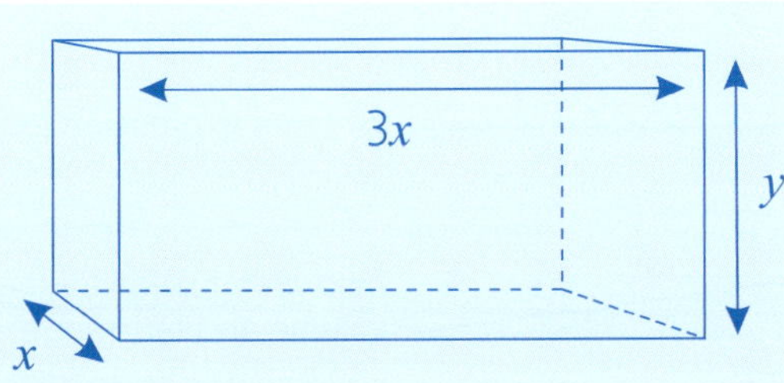

$V = \text{length} \times \text{width} \times \text{height} = 3x \times x \times y = 3x^2y$ ← You know the basic equation for volume.

Surface area $= 2 \times [(3x \times x) + (3x \times y) + (x \times y)] = 450$

$\Rightarrow 6x^2 + 8xy = 450 \Rightarrow y = \dfrac{450 - 6x^2}{8x} = \dfrac{225 - 3x^2}{4x}$

← Use the information about the total amount of wood to write an equation for the surface area, and rearrange to write y in terms of x.

$V = 3x^2y = 3x^2\left(\dfrac{225 - 3x^2}{4x}\right) = \dfrac{675x - 9x^3}{4}$ ← Now substitute this into the expression for the volume of the box.

$V = \dfrac{675x - 9x^3}{4} \Rightarrow \dfrac{dV}{dx} = \dfrac{675 - 27x^2}{4}$

When $\dfrac{dV}{dx} = 0$, $\dfrac{675 - 27x^2}{4} = 0$

$\Rightarrow x^2 = \dfrac{675}{27} = 25 \Rightarrow x = 5$

← Now just differentiate and find x at the stationary point(s).

Problem Solving x is a length so it can't have a negative value.

$\dfrac{d^2V}{dx^2} = -\dfrac{27x}{2}$ ← Check that V is actually a maximum at $x = 5$.

So when $x = 5$, $\dfrac{d^2V}{dx^2} = -\dfrac{135}{2}$ (so V is a maximum)

$V = \dfrac{675x - 9x^3}{4}$

So when $x = 5$, $V = \dfrac{675(5) - 9(5^3)}{4} = 562.5 \text{ cm}^3$ ← Then just calculate V with $x = 5$.

Differentiation isn't limited to rectangles and cuboids — it can be used on **any shape** as long as you can describe its (surface) area or volume with variables (e.g. x, y).

Example 3 

A cylindrical pie tin is t cm high with a diameter of d cm. The volume of the pie tin is 1000 cm^3.

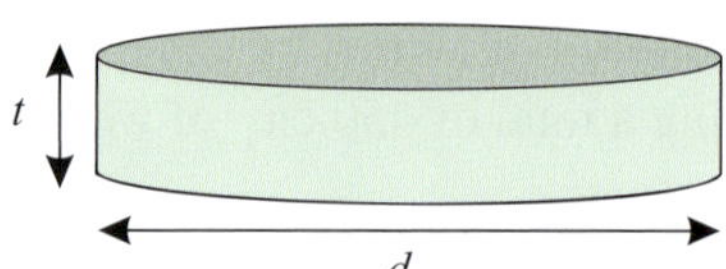

Show that the surface area of the tin is given by $A = \frac{\pi}{4}d^2 + \frac{4000}{d}$ and find the minimum surface area.

A = area of tin's base + area of tin's curved face

$= \pi\left(\frac{d}{2}\right)^2 + (\pi d \times t) = \frac{\pi d^2}{4} + \pi dt$ ← Write an expression for A.

$V = \pi\left(\frac{d}{2}\right)^2 t = 1000 \Rightarrow t = \frac{1000}{\pi\left(\frac{d}{2}\right)^2} = \frac{4000}{\pi d^2}$

$A = \frac{\pi d^2}{4} + \pi dt = \frac{\pi d^2}{4} + \left(\pi d \times \frac{4000}{\pi d^2}\right) = \frac{\pi d^2}{4} + \frac{4000}{d}$

Find an equation for the volume and rearrange it to make t the subject. Then put that into the equation for surface area.

$\frac{dA}{dd} = \frac{\pi d}{2} - \frac{4000}{d^2}$ so when $\frac{dA}{dd} = 0$,

$\frac{\pi d}{2} - \frac{4000}{d^2} = 0 \Rightarrow d^3 = \frac{2 \times 4000}{\pi} \Rightarrow d = \frac{20}{\sqrt[3]{\pi}}$ ← Next, differentiate with respect to d and find the values of d that make $\frac{dA}{dd} = 0$.

$\frac{d^2A}{dd^2} = \frac{\pi}{2} + \frac{8000}{d^3} = \frac{\pi}{2} + \frac{8000}{\left(\frac{8000}{\pi}\right)} = \frac{3\pi}{2}$, so it's a minimum. ← Check to see if this value of d gives a minimum for A.

$A = \frac{\pi}{4}\left(\frac{20}{\sqrt[3]{\pi}}\right)^2 + \frac{4000}{\left(\frac{20}{\sqrt[3]{\pi}}\right)} = 439$ cm^2 (to 3 s.f.) ← Now calculate the surface area for that value of d.

Exercise 10.12

P M Q1 A farmer wants to enclose a rectangular area of 100 m^2 with a fence. Find the minimum length of fencing he needs to use.

P M Q2 A rectangular vegetable patch is enclosed by a wall on one side and fencing on three sides, as shown in the diagram.

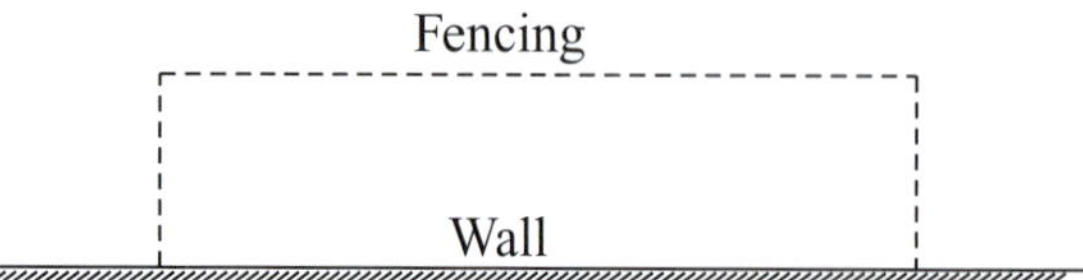

Use calculus to show that the maximum possible area that can be enclosed by 66 m of fencing is 544.5 m^2.

Problem Solving

It might look like you're not given enough information here, but just call the length x and the width y and you're on your way.

P M **Q3** A pet food manufacturer designs tins of cat food of capacity 500 cm³ as shown below. The radius of the tin is r cm and the height is h cm.

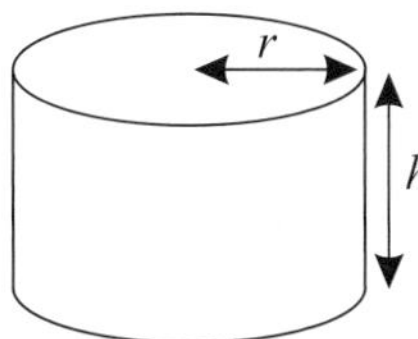

a) Show that the surface area A of the tin is given by $A = 2\pi r^2 + \frac{1000}{r}$.

b) Find the value of r which minimises the surface area (to 3 s.f.).

c) Find the minimum possible surface area for the tin (to 3 s.f.).

P M **Q4** A child makes a box by taking a piece of card measuring 40 × 40 cm and cutting squares with side length x cm, as shown in the diagram. The sides are then folded up to make a box.

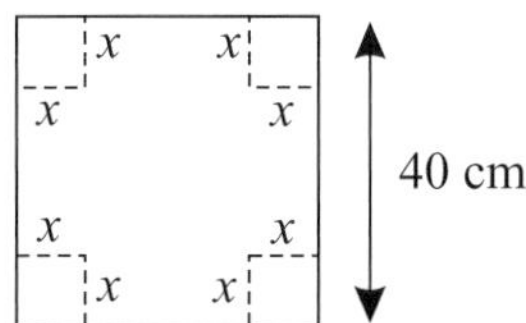

a) Write down a formula for the volume of the box, V.

b) Find the maximum possible volume of the box to 3 s.f.

P M **Q5** A chocolate manufacturer designs a box which is a triangular prism, as shown in the diagram. The cross-section of the prism is a right-angled triangle with sides of x cm, x cm and h cm. The length of the prism is l cm and the volume is 300 cm³.

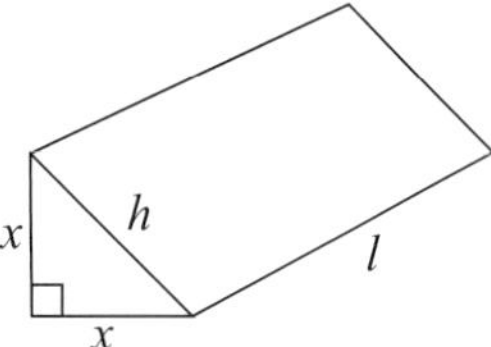

a) Show that the surface area of the prism is given by $A = x^2 + \frac{600(2+\sqrt{2})}{x}$.

b) Show that the value of x which minimises the surface area of the box is $\sqrt[3]{600 + 300\sqrt{2}}$.

P M **Q6** The diagram shows a box with dimensions x cm, $2x$ cm and y cm, and volume 200 cm³.

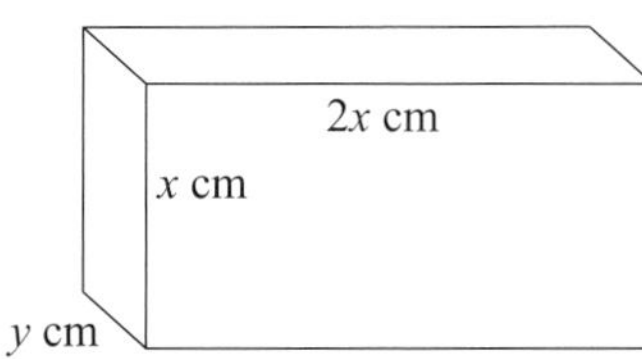

a) Show that the surface area A of the box is given by $A = 4x^2 + \frac{600}{x}$.

b) Use calculus to find the value of x that gives the minimum value of A (to 3 s.f.).

c) Hence find the minimum possible surface area of the box, correct to 3 s.f.

E P M Q7 A plant pot has a vertical cross-section in the shape of a trapezium, as shown in the diagram below.

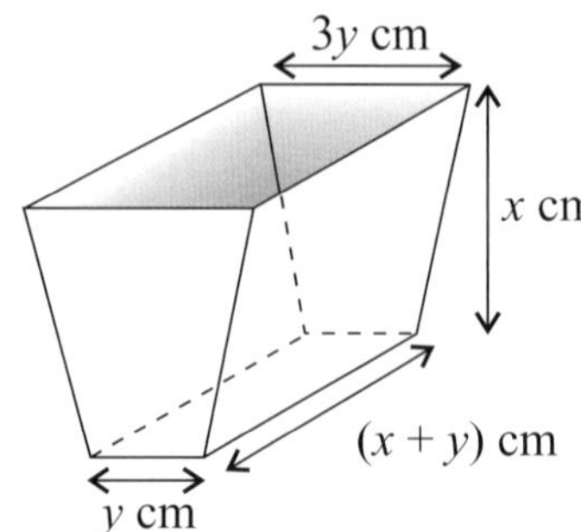

The vertical height of the plant pot is x cm and the two parallel sides of the trapezium cross-section have widths of y cm and $3y$ cm respectively. The length of the plant pot is $(x + y)$ cm.

a) Given that the area of the vertical cross-section of the plant pot is 20 cm^2, show that the volume is given by $V = 20x + \frac{200}{x}$. *[4 marks]*

b) Use calculus to find the value of x that minimises the volume V, and prove that this value of x minimises V. *[7 marks]*

c) Find the minimum volume of the plant pot. *[1 mark]*

E P M Q8 A closed cuboid box has dimensions x cm, $3x$ cm and $(40 – 2x)$ cm, as shown in the diagram below.

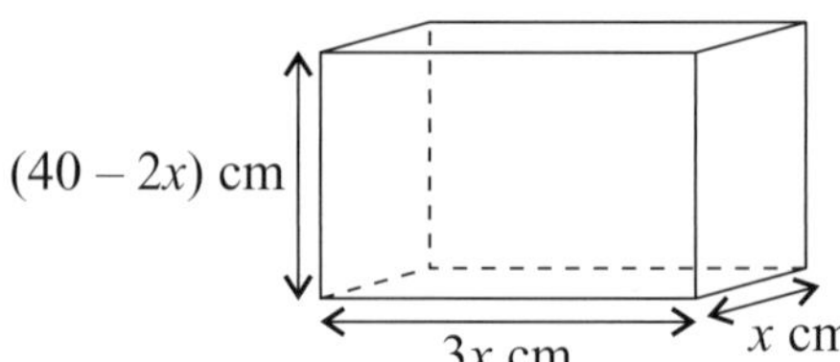

a) Find an expression for the surface area of the box in terms of x. *[3 marks]*

b) Find the value of x for which the surface area of the box is maximised and find the maximum surface area. *[3 marks]*

c) The costs of the materials used to produce the box are as follows:
- £0.50 per cm^2 for the sides
- £0.75 per cm^2 for the top and base.

(i) Explain why the value of x found in part b) will not necessarily be the value for which the cost of the box is maximised. *[1 mark]*

(ii) Find the maximum possible cost of the box. *[5 marks]*

d) Suggest one reason why the maximum cost might differ from the value found in part c). *[1 mark]*

10 Review Exercise

Q1 Differentiate the following functions from first principles:

a) $y = x + 1$ b) $y = 4x^2$ c) $y = 3 - x^3$

E Q2 Differentiate $y = x^3 + 4x$ from first principles to find $\frac{dy}{dx}$. *[5 marks]*

Q3 Differentiate these functions with respect to x:

a) $y = x^2 + 2$ b) $y = x^4 + \sqrt{x}$ c) $y = \frac{7}{x^2} - \frac{3}{\sqrt{x}} + 12x^3$

Q4 Find the gradients of these graphs at $x = 2$:

a) 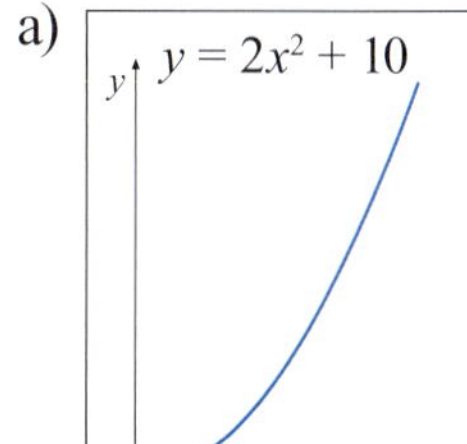

b) 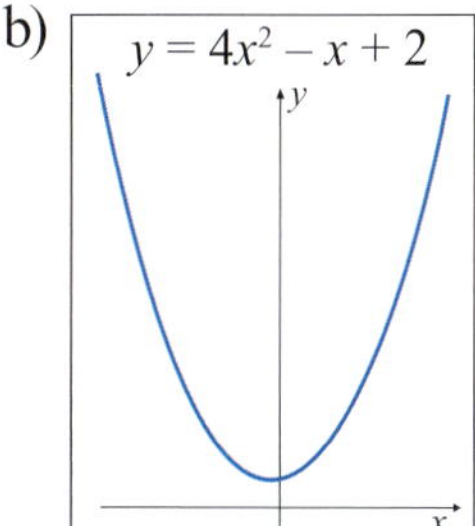

c) 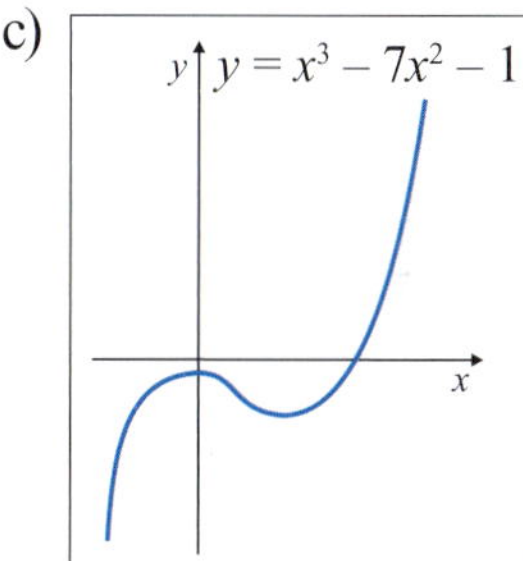

M Q5 Water is poured into a bowl. The volume (v) of water in the bowl (in ml) after t seconds is given by the function: $v = 3t^2 + 4$.

a) How much water is in the bowl initially?

b) Find the rate at which water is being poured into the bowl when $t = 4$ seconds.

E P Q6 $f(x) = 4\sqrt{x} + \frac{a}{x^2} - 6x + b$

If $f(4) = \frac{-97}{8}$ and $f'(1) = -64$ find the values of a and b. *[4 marks]*

Q7 Find the equations of the tangent and the normal to the curve $y = \sqrt{x^3} - 3x - 10$ at $x = 16$.

P Q8 Show that the graphs of $y = \frac{x^3}{3} - 2x^2 - 4x + \frac{86}{3}$ and $y = \sqrt{x}$ both go through the point (4, 2), and are perpendicular at that point.

P Q9 Consider the curve C given by the equation $y = x^2 - 6$ and the line L given by the equation $y = 3$.

a) Find the coordinates of the points, A and B, where C and L intersect.

b) Find the gradient of C at points A and B.

c) Find the equations of the normals to C at A and B.

d) The normals at points A and B meet at the point D. Find the coordinates of the point D.

E Q10 A curve has the equation $y = x^2 + 4x - 2$. Find the following:

a) the equation of the tangent, when $x = 2$, *[3 marks]*

b) the equation of the normal, when $x = -1$, *[3 marks]*

c) the point V, where the tangent at $x = 2$ and the normal at $x = -1$ intersect. *[2 marks]*

P Q11 Consider the curve C given by the equation $y = x^3 - 2x^2 + 1, x > 0$, and the line L given by the equation $y = 1$.

a) Write down the gradient of the line L for any x.

b) Find the point at which the curve C has the same gradient as the line L.

c) Hence give the equation of the tangent to C at this point.

Q12 Find the equation of the tangent to the curve $y = x^3 + \frac{4}{x} + 2\sqrt{x}$ at $x = 1$.

Q13 Find the equations of the tangent and the normal to the curve $y = 1 + \sqrt{x^3}$ at $x = 16$.

E Q14 The curve C has equation $y = x - x^3$.

a) Show that the point $P(0, 0)$ lies on C. *[1 mark]*

b) Find the equation of the normal to C at the point P. *[4 marks]*

c) The normal to C at P intersects C again at the points A and B. Find the coordinates of A and B. *[3 marks]*

E Q15 The points P and Q lie on the curve C with equation $y = x^2 - 1$. The tangent to the curve C at P has a gradient of -8, and the tangent at Q has a gradient of 4.

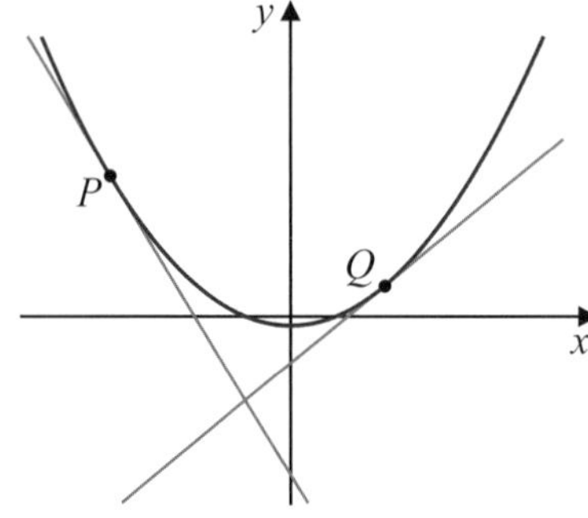

a) Find the coordinates of P and Q. *[3 marks]*

b) Find the equations of the tangents to C at P and Q. *[3 marks]*

The tangents to the curve C at points P and Q meet at the point R.

c) Find the coordinates of R. *[2 marks]*

P Q16 Consider the curve with equation $y = f(x)$, where $f(x) = x^3 - 3x$.

a) Work out the gradient of this curve when $x = -1$.

b) Show that $2f''(x) - 3f'(x) + f(x) = x^3 + 9(1 + x - x^2)$.

P Q17 Let $f(x) = x^4$. Find $f''(x) + 2f'(x) - 4f(x)$, expressing your answer as the product of factors.

E Q18 When $y = \frac{x-1}{x^2}$, show that $\frac{d^2y}{dx^2} + \frac{4}{x}\left(\frac{dy}{dx}\right) + \frac{2}{x^2}y = 0$. *[5 marks]*

Q19 a) Find the stationary points of the graph of the function $y = x^3 + \frac{3}{x}$.
b) Work out whether each stationary point is a maximum or a minimum.

Q20 Find all the stationary points of the graph of $y = 2x^4 - x^2 + 4$ and determine their nature.

E Q21 If $y = x^2(x-3)^2$
a) Find the coordinates of the stationary points of $y = x^2(x-3)^2$. *[4 marks]*
b) Describe the nature of each stationary point. *[3 marks]*
c) Sketch $y = x^2(x-3)^2$. *[3 marks]*

E Q22 A function is defined as $f(x) = \frac{x^5}{100} - \frac{13}{60}x^3 + \frac{9}{5}x$.
a) Find $f'(x)$. *[2 marks]*
b) Hence show that $y = f(x)$ has four stationary points. *[4 marks]*
c) Show that two of the stationary points are maximum points and two are minimum points. *[3 marks]*

E P Q23 A curve has equation $y = ax^3 + bx^2 + cx + d$, where a, b, c and d are constants, and $a \neq 0$.
a) Show that the curve has two stationary points when $b^2 > 3ac$. *[5 marks]*
b) State how many stationary points the curve will have when $b^2 < 3ac$. *[1 mark]*
c) Hence, or otherwise, determine how many stationary points the following curves have:
(i) $y = 2x^3 + 4x^2 - x + 7$ (ii) $y = 2 - 5x - 2x^2 - x^3$ *[2 marks]*

Q24 Find when each of the functions below is increasing and decreasing:
a) $y = 6(x+2)(x-3)$ b) $y = \frac{1}{x^2}$

E Q25 Determine the x-values for which the function $f(x) = x^4 - 14x^2 + 24x$ is increasing and the x-values for which it is decreasing. *[7 marks]*

E Q26 For a function $f(x)$, $f'(x) = (x+1)(x^2-4)$.
a) State the x-values of any stationary points of the graph of $y = f(x)$. *[1 mark]*
b) Find the set of values of x for which $f(x)$ is an increasing function. *[3 marks]*

E P Q27 Prove that $g(x) = x + 3 - \frac{4}{x}$ is increasing for all real values of x, $x \neq 0$. *[3 marks]*

Q28 Sketch the graph of $y = 3x^3 - 16x$, clearly showing the coordinates of any turning points.

Q29 Sketch the graph of $y = -3x^3 + 6x^2$, clearly showing the coordinates of any turning points.

E Q30 A curve has equation $y = 8x^2 - \frac{1}{x}$, $x \neq 0$.

a) Find the coordinates of the point at which the curve crosses the x-axis. *[2 marks]*

b) Find the coordinates of the stationary point of the curve, giving your answer to 3 significant figures. *[4 marks]*

c) Show that y is an increasing function for $x > 0$. *[2 marks]*

d) Hence sketch the curve, labelling the coordinates of the stationary point and any points of intersection with the coordinate axes. *[5 marks]*

P Q31 Given that $xy = 20$ and that both x and y are positive, find the least possible value of $x^2 + y^2$.

E P M Q32 A cylinder with radius r cm and height $10h$ cm fits perfectly inside a sphere with radius 15 cm.

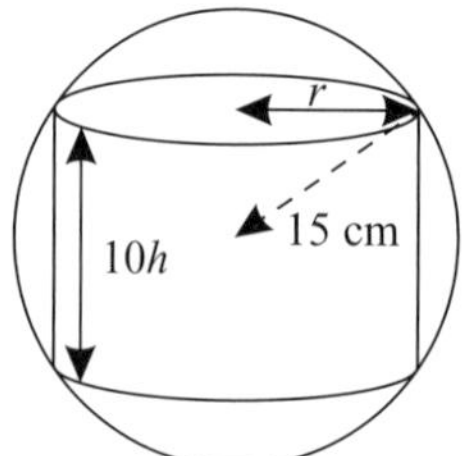

a) Express r in terms of h. *[2 marks]*

b) Find the volume of the cylinder, V in terms of h. *[2 marks]*

c) Find the maximum volume of the cylinder as h varies to the nearest cm^3. *[5 marks]*

M Q33 A particle moves along a path described by the equation $x = t^3 - 8t$, $t > 0$, where t is the time in seconds and x is the displacement in metres.

a) Find $\frac{dx}{dt}$, the velocity of the particle as a function of t.

b) Find x and t when the velocity is 19 ms^{-1}.

c) Find the acceleration $\frac{d^2x}{dt^2}$ of the particle as a function of t.

d) Find the acceleration, in ms^{-2}, after 2 seconds.

e) Find the velocity, in ms^{-1}, when the acceleration is 18 ms^{-2}.

E M Q34 A particle moves such that its displacement s metres, at time t seconds is given by:

$$s = 4 + 12t^2 - t^3$$

Find the acceleration when $t = 4.5$ seconds. *[4 marks]*

P M Q35 The height (h m) a firework can reach is related to the mass (m g) of fuel it carries as shown:

$$h = \frac{m^2}{10} - \frac{m^3}{800}$$

Find the mass of fuel required to achieve the maximum height and state what the maximum height is to 3 s.f.

E M Q36 A constant force, F newtons, acts on a particle moving in a straight line with velocity v ms^{-1} over a distance x m. The work done by the force, W, is given by $W = Fx$ and the power, P, is given by $P = Fv$.

a) Show that $\frac{dW}{dt} = P$ for a constant force. *[1 mark]*

$\frac{dW}{dt} = P$ for non-constant forces as well.
The net work done by a force acting on a particle is given by $W = -\frac{3}{2}t^2 + 8t$.

b) Find the power when $t = 2$. *[3 marks]*

c) Find the maximum value of net work done. *[3 marks]*

d) Prove that the value found in part c) is a maximum. *[2 marks]*

E M Q37 The displacement of a particle, x metres, at time t seconds is given by:

$$x = 6t + 6t^2 - t^4,\ 0 \le t \le 2$$

a) Find the acceleration of the particle in terms of t. *[3 marks]*

b) The particle decelerates for $t > k$, where k is a constant. Find the value of k. *[3 marks]*

c) Find the maximum speed of the particle. *[2 marks]*

E P M Q38 A piece of paper of width x cm and perimeter 60 cm is rolled up to make a cylinder, as shown in the diagram below.

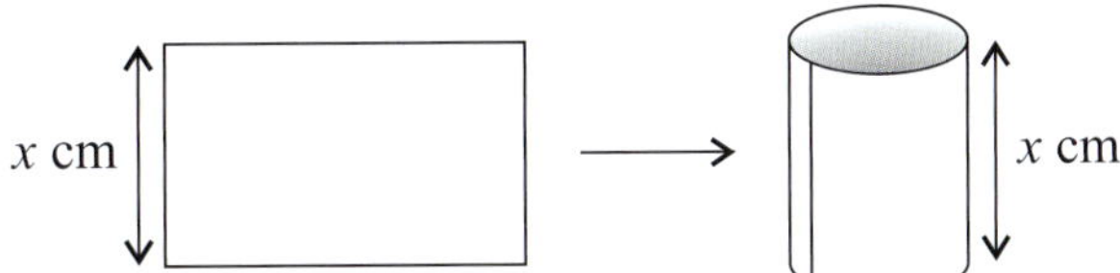

a) Find the radius of the cylinder in terms of x. *[2 marks]*

b) Show that the volume of the cylinder is given by $V = \frac{1}{4\pi}x(30 - x)^2$. *[2 marks]*

c) Use calculus to find the maximum possible volume of the cylinder as x varies. *[5 marks]*

d) Prove that the value found in part c) is a maximum. *[3 marks]*

The outside curved surface area of the cylinder is painted.
1 litre of paint covers an area of 1.2 m^2.

e) Find the smallest amount of paint that will ensure, regardless of the value of x, that all of the outside curved surface area of the cylinder can be painted. *[5 marks]*

Challenge

E P Q39 The curve C has equation $y = k\sqrt{x} - \frac{1}{k\sqrt{x}}$.

a) Show that $\frac{dy}{dx} = \frac{k^2x + 1}{2kx\sqrt{x}}$. *[4 marks]*

b) The gradient of the curve C is $\frac{1}{4}$ at the point where $x = 4$.

(i) Show that $4k^2 - 4k + 1 = 0$. *[2 marks]*

(ii) Hence find the value of k. *[2 marks]*

E P Q40 The curve C has equation $x = ay^2$, $y > 0$, where a is a non-zero constant.

a) Find $\frac{dy}{dx}$ in terms of a. *[3 marks]*

b) Find the equation of the tangent to C at the point $\left(\frac{1}{a}, \frac{1}{a}\right)$, giving your answer in the form $y = mx + c$. *[3 marks]*

P Q41 At points P and Q, the curve $y = x^3$ has a gradient of 3. The tangents and normals to the curve at points P and Q cross at points R and S, as shown in the diagram below.

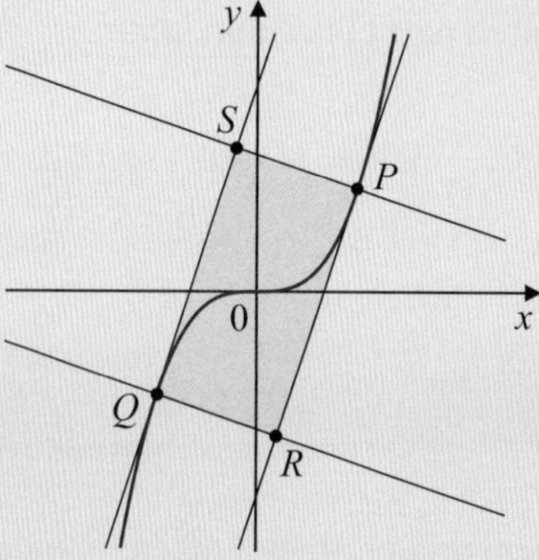

Find the area of the quadrilateral $PRQS$.

E P Q42 A function is defined as $f(x) = x^2 - \frac{2}{x}$, $x \neq 0$.

a) Work out $f''(x)$. *[3 marks]*

b) Prove that $f'(x)$ is increasing when $x < 0$. *[2 marks]*

c) Find the values of x for which $f(x)$ is increasing. *[3 marks]*

P M Q43 A manufacturer is creating a design for a solid glass prism. The length of the prism is y cm, and the cross-section of the prism is an equilateral triangle with sides of length x cm, as shown in the diagram below.

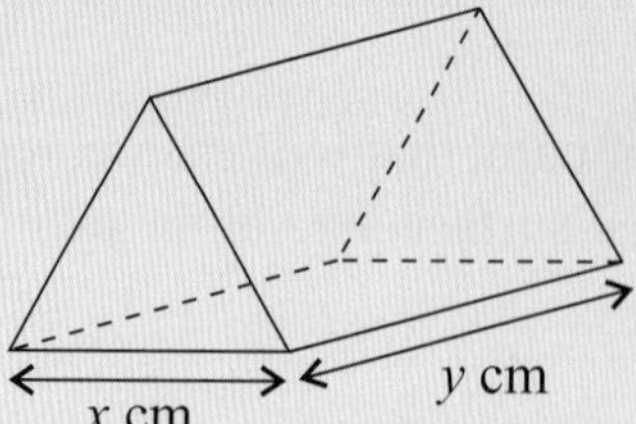

Given that the prism will be made using 50 cm^3 of glass, find the values of x and y that maximise its surface area. Give your answers to 3 s.f.

10 Chapter Summary

1 To find the gradient of a curve at a point, you need to use differentiation.

2 The derivative of y with respect to x is written as $\frac{dy}{dx}$.

3 The derivative of a function $f(x)$ is denoted $f'(x)$.

4 To differentiate from first principles, use this formula: $f'(x) = \lim_{h\to 0}\left[\frac{f(x+h)-f(x)}{(x+h)-x}\right]$

5 You can differentiate powers of x with an easier formula: if $y = x^n$, then $\frac{dy}{dx} = nx^{n-1}$

6 For a function with multiple terms, use this formula: $\frac{d}{dx}(x^m + x^n) = \frac{d}{dx}(x^m) + \frac{d}{dx}(x^n)$

7 To find the equation of a tangent to a curve at a point:
- Differentiate the function and find the gradient at that point.
- The gradient, m, of the tangent is equal to the gradient of the curve.
- Write the equation of the tangent in the form $y = mx + c$.
- Work out the value of c using the point on the curve.

8 A normal is a straight line that is perpendicular to the curve at a point:
- The gradient of the normal $= \frac{-1}{\text{gradient of the curve}} = \frac{-1}{\text{gradient of the tangent}}$
- You can find the equation of the normal in the form $y = mx + c$ like you do with the tangent.

9 The second derivative is denoted $\frac{d^2y}{dx^2}$. You find it by differentiating $\frac{dy}{dx}$ again.
A function's second derivative is denoted $f''(x)$.

10 Stationary points occur when the gradient of a graph is zero. There are 3 types:
- Maximum — when the gradient changes from positive to negative.
- Minimum — when the gradient changes from negative to positive.
- Point of inflection — when the gradient doesn't change sign either side of the point.

11 You can find stationary points by differentiating the function and setting the derivative equal to zero.

12 A function's second derivative at a stationary point can tell you if the stationary point is a maximum or a minimum — if it's negative it's a maximum and if it's positive it's a minimum.

13 If a curve's gradient at a point is positive then the function is increasing.
If the gradient is negative then the function is decreasing.

14 To sketch a graph, determine where it crosses the axes, its shape and its stationary points.

15 In real-life problems you apply the same skills to different variables like time or distance. You might be asked to find the maximum or minimum value of a quantity like area or volume by finding stationary points.

Integration

11

Learning Objectives

Once you've completed this chapter, you should be able to:

- Use the integral symbol $\int$.
- Integrate powers of x.
- Integrate more complicated functions containing powers of x.
- Find the equation of a curve, given the gradient and a point on the curve.
- Evaluate definite integrals.
- Find the area between a curve and the x-axis using definite integration.

Prior Knowledge Check

1 Simplify these expressions: a) $x^2 \times x^5$ b) $\frac{x^9}{x^{-3}}$ c) $(x^6)^3$ see pages 25-26

2 Factorise the following: a) $x^2 - 4x + 4$ b) $5x^2 + 31x + 6$ see pages 39-41

3 Given that $(x + 2)$ is a factor of $x^3 + 5x^2 + 2x - 8$, sketch the graph of $y = x^3 + 5x^2 + 2x - 8$, labelling any intersections with the axes. see pages 70-71, 123-125

4 Differentiate the following to find $\frac{dy}{dx}$:

a) $y = 3x^5$ b) $y = 2x^2 + 3x^{-2}$ c) $y = (2x^3 - 2)(x^2 - 2x^{-6})$ see pages 252-255

11.1 Integration

Integration is just the process of getting from $\frac{dy}{dx}$ back to y itself.

Integration is the '**opposite**' of differentiation. When you integrate something, you're trying to find a function that returns to **what you started with** when you differentiate it. This function is called an **integral**. The integral of a **function** f(x) with respect to x is written:

$\int$ means **the integral of** → $\int \mathbf{f(x)\,dx}$ ← dx means **with respect to x**.

For example, 'the integral of $2x$ with respect to x' is written $\int \mathbf{2x\,dx}$.

The answer could be **any function** which differentiates to give $2x$.

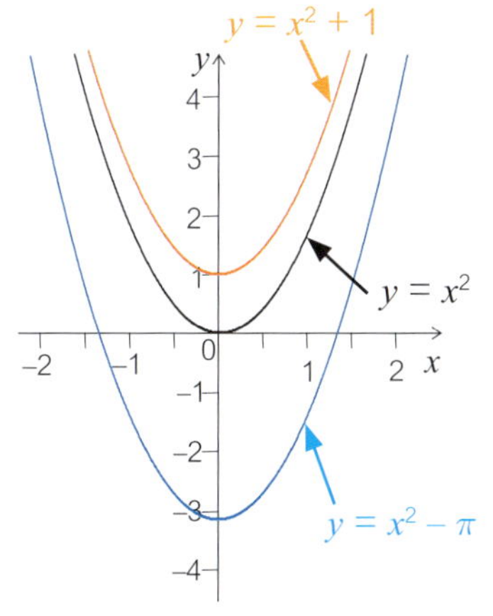

From Chapter 10, we know that:

$$\frac{d}{dx}(x^2) = 2x \qquad \frac{d}{dx}(x^2 + 1) = 2x \qquad \frac{d}{dx}(x^2 - \pi) = 2x$$

If you differentiate any of these functions, you get $2x$ — they're **all possible integrals** because they all have the **same gradient**.

In fact, if you differentiate **any** function which is of the form $\boldsymbol{x^2}$ **+ 'a constant'** you'll get $2x$ because differentiating a constant always gives zero.

So the answer to this integral is actually $\int 2x\,dx = x^2 + C$.

C is a constant representing 'any number' — it's known as the **constant of integration**.

This is an example of **indefinite integration** — a good way to remember this is that C can take an **indefinite number** of values. There are **lots of answers** to an indefinite integral, so you need to add a **constant of integration** to show that it could be **any number**.

Tip **Definite** integrals only have one possible answer — you'll learn about these later in this chapter.

Formally, the **Fundamental Theorem of Calculus** states that:

$$\int f(x)\,dx = F(x) + C \iff f(x) = \frac{d}{dx}(F(x))$$

Or, more simply, it says that if differentiating takes you from one function to another, then integrating the second function will take you back to the first (with a constant of integration).

11.2 Integrating x^n

The formula to the right tells you how to integrate any power of x (except x^{-1}):

$$\int x^n\,dx = \frac{x^{n+1}}{n+1} + C$$

This means to integrate a power of x: (i) **Increase the power** by one — then divide by it.
(ii) Add a **constant**.

You can't use this formula for $\frac{1}{x} = x^{-1}$. When you increase the power by 1 and then divide by the power you get $\int x^{-1}\,dx = \frac{x^0}{0}$. This is undefined since you can't divide by 0.

Tip It's easy to forget the constant of integration and lose easy marks. Make sure you get used to adding it on.

Example 1

Find the following integrals:

a) $\int x^3\,dx$

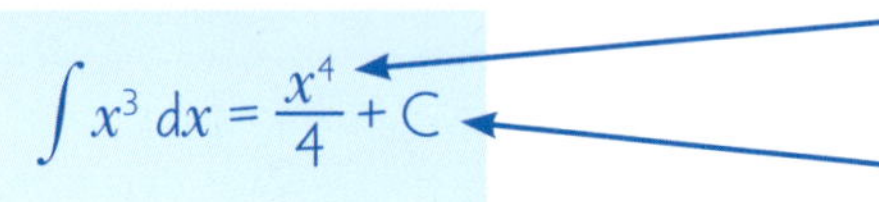

$$\int x^3\,dx = \frac{x^4}{4} + C$$

Increase the power to 4, then divide by 4.

Add a constant of integration.

You can check you've got the right answer by differentiating it — you should end up with what you started with: $\frac{d}{dx}\left(\frac{x^4}{4} + C\right) = \frac{d}{dx}\left(\frac{x^4}{4}\right) + \frac{d}{dx}(C) = x^3 + 0 = x^3$

b) $\int \frac{1}{x^3}\,dx$

$$\int \frac{1}{x^3}\,dx = \int x^{-3}\,dx = \frac{x^{-2}}{-2} + C = -\frac{1}{2x^2} + C$$

Increase the power by 1 to –2, then divide by –2.

Add a constant of integration.

Differentiate to check your answer: $\frac{d}{dx}\left(-\frac{1}{2x^2} + C\right) = \frac{d}{dx}\left(-\frac{1}{2}x^{-2}\right) + \frac{d}{dx}(C) = x^{-3} + 0 = \frac{1}{x^3}$

c) $\int \sqrt[3]{x^4}\,dx$

$$\int \sqrt[3]{x^4}\,dx = \int x^{\frac{4}{3}}\,dx = \frac{x^{\frac{7}{3}}}{\left(\frac{7}{3}\right)} + C = \frac{3\sqrt[3]{x^7}}{7} + C$$

Add 1 to the power, then divide by $\frac{7}{3}$.

Add a constant of integration.

Differentiate to check your answer: $\frac{d}{dx}\left(\frac{3\sqrt[3]{x^7}}{7} + C\right) = \frac{d}{dx}\left(\frac{3}{7}x^{\frac{7}{3}}\right) + \frac{d}{dx}(C) = x^{\frac{4}{3}} + 0 = \sqrt[3]{x^4}$

d) $\int 4\,dx$

$$\int 4\,dx = \int 4x^0\,dx = \frac{4x^1}{1} + C = 4x + C$$

Increase the power from 0 to 1, then divide by the power.

Add a constant of integration.

Exercise 11.1-11.2

Q1 Find an expression for y when $\frac{dy}{dx}$ is the following:

a) x^7 b) $2x^3$ c) $8x$

d) $-5x^4$ e) $200x^{99}$ f) x^{-3}

g) $4x^{-4}$ h) $-6x^{-5}$ i) -12

j) $x^{\frac{1}{2}}$ k) $x^{\frac{1}{3}}$ l) $12\sqrt{x^3}$

Q1 Hint When the x^n term is multiplied by a constant, the integral of the x^n term is multiplied by the same constant — just like when you differentiate. Look at the formula and examples on page 292 if you need to.

Q2 Find f(x) when f′(x) is the following:

a) x^5 b) $-6x$ c) $\frac{4}{3}$ d) $2x^{-2}$

e) $-9x^{-19}$ f) $\frac{x}{5}$ g) $-x^{-6}$ h) $\frac{5}{\sqrt{x}}$

i) $x^{-\frac{4}{3}}$ j) $30x^{-0.8}$ k) $-\frac{2}{3}x^{\frac{7}{3}}$ l) $-\frac{3}{4}x^{-\frac{5}{2}}$

Q3 For each of the following, find the value of a:

a) $\int 12x^2\,dx = ax^3 + C$ b) $\int 20x^{-9}\,dx = \frac{a}{2}x^{-8} + C$ c) $\int \frac{4}{5}x^a\,dx = \frac{8}{15}x^{\frac{3}{2}} + C$

d) $\int \frac{(\sqrt[3]{x})}{6}\,dx = \frac{x^a}{8} + C$ e) $\int -9x^{-4}\,dx = \frac{a}{x^a} + C$ f) $\int \left(-\frac{1}{3}\right)^3 dx = -\frac{1}{27}x^a + C$

Q4 Find the following:

a) $\int x^{\frac{2}{3}}\,dx$ b) $\int 7x^{\frac{4}{3}}\,dx$ c) $\int x^{-\frac{1}{2}}\,dx$

d) $\int 2x^{-\frac{1}{3}}\,dx$ e) $\int 14x^{0.4}\,dx$ f) $\int -1.2x^{-0.6}\,dx$

g) $\int -2x^{-\frac{5}{4}}\,dx$ h) $\int -\frac{3}{2}x^{-\frac{1}{2}}\,dx$ i) $\int -\frac{4}{3}x^{-\frac{4}{3}}\,dx$

j) $\int \frac{1}{2}\sqrt{x^5}\,dx$ k) $\int \frac{2}{3}x^{\frac{7}{5}}\,dx$ l) $\int 50.5x^{0.01}\,dx$

P Q5 Find an expression for each of these integrals in terms of x and k, where k is a constant.

a) $\int kx^9\,dx$ b) $\int \frac{k}{2}x^{-3}\,dx$ c) $\int \frac{1}{5}x^{2k}\,dx,\ k \neq -\frac{1}{2}$

d) $\int (k-1)x^{-\frac{1}{2}}\,dx$ e) $\int -x^{-(k+1)}\,dx,\ k \neq 0$ f) $\int (kx)^{-\frac{3}{2}}\,dx$

Challenge

P Q6 Find an expression for each of these integrals in terms of y and b, where b is a constant.

a) $\int \frac{7y^b}{y}\,dy,\ b \neq 0$ b) $\int \frac{y^b}{(b-1)}\,dy,\ b \neq -1, 1$ c) $\int (b^2 + b - 2)y^{b-2}\,dy,\ b \neq 1$

P Q7 Given that a is a constant, find the value of x where $\int 4ax^{a-1}\,dx = \int (a+1)x^a\,dx$. Assume that C = 0 for both integrations.

11.3 Integrating Functions

Like differentiating, if there are **lots of terms** in an expression, you can just integrate each bit **separately**. If the terms are multiplied by **constants**, take them **outside** the integral like this:

$$\int ax^n \, dx = a\int x^n \, dx$$

When you're integrating an expression with multiple terms, you only need **one constant** of integration for the whole expression — each integral gives a constant, so you can **add** them up to get a **new constant**.

Example 1

a) Find $\int \left(3x^2 - \frac{2}{\sqrt{x}} + \frac{7}{x^2}\right) dx$.

$$\int \left(3x^2 - \frac{2}{\sqrt{x}} + \frac{7}{x^2}\right) dx = \int (3x^2 - 2x^{-\frac{1}{2}} + 7x^{-2})\, dx$$ ← Write all the terms as powers of x.

$$= 3\int x^2\, dx - 2\int x^{-\frac{1}{2}}\, dx + 7\int x^{-2}\, dx$$ ← Take the constants outside each integral.

$$= \frac{3x^3}{3} - \frac{2x^{\frac{1}{2}}}{\left(\frac{1}{2}\right)} + \frac{7x^{-1}}{-1} + C = x^3 - 4\sqrt{x} - \frac{7}{x} + C$$ ← Integrate each term separately and just add one constant of integration.

b) Find y if $\frac{dy}{dx} = \frac{1}{2}x^3 - 4x^{\frac{3}{2}}x$.

$$y = \int \frac{dy}{dx}\, dx = \int \left(\frac{1}{2}x^3 - 4x^{\frac{3}{2}}x\right) dx$$ ← You need to integrate the derivative of y to get y.

$$= \int \left(\frac{1}{2}x^3 - 4x^{\frac{5}{2}}\right) dx = \frac{1}{2}\int x^3\, dx - 4\int x^{\frac{5}{2}}\, dx$$ ← First take the constants outside each integral.

$$= \frac{1}{2} \times \frac{x^4}{4} + (-4) \times \frac{x^{\frac{7}{2}}}{\frac{7}{2}} + C = \frac{x^4}{8} - \frac{8}{7}x^{\frac{7}{2}} + C$$ ← Then integrate each term separately and add one constant of integration.

c) Find $\int \left(\frac{(x-1)^2}{\sqrt{x}}\right) dx$.

Problem Solving Some expressions will need simplifying before you integrate.

$$\int \left(\frac{(x-1)^2}{\sqrt{x}}\right) dx = \int \left(\frac{x^2 - 2x + 1}{x^{\frac{1}{2}}}\right) dx$$ ← Expand the bracket.

$$= \int \left(\frac{x^2}{x^{\frac{1}{2}}} - \frac{2x}{x^{\frac{1}{2}}} + \frac{1}{x^{\frac{1}{2}}}\right) dx = \int (x^{\frac{3}{2}} - 2x^{\frac{1}{2}} + x^{-\frac{1}{2}})\, dx$$ ← Split into separate terms. Write all terms as powers of x.

$$= \int x^{\frac{3}{2}}\, dx - 2\int x^{\frac{1}{2}}\, dx + \int x^{-\frac{1}{2}}\, dx$$ ← Take the constants outside each integral.

$$= \frac{x^{\frac{5}{2}}}{\left(\frac{5}{2}\right)} - \frac{2x^{\frac{3}{2}}}{\left(\frac{3}{2}\right)} + \frac{x^{\frac{1}{2}}}{\left(\frac{1}{2}\right)} + C = \frac{2(\sqrt{x})^5}{5} - \frac{4(\sqrt{x})^3}{3} + 2\sqrt{x} + C$$ ← Integrate each term separately and add one constant of integration.

Exercise 11.3

Q1 Find f(x) when f′(x) is given by the following:

a) $5x + 3x^{-4}$ b) $4x(x^2 - 1)$ c) $(x - 3)^2$

d) $x\left(6x + \frac{4}{x^4}\right)$ e) $\left(x + \frac{2}{x}\right)^2$ f) $x\left(3x^{\frac{1}{2}} - \frac{2}{x^{\frac{4}{3}}}\right)$

g) $6\sqrt{x} - \frac{1}{x^2}$ h) $\frac{2}{\sqrt{x}} - 7x^2\sqrt{x}$ i) $5(\sqrt{x})^3 - \frac{3x}{\sqrt{x}}$

j) $\sqrt{x}(1 - x)$ k) $3\sqrt[6]{x} - \frac{\sqrt{x}}{\sqrt[3]{x}}$ l) $\frac{x^3 - 2x^2}{\sqrt{x}}$

Q2 Integrate with respect to x:

a) $\frac{5}{7}x^4 + \frac{2}{3}x + \frac{1}{4}$ b) $\frac{1}{\sqrt{x}} + \sqrt{x}$ c) $\frac{3}{x^2} + \frac{3}{\sqrt[3]{x}}$

d) $x^{\frac{5}{4}} + x^{\frac{4}{5}}$ e) $\frac{1}{2}x^{-\frac{1}{2}} + 3x^{-\frac{2}{3}} + 4x^{-\frac{3}{4}}$ f) $-\frac{4}{x^3} + \frac{1}{\sqrt{x^3}}$

E Q3 Integrate the following expressions with respect to x:

a) $\frac{2 - \sqrt{x}}{\sqrt{x}}$ *[3 marks]*

b) $\sqrt{x}(3 - 2x)$ *[3 marks]*

Q4 Find the following integrals:

a) $\int (0.55x^{0.1} - 3x^{-1.5}x)\,dx$ b) $\int \left(8x^3 - \frac{2}{\sqrt{x}} + \frac{5}{x^2}\right) dx$

c) $\int \left((\sqrt{x})^5 + \frac{1}{2\sqrt{x}}\right) dx$ d) $\int \left(\sqrt{x}\left(7x^2 - 1 - \frac{2}{x}\right)\right) dx$

e) $\int (3x - 5\sqrt{x})^2\,dx$ f) $\int \left(\frac{2x^3 - \sqrt{x}}{x}\right) dx$

g) $\int \left(\frac{(5x - 3)^2}{\sqrt{x}}\right) dx$ h) $\int (x^{\frac{1}{2}} + 1)(x^{-\frac{1}{2}} - 3)\,dx$

i) $\int x(2x + \sqrt{x})^2\,dx$ j) $\int (\sqrt{x} + 2\sqrt[3]{x})^2\,dx$

E Q5 Given that $y = 2x - 1 + \frac{5}{\sqrt{x}}$, find $\int y\,dx$. *[3 marks]*

Q6 Given that $\frac{dy}{dx} = 1.5x^2 - \frac{4}{x^3}$, find y.

Q7 Given that $f'(x) = \frac{4}{3(x^{\frac{1}{3}})^4} + 5x^{\frac{3}{2}}$, find f($x$).

Q8 Find: a) $\int \left(4x^2 + \frac{3}{\sqrt{x}} - 2\right) dx$ b) $\int (3\sqrt{x} + 3)^2\, dx$

c) $\int \left(\frac{(\sqrt{x}+3)(\sqrt{x}-1)}{\sqrt{x}}\right) dx$ d) $\int \left(\sqrt{x}\left(\sqrt{x} - \frac{1}{\sqrt{x}}\right)^2\right) dx$

e) $\int \left(\frac{(\sqrt{x^3}+6)(\sqrt{x^3}-6)}{\sqrt{x^3}}\right) dx$ f) $\int \left(\frac{3x - \sqrt{x} - 2}{\sqrt{x} - 1}\right) dx$

Q8f) Hint

Factorise the numerator first and then cancel with the denominator.

E Q9 $f(x) = (2 - \sqrt{x})^2, x > 0$

a) Solve the equation $f(x) = 0$. *[2 marks]*

b) Find f(2), giving your answer in the form $a - b\sqrt{2}$, where a and b are integer values to be found. *[2 marks]*

c) Find $\int f(x)\, dx$. *[3 marks]*

Challenge

P Q10 Integrate $\frac{2n^2x^2 + 3x^3}{nx}$ with respect to x, given that n is a constant.

11.4 Integrating to Find Equations of Curves

As you saw in Chapter 10, **differentiating** the equation of a curve gives its **gradient**. **Integrating** the gradient function of a curve does the **opposite** — it gives you the **equation** of the curve.

But integrating actually gives you **many** possible curves because of the **constant of integration**, C. C can take any value and each different value represents a different curve (all vertically translated copies of each other).

So to find the equation of a **particular curve** by integration, you need to know the coordinates of **one point** on it, which you can use to find C.

Tip Have a look at page 129 for more on translations of graphs.

Example 1

a) The curve $y = f(x)$ goes through the point (2, 16) and $\frac{dy}{dx} = 2x^3$. Find the equation of the curve.

$y = \int 2x^3\, dx = \frac{2x^4}{4} + C = \frac{x^4}{2} + C$ ← You know the derivative $\frac{dy}{dx} = 2x^3$ and need to find y. So integrate the derivative.

$y = \frac{x^4}{2} + C$, $\frac{dy}{dx} = \frac{1}{2}(4x^3) + 0 = 2x^3$ ← Check this is correct by differentiating it and making sure you get what you started with.

$y = \frac{x^4}{2} + C$

$\Rightarrow 16 = \frac{2^4}{2} + C = 23 + C$ ← So this function has the correct derivative — but you haven't finished yet. You now need to find C — and you do this by using the fact that it goes through the point (2, 16). Put $x = 2$ and $y = 16$ in the equation.

$\Rightarrow C = 8$

$y = \frac{x^4}{2} + 8$ ← Put the value of C back in the equation.

b) The curve $y = f(x)$ goes through the point (2, 8) and $f'(x) = 6x(x - 1)$. Find $f(x)$.

$f'(x) = 6x(x - 1) = 6x^2 - 6x$ ← Expand the brackets of $f'(x)$.

$f(x) = \int (6x^2 - 6x)\,dx = \frac{6x^3}{3} - \frac{6x^2}{2} + C = 2x^3 - 3x^2 + C$ ← Integrate to find $f(x)$.

$f(x) = 2x^3 - 3x^2 + C$
$f'(x) = 2(3x^2) - 3(2x^1) = 6x^2 - 6x$ ← Check that this is correct by differentiating.

$8 = (2 \times 2^3) - (3 \times 2^2) + C$ ← You now need to find C using the point (2, 8). Put $x = 2$ and $y = 8$ into $f(x) = 2x^3 - 3x^2 + C$.
$\Rightarrow 8 = 16 - 12 + C$
$\Rightarrow C = 4$

$f(x) = 2x^3 - 3x^2 + 4$ ← Put C in the equation.

Exercise 11.4

Q1 For each of the following, the curve $y = f(x)$ passes through the given point. Find $f(x)$.

a) $f'(x) = 4x^3$, (0, 5)

b) $f'(x) = 3x^2 - 4x + 3$, (1, –3)

c) $f'(x) = 6x(x + 2)$, (–1, 1)

d) $f'(x) = \frac{5}{x^2} + 2x$, (5, 4)

e) $f'(x) = 3x^2(x - 4)$, (2, –10)

f) $f'(x) = (3x + 1)(x - 1)$, (3, –3)

g) $f'(x) = x(x + \frac{3}{x^3})$, (–3, 5)

h) $f'(x) = \frac{9x^3 + 2x^{-2}}{x}$, (–1, 2)

i) $f'(x) = \sqrt{x}(3 + x)$, (1, 4)

j) $f'(x) = \frac{2 - 3\sqrt[6]{x}}{\sqrt{x}}$, (64, –33)

Q2 A curve $y = f(x)$ that passes through the origin has derivative $f'(x) = 6x^2 + 6x - 5$.

a) Find the equation of the curve.

b) Factorise and hence sketch the curve, showing the points where the curve cuts the axes.

E Q3 The curve $y = f(x)$ has the gradient function $\frac{dy}{dx} = \frac{3x - x^2}{x}$, $x \neq 0$.
Given that the point (4, 5) lies on the curve $y = f(x)$, find an expression for $f(x)$. *[4 marks]*

Q4 A curve $y = f(x)$ that passes through the point (4, 9) has gradient function $f'(x) = \frac{3}{\sqrt{x}} + 2x$. Find the equation of the curve.

Q5 The gradient function of a curve is given by $\frac{dy}{dx} = 3\sqrt{x} + \frac{1}{x^2}$.
Find the equation of the curve if it passes through the point (1, 7).

Q3-5 Hint The gradient function is just the function which tells you the gradient — the derivative.

Q6 Consider $\frac{dy}{dt} = (\sqrt{t} - 3)^2$. Given that $y = 9$ when $t = 4$, find y as a function of t.

Q7 The curve $y = f(x)$ goes through the point $\left(1, \frac{1}{3}\right)$ and $f'(x) = \sqrt{x}(5x - 1)$. Find $f(x)$.

Q8 The curve $y = f(x)$ has derivative $f'(x) = x^2 + \frac{2}{x^{\frac{3}{2}}}$ and passes through the point $\left(1, -\frac{5}{3}\right)$.
Find the equation of the curve.

Q9 The gradient function of a curve is given by $\frac{dy}{dx} = \frac{x-6}{x^3} + 2$.
Find the equation of the curve if it passes through the point (3, –1).

Q10 The gradient of a curve C is given by $\frac{dy}{dx} = \frac{(x+2)(x-2)}{\sqrt{x}}, x > 0$.

a) Show that $\frac{dy}{dx}$ can be written in the form $Ax^{\frac{3}{2}} + Bx^{-\frac{1}{2}}$, where A and B are integers.

b) The point $\left(1, \frac{7}{5}\right)$ lies on C. Find the equation of C.

E Q11 The curve C has equation $y = f(x)$, where $f'(x) = 2 + \frac{3}{\sqrt{x}}, x > 0$. The line $y - 3x = 1$ is a tangent to the curve C at the point P.

a) Find gradient of the curve C at the point P. *[1 mark]*

b) Find the coordinates of the point P. *[3 marks]*

c) Find the equation of the curve C. *[5 marks]*

Challenge

E Q12 The curve $y = f(x)$ passes through a point with coordinates (–1, 4).
Given that $\frac{dy}{dx} = -\frac{2}{x^2}, x \neq 0$,

a) Find an expression for f(x). *[4 marks]*

b) Sketch the graph of $y = f(x)$, clearly labelling the equations of any asymptotes and coordinates of any intersections with the axes. *[3 marks]*

E P Q13 The diagram on the right shows the curve $y = f(x)$.
The curve passes through the origin and the point P on the x-axis.
Given that $f'(x) = 3\sqrt{x} - \frac{2}{\sqrt{x}}, x > 0$,

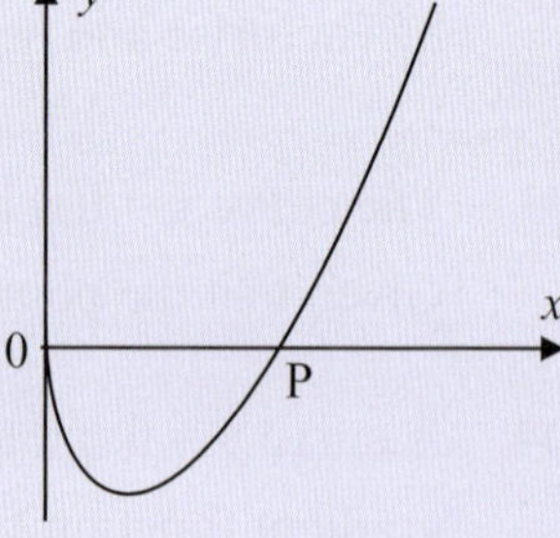

a) Find an expression for f(x). *[5 marks]*

b) Find the coordinates of the point P. *[2 marks]*

P M Q14 A toy car is moving such that its acceleration, in ms^{-2}, is given by the function $\frac{dv}{dt} = 6t - t^2$, for $0 \leq t \leq 10$, (t = time, measured in seconds).
Given that the car comes to rest after 10 seconds, find its initial velocity.

P Q15 A function has a gradient given by $f'(x) = 3x^2 + kx - k$, where k is a constant.
Given that f(x) passes through the point (2, 7) with a gradient of 18,
find the value of k, and hence the equation of f(x).

11.5 Evaluating Definite Integrals

Definite integrals have **limits** (little numbers) next to the integral sign. The limits just tell you the **x-values** to integrate the function between.

If you're integrating with respect to a different variable, such as t, then the limits tell you the range of that variable instead.

The definite integral of **f(x)** with respect to x between the limits $x = a$ and $x = b$ is written:

$$\int_a^b f(x)\,dx$$

The lower limit goes here. The upper limit goes here.

Finding a definite integral isn't really any harder than an indefinite one — there's just an **extra stage** you have to do. Integrate the function as normal but **don't** add a **constant of integration**. Once you've integrated the function, work out the **value** of the definite integral by **putting in the limits**.

Problem Solving

You might be asked to 'evaluate' an integral — this just means find the value. A definite integral always comes out as a number.

The proper way to write out definite integrals is to use square brackets with the limits to the right as shown below.

If you know that the integral of f(x) is $\int f(x)\,dx = g(x) + C$ then:

$$\int_a^b f(x)\,dx = [g(x)]_a^b = g(b) - g(a)$$

Subtract the value of g at the **lower** limit from the value of g at the **upper** limit.

This is the second part of the **Fundamental Theorem of Calculus**.

Example 1

Evaluate $\int_1^3 (x^2 + 2)\,dx$.

$$\int_1^3 (x^2+2)\,dx = \left[\frac{x^3}{3} + 2x\right]_1^3$$

Find the integral in the normal way — but put the integrated function in square brackets and rewrite the limits on the right-hand side. Notice that there's no constant of integration.

$$\left[\frac{x^3}{3} + 2x\right]_1^3 = \left(\frac{3^3}{3} + 6\right) - \left(\frac{1^3}{3} + 2\right)$$

$$= 15 - \frac{7}{3} = \frac{38}{3}$$

Put the upper limit into the integral and subtract the value of the integral at the lower limit.

The area under a curve

The value of a **definite integral** represents the **area** between the x-axis and the graph of the function you're integrating between the two limits.

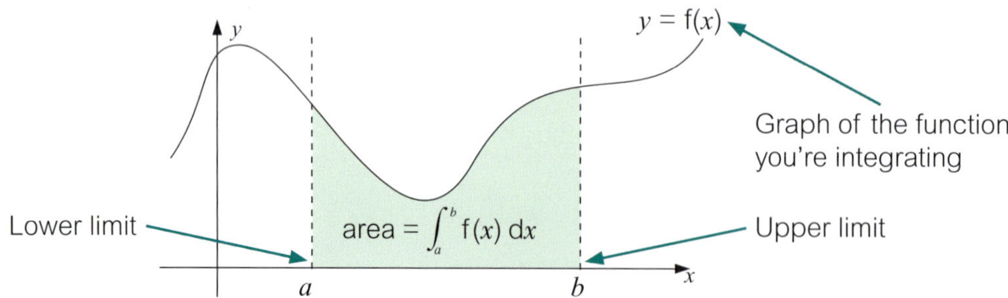

Example 2

Find the area between the graph of $y = x^2$, the x-axis and the lines $x = -1$ and $x = 2$.

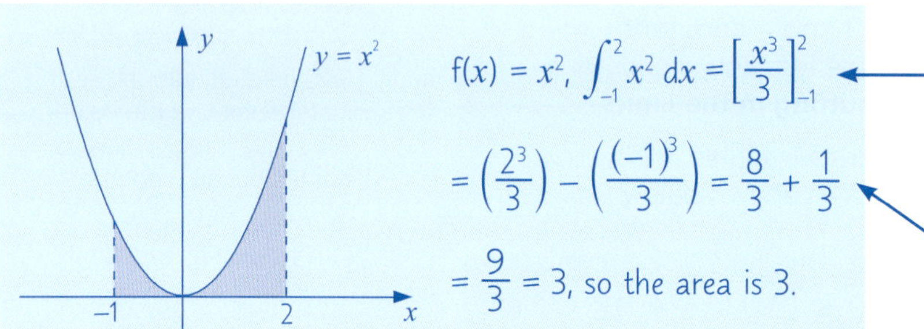

$f(x) = x^2$, $\int_{-1}^{2} x^2\,dx = \left[\frac{x^3}{3}\right]_{-1}^{2}$

$= \left(\frac{2^3}{3}\right) - \left(\frac{(-1)^3}{3}\right) = \frac{8}{3} + \frac{1}{3}$

$= \frac{9}{3} = 3$, so the area is 3.

You just need to integrate the function $f(x) = x^2$ between -1 and 2 with respect to x.

Put the upper limit into the integral and subtract the value of the integral at the lower limit.

If you integrate a function to find an area that lies **below** the x-axis, it'll give a **negative** value.

If you need to find an area like this, you'll need to make your answer **positive** at the end as you can't have **negative area**.

It's important to note that you're actually finding the area between the curve and the ***x*-axis**, not the area under the curve (the area below a curve that lies under the x-axis will be **infinite**).

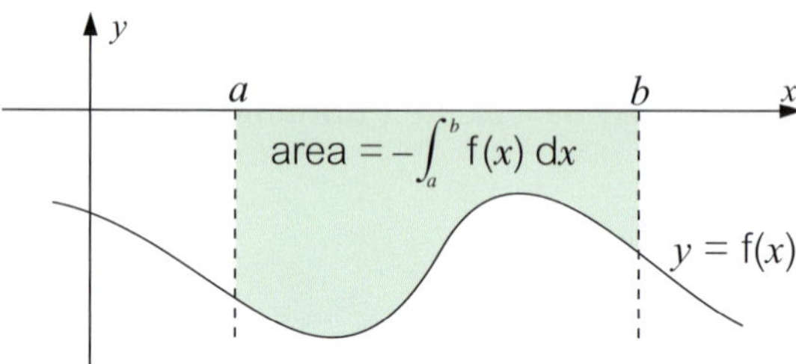

Example 3

Find the area between the graph of $y = 4x - 3x^2 - x^3$ and the x-axis between $x = -4$ and $x = 0$.

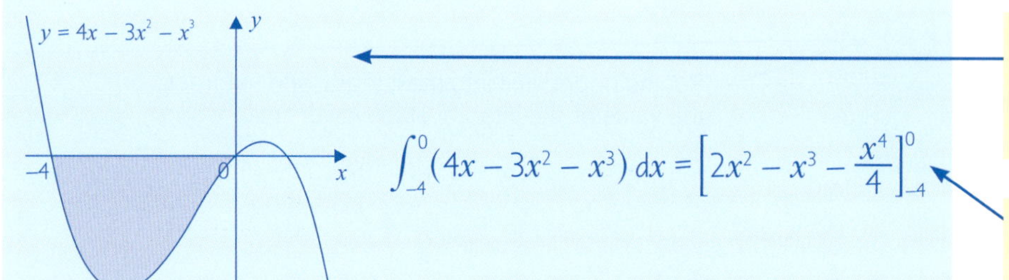

$\int_{-4}^{0} (4x - 3x^2 - x^3)\,dx = \left[2x^2 - x^3 - \frac{x^4}{4}\right]_{-4}^{0}$

You can see from the sketch of the graph that the area you're trying to find lies below the x-axis.

Integrate the curve between the given limits.

$= (0) - \left(2(-4)^2 - (-4)^3 - \frac{(-4)^4}{4}\right) = 0 - (32 + 64 - 64) = -32$ ← Put the limits into the integral and subtract.

So the area between the curve and the x-axis between $x = -4$ and $x = 0$ is 32. ← Make the area positive.

If you need to find the area for a portion of a curve which lies both **above** and **below** the x-axis, you'll need to find the areas above and below **separately** and add them up at the end so that the negative and positive integrals don't **cancel each other out**.

Example 4

a) Evaluate $\int_{-2}^{2} x^3\,dx$.

$$\int_{-2}^{2} x^3\,dx = \left[\frac{x^4}{4}\right]_{-2}^{2} = \left(\frac{2^4}{4}\right) - \left(\frac{(-2)^4}{4}\right) = \frac{16}{4} - \frac{16}{4} = 0$$

Integrate the function and put in the limits to find its value.

b) Find the area between the graph of $y = x^3$, the x-axis and the lines $x = -2$ and $x = 2$.

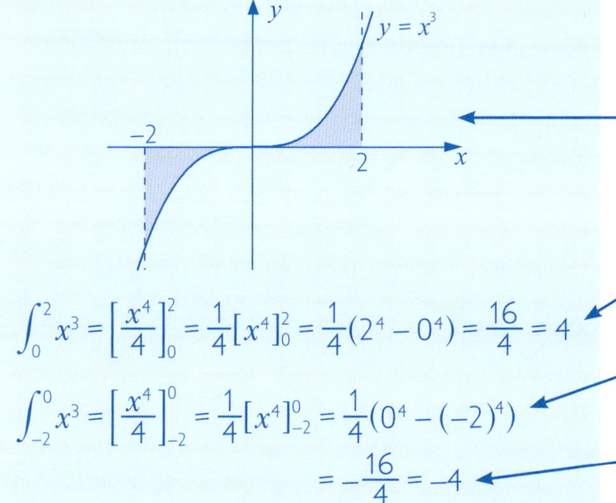

You'd usually just integrate the function between the limits, which gave 0 in part a). But you can see from the diagram that the area is not 0. The 'negative area' below the axis has cancelled out the positive area. So to work out the total area, you need to work out the positive and negative areas separately and then **add** them together.

$$\int_{0}^{2} x^3 = \left[\frac{x^4}{4}\right]_{0}^{2} = \frac{1}{4}[x^4]_{0}^{2} = \frac{1}{4}(2^4 - 0^4) = \frac{16}{4} = 4$$

The area **above** the x-axis is between 0 and 2.

$$\int_{-2}^{0} x^3 = \left[\frac{x^4}{4}\right]_{-2}^{0} = \frac{1}{4}[x^4]_{-2}^{0} = \frac{1}{4}(0^4 - (-2)^4)$$

$$= -\frac{16}{4} = -4$$

The area **below** the x-axis is between –2 and 0.

The area below the x-axis is the positive value of this integral, so it's 4.

Area = 4 + 4 = 8 ← Add these areas together to get the total area.

Some questions might give you an expression for the area in terms of an unknown and ask you to find its value (or possible values).

Example 5 P

Find the two possible values for A that satisfy: $\int_{1}^{4}\left(\frac{3}{7}x^2 + \frac{2A}{\sqrt{x}}\right)dx = 5A^2$

$$\int_{1}^{4}\left(\frac{3}{7}x^2 + 2Ax^{-\frac{1}{2}}\right)dx = \left[\frac{1}{7}x^3 + 4Ax^{\frac{1}{2}}\right]_{1}^{4} = \left(\frac{64}{7} + 8A\right) - \left(\frac{1}{7} + 4A\right)$$

$$= \frac{63}{7} + 4A = 9 + 4A$$

First, you need to evaluate the integral. Treat the A as a constant for now.

$9 + 4A = 5A^2$
$5A^2 - 4A - 9 = 0$
$(5A - 9)(A + 1) = 0$
$5A - 9 = 0 \Rightarrow A = \frac{9}{5}$
or $A + 1 = 0 \Rightarrow A = -1$
So the solutions are $A = \frac{9}{5}$ and $A = -1$.

You know this is equal to $5A^2$, so form a quadratic in A and solve it.

Factorise the equation. (You could also use the quadratic formula.)

Exercise 11.5

Q1 Find the value of the following, giving exact answers:

a) $\int_{-2}^{0} (4x^3 + 2x)\,dx$ b) $\int_{-2}^{5} (x^3 + x)\,dx$ c) $\int_{-5}^{-2} (x+1)^2\,dx$

d) $\int_{3}^{4} (6x^{-4} + x^{-2})\,dx$ e) $\int_{1}^{2} \left(x^2 + \frac{1}{x^2}\right) dx$ f) $\int_{1}^{4} (3x^{-4} + \sqrt{x})\,dx$

g) $\int_{0}^{1} ((2x+3)(x+2))\,dx$ h) $\int_{1}^{4} \left(\frac{x^2+2}{\sqrt{x}}\right) dx$ i) $\int_{4}^{9} \left(\frac{1}{x} + \sqrt{x}\right)^2 dx$

j) $\int_{4}^{16} \left(\frac{\sqrt{x}-1}{x^2}\right) dx$ k) $\int_{1}^{9} x^{\frac{1}{2}}(5x - x^{-\frac{1}{2}})\,dx$ l) $\int_{1}^{4} (1+x^2)(1+\sqrt{x})\,dx$

E Q2 Evaluate each of the following definite integrals:

a) $\int_{1}^{3} (2x-1)(x+2)\,dx$ *[5 marks]*

b) $\int_{1}^{4} \frac{1}{2}\sqrt{x}\,dx$ *[4 marks]*

Q3 Integrate the function $4x - 5x^3 + 7$ between the limits $x = -1$ and $x = 3$.

Q4 Find the integral of f(x) between $x = 0$ and $x = 1$, if $f(x) = 3 - 4\sqrt{x} + \frac{1}{2}x^2$.

E P Q5 Given that $\int_{1}^{3} (x^2 - 2x + k)\,dx = \frac{26}{3}$, find the value of the constant k. *[6 marks]*

P Q6 Find a, where $a > 0$, given that:

a) $\int_{0}^{a} x^3\,dx = 64$ b) $\int_{0}^{a} 2x^4\,dx = 4a^4$

Q7 Calculate the exact shaded area in the following diagrams:

a)

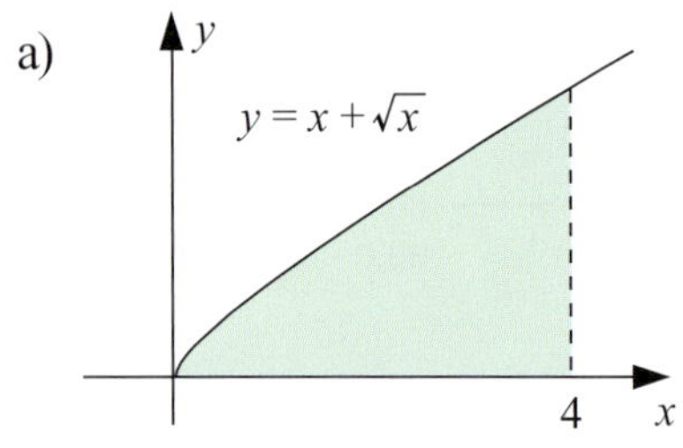

b)

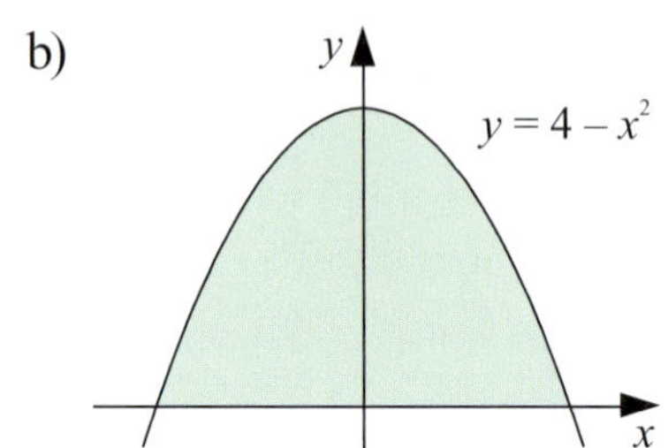

Q7 Hint

You'll need to work out where the graphs cross the x-axis.

c) 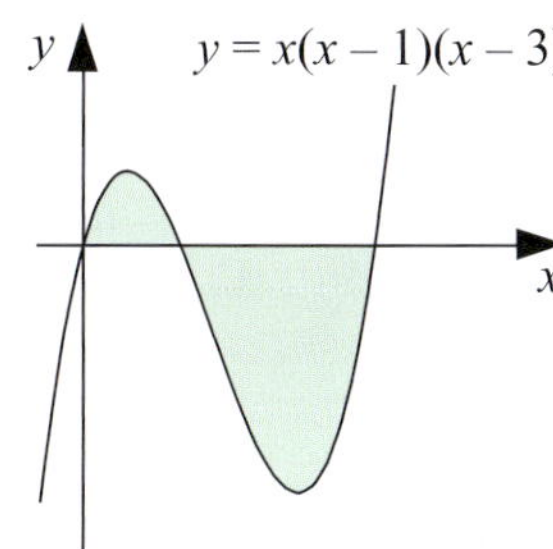

d) 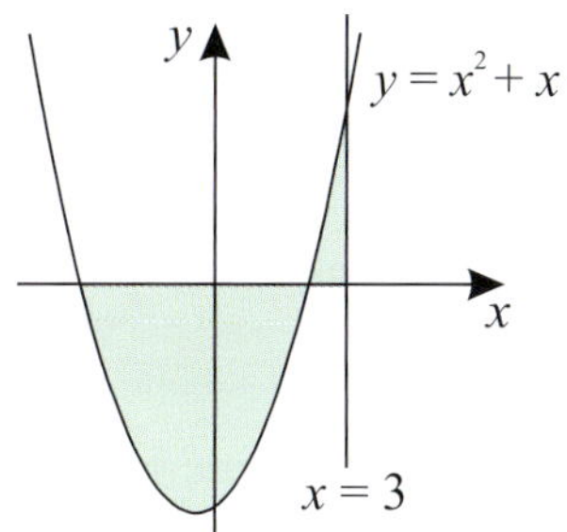

E Q8 The figure below shows the curve with equation $y = 3x^{\frac{1}{2}} - 2x, x \geq 0$.

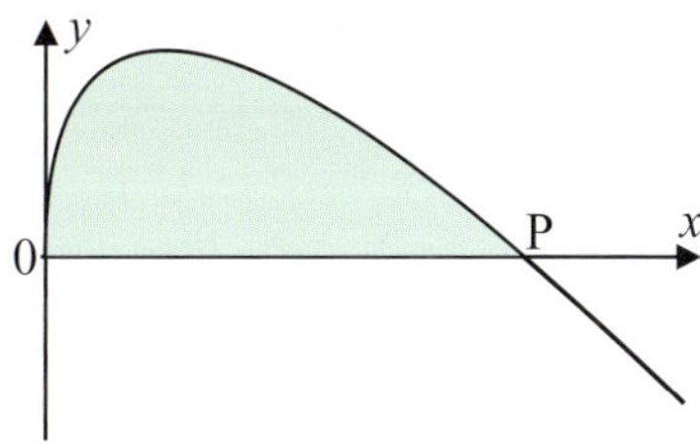

The curve meets the x-axis at the origin and the point P with coordinates $(p, 0)$.

a) Show that $p = \frac{9}{4}$. *[3 marks]*

b) Find the area of the finite region bounded by the curve and the positive x-axis. *[5 marks]*

Q9 Find the area enclosed by the curve with equation $y = (x - 1)(3x + 9)$, the x-axis and the lines:

a) $x = 1$ and $x = 5$

b) $x = -3$ and $x = -4$

c) $x = -2$ and $x = 2$

d) $x = -6$ and $x = 0$

Q9-10 Hint

It may help to sketch the graphs so that you can see what's happening.

Q10 Find the area enclosed by the graph of $y = \frac{20}{x^5}$, the x-axis and the lines $x = 1$ and $x = 2$.

P Q11 Calculate the area enclosed by the line $y = 3x$, the curve $y = (x - 6)^2$ and the x-axis.

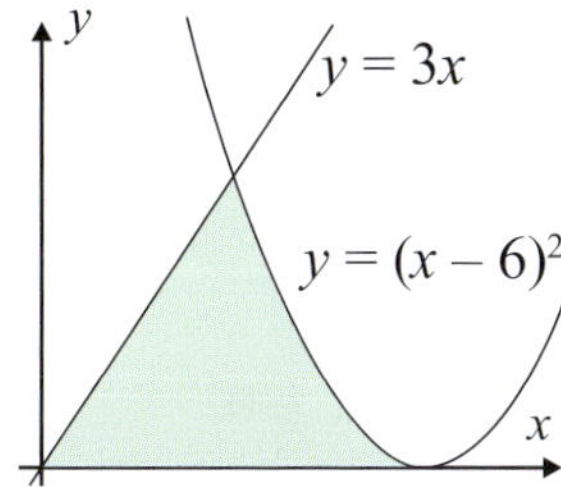

Q12 By first sketching the graph, find the total area between the graph of $y = x^3 + 4x^2 + 3x$ and the x-axis between $x = 0$ and $x = -2$.

P Q13 Find the possible values of A that satisfy:

a) $\int_2^3 (1 - 2Ax)\,dx = 6A^2$

b) $\int_{-2}^2 \left(\frac{21}{8}x^2 + \frac{A}{x^2}\right)dx = 3A^2$

c) $\int_4^5 2A^2 - 6x^2\,dx = 120A$

d) $\int_1^4 (A - 2\sqrt{x})^2\,dx = 10 - A^2$

P **M** Q14 The area under a velocity-time graph gives the distance travelled. An object's motion is tracked as it speeds up, and then slows to rest. Its velocity, v, at time t is modelled by the function below.

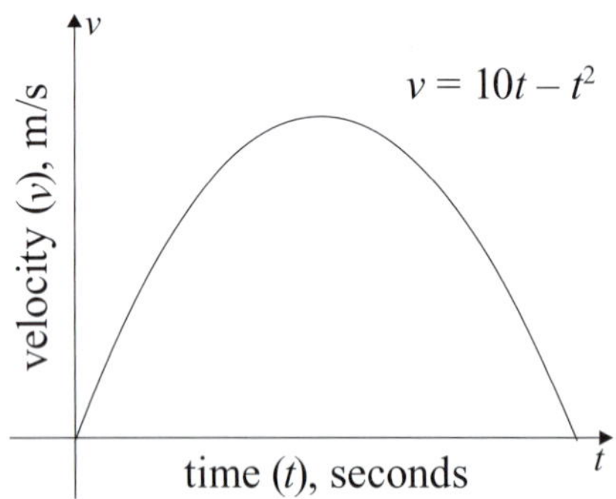

Problem Solving

All question 14 is asking you to do is to find the area under the graph between these limits. Remember that you're integrating with respect to t and not x.

How far does the object travel:

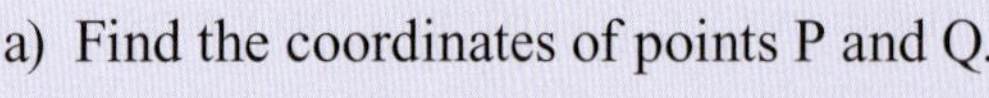

a) between $t = 1$ and $t = 3$?

b) in total?

E Q15 Find the exact value of $\int_1^3 \frac{x^3 + \sqrt{x}}{x^2}\,dx$. *[5 marks]*

Challenge

E **P** Q16 The diagram on the right shows the curve with equation $y = 12 + 4x - x^2$ and the line $y = 3x$.

The curve and line intersect at points P and Q.

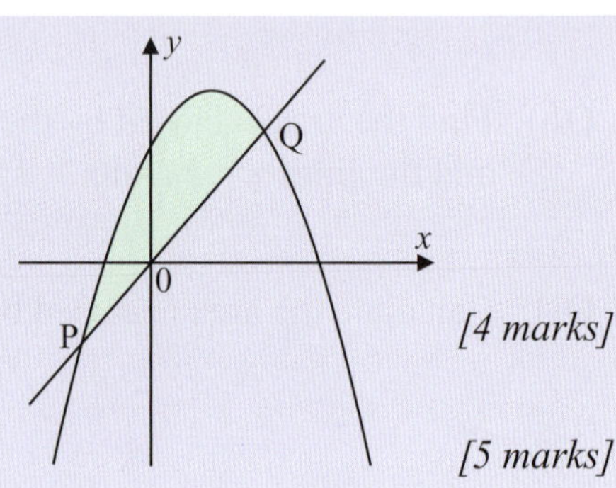

a) Find the coordinates of points P and Q. *[4 marks]*

b) The area of the shaded region below the x-axis is $\frac{55}{6}$. Find the exact value of the total shaded region. *[5 marks]*

E **P** Q17 The diagram on the right shows sections of the curves $y = x^2$ and $y = x^2 - 6x + 9$, for $x \geq 0$.

The two curves intersect at point A.

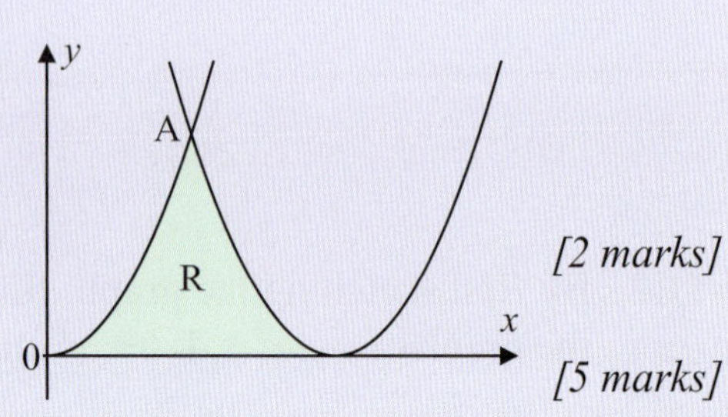

a) Find the coordinates of point A. *[2 marks]*

b) Hence or otherwise find the area of the region R bounded by the two curves and the positive x-axis. *[5 marks]*

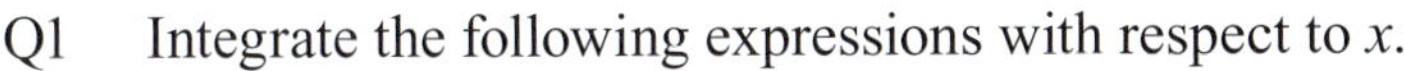

11 Review Exercise

Q1 Integrate the following expressions with respect to x.

a) $18x$ b) $-x^4$ c) $\frac{1}{\sqrt{2}}$ d) $6\sqrt{x}$

e) $\frac{1}{2}x^{-2}$ f) $15x^{\frac{3}{2}}$ g) $-\frac{2}{x^3}$ h) $-27x^{-10}$

i) $-9x^{-\frac{1}{2}}$ j) $(3x)^{-4}$ k) $-\frac{3}{5}x^{-0.9}$ l) $-\frac{11}{6(\sqrt[3]{x^2})}$

P Q2 Find the value of a in each of the following, where $a \neq 0$.

a) $\int 10x^{-6}\,dx = ax^{-5} + C$ b) $\int 4x^{15}\,dx = \frac{1}{a}x^{16} + C$ c) $\int -\frac{a^2}{x^3}\,dx = \frac{a}{x^2} + C$

d) $\int \frac{1}{2\sqrt{x}}\,dx = x^a + C$ e) $\int 14x^a\,dx = 6(\sqrt[3]{x^7}) + C$ f) $\int \frac{24}{5}x^a\,dx = \frac{8}{15}x^{a+1} + C$

Q3 Find f(x) in each case below. Give each term in its simplest form.

a) $f'(x) = x^{-\frac{1}{2}} + 4 - 5x^3$ b) $f'(x) = 2x + \frac{3}{x^2}$ c) $f'(x) = 6x^2 - \frac{1}{3\sqrt{x}}$

E Q4 Find $\int 3x^2 - \frac{1}{x^2}\,dx$. *[3 marks]*

E Q5 Find $\int \left(\frac{5}{3}x^{\frac{2}{3}} - \frac{4}{\sqrt{x}} + (2x)^3 - \frac{3}{2x^2}\right)dx$. *[5 marks]*

E P Q6 Find $\int \frac{(1-\sqrt{x})(1+\sqrt{x})}{x^3}\,dx$. *[5 marks]*

E Q7 For each of the following gradient functions, find the equation of the original curve that passes through the given point.

a) $\frac{dy}{dx} = (x+3)(x-3)$, (3, 4) *[4 marks]*

b) $\frac{dy}{dx} = \frac{2}{3x^2}$, (1, 1) *[3 marks]*

Q8 Work out the equation of the curve that has derivative $\frac{dy}{dx} = 3x^2 - \frac{7}{\sqrt{x}}$ and goes through the point (1, 0).

E Q9 The curve $y = f(x)$ passes through the point with coordinates (–1, 4). Given that $f'(x) = 3x^2 + 2x - 1$, find the equation for the curve $y = f(x)$. *[4 marks]*

E Exam Style P Problem Solving M Modelling

Q10 The gradient function of a curve is given by $\frac{dy}{dx} = 2(3x - 6.5)$.
The curve passes through the point (1, 2).

a) Find the equation of the curve.

b) Sketch the curve, stating the coordinates of the points where the curve crosses the axes.

E Q11 The curve $y = f(x)$, where $f'(x) = -2x + 5$, crosses the x-axis when $x = 1$.

a) Find the equation of the curve $y = f(x)$. *[3 marks]*

b) Sketch the graph of $y = f(x)$, labelling all intersections with the coordinate axes. *[3 marks]*

Q12 The curve C with equation $y = f(x)$ has derivative $f'(x) = 6x^2 - 12 - \frac{8}{x^2}$, $x > 0$ and passes through the point P with coordinates (–2, 5).
Find the equation of the curve C.

Q13 The curve $y = f(x)$ passes through the point P with coordinates (1, –9).
Given that $f'(x) = \frac{5x^2 + 1}{x^{\frac{1}{2}}} - 10$, $x > 0$, find the equation of the curve.

E P Q14 The point A (–2, –13) lies on the curve $y = f(x)$. If the gradient at A is –8 and $\frac{d^2y}{dx^2} = 12x$, use the fact that $\int \frac{d^2y}{dx^2} = \frac{dy}{dx}$ to find the equation of the curve $y = f(x)$. *[7 marks]*

Q15 Evaluate the following definite integrals:

a) $\int_0^1 (4x^3 + 3x^2 + 2x + 1)\,dx$

b) $\int_1^6 \frac{3}{x^2}\,dx$

c) $\int_1^2 \left(\frac{8}{x^5} + \frac{3}{\sqrt{x}}\right) dx$

d) $\int_4^9 \sqrt{x}(1 - 2\sqrt{x})\,dx$

e) $\int_1^4 \frac{3\sqrt{x} + 2x^4}{x^2}\,dx$

f) $\int_{-1}^{0.5} \frac{2x^5 + 4x^4}{5x^3}\,dx$

E Q16 Evaluate $\int_{-2}^{0} (3x - 2)^2\,dx$. *[5 marks]*

E P Q17 $I = \int_a^6 (4x - 5)\,dx$. Find the possible values of a, if $I = 24$. *[6 marks]*

E Q18 Given the value of each definite integral, find the value of the constant k, for $k > 0$.

a) $\int_1^k (2x^3 - x)\,dx = 36$ *[6 marks]*

b) $\int_2^5 (x^2 + kx - 2)\,dx = \frac{129}{2}$ *[4 marks]*

Q19 a) Evaluate $\int_{-3}^{3} (9 - x^2)\,dx$.

b) Sketch the area represented by this integral.

Q20 Find the shaded area in the diagrams below:

a)

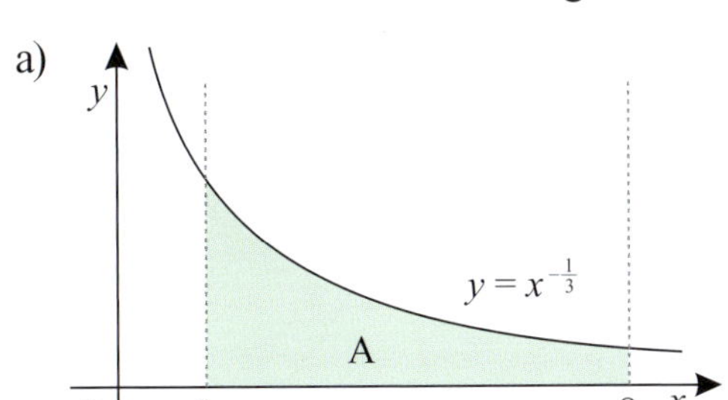

b)

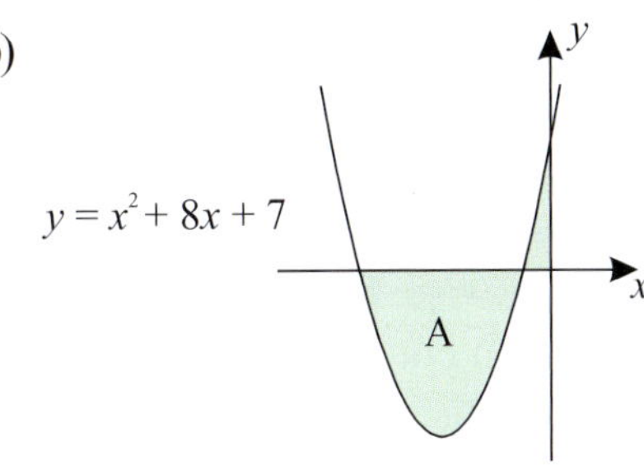

P Q21 Use integration to find the shaded area in each of these graphs:

a)

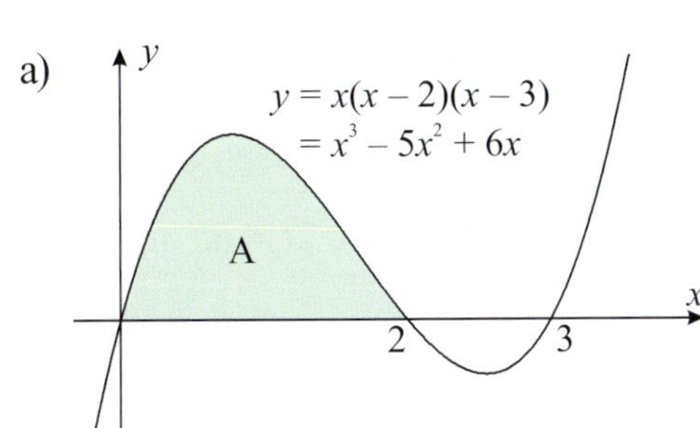

b)

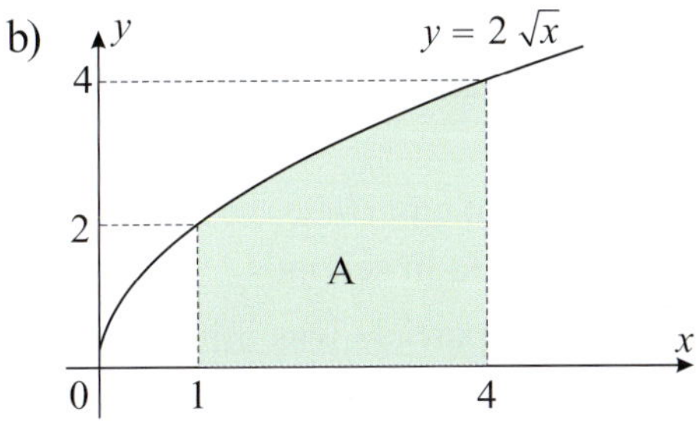

c)

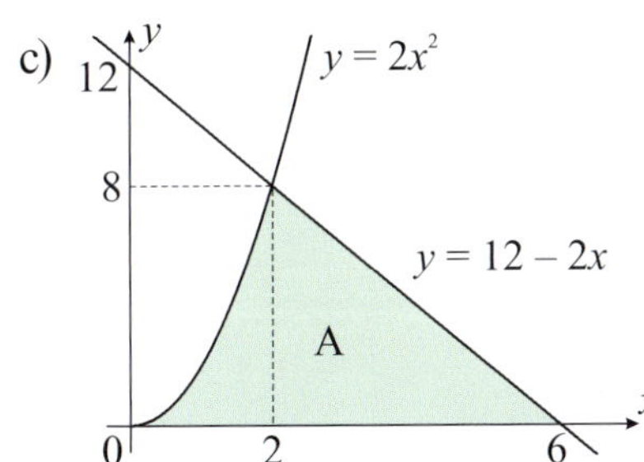

d)

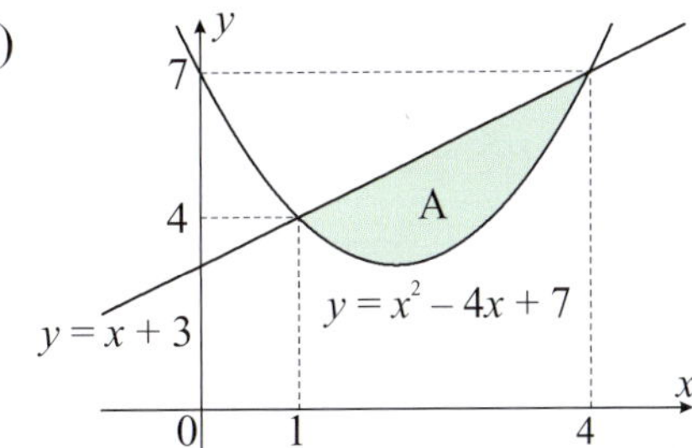

E P Q22 The diagram on the right shows the curve with equation $y = x^3 - \frac{15}{2}x^2 + 12x + 10$.

A and B are stationary points on the curve.

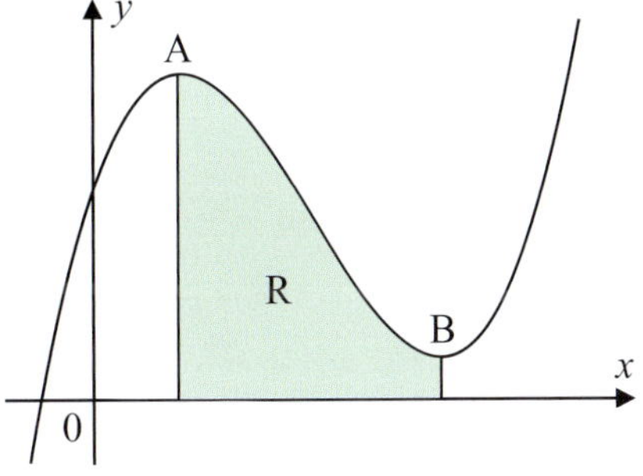

a) Find the x-coordinates of points A and B. *[4 marks]*

b) Hence or otherwise, find the area of the finite region bounded by the curve, the x-axis and the normals at points A and B. *[6 marks]*

P Q23 Find the total shaded area on each of the following graphs:

a)

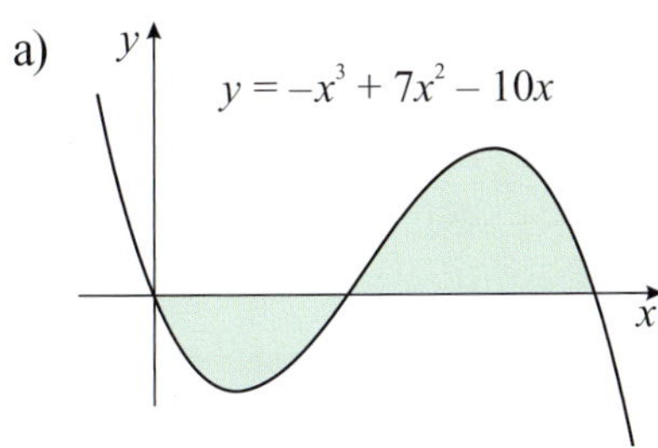

b)

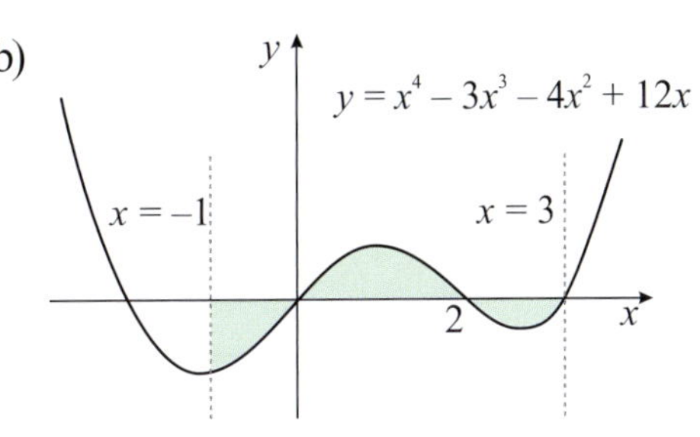

E P Q24 The diagram on the right shows the curve with equation $y = x^3 - 4x^2 + 3x$.

It has roots at the origin and at points A and B.

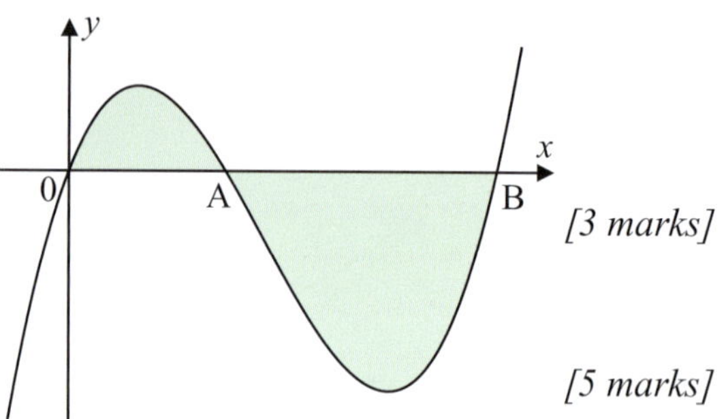

a) Find the x-coordinates of the points A and B. *[3 marks]*

b) Hence or otherwise, find the total area of the finite region bounded by the curve and the positive x-axis between the origin and B. *[5 marks]*

E P Q25 a) Sketch the graph $y = (x + 1)(2x - 1)(x - 3)$, labelling where the curve intersects each axis. *[3 marks]*

b) Find the area above the x-axis enclosed by $y = (x + 1)(2x - 1)(x - 3)$. *[4 marks]*

c) Find the total area enclosed between $y = (x + 1)(2x - 1)(x - 3)$ and the x-axis. *[4 marks]*

E P Q26 The acceleration of a particle, in ms^{-2}, is given by the function $\frac{dV}{dt} = 2t - 3t^2$ for $t \geq 0$, where t is measured in seconds.

a) Given that the particle was initially at rest, find an expression for V. *[4 marks]*

b) Find the velocity of the particle after 10 seconds of motion. *[2 marks]*

Challenge

P Q27 Integrate and solve each of the following equations for x:

a) $\int 2x^3\, dx = \int \frac{1}{4}x\, dx$, where C = 0 for both integrations.

b) $\int x^0\, dx = \int \frac{3}{2x^{\frac{1}{2}}}\, dx$, where C = –3 and C = 15 respectively.

c) $\int 3x^2\, dx = \int 13\, dx$, where C = –4 and C = 8 respectively.

P Q28 For a constant $k > 0$, it is given that $\int \frac{(k^2 + 2k - 15)x^k}{x^4}\, dx = \frac{6}{x^2} + C$. What is the value of k?

E P Q29 A curve has the equation $y = f(x)$, where $f'(x) = (x + \alpha)^2$ and $\alpha > 0$.
Given that the curve $y = f(x)$ passes through the points (3, 18) and $\left(1, -\frac{2}{3}\right)$, find the value of α. *[7 marks]*

E P Q30 A curve $y = f(x)$ has the gradient function $\frac{dy}{dx} = 2x - \frac{4}{x^3}$, $x \neq 0$, and passes through the point P(1, 0).

a) Find the equation of the normal to the curve at point P, giving your answer in the form $ax + by + c = 0$, where a, b and c are integers. *[4 marks]*

b) Find the equation of the curve $y = f(x)$. *[5 marks]*

c) The curve crosses the x-axis at another point, Q. Find the exact value of the x-coordinate of Q, given that it is greater than the x-coordinate of P. *[5 marks]*

E P Q31 Show that $\int_2^3 \left(3\sqrt{x} - \frac{2}{\sqrt{x}}\right) dx = k\sqrt{3}$, where k is a constant to be found. *[5 marks]*

P Q32 The graph of $y = 2x^3 - 15x^2 + 36x - 28$ has a double root at $x = a$, where a is a positive integer. Find the value of a and hence find the area bounded by the graph, the x-axis, the y-axis and the line $x = a$.

P M Q33 An architect is designing a floor plan for a new art gallery. He sketches the plan on a set of axes, with the x- and y-axes forming two walls and the third given by the function $y = 9 - \frac{1}{3}\sqrt{x^3}$ for $0 \leq x \leq 9$, measured in metres.

a) The room needs at least 40 m^2 of floor space. Does the plan meet this requirement?

b) An area bounded by the x-axis, the y-axis and the curve $y = 2 - \frac{1}{2}x^2$, $0 \leq x \leq 2$, is reserved for an information kiosk. How much floor space is left?

E P Q34

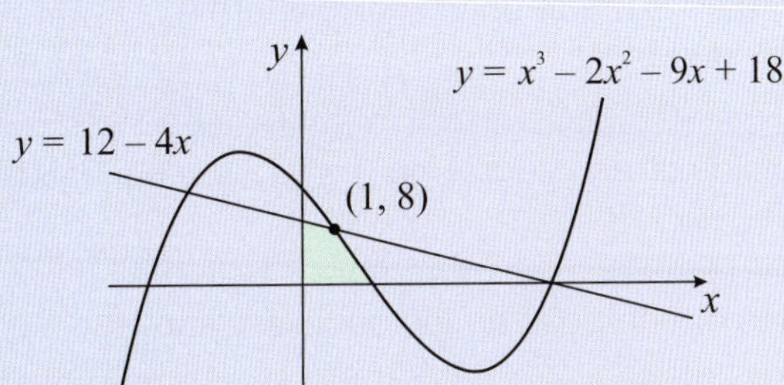

The graph above shows the curve $y = x^3 - 2x^2 - 9x + 18$ and the line $y = 12 - 4x$ intersecting at the point (1, 8).

a) Find the x-coordinates where the curve $y = x^3 - 2x^2 - 9x + 18$ crosses the x-axis. *[3 marks]*

b) Find the size of the shaded area on the diagram. *[7 marks]*

E P Q35

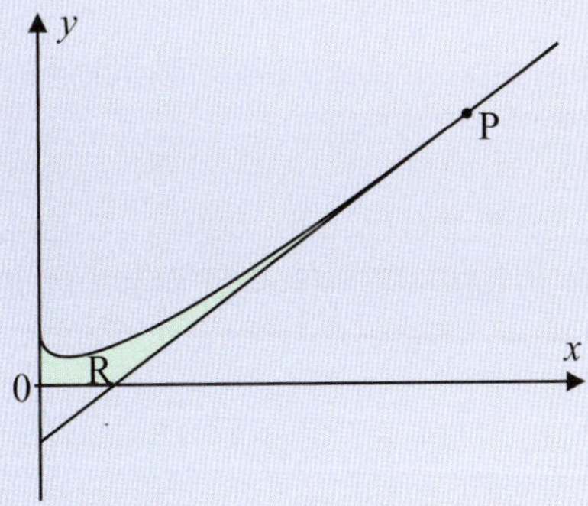

The figure above shows the curve with equation $y = 2x - 2\sqrt{x} + 1$ and a tangent to the curve at point P. The x-coordinate of P is 4.

a) Show the that tangent at point P has the equation $3x - 2y - 2 = 0$. *[4 marks]*

The shaded region, R, is bounded by the curve, the tangent at P and the positive coordinate axes.

b) Find the exact area of R. *[7 marks]*

11 Chapter Summary

1 The indefinite integral of $\mathrm{f}(x)$ with respect to x is written as $\int \mathrm{f}(x)\,\mathrm{d}x$.

2 Since there are multiple potential answers to an indefinite integral, the constant of integration (C) must be included for the answer to be correct.

3 The first part of the Fundamental Theorem of Calculus shows how integration is related to differentiation:

$$\int \mathrm{f}(x)\,\mathrm{d}x = \mathrm{F}(x) + \mathrm{C} \Leftrightarrow \mathrm{f}(x) = \frac{\mathrm{d}}{\mathrm{d}x}(\mathrm{F}(x))$$

4 The formula $\int x^n\,\mathrm{d}x = \frac{x^{n+1}}{n+1} + \mathrm{C}$ gives the integral of any function of the form x^n.

5 If an expression being integrated is made up of multiple terms, each term can be integrated separately.

6 Constants can be moved outside of an integral, so $\int a\mathrm{f}(x)\,\mathrm{d}x = a\int \mathrm{f}(x)\,\mathrm{d}x$ for a constant a.

7 Integration can be used to find the equation of a curve if both the derivative and the coordinates of one point on the curve are known.

8 The definite integral of $\mathrm{f}(x)$ with respect to x between the limits $x = a$ and $x = b$ is written as $\int_a^b \mathrm{f}(x)\,\mathrm{d}x$.

9 The second part of the Fundamental Theorem of Calculus shows how definite and indefinite integration are related:

If $\int \mathrm{f}(x)\,\mathrm{d}x = \mathrm{g}(x) + \mathrm{C}$, then $\int_a^b \mathrm{f}(x)\,\mathrm{d}x = [\mathrm{g}(x)]_a^b = \mathrm{g}(b) - \mathrm{g}(a)$.

10 The area between the graph of a function and the x-axis between two limits can be found with a definite integral of the function.

11 Area cannot be negative, so the value found by integrating a function over an interval where its graph is below the x-axis must be made positive.

Vectors

12

Learning Objectives

Once you've completed this chapter, you should be able to:

- Understand what vectors are and how to represent them.
- Add and subtract vectors and multiply them by scalars.
- Understand position vectors and use them to find a vector from one point to another.
- Convert between unit vector form and column vectors.
- Find the magnitude and direction of any vector in two dimensions.
- Use vectors to solve problems in different contexts including modelling forces as vectors.

Prior Knowledge Check

1 Calculate the following: a) $\begin{pmatrix}3\\2\end{pmatrix}+\begin{pmatrix}4\\-3\end{pmatrix}$ b) $\begin{pmatrix}5\\-2\end{pmatrix}-\begin{pmatrix}-1\\6\end{pmatrix}$ c) $5\begin{pmatrix}4\\-3\end{pmatrix}$ *see GCSE Maths*

2 Use Pythagoras' theorem to find the missing length in this triangle. (5 cm, 12 cm) *see GCSE Maths*

3 Calculate the value of x in these right-angled triangles to 3 s.f.

a) 3 cm, 5 cm, x b) x, 20°, 7 cm c) 11 cm, x, 4 cm

see page 175

4 Use the cosine rule to find angle θ in this triangle to 3 s.f. (4 cm, 5 cm, 6 cm, θ) *see page 180*

Chapter 12

12.1 Introducing Vectors

Scalars are quantities **without a direction** — e.g. a speed of 2 ms^{-1}.

Vectors have both **size and direction** — e.g. a velocity of 2 ms^{-1} on a bearing of 050°.

Vectors are drawn as **lines** with **arrowheads** on them.

The **length** of the line represents the **magnitude** (size) of the vector.

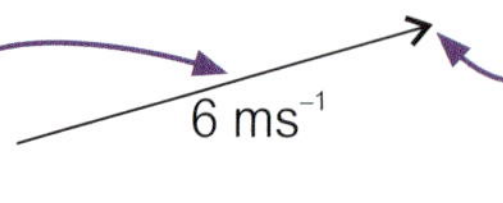

The **direction** of the arrowhead shows the direction of the vector.

Sometimes vectors are drawn to **scale**:

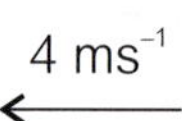

8 ms^{-1}

> **Tip** When a vector is typed it's usually bold, but if you're handwriting a vector you should write it underlined, e.g. <u>a</u>.

Vectors are usually **written** using either a **lowercase bold** letter or a **lowercase underlined** letter. When the **endpoints** of a vector are labelled, the vector can also be written by putting an **arrow** over the endpoints:

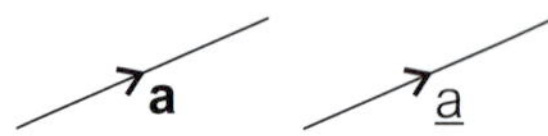

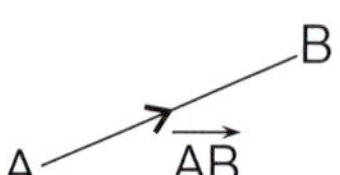

Adding vectors

You can **add** vectors together by drawing the arrows **nose to tail**.

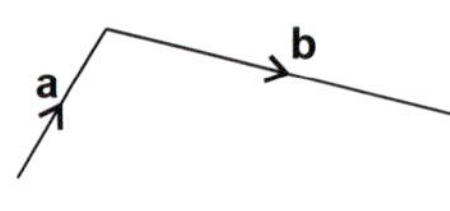

The single vector that goes from the start to the end of the combined vectors is called the **resultant vector**.

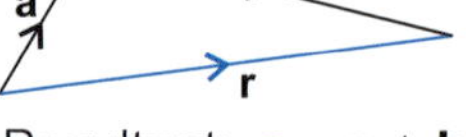

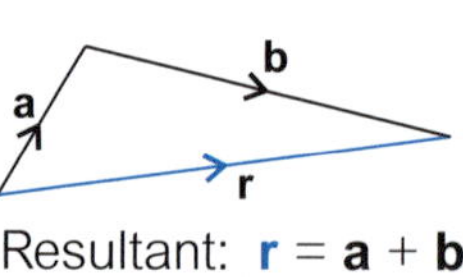

Resultant: **r** = **a** + **b**

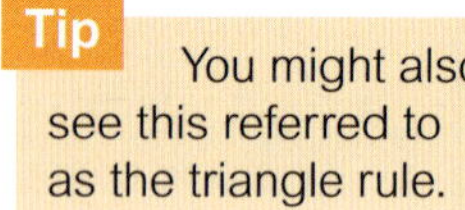

This method of adding is called the **parallelogram rule** because **a** and **b** form the sides of a parallelogram which has the resultant vector **r** = **a** + **b** as its diagonal.

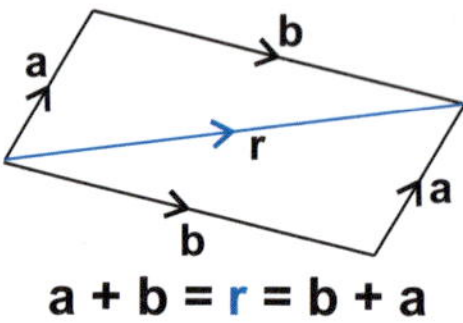

a + b = r = b + a

When you add two vectors you're really **combining** two **translations**:

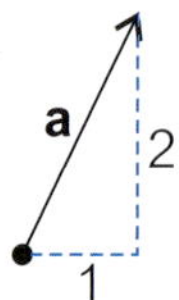

a is a translation of 1 across and 2 up.

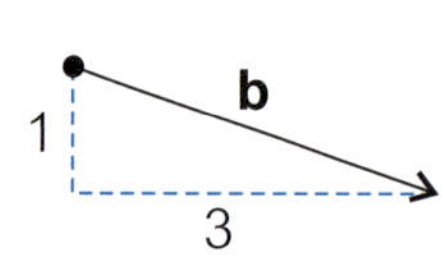

b is a translation of 3 across and 1 down (or –1 up).

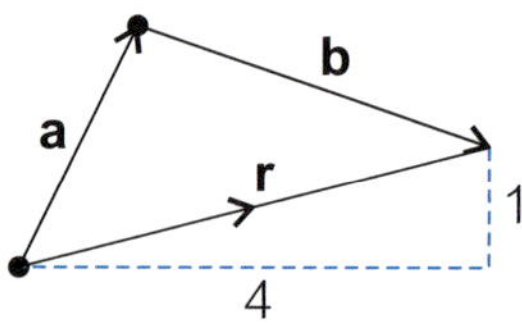

So doing **a** then **b** gives you a combined translation of (1 + 3) = 4 across and (2 – 1) = 1 up.

Subtracting vectors

The vector –**a** points in the opposite direction to the vector **a**, and they're both exactly the **same size**. So **subtracting** a vector is the same as **adding the negative vector**:

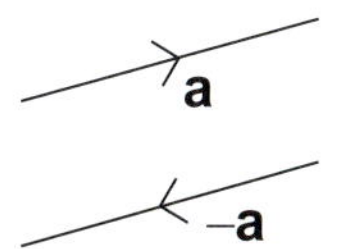

To go from Q to P, you can't just add the vectors **a** and **b** because the arrows don't run from end to end.

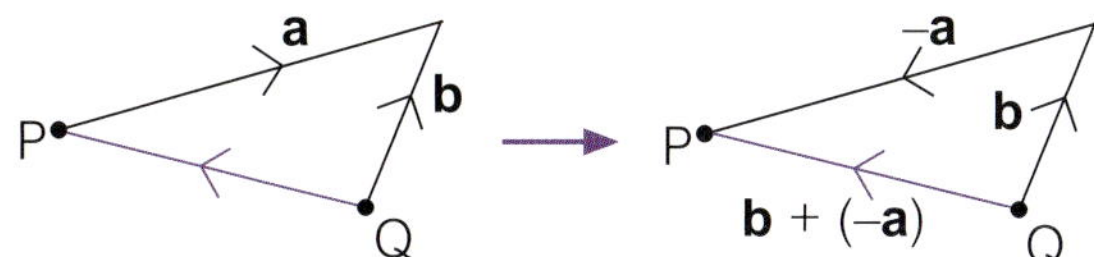

But replace vector **a** with –**a** (which goes in the opposite direction) and now you can add.

So $\overrightarrow{QP}$ = **b** + (–**a**) = **b** – **a**

You can use these rules to find a vector in terms of **other vectors**.

Example 1

Find $\overrightarrow{WZ}$ and $\overrightarrow{ZX}$ in terms of **p**, **q** and **r**.

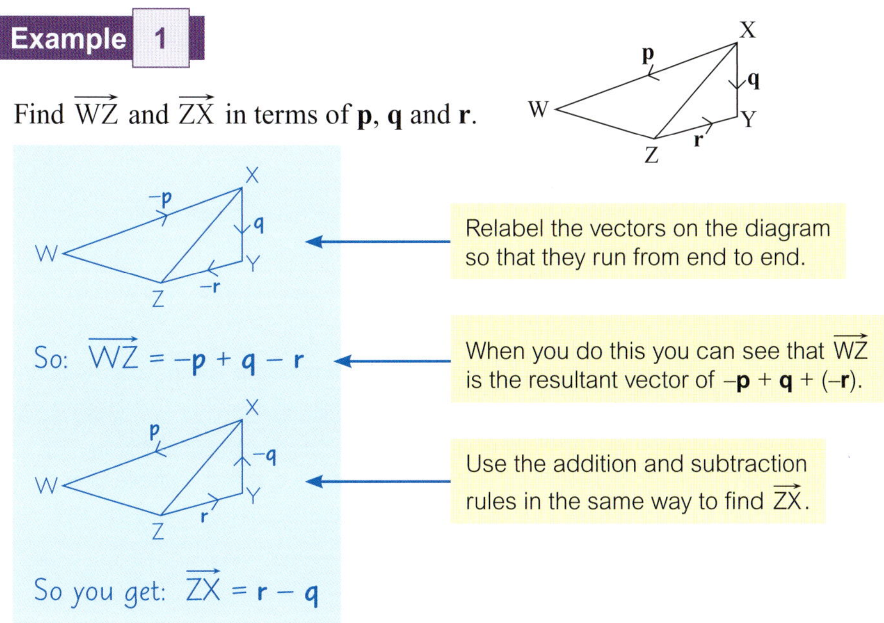

Relabel the vectors on the diagram so that they run from end to end.

When you do this you can see that $\overrightarrow{WZ}$ is the resultant vector of –**p** + **q** + (–**r**).

Use the addition and subtraction rules in the same way to find $\overrightarrow{ZX}$.

Tip You don't have to draw this diagram out — it's enough to know that if you want your vector to go from W to X and the vector **p** goes from X to W then you need to use –**p** instead.

Scalar multiplication

You can **multiply** a vector by a **scalar** (just a number).

When you do this the **length changes** but the **direction** stays the **same**...

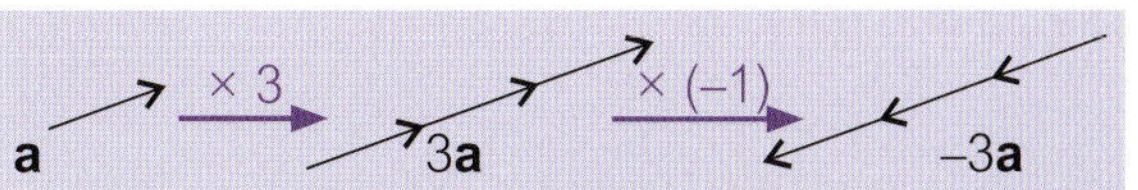

...unless the scalar is **negative**, then the direction's **reversed**.

You can **divide** a vector by a scalar as well — the result is the same as **multiplying** the vector by the **reciprocal** of the scalar. E.g. $\frac{\mathbf{a}}{3} = \frac{1}{3}\mathbf{a}$. **Multiplying** or **dividing** a vector by a **non-zero** scalar always produces a **parallel** vector.

All **parallel** vectors are **scalar multiples** of each other, so showing that one vector is a scalar multiple of another is the same as showing they're parallel.

If two vectors have the same components, e.g. **a** and **b**, then you can check the **scale factor** for each component. If they're all the **same**, then the vectors are parallel, if not then they're not.

> **Tip**
> A 'scale factor' is the scalar used when one vector is multiplied to give another. E.g. 1.5 is the scale factor in $9\mathbf{a} = 1.5 \times (6\mathbf{a})$.

Example 2

Show that the vector $9\mathbf{a} + 15\mathbf{b}$ is parallel to the vector $6\mathbf{a} + 10\mathbf{b}$.

$\mathbf{a}: \frac{9}{6} = 1.5 \quad \mathbf{b}: \frac{15}{10} = 1.5$ — Divide the coefficients of corresponding components to find the scale factors.

$9\mathbf{a} + 15\mathbf{b} = 1.5(6\mathbf{a} + 10\mathbf{b})$, so the vectors are parallel — The scale factor is the same for **a** and **b**, so it's possible to write the first vector as a scalar multiple of the second.

Example 3

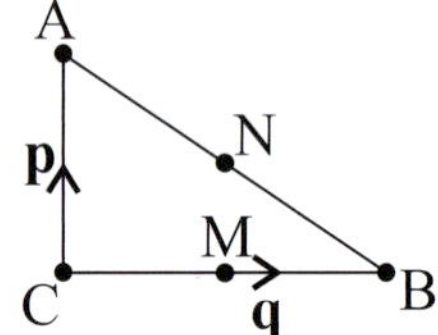

$\overrightarrow{CA} = \mathbf{p}$, $\overrightarrow{CB} = \mathbf{q}$, point M lies halfway along $\overrightarrow{CB}$, point N lies halfway along $\overrightarrow{AB}$. Show that $\overrightarrow{MN}$ is parallel to $\overrightarrow{CA}$.

$\overrightarrow{MN} = \overrightarrow{MB} + \overrightarrow{BN} = \frac{1}{2}\overrightarrow{CB} + \frac{1}{2}\overrightarrow{BA}$ — Write $\overrightarrow{MN}$ in terms of other vectors.

$\overrightarrow{BA} = -\mathbf{q} + \mathbf{p}$ and $\overrightarrow{CB} = \mathbf{q}$ — Write $\overrightarrow{BA}$ and $\overrightarrow{CB}$ in terms of **p** and **q**.

So $\overrightarrow{MN} = \frac{1}{2}\mathbf{q} + \frac{1}{2}(-\mathbf{q} + \mathbf{p})$ — Write $\overrightarrow{MN}$ in terms of **p** and **q**.

$= \frac{1}{2}\mathbf{p} = \frac{1}{2}\overrightarrow{CA}$ — To show that $\overrightarrow{MN}$ is parallel to $\overrightarrow{CA}$ you need to show it's a scalar multiple of **p**

$\overrightarrow{MN}$ is a scalar multiple of $\overrightarrow{CA}$, so they're parallel.

A vector can be **anywhere** in **space**.

This means that vectors of the **same size** which are **parallel** and pointing in the **same direction** are the **same**, even if they're not in the same place.

E.g. in a parallelogram, opposite sides have the **same vector**, so knowing one means you know the other:

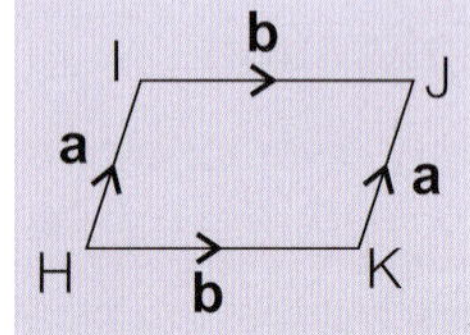

Look out for questions where you have to recognise that two lines are parallel in order to find a vector.

Collinear points

You can also use **vector addition** to show that three points are **collinear** — i.e. they all lie on a **single straight line**. If vectors $\overrightarrow{AB}$ and $\overrightarrow{BC}$ are **parallel**, then the points A, B and C are collinear.

Example 4 

$\overrightarrow{AP} = \mathbf{m}$, $\overrightarrow{AQ} = \mathbf{m} + 2\mathbf{n}$, $\overrightarrow{AR} = \mathbf{m} + 6\mathbf{n}$. Show that P, Q and R are collinear.

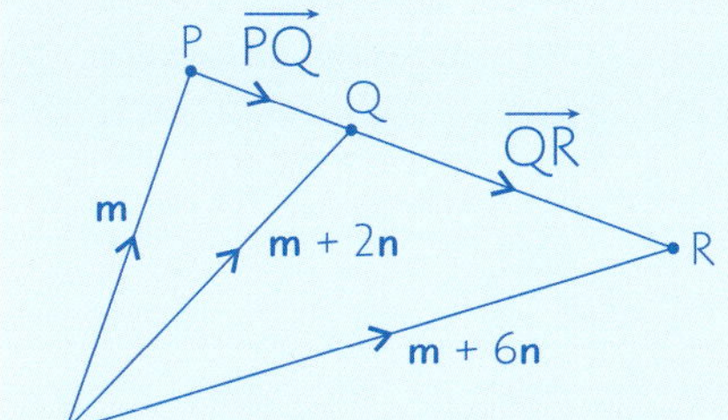

$\overrightarrow{PQ} = -\overrightarrow{AP} + \overrightarrow{AQ}$
$= -\mathbf{m} + \mathbf{m} + 2\mathbf{n} = 2\mathbf{n}$

$\overrightarrow{QR} = -\overrightarrow{AQ} + \overrightarrow{AR}$
$= -\mathbf{m} - 2\mathbf{n} + \mathbf{m} + 6\mathbf{n} = 4\mathbf{n}$

Find $\overrightarrow{PQ}$ and $\overrightarrow{QR}$ in terms of **m** and **n**.

$\overrightarrow{QR} = 4\mathbf{n} = 2(2\mathbf{n}) = 2(\overrightarrow{PQ})$

Now show that $\overrightarrow{QR}$ is a scalar multiple of $\overrightarrow{PQ}$.

The vectors are parallel and share a point (Q), this means the points P, Q and R lie on a straight line — i.e. they are collinear.

Exercise 12.1

M Q1 State whether each of these real-world examples refers to a scalar quantity, a vector quantity or neither.

a) A pilot flies due south for a distance of 200 kilometres.

b) The time taken to travel from London to Exeter is 3 hours.

c) A force of 20 newtons is required to pull a sledge up the steepest section of a hill — the slope is at an angle of 5° to the horizontal.

Q2 Vectors **a** and **b** are represented by the lines to the right. Draw and label sketches that represent the following vectors:

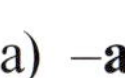
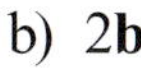

a) $-\mathbf{a}$ b) $2\mathbf{b}$ c) $\mathbf{a} + \mathbf{b}$ d) $\mathbf{a} - \mathbf{b}$

Q3 For the rectangle ABCD shown on the right, write down single vectors that are equivalent to:

a) $\overrightarrow{AB} + \overrightarrow{BC}$ b) $\overrightarrow{BC} + \overrightarrow{CD} + \overrightarrow{DA}$ c) $\overrightarrow{DC} - \overrightarrow{BC}$

Q4 In the triangle XYZ, the vector **p** represents $\overrightarrow{XZ}$ and the vector **q** represents $\overrightarrow{YX}$. Express the following in terms of **p** or **q** or both:

a) $\overrightarrow{XY}$ b) $\overrightarrow{YZ}$ c) $\overrightarrow{ZY}$

E Q5 The parallelogram ABCD is defined by the vectors, $\overrightarrow{AB} = \mathbf{p}$ and $\overrightarrow{BC} = \mathbf{q}$, where $\overrightarrow{AB} = \overrightarrow{DC}$ and $\overrightarrow{BC} = \overrightarrow{AD}$. Express in terms of **p** and **q**:

a) $\overrightarrow{AB} + \overrightarrow{AC}$ *[2 marks]*

b) $2(\overrightarrow{AD} + \overrightarrow{BA})$ *[2 marks]*

Q6 ABCD is a parallelogram. The vector $\overrightarrow{BA} = \mathbf{n}$ and $\overrightarrow{BD} = \mathbf{m}$. Find $\overrightarrow{BC}$ in terms of **n** and **m**.

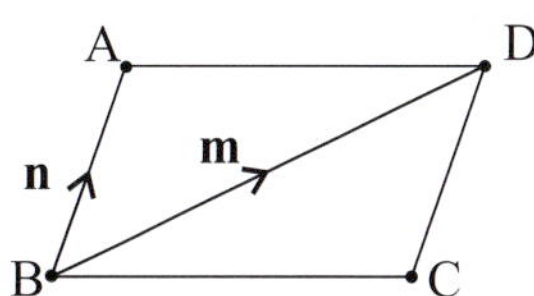

Q7 In the rectangle ABCD, E is the midpoint of AD and F divides DC in the ratio 2 : 1. If $\overrightarrow{AB} = \mathbf{b}$ and $\overrightarrow{AD} = \mathbf{d}$, find the following vectors in terms of **b** and **d**.

a) $\overrightarrow{DF}$ b) $\overrightarrow{BE}$ c) $\overrightarrow{EF}$

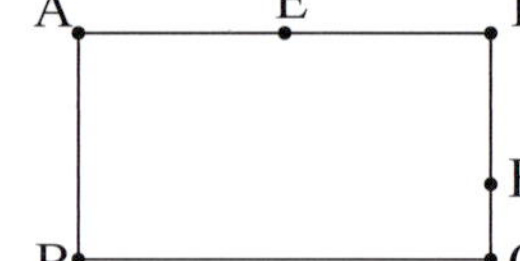

Q8 CDEFGH is a regular hexagon whose centre is O. If $\overrightarrow{OE} = \mathbf{e}$ and $\overrightarrow{OD} = \mathbf{d}$, express in terms of **e** and **d**:

a) $\overrightarrow{HE}$ b) $\overrightarrow{DG}$

c) $\overrightarrow{ED}$ d) $\overrightarrow{CE}$

e) $\overrightarrow{DF}$ f) $\overrightarrow{EG}$

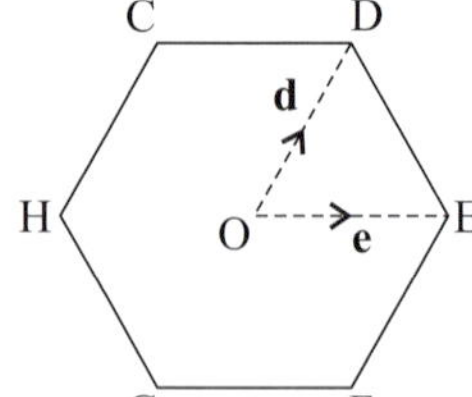

P Q9 In triangle DEF, J and L are midpoints of ED and FD respectively. Given that $\overrightarrow{EF} = \mathbf{f}$ and $\overrightarrow{ED} = \mathbf{d}$, prove that $\overrightarrow{JL} = \frac{1}{2}\mathbf{f}$.

E Q10 In the diagram on the right, BC = 3AB. $\overrightarrow{AB}$ and $\overrightarrow{BC}$ lie along the same straight line. Find the following vectors in terms of **p** and **q**:

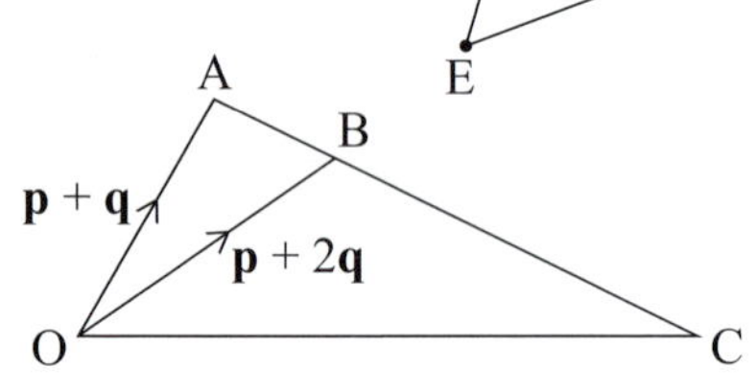

a) $\overrightarrow{AB}$ *[1 mark]*

b) $\overrightarrow{OC}$ *[2 marks]*

E P Q11 ABCD is a right-angled trapezium, where $\overrightarrow{AB} = 2\overrightarrow{DC}$ and M is the midpoint of $\overrightarrow{AD}$. Point P lies at the intersection of the diagonals, such that the ratio $\overrightarrow{BP} : \overrightarrow{PD}$ is 3 : 1. $\overrightarrow{AB} = \mathbf{a}$ and $\overrightarrow{BC} = \mathbf{b}$. Express the following vectors in terms of **a** and **b**:

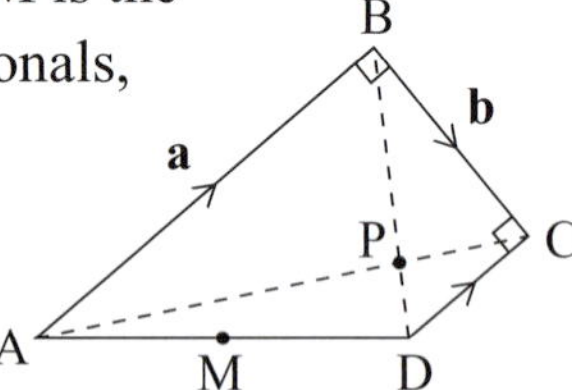

a) $\overrightarrow{AM}$ *[2 marks]*

b) $\overrightarrow{BP}$ *[2 marks]*

c) $\overrightarrow{PM}$ *[2 marks]*

Q12 Give two vectors that are parallel to $3\mathbf{t} - 2\mathbf{u}$.

Q13 $\overrightarrow{XY} = \mathbf{a}$, $\overrightarrow{XZ} = \mathbf{b}$. P is the midpoint of $\overrightarrow{YZ}$, and Q is the midpoint of $\overrightarrow{XY}$. Show that $\overrightarrow{PQ}$ is parallel to $\overrightarrow{XZ}$.

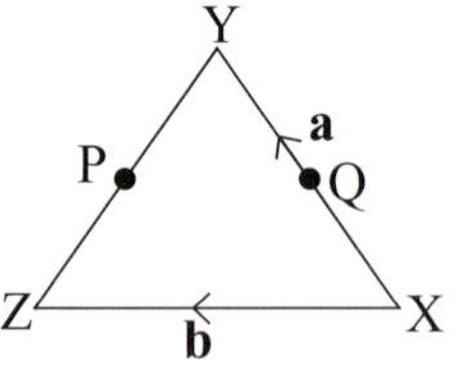

P Q14 Given that $\overrightarrow{TU} = \mathbf{v} - \mathbf{w}$ and $\overrightarrow{ST} = 2\mathbf{v} + \mathbf{w}$, show that $\overrightarrow{US}$ is parallel to **v**.

Problem Solving

Drawing diagrams will help you to visualise the vectors that you need to find.

P Q15 Given that $\overrightarrow{XY} = 3\mathbf{a} - 4\mathbf{b} + 2\mathbf{c}$ and $\overrightarrow{XZ} = \mathbf{a} - 2\mathbf{b} - 2\mathbf{c}$, show that $\overrightarrow{YZ}$ is parallel to $\mathbf{a} - \mathbf{b} + 2\mathbf{c}$.

P Q16 $\overrightarrow{XY} = \mathbf{t} + \mathbf{u}$, $\overrightarrow{AY} = -\mathbf{t}$, $\overrightarrow{AZ} = \mathbf{u}$. Show that X, Y and Z are collinear.

Q17 Group the following into sets of parallel vectors:

$2\mathbf{a} + \mathbf{b}$ $\quad 10\mathbf{a} - 5\mathbf{b}$ $\quad 2\mathbf{p} + \mathbf{q}$ $\quad -\mathbf{b} - 2\mathbf{a}$ $\quad 2\mathbf{a} - \mathbf{b}$ $\quad \frac{1}{2}\mathbf{q} + \mathbf{p}$ $\quad 4\mathbf{b} + 8\mathbf{a}$

P Q18 $\overrightarrow{OA} = \mathbf{a}$, $\overrightarrow{OB} = \mathbf{b}$, $\overrightarrow{OC} = 5\mathbf{a} - 4\mathbf{b}$. Show that A, B and C are collinear.

P Q19 $\overrightarrow{PQ} = -(\mathbf{m} + \frac{9}{2}\mathbf{n})$, $\overrightarrow{PR} = \mathbf{m} - \frac{3}{2}\mathbf{n}$, $\overrightarrow{PS} = 2\mathbf{m}$. Show that Q, R and S are collinear.

P Q20 In the diagram on the right, $\overrightarrow{OB} = 4\mathbf{a}$, $\overrightarrow{AB} = 2\mathbf{b}$, $\overrightarrow{BD} = 4\mathbf{a} - \mathbf{b}$ and $\overrightarrow{DC} = -\frac{5}{2}\mathbf{b} - \mathbf{a}$. Show that OAC is a straight line.

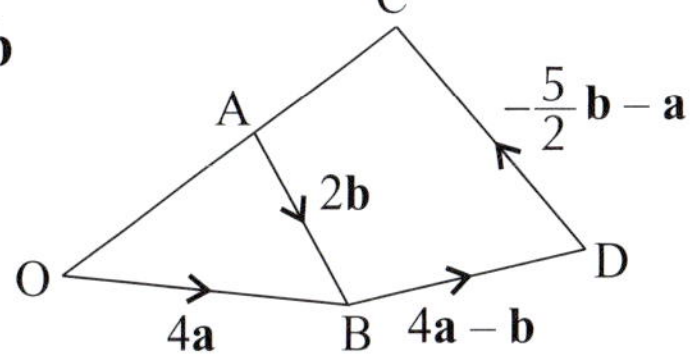

P Q21 $\overrightarrow{AB} = \mathbf{q} - \frac{1}{2}\mathbf{p}$, $\overrightarrow{AC} = \mathbf{p}$, $\overrightarrow{AD} = -5\mathbf{p} + 4\mathbf{q}$.
Show that B, C and D are collinear.

P Q22 A quadrilateral PQRS has sides $\overrightarrow{PQ} = -\mathbf{a}$, $\overrightarrow{QR} = -\frac{1}{2}\mathbf{a} + \mathbf{b}$ and $\overrightarrow{RS} = \frac{5}{2}\mathbf{a} - 3\mathbf{b}$.

a) Express $\overrightarrow{PS}$ in terms of **a** and **b**.

b) Show that PQRS is a trapezium.

P Q23 ABCD is a quadrilateral and X is the midpoint of the line AC. $\overrightarrow{DA} = \mathbf{a} - \mathbf{b}$, $\overrightarrow{AB} = 3\mathbf{a} - 2\mathbf{b}$ and $\overrightarrow{XC} = \mathbf{a}$. Is DXB a straight line? Give reasons for your answer.

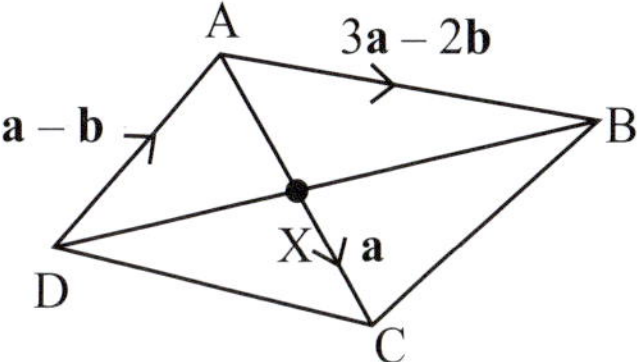

P Q24 In the diagram on the right,
$\overrightarrow{AB} = \mathbf{b} - \mathbf{a}$, $\overrightarrow{BC} = \mathbf{a}$, $\overrightarrow{AD} = \frac{3}{2}\mathbf{a}$ and $\overrightarrow{AE} = 2\mathbf{a} - \mathbf{b}$.

a) Show that BE is parallel to CD.

b) The point O divides $\overrightarrow{BE}$ in the ratio 1 : 2.
Show that AOC is a straight line.

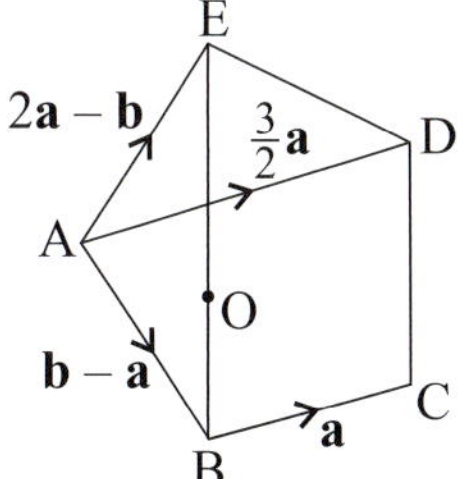

Problem Solving

Showing three points form a straight line is the same as showing the points are collinear.

E P Q25 The diagram on the right shows a regular hexagon ABCDEF, where $\overrightarrow{AB} = \mathbf{p}$, $\overrightarrow{BC} = \mathbf{q}$ and $\overrightarrow{CD} = \mathbf{r}$. Point P is such that $\overrightarrow{AD} = \overrightarrow{DP}$ and point M is such that the ratio $\overrightarrow{CM} : \overrightarrow{MF}$ is 3 : 1.

a) Show that $\overrightarrow{PM} = -\frac{7}{4}\mathbf{p} - \frac{7}{4}\mathbf{q} - \frac{5}{4}\mathbf{r}$. *[6 marks]*

b) Hence, or otherwise, write $\overrightarrow{PM}$ in terms of **p** and **q**. *[2 marks]*

Challenge

P Q26 In the quadrilateral on the right,
$\overrightarrow{PQ} = \mathbf{a} + 2\mathbf{b}$, $\overrightarrow{QR} = 3\mathbf{a} + \mathbf{b}$, $\overrightarrow{MS} = \frac{1}{2}(\mathbf{a} - \frac{1}{2}\mathbf{b})$
and the point M is the midpoint of $\overrightarrow{PR}$.
Lines PS and QR are extended to meet at point T.
Give the vector $\overrightarrow{PT}$ in terms and **a** and **b**.

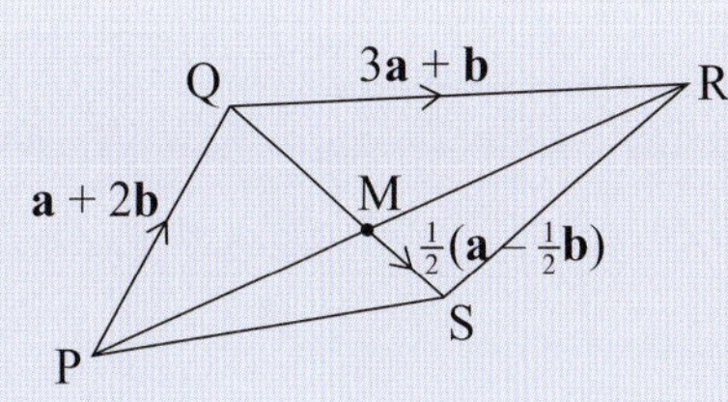

12.2 Position Vectors

You can use a vector to describe the **position** of a point in relation to the **origin**, O. This vector is called a **position vector** and they always **start** at the origin and finish at the point they're describing.

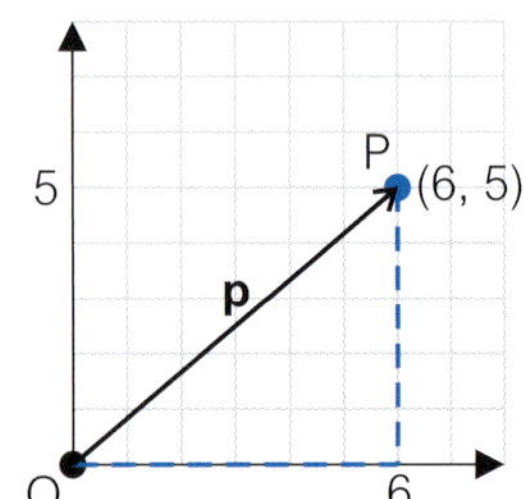

One way of describing the position of the point P is with its **Cartesian coordinates**, which are e.g. (6, 5).

This just tells you how far P is vertically and horizontally from the **origin** O.

Another way of describing how far P is from the origin is using the **position vector** $\overrightarrow{OP} = \mathbf{p}$, which has **horizontal** and **vertical** components.

The position vector of any point A is $\overrightarrow{OA}$. It's usually called vector **a**.

You can write the vector from one point to another in **terms** of their **position vectors**:

$$\overrightarrow{AB} = -\overrightarrow{OA} + \overrightarrow{OB} = \overrightarrow{OB} - \overrightarrow{OA}$$
$$= -\mathbf{a} + \mathbf{b} = \mathbf{b} - \mathbf{a}$$

Tip This result will be used time after time for finding the vector from one point to another in this chapter. Make sure you learn it in both its forms: $\overrightarrow{AB} = \overrightarrow{OB} - \overrightarrow{OA} = \mathbf{b} - \mathbf{a}$

The unit vectors i and j

A **unit vector** is any vector with a **length of 1 unit**.

The vectors **i** and **j** are **standard unit vectors**, so they each have a length of 1 unit.
i is in the direction of the **positive x-axis**, and **j** is in the direction of the **positive y-axis**.

Every vector in two dimensions is made up of **horizontal** and **vertical components**, so you can express any vector as a **sum** of **i** and **j** unit vectors.

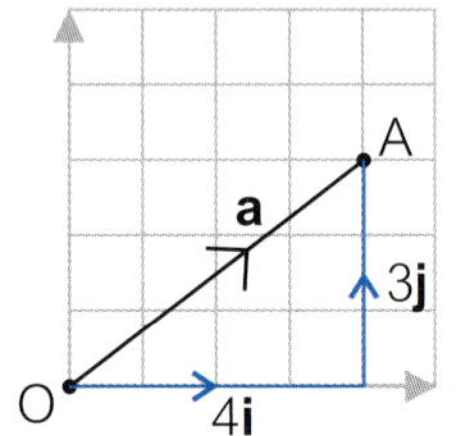

Vector **a** goes from the origin O to the point A.

To get from O to A you move **4** units **to the right** and **3** units **up**.

So **a** is the **resultant** vector when you add a **horizontal vector** that goes **4 units** in the positive x direction and a **vertical vector** that goes **3 units** in the positive y direction. **i** and **j** are the **standard** unit vectors used to express horizontal and vertical components. So $\mathbf{a} = 4\mathbf{i} + 3\mathbf{j}$

Example 1

a) Write down the position vectors of A and B in terms of **i** and **j**.

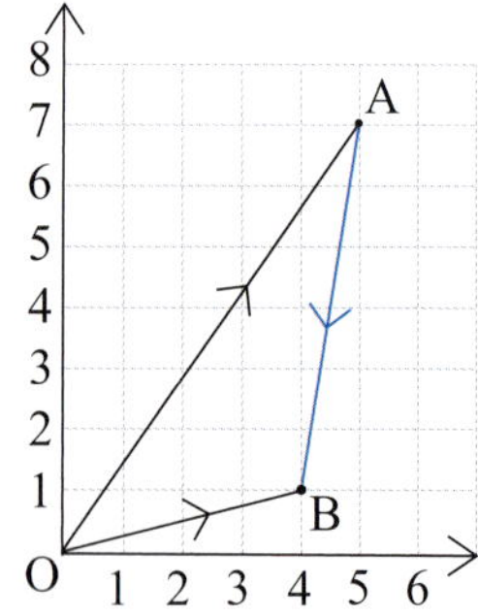

Point A lies 5 units to the right and 7 units above the origin ← Look at the position of point A.

$\mathbf{a} = 5\mathbf{i} + 7\mathbf{j}$ ← Use this to write A in the form $x\mathbf{i} + y\mathbf{j}$.

Point B lies 4 units to the right and 1 unit above the origin

$\mathbf{b} = 4\mathbf{i} + \mathbf{j}$ ← Repeat for point B.

b) Hence find $\overrightarrow{AB}$ in terms of **i** and **j**.

$\overrightarrow{AB} = -\overrightarrow{OA} + \overrightarrow{OB} = \overrightarrow{OB} - \overrightarrow{OA}$ ← Find $\overrightarrow{AB}$ in terms of $\overrightarrow{OA}$ and $\overrightarrow{OB}$.

$= -\mathbf{a} + \mathbf{b} = \mathbf{b} - \mathbf{a}$ ← Write $\overrightarrow{AB}$ in terms of **a** and **b**.

$= (4\mathbf{i} + \mathbf{j}) - (5\mathbf{i} + 7\mathbf{j})$

$= -\mathbf{i} - 6\mathbf{j}$ ← Add or subtract the **i** and **j** components separately.

In this example, the answer just means that to go from A to B, you **move** 1 unit left and 6 units down. Vectors like this are just like a **translation**.

Column vectors

Column vectors are another way of writing vectors in terms of their **horizontal** and **vertical components**.

You just write the **horizontal** (**i**) **component** on **top** of the **vertical** (**j**) **component** and put a bracket around them:

$$x\mathbf{i} + y\mathbf{j} = \begin{pmatrix} x \\ y \end{pmatrix}$$

Tip Using column vectors is often quicker and easier than working with sums of **i** and **j** components.

Calculating with them is simple. Just add or subtract the **top** row, then add or subtract the **bottom** row **separately**:

$$\mathbf{a} = 5\mathbf{i} + 7\mathbf{j} = \begin{pmatrix} 5 \\ 7 \end{pmatrix} \quad \mathbf{b} = 4\mathbf{i} + \mathbf{j} = \begin{pmatrix} 4 \\ 1 \end{pmatrix} \quad \mathbf{b} - \mathbf{a} = \begin{pmatrix} 4 \\ 1 \end{pmatrix} - \begin{pmatrix} 5 \\ 7 \end{pmatrix} = \begin{pmatrix} 4-5 \\ 1-7 \end{pmatrix} = \begin{pmatrix} -1 \\ -6 \end{pmatrix}$$

When you're **multiplying** a column vector by a **scalar** you multiply **each number** in the column vector by the scalar:

$$2\mathbf{b} - 3\mathbf{a} = 2\begin{pmatrix} 4 \\ 1 \end{pmatrix} - 3\begin{pmatrix} 5 \\ 7 \end{pmatrix} = \begin{pmatrix} 2\times4 \\ 2\times1 \end{pmatrix} - \begin{pmatrix} 3\times5 \\ 3\times7 \end{pmatrix} = \begin{pmatrix} 8 \\ 2 \end{pmatrix} - \begin{pmatrix} 15 \\ 21 \end{pmatrix} = \begin{pmatrix} -7 \\ -19 \end{pmatrix}$$

Exercise 12.2

M Q1 On a map, Jack's house has coordinates (2, 3) and his school has coordinates (4, –5). Write down the position vectors of Jack's house and Jack's school, giving your answers as column vectors.

Q2 Give, in **i** and **j** form, the position vectors of the following points:
a) (2, –4) b) (–1, –2) c) (5, 7) d) (3, –7)

Q3 C has position vector –**i** + 2**j** and D has position vector 4**i** – 3**j**.
a) What are the Cartesian coordinates of the points C and D?
b) Write the vectors $\overrightarrow{CD}$ and $\overrightarrow{DC}$ in unit vector form.

Q4 Given that $\mathbf{a} = \begin{pmatrix} -1 \\ -2 \end{pmatrix}$, $\mathbf{b} = \begin{pmatrix} 3 \\ -2 \end{pmatrix}$ and $\mathbf{c} = \begin{pmatrix} 4 \\ 3 \end{pmatrix}$, calculate the following:
a) $\mathbf{a} + \mathbf{b} + \mathbf{c}$ b) $\mathbf{c} - 2\mathbf{b}$ c) $3\mathbf{a} - \mathbf{b} + 2\mathbf{c}$ d) $5\mathbf{a} - 5\mathbf{c}$

E Q5 Given the vectors $\mathbf{a} = \begin{pmatrix}-2\\3\end{pmatrix}$, $\mathbf{a} + 3\mathbf{b} = \begin{pmatrix}1\\6\end{pmatrix}$ and $\mathbf{a} + \mathbf{b} - \mathbf{c} = \begin{pmatrix}-1\\-3\end{pmatrix}$, calculate:

a) **b** *[2 marks]*

b) **c** *[2 marks]*

P Q6 Given that $\mathbf{p} = \begin{pmatrix}-1\\-2\end{pmatrix}$, $\mathbf{q} = \begin{pmatrix}3\\-2\end{pmatrix}$ and $\mathbf{r} = \begin{pmatrix}-4\\5\end{pmatrix}$, show that $\mathbf{p} + 3\mathbf{q} + \mathbf{r}$ is parallel to $12\mathbf{i} - 9\mathbf{j}$.

Q6 Problem Solving

Remember that parallel vectors are scalar multiples of each other.

E Q7 $\overrightarrow{OP} = \begin{pmatrix}2\\-3\end{pmatrix}$, $\overrightarrow{OQ} = \begin{pmatrix}-2\\3\end{pmatrix}$ and $\overrightarrow{OR} = \begin{pmatrix}4\\-6\end{pmatrix}$.

By first finding vectors $\overrightarrow{PR}$ and $\overrightarrow{QR}$, show that points P, Q and R all lie on the same straight line. *[3 marks]*

E **P** Q8 Points A and B have position vectors $3\mathbf{i} - 3\mathbf{j}$ and $4\mathbf{i}$ respectively.

a) Find vector $\overrightarrow{AB}$. *[2 marks]*

b) Point C has position vector $\begin{pmatrix}-4\\2\end{pmatrix}$ and $2\overrightarrow{CD} = 3\overrightarrow{AB}$.

Find the position vector of point D in **i** and **j** form. *[3 marks]*

Q9 Triangle ABC is shown on the right.

Find the vectors $\overrightarrow{AB}$, $\overrightarrow{BC}$ and $\overrightarrow{CA}$.

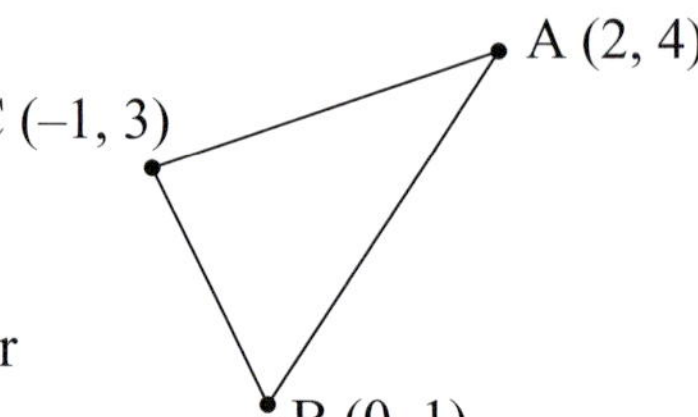

Q10 ABCD is a square, where A has position vector $-4\mathbf{i} + 6\mathbf{j}$ and C has position vector $3\mathbf{i} - \mathbf{j}$. Find the position vectors of B and D.

P Q11 M is the midpoint of the line PQ, where P has position vector $-3\mathbf{i} + \mathbf{j}$ and M has position vector $2\mathbf{i} - 5\mathbf{j}$. Find the position vector of Q.

P Q12 A point P divides the line AB in the ratio 2 : 1, where $\overrightarrow{OA} = \begin{pmatrix}-2\\4\end{pmatrix}$ and $\overrightarrow{OB} = \begin{pmatrix}4\\-5\end{pmatrix}$.

a) Find the position vector of P.

b) Find the vector $\overrightarrow{PB}$.

E **P** Q13 The parallelogram ABCD is shown below.

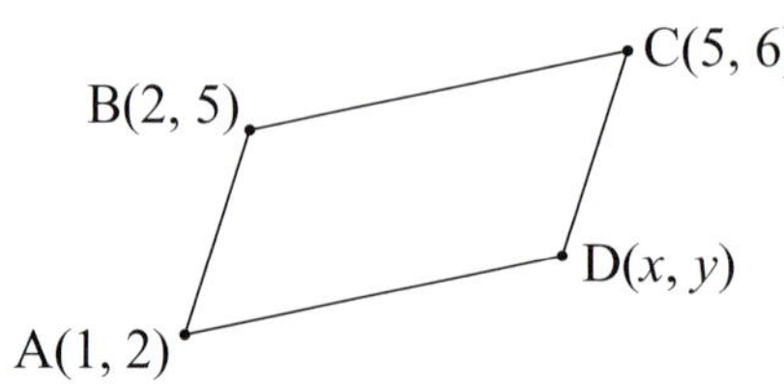

a) Find the column vector $\overrightarrow{BC}$. *[2 marks]*

b) Find the coordinates of point D. *[2 marks]*

The parallelogram is translated such that the position vector of A is now $4\mathbf{i} + \mathbf{j}$.

c) Find the new position vector of point C in terms of **i** and **j**. *[2 marks]*

E Q14 The four vertices of quadrilateral PQRS have position vectors $\overrightarrow{OP} = \mathbf{i} + \mathbf{j}$, $\overrightarrow{OQ} = 2\mathbf{i} + 3\mathbf{j}$, $\overrightarrow{OR} = 3\mathbf{i} - 2\mathbf{j}$ and $\overrightarrow{OS} = -\mathbf{i} - \mathbf{j}$. Find the following vectors:

a) $\overrightarrow{PR}$ *[2 marks]*

b) $\overrightarrow{SQ}$ *[2 marks]*

E P Q15 The points A and B have position vectors such that $\overrightarrow{OA} = -\mathbf{i} + \mathbf{j}$ and $\overrightarrow{OB} = 5\mathbf{i} - 2\mathbf{j}$. A third point, C, lies on the straight line through A and B such that AB : BC = 3 : 1.

a) Find the vector $\overrightarrow{AB}$. *[2 marks]*

b) (i) Find the vector $\overrightarrow{AC}$. *[3 marks]*

(ii) Hence find the position vector of point C. *[2 marks]*

P M Q16 A robotic vacuum cleaner models a room using a quadrilateral DEFG, with vertices at the points D (–7, –2), E (–3, –1), F (–1, 5) and G (–3, 10).

a) Give the vectors for the room's walls $\overrightarrow{DE}$, $\overrightarrow{EF}$, $\overrightarrow{FG}$ and $\overrightarrow{GD}$.

b) The vacuum cleaner follows the wall from D to E, then E to F. Give a single vector that the vacuum cleaner could have followed to get from D to F more efficiently.

Problem Solving

Sketching the points and vectors given in the question will help you to see the vectors you need to find.

P Q17 PQR is a triangle. Given that $\overrightarrow{OQ} = \begin{pmatrix} 3 \\ 3 \end{pmatrix}$, $\overrightarrow{OP} = \begin{pmatrix} 3 \\ 0 \end{pmatrix}$ and $\overrightarrow{PR} = \begin{pmatrix} 4 \\ 7 \end{pmatrix}$, find the Cartesian coordinates of R and give the vector $\overrightarrow{QR}$.

P Q18 The position vectors of the vertices of a quadrilateral ABCD are: $\overrightarrow{OA} = \mathbf{i} - \mathbf{j}$, $\overrightarrow{OB} = -4\mathbf{j}$, $\overrightarrow{OC} = 4\mathbf{i} - 2\mathbf{j}$ and $\overrightarrow{OD} = 3\mathbf{i} + \mathbf{j}$. Find the vectors for the diagonals of the quadrilateral.

E P Q19 In the diagram below, points A, B, C and D have position vectors $\mathbf{i} - \mathbf{j}$, $7\mathbf{i} + 3\mathbf{j}$, $8\mathbf{i}$ and $5\mathbf{i} - 2\mathbf{j}$ respectively.

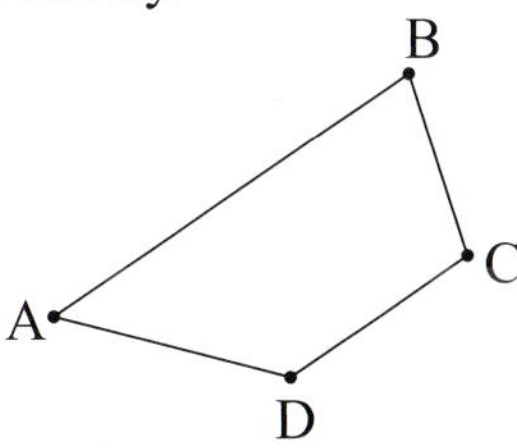

a) Show that the vectors $\overrightarrow{AB}$ and $\overrightarrow{CD}$ are parallel. *[4 marks]*

b) M is the midpoint of $\overrightarrow{BD}$. Find the position vector $\overrightarrow{OM}$. *[3 marks]*

Challenge

E P Q20 Naomi marks 4 points on a map that form a parallelogram with corners A, B, C and D. Points A, B and C have position vectors $-2\mathbf{i} - 3\mathbf{j}$, $\mathbf{i} + \mathbf{j}$ and $6\mathbf{i} + \mathbf{j}$ respectively.

a) Find all possible position vectors of point D. *[4 marks]*

b) The point P is the intersection of the diagonals of the parallelogram. Find the position vector of P in the form $a\mathbf{i} + b\mathbf{j}$ where $a < 0$. *[4 marks]*

12.3 Calculating with Vectors

Calculating the magnitude of a vector

The **magnitude** of a vector is the **distance** between its start point and end point.
It's sometimes called **modulus** instead of magnitude.

The **magnitude** of a vector $\boldsymbol{a}$ is written $|\boldsymbol{a}|$.

The **magnitude** of a vector $\overrightarrow{AB}$ is written $|\overrightarrow{AB}|$.

Magnitude is a **scalar**, and it's **always positive**. The **i** and **j** components of a vector form a convenient **right-angled triangle**, so you can use **Pythagoras' theorem** to find a vector's magnitude.

Example 1

Find the magnitude of the vector $\mathbf{a} = 5\mathbf{i} + 3\mathbf{j}$.

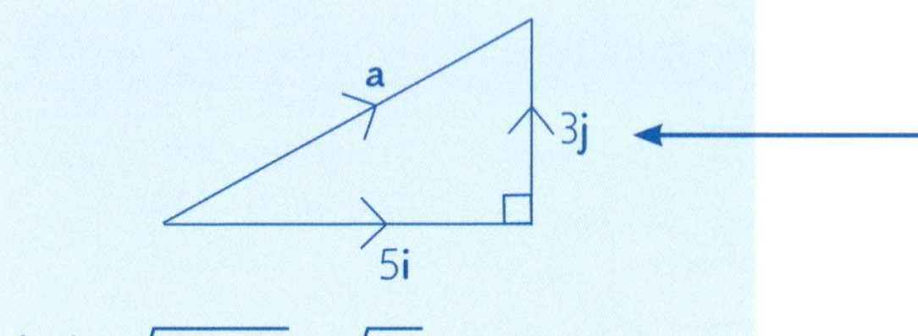

You know the length of two sides of the right-angled triangle formed by **a** and its **horizontal** and **vertical** components.

$|\mathbf{a}| = \sqrt{5^2 + 3^2} = \sqrt{34} = 5.83$ to 3 s.f.

The magnitude of **a** is the length of the **hypotenuse** of this triangle. So find $|\mathbf{a}|$ using **Pythagoras**.

You can use a vector's magnitude to find the **distance** between two **points**:

Example 2

$\overrightarrow{JK} = \begin{pmatrix} 4 \\ 7 \end{pmatrix}$. Find the distance between J and K. Give your answer in surd form.

The distance between J and K is $|\overrightarrow{JK}| = \sqrt{4^2 + (-7)^2} = \sqrt{65}$

The question asks for surd form so leave the root sign in.

You can find **missing components** of the vector using its magnitude:

Example 3 P

$\overrightarrow{OP} = \begin{pmatrix} 3 \\ 5 \end{pmatrix}$, $\overrightarrow{OQ} = \begin{pmatrix} -2 \\ b \end{pmatrix}$, given that $|\overrightarrow{PQ}| = \sqrt{29}$ and $|\overrightarrow{OQ}| = \sqrt{13}$, find b.

$\overrightarrow{PQ} = \overrightarrow{OQ} - \overrightarrow{OP} = \begin{pmatrix} -2 \\ b \end{pmatrix} - \begin{pmatrix} 3 \\ 5 \end{pmatrix} = \begin{pmatrix} -5 \\ b-5 \end{pmatrix}$

First find $\overrightarrow{PQ}$.

continued on the next page...

$|\overrightarrow{PQ}| = \sqrt{25+(b-5)^2} \Rightarrow 29 = 25 + (b-5)^2$
$\Rightarrow 4 = (b-5)^2 \Rightarrow \pm 2 = b - 5$
$\Rightarrow b = 3$ or $b = 7$

Now find the magnitude of $\overrightarrow{PQ}$ in terms of b and compare it with the value given.

$|\overrightarrow{OQ}| = \sqrt{(-2)^2 + b^2} \Rightarrow 13 = 4 + b^2$
$\Rightarrow 9 = b^2 \Rightarrow b = \pm 3$

Do the same with $\overrightarrow{OQ}$.

The only value of b which satisfies both conditions is $b = 3$

To find a **unit vector** in the direction of a particular vector you just **divide** the vector by its **magnitude** (i.e. multiply by the magnitude's reciprocal).

The **unit vector** in the direction of the vector **a** is: $\frac{1}{|\mathbf{a}|}\mathbf{a} = \frac{\mathbf{a}}{|\mathbf{a}|}$.

A unit vector always has a **magnitude** of $\frac{1}{|\mathbf{a}|} \times |\mathbf{a}| = 1$.

It's a **positive scalar multiple** of **a** (as magnitude is always positive), so it has the **same direction** as **a**.

Example 4

Find the unit vector in the direction of $\mathbf{q} = 5\mathbf{i} - 12\mathbf{j}$.

$|\mathbf{q}| = \sqrt{5^2 + (-12)^2} = \sqrt{169} = 13$

First find the magnitude of **q**.

$\frac{\mathbf{q}}{|\mathbf{q}|} = \frac{1}{13}(5\mathbf{i} - 12\mathbf{j}) = \frac{5}{13}\mathbf{i} - \frac{12}{13}\mathbf{j}$

Use the magnitude to work out the unit vector.

Calculating the direction of a vector

The direction of a vector **a** is the **angle** between a line parallel to the x-axis and **a**. It is usually measured **anticlockwise** from the x-axis.

If you know the **i** and **j** components of a vector, then you can find the **direction** of the vector by using **trigonometry**.

Problem Solving You may see questions asking you to calculate other angles too — like the angle between a vector and the vertical y-axis.

Example 5

The diagram shows the vector $\mathbf{a} = 2\mathbf{i} + 3\mathbf{j}$.
Find the magnitude and direction of the vector.

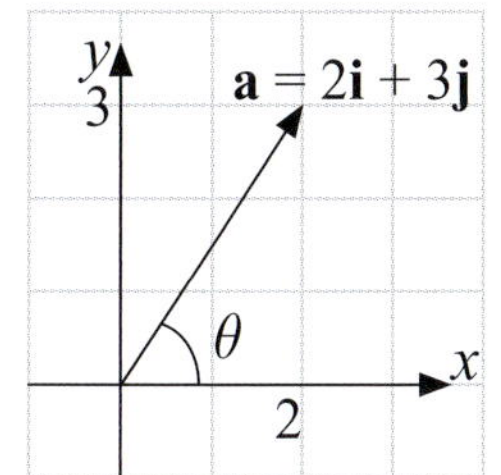

$|\mathbf{a}| = \sqrt{2^2 + 3^2} = \sqrt{13}$

Use Pythagoras' theorem as before to find the magnitude.

$\tan\theta = \frac{3}{2}$

$\Rightarrow \theta = \tan^{-1}\left(\frac{3}{2}\right) = 56.3°$ (3 s.f.)

Use trigonometry to find the angle θ.

In general, a vector $\begin{pmatrix} x \\ y \end{pmatrix}$ has magnitude $\sqrt{x^2 + y^2}$ and makes an angle of $\tan^{-1}\left(\frac{y}{x}\right)$ with the horizontal.

Similarly, if you know the **magnitude** and **direction** of a vector then you can use **trigonometry** to calculate its horizontal and vertical components.

The direction is measured **anticlockwise** from the positive ***x*-axis**, so the direction isn't always the same as the angle with the **horizontal**. E.g. in the diagram on the right, the direction of the vector is $360° - \theta$.

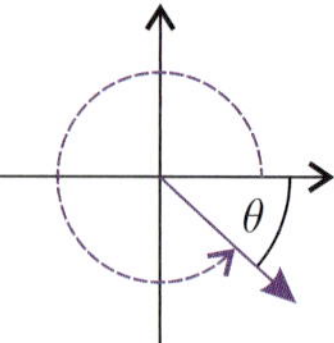

Example 6

Given a vector $\mathbf{v} = a\mathbf{i} + b\mathbf{j}$, with direction 30° and magnitude $|\mathbf{v}| = 5$, calculate a and b.

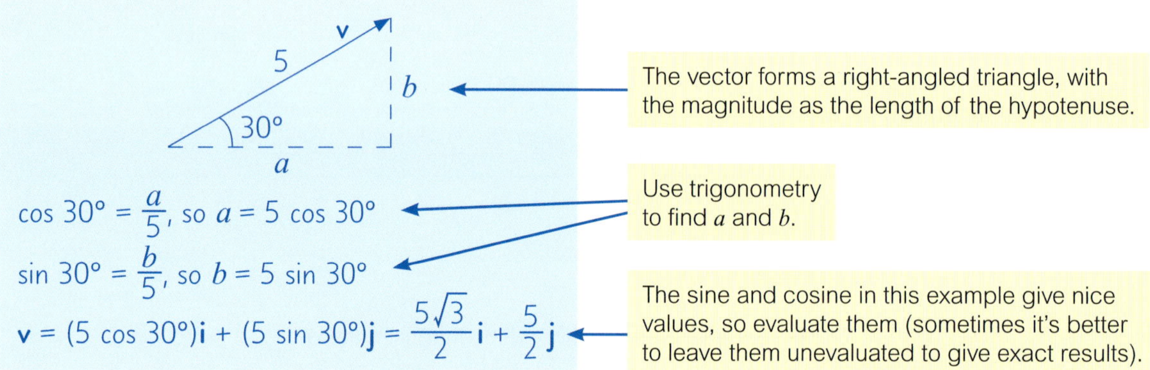

The vector forms a right-angled triangle, with the magnitude as the length of the hypotenuse.

$\cos 30° = \frac{a}{5}$, so $a = 5\cos 30°$

$\sin 30° = \frac{b}{5}$, so $b = 5\sin 30°$

Use trigonometry to find a and b.

$\mathbf{v} = (5\cos 30°)\mathbf{i} + (5\sin 30°)\mathbf{j} = \frac{5\sqrt{3}}{2}\mathbf{i} + \frac{5}{2}\mathbf{j}$

The sine and cosine in this example give nice values, so evaluate them (sometimes it's better to leave them unevaluated to give exact results).

Calculating the angle between two vectors

The angle between two vectors **a** and **b** can be calculated by constructing a triangle with **a** and **b** as two of its sides. First calculate the **magnitude** of these vectors, and then use the **cosine rule** to find the angle between them.

Example 7

Find the angle θ between the vectors $\overrightarrow{PQ} = 3\mathbf{i} - \mathbf{j}$ and $\overrightarrow{PR} = -\mathbf{i} + 4\mathbf{j}$.

$|\overrightarrow{PQ}| = \sqrt{3^2 + (-1)^2} = \sqrt{10}$ and $|\overrightarrow{PR}| = \sqrt{(-1)^2 + 4^2} = \sqrt{17}$

Work out the lengths of $\overrightarrow{PQ}$ and $\overrightarrow{PR}$.

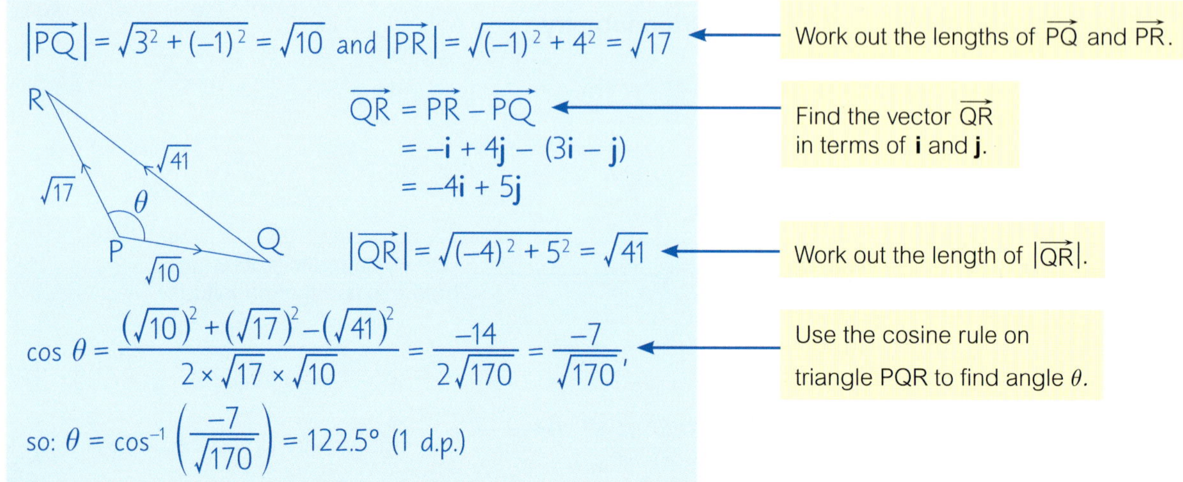

$\overrightarrow{QR} = \overrightarrow{PR} - \overrightarrow{PQ}$
$= -\mathbf{i} + 4\mathbf{j} - (3\mathbf{i} - \mathbf{j})$
$= -4\mathbf{i} + 5\mathbf{j}$

Find the vector $\overrightarrow{QR}$ in terms of **i** and **j**.

$|\overrightarrow{QR}| = \sqrt{(-4)^2 + 5^2} = \sqrt{41}$

Work out the length of $|\overrightarrow{QR}|$.

$$\cos\theta = \frac{(\sqrt{10})^2 + (\sqrt{17})^2 - (\sqrt{41})^2}{2 \times \sqrt{17} \times \sqrt{10}} = \frac{-14}{2\sqrt{170}} = \frac{-7}{\sqrt{170}},$$

Use the cosine rule on triangle PQR to find angle θ.

so: $\theta = \cos^{-1}\left(\frac{-7}{\sqrt{170}}\right) = 122.5°$ (1 d.p.)

Exercise 12.3

Q1 For each of the following vectors, find: (i) the exact magnitude, (ii) the direction (to 2 d.p.)

a) $6\mathbf{i} + 8\mathbf{j}$ b) $12\mathbf{i} - 5\mathbf{j}$ c) $\begin{pmatrix} 2 \\ 4 \end{pmatrix}$ d) $\begin{pmatrix} -3 \\ -1 \end{pmatrix}$

e) $\begin{pmatrix} 24 \\ -7 \end{pmatrix}$ f) $\begin{pmatrix} -\sqrt{13} \\ 6 \end{pmatrix}$ g) $3\mathbf{i} + \sqrt{7}\,\mathbf{jw}$ h) $-7\mathbf{j}$

Q2 S has position vector $10\mathbf{i} + 5\mathbf{j}$. Find the exact length of the line that joins point S to the origin.

Q3 Find the distance between each of the following pairs of points using position vectors:

a) (0, 1) and (2, 2) b) (–3, 2) and (4, 3) c) (–1, –1) and (0, 4)

Q4 For each of the pairs of vectors given below, find the exact magnitude of the resultant when the two vectors are added together.

a) $\mathbf{a} = 2\mathbf{i} + \mathbf{j}$ and $\mathbf{b} = 2\mathbf{i} - 4\mathbf{j}$ b) $\mathbf{u} = -5\mathbf{i} + \mathbf{j}$ and $\mathbf{v} = 9\mathbf{i} - 5\mathbf{j}$

c) $\mathbf{f} = \begin{pmatrix} 7 \\ 2 \end{pmatrix}$ and $\mathbf{g} = \begin{pmatrix} 17 \\ -12 \end{pmatrix}$ d) $\mathbf{d} = \begin{pmatrix} 4 \\ -2 \end{pmatrix}$ and $\mathbf{e} = \begin{pmatrix} -1 \\ -4 \end{pmatrix}$

e) $\mathbf{s} = 3\mathbf{i} - 4\mathbf{j}$ and $\mathbf{t} = -(3\mathbf{i} + \mathbf{j})$ f) $\mathbf{w} = \begin{pmatrix} -3 \\ -5 \end{pmatrix}$ and $\mathbf{x} = \begin{pmatrix} -6 \\ 5 \end{pmatrix}$

Q5 For each of the following vectors, give the unit vector in the same direction:

a) $3\mathbf{i}$ b) $\begin{pmatrix} 1 \\ 2 \end{pmatrix}$ c) $5\mathbf{i} - 4\mathbf{j}$ d) $\begin{pmatrix} -2 \\ -6 \end{pmatrix}$

E Q6 The points A and B have position vectors $\overrightarrow{OA} = \mathbf{i} + \mathbf{j}$ and $\overrightarrow{OB} = 3\mathbf{i} - 2\mathbf{j}$.

a) Find the vector $\overrightarrow{AB}$. *[2 marks]*

b) (i) Find the magnitude of the vector $\overrightarrow{AB}$ as a surd. *[2 marks]*

(ii) Find the direction of the vector $\overrightarrow{AB}$.
Give your answer in degrees to 1 decimal place. *[2 marks]*

c) Find the exact unit vector in the direction of $\overrightarrow{AB}$.
Give your answer in the form $a\mathbf{i} + b\mathbf{j}$. *[1 mark]*

Q7 $\overrightarrow{AB} = 3\mathbf{i} - 2\mathbf{j}$ and $\overrightarrow{BC} = \mathbf{i} + 5\mathbf{j}$. Find the unit vector in the direction of $\overrightarrow{AC}$.

Q8 Point A has position vector $2\mathbf{i} - \mathbf{j}$, and point B has position vector $7\mathbf{i} - 13\mathbf{j}$.
Find the unit vector in the direction of $\overrightarrow{BA}$.

E P Q9 Points A and B have position vectors $7\mathbf{i}$ and $5\mathbf{i} - 2\mathbf{j}$ respectively.

a) Find vector $\overrightarrow{AB}$. *[2 marks]*

b) (i) Find the position vector for M, the midpoint of the line joining A and B. *[2 marks]*

(ii) Hence find the unit vector in the direction $\overrightarrow{OM}$.
Give your answer in the form $a\mathbf{i} + b\mathbf{j}$. *[3 marks]*

Q10 By finding the horizontal and vertical components, express these vectors in exact **i**, **j** form:

a) **a** has direction 45° and magnitude $\sqrt{2}$ b) **b** has direction 60° and magnitude $\sqrt{7}$

c) **c** has direction 33° and magnitude 3 d) **d** has direction 76° and magnitude 5

P Q11 Vector **c** has the same direction as vector **d**. Given that $\mathbf{d} = 8\mathbf{i} - 6\mathbf{j}$ and $|\mathbf{c}| = 70$, find vector **c**.

E P Q12 Point Q has position vector $3\mathbf{i} + n\mathbf{j}$.
Given that the vector makes an angle of 30° above the x-axis, find the value of n. *[2 marks]*

P Q13 The vector $\mathbf{v} = a\mathbf{i} - 4\mathbf{j}$ makes an angle of 51° below the x-axis. Find $|\mathbf{v}|$ to 2 d.p.

E P Q14 Point P has position vector $\overrightarrow{OP} = m\mathbf{i} + n\mathbf{j}$, where both $m, n > 0$.
Given that the vector makes an angle of 30° above the x-axis, and $|\overrightarrow{OP}| = 6$, find the exact values of m and n. *[3 marks]*

P Q15 $|\overrightarrow{AB}| = 12$ and $|\overrightarrow{BC}| = 14$ and the angle between vectors $\overrightarrow{AB}$ and $\overrightarrow{BC}$ is 115°.
Find $|\overrightarrow{CA}|$ to 2 d.p.

E P Q16 PQRS is a quadrilateral where $\overrightarrow{OP} = \begin{pmatrix} -4 \\ -5 \end{pmatrix}$, $\overrightarrow{OQ} = \begin{pmatrix} -5 \\ 1 \end{pmatrix}$, $\overrightarrow{OR} = \begin{pmatrix} 1 \\ 5 \end{pmatrix}$ and $\overrightarrow{OS} = \begin{pmatrix} 8 \\ 3 \end{pmatrix}$.

a) Find the exact lengths of the diagonals of PQRS. *[3 marks]*

b) Show that QR is parallel to PS, and hence show that PQRS is a trapezium. *[4 marks]*

P M Q17 Two boats set off from a harbour. Each boat's course is modelled by a vector.
Boat A's course is given by $\mathbf{a} = \begin{pmatrix} 3 \\ 3 \end{pmatrix}$ and Boat B's by $\mathbf{b} = \begin{pmatrix} -2 \\ 5 \end{pmatrix}$.
What is the angle (to 2 d.p.) between the two boats' courses?

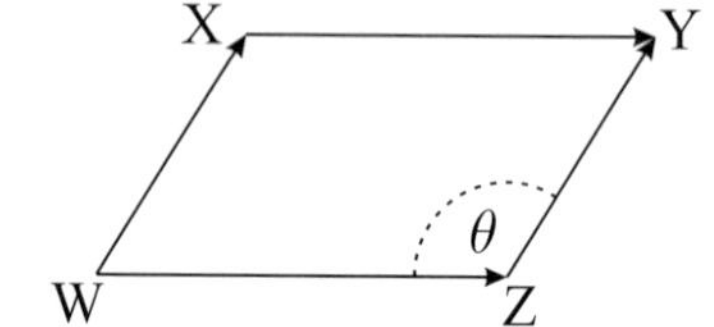

P Q18 The diagram to the right shows a parallelogram WXYZ.
Given $\overrightarrow{WX} = 2\mathbf{i} + 5\mathbf{j}$ and $\overrightarrow{WZ} = 8\mathbf{i}$, what is angle θ (to 1 d.p.)?

Challenge

E P Q19 Points A and B have position vectors, $\overrightarrow{OA} = \begin{pmatrix} 5 \\ 2 \end{pmatrix}$ and $\overrightarrow{OB} = \begin{pmatrix} 7 \\ \alpha \end{pmatrix}$.
Given that $|\overrightarrow{AB}| = 2\sqrt{5}$, find the two possible values of α. *[6 marks]*

E P Q20 Points P, Q and R form a triangle and have position vectors $\begin{pmatrix} 2 \\ -1 \end{pmatrix}$, $\begin{pmatrix} 5 \\ 2 \end{pmatrix}$ and $\begin{pmatrix} 6 \\ -3 \end{pmatrix}$ respectively.
Find angle PQR, giving your answer to 1 decimal place. *[6 marks]*

P Q21 Points A, B and C have position vectors $\begin{pmatrix} 1 \\ -2 \end{pmatrix}$, $\begin{pmatrix} 4 \\ -1 \end{pmatrix}$ and $\begin{pmatrix} 3 \\ -4 \end{pmatrix}$ respectively.

a) Show that ABC is an isosceles triangle.

b) Find angle ABC.

c) Hence or otherwise, find the area of the triangle ABC.

12.4 Modelling with Vectors

M

An object's **motion** will have a **magnitude** and **direction**, so can be modelled using vectors:

Displacement is the **distance** an object has travelled in a given **direction**.

- **Velocity** is the **speed** of an object with a **direction**.
- **Acceleration** is the rate at which an object's **velocity changes**.
- **Forces** can also be modelled with vectors.

Tip Be careful — the word acceleration could refer to the vector **a** or its magnitude |**a**|.

Example 1

The acceleration of a particle is given by the vector $\mathbf{a} = (6\mathbf{i} - 2\mathbf{j})\ \text{ms}^{-2}$.
Find the magnitude of the acceleration, and the angle this vector makes with the horizontal axis.

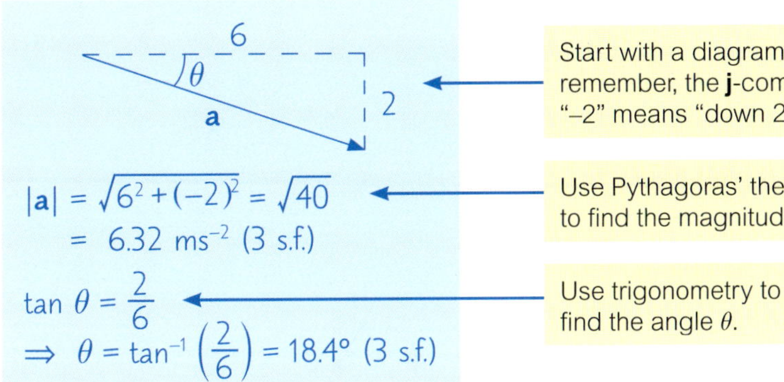

$|\mathbf{a}| = \sqrt{6^2 + (-2)^2} = \sqrt{40}$
$= 6.32\ \text{ms}^{-2}$ (3 s.f.)

$\tan\theta = \frac{2}{6}$
$\Rightarrow \theta = \tan^{-1}\left(\frac{2}{6}\right) = 18.4°$ (3 s.f.)

Start with a diagram — remember, the **j**-component "–2" means "down 2".

Use Pythagoras' theorem to find the magnitude.

Use trigonometry to find the angle θ.

Problem Solving Make sure you pay attention to whether the components are positive or negative — this tells you which direction the vector acts in.

Example 2

A ball's velocity is modelled by vector $\mathbf{v} = (x\mathbf{i} - y\mathbf{j})\ \text{ms}^{-1}$, with a magnitude of $4\ \text{ms}^{-1}$ and direction of 40° below the positive x-axis. Find the x and y components of vector **v**, giving your answer to 4 s.f.

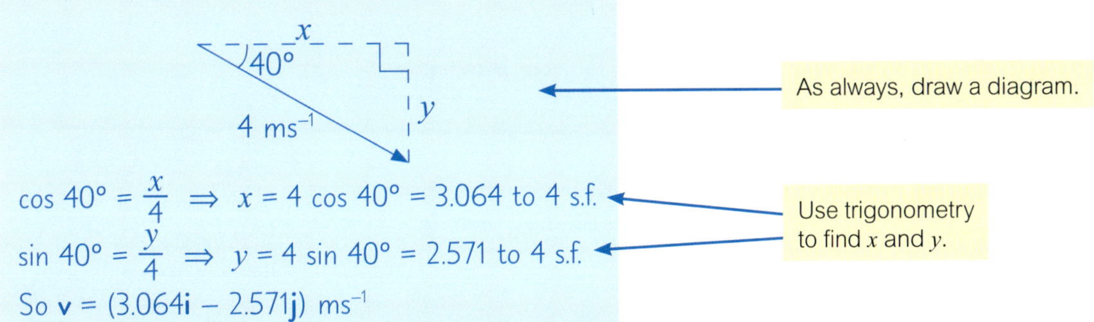

$\cos 40° = \frac{x}{4} \Rightarrow x = 4\cos 40° = 3.064$ to 4 s.f.

$\sin 40° = \frac{y}{4} \Rightarrow y = 4\sin 40° = 2.571$ to 4 s.f.

So $\mathbf{v} = (3.064\mathbf{i} - 2.571\mathbf{j})\ \text{ms}^{-1}$

As always, draw a diagram.

Use trigonometry to find x and y.

The effect of **two forces** working together can also be modelled by vectors.

These two vectors will probably form a triangle **without** a **right angle**, so you will need to use the **sine rule** (p.177) and **cosine rule** (p.180) for the trigonometry involved.

The size of a force is the magnitude of the vector that represents it.

Example 3

Two tug boats are pulling a ship with an angle of 30° between them. One tug boat exerts a force of 10 kN and is modelled with vector **a**. The other boat exerts a force of 12 kN and is modelled with vector **b**.

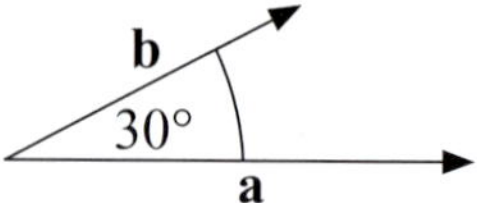

The resultant force on the ship, **r**, is the resultant vector of these two forces. Calculate the size of the resultant force.

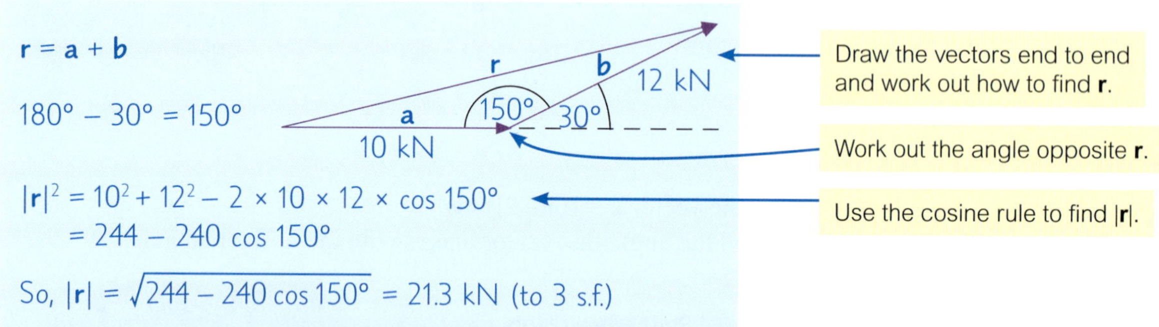

Vectors can also be used to model **lines** and the **sides of polygons** when investigating problems in geometry.

Example 4

The routes from Ayeside to Beesville ($\overrightarrow{AB}$) and to Ceeston ($\overrightarrow{AC}$) are modelled by the vectors **p** and **q** respectively. Shazia's house lies between Beesville and Ceeston such that its position, X, divides the line BC in the ratio 2 : 5.

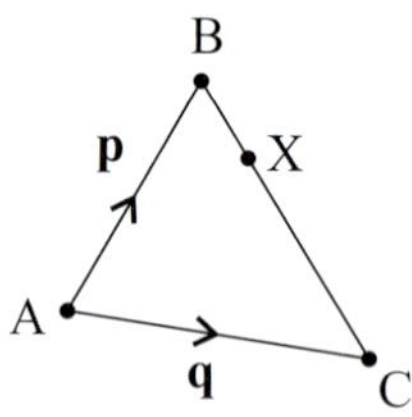

Find the vector $\overrightarrow{AX}$ in terms of **p** and **q**.

$\overrightarrow{AX} = \overrightarrow{AB} + \overrightarrow{BX}$ ← Work out how to find $\overrightarrow{AX}$.

$\overrightarrow{BC} = \overrightarrow{BA} + \overrightarrow{AC} = -\overrightarrow{AB} + \overrightarrow{AC}$

$= -\mathbf{p} + \mathbf{q}$ ← Find $\overrightarrow{BC}$ in terms of **p** and **q**.

BX is $\frac{2}{2+5} = \frac{2}{7}$ of BC,

so $\overrightarrow{BX} = \frac{2}{7}\overrightarrow{BC}$ ← X divides BC in the ratio 2 : 5, so work out $\overrightarrow{BX}$ in terms of $\overrightarrow{BC}$.

$\overrightarrow{AX} = \overrightarrow{AB} + \overrightarrow{BX} = \overrightarrow{AB} + \frac{2}{7}\overrightarrow{BC}$

$= \mathbf{p} + \frac{2}{7}(-\mathbf{p} + \mathbf{q}) = \frac{5}{7}\mathbf{p} + \frac{2}{7}\mathbf{q}$ ← You know $\overrightarrow{AB} = \mathbf{p}$, so plug all this into your equation for $\overrightarrow{AX}$.

Problem Solving

'X divides BC in the ratio 2 : 5' means X is $\frac{2}{7}$ of the way from B to C.
'X divides CB in the ratio 2 : 5' would mean X is $\frac{2}{7}$ of the way from C to B.

You might also come across ratio questions **without** contexts — e.g. "P divides the vector $\overrightarrow{QR}$ in the ratio 1 : 3".

Example 5

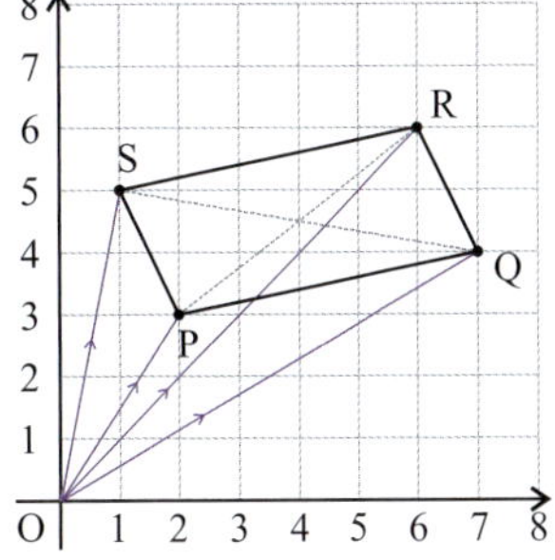

The position vectors of the vertices of the parallelogram PQRS are: $\overrightarrow{OP} = 2\mathbf{i} + 3\mathbf{j}$, $\overrightarrow{OQ} = 7\mathbf{i} + 4\mathbf{j}$, $\overrightarrow{OR} = 6(\mathbf{i} + \mathbf{j})$ and $\overrightarrow{OS} = \mathbf{i} + 5\mathbf{j}$.
What are the exact lengths of this parallelogram's diagonals?

$\overrightarrow{PR} = \overrightarrow{OR} - \overrightarrow{OP} = 6(\mathbf{i} + \mathbf{j}) - (2\mathbf{i} + 3\mathbf{j})$
$= 4\mathbf{i} + 3\mathbf{j}$

$\overrightarrow{SQ} = \overrightarrow{OQ} - \overrightarrow{OS} = (7\mathbf{i} + 4\mathbf{j}) - (\mathbf{i} + 5\mathbf{j})$
$= 6\mathbf{i} - \mathbf{j}$

Find the diagonals in terms of **i** and **j**.

$|\overrightarrow{PR}| = \sqrt{4^2 + 3^2} = \sqrt{25} = 5$

$|\overrightarrow{SQ}| = \sqrt{6^2 + (-1)^2} = \sqrt{37}$

Use Pythagoras' theorem to find the lengths of the diagonals.

Vectors are also really useful for modelling the **direction** something is **travelling** in — like the course of a ship or a plane's flight path.

The **bearing** the vehicle travels on can be used to calculate the vector's **direction**. The **distance** it travels is the **magnitude** of its **displacement vector**, and its **speed** is the magnitude of its **velocity vector**.

Example 6

A ship travels 75 km on a bearing of 140°. The ship's displacement is modelled by the vector $\mathbf{d} = \begin{pmatrix} x \\ y \end{pmatrix}$.
Calculate x and y (to 2 d.p.).

140°
x
50°
y
d
75 km

Draw a diagram.

$140° - 90° = 50°$

This shows you that the angle **d** makes with the positive x-axis is 50°.

$\cos 50° = \frac{x}{75} \Rightarrow x = 75 \cos 50°$
$= 48.21$ (2 d.p.)

$\sin 50° = \frac{y}{75} \Rightarrow y = 75 \sin 50°$
$= 57.45$ (2 d.p.)

Use trigonometry to find x and y.

$\mathbf{d} = \begin{pmatrix} 48.21 \\ -57.45 \end{pmatrix}$ km

The y component of **d** should be negative.

Exercise 12.4

Give all answers to 1 decimal place unless otherwise stated.

M Q1 The accelerations of various particles are given by the vectors below. Calculate the exact magnitude of each particle's acceleration.

a) $\mathbf{a} = (\mathbf{i} + 2\mathbf{j})$ ms^{-2} b) $\mathbf{b} = (-\mathbf{i} - \mathbf{j})$ ms^{-2}

c) $\mathbf{c} = (3\mathbf{i} + 2\mathbf{j})$ ms^{-2} d) $\mathbf{d} = (-2\mathbf{i} + 3\mathbf{j})$ ms^{-2}

M Q2 The quadrilateral ABCD on the right is used to model a garden. There is a straight path that crosses the garden. Its start point divides $\overrightarrow{AB}$ in the ratio 7 : 3, and it ends at the midpoint of $\overrightarrow{CD}$.

The path is modelled by vector $\mathbf{p} = \begin{pmatrix} x \\ y \end{pmatrix}$. Calculate x and y.

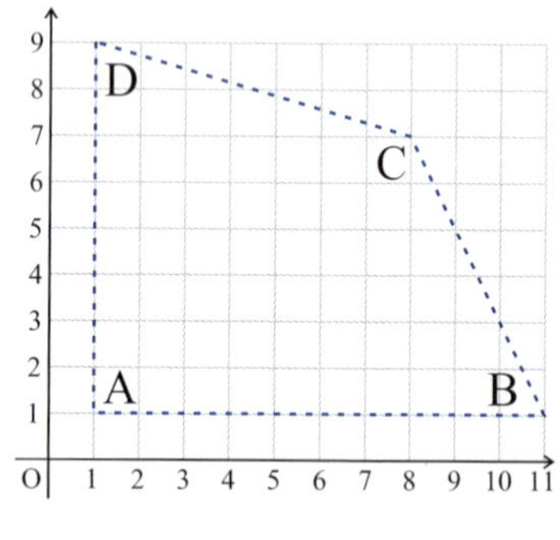

P M Q3 A simple mathematical model of a ball bouncing off the side of a pool table is constructed using vectors. The ball's velocity has vector $\mathbf{v}_1 = \begin{pmatrix} 3 \\ -2 \end{pmatrix}$ before it hits the side, and vector $\mathbf{v}_2 = \begin{pmatrix} 1 \\ 3 \end{pmatrix}$ afterwards. Find the acute angle θ between $\mathbf{v}_1$ and $\mathbf{v}_2$. Give your answer to 2 d.p.

M Q4 The velocity of a fish swimming in the horizontal plane is modelled by a vector $\mathbf{v} = 2t(2\mathbf{i} - \mathbf{j})$ ms^{-1}, where t is time in seconds.

a) State the fish's velocity after 2 seconds.

b) Calculate the fish's exact speed after 3 seconds.

c) Find the direction of the vector $\mathbf{v}$.

Tip The direction of a vector is usually measured anticlockwise from the positive horizontal.

P M Q5 A firework's displacement is modelled by the vector $\mathbf{s} = 2t^2(-\mathbf{i} + 7\mathbf{j})$ m, where t is time in seconds, $\mathbf{i}$ is horizontal and $\mathbf{j}$ is vertical (pointing upwards).

a) Find the firework's displacement after 1.5 seconds.

b) Calculate, to 3 s.f., the direction of the firework above the horizontal.

The firework explodes after 2.5 seconds.

c) What is the firework's vertical distance from the ground when it goes off?

M Q6 A roller coaster is accelerating at 30 ms^{-2} at an angle of 35° above the negative horizontal. Express this acceleration as a vector of the form $\mathbf{a} = x\mathbf{i} + y\mathbf{j}$, giving x and y to 2 decimal places.

P M Q7 A park is modelled as a quadrilateral EFGH, with sides given by the vectors $\overrightarrow{EF} = 2\mathbf{i} + 3\mathbf{j}$, $\overrightarrow{FG} = \mathbf{i} - \frac{1}{2}\mathbf{j}$, $\overrightarrow{GH} = -\mathbf{i} - \frac{3}{2}\mathbf{j}$ and $\overrightarrow{HE} = -2\mathbf{i} - \mathbf{j}$. Show that the park is a trapezium.

E P M Q8 Points P, Q and R form a triangle and have position vectors $(2\mathbf{i} + \mathbf{j})$ m, $(3\mathbf{i} - 2\mathbf{j})$ m and $(3\mathbf{i} - 4\mathbf{j})$ m respectively. The three points model the shape of a flowerbed.

a) Find the perimeter of the flowerbed. *[5 marks]*

b) Find the largest angle in PQR. *[3 marks]*

c) Hence or otherwise, find the area of the flowerbed. *[2 marks]*

P M Q9 An aircraft is attempting to fly due north at 600 km/h, but there is a wind from the west at 75 km/h. The aircraft's actual course is modelled by the resultant of these two vectors. Calculate:

a) the actual bearing the plane is flying on.

b) the aircraft's resultant speed in km/h (to 2 d.p.).

P M Q10 Two lumberjacks are pulling ropes attached to a tree. The angle between the ropes is 100°, and the lumberjacks exert forces of 250 N and 210 N respectively. The resultant force, **f**, is modelled by the resultant of these two vectors. Calculate the magnitude of **f**.

E P M Q11 Shoaib is parachuting and is slowly descending vertically with a constant velocity of 4.8 ms^{-1}. A cross wind starts to blow him westwards at a speed of 2 ms^{-1} while he continues to descend.

a) Express the velocity vector that models Shoaib's descent in the form $(a\mathbf{i} + b\mathbf{j})$ ms^{-1}, where **i** is due East and **j** is vertically upwards. *[1 mark]*

b) Find the angle Shoaib's motion makes with the positive **j** direction. *[3 marks]*

P M Q12 The position vectors of the vertices of the parallelogram PQRS are $\overrightarrow{OP} = 2\mathbf{i} + 3\mathbf{j}$, $\overrightarrow{OQ} = 7\mathbf{i} + 4\mathbf{j}$, $\overrightarrow{OR} = 6(\mathbf{i} + \mathbf{j})$ and $\overrightarrow{OS} = \mathbf{i} + 5\mathbf{j}$. What are the exact lengths of this parallelogram's diagonals?

M Q13 Ray is attempting to paddle his canoe due north at 4 ms^{-1}, but there is a current travelling west at 3 ms^{-1}. Ray's actual course is modelled by the resultant of these two vectors. Calculate:

a) the actual bearing Ray is travelling on.

b) Ray's resultant speed in ms^{-1}.

Challenge

P M Q14 In the diagram to the right, W divides QR in the ratio $a:b$. Given that $\overrightarrow{PW} = \frac{5}{9}\mathbf{s} + \frac{4}{9}\mathbf{t}$, find a and b.

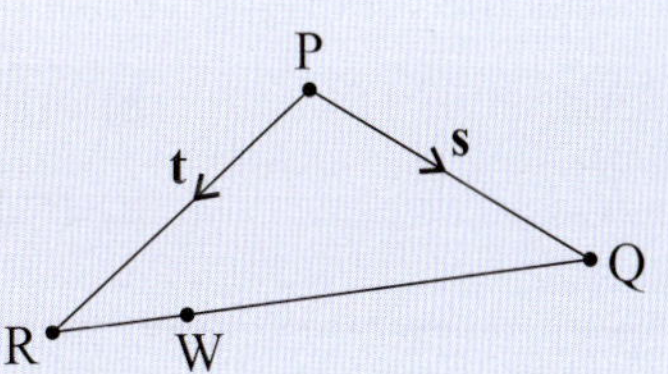

E P M Q15 The diagram below shows two particles moving from the same point with constant velocities, given by $\mathbf{a} = (-3\mathbf{i} + 2\mathbf{j})$ ms^{-1} and $\mathbf{b} = (2\mathbf{i} + 4\mathbf{j})$ ms^{-1}.

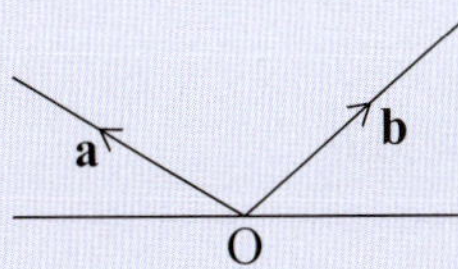

a) Find the angle between vectors **a** and **b**. *[3 marks]*

b) Find the distance separating the particles after 3 seconds of motion. *[4 marks]*

12 Review Exercise

Give all answers to 1 decimal place unless otherwise stated.

Q1 Vectors **a** and **b** are represented by the lines to the right. Draw and label sketches that represent the following vectors:

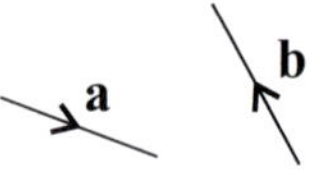

a) –**b** b) 3**a** c) **a** + **b** d) 2**a** – **b** e) **b** – **a**

Q2 Using the diagram on the right, find these vectors in terms of vectors **a**, **b** and **c**.

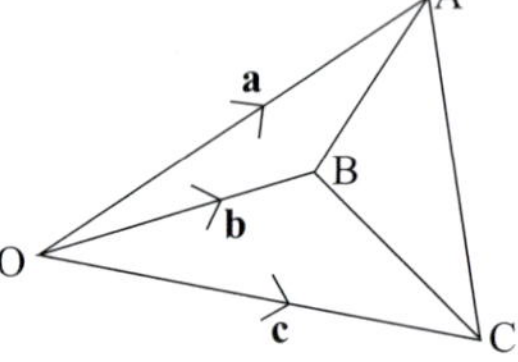

a) $\overrightarrow{AB}$ b) $\overrightarrow{BA}$ c) $\overrightarrow{CB}$ d) $\overrightarrow{AC}$

E Q3 A triangle PQR is defined by the vectors: $\overrightarrow{PQ} = \mathbf{a}$ and $\overrightarrow{RQ} = \mathbf{b}$. Express the following vectors in terms of **a** and **b**:

a) $\overrightarrow{QR}$ *[1 mark]*

b) $\overrightarrow{RP}$ *[1 mark]*

c) $\overrightarrow{PR}$ *[1 mark]*

Q4 Give two vectors that are parallel to each of the following:

a) 2**a** b) 3**i** + 4**j** c) 3**i** – **j** d) $\begin{pmatrix} 3 \\ 5 \end{pmatrix}$

Q5 In the triangle on the right, M is the midpoint of $\overrightarrow{AB}$ and P is the midpoint of $\overrightarrow{AC}$. $\overrightarrow{CB} = 6\mathbf{p}$ and $\overrightarrow{CA} = 4\mathbf{q}$. Express the following vectors in terms of **p** and **q**:

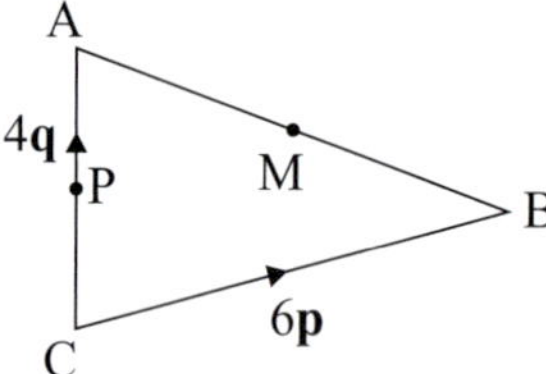

a) $\overrightarrow{AB}$ b) $\overrightarrow{AP}$

c) $\overrightarrow{AM}$ d) $\overrightarrow{PM}$

P Q6 STU is a triangle, where $\overrightarrow{ST} = 4\mathbf{a}$ and $\overrightarrow{UT} = 3\mathbf{b} - \mathbf{a}$. Point M is the midpoint of line ST and point P divides line SU in the ratio 3 : 1.

Find the vector $\overrightarrow{PM}$ in terms of **a** and **b**.

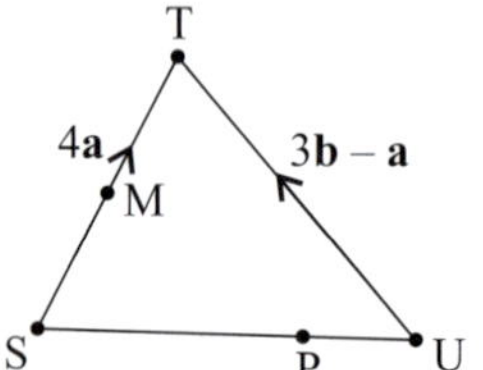

E P Q7 $\overrightarrow{AC} = \mathbf{q}$, $\overrightarrow{BC} = \mathbf{q} - \mathbf{p}$ and $\overrightarrow{AD} = \mathbf{p}$. Show that the points B, C and D are collinear. *[3 marks]*

E P **Q8** In the triangle on the right, $\overrightarrow{AB} = \mathbf{p}$ and $\overrightarrow{AC} = \mathbf{q}$.
It is given that $2\overrightarrow{BM} = 3\overrightarrow{MC}$ and $\overrightarrow{AN}:\overrightarrow{AC} = 3:5$.

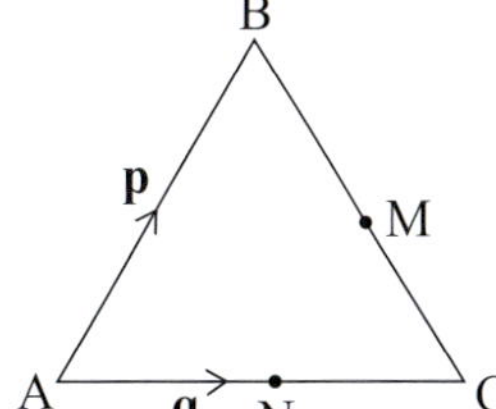

a) Show that $\overrightarrow{AB}$ is parallel to $\overrightarrow{NM}$. *[4 marks]*

b) Hence find the ratio $\overrightarrow{AB}:\overrightarrow{NM}$. *[1 mark]*

Q9 Show that the points X, Y and Z are collinear for each of the following sets of vectors:

a) $\overrightarrow{XY} = 2\mathbf{b} - \mathbf{a}$, $\overrightarrow{OY} = 2\mathbf{b}$, $\overrightarrow{OZ} = 2(\mathbf{a} - \mathbf{b})$

b) $\overrightarrow{OX} = 3\mathbf{p}$, $\overrightarrow{OY} = \mathbf{q}$, $\overrightarrow{OZ} = 4\mathbf{q} - 9\mathbf{p}$

Q10 Given that $\mathbf{d} = \begin{pmatrix} 3 \\ 2 \end{pmatrix}$, $\mathbf{e} = \begin{pmatrix} -1 \\ -2 \end{pmatrix}$, and $\mathbf{f} = \begin{pmatrix} 3 \\ -1 \end{pmatrix}$, find the following vectors:

a) $2\mathbf{d} - \mathbf{f}$

b) $\mathbf{d} - \mathbf{e} - \mathbf{f}$

c) $\mathbf{f} - 3\mathbf{d} + \mathbf{e}$

d) $-2\mathbf{e} + \mathbf{d} - \mathbf{f}$

Q11 X is the point (6, –1) and Y is the point (–4, 7).
Write the vectors $\overrightarrow{XO}$ and $\overrightarrow{YO}$ in **i** and **j** form and in column vector form.

E **Q12** Points P and Q have position vectors $\mathbf{i} - 2\mathbf{j}$ and $3\mathbf{i} + 5\mathbf{j}$ respectively.

a) Find vector $\overrightarrow{PQ}$. *[2 marks]*

b) Find the unit vector in the direction of $\overrightarrow{PQ}$.
Give your answer in the form $a\mathbf{i} + b\mathbf{j}$ with exact values of a and b. *[3 marks]*

Q13 R has position vector $\begin{pmatrix} 3 \\ -1 \end{pmatrix}$ and S has position vector $\begin{pmatrix} -5 \\ -7 \end{pmatrix}$.
Find the magnitude of $\overrightarrow{RS}$.

E **Q14** Given $\overrightarrow{OM} = -7\mathbf{i} + 6\mathbf{j}$ and $\overrightarrow{ON} = 3\mathbf{i} + 3\mathbf{j}$, find:

a) $\overrightarrow{MN}$ *[2 marks]*

b) $|\overrightarrow{MN}|$ *[2 marks]*

E P **Q15** Given $\overrightarrow{BA} = \mathbf{i} + \mathbf{j}$ and $\overrightarrow{BC} = 3\mathbf{i} - 2\mathbf{j}$, find the exact magnitude of vector $\overrightarrow{AC}$. *[4 marks]*

P **Q16** If $\mathbf{p} = 5\mathbf{i} - 12\mathbf{j}$ and vector **q** is parallel to **p** with magnitude 65, find the vector **q**.

E Q17 Given that $|\overrightarrow{AB}| = 10$, $|\overrightarrow{AC}| = 12$ and angle BAC is 50°:

a) Find the area of triangle ABC. Give your answer to 2 decimal places. *[2 marks]*

b) Find $|\overrightarrow{CB}|$. Give your answer to 2 decimal places. *[2 marks]*

E P Q18 Vector **c** is parallel to vector **d**. Given that $\mathbf{d} = 6\mathbf{i} - 9\mathbf{j}$ and $|\mathbf{c}| = \sqrt{13}$, find **c**. *[4 marks]*

E Q19 Given $\mathbf{a} = -3\mathbf{i} + 4\mathbf{j}$ and $\mathbf{b} = \mathbf{i} + 2\mathbf{j}$:

a) Work out $-5\mathbf{a} + 2\mathbf{b}$. *[2 marks]*

b) Find the magnitude and direction of **a**. *[4 marks]*

P Q20 A has position vector $\begin{pmatrix} 2 \\ -3 \end{pmatrix}$ and B has position vector $\begin{pmatrix} x \\ 1 \end{pmatrix}$.

Given that $|\overrightarrow{AB}| = 5$, and the direction of $\overrightarrow{OB}$ is less than 90°, find x.

Q21 $\mathbf{v} = 4\mathbf{i} - 6\mathbf{j}$ and $\mathbf{u} = -\mathbf{i} - 3\mathbf{j}$. Find the angle between **v** and **u** to two decimal places.

E M Q22 The velocity of a particle can be modelled by the vectors $\mathbf{u} = \begin{pmatrix} 6 \\ -2 \end{pmatrix}$ ms^{-1}

before striking the horizontal floor and $\mathbf{v} = \begin{pmatrix} 3 \\ 1 \end{pmatrix}$ ms^{-1} after rebounding.

a) Find the acute angle at which the particle strikes the horizontal floor. *[2 marks]*

b) Find the exact magnitude of velocity **v**. *[2 marks]*

c) Find the angle θ between **u** and **v**. *[2 marks]*

E P M Q23 The acceleration of a pigeon as it descends from the top of a skyscraper can be modelled by the vector $\mathbf{a} = (5\mathbf{i} - 2\mathbf{j})$ ms^{-2}.

a) Find the angle of the pigeon's acceleration measured clockwise from the positive **i** direction. *[2 marks]*

The pigeon's velocity is modelled by the vector $\begin{pmatrix} 5t \\ -2t \end{pmatrix}$ ms^{-1} where t is the time in seconds.

b) Find the exact speed of the pigeon after 5 seconds. Give your answer as a simplified surd. *[3 marks]*

E P M Q24 After releasing the brake, the velocity of a mobility vehicle can be modelled by the vector $\mathbf{v} = \left(2t\mathbf{i} + \frac{1}{3}t\mathbf{j}\right)$ ms^{-1}, where t is measured in seconds.

a) Find the exact speed of the mobility vehicle after 3 seconds. *[2 marks]*

b) Find the direction of the mobility vehicle as a bearing where vector **j** is north. *[3 marks]*

M Q25 A girl cycles along a bearing of 171° with speed 16 km/h.
Find her velocity in terms of **i** and **j**, where **i** and **j** are the unit vectors directed due east and due north respectively. Give your answer to 3 significant figures.

E P M Q26 Davina is swimming due east at 1.5 ms^{-1}. At the same time there is a water current moving Davina south at 1 ms^{-1}. Her velocity and position can be modelled using vectors.

a) Express her velocity as a column vector, where north is parallel to $\begin{pmatrix} 0 \\ 1 \end{pmatrix}$. *[1 mark]*

b) Find the bearing of Davina's direction of motion. *[3 marks]*

c) Assuming her velocity remains constant, find the exact distance Davina travels during the first 10 seconds. Give your answer as a simplified surd. *[3 marks]*

E P M Q27 The motion of a glider can be modelled as travelling due south at 20 ms^{-1} with a crosswind blowing the glider west with a velocity of 4 ms^{-1}. North is in the positive **j** direction.

a) Express the velocity of the glider in the form $\mathbf{v} = (n\mathbf{i} + m\mathbf{j})$ ms^{-1}. *[1 mark]*

b) Calculate the speed of the glider, giving your answer to 3 significant figures. *[2 marks]*

c) Calculate the distance travelled by the glider after 8 seconds, giving your answer to 3 significant figures. *[2 marks]*

E P M Q28 Points A, B and C form a triangle with position vectors $\overrightarrow{OA} = \mathbf{i} + \mathbf{j}$, $\overrightarrow{OB} = 2\mathbf{i} - 1.5\mathbf{j}$ and $\overrightarrow{OC} = 1.5\mathbf{i} - 2.5\mathbf{j}$ respectively. The three points form a triangle, modelling the design for a table top. The units of the vectors are in metres.

a) Find the perimeter of the table top, to 3 significant figures. *[5 marks]*

b) Find the largest angle in ABC, to 3 significant figures. *[3 marks]*

c) Hence or otherwise, find the exact area of the table top. *[2 marks]*

E P M Q29 Two forces are acting on a particle P. The magnitude in newtons (N) and the direction of each force is shown on the diagram on the right.

Find the magnitude of the resultant force, R, to 3 signifcant figures. *[3 marks]*

Challenge

P Q30 Given the vectors $3\mathbf{a} + 2\mathbf{b} = \begin{pmatrix} 4 \\ 9 \end{pmatrix}$ and $-\mathbf{a} + 4\mathbf{b} = \begin{pmatrix} -6 \\ 11 \end{pmatrix}$,

find the values of p and q such that $p\mathbf{a} + q\mathbf{b} = \begin{pmatrix} 1 \\ 32 \end{pmatrix}$.

E P M Q31 A man wants to swim across a river. The current is flowing at 1.8 ms^{-1} parallel to the riverbank. Find the speed and direction that he needs to swim at for his resultant speed to be 1.2 ms^{-1} perpendicular to the riverbank. *[4 marks]*

12 Chapter Summary

1 Vectors are quantities with both magnitude and direction. They can be drawn as straight lines with arrowheads.

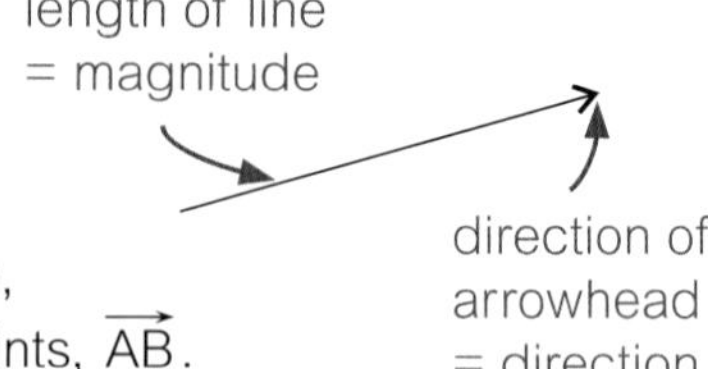

2 Vectors can be written as either a lowercase bold letter, **a**, or a lowercase underlined letter, $\underline{a}$. When the endpoints are given, the vector can also be written by putting an arrow over the endpoints, $\overrightarrow{AB}$.

3 Adding two vectors nose to tail creates a single resultant vector.

4 Multiplying a vector by a scalar changes the length:
- If the scalar is positive, the direction stays the same
- If the scalar is negative, the new vector points in the opposite direction

To 'divide' a vector, you multiply by the reciprocal of the scalar.

5 All parallel vectors are scalar multiples of each other.

6 Three points A, B and C are collinear (i.e. lie on a single straight line) if vectors $\overrightarrow{AB}$ and $\overrightarrow{BC}$ are parallel.

7 A position vector describes the position of a point in relation to the origin, O.

8 The standard unit vectors **i** and **j** each have length 1 in the directions of the positive x and y-axes respectively. Any 2D vector can be written as a sum of **i** and **j** vectors, e.g. $3\mathbf{i} + 4\mathbf{j}$.

9 You can also write the horizontal and vertical components of a vector in a column, e.g. $\begin{pmatrix} 3 \\ 4 \end{pmatrix}$

10 The magnitude (or modulus) of vector **a**, written $|\mathbf{a}|$, is the distance between its start point and end point. If you know the **i** and **j** components, you can calculate the modulus using Pythagoras' theorem.

11 The unit vector (of length 1) in the direction of the vector **a** is: $\frac{1}{|\mathbf{a}|}\mathbf{a} = \frac{\mathbf{a}}{|\mathbf{a}|}$.

12 The direction of a vector is usually measured anticlockwise from the positive x-axis. If you know the **i** and **j** components, you can find the direction by using trigonometry.

13 In general, a vector $\begin{pmatrix} x \\ y \end{pmatrix}$ has magnitude $\sqrt{x^2 + y^2}$ and makes an angle of $\tan^{-1}\left(\frac{y}{x}\right)$ with the horizontal.

14 An object's motion will have a magnitude and direction, so can be modelled using vectors.

Edexcel AS-Level Mathematics

Paper 1: Pure Mathematics

Time allowed: 2 hours

Centre name					
Centre number					
Candidate number					

Surname
Other names
Candidate signature

In addition to this paper you should have:

- An Edexcel booklet of Mathematical Formulae
- A calculator

Instructions to candidates

- Use black ink or ball-point pen.
- A pencil may be used for diagrams, sketches and graphs.
- Write your name and other details in the spaces provided above.
- Answer all questions in the spaces provided.
- Show clearly how you worked out your answers.
- Round answers to 3 significant figures unless otherwise stated.

Information for candidates

- There are 16 questions in this paper.
- There are 100 marks available for this paper.
- The marks available are given in brackets at the end of each question.
- You may get marks for method, even if your answer is incorrect.

Advice to candidates

- Work steadily through the paper and try to answer every question.
- Don't spend too long on one question.
- If you have time at the end, go back and check your answers.

For examiner's use			
Q	Mark	Q	Mark
1		9	
2		10	
3		11	
4		12	
5		13	
6		14	
7		15	
8		16	
Total			

Answer ALL the questions.

Q1 Given that $\mathbf{p} = \begin{pmatrix} -3 \\ 2 \end{pmatrix}$, $\mathbf{q} = \begin{pmatrix} 6 \\ 10 \end{pmatrix}$ and $\mathbf{r} = \begin{pmatrix} 3 \\ 2 \end{pmatrix}$, show that $3\mathbf{p} - 2\mathbf{q}$ is parallel to $\mathbf{r}$.

(2)

Q2 a) A student says that $\sqrt{x^2} = x$ for all x.
Prove by counter-example that the student's statement is incorrect.

(1)

b) Prove that when n is a positive even number,
$2n^2 + 2n + 6$ is never exactly divisible by 4.

(3)

Q3 Differentiate $f(x) = 4x^2 - 4x + 3$ from first principles.

(4)

Q4 Clearly showing your working, find the exact solution(s) of the equation:

$$2\log_5(2x - 1) = 1 + \log_5(3 - x)$$

(4)

Q5 $p(x) = 2x^3 + ax^2 + bx + 18$ is exactly divisible by $(x - 3)$ and $(x + 2)$, where a and b are integers.

a) By using the Factor Theorem, find the values of a and b.

(3)

b) Hence, fully factorise $p(x)$.

(1)

Q6 a) Find the integral $\int \frac{9x^2 - 3x^3}{\sqrt{x^3}}\,dx$. **(3)**

The diagram shows part of the graph of $f(x) = \frac{9x^2 - 3x^3}{\sqrt{x^3}}$.

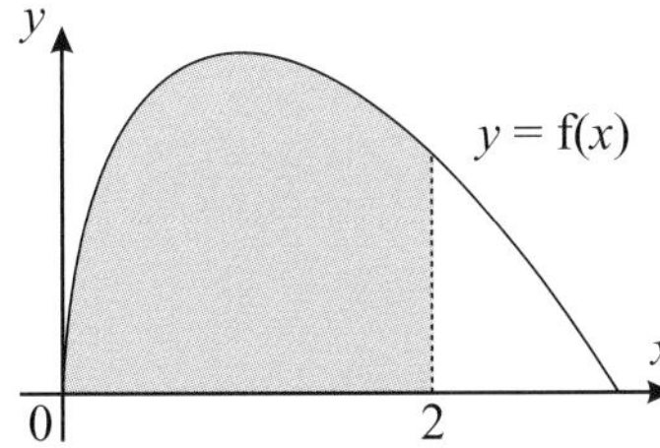

b) Given that f(x) passes through the origin, find the exact value of the area of the shaded region bounded by the curve f(x), the x-axis and the line $x = 2$. Give your answer in the form $p\sqrt{q}$, where p and q are rational numbers. **(3)**

Q7 A, B and C are the vertices of a triangle.

The position vectors of A and B are $\begin{pmatrix}1\\1\end{pmatrix}$ and $\begin{pmatrix}3\\7\end{pmatrix}$ respectively.

a) Find $\overrightarrow{AB}$ and $|\overrightarrow{AB}|$, giving your answer as a simplified surd where appropriate. **(3)**

b) Given that $|\overrightarrow{AC}| = 2\sqrt{3}$ and $|\overrightarrow{BC}| = 4$, find the angle at vertex A in degrees to one decimal place. **(2)**

c) Hence, find the area of the triangle ABC to one decimal place. **(2)**

Q8 The straight line l intersects the curve $f(x) = 2 - 6x + 8x^2 - 2x^3$ at two distinct points, P and Q. Given that l is a tangent to f(x) at P and the coordinates of P are (1, 2):

a) find the equation of line l, **(4)**

b) find the coordinates of point Q. **(3)**

Q9 a) Find the binomial expansion of $(2x + 3)^5$.

(4)

b) State the binomial expansion of $(2x - 3)^5$.

(1)

c) Hence solve the equation

$$(2x + 3)^5 - (2x - 3)^5 = 475x^4 + 2138x^2 + 501$$

(3)

Q10 Given that $f(x) = \dfrac{2x - 4}{4 - x}$

a) Show that $f(x) = a + \dfrac{b}{4 - x}$,
where a and b are integers to be found, clearly showing your working.

(2)

b) Sketch the graph of $y = f(x)$, clearly indicating on your diagram any points of intersection with the coordinate axes and any horizontal and vertical asymptotes.

(3)

Q11 During an experiment, the pressure inside two separate tanks filled with gas varies over time.

The pressure in tank P is modelled by the equation $p(t) = 72 + 10t - 2t^2$ and the pressure in tank Q is modelled by $q(t) = a + bt$. The pressure in each tank is measured in kilopascals (kPa) and t is measured in minutes after the start of the experiment.

When $t = 0$, the pressure in tank Q is measured as 90 kPa.
When $t = 7$, the pressure in tank Q is measured as 34 kPa.

a) Determine the values of a and b.

(2)

b) For how long during the experiment is the pressure in tank P greater than or equal to the pressure in tank Q?
Give your answer in minutes and seconds to the nearest second.

(4)

c) Give a suitable reason why these models are not valid for all values of t.

(1)

Q12 a) Prove the identity $\dfrac{\sin^4 x - \cos^4 x}{\cos^2 x} + \tan^2 x \equiv 2\tan^2 x - 1$ **(3)**

b) Hence, for $-180° \leq x \leq 180°$, solve the equation

$$\frac{\sin^4 x - \cos^4 x}{\cos^2 x} + \tan^2 x = 3\tan x - 1$$

Give your answers to one decimal place where appropriate. **(4)**

Q13 The points $A(0, 0)$, $B(-2, 4)$, $C(4, 4)$ and $D(6, 0)$ are the vertices of a parallelogram.
A line l_1 is drawn through C and the midpoint M of the side AB.
A second line l_2 is drawn through D and perpendicular to l_1.
T is the point of intersection of l_1 and l_2 as shown in the diagram.

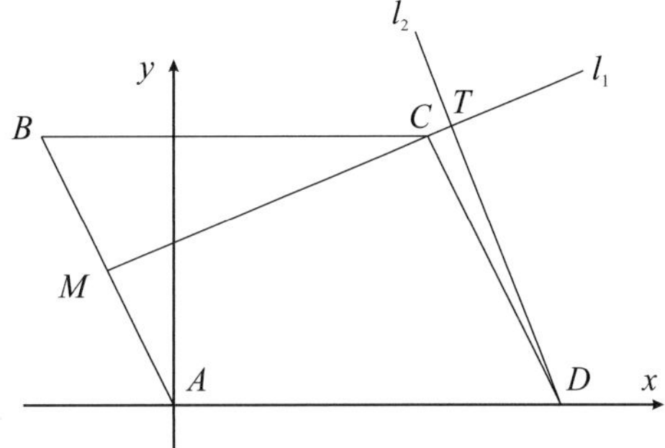

a) Find the exact coordinates of the point T. **(6)**

b) Hence show that the points A, T and D are the vertices of an isosceles triangle. **(2)**

Q14 A closed cylinder made from a thin sheet of metal has radius r cm, length h cm and volume 128π cm^3.

a) Show that $h = \dfrac{128}{r^2}$ and use this to find an expression for the surface area, S, of the cylinder in terms of r. **(2)**

b) Find the exact minimum value of the surface area of the cylinder and prove that the value is a minimum. **(5)**

Q15 The population of a rapidly expanding town is thought to be modelled by the equation $P = ab^t$, where t is measured in years and $t = 0$ corresponds to 1st January 2000.
Some data relating to the population of the town is given in the table.

Year (1st January)	2000	2020
$\log_{10}P$	4.762	5.012

Using data from the table:

a) Write down an equation for $\log_{10}P$ in terms of t.

(3)

b) Find the values of a and b, and the population predicted by the model for 1st January 2012 (to the nearest hundred).

(3)

c) In which year did the population reach 100 000 according to the model?

(2)

Q16 a) Explain why points $A(10, 4)$, $B(10, 10)$ and $C(2, 10)$ are the vertices of a right-angled triangle.

(1)

b) Hence find the equation of the circle D_1 which passes through the points A, B and C.

(3)

A second circle D_2 with the centre on the same vertical line as the centre of D_1 has equation $(x - 6)^2 + (y - 12)^2 = 10$. The circles D_1 and D_2 intersect at two distinct points.

c) Show that the point $M(9, 11)$ is a point of intersection of the circles and find the coordinates of the second point of intersection N.

(2)

d) Show that the tangent lines to D_2 at the points M and N intersect on the circumference of the circle D_1.

(6)

Chapter 2: Proof

Prior Knowledge Check

Q1 The product of two consecutive square numbers can be written as $x^2(x + 1)^2$, where x is an integer.

Q2 Let the smallest side be x. Then the other two sides are $(x + 2)$ and $(x + 4)$. So the perimeter is $x + (x + 2) + (x + 4) = 3x + 6$.

Q3 Yes: if y is negative, then y^2 could be greater than x^2. E.g. Let $x = 3$ and $y = -4$. Then $9 < 16$, i.e. $x^2 < y^2$.

Chapter 2 Review Exercise

Q1 a) Take two odd numbers $2l + 1$ and $2m + 1$ (where l and m are integers), then their sum is $2l + 1 + 2m + 1 = 2l + 2m + 2 = 2(l + m + 1) =$ even.

b) Take two even numbers, $2j$ and $2k$ (where j and k are integers), then their product is $2j \times 2k = 4jk = 2(2jk) =$ even.

c) Take one even number, $2l$ and one odd number $2m + 1$ (where l and m are integers), then their product is $2l \times (2m + 1) = 4lm + 2l = 2(2lm + l) =$ even.

Q2 Take one even number $2l$ and one odd number $2m + 1$ (where l and m are integers), then subtracting the odd number from the even number gives $2l - (2m + 1) = 2l - 2m - 1 = 2(l - m) - 1$
$= 2(l - m - 1) + 1$

Q3 $f(x) = 2x^2 + 2x + 3 = 2x^2 + 2x + 2 + 1$
$= 2(x^2 + x + 1) + 1$
x is an integer $\Rightarrow x^2 + x + 1$ is an integer
$\Rightarrow 2(x^2 + x + 1)$ is even
$\Rightarrow 2(x^2 + x + 1) + 1$ is odd
So $f(x)$ is odd for all integer values of x.
[2 marks available — 1 mark for rearranging each expression into the form of an odd number, 1 mark for correct interpretation]
You could also do this by expressing x as a general odd or even integer and showing that f(x) is odd in both cases.

Q4 Let the first odd integer be $2n + 1$, then the next consecutive odd integer is $2n + 3$. The sum of the squares of these two numbers is: $(2n + 1)^2 + (2n + 3)^2 = 4n^2 + 4n + 1 + 4n^2 + 12n + 9$
$= 8n^2 + 16n + 10$
$= 2(4n^2 + 8n + 5)$
The expression in the brackets is an integer, and since it's multiplied by 2 the full expression must be even.
[4 marks available — 1 mark for appropriate expressions for consecutive odd numbers, 1 mark for expanding the sum of squares, 1 mark for simplifying the expression, 1 mark for correct interpretation]

Q5 Take one even number $2l$ and one odd number $2m + 1$ (where l and m are integers), then:
$(2l)^{2m+1} = 2l \times 2l \times 2l \times \ldots \times 2l$ (this is $2m + 1$ lots of $2l$)
$= 2(l \times 2l \times 2l \times \ldots \times 2l)$
The expression in the brackets is an integer, and since it's multiplied by 2 the full expression must be even.

Q6 Let the odd numbers be $2n - 1$ and $2n + 1$, where n is an integer. Then $(2n + 1)(2n - 1) + 1 = 4n^2 - 1 + 1 = 4n^2 = (2n)^2$, so one more than the product of two consecutive odd numbers is a square number.
[3 marks available — 1 mark for 2n – 1 and 2n + 1, 1 mark for expanding the brackets, 1 mark for correct interpretation]
As with a lot of these questions, you could have represented the odd numbers differently, e.g. $(2n + 1)(2n + 3)$ leads to the result $(2n + 2)^2$.

Q7 $(4n + 1)^2 - (2n - 1) = 16n^2 + 8n + 1 - 2n + 1$
$= 16n^2 + 6n + 2 = 2(8n^2 + 3n + 1)$
The expression in the brackets is an integer, and since it's multiplied by 2, the full expression must be even.
[3 marks available — 1 mark for expanding the brackets, 1 mark for simplifying the expression, 1 mark for correct interpretation]

Q8 $5(n + 5)^2 + 3n^2 - 15(2n - 3)$
$= 5(n^2 + 10n + 25) + 3n^2 - 30n + 45$
$= 5n^2 + 50n + 125 + 3n^2 - 30n + 45$
$= 8n^2 + 20n + 170 = 2(4n^2 + 10n + 85)$
The expression in the brackets is an integer, and since it's multiplied by 2, the full expression must be even.
[3 marks available — 1 mark for expanding the brackets, 1 mark for simplifying the expression, 1 mark for correct interpretation]

Q9 Let the odd integer $y = 2n + 1$.
The angles in a triangle add up to 180°, so:
$2y + x = 180 \Rightarrow 2(2n + 1) + x = 180$
$\Rightarrow x = 180 - 4n - 2 = 178 - 4n = 2(89 - 2n)$
The expression in the brackets is an integer, and since it's multiplied by 2, the full expression must be even.
[3 marks available — 1 mark for using a correct expression for an odd number in a suitable equation, 1 mark for rearranging into the form of an even number, 1 mark for correct interpretation]

Q10 a) (i) $(n + 1)^3 = (n + 1)(n + 1)(n + 1)$
$= (n + 1)(n^2 + 2n + 1) = n^3 + 3n^2 + 3n + 1$
[2 marks available — 1 mark for a correct method to expand the brackets, 1 mark for a correct simplified expression]

(ii) Similar to a), $(n - 1)^3 = (n - 1)(n - 1)(n - 1)$
$= (n - 1)(n^2 - 2n + 1) = n^3 - 3n^2 + 3n - 1$
[1 mark for a correct simplified expansion]

b) Let the three consecutive cube numbers be $(n - 1)^3$, n^3 and $(n + 1)^3$.
Then $(n - 1)^3 + n^3 + (n + 1)^3$
$= (n^3 - 3n^2 + 3n - 1) + n^3 + (n^3 + 3n^2 + 3n + 1)$
$= 3n^3 + 6n = 3(n^3 + 2n) = 3k$, where $k = n^3 + 2n$ is an integer, so it must be divisible by 3.
[2 marks available — 1 mark for an expression for the sum of three consecutive cube numbers, 1 mark for a correct interpretation]

Q11 $a^m = a \times a \times a \times \ldots \times a$ (m lots of a multiplied together)
$a^n = a \times a \times a \ldots \times a$ (n lots of a multiplied together)
$a^m \times a^n = a \times a \times a \ldots \times a \times a \times a \times \ldots a$
There are $m + n$ lots of a multiplied together, so $a^m \times a^n = a^{m+n}$.

Q12 Let $x = a + b$, then $x^2 \geq 0 \Rightarrow (a + b)^2 \geq 0 \Rightarrow a^2 + 2ab + b^2 \geq 0$.

Q13 $x < y \Rightarrow x + y < y + y \Rightarrow x + y < 2y \Rightarrow \frac{x+y}{2} < y$
Similarly $x < y \Rightarrow x + x < x + y \Rightarrow 2x < x + y \Rightarrow x < \frac{x+y}{2}$
So $x < \frac{x+y}{2} < y$
[3 marks available — 1 mark for deriving the inequality $\frac{x+y}{2} < y$, 1 mark for deriving the inequality $x < \frac{x+y}{2}$, 1 mark for a correct interpretation]

Q14 Let N^2 be a square number with positive square root N. N has a finite number of prime factors (where some prime numbers may be repeated), so write its prime factorisation as $N = abc\ldots$ Then, $N^2 = (abc\ldots)(abc\ldots) = a^2b^2c^2\ldots$
Each prime factor of N is included twice in the prime factorisation of N^2, so N^2 has an even number of prime factors.

Q15 n divisible by $k \Rightarrow n = ka$ for some positive integer a
m divisible by $k \Rightarrow m = kb$ for some positive integer b
So $pn + qm = pka + qkb = k(pa + qb)$, where $pa + qb$ is a positive integer. So $pn + qm$ is divisible by k.

Q16 The product of two numbers with 1 in the units position will also have a 1 in the units position.
$\Rightarrow 11^n$ has a 1 in the units position for all integers $n \geq 1$
$\Rightarrow 11^n - 1$ has a 0 in the units position for all integers $n \geq 1$
$\Rightarrow 11^n - 1$ is divisible by 10 for all integers $n \geq 1$

Q17 $(x+5)^2+3(x-1)^2 = x^2+10x+25+3(x^2-2x+1)$
$= x^2+10x+25+3x^2-6x+3$
$= 4x^2+4x+28$
$= 4(x^2+x+7)$
This has a factor of 4 outside the brackets, so it is always divisible by 4.

Q18 Take two rational numbers $a = \frac{p}{q}$ and $b = \frac{r}{s}$.
The difference between them is $\frac{p}{q} - \frac{r}{s} = \frac{ps-qr}{qs}$
p, q, r and s are all integers, so $ps - qr$ is an integer.
q and s are non-zero integers, so qs is a non-zero integer.
So $\frac{ps-qr}{qs}$ is a rational number.
[3 marks available — 1 mark for expressing a and b as algebraic fractions, 1 mark for finding an algebraic expression for their difference, 1 mark for correct interpretation]

Q19 Proof by exhaustion:
Take three consecutive integers $(n-1)$, n and $(n+1)$.
Their product is $(n-1)n(n+1) = n(n^2-1) = n^3-n$.
Consider the two cases — n even and n odd.
For n even, n^3 is even (as even × even = even) so n^3-n is also even (as even – even = even). For n odd, n^3 is odd (as odd × odd = odd) so n^3-n is even (as odd – odd = even). So n^3-n is even when n is even and when n is odd, and n must be either odd or even, so the product of three consecutive integers is always even.
Another approach to this proof is to take the product of three consecutive integers n(n + 1)(n + 2) and consider n odd and n even.
If n is odd:
n(n + 1)(n + 2) = (odd × even) × odd = even × odd = even.
If n is even:
n(n + 1)(n + 2) = (even × odd) × even = even × even = even.

Q20 If n is even:
Let $n = 2k$, where k is an integer. Then $n^2-6 = 4k^2-6$
$= 4(k^2-1)-2$, so it is two less than a multiple of 4.
If n is odd:
Let $n = 2k+1$, where k is an integer.
Then $n^2-6 = (2k+1)^2-6 = 4k^2+4k+1-6 = 4k^2+4k-5$
$= 4(k^2+k-1)-1$, so it is one less than a multiple of 4.
Therefore, n^2-6 is never a multiple of 4 when n is an integer.
[4 marks available — 1 mark for writing n = 2k or n = 2k + 1, 1 mark for correct proof in the even case, 1 mark for correct proof in the odd case, 1 mark for complete proof]

Q21 **a)** Proof by exhaustion:
Consider the two cases — n even and n odd.
Let n be even. $n^2-n = n(n-1)$.
If n is even, $n-1$ is odd so $n(n-1)$ is even (as even × odd = even). This means that $n(n-1)-1$ is odd.
Let n be odd. If n is odd, $n-1$ is even, so $n(n-1)$ is even (as odd × even = even). This means that $n(n-1)-1$ is odd.
As any integer n has to be either odd or even, n^2-n-1 is odd for any value of n.

b) As n^2-n-1 is odd, n^2-n-2 is even. The product of even numbers is also even, so as $(n^2-n-2)^3$ is the product of 3 even numbers, it will always be even.

Q22 E.g. Let $p = 1 \Rightarrow \frac{1}{p^2} = \frac{1}{p}$, so the statement is not true.
You could have also taken p to be a negative integer.

Q23 E.g. If $x = -2$, $x^3 = (-2)^3 = -8$
$-8 < -2$, so here $x^3 < x$.
So the statement is not true for all $x \neq 0$.
[2 marks available — 1 mark for using an appropriate x-value, 1 mark for correct interpretation]

Q24 The simplest way to disprove the statement is to find a counter-example. Try some values of n and see if the statement is true for them:
$n = 3 \Rightarrow n^2-n-1 = 3^2-3-1 = 5$ — prime
$n = 4 \Rightarrow n^2-n-1 = 4^2-4-1 = 11$ — prime
$n = 5 \Rightarrow n^2-n-1 = 5^2-5-1 = 19$ — prime
$n = 6 \Rightarrow n^2-n-1 = 6^2-6-1 = 29$ — prime
$n = 7 \Rightarrow n^2-n-1 = 7^2-7-1 = 41$ — prime
$n = 8 \Rightarrow n^2-n-1 = 8^2-8-1 = 55$ — not prime
n^2-n-1 is not prime when $n = 8$. So the statement is false.
Sometimes trial and error is the easiest way to find a counter-example. Don't forget, if you've been told to disprove a statement like this, then a counter-example must exist.

Q25 E.g. If $x = 0$, $a = 1$ and $b = 2$:
$ax = 1 \times 0 = 0$ and $bx = 2 \times 0 = 0$, so $ax = bx$
But $1 \neq 2$, so $a \neq b$. So the statement is not correct.
[2 marks available — 1 mark for setting x, a and b as appropriate values, 1 mark for correct interpretation]

Q26 Find a counter-example for which the statement isn't true.
Take $x = -1$ and $y = 2$. Then
$\sqrt{x^2+y^2} = \sqrt{(-1)^2+2^2} = \sqrt{1+4} = \sqrt{5} = 2.236...$
and $x + y = -1 + 2 = 1$. $2.236... > 1$, so the statement is not true.

Q27 E.g. If $x = 3$, $y = 5$, $z = 7$, then 4 is a factor of $x + y = 8$ and $y + z = 12$, but not of $x + 4y + z = 30$.

Q28 E.g. If $n = 17$, $n^3+n^2+17 = 17^3+17^2+17 = 17(17^2+17+1)$, which is a multiple of 17 and therefore not prime.
[2 marks available — 1 mark for an appropriate value of n, 1 mark for correct interpretation]

Q29 E.g. $N = 64$ is a square number since $64 = 8^2$, but 64 is also a cube number since $64 = 4^3$.
Any integer to the sixth power could be used as a counter-example — note that $64 = 2^6$.

Q30 **a)** E.g. If $x = 0$, $y = -1$, then $x^2+xy+y^2 = 1$ but $3y^2 = 3$.
$1 < 3$ so Ananthi is wrong.
[2 marks available — 1 mark for setting x and y as appropriate values, 1 mark for correct interpretation]

b) E.g. If $x = 0.1$ and $y = 0.1$, then $x^2+xy+y^2 = 0.03 < 1$, so Alan is wrong.
[2 marks available — 1 mark for setting x and y as appropriate values, 1 mark for correct interpretation]

Q31 E.g. If $y = -2$, then $y^2+5y+4 = (-2)^2+5(-2)+4$
$= 4-10+4 = -2$, which is not positive.
Therefore, y^2+5y+4 is not always positive.

Q32 E.g. $\sqrt{2}$ and $\sqrt{8} \Rightarrow \sqrt{2}\sqrt{8} = \sqrt{2 \times 8} = \sqrt{16} = 4$
[2 marks available — 1 mark for two appropriate irrational numbers, 1 mark for correct interpretation]

Q33 Disproof by counter-example: Zero is a rational number, but dividing by zero does not give a rational result.

Q34 Any real number squared is either positive or zero, so
$\left(x - \frac{2}{x}\right)^2 \geq 0$. So $x^2 + \frac{4}{x^2} - 4 \geq 0 \Leftrightarrow x^2 + \frac{4}{x^2} \geq 4$.
[3 marks available — 1 mark for a suitable square ≥ 0, 1 mark for correct expansion of brackets, 1 mark for complete proof]
Alternatively, as $x \neq 0$, you could prove $x^4 + 4 \geq 4x^2$. Consider $(x^2-2)^2 \geq 0$. Expanding the brackets, we have $x^4 - 4x^2 + 4 \geq 0$, so $x^4 + 4 \geq 4x^2$. Dividing by x^2 (as $x \neq 0$), we have $x^2 + \frac{4}{x^2} \geq 4$.

Q35 **a)** If n is not a multiple of 3, then either $n = 3k+1$ or $n = 3k-1$, where k is an integer.
Case 1: $n = 3k+1$. Then $2n^2+1 = 2(3k+1)^2+1$
$= 2(9k^2+6k+1)+1 = 18k^2+12k+3 = 3(6k^2+4k+1)$,
so $2n^2+1$ is a multiple of 3.
Case 2: $n = 3k-1$. Then $2n^2+1 = 2(3k-1)^2+1$
$= 2(9k^2-6k+1)+1 = 18k^2-12k+3 = 3(6k^2-4k+1)$,
so $2n^2+1$ is a multiple of 3. Therefore, when n is an integer that is not a multiple of 3, $2n^2+1$ is a multiple of 3.
[4 marks available — 1 mark for correct cases, 1 mark for one of $2(3k \pm 1)^2 + 1$, 1 mark for correct proof in one of the two cases, 1 mark for complete proof]

b) Since n is an integer, $-6n^2 = 3(-2n^2)$ is divisible by 3.
That means $1 - 6n^2$ is always one more than a multiple of 3, so it can't be divisible by 3.
[1 mark available for correct explanation]

Q36 If $10a + b$ is divisible by 9, then $10a + b = 9k$ for some integer k.
So $9a + a + b = 9k \Rightarrow a + b = 9k - 9a \Rightarrow a + b = 9(k - a)$.
$(k - a)$ is an integer, so $a + b$ is a multiple of 9.
[3 marks available — 1 mark for stating that $10a + b = 9k$ or equivalent, 1 mark for correctly showing that $a + b = 9(k - a)$ or equivalent, 1 mark for a written conclusion]

Q37 **a)** $n^2 + 3n = n(n + 3)$. If n is odd, then $n + 3$ is even.
So $n(n + 3) = \text{odd} \times \text{even} = \text{even}$, so $n^2 + 3n$ is even.
If n is even, then $n + 3$ is odd.
So $n(n + 3) = \text{even} \times \text{odd} = \text{even}$, so $n^2 + 3n$ is even.
So $n^2 + 3n$ is even for all integer values of n.
[3 marks available — 1 mark for a proof in the case where n is odd, 1 mark for a proof in the case where n is even, 1 mark for a correct interpretation]
Alternative proofs are possible — for example, you could have written $n = 2k$ and $n = 2k + 1$, where k is an integer, and completed the proof using algebra.

b) From part a), you know that $n^2 + 3n$ is even for all integer values of n, so you only need to show that $n^4 + 3n^2$ is a multiple of 4 to complete the proof. $n^4 + 3n^2 = n^2(n^2 + 3)$

If n is odd: Write $n = 2k + 1$, where k is an integer.
$n^2 + 3 = (2k + 1)^2 + 3 = 4k^2 + 4k + 1 + 3$
$= 4k^2 + 4k + 4 = 4(k^2 + k + 1)$.
So $n^2(n^2 + 3) = 4n^2(k^2 + k + 1) \Rightarrow n^4 + 3n^2$ is a multiple of 4.

If n is even: Write $n = 2k$, where k is an integer. $n^2 = 4k^2$, so $n^2(n^2 + 3) = 4k^2(n^2 + 3) \Rightarrow n^4 + 3n^2$ is a multiple of 4.

Therefore, $n^4 + 3n^2$ is a multiple of 4 for all integers n.
So $(n^4 + 3n^2)(n^2 + 3n) = (4p)(2q) = 8pq$ for some integers p and q, so it must be a multiple of 8.
[5 marks available — 1 mark for using part a) to justify that $n^4 + 3n^2$ needs to be a multiple of 4, 1 mark for writing $n = 2k$ or $n = 2k + 1$, 1 mark for a correct proof in the case where n is odd, 1 mark for a correct proof in the case where n is even, 1 mark for a correct interpretation]

Chapter 3: Algebra

Prior Knowledge Check

Q1 **a)** $4x - 28$ **b)** $3a - 2ab$

Q2 **a)** $3(x + 2y)$ **b)** $x(9x - 5)$

Q3 $\frac{x(x+2)}{x^2} + \frac{3}{x^2} = \frac{x^2 + 2x + 3}{x^2}$

Q4 **a)** 3^{11} **b)** 2^{-6} **c)** 5^8

Q5 **a)** 8 **b)** $\sqrt{15}$ **c)** $5\sqrt{7}$

Exercise 3.1 — Expanding Brackets

Q1 **a)** $5(x + 4) = 5x + (5 \times 4) = 5x + 20$

b) $a(4 - 2b) = 4a + (a \times -2b) = 4a - 2ab$

c) $-2(x^2 + y) = -2x^2 - 2y$

d) $6mn(m + 1) = 6mnm + 6mn = 6m^2n + 6mn$

e) $-4ht(t^2 - 2ht - 3h^3)$
$= -4ht \times t^2 + (-4ht \times -2ht) + (-4ht \times -3h^3)$
$= -4ht^3 + 8h^2t^2 + 12h^4t$

f) $7z^2(2 + z) = 14z^2 + 7z^2z = 14z^2 + 7z^3$

g) $4(x + 2) + 3(x - 5) = 4x + 8 + 3x - 15 = 7x - 7$

h) $p(3p^2 - 2q) + (q + 4p^3) = (p \times 3p^2) + (p \times -2q) + q + 4p^3$
$= 3p^3 - 2pq + q + 4p^3 = 7p^3 - 2pq + q$

i) $7xy(x^2 + z^2) = (7xy \times x^2) + (7xy \times z^2) = 7x^3y + 7xyz^2$
Don't forget to simplify your answer if possible.

Q2 **a)** $(x + 5)(x - 3) = x^2 - 3x + 5x - 15 = x^2 + 2x - 15$

b) $(2z + 3)(3z - 2) = 6z^2 - 4z + 9z - 6 = 6z^2 + 5z - 6$

c) $(u + 8)^2 = (u + 8)(u + 8) = u^2 + 8u + 8u + 64 = u^2 + 16u + 64$

d) $(ab + cd)(ac + bd) = abac + abbd + cdac + cdbd$
$= a^2bc + ab^2d + ac^2d + bcd^2$

e) $(10 + f)(2f^2 - 3g) = 20f^2 - 30g + 2f^3 - 3fg$

f) $(7 + q)(7 - q) = 49 - 7q + 7q - q^2 = 49 - q^2$

g) $(2 - 3w)^2 = (2 - 3w)(2 - 3w) = 2^2 - 6w - 6w + 9w^2$
$= 4 - 12w + 9w^2$

h) $(4rs^2 + 3)^2 = (4rs^2 + 3)(4rs^2 + 3) = 16r^2s^4 + 12rs^2 + 12rs^2 + 9$
$= 16r^2s^4 + 24rs^2 + 9$

i) $(5k^2l - 2kn)^2 = (5k^2l - 2kn)(5k^2l - 2kn)$
$= 25k^4l^2 - 10k^3nl - 10k^3nl + 4k^2n^2$
$= 25k^4l^2 - 20k^3ln + 4k^2n^2$
In parts c), g), h) and i), you could get straight to the answer by using $(a + b)^2 = a^2 + 2ab + b^2$.

Q3 **a)** $(l + 5)(l^2 + 2l + 3) = l(l^2 + 2l + 3) + 5(l^2 + 2l + 3)$
$= l^3 + 2l^2 + 3l + 5l^2 + 10l + 15$
$= l^3 + 7l^2 + 13l + 15$

b) $(2 + q)(3 - q + 4q^2) = 2(3 - q + 4q^2) + q(3 - q + 4q^2)$
$= 6 - 2q + 8q^2 + 3q - q^2 + 4q^3 = 6 + q + 7q^2 + 4q^3$

c) $(m + 1)(m + 2)(m - 4) = (m^2 + 2m + m + 2)(m - 4)$
$= (m^2 + 3m + 2)(m - 4) = m^2(m - 4) + 3m(m - 4) + 2(m - 4)$
$= m^3 - 4m^2 + 3m^2 - 12m + 2m - 8 = m^3 - m^2 - 10m - 8$

d) $(r + s)^3 = (r + s)(r + s)(r + s) = (r^2 + rs + sr + s^2)(r + s)$
$= (r^2 + 2rs + s^2)(r + s)$
$= r^2(r + s) + 2rs(r + s) + s^2(r + s)$
$= r^3 + r^2s + 2r^2s + 2rs^2 + rs^2 + s^3 = r^3 + 3r^2s + 3rs^2 + s^3$

e) $(3x + 2)(x - 4)(2x + 1) = (3x^2 - 12x + 2x - 8)(2x + 1)$
$= (3x^2 - 10x - 8)(2x + 1)$
$= 3x^2(2x + 1) - 10x(2x + 1) - 8(2x + 1)$
$= 6x^3 + 3x^2 - 20x^2 - 10x - 16x - 8$
$= 6x^3 - 17x^2 - 26x - 8$

f) $(4 + x + y)(1 - x - y) = 4(1 - x - y) + x(1 - x - y) + y(1 - x - y)$
$= 4 - 4x - 4y + x - x^2 - xy + y - xy - y^2$
$= 4 - 3x - 3y - 2xy - x^2 - y^2$

g) $(j + 2k - 3)(j^2 + 2j + 1)$
$= j(j^2 + 2j + 1) + 2k(j^2 + 2j + 1) - 3(j^2 + 2j + 1)$
$= j^3 + 2j^2 + j + 2j^2k + 4jk + 2k - 3j^2 - 6j - 3$
$= j^3 - j^2 - 5j + 2j^2k + 4jk + 2k - 3$

h) $(2c^2 - cd + d)(2d - c - 5c^2)$
$= 2c^2(2d - c - 5c^2) - cd(2d - c - 5c^2) + d(2d - c - 5c^2)$
$= 4c^2d - 2c^3 - 10c^4 - 2cd^2 + c^2d + 5c^3d + 2d^2 - dc - 5c^2d$
$= -10c^4 - 2c^3 + 5c^3d - 2cd^2 - cd + 2d^2$

i) $(2f^3 - 4f - 1)(f^2 + 3f + 2)$
$= 2f^3(f^2 + 3f + 2) - 4f(f^2 + 3f + 2) - (f^2 + 3f + 2)$
$= 2f^5 + 6f^4 + 4f^3 - 4f^3 - 12f^2 - 8f - f^2 - 3f - 2$
$= 2f^5 + 6f^4 - 13f^2 - 11f - 2$

Q4 **a)** $(2x + 1)(3x - 4)(x + 7) - 2(x + 2)(2x - 3)$
$= (2x + 1)(3x^2 + 17x - 28) - 2(2x^2 + x - 6)$
$= (6x^3 + 34x^2 - 56x + 3x^2 + 17x - 28) - 4x^2 - 2x + 12$
$= 6x^3 + 33x^2 - 41x - 16$

b) $(2x - 1)(x^2 + x + 1) + 2(x - 3)((x + 1)(x + 2) + 5)$
$(2x^3 + 2x^2 + 2x - x^2 - x - 1) + 2(x - 3)(x^2 + 3x + 7)$
$= 2x^3 + x^2 + x - 1 + 2(x^3 + 3x^2 + 7x - 3x^2 - 9x - 21)$
$= 2x^3 + x^2 + x - 1 + 2x^3 - 4x - 42 = 4x^3 + x^2 - 3x - 43$

Q5 $\frac{2}{3}(x + 3)(x^2 + 1) + \frac{1}{4}(x^2 + 4x - 7)$
$= \frac{1}{12}(8(x + 3)(x^2 + 1) + 3(x^2 + 4x - 7))$
$= \frac{1}{12}(8(x^3 + x + 3x^2 + 3) + 3(x^2 + 4x - 7))$
$= \frac{1}{12}(8x^3 + 8x + 24x^2 + 24 + 3x^2 + 12x - 21)$
$= \frac{1}{12}(8x^3 + 27x^2 + 20x + 3) = \frac{2}{3}x^3 + \frac{9}{4}x^2 + \frac{5}{3}x + \frac{1}{4}$
[4 marks available — 4 marks for the correct simplified answer, otherwise 3 marks for collecting like terms but coefficients not simplified, or 2 marks for correctly expanding brackets, or 1 mark for using the correct method]

Q6 Radius $= 3h - 2$ cm
Volume $= \pi r^2h = \pi(3h - 2)^2h = \pi h(9h^2 - 12h + 4)$
$= 9\pi h^3 - 12\pi h^2 + 4\pi h$ cm^3

Q7 Carole's garden: $x \times x = x^2$ m²
Mark's garden: $(x + 3)(2x + 1) = 2x^2 + x + 6x + 3$
$= 2x^2 + 7x + 3$ m²

Difference: $2x^2 + 7x + 3 - x^2 = x^2 + 7x + 3$ m²
For Mark's garden, use the information given to find the length of the sides. Then multiply the brackets and expand.

Q8 $(ax + b)(x^2 - 4x - 12) = ax^3 + (b - 4a)x^2 + (-12a - 4b)x - 12b.$
Compare this to $2x^3 - 7x^2 + cx - 12$.
Matching coefficients of x^3: $a = 2$
Matching constant terms: $-12 = -12b \Rightarrow b = 1$
Matching coefficients of x terms:
$c = -12a - 4b \Rightarrow c = -12 \times 2 - 4 \times 1 \Rightarrow c = -28$
[4 marks available — 4 marks for finding the correct values of all three unknowns (a, b and c), otherwise 3 marks for finding two correct values, or 2 marks for expanding brackets correctly, or 1 mark for using the correct method]

Q9 **a)** $(a + b)^3 = (a + b)(a + b)(a + b) = (a + b)(a^2 + 2ab + b^2)$
$= a^3 + 2a^2b + ab^2 + a^2b + 2ab^2 + b^3$
$= a^3 + 3a^2b + 3ab^2 + b^3$
[2 marks available — 1 mark for expanding brackets correctly, 1 mark for the correct simplified answer]

b) Let $a = 2x$ and $b = 3y$, then
$(2x + 3y)^3 = (2x)^3 + 3(2x)^2(3y) + 3(2x)(3y)^2 + (3y)^3$
$= 8x^3 + 36x^2y + 54xy^2 + 27y^3$
[3 marks available — 3 marks for the correct answer, otherwise 2 marks for correct substitution of a and b, or 1 mark for using the correct method]

Q10 $(2x + y - 1)^2 + (2 - 4x)(y - 1)$
$= (2x + y - 1)(2x + y - 1) + (2y - 2 - 4xy + 4x)$
$= (4x^2 + 2xy - 2x + 2xy + y^2 - y - 2x - y + 1) + (2y - 2 - 4xy + 4x)$
$= (4x^2 + y^2 + 4xy - 4x - 2y + 1) + (2y - 2 - 4xy + 4x)$
$= 4x^2 + y^2 - 1$
[4 marks available — 4 marks for the correct simplified answer, otherwise 3 marks for correctly expanding both sets of brackets in the given expression, or 2 marks for correctly expanding one set of brackets, or 1 mark for using the correct method]

Q11 $2x^3 \times 2 \times 5 = 20x^3$ $\quad$ $5x \times -4x^2 \times 5 = -100x^3$
$5x \times 2 \times -x^2 = -10x^3$ $\quad$ $-8 \times x \times -x^2 = 8x^3$
$20x^3 - 100x^3 - 10x^3 + 8x^3 = -82x^3$, so the coefficient of x^3 is -82.
[3 marks available — 3 marks for the correct answer, otherwise 2 marks for at least three correct coefficients, or 1 mark for at least two correct coefficients]
You don't need to expand the whole expression to find the coefficient of x^3, only the parts that will give terms in x^3.

Exercise 3.2 — Factorising

Q1 **a)** $9k + 15l = (3 \times 3k) + (3 \times 5l) = 3(3k + 5l)$

b) $u^2 - uv = u(u - v)$

c) $2x^2y - 12xy^2 = (2xy \times x) - (2xy \times 6y) = 2xy(x - 6y)$

d) $f^2g^2 - fg = (fg \times fg) - (fg \times 1) = fg(fg - 1)$

e) $p^3 + 3pq^3 + 2p = (p \times p^2) + (p \times 3q^3) + (p \times 2)$
$= p(p^2 + 3q^3 + 2)$

f) $mnp^2 + 7m^2np^3 = (mnp^2 \times 1) + (mnp^2 \times 7mp)$
$= mnp^2(1 + 7mp)$

g) $2ab^4 + 3a^3b^2 - 4ab = (ab \times 2b^3) + (ab \times 3a^2b) - (ab \times 4)$
$= ab(2b^3 + 3a^2b - 4)$

h) $36xyz - 8x^2z^2 + 20y^2z^2 = (4z \times 9xy) - (4z \times 2x^2z) + (4z \times 5y^2z)$
$= 4z(9xy - 2x^2z + 5y^2z)$

Q2 **a)** $x^2 - y^2 = (x + y)(x - y)$
This is just using the formula for the 'difference of two squares'.

b) $9a^2 - 4b^2 = (3a)^2 - (2b)^2 = (3a + 2b)(3a - 2b)$

c) $25x^2 - 49z^2 = (5x)^2 - (7z)^2 = (5x + 7z)(5x - 7z)$

d) $a^2c - 16b^2c = c(a^2 - 16b^2) = c(a^2 - (4b)^2) = c(a + 4b)(a - 4b)$

e) $y^2 - 2 = y^2 - (\sqrt{2})^2 = (y + \sqrt{2})(y - \sqrt{2})$

f) $m^2 - 11 = m^2 - (\sqrt{11})^2 = (m + \sqrt{11})(m - \sqrt{11})$

g) $4x^2 - 3 = (2x)^2 - (\sqrt{3})^2 = (2x + \sqrt{3})(2x - \sqrt{3})$

h) $7p^2 - 13 = (\sqrt{7}p)^2 - (\sqrt{13})^2 = (\sqrt{7}p + \sqrt{13})(\sqrt{7}p - \sqrt{13})$
Parts e) - h) use the fact that any number can be written as its square root squared.

Q3 **a)** $(4 - z)^2(2 - z) + p(2 - z) = (2 - z)[(4 - z)^2 + p]$

b) $(r - d)^3 + 5(r - d)^2 = (r - d)^2[(r - d) + 5] = (r - d)^2(r - d + 5)$

c) $(b + c)^5(a + b) - (b + c)^5 = (b + c)^5[(a + b) - 1]$
$= (b + c)^5(a + b - 1)$

d) $l^2m(a - 2x) + rp^2(2x - a) = l^2m(a - 2x) + rp^2(-(a - 2x))$
$= l^2m(a - 2x) - rp^2(a - 2x)$
$= (a - 2x)(l^2m - rp^2)$
You might have factorised this slightly differently and ended up with $(2x - a)(rp^2 - l^2m)$ instead.

Q4 **a)** $(p + q)^2 + 2q(p + q) = (p + q)[(p + q) + 2q] = (p + q)(p + 3q)$

b) $2(2x - y)^2 - 6x(2x - y) = 2(2x - y)[(2x - y) - 3x]$
$= -2(2x - y)(x + y)$

c) $(l + w + h)^2 - l(l + w + h) = (l + w + h)[(l + w + h) - l]$
$= (l + w + h)(w + h)$

Q5 **a)** $(2x + 1)$ and $(x - 3)$ are common factors, so
$(2x + 1)(x - 3)(3x - 1) - 2(x - 3)(x + 2)(2x + 1)$
$= (2x + 1)(x - 3)((3x - 1) - 2(x + 2))$
$= (2x + 1)(x - 3)(3x - 1 - 2x - 4) = (2x + 1)(x - 3)(x - 5)$
[3 marks available — 3 marks for the correct answer, otherwise 2 marks for correctly factoring out (2x + 1)(x – 3), or 1 mark for an attempt to factorise]

b) $(2x + 1)(x - 3)(3x - 1) - 2(x - 3)(x + 2)(2x + 1) = 0$
$\Rightarrow (2x + 1)(x - 3)(x - 5) = 0 \Rightarrow x = -\frac{1}{2}, x = 3$ or $x = 5$
[1 mark for all three correct solutions]

Q6 $2(5x - 7y)^2$ is a common factor, so $6(5x - 7y)^3 - 4(x + y)(5x - 7y)^2$
$= 2(5x - 7y)^2(3(5x - 7y) - 2(x + y))$
$= 2(5x - 7y)^2(15x - 21y - 2x - 2y) = 2(5x - 7y)^2(13x - 23y)$
[3 marks available — 3 marks for the correct answer, otherwise 2 marks for correctly factoring out 2(5x – 7y)², or 1 mark for attempting to factorise]

Q7 $12m^3n^6(1 + 6n^2) + 18m^2n^7(1 - 4mn)$
$= 6m^2n^6(2m(1 + 6n^2) + 3n(1 - 4mn))$
$= 6m^2n^6(2m + 12mn^2 + 3n - 12mn^2) = 6m^2n^6(2m + 3n)$
[2 marks available — 2 marks for the correct answer, otherwise 1 mark for an incomplete factorisation]

Q8 **a)** $(m + 5)(m^2 - 5m + 25) = m(m^2 - 5m + 25) + 5(m^2 - 5m + 25)$
$= m^3 - 5m^2 + 25m + 5m^2 - 25m + 125 = m^3 + 125$

b) $(p - 2q)(p^2 + 2pq + 4q^2)$
$= p(p^2 + 2pq + 4q^2) - 2q(p^2 + 2pq + 4q^2)$
$= p^3 + 2p^2q + 4pq^2 - 2p^2q - 4pq^2 - 8q^3 = p^3 - 8q^3$
Parts a) and b) were likely to need the brackets expanding because the quadratic in the second bracket won't factorise.

c) $(u - v)(u + v) - (u + v)^2 = (u + v)[(u - v) - (u + v)]$
$= (u + v)(-2v) = -2v(u + v)$

d) $(c + d)^3 - c(c + d)^2 - d(c + d)^2 = (c + d)^2[(c + d) - c - d]$
$= (c + d)^2(0) = 0$

Exercise 3.3 — Algebraic Fractions

Q1 **a)** The common denominator is 3×4:
$\frac{x}{3} + \frac{x}{4} = \frac{4x}{12} + \frac{3x}{12} = \frac{7x}{12}$

b) The common denominator is t^2:
$\frac{2}{t} + \frac{13}{t^2} = \frac{2t}{t^2} + \frac{13}{t^2} = \frac{2t + 13}{t^2}$

c) The common denominator is $2 \times p \times 5 \times q = 10pq$:
$\frac{1}{2p} - \frac{1}{5q} = \frac{5q}{10pq} - \frac{2p}{10pq} = \frac{5q - 2p}{10pq}$

d) 12 is the lowest common multiple of 3, 2 and 4, so the common denominator is $12h$:
$\frac{2}{3h} + \frac{1}{2h} - \frac{3}{4h} = \frac{8}{12h} + \frac{6}{12h} - \frac{9}{12h} = \frac{5}{12h}$

e) The common denominator is $a \times b \times c$:

$$\frac{ab}{c} + \frac{bc}{a} + \frac{ca}{b} = \frac{abab}{abc} + \frac{bcbc}{abc} + \frac{caca}{abc}$$
$$= \frac{a^2b^2 + b^2c^2 + c^2a^2}{abc}$$

f) The common denominator is mn:

$$\frac{2}{mn} - \frac{3m}{n} + \frac{n^2}{m} = \frac{2}{mn} - \frac{3m^2}{mn} + \frac{n^3}{mn}$$
$$= \frac{2 - 3m^2 + n^3}{mn}$$

g) The common denominator is $a^3 \times b^3 = a^3b^3$:

$$\frac{2}{ab^3} - \frac{9}{a^3b} = \frac{2a^2}{a^3b^3} - \frac{9b^2}{a^3b^3} = \frac{2a^2 - 9b^2}{a^3b^3}$$

h) The common denominator is $x^2 \times y = x^2y$:

$$\frac{1}{x} + \frac{2x}{y} + \frac{4}{x^2} = \frac{xy}{x^2y} + \frac{2x^3}{x^2y} + \frac{4y}{x^2y} = \frac{xy + 2x^3 + 4y}{x^2y}$$

i) The common denominator is $a^2 \times b = a^2b$:

$$2 + \frac{a^2}{b} - \frac{2b}{a^2} = \frac{2a^2b}{a^2b} + \frac{a^4}{a^2b} - \frac{2b^2}{a^2b} = \frac{2a^2b + a^4 - 2b^2}{a^2b}$$

Q2 a) The common denominator is $(y-1)(y-2)$:

$$\frac{5}{y-1} + \frac{3}{y-2} = \frac{5(y-2)}{(y-1)(y-2)} + \frac{3(y-1)}{(y-1)(y-2)}$$
$$= \frac{5(y-2) + 3(y-1)}{(y-1)(y-2)}$$
$$= \frac{5y - 10 + 3y - 3}{(y-1)(y-2)}$$
$$= \frac{8y - 13}{(y-1)(y-2)}$$

b) The common denominator is $(r-5)(r+3)$:

$$\frac{7}{r-5} - \frac{4}{r+3} = \frac{7(r+3)}{(r-5)(r+3)} - \frac{4(r-5)}{(r-5)(r+3)}$$
$$= \frac{7(r+3) - 4(r-5)}{(r-5)(r+3)}$$
$$= \frac{7r + 21 - 4r + 20}{(r-5)(r+3)}$$
$$= \frac{3r + 41}{(r-5)(r+3)}$$

c) The common denominator is $p(p-3)$:

$$\frac{8}{p} - \frac{1}{p-3} = \frac{8(p-3)}{p(p-3)} - \frac{p}{p(p-3)}$$
$$= \frac{8p - 24 - p}{p(p-3)} = \frac{7p - 24}{p(p-3)}$$

d) The common denominator is $2(w-2)(w-7)$:

$$\frac{w}{2(w-2)} + \frac{3w}{w-7}$$
$$= \frac{w(w-7)}{2(w-2)(w-7)} + \frac{3w \times 2(w-2)}{2(w-2)(w-7)}$$
$$= \frac{w^2 - 7w}{2(w-2)(w-7)} + \frac{6w(w-2)}{2(w-2)(w-7)}$$
$$= \frac{w^2 - 7w + 6w(w-2)}{2(w-2)(w-7)}$$
$$= \frac{w^2 - 7w + 6w^2 - 12w}{2(w-2)(w-7)}$$
$$= \frac{7w^2 - 19w}{2(w-2)(w-7)} = \frac{w(7w-19)}{2(w-2)(w-7)}$$

e) The common denominator is $(z+2)(z+4)$:

$$\frac{z+1}{z+2} - \frac{z+3}{z+4} = \frac{(z+1)(z+4)}{(z+2)(z+4)} - \frac{(z+2)(z+3)}{(z+2)(z+4)}$$
$$= \frac{(z+1)(z+4) - (z+2)(z+3)}{(z+2)(z+4)}$$
$$= \frac{(z^2 + 5z + 4) - (z^2 + 5z + 6)}{(z+2)(z+4)}$$
$$= \frac{-2}{(z+2)(z+4)}$$

f) The common denominator is $(q+1)(q-2)$:

$$\frac{1}{q+1} + \frac{3}{q-2} = \frac{(q-2)}{(q+1)(q-2)} + \frac{3(q+1)}{(q+1)(q-2)}$$
$$= \frac{(q-2) + 3(q+1)}{(q+1)(q-2)}$$
$$= \frac{q - 2 + 3q + 3}{(q+1)(q-2)}$$
$$= \frac{4q + 1}{(q+1)(q-2)}$$

g) The common denominator is $(x+z)(x-z)$:

$$\frac{x}{x+z} + \frac{2z}{x-z} = \frac{x(x-z)}{(x+z)(x-z)} + \frac{2z(x+z)}{(x+z)(x-z)}$$
$$= \frac{x^2 - xz + 2xz + 2z^2}{(x+z)(x-z)} = \frac{x^2 + xz + 2z^2}{(x+z)(x-z)}$$

h) The common denominator is $(2x+3)(3-x)$:

$$\frac{y}{2x+3} - \frac{2y}{3-x} = \frac{y(3-x)}{(2x+3)(3-x)} - \frac{2y(2x+3)}{(2x+3)(3-x)}$$
$$= \frac{3y - xy - 4xy - 6y}{(2x+3)(3-x)}$$
$$= \frac{-3y - 5xy}{(2x+3)(3-x)} = \frac{3y + 5xy}{(2x+3)(x-3)}$$

In the final step, top and bottom have been multiplied by −1 to make the answer a bit neater.

i) The common denominator is $r(r-4)(r+1)$:

$$\frac{5}{r-4} + \frac{3}{r} - \frac{r}{r+1}$$
$$= \frac{5r(r+1)}{r(r-4)(r+1)} + \frac{3(r-4)(r+1)}{r(r-4)(r+1)} - \frac{r^2(r-4)}{r(r-4)(r+1)}$$
$$= \frac{5r^2 + 5r + 3(r^2 + r - 4r - 4) - (r^3 - 4r^2)}{r(r-4)(r+1)}$$
$$= \frac{5r^2 + 5r + 3r^2 - 9r - 12 - r^3 + 4r^2}{r(r-4)(r+1)}$$
$$= \frac{-r^3 + 12r^2 - 4r - 12}{r(r-4)(r+1)}$$

Q3 a) $\frac{2x+10}{6} = \frac{2(x+5)}{6} = \frac{x+5}{3}$

b) $\frac{6a - 12b - 15c}{3} = \frac{3(2a - 4b - 5c)}{3} = 2a - 4b - 5c$

c) $\frac{np^2 - 2n^2p}{np} = \frac{np(p - 2n)}{np} = p - 2n$

d) $\frac{4st + 6s^2t + 9s^3t}{2t} = \frac{st(4 + 6s + 9s^2)}{2t}$

$$= \frac{s(4 + 6s + 9s^2)}{2}$$

e) $\frac{10yz^3 - 40y^3z^3 + 60y^2z^3}{10z^2} = \frac{10yz^3(1 - 4y^2 + 6y)}{10z^2}$

$$= yz(1 - 4y^2 + 6y)$$

f) $\frac{12cd - 6c^2d + 3c^3d^2}{12c^2de} = \frac{3cd(4 - 2c + c^2d)}{12c^2de}$

$$= \frac{4 - 2c + c^2d}{4ce}$$

g) $\frac{2x + x^2y - x^2}{x^2 + 3x} = \frac{x(2 + xy - x)}{x(x+3)} = \frac{2 + xy - x}{x+3}$

h) $\frac{2w^3 + 14w^2}{w^2 - 49} = \frac{2w^2(w+7)}{(w+7)(w-7)} = \frac{2w^2}{w-7}$

i) $\frac{4g^2 - 4h^2}{g^2 + gh} = \frac{4(g^2 - h^2)}{g(g+h)} = \frac{4(g+h)(g-h)}{g(g+h)} = \frac{4(g-h)}{g}$

Q4 a) $\frac{x+3}{(2x+1)^2(x-1)} - \frac{1}{(2x+1)(x-1)^2}$

$$= \frac{(x+3)(x-1) - (2x+1)}{(2x+1)^2(x-1)^2} = \frac{x^2 + 2x - 3 - 2x - 1}{(2x+1)^2(x-1)^2}$$
$$= \frac{x^2 - 4}{(2x+1)^2(x-1)^2} = \frac{(x+2)(x-2)}{(2x+1)^2(x-1)^2}$$

b) $\frac{8}{x}-\left(\frac{5}{2x-1}+\frac{x+4}{x}\right)=\frac{8}{x}-\frac{5}{2x-1}-\frac{x+4}{x}$

$=\frac{8(2x-1)-5x-(x+4)(2x-1)}{x(2x-1)}$

$=\frac{16x-8-5x-2x^2-7x+4}{x(2x-1)}=\frac{-2x^2+4x-4}{x(2x-1)}$

$=\frac{2(x^2-2x+2)}{x(1-2x)}$

c) $\frac{2x+3}{(x-5)(x+9)}+\frac{x}{(x-3)(x-5)}$

$=\frac{(2x+3)(x-3)+x(x+9)}{(x-5)(x-3)(x+9)}=\frac{2x^2-6x+3x-9+x^2+9x}{(x-5)(x-3)(x+9)}$

$=\frac{3x^2+6x-9}{(x-5)(x-3)(x+9)}$

d) $\left(\frac{3}{x+1}\right)^2-\frac{2}{x+1}=\frac{9}{(x+1)^2}-\frac{2}{x+1}$

$=\frac{9-2(x+1)}{(x+1)^2}=\frac{7-2x}{(x+1)^2}$

Q5 $\frac{8}{2x+1}-4\left(\frac{3}{x+4}+\frac{1}{2}\right)=\frac{8}{2x+1}-2\left(\frac{6+(x+4)}{x+4}\right)$

$=\frac{8}{2x+1}-\frac{12+2x+8}{x+4}=\frac{8(x+4)-(20+2x)(2x+1)}{(x+4)(2x+1)}$

$=\frac{8x+32-40x-20-4x^2-2x}{(x+4)(2x+1)}=\frac{12-34x-4x^2}{(x+4)(2x+1)}$

$=\frac{2(6-17x-2x^2)}{(x+4)(2x+1)}$

[4 marks available — 1 mark for simplifying the brackets to a single fraction, 1 mark for writing as a single fraction with the correct common denominator, 1 mark for simplifying the numerator, 1 mark for the fully correct simplified fraction]

Q6 Maya's pieces are $\frac{10}{x}$ cm long. Hal's pieces are $\frac{15}{x+3}$ cm long.

So the total length of one of Maya's pieces and one of Hal's pieces is: $\frac{10}{x}+\frac{15}{x+3}=\frac{10(x+3)}{x(x+3)}+\frac{15x}{x(x+3)}$

$=\frac{10x+30+15x}{x(x+3)}=\frac{25x+30}{x(x+3)}=\frac{5(5x+6)}{x(x+3)}$ cm

Q7 $\frac{12}{2(x-3)}-\frac{6}{3(x+4)}=\frac{6}{x-3}-\frac{2}{x+4}=\frac{6(x+4)-2(x-3)}{(x-3)(x+4)}$

$=\frac{6x+24-2x+6}{(x-3)(x+4)}=\frac{4x+30}{(x-3)(x+4)}\Rightarrow A=4$ and $B=30$

[3 marks available — 1 mark for finding the correct common denominator, 1 mark for simplifying the numerator, 1 mark for both correct values of A and B]

Q8 a) $\frac{a}{2x+1}+\frac{b}{x-3}\equiv\frac{a(x-3)}{(2x+1)(x-3)}+\frac{b(2x+1)}{(2x+1)(x-3)}$

$\equiv\frac{a(x-3)+b(2x+1)}{(2x+1)(x-3)}\equiv\frac{ax-3a+2bx+b}{(2x+1)(x-3)}$

$\equiv\frac{(a+2b)x+(b-3a)}{(2x+1)(x-3)}$

[3 marks available — 3 marks for the correct working to show the required result, otherwise 2 marks for correctly adding the fractions, or 1 mark for attempting to find the common denominator]

b) Equate corresponding coefficients:
$a+2b=1$ and $b-3a=-17\Rightarrow a=5$ and $b=-2$
[2 marks available — 1 mark for equating coefficients, 1 mark for the correct values for a and b]

Exercise 3.4 — Laws of Indices

Q1 a) $10\times10^4=10^{1+4}=10^5$

b) $y^{-1}\times y^{-2}\times y^7=y^{-1-2+7}=y^4$

c) $5^{\frac{1}{2}}\times5^3\times5^{-\frac{3}{2}}=5^{\frac{1}{2}+3-\frac{3}{2}}=5^2$

d) $6^5\div6^2=6^{5-2}=6^3$

e) $3^4\div3^{-1}=3^{4-(-1)}=3^{4+1}=3^5$

f) $\frac{6^{11}}{6}=6^{11-1}=6^{10}$

g) $\frac{r^2}{r^6}=r^{2-6}=r^{-4}$

h) $(3^2)^3=3^{2\times3}=3^6$

i) $(k^{-2})^5=k^{(-2)\times5}=k^{-10}$

j) $(z^4)^{-\frac{1}{8}}=z^{4\times\left(-\frac{1}{8}\right)}=z^{-\frac{4}{8}}=z^{-\frac{1}{2}}$

k) $(8^{-6})^{-\frac{1}{2}}=8^{-6\times-\frac{1}{2}}=8^{\frac{6}{2}}=8^3$

l) $\frac{p^5q^4}{p^4q}=(p^{5-4})(q^{4-1})=p^1q^3=pq^3$

m) $\frac{c^{-1}d^{-2}}{c^2d^4}=c^{-1-2}d^{-2-4}=c^{-3}d^{-6}=\frac{1}{c^3d^6}$

n) $(ab^2)^2=(a)^2(b^2)^2=a^2b^{2\times2}=a^2b^4$

o) $\frac{12yz^{-\frac{1}{2}}}{4yz^{\frac{1}{2}}}=\left(\frac{12}{4}\right)(y^{1-1})\left(z^{-\frac{1}{2}-\frac{1}{2}}\right)=3y^0z^{-1}=\frac{3}{z}$

p) $(mn^{\frac{1}{2}})^4=m^4n^{\frac{1}{2}\times4}=m^4n^2$

Q2 a) $4^{\frac{1}{2}}\times4^{\frac{3}{2}}=4^{\frac{1}{2}+\frac{3}{2}}=4^2=16$

b) $\frac{2^3\times2}{2^5}=\frac{2^{3+1}}{2^5}=\frac{2^4}{2^5}=2^{4-5}=2^{-1}=\frac{1}{2}$

c) $\frac{7^5\times7^3}{7^6}=\frac{7^{5+3}}{7^6}=\frac{7^8}{7^6}=7^{8-6}=7^2=49$

d) $\frac{6^4}{6^{\frac{5}{4}}\times6^{\frac{3}{4}}}=\frac{6^4}{6^{\frac{5}{4}+\frac{3}{4}}}=\frac{6^4}{6^{\frac{8}{4}}}=\frac{6^4}{6^2}=6^{4-2}=6^2=36$

e) $(3^2)^5\div(3^3)^3=3^{2\times5}\div3^{3\times3}$
$=3^{10}\div3^9=3^{10-9}=3^1=3$

f) $(4^{-\frac{1}{2}})^2\times(4^{-3})^{-\frac{1}{3}}=4^{-\frac{1}{2}\times2}\times4^{(-3)\times\left(-\frac{1}{3}\right)}$
$=4^{-1}\times4^1=4^{-1+1}=4^0=1$

g) $\frac{(2^{\frac{1}{2}})^6\times(2^{-2})^{-2}}{(2^{-1})^{-1}}=\frac{2^{\frac{1}{2}\times6}\times2^{(-2)\times(-2)}}{2^{(-1)\times(-1)}}=\frac{2^3\times2^4}{2^1}=\frac{2^{3+4}}{2^1}$
$=\frac{2^7}{2^1}=2^6=64$

h) $1^0=1$

i) $\left(\frac{4}{5}\right)^0=1$

j) $(-5.726324)^0=1$

k) $8.374936^1=8.374936$

l) $\frac{(3^3)^2}{(9^{\frac{1}{2}})^4\times(9^{\frac{1}{4}})^8}=\frac{3^{3\times2}}{9^{\frac{1}{2}\times4}\times9^{\frac{1}{4}\times8}}=\frac{3^6}{9^2\times9^2}$
$=\frac{3^6}{9^{2+2}}=\frac{3^6}{9^4}=\frac{(3^2)^3}{9^4}=\frac{9^3}{9^4}=9^{3-4}=9^{-1}=\frac{1}{9}$

Q3 a) $\frac{1}{p}=p^{-1}$

b) $\frac{5}{y^4}=5y^{-4}$

c) $\sqrt{q}=q^{\frac{1}{2}}$

d) $\sqrt{r^3}=(r^3)^{\frac{1}{2}}=r^{3\times\frac{1}{2}}=r^{\frac{3}{2}}$

e) $\sqrt[4]{s^5}=(s^5)^{\frac{1}{4}}=s^{5\times\frac{1}{4}}=s^{\frac{5}{4}}$

f) $\frac{1}{\sqrt[3]{t}}=\frac{1}{(t^{\frac{1}{3}})}=t^{-\frac{1}{3}}$

g) $\left(\frac{1}{\sqrt[3]{x}}\right)^4=\left(\frac{1}{x^{\frac{1}{3}}}\right)^4=\left(x^{-\frac{1}{3}}\right)^4=x^{-\frac{1}{3}\times4}=x^{-\frac{4}{3}}$

h) $\frac{\sqrt{z}}{z^3}=\frac{z^{\frac{1}{2}}}{z^3}=z^{\frac{1}{2}-3}=z^{-\frac{5}{2}}$

Q4 a) $9^{\frac{1}{2}}=\sqrt{9}=3$

b) $8^{\frac{1}{3}}=\sqrt[3]{8}=2$

c) $4^{\frac{3}{2}}=4^{\frac{1}{2}\times3}=(4^{\frac{1}{2}})^3=(\sqrt{4})^3=(2)^3=8$

d) $27^{-\frac{1}{3}}=\frac{1}{27^{\frac{1}{3}}}=\frac{1}{\sqrt[3]{27}}=\frac{1}{3}$

e) $16^{-\frac{3}{4}}=\frac{1}{16^{\frac{3}{4}}}=\frac{1}{(16^{\frac{1}{4}})^3}=\frac{1}{(\sqrt[4]{16})^3}=\frac{1}{(2)^3}=\frac{1}{8}$

f) $125^{\frac{2}{3}}=125^{\frac{1}{3}\times2}=(125^{\frac{1}{3}})^2=(\sqrt[3]{125})^2=5^2=25$

g) $81^{\frac{1}{4}}=\sqrt[4]{81}=3$

h) $64^{\frac{1}{2}}\times64^{-\frac{1}{3}}=64^{\frac{1}{2}}\times\frac{1}{64^{\frac{1}{3}}}=\sqrt{64}\times\frac{1}{\sqrt[3]{64}}=8\times\frac{1}{4}=2$

Q5 Taking the cube root gives: $x^{\frac{1}{3}}$
Raising this to the power 6 gives: $(x^{\frac{1}{3}})^6=x^{\frac{1}{3}\times6}=x^2$
Dividing by x gives: $x^2\div x=x$

Q6 a) $p^{\frac{1}{2}}=\left(\frac{1}{16}q^2\right)^{\frac{1}{2}}=\left(\frac{1}{16}\right)^{\frac{1}{2}}(q^2)^{\frac{1}{2}}$
$=\sqrt{\frac{1}{16}}q^{2\times\frac{1}{2}}=\frac{1}{\sqrt{16}}q=\frac{1}{4}q$

b) $2p^{-1} = 2\left(\frac{1}{16}q^2\right)^{-1} = 2\left(\frac{1}{16}\right)^{-1}(q^2)^{-1}$

$= 2 \times 16 \times q^{2\times -1} = 32q^{-2} = \frac{32}{q^2}$

c) $p^{\frac{1}{2}} \div 2p^{-1} = \frac{1}{4}q \div \left(\frac{32}{q^2}\right) = \frac{1}{4}q \times \frac{q^2}{32}$

$= \frac{q^3}{128} = \frac{1}{128}q^3$

Substitute the answers from a) and b) into the division and use the rule for dividing by fractions. You could also simplify the expression to $\frac{1}{2}p^{\frac{3}{2}}$ first.

d) $p^2q = \left(\frac{1}{16}q^2\right)^2 q = \frac{1}{256}q^4 \times q = \frac{1}{256}q^5$

e) $\frac{4p}{q^3} = \frac{4\left(\frac{1}{16}q^2\right)}{q^3} = \frac{\frac{1}{4}q^2}{q^3} = \frac{1}{4q}$

f) $\frac{q^2}{4p^2} = \frac{q^2}{4\left(\frac{1}{16}q^2\right)^2} = \frac{q^2}{4\left(\frac{1}{256}q^4\right)} = \frac{q^2}{\frac{1}{64}q^4} = \frac{64}{q^2}$

Q7 Start by writing b as a power of 8: $b = 64^3 = (8^2)^3 = 8^6$

Then: $\frac{a^{-5}}{b^{\frac{1}{2}} \times c^4} = \frac{(8^{-3})^{-5}}{(8^6)^{\frac{1}{2}} \times (8^{\frac{1}{2}})^4} = \frac{8^{15}}{8^3 \times 8^2} = \frac{8^{15}}{8^{3+2}}$

$= \frac{8^{15}}{8^5} = 8^{15-5} = 8^{10}$

Q8 a) Write the RHS as 4 to the power 'something':
$\sqrt[3]{16} = (16)^{\frac{1}{3}} = (4^2)^{\frac{1}{3}} = 4^{2\times\frac{1}{3}} = 4^{\frac{2}{3}}$, so $x = \frac{2}{3}$.

b) Write the RHS as 9 to the power 'something':
$\frac{1}{3} = \frac{1}{\sqrt{9}} = \frac{1}{9^{\frac{1}{2}}} = 9^{-\frac{1}{2}}$, so $x = -\frac{1}{2}$.

c) Write the LHS as 5 to the power 'something':
$\sqrt{5} \times 5^x = 5^{\frac{1}{2}} \times 5^x = 5^{x+\frac{1}{2}}$
Write the RHS as 5 to the power 'something':
$\frac{1}{25} = \frac{1}{5^2} = 5^{-2}$
Then equate the two 'something's:
$x + \frac{1}{2} = -2$. So $x = -2 - \frac{1}{2} = -\frac{5}{2}$.

d) Write the LHS as 16 to the power 'something':
$(16^x)^2 = 16^{2x}$
Write the RHS as 16 to the power 'something':
$\frac{1}{4} = \frac{1}{16^{\frac{1}{2}}} = 16^{-\frac{1}{2}}$
Then equate the two 'something's:
$2x = -\frac{1}{2}$, so $x = -\frac{1}{4}$.

e) Write the LHS as 'something' to the power 3:
$x^{-3} = \frac{1}{x^3} = \left(\frac{1}{x}\right)^3$
Write the RHS as 'something' to the power 3:
$-8 = (-2)^3$
Then equate the two 'something's:
$\frac{1}{x} = -2$, so $x = -\frac{1}{2}$.

f) Square both sides:
$\sqrt{100^x} = 0.001 \Rightarrow 100^x = 0.001^2$
$\Rightarrow 100^x = 0.000001$
Write the RHS as a power of 100:
$0.000001 = 10^{-6} = (100^{\frac{1}{2}})^{-6} = 100^{-3}$
Then equate the powers on each side: $x = -3$
In each of the parts of this question, you could have used the laws in a different order to get the same answer.

Exercise 3.5 — The Laws of Surds

Q1 a) $\sqrt{8} = \sqrt{4 \times 2} = \sqrt{4}\sqrt{2} = 2\sqrt{2}$

b) $\sqrt{24} = \sqrt{4 \times 6} = \sqrt{4}\sqrt{6} = 2\sqrt{6}$

c) $\sqrt{50} = \sqrt{25 \times 2} = \sqrt{25}\sqrt{2} = 5\sqrt{2}$

d) $\sqrt{63} = \sqrt{9 \times 7} = \sqrt{9}\sqrt{7} = 3\sqrt{7}$

e) $\sqrt{72} = \sqrt{36 \times 2} = \sqrt{36}\sqrt{2} = 6\sqrt{2}$

f) $\sqrt{\frac{5}{4}} = \frac{\sqrt{5}}{\sqrt{4}} = \frac{\sqrt{5}}{2}$

g) $\sqrt{\frac{7}{100}} = \frac{\sqrt{7}}{\sqrt{100}} = \frac{\sqrt{7}}{10}$

h) $\sqrt{\frac{11}{9}} = \frac{\sqrt{11}}{\sqrt{9}} = \frac{\sqrt{11}}{3}$

Q2 a) $2\sqrt{3} \times 4\sqrt{3} = 2 \times 4 \times \sqrt{3} \times \sqrt{3}$
$= 8\sqrt{3}\sqrt{3} = 8 \times 3 = 24$

b) $\sqrt{5} \times 3\sqrt{5} = 3\sqrt{5}\sqrt{5} = 3 \times 5 = 15$

c) $(\sqrt{7})^2 = \sqrt{7}\sqrt{7} = 7$

d) $2\sqrt{2} \times 3\sqrt{5} = 2 \times 3 \times \sqrt{2} \times \sqrt{5} = 6\sqrt{2}\sqrt{5} = 6\sqrt{10}$

e) $(2\sqrt{11})^2 = (2\sqrt{11})(2\sqrt{11})$
$= 4\sqrt{11}\sqrt{11} = 4 \times 11 = 44$

f) $5\sqrt{8} \times 2\sqrt{2} = 5\sqrt{4 \times 2} \times 2\sqrt{2}$
$= 5 \times 2\sqrt{2} \times 2\sqrt{2}$
$= 5 \times 4 \times \sqrt{2} \times \sqrt{2} = 20 \times 2 = 40$

g) $4\sqrt{3} \times 2\sqrt{27} = 4 \times 2 \times \sqrt{3}\sqrt{27}$
$= 8\sqrt{3 \times 27} = 8\sqrt{81} = 8 \times 9 = 72$

h) $2\sqrt{6} \times 5\sqrt{24} = 2 \times 5 \times \sqrt{6} \times \sqrt{24}$
$= 10\sqrt{6 \times 24} = 10\sqrt{144}$
$= 10 \times 12 = 120$

i) $\frac{6}{\sqrt{11}} \times \sqrt{44} = \frac{6}{\sqrt{11}} \times \sqrt{4 \times 11}$
$= \frac{6}{\sqrt{11}} \times \sqrt{4}\sqrt{11} = 6 \times 2 = 12$

j) $2\sqrt{18} \times \frac{5}{\sqrt{8}} = 2\sqrt{9 \times 2} \times \frac{5}{\sqrt{4 \times 2}}$
$= 2\sqrt{9}\sqrt{2} \times \frac{5}{\sqrt{4}\sqrt{2}} = 2 \times 3\sqrt{2} \times \frac{5}{2\sqrt{2}} = 15$

k) $\frac{\sqrt{10}}{6} \times \frac{12}{\sqrt{5}} = \frac{12\sqrt{10}}{6\sqrt{5}}$
$= \frac{12}{6} \times \frac{\sqrt{10}}{\sqrt{5}} = 2 \times \sqrt{\frac{10}{5}} = 2\sqrt{2}$

l) $\frac{\sqrt{12}}{3} \times \frac{2}{\sqrt{27}} = \frac{2\sqrt{12}}{3\sqrt{27}} = \frac{2}{3} \times \frac{\sqrt{12}}{\sqrt{27}}$
$= \frac{2}{3} \times \frac{\sqrt{4 \times 3}}{\sqrt{9 \times 3}} = \frac{2}{3} \times \frac{\sqrt{4}\sqrt{3}}{\sqrt{9}\sqrt{3}}$
$= \frac{2}{3} \times \frac{2\sqrt{3}}{3\sqrt{3}} = \frac{2}{3} \times \frac{2}{3} = \frac{4}{9}$

Q3 a) $\sqrt{20} + \sqrt{5} = \sqrt{4 \times 5} + \sqrt{5} = \sqrt{4}\sqrt{5} + \sqrt{5}$
$= 2\sqrt{5} + \sqrt{5} = 3\sqrt{5}$

b) $\sqrt{32} - \sqrt{8} = \sqrt{16 \times 2} - \sqrt{4 \times 2}$
$= \sqrt{16}\sqrt{2} - \sqrt{4}\sqrt{2} = 4\sqrt{2} - 2\sqrt{2} = 2\sqrt{2}$

c) $\sqrt{27} + 4\sqrt{3} = \sqrt{9 \times 3} + 4\sqrt{3} = \sqrt{9}\sqrt{3} + 4\sqrt{3}$
$= 3\sqrt{3} + 4\sqrt{3} = 7\sqrt{3}$

d) $2\sqrt{8} - 3\sqrt{2} = 2\sqrt{4 \times 2} - 3\sqrt{2}$
$= 2\sqrt{4}\sqrt{2} - 3\sqrt{2} = 4\sqrt{2} - 3\sqrt{2} = \sqrt{2}$

e) $3\sqrt{10} + \sqrt{250} = 3\sqrt{10} + \sqrt{25 \times 10}$
$= 3\sqrt{10} + \sqrt{25}\sqrt{10}$
$= 3\sqrt{10} + 5\sqrt{10} = 8\sqrt{10}$

f) $4\sqrt{27} + 2\sqrt{48} + 5\sqrt{108}$
$= 4\sqrt{9 \times 3} + 2\sqrt{16 \times 3} + 5\sqrt{36 \times 3}$
$= 4\sqrt{9}\sqrt{3} + 2\sqrt{16}\sqrt{3} + 5\sqrt{36}\sqrt{3}$
$= 12\sqrt{3} + 8\sqrt{3} + 30\sqrt{3} = 50\sqrt{3}$

Q4 a) $(1 + \sqrt{2})(2 + \sqrt{2}) = 2 + \sqrt{2} + 2\sqrt{2} + \sqrt{2}\sqrt{2}$
$= 2 + 3\sqrt{2} + 2 = 4 + 3\sqrt{2}$

b) $(3 + 4\sqrt{3})(2 - \sqrt{3}) = 6 - 3\sqrt{3} + 8\sqrt{3} - 4\sqrt{3}\sqrt{3}$
$= 6 + 5\sqrt{3} - 12 = 5\sqrt{3} - 6$

c) By the difference of two squares rule:
$(\sqrt{11} + 2)(\sqrt{11} - 2) = (\sqrt{11})^2 - 2^2 = 11 - 4 = 7$

d) By the difference of two squares rule:
$(9-2\sqrt{5})(9+2\sqrt{5}) = 9^2 - (2\sqrt{5})^2 = 81 - 20 = 61$

e) $(\sqrt{3}+2)^2 = (\sqrt{3}+2)(\sqrt{3}+2)$
$= \sqrt{3}\sqrt{3} + 2\sqrt{3} + 2\sqrt{3} + 4$
$= 3 + 4\sqrt{3} + 4 = 7 + 4\sqrt{3}$

f) $(3\sqrt{5}-4)^2 = (3\sqrt{5}-4)(3\sqrt{5}-4)$
$= (3\sqrt{5})^2 - 12\sqrt{5} - 12\sqrt{5} + 16$
$= 45 - 24\sqrt{5} + 16$
$= 61 - 24\sqrt{5}$

You could have used the rule $(a+b)^2 = a^2 + 2ab + b^2$ for parts e and f.

Q5 Area of parallelogram = base length × vertical height
$= 2\sqrt{6} \times \sqrt{3} = 2\sqrt{2\times3}\sqrt{3} = 2\sqrt{2}\sqrt{3}\sqrt{3}$
$= 2\sqrt{2} \times 3 = 6\sqrt{2}\text{ cm}^2$

Q6 Perimeter $= 2(3\sqrt{28} + \sqrt{63}) = 2(3\sqrt{4\times7} + \sqrt{9\times7})$
$= 2(3\sqrt{4}\sqrt{7} + \sqrt{9}\sqrt{7}) = 2(3\times2\times\sqrt{7} + 3\sqrt{7})$
$= 2(6\sqrt{7} + 3\sqrt{7}) = 2(9\sqrt{7}) = 18\sqrt{7}\text{ m}$

Q7 You may want to draw the triangle:
Using Pythagoras:
$(\sqrt{2})^2 + (BC)^2 = (5\sqrt{2})^2$
$2 + (BC)^2 = 50$
$\Rightarrow (BC)^2 = 48$
$\Rightarrow BC = \sqrt{48} = \sqrt{16\times3} = 4\sqrt{3}\text{ cm}$

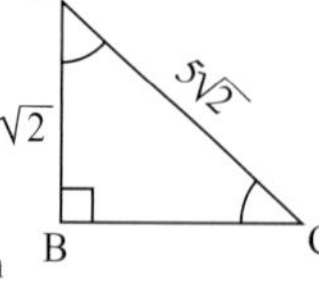

Exercise 3.6 — Rationalising the Denominator

Q1 a) $\frac{6}{\sqrt{3}} = \frac{6\sqrt{3}}{\sqrt{3}\sqrt{3}} = \frac{6\sqrt{3}}{3} = 2\sqrt{3}$

b) $\frac{21}{\sqrt{7}} = \frac{21\sqrt{7}}{\sqrt{7}\sqrt{7}} = \frac{21\sqrt{7}}{7} = 3\sqrt{7}$

c) $\frac{30}{\sqrt{5}} = \frac{30\sqrt{5}}{\sqrt{5}\sqrt{5}} = \frac{30\sqrt{5}}{5} = 6\sqrt{5}$

d) $\sqrt{45} + \frac{15}{\sqrt{5}} = \sqrt{45} + \frac{15\sqrt{5}}{\sqrt{5}\sqrt{5}} = \sqrt{45} + \frac{15\sqrt{5}}{5}$
$= \sqrt{9\times5} + 3\sqrt{5}$
$= \sqrt{9}\sqrt{5} + 3\sqrt{5}$
$= 3\sqrt{5} + 3\sqrt{5} = 6\sqrt{5}$

e) $\frac{\sqrt{54}}{3} - \frac{12}{\sqrt{6}} = \frac{\sqrt{9\times6}}{3} - \frac{12\sqrt{6}}{\sqrt{6}\sqrt{6}}$
$= \frac{\sqrt{9}\sqrt{6}}{3} - \frac{12\sqrt{6}}{6}$
$= \frac{3\sqrt{6}}{3} - \frac{12\sqrt{6}}{6} = \sqrt{6} - 2\sqrt{6} = -\sqrt{6}$

f) $\frac{\sqrt{300}}{5} + \frac{30}{\sqrt{12}} = \frac{\sqrt{100\times3}}{5} + \frac{30\sqrt{12}}{\sqrt{12}\sqrt{12}}$
$= \frac{\sqrt{100}\sqrt{3}}{5} + \frac{30\sqrt{4\times3}}{12}$
$= \frac{10\sqrt{3}}{5} + \frac{30\sqrt{4}\sqrt{3}}{12}$
$= 2\sqrt{3} + \frac{60\sqrt{3}}{12} = 2\sqrt{3} + 5\sqrt{3} = 7\sqrt{3}$

g) $\frac{1}{\sqrt{18}} - \frac{1}{\sqrt{2}} = \frac{1}{\sqrt{9\times2}} - \frac{1}{\sqrt{2}} = \frac{1}{3\sqrt{2}} - \frac{1}{\sqrt{2}}$
$= \frac{1-3}{3\sqrt{2}} = \frac{-2}{3\sqrt{2}} = \frac{-2\sqrt{2}}{3\times2} = -\frac{2\sqrt{2}}{6} = -\frac{1}{3}\sqrt{2}$

h) $\frac{1}{\sqrt{28}} + \frac{3}{\sqrt{7}} = \frac{1}{\sqrt{4\times7}} + \frac{3}{\sqrt{7}} = \frac{1}{2\sqrt{7}} + \frac{3}{\sqrt{7}}$
$= \frac{1+6}{2\sqrt{7}} = \frac{7}{2\sqrt{7}} = \frac{7\sqrt{7}}{2\times7} = \frac{1}{2}\sqrt{7}$

i) $\frac{2}{\sqrt{72}} - \frac{5}{\sqrt{8}} = \frac{2}{\sqrt{9\times8}} - \frac{5}{\sqrt{8}} = \frac{2}{3\sqrt{8}} - \frac{5}{\sqrt{8}} = \frac{2-15}{3\sqrt{8}}$
$= \frac{-13}{3\sqrt{8}} = \frac{-13\sqrt{8}}{3\times8} = -\frac{13}{24}\sqrt{8} = -\frac{13}{24}\times2\sqrt{2} = -\frac{13}{12}\sqrt{2}$

Q2 a) $\frac{4}{1+\sqrt{3}} = \frac{4(1-\sqrt{3})}{(1+\sqrt{3})(1-\sqrt{3})}$
$= \frac{4-4\sqrt{3}}{1-3} = \frac{4-4\sqrt{3}}{-2} = -2+2\sqrt{3}$

The denominator was simplified by using the difference of two squares rule. It will be used in almost every question in the rest of this exercise, so watch out for it and make sure you understand what's going on.

b) $\frac{8}{-1+\sqrt{5}} = \frac{8(-1-\sqrt{5})}{(-1+\sqrt{5})(-1-\sqrt{5})}$
$= \frac{-8-8\sqrt{5}}{1-5} = \frac{-8-8\sqrt{5}}{-4} = 2+2\sqrt{5}$

c) $\frac{18}{\sqrt{10}-4} = \frac{18(\sqrt{10}+4)}{(\sqrt{10}-4)(\sqrt{10}+4)} = \frac{18\sqrt{10}+72}{10-16}$
$= \frac{18\sqrt{10}+72}{-6} = -12-3\sqrt{10}$

d) $\frac{\sqrt{6}}{2-\sqrt{6}} = \frac{\sqrt{6}(2+\sqrt{6})}{(2-\sqrt{6})(2+\sqrt{6})} = \frac{2\sqrt{6}+6}{4-6}$
$= \frac{2\sqrt{6}+6}{-2} = -3-\sqrt{6}$

e) $\frac{3}{5+2\sqrt{7}} = \frac{3(5-2\sqrt{7})}{(5+2\sqrt{7})(5-2\sqrt{7})} = \frac{15-6\sqrt{7}}{25-(2\sqrt{7})^2}$
$= \frac{15-6\sqrt{7}}{25-28} = \frac{15-6\sqrt{7}}{-3} = -5+2\sqrt{7}$

f) $\frac{6}{3\sqrt{2}-4} = \frac{6(3\sqrt{2}+4)}{(3\sqrt{2}-4)(3\sqrt{2}+4)} = \frac{18\sqrt{2}+24}{(3\sqrt{2})^2-16}$
$= \frac{18\sqrt{2}+24}{18-16} = \frac{18\sqrt{2}+24}{2} = 12+9\sqrt{2}$

Q3 a) $\frac{\sqrt{2}+1}{\sqrt{2}-1} = \frac{(\sqrt{2}+1)(\sqrt{2}+1)}{(\sqrt{2}-1)(\sqrt{2}+1)}$
$= \frac{2+\sqrt{2}+\sqrt{2}+1}{2-1} = \frac{2\sqrt{2}+3}{1} = 3+2\sqrt{2}$

b) $\frac{\sqrt{5}+3}{\sqrt{5}-2} = \frac{(\sqrt{5}+3)(\sqrt{5}+2)}{(\sqrt{5}-2)(\sqrt{5}+2)}$
$= \frac{5+2\sqrt{5}+3\sqrt{5}+6}{5-4}$
$= \frac{11+5\sqrt{5}}{1} = 11+5\sqrt{5}$

c) $\frac{3-\sqrt{3}}{4+\sqrt{3}} = \frac{(3-\sqrt{3})(4-\sqrt{3})}{(4+\sqrt{3})(4-\sqrt{3})} = \frac{12-3\sqrt{3}-4\sqrt{3}+3}{16-3}$
$= \frac{15-7\sqrt{3}}{13} = \frac{15}{13} - \frac{7}{13}\sqrt{3}$

d) $\frac{3\sqrt{5}-1}{2\sqrt{5}-3} = \frac{(3\sqrt{5}-1)(2\sqrt{5}+3)}{(2\sqrt{5}-3)(2\sqrt{5}+3)}$
$= \frac{(2\sqrt{5})(3\sqrt{5})+9\sqrt{5}-2\sqrt{5}-3}{(2\sqrt{5})^2-9}$
$= \frac{27+7\sqrt{5}}{(2\sqrt{5})^2-9} = \frac{27+7\sqrt{5}}{11} = \frac{27}{11} + \frac{7}{11}\sqrt{5}$

e) $\frac{\sqrt{2}+\sqrt{3}}{3\sqrt{2}-\sqrt{3}} = \frac{(\sqrt{2}+\sqrt{3})(3\sqrt{2}+\sqrt{3})}{(3\sqrt{2}-\sqrt{3})(3\sqrt{2}+\sqrt{3})}$
$= \frac{3\sqrt{2}\sqrt{2}+\sqrt{2}\sqrt{3}+3\sqrt{3}\sqrt{2}+3}{(3\sqrt{2})^2-(\sqrt{3})^2}$
$= \frac{6+\sqrt{6}+3\sqrt{6}+3}{18-3}$
$= \frac{9+4\sqrt{6}}{15} = \frac{9}{15} + \frac{4}{15}\sqrt{6}$
$= \frac{3}{5} + \frac{4}{15}\sqrt{6}$

f) $\frac{2\sqrt{7}-\sqrt{5}}{\sqrt{7}+2\sqrt{5}} = \frac{(2\sqrt{7}-\sqrt{5})(\sqrt{7}-2\sqrt{5})}{(\sqrt{7}+2\sqrt{5})(\sqrt{7}-2\sqrt{5})}$
$= \frac{2\sqrt{7}\sqrt{7}-4\sqrt{7}\sqrt{5}-\sqrt{5}\sqrt{7}+10}{7-(2\sqrt{5})^2}$
$= \frac{14-4\sqrt{35}-\sqrt{35}+10}{7-20}$
$= \frac{24-5\sqrt{35}}{-13} = -\frac{24}{13} + \frac{5}{13}\sqrt{35}$

g) $\frac{2\sqrt{2}+\sqrt{3}}{\sqrt{3}-\sqrt{12}} = \frac{(2\sqrt{2}+\sqrt{3})(\sqrt{3}+\sqrt{12})}{(\sqrt{3}-\sqrt{12})(\sqrt{3}+\sqrt{12})}$
$= \frac{2\sqrt{2}\sqrt{3}+2\sqrt{2}\sqrt{12}+3+\sqrt{3}\sqrt{12}}{3-12}$
$= \frac{2\sqrt{2}\sqrt{3}+2\sqrt{2}\sqrt{4\times3}+3+\sqrt{3}\sqrt{4\times3}}{-9}$
$= -\frac{2\sqrt{2}\sqrt{3}+4\sqrt{2}\sqrt{3}+3+2\sqrt{3}\sqrt{3}}{9}$
$= -\frac{6\sqrt{2}\sqrt{3}+3+2\times3}{9} = -\frac{6\sqrt{6}+9}{9} = -1-\frac{2}{3}\sqrt{6}$

h) $\frac{6-4\sqrt{2}}{5\sqrt{2}-\sqrt{8}} = \frac{(6-4\sqrt{2})(5\sqrt{2}+\sqrt{8})}{(5\sqrt{2}-\sqrt{8})(5\sqrt{2}+\sqrt{8})}$
$= \frac{30\sqrt{2}+6\sqrt{8}-20\sqrt{2}\sqrt{2}-4\sqrt{2}\sqrt{8}}{(5\sqrt{2})^2-8}$
$= \frac{30\sqrt{2}+6\sqrt{4\times2}-40-4\sqrt{2}\sqrt{4\times2}}{42}$
$= \frac{30\sqrt{2}+12\sqrt{2}-40-4\sqrt{2}\times2\sqrt{2}}{42}$
$= \frac{42\sqrt{2}-40-16}{42} = \frac{42\sqrt{2}-56}{42} = -\frac{4}{3}+\sqrt{2}$

i) $\frac{\sqrt{3}+3}{\sqrt{5}+\sqrt{15}} = \frac{(\sqrt{3}+3)(\sqrt{5}-\sqrt{15})}{(\sqrt{5}+\sqrt{15})(\sqrt{5}-\sqrt{15})}$
$= \frac{\sqrt{3}\sqrt{5}-\sqrt{3}\sqrt{15}+3\sqrt{5}-3\sqrt{15}}{-10}$
$= \frac{\sqrt{15}-\sqrt{3}\sqrt{15}+\sqrt{3}\sqrt{3}\sqrt{5}-3\sqrt{15}}{-10}$
$= \frac{\sqrt{15}-\sqrt{3}\sqrt{15}+\sqrt{3}\sqrt{15}-3\sqrt{15}}{-10} = \frac{-2\sqrt{15}}{-10} = \frac{1}{5}\sqrt{15}$

Q4 **a)** $\frac{4}{\sqrt{7}-\sqrt{3}} = \frac{4(\sqrt{7}+\sqrt{3})}{(\sqrt{7}-\sqrt{3})(\sqrt{7}+\sqrt{3})}$
$= \frac{4(\sqrt{7}+\sqrt{3})}{7-3} = \frac{4(\sqrt{7}+\sqrt{3})}{4} = \sqrt{7}+\sqrt{3}$

b) $\frac{24}{\sqrt{11}-\sqrt{17}} = \frac{24(\sqrt{11}+\sqrt{17})}{(\sqrt{11}-\sqrt{17})(\sqrt{11}+\sqrt{17})}$
$= \frac{24(\sqrt{11}+\sqrt{17})}{11-17} = \frac{24(\sqrt{11}+\sqrt{17})}{-6}$
$= -4(\sqrt{11}+\sqrt{17})$

c) $\frac{2}{\sqrt{13}+\sqrt{5}} = \frac{2(\sqrt{13}-\sqrt{5})}{(\sqrt{13}+\sqrt{5})(\sqrt{13}-\sqrt{5})}$
$= \frac{2(\sqrt{13}-\sqrt{5})}{13-5} = \frac{2(\sqrt{13}-\sqrt{5})}{8} = \frac{1}{4}(\sqrt{13}-\sqrt{5})$

d) $\frac{\sqrt{5}}{\sqrt{6}+\sqrt{3}} = \frac{\sqrt{5}(\sqrt{6}-\sqrt{3})}{(\sqrt{6}+\sqrt{3})(\sqrt{6}-\sqrt{3})}$
$= \frac{\sqrt{5}\sqrt{6}-\sqrt{5}\sqrt{3}}{6-3} = \frac{1}{3}(\sqrt{30}-\sqrt{15})$

e) $\frac{\sqrt{3}}{\sqrt{21}-3\sqrt{5}} = \frac{\sqrt{3}(\sqrt{21}+3\sqrt{5})}{(\sqrt{21}-3\sqrt{5})(\sqrt{21}+3\sqrt{5})}$
$= \frac{\sqrt{3}\sqrt{21}+3\sqrt{3}\sqrt{5}}{21-(3\sqrt{5})^2} = \frac{\sqrt{3}\sqrt{21}+3\sqrt{3}\sqrt{5}}{21-45}$
$= \frac{\sqrt{3}\sqrt{3\times7}+3\sqrt{3}\sqrt{5}}{-24} = -\frac{3\sqrt{7}+3\sqrt{15}}{24}$
$= -\frac{3}{24}(\sqrt{7}+\sqrt{15}) = -\frac{1}{8}(\sqrt{7}+\sqrt{15})$

f) $\frac{3\sqrt{2}}{2\sqrt{3}+\sqrt{20}} = \frac{3\sqrt{2}(2\sqrt{3}-\sqrt{20})}{(2\sqrt{3}+\sqrt{20})(2\sqrt{3}-\sqrt{20})}$
$= \frac{6\sqrt{2}\sqrt{3}-3\sqrt{2}\sqrt{20}}{(2\sqrt{3})^2-20} = \frac{6\sqrt{6}-3\sqrt{2}\sqrt{4\times5}}{12-20}$
$= \frac{6\sqrt{6}-3\sqrt{2}\times2\sqrt{5}}{-8} = -\frac{6\sqrt{6}-6\sqrt{10}}{8}$
$= -\frac{3}{4}(\sqrt{6}-\sqrt{10}) = \frac{3}{4}(\sqrt{10}-\sqrt{6})$

Q5 $\frac{1}{4\sqrt{3}-2\sqrt{5}} = \frac{4\sqrt{3}+2\sqrt{5}}{(4\sqrt{3}-2\sqrt{5})(4\sqrt{3}+2\sqrt{5})}$
$= \frac{4\sqrt{3}+2\sqrt{5}}{48-20} = \frac{4\sqrt{3}+2\sqrt{5}}{28}$
$= \frac{2\sqrt{3}+\sqrt{5}}{14} = \frac{\sqrt{4}\sqrt{3}+\sqrt{5}}{14} = \frac{1}{14}(\sqrt{12}+\sqrt{5})$

Q6 $12 = \sqrt{3}z \Rightarrow z = \frac{12}{\sqrt{3}} = \frac{12\sqrt{3}}{3} = 4\sqrt{3}$

Q7 $8 = (\sqrt{5}-1)x \Rightarrow x = \frac{8}{(\sqrt{5}-1)} = \frac{8(\sqrt{5}+1)}{(\sqrt{5}-1)(\sqrt{5}+1)}$
$= \frac{8\sqrt{5}+8}{5-1} = \frac{8\sqrt{5}+8}{4} = 2+2\sqrt{5}$

Q8 $5+\sqrt{7} = (3-\sqrt{7})y$
$\Rightarrow y = \frac{5+\sqrt{7}}{3-\sqrt{7}} = \frac{(5+\sqrt{7})(3+\sqrt{7})}{(3-\sqrt{7})(3+\sqrt{7})}$
$= \frac{15+5\sqrt{7}+3\sqrt{7}+7}{9-7} = \frac{22+8\sqrt{7}}{2} = 11+4\sqrt{7}$

Q9 The area of a rectangle is given by
area (A) = length (l) × width (w) so:
$(2+\sqrt{2}) = l\times(3\sqrt{2}-4)$
$\Rightarrow l = \frac{(2+\sqrt{2})}{(3\sqrt{2}-4)} = \frac{(2+\sqrt{2})(3\sqrt{2}+4)}{(3\sqrt{2}-4)(3\sqrt{2}+4)} = \frac{6\sqrt{2}+8+6+4\sqrt{2}}{(3\sqrt{2})^2-16}$
$= \frac{14+10\sqrt{2}}{18-16} = \frac{14+10\sqrt{2}}{2} = (7+5\sqrt{2})$ cm
Don't forget the units here.

Chapter 3 Review Exercise

Q1 **a)** $(a+b)(a-b) = a^2-ab+ba-b^2 = a^2-b^2$

b) $(p+q)(p+q) = p^2+pq+qp+q^2 = p^2+2pq+q^2$

c) $35xy+25y(5y+7x)-100y^2$
$= 35xy+125y^2+175xy-100y^2 = 25y^2+210xy$

d) $(x+3y+2)(3x+y+7)$
$= x(3x+y+7)+3y(3x+y+7)+2(3x+y+7)$
$= 3x^2+xy+7x+9xy+3y^2+21y+6x+2y+14$
$= 3x^2+10xy+3y^2+13x+23y+14$

e) $(c+2d)(c-d)(2d-3c)$
$= (c^2-cd+2dc-2d^2)(2d-3c)$
$= c^2(2d-3c)-cd(2d-3c)+2dc(2d-3c)-2d^2(2d-3c)$
$= 2c^2d-3c^3-2cd^2+3c^2d+4cd^2-6c^2d-4d^3+6cd^2$
$= -c^2d-3c^3+8cd^2-4d^3$

f) $[(s-2t)(s+2t)]^2 = [s^2+2st-2ts-4t^2]^2$
$= [s^2-4t^2]^2 = (s^2-4t^2)(s^2-4t^2)$
$= s^4-4s^2t^2-4t^2s^2+16t^4 = s^4-8s^2t^2+16t^4$

Q2 **a)** $(2x^2+7x-8)(6x^2-5x-10)$
$= 12x^4-10x^3-20x^2+42x^3-35x^2-70x-48x^2+40x+80$
$= 12x^4+32x^3-103x^2-30x+80$

b) $3p(q-5r)+4q(p+2r)-7r(2p-3q)$
$= 3pq-15pr+4pq+8qr-14pr+21qr$
$= 7pq-29pr+29qr$

Q3 The side lengths of the box are x cm, $(x-10)$ cm and $(x-8)$ cm.
So the volume of one box is $x(x-10)(x-8)$ cm^3.
$x(x-10)(x-8) = x(x^2-8x-10x+80)$
$= x^3-18x^2+80x$ cm^3
So the volume of 5 boxes is:
$5(x^3-18x^2+80x) = 5x^3-90x^2+400x$ cm^3

Q4 $p(x)-(2-3x)q(x) = 3x^3-7x+5-(2-3x)(x^2-3x+1)$
$= 3x^3-7x+5-(2x^2-6x+2-3x^3+9x^2-3x)$
$= 6x^3-11x^2+2x+3 \Rightarrow a=6, b=-11, c=2$ and $d=3$
[3 marks available — 1 mark for correctly expanding brackets, 1 mark for correctly simplifying, 1 mark for all four correct values of a, b, c and d]

Q5 $N = ((3n+m)^2-2mn)^2 = (9n^2+4nm+m^2)^2$
$= 81n^4+36n^3m+9n^2m^2+36n^3m$
$+16n^2m^2+4nm^3+9n^2m^2+4nm^3+m^4$
$= 81n^4+72n^3m+34n^2m^2+8nm^3+m^4 \Rightarrow a=8$ and $b=34$
[3 marks available — 3 marks for the correct values of a and b, otherwise 2 marks for expanding brackets correctly, or 1 mark for the correct initial expression for N]

Q6 **a)** $(2p+q)(p-3) = 2p^2-6p+pq-3q$ *[1 mark]*

b) Expanding the brackets gives
$q^3((6p-18)p^5+(3p-9)p^4q) = q^3(6p^6-18p^5+3p^5q-9p^4q)$
$= 6p^6q^3 - 18p^5q^3 + 3p^5q^4 - 9p^4q^4 = 3p^4q^3(2p^2-6p+pq-3q)$
Using the result from a) gives $3p^4q^3(2p+q)(p-3)$.
[3 marks available — 3 marks for the correct answer, otherwise 2 marks for a correct partial factorisation, or 1 mark for the correct expansion of brackets]

Q7 a) $2x^2y + axy + 2xy^2 = (xy \times 2x) + (xy \times a) + (xy \times 2y)$
$= xy(2x + a + 2y)$

b) $a^2x + a^2b^2x^2 = (a^2x \times 1) + (a^2x \times b^2x) = a^2x(1 + b^2x)$

c) $16y + 8yx + 56x = (8 \times 2y) + (8 \times yx) + (8 \times 7x)$
$= 8(2y + xy + 7x)$

d) $24s + 60st + 15s^2t^2 = (3s \times 8) + (3s \times 20t) + (3s \times 5st^2)$
$= 3s(8 + 20t + 5st^2)$

e) $27c - 9c^3d - 45cd^2 = (9c \times 3) - (9c \times c^2d) - (9c \times 5d^2)$
$= 9c(3 - c^2d - 5d^2)$

f) $x^2y^2z^2 + x^3y^3 - x^2yz = (x^2y \times yz^2) + (x^2y \times xy^2) - (x^2y \times z)$
$= x^2y(yz^2 + xy^2 - z)$

Q8 a) $(x+1) - y(x+1) = (x+1)(1-y)$

b) $z^4 + z^2(3-z) = z^2(z^2+3-z)$

c) $(x+y)^2 + x(x+y) = (x+y)(x+y+x) = (x+y)(2x+y)$

d) $x(x-2) + 3(2-x) = x(x-2) - 3(x-2) = (x-2)(x-3)$

e) $25 - x^4 = (5+x^2)(5-x^2)$

f) $9b^2c^4 - 4c^2d^6 = c^2(9b^2c^2 - 4d^6) = c^2((3bc)^2 - (2d^3)^2)$
$= c^2(3bc + 2d^3)(3bc - 2d^3)$

Q9 a) Area of $S = (2x+3)^2$, area of $R = (2x+3)(y+2)$,
so $A = 8S + 12R = 8(2x+3)^2 + 12(2x+3)(y+2)$
$= 4(2x+3)(2(2x+3) + 3(y+2))$
$= 4(2x+3)(4x+3y+12)\text{ cm}^2$
[3 marks available — 3 marks for the correct fully factorised answer, otherwise 2 marks for the correct initial expression for A, or 1 mark for using the correct method]

b) The side length of the S paving stones is 40 cm, so
$2x + 3 = 40 \Rightarrow x = 18.5$
$4(2 \times 18.5 + 3)(4 \times 18.5 + 3y + 12) = 24\,800$
$\Rightarrow 160(86 + 3y) = 24\,800 \Rightarrow 86 + 3y = 155 \Rightarrow y = 23$
[3 marks available — 1 mark for the correct value of x, 1 mark for the correct value of y, 1 mark for correct working to find y]

Q10 a) 60 is the lowest common multiple of 3, 12 and 5, so the common denominator is 60:
$$\frac{2x}{3} + \frac{y}{12} + \frac{x}{5} = \frac{40x}{60} + \frac{5y}{60} + \frac{12x}{60} = \frac{52x + 5y}{60}$$

b) The common denominator is $x^2 \times y^2 = x^2y^2$:
$$\frac{5}{xy^2} - \frac{2}{x^2y} = \frac{5x}{x^2y^2} - \frac{2y}{x^2y^2} = \frac{5x - 2y}{x^2y^2}$$

c) The common denominator is $x(x+y)(x-y)$:
$$\frac{1}{x} + \frac{x}{x+y} + \frac{y}{x-y}$$
$$= \frac{(x+y)(x-y)}{x(x+y)(x-y)} + \frac{x^2(x-y)}{x(x+y)(x-y)} + \frac{xy(x+y)}{x(x+y)(x-y)}$$
$$= \frac{x^2 - xy + yx - y^2 + x^3 - x^2y + x^2y + xy^2}{x(x^2 - y^2)}$$
$$= \frac{x^3 + x^2 - y^2 + xy^2}{x(x^2 - y^2)}$$

d) The common denominator is $a^2 \times b = a^2b$:
$$\frac{a}{b} + \frac{4}{a} - \frac{7}{a^2} = \frac{a^3}{a^2b} + \frac{4ab}{a^2b} - \frac{7b}{a^2b} = \frac{a^3 + 4ab - 7b}{a^2b}$$

e) The common denominator is $3xy$:
$$3x - \frac{4}{3xy} = \frac{9x^2y}{3xy} - \frac{4}{3xy} = \frac{9x^2y - 4}{3xy}$$

f) The common denominator is $2 \times s^2 \times t^2 = 2s^2t^2$:
$$\frac{2s}{t^2} + \frac{5}{2t} - \frac{t}{s^2} = \frac{4s^3}{2s^2t^2} + \frac{5s^2t}{2s^2t^2} - \frac{2t^3}{2s^2t^2}$$
$$= \frac{4s^3 + 5s^2t - 2t^3}{2s^2t^2}$$

Q11 a) The common denominator is $2b$:
$$\frac{2a}{b} - \frac{a}{2b} = \frac{4a}{2b} - \frac{a}{2b} = \frac{3a}{2b}$$

b) The common denominator is $(p+q)(p-q)$:
$$\frac{2p}{p+q} + \frac{2q}{p-q} = \frac{2p(p-q)}{(p+q)(p-q)} + \frac{2q(p+q)}{(p+q)(p-q)}$$
$$= \frac{2p^2 - 2pq}{p^2 - q^2} + \frac{2qp + 2q^2}{p^2 - q^2} = \frac{2(p^2 + q^2)}{p^2 - q^2}$$

c) The common denominator is $(c-d)^2(c+d)$:
$$\frac{c+d}{(c-d)^2} + \frac{1}{c+d} = \frac{(c+d)^2}{(c-d)^2(c+d)} + \frac{(c-d)^2}{(c-d)^2(c+d)}$$
$$= \frac{c^2 + 2cd + d^2 + c^2 - 2cd + d^2}{(c-d)^2(c+d)} = \frac{2c^2 + 2d^2}{(c-d)^2(c+d)}$$
$$= \frac{2(c^2 + d^2)}{(c-d)^2(c+d)}$$

d) The common denominator is $2x^2(1+x)$:
$$\frac{1}{1+x} - \frac{1-x}{2x^2} = \frac{2x^2}{2x^2(1+x)} - \frac{(1-x)(1+x)}{2x^2(1+x)}$$
$$= \frac{2x^2 - (1-x^2)}{2x^2(1+x)} = \frac{3x^2 - 1}{2x^2(1+x)}$$

e) The two denominators in the expression are $k^2 - 1 = (k+1)(k-1)$ and $(k-1)$. So the common denominator is $(k+1)(k-1)$.
$$\frac{2k}{k^2-1} + \frac{k^2}{k-1} = \frac{2k}{(k+1)(k-1)} + \frac{k^2}{k-1}$$
$$= \frac{2k}{(k+1)(k-1)} + \frac{k^2(k+1)}{(k-1)(k+1)}$$
$$= \frac{2k + k^3 + k^2}{(k+1)(k-1)} = \frac{k(k^2 + k + 2)}{k^2 - 1}$$

f) The common denominator is $(z+1)(y+z)(y-1)$.
$$\frac{4}{z+1} + \frac{2}{y+z} - \frac{6}{y-1}$$
$$= \frac{4(y+z)(y-1)}{(z+1)(y+z)(y-1)} + \frac{2(z+1)(y-1)}{(z+1)(y+z)(y-1)} - \frac{6(z+1)(y+z)}{(z+1)(y+z)(y-1)}$$
$$= \frac{4(y^2 - y + zy - z)}{(z+1)(y+z)(y-1)} + \frac{2(zy - z + y - 1)}{(z+1)(y+z)(y-1)} - \frac{6(zy + z^2 + y + z)}{(z+1)(y+z)(y-1)}$$
$$= \frac{4y^2 - 4y + 4zy - 4z}{(z+1)(y+z)(y-1)} + \frac{2zy - 2z + 2y - 2}{(z+1)(y+z)(y-1)} - \frac{6zy + 6z^2 + 6y + 6z}{(z+1)(y+z)(y-1)}$$
$$= \frac{4y^2 - 8y - 12z - 2 - 6z^2}{(z+1)(y+z)(y-1)}$$

Q12
$$\frac{4}{3} + \frac{x+2}{x} + \frac{x-3}{5} = \frac{20x + 15(x+2) + 3x(x-3)}{15x}$$
$$= \frac{20x + 15x + 30 + 3x^2 - 9x}{15x} = \frac{3x^2 + 26x + 30}{15x}$$
[3 marks available — 3 marks for the correct answer, otherwise 2 marks for partially simplifying the numerator, or 1 mark for the correct denominator]

Q13
$$\frac{4}{5}\left(\frac{x+1}{x}\right) - \frac{1}{4}\left(\frac{1-2x}{3x+1}\right) = \frac{4(x+1)}{5x} - \frac{1-2x}{4(3x+1)}$$
$$= \frac{16(3x+1)(x+1) - 5x(1-2x)}{20x(3x+1)}$$
$$= \frac{16(3x^2 + 4x + 1) - 5x + 10x^2}{20x(3x+1)} = \frac{58x^2 + 59x + 16}{20x(3x+1)}$$
[3 marks available — 3 marks for the correct answer, otherwise 2 marks for partially simplifying the numerator, or 1 mark for the correct denominator]

Q14
$$\frac{3}{x+1} - \frac{x+2}{(x+1)^2} - \frac{2x+1}{(x+1)^3}$$
$$= \frac{3(x+1)^2 - (x+2)(x+1) - 2x - 1}{(x+1)^3}$$

$= \frac{3x^2 + 6x + 3 - x^2 - 3x - 2 - 2x - 1}{(x+1)^3} = \frac{2x^2 + x}{(x+1)^3} = \frac{x(2x+1)}{(x+1)^3}$

[3 marks available — 3 marks for the correct answer, otherwise 2 marks for partially simplifying the numerator, or 1 mark for correctly subtracting the algebraic fractions without simplifying]

Q15 Call the unknown side of the flower bed z.

Then $z = \frac{x^2}{x-3}$ and $y + z = \frac{3x^2}{x+6}$.

So $y = \frac{3x^2}{x+6} - z = \frac{3x^2}{x+6} - \frac{x^2}{x-3} = \frac{3x^2(x-3) - x^2(x+6)}{(x+6)(x-3)}$

$= \frac{3x^3 - 9x^2 - x^3 - 6x^2}{(x+6)(x-3)} = \frac{2x^3 - 15x^2}{(x+6)(x-3)} = \frac{x^2(2x-15)}{(x+6)(x-3)}$

Q16 a) $x^3 \cdot x^5 = x^{3+5} = x^8$ **b)** $a^7 \cdot a^8 = a^{7+8} = a^{15}$

c) $\frac{x^8}{x^2} = x^{8-2} = x^6$ **d)** $(a^2)^4 = a^{2\times4} = a^8$

e) $(xy^2)\cdot(x^3yz) = x^{1+3}y^{2+1}z = x^4y^3z$

f) $\frac{a^2b^4c^6}{a^3b^2c} = a^{2-3}b^{4-2}c^{6-1} = a^{-1}b^2c^5 = \frac{b^2c^5}{a}$

Q17 a) $g^2 \times g^{-5} = g^{2-5} = g^{-3}$

b) $p^4r^2 \div p^5r^{-6} = p^{4-5}r^{2-(-6)} = p^{-1}r^8$

c) $\left(k^{\frac{1}{3}}\right)^6 = k^{\frac{1}{3}\times6} = k^2$

d) $(mn^8 \times m^4n^{-11})^{-2} = (m^{1+4}n^{8-11})^{-2} = (m^5n^{-3})^{-2}$
$= m^{5\times(-2)}n^{(-3)\times(-2)} = m^{-10}n^6$

e) $s^4t^3\left(\frac{1}{s^2t^5}\right)^{-3} = s^4t^3(s^2t^5)^3 = s^4t^3(s^2)^3(t^5)^3 = s^4t^3s^{2\times3}t^{5\times3}$
$= s^4t^3s^6t^{15} = s^{4+6}t^{3+15} = s^{10}t^{18}$

f) $\frac{a^2}{b^2c} \times \frac{b^6}{a^4c^{-2}} \div \frac{c^2}{a^3b} = \frac{a^2}{b^2c} \times \frac{b^6}{a^4c^{-2}} \times \frac{a^3b}{c^2}$
$= \frac{a^{2+3}b^{6+1}}{a^4b^2c^{1-2+2}} = \frac{a^5b^7}{a^4b^2c} = a^{5-4}b^{7-2}c^{-1} = ab^5c^{-1}$

Q18 $\frac{(3a^3b^2)^2 \times (2a^2b)^2}{(8a^6b^{-3})^{\frac{1}{3}}} = \frac{9a^6b^4 \times 4a^4b^2}{8^{\frac{1}{3}}a^2b^{-1}} = \frac{36a^{10}b^6}{2a^2b^{-1}} = 18a^8b^7$

[2 marks available — 1 mark for fully simplifying the numerator correctly, 1 mark for the correct answer]

Q19 a) Write the RHS as 9 to the power 'something': $3 = \sqrt{9} = 9^{\frac{1}{2}}$

So $x = \frac{1}{2}$ *[1 mark]*

b) $9^{3x} = (3^2)^{3x} = 3^{6x}$

$81 = 9^2 = 3^4$, so $81^{2x-1} = (3^4)^{2x-1} = 3^{8x-4}$

[1 mark for expressing both terms on the left-hand side of the equation as powers of 3]

So $9^{3x} \cdot 81^{2x-1} = 3^{6x} \times 3^{8x-4} = 3^{6x+8x-4} = 3^{14x-4}$

So $9^{3x} \cdot 81^{2x-1} = 27 \Rightarrow 3^{14x-4} = 3^3$

[1 mark for writing both sides of the equation as a single power of 3]

So $14x - 4 = 3 \Rightarrow 14x = 7 \Rightarrow x = \frac{1}{2}$

[1 mark for the correct value of x]

Q20 a) $16^{\frac{1}{2}} = \sqrt{16} = 4$ **b)** $8^{\frac{1}{3}} = \sqrt[3]{8} = 2$

c) $81^{\frac{3}{4}} = \left(81^{\frac{1}{4}}\right)^3 = 3^3 = 27$ **d)** $x^0 = 1$

e) $49^{-\frac{1}{2}} = \frac{1}{\sqrt{49}} = \frac{1}{7}$

f) $\frac{1}{27^{-\frac{2}{3}}} = 27^{\frac{2}{3}} = \left(27^{\frac{1}{3}}\right)^2 = 3^2 = 9$

Q21 $6^{\frac{1}{3}} + 6^{\frac{1}{3}} + 6^{\frac{1}{3}} = 3 \times 6^{\frac{1}{3}} = 3 \times (2 \times 3)^{\frac{1}{3}}$
$= 3 \times 2^{\frac{1}{3}} \times 3^{\frac{1}{3}} = 2^{\frac{1}{3}}3^{1+\frac{1}{3}} = 2^{\frac{1}{3}}3^{\frac{4}{3}}$

[2 marks available — 1 mark for writing $6^{\frac{1}{3}}$ as $2^{\frac{1}{3}} \times 3^{\frac{1}{3}}$, 1 mark for the correct answer]

Q22 Using laws of indices, $\frac{(ab^5)^x}{a^y\sqrt{b^{3-2x}}} = \frac{a^x(b^5)^x}{a^y(b^{3-2x})^{\frac{1}{2}}} = \frac{a^xb^{5x}}{a^yb^{\frac{3}{2}-x}}$

$= \frac{a^x}{a^y} \times \frac{b^{5x}}{b^{\frac{3}{2}-x}} = a^{x-y} \times b^{5x-\left(\frac{3}{2}-x\right)} = a^{x-y}b^{6x-\frac{3}{2}}$

[4 marks available — 1 mark for using the correct method, 1 mark for correctly using laws of indices, 1 mark for the correct power for a, 1 mark for the correct power for b]

Q23 $xy = 2^{10} \times 3^6 \times 5^7 \times 11 \times 2^8 \times 5^5 \times 7^{12} \times 11^8$
$= 2^{10} \times 2^8 \times 3^6 \times 5^7 \times 5^5 \times 7^{12} \times 11^1 \times 11^8$
$= 2^{18} \times 3^6 \times 5^{12} \times 7^{12} \times 11^9$
$\Rightarrow \sqrt[3]{xy} = \sqrt[3]{2^{18} \times 3^6 \times 5^{12} \times 7^{12} \times 11^9}$
$= \sqrt[3]{2^{18}} \times \sqrt[3]{3^6} \times \sqrt[3]{5^{12}} \times \sqrt[3]{7^{12}} \times \sqrt[3]{11^9}$
$= 2^6 \times 3^2 \times 5^4 \times 7^4 \times 11^3$

[3 marks available — 3 marks for the correct answer, otherwise 2 marks for attempting to find $\sqrt[3]{xy}$ with the correct xy, or 1 mark for attempting to find xy]

Q24 a) $\sqrt{28} = \sqrt{4 \times 7} = \sqrt{4}\sqrt{7} = 2\sqrt{7}$

b) $\sqrt{\frac{5}{36}} = \frac{\sqrt{5}}{\sqrt{36}} = \frac{\sqrt{5}}{6}$

c) $\sqrt{18} = \sqrt{9 \times 2} = \sqrt{9}\sqrt{2} = 3\sqrt{2}$

d) $\sqrt{\frac{9}{16}} = \frac{\sqrt{9}}{\sqrt{16}} = \frac{3}{4}$

Q25 a) $\sqrt{3} - \sqrt{12} = \sqrt{3} - \sqrt{4 \times 3} = \sqrt{3} - 2\sqrt{3} = -\sqrt{3}$

b) $3\sqrt{5} + \sqrt{45} = 3\sqrt{5} + \sqrt{9 \times 5} = 3\sqrt{5} + 3\sqrt{5} = 6\sqrt{5}$

c) $\sqrt{7} + \sqrt{448} = \sqrt{7} + \sqrt{64 \times 7} = \sqrt{7} + 8\sqrt{7} = 9\sqrt{7}$

d) $\sqrt{52} + \sqrt{117} = \sqrt{4 \times 13} + \sqrt{9 \times 13}$
$= 2\sqrt{13} + 3\sqrt{13} = 5\sqrt{13}$

e) $4\sqrt{150} + \sqrt{54} - \sqrt{5}\sqrt{120}$
$= 4\sqrt{25 \times 6} + \sqrt{9 \times 6} - \sqrt{5}\sqrt{20 \times 6}$
$= 4 \times 5\sqrt{6} + 3\sqrt{6} - \sqrt{5}\sqrt{4 \times 5}\sqrt{6}$
$= 20\sqrt{6} + 3\sqrt{6} - 2\sqrt{5}\sqrt{5}\sqrt{6}$
$= 20\sqrt{6} + 3\sqrt{6} - 10\sqrt{6} = 13\sqrt{6}$

Q26 The larger square has side length $\sqrt{1920}$ cm and the smaller square has side length $\sqrt{1080}$ cm.
a is the difference between the side lengths of the two squares, so:
$a = \sqrt{1920} - \sqrt{1080} = \sqrt{64 \times 30} - \sqrt{36 \times 30}$
$= 8\sqrt{30} - 6\sqrt{30} = 2\sqrt{30}$

Q27 a) $\frac{(5 - 2\sqrt{m}) + (10 + 9\sqrt{m}) + n\sqrt{m}}{3} = 5 + 4\sqrt{m}$

$\Rightarrow \frac{15 + (7+n)\sqrt{m}}{3} = 5 + 4\sqrt{m}$ *[1 mark]*

$\Rightarrow 15 + (7+n)\sqrt{m} = 15 + 12\sqrt{m}$

$\Rightarrow 7 + n = 12$

$\Rightarrow n = 5$ *[1 mark]*

b) $10 + 9\sqrt{m}$ must be the largest number *[1 mark]*, so the range is either:
$10 + 9\sqrt{m} - (5 - 2\sqrt{m}) = 5 + 11\sqrt{m}$
or $10 + 9\sqrt{m} - 5\sqrt{m} = 10 + 4\sqrt{m}$
[1 mark for both expressions]
You're told the range is $5 + 11\sqrt{m}$,
so $5 - 2\sqrt{m}$ must be the smallest number *[1 mark]*.
So $5 - 2\sqrt{m} < 5\sqrt{m} \Rightarrow 5 < 7\sqrt{m} \Rightarrow \frac{5}{7} < \sqrt{m}$ *[1 mark]*
So $m > \frac{25}{49}$ *[1 mark]*

Q28 Let the radius of the pond be p m.
Circumference of pond $= 10\pi = 2\pi p \Rightarrow p = 5$ *[1 mark]*

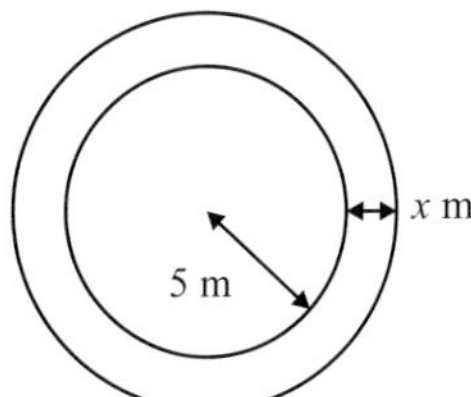

Area of path $= \pi(x+5)^2 - \pi \times 5^2$
$= \pi((x+5)^2 - 25)$ m^2 *[1 mark]*

Maximum area of material = 20π m^2, so the maximum value of x is the solution to: $\pi((x+5)^2 - 25) = 20\pi$ *[1 mark]*
$\Rightarrow (x+5)^2 - 25 = 20 \Rightarrow (x+5)^2 = 45$
$\Rightarrow x + 5 = \pm\sqrt{45} = \pm\sqrt{9\times5} = \pm 3\sqrt{5}$ *[1 mark]*
$\Rightarrow x = 3\sqrt{5} - 5$ or $x = -3\sqrt{5} - 5$ *[1 mark]*
But x must be positive, so the second solution isn't possible.
So the maximum value of x is: $x = 3\sqrt{5} - 5$ *[1 mark]*.
The maximum possible width of the path is approximately 1.7 m.

Q29 $(6\sqrt{3}+2\sqrt{7})^2$
$= (6\sqrt{3}+2\sqrt{7})(6\sqrt{3}+2\sqrt{7})$
$= 36\sqrt{3}\sqrt{3} + 12\sqrt{3}\sqrt{7} + 12\sqrt{7}\sqrt{3} + 4\sqrt{7}\sqrt{7}$
$= 36\times3 + 24\sqrt{3}\sqrt{7} + 4\times7$
$= 108 + 24\sqrt{21} + 28$
$= 136 + 24\sqrt{21}$

Q30 $(3\sqrt{5}-5\sqrt{3})^2 = (3\sqrt{5}-5\sqrt{3})(3\sqrt{5}-5\sqrt{3})$
$= 9\sqrt{5}\sqrt{5} - 15\sqrt{5}\sqrt{3} - 15\sqrt{3}\sqrt{5} + 25\sqrt{3}\sqrt{3}$
$= 45 - 15\sqrt{15} - 15\sqrt{15} + 75 = 120 - 30\sqrt{15} = 30(4-\sqrt{15})$
[3 marks available — 3 marks for the correct answer, otherwise 2 marks for any two correctly simplified terms (45, $-15\sqrt{15}$ or 75), or 1 mark for attempting to expand the brackets and getting one term correct]

Q31 a) $\frac{8}{\sqrt{2}} = \frac{8}{\sqrt{2}}\times\frac{\sqrt{2}}{\sqrt{2}} = \frac{8\sqrt{2}}{2} = 4\sqrt{2}$

b) $\frac{\sqrt{2}}{2} = \frac{\sqrt{2}}{(\sqrt{2})^2} = \frac{1}{\sqrt{2}}$

Q32 $\frac{2}{3+\sqrt{7}} = \frac{2(3-\sqrt{7})}{(3+\sqrt{7})(3-\sqrt{7})}$
$= \frac{6-2\sqrt{7}}{9-7} = \frac{6-2\sqrt{7}}{2} = 3 - \sqrt{7}$

Q33 a) $(2\sqrt{2}+\sqrt{3})^2 = 4\times2 + 4\sqrt{2}\sqrt{3} + 3 = 11 + 4\sqrt{6}$
[2 marks available — 1 mark for correctly expanding the brackets, 1 mark for the correct simplified answer]

b) Using the result from a), $\frac{1}{(2\sqrt{2}+\sqrt{3})^2} = \frac{1}{11+4\sqrt{6}}$
$= \frac{1}{11+4\sqrt{6}}\times\frac{11-4\sqrt{6}}{11-4\sqrt{6}} = \frac{11-4\sqrt{6}}{121-96} = \frac{11-4\sqrt{6}}{25}$
[2 marks available — 2 marks for the correct answer, otherwise 1 mark for using the correct method]

Q34 a) $\frac{11+\sqrt{13}}{5-\sqrt{13}} = \frac{(11+\sqrt{13})(5+\sqrt{13})}{(5-\sqrt{13})(5+\sqrt{13})}$
$= \frac{55+11\sqrt{13}+5\sqrt{13}+13}{25-13}$
$= \frac{68+16\sqrt{13}}{12} = \frac{17}{3} + \frac{4}{3}\sqrt{13}$

b) $\frac{2\sqrt{7}+9}{3-\sqrt{7}} = \frac{(2\sqrt{7}+9)(3+\sqrt{7})}{(3-\sqrt{7})(3+\sqrt{7})}$
$= \frac{6\sqrt{7}+14+27+9\sqrt{7}}{9-7}$
$= \frac{15\sqrt{7}+41}{2} = \frac{41}{2} + \frac{15}{2}\sqrt{7}$

c) $\frac{3\sqrt{5}+\sqrt{15}}{\sqrt{60}-\sqrt{20}} = \frac{(3\sqrt{5}+\sqrt{15})(\sqrt{60}+\sqrt{20})}{(\sqrt{60}-\sqrt{20})(\sqrt{60}+\sqrt{20})}$
$= \frac{3\sqrt{5}\sqrt{60}+3\sqrt{5}\sqrt{20}+\sqrt{15}\sqrt{60}+\sqrt{15}\sqrt{20}}{60-20}$
$= \frac{3\sqrt{5}\sqrt{5}\sqrt{3}\sqrt{4}+3\sqrt{5}\sqrt{5}\sqrt{4}}{40}$
$+ \frac{\sqrt{3}\sqrt{5}\sqrt{5}\sqrt{3}\sqrt{4}+\sqrt{3}\sqrt{5}\sqrt{5}\sqrt{4}}{40}$
$= \frac{30\sqrt{3}+30+30+10\sqrt{3}}{40}$
$= \frac{40\sqrt{3}+60}{40} = \frac{3}{2} + \sqrt{3}$

Q35 $(\sqrt{32}+\sqrt{128})^2 = (4\sqrt{2}+8\sqrt{2})^2 = (12\sqrt{2})^2 = 144\times2 = 288$
$\Rightarrow \frac{(\sqrt{32}+\sqrt{128})^2}{\sqrt{5}+\sqrt{3}} = \frac{288}{\sqrt{5}+\sqrt{3}} = \frac{288}{\sqrt{5}+\sqrt{3}}\times\frac{\sqrt{5}-\sqrt{3}}{\sqrt{5}-\sqrt{3}}$
$= \frac{288(\sqrt{5}-\sqrt{3})}{5-3} = 144(\sqrt{5}-\sqrt{3})$ or $144\sqrt{5} - 144\sqrt{3}$
[3 marks available — 1 mark for using the correct method to rationalise the denominator, 1 mark for showing that the numerator is equal to 288, 1 mark for the correct answer]

Q36 a) $(a+b+c)(a-b-c)$
$= a^2 - ab - ac + ba - b^2 - bc + ca - cb - c^2$
$= a^2 - b^2 - c^2 - 2bc$
[2 marks available — 1 mark for correctly expanding the brackets, 1 mark for correctly simplifying to the answer]

b) Set $a = \sqrt{11}$, $b = \sqrt{3}$ and $c = \sqrt{2}$
Then using the result from a)
$(\sqrt{11}+\sqrt{3}+\sqrt{2})(\sqrt{11}-\sqrt{3}-\sqrt{2})$
$= (\sqrt{11})^2 - (\sqrt{3})^2 - (\sqrt{2})^2 - 2\sqrt{3}\sqrt{2}$
$= 11 - 3 - 2 - 2\sqrt{6} = 6 - 2\sqrt{6}$
$\Rightarrow \frac{1}{(\sqrt{11}+\sqrt{3}+\sqrt{2})(\sqrt{11}-\sqrt{3}-\sqrt{2})} = \frac{1}{6-2\sqrt{6}}$
$\Rightarrow \frac{1}{6-2\sqrt{6}}\times\frac{3+\sqrt{6}}{3+\sqrt{6}} = \frac{3+\sqrt{6}}{6}$
[3 marks available — 3 marks for the correct answer, otherwise 2 marks for a clear attempt at rationalising the denominator, or 1 mark for correctly using the result from a)]

Q37 a) $\frac{1}{2(x-1)} - \frac{1}{2(x+1)} \equiv \frac{x+1}{2(x-1)(x+1)} - \frac{x-1}{2(x+1)(x-1)}$
$\equiv \frac{x+1}{2(x^2-1)} - \frac{x-1}{2(x^2-1)} \equiv \frac{2}{2(x^2-1)} \equiv \frac{1}{x^2-1}$
[2 marks available — 1 mark for using the correct method of subtraction of algebraic expressions, 1 mark for the correct simplified answer]

b) $\frac{1}{\sqrt{32}-2} = \frac{1}{2\sqrt{8}-2} = \frac{1}{2(\sqrt{8}-1)}$ and
$\frac{1}{\sqrt{32}+2} = \frac{1}{2(\sqrt{8}+1)}$. So $\frac{1}{\sqrt{32}-2} - \frac{1}{\sqrt{32}+2}$
$= \frac{1}{2(\sqrt{8}-1)} - \frac{1}{2(\sqrt{8}+1)} = \frac{1}{(\sqrt{8})^2-1} = \frac{1}{7}$
[2 marks available — 2 marks for the correct answer, otherwise 1 mark for correctly expressing one of the denominators in the form from part a)]

Q38 Let $a = 2x^2 + 3x - 1$ and $b = x^2 + x + 3$
$\Rightarrow a^2 - b^2 = (2x^2+3x-1)^2 - (x^2+x+3)^2$
$= ((2x^2+3x-1) + (x^2+x+3))((2x^2+3x-1) - (x^2+x+3))$
$= (3x^2+4x+2)(x^2+2x-4)$
[3 marks available — 3 marks for the correct answer, otherwise 2 marks for correct use of $a^2 - b^2 \equiv (a+b)(a-b)$, or 1 mark for attempting to use $a^2 - b^2 \equiv (a+b)(a-b)$]

Q39 $\frac{\sqrt{x}}{\sqrt{x}+\sqrt{y}} + \frac{\sqrt{y}}{\sqrt{x}-\sqrt{y}}$
$= \frac{\sqrt{x}(\sqrt{x}-\sqrt{y})}{(\sqrt{x}+\sqrt{y})(\sqrt{x}-\sqrt{y})} + \frac{\sqrt{y}(\sqrt{x}+\sqrt{y})}{(\sqrt{x}+\sqrt{y})(\sqrt{x}-\sqrt{y})}$
$= \frac{\sqrt{x}\sqrt{x}-\sqrt{x}\sqrt{y}+\sqrt{y}\sqrt{x}+\sqrt{y}\sqrt{y}}{x-y} = \frac{x+y}{x-y}$
The common denominator is in the form $(a+b)(a-b) = a^2 - b^2$.
[3 marks available — 1 mark for putting the fractions over a suitable common denominator, 1 mark for at least three correct terms in the expansion of the numerator, 1 mark for the correct answer]

Q40 $(\sqrt{x}-\sqrt{y})(3\sqrt{x}+7\sqrt{y}) + k\sqrt{x}(2\sqrt{y}+\sqrt{x})$
$= (3x + 7\sqrt{xy} - 3\sqrt{xy} - 7y) + (2k\sqrt{xy} + xk)$
$= (3+k)x - 7y + (4+2k)\sqrt{xy}$
Since xy is not a square number then $\sqrt{xy}$ is irrational,
so $4 + 2k = 0 \Rightarrow k = -2$
[3 marks available — 1 mark for correctly expanding brackets, 1 mark for recognising that the expression will be rational provided $4 + 2k = 0$, 1 mark for the correct value of k]

Q41 $\frac{125}{216} = \frac{5^3}{6^3} = \left(\frac{5}{6}\right)^3$, so $\left(\frac{5}{6}\right)^{x+3} = \left(\frac{125}{216}\right)^{x-4}$

$\Rightarrow \left(\frac{5}{6}\right)^{x+3} = \left(\left(\frac{5}{6}\right)^3\right)^{x-4} \Rightarrow \left(\frac{5}{6}\right)^{x+3} = \left(\frac{5}{6}\right)^{3x-12}$

Hence $x + 3 = 3x - 12 \Rightarrow 2x = 15 \Rightarrow x = \frac{15}{2}$

[4 marks available — 4 marks for finding the correct value of x, otherwise 3 marks for deriving the correct linear equation, or 2 marks for correctly using laws of indices, or 1 mark for replacing $\frac{125}{216}$ with $\left(\frac{5}{6}\right)^3$]

Q42 $\left(\frac{125}{64}\right)^{-\frac{1}{3}} = \left(\left(\frac{125}{64}\right)^{-1}\right)^{\frac{1}{3}} = \left(\frac{125^{-1}}{64^{-1}}\right)^{\frac{1}{3}} = \left(\frac{\left(\frac{1}{125}\right)}{\left(\frac{1}{64}\right)}\right)^{\frac{1}{3}} = \left(\frac{64}{125}\right)^{\frac{1}{3}}$

$= \frac{64^{\frac{1}{3}}}{125^{\frac{1}{3}}} = \frac{\sqrt[3]{64}}{\sqrt[3]{125}} = \frac{4}{5}$

Similarly, $\left(\frac{64}{49}\right)^{-\frac{1}{2}}$ can be shown to be equal to $\frac{7}{8}$.

Hence $\left(\frac{125}{64}\right)^{-\frac{1}{3}} \div \left(\frac{64}{49}\right)^{-\frac{1}{2}} = \frac{4}{5} \div \frac{7}{8} = \frac{4}{5} \times \frac{8}{7} = \frac{32}{35}$

[4 marks available — 1 mark for correctly using laws of indices in part of the working, 1 mark for correctly simplifying one of the two parts, 1 mark for correctly simplifying both $\left(\frac{125}{64}\right)^{-\frac{1}{3}}$ and $\left(\frac{64}{49}\right)^{-\frac{1}{2}}$, 1 mark for the correct answer]

Q43 $3x + 2y = 23 + 5\sqrt{5}$ ①

$\sqrt{5}x + y = 12 + 4\sqrt{5}$ ②

② × 2: $2\sqrt{5}x + 2y = 24 + 8\sqrt{5}$ ③

① – ③:

$(3 - 2\sqrt{5})x = 23 + 5\sqrt{5} - (24 + 8\sqrt{5})$

$(3 - 2\sqrt{5})x = -1 - 3\sqrt{5}$

$x = -\frac{1 + 3\sqrt{5}}{3 - 2\sqrt{5}} = -\frac{(1 + 3\sqrt{5})(3 + 2\sqrt{5})}{(3 - 2\sqrt{5})(3 + 2\sqrt{5})}$

$= -\frac{3 + 2\sqrt{5} + 9\sqrt{5} + 6\sqrt{5}\sqrt{5}}{9 - (2\sqrt{5})^2}$

$= -\frac{33 + 11\sqrt{5}}{9 - 20} = -\frac{33 + 11\sqrt{5}}{-11} = 3 + \sqrt{5}$

Substitute into ②:

$\sqrt{5}(3 + \sqrt{5}) + y = 12 + 4\sqrt{5}$

$\Rightarrow 3\sqrt{5} + 5 + y = 12 + 4\sqrt{5}$

$\Rightarrow y = 7 + \sqrt{5}$

[7 marks available — 1 mark for eliminating y, 1 mark for rearranging to get an expression for x, 1 mark for attempting to rationalise the denominator, 1 mark for at least three correct terms in the numerator, 1 mark for finding the correct value of x, 1 mark for substituting to find the value of y, 1 mark for the correct value of y.]

You could eliminate x instead — then you'd find the value of y first, and substitute it back in to find x.

Q44 a) $\frac{(\sqrt{2})^{4x}}{64^y} = 2\left(\frac{1}{4}\right)^y \times 2^{7x} \Rightarrow \frac{2^{2x}}{2^{6y}} = 2^1 \times 2^{-2y} \times 2^{7x}$

$\Rightarrow 2^{2x-6y} = 2^{1-2y+7x} \Rightarrow 2x - 6y = 1 - 2y + 7x$

$\Rightarrow 5x + 4y + 1 = 0$

[3 marks available — 3 marks for the correct answer, otherwise 2 marks for deriving the correct linear equation, or 1 mark for correctly using laws of indices in working]

b) Using the answer from part a), the simultaneous equations are:

$5x + 4y + 1 = 0$ ①

and $2x + y = 8 \Rightarrow 2x + y - 8 = 0$ ②

① – 4 × ② = $-3x + 33 = 0 \Rightarrow x = 11$

Substitute x into one equation to find $y = -14$

[3 marks available — 1 mark for using the correct method to solve simultaneous equations, 1 mark for attempting to solve the simultaneous equations with the result from a), 1 mark for the correct answer]

Q45 $\frac{3 - \sqrt{5}}{3 + \sqrt{5}} \times \frac{3 - \sqrt{5}}{3 - \sqrt{5}} = \frac{(3 - \sqrt{5})^2}{9 - 5} = \frac{(3 - \sqrt{5})^2}{4}$

So $\sqrt{\frac{3 - \sqrt{5}}{3 + \sqrt{5}}} = \sqrt{\frac{(3 - \sqrt{5})^2}{4}} = \frac{3 - \sqrt{5}}{2} = \frac{3}{2} - \frac{1}{2}\sqrt{5}$

[3 marks available — 1 mark for attempting to rationalise the denominator, 1 mark for taking the square root of the rationalised denominator form of $\frac{3 - \sqrt{5}}{3 + \sqrt{5}}$, 1 mark for the correct answer]

Q46 a) $\frac{1 - \sqrt{3}}{1 + \sqrt{3}} = \frac{1 - \sqrt{3}}{1 + \sqrt{3}} \times \frac{1 - \sqrt{3}}{1 - \sqrt{3}} = \frac{(1 - \sqrt{3})^2}{1 - 3} = \frac{1 - 2\sqrt{3} + 3}{-2}$

$= \frac{4 - 2\sqrt{3}}{-2} = -2 + \sqrt{3}$

[2 marks available — 2 marks for the correct answer, otherwise 1 mark for a clear attempt to rationalise the denominator]

b) If $x = \frac{1 - \sqrt{3}}{1 + \sqrt{3}}$ then by a), $x = \frac{1 - \sqrt{3}}{1 + \sqrt{3}} = -2 + \sqrt{3}$

So, $x^2 = (-2 + \sqrt{3})^2 = 4 - 4\sqrt{3} + 3 = 7 - 4\sqrt{3}$

Therefore $x^2 + 4x + 1 = (7 - 4\sqrt{3}) + 4(-2 + \sqrt{3}) + 1$

$= 7 - 4\sqrt{3} - 8 + 4\sqrt{3} + 1 = 0$

[2 marks available — 2 marks for a fully correct answer, otherwise 1 mark for using the correct method]

c) $x = -2 - \sqrt{3}$ *[1 mark]*

Chapter 4: Quadratics and Cubics

Prior Knowledge Check

Q1 a) $x = 0$ or $x = -1$ **b)** $x = -6$ or $x = -5$

c) $3x = -5 \Rightarrow x = -\frac{5}{3}$ **d)** $x \leq -2$

Q2 a) $4x^3 - 8x^2$ **b)** $p^2 - 7p + 4p - 28 = p^2 - 3p - 28$

c) $(mn + 3)(mn + 3) = m^2n^2 + 6mn + 9$

Q3 $(1 + \sqrt{5})(1 - 2\sqrt{5}) = 1 - 2\sqrt{5} + \sqrt{5} - 10 = -9 - \sqrt{5}$

Exercise 4.1 — Factorising a Quadratic

Q1 a) $x^2 - 6x + 5 = (x - 5)(x - 1)$

b) $x^2 - 3x - 18 = (x - 6)(x + 3)$

c) $x^2 + 22x + 121 = (x + 11)(x + 11) = (x + 11)^2$

d) $x^2 - 12x = x(x - 12)$

Note that if every term contains an x, you can just take a factor of x out of the bracket.

e) $y^2 - 13y + 42 = (y - 6)(y - 7)$

f) $x^2 + 51x + 144 = (x + 48)(x + 3)$

g) $x^2 - 121 = (x + 11)(x - 11)$

If there is no 'b' term, see if the expression is a 'difference of two squares' (chances are it will be).

h) $x^2 - 35x + 66 = (x - 2)(x - 33)$

Q2 a) $x^2 - 3x - 10 = 0 \Rightarrow (x - 5)(x + 2) = 0$

$\Rightarrow x - 5 = 0$ or $x + 2 = 0 \Rightarrow x = 5$ or $x = -2$

b) $2x^2 + 2x - 40 = 0 \Rightarrow 2(x^2 + x - 20) = 0$

This is an example of a question where you can simplify the equation before factorising. You can divide through by 2.

$x^2 + x - 20 = 0 \Rightarrow (x + 5)(x - 4) = 0$

$\Rightarrow x + 5 = 0$ or $x - 4 = 0 \Rightarrow x = -5$ or $x = 4$

c) $p^2 + 21p + 38 = 0 \Rightarrow (p + 19)(p + 2) = 0$

$\Rightarrow p + 19 = 0$ or $p + 2 = 0 \Rightarrow p = -19$ or $p = -2$

d) $x^2 - 15x + 54 = 0 \Rightarrow (x - 9)(x - 6) = 0$

$\Rightarrow x - 9 = 0$ or $x - 6 = 0 \Rightarrow x = 9$ or $x = 6$

e) $x^2 + 18x = -65 \Rightarrow x^2 + 18x + 65 = 0$

$(x + 5)(x + 13) = 0 \Rightarrow x + 5 = 0$ or $x + 13 = 0$

$\Rightarrow x = -5$ or $x = -13$

f) $x^2 - x = 42 \Rightarrow x^2 - x - 42 = 0 \Rightarrow (x-7)(x+6) = 0$
$\Rightarrow x - 7 = 0$ or $x + 6 = 0 \Rightarrow x = 7$ or $x = -6$

g) $x^2 + 1100x + 100\,000 = 0 \Rightarrow (x+100)(x+1000) = 0$
$\Rightarrow x + 100 = 0$ or $x + 1000 = 0 \Rightarrow x = -100$ or $x = -1000$

h) $3x^2 - 3x - 6 = 0 \Rightarrow 3(x^2 - x - 2) = 0$
$\Rightarrow x^2 - x - 2 = 0 \Rightarrow (x-2)(x+1) = 0$
$\Rightarrow x - 2 = 0$ or $x + 1 = 0 \Rightarrow x = 2$ or $x = -1$

Q3 a) $4x^2 - 4x - 3 = (2x+1)(2x-3)$

b) $2x^2 + 23x + 11 = (2x+1)(x+11)$

c) $7x^2 - 19x - 6 = (7x+2)(x-3)$

d) $-x^2 - 5x + 36 = -(x^2 + 5x - 36) = -(x-4)(x+9)$

e) $6x^2 - 7x - 3 = (3x+1)(2x-3)$

f) $2x^2 - 2 = 2(x^2 - 1) = 2(x+1)(x-1)$

g) $3x^2 - 3 = 3(x^2 - 1) = 3(x+1)(x-1)$

h) $-x^2 + 9x - 14 = -(x^2 - 9x + 14) = -(x-7)(x-2)$

Q4 a) $-5x^2 - 22x + 15 = 0 \Rightarrow 5x^2 + 22x - 15 = 0$
$\Rightarrow (5x-3)(x+5) = 0 \Rightarrow x = \frac{3}{5}$ or $x = -5$

If you want to get rid of the minus sign in front of the x^2 just multiply through by -1 — the right-hand side will remain 0 and the left-hand side will change signs.

b) $32x^2 + 60x + 13 = 0 \Rightarrow (4x+1)(8x+13) = 0$
$\Rightarrow 4x + 1 = 0$ or $8x + 13 = 0 \Rightarrow x = -\frac{1}{4}$ or $x = -\frac{13}{8}$

c) $5a^2 + 12a = 9 \Rightarrow 5a^2 + 12a - 9 = 0$
$\Rightarrow (5a-3)(a+3) = 0$
$\Rightarrow 5a - 3 = 0$ or $a + 3 = 0 \Rightarrow a = \frac{3}{5}$ or $a = -3$

d) $8x^2 + 22x + 15 = 0 \Rightarrow (4x+5)(2x+3) = 0$
$\Rightarrow 4x + 5 = 0$ or $2x + 3 = 0 \Rightarrow x = -\frac{5}{4}$ or $x = -\frac{3}{2}$

e) $4q^2 + 6 = 11q \Rightarrow 4q^2 - 11q + 6 = 0$
$\Rightarrow (4q-3)(q-2) = 0$
$\Rightarrow 4q - 3 = 0$ or $q - 2 = 0 \Rightarrow q = \frac{3}{4}$ or $q = 2$

f) $24y^2 + 23y - 12 = 0 \Rightarrow (3y+4)(8y-3) = 0$
$\Rightarrow 3y + 4 = 0$ or $8y - 3 = 0 \Rightarrow y = -\frac{4}{3}$ or $y = \frac{3}{8}$

Q5 $(x-1)(x-2) = 37 - x \Rightarrow x^2 - 3x + 2 = 37 - x$
$\Rightarrow x^2 - 2x - 35 = 0 \Rightarrow (x-7)(x+5) = 0$
$\Rightarrow x - 7 = 0$ or $x + 5 = 0 \Rightarrow x = 7$ or $x = -5$

Q6 a) $2x^2 - x - 15 = (2x+5)(x-3)$ *[1 mark]*

b) From part a), $2x^2 - x - 15 = (x+7)(x-3)$
becomes $(2x+5)(x-3) = (x+7)(x-3)$
$\Rightarrow (2x+5)(x-3) - (x+7)(x-3) = 0$
$\Rightarrow (x-3)((2x+5) - (x+7)) = 0$
$\Rightarrow (x-3)(x-2) = 0 \Rightarrow x = 3$ or $x = 2$
[3 marks available — 1 mark for clear attempt at solution, 1 mark for correct method of solution, 1 mark for both correct solutions]
Alternatively you could expand $(x + 7)(x - 3)$, collect like terms and then factorise.

Q7 The function f(x) meets the x-axis when f(x) = 0 so set the expression for f(x) equal to 0.
$-x^2 + 7x + 30 = 0 \Rightarrow x^2 - 7x - 30 = 0$
$\Rightarrow (x-10)(x+3) = 0$
$\Rightarrow x - 10 = 0$ or $x + 3 = 0 \Rightarrow x = 10$ or $x = -3$
So the graph of f(x) meets the x-axis when $x = 10$ and $x = -3$.

Q8 The functions intersect when f(x) = g(x), so:
$(x-8)(x+10) = (3x+2)(x-11)$
$\Rightarrow x^2 + 2x - 80 = 3x^2 - 31x - 22$
$\Rightarrow 0 = 2x^2 - 33x + 58 \Rightarrow 0 = (2x-29)(x-2)$
$\Rightarrow 0 = 2x - 29$ or $0 = x - 2 \Rightarrow x = \frac{29}{2} = 14.5$ or $x = 2$
So the functions intersect when $x = 14.5$ and $x = 2$.

Q9 Form an equation using the dimensions and area of the rectangle:
$(3x+1)(2x-3) = 2 \Rightarrow 6x^2 - 7x - 3 = 2 \Rightarrow 6x^2 - 7x - 5 = 0$
$\Rightarrow (2x+1)(3x-5) = 0 \Rightarrow x = -\frac{1}{2}$ or $x = \frac{5}{3}$.
But x cannot be equal to $-\frac{1}{2}$ as the length $(3x + 1)$ m would be negative, so $x = \frac{5}{3}$.
So the rectangle has a length of $3 \times \frac{5}{3} + 1 = 6$ m and a width of $2 \times \frac{5}{3} - 3 = \frac{1}{3}$ m.
[4 marks available — 1 mark for forming the equation, 1 mark for expanding the brackets and factorising the quadratic, 1 mark for identifying the valid x-value, 1 mark for the correct length and width]

Q10 Here, you have to set T equal to 0 and solve the quadratic equation to find the values of h:
$0 = -2h^2 + 13h - 20 \Rightarrow 0 = 2h^2 - 13h + 20$
$0 = (2h-5)(h-4) \Rightarrow 0 = 2h - 5$ or $0 = h - 4$
$\Rightarrow h = \frac{5}{2} = 2.5$ or $h = 4$
So the temperature is 0 °C after 2.5 hours and again after 4 hours.

Q11 *This question looks harder because it has y's in it as well as x's — just treat the y as a constant. You'll need two numbers which multiply to give $8y^2$ and add or subtract to give 6y.*
$4y$ and $2y$ multiply to $8y^2$ and add to give $6y$ so these are the numbers you need. $x^2 + 6xy + 8y^2 = (x+4y)(x+2y)$

Q12 Width of the square $= \frac{2z+5}{4}$, so area $= \left(\frac{2z+5}{4}\right)^2$.
$\left(\frac{2z+5}{4}\right)^2 = \frac{9z}{2} \Rightarrow \frac{(2z+5)^2}{16} = \frac{9z}{2}$
$\Rightarrow (2z+5)^2 = 72z \Rightarrow (2z+5)(2z+5) = 72z$
$\Rightarrow 4z^2 + 20z + 25 = 72z \Rightarrow 4z^2 - 52z + 25 = 0$
$\Rightarrow (2z-1)(2z-25) = 0 \Rightarrow 2z - 1 = 0$ or $2z - 25 = 0$
$\Rightarrow z = \frac{1}{2} = 0.5$ or $z = \frac{25}{2} = 12.5$

Q13 *First, set up and solve a quadratic equation in x.*
Area of the triangle $= \frac{1}{2}(5x-3)(x+2) = (9x+3)$
$\Rightarrow (5x-3)(x+2) = 2(9x+3) \Rightarrow 5x^2 + 7x - 6 = 18x + 6$
$\Rightarrow 5x^2 - 11x - 12 = 0 \Rightarrow (5x+4)(x-3) = 0$
$\Rightarrow 5x + 4 = 0$ or $x - 3 = 0 \Rightarrow x = -\frac{4}{5}$ or $x = 3$
The lengths must be positive, and when $x = -\frac{4}{5}$,
$5x - 3 = -4 - 3 = -7$. So x must be 3, and the lengths are $5(3) - 3 = 12$ m, and $3 + 2 = 5$ m.
Using Pythagoras, hypotenuse $= \sqrt{12^2 + 5^2} = 13$ m.

Q14 a) $18x^2 + 39x - 70 = 0 \Rightarrow (6x-7)(3x+10) = 0$
$\Rightarrow x = \frac{7}{6}$ or $x = -\frac{10}{3}$. $b < a$, so $a = \frac{7}{6}$ and $b = -\frac{10}{3}$.
[2 marks available — 1 mark for correct factorisation, 1 mark for both correct solutions]

b) The roots of q(x) are $2 \times \frac{7}{6} - 2 = \frac{1}{3}$ and $-\frac{10}{3} + 4 = \frac{2}{3}$.
So $q(x) = 9\left(x - \frac{1}{3}\right)\left(x - \frac{2}{3}\right)$ or $(3x-1)(3x-2)$.
[2 marks available — 1 mark for correct values of roots of q(x), 1 mark for correct factorisation of q(x)]

Q15 a) Notice that $\sqrt{15} = \sqrt{5}\sqrt{3}$.
So $10x^2 - 7\sqrt{15}x - 12 = 2(\sqrt{5})^2x^2 - 7\sqrt{5}\sqrt{3}x - 4(\sqrt{3})^2$
$= (2\sqrt{5}x + \sqrt{3})(\sqrt{5}x - 4\sqrt{3})$

b) $10x^2 - 7\sqrt{15}x - 12 = 0 \Rightarrow (2\sqrt{5}x + \sqrt{3})(\sqrt{5}x - 4\sqrt{3}) = 0$
$\Rightarrow x = -\frac{\sqrt{3}}{2\sqrt{5}}$ or $x = \frac{4\sqrt{3}}{\sqrt{5}}$
Rationalising the denominators gives
$x = -\frac{\sqrt{15}}{10}$ or $x = \frac{4\sqrt{15}}{5}$.

Exercise 4.2 — The Quadratic Formula

Q1 a) $x^2 - 4x = -2 \Rightarrow x^2 - 4x + 2 = 0 \Rightarrow a = 1, b = -4, c = 2$

$$x = \frac{-b \pm \sqrt{b^2 - 4ac}}{2a} = \frac{-(-4) \pm \sqrt{(-4)^2 - 4 \times 1 \times 2}}{2 \times 1}$$
$$= \frac{4 \pm \sqrt{16 - 8}}{2} = \frac{4 \pm \sqrt{8}}{2} = \frac{4 \pm 2\sqrt{2}}{2} = 2 \pm \sqrt{2}$$

b) $x^2 - 2x - 44 = 0 \Rightarrow a = 1, b = -2, c = -44$

$$x = \frac{-b \pm \sqrt{b^2 - 4ac}}{2a} = \frac{-(-2) \pm \sqrt{(-2)^2 - 4 \times 1 \times (-44)}}{2 \times 1} = \frac{2 \pm \sqrt{4 + (4 \times 1 \times 44)}}{2} = \frac{2 \pm \sqrt{180}}{2} = \frac{2 \pm \sqrt{36 \times 5}}{2} = \frac{2 \pm 6\sqrt{5}}{2} = 1 \pm 3\sqrt{5}$$

c) $x^2 + 3x - 12 = 0 \Rightarrow a = 1, b = 3, c = -12$

$$x = \frac{-b \pm \sqrt{b^2 - 4ac}}{2a} = \frac{-3 \pm \sqrt{3^2 - 4 \times 1 \times (-12)}}{2 \times 1} = \frac{-3 \pm \sqrt{9 + (4 \times 1 \times 12)}}{2} = \frac{-3 \pm \sqrt{57}}{2} = -\frac{3}{2} \pm \frac{1}{2}\sqrt{57}$$

d) $x^2 - 14x + 42 = 0 \Rightarrow a = 1, b = -14, c = 42$

$$x = \frac{-b \pm \sqrt{b^2 - 4ac}}{2a} = \frac{-(-14) \pm \sqrt{(-14)^2 - 4 \times 1 \times 42}}{2 \times 1} = \frac{14 \pm \sqrt{196 - 168}}{2} = \frac{14 \pm \sqrt{28}}{2} = \frac{14 \pm \sqrt{4 \times 7}}{2} = \frac{14 \pm 2\sqrt{7}}{2} = 7 \pm \sqrt{7}$$

e) $4x^2 + 4x - 1 = 0 \Rightarrow a = 4, b = 4, c = -1$

$$x = \frac{-b \pm \sqrt{b^2 - 4ac}}{2a} = \frac{-4 \pm \sqrt{(4)^2 - 4 \times 4 \times (-1)}}{2 \times 4} = \frac{-4 \pm \sqrt{16 + 16}}{8} = \frac{-4 \pm \sqrt{32}}{8} = \frac{-4 \pm \sqrt{16 \times 2}}{8} = \frac{-4 \pm 4\sqrt{2}}{8} = -\frac{1}{2} \pm \frac{1}{2}\sqrt{2}$$

f) $-x^2 + 4x - 3 = 0 \Rightarrow a = -1, b = 4, c = -3$

$$x = \frac{-b \pm \sqrt{b^2 - 4ac}}{2a} = \frac{-4 \pm \sqrt{4^2 - 4 \times (-1) \times (-3)}}{2 \times (-1)} = \frac{-4 \pm \sqrt{16 - (4 \times 1 \times 3)}}{-2} = \frac{-4 \pm \sqrt{4}}{-2} = \frac{-4 \pm 2}{-2} = 1 \text{ or } 3$$

g) $x^2 - \frac{5}{6}x + \frac{1}{6} = 0 \Rightarrow 6x^2 - 5x + 1 = 0$
$\Rightarrow a = 6, b = -5, c = 1$

$$x = \frac{-b \pm \sqrt{b^2 - 4ac}}{2a} = \frac{-(-5) \pm \sqrt{(-5)^2 - 4 \times 6 \times 1}}{2 \times 6} = \frac{5 \pm \sqrt{25 - 24}}{12} = \frac{5 \pm 1}{12} = \frac{1}{2} \text{ or } \frac{1}{3}$$

Removing the fractions right at the start here saves you lots of fraction headaches in the working. This one wasn't actually too hard to factorise — you'd get (3x − 1)(2x − 1).

h) $x^2 - 2\sqrt{11}x + 11 = 0 \Rightarrow a = 1, b = -2\sqrt{11}, c = 11$

$$x = \frac{-b \pm \sqrt{b^2 - 4ac}}{2a} = \frac{-(-2\sqrt{11}) \pm \sqrt{(-2\sqrt{11})^2 - 4 \times 1 \times 11}}{2 \times 1} = \frac{2\sqrt{11} \pm \sqrt{44 - 44}}{2} = \frac{2\sqrt{11} \pm \sqrt{0}}{2} = \frac{2\sqrt{11}}{2} = \sqrt{11}$$

There's only one solution to this quadratic — it factorises to give $(x - \sqrt{11})^2 = 0$.

Q2 a) $(x - 2 + \sqrt{5})(x - 2 - \sqrt{5})$
$= x(x - 2 - \sqrt{5}) - 2(x - 2 - \sqrt{5}) + \sqrt{5}(x - 2 - \sqrt{5})$
$= x^2 - 2x - \sqrt{5}x - 2x + 4 + 2\sqrt{5} + \sqrt{5}x - 2\sqrt{5} - 5$
$= x^2 - 4x - 1$

Use the method for multiplying out long brackets from Chapter 3.

b) $x^2 - 4x - 1 = 0 \Rightarrow a = 1, b = -4, c = -1$

$$x = \frac{-b \pm \sqrt{b^2 - 4ac}}{2a} = \frac{-(-4) \pm \sqrt{(-4)^2 - 4 \times 1 \times (-1)}}{2 \times 1} = \frac{4 \pm \sqrt{16 + 4}}{2} = \frac{4 \pm \sqrt{20}}{2} = \frac{4 \pm 2\sqrt{5}}{2} = 2 \pm \sqrt{5}$$

c) The roots produced by the quadratic formula in part b) are the same as the numbers subtracted from x in the expression from a) — this is because it's just the factorised version of the same quadratic. If you put the factorised version equal to zero and solved the equation, you'd get the same roots.

Q3 $x^2 + 8x + 13 = 0 \Rightarrow a = 1, b = 8, c = 13$

$$x = \frac{-b \pm \sqrt{b^2 - 4ac}}{2a} = \frac{-8 \pm \sqrt{8^2 - 4 \times 1 \times 13}}{2 \times 1} = \frac{-8 \pm \sqrt{64 - 52}}{2} = \frac{-8 \pm \sqrt{12}}{2} = \frac{-8 \pm 2\sqrt{3}}{2} = -4 \pm \sqrt{3}$$

So A = – 4 and B = 3.

Q4 a) $x^2 + x + \frac{1}{4} = 0 \Rightarrow a = 1, b = 1, c = \frac{1}{4}$

$$x = \frac{-b \pm \sqrt{b^2 - 4ac}}{2a} = \frac{-1 \pm \sqrt{1^2 - 4 \times 1 \times \frac{1}{4}}}{2 \times 1} = \frac{-1 \pm \sqrt{1 - 1}}{2} = \frac{-1 \pm 0}{2} = -\frac{1}{2}$$

Multiplying the first equation by 4 gives $4x^2 + 4x + 1 = 0$. This factorises to $(2x + 1)^2 = 0$, giving the same answer.

b) $x^2 - \frac{7}{4}x + \frac{2}{3} = 0 \Rightarrow 12x^2 - 21x + 8 = 0$
$\Rightarrow a = 12, b = -21, c = 8$

$$x = \frac{-b \pm \sqrt{b^2 - 4ac}}{2a} = \frac{-(-21) \pm \sqrt{(-21)^2 - 4 \times 12 \times 8}}{2 \times 12} = \frac{21 \pm \sqrt{441 - 384}}{24} = \frac{21 \pm \sqrt{57}}{24} = \frac{21}{24} \pm \frac{\sqrt{57}}{24} = \frac{7}{8} \pm \frac{1}{24}\sqrt{57}$$

c) $25x^2 - 30x + 7 = 0 \Rightarrow a = 25, b = -30, c = 7$

$$x = \frac{-b \pm \sqrt{b^2 - 4ac}}{2a} = \frac{-(-30) \pm \sqrt{(-30)^2 - 4 \times 25 \times 7}}{2 \times 25} = \frac{30 \pm \sqrt{900 - 700}}{2 \times 25} = \frac{30 \pm \sqrt{200}}{50} = \frac{30 \pm 10\sqrt{2}}{50} = \frac{30}{50} \pm \frac{10}{50}\sqrt{2} = \frac{3}{5} \pm \frac{1}{5}\sqrt{2}$$

d) $60x - 5 = -100x^2 - 3 \Rightarrow 100x^2 + 60x - 2 = 0$
$a = 100, b = 60, c = -2$

$$x = \frac{-b \pm \sqrt{b^2 - 4ac}}{2a} = \frac{-60 \pm \sqrt{60^2 - 4 \times 100 \times (-2)}}{2 \times 100} = \frac{-60 \pm \sqrt{3600 + 800}}{200} = \frac{-60 \pm \sqrt{4400}}{200} = \frac{-60 \pm \sqrt{44 \times 100}}{200} = \frac{-60 \pm \sqrt{4 \times 11 \times 100}}{200} = \frac{-60 \pm \sqrt{4}\sqrt{100}\sqrt{11}}{200} = \frac{-60 \pm 20\sqrt{11}}{200} = -\frac{3}{10} \pm \frac{1}{10}\sqrt{11}$$

e) $2x(x-4) = 7 - 3x \Rightarrow 2x^2 - 8x = 7 - 3x$
$\Rightarrow 2x^2 - 5x - 7 = 0 \Rightarrow a = 2, b = -5, c = -7$

$$x = \frac{-b \pm \sqrt{b^2 - 4ac}}{2a} = \frac{-(-5) \pm \sqrt{(-5)^2 - 4 \times 2 \times (-7)}}{2 \times 2} = \frac{5 \pm \sqrt{25+56}}{4} = \frac{5 \pm \sqrt{81}}{4} = \frac{5 \pm 9}{4}$$
$$= \frac{5+9}{4} \text{ or } \frac{5-9}{4} = \frac{14}{4} \text{ or } \frac{-4}{4} = \frac{7}{2} \text{ or } -1$$

This factorises to $(2x - 7)(x + 1) = 0$.

f) $(3x-5)(x+2) = 3x - 2 \Rightarrow 3x^2 + x - 10 = 3x - 2$
$\Rightarrow 3x^2 - 2x - 8 = 0 \Rightarrow a = 3, b = -2, c = -8$

$$x = \frac{-b \pm \sqrt{b^2 - 4ac}}{2a} = \frac{-(-2) \pm \sqrt{(-2)^2 - 4 \times 3 \times (-8)}}{2 \times 3} = \frac{2 \pm \sqrt{4+96}}{6} = \frac{2 \pm \sqrt{100}}{6} = \frac{2 \pm 10}{6}$$
$$= 2 \text{ or } -\frac{4}{3}$$

Q5 a) Multiply both sides of the equation by $(x - 1)(x + 2)$:
$$\frac{(3x-5)(x-1)(x+2)}{x-1} = \frac{(x+3)(x-1)(x+2)}{x+2}$$
$\Rightarrow (3x-5)(x+2) = (x+3)(x-1)$
$\Rightarrow 3x^2 + x - 10 = x^2 + 2x - 3 \Rightarrow 2x^2 - x - 7 = 0$

b) From part a), you can find the solutions to $2x^2 - x - 7 = 0$.
Using the quadratic formula: $a = 2, b = -1, c = -7$
$$x = \frac{-b \pm \sqrt{b^2 - 4ac}}{2a} = \frac{-(-1) \pm \sqrt{(-1)^2 - 4 \times 2 \times (-7)}}{2 \times 2} = \frac{1 \pm \sqrt{1+56}}{4} = \frac{1 \pm \sqrt{57}}{4}$$
So $x = \frac{1+\sqrt{57}}{4}$ or $x = \frac{1-\sqrt{57}}{4}$

Q6 Multiply through by $(3x - 2)(x - 3)$:
$$\frac{x}{3x-2} = \frac{4}{x-3} + 1 \Rightarrow x(x-3) = 4(3x-2) + (3x-2)(x-3)$$
$\Rightarrow x^2 - 3x = 12x - 8 + 3x^2 - 11x + 6$
$\Rightarrow x^2 + 2x - 1 = 0 \Rightarrow a = 1, b = 2, c = -1$
$$x = \frac{-b \pm \sqrt{b^2 - 4ac}}{2a} = \frac{-2 \pm \sqrt{2^2 - 4 \times 1 \times (-1)}}{2 \times 1} = \frac{-2 \pm \sqrt{4+4}}{2} = \frac{-2 \pm \sqrt{8}}{2}$$
So $x = -1 + \sqrt{2}$ or $x = -1 - \sqrt{2}$

[4 marks available — 1 mark for a correct method to remove the fractions in the equation, 1 mark for derivation of the correct quadratic to solve, 1 mark for a correct method to solve the quadratic, 1 mark for both correct values of x]

Q7 a) The ball will bounce when it hits the ground, and the ball hits the ground when $h = 0$, so find t when $h = 0$.
$10t - 5t^2 = 0 \Rightarrow t(2 - t) = 0 \Rightarrow t = 0$ or $t = 2$.
But $t = 0$ corresponds to the time when the ball is kicked, therefore, the ball first bounces when $t = 2$ seconds.
[2 marks available — 1 mark for recognising that the ball bounces when h = 0 and forming an equation, 1 mark for the correct answer]

b) The ball is at least 3 metres above the ground when $h \geq 3$
$\Rightarrow 10t - 5t^2 \geq 3 \Rightarrow 5t^2 - 10t + 3 \leq 0$
Using the quadratic formula, with $a = 5, b = -10, c = 3$:
$$t = \frac{-(-10) \pm \sqrt{(-10)^2 - 4 \times 5 \times 3}}{2 \times 5} = \frac{10 \pm \sqrt{100-60}}{10}$$
$$= \frac{10 \pm 2\sqrt{10}}{10} \Rightarrow t = 1.632... \text{ or } t = 0.367...$$
Since the ball is projected upwards, the ball will be at least 3 metres above the ground for $0.367... \leq t \leq 1.632...$
So, the ball is at least 3 metres above the ground for $1.632... - 0.367... = 1.264...$ seconds = 1.3 seconds (to 1 d.p.)
[3 marks available — 1 mark for attempting to solve the correct quadratic, 1 mark for finding the times when h = 3, 1 mark for the correct answer]

Q8 Using the quadratic formula:
$kx^2 + 4x - 2 = 0 \Rightarrow a = k, b = 4, c = -2$:
$$x = \frac{-b \pm \sqrt{b^2 - 4ac}}{2a} = \frac{-4 \pm \sqrt{4^2 - 4 \times k \times (-2)}}{2k} = \frac{-4 \pm \sqrt{16+8k}}{2k} = -\frac{4}{2k} \pm \frac{\sqrt{16+8k}}{2k}$$
Comparing with the given root:
$-\frac{4}{2k} = -\frac{2}{5} \Rightarrow 4k = 20 \Rightarrow k = 5$
Check that this works for the other part of the root:
If $k = 5$, $\frac{\sqrt{16+8k}}{2k} = \frac{\sqrt{16+8 \times 5}}{2 \times 5} = \frac{\sqrt{56}}{10}$
$$= \frac{\sqrt{4 \times 14}}{10} = \frac{2\sqrt{14}}{10} = \frac{\sqrt{14}}{5}.$$
So the other root will be $x = -\frac{2}{5} - \frac{\sqrt{14}}{5}$.

Q9 The shopper will arrive home at the first point when $d = 0$, so use the quadratic formula to find the smallest root of the equation $2t^2 - 5t + 1 = 0 \Rightarrow a = 2, b = -5, c = 1$
$$t = \frac{-b \pm \sqrt{b^2 - 4ac}}{2a} = \frac{-(-5) \pm \sqrt{(-5)^2 - 4 \times 2 \times 1}}{2 \times 2} = \frac{5 \pm \sqrt{25-8}}{4} = \frac{5 \pm \sqrt{17}}{4}$$
$= 0.2192...$ or $2.2807...$
The smallest root is $t = 0.2192...$ hours = 13.1534... minutes.
So they arrive home at 2.13 pm to the nearest minute.

Q10 Surface area of closed cylinder = $2\pi r^2 + 2\pi rh$,
where r is the radius and h is the height.
So $2\pi r^2 + 2\pi r(14) = 200 \Rightarrow \pi r^2 + 14\pi r - 100 = 0$
Using the quadratic formula, with $a = \pi, b = 14\pi, c = -100$:
$$r = \frac{-14\pi \pm \sqrt{(14\pi)^2 - 4 \times \pi \times -100}}{2 \times \pi} = \frac{-14\pi \pm \sqrt{(14\pi)^2 + 400\pi}}{2\pi}$$
So $r = 1.9906...$ or $r = -15.9906...$
But the radius must be positive, so $r = 1.9906... = 2.0$ cm to the nearest tenth of a centimetre.
[4 marks available — 1 mark for use of correct formula for surface area, 1 mark for deriving an appropriate quadratic equation in r, 1 mark for an appropriate method to solve the quadratic, 1 mark for correct value of r]

Exercise 4.3 — Completing the Square

Q1 a) Take the square root of both sides to get: $x + 4 = \pm\sqrt{25}$
$\Rightarrow x = -4 \pm \sqrt{25} = -4 \pm 5$. So $x = 1$ or -9

b) Take the square root of both sides to get: $2x + 5 = \pm\sqrt{9}$
$\Rightarrow 2x = -5 \pm \sqrt{9} = -5 \pm 3$. So $2x = -2$ or $-8 \Rightarrow x = -1$ or -4

c) Take the square root of both sides to get: $5x - 3 = \pm\sqrt{21}$
$\Rightarrow 5x = 3 \pm \sqrt{21} \Rightarrow x = \frac{3}{5} \pm \frac{\sqrt{21}}{5}$

Q2 a) $x^2 + 6x + 8 = (x + 3)^2 - 9 + 8 = (x + 3)^2 - 1$

b) $x^2 + 8x - 10 = (x + 4)^2 - 16 - 10 = (x + 4)^2 - 26$

c) $x^2 - 3x - 10 = \left(x - \frac{3}{2}\right)^2 - \frac{9}{4} - 10$
$$= \left(x - \frac{3}{2}\right)^2 - \frac{9}{4} - \frac{40}{4} = \left(x - \frac{3}{2}\right)^2 - \frac{49}{4}$$

d) $x^2 - 20x + 15 = (x - 10)^2 - 100 + 15 = (x - 10)^2 - 85$

e) $x^2 - 2mx + n = (x - m)^2 - m^2 + n = (x - m)^2 + (-m^2 + n)$

f) $x^2 + 6tx + s = (x + 3t)^2 - 9t^2 + s = (x + 3t)^2 + (-9t^2 + s)$

g) $3x^2 - 12x + 7 = 3(x-2)^2 - 12 + 7 = 3(x-2)^2 - 5$

h) $2x^2 - 4x - 3 = 2(x-1)^2 - 2 - 3 = 2(x-1)^2 - 5$

i) $6x^2 + 30x - 20 = 6\left(x+\frac{5}{2}\right)^2 - \frac{75}{2} - 20 = 6\left(x+\frac{5}{2}\right)^2 - \frac{115}{2}$

j) $-x^2 - 9x + 9 = -\left(x+\frac{9}{2}\right)^2 + \frac{81}{4} + 9 = -\left(x+\frac{9}{2}\right)^2 + \frac{117}{4}$

k) $4x^2 - 22x + 5 = 4\left(x-\frac{11}{4}\right)^2 - \frac{121}{4} + 5 = 4\left(x-\frac{11}{4}\right)^2 - \frac{101}{4}$

l) $-3x^2 + 9x + 1 = -3\left(x-\frac{3}{2}\right)^2 + \frac{27}{4} + 1 = -3\left(x-\frac{3}{2}\right)^2 + \frac{31}{4}$

Q3 a) First complete the square of the expression:
$x^2 - 6x - 16 = (x-3)^2 - 9 - 16 = (x-3)^2 - 25$
Now set the completed square equal to zero:
$(x-3)^2 - 25 = 0 \Rightarrow (x-3)^2 = 25$
$\Rightarrow x - 3 = \pm\sqrt{25} \Rightarrow x = 3 \pm \sqrt{25} = 3 \pm 5 \Rightarrow x = 8$ or -2

b) Write the equation in standard quadratic form:
$p^2 - 10p = 200 \Rightarrow p^2 - 10p - 200 = 0$
Then complete the square of the expression:
$p^2 - 10p - 200 = (p-5)^2 - 25 - 200 = (p-5)^2 - 225$
Now set the completed square equal to zero:
$(p-5)^2 - 225 = 0 \Rightarrow (p-5)^2 = 225 \Rightarrow p - 5 = \pm\sqrt{225}$
$\Rightarrow p = 5 \pm \sqrt{225} = 5 \pm 15 \Rightarrow p = 20$ or -10

c) First complete the square of the expression:
$x^2 + 2x + k = (x+1)^2 - 1 + k = (x+1)^2 + (k-1)$
Now set the completed square equal to zero:
$(x+1)^2 + (k-1) = 0 \Rightarrow (x+1)^2 = 1 - k$
$\Rightarrow x + 1 = \pm\sqrt{1-k} \Rightarrow x = -1 \pm \sqrt{1-k}$

d) First complete the square of the expression:
$x^2 + 4x - 8 = (x+2)^2 - 4 - 8 = (x+2)^2 - 12$
Now set the completed square equal to zero:
$(x+2)^2 - 12 = 0 \Rightarrow (x+2)^2 = 12$
$\Rightarrow x + 2 = \pm\sqrt{12} \Rightarrow x = \pm\sqrt{12} - 2$. So $x = -2 \pm 2\sqrt{3}$

e) First complete the square of the expression:
$4x^2 + 24x - 13 = 4(x+3)^2 - 36 - 13 = 4(x+3)^2 - 49$
Now set the completed square equal to zero:
$4(x+3)^2 - 49 = 0 \Rightarrow 4(x+3)^2 = 49 \Rightarrow x + 3 = \pm\sqrt{\frac{49}{4}}$
$\Rightarrow x = -3 \pm\sqrt{\frac{49}{4}} \Rightarrow x = -3 \pm \frac{7}{2}$, so $x = \frac{1}{2}$ or $-\frac{13}{2}$

f) Write the equation in standard quadratic form:
$9x^2 + 18x = 16 \Rightarrow 9x^2 + 18x - 16 = 0$
Then complete the square of the expression:
$9x^2 + 18x - 16 = 9(x+1)^2 - 9 - 16 = 9(x+1)^2 - 25$
Now set the completed square equal to zero:
$9(x+1)^2 - 25 = 0 \Rightarrow 9(x+1)^2 = 25$
$\Rightarrow (x+1)^2 = \frac{25}{9} \Rightarrow x + 1 = \pm\sqrt{\frac{25}{9}}$
$\Rightarrow x = -1 \pm\sqrt{\frac{25}{9}} \Rightarrow x = -1 \pm \frac{5}{3}$. So $x = \frac{2}{3}$ or $-\frac{8}{3}$

g) First complete the square of the expression:
$2x^2 - 12x + 9 = 2(x-3)^2 - 18 + 9 = 2(x-3)^2 - 9$
Now set the completed square equal to zero:
$2(x-3)^2 - 9 = 0 \Rightarrow 2(x-3)^2 = 9 \Rightarrow (x-3)^2 = \frac{9}{2}$
$\Rightarrow x - 3 = \pm\sqrt{\frac{9}{2}} \Rightarrow x = 3 \pm\sqrt{\frac{9}{2}}$
$\Rightarrow x = 3 \pm \frac{3}{\sqrt{2}} = 3 \pm \frac{3\sqrt{2}}{2}$
Here you should rationalise the denominator by multiplying the top and bottom of the fraction by $\sqrt{2}$.

h) First divide through by 2:
$x^2 - 6x - 27 = (x-3)^2 - 9 - 27 = (x-3)^2 - 36$
Now set the completed square equal to zero:
$(x-3)^2 - 36 = 0 \Rightarrow (x-3)^2 = 36$
$\Rightarrow x - 3 = \pm 6 \Rightarrow x = 3 \pm 6$. So $x = 9$ or -3

i) Write the equation in standard quadratic form:
$5x^2 + 10x = 1 \Rightarrow 5x^2 + 10x - 1 = 0$
Then complete the square of the expression:
$5x^2 + 10x - 1 = 5(x+1)^2 - 5 - 1 = 5(x+1)^2 - 6$
Now set the completed square equal to zero:
$5(x+1)^2 - 6 = 0 \Rightarrow 5(x+1)^2 = 6$
$\Rightarrow (x+1)^2 = \frac{6}{5} \Rightarrow x + 1 = \pm\sqrt{\frac{6}{5}} \Rightarrow x = -1 \pm\sqrt{\frac{6}{5}}$
$\Rightarrow x = -1 \pm \frac{\sqrt{6}\times\sqrt{5}}{\sqrt{5}\times\sqrt{5}}$. So $x = -1 \pm \frac{\sqrt{30}}{5}$

j) First complete the square of the expression:
$-3x^2 - 18x + 2 = -3(x+3)^2 + 27 + 2 = -3(x+3)^2 + 29$
Now set the completed square equal to zero:
$-3(x+3)^2 + 29 = 0 \Rightarrow -3(x+3)^2 = -29$
$\Rightarrow (x+3)^2 = \frac{-29}{-3} \Rightarrow x + 3 = \pm\sqrt{\frac{29}{3}}$
$\Rightarrow x = -3 \pm\sqrt{\frac{29}{3}} = -3 \pm \frac{\sqrt{29}\times\sqrt{3}}{\sqrt{3}\times\sqrt{3}} = -3 \pm \frac{\sqrt{87}}{3}$

k) Write the equation in standard quadratic form:
$3x^2 + 2x = \frac{7}{6} \Rightarrow 3x^2 + 2x - \frac{7}{6} = 0$
Then complete the square of the expression:
$3x^2 + 2x - \frac{7}{6} = 3\left(x+\frac{1}{3}\right)^2 - \frac{1}{3} - \frac{7}{6} = 3\left(x+\frac{1}{3}\right)^2 - \frac{3}{2}$
Now set the completed square equal to zero:
$3\left(x+\frac{1}{3}\right)^2 - \frac{3}{2} = 0 \Rightarrow 3\left(x+\frac{1}{3}\right)^2 = \frac{3}{2}$
$\Rightarrow \left(x+\frac{1}{3}\right)^2 = \frac{1}{2} \Rightarrow x + \frac{1}{3} = \pm\sqrt{\frac{1}{2}}$
$\Rightarrow x = -\frac{1}{3} \pm \frac{\sqrt{1}\times\sqrt{2}}{\sqrt{2}\times\sqrt{2}} \Rightarrow x = -\frac{1}{3} \pm \frac{\sqrt{2}}{2}$

l) First complete the square of the expression:
$5x^2 - 3x + \frac{2}{5} = 5\left(x-\frac{3}{10}\right)^2 - \frac{9}{20} + \frac{2}{5}$
$= 5\left(x-\frac{3}{10}\right)^2 + \frac{-9+8}{20} = 5\left(x-\frac{3}{10}\right)^2 - \frac{1}{20}$
Now set the completed square equal to zero:
$5\left(x-\frac{3}{10}\right)^2 - \frac{1}{20} = 0 \Rightarrow 5\left(x-\frac{3}{10}\right)^2 = \frac{1}{20}$
$\Rightarrow \left(x-\frac{3}{10}\right)^2 = \frac{1}{100} \Rightarrow x - \frac{3}{10} = \pm\sqrt{\frac{1}{100}}$
$\Rightarrow x - \frac{3}{10} = \pm\frac{1}{10} \Rightarrow x = \frac{3}{10} \pm \frac{1}{10}$. So $x = \frac{2}{5}$ or $\frac{1}{5}$

Q4 Complete the square of the expression:
$3x^2 - 12x + 14 = 3(x-2)^2 - 12 + 14 = 3(x-2)^2 + 2$
Since $(x-2)^2 \geq 0$ for all x, $3(x-2)^2 + 2 \geq 2$
So $3x^2 - 12x + 14 > 0$ for all x, as required.

Q5 First complete the square of the expression:
$ax^2 + bx + c = a(x^2 + \frac{b}{a}x + \frac{c}{a}) = a\left(x+\frac{b}{2a}\right)^2 - \frac{b^2}{4a} + c$
Now set the completed square equal to zero and rearrange to find the roots:
$a\left(x+\frac{b}{2a}\right)^2 - \frac{b^2}{4a} + c = 0 \Rightarrow \left(x+\frac{b}{2a}\right)^2 = \frac{b^2}{4a^2} - \frac{c}{a}$
$\Rightarrow \left(x+\frac{b}{2a}\right)^2 = \frac{b^2-4ac}{4a^2} \Rightarrow x + \frac{b}{2a} = \pm\sqrt{\frac{b^2-4ac}{4a^2}}$
$\Rightarrow x = -\frac{b}{2a} \pm \frac{\sqrt{b^2-4ac}}{2a} \Rightarrow x = \frac{-b\pm\sqrt{b^2-4ac}}{2a}$
This last question was quite tricky, but if you got there you should have noticed something quite special — you've just proved the quadratic formula.

Exercise 4.4 — Quadratics Involving Functions of x

Q1 a) $u = x^{\frac{1}{2}} (= \sqrt{x})$

b) $3^x(3^x - 6) = 8 \Rightarrow 3^{2x} - 6(3^x) - 8 = 0$
$\Rightarrow (3^x)^2 - 6(3^x) - 8 = 0$. So $u = 3^x$

c) $5^x + 5^{2x} = 4 \Rightarrow 5^{2x} + 5^x - 4 = 0$
$\Rightarrow (5^x)^2 + (5^x) - 4 = 0$. So $u = 5^x$.

d) $2\cos^2 x + 3 = 5\cos x \Rightarrow 2\cos^2 x - 5\cos x + 3 = 0$
$\Rightarrow 2(\cos x)^2 - 5(\cos x) + 3 = 0$. So $u = \cos x$

Q2 a) $x^2 + 6x + 7 = (x+3)^2 - 9 + 7 = (x+3)^2 - 2$
This is just completing the square.

b) Let $u = (2x + 1)$
So $(2x + 1)^2 + 6(2x + 1) + 7$ becomes
$u^2 + 6u + 7$, which can be written as $(u + 3)^2 - 2$.
$(u + 3)^2 - 2 = 0 \Rightarrow (u + 3)^2 = 2 \Rightarrow u + 3 = \pm\sqrt{2}$
$\Rightarrow u = -3 \pm \sqrt{2}$
Now replace u with $(2x + 1)$:
$(2x + 1) = -3 \pm \sqrt{2} \Rightarrow 2x = -4 \pm \sqrt{2}$
So $x = -2 \pm \frac{\sqrt{2}}{2}$

Q3 **a)** $2x^2 + 3x - 9 = 0 \Rightarrow (2x - 3)(x + 3) = 0 \Rightarrow x = \frac{3}{2}$ or $x = -3$
[2 marks available — 1 mark for correct method of solution, 1 mark for both correct solutions]

b) Let $u = x^2$. So $2x^4 + 3x^2 - 9 = 0$ becomes $2u^2 + 3u - 9 = 0$.
Using part a), $u = \frac{3}{2}$ or $u = -3$, so $x^2 = \frac{3}{2}$ or $x^2 = -3$.
$x^2 = -3$ has no real solutions, so the solutions are:
$x^2 = \frac{3}{2} \Rightarrow x = \sqrt{\frac{3}{2}}$ or $x = -\sqrt{\frac{3}{2}}$
$\Rightarrow x = \frac{1}{2}\sqrt{6}$ or $x = -\frac{1}{2}\sqrt{6}$.
[3 marks available — 1 mark for substituting to form an equation, 1 mark for a reason why $x^2 = -3$ gives no solutions, 1 mark for the correct solution]

Q4 Let $u = x - 2$.
So $3(x - 2)^2 - 2(x - 2) - 6 = 0$ becomes $3u^2 - 2u - 6 = 0$
$u = \frac{2 \pm \sqrt{(-2)^2 - 4 \times 3 \times -6}}{2 \times 3}$
$\Rightarrow u = \frac{2 \pm \sqrt{76}}{6} \Rightarrow u = \frac{1 \pm \sqrt{19}}{3}$
This means $x = 2 + \frac{1 \pm \sqrt{19}}{3} \Rightarrow x = \frac{7 + \sqrt{19}}{3}$ or $x = \frac{7 - \sqrt{19}}{3}$

Q5 Let $u = x^2$
So $x^4 - 17x^2 + 16 = 0$ becomes $u^2 - 17u + 16 = 0$
$(u - 1)(u - 16) = 0 \Rightarrow u = 1$ or $u = 16$
This means $x^2 = 1$ or $x^2 = 16$, so $x = \pm 1$ or $x = \pm 4$
So the four solutions are $x = 1, x = -1, x = 4$ and $x = -4$.

Q6 **a)** Let $u = \frac{1}{5x + 2}$
So $\frac{3}{(5x + 2)^2} + \frac{1}{5x + 2} = 10$ becomes $3u^2 + u - 10 = 0$
$(3u - 5)(u + 2) = 0 \Rightarrow u = \frac{5}{3}$ or $u = -2$
This means $\frac{1}{5x + 2} = \frac{5}{3} \Rightarrow 3 = 5(5x + 2)$
$\Rightarrow 3 = 25x + 10 \Rightarrow 25x = -7 \Rightarrow x = -\frac{7}{25}$ or $\frac{1}{5x + 2} = -2$
$\Rightarrow 1 = -2(5x + 2) \Rightarrow 1 = -10x - 4 \Rightarrow 10x = -5 \Rightarrow x = -\frac{1}{2}$

b) Let $u = \sqrt{x}$
So $3x + \sqrt{x} = 14$ becomes $3u^2 + u = 14 \Rightarrow 3u^2 + u - 14 = 0$
$(3u + 7)(u - 2) = 0 \Rightarrow u = -\frac{7}{3}$ or $u = 2$
This means $\sqrt{x} = -\frac{7}{3} \Rightarrow x = \left(-\frac{7}{3}\right)^2 = \frac{49}{9}$ or $\sqrt{x} = 2 \Rightarrow x = 4$.

Q7 **a)** $(2x^2 + x + 3)(2x^2 - x + 3)$
$\equiv 4x^4 - 2x^3 + 6x^2 + 2x^3 - x^2 + 3x + 6x^2 - 3x + 9$
$\equiv 4x^4 + 11x^2 + 9$
[2 marks available — 1 mark for correct expansion of brackets, 1 mark for correct simplification]

b) $(2x^2 + x + 3)(2x^2 - x + 3) = 12$
$\Rightarrow 4x^4 + 11x^2 + 9 = 12 \Rightarrow 4x^4 + 11x^2 - 3 = 0$.
Let $u = x^2$, then $4u^2 + 11u - 3 = 0 \Rightarrow (4u - 1)(u + 3) = 0$
$\Rightarrow u = \frac{1}{4}$ or $u = -3 \Rightarrow x^2 = \frac{1}{4}$ or $x^2 = -3$
But $x^2 = -3$ has no real solutions,
so $x^2 = \frac{1}{4} \Rightarrow x = \frac{1}{2}$ or $x = -\frac{1}{2}$
[3 marks available — 1 mark for substituting to form an equation, 1 mark for a reason why $x^2 = -3$ gives no solutions, 1 mark for the correct solution]

Q8 **a)** Using laws of indices, $2^{2x+1} = 2 \times 2^{2x} = 2 \times (2^x)^2$. Let $u = 2^x$, then $2^{2x+1} - 33(2^x) + 16 = 0$ becomes $2 \times u^2 - 33u + 16 = 0$
$\Rightarrow 2u^2 - 33u + 16 = 0$.
[2 marks available — 1 mark for correct manipulation of indices, 1 mark for correct substitution of u leading to result]

b) $2^{2x+1} - 33(2^x) + 16 = 0 \Rightarrow 2u^2 - 33u + 16 = 0$
$\Rightarrow (2u - 1)(u - 16) = 0 \Rightarrow u = \frac{1}{2}$ or $u = 16$
$\Rightarrow 2^x = \frac{1}{2}$ or $2^x = 16$.
When $2^x = \frac{1}{2}$, $2^x = 2^{-1} \Rightarrow x = -1$
When $2^x = 16$, $2^x = 2^4 \Rightarrow x = 4$
[3 marks available — 1 mark for substituting to form an equation, 1 mark for a method to solve the equation, 1 mark for the correct solutions]

Q9 Let $u = x^{\frac{3}{2}}$.
So $8x^3 - 117x^{\frac{3}{2}} - 125 = 0$ becomes $8u^2 - 117u - 125 = 0$
$\Rightarrow (8u - 125)(u + 1) = 0 \Rightarrow u = \frac{125}{8}$ or $u = -1$
$\Rightarrow x^{\frac{3}{2}} = \frac{125}{8}$ or $x^{\frac{3}{2}} = -1$.
However, $x \geq 0$, so $x^{\frac{3}{2}} = -1$ is not a valid solution.
So $x^{\frac{3}{2}} = \frac{125}{8} \Rightarrow x = \left(\sqrt[3]{\frac{125}{8}}\right)^2 \Rightarrow x = \frac{25}{4}$.
[3 marks available — 1 mark for substituting to form an equation, 1 mark for a reason why $x^{\frac{3}{2}} = -1$ gives no solutions, 1 mark for correct value of x]

Q10 At the point at which there are 1000 more birds, $p = 1$, so $5y^3 - y^6 = 1$.
Let $u = y^3$, so $5y^3 - y^6 = 1$ becomes $5u - u^2 = 1$
$\Rightarrow u^2 - 5u + 1 = 0$. This won't factorise, so use the quadratic formula: $a = 1, b = -5, c = 1$.
$u = \frac{-b \pm \sqrt{b^2 - 4ac}}{2a} = \frac{-(-5) \pm \sqrt{(-5)^2 - 4 \times 1 \times 1}}{2 \times 1}$
$= \frac{5 \pm \sqrt{25 - 4}}{2} = \frac{5 \pm \sqrt{21}}{2}$
You could also complete the square to solve the quadratic instead of using the formula.
So $u = 0.2087...$ or $4.7912...$, which means that
$y^3 = 0.2087... \Rightarrow y = \sqrt[3]{0.2087...} = 0.5931...$
or $y^3 = 4.7912... \Rightarrow y = \sqrt[3]{4.7912...} = 1.6858...$
You need the smallest amount of time, so $y = 0.5931... \times 100$
$= 59$ years to the nearest year.
Be careful with the units — p is in 1000s of birds and y is in 100s of years.

Q11 Let $u = \sqrt{x}$. Then $2x - 9\sqrt{x} + 5 = 0$ becomes $2u^2 - 9u + 5 = 0$
$\Rightarrow u = \frac{9 \pm \sqrt{(-9)^2 - 4 \times 2 \times 5}}{2 \times 2} \Rightarrow u = \frac{9 \pm \sqrt{41}}{4}$
This means $\sqrt{x} = \frac{9 \pm \sqrt{41}}{4} \Rightarrow x = \left(\frac{9 \pm \sqrt{41}}{4}\right)^2$
$\Rightarrow x = \frac{81 + 18\sqrt{41} + 41}{16} \Rightarrow x = \frac{61}{8} + \frac{9}{8}\sqrt{41}$
or $x = \frac{81 - 18\sqrt{41} + 41}{16} \Rightarrow x = \frac{61}{8} - \frac{9}{8}\sqrt{41}$
[4 marks available — 1 mark for an appropriate method to solve the equation, 1 mark for both correct values of $\sqrt{x}$ in an exact form, 1 mark for both correct values of x, 1 mark for rearranging solutions into the correct form]

Exercise 4.5 — The Roots of a Quadratic Function

Q1 **a)** 2 real roots. **b)** 1 real root.
c) no real roots. **d)** 2 real roots.

Q2 Completing the square:
$f(x) = x^2 + 6x + 10 = (x + 3)^2 - 9 + 10 = (x + 3)^2 + 1$
The smallest the $(x + 3)^2$ bit can be is 0, and 1 is positive which means that f(x) is always positive and the smallest it can be is 1.
So f(x) has no real roots.
$q = 3$, so the graph has a line of symmetry at $x = -3$.

Q3 Comparing $f(x) = -\left(x + \frac{7}{2}\right)^2 + \frac{25}{4}$ to $p(x + q)^2 + r$ gives
$p = -1, r = \frac{25}{4}$
These have different signs, so f(x) has two real roots.

Alternatively, $-\left(x+\frac{7}{2}\right)^2+\frac{25}{4}=0 \Rightarrow \left(x+\frac{7}{2}\right)^2=\frac{25}{4}$.
This can be solved by taking the square root (since the RHS is positive) — so it has real roots.

Q4 Completing the square:
$g(x)=4x^2-3x-5=4\left(x-\frac{3}{8}\right)^2-\frac{9}{16}-5$
$=4\left(x-\frac{3}{8}\right)^2-\frac{89}{16}$, so $p=4$ and $r=-\frac{89}{16}$.
p and r have different signs, so $g(x)$ has two real roots.
The turning point has coordinates $(-q, r)=\left(\frac{3}{8}, -\frac{89}{16}\right)$

Q5 **a)** Completing the square gives $p(x)=-2\left(x^2-\frac{7}{2}x\right)-10$
$=-2\left(\left(x-\frac{7}{4}\right)^2-\frac{49}{16}\right)-10=-2\left(x-\frac{7}{4}\right)^2-\frac{31}{8}$
[2 marks available — 1 mark for $\left(x-\frac{7}{4}\right)^2$*, 1 mark for the correct answer]*

b) The turning point of $y=p(x)$ is $\left(\frac{7}{4}, -\frac{31}{8}\right)$.
[1 mark for correct coordinates]

c) $p(x)$ is a negative quadratic, so the turning point of the graph of $y=p(x)$ will be a maximum point.
The y-coordinate of the turning point is $-\frac{31}{8}$, which is below the x-axis, so $y=p(x)$ lies entirely below the x-axis.
[2 marks available — 1 mark for stating that the turning point is a maximum, 1 mark for correct conclusion]

Q6 **a)** Completing the square:
$f(x)=-2x^2+3x+k=-2\left(x-\frac{3}{4}\right)^2+\frac{9}{8}+k$.
There is exactly one real root, so $\frac{9}{8}+k=0 \Rightarrow k=-\frac{9}{8}$.

b) The graph is symmetrical about the single root, i.e. where $-2\left(x-\frac{3}{4}\right)^2=0 \Rightarrow x=\frac{3}{4}$ is the line of symmetry.
This is the value of $-q$ when the equation is in the form $p(x+q)^2+r$.

c) The turning point has coordinates $(-q, r)$ when the equation is in the form $p(x+q)^2+r$.
$f(x)=-2\left(x-\frac{3}{4}\right)^2$, so the turning point is at $\left(\frac{3}{4}, 0\right)$.
p is negative, so the graph is n-shaped and the turning point is a maximum.

Q7 Completing the square:
$f(x)=x^2+6kx+5k^2=(x+3k)^2-9k^2+5k^2=(x+3k)^2-4k^2$
The coefficient of x^2 is positive for $f(x)$, so its turning point at $(-3k, -4k^2)$ is a minimum. That means it will have real roots if $-4k^2\le 0$. For all real values of k, $k^2\ge 0$, so $-4k^2\le 0$, so $f(x)$ has real roots for all real values of k.
[4 marks available — 1 mark for correctly completing the square, 1 mark for stating that f(x) has a minimum value of $-4k^2$, 1 mark for using $-4k^2\le 0$, 1 mark for correct conclusion with justification]

Q8 **a)** Completing the square:
$x^2+2(3k+1)x+3(k+7)$
$=(x+(3k+1))^2-(3k+1)^2+3(k+7)$
$=(x+(3k+1))^2-(9k^2+6k+1)+(3k+21)$
$=(x+(3k+1))^2-(9k^2+3k-20)$
[2 marks available — 1 mark for $(x+(3k+1))^2$, 1 mark for correct answer]

b) Using part a), $x^2+2(3k+1)x+3(k+7)=0$ is equivalent to $(x+(3k+1))^2-(9k^2+3k-20)=0$, so it will have real solutions when $9k^2+3k-20\ge 0$.
$\Rightarrow (3k+5)(3k-4)\ge 0 \Rightarrow k\le -\frac{5}{3}$ or $k\ge \frac{4}{3}$
[3 marks available — 1 mark for derivation of appropriate quadratic inequality in k to solve, 1 mark for use of an appropriate method of solution, 1 mark for correct solution]

c) $3x^2-5x+14=7x-40 \Rightarrow 3x^2-12x+54=0$
$\Rightarrow x^2-4x+18=0$. This is the same as the previous expression when $k=-1$.
From part b), there are only real solutions when $k\le -\frac{5}{3}$ or $k\ge \frac{4}{3}$, so when $k=-1$, there are no real solutions.
[3 marks available — 1 mark for rearrangement of the equation, 1 mark for realising that k = –1 , 1 mark for use of result from b) to arrive at a correct, written conclusion]

Exercise 4.6 — Using the Discriminant

Q1 **a)** $a=1, b=8, c=15$.
So $b^2-4ac=8^2-4\times 1\times 15=64-60=4$.
Discriminant >0 so the equation has 2 real roots.

b) $a=1, b=2\sqrt{3}, c=3$.
So $b^2-4ac=(2\sqrt{3})^2-4\times 1\times 3=12-12=0$.
Discriminant $=0$ so the equation has 1 real root.

c) Write in standard form: $(2x+1)(5x-3)=10x^2-x-3$
so $a=10$, $b=-1$ and $c=-3$.
$b^2-4ac=(-1)^2-4\times 10\times -3=1+120=121$
Discriminant >0 so the equation has 2 real roots.

d) $a=-3, b=-\frac{11}{5}, c=-\frac{2}{5}$.
So $b^2-4ac=\left(-\frac{11}{5}\right)^2-4\times(-3)\times\left(-\frac{2}{5}\right)$
$=\frac{121}{25}-\frac{24}{5}=\frac{121}{25}-\frac{120}{25}=\frac{1}{25}$
Discriminant >0 so the equation has 2 real roots.

e) $a=9, b=20, c=0$.
So $b^2-4ac=20^2-4\times 9\times 0=400-0=400$.
Discriminant >0 so the equation has 2 real roots.

f) $a=\frac{19}{16}, b=0, c=-4$.
So $b^2-4ac=0^2-4\times\frac{19}{16}\times(-4)=0+19=19$.
Discriminant >0 so the equation has 2 real roots.

Q2 Find the discriminant of the equation by first writing it in standard form: $15x^2+bx=2 \Rightarrow 15x^2+bx-2=0$
$a=15, b=b, c=-2$.
So $b^2-4ac=b^2-4\times 15\times(-2)=b^2+120$.
Now you know that the discriminant is 169 so let $b^2+120=169 \Rightarrow b^2=49 \Rightarrow b=\pm 7$.

Q3 First find the discriminant: $a=a, b=7, c=\frac{1}{4}$.
So $b^2-4ac=7^2-4\times a\times\frac{1}{4}=49-a$.
The equation has one real root which means its discriminant must be 0. So $49-a=0 \Rightarrow a=49$.

Q4 **a)** $a=13, b=8, c=2$
so $b^2-4ac=8^2-4\times 13\times 2=64-104=-40$.
The discriminant is negative so the equation has no real roots.

b) $a=\frac{1}{3}, b=\frac{5}{2}, c=3$
so $b^2-4ac=\left(\frac{5}{2}\right)^2-4\times\frac{1}{3}\times 3=\frac{25}{4}-4=\frac{25}{4}-\frac{16}{4}=\frac{9}{4}$
The discriminant is positive so there are two real roots.

c) $a=-\frac{1}{2}, b=-\frac{1}{3}, c=4$
Don't get caught out by the order of the terms in the equation here.
$b^2-4ac=\left(-\frac{1}{3}\right)^2-4\times\left(-\frac{1}{2}\right)\times 4=\frac{1}{9}+8=\frac{73}{9}$
The discriminant is positive so there are two real roots.

Q5 $a=1, b=-12, c=27+p$.
So $b^2-4ac=(-12)^2-4\times 1\times(27+p)$
$=144-(108+4p)=36-4p$
If the equation has two distinct real roots, the discriminant must be positive so $36-4p>0 \Rightarrow 36>4p \Rightarrow p<9$.

Q6 $a=10, b=-10, c=\frac{q}{2}$.
So $b^2-4ac=(-10)^2-4\times 10\times\frac{q}{2}=100-20q$
If the equation has two distinct real roots, the discriminant must be positive so $100-20q>0 \Rightarrow 100>20q \Rightarrow q<5$

Q7 $a = 2, b = 10p + 1, c = 5$
So $b^2 - 4ac = (10p + 1)^2 - 4 \times 2 \times 5$
$= (100p^2 + 20p + 1) - 40 = 100p^2 + 20p - 39$

If the equation has no real roots, the discriminant must be negative so $100p^2 + 20p - 39 < 0 \Rightarrow 100p^2 + 20p < 39$
$\Rightarrow 20p(5p + 1) < 39 \Rightarrow p(5p + 1) < \frac{39}{20}$

Q8 First find the discriminant of the equation. $a = -2, b = -2, c = k$.
So $b^2 - 4ac = (-2)^2 - 4 \times (-2) \times k = 4 + 8k$.

a) If the equation has two distinct real roots, the discriminant must be positive so $4 + 8k > 0 \Rightarrow 8k > -4 \Rightarrow k > -\frac{1}{2}$

b) If the equation has one real root, the discriminant must be zero so $4 + 8k = 0 \Rightarrow k = -\frac{1}{2}$

c) If the equation has no real roots, the discriminant must be negative so $4 + 8k < 0 \Rightarrow k < -\frac{1}{2}$.

Q9 a) First work out the discriminant: $a = 1, b = k + 5, c = \frac{k^2}{4}$
So $b^2 - 4ac = (k + 5)^2 - 4 \times 1 \times \frac{k^2}{4}$
$= (k^2 + 10k + 25) - k^2 = 10k + 25$

The equation has no real roots so the discriminant is negative so $10k + 25 < 0$.

b) To find the range of values of k, solve the inequality in part a).
$10k + 25 < 0 \Rightarrow 10k < -25 \Rightarrow k < -\frac{25}{10} = -\frac{5}{2}$.
So $k < -\frac{5}{2}$

Q10 a) $a = k - \frac{6}{5}, b = \sqrt{k}, c = \frac{5}{4}$
$b^2 - 4ac = (\sqrt{k})^2 - 4 \times \left(k - \frac{6}{5}\right) \times \frac{5}{4} = k - 5\left(k - \frac{6}{5}\right)$
$= k - 5k + 6 = -4k + 6$

b) (i) For one real root, discriminant = 0:
$-4k + 6 = 0 \Rightarrow k = \frac{6}{4} = \frac{3}{2}$

(ii) For no real roots, discriminant is negative:
$-4k + 6 < 0$ so $k > \frac{3}{2}$

(iii) For two real roots, discriminant is positive:
$-4k + 6 > 0$ so $k < \frac{3}{2}$

Q11 Find the discriminant: $a = \frac{m}{2}, b = \left(\frac{m}{\sqrt{3}} + 1\right), c = \frac{m}{6}$
$b^2 - 4ac = \left(\frac{m}{\sqrt{3}} + 1\right)^2 - 4 \times \frac{m}{2} \times \frac{m}{6}$
$= \frac{m^2}{3} + \frac{2m}{\sqrt{3}} + 1 - \frac{m^2}{3} = \frac{2m}{\sqrt{3}} + 1$

a) For one real root, discriminant = 0:
$\frac{2m}{\sqrt{3}} + 1 = 0 \Rightarrow m = -\frac{\sqrt{3}}{2}$

b) For no real roots, discriminant is negative:
$\frac{2m}{\sqrt{3}} + 1 < 0$ so $m < -\frac{\sqrt{3}}{2}$

c) For two real roots, discriminant is positive:
$\frac{2m}{\sqrt{3}} + 1 > 0$ so $m > -\frac{\sqrt{3}}{2}$

Q12 a) Find the discriminant: $a = (k - 1), b = (k^2 - 5), c = \frac{1}{2}(k + 1)$.
$b^2 - 4ac = (k^2 - 5)^2 - 4(k - 1)\left(\frac{1}{2}(k + 1)\right)$
$= k^4 - 10k^2 + 25 - 2(k^2 - 1) = k^4 - 12k^2 + 27$
[2 marks available — 1 mark for a method to calculate the discriminant, 1 mark for the correct expression]

b) $p(x)$ has a repeated root when the discriminant = 0.
$k^4 - 12k^2 + 27 = 0 \Rightarrow (k^2 - 9)(k^2 - 3) = 0$
$\Rightarrow k^2 = 9$ or $k^2 = 3 \Rightarrow k = -3, 3, -\sqrt{3}$ or $\sqrt{3}$.
[4 marks available — 1 mark for setting discriminant equal to zero, 1 mark for factorising the quartic equation, 1 mark for both correct values of k^2, 1 mark for all four correct values of k]

Q13 a) The original rectangle has dimensions of $2w$ by w, so the new rectangle has an area of:
$(2w - 5)(w + 5) = 2w^2 + 5w - 25$.

b) (i) $2w^2 + 5w - 25 = 25$, so $2w^2 + 5w - 50 = 0$.
Find the discriminant: $a = 2, b = 5, c = -50$.
$b^2 - 4ac = 5^2 - 4 \times 2 \times (-50) = 25 + 400 = 425$
The discriminant is positive, so the equation has two real roots.

(ii) In practice, the value of w needs to be a positive number, and $2w - 5$ needs to be greater than 0.
The discriminant only tells us the number of real roots, not the number of positive roots.
There is only one possible solution in practice: $w = 3.9$ m to 1 d.p.

Q14 a) For each point, the x-coordinate equals the y-coordinate, so $y = 2x^2 + 4x - 5 \Rightarrow x = 2x^2 + 4x - 5 \Rightarrow 2x^2 + 3x - 5 = 0$
$\Rightarrow (x - 1)(2x + 5) \Rightarrow x = 1$ or $x = -\frac{5}{2}$
So the coordinates of P and Q are $(1, 1)$ and $\left(-\frac{5}{2}, -\frac{5}{2}\right)$.
[4 marks available — 1 mark for deriving an equation to solve, 1 mark for an appropriate method to solve the equation, 1 mark for both correct x-values, 1 mark for the coordinates of P and Q]

b) The x-coordinate equals the y-coordinate, so
$y = ax^2 + bx + c \Rightarrow x = ax^2 + bx + c$
$\Rightarrow 0 = ax^2 + bx - x + c \Rightarrow ax^2 + (b - 1)x + c = 0$
This equation will have at least one solution whenever the discriminant $\geq 0 \Rightarrow (b - 1)^2 - 4ac \geq 0$
[2 marks available — 1 mark for deriving the equation, 1 mark for using the discriminant to find the inequality]

Q15 Set the equations equal to each other:
$x^2 - 3x + 3 = kx + 1 \Rightarrow x^2 - (k + 3)x + 2 = 0$
Find the discriminant: $a = 1, b = -(k + 3), c = 2$
$b^2 - 4ac = (-(k + 3))^2 - 4 \times 1 \times 2 = (k + 3)^2 - 8$
The simultaneous equations will have two distinct solutions when this discriminant > 0. First solve discriminant = 0:
$(k + 3)^2 - 8 = 0 \Rightarrow k + 3 = \pm\sqrt{8}$
$\Rightarrow k = -3 + 2\sqrt{2}$ or $k = -3 - 2\sqrt{2}$
$(k + 3)^2 - 8 = k^2 + 6k + 1$ is a positive quadratic, so the discriminant will be > 0 for $k < (-3 - 2\sqrt{2})$ or $k > (-3 + 2\sqrt{2})$.
So the simultaneous equations will have two distinct solutions when $k < (-3 - 2\sqrt{2})$ or $k > (-3 + 2\sqrt{2})$.
[5 marks available — 1 mark for finding $x^2 - (k + 3)x + 2 = 0$, 1 mark for finding the discriminant, 1 mark for finding a quadratic inequality in k, 1 mark for a method to solve the quadratic inequality, 1 mark for the correct range of values]

Q16 a) Find the discriminant: $a = \frac{1}{2\sqrt{2}}, b = -(k + 1), c = -\frac{1}{\sqrt{2}}k^2$
$b^2 - 4ac = (-(k + 1))^2 - 4 \times \frac{1}{2\sqrt{2}} \times -\frac{1}{\sqrt{2}}k^2$
$= (k + 1)^2 + k^2 = 2k^2 + 2k + 1$
[2 marks available — 1 mark for a method to calculate the discriminant, 1 mark for correct answer]

b) Find the discriminant of $2k^2 + 2k + 1$: $a = 2, b = 2, c = 1$
$2^2 - 4 \times 2 \times 1 = -4 < 0$, so $2k^2 + 2k + 1$ has no real roots.
$2k^2 + 2k + 1$ has a positive coefficient of x^2, so it must lie above the horizontal axis — it is positive for all values of k.
Since the discriminant of $p(x) > 0$ for all k, $p(x)$ has two distinct real solutions for all k.
[3 marks available — 1 mark for calculating the discriminant, 1 mark for a correct interpretation of the discriminant, 1 mark for a correct conclusion about p(x)]
Alternatively you could complete the square to find the turning point and see that the y-coordinate is positive.

Q17 a) Substitute $y = kx + 9$ into $(x - 4)^2 + (y - 5)^2 = 9$:
$(x - 4)^2 + ((kx + 9) - 5)^2 = 9$
$\Rightarrow (x - 4)^2 + (kx + 4)^2 = 9$
$\Rightarrow x^2 - 8x + 16 + k^2x^2 + 8kx + 16 = 9$
$\Rightarrow (1 + k^2)x^2 + (8k - 8)x + 23 = 0$
If l is a tangent to C, the quadratic equation will have a repeated solution, i.e. the discriminant will equal 0.

Find the discriminant: $a = (1 + k^2)$, $b = (8k - 8)$, $c = 23$
$b^2 - 4ac = 0 \Rightarrow (8k - 8)^2 - 4(1 + k^2) \times 23 = 0$
$\Rightarrow 64k^2 - 128k + 64 - 92 - 92k^2 = 0$
$\Rightarrow -28k^2 - 128k - 28 = 0 \Rightarrow 28k^2 + 128k + 28 = 0$
$\Rightarrow 7k^2 + 32k + 7 = 0 \Rightarrow k = \frac{-32 \pm \sqrt{(32)^2 - 4 \times 7 \times 7}}{2 \times 7}$
$\Rightarrow k = \frac{-16 \pm \sqrt{207}}{7} = k = \frac{-16 \pm 3\sqrt{23}}{7}$
So the values of k for which l is tangent to C are,
$k = \frac{-16 + 3\sqrt{23}}{7}$ and $k = \frac{-16 - 3\sqrt{23}}{7}$.

b) If l doesn't intersect C, $(1 + k^2)x^2 + (8k - 8)x + 23 = 0$ has no real solutions, so the discriminant $< 0 \Rightarrow -7k^2 - 32k - 7 < 0$
$\Rightarrow 7k^2 + 32k + 7 > 0$. This has a positive coefficient of x^2,
so $k < \frac{-16 - 3\sqrt{23}}{7}$ or $k > \frac{-16 + 3\sqrt{23}}{7}$.

Exercise 4.7 — Sketching Quadratic Graphs

Q1 a) & b)

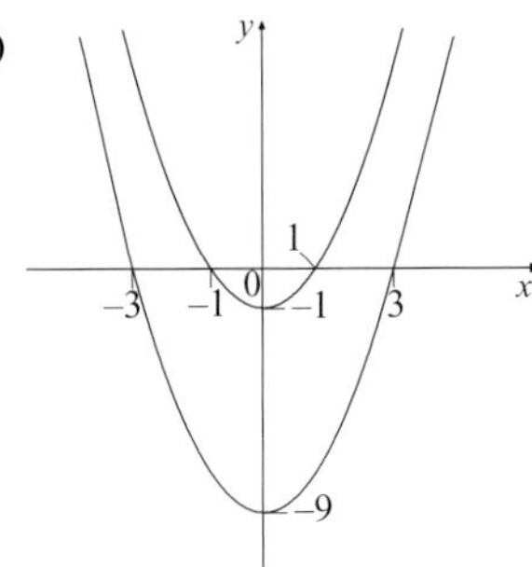

Q2 a) $f(x) = x^2 - 10x + 9 = (x - 9)(x - 1)$

b) & c)

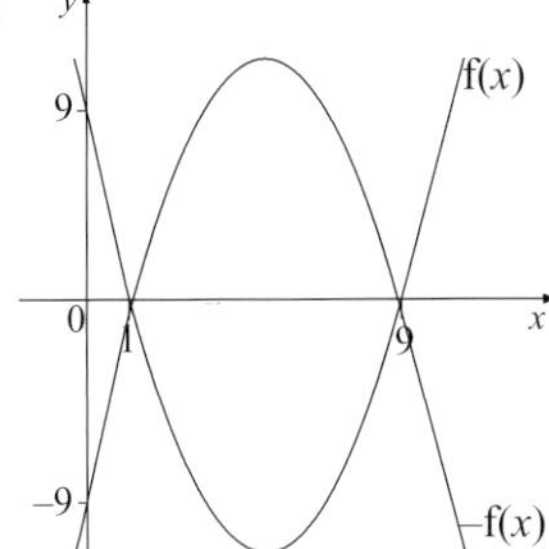

Q3 a) $y = -x^2 + 2x + 1$

(i) The x^2 coefficient is −1 so it is n-shaped.

(ii) Letting $x = 0$, $y = 1$ is the y-intercept.

(iii) Calculate the discriminant to work out the number of roots: $a = -1$, $b = 2$, $c = 1$.
$b^2 - 4ac = 2^2 - 4 \times (-1) \times 1 = 4 + 4 = 8$
The discriminant is positive so there are 2 distinct real roots.

(iv) To find the x-intercepts — find the roots:
$y = -x^2 + 2x + 1 = -(x - 1)^2 + 2$ by completing the square.
Setting this equal to zero: $-(x - 1)^2 + 2 = 0$
$\Rightarrow (x - 1)^2 = 2 \Rightarrow x - 1 = \pm\sqrt{2} \Rightarrow x = 1 \pm \sqrt{2}$

(v) The vertex is a maximum since the graph's n-shaped. The maximum can be found by looking at the completed square $y = -(x - 1)^2 + 2$.
The highest value $-(x - 1)^2$ can take is 0, so the maximum is at $y = 2$ and $x = 1$ (to make the bracket 0) — i.e. the maximum has coordinates (1, 2).

(vi)

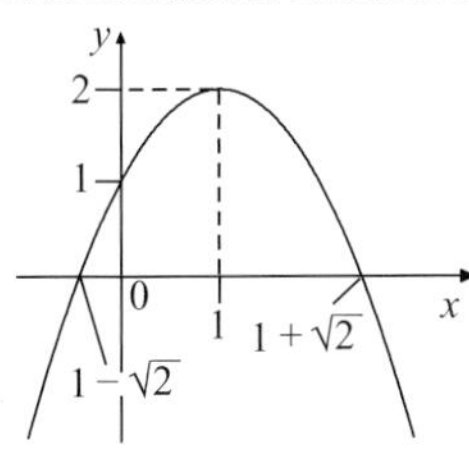

b) $y = x^2 - 7x + 15$

(i) The x^2 coefficient is 1 so the graph's u-shaped.

(ii) Letting $x = 0$, $y = 15$ is the y-intercept.

(iii) Calculate the discriminant to work out the number of roots: $a = 1$, $b = -7$, $c = 15$.
$b^2 - 4ac = (-7)^2 - 4 \times 1 \times 15 = 49 - 60 = -11$
The discriminant is negative so there are no real roots.

(iv) There are no real roots so the graph does not intersect the x-axis.

(v) The vertex is a minimum since the graph's u-shaped. The minimum can be found by completing the square.
$y = x^2 - 7x + 15 = \left(x - \frac{7}{2}\right)^2 + \frac{11}{4}$
The lowest value $\left(x - \frac{7}{2}\right)^2$ can take is zero — so the minimum is at $y = \frac{11}{4}$ and so $x = \frac{7}{2}$ (to make the bracket 0) — i.e. it has coordinates $\left(\frac{7}{2}, \frac{11}{4}\right)$.

(vi)

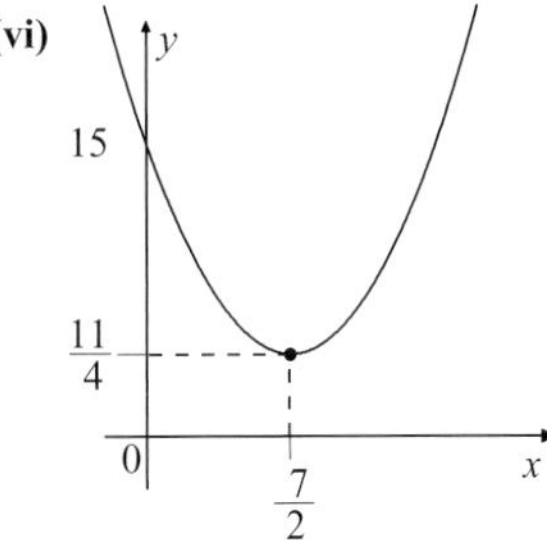

c) $y = 2x^2 + 4x - 9$

(i) The x^2 coefficient is 2 so it is u-shaped.

(ii) Letting $x = 0$, $y = -9$ is the y-intercept.

(iii) Calculate the discriminant to work out the number of roots: $a = 2$, $b = 4$, $c = -9$.
$b^2 - 4ac = 4^2 - 4 \times 2 \times (-9) = 16 + 72 = 88$
The discriminant is positive so there are 2 distinct real roots.

(iv) To find the x-intercepts, find the roots:
$2x^2 + 4x - 9 = 0$
Completing the square gives:
$2(x + 1)^2 - 2 - 9 = 0 \Rightarrow 2(x + 1)^2 - 11 = 0$
Solving: $(x + 1)^2 = \frac{11}{2} \Rightarrow x = -1 \pm \sqrt{\frac{11}{2}}$

(v) The vertex is a minimum since the graph is u-shaped. The minimum occurs when the square is 0, so it's (−1, −11).

(vi)

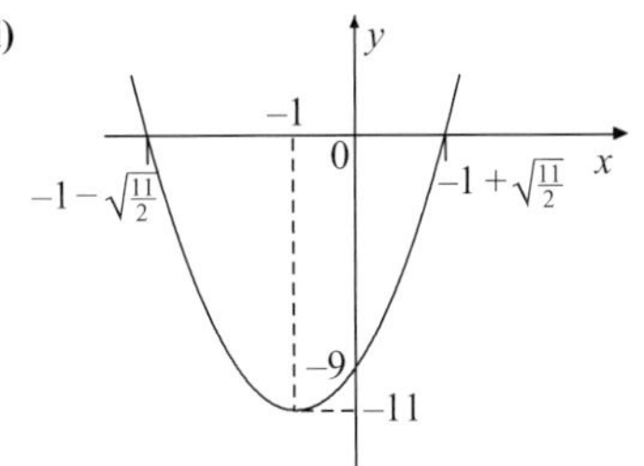

d) $y = -x^2 + 4x - 7$

(i) The x^2 coefficient is −1 so it is n-shaped.

(ii) Letting $x = 0$, $y = -7$ is the y-intercept.

(iii) Calculate the discriminant to work out the number of roots: $a = -1$, $b = 4$, $c = -7$.
$b^2 - 4ac = 4^2 - 4 \times (-1) \times (-7) = 16 - 28 = -12$
The discriminant is negative so there are no real roots.

(iv) There are no real roots so the graph does not intersect the x-axis.

(v) The vertex is a maximum since the graph is n-shaped. The maximum can be found by completing the square.
$y = -x^2 + 4x - 7 = -(x-2)^2 + 4 - 7 \Rightarrow y = -(x-2)^2 - 3$
The highest value $-(x-2)^2$ can take is 0 — so the maximum is at $y = -3$ and $x = 2$ (to make the bracket 0) – i.e. it has coordinates (2, –3).

(vi)

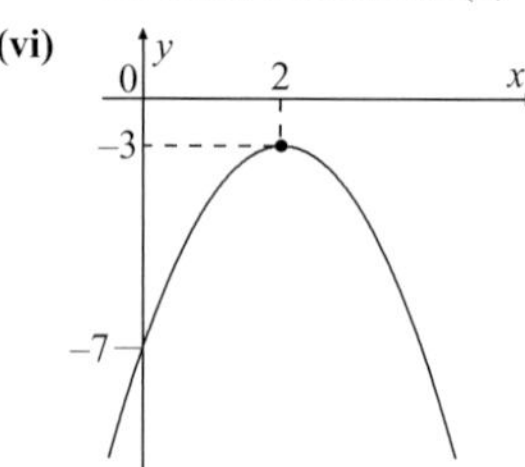

Q4 a) The minimum point is shown on the graph as (–4, 2). The coordinates of the vertex of the function $f(x) = p(x+q)^2 + r$ are $(-q, r)$. In this case $p = 1$ and from the minimum on the graph you can see $-q = -4$, so $q = 4$ and $r = 2$. So you can write the function $f(x) = (x+4)^2 + 2$.

b) $g(x) = (x+4)^2$ is in the form $p(x+q)^2 + r$ with $p = 1$ so the graph is u-shaped and the minimum is at $(-q, r) = (-4, 0)$.

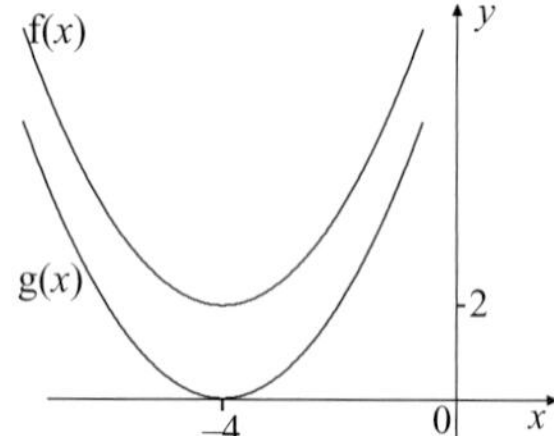

c) f(x) does not have any real roots as its graph does not touch the x-axis. g(x) has one real root as its graph touches the x-axis once (at $x = -4$).

Q5 a) $x^2 - 6x + 5 = (x-3)^2 - 9 + 5 = (x-3)^2 - 4$

b) $x^2 - 6x + 5 = 0 \Rightarrow (x-3)^2 - 4 = 0 \Rightarrow (x-3)^2 = 4$
$\Rightarrow x - 3 = \pm\sqrt{4} \Rightarrow x = 3 \pm \sqrt{4} = 3 \pm 2 = 5$ or 1

c) The graph is u-shaped. The function has roots $x = 1$ and 5 so these are the x-intercepts. Putting $x = 0$ into the original equation gives $y = 5$, so this is the y-intercept. Completing the square gives the minimum as (3, –4). Putting all this together gives the following graph:

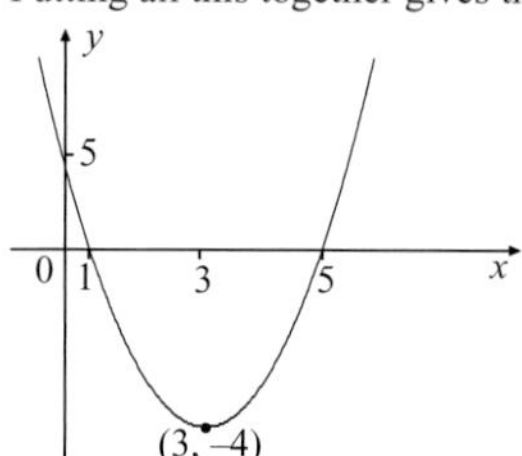

Q6 a) $f(x) = x^2 - 2x + 1 = (x-1)^2$ so the function has one repeated root at $x = 1$. Letting $x = 0$ gives $f(x) = 1$ so the y-intercept is at 1. The graph is u-shaped.

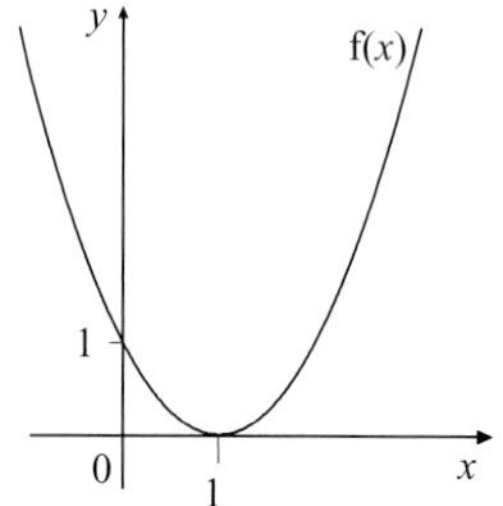

b) $f(x) = x^2 + x - 1 = \left(x + \frac{1}{2}\right)^2 - \frac{5}{4}$ and solving $f(x) = 0$ gives $x = -\frac{1}{2} \pm \frac{\sqrt{5}}{2}$ as the x-intercepts. Letting $x = 0$ we get $f(x) = -1$ so this is the y-intercept. The graph is u-shaped.

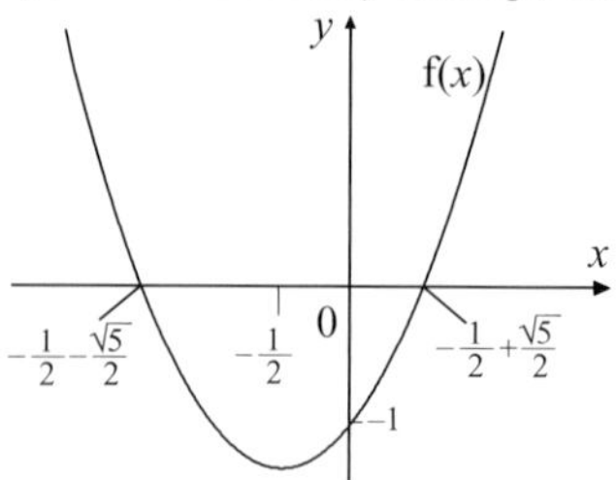

c) $f(x) = x^2 - 8x + 18 = (x-4)^2 + 2$. Solving $f(x) = 0$ gives $x = 4 \pm \sqrt{-2}$ so there are no x-intercepts as you cannot take the square root of –2.

You could have worked out the discriminant to see that there were no real roots to save you trying to solve the equation.

Letting $x = 0$ gives $f(x) = 18$. The graph is u-shaped but it could be one of two graphs which are u-shaped with a y-intercept of 18. To find out which, work out the vertex. It has a minimum as it is u-shaped and from completing the square, the minimum is at (4, 2).

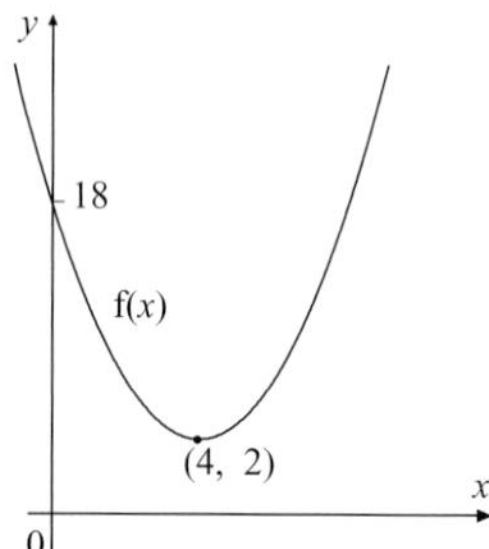

d) $f(x) = -x^2 + 3$ so setting $f(x) = 0$ gives $x = \pm\sqrt{3}$ as the x-intercepts. Letting $x = 0$ gives $f(x) = 3$ so 3 is the y-intercept. The graph is n-shaped.

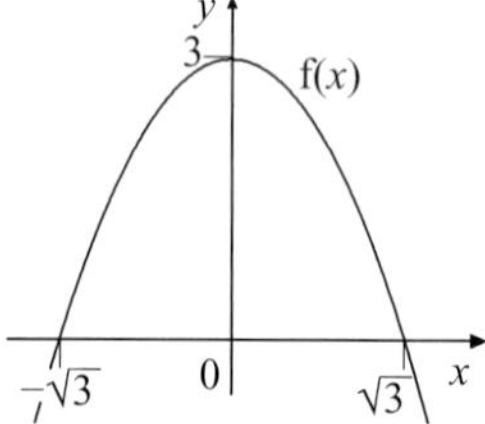

e) $f(x) = 2x^2 + 5x + 2 = 2\left(x + \frac{5}{4}\right)^2 - \frac{9}{8}$ and solving $f(x) = 0$ gives $x = -\frac{5}{4} \pm \frac{3}{4} = -2$ and $-\frac{1}{2}$ as the x-intercepts. $f(0) = 2$ so this is the y-intercept. The graph is u-shaped.

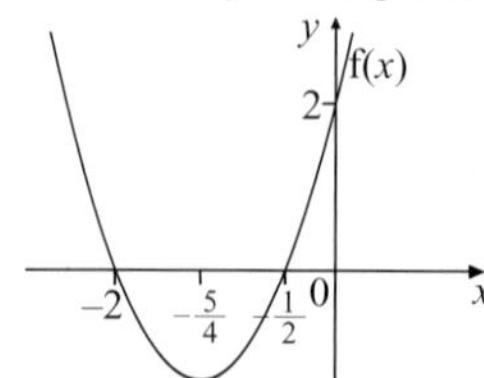

f) $f(x) = 2x^2 - 5x - 1 = 2\left(x - \frac{5}{4}\right)^2 - \frac{33}{8}$ and solving $f(x) = 0$ gives $x = \frac{5}{4} \pm \frac{\sqrt{33}}{4}$ as the x-intercepts. Letting $x = 0$ we get $f(x) = -1$ so this is the y-intercept. The graph is u-shaped.

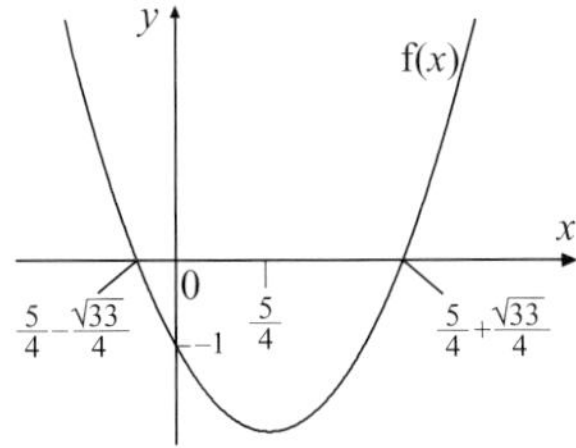

Q7 $f(x) = (x + 3)^2$ so setting $f(x) = 0$ gives $x = -3$ as the x-intercept, which means the graph just touches the x-axis at this point. $f(0) = 9$ so 9 is the y-intercept. The graph is u-shaped, so the vertex is a minimum, and occurs when $(x + 3) = 0$, at $(-3, 0)$:

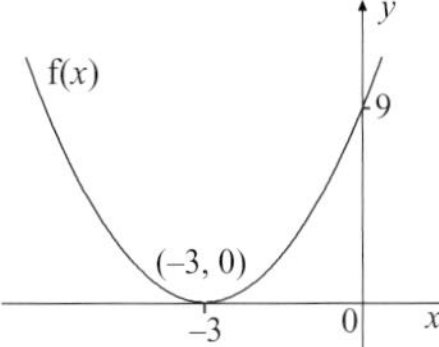

Q8 $g(x) = x^2 - 2x - 15 = (x - 1)^2 - 16$. Setting $g(x) = 0$ gives $x = -3$ and 5 as the x-intercepts. Letting $x = 0$ gives $g(x) = -15$ so -15 is the y-intercept. The graph is u-shaped, so the vertex is a minimum, and occurs when $(x - 1) = 0$, at $(1, -16)$:

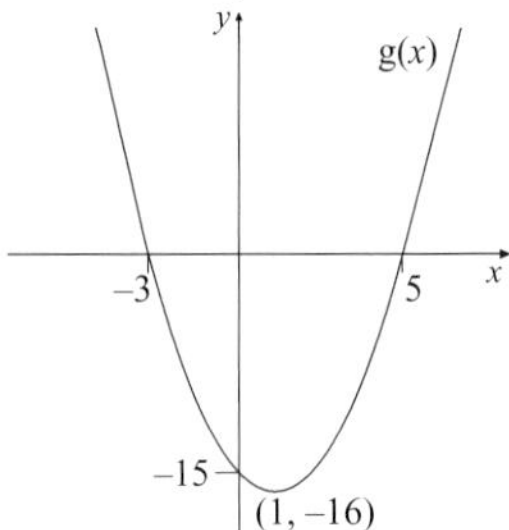

Q9 a) $x^2 - 5x + 8 = \left(x - \frac{5}{2}\right)^2 - \frac{25}{4} + 8 \Rightarrow \left(x - \frac{5}{2}\right)^2 + \frac{7}{4}$

The coordinates of the minimum point are $\left(\frac{5}{2}, \frac{7}{4}\right)$.

[2 marks available — 1 mark for completing the square correctly, 1 mark for correct coordinates for minimum point]

b)

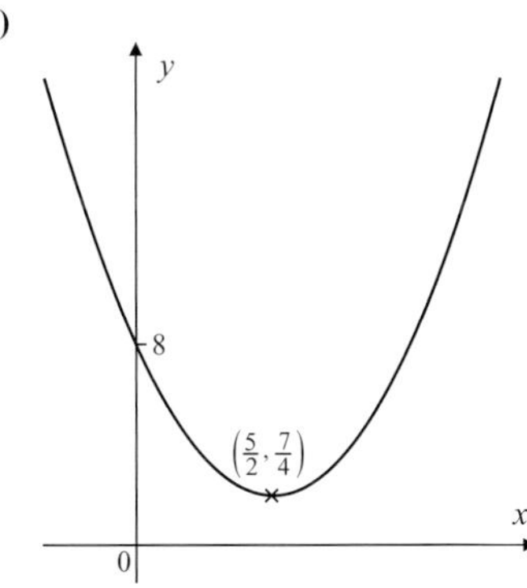

[3 marks available — 1 mark for correct shape, 1 mark for correct vertex, 1 mark for correct intersection with y-axis]

c) The graph of $y = -p(x)$ is a reflection of the graph of $y = p(x)$ in the x-axis. $p(x)$ is a positive quadratic, so $-p(x)$ is a negative quadratic. So the coordinates of the maximum point on the graph of $y = -p(x)$ are $\left(\frac{5}{2}, -\frac{7}{4}\right)$.

[1 mark for the correct coordinates]

Q10 a) $2x^2 + 3x - 6 = 0 \Rightarrow x = \frac{-3 \pm \sqrt{3^2 - 4 \times 2 \times -6}}{2 \times 2}$

$\Rightarrow x = -\frac{3}{4} + \frac{1}{4}\sqrt{57}$ or $-\frac{3}{4} - \frac{1}{4}\sqrt{57}$

[2 marks available — 1 mark for an appropriate method to solve the quadratic equation, 1 mark for both correct solutions in the correct form]

b) The x-coordinate of the vertex is halfway between the roots, so it is $-\frac{3}{4}$.

So the y-coordinate of the vertex is:

$y = 2\left(-\frac{3}{4}\right)^2 + 3\left(-\frac{3}{4}\right) - 6 = -\frac{57}{8}$

$\Rightarrow$ coordinates of the vertex are $\left(-\frac{3}{4}, -\frac{57}{8}\right)$

[2 marks available — 1 mark for an appropriate method, 1 mark for correct coordinates of the vertex]

You could have found the minimum by completing the square.

c)

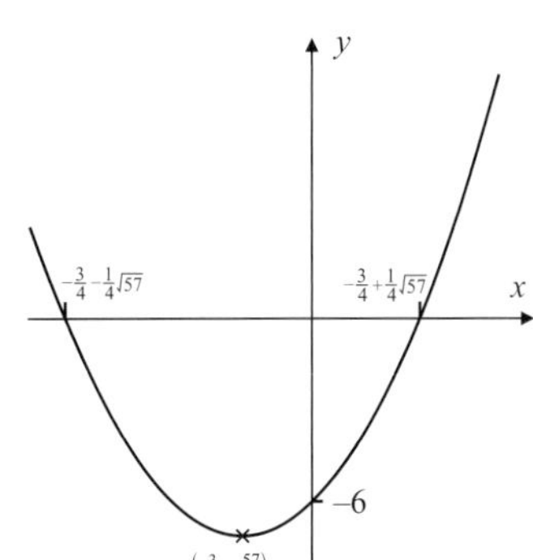

[3 marks available — 1 mark for correct curve shape, 1 mark for correct vertex, 1 mark for correct intersections with axes]

Q11 a) The roots of the quadratic function are the values of x where the graph crosses the x-axis. So the roots are $x = -2$ and $x = 1$.

b) One root of the equation is $x = -2$ which means $x + 2$ will be a factor. The other root $x = 1$ means that $x - 1$ will be a factor. So the quadratic function should be of the form $y = a(x + 2)(x - 1)$ for some value of a. But you know the equation has the form $y = -x^2 + px + q$. So a should be -1 to produce the term $-x^2$. So $y = -(x + 2)(x - 1)$ which gives $y = -x^2 - x + 2$, so $p = -1$ and $q = 2$.

The trickiest part of this question is realising you might also need a number factor, a, to form the factorised quadratic. Without it, you'd have got the wrong answer of $x^2 + x - 2$.

Q12 a) $h = 24t - 16t^2 = 8t(3 - 2t)$. Setting $h = 0$ gives $t = 0$ and $\frac{3}{2}$ as the t-intercepts. Letting $t = 0$ gives $h = 0$ so the h-intercept is $(0, 0)$. The coefficient of t^2 is -16 so the graph is n-shaped:

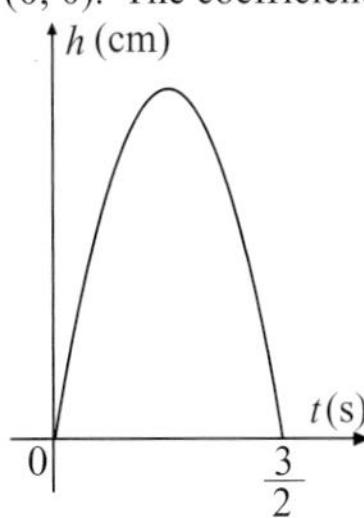

b) The maximum point on the graph occurs halfway between the t-intercepts, when $t = \frac{3}{4}$ s.

So the maximum height $= 24\left(\frac{3}{4}\right) - 16\left(\frac{3}{4}\right)^2 = 9$ cm.

Q13 a) Setting $t = 0$ gives the h-intercept at $h = 4$.
Setting $h = 0$ gives $0.25t^2 - 2.5t + 4 = 0$, so
$t^2 - 10t + 16 = 0 \Rightarrow (t - 2)(t - 8) = 0$
so the t-intercepts are at $t = 2$ or $t = 8$.

Setting $t = 10$ gives $h = 25 - 25 + 4 = 4$.
So the graph is u-shaped and looks like this:

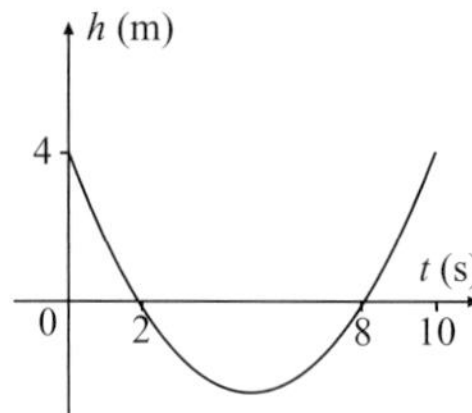

b) (i) The height of the raised platform is where the roller coaster sets off from (i.e. at $t = 0$). From part a), this is 4 m.

(ii) The lowest point of the roller coaster is the value of h at the minimum point of the graph. Using the symmetry of the graph, this point occurs halfway between $t = 2$ and $t = 8$ (i.e. at $t = 5$).
When $t = 5$, $h = 0.25(5)^2 - 2.5(5) + 4 = -2.25$ m.

(iii) The roller coaster is underground when $h < 0$. From the graph, you can see that this is between $t = 2$ and $t = 8$, so it is underground for $8 - 2 = 6$ seconds.

Q14 a) $h = 0.5t^2 - 13t + 100$. Setting $t = 0$ gives the starting height $h = 100$, which is the intercept with the h-axis. To find the time taken to complete the stunt, set $h = 100$ and find the non-zero solution for t: $0.5t^2 - 13t + 100 = 100$
$\Rightarrow 0.5t(t - 26) = 0 \Rightarrow t = 0$ and 26, so the stunt is complete at $t = 26$ seconds. The coefficient of t^2 is 0.5 so the graph is u-shaped. The discriminant
$b^2 - 4ac = (-13)^2 - 4 \times 0.5 \times 100 = -31$, so there are no real roots and the graph will not touch the t-axis:

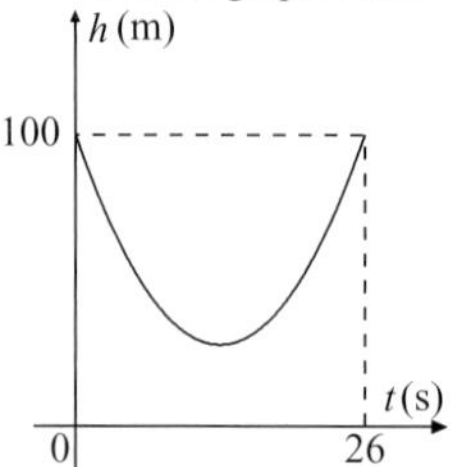

b) The graph is symmetrical so the minimum occurs when $t = 26 \div 2 = 13$ s. This gives a minimum height of $0.5(13)^2 - 13(13) + 100 = 15.5$ m.

Q15 a) Completing the square: $2x^2 + ax + b = 2\left(x^2 + \frac{a}{2}x\right) + b$
$= 2\left(\left(x + \frac{a}{4}\right)^2 - \frac{a^2}{16}\right) + b = 2\left(x + \frac{a}{4}\right)^2 - \frac{a^2}{8} + b$
The minimum has coordinates (2, 3), so using the completed square form, $-\frac{a}{4} = 2 \Rightarrow a = -8$
and $-\frac{a^2}{8} + b = 3 \Rightarrow -\frac{(-8)^2}{8} + b = 3 \Rightarrow b = 11$.
So the equation of the quadratic is $y = 2x^2 - 8x + 11$.
When $x = 0$, $y = 11$, so the coordinates of A are (0, 11).
[4 marks available — 1 mark for completing the square, 1 mark for the correct value of a, 1 mark for the correct value of b, 1 mark for the correct coordinates for A]

b)

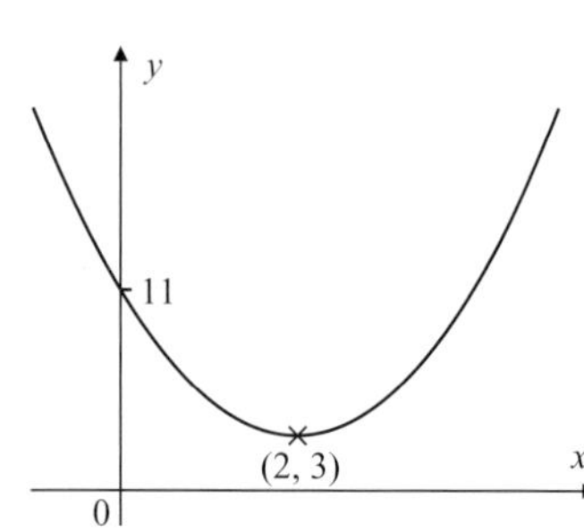

[2 marks available — 1 mark for the correct curve shape, 1 mark for all relevant coordinates correctly labelled]

Q16 a) Completing the square: $p(x) = 2(x^2 - 5x) + 8$
$= 2\left(x - \frac{5}{2}\right)^2 - \frac{25}{2} + 8 = 2\left(x - \frac{5}{2}\right)^2 - \frac{9}{2}$
So the coordinates of minimum point of C are $\left(\frac{5}{2}, -\frac{9}{2}\right)$.
[2 marks available — 1 mark for completing the square correctly, 1 mark for the correct coordinates]

b) C intersects the y-axis at $y = 8$, and intersects the x-axis when $2x^2 - 10x + 8 = 0 \Rightarrow x^2 - 5x + 4 = 0$
$\Rightarrow (x - 1)(x - 4) = 0 \Rightarrow x = 1$ or $x = 4$.
The coefficient of x^2 is positive so the graph is u-shaped:

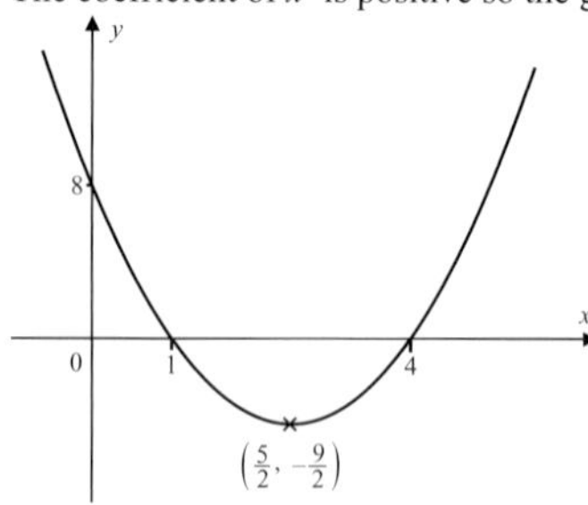

[3 marks available — 1 mark for correct curve shape, 1 mark for correct vertex, 1 mark for correct intersections with axes]

c) The minimum point of C is 1.5 units to the right of the line of reflection, $x = 1$, so after it has been reflected, the minimum point will be 1.5 units to the left of the line. The y-coordinate doesn't change, so the coordinates of minimum point of C' are $\left(-\frac{1}{2}, -\frac{9}{2}\right)$.
[1 mark for correct coordinates]

d) q(x) can be written in the general form
$q(x) = 2(x + a)^2 + b$, where $(-a, b)$ is the vertex.
From part c), you know the minimum point is $\left(-\frac{1}{2}, -\frac{9}{2}\right)$,
so $q(x) = 2\left(x + \frac{1}{2}\right)^2 - \frac{9}{2} \Rightarrow q(x) = 2x^2 + 2x - 4$
[1 mark for correct equation of q(x)]

Exercise 4.8 — Factorising a Cubic (When x is a Factor)

Q1
- **a)** $x(x^2 + 5x + 6) = x(x + 2)(x + 3)$
- **b)** $x(x^2 + 6x - 7) = x(x + 7)(x - 1)$
- **c)** $x(x^2 - 18x + 81) = x(x - 9)(x - 9) = x(x - 9)^2$
- **d)** $x(x^2 + 7x + 10) = x(x + 5)(x + 2)$
- **e)** $-x(x^2 - 4x + 3) = -x(x - 3)(x - 1)$
- **f)** $x(x^2 + 4x + 3) = x(x + 1)(x + 3)$
- **g)** $x(x^2 + 2x - 35) = x(x + 7)(x - 5)$
- **h)** $x(x^2 - 6x - 16) = x(x + 2)(x - 8)$
- **i)** $-x(x^2 + 3x - 4) = -x(x + 4)(x - 1)$
- **j)** $x(2x^2 + 15x + 25) = x(2x + 5)(x + 5)$
- **k)** $x(2x^2 - 7x + 6) = x(2x - 3)(x - 2)$
- **l)** $x(4x^2 + 13x - 12) = x(4x - 3)(x + 4)$
- **m)** $x\left(x^2 - \frac{4}{25}\right) = x\left(x + \frac{2}{5}\right)\left(x - \frac{2}{5}\right)$
- **n)** $x(x^2 - 49) = x(x + 7)(x - 7)$
- **o)** $x\left(x^2 - \frac{9}{4}\right) = x\left(x + \frac{3}{2}\right)\left(x - \frac{3}{2}\right)$

Q2 a) $-x^3 + 2x^2 + 24x = 0 \Rightarrow -x(x^2 - 2x - 24) = 0$
$\Rightarrow -x(x - 6)(x + 4) = 0 \Rightarrow -x = 0, x - 6 = 0$ or $x + 4 = 0$.
So $x = 0$, $x = 6$ or $x = -4$.

b) $x^3 - \frac{7}{9}x^2 + \frac{10}{81}x = 0 \Rightarrow x\left(x^2 - \frac{7}{9}x + \frac{10}{81}\right) = 0$
$\Rightarrow x\left(x - \frac{5}{9}\right)\left(x - \frac{2}{9}\right) = 0 \Rightarrow x = 0, x - \frac{5}{9} = 0$ or $x - \frac{2}{9} = 0$.
So $x = 0$, $x = \frac{5}{9}$ or $x = \frac{2}{9}$.

c) $2x^3 + 9x^2 + 4x = 0 \Rightarrow x(2x^2 + 9x + 4) = 0$
$\Rightarrow x(2x + 1)(x + 4) = 0 \Rightarrow x = 0, 2x + 1 = 0$ or $x + 4 = 0$.
So $x = 0$, $x = -\frac{1}{2}$ or $x = -4$.

d) $3x^3 - 3x^2 + 4x = 0 \Rightarrow x(3x^2 - 3x + 4) = 0$
This quadratic won't factorise — so use the quadratic formula: $a = 3$, $b = -3$, $c = 4$

$$x = \frac{-b \pm \sqrt{b^2 - 4ac}}{2a} = \frac{3 \pm \sqrt{(-3)^2 - 4 \times 3 \times 4}}{2 \times 3}$$
$$= \frac{3 \pm \sqrt{9 - 48}}{6} = \frac{3 \pm \sqrt{-39}}{6}$$

These aren't possible solutions as you can't take the square root of a negative number, so the only real solution is $x = 0$.

e) $4x - x^3 = 0 \Rightarrow x^3 - 4x = 0 \Rightarrow x(x^2 - 4) = 0$
$\Rightarrow x(x - 2)(x + 2) = 0 \Rightarrow x = 0, x - 2 = 0$ or $x + 2 = 0$.
So $x = 0$, $x = 2$ or $x - 2$.

f) $5x^3 + 7x^2 - 3x = 0 \Rightarrow x(5x^2 + 7x - 3) = 0$
The quadratic won't factorise — so use the quadratic formula: $a = 5$, $b = 7$, $c = -3$

$$x = \frac{-b \pm \sqrt{b^2 - 4ac}}{2a} = \frac{-7 \pm \sqrt{7^2 - 4 \times 5 \times (-3)}}{2 \times 5}$$
$$= \frac{-7 \pm \sqrt{49 + 60}}{10} = \frac{-7 \pm \sqrt{109}}{10}$$

So $x = 0$ or $x = -\frac{7}{10} \pm \frac{\sqrt{109}}{10}$.

g) $3x^3 + 26x^2 - 9x = 0 \Rightarrow x(3x^2 + 26x - 9) = 0$
$\Rightarrow x(3x - 1)(x + 9) = 0 \Rightarrow x = 0, 3x - 1 = 0$, or $x + 9 = 0$.
So $x = 0$, $x = \frac{1}{3}$ or $x = -9$

h) $x^3 + \frac{2}{3}x^2 - \frac{8}{9}x = 0 \Rightarrow 9x^3 + 6x^2 - 8x = 0$
$\Rightarrow x(9x^2 + 6x - 8) = 0 \Rightarrow x(3x - 2)(3x + 4) = 0$
$\Rightarrow x = 0, 3x - 2 = 0$, or $3x + 4 = 0$.
So $x = 0$, $x = \frac{2}{3}$ or $x = -\frac{4}{3}$

i) $x^2(4x + 3) = x \Rightarrow 4x^3 + 3x^2 = x \Rightarrow 4x^3 + 3x^2 - x = 0$
$\Rightarrow x(4x^2 + 3x - 1) = 0 \Rightarrow x(4x - 1)(x + 1) = 0$
$\Rightarrow x = 0, 4x - 1 = 0$ or $x + 1 = 0$.
So $x = 0$, $x = \frac{1}{4}$ or $x = -1$.

j) $2x^3 + 8x^2 = -3x \Rightarrow 2x^3 + 8x^2 + 3x = 0 \Rightarrow x(2x^2 + 8x + 3) = 0$
This quadratic won't factorise, so use the quadratic formula.
Now $a = 2$, $b = 8$ and $c = 3$.

$$x = \frac{-b \pm \sqrt{b^2 - 4ac}}{2a} = \frac{-8 \pm \sqrt{8^2 - 4 \times 2 \times 3}}{2 \times 2}$$
$$= \frac{-8 \pm \sqrt{40}}{4} = -2 \pm \frac{1}{2}\sqrt{10}$$

So $x = 0$ or $x = -2 \pm \frac{1}{2}\sqrt{10}$.

Q3 a) $-x^3 + 36x = -x(x^2 - 36) = -x(x + 6)(x - 6)$

b) $f(x) = 0 \Rightarrow -x(x + 6)(x - 6) = 0$
So the roots are $x = 0$, $x = -6$ and $x = 6$

Q4 $2x^3 + 3x = x^2 \Rightarrow 2x^3 + 3x - x^2 = 0 \Rightarrow x(2x^2 - x + 3) = 0$
So $x = 0$ is one solution.
Find the discriminant of the quadratic factor:
$a = 2$, $b = -1$, $c = 3$. $b^2 - 4ac = (-1)^2 - 4 \times 2 \times 3 = -23$
The discriminant is negative, so the quadratic has no real roots.
So the only real solution to the cubic is $x = 0$.

Exercise 4.9 — The Factor Theorem

Q1 a) $a = 1$, find $f(a)$ and show the result is 0:
$f(1) = (1)3 - (1)2 - 3(1) + 3 = 1 - 1 - 3 + 3 = 0$
So by the Factor Theorem, $(x - 1)$ is a factor.
The question asked you to use the Factor Theorem, but you could also show it was a factor by adding the coefficients (1, –1, –3, 3) to get 0. (If the coefficients in a polynomial add up to 0, then (x – 1) is a factor.)

b) $a = -1$, find $f(a)$ and show the result is 0:
$f(-1) = (-1)^3 + 2(-1)^2 + 3(-1) + 2 = -1 + 2 - 3 + 2 = 0$
So by the Factor Theorem, $(x + 1)$ is a factor.

c) $a = -2$, find $f(a)$ and show the result is 0:
$f(-2) = (-2)^3 + 3(-2)^2 - 10(-2) - 24 = -8 + 12 + 20 - 24 = 0$
So by the Factor Theorem, $(x + 2)$ is a factor.

d) $a = 3$, find $f(a)$ and show the result is 0:
$f(3) = (3)^3 + 2(3)^2 - 9(3) - 18 = 0$
So by the Factor Theorem, $(x - 3)$ is a factor.

Q2 a) Substitute $x = \frac{1}{2}$ and show the result is 0:
$$f\left(\frac{1}{2}\right) = 2\left(\frac{1}{2}\right)^3 - \left(\frac{1}{2}\right)^2 - 8\left(\frac{1}{2}\right) + 4 = \frac{2}{8} - \frac{1}{4} - 4 + 4 = 0$$
So by the Factor Theorem, $(2x - 1)$ is a factor.

b) Substitute $x = \frac{2}{3}$ and show the result is 0:
$$f\left(\frac{2}{3}\right) = 3\left(\frac{2}{3}\right)^3 - 5\left(\frac{2}{3}\right)^2 - 16\left(\frac{2}{3}\right) + 12$$
$$= \frac{8}{9} - \frac{20}{9} - \frac{32}{3} + 12$$
$$= \frac{8}{9} - \frac{20}{9} - \frac{96}{9} + 12 = 0$$
So by the Factor Theorem, $(3x - 2)$ is a factor.

Q3 a) Substitute $x = -\frac{1}{5}$ and show the result is 0:
$$f\left(-\frac{1}{5}\right) = 5\left(-\frac{1}{5}\right)^3 - 44\left(-\frac{1}{5}\right)^2 + 61\left(-\frac{1}{5}\right) + 14$$
$$= -\frac{1}{25} - \frac{44}{25} - \frac{61}{5} + 14 = 0$$
So by the Factor Theorem, $(5x + 1)$ is a factor.

b) Substitute $x = \frac{1}{2}$ and show the result is 0:
$$f\left(\frac{1}{2}\right) = -2\left(\frac{1}{2}\right)^3 + 3\left(\frac{1}{2}\right)^2 + 11\left(\frac{1}{2}\right) - 6$$
$$= -\frac{1}{4} + \frac{3}{4} + \frac{11}{2} - 6 = 0$$
So by the Factor Theorem, $(1 - 2x)$ is a factor.

Q4 a) $f(3) = (3)^3 - 2(3)^2 - 5(3) + 6 = 27 - 18 - 15 + 6 = 0$
So by the Factor Theorem, $(x - 3)$ is a factor.

b) $1 - 2 - 5 + 6 = 0$
The coefficients add up to 0, so by the Factor Theorem, $(x - 1)$ is a factor.

Q5 a) $f(-4) = 3(-4)^3 - 5(-4)^2 - 58(-4) + 40$
$= -192 - 80 + 232 + 40 = 0$
So by the Factor Theorem, $(x + 4)$ is a factor.

b)
$$f\left(\frac{2}{3}\right) = 3\left(\frac{2}{3}\right)^3 - 5\left(\frac{2}{3}\right)^2 - 58\left(\frac{2}{3}\right) + 40$$
$$= \frac{8}{9} - \frac{20}{9} - \frac{116}{3} + 40 = -\frac{120}{3} + 40 = 0$$
So by the Factor Theorem, $(3x - 2)$ is a factor.

c) $f(5) = 3(5)^3 - 5(5)^2 - 58(5) + 40$
$= 375 - 125 - 290 + 40 = 0$
So by the Factor Theorem, $(x - 5)$ is a factor.

Q6 $(x - 2)$ is a factor of $f(x) = 2x^3 - 7x^2 + px + 20$,
so $f(2) = 0$. Using the Factor Theorem in reverse:
$f(2) = 2(2)^3 - 7(2)^2 + p(2) + 20 = 16 - 28 + 2p + 20 = 2p + 8$
$\Rightarrow 2p + 8 = 0 \Rightarrow 2p = -8 \Rightarrow p = -4$
So $f(x) = 2x^3 - 7x^2 - 4x + 20$

Q7 $(x - 3)$ is a factor of $f(x) = qx^3 - 4x^2 - 7qx + 12$,
so $f(3) = 0$. Using the Factor Theorem in reverse:
$f(3) = q(3)^3 - 4(3)^2 - 7q(3) + 12 = 27q - 36 - 21q + 12 = 6q - 24$
$\Rightarrow 6q - 24 = 0 \Rightarrow 6q = 24 \Rightarrow q = 4$
So $f(x) = 4x^3 - 4x^2 - 28x + 12$

Q8 $(x - 2)$ is a factor of $p(x)$, so by the Factor Theorem, $p(2) = 0$.
So $b \times 2^3 - (b + 1) \times 2^2 + b^2 \times 2 + b + 1 = 0$
$\Rightarrow 8b - 4(b + 1) + 2b^2 + b + 1 = 0 \Rightarrow 2b^2 + 5b - 3 = 0$
$\Rightarrow (2b - 1)(b + 3) = 0 \Rightarrow b = \frac{1}{2}$ or $b = -3$
[3 marks available — 1 mark for using the Factor Theorem, 1 mark for finding the quadratic equation in b, 1 mark for both correct solutions]

Q9 a) Substitute $x = -\frac{2}{3}$, $x = -\frac{1}{2}$ and $x = -5$ into $V(x)$ and show the result is 0 in each case:
$$V\left(-\frac{2}{3}\right) = 6\left(-\frac{2}{3}\right)^3 + 37\left(-\frac{2}{3}\right)^2 + 37\left(-\frac{2}{3}\right) + 10$$
$$= -\frac{16}{9} + \frac{148}{9} - \frac{74}{3} + 10 = 0$$
$$V\left(-\frac{1}{2}\right) = 6\left(-\frac{1}{2}\right)^3 + 37\left(-\frac{1}{2}\right)^2 + 37\left(-\frac{1}{2}\right) + 10$$
$$= -\frac{6}{8} + \frac{37}{4} - \frac{37}{2} + 10 = 0$$

$V(-5) = 6(-5)^3 + 37(-5)^2 + 37(-5) + 10$
$= -750 + 925 - 185 + 10 = 0$

By the Factor Theorem, $(3x + 2)$, $(2x + 1)$ and $(x + 5)$ are the three factors of $V(x)$. So $V(x) = (3x + 2)(2x + 1)(x + 5)$, and the volume of a cuboid is length × width × height, so the three factors are the length, width and height of the cuboid.

You can see that there are no constant numerical factors of V(x) by considering the product of the x-coefficients of the factors — $3x \times 2x \times x = 6x^3$, which is the required x^3 term in V(x).

b) You're told that x is a positive integer, so the smallest value of x is 1. Substituting $x = 1$ into $V(x)$ gives $V(x) = (3 + 2)(2 + 1)(1 + 5) = 5 \times 3 \times 6 = 90$ cm³.

You could substitute x = 1 into the original equation:
$V(1) = 6(1)^3 + 37(1)^2 + 37(1) + 10$
$= 6 + 37 + 37 + 10 = 90$ cm³

Q10 $(x - 1)$ and $(x - 2)$ are factors, so using the Factor Theorem in reverse, $f(1) = 0$ and $f(2) = 0$.
$f(1) = (1)^3 + c(1)^2 + d(1) - 2 = 1 + c + d - 2 = 0$
$c + d = 1$ (equation 1)

$f(2) = (2)^3 + c(2)^2 + d(2) - 2 = 8 + 4c + 2d - 2 = 0$
$4c + 2d = -6$ (equation 2)

Rearrange (1) to get $d = 1 - c$, and sub into (2):
$\Rightarrow 4c + 2(1 - c) = -6 \Rightarrow 4c + 2 - 2c = -6$
$\Rightarrow 2c = -8 \Rightarrow c = -4$

Sub c into rearranged (1): $d = 1 - c = 1 + 4 = 5$
So $f(x) = x^3 - 4x^2 + 5x - 2$

Q11 Using the Factor Theorem, the repeated root at $x = -1$ means that $(x + 1)$ is a repeated factor of f(x), and the root at $x = \frac{5}{2}$ means that $(2x - 5)$ is a factor of f(x).
f(x) is cubic, so $f(x) = k(2x - 5)(x + 1)^2$ for some constant k.
From the graph, $f(0) = -10$, so $k(2(0) - 5)(0 + 1)^2 = -10$
$\Rightarrow k(-5)(1)^2 = -10 \Rightarrow -5k = -10 \Rightarrow k = 2$
So $f(x) = 2(2x - 5)(x + 1)^2$.
[3 marks available — 1 mark for identifying (x + 1) is a repeated factor of f(x), 1 mark for identifying (2x – 5) is a factor of f(x), 1 mark for an expression for f(x) in the correct form]

Exercise 4.10 — Factorising a Cubic (When x isn't a Factor)

Q1 a) x is a common factor, so you get:
$x(x^2 - 3x + 2) = x(x - 1)(x - 2)$

b) Adding the coefficients gives you –12, so $(x - 1)$ is not a factor. Using trial and error, $f(2) = 0$, so $(x - 2)$ is a factor.
Factorise to get: $(x - 2)(2x^2 + 7x + 3) = (x - 2)(x + 3)(2x + 1)$

c) Add the coefficients $(1 - 3 + 3 - 1)$ to get 0, so $(x - 1)$ is a factor. Factorise to get: $(x - 1)(x^2 - 2x + 1) = (x - 1)^3$

d) Adding the coefficients gives you 2, so $(x - 1)$ is not a factor. Using trial and error, $f(2) = 0$, so $(x - 2)$ is a factor.
Factorise to get:
$(x - 2)(x^2 - x - 2) = (x - 2)(x - 2)(x + 1) = (x - 2)^2(x + 1)$

e) Add the coefficients $(1 - 1 - 7 + 7)$ to get 0, so $(x - 1)$ is a factor. Factorise to get:
$(x - 1)(x^2 - 7) = (x - 1)(x + \sqrt{7})(x - \sqrt{7})$

f) Adding the coefficients gives you –8, so $(x - 1)$ is not a factor. Using trial and error, $f(2) = 0$, so $(x - 2)$ is a factor.
Factorise to get: $(x - 2)(x^2 + 4x + 3) = (x - 2)(x + 1)(x + 3)$

Q2 a) Adding the coefficients gives you 0, so $(x - 1)$ is a factor.
Factorise to get: $(x - 1)(x^2 - 2x - 35) = (x - 1)(x + 5)(x - 7)$
So the solutions are $x = 1$, $x = -5$ and $x = 7$.

b) Adding the coefficients gives you 21, so $(x - 1)$ is not a factor. Using trial and error, $f(2) = 0$, so $(x - 2)$ is a factor.
Factorise to get: $(x - 2)(x^2 + 2x - 24) = (x - 2)(x - 4)(x + 6)$
So the solutions are $x = 2$, $x = 4$ and $x = -6$.

Q3 a) Adding the coefficients gives you –3, so $(x - 1)$ is not a factor. Using trial and error, $f(-2) = 0$, so $(x + 2)$ is a factor.
Factorise to get: $(x + 2)(x^2 + 2x - 4)$
You're asked for the product of a linear factor and a quadratic factor, so you don't need to try to factorise the quadratic.

b) There is one solution at $x = -2$. The quadratic doesn't factorise, so use the quadratic formula: $a = 1$, $b = 2$, $c = -4$

$$x = \frac{-b \pm \sqrt{b^2 - 4ac}}{2a} = \frac{-2 \pm \sqrt{2^2 - 4 \times 1 \times (-4)}}{2 \times 1}$$
$$= \frac{-2 \pm \sqrt{4 + 16}}{2} = \frac{-2 \pm \sqrt{20}}{2} = -1 \pm \sqrt{5}$$

So the solutions are $x = -2$, $x = -1 + \sqrt{5}$ and $x = -1 - \sqrt{5}$.

Q4 Add the coefficients $(1 - 2 - 1 + 2)$ to get 0, so $(x - 1)$ is a factor.
Factorise to get: $(x - 1)(x^2 - x - 2) = (x - 1)(x + 1)(x - 2)$.
So the roots are $x = 1$, $x = -1$ and $x = 2$.

Q5 Add the coefficients $(1 - 1 - 3 + 3)$ to get 0, so $(x - 1)$ is a factor.
Factorise to get: $(x - 1)(x^2 - 3)$.
So the roots are $x = 1$ and $x = \pm\sqrt{3}$.

Q6 $(3x - 1)(2x^2 + 13x + 6) = (3x - 1)(2x + 1)(x + 6)$

Q7 a) $(x - 5)$ is a factor, so $f(5) = 0$
$f(5) = (5)^3 - p(5)^2 + 17(5) - 10$
$= 125 - 25p + 85 - 10 = 200 - 25p$
$\Rightarrow 200 - 25p = 0 \Rightarrow 200 = 25p \Rightarrow p = 8$

b) $(x - 5)(x^2 - 3x + 2) = (x - 5)(x - 1)(x - 2)$

c) So the solutions are $x = 5$, 1 and 2.

Q8 a) Adding the coefficients gives you 0, so $(x - 1)$ is a factor.
Factorise to get: $(x - 1)(3x^2 + 5x - 2) = (x - 1)(3x - 1)(x + 2)$

b) Adding the coefficients gives you 0, so $(x - 1)$ is a factor.
Factorise to get: $(x - 1)(5x^2 - 8x - 4) = (x - 1)(5x + 2)(x - 2)$

Q9 Rearrange to give $4x^3 - 7x + 3 = 0$. Adding the coefficients gives you 0, so $(x - 1)$ is a factor. Factorise to get:
$(x - 1)(4x^2 + 4x - 3) = (x - 1)(2x + 3)(2x - 1)$.
$(x - 1)(2x + 3)(2x - 1) = 0$, so $x - 1 = 0$, or $2x + 3 = 0$, or $2x - 1 = 0$. So the solutions are $x = 1$, $-\frac{3}{2}$ and $\frac{1}{2}$.

Q10 If $x = 2$ is a root, $f(2) = 0$:
$f(2) = 2(2)^3 - 2^2 - 2(2) - 8 = 16 - 4 - 4 - 8 = 0$
So $x = 2$ is a root, and $(x - 2)$ is a factor.
Now factorise: $(x - 2)(2x^2 + 3x + 4) = 0$.
The discriminant of the quadratic factor is $b^2 - 4ac$, which is $3^2 - 4 \times 2 \times 4 = 9 - 32 = -23$.
The discriminant is negative so the quadratic has no real roots.
Hence the only real root of the cubic is $x = 2$.
You could have put the values of a, b and c into the quadratic formula here — you'd end up with a negative number inside the square root, which would mean the quadratic has no real roots.

Q11 a) $p(2) = 3(2)^3 - 4(2)^2 - 5(2) + 2 = 24 - 16 - 10 + 2 = 0$, so by the Factor Theorem, $(x - 2)$ is a factor of p(x).
[1 mark for correct working with justification]

b) Set the expressions equal to each other:
$3x^3 - 4x^2 - 8x + 6 = 4 - 3x \Rightarrow 3x^3 - 4x^2 - 5x + 2 = 0$
From part a), $(x - 2)$ is a factor of $3x^3 - 4x^2 - 5x + 2$, so factorise to get $3x^3 - 4x^2 - 5x + 2 = (x - 2)(3x^2 + 2x - 1)$
$= (x - 2)(3x - 1)(x + 1)$.
So $3x^3 - 4x^2 - 5x + 2 = 0 \Rightarrow (x - 2)(3x - 1)(x + 1) = 0$
$\Rightarrow x = 2$, $x = \frac{1}{3}$ or $x = -1$.
$x = 2 \Rightarrow y = 4 - 3(2) = -2$
$x = \frac{1}{3} \Rightarrow y = 4 - 3(\frac{1}{3}) = 3$
$x = -1 \Rightarrow y = 4 - 3(-1) = 7$
So the solutions are:
$x = 2, y = -2$, $x = \frac{1}{3}, y = 3$ and $x = -1, y = 7$.
[5 marks available — 1 mark for deriving a cubic equation to solve, 1 mark for correct partial factorisation, 1 mark for correct complete factorisation, 1 mark for all three correct x-values, 1 mark for all three correct solutions]

Q12 a) $p(a) = k \Rightarrow p(a) - k = 0 \Rightarrow q(a) = 0$
so by the Factor Theorem, $(x - a)$ is a factor of q(x).
[2 marks available — 1 mark for showing that q(a) = 0, 1 mark for justification]

b) $f(-4) = (-4)^3 - 6(-4)^2 - 19(-4) + 87 = -64 - 96 + 76 + 87 = 3$
[1 mark for correct calculation]

c) $f(x) = 3 \Rightarrow f(x) - 3 = 0 \Rightarrow x^3 - 6x^2 - 19x + 84 = 0$
From parts a) and b), $(x + 4)$ is a factor of $f(x) - 3$
$\Rightarrow (x + 4)$ is a factor of $x^3 - 6x^2 - 19x + 84$.
Equating coefficients gives $x^3 - 6x^2 - 19x + 84$
$= (x + 4)(x^2 - 10x + 21) = (x + 4)(x - 3)(x - 7)$.
So the solutions are $x = -4$, $x = 3$ and $x = 7$.
[4 marks available — 1 mark for recognising that (x + 4) is a factor of f(x) – 3, 1 mark for correct partial factorisation of f(x) – 3, 1 mark for correct complete factorisation, 1 mark for all three correct solutions]

Q13 a) $p(4) = 2 \times 4^3 - 17 \times 4^2 + 40 \times 4 - 16 = 0$,
so by the Factor Theorem, $(x - 4)$ is a factor of $p(x)$.
[1 mark for correct working with justification]

b) $(x - 4)$ is a factor of $q(x)$, so by the Factor Theorem, $q(4) = 0$
$\Rightarrow 4^3 - 8 \times 4^2 + 22 \times 4 + k = 0 \Rightarrow 24 + k = 0 \Rightarrow k = -24$
[1 mark for correct value of k]

c) $p(x) = q(x) \Rightarrow 2x^3 - 17x^2 + 40x - 16 = x^3 - 8x^2 + 22x - 24$
$\Rightarrow x^3 - 9x^2 + 18x + 8 = 0 \Rightarrow (x - 4)(x^2 - 5x - 2) = 0$,
since $(x - 4)$ is a factor of both $p(x)$ and $q(x)$.
Now, solve $x^2 - 5x - 2 = 0$:
$$\Rightarrow x = \frac{5 \pm \sqrt{(-5)^2 - 4 \times 1 \times -2}}{2} \Rightarrow x = \frac{5 \pm \sqrt{33}}{2}$$
So the solutions of the equation $p(x) = q(x)$ are:
$$x = 4,\ x = \frac{5 + \sqrt{33}}{2} \text{ and } x = \frac{5 - \sqrt{33}}{2}$$
[4 marks available — 1 mark for deriving a cubic equation to solve, 1 mark for correct partial factorisation, 1 mark for correct method to solve the quadratic factor, 1 mark for all three correct solutions]

Q14 a) $p\left(\frac{1}{3}\right) = 3\left(\frac{1}{3}\right)^3 - 7\left(\frac{1}{3}\right)^2 - 22\left(\frac{1}{3}\right) + 8 = \frac{1}{9} - \frac{7}{9} - \frac{22}{3} + 8$
$= 0$, so by the Factor Theorem, $(3x - 1)$ is a factor of $p(x)$.
[1 mark for correct working with justification]

b) $(3x - 1)$ is a factor of $p(x)$, so $p(x) = (3x - 1)f(x)$,
for some function $f(x)$. By equating coefficients:
$p(x) = (3x - 1)(x^2 - 2x - 8) = (3x - 1)(x - 4)(x + 2)$
The graph of $y = p(x)$ crosses the x-axis at $x = \frac{1}{3}$, 4 and -2,
and crosses the y-axis at $y = 3(0)^3 - 7(0)^2 - 22(0) + 8 = 8$.

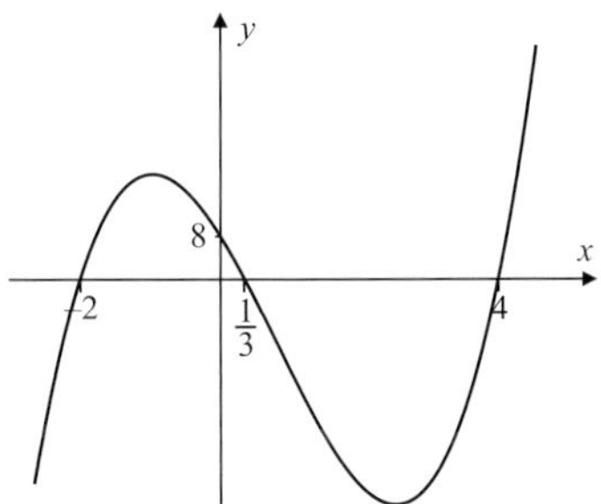

[4 marks available — 1 mark for correct curve shape, 1 mark for correct y-intercept, 1 mark for one correct x-intercept, 1 mark for other two correct x-intercepts]

c) $p(x) > 0$ when the graph of $y = p(x)$ is above the x-axis,
so $-2 < x < \frac{1}{3}$ or $x > 4$
[1 mark for the correct ranges of x-values]

Exercise 4.11 — Algebraic Division

Q1 a)
$$\begin{array}{r} x^2 + x - 12 \\ x - 3 \overline{\smash{)}\, x^3 - 2x^2 - 15x + 36} \\ -(x^3 - 3x^2) \\ \hline x^2 - 15x \\ -(x^2 - 3x) \\ \hline -12x + 36 \\ -(-12x + 36) \\ \hline 0 \end{array}$$
Factorise the quadratic: $x^2 + x - 12 = (x - 3)(x + 4)$
So $x^3 - 2x^2 - 15x + 36 = (x - 3)(x - 3)(x + 4) = (x - 3)^2(x + 4)$

b)
$$\begin{array}{r} x^2 - 3x - 5 \\ x + 2 \overline{\smash{)}\, x^3 - x^2 - 11x - 10} \\ -(x^3 + 2x^2) \\ \hline -3x^2 - 11x \\ -(-3x^2 - 6x) \\ \hline -5x - 10 \\ -(-5x - 10) \\ \hline 0 \end{array}$$
The quadratic doesn't factorise, so the full factorisation is:
$x^3 - x^2 - 11x - 10 = (x + 2)(x^2 - 3x - 5)$

c)
$$\begin{array}{r} 2x^2 + 15x + 7 \\ x - 2 \overline{\smash{)}\, 2x^3 + 11x^2 - 23x - 14} \\ -(2x^3 - 4x^2) \\ \hline 15x^2 - 23x \\ -(15x^2 - 30x) \\ \hline 7x - 14 \\ -(7x - 14) \\ \hline 0 \end{array}$$
Factorise the quadratic: $2x^2 + 15x + 7 = (2x + 1)(x + 7)$
So $2x^3 + 11x^2 - 23x - 14 = (x - 2)(2x + 1)(x + 7)$

d)
$$\begin{array}{r} x^2 + 5x + 6 \\ x + 5 \overline{\smash{)}\, x^3 + 10x^2 + 31x + 30} \\ -(x^3 + 5x^2) \\ \hline 5x^2 + 31x \\ -(5x^2 + 25x) \\ \hline 6x + 30 \\ -(6x + 30) \\ \hline 0 \end{array}$$
Factorise the quadratic: $x^2 + 5x + 6 = (x + 2)(x + 3)$
So $x^3 + 10x^2 + 31x + 30 = (x + 5)(x + 2)(x + 3)$

Q2 Add the coefficients $(1 - 5 + 4)$ to get 0, so $(x - 1)$ is a factor. Now factorise using long division:
$$\begin{array}{r} x^2 + x - 4 \\ x - 1 \overline{\smash{)}\, x^3 + 0x^2 - 5x + 4} \\ -(x^3 - x^2) \\ \hline x^2 - 5x \\ -(x^2 - x) \\ \hline -4x + 4 \\ -(-4x + 4) \\ \hline 0 \end{array}$$
Finally, write the cubic as the product of a linear factor and a quadratic factor: $(x^3 - 5x + 4) = (x - 1)(x^2 + x - 4)$

Q3
$$\begin{array}{r} x^2 + 4x + 1 \\ x - 2 \overline{\smash{)}\, x^3 + 2x^2 - 7x - 2} \\ -(x^3 - 2x^2) \\ \hline 4x^2 - 7x \\ -(4x^2 - 8x) \\ \hline x - 2 \\ -(x - 2) \\ \hline 0 \end{array}$$
So $f(x) = (x - 2)(x^2 + 4x + 1)$.

Q4 If $f(-2) = 0$ then $(x + 2)$ is a factor.
Now factorise using long division:
$$\begin{array}{r} x^2 - 2x - 3 \\ x + 2 \overline{\smash{)}\, x^3 + 0x^2 - 7x - 6} \\ -(x^3 + 2x^2) \\ \hline -2x^2 - 7x \\ -(-2x^2 - 4x) \\ \hline -3x - 6 \\ -(-3x - 6) \\ \hline 0 \end{array}$$
Then factorise the quadratic: $x^2 - 2x - 3 = (x - 3)(x + 1)$
So $f(x) = (x + 2)(x - 3)(x + 1)$
So the solutions to $f(x) = 0$ are $x = -2$, $x = 3$ and $x = -1$.

Q5 Adding the coefficients gives you –10, so $(x-1)$ is not a factor. Using trial and error, $f(2)=0$, so $(x-2)$ is a factor. Factorise using long division:

$$
\begin{array}{r}
x^2+3x+6 \\
x-2\,\overline{)\,x^3+x^2+0x-12} \\
-(x^3-2x^2) \\
3x^2+0x \\
-(3x^2-6x) \\
6x-12 \\
-(6x-12) \\
0
\end{array}
$$

So $x^3+x^2-12=(x-2)(x^2+3x+6)$

Q6 **a)**

$$
\begin{array}{r}
x^2-5x+16 \\
x+3\,\overline{)\,x^3-2x^2+x-1} \\
-(x^3+3x^2) \\
-5x^2+x \\
-(-5x^2-15x) \\
16x-1 \\
-(16x+48) \\
-49
\end{array}
$$

So the remainder is –49.

b) $f(x)=(x+3)(x^2-5x+16)-49$

If you expand the brackets and simplify, you'll end up with f(x) back in its original form. This is a good way to check your answer.

Q7 **a)**

$$
\begin{array}{r}
x^2-6x+8 \\
x-2\,\overline{)\,x^3-8x^2+20x-3} \\
-(x^3-2x^2) \\
-6x^2+20x \\
-(-6x^2+12x) \\
8x-3 \\
-(8x-16) \\
13
\end{array}
$$

So the remainder is 13.

b) From part a), $f(x)=(x-2)(x^2-6x+8)+13$.
So if $f(x)-13=0$, then: $(x-2)(x^2-6x+8)+13-13=0$
$\Rightarrow (x-2)(x^2-6x+8)=0 \Rightarrow (x-2)(x-2)(x-4)=0$
$\Rightarrow (x-2)^2(x-4)=0$. So either $x-2=0$ or $x-4=0$, and so the solutions are $x=2$ and $x=4$.

Q8 Rearrange to give $x^3-15x^2+75x-125=0$. $x=5$ is a solution, so $x-5$ must be a factor, so divide by $x-5$ to get the other factors:

$$
\begin{array}{r}
x^2-10x+25 \\
x-5\,\overline{)\,x^3-15x^2+75x-125} \\
-(x^3-5x^2) \\
-10x^2+75x \\
-(-10x^2+50x) \\
25x-125 \\
-(25x-125) \\
0
\end{array}
$$

So: $(x-5)(x^2-10x+25)=0 \Rightarrow (x-5)(x-5)(x-5)=0$
$\Rightarrow (x-5)^3=0$. So $x=5$ is the only solution.

Q9 Use algebraic division to factorise the equation, taking care with the negative coefficient of t^3:

$$
\begin{array}{r}
-t^2+3t+10 \\
t+1\,\overline{)\,-t^3+2t^2+13t+10} \\
-(-t^3-t^2) \\
3t^2+13t \\
-(3t^2+3t) \\
10t+10 \\
-(10t+10) \\
0
\end{array}
$$

The car stops when $S=0$, so solve: $(t+1)(-t^2+3t+10)=0$
$\Rightarrow -(t+1)(t^2-3t-10)=0 \Rightarrow (t+1)(t^2-3t-10)=0$
$\Rightarrow (t+1)(t-5)(t+2)=0$. So either $t+1=0$, $t-5=0$ or $t+2=0$, and so the solutions are $t=-1$, 5 and –2.
But T must be greater than zero, so $T=5$ minutes.
Don't forget to link it back to the actual question — you're asked for the value of T, not just the possible solutions.

Chapter 4 Review Exercise

Q1 **a)** $x^2+2x+1=(x+1)(x+1)=(x+1)^2$

b) $x^2-13x+30=(x-10)(x-3)$

c) $x^2-4=(x+2)(x-2)$

d) $3+2x-x^2=(3-x)(x+1)$

e) $2x^2-7x-4=(2x+1)(x-4)$

f) $5x^2+7x-6=(5x-3)(x+2)$

Q2 **a)** $x^2-3x+2=0 \Rightarrow (x-2)(x-1)=0$
$\Rightarrow x-2=0$ or $x-1=0$, so $x=2$ or 1

b) $x^2+x-12=0 \Rightarrow (x+4)(x-3)=0$
$\Rightarrow x+4=0$ or $x-3=0$, so $x=-4$ or 3

c) $2+x-x^2=0 \Rightarrow x^2-x-2=0$
$\Rightarrow (x-2)(x+1)=0$
$\Rightarrow x-2=0$ or $x+1=0$, so $x=2$ or -1

d) $x^2+x-16=x \Rightarrow x^2-16=0$
$\Rightarrow (x+4)(x-4)=0 \Rightarrow x+4=0$ or $x-4=0$, so $x=\pm 4$

e) $3x^2-15x-14=4x \Rightarrow 3x^2-19x-14=0$
$\Rightarrow (3x+2)(x-7)=0$
$\Rightarrow 3x+2=0$ or $x-7=0$, so $x=-\frac{2}{3}$ or 7

f) $4x^2-1=0 \Rightarrow (2x+1)(2x-1)=0$
$\Rightarrow 2x+1=0$ or $2x-1=0$, so $x=\pm\frac{1}{2}$

g) $6x^2-11x+9=2x^2-x+3 \Rightarrow 4x^2-10x+6=0$
$\Rightarrow 2x^2-5x+3=0 \Rightarrow (2x-3)(x-1)=0$
$\Rightarrow 2x-3=0$ or $x-1=0$, so $x=\frac{3}{2}$ or 1

h) $3x^2+10x-8=2-x-3x^2$
$\Rightarrow 6x^2+11x-10=0 \Rightarrow (3x-2)(2x+5)=0$
$\Rightarrow 3x-2=0$ or $2x+5=0$, so $x=\frac{2}{3}$ or $-\frac{5}{2}$

i) $4-9x^2=0 \Rightarrow (2+3x)(2-3x)=0$
$\Rightarrow 2+3x=0$ or $2-3x=0$, so $x=\pm\frac{2}{3}$

Q3 These solutions use the quadratic formula, but you could complete the square to get the same answers.

a) $3x^2-7x+3=0$, so $a=3$, $b=-7$, $c=3$

$$x=\frac{-b\pm\sqrt{b^2-4ac}}{2a}=\frac{-(-7)\pm\sqrt{(-7)^2-4\times 3\times 3}}{2\times 3}$$
$$=\frac{7\pm\sqrt{49-36}}{6}=\frac{7\pm\sqrt{13}}{6}$$

b) $2x^2-6x-2=0 \Rightarrow x^2-3x-1=0$, so $a=1$, $b=-3$, $c=-1$

$$x=\frac{-b\pm\sqrt{b^2-4ac}}{2a}$$
$$=\frac{-(-3)\pm\sqrt{(-3)^2-4\times 1\times(-1)}}{2\times 1}$$
$$=\frac{3\pm\sqrt{9+4}}{2}=\frac{3\pm\sqrt{13}}{2}$$

c) $x^2+4x+6=12 \Rightarrow x^2+4x-6=0$, so $a=1$, $b=4$, $c=-6$

$$x=\frac{-b\pm\sqrt{b^2-4ac}}{2a}=\frac{-4\pm\sqrt{4^2-4\times 1\times(-6)}}{2\times 1}$$
$$=\frac{-4\pm\sqrt{16+24}}{2}=\frac{-4\pm\sqrt{40}}{2}$$
$$=\frac{-4\pm 2\sqrt{10}}{2}=-2\pm\sqrt{10}$$

Q4 **a)** Using the quadratic formula with $a=1$, $b=4$ and $c=-11$:

$$x=\frac{-b\pm\sqrt{b^2-4ac}}{2a}=\frac{-4\pm\sqrt{4^2-4\times 1\times(-11)}}{2\times 1}$$
$$=\frac{-4\pm\sqrt{60}}{2}=\frac{-4\pm 2\sqrt{15}}{2}$$

$\Rightarrow x=-2+\sqrt{15}$ or $x=-2-\sqrt{15}$
[2 marks available — 1 mark for a correct method, 1 mark for both solutions in the correct form]

b) Using the result from a):
$x^2+4x-11=(x-(-2+\sqrt{15}))(x-(-2-\sqrt{15}))$
$=(x+(2-\sqrt{15}))(x+(2+\sqrt{15}))$ *[1 mark]*

Q5 **a)** $x^2 + 6x + 7 = (x + 3)^2 - 9 + 7 = (x + 3)^2 - 2$

b) Let $u = 2x + 1$. From a), $(u + 3)^2 - 2 = 0$
$\Rightarrow (u + 3)^2 = 2 \Rightarrow u + 3 = \pm\sqrt{2} \Rightarrow u = -3 \pm \sqrt{2}$
$\Rightarrow 2x + 1 = -3 \pm \sqrt{2} \Rightarrow x = -2 \pm \frac{\sqrt{2}}{2}$

Q6 **a)** When $t = 0$, $d = \frac{15}{2} = 7.5$,
so the car is initially 7.5 km from O. *[1 mark]*

b) When $d = 0$, $\frac{15}{2} + t - \frac{1}{10}t^2 = 0 \Rightarrow t^2 - 10t - 75 = 0$
$\Rightarrow (t - 15)(t + 5) = 0 \Rightarrow t = 15$ or $t = -5$. Time can't be negative, so $t = 15$, so the car reaches O after 15 minutes.
[3 marks available — 1 mark for using d = 0 to form an equation, 1 mark for an appropriate method, 1 mark for the correct answer]

c) Completing the square:
$d = -\frac{1}{10}(t^2 - 10t) + \frac{15}{2} = -\frac{1}{10}(t - 5)^2 + \frac{25}{10} + \frac{15}{2}$
$= -\frac{1}{10}(t - 5)^2 + 10 \Rightarrow -\frac{1}{10}(t - 5)^2 \leq 0$, so the car is furthest from O when $t = 5$, i.e. when $d = 10$ km.
[2 marks available — 1 mark for completing the square, 1 mark for the correct distance with explanation]

Q7 Let $u = x^2$: $u^2 - 17u + 16 = 0 \Rightarrow (u - 16)(u - 1) = 0$
So $u - 16 = 0$ or $u - 1 = 0$, so $u = 16$ or $u = 1$.
$x^2 = 16 \Rightarrow x = 4$ or $x = -4$
$x^2 = 1 \Rightarrow x = 1$ or $x = -1$

Q8 **a)** $2x^2 - 5x - 3 = 0 \Rightarrow (2x + 1)(x - 3) = 0 \Rightarrow x = -\frac{1}{2}$ or $x = 3$
[2 marks available — 1 mark for correct factorisation, 1 mark for both correct solutions]

b) Let $u = \sqrt{x}$, then $2x - 5\sqrt{x} - 3 = 2u^2 - 5u - 3$
$2u^2 - 5u - 3 = 0 \Rightarrow u = -\frac{1}{2}$ or $u = 3$
$\Rightarrow \sqrt{x} = -\frac{1}{2}$ or $\sqrt{x} = 3$
$\sqrt{x} = -\frac{1}{2}$ gives no solution as $\sqrt{x} \geq 0$
$\sqrt{x} = 3 \Rightarrow x = 3^2 = 9$
[3 marks available — 1 mark for substituting to form a quadratic, 1 mark for reason why $\sqrt{x} = -\frac{1}{2}$ gives no solution, 1 mark for correct solution]

Q9 **a)** $d(t) = r(t) - f(t) \Rightarrow d(t) = \frac{1}{4}t^2 - 3t + 17 - t$
$\Rightarrow d(t) = \frac{1}{4}t^2 - 4t + 17$
[1 mark for correct expression for d(t)]

b) The fox catches the rabbit when $d(t) = 0$.
Find the discriminant: $a = \frac{1}{4}$, $b = -4$, $c = 17$
$b^2 - 4ac = (-4)^2 - 4 \times \frac{1}{4} \times 17 = 16 - 17 = -1 < 0$,
so $d(t)$ has no real roots, so the fox doesn't catch the rabbit.
[2 marks available — 1 mark for recognising that the fox will catch the rabbit when d(t) = 0, 1 mark for showing that d(t) = 0 has no solutions]

c) The smallest distance between the fox and rabbit is at the minimum point of $d(t)$. Completing the square:
$\frac{1}{4}t^2 - 4t + 17 = \frac{1}{4}(t^2 - 16t) + 17 = \frac{1}{4}((t - 8)^2 - 64) + 17$
$= \frac{1}{4}(t - 8)^2 - 16 + 17 = \frac{1}{4}(t - 8)^2 + 1$
So the minimum occurs when $t = 8$.
$d(8) = \frac{1}{4}(8)^2 - 4(8) + 17 = 16 - 32 + 17 = 1$, so the smallest distance between the fox and rabbit is 1 m.
[2 marks available — 1 mark for completing the square, 1 mark for the correct distance with explanation]
The minimum value of d is the y-coordinate of the vertex, so you could also see from the completed square that the minimum value is 1.

Q10 $a = 1$, $b = k$, $c = 4$.
So $b^2 - 4ac = k^2 - 4 \times 1 \times 4 = k^2 - 16$
If the equation has two distinct real roots, the discriminant must be positive so $k^2 - 16 > 0 \Rightarrow k^2 > 16 \Rightarrow k > 4$ or $k < -4$.

Q11 For a quadratic with repeated roots, the discriminant equals zero, so $b^2 - 4ac = 0 \Rightarrow 5^2 - 4 \times 2k \times k = 0 \Rightarrow 25 - 8k^2 = 0$
$\Rightarrow 8k^2 = 25 \Rightarrow k^2 = \frac{25}{8} \Rightarrow k = \pm\sqrt{\frac{25}{8}} = \pm\frac{5\sqrt{2}}{4}$
[5 marks available — 1 mark for using the discriminant, 1 mark for correctly substituting in a, b and c, 1 mark for attempting to solve quadratic to find k, 1 mark for unsimplified answer, 1 mark for simplifying and rationalising denominator]

Q12 **a)** $x^2 - 4x - 3 = (x - 2)^2 - 4 - 3 = (x - 2)^2 - 7$.
The lowest value $(x - 2)^2$ can take is zero — so the minimum value $= -7$ at $x = 2$ (to make the bracket 0). The graph crosses the x-axis at $(x - 2)^2 - 7 = 0 \Rightarrow x = 2 \pm \sqrt{7}$.

b) $x^2 + 5x + 8 = \left(x + \frac{5}{2}\right)^2 - \frac{25}{4} + 8 = \left(x + \frac{5}{2}\right)^2 + \frac{7}{4}$.
The lowest value $\left(x + \frac{5}{2}\right)^2$ can take is zero — so the minimum value $= \frac{7}{4}$ at $x = -\frac{5}{2}$ (to make the bracket 0), and the graph doesn't cross the x-axis.

c) $3 - 3x - x^2 = -\left(x + \frac{3}{2}\right)^2 + \frac{9}{4} + 3 = \frac{21}{4} - \left(x + \frac{3}{2}\right)^2$.
The lowest value $\left(x + \frac{3}{2}\right)^2$ can take is zero — so the maximum value $= \frac{21}{4}$ at $x = -\frac{3}{2}$ (to make the bracket 0). The graph crosses the x-axis at $\frac{21}{4} - \left(x + \frac{3}{2}\right)^2 = 0 \Rightarrow x = -\frac{3}{2} \pm \frac{\sqrt{21}}{2}$.

d) $2x^2 - 4x + 11 = 2(x - 1)^2 - 2 + 11 = 2(x - 1)^2 + 9$.
The lowest value $(x - 1)^2$ can take is zero — so the minimum value $= 9$ at $x = 1$ (to make the bracket 0), and the graph doesn't cross the x-axis.

e) $4x^2 - 28x + 48 = 4\left(x - \frac{7}{2}\right)^2 - 49 + 48 = 4\left(x - \frac{7}{2}\right)^2 - 1$.
The lowest value $\left(x - \frac{7}{2}\right)^2$ can take is zero — so the minimum value $= -1$ at $x = \frac{7}{2}$ (to make the bracket 0).
The graph crosses the x-axis at $4\left(x - \frac{7}{2}\right)^2 - 1 = 0$
$\Rightarrow x = 4$ or $x = 3$.

f) $-3x^2 + 12x + 14 = -3(x - 2)^2 + 12 + 14 = -3(x - 2)^2 + 26$.
The lowest value $(x - 2)^2$ can take is zero — so the maximum value $= 26$ at $x = 2$ (to make the bracket 0). The graph crosses the x-axis at $-3(x - 2)^2 + 26 = 0 \Rightarrow x = 2 \pm \frac{\sqrt{78}}{3}$.

Q13 **a)** $y = \frac{1}{2}x^2 + kx + 25 = \frac{1}{2}(x^2 + 2kx) + 25$
$= \frac{1}{2}((x + k)^2 - k^2) + 25 = \frac{1}{2}(x + k)^2 - \frac{1}{2}k^2 + 25$
[2 marks available — 1 mark for $\frac{1}{2}(x + k)^2$, 1 mark for the correct answer]

b) The coefficient of x^2 is positive, so the graph is u-shaped and the vertex will be a minimum. From part a), the y-coordinate of the minimum point is $25 - \frac{1}{2}k^2$.
The graph will intersect the x-axis at exactly two points when $25 - \frac{1}{2}k^2 < 0 \Rightarrow \frac{1}{2}k^2 > 25 \Rightarrow k^2 > 50$
$\Rightarrow k < -5\sqrt{2}$ or $k > 5\sqrt{2}$
[3 marks available — 1 mark for mentioning that the vertex is a minimum, 1 mark for using part a) to find a quadratic inequality in k, 1 mark for correct range of values of k]

Q14 **a)** $x^2 - 2x - 3 = 0 \Rightarrow (x - 1)^2 - 4 = 0$
$\Rightarrow (x - 1)^2 = 4$, so there are 2 roots, at $x = -2 + 1 = -1$ and $x = 2 + 1 = 3$.
At $x = 0$, $y = -3$. The graph is u-shaped:

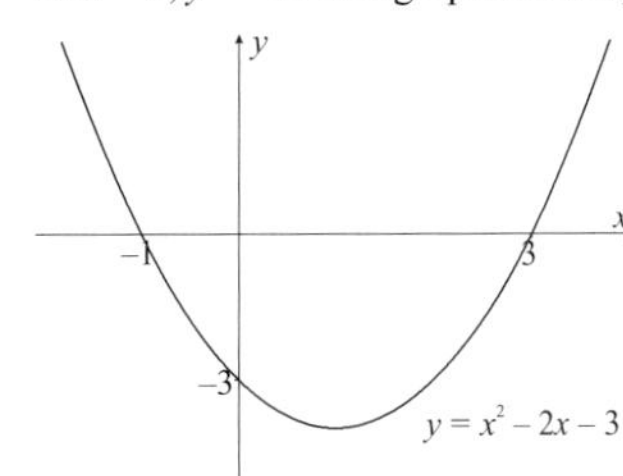

b) $x^2 - 6x + 9 = 0 \Rightarrow (x-3)^2 = 0$, so there is 1 root, at $x = 3$.
Letting $x = 0$ gives 9 as the y-intercept.
The graph is u-shaped:

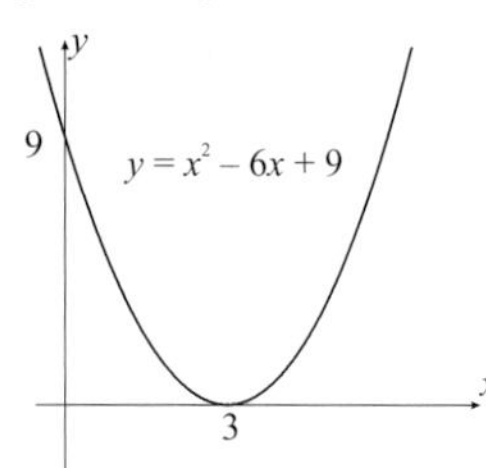

c) $2x^2 + 4x + 3 = 0 \Rightarrow 2(x+1)^2 + 1 = 0$, so there are no real roots. Letting $x = 0$ gives 3 as the y-intercept. The graph is u-shaped, and the lowest value $(x+1)^2$ can take is zero — so the minimum value = 1 at $x = -1$ (to make the bracket 0):

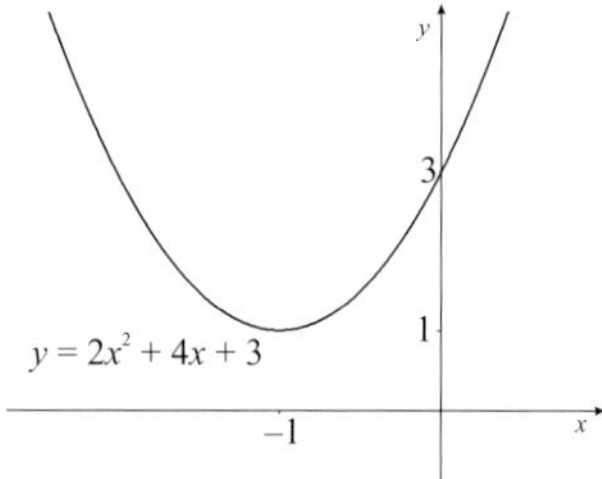

Q15 a) (i) $f(x) = x^2 - 2x - 14 = (x-1)^2 - 1 - 14 = (x-1)^2 - 15$
[2 marks available — 1 mark for correct a, 1 mark for correct b]

(ii) When $f(x) = 0$, $(x-1)^2 - 15 = 0 \Rightarrow (x-1)^2 = 15$
$\Rightarrow x - 1 = \pm\sqrt{15} \Rightarrow x = 1 + \sqrt{15}$ or $x = 1 - \sqrt{15}$
[2 marks available — 1 mark for each correct solution]

b)

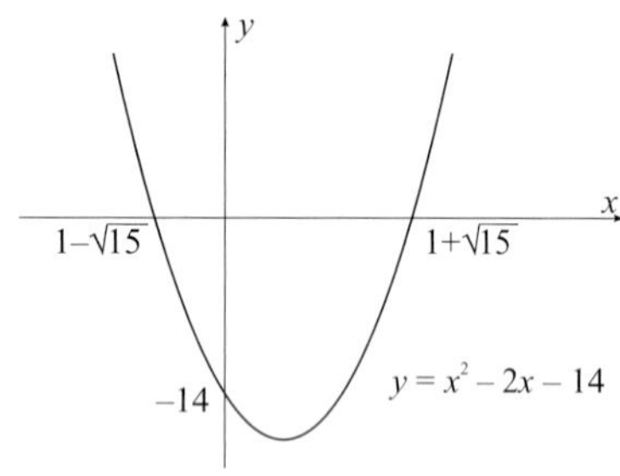

[3 marks available — 1 mark for correct curve shape, 1 mark for both correct x-intercepts, 1 mark for correct y-intercept]

Q16 a) $28 - 13x - 6x^2 = (7 + 2x)(4 - 3x)$ *[1 mark]*

b) $28 - 13x - 6x^2 = 0 \Rightarrow (7 + 2x)(4 - 3x) = 0$
$\Rightarrow x = -\frac{7}{2}$ or $x = \frac{4}{3}$ *[1 mark]*

c)

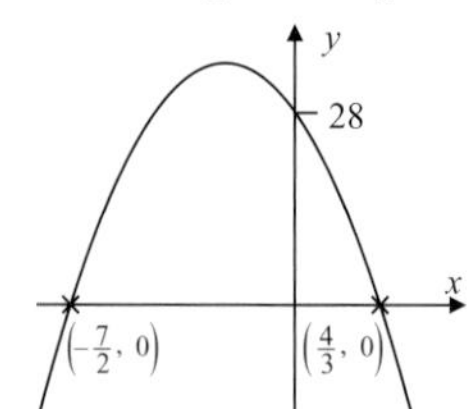

[3 marks available — 1 mark for correct curve shape, 1 mark for both correct x-intercepts, 1 mark for correct y-intercept]

Q17 a) $a = 2$, $b = 12$, $c = 21$, so $b^2 - 4ac = 12^2 - 4 \times 2 \times 21 = -24 < 0$
$2x^2 + 12x + 21$ has no real roots, so $y = 2x^2 + 12x + 21$ does not intersect the x-axis.
[2 marks available — 1 mark for a correct method, 1 mark for a correct conclusion]

b) $2x^2 + 12x + 21 = 2(x^2 + 6x) + 21$
$= 2(x+3)^2 - 18 + 21 = 2(x+3)^2 + 3$
[2 marks available — 1 mark for correct values of a and b, 1 mark for the full correct expression]

c) From part a), $2x^2 + 12x + 21$ has no roots,
so $y = \frac{10}{2x^2 + 12x + 21}$ is valid for all values of x.
The maximum value of $y = \frac{10}{2x^2 + 12x + 21}$ occurs at the minimum value of $2x^2 + 12x + 21$. From part b), $2x^2 + 12x + 21$ is at its minimum when $x = -3$ and $y = 3$.
So the maximum value of $y = \frac{10}{2x^2 + 12x + 21}$ is $y = \frac{10}{3}$, which occurs when $x = -3$.
[3 marks available — 1 mark for recognising that the maximum occurs at the minimum value of the denominator, 1 mark for correct value of maximum, 1 mark for correct x-value at the maximum]

Q18 a) When $t = 0$, $h = 6$, so the h-intercept = 6.
When $h = 0$, $0.25t^2 - 2.75t + 6 = 0$
$\Rightarrow t^2 - 11t + 24 = 0 \Rightarrow (t-8)(t-3) = 0$, so there are 2 roots, at $t = 8$ and $t = 3$. The graph is u-shaped:

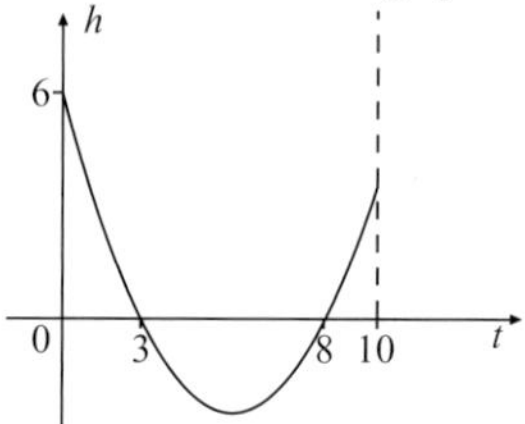

b) (i) Initial height when $t = 0$ is 6 m.

(ii) The vertex is halfway between the roots, i.e. when $t = (3 + 8) \div 2 = 5.5$ s, and
$h = 0.25(5.5)^2 - 2.75(5.5) + 6 = -1.5625$ m

(iii) The car is underground between 3 and 8 seconds, so for $8 - 3 = 5$ seconds.

Q19 a) $3x^2 + 2x + 1 = 3\left(x^2 + \frac{2}{3}x\right) + 1 = 3\left(\left(x + \frac{1}{3}\right)^2 - \frac{1}{9}\right) + 1$
$= 3\left(x + \frac{1}{3}\right)^2 - \frac{1}{3} + 1 = 3\left(x + \frac{1}{3}\right)^2 + \frac{2}{3}$
[2 marks available — 1 mark for correct values of a and b, 1 mark for the correct answer]

b) The coefficient of x^2 is positive, so the graph is u-shaped. When $x = 0$, $y = 1$, so the y-intercept is 1. The coordinates of the minimum point of the graph are $\left(-\frac{1}{3}, \frac{2}{3}\right)$, so the graph won't cross the x-axis.

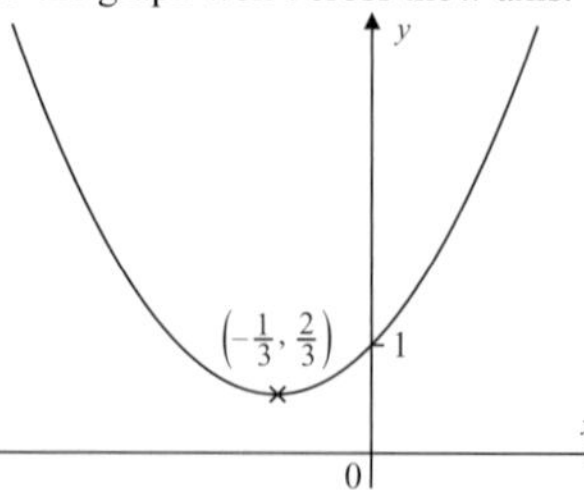

[3 marks available — 1 mark for correct curve shape, 1 mark for correct vertex, 1 mark for correct y-intercept]

Q20 a) The y-intercept is $-\frac{5}{2}$, so $c = -\frac{5}{2}$.
Completing the square on $y = 2x^2 + bx - \frac{5}{2}$ gives
$y = 2\left(x^2 + \frac{b}{2}x\right) - \frac{5}{2} = 2\left(x + \frac{b}{4}\right)^2 - \frac{b^2}{8} - \frac{5}{2}$
The minimum occurs at $x = -\frac{7}{2}$, so $-\frac{b}{4} = -\frac{7}{2} \Rightarrow b = 14$.
[3 marks available — 1 mark for using the y-intercept to find c, 1 mark for a correct method to find b, 1 mark for correct value of b]

b) $2x^2 + bx + c = 0 \Rightarrow 2x^2 + 14x - \frac{5}{2} = 0$
Using the quadratic formula with $a = 2$, $b = 14$ and $c = -\frac{5}{2}$:

$$x = \frac{-b \pm \sqrt{b^2 - 4ac}}{2a} = \frac{-14 \pm \sqrt{14^2 - 4 \times 2 \times -\frac{5}{2}}}{2 \times 2}$$

$\Rightarrow x = \frac{-7 + 3\sqrt{6}}{2}$ or $x = \frac{-7 - 3\sqrt{6}}{2}$

[2 marks available — 1 mark for a correct method, 1 mark for both correct solutions]

Q21 a) $\frac{1}{7}x^2 - \frac{62}{21}x - 1 = \left(\frac{1}{7}x - 3\right)\left(x + \frac{1}{3}\right)$

b) The x-value of the minimum of a quadratic is exactly halfway between the roots. Here, the roots are $x = 21$ and $x = -\frac{1}{3}$, so the x-value of the minimum is $\frac{1}{2}\left(21 + \left(-\frac{1}{3}\right)\right) = \frac{31}{3}$.

So the minimum value is $\frac{1}{7}\left(\frac{31}{3}\right)^2 - \frac{62}{21}\left(\frac{31}{3}\right) - 1 = -\frac{1024}{63}$.

Q22 a) $-10 + 7x - x^2 = 0 \Rightarrow x^2 - 7x + 10 = 0$
$\Rightarrow (x - 5)(x - 2) = 0 \Rightarrow x = 5$ or $x = 2$
The x-coordinate of B is greater than A, so A has coordinates (2, 0), and B has coordinates (5, 0).
[2 marks available — 1 mark for setting the equation equal to 0, 1 mark for both correct sets of coordinates]

b) The x-coordinate of the vertex is the midpoint of AB, so C has x-coordinate $\frac{2+5}{2} = \frac{7}{2}$, and y-coordinate
$y = -10 + 7\left(\frac{7}{2}\right) - \left(\frac{7}{2}\right)^2 = -10 + \frac{49}{2} - \frac{49}{4} = \frac{9}{4}$
So the coordinates of C are $\left(\frac{7}{2}, \frac{9}{4}\right)$.
[2 marks available — 1 mark for using symmetry to find the x-coordinate, 1 mark for the correct coordinates of C]

c) Let X be the midpoint of AB. Draw a straight line from X to C.

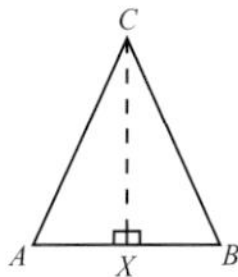

For triangle ABC to be isosceles, it needs to have two sides of equal length. XC is perpendicular to AB, so triangles AXC and BXC are right-angled triangles. $AX = XB$, the triangles share a common side XC, and they have corresponding right-angles, so triangles AXC and BXC are congruent. This means that $BC = AC$, so triangle ABC has two equal length sides, so triangle ABC is isosceles.

For the area:
ABC has a base of length $5 - 2 = 3$ and perpendicular height $\frac{9}{4}$, so the area of triangle ABC is $\frac{1}{2} \times 3 \times \frac{9}{4} = \frac{27}{8}$.
[3 marks available — 1 mark for a sensible argument about angles and side lengths, 1 mark for a valid conclusion that ABC is isosceles, 1 mark for the correct area]
You could have shown the triangle to be isosceles by a different method, e.g. by using angles or Pythagoras' theorem.

Q23 $f(x) = x^3 + x^2 = x^2(x + 1)$
Where $y = f(x)$ intersects the x-axis, $y = f(x) = 0$, so $x^2(x + 1) = 0 \Rightarrow x = 0$ or $x = -1$
So the curve intersects the x-axis more than once, at (0, 0) and (–1, 0).
[3 marks available — 1 mark for factorising f(x), 1 mark for setting f(x) equal to zero, 1 mark for both correct coordinate pairs]

Q24 a) $x^3 - 4x^2 = 0 \Rightarrow x^2(x - 4) = 0 \Rightarrow x = 0$ or $x = 4$

b) $x^3 + 5x^2 - 6x = 0 \Rightarrow x(x^2 + 5x - 6) = 0$
$\Rightarrow x(x - 1)(x + 6) = 0 \Rightarrow x = 0, x = 1$ or $x = -6$

c) $x^3 - 6x^2 + 9x = 0 \Rightarrow x(x^2 - 6x + 9) = 0$
$\Rightarrow x(x - 3)^2 = 0 \Rightarrow x = 0$ or $x = 3$

d) $2x^3 + 5x^2 + 15x = x^3 - 3x^2$
$\Rightarrow x^3 + 8x^2 + 15x = 0 \Rightarrow x(x^2 + 8x + 15) = 0$
$\Rightarrow x(x + 3)(x + 5) = 0 \Rightarrow x = 0, x = -3$ or $x = -5$

e) $2x^3 + 20x^2 + 12x = 9x^3 - 20x^2$
$\Rightarrow 7x^3 - 40x^2 - 12x = 0 \Rightarrow x(7x^2 - 40x - 12) = 0$
$\Rightarrow x(x - 6)(7x + 2) = 0 \Rightarrow x = 0, x = 6$ or $x = -\frac{2}{7}$

f) $6x^3 - 5x^2 - 4x = 0 \Rightarrow x(6x^2 - 5x - 4) = 0$
$\Rightarrow x(3x - 4)(2x + 1) = 0 \Rightarrow x = 0, x = \frac{4}{3}$ or $x = -\frac{1}{2}$

Q25 $2x^3 + 4x^2 - x + 4 = x^2 + 4x + 4 \Rightarrow 2x^3 + 3x^2 - 5x = 0$
$\Rightarrow x(2x^2 + 3x - 5) = 0 \Rightarrow x(x - 1)(2x + 5) = 0$
So the solutions are $x = 0$, $x = 1$ and $x = -\frac{5}{2}$.
[4 marks available — 1 mark for correct expansion and simplification, 1 mark for factorising x out of equation, 1 mark for an appropriate method to solve the equation, 1 mark for all three correct solutions]

Q26 a) $5x^3 - 13x^2 + 6x = -5x^3 + 7x^2 + 6x \Rightarrow 10x^3 - 20x^2 = 0$
$\Rightarrow 10x^2(x - 2) = 0 \Rightarrow 10x^2 = 0$ or $x - 2 = 0$, $x = 0$ or $x = 2$.
When $x = 0$, $y = 0 - 0 + 0 = 0$.
When $x = 2$, $y = 40 - 52 + 12 = 0$.
So they intersect at (0, 0) and (2, 0).

b) $f(x) = 5x^3 - 13x^2 + 6x = x(5x^2 - 13x + 6) = x(x - 2)(5x - 3)$.

Q27 a) Set the equations equal to each other:
$x(x - 6)^2 = -x(2x - 31) \Rightarrow x(x^2 - 12x + 36) = -2x^2 + 31x$
$\Rightarrow x^3 - 12x^2 + 36x = -2x^2 + 31x \Rightarrow x^3 - 10x^2 + 5x = 0$

b) $x^3 - 10x^2 + 5x = 0 \Rightarrow x(x^2 - 10x + 5)$
So the curves meet at $x = 0$ and at
$x^2 - 10x + 5 = 0 \Rightarrow (x - 5)^2 - 20 = 0 \Rightarrow x = 5 \pm 2\sqrt{5}$.
You can also use the quadratic formula.

Q28 a) Using the x-intercepts, you know that:
$f(x) = (x + 1)(x - 2)(mx + n)$, where m and n are constants.
You're told that the coefficient of $x^3 = 1$, so $m = 1$.
So $f(x) = (x + 1)(x - 2)(x + n)$.
The y-intercept of the curve is –10 (i.e. when $x = 0$, $y = -10$) so:
$f(0) = (1)(-2)(n) = -10 \Rightarrow n = 5$
So the coordinates of the x-intercept are (–5, 0).
[3 marks available — 1 mark for correct f(x) in terms of m and n (or other constants), 1 mark for showing n = 5, 1 mark for correct coordinate pair]

b) $f(x) = (x + 5)(x + 1)(x - 2) = (x + 5)(x^2 - x - 2)$
$= x^3 - x^2 - 2x + 5x^2 - 5x - 10 = x^3 + 4x^2 - 7x - 10$
[2 marks available — 1 mark for expanding to correct linear factor and quadratic, 1 mark for all correct terms, a maximum of 1 mark if error carried forward from part a) (but correctly expanded)]

Q29 a) $f(1) = 1^5 - 4(1)^4 + 3(1)^3 + 2(1)^2 - 2 = 0$, so $(x - 1)$ is a factor.

b) $f(-1) = (-1)^5 - 4(-1)^4 + 3(-1)^3 + 2(-1)^2 - 2 = -8$, so $(x + 1)$ is not a factor.

c) $f(2) = 2^5 - 4(2)^4 + 3(2)^3 + 2(2)^2 - 2 = -2$, so $(x - 2)$ is not a factor.

d) $f\left(\frac{2}{2}\right) = f(1) = 0$ (from a)), so $(2x - 2)$ is a factor.

Q30 a) $p(2) = 4(2)^3 + 4(2)^2 - 5(2) - 3 = 32 + 16 - 10 - 3 = 35$
$p(2) \neq 0$, so by the Factor Theorem, $(x - 2)$ is not a factor of $p(x)$. *[1 mark]*

b) $p\left(-\frac{3}{2}\right) = 4\left(-\frac{3}{2}\right)^3 + 4\left(-\frac{3}{2}\right)^2 - 5\left(-\frac{3}{2}\right) - 3$
$= 4\left(-\frac{27}{8}\right) + 4\left(\frac{9}{4}\right) + \frac{15}{2} - 3 = 0$, so by the Factor Theorem, $(2x + 3)$ is a factor of $p(x)$. *[1 mark]*

Q31 a) $x^2 - 1 = (x + 1)(x - 1)$
If $(x^2 - 1)$ is a factor of $f(x)$, both $(x + 1)$ and $(x - 1)$ must be factors of $f(x)$.
Substitute $x = -1$ into $f(x)$ and show the result is 0:
$f(-1) = 2(-1)^3 + 3(-1)^2 - 2(-1) - 3$
$= -2 + 3 + 2 - 3 = 0$
So by the Factor Theorem, $(x + 1)$ is a factor.

Substitute $x = 1$ into f(x) and show the result is 0:
$f(1) = 2(1)^3 + 3(1)^2 - 2(1) - 3 = 2 + 3 - 2 - 3 = 0$
So by the Factor Theorem, $(x - 1)$ is a factor.
So $(x^2 - 1)$ is a factor of f(x).
[3 marks available — 1 mark for factorising $x^2 - 1$, 1 mark for substituting $x = -1$ and $x = 1$ into f(x), 1 mark for correct interpretation]

b) From part a), you know that:
$f(x) = 2x^3 + 3x^2 - 2x - 3 = (x^2 - 1)(mx + n)$
The coefficient of x^3 in f(x) is 2, so $m = 2$.
So $y = f(x) = (x^2 - 1)(2x + n)$
The y-intercept is -3 (i.e. when $x = 0$, $y = -3$), so:
$f(0) = (-1)(n) = -3 \Rightarrow n = 3$
$\Rightarrow f(x) = (x + 1)(x - 1)(2x + 3) = 0$
$\Rightarrow x = -1$ or $x = 1$ or $x = -\frac{3}{2}$

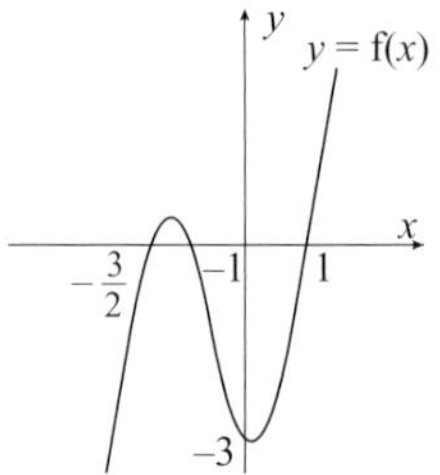

[4 marks available — 1 mark for correct factorisation of f(x), 1 mark for correct curve shape, 1 mark for correct y-intercept, 1 mark for correct x-intercepts]

Q32 p(x) is divisible by $(x - 5)$, so by the Factor Theorem,
$p(5) = 0 \Rightarrow a \times 5^3 - 9(5^2) + 23 \times 5 + b = 0$
$\Rightarrow 125a - 225 + 115 + b = 0 \Rightarrow 125a + b = 110$ (1)
Similarly, p(x) is divisible by $(x - 3)$, so by the Factor Theorem,
$p(3) = 0 \Rightarrow a \times 3^3 - 9(3^2) + 23 \times 3 + b = 0 \Rightarrow 27a + b = 12$ (2)
To solve simultaneously, calculate (1) – (2):
$98a = 98 \Rightarrow a = 1$, and then $27(1) + b = 12 \Rightarrow b = -15$.
[3 marks available — 1 mark for correct use of Factor Theorem, 1 mark for derivation of correct simultaneous equations, 1 mark for correct solution to simultaneous equations]

Q33 a) $(p - q)(p^2 + pq + q^2) \equiv p^3 + p^2q + pq^2 - p^2q - pq^2 - q^3 \equiv p^3 - q^3$
[2 marks available — 1 mark for correct expansion of brackets, 1 mark for correct simplification]

b) Let $p = x - 1$ and $q = 3 - 2x$. Using the result from part a):
$(x - 1)^3 - (3 - 2x)^3$
$= ((x - 1) - (3 - 2x))((x - 1)^2 + (x - 1)(3 - 2x) + (3 - 2x)^2)$
$= (3x - 4)((x^2 - 2x + 1) + (-2x^2 + 5x - 3) + (9 - 12x + 4x^2))$
$= (3x - 4)(3x^2 - 9x + 7)$
$(x - 1)^3 - (3 - 2x)^3 = 0 \Rightarrow (3x - 4) = 0$ or $(3x^2 - 9x + 7) = 0$
So $x = \frac{4}{3}$ is a solution.
Consider $3x^2 - 9x + 7$: $b^2 - 4ac = (-9)^2 - 4 \times 3 \times 7 = -3 < 0$,
so $3x^2 - 9x + 7$ has no real roots.
So the equation has only one solution, at $x = \frac{4}{3}$.
[4 marks available — 1 mark for attempting to simplify the equation, 1 mark for correct partial factorisation, 1 mark for showing that the quadratic factor gives no solutions, 1 mark for correct solution]

Q34 $(x + 2)$ is a factor, so $f(-2) = 0$
$\Rightarrow (-2 + 5)(-2 - 2)(-2 - 1) + k = 0$
$\Rightarrow 3 \times (-4) \times (-3) + k = 0 \Rightarrow 36 + k = 0 \Rightarrow k = -36$

Q35 $f(2) = 0 \Rightarrow 2(2)^4 + 3(2)^3 + 5(2)^2 + 2c + d = 0$
$2c + d = -76$ — equation 1
$f(-3) = 0 \Rightarrow 2(-3)^4 + 3(-3)^3 + 5(-3)^2 - 3c + d = 0$
$-3c + d = -126$ — equation 2
Subtract equation 2 from equation 1: $5c = 50 \Rightarrow c = 10$.
In equation 1: $2 \times 10 + d = -76 \Rightarrow d = -96$.

Q36 Use algebraic long division or another method to get:
$f(x) = (x - 3)(x^2 - 6x - 11) = 0$
So $x - 3 = 0 \Rightarrow x = 3$, or $x^2 - 6x - 11 = 0$.
Using the quadratic formula, $a = 1$, $b = -6$, $c = -11$:
$$x = \frac{-b \pm \sqrt{b^2 - 4ac}}{2a} = \frac{-(-6) \pm \sqrt{(-6)^2 - 4 \times 1 \times (-11)}}{2 \times 1}$$
$$= \frac{6 \pm \sqrt{36 + 44}}{2} = \frac{6 \pm \sqrt{80}}{2} = \frac{6 \pm 4\sqrt{5}}{2} = 3 \pm 2\sqrt{5}$$
So the solutions are $x = 3$, $x = 3 - 2\sqrt{5}$ and $x = 3 + 2\sqrt{5}$.

Q37 a) Adding the coefficients gives you 0, so $(x - 1)$ is a factor of p(x). By comparing coefficients:
$p(x) = 2x^3 + 3x^2 - 3x - 2 = (x - 1)(2x^2 + 5x + 2)$
So $p(x) = (x - 1)(2x + 1)(x + 2)$
[3 marks available — 1 mark for using the Factor Theorem to identify a factor, 1 mark for correct partial factorisation, 1 mark for the complete factorisation]

b) $p(x) = 0 \Rightarrow (x - 1)(2x + 1)(x + 2) = 0$
$\Rightarrow x = 1, x = -\frac{1}{2}$ and $x = -2$
[2 marks available — 1 mark for correct use of the result from part a), 1 mark for all three correct solutions]

Q38 a) Using the Factor Theorem, $(x - 2)$ is a factor of p(x)
$\Rightarrow p(2) = 0 \Rightarrow -2^3 + 7 \times 2^2 + 2a + 12 = 0 \Rightarrow a = -16$
[2 marks available — 1 mark for a correct method, 1 mark for correct value of a]

b) By comparing coefficients:
$p(x) = -x^3 + 7x^2 - 16x + 12 = (x - 2)(-x^2 + 5x - 6)$
$\Rightarrow p(x) = (x - 2)(-x + 3)(x - 2) = -(x - 2)^2(x - 3)$
[2 marks available — 1 mark for a correct method, 1 mark for correct complete factorisation]

c) When $x = 0$, $y = 12$, so the y-intercept is 12.

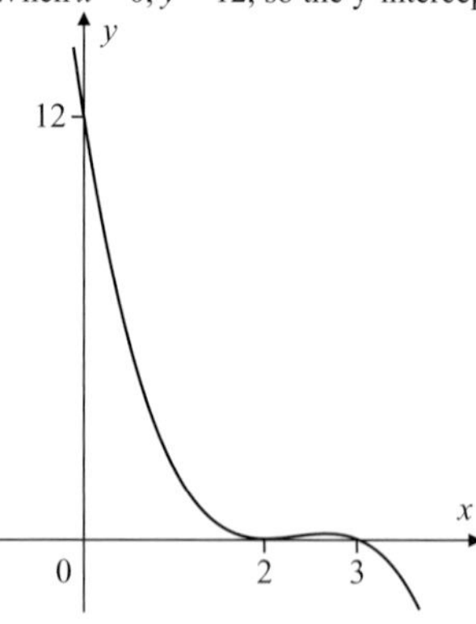

[3 marks available — 1 mark for correct curve shape, 1 mark for both x-intercepts labelled, 1 mark for y-intercept labelled]

Q39 Adding the coefficients gives you 24, so $(x - 1)$ is not a factor. Using trial and error, $f(-1) = 0$, so $(x + 1)$ is a factor. Factorise using algebraic long division or another method to get:
$f(x) = (x + 1)(x^2 + 5x + 6) = (x + 1)(x + 2)(x + 3) = 0$
So the roots are $x = -1$, -2 and -3.

Q40 $f(x) = 4x^3 - 6x^2 - 3x + 5$
$f(1) = 4 - 6 - 3 + 5 = 0$, so $(x - 1)$ is a factor.
Use algebraic division to find the quadratic factor:
$$\begin{array}{r} 4x^2 - 2x - 5 \\ x - 1 \overline{\smash{)}\,4x^3 - 6x^2 - 3x + 5} \\ -\underline{(4x^3 - 4x^2)} \\ -2x^2 - 3x \\ -\underline{(-2x^2 + 2x)} \\ -5x + 5 \\ -\underline{(-5x + 5)} \\ 0 \end{array}$$
So $f(x) = (x - 1)(4x^2 - 2x - 5)$
Use the quadratic formula to solve $4x^2 - 2x - 5 = 0$:

$$x = \frac{-b \pm \sqrt{b^2 - 4ac}}{2a} = \frac{-(-2) \pm \sqrt{(-2)^2 - 4 \times 4 \times (-5)}}{2 \times 4}$$
$$= \frac{2 \pm \sqrt{4 + 80}}{8} = \frac{1 \pm \sqrt{21}}{4}$$

So $f(x) = 0$ when $x = 1$ and $x = \frac{1 \pm \sqrt{21}}{4}$.

[4 marks available — 1 mark for correct linear factor, 1 mark for correct quadratic factor, 1 mark for correctly substituting into quadratic formula, 1 mark for correct x-values]

Q41 a) (i) $f(-2) = (-2)^3 + 3(-2)^2 - 4(-2) - 12$
$= -8 + 12 + 8 - 12 = 0$

[2 marks available — 1 mark for correctly substituting in x = –2, 1 mark for correct answer]

(ii) $f(x) = x^3 + 3x^2 - 4x - 12 = (x + 2)(x^2 + nx - 6)$
$\Rightarrow nx^2 + 2x^2 = 3x^2 \Rightarrow n = 1$

So $f(x) = (x + 2)(x^2 + x - 6) = (x + 2)(x + 3)(x - 2)$

[3 marks available — 1 mark for suitable method, 1 mark for one correct factor, 1 mark for other two correct factors]

b)

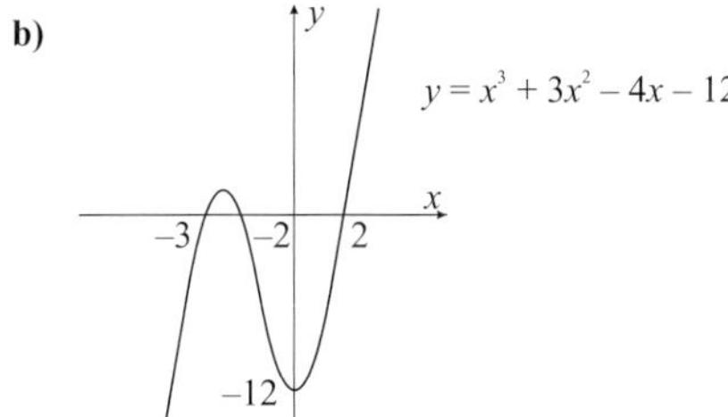

[4 marks available — 1 mark for correct curve shape, 1 mark for correct y-intercept, 1 mark for one correct x-intercept, 1 mark for other two correct x-intercepts]

Q42 $f(x) = 2x^3 - 5x^2 - 4x + 3 = (2x - 1)(x^2 + nx - 3)$
$\Rightarrow 2nx^2 - x^2 = -5x^2 \Rightarrow 2nx^2 = -4x^2 \Rightarrow n = -2$

So $f(x) = 2x^3 - 5x^2 - 4x + 3 = (2x - 1)(x^2 - 2x - 3)$
$= (2x - 1)(x + 1)(x - 3)$

[3 marks available — 1 mark for suitable method, 1 mark each for the correct factors]

Q43 $(3x - 1)(2x + 1) = 6x^2 + x - 1$

$6x^3 - 29x^2 + Px + Q = (6x^2 + x - 1)(ax + b)$

Find a: $6x^3 = 6ax^3 \Rightarrow a = 1$

Find b: $-29x^2 = ax^2 + 6bx^2 = x^2 + 6bx^2$
$\Rightarrow 6bx^2 = -30x^2 \Rightarrow b = -5$

$(6x^2 + x - 1)(x - 5) = 6x^3 - 30x^2 + x^2 - 5x - x + 5$
$= 6x^3 - 29x^2 - 6x + 5$

So $P = -6$ and $Q = 5$.

[4 marks available — 1 mark for suitable method, 1 mark for one correct term of quotient, 1 mark for other correct terms of quotient, 1 mark for correct values of both P and Q]

Q44 a)

$$\begin{array}{r} x^2 - 4x + 9 \\ x + 3\overline{)\,x^3 - x^2 - 3x + 3} \\ -\underline{(x^3 + 3x^2)} \\ -4x^2 - 3x \\ -\underline{(-4x^2 - 12x)} \\ 9x + 3 \\ -\underline{(9x + 27)} \\ -24 \end{array}$$

Quotient: $x^2 - 4x + 9$, remainder: –24

b)

$$\begin{array}{r} x^2 - x - 7 \\ x - 2\overline{)\,x^3 - 3x^2 - 5x + 6} \\ -\underline{(x^3 - 2x^2)} \\ -x^2 - 5x \\ -\underline{(-x^2 + 2x)} \\ -7x + 6 \\ -\underline{(-7x + 14)} \\ -8 \end{array}$$

Quotient: $x^2 - x - 7$, remainder: –8

c)

$$\begin{array}{r} x^2 + 0x + 3 \\ x + 2\overline{)\,x^3 + 2x^2 + 3x + 2} \\ -\underline{(x^3 + 2x^2)} \\ 0x^2 + 3x \\ -\underline{(0x^2 + 0x)} \\ 3x + 2 \\ -\underline{(3x + 6)} \\ -4 \end{array}$$

Quotient: $x^2 + 3$, remainder: –4

Q45 a)

$$\begin{array}{r} 3x^2 - 10x + 15 \\ x + 2\overline{)\,3x^3 - 4x^2 - 5x - 6} \\ -\underline{(3x^3 + 6x^2)} \\ -10x^2 - 5x \\ -\underline{(-10x^2 - 20x)} \\ 15x - 6 \\ -\underline{(15x + 30)} \\ -36 \end{array}$$

So $f(x) = (x + 2)(3x^2 - 10x + 15) - 36$

b)

$$\begin{array}{r} x^2 - 0x - 3 \\ x + 2\overline{)\,x^3 + 2x^2 - 3x + 4} \\ -\underline{(x^3 + 2x^2)} \\ 0x^2 - 3x \\ -\underline{(0x^2 + 0x)} \\ -3x + 4 \\ -\underline{(-3x - 6)} \\ 10 \end{array}$$

So $f(x) = (x + 2)(x^2 - 3) + 10$

c)

$$\begin{array}{r} 2x^2 - 4x + 14 \\ x + 2\overline{)\,2x^3 + 0x^2 + 6x - 3} \\ -\underline{(2x^3 + 4x^2)} \\ -4x^2 + 6x \\ -\underline{(-4x^2 - 8x)} \\ 14x - 3 \\ -\underline{(14x + 28)} \\ -31 \end{array}$$

So $f(x) = (x + 2)(2x^2 - 4x + 14) - 31$

Q46 a)

$$\begin{array}{r} x^2 + 4x + 3 \\ x + 3\overline{)\,x^3 + 7x^2 + 15x + 9} \\ -\underline{(x^3 + 3x^2)} \\ 4x^2 + 15x \\ -\underline{(4x^2 + 12x)} \\ 3x + 9 \\ -\underline{(3x + 9)} \\ 0 \end{array}$$

So the quotient is $x^2 + 4x + 3$.

[2 marks available — 1 mark for a suitable method, 1 mark for correct quotient]

b) From part a), $x^3 + 7x^2 + 15x + 9 = (x + 3)(x^2 + 4x + 3)$, so $x^3 + 7x^2 + 15x + 9 = 0 \Rightarrow (x + 3)(x^2 + 4x + 3) = 0$
$\Rightarrow (x + 3)(x + 3)(x + 1) = 0$.

So the solutions are $x = -3$ and $x = -1$.

[3 marks available — 1 mark for correct partial factorisation, 1 mark for correct complete factorisation, 1 mark for both correct solutions]

Q47 a)

$$\begin{array}{r} x^2 - 7x + 14 \\ x + 2\overline{)\,x^3 - 5x^2 + 0x - 2} \\ -\underline{(x^3 + 2x^2)} \\ -7x^2 + 0x \\ -\underline{(-7x^2 - 14x)} \\ 14x - 2 \\ -\underline{(14x + 28)} \\ -30 \end{array}$$

So $f(x) = (x + 2)(x^2 - 7x + 14) - 30$

b) $f(x) + 30 = (x + 2)(x^2 - 7x + 14)$

So when $f(x) + 30 = 0$, $x = -2$ is a solution.

Show that $x^2 - 7x + 14 = 0$ has no real solutions:
$b^2 - 4ac = (-7)^2 - 4 \times 1 \times 14 = -7 < 0$.

Hence $x = -2$ is the only solution to $f(x) + 30 = 0$.

Q48 a) The graph of $p(x) = x^2 + 6$ is symmetrical about the y-axis, so the x-coordinate of the vertex is 0.
When $x = 0$, $y = 6$, so the vertex has coordinates (0, 6).
$q(0) = 6 + 5(0) - 0^2 = 6$, so the graph of $y = q(x)$ passes through the vertex of $y = p(x)$.
Completing the square on $q(x)$:
$q(x) = -(x^2 - 5x) + 6 = -\left(x - \frac{5}{2}\right)^2 + \frac{49}{4}$,
so the vertex of $y = q(x)$ has coordinates $\left(\frac{5}{2}, \frac{49}{4}\right)$.
$p\left(\frac{5}{2}\right) = \left(\frac{5}{2}\right)^2 + 6 = \frac{49}{4}$, so the graph of $y = p(x)$ passes through the vertex of $y = q(x)$.
[4 marks available — 1 mark for finding the vertex of p(x), 1 mark for showing q(x) passes through this point, 1 mark for finding the vertex of q(x), 1 mark for showing p(x) passes through this point]

b) $q(x) = 6 + 5x - x^2 = (-x + 6)(x + 1)$,
so the roots are $x = 6$ and $x = -1$.

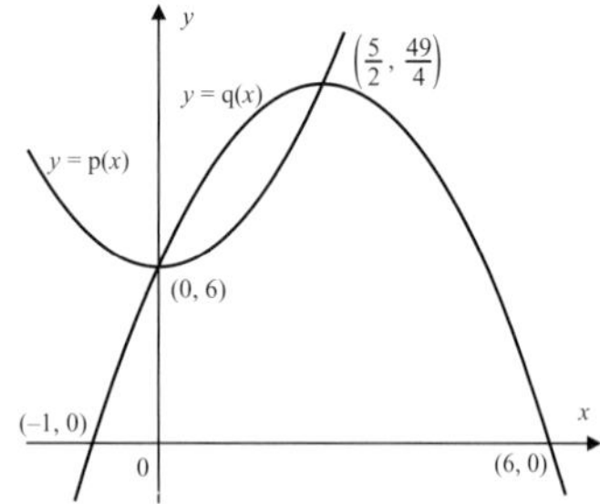

[3 marks available — 1 mark for correct shape of each of y = p(x) and y = q(x), 1 mark for each graph passing through the vertex of the other with coordinates marked, 1 mark for correctly labelled intersections with axes]

Q49 a) The solutions are $x = a$, $x = a + 2$ and $x = a + 5$.

b) As $-5 < a < -2$, a and $a + 2$ are negative and $a + 5$ is positive.
It intersects the y-axis when y is negative,
so it must be a positive cubic graph.

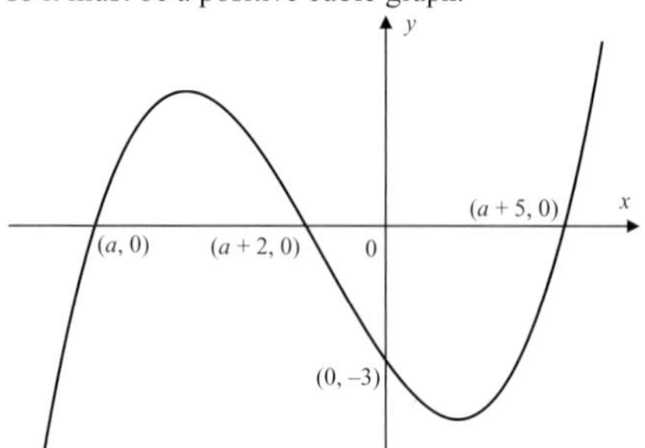

Q50 a) $p(10) = 8 \times 10^3 + 60 \times 10^2 + 142 \times 10 + 105$
$= 8000 + 6000 + 1420 + 105 = 15\,525$ *[1 mark]*

b)

$$\begin{array}{r} 4n^2 + 20n + 21 \\ 2n+5\overline{)\,8n^3 + 60n^2 + 142n + 105} \\ -(8n^3 + 20n^2) \\ 40n^2 + 142n \\ -(40n^2 + 100n) \\ 42n + 105 \\ -(42n + 105) \\ 0 \end{array}$$

So the quotient is $4n^2 + 20n + 21$.
[2 marks available — 1 mark for a suitable method, 1 mark for the correct quotient]

c) From part b):
$p(n) = (2n + 5)(4n^2 + 20n + 21) = (2n + 5)(2n + 3)(2n + 7)$
$(2n + 3)$, $(2n + 5)$ and $(2n + 7)$ can be written in the form $2m + 1$, where m is an integer, and the values of m are consecutive, so $p(n)$ is a product of three consecutive odd numbers.
[3 marks available — 1 mark for correct partial factorisation of p(n), 1 mark for correct complete factorisation, 1 mark for showing the factors of p(n) are consecutive odd numbers]

d) $p(10) = (2 \times 10 + 3)(2 \times 10 + 5)(2 \times 10 + 7)$
$= 23 \times 25 \times 27 = 15\,525$
So the numbers are 23, 25 and 27.
[1 mark for all three correct odd numbers]

Q51 a)

$$\begin{array}{r} 3x^2 - 5x - 2 \\ x-2\overline{)\,3x^3 - 11x^2 + 8x + 4} \\ -(3x^3 - 6x^2) \\ -5x^2 + 8x \\ -(-5x^2 + 10x) \\ -2x + 4 \\ -2x + 4 \\ 0 \end{array}$$

So the quotient is $3x^2 - 5x - 2$.
[2 marks available — 1 mark for a suitable method, 1 mark for the correct quotient]

b) The graphs intersect when
$3x^3 - 11x^2 + 11x + 2 = 3x - 2 \Rightarrow 3x^3 - 11x^2 + 8x + 4 = 0$
Using the result from part a),
$(x - 2)(3x^2 - 5x - 2) = 0 \Rightarrow (x - 2)(3x + 1)(x - 2) = 0$.
The line is tangent to the curve when there is a repeated root.
Since $(x - 2)$ is a repeated factor, the x-coordinate of P is 2.
When $x = 2$, $y = 3(2) - 2 = 4$, so P has coordinates (2, 4).
[4 marks available — 1 mark for using the result from part a), 1 mark for correct factorisation, 1 mark for correct interpretation of repeated root, 1 mark for correct coordinates of P]

Q52 a) $(x - 1)(x^2 - (k - 1)x - (k^2 - 1))$
$\equiv x^3 - (k - 1)x^2 - (k^2 - 1)x - x^2 + (k - 1)x + (k^2 - 1)$
$\equiv x^3 - kx^2 + x^2 - k^2x + x - x^2 + kx - x + k^2 - 1$
$\equiv x^3 - kx^2 - k^2x + kx + k^2 - 1$
$\equiv x^3 - kx^2 + k(1 - k)x + (k^2 - 1)$
[2 marks available — 1 mark for expanding correctly, 1 mark for correctly rearranging into the required form]

b) From part a), $y = (x - 1)(x^2 - (k - 1)x - (k^2 - 1))$,
so the graph of $y = x^3 - kx^2 + k(1 - k)x + (k^2 - 1)$ crosses the x-axis at $x = 1$.
There will be no additional intersections with the x-axis if $(x^2 - (k - 1)x - (k^2 - 1))$ has no roots,
i.e. if $b^2 - 4ac < 0$. $a = 1$, $b = -(k - 1)$, $c = -(k^2 - 1)$,
so $b^2 - 4ac < 0 \Rightarrow (-(k - 1))^2 + 4(k^2 - 1) < 0$
$\Rightarrow k^2 - 2k + 1 + 4k^2 - 4 < 0 \Rightarrow 5k^2 - 2k - 3 < 0$
$\Rightarrow (5k + 3)(k - 1) < 0 \Rightarrow -\frac{3}{5} < k < 1$
[4 marks available — 1 mark for using the result from part a), 1 mark for calculating the discriminant of the quadratic factor, 1 mark for an appropriate method to solve the quadratic inequality, 1 mark for correct range of values of k]

Chapter 5: Inequalities and Simultaneous Equations

Prior Knowledge Check

Q1 a) 2, 3, 5, 7 **b)** 2, 4, 6, 8, 10
c) $A \cap B$ is the intersection of A and B, so C = 2.
d) $A \cup B$ is the union of A and B, so D = 2, 3, 4, 5, 6, 7, 8, 10.

Q2 a) $3x - 3$ **b)** $-16x + 40y$ **c)** $a^3 + ab$

Q3 a) $4(2c - 9d)$ **b)** $m(m^2 + 2n)$ **c)** $3pq(2q + 3p)$

Q4 a) $(x + 7)(x - 4) = 0 \Rightarrow x = -7$ or $x = 4$
b) $(2x + 3)(x + 5) = 0 \Rightarrow x = -\frac{3}{2}$ or $x = -5$
c) $(5x - 2)(x + 2) = 0 \Rightarrow x = \frac{2}{5}$ or $x = -2$

Exercise 5.1 — Linear Inequalities

Q1 a) $2x - 1 < x + 4 \Rightarrow x < 5$
b) $4 - 3x \geq 10 - 5x \Rightarrow 2x \geq 6 \Rightarrow x \geq 3$

c) $5x + 7 > 3x + 1 \Rightarrow 2x > -6 \Rightarrow x > -3$

d) $3 - 2x \le 5x - 4 \Rightarrow -7x \le -7 \Rightarrow x \ge 1$

e) $9 - x \ge 7x + 5 \Rightarrow -8x \ge -4 \Rightarrow x \le \frac{1}{2}$

f) $12x - 9 \le 4x + 11 \Rightarrow 8x \le 20 \Rightarrow x \le 2.5$

g) $3x - 6 > 6 - 3x \Rightarrow 6x > 12 \Rightarrow x > 2$

h) $-4x < 16 - 7x \Rightarrow 3x < 16 \Rightarrow x < \frac{16}{3}$

Q2 **a)** $2(x + 3) > 3(x + 2) \Rightarrow 2x + 6 > 3x + 6 \Rightarrow -x > 0 \Rightarrow x < 0$
In set notation, this is $\{x : x < 0\}$

b) $5(1 + 3x) \le 7 \Rightarrow 5 + 15x \le 7 \Rightarrow 15x \le 2 \Rightarrow x \le \frac{2}{15}$
In set notation, this is $\left\{x : x \le \frac{2}{15}\right\}$

c) $12 \ge 2(5 - 2x) \Rightarrow 6 \ge 5 - 2x \Rightarrow 1 \ge -2x \Rightarrow x \ge -\frac{1}{2}$
In set notation, this is $\left\{x : x \ge -\frac{1}{2}\right\}$

Q3 **a)** $\frac{6-5x}{2} < \frac{4-8x}{3} \Rightarrow 3(6 - 5x) < 2(4 - 8x)$
$\Rightarrow 18 - 15x < 8 - 16x \Rightarrow x < -10$

b) $\frac{3x-1}{4} \ge 2x \Rightarrow 3x - 1 \ge 8x \Rightarrow x \le -\frac{1}{5}$

c) $\frac{x-2}{2} - \frac{2x+3}{3} < 7 \Rightarrow 3(x - 2) - 2(2x + 3) < 42$
$\Rightarrow 3x - 6 - 4x - 6 < 42 \Rightarrow -x < 54 \Rightarrow x > -54$

Q4 **a)** $-5 < 2x - 3 < 15 \Rightarrow -2 < 2x < 18 \Rightarrow -1 < x < 9$
In set notation, this is either $\{x : -1 < x < 9\}$
or $\{x : x > -1\} \cap \{x : x < 9\}$

b) $-5 \le 4 - 3x < 19 \Rightarrow -9 \le -3x < 15$
$\Rightarrow 3 \ge x > -5 \Rightarrow -5 < x \le 3$
In set notation, this is either $\{x : -5 < x \le 3\}$
or $\{x : x > -5\} \cap \{x : x \le 3\}$

c) $5 \le 7 + 6x \le 11 \Rightarrow -2 \le 6x \le 4 \Rightarrow -\frac{1}{3} \le x \le \frac{2}{3}$
In set notation, this is either $\left\{x : -\frac{1}{3} \le x \le \frac{2}{3}\right\}$
or $\left\{x : x \ge -\frac{1}{3}\right\} \cap \left\{x : x \le \frac{2}{3}\right\}$

Q5 **a)** $2x \ge 3 - x \Rightarrow 3x \ge 3 \Rightarrow x \ge 1$

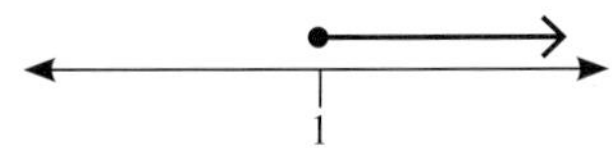

b) $5x - 1 < 3x + 5 \Rightarrow 2x < 6 \Rightarrow x < 3$

c) $2x + 1 \ge 3x + 2 \Rightarrow -x \ge 1 \Rightarrow x \le -1$

d) $3(x - 3) \le 5(x - 1) \Rightarrow 3x - 9 \le 5x - 5$
$\Rightarrow -2x \le 4 \Rightarrow x \ge -2$

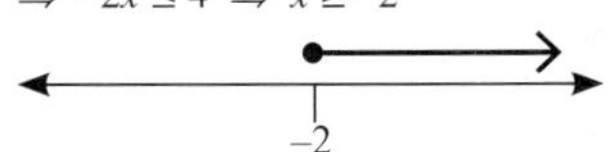

e) $9 - x \le 3 - 4x \Rightarrow 3x \le -6 \Rightarrow x \le -2$

f) $\frac{2(x-3)}{3} + 1 < \frac{2x-1}{2}$
$\Rightarrow 4(x - 3) + 6 < 3(2x - 1)$
$\Rightarrow 4x - 12 + 6 < 6x - 3 \Rightarrow -2x < 3 \Rightarrow x > -\frac{3}{2}$

Q6 **a)** $7 \le 3x - 2 < 16 \Rightarrow 9 \le 3x < 18 \Rightarrow 3 \le x < 6$

b)

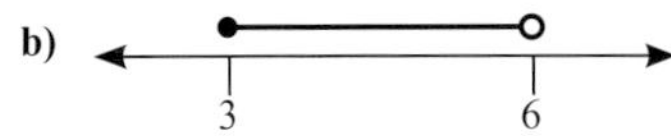

Q7 $4 - 2x < 10 \Rightarrow -2x < 6 \Rightarrow x > -3$
$3x - 1 < x + 7 \Rightarrow 2x < 8 \Rightarrow x < 4$

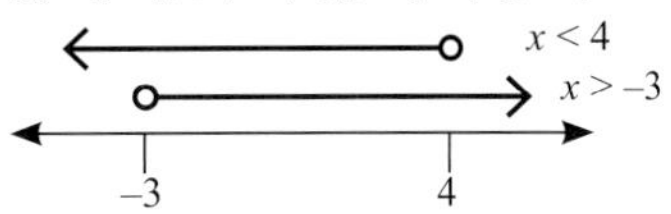

The answer will be the intersection of these solutions, i.e. $\{x : x < 4\} \cap \{x : x > -3\}$

The solutions overlap between –3 and 4, so this is the same as $\{x : -3 < x < 4\}$

Q8 **a)** $2x \ge 3x - 5 \Rightarrow -x \ge -5 \Rightarrow x \le 5$
$3x - 2 \ge x - 6 \Rightarrow 2x \ge -4 \Rightarrow x \ge -2$

Solution: $-2 \le x \le 5$

b) $5x + 1 \le 11 \Rightarrow 5x \le 10 \Rightarrow x \le 2$
$2x - 3 < 5x - 6 \Rightarrow -3x < -3 \Rightarrow x > 1$

Solution: $1 < x \le 2$

c) $2x - 1 \le 3x - 5 \Rightarrow -x \le -4 \Rightarrow x \ge 4$
$5x - 6 > x + 22 \Rightarrow 4x > 28 \Rightarrow x > 7$

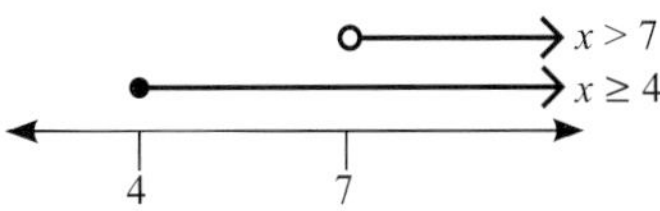

Solution: $x > 7$
Only these values satisfy both of the inequalities.

d) $3x + 5 < x + 1 \Rightarrow 2x < -4 \Rightarrow x < -2$
$6x - 1 \ge 3x + 5 \Rightarrow 3x \ge 6 \Rightarrow x \ge 2$

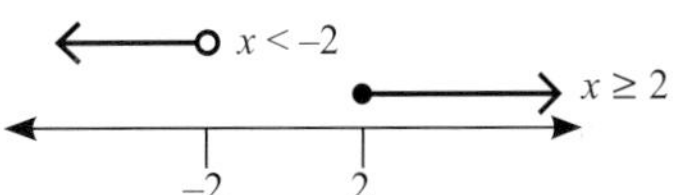

There is no solution that satisfies both inequalities.
The solutions don't overlap on the number line.

Q9 $4x - 2 > x + 4 \Rightarrow 3x > 6 \Rightarrow x > 2$
$4x - 16 < 19 - 3x \Rightarrow 7x < 35 \Rightarrow x < 5$
The set of values which satisfy both inequalities is $\{x : x > 2 \text{ and } x < 5\} = \{x : 2 < x < 5\}$
[3 marks available — 1 mark for solving one inequality, 1 mark for solving the second inequality, 1 mark for the correct answer (expressed as a single inequality, with or without set notation)]

Q10 $P > 73 \Rightarrow \frac{3t+5}{4} + \frac{2t-1}{5} > 73$
$\Rightarrow 5(3t + 5) + 4(2t - 1) > 1460$
$\Rightarrow 23t + 21 > 1460 \Rightarrow t > \frac{1439}{23}$
[3 marks available — 1 mark for a correct method, 1 mark for a correct simplification, 1 mark for the correct answer]

Q11 $\frac{6x+5}{3} < \frac{3-2x}{5} + 2(x + 7)$
$\Rightarrow 5(6x + 5) < 3(3 - 2x) + 30(x + 7)$
$\Rightarrow 30x + 25 < 9 - 6x + 30x + 210$
$\Rightarrow 6x < 194 \Rightarrow x < \frac{97}{3}$
In set notation, this is $\{x : x < \frac{97}{3}\}$
[3 marks available — 1 mark for a correct method, 1 mark for a correct simplification, 1 mark for the correct answer in set notation]

Q12 $3 + x\sqrt{7} < 2x - 3 \Rightarrow x(\sqrt{7} - 2) < -6 \Rightarrow x < -\frac{6}{\sqrt{7} - 2}$

$\Rightarrow x < -\frac{6}{\sqrt{7}-2} \times \frac{\sqrt{7}+2}{\sqrt{7}+2} \Rightarrow x < -\frac{6(\sqrt{7}+2)}{7-4}$

$\Rightarrow x < -2\sqrt{7} - 4$

[3 marks available — 1 mark for rearranging to an inequality with x on one side, 1 mark for attempting to rationalise the denominator, 1 mark for the correct answer]

Q13 a) $a, b > 0$, so $ab > 0$. So multiplying both sides of the inequality by ab does not change the direction of the inequality symbol.

So: $\frac{1}{a} < \frac{1}{b} \Rightarrow \frac{ab}{a} < \frac{ab}{b} \Rightarrow b < a \Rightarrow a > b$

[2 marks available — 1 mark for multiplication by ab (or by a and b in two steps) with justification, 1 mark for simplifying to show the correct result]

b) $\frac{1}{3x+2} < \frac{3}{5x+11} \Rightarrow \frac{1}{3x+2} < \frac{1}{\left(\frac{5x+11}{3}\right)}$

As $x > 0$, both denominators are > 0, so using part a):

$3x + 2 > \frac{5x+11}{3} \Rightarrow 9x + 6 > 5x + 11$

$\Rightarrow 4x > 5 \Rightarrow x > \frac{5}{4}$

[3 marks available — 1 mark for correctly using part a), 1 mark for a correct method of simplifying, 1 mark for the correct answer]

Q14 $3x - 2y + 7 = 0 \Rightarrow y = \frac{3x+7}{2}$

$5y + 3 = 9x \Rightarrow y = \frac{9x-3}{5}$

The graph of $3x - 2y + 7 = 0$ is above the graph of $5y + 3 = 9x$ when $\frac{3x+7}{2} > \frac{9x-3}{5}$

$\Rightarrow 15x + 35 > 18x - 6 \Rightarrow 3x < 41 \Rightarrow x < \frac{41}{3}$

[3 marks available — 1 mark for a correct method, 1 mark for a correct simplification, 1 mark for the correct answer]

Exercise 5.2 — Quadratic Inequalities

Q1 a) $-3 < x < 1$

b) $x < 0$ or $x > 4$

c) $2x^2 \geq 5 - 9x \Rightarrow 2x^2 + 9x - 5 \geq 0$

$\Rightarrow x \leq -5$ or $x \geq \frac{1}{2}$

d) $x < 1 - \sqrt{6}$ or $x > 1 + \sqrt{6}$

Q2 a) Solve the equation $x^2 = 4$ to find the x-intercepts:

$x^2 = 4 \Rightarrow x^2 - 4 = 0 \Rightarrow (x-2)(x+2) = 0$

$x = -2$ or $x = 2$

Solution: $x^2 \leq 4 \Rightarrow x^2 - 4 \leq 0 \Rightarrow -2 \leq x \leq 2$

In set notation, this is either $\{x : -2 \leq x \leq 2\}$ or $\{x : x \geq -2\} \cap \{x : x \leq 2\}$

b) $13x = 3x^2 + 4 \Rightarrow -3x^2 + 13x - 4 = 0 \Rightarrow 3x^2 - 13x + 4 = 0$

$\Rightarrow (3x-1)(x-4) = 0 \Rightarrow x = \frac{1}{3}$ or $x = 4$

Solution: $13x < 3x^2 + 4 \Rightarrow -3x^2 + 13x - 4 < 0$

$\Rightarrow x < \frac{1}{3}$ or $x > 4$

In set notation, this is $\left\{x : x < \frac{1}{3}\right\} \cup \{x : x > 4\}$

c) $x^2 + 4 = 6x \Rightarrow x^2 - 6x + 4 = 0$

$\Rightarrow x = \frac{6 \pm \sqrt{36-16}}{2} = \frac{6 \pm \sqrt{20}}{2} = \frac{6 \pm 2\sqrt{5}}{2}$

$\Rightarrow x = 3 \pm \sqrt{5}$

Solution: $x^2 + 4 < 6x \Rightarrow x^2 - 6x + 4 < 0$

$\Rightarrow 3 - \sqrt{5} < x < 3 + \sqrt{5}$

In set notation, this is either $\{x : 3 - \sqrt{5} < x < 3 + \sqrt{5}\}$ or $\{x : x > 3 - \sqrt{5}\} \cap \{x : x < 3 + \sqrt{5}\}$

d) $7x = 4 - 2x^2 \Rightarrow -2x^2 - 7x + 4 = 0$

$\Rightarrow (x+4)(-2x+1) = 0 \Rightarrow x = -4$ or $x = \frac{1}{2}$

Solution: $7x > 4 - 2x^2 \Rightarrow 0 > -2x^2 - 7x + 4$

$\Rightarrow x < -4$ or $x > \frac{1}{2}$

In set notation, this is $\{x : x < -4\} \cup \left\{x : x > \frac{1}{2}\right\}$

Q3 a) $x^2 + 5x - 6 = 0 \Rightarrow (x+6)(x-1) = 0$

$\Rightarrow x = -6$ or $x = 1$

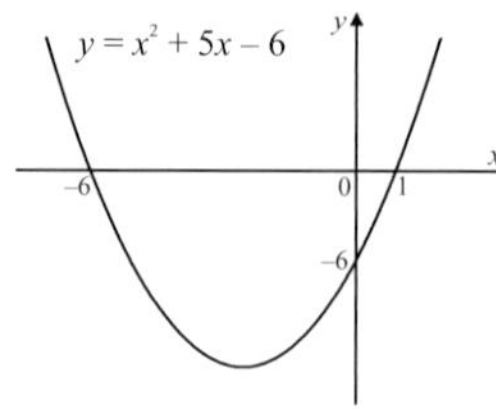

$x^2 + 5x - 6 \geq 0 \Rightarrow x \leq -6$ or $x \geq 1$

b) $x^2 - 3x + 2 = 0 \Rightarrow (x-1)(x-2) = 0 \Rightarrow x = 1$ or $x = 2$

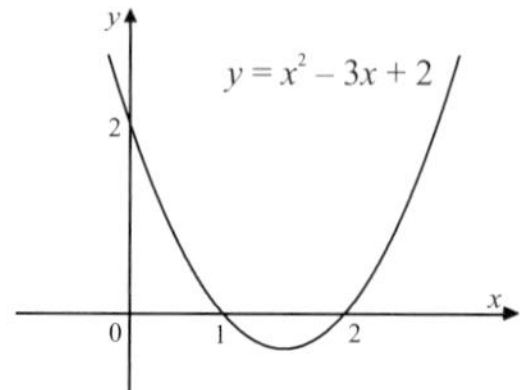

$x^2 - 3x + 2 < 0 \Rightarrow 1 < x < 2$

c) $6 - 5x = 6x^2 \Rightarrow -6x^2 - 5x + 6 = 0 \Rightarrow 6x^2 + 5x - 6 = 0$

$\Rightarrow (3x-2)(2x+3) = 0 \Rightarrow x = \frac{2}{3}$ or $x = -\frac{3}{2}$

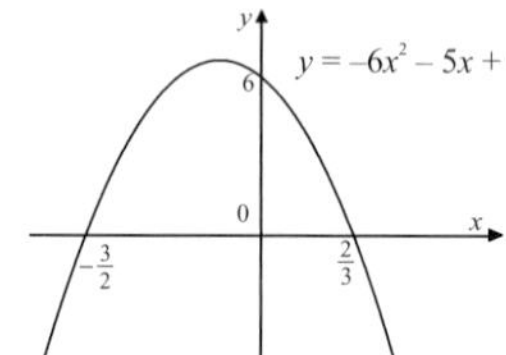

$6 - 5x > 6x^2 \Rightarrow -6x^2 - 5x + 6 > 0 \Rightarrow -\frac{3}{2} < x < \frac{2}{3}$

You could have rearranged the inequality into $6x^2 + 5x - 6 < 0$ and sketched the corresponding graph. You'd get the same final answer, but the graph would be the other way up.

d) $x^2 - 5x + 24 = 5x + 3 \Rightarrow x^2 - 10x + 21 = 0$

$\Rightarrow (x-3)(x-7) = 0 \Rightarrow x = 3$ or $x = 7$

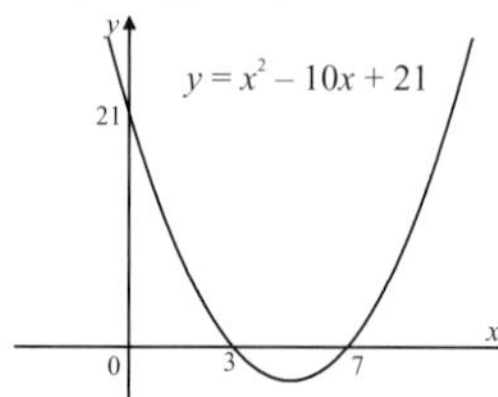

$x^2 - 5x + 24 \leq 5x + 3 \Rightarrow x^2 - 10x + 21 \leq 0 \Rightarrow 3 \leq x \leq 7$

e) $36 - 4x^2 = 0 \Rightarrow 9 - x^2 = 0 \Rightarrow (3-x)(3+x) = 0 \Rightarrow x = \pm 3$

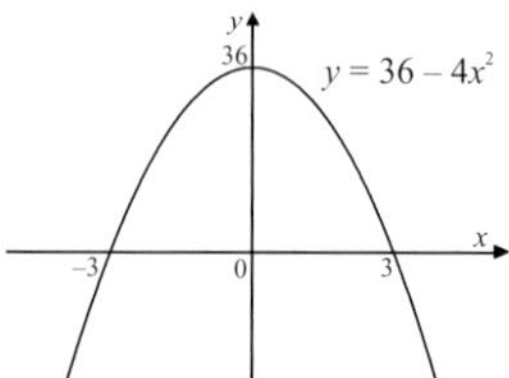

$36 - 4x^2 \leq 0 \Rightarrow x \leq -3$ or $x \geq 3$

f) $x^2 - 6x + 3 = 0 \Rightarrow x = \frac{6 \pm \sqrt{36-12}}{2}$

$\Rightarrow x = \frac{6 \pm \sqrt{24}}{2} = \frac{6 \pm 2\sqrt{6}}{2} = 3 \pm \sqrt{6}$

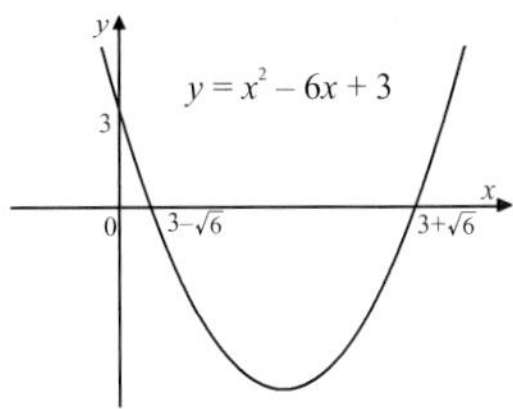

$x^2 - 6x + 3 > 0 \Rightarrow x < 3 - \sqrt{6}$ or $x > 3 + \sqrt{6}$

g) $x^2 - x + 3 = 0 \Rightarrow x = \dfrac{1 \pm \sqrt{1-12}}{2}$

$\Rightarrow$ no root because ($\sqrt{-11}$ is not real) so the graph doesn't cross the x-axis.

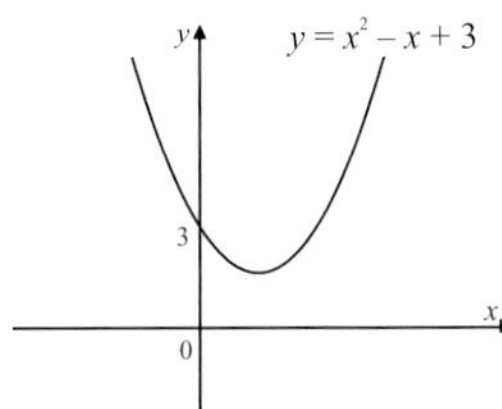

$x^2 - x + 3 > 0 \Rightarrow x$ can take any real value

h) $6 = 5x^2 + 13x \Rightarrow -5x^2 - 13x + 6 = 0 \Rightarrow 5x^2 + 13x - 6 = 0$

$\Rightarrow (5x - 2)(x + 3) = 0 \Rightarrow x = \frac{2}{5}$ or $x = -3$

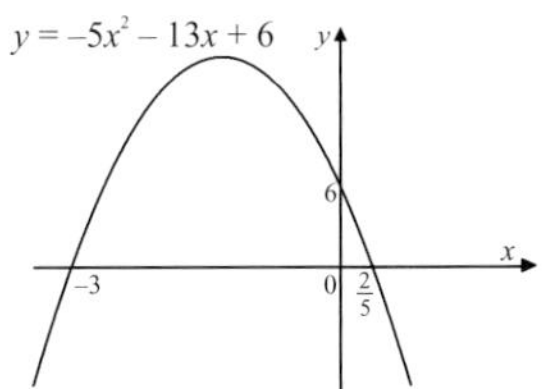

$6 \geq 5x^2 + 13x \Rightarrow -5x^2 - 13x + 6 \geq 0 \Rightarrow -3 \leq x \leq \frac{2}{5}$

Again, you might have rearranged the inequality differently and ended up with the graph the other way up.

i) $2x^2 = 3(x + 3) \Rightarrow 2x^2 - 3x - 9 = 0$

$\Rightarrow (2x + 3)(x - 3) = 0 \Rightarrow x = -\frac{3}{2}$ or $x = 3$

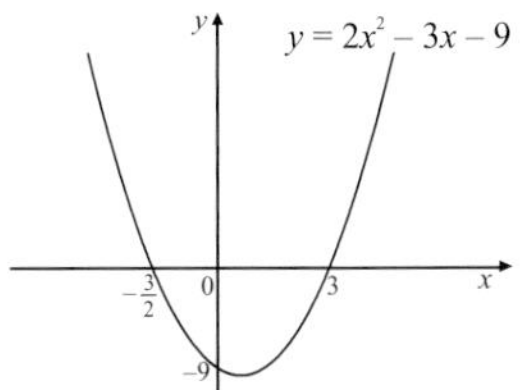

$2x^2 > 3(x + 3) \Rightarrow 2x^2 - 3x - 9 > 0 \Rightarrow x < -\frac{3}{2}$ or $x > 3$

j) $(x + 4)^2 = 5x \Rightarrow x^2 + 8x + 16 = 5x$

$\Rightarrow x^2 + 3x + 16 = 0 \Rightarrow x = \dfrac{-3 \pm \sqrt{9-64}}{2}$

$\Rightarrow$ no root because ($\sqrt{-55}$) is not real, so the graph doesn't cross the x-axis

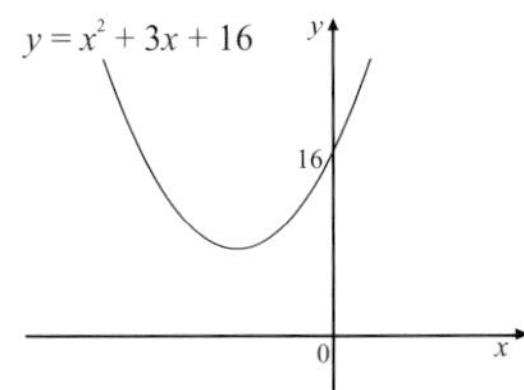

$(x + 4)^2 \leq 5x \Rightarrow x^2 + 3x + 16 \leq 0$

$\Rightarrow$ there are no real solutions for x

k) $x^2 + 5x = \frac{1}{2} \Rightarrow x^2 + 5x - \frac{1}{2} = 0 \Rightarrow x = \dfrac{-5 \pm \sqrt{25+2}}{2}$

$\Rightarrow x = -\frac{5}{2} - \frac{3}{2}\sqrt{3}$ or $x = -\frac{5}{2} + \frac{3}{2}\sqrt{3}$

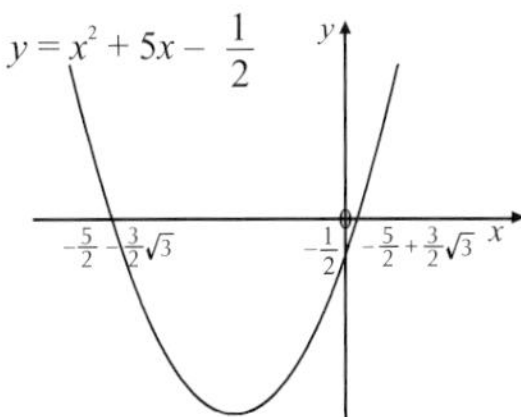

$x^2 + 5x < \frac{1}{2} \Rightarrow x^2 + 5x - \frac{1}{2} < 0$

$\Rightarrow -\frac{5}{2} - \frac{3}{2}\sqrt{3} < x < -\frac{5}{2} + \frac{3}{2}\sqrt{3}$

l) $\frac{3}{4}x^2 = 1 + \frac{1}{4}x \Rightarrow \frac{3}{4}x^2 - \frac{1}{4}x - 1 = 0$

$\Rightarrow (x + 1)(\frac{3}{4}x - 1) = 0 \Rightarrow x = -1$ or $x = \frac{4}{3}$

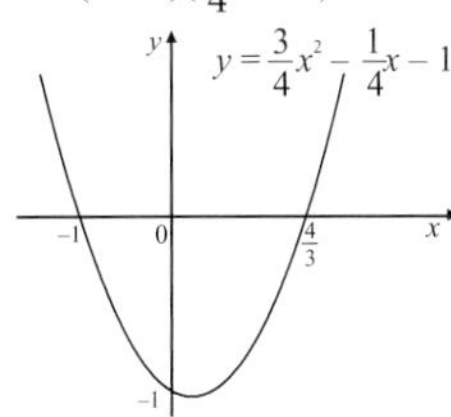

$\frac{3}{4}x^2 \geq 1 + \frac{1}{4}x \Rightarrow (x + 1)(\frac{3}{4}x - 1) \geq 0 \Rightarrow x \leq 1$ or $x \geq \frac{4}{3}$

Q4 **a)** $\frac{1}{x} > 5 \Rightarrow x > 5x^2 \Rightarrow 5x^2 - x < 0 \Rightarrow x(5x - 1) < 0$

$\Rightarrow 0 < x < \frac{1}{5}$, or in set notation, $\{x : 0 < x < \frac{1}{5}\}$

b) $7 > \frac{3}{x} \Rightarrow 7x^2 > 3x \Rightarrow 7x^2 - 3x > 0$

$\Rightarrow x(7x - 3) > 0 \Rightarrow x < 0$ or $x > \frac{3}{7}$,

or in set notation, $\{x : x < 0\} \cup \{x : x > \frac{3}{7}\}$

c) $-5 > \frac{2}{x} \Rightarrow -5x^2 > 2x \Rightarrow 0 > 5x^2 + 2x$

$\Rightarrow 0 > x(5x + 2) \Rightarrow -\frac{2}{5} < x < 0$

or in set notation, $\{x : -\frac{2}{5} < x < 0\}$

d) $-\frac{6}{x} > 1 \Rightarrow -6x > x^2 \Rightarrow 0 > x^2 + 6x$

$\Rightarrow 0 > x(x + 6) \Rightarrow -6 < x < 0$

or in set notation, $\{x : -6 < x < 0\}$

Q5 **a)** $x^2 - 6x - 7 < 0 \Rightarrow -1 < x < 7$

But $x \leq 4$, so the solution is $-1 < x \leq 4$. This is either $\{x : -1 < x \leq 4\}$ or $\{x : x > -1\} \cap \{x : x \leq 4\}$ in set notation.

b) $-2x^2 + 19x - 30 > 0 \Rightarrow 2 < x < \frac{15}{2}$

But $x > 5$, so the solution is $5 < x < \frac{15}{2}$. This is either $\left\{x : 5 < x < \frac{15}{2}\right\}$ or $\{x : x > 5\} \cap \left\{x : x < \frac{15}{2}\right\}$ in set notation.

c) $x^2 - x \leq 56 \Rightarrow x^2 - x - 56 \leq 0 \Rightarrow -7 \leq x \leq 8$

But $\frac{1}{x} + \frac{1}{x^2} > 0 \Rightarrow x + 1 > 0 \Rightarrow x > -1$,

so the solution is $-1 < x \leq 8$. This is either $\{x : -1 < x \leq 8\}$ or $\{x : x > -1\} \cap \{x : x \leq 8\}$ in set notation.

d) $4x \leq \frac{x^2}{3} \Rightarrow -\frac{x^2}{3} + 4x \leq 0 \Rightarrow x \leq 0$ or $x \geq 12$

$5x - 2 < 4x + 8 \Rightarrow x < 10$

So the solution is $x \leq 0$. This is $\{x : x \leq 0\}$ in set notation.

Q6 The area of the office will be $(x - 9)(x - 6)$ m^2, so use this to form an inequality for the necessary floor space:

$(x - 9)(x - 6) \geq 28 \Rightarrow x^2 - 15x + 54 \geq 28 \Rightarrow x^2 - 15x + 26 \geq 0$

Find the x-intercepts of the graph:

$x^2 - 15x + 26 = 0 \Rightarrow (x - 2)(x - 13) = 0 \Rightarrow x = 2$ and $x = 13$

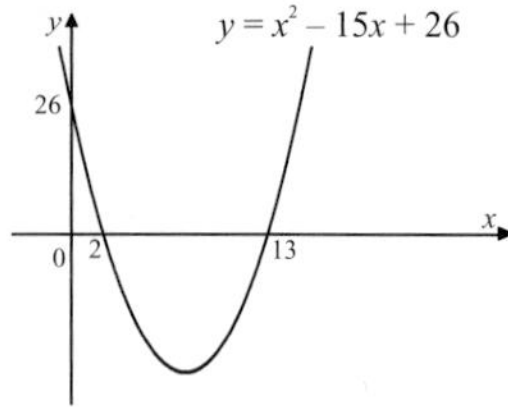

$x^2 - 15x + 26 \geq 0 \Rightarrow x \leq 2$ or $x \geq 13$
But $x \leq 2$ would mean that the sides of the office would have negative lengths, so the only possible values of x are $x \geq 13$ m.

Q7 **a)** $kx^2 - 6x + k = 0 \Rightarrow a = k, b = -6, c = k$
$b^2 - 4ac = (-6)^2 - (4 \times k \times k) = 36 - 4k^2$
The original equation has two distinct real solutions, so the discriminant must be > 0. So $36 - 4k^2 > 0$.
Factorise the quadratic: $36 - 4k^2 = 4(3 + k)(3 - k)$
So the graph is n-shaped and crosses the k-axis at $k = 3$ and $k = -3$.

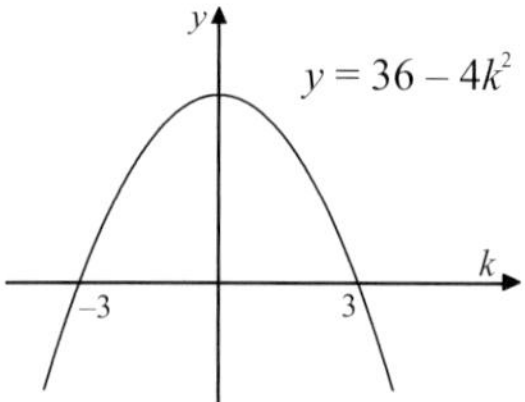

Solution: $-3 < k < 3$

b) $x^2 - kx + k = 0 \Rightarrow a = 1, b = -k, c = k$
$b^2 - 4ac = (-k)^2 - (4 \times 1 \times k) = k^2 - 4k$
The original equation has no real solutions, so the discriminant must be < 0. So $k^2 - 4k < 0$
Factorise the quadratic: $k^2 - 4k = k(k - 4)$
So the graph is u-shaped and crosses the k-axis at $k = 0$ and $k = 4$.

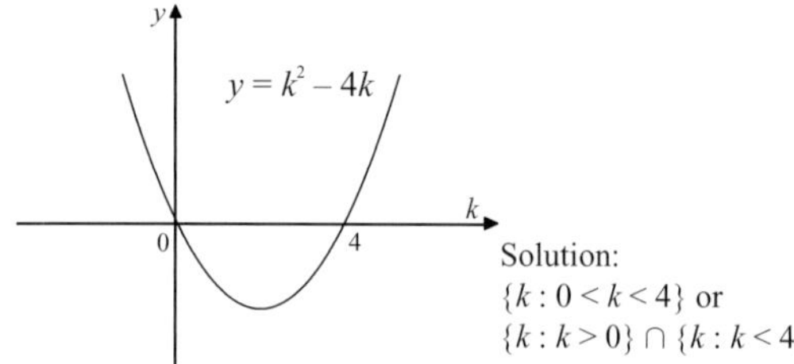

Solution:
$\{k : 0 < k < 4\}$ or
$\{k : k > 0\} \cap \{k : k < 4\}$

Q8 $4(3 - x) \geq 13 - 5x \Rightarrow 12 - 4x \geq 13 - 5x \Rightarrow x \geq 1$
$7x + 6 \geq 3x^2 \Rightarrow -3x^2 + 7x + 6 \geq 0$
$-3x^2 + 7x + 6 = 0 \Rightarrow 3x^2 - 7x - 6 = 0 \Rightarrow (3x + 2)(x - 3) = 0$
$\Rightarrow x = -\frac{2}{3}$ or $x = 3$

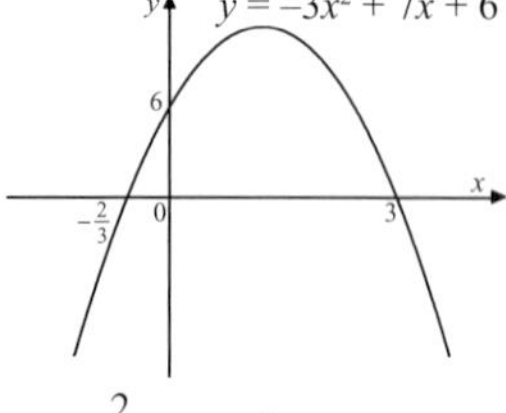

$\Rightarrow -\frac{2}{3} \leq x \leq 3$
So, for both inequalities:

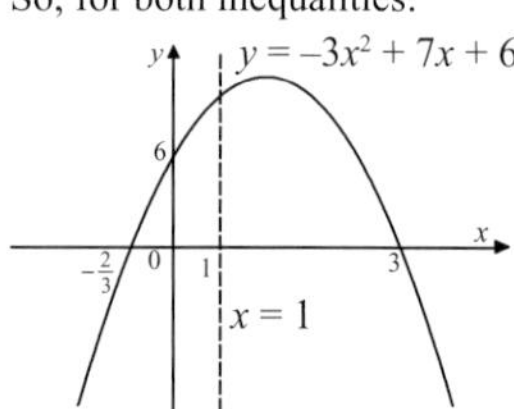

Solution that satisfies both inequalities: $1 \leq x \leq 3$
Your graphs might be the other way up if you rearranged the inequality differently at the start.

Exercise 5.3 — Graphing Inequalities

Q1 **a)** If (2, 4) lies in the region that satisfies $3y > 8x - 3$ then $3(4) > 8(2) - 3 \Rightarrow 12 > 13$.
This is false so the statement is false.

b) If (–3, –5) lies outside the region that satisfies $4y + x^2 \leq 3$ then it lies within the region that satisfies $4y + x^2 > 3$, so $4(-5) + (-3)^2 > 3 \Rightarrow -20 + 9 > 3 \Rightarrow -11 > 3$.
This is false so the statement is false.

c) If (8, –4) lies in the region that satisfies $y^2 + (x + 6)^2 \geq 68$ then $(-4)^2 + (8 + 6)^2 \geq 68$
$\Rightarrow 16 + 196 \geq 68 \Rightarrow 212 \geq 68$.
This is true so the statement is true.

d) If (1, 3) lies in the region that satisfies $x + 2y > 4$ then $1 + 2(3) > 4 \Rightarrow 7 > 4$.
If (1, 3) is in the region that satisfies $3x^2 > 20 - 4y$ then $3(1)^2 > 20 - 4(3) \Rightarrow 3 > 8$.
The first part of the statement is true, but the second part is false, so the statement is false.
If the point isn't in the region that satisfies all the inequalities in the statement then the statement is false.

e) If $\left(\frac{1}{2}, \frac{3}{2}\right)$ lies outside the region that satisfies $y^2 < 10 - 8x^2$ then it lies within the region that satisfies $y^2 \geq 10 - 8x^2$,
so $\left(\frac{3}{2}\right)^2 \geq 10 - 8\left(\frac{1}{2}\right)^2 \Rightarrow \frac{9}{4} \geq 10 - 2 \Rightarrow \frac{9}{4} \geq 8$.
If $\left(\frac{1}{2}, \frac{3}{2}\right)$ lies outside the region that satisfies $3x + 4y \geq 6$ then it lies within the region that satisfies $3x + 4y < 6$,
so $3\left(\frac{1}{2}\right) + 4\left(\frac{3}{2}\right) < 6 \Rightarrow \frac{3}{2} + \frac{12}{2} < 6 \Rightarrow \frac{15}{2} < 6$.
Both parts of the statement are false, so the statement is false.
It isn't strictly necessary to show that the second part is also false — the statement is shown to be false from the first inequality.

Q2 **a)** The shaded region is above the solid line $y = -\frac{1}{4}x + 1$ and below the dotted curve $y = 6 - x + x^2$. So the shaded region is defined by $y \geq -\frac{1}{4}x + 1$ and $y < 6 + x - x^2$.

b) The shaded region is above the solid line $y = \frac{3}{2}x + 2$, below the dotted line $y = 14 - \frac{1}{2}x$ and above the curve $y = \frac{1}{2}x^2 - 5x + \frac{9}{2}$. So the shaded region is defined by $y \geq \frac{3}{2}x + 2$, $y < 14 - \frac{1}{2}x$ and $y > \frac{1}{2}x^2 - 5x + \frac{9}{2}$.

Q3 **a)** Write as equations and rearrange: $y = -x + 5$ (dotted), $y = -2x + 4$ (solid), $y = -\frac{1}{2}x + 3$ (dotted)

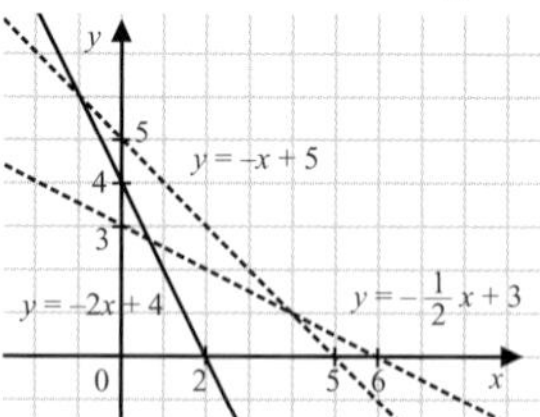

Try (0, 0) in each inequality: $x + y < 5 \Rightarrow 0 < 5$ — this is true so shade this side.
$2x + y \geq 4 \Rightarrow 0 \geq 4$ — this is false so shade the other side.
$x + 2y > 6 \Rightarrow 0 > 6$ — this is false so shade the other side.
So the final region is:

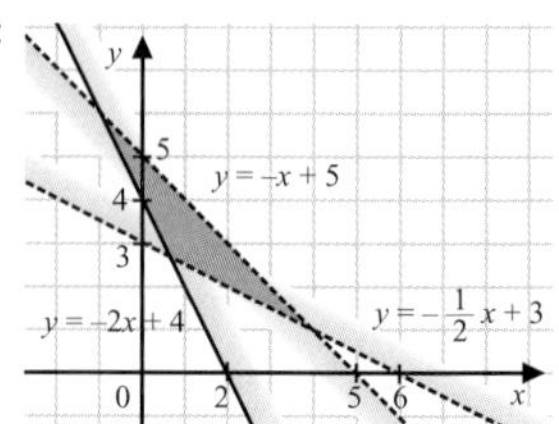

b) Write as equations and rearrange:
$x = 4$ (solid), $y = 7$ (solid), $y = -x + 4$ (dotted)

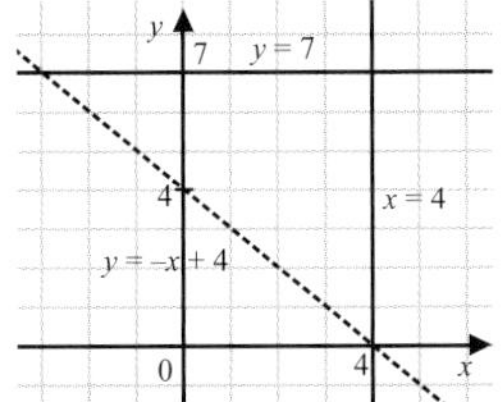

Try (0, 0) in each inequality: $x \leq 4 \Rightarrow 0 \leq 4$
— this is true so shade this side.
$y \leq 7 \Rightarrow 0 \leq 7$ — this is true so shade this side.
$x + y > 4 \Rightarrow 0 > 4$ — this is false so shade the other side.

So the final region is:

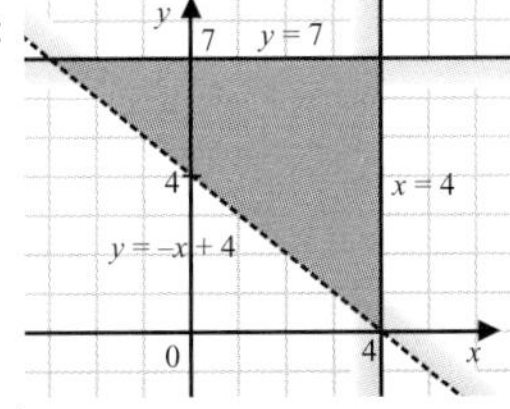

c) Write as equations and rearrange:
$y = x^2$ (dotted), $y = x + 3$ (solid)

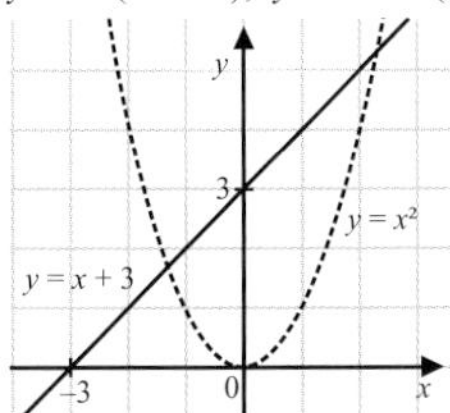

You can't use (0, 0) as it lies on one of the lines, so try (0, 1) in each inequality: $y > x^2 \Rightarrow 1 > 0$
— this is true so shade this side.
$x - y \geq -3 \Rightarrow -1 \geq -3$ — this is true so shade this side.

So the final region is:

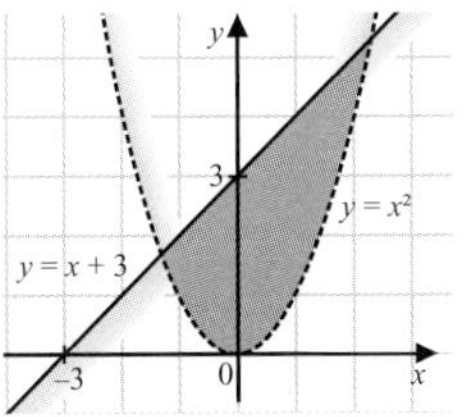

d) Write as equations and rearrange:
$y = x^2 + 2$ (solid), $y = 2x^2 - 2$ (dotted)

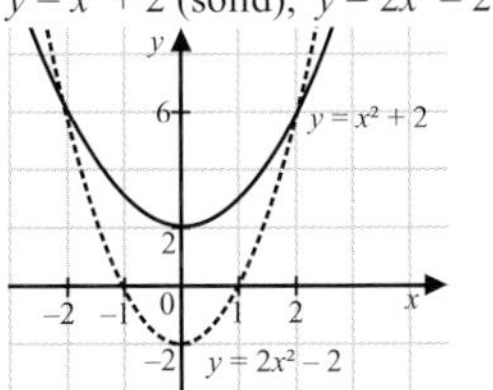

Try (0, 0) in each inequality: $y - 2 \leq x^2 \Rightarrow -2 \leq 0$
— this is true so shade this side.
$2x^2 - y < 2 \Rightarrow 0 < 2$ — this is true so shade this side.

So the final region is:

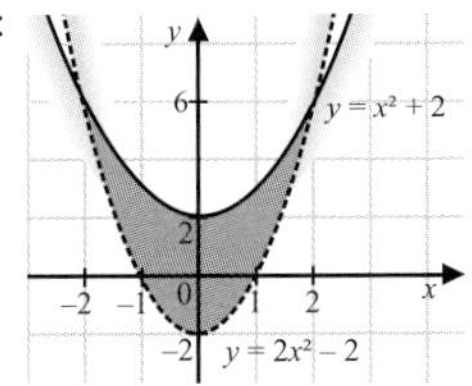

e) Write as equations and rearrange:
$y = 4x^2 + 5$ (dotted), $y = -\frac{3}{5}x + 8$ (solid)

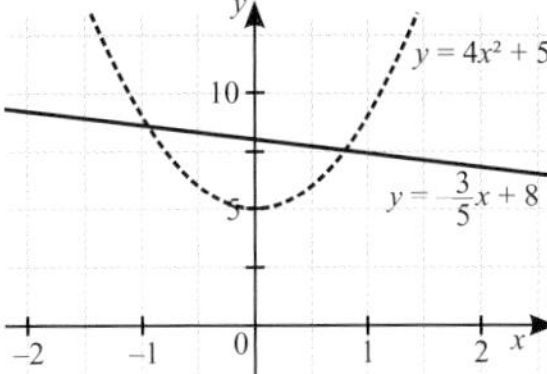

Try (0, 0) in each inequality: $4x^2 > y - 5 \Rightarrow 0 > -5$
— this is true so shade this side.
$3x + 5y \leq 40 \Rightarrow 0 \leq 40$ — this is true so shade this side.

So the final region is:

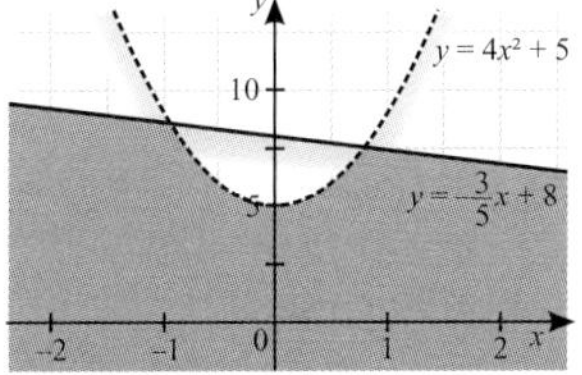

f) Write as equations and rearrange:
$y = -2x^2 + 3x + 5$ (dotted), $y = \frac{2}{5}x + 1$ (dotted)

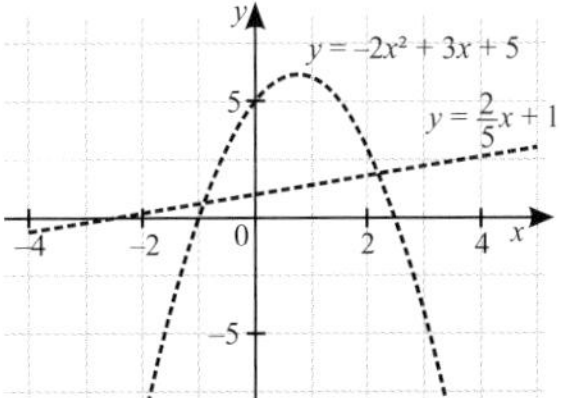

Try (0, 0) in each inequality: $5y > 2x + 5 \Rightarrow 0 > 5$
— this is false so shade the other side.
$2y + 4x^2 < 6x + 10 \Rightarrow 0 < 10$ — this is true so shade this side.

So the final region is:

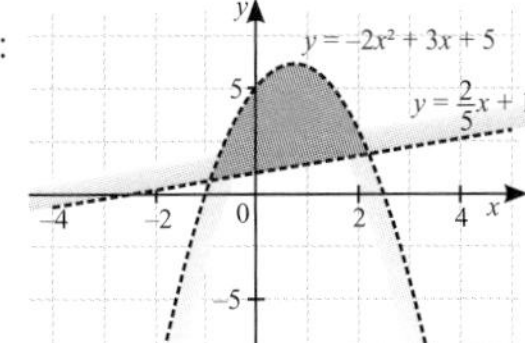

Q4 a) A and B both lie on the line $y = 2x + 2$,
so they both satisfy the inequality $y \geq 2x + 2$.
A lies on the line $x + y - 7 = 0$,
so it doesn't satisfy the inequality $x + y - 7 > 0$.
Therefore, A does not lie in the region R.
B lies on the line $x = 5$,
so it also satisfies the inequality $x \leq 5$.
$x = 5 \Rightarrow y = 2 \times 5 + 2 = 12$, so B has coordinates (5, 12).
$5 + 12 - 7 = 10 > 0$, so B satisfies $x + y - 7 > 0$.
Therefore, B lies in the region R.
[2 marks available — 1 mark for stating A is not in R with correct justification, 1 mark for stating that B is in R with correct justification]

b)

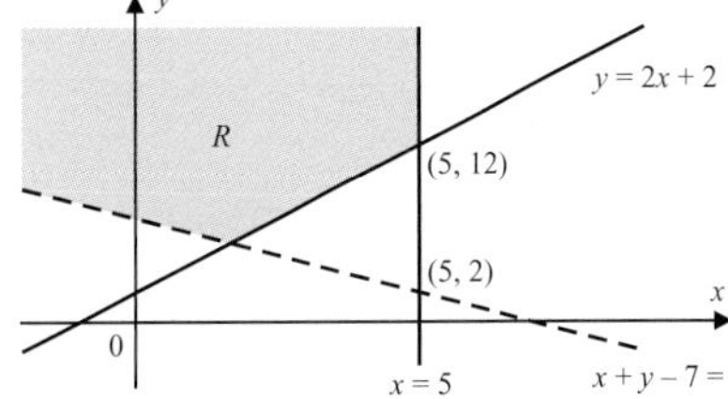

[4 marks available — 1 mark for each correct line (solid or dotted as appropriate), 1 mark for the correct shaded region]

Q5 a) $x = 0 \Rightarrow y + 2 \times 0 = 6 \Rightarrow y = 6$
$y = 0 \Rightarrow 0 + 2x = 6 \Rightarrow x = 3$
So $y + 2x = 6$ intercepts the axes at (0, 6) and (3, 0).
[1 mark for both correct intercepts]

b) Completing the square on $y = 2x^2 + 5x - 9$ gives
$y = 2\left(x + \frac{5}{4}\right)^2 - \frac{97}{8} \Rightarrow$ turning point is $\left(-\frac{5}{4}, -\frac{97}{8}\right)$
Setting $x = 0$ gives $y = -9$, so the y-intercept is $(0, -9)$.
[2 marks available — 1 mark for correct turning point, 1 mark for correct y-intercept]

c)

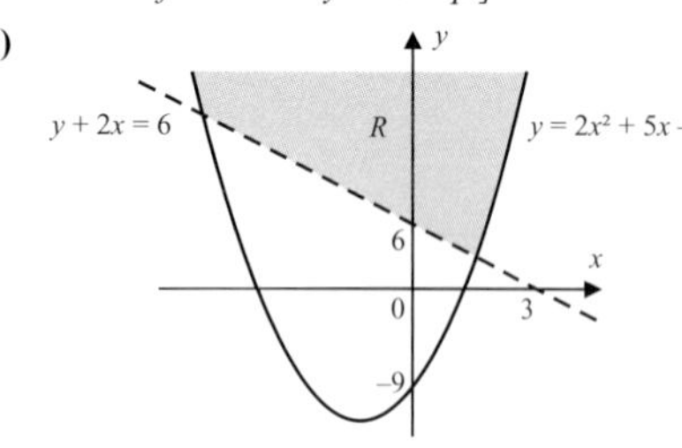

[3 marks available — 1 mark for the correct quadratic graph using a solid line, 1 mark for the correct straight-line graph using a dotted line, 1 mark for the correct region shaded]

Q6 *A*: Write as equations and rearrange:
$y = 6 - \frac{1}{2}x,\ y = \frac{3}{2}x + 2,\ y = 2$
Then plot these lines (all solid):

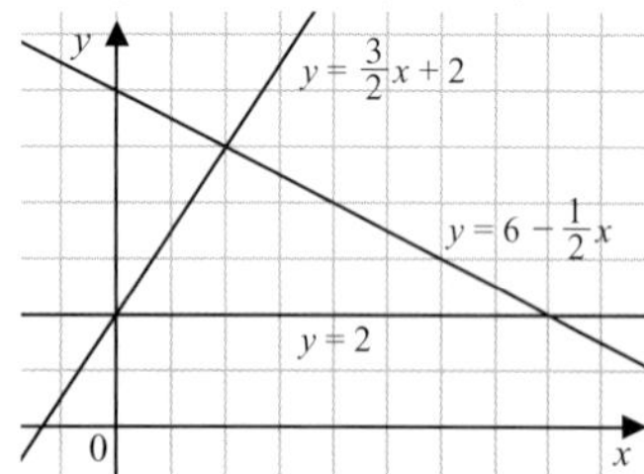

Try (0, 0) in each inequality:
$x + 2y \leq 12 \Rightarrow 0 \leq 12$ — this is true so shade the other side.
$2y - 3x \leq 4 \Rightarrow 0 \leq 4$ — this is true so shade the other side.
$y \geq 2 \Rightarrow 0 \geq 2$ — this is false so shade this side.

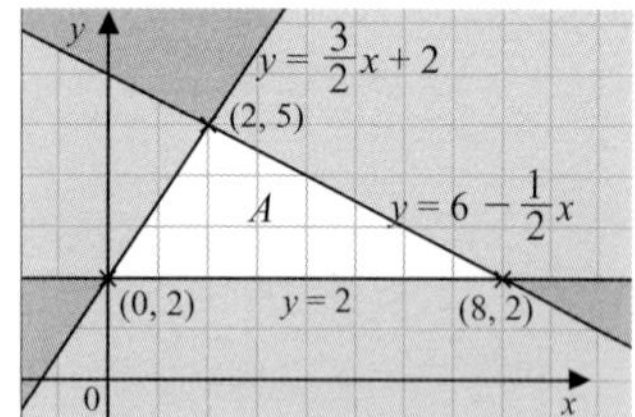

B: Write as equations and rearrange: $x = 3,\ y = 2x - 9,$
$y = 5 - \frac{1}{3}x$. Then plot these lines (all solid):

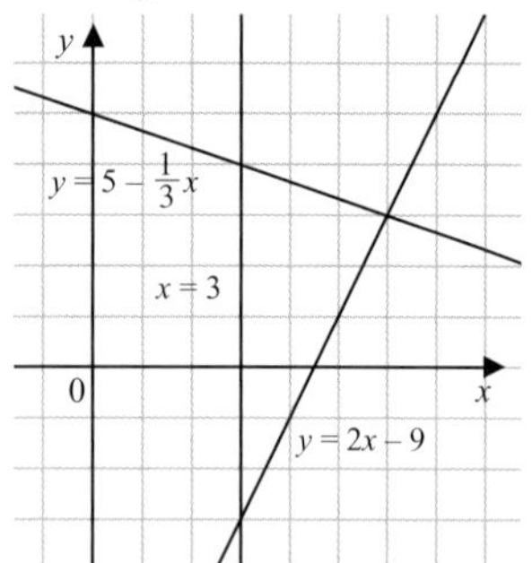

Try (0, 0) in each inequality: $x \geq 3 \Rightarrow 0 \geq 3$
This is false so shade this side.
$2x \leq y + 9 \Rightarrow 0 \leq 9$. This is true so shade the other side.
$x + 3y \leq 15 \Rightarrow 0 \leq 15$. This is true so shade the other side.

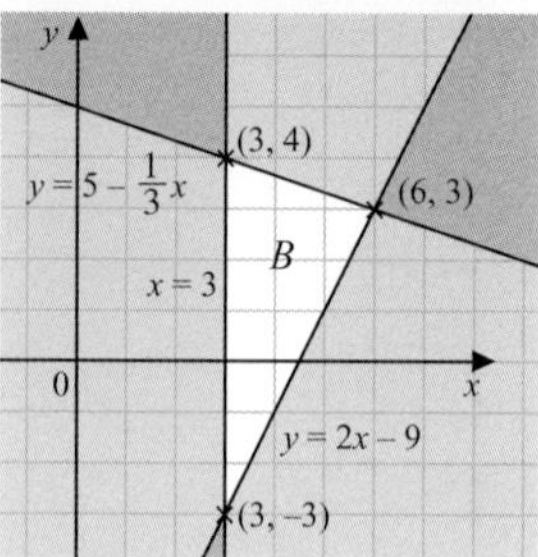

The coordinates of the vertices of triangles *A* and *B* can be read off the graphs. In order to decide which region is larger, calculate the area of each triangle.
You can also find the vertices by equating the lines to find their points of intersection.
A has base $8 - 0 = 8$ and height $5 - 2 = 3$
$\Rightarrow$ Area $A = \frac{1}{2} \times 8 \times 3 = 12$
B has base $4 - (-3) = 7$ and height $6 - 3 = 3$
$\Rightarrow$ Area $B = \frac{1}{2} \times 7 \times 3 = 10.5$
So region *A* is larger.

Q7 a) Completing the square gives:
$y = 2x^2 - 10x + \frac{21}{2} \Rightarrow y = 2\left(x - \frac{5}{2}\right)^2 - 2$
$y = \frac{3}{4} + 5x - x^2 \Rightarrow y = -\left(x - \frac{5}{2}\right)^2 + 7$
So the turning points are $\left(\frac{5}{2}, -2\right)$ and $\left(\frac{5}{2}, 7\right)$ respectively.
[3 marks available — 1 mark for a correct method, 1 mark for one correct turning point, 1 mark for the second correct turning point]

b)

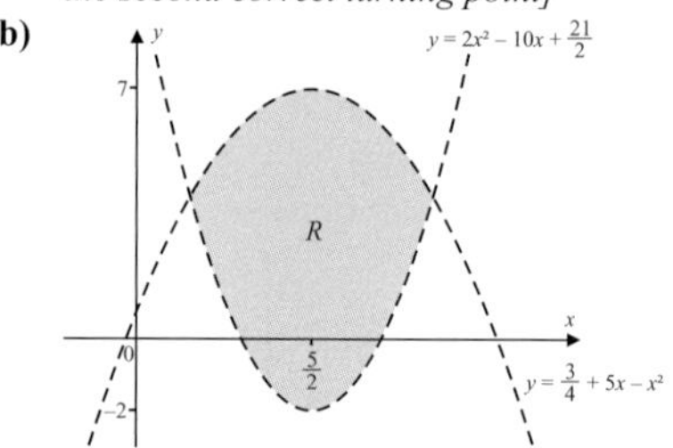

[3 marks available — 1 mark for each quadratic with correct curve shape using dotted lines, 1 mark for the correct region shaded]

Q8 a)

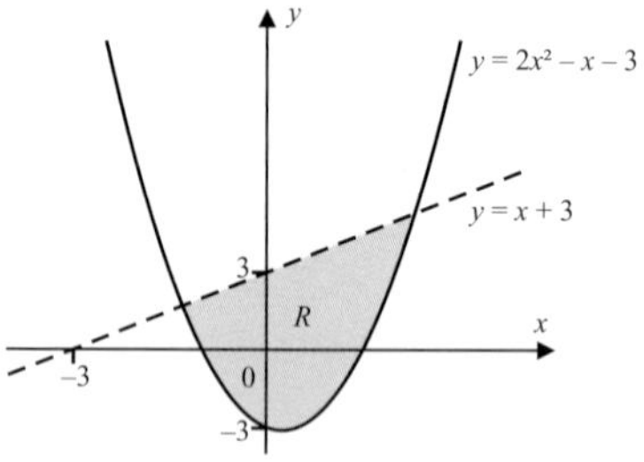

[3 marks available — 1 mark for the correct quadratic graph using a solid line, 1 mark for the correct straight-line graph using a dotted line, 1 mark for the correct region shaded]

b) *S* is the part of region *R* that lies to the right of (but not on) the line $x = k$. Using the given x-coordinates for the points of intersection and the diagram in part a), *S* is empty when
$k \geq \frac{1+\sqrt{13}}{2}$, so it is only non-empty when $k < \frac{1+\sqrt{13}}{2}$.
[1 mark for correct range of values for k]

Q9 a) $3x + y \leq 42$

b) Write as equations and rearrange: $y = 12 - \frac{1}{2}x$, $y = 42 - 3x$

Plotting the graphs and testing the point (1, 1) in each inequality gives the region labelled R:

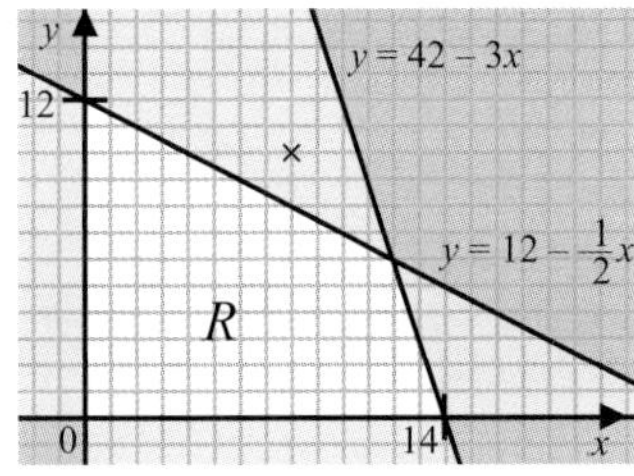

c) Checking the point (8, 10) on the graph (marked in b)) shows that it isn't in the possible region.

Test $x = 8$ and $y = 10$ in both inequalities:

Flour: $x + 2y = 8 + 20 = 28 > 24$

Eggs: $3x + y = 24 + 10 = 34 \leq 42$

So the bakery has enough eggs, but not enough flour to meet the order.

Exercise 5.4 — Simultaneous Equations — Both Linear

Q1 a)
① $2x - 3y = 3$
② $x + 3y = 6$
①+② $3x = 9 \Rightarrow x = 3$
$x = 3$ in ② $3 + 3y = 6 \Rightarrow 3y = 3 \Rightarrow y = 1$
So the solution is $x = 3$, $y = 1$

b)
① $3x + 2y = 7$
② $7x - y = -12$
②×2 $14x - 2y = -24$ ③
①+③ $17x = -17 \Rightarrow x = -1$
$x = -1$ in ① $-3 + 2y = 7 \Rightarrow 2y = 10 \Rightarrow y = 5$
So the solution is $x = -1$, $y = 5$

c)
① $4x + 3y = -4$
② $6x - 4y = 11$
①×3 $12x + 9y = -12$ ③
②×2 $12x - 8y = 22$ ④
③–④ $17y = -34 \Rightarrow y = -2$
$y = -2$ in ② $6x + 8 = 11 \Rightarrow 6x = 3 \Rightarrow x = \frac{1}{2}$
So the solution is $x = \frac{1}{2}$, $y = -2$

d)
① $7x - 6y = 4$
② $11x + 9y = -6$
①×3 $21x - 18y = 12$ ③
②×2 $22x + 18y = -12$ ④
③+④ $43x = 0 \Rightarrow x = 0$
$x = 0$ in ② $0 + 9y = -6 \Rightarrow y = -\frac{6}{9} = -\frac{2}{3}$
So the solution is $x = 0$, $y = -\frac{2}{3}$

e)
Rearrange ① $6x + 2y = 8$
Rearrange ② $4x + 3y = -3$
①×2 $12x + 4y = 16$ ③
②×3 $12x + 9y = -9$ ④
③–④ $-5y = 25 \Rightarrow y = -5$
$y = -5$ in ② $4x - 15 = -3 \Rightarrow 4x = 12 \Rightarrow x = 3$
So the solution is $x = 3$, $y = -5$

f)
Rearrange ① $2x + 18y = 21$
Rearrange ② $-3x - 14y = 14$
①×3 $6x + 54y = 63$ ③
②×2 $-6x - 28y = 28$ ④
③+④ $26y = 91 \Rightarrow y = \frac{7}{2}$
$y = \frac{7}{2}$ in ① $2x + 63 = 21 \Rightarrow 2x = -42$
$\Rightarrow x = -21$
So the solution is $x = -21$, $y = \frac{7}{2}$

g)
① $2x + 16y = 10$
Rearrange ② $3x + 64y = 5$
①×4 $8x + 64y = 40$ ③
②–③ $-5x = -35 \Rightarrow x = 7$
$x = 7$ in ① $14 + 16y = 10 \Rightarrow 16y = -4$
$\Rightarrow y = -\frac{1}{4}$
So the solution is $x = 7$, $y = -\frac{1}{4}$

h)
① $4x - 3y = 15$
Rearrange ② $-9x + 5y = 12$
①×5 $20x - 15y = 75$ ③
②×3 $-27x + 15y = 36$ ④
③+④ $-7x = 111 \Rightarrow x = -\frac{111}{7}$
$x = -\frac{111}{7}$ in ① $-\frac{444}{7} - 3y = 15$
$\Rightarrow 3y = -\frac{549}{7} \Rightarrow y = -\frac{183}{7}$
So the solution is $x = -\frac{111}{7}$, $y = -\frac{183}{7}$

Q2 a)
① $y = 2x - 3$
② $y = \frac{1}{2}x + 3$
②×4 $4y = 2x + 12$ ③
①–③ $-3y = -15 \Rightarrow y = 5$
$y = 5$ in ① $5 = 2x - 3 \Rightarrow 8 = 2x \Rightarrow x = 4$
So they intersect at (4, 5)

b)
① $y = -\frac{2}{3}x + 7$
② $y = \frac{1}{2}x + \frac{21}{2}$
①×3 $3y = -2x + 21$ ③
②×4 $4y = 2x + 42$ ④
③+④ $7y = 63 \Rightarrow y = 9$
$y = 9$ in ① $9 = -\frac{2}{3}x + 7$
$\Rightarrow 2 = -\frac{2}{3}x \Rightarrow x = -3$
So they intersect at (–3, 9)

c)
Rearrange ① $x + 2y = -5$
Rearrange ② $3x - 5y = 7$
①×3 $3x + 6y = -15$ ③
②–③ $-11y = 22 \Rightarrow y = -2$
$y = -2$ in ① $x - 4 = -5 \Rightarrow x = -1$
So they intersect at (–1, –2)

d)
① $2x - 3y = 7$
② $5x - \frac{15}{2}y = 9$
①×5 $10x - 15y = 35$ ③
②×2 $10x - 15y = 18$ ④
③–④ $0 = 17$
This is not possible — so these lines do not intersect.
The lines are actually parallel.

e)
Rearrange ① $8x + 3y = 10$
Rearrange ② $6x + 9y = 3$
①×3 $24x + 9y = 30$ ③
②–③ $-18x = -27 \Rightarrow x = \frac{3}{2}$
$x = \frac{3}{2}$ in ② $9 + 9y = 3$
$\Rightarrow 9y = -6 \Rightarrow y = -\frac{2}{3}$
So they intersect at $\left(\frac{3}{2}, -\frac{2}{3}\right)$

f) ① $7x - 5y = 15$

Rearrange ② $2x - 3y = 9$

① × 2 $14x - 10y = 30$ ③

② × 7 $14x - 21y = 63$ ④

③ – ④ $11y = -33 \Rightarrow y = -3$

$y = -3$ in ② $2x + 9 = 9 \Rightarrow 2x = 0 \Rightarrow x = 0$

So they intersect at (0, –3)

g) ① $6x + 3y = 10$

Rearrange ② $-4x + 8y = -9$

① × 2 $12x + 6y = 20$ ③

② × 3 $-12x + 24y = -27$ ④

③ + ④ $30y = -7 \Rightarrow y = -\frac{7}{30}$

$y = -\frac{7}{30}$ in ① $6x + -\frac{7}{10} = 10 \Rightarrow 6x = \frac{107}{10}$

$\Rightarrow x = \frac{107}{60}$

So they intersect at $\left(\frac{107}{60}, -\frac{7}{30}\right)$

h) Rearrange ① $x + 10y = 3$

Rearrange ② $-6x + 5y = 5$

① × 6 $6x + 60y = 18$ ③

② + ③ $65y = 23 \Rightarrow y = \frac{23}{65}$

y in ① $x + \frac{46}{13} = 3 \Rightarrow x = -\frac{7}{13}$

So they intersect at $\left(-\frac{7}{13}, \frac{23}{65}\right)$

i) Rearrange ① $\frac{7}{3}x - \frac{5}{3}y = 2$

Rearrange ② $-\frac{3}{4}x + y = \frac{1}{3}$

② × $\frac{5}{3}$ $-\frac{5}{4}x + \frac{5}{3}y = \frac{5}{9}$ ③

① + ③ $\frac{13}{12}x = \frac{23}{9} \Rightarrow x = \frac{92}{39}$

x in ② $-\frac{23}{13} + y = \frac{1}{3} \Rightarrow y = \frac{82}{39}$

So they intersect at $\left(\frac{92}{39}, \frac{82}{39}\right)$

j) Rearrange ① $-\frac{9}{5}x + \frac{3}{4}y = -10$

Rearrange ② $\frac{3}{2}x - \frac{3}{5}y = -10$

① × $\frac{3}{5}$ $-\frac{27}{25}x + \frac{9}{20}y = -6$ ③

② × $\frac{3}{4}$ $\frac{9}{8}x - \frac{9}{20}y = -\frac{15}{2}$ ④

③ + ④ $\frac{9}{200}x = -\frac{27}{2} \Rightarrow x = -300$

x in ① $540 + \frac{3}{4}y = -10 \Rightarrow \frac{3}{4}y = -550$

$\Rightarrow y = -\frac{2200}{3}$

So they intersect at $\left(-300, -\frac{2200}{3}\right)$

Q3 There will be a signpost at the point of intersection of each pair of straight lines:

A and B: ① $5x + 2y = -11$

Rearrange ② $2x - y = 1$

② × 2 $4x - 2y = 2$ ③

① + ③ $9x = -9 \Rightarrow x = -1$

$x = -1$ in ② $-2 - y = 1 \Rightarrow y = -3$

So they intersect at (–1, –3)

B and C: Rearrange ① $2x - y = 1$

Rearrange ② $-x + 5y = 13$

② × 2 $-2x + 10y = 26$ ③

① + ③ $9y = 27 \Rightarrow y = 3$

$y = 3$ in ① $2x - 3 = 1 \Rightarrow 2x = 4$

$\Rightarrow x = 2$

So they intersect at (2, 3)

A and C: ① $5x + 2y = -11$

Rearrange ② $-x + 5y = 13$

② × 5 $-5x + 25y = 65$ ③

① + ③ $27y = 54 \Rightarrow y = 2$

$y = 2$ in ② $-x + 10 = 13$

$\Rightarrow -x = 3 \Rightarrow x = -3$

So they intersect at (–3, 2)

So the three signposts are at (–1, –3), (2, 3) and (–3, 2).

Q4 a) $5x + 10y = 36$ and $10x + 2y = 18$

[1 mark for both equations correct]

b) ①: $5x + 10y = 36$

②: $10x + 2y = 18$

① × 2: $10x + 20y = 72$ ③

③ – ②: $18y = 54 \Rightarrow y = 3$

$y = 3$ in ②: $10x + 6 = 18 \Rightarrow 10x = 12 \Rightarrow x = 1.2$

So the small blocks have a mass of 1.2 kg, and the large blocks have a mass of 3 kg.

[3 marks available — 1 mark for a correct method, 1 mark for correct x-value, 1 mark for correct y-value]

Q5 a) (i) ①: $2c - t = 64$

②: $6c - 2t = 291$

① × 3: $6c - 3t = 192$ ③

② – ③: $t = 99$

So in $t = 99$ months = 8 years and 3 months, the prices of the two stocks will be the same.
This will happen in the year 2015 + 8 = 2023.

[3 marks available — 1 mark for a correct method, 1 mark for correct value of t, 1 mark for correct year]

(ii) $t = 99$ in ① $\Rightarrow 2c - 99 = 64 \Rightarrow c = 81.5$

So the price will be £81.50. *[1 mark]*

b) E.g. The prices of the stocks may significantly increase or decrease over time. / The prices of the stocks are unlikely to change in a continuous way. / The prices of the stocks may go down as well as up.

[1 mark for an appropriate reason]

Q6 a) ①: $3x + 2y = k$

②: $x - y = 3k + 2$

② × 3: $3x - 3y = 9k + 6$ ③

① – ③: $5y = -8k - 6 \Rightarrow y = -\frac{8k+6}{5}$

Sub in ②: $x = 3k + 2 - \frac{8k+6}{5} \Rightarrow x = \frac{7k+4}{5}$

[3 marks available — 1 mark for a correct method, 1 mark for correct expression for x, 1 mark for correct expression for y]

b) From part a), the coordinates of A are $\left(\frac{7k+4}{5}, -\frac{8k+6}{5}\right)$.

The x-coordinate is equal to the y-coordinate, so

$\frac{7k+4}{5} = -\frac{8k+6}{5} \Rightarrow 7k + 4 = -8k - 6$

$\Rightarrow 15k = -10 \Rightarrow k = -\frac{2}{3}$

Hence $x = \frac{7\left(-\frac{2}{3}\right)+4}{5} = -\frac{2}{15}$, so $y = -\frac{2}{15}$.

So the coordinates of A are $\left(-\frac{2}{15}, -\frac{2}{15}\right)$.

[3 marks available — 1 mark for attemptng to solve the correct equation, 1 mark for the correct value of k, 1 mark for correct coordinates of A]

Q7 ① $2x - y = 2$

② $5x - y\sqrt{5} = 3\sqrt{5}$

① × 5 $10x - 5y = 10$ ③

② × 2 $10x - 2y\sqrt{5} = 6\sqrt{5}$ ④

③ – ④ $\quad -5y + 2y\sqrt{5} = 10 - 6\sqrt{5} \Rightarrow y = \frac{10 - 6\sqrt{5}}{2\sqrt{5} - 5}$

$$\Rightarrow y = \frac{10 - 6\sqrt{5}}{2\sqrt{5} - 5} \times \frac{2\sqrt{5} + 5}{2\sqrt{5} + 5}$$
$$= \frac{20\sqrt{5} + 50 - 60 - 30\sqrt{5}}{20 - 25}$$
$$= \frac{-10 - 10\sqrt{5}}{-5} = 2 + 2\sqrt{5}$$

Sub y in ① $\quad 2x - (2 + 2\sqrt{5}) = 2 \Rightarrow x = 2 + \sqrt{5}$

So the solution is $x = 2 + \sqrt{5}$ and $y = 2 + 2\sqrt{5}$.

[4 marks available — 1 mark for a correct method, 3 marks for both correct x- and y-values in the correct simplified form, otherwise 2 marks for one correct x- or y-value in the correct simplified form, or 1 mark for a correct x- or y-value not in the correct simplified form]

Exercise 5.5 — Simultaneous Equations — if One is not Linear

Q1 a) ① $y = 4x + 3$

② $2y - 3x = 1$

Sub ① in ② $\quad 2(4x + 3) - 3x = 1$
$8x + 6 - 3x = 1$
$5x = -5 \Rightarrow x = -1$

$x = -1$ in ① $\quad y = 4 \times -1 + 3 = -1$

So the solution is $x = -1$, $y = -1$

b) ① $5x + 2y = 16$

Rearrange ② $\quad x = 2y - 4$

Sub ② in ① $\quad 5(2y - 4) + 2y = 16$
$12y - 20 = 16$
$12y = 36 \Rightarrow y = 3$

$y = 3$ in ② $\quad x = 2 \times 3 - 4 = 2$

So the solution is $x = 2$, $y = 3$

Q2 a) ① $y = 2x + 5$

② $y = x^2 - x + 1$

Sub ① in ② $\quad 2x + 5 = x^2 - x + 1$
$x^2 - 3x - 4 = 0$
$(x - 4)(x + 1) = 0 \Rightarrow x = 4$ or $x = -1$

From ①, when $x = 4$, $\quad y = 8 + 5 = 13$, and
when $x = -1$, $\quad y = -2 + 5 = 3$

So $x = 4$, $y = 13$ or $x = -1$, $y = 3$

b) ① $y = 2x^2 - 3$

② $y = 3x + 2$

Sub ② in ① $\quad 3x + 2 = 2x^2 - 3$
$2x^2 - 3x - 5 = 0$
$(2x - 5)(x + 1) = 0 \Rightarrow x = \frac{5}{2}$ or $x = -1$

From ②, when $x = \frac{5}{2}$, $\quad y = \frac{15}{2} + 2 = \frac{19}{2}$, and
when $x = -1$, $\quad y = -3 + 2 = -1$

So $x = \frac{5}{2}$, $y = \frac{19}{2}$ or $x = -1$, $y = -1$

c) ① $2x^2 - xy = 6$

Rearrange ② $\quad y = 3x - 7$

Sub ② in ① $\quad 2x^2 - x(3x - 7) = 6$
$2x^2 - 3x^2 + 7x - 6 = 0$
$-x^2 + 7x - 6 = 0$
$x^2 - 7x + 6 = 0$
$(x - 6)(x - 1) = 0$
$\Rightarrow x = 6$ or $x = 1$

From ②, when $x = 6$, $\quad y = 18 - 7 = 11$, and
when $x = 1$, $\quad y = 3 - 7 = -4$

So $x = 6$, $y = 11$ or $x = 1$, $y = -4$

d) ① $xy = 6$

Rearrange ② $\quad 2y + 4 = x$

Sub ② in ① $\quad y(2y + 4) = 6$
$2y^2 + 4y - 6 = 0$
$y^2 + 2y - 3 = 0$
$(y + 3)(y - 1) = 0$
$\Rightarrow y = -3$ or $y = 1$

From ②, when $y = -3$, $\quad x = -6 + 4 = -2$, and
when $y = 1$, $\quad x = 2 + 4 = 6$

So $x = -2$, $y = -3$ or $x = 6$, $y = 1$

e) ① $y = x^2 - 2x - 3$

Rearrange ② $\quad y = -x - 8$

Sub ② in ① $\quad -x - 8 = x^2 - 2x - 3$
$x^2 - x + 5 = 0$

Check discriminant: $b^2 - 4ac = 1 - 20 = -19$, which is negative so there are no real roots.
So there are no solutions for the simultaneous equations.

f) ① $y = 2x^2 - 3x + 5$

Rearrange ② $\quad 5x - 3 = y$

Sub ② in ① $\quad 5x - 3 = 2x^2 - 3x + 5$
$2x^2 - 8x + 8 = 0$
$x^2 - 4x + 4 = 0$
$(x - 2)^2 = 0 \Rightarrow x = 2$

From ②, when $x = 2$, $\quad y = 10 - 3 = 7$

So $x = 2$, $y = 7$

There is only one solution here, so the straight line is a tangent to the curve.

g) ① $2x^2 + 3y^2 + 18x = 347$

Rearrange ② $\quad y = -4x + 7$

Sub ② in ① $\quad 2x^2 + 3(-4x + 7)^2 + 18x = 347$
$2x^2 + 3(16x^2 - 56x + 49) + 18x - 347 = 0$
$2x^2 + 48x^2 - 168x + 147 + 18x - 347 = 0$
$50x^2 - 150x - 200 = 0$
$x^2 - 3x - 4 = 0$
$(x + 1)(x - 4) = 0 \Rightarrow x = -1$ or $x = 4$

From ②, when $x = -1$, $\quad y = 4 + 7 = 11$, and
when $x = 4$, $\quad y = -16 + 7 = -9$

So $x = -1$, $y = 11$ or $x = 4$, $y = -9$

h) ① $2y = 2x^2 + x + 1$

Rearrange ② $\quad y = 2 - 2x$

Sub ② in ① $\quad 2(2 - 2x) = 2x^2 + x + 1$
$4 - 4x = 2x^2 + x + 1$
$2x^2 + 5x - 3 = 0$
$(2x - 1)(x + 3) = 0$
$\Rightarrow x = -3$ or $x = \frac{1}{2}$

From ②, when $x = -3$, $y = 2 + 6 = 8$, and
when $x = \frac{1}{2}$, $y = 2 - 1 = 1$

So $x = -3$, $y = 8$ or $x = \frac{1}{2}$, $y = 1$

i) ① $x^2 + 4x = 4y + 40$

Rearrange ② $\quad y = -\frac{5}{12}x - \frac{5}{2}$

Sub ② in ① $\quad x^2 + 4x = 4\left(-\frac{5}{12}x - \frac{5}{2}\right) + 40$
$x^2 + 4x = -\frac{5}{3}x - 10 + 40$
$x^2 + \frac{17}{3} - 30 = 0$
$3x^2 + 17x - 90 = 0$
$\Rightarrow (3x - 10)(x + 9) = 0$
$\Rightarrow x = -9$ or $x = \frac{10}{3}$

From ②, when $x = -9$, $y = \frac{45}{12} - \frac{5}{2} = \frac{5}{4}$, and
when $x = \frac{10}{3}$, $y = -\frac{50}{36} - \frac{5}{2} = -\frac{35}{9}$

So $x = -9$, $y = \frac{5}{4}$ or $x = \frac{10}{3}$, $y = -\frac{35}{9}$

j) Rearrange ① $y = 2x + 2$

② $\frac{1}{4}y^2 + 25 = 3x^2 + 11x$

Sub ① in ② $\frac{1}{4}(2x + 2)^2 + 25 = 3x^2 + 11x$

$x^2 + 2x + 1 + 25 = 3x^2 + 11x$

$2x^2 + 9x - 26 = 0$

$\Rightarrow (2x + 13)(x - 2) = 0$

$\Rightarrow x = -\frac{13}{2}$ or $x = 2$

From ①, when $x = -\frac{13}{2}$, $y = -13 + 2 = -11$, and
when $x = 2$, $y = 4 + 2 = 6$

So $x = -\frac{13}{2}$, $y = -11$ or $x = 2$, $y = 6$

Q3 ① $x^2 + 2xy = y + 1$

② $2x + 5y - 2 = 0$

① × 5 $5x^2 + 10xy = 5y + 5$ ③

Rearrange ②: $5y = 2 - 2x$ ④

Sub ④ in ③: $5x^2 + 2x(2 - 2x) = (2 - 2x) + 5$

$\Rightarrow 5x^2 + 4x - 4x^2 = 7 - 2x \Rightarrow x^2 + 6x - 7 = 0$

$\Rightarrow (x + 7)(x - 1) = 0 \Rightarrow x = -7$ or $x = 1$

From ②, when $x = -7$, $2(-7) + 5y - 2 = 0 \Rightarrow y = \frac{16}{5}$
when $x = 1$, $2(1) + 5y - 2 = 0 \Rightarrow y = 0$

The solutions are $x = -7$, $y = \frac{16}{5}$ or $x = 1$, $y = 0$.

[5 marks available — 1 mark for forming an equation by substituting x or y, 1 mark for simplifying quadratic equation, 1 mark for solving quadratic equation, 1 mark for one correct pair of solutions, 1 mark for other correct pair of solutions]

Q4 a) ① $y = x^2 - 5x + 7$

Rearrange ② $y = -2x + 11$

Sub ② in ① $-2x + 11 = x^2 - 5x + 7$

$x^2 - 3x - 4 = 0$

$(x + 1)(x - 4) = 0$

$\Rightarrow x = -1$ or $x = 4$

From ②, when $x = -1$, $y = 2 + 11 = 13$, and
when $x = 4$, $y = -8 + 11 = 3$

So the points of intersection are $(-1, 13)$ and $(4, 3)$

b) ① $y = -2x^2 + 2x + 12$

Rearrange ② $y = 2x + 4$

Sub ② in ① $2x + 4 = -2x^2 + 2x + 12$

$2x^2 = 8 \Rightarrow x = -2$ or $x = 2$

From ②, when $x = -2$, $y = -4 + 4 = 0$ and
when $x = 2$, $y = 4 + 4 = 8$

So the points of intersection are $(-2, 0)$ and $(2, 8)$

Q5 a) ① $y = \frac{1}{2}x^2 + 4x - 8$

② $y = 4 + \frac{3}{2}x$

Sub ② in ① $4 + \frac{3}{2}x = \frac{1}{2}x^2 + 4x - 8$

$8 + 3x = x^2 + 8x - 16$

$0 = x^2 + 5x - 24$

$(x + 8)(x - 3) = 0 \Rightarrow x = -8$ or $x = 3$

From ②, when $x = -8$, $y = 4 - 12 = -8$, and
when $x = 3$, $y = 4 + \frac{9}{2} = \frac{17}{2}$

So they intersect at $(-8, -8)$ and $\left(3, \frac{17}{2}\right)$

b) ① $y = 2x^2 + x - 6$

Rearrange ② $y = 5x + 10$

Sub ② in ① $2x^2 + x - 6 = 5x + 10$

$2x^2 - 4x - 16 = 0$

$x^2 - 2x - 8 = 0$

$(x - 4)(x + 2) = 0 \Rightarrow x = 4$ or $x = -2$

From ②, when $x = 4$, $y = 20 + 10 = 30$, and
when $x = -2$, $y = -10 + 10 = 0$

So they intersect at $(4, 30)$ and $(-2, 0)$

c) ① $x^2 + y^2 = 50$

Rearrange ② $x = -2y + 5$

Sub ② in ① $(-2y + 5)^2 + y^2 = 50$

$4y^2 - 20y + 25 + y^2 - 50 = 0$

$5y^2 - 20y - 25 = 0$

$y^2 - 4y - 5 = 0$

$(y - 5)(y + 1) = 0 \Rightarrow y = 5$ or $y = -1$

From ②, when $y = 5$, $x = -10 + 5 = -5$, and
when $y = -1$, $x = 2 + 5 = 7$

So they intersect at $(-5, 5)$ and $(7, -1)$

d) ① $2x^2 - y + 3x + 1 = 0$

Rearrange ② $y = x + 5$

Sub ② in ① $2x^2 - (x + 5) + 3x + 1 = 0$

$2x^2 + 2x - 4 = 0$

$x^2 + x - 2 = 0$

$(x + 2)(x - 1) = 0 \Rightarrow x = -2$ or $x = 1$

From ②, when $x = -2$, $y = -2 + 5 = 3$, and
when $x = 1$, $y = 1 + 5 = 6$

So they intersect at $(-2, 3)$ and $(1, 6)$

e) ① $3x^2 + 9x + 1 = 6y$

Rearrange ② $y = \frac{11}{6} - \frac{2}{3}x$

Sub ② in ① $3x^2 + 9x + 1 = 6\left(\frac{11}{6} - \frac{2}{3}x\right)$

$3x^2 + 9x + 1 = 11 - 4x$

$3x^2 + 13x - 10 = 0$

$(3x - 2)(x + 5) = 0$

$\Rightarrow x = -5$ or $x = \frac{2}{3}$

From ②, when $x = -5$, $y = \frac{11}{6} + \frac{10}{3} = \frac{31}{6}$

when $x = \frac{2}{3}$, $y = \frac{11}{6} - \frac{4}{9} = \frac{25}{18}$

So they intersect at $\left(-5, \frac{31}{6}\right)$ and $\left(\frac{2}{3}, \frac{25}{18}\right)$

f) Rearrange ① $y = 4x + 10$

② $2y - 19 = 4x^2 + 8x$

Sub ① in ② $2(4x + 10) - 19 = 4x^2 + 8x$

$8x + 20 - 19 = 4x^2 + 8x$

$4x^2 = 1 \Rightarrow x = -\frac{1}{2}$ or $x = \frac{1}{2}$

From ①, when $x = -\frac{1}{2}$, $y = -2 + 10 = 8$, and

when $x = \frac{1}{2}$, $y = 2 + 10 = 12$

So they intersect at $\left(-\frac{1}{2}, 8\right)$ and $\left(\frac{1}{2}, 12\right)$

Q6 a) ① $x^2 + y^2 = 10$

Rearrange ② $x = 3y - 10$

Sub ② in ① $(3y - 10)^2 + y^2 = 10$

$9y^2 - 60y + 100 + y^2 - 10 = 0$

$10y^2 - 60y + 90 = 0$

$y^2 - 6y + 9 = 0$

$(y - 3)^2 = 0 \Rightarrow y = 3$

From ②, when $y = 3$, $x = 9 - 10 = -1$

So $x = -1$, $y = 3$.

b) $x^2 + y^2 = 10$ is a circle and $x - 3y + 10 = 0$ is a straight line. Part a) tells us that they intersect at a single point, so the line must actually be a tangent to the circle.

Q7 **a)** ① $y = x^2 + 6x - 7$
② $y = 2x - 3$
Sub ② in ① $2x - 3 = x^2 + 6x - 7$
$x^2 + 4x - 4 = 0$
So $b^2 - 4ac = 16 + 16 = 32 > 0$
So they will intersect at two points.

b) ① $3x^2 + 4y^2 + 6x = 9$
Rearrange ② $x = 3 - 2y$
Sub ② in ① $3(3 - 2y)^2 + 4y^2 + 6(3 - 2y) = 9$
$27 - 36y + 12y^2 + 4y^2 + 18 - 12y - 9 = 0$
$16y^2 - 48y + 36 = 0$
$4y^2 - 12y + 9 = 0$
Now $b^2 - 4ac = 144 - 144 = 0$
So they will intersect only once — ② is a tangent to the curve ①.
You could have rearranged differently to get an equation in terms of x — you would still get a discriminant of 0.

c) ① $xy + 2x - y = 8$
Rearrange ② $x = 1 - y$
Sub ② in ① $(1 - y)y + 2(1 - y) - y = 8$
$y - y^2 + 2 - 2y - y = 8$
$-y^2 - 2y - 6 = 0$
$y^2 + 2y + 6 = 0$
So $b^2 - 4ac = 4 - 24 = -20 < 0$
So the graphs will not intersect.

Q8 **a)** ① $p - 2q = 4$
② $q = \frac{1}{4}p^2 - 2p + 4$
Rearrange ①: $q = \frac{1}{2}p - 2 \Rightarrow q^2 = \left(\frac{1}{2}p - 2\right)^2$
Factorise ②: $q = \left(\frac{1}{2}p - 2\right)^2$
Therefore $q = \left(\frac{1}{2}p - 2\right)^2 = q^2$.
[2 marks available — 2 marks for fully deriving the result with correct working, otherwise 1 mark for a partial attempt using a correct method]

b) From part a), $q = q^2 \Rightarrow q = 0$ or $q = 1$.
When $q = 0$, $p = 4$. When $q = 1$, $p = 4 + 2 = 6$.
So the solutions are $p = 4$, $q = 0$ and $p = 6$, $q = 1$.
[3 marks available — 1 mark for correct use of result from a), 1 mark for both correct q-values, 1 mark for both correct solution pairs]

Q9 **a)** $T = t - 2$ *[1 mark]*

b) $q(T) = q(t - 2)$, so the expression is:
$20 + 8(t - 2) - (t - 2)^2 = 20 + 8t - 16 - t^2 + 4t - 4 = 12t - t^2$
$q(T)$ is valid for $T \geq 0$, so this expression is valid for $t \geq 2$.
[3 marks available — 1 mark for correct substitution of the result from part a), 1 mark for correct expression, 1 mark for correct range of values for t]

c) The times at which the temperature of both tanks is the same can be found by setting $p(t)$ equal to the expression from b):
$20 + t = 12t - t^2 \Rightarrow t^2 - 11t + 20 = 0 \Rightarrow t = \frac{11 \pm \sqrt{41}}{2}$
$\Rightarrow t = 2.298...$ or $t = 8.701...$
$\Rightarrow t \approx 2$ hours 18 mins or $t \approx 8$ hours 42 mins
So the times at which the temperature is the same in each tank are 10:18 and 16:42 to the nearest minute.
[3 marks available, 1 mark for deriving the correct equation, 1 mark for finding the correct values of t, 1 mark for both correct clock times to the nearest minute]

d) E.g. The temperature of P rises without bound according to the model, which means that the water would eventually boil. / The temperature of Q will decrease without bound according to the model and the water will eventually freeze.
[1 mark for an appropriate limitation with explanation]

Chapter 5 Review Exercise

Q1 **a)** $7x - 4 > 2x - 42 \Rightarrow 5x > -38 \Rightarrow x > -\frac{38}{5}$

b) $12y - 3 \leq 4y + 4 \Rightarrow 8y \leq 7 \Rightarrow y \leq \frac{7}{8}$

c) $9y - 4 \geq 17y + 2 \Rightarrow -8y \geq 6 \Rightarrow y \leq -\frac{3}{4}$

d) $x + 6 < 5x - 4 \Rightarrow -4x < -10 \Rightarrow x > \frac{5}{2}$

e) $4x - 2 > x - 14 \Rightarrow 3x > -12 \Rightarrow x > -4$

f) $7 - x \leq 4 - 2x \Rightarrow x \leq -3$

g) $11x - 4 < 4 - 11x \Rightarrow 22x < 8 \Rightarrow x < \frac{4}{11}$

h) $1 + 10y \geq 7y - 12 \Rightarrow 3y \geq -13 \Rightarrow y \geq -\frac{13}{3}$

i) $8y - 6 \leq 6 - 8y \Rightarrow 16y \leq 12 \Rightarrow y \leq \frac{3}{4}$

Q2 $3(2x - 5) + 2(4 - x) \geq x + 7 \Rightarrow 6x - 15 + 8 - 2x \geq x + 7$
$\Rightarrow 4x - 7 \geq x + 7 \Rightarrow 3x \geq 14 \Rightarrow x \geq \frac{14}{3}$
[3 marks available — 1 mark for expanding brackets, 1 mark for simplifying, 1 mark for correct answer]

Q3 **a)** $3x^2 - 5x - 2 = 0 \Rightarrow (3x + 1)(x - 2) = 0$
$\Rightarrow x = -\frac{1}{3}$ or $x = 2$

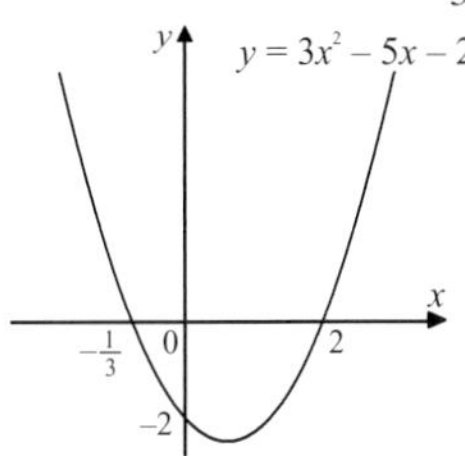

So: $3x^2 - 5x - 2 \leq 0 \Rightarrow -\frac{1}{3} \leq x \leq 2$

b) $x^2 + 2x + 7 = 4x + 9 \Rightarrow x^2 - 2x - 2 = 0$
$\Rightarrow x = \frac{2 \pm \sqrt{4 + 8}}{2} \Rightarrow x = 1 \pm \sqrt{3}$

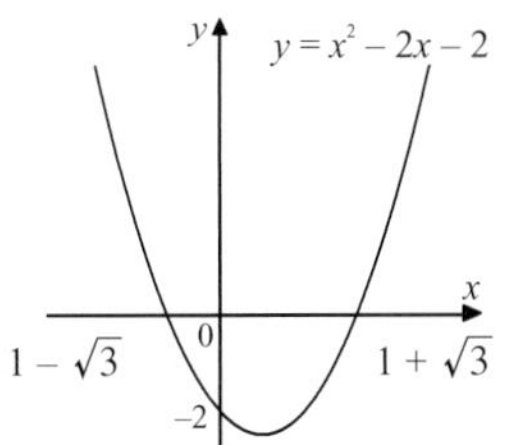

So: $x^2 + 2x + 7 > 4x + 9 \Rightarrow x^2 - 2x - 2 > 0$
$\Rightarrow x < 1 - \sqrt{3}$ or $x > 1 + \sqrt{3}$

c) $3x^2 + 7x + 4 = 2(x^2 + x - 1) \Rightarrow x^2 + 5x + 6 = 0$
$\Rightarrow (x + 3)(x + 2) = 0 \Rightarrow x = -3$ or $x = -2$

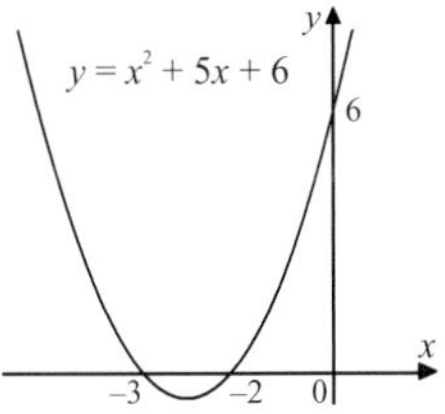

So: $3x^2 + 7x + 4 \geq 2(x^2 + x - 1)$
$\Rightarrow (x + 3)(x + 2) \geq 0 \Rightarrow x \leq -3$ or $x \geq -2$

d) $x^2 + 3x - 1 = x + 2 \Rightarrow x^2 + 2x - 3 = 0$
$\Rightarrow (x + 3)(x - 1) = 0 \Rightarrow x = -3$ or $x = 1$

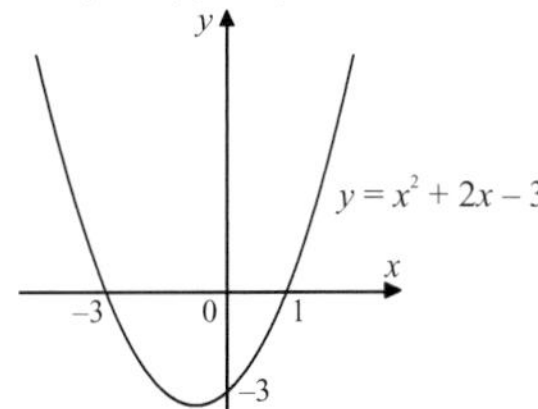

So: $x^2 + 3x - 1 \geq x + 2 \Rightarrow (x + 3)(x - 1) \geq 0$
$\Rightarrow x \leq -3$ or $x \geq 1$

e) $2x^2 = x + 1 \Rightarrow 2x^2 - x - 1 = 0$
$\Rightarrow (2x + 1)(x - 1) = 0 \Rightarrow x = -\frac{1}{2}$ or $x = 1$

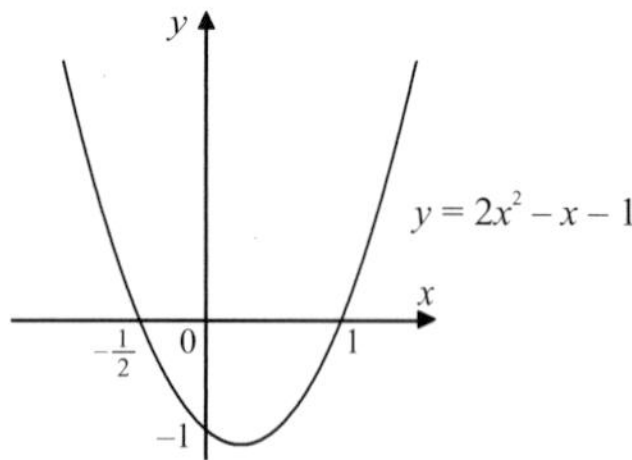

So: $2x^2 > x + 1 \Rightarrow (2x + 1)(x - 1) > 0 \Rightarrow x < -\frac{1}{2}$ or $x > 1$

f) $3x^2 - 12 = x^2 - 2x \Rightarrow 2x^2 + 2x - 12 = 0$
$\Rightarrow (2x - 4)(x + 3) = 0 \Rightarrow x = 2$ or $x = -3$

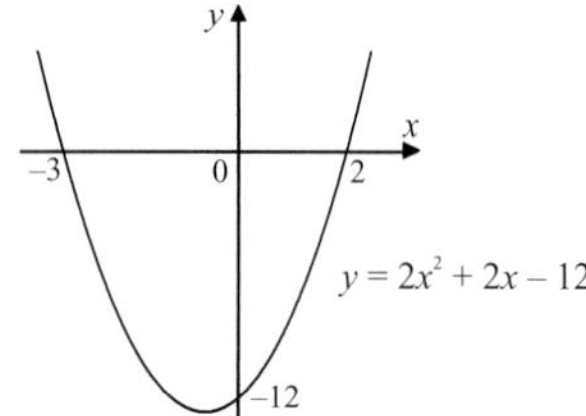

So: $3x^2 - 12 < x^2 - 2x \Rightarrow (2x - 4)(x + 3) < 0 \Rightarrow -3 < x < 2$

g) $3x^2 + 6x = 2x^2 + 3 \Rightarrow x^2 + 6x - 3 = 0$
$\Rightarrow x = \dfrac{-6 \pm \sqrt{36 + 12}}{2} = -3 \pm 2\sqrt{3}$

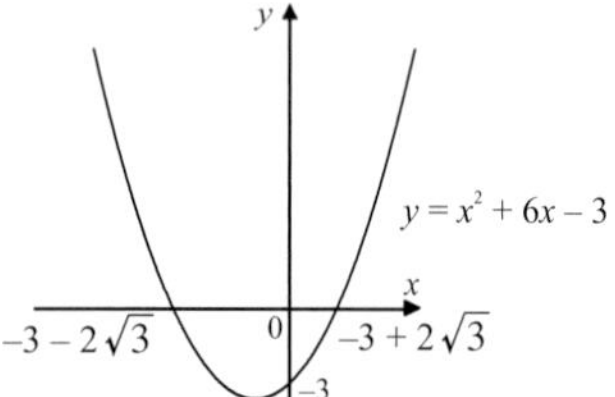

So: $3x^2 + 6x \leq 2x^2 + 3 \Rightarrow x^2 + 6x - 3 \leq 0$
$\Rightarrow -3 - 2\sqrt{3} \leq x \leq -3 + 2\sqrt{3}$

h) $(x + 2)(x - 3) = 8 - 3x^2 \Rightarrow x^2 - x - 6 = 8 - 3x^2$
$\Rightarrow 4x^2 - x - 14 = 0 \Rightarrow (4x + 7)(x - 2) = 0$
$\Rightarrow x = -\frac{7}{4}$ or $x = 2$

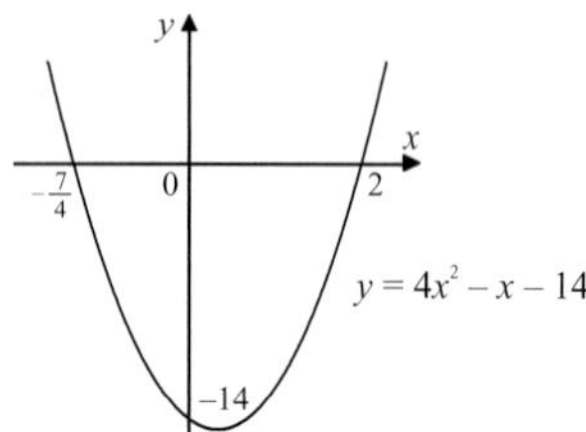

So: $(x + 2)(x - 3) \geq 8 - 3x^2 \Rightarrow (4x + 7)(x - 2) \geq 0$
$\Rightarrow x \leq -\frac{7}{4}$ or $x \geq 2$

Q4 $2x^2 - 5x - 3 = 0 \Rightarrow (2x + 1)(x - 3) = 0$
$\Rightarrow x = -\frac{1}{2}$ or $x = 3$

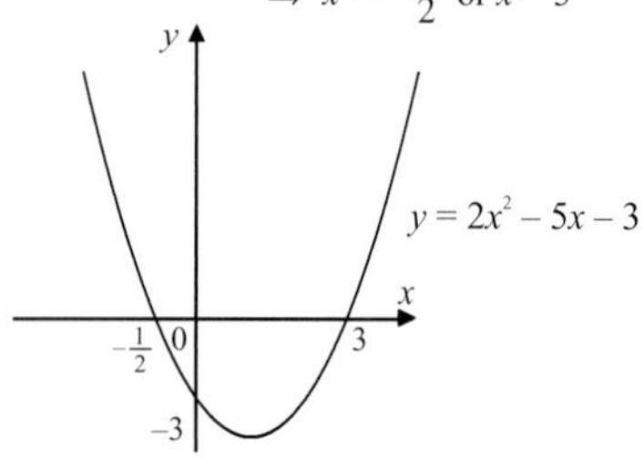

Solution: $2x^2 - 5x - 3 > 0 \Rightarrow (2x + 1)(x - 3) > 0$
$\Rightarrow x < -\frac{1}{2}$ or $x > 3$

In set notation, this is $\left\{x : x < -\frac{1}{2}\right\} \cup \{x : x > 3\}$
[4 marks available — 1 mark for factorising quadratic equation, 1 mark for correct root values, 2 marks for correct solution in set notation, otherwise 1 mark for correct solution not in set notation]

Q5 $x^2 - 23x - 472 = 0 \Rightarrow x = \dfrac{-(-23) \pm \sqrt{23^2 - 4 \times 1 \times -472}}{2}$
$\Rightarrow x = \dfrac{23 \pm \sqrt{2417}}{2} \Rightarrow x = 36.081...$ or $x = -13.081...$
The coefficient of x^2 is positive, so the graph is above the x-axis when $x \geq 36.081...$ or $x \leq -13.081...$
N is a positive integer, so $N \geq 36.081$. The smallest positive integer greater than 36.081... is $N = 37$.
[4 marks available — 1 mark for a method to solve the quadratic equation, 1 mark for correct root values, 1 mark for using $N \geq 36.081...$, 1 mark for correct value of N]

Q6 a) $8 \leq y - x \Rightarrow y \geq x + 8$
$y < 12 - x$
$9x + 2y < -4 \Rightarrow y < -\frac{9}{2}x - 2$

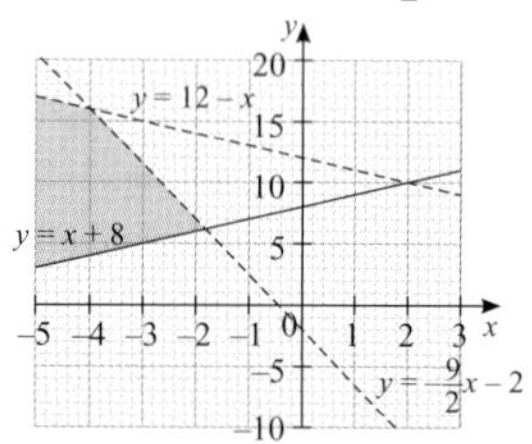

b) $x + 3y > 15 \Rightarrow y > -\frac{1}{3}x + 5$
$3x + y < 12 \Rightarrow y < 12 - 3x$
$4y \leq x + 36 \Rightarrow y \leq \frac{1}{4}x + 9$

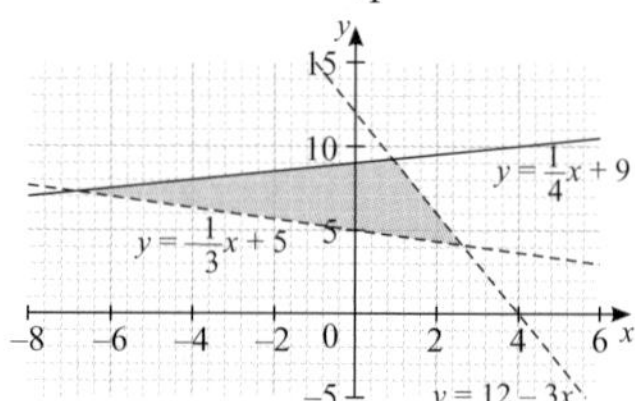

c) $10y + 10x > x^2 \Rightarrow y > \frac{1}{10}x^2 - x$
$y < -x^2 + 8x - 12$

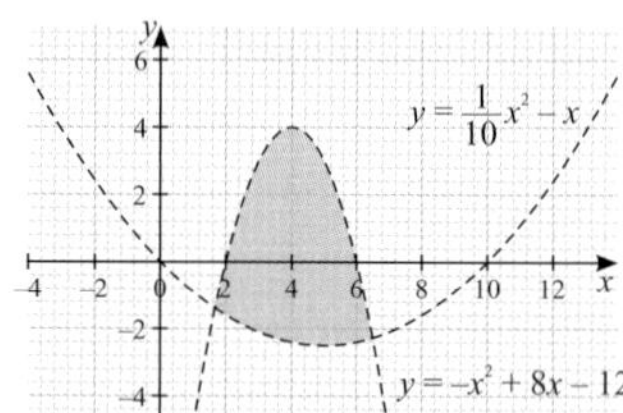

Q7 The graph is below the x-axis when $\frac{1}{2}x^2 + 4x - \frac{5}{2} < 0$.
$\frac{1}{2}x^2 + 4x - \frac{5}{2} = 0 \Rightarrow x = \dfrac{-4 \pm \sqrt{4^2 - 4 \times \frac{1}{2} \times -\frac{5}{2}}}{2 \times \frac{1}{2}}$
$\Rightarrow x = -4 \pm \sqrt{21}$
The coefficient of x^2 is positive, so the graph is u-shaped.
So the graph is below the x-axis for $-4 - \sqrt{21} < x < -4 + \sqrt{21}$.
[2 marks available — 1 mark for solving the equation with an appropriate method, 1 mark for correct set of x-values]

Q8 a) The car engine must be stopped when $T \geq 100$.
$-\frac{1}{18}t^2 + \frac{18}{5}t + 55 \geq 100 \Rightarrow -\frac{1}{18}t^2 + \frac{18}{5}t - 45 \geq 0$
$\Rightarrow t^2 - \frac{324}{5}t + 810 \leq 0 \Rightarrow 5t^2 - 324t + 4050 \leq 0$
Using the quadratic formula:
$t = \dfrac{-(-324) \pm \sqrt{324^2 - 4 \times 5 \times 4050}}{2 \times 5}$
$\Rightarrow t = 47.884...$ or $t = 16.915...$

So the car must be stopped between
$16.915... < t < 47.884...$
The car must be stopped for at least
$47.884... - 16.915... = 30.968... \approx 31$ minutes
[4 marks available — 1 mark for forming an inequality to solve, 1 mark for a method to solve the quadratic equation, 1 mark for correct root values, 1 mark for the correct duration of time given to nearest minute]

b) E.g. In reality, Barry will need to wait for the car engine to cool to a temperature below 100 °C before setting off again, so the engine will have to be off for more than 31 minutes.
[1 mark for a suitable answer with explanation]

Q9 The inequalities are $3x + y < 10$, $x + y \leq 6$ and $y > \frac{1}{4}x^2 - \frac{5}{2}x + 4$.
[2 marks available — 2 marks for all three inequalities correct, otherwise 1 mark for at least two inequalities correct]

Q10 a-c)

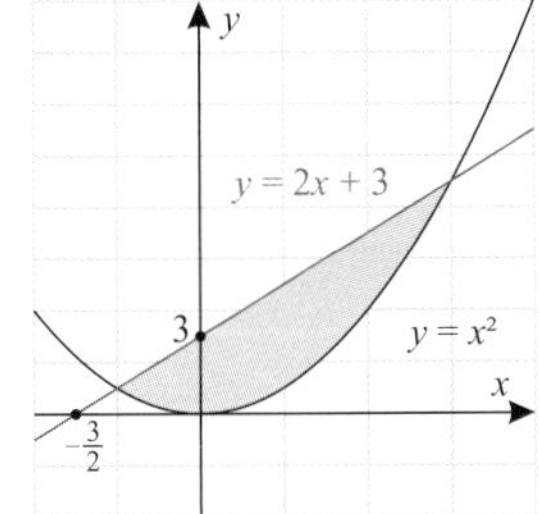

a) *[1 mark for correctly drawn graph of $y = x^2$]*

b) *[2 marks available — 1 mark for straight line with a positive gradient, 1 mark for two correctly labelled axis intercepts]*

c) *[1 mark for correct shading]*

Q11 a)

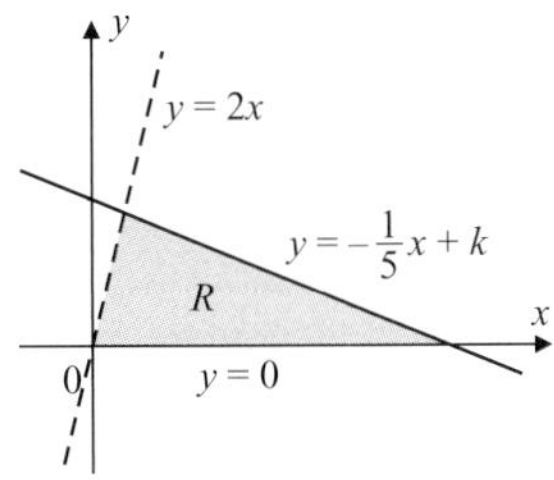

[4 marks available — 1 mark for each line drawn correctly with a dotted or solid line as appropriate, 1 mark for the correct region shaded]

b) There are no solutions to the inequalities $y \geq 0$, $y < 2x$ and $y \leq -\frac{1}{5}x + k$ when $k < 0$. So the region R will not contain any points and the machine cannot cut an empty region.
[1 mark for correct possible reason with explanation]

c) Substituting $y = 2x$ into $y = -\frac{1}{5}x + k$:
$2x = -\frac{1}{5}x + k \Rightarrow 10x = -x + 5k \Rightarrow x = \frac{5k}{11}$
Then $y = 2 \times \frac{5k}{11} = \frac{10k}{11}$, so the lines intersect at $\left(\frac{5k}{11}, \frac{10k}{11}\right)$.
$y = -\frac{1}{5}x + k$ intersects the x-axis when $x = 5k$, so the region R is a triangle with base of length $5k$ and height $\frac{10k}{11}$.
So $\frac{1}{2} \times 5k \times \frac{10k}{11} = 4 \Rightarrow k^2 = \frac{44}{25} \Rightarrow k = \frac{2\sqrt{11}}{5}$ (as $k > 0$)
[3 marks available — 1 mark for the correct height of the triangle in terms of k, 1 mark for correct base of the triangle in terms of k, 1 mark for the correct answer]

Q12 a) Completing the square gives
$y = -(x - 3)^2 + 12 \Rightarrow p = 3$ and $q = 12$
[2 marks available — 1 mark for a correct method, 1 mark for both correct values of p and q]

b) Substituting $x = 3$ into $y = 4x - 5$ gives $y = 7$.
Substituting $x = 3$ into $3y - x = 18$ gives $y = 7$.
So both lines pass through the point at (3, 7).
[1 mark for showing x = 3, y = 7 satisfies both equations]

c)

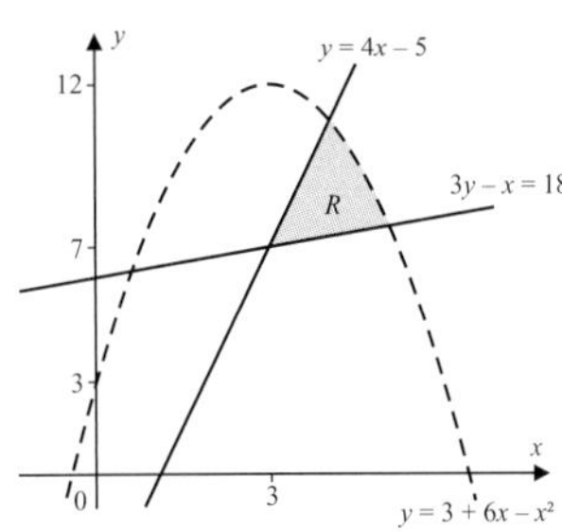

[3 marks available — 1 mark for the correct quadratic graph with a dotted line, 1 mark for the correct straight-line graphs with solid lines, 1 mark for the correct region shaded]

Q13 a)
①	$3x - 4y = 7$	
②	$-2x + 7y = -22$	
① × 2	$6x - 8y = 14$	③
② × 3	$-6x + 21y = -66$	④
③ + ④	$13y = -52 \Rightarrow y = -4$	

$y = -4$ in ① $3x + 16 = 7 \Rightarrow x = -3$
So the solution is $x = -3$, $y = -4$.

b)
①	$2x - 3y = \frac{11}{12}$	
②	$x + y = -\frac{7}{12}$	
② × 3	$3x + 3y = -\frac{7}{4}$	③
① + ③	$5x = -\frac{5}{6} \Rightarrow x = -\frac{1}{6}$	
$x = -\frac{1}{6}$ in ②	$-\frac{1}{6} + y = -\frac{7}{12} \Rightarrow y = -\frac{5}{12}$	

So the solution is $x = -\frac{1}{6}$, $y = -\frac{5}{12}$.

c)
①	$2x + 3y = 8$	
Rearrange ②	$4x + 6y = 5$	
① × 2	$4x + 6y = 16$	③
② – ③	$0 = -11$	

This is not possible — so there are no solutions.

d)
Rearrange ①	$9x - 11y = -4$	
②	$3x - 2y = 7$	
② × 3	$9x - 6y = 21$	③
① – ③	$-5y = -25 \Rightarrow y = 5$	
$y = 5$ in ②	$3x - 10 = 7 \Rightarrow x = \frac{17}{3}$	

So the solution is $x = \frac{17}{3}$, $y = 5$.

e)
①	$\frac{1}{2}x + \frac{1}{3}y = 50$	
②	$x + 4y = 25$	
① × 2	$x + \frac{2}{3}y = 100$	③
② – ③	$\frac{10}{3}y = -75 \Rightarrow y = -\frac{45}{2}$	
$y = -\frac{45}{2}$ in ②	$x - 90 = 25 \Rightarrow x = 115$	

So the solution is $x = 115$, $y = -\frac{45}{2}$.

f)
①	$x + 4y = \frac{1}{4}$	
Rearrange ②	$2x + y = \frac{1}{5}$	
① × 2	$2x + 8y = \frac{1}{2}$	③
③ – ②	$7y = \frac{3}{10} \Rightarrow y = \frac{3}{70}$	
$y = \frac{3}{70}$ in ①	$x + \frac{6}{35} = \frac{1}{4} \Rightarrow x = \frac{11}{140}$	

So the solution is $x = \frac{11}{140}$, $y = \frac{3}{70}$.

Q14 a)
①	$y = 3x - 4$
②	$y = 7x - 5$
Sub ① in ②	$3x - 4 = 7x - 5 \Rightarrow x = \frac{1}{4}$

$x = \frac{1}{4}$ in ① $\quad y = \frac{3}{4} - 4 \Rightarrow y = -\frac{13}{4}$

So the lines intersect at the point $\left(\frac{1}{4}, -\frac{13}{4}\right)$

b) ① $\quad y = 13 - 2x$

② $\quad 7x - y - 23 = 0$

Sub ① in ② $\quad 7x - (13 - 2x) - 23 = 0$
$\Rightarrow 9x = 36 \Rightarrow x = 4$

$x = 4$ in ① $\quad y = 13 - 8 = 5$

So the lines intersect at the point (4, 5)

c) Rearrange ① $\quad 2x - 3y = -4$

Rearrange ② $\quad x - 2y = -1$

② × 2 $\quad 2x - 4y = -2$ ③

① – ③ $\quad y = -2$

$y = -2$ in ② $\quad x + 4 = -1 \Rightarrow x = -5$

So the lines intersect at the point (–5, –2)

d) ① $\quad 5x - 7y = 22$

Rearrange ② $\quad -4x + 3y = 13$

① × 4 $\quad 20x - 28y = 88$ ③

② × 5 $\quad -20x + 15y = 65$ ④

③ + ④ $\quad -13y = 153 \Rightarrow y = -\frac{153}{13}$

$y = -\frac{153}{13}$ in ① $\quad 5x + \frac{1071}{13} = 22$
$\Rightarrow x = -\frac{157}{13}$

So the lines intersect at the point $\left(-\frac{157}{13}, -\frac{153}{13}\right)$

e) Rearrange ① $\quad -\frac{2}{3}x - 8y = -9$

② $\quad \frac{1}{3}x + \frac{2}{3}y = 10$

② × 2 $\quad \frac{2}{3}x + \frac{4}{3}y = 20$ ③

① + ③ $\quad -\frac{20}{3}y = 11 \Rightarrow y = -\frac{33}{20}$

$y = -\frac{33}{20}$ in ② $\quad \frac{1}{3}x - \frac{66}{60} = 10 \Rightarrow x = \frac{333}{10}$

So the lines intersect at the point $\left(\frac{333}{10}, -\frac{33}{20}\right)$

f) ① $\quad 24x + 15y = 2$

② $\quad 18x + 36y = 5$

① × 3 $\quad 72x + 45y = 6$ ③

② × 4 $\quad 72x + 144y = 20$ ④

④ – ③ $\quad 99y = 14 \Rightarrow y = \frac{14}{99}$

$y = \frac{14}{99}$ in ① $\quad 24x + \frac{210}{99} = 2 \Rightarrow x = -\frac{1}{198}$

So the lines intersect at the point $\left(-\frac{1}{198}, \frac{14}{99}\right)$

Q15 Let the volume of large pots = L and volume of small pots = S.

① $\quad 14L + 18S = 39.5$

② $\quad 12L + 21S = 39.15$

① × 6 $\quad 84L + 108S = 237$ ③

② × 7 $\quad 84L + 147S = 274.05$ ④

④ – ③ $\quad 39S = 37.05 \Rightarrow S = 0.95$

Sub S in ① $\quad 14L + 18 \times 0.95 = 39.5 \Rightarrow L = 1.6$

So the volume of a large pot is 1.6 litres and the volume of a small pot is 0.95 litres.

[4 marks available — 1 mark for setting up both equations, 1 mark for multiplying both equations to get same coefficient of L or S, 1 mark for one correct volume, 1 mark for the other correct volume]

Q16 a) ① $\quad 2x + ay = 4$

② $\quad 3x - 2y = 1$

① × 3 $\quad 6x + 3ay = 12$ ③

② × 2 $\quad 6x - 4y = 2$ ④

③ – ④ $\quad 3ay + 4y = 10 \Rightarrow y(3a + 4) = 10$
$\Rightarrow y = \frac{10}{3a + 4}$

Sub $y = \frac{10}{3a+4}$ in ②, $3x - 2\left(\frac{10}{3a+4}\right) = 1$

$\Rightarrow 3x = 1 + \frac{20}{3a+4} \Rightarrow 3x = \frac{3a + 4 + 20}{3a + 4} \Rightarrow x = \frac{a+8}{3a+4}$

[4 marks available — 1 mark for multiplying both equations to get same coefficient of x or y, 1 mark for adding or subtracting equations to eliminate x or y, 1 mark for correct x or y value, 1 mark for other correct value]

b) The denominator of both x and y is $3a + 4$. This can never be zero, so no solution exists when $3a + 4 = 0 \Rightarrow a = -\frac{4}{3}$

[2 marks available — 1 mark for explanation, 1 mark for correct value]

c) If $a = -\frac{4}{3}$, then ① is $2x - \frac{4}{3}y = 4 \Rightarrow 3x - 2y = 6$.
$3x - 2y = 6$ and ② $3x - 2y = 1$ cannot be simultaneously true as both represent parallel lines.

[2 marks available — 1 mark for substituting a into equation 1 and rearranging, 1 mark for identifying parallel lines]

Q17 a) Substituting $y = 2x - 7$ into $4x + 3y = 7$:
$4x + 3(2x - 7) = 7 \Rightarrow 4x + 6x - 21 = 7$
$\Rightarrow 10x = 28 \Rightarrow x = \frac{14}{5}$

So $y = 2 \times \frac{14}{5} - 7 = -\frac{7}{5}$

Hence the lines intersect at $\left(\frac{14}{5}, -\frac{7}{5}\right)$.

[3 marks available — 1 mark for substituting one equation into the other, 1 mark for correct x or y value, 1 mark for other correct value]

b) Substituting $y = 2x - 7$ into $5y - 10x = 1$:
$5(2x - 7) - 10x = 1 \Rightarrow 10x - 35 - 10x = 1 \Rightarrow -35 = 1$
This is false, so no values for x and y can satisfy both equations at the same time. Therefore the graphs of the two lines do not intersect.

[2 marks available — 1 mark for an attempt to solve the equations simultaneously, 1 mark for deriving a false identity and stating the correct conclusion]

Q18 a) ① $\quad y = x^2 - 7x + 4$

Rearrange ② $\quad y = 2x - 10$

Sub ① in ② $\quad x^2 - 7x + 4 = 2x - 10$
$\Rightarrow x^2 - 9x + 14 = 0$
$\Rightarrow (x - 2)(x - 7) = 0$
$\Rightarrow x = 2$ or $x = 7$

From ②, when $x = 2$, $y = 4 - 10 = -6$, and when $x = 7$, $y = 14 - 10 = 4$

So the line and the curve meet at the points (2, –6) and (7, 4).

b) Rearrange ① $\quad y = 2x^2 - 6x + 30$

Expand ② $\quad y = 2x + 22$

Sub ① in ② $\quad 2x^2 - 6x + 30 = 2x + 22$
$\Rightarrow 2x^2 - 8x + 8 = 0$
$\Rightarrow x^2 - 4x + 4 = 0$
$\Rightarrow (x - 2)^2 = 0 \Rightarrow x = 2$

$x = 2$ in ② $\quad y = 4 + 22 = 26$

So the line is a tangent to the parabola at the point (2, 26).

c) ① $\quad 2x^2 + 2y^2 - 3 = 0$

② $\quad y = x + 4$

Sub ② in ① $\quad 2x^2 + 2(x + 4)^2 - 3 = 0$
$\Rightarrow 2x^2 + 2x^2 + 16x + 32 - 3 = 0$
$\Rightarrow 4x^2 + 16x + 29 = 0$

Check discriminant: $b^2 - 4ac = 256 - 464 = -208$, which is negative so there are no real roots.
So the line and the curve never meet.

d) Rearrange ① $y = 2 - \frac{3}{4}x$

② $2y - 2x^2 - 4x = 7$

Sub ① in ② $2(2 - \frac{3}{4}x) - 2x^2 - 4x = 7$

$\Rightarrow 4 - \frac{3}{2}x - 2x^2 - 4x = 7$

$\Rightarrow 2x^2 + \frac{11}{2}x + 3 = 0$

$\Rightarrow 4x^2 + 11x + 6 = 0$

$\Rightarrow (4x + 3)(x + 2) = 0$

$\Rightarrow x = -\frac{3}{4}$ or $x = -2$

From ①, when $x = -\frac{3}{4}$, $y = 2 + \frac{9}{16} = \frac{41}{16}$, and when $x = -2$, $y = 2 + \frac{3}{2} = \frac{7}{2}$

So they meet at the points $\left(-\frac{3}{4}, \frac{41}{16}\right)$ and $\left(-2, \frac{7}{2}\right)$

e) ① $\frac{1}{4}x^2 + 3x + 15 = 4y$

② $2y = 3x + 3$

② × 2 $4y = 6x + 6$ ③

Sub ③ in ① $\frac{1}{4}x^2 + 3x + 15 = 6x + 6$

$\Rightarrow \frac{1}{4}x^2 - 3x + 9 = 0$

$\Rightarrow x^2 - 12x + 36 = 0$

$\Rightarrow (x - 6)^2 = 0 \Rightarrow x = 6$

$x = 6$ in ② $2y = 18 + 3 \Rightarrow y = \frac{21}{2}$

So the line is a tangent to the parabola at the point $\left(6, \frac{21}{2}\right)$.

f) ① $(x - 3)^2 + (y + 4)^2 = 25$

Rearrange ② $x = 7y + 6$

Sub ② in ① $(7y + 3)^2 + (y + 4)^2 = 25$

$\Rightarrow 49y^2 + 42y + 9 + y^2 + 8y + 16 = 25$

$\Rightarrow 50y^2 + 50y = 0$

$\Rightarrow 50y(y + 1) = 0 \Rightarrow y = -1$ or $y = 0$

From ②, when $y = -1$, $x = -7 + 6 = -1$, and when $y = 0$, $x = 6$

So the line crosses the circle at the points (–1, –1) and (6, 0)

Q19 ① $y = x^2 - 2x - 3$

② $y = 3x + 11$

Sub ① in ② $x^2 - 2x - 3 = 3x + 11$

$\Rightarrow x^2 - 5x - 14 = 0$

$\Rightarrow (x + 2)(x - 7) = 0 \Rightarrow x = -2$ or 7

So the line and curve will intersect at two points.

Q20 a) ① $2x - y + 3 = 0$

② $y = -x^2 + 3x - 2$

Rearrange ①: $y = 2x + 3$ ③

Sub ③ in ②: $2x + 3 = -x^2 + 3x - 2 \Rightarrow x^2 - x + 5 = 0$

[2 marks available — 1 mark for forming an equation, 1 mark for simplifying quadratic equation to give the result]

b) Find the discriminant: a = 1, b = –1, c = 5, so $b^2 - 4ac = (-1)^2 - 4 \times 1 \times 5 = 1 - 20 = -19 < 0$

So $x^2 - x + 5 = 0$ has no solutions, therefore there are no solutions to the simultaneous equations.

[2 marks available — 1 mark for calculating the discriminant, 1 mark for a correct conclusion]

Q21 a) ① $y = 3x^2 + 7x + 15$

② $y = 6x + 25$

Sub ① in ② $3x^2 + 7x + 15 = 6x + 25$

$\Rightarrow 3x^2 + x - 10 = 0$

$\Rightarrow (3x - 5)(x + 2) = 0$

$\Rightarrow x = \frac{5}{3}$ or $x = -2$

From ②, when $x = \frac{5}{3}$, $y = 6\left(\frac{5}{3}\right) + 25 = 35$, and when $x = -2$, $y = 6(-2) + 25 = 13$.

So they meet at the points $(\frac{5}{3}, 35)$ and (–2, 13).

[5 marks available — 1 mark for setting equations equal to one another, 1 mark for simplifying quadratic equation, 1 mark for solving quadratic equation, 1 mark for one correct coordinate pair, 1 mark for other correct coordinate pair]

b) Using part a):

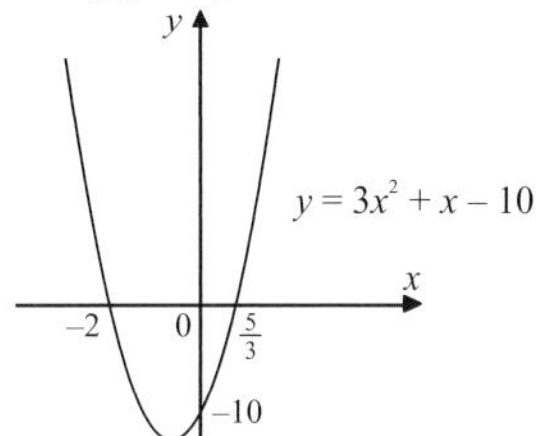

So $3x^2 + 7x + 15 > 6x + 25 \Rightarrow 3x^2 + x - 10 > 0$

$\Rightarrow x < -2$ or $x > \frac{5}{3}$

[2 marks available — 1 mark for using root values from part a), 1 mark for correct solution]

Q22 ① $3x^2 + 5y = 14$

② $5x - 10y = -38$

① × 2: $3x^2 + 5y = 14 \Rightarrow 10y = 28 - 6x^2$ ③

Rearrange ②: $10y = 5x + 38$ ④

Equating ③ and ④: $28 - 6x^2 = 5x + 38 \Rightarrow 6x^2 + 5x + 10 = 0$

Check discriminant: $b^2 - 4ac = 25 - (4 \times 6 \times 10) = 25 - 240$ which is negative so there are no real roots.

So the line l and curve C never meet.

[4 marks available — 1 mark for rearranging and substituting to eliminate y (or x), 1 mark for simplifying quadratic equation, 1 mark for negative discriminant value, 1 mark for correct explanation]

Q23 ① $y = 2x + 7$

② $(x - 9)^2 + (y - 5)^2 = 160$

Sub ① in ② $(x - 9)^2 + (2x + 7 - 5)^2 = 160$

$\Rightarrow x^2 - 18x + 81 + 4x^2 + 8x + 4 = 160$

$\Rightarrow 5x^2 - 10x - 75 = 0$

$\Rightarrow x^2 - 2x - 15 = 0$

$\Rightarrow (x + 3)(x - 5) = 0$

$\Rightarrow x = -3$ or $x = 5$

From ①, when $x = -3$, $y = 2(-3) + 7 = 1$, and when $x = 5$, $y = 2(5) + 7 = 17$.

So the line and the circle meet at the points (–3, 1) and (5, 17).

[5 marks available — 1 mark for forming an equation by substituting x or y, 1 mark for simplifying quadratic equation, 1 mark for solving quadratic equation, 1 mark for one correct coordinate pair, 1 mark for other correct coordinate pair]

Q24 ① $y = 2x + k$

② $y = x^2 - 4x + 6$

Sub ② in ① $x^2 - 4x + 6 = 2x + k$

$\Rightarrow x^2 - 6x + (6 - k) = 0$

The line is a tangent to the curve so there is only one solution and the discriminant $b^2 - 4ac = 0$. So:

$(-6)^2 - 4 \times 1 \times (6 - k) = 0 \Rightarrow 36 - 24 + 4k = 0 \Rightarrow k = -3$

So $x^2 - 6x + 9 = 0 \Rightarrow (x - 3)^2 = 0 \Rightarrow x = 3$

From ①, $y = 2(3) + (-3) \Rightarrow y = 3$

So the line is a tangent to the curve at (3, 3).

[6 marks available — 1 mark for setting equations 1 and 2 equal to one another, 1 mark for simplifying quadratic equation, 1 mark for using the discriminant, 1 mark for correct value of k, 1 mark for correct value of x, 1 mark for correct value of y]

Q25 a) ① $4x + y + 6 = 0$

② $y = 4x^2 + 16x + 15$

Rearrange ①: $y = -4x - 6$ ③

Sub ② in ③: $4x^2 + 16x + 15 = -4x - 6$

$\Rightarrow 4x^2 + 20x + 21 = 0$

$\Rightarrow (2x + 7)(2x + 3) = 0$

$\Rightarrow x = -\frac{7}{2}$ or $x = -\frac{3}{2}$

From ③, when $x = -\frac{7}{2}$, $y = -(4 \times -\frac{7}{2}) - 6 = 8$

when $x = -\frac{3}{2}$, $y = -(4 \times -\frac{3}{2}) - 6 = 0$

So the points of intersection are $\left(-\frac{7}{2}, 8\right)$ and $\left(-\frac{3}{2}, 0\right)$.

[5 marks available — 1 mark for correct method of solving simultaneous equations, 1 mark for simplifying the quadratic equation, 1 mark for solving the quadratic equation, 1 mark for one correct coordinate pair, 1 mark for other correct coordinate pair]

b)

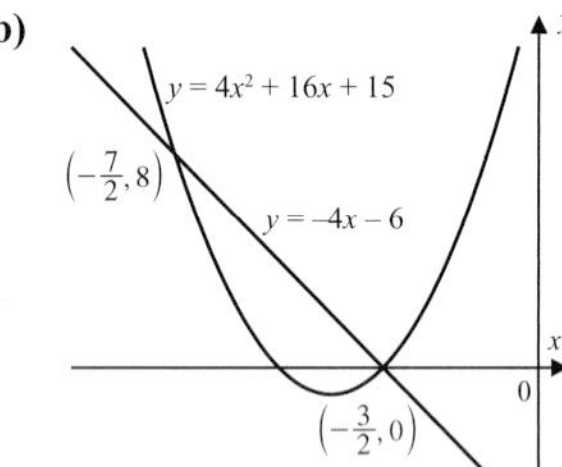

[3 marks available — 1 mark for correct shape of quadratic, 1 mark for correct straight line drawn, 1 mark for both points of intersection correctly labelled]

Q26 a) When $t = 0$, $a(0) = 23$ and $b(0) = 28$, so supplier A is cheaper initially. *[1 mark]*

b) Set the equations equal to each other: $a(t) = b(t)$

$\Rightarrow \frac{1}{10}t^2 - 2t + 28 = 23 + \frac{1}{2}t \Rightarrow t^2 - 25t + 50 = 0$

Using the quadratic formula: $a = 1$, $b = -25$, $c = 50$

$t = \frac{-(-25) \pm \sqrt{(-25)^2 - 4 \times 1 \times 50}}{2 \times 1} = \frac{25 \pm \sqrt{425}}{2}$

$\Rightarrow t = 2.192...$ or $t = 22.807...$

So the prices are equal for the first time at $t = 2.192...$

$a(2.192...) = 23 + \frac{1}{2} \times 2.192... = 24.096...$

So the price at this time is £24.10 (nearest pence).

[4 marks available — 1 mark for setting up the correct equation, 1 mark for a correct method of solving, 1 mark for the correct value of t for the first time the prices are equal, 1 mark for the correct price]

Q27 a) The graphs intersect when $2x^2 - 9x + 14 = 2x + 2$

$\Rightarrow 2x^2 - 11x + 12 = 0 \Rightarrow (2x - 3)(x - 4) = 0$

$\Rightarrow x = \frac{3}{2}$ or $x = 4$

When $x = \frac{3}{2}$, $y = 2 \times \frac{3}{2} + 2 = 5$

When $x = 4$, $y = 2 \times 4 + 2 = 10$

So A has coordinates $\left(\frac{3}{2}, 5\right)$ and B has coordinates $(4, 10)$.

[5 marks available — 1 mark for setting equations equal to one another, 1 mark for simplifying quadratic equation, 1 mark for solving quadratic equation, 1 mark for one correct coordinate pair, 1 mark for other correct coordinate pair]

b) AD and BC are parallel, so from part a), the quadrilateral is a trapezium, where AD has length 5 and BC has length 10.

The width of the trapezium is $CD = 4 - \frac{3}{2} = \frac{5}{2}$.

So the area is $\frac{1}{2}(5 + 10) \times \frac{5}{2} = \frac{75}{4}$ units².

[3 marks available — 1 mark for finding the dimensions of the trapezium, 1 mark for setting an equation to solve, 1 mark for the correct area]

Q28 a) ① $2y - z = -5$

② $2x - y + 3z = 4$

Rearrange ①: $z = 2y + 5$ ③

Sub ③ in ②: $2x - y + 3(2y + 5) = 4$

$\Rightarrow 2x - y + 6y + 15 = 4$

$\Rightarrow 2x + 5y = -11$

[2 marks available — 1 mark for a correct method, 1 mark for deriving the correct result]

b) Using the result from a):

① $2x + 5y = -11$

② $4y + 5x + 2 = 0$

① × 4 $8x + 20y = -44$ ③

② × 5 $20y + 25x + 10 = 0$ ④

④ − ③ $17x + 10 = 44 \Rightarrow x = 2$

$x = 2$ in ① $2(2) + 5y = -11 \Rightarrow y = -3$

When $y = -3$, $z = 2 \times (-3) + 5 = -1$.

So the solution is $x = 2$, $y = -3$ and $z = -1$.

[4 marks available — 1 mark for multiplying both equations to get same coefficient of x or y, 1 mark for adding or subtracting equations to eliminate x or y, 2 marks for three correct values, otherwise 1 mark for two correct values]

Q29 a) $\frac{(\sqrt{2})^{3x} \times 9^{2x-y}}{18^{y+\frac{1}{2}x}} = \frac{(2^{\frac{1}{2}})^{3x} \times (3^2)^{2x-y}}{(2 \times 3^2)^{y+\frac{1}{2}x}} = \frac{2^{\frac{3}{2}x} \times 3^{4x-2y}}{2^{y+\frac{1}{2}x} \times 3^{2y+x}}$

$= \frac{2^{\frac{3}{2}x}}{2^{y+\frac{1}{2}x}} \times \frac{3^{4x-2y}}{3^{2y+x}} = 2^{\frac{3}{2}x-(y+\frac{1}{2}x)} \times 3^{4x-2y-(2y+x)} = 2^{x-y} \times 3^{3x-4y}$

[3 marks available — 1 mark for an attempt to simplify, 1 mark for correct use of laws of indices, 1 mark for the correct answer]

b) $\frac{(\sqrt{2})^{3x} \times 9^{2x-y}}{18^{y+\frac{1}{2}x}} = 6^{10} \Rightarrow 2^{x-y} \times 3^{3x-4y} = (2 \times 3)^{10}$

$\Rightarrow 2^{x-y} \times 3^{3x-4y} = 2^{10} \times 3^{10}$

Equating indices gives:

① $x - y = 10$

② $3x - 4y = 10$

Rearrange ①: $y = x - 10$ ③

Sub ③ in ②: $3x - 4(x - 10) = 10$

$\Rightarrow 3x - 4x + 40 = 10 \Rightarrow x = 30$

When $x = 30$, $y = 30 - 10 = 20$.

[4 marks available — 1 mark for using result from part a), 1 mark for a correct method, 1 mark for correct x or y value, 1 mark for other correct value]

Chapter 6: Coordinate Geometry, Graphs and Circles

Prior Knowledge Check

Q1 a) Gradient = 2, y-intercept = −4

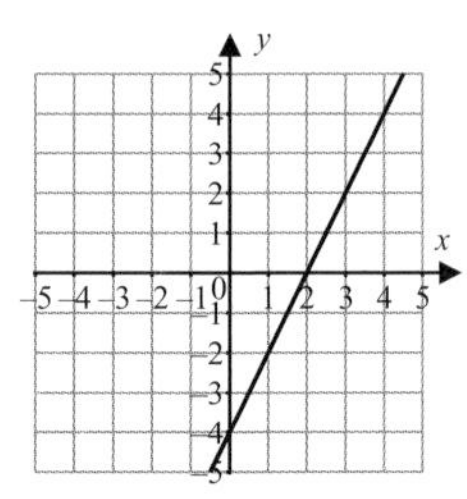

b) Gradient = −3, y-intercept = 4

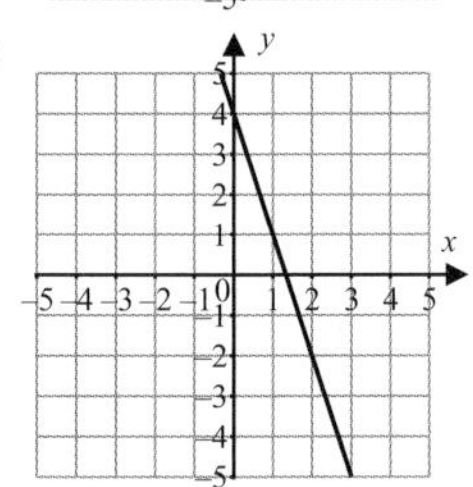

c) Gradient = 5, y-intercept = –2

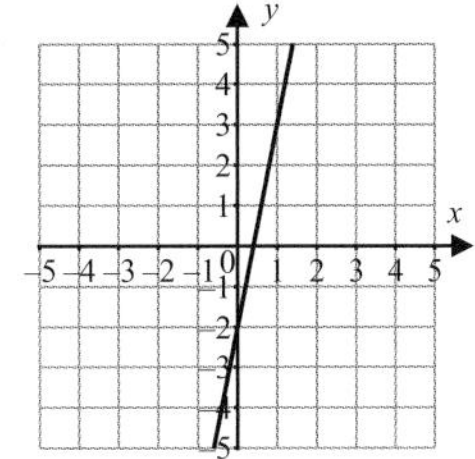

Q2 a) $y = \frac{k}{x}$ b) $x = ky$

Q3 a) $3x^2 - 11x - 20 = (3x + 4)(x - 5)$

b) Sum the coefficients: $1 - 3 - 6 + 8 = 0$, so $(x - 1)$ is a factor.
Using algebraic division,
$x^3 - 3x^2 - 6x + 8 \div (x - 1) = x^2 - 2x - 8$
So $x^3 - 3x^2 - 6x + 8 = (x - 1)(x^2 - 2x - 8)$
$= (x - 1)(x - 4)(x + 2)$

Q4 Using Pythagoras' theorem, length = $\sqrt{(3-1)^2 + (-2-6)^2}$
$= \sqrt{4 + 64} = \sqrt{68} = 2\sqrt{17}$

Midpoint = $\left(\frac{3+1}{2}, \frac{-2+6}{2}\right) = (2, 2)$

Q5 a) $f(2) = (2)^2 + 4(2) - 7 = 5$

b) $f(x) = x^2 + 4x - 7 \Rightarrow ((x + 2)^2 - 4) - 7 \Rightarrow (x + 2)^2 - 11$

Exercise 6.1-6.2 — Equations of the Form $y - y_1 = m(x - x_1)$ and $y = mx + c$

Q1 a) gradient = –4, y-intercept = (0, 11)

b) gradient = –1, y-intercept = (0, 4)

c) gradient = 1.7, y-intercept = (0, –2.3)

Q2 a) $y = -3x + 2$

b) $y = 5x - 3$

c) $y = \frac{1}{2}x + 6$

d) $y = 0.8x + 1.2$

e) $y = -0.4x - 7$

f) $y = -\frac{5}{3}x + \frac{1}{2}$

Q3 a) $c = 8$
$(x_1, y_1) = (-4, 0), (x_2, y_2) = (0, 8)$
$m = \frac{8-0}{0-(-4)} = \frac{8}{4} = 2 \Rightarrow y = 2x + 8$

b) $c = -5$
$(x_1, y_1) = (-2, 11), (x_2, y_2) = (0, -5)$
$m = \frac{-5-11}{0-(-2)} = \frac{-16}{2} = -8 \Rightarrow y = -8x - 5$

Q4 a) $(x_1, y_1) = (2, -2), (x_2, y_2) = (6, 10)$
$m = \frac{10-(-2)}{6-2} = \frac{12}{4} = 3$
(i) $y - (-2) = 3(x - 2) \Rightarrow y + 2 = 3(x - 2)$
(ii) $y = 3x - 8$

b) $(x_1, y_1) = (-1, -6), (x_2, y_2) = (3, 4)$
$m = \frac{4-(-6)}{3-(-1)} = \frac{10}{4} = 2.5$
(i) $y - (-6) = 2.5(x - (-1)) \Rightarrow y + 6 = 2.5(x + 1)$
(ii) $y = 2.5x - 3.5$

c) $(x_1, y_1) = (4, 1), (x_2, y_2) = (0, -3)$
$m = \frac{-3-1}{0-4} = \frac{-4}{-4} = 1$
(i) $y - 1 = 1(x - 4) \Rightarrow y - 1 = x - 4$
(ii) $y = x - 3$

d) $(x_1, y_1) = (12, -3), (x_2, y_2) = (14, 1)$
$m = \frac{1-(-3)}{14-12} = \frac{4}{2} = 2$
(i) $y - (-3) = 2(x - 12) \Rightarrow y + 3 = 2(x - 12)$
(ii) $y = 2x - 27$

e) $(x_1, y_1) = (5, 7), (x_2, y_2) = (-2, 5)$
$m = \frac{5-7}{-2-5} = \frac{-2}{-7} = \frac{2}{7}$
(i) $y - 7 = \frac{2}{7}(x - 5)$
(ii) $y = \frac{2}{7}x + \frac{39}{7}$

f) $(x_1, y_1) = (-3, 6), (x_2, y_2) = (4, -2)$
$m = \frac{-2-6}{4-(-3)} = -\frac{8}{7}$
(i) $y - 6 = -\frac{8}{7}(x - (-3)) \Rightarrow y - 6 = -\frac{8}{7}(x + 3)$
(ii) $y = -\frac{8}{7}x + \frac{18}{7}$

Q5 a) $m = \frac{0.65-(-1.85)}{-0.3-0.2} = \frac{2.5}{-0.5} = -5$

b) $y - 0.65 = -5(x + 0.3) \Rightarrow y = -5x - 1.5 + 0.65$
$\Rightarrow y = -5x - 0.85$

Q6 $y = mx + c \Rightarrow -3 = \frac{1}{4} \times (-4) + c \Rightarrow -3 = -1 + c \Rightarrow c = -2$
So $y = \frac{1}{4}x - 2$

Q7 $y - y_1 = m(x - x_1) \Rightarrow y - 2 = -\frac{2}{5}(x - (-8))$
$\Rightarrow y - 2 = -\frac{2}{5}(x + 8)$
Rearrange into $y = mx + c$ form:
$y - 2 = -\frac{2}{5}(x + 8) \Rightarrow y = -\frac{2}{5}x - \frac{16}{5} + 2 \Rightarrow y = -\frac{2}{5}x - \frac{6}{5}$

Q8 Find the equation of the line first.
$m = 3$, find c using the point (2, –7) on the line:
$y = mx + c \Rightarrow -7 = 3 \times 2 + c \Rightarrow -7 = 6 + c \Rightarrow c = -13$
So $y = 3x - 13$ — the points a), c) and e) lie on the line.
Sub in the x value from each point — if the resulting value for y matches the value of y in the original point, then the point lies on that line.

Q9 Find the equation of the line first: $m = \frac{20-6}{-1-6} = \frac{14}{-7} = -2$
Then $y - 6 = -2(x - 6) \Rightarrow y = -2x + 18$.
So the points a), c), d) and f) lie on the line.

Q10 a) The gradient (m) is given as 32. To find c, substitute in the conditions $t = 0$ and $d = 0$:
$d = 32t + c \Rightarrow 0 = 32(0) + c \Rightarrow c = 0$
So the equation is $d = 32t$.

b) Solve the equation where $d = 9.6$:
$9.6 = 32t \Rightarrow t = 9.6 \div 32 = 0.3$ hours
$0.3 \times 60 = 18$ minutes

c) Some possible answers include:
- It is unrealistic that the car would travel at exactly the same speed for any length of time — it would probably vary slightly, which would make the model less accurate.
- In practice, external factors would probably affect the speed of the car during its journey, such as bends in the road, or other vehicles.
- The car wouldn't start at 32 km/h — it would take time for it to reach this speed.

Q11 a) a is the gradient of the straight-line equation, i.e. how much W changes by per unit change in t, or per day.
W decreases by 650 g = 0.65 kg per day, so $a = -0.65$.
When $t = 6$, $W = 16.1 \Rightarrow 16.1 = -0.65 \times 6 + b \Rightarrow b = 20$
a is the change in weight of the dog food in the bag per day, and b is the initial weight of the dog food in the bag.
[4 marks available — 1 mark for correct value of a, 1 mark for correct value of b, 1 mark for correct interpretation of a, 1 mark for correct interpretation of b]

b) $W = 0 \Rightarrow -0.65t + 20 = 0 \Rightarrow t = 30.769...$
$30.5 < t < 31$ corresponds to the time period from midnight at the start of 16th August to midday on 16th August.
So Sally will have to open a new bag on 16th August.
[2 marks available — 1 mark for calculating the correct value of t, 1 mark for correct interpretation of value of t found]

c) E.g. The dog food will not be removed from the bag at a constant rate like the model suggests. Sally will only take food from the bag at certain times, since the dog will not eat when it is asleep, for example.
[1 mark for a suitable limitation with a reason]

Q12 a) Gradient of $l = \frac{7-4}{3-(-2)} = \frac{3}{5}$

$y - y_1 = m(x - x_1) \Rightarrow y - 7 = \frac{3}{5}(x-3)$

$\Rightarrow y = \frac{3}{5}x - \frac{9}{5} + 7 \Rightarrow y = \frac{3}{5}x + \frac{26}{5}$

[2 marks available — 1 mark for a correct method, 1 mark for a correct answer]

b) $x = k \Rightarrow y = \frac{3k+26}{5}$

So the coordinates of C in terms of k are $\left(k, \frac{3k+26}{5}\right)$

Distance from C to A

$= \sqrt{(k-(-2))^2 + \left(\frac{3k+26}{5} - 4\right)^2} = 2\sqrt{34}$

$\Rightarrow (k+2)^2 + \frac{(3k+6)^2}{25} = (2\sqrt{34})^2$

$\Rightarrow (k+2)^2 + \frac{(3(k+2))^2}{25} = 136$

$\Rightarrow 25(k+2)^2 + 9(k+2)^2 = 25 \times 136$

$\Rightarrow 34(k+2)^2 = 3400$

$\Rightarrow (k+2)^2 = 100$

$\Rightarrow k+2 = 10$ or $k+2 = -10$

$\Rightarrow k = 8$ or $k = -12$

[4 marks available — 1 mark for coordinates of C correctly expressed in terms of k, 1 mark for use of formula for distance between two points, 1 mark for an appropriate quadratic in k, 1 mark for both correct values of k]

c) When $k = 8$, the coordinates of C are $\left(8, \frac{24+26}{5}\right) = (8, 10)$

When $k = -12$, the coordinates of C are

$\left(-12, \frac{-36+26}{5}\right) = (-12, -2)$

[2 marks available — 1 mark for each pair of correct coordinates]

Exercise 6.3 — Equations of the Form $ax + by + c = 0$

Q1 a) $5x - y + 2 = 0$

b) $3y = -\frac{1}{2}x + 3 \Rightarrow \frac{1}{2}x + 3y - 3 = 0 \Rightarrow x + 6y - 6 = 0$

c) $2(x-1) = 4y - 1 \Rightarrow 2x - 2 = 4y - 1 \Rightarrow 2x - 4y - 1 = 0$

d) $7x - 2y - 9 = 0$

e) $\frac{1}{2}(4x+3) = 3(y-2) \Rightarrow 2x + \frac{3}{2} = 3y - 6$

$\Rightarrow 2x - 3y + \frac{15}{2} = 0 \Rightarrow 4x - 6y + 15 = 0$

f) $3(y-4) = 4(x-3) \Rightarrow 3y - 12 = 4x - 12 \Rightarrow 4x - 3y = 0$

Q2 a) $6x - 2y + 3 = 0 \Rightarrow 2y = 6x + 3 \Rightarrow y = 3x + \frac{3}{2}$

$m = 3$, y-intercept $= \left(0, \frac{3}{2}\right)$

b) $-9x + 3y - 12 = 0 \Rightarrow 3y = 9x + 12 \Rightarrow y = 3x + 4$

$m = 3$, y-intercept $= (0, 4)$

c) $-x - 4y - 2 = 0 \Rightarrow -4y = x + 2 \Rightarrow y = -\frac{1}{4}x - \frac{1}{2}$

$m = -\frac{1}{4}$, y-intercept $= \left(0, -\frac{1}{2}\right)$

d) $7x + 8y + 11 = 0 \Rightarrow 8y = -7x - 11 \Rightarrow y = -\frac{7}{8}x - \frac{11}{8}$

$m = -\frac{7}{8}$, y-intercept $= \left(0, -\frac{11}{8}\right)$

e) $2x - 14y + 1 = 0 \Rightarrow 14y = 2x + 1 \Rightarrow y = \frac{1}{7}x + \frac{1}{14}$

$m = \frac{1}{7}$, y-intercept $= \left(0, \frac{1}{14}\right)$

f) $-3x + 28y - 16 = 0 \Rightarrow 28y = 3x + 16 \Rightarrow y = \frac{3}{28}x + \frac{4}{7}$

$m = \frac{3}{28}$, y-intercept $= \left(0, \frac{4}{7}\right)$

g) $0.1x + 0.2y + 0.3 = 0 \Rightarrow 0.2y = -0.1x - 0.3$

$\Rightarrow y = -0.5x - 1.5$

$m = -0.5$, y-intercept $= (0, -1.5)$

h) $-10x + 0.1y + 11 = 0 \Rightarrow 0.1y = 10x - 11 \Rightarrow y = 100x - 110$

$m = 100$, y-intercept $= (0, -110)$

i) $\frac{6}{7}x - 3y + \frac{3}{4} = 0 \Rightarrow 3y = \frac{6}{7}x + \frac{3}{4} \Rightarrow y = \frac{2}{7}x + \frac{1}{4}$

$m = \frac{2}{7}$, y-intercept $= \left(0, \frac{1}{4}\right)$

Q3 a) $(x_1, y_1) = (0, 1), (x_2, y_2) = (-1, -1)$

$m = \frac{-1-1}{-1-0} = \frac{-2}{-1} = 2$

Since you are given the y-intercept (0, 1), you can just use the $y = mx + c$ method before rearranging:

$y = mx + c \Rightarrow y = 2x + 1 \Rightarrow 2x - y + 1 = 0$

b) $(x_1, y_1) = (5, 5), (x_2, y_2) = (0, 0.2)$

$m = \frac{0.2-5}{0-5} = \frac{-4.8}{-5} = \frac{24}{25}$

$y = mx + c \Rightarrow y = \frac{24}{25}x + 0.2 \Rightarrow y = \frac{24}{25}x + \frac{5}{25}$

$\Rightarrow 25y = 24x + 5 \Rightarrow 24x - 25y + 5 = 0$

c) $(x_1, y_1) = (5, 2), (x_2, y_2) = (3, 4)$

$m = \frac{4-2}{3-5} = \frac{2}{-2} = -1$

Here you don't have the y-intercept, so use one of the given points with the $y - y_1 = m(x - x_1)$ method:

$y - y_1 = m(x - x_1) \Rightarrow y - 2 = -1(x - 5)$

$\Rightarrow y - 2 = -x + 5 \Rightarrow x + y - 7 = 0$

d) $(x_1, y_1) = (9, -1), (x_2, y_2) = (7, 2)$

$m = \frac{2-(-1)}{7-9} = -\frac{3}{2}$

$y - y_1 = m(x - x_1)$

$\Rightarrow y - (-1) = -\frac{3}{2}(x-9) \Rightarrow y + 1 = -\frac{3}{2}x + \frac{27}{2}$

$\Rightarrow \frac{3}{2}x + y - \frac{25}{2} = 0 \Rightarrow 3x + 2y - 25 = 0$

e) $(x_1, y_1) = (-6, 1), (x_2, y_2) = (4, 0)$

$m = \frac{0-1}{4-(-6)} = -\frac{1}{10}$

$y - y_1 = m(x - x_1)$

$\Rightarrow y - 1 = -\frac{1}{10}(x-(-6)) \Rightarrow y - 1 = -\frac{1}{10}x - \frac{6}{10}$

$\Rightarrow \frac{1}{10}x + y - \frac{4}{10} = 0 \Rightarrow x + 10y - 4 = 0$

f) $(x_1, y_1) = (-12, 3), (x_2, y_2) = (5, 7)$

$m = \frac{7-3}{5-(-12)} = \frac{4}{17}$

$y - y_1 = m(x - x_1) \Rightarrow y - 3 = \frac{4}{17}(x - (-12))$

$\Rightarrow y - 3 = \frac{4}{17}x + \frac{48}{17} \Rightarrow -\frac{4}{17}x + y - \frac{99}{17} = 0$

$\Rightarrow -4x + 17y - 99 = 0 \Rightarrow 4x - 17y + 99 = 0$

Q4 a) $(x_1, y_1) = (0, -5), (x_2, y_2) = (-5, 0)$

$m = \frac{0-(-5)}{-5-0} = -1$

$y - y_1 = m(x - x_1) \Rightarrow y - (-5) = -1(x - 0)$

$\Rightarrow y + 5 = -x \Rightarrow x + y + 5 = 0$

You can also use the y = mx + c method because you know the y-intercept.

b) $(x_1, y_1) = (0, -2), (x_2, y_2) = (3, 0)$

$m = \frac{0-(-2)}{3-0} = \frac{2}{3}$

$y - y_1 = m(x - x_1)$

$\Rightarrow y - (-2) = \frac{2}{3}(x - 0) \Rightarrow y + 2 = \frac{2}{3}x$

$\Rightarrow -\frac{2}{3}x + y + 2 = 0 \Rightarrow 2x - 3y - 6 = 0$

Q5 $(x_1, y_1) = (-6, 1), (x_2, y_2) = (-2, 7)$

$m = \frac{7-1}{-2-(-6)} = \frac{6}{4} = \frac{3}{2}$

$y - y_1 = m(x - x_1) \Rightarrow y - 7 = \frac{3}{2}(x - (-2)) \Rightarrow y - 7 = \frac{3}{2}x + 3$

$\Rightarrow 2y - 14 = 3x + 6 \Rightarrow 3x - 2y + 20 = 0$

Q6 **a)** The gradient of l is $\frac{-2-5}{6-2} = -\frac{7}{4}$

$y - y_1 = m(x - x_1) \Rightarrow y - 5 = -\frac{7}{4}(x - 2)$
$\Rightarrow 4y - 20 = -7x + 14$
$\Rightarrow 7x + 4y - 34 = 0$

[2 marks available — 1 mark for a correct method, 1 mark for correct equation in the correct form]

b) l intersects the y-axis when $x = 0$:
$7(0) + 4y - 34 = 0 \Rightarrow 4y - 34 = 0 \Rightarrow y = \frac{17}{2}$

So l intersects the y-axis at the point $\left(0, \frac{17}{2}\right)$

l intersects the x-axis when $y = 0$:
$7x + 4(0) - 34 = 0 \Rightarrow 7x - 34 = 0 \Rightarrow x = \frac{34}{7}$

So l intersects the x-axis at the point $\left(\frac{34}{7}, 0\right)$

[2 marks available — 1 mark for correct y-intercept, 1 mark for correct x-intercept]

Q7 **a)** B **b)** A
c) D **d)** C

Q8 **a)** $y - y_1 = m(x - x_1) \Rightarrow y - 5 = \frac{2}{3}(x - 6)$
$\Rightarrow 3y - 15 = 2x - 12 \Rightarrow 2x - 3y + 3 = 0$

[2 marks available — 1 mark for a correct method, 1 mark for correct equation in the correct form]

b) Substitute $x = \frac{3}{4}$ and $y = k$ into the equation for l:
$\Rightarrow 2 \times \frac{3}{4} - 3k + 3 = 0 \Rightarrow k = \frac{3}{2}$

[2 marks available — 1 mark for a correct method, 1 mark for the correct value of k]

Q9 For diagonal AC: $m_{AC} = \frac{5-2}{6-(-3)} = \frac{3}{9} = \frac{1}{3}$

$y - y_1 = m(x - x_1) \Rightarrow y - 2 = \frac{1}{3}(x - (-3)) \Rightarrow y - 2 = \frac{1}{3}x + 1$
$\Rightarrow 3y - 6 = x + 3 \Rightarrow x - 3y + 9 = 0$

For diagonal BD: $m_{BD} = \frac{2-5}{6-(-3)} = \frac{-3}{9} = -\frac{1}{3}$

$y - y_1 = m(x - x_1) \Rightarrow y - 2 = -\frac{1}{3}(x - 6) \Rightarrow y - 2 = -\frac{1}{3}x + 2$
$\Rightarrow 3y - 6 = -x + 6 \Rightarrow x + 3y - 12 = 0$

Q10 **a)** $m = \frac{\left(-\frac{11}{6}\right) - \left(-\frac{2}{15}\right)}{\frac{25}{8} - 1} = \frac{\left(-\frac{55}{30}\right) + \frac{4}{30}}{\frac{25}{8} - \frac{8}{8}} = \frac{-\frac{51}{30}}{\frac{17}{8}}$

$= -\frac{51}{30} \times \frac{8}{17} = -\frac{4}{5}$

$y - y_1 = m(x - x_1) \Rightarrow y - \left(-\frac{2}{15}\right) = -\frac{4}{5}(x - 1)$
$\Rightarrow 15y + 2 = -12x + 12 \Rightarrow 12x + 15y - 10 = 0$

[2 marks available — 1 mark for use of an appropriate formula, 1 mark for correct equation in the correct form]

b) If A, B and C lie on the same straight line, then C must also lie on l. Substituting $x = \frac{5}{3}$ into the equation of l gives:

$12 \times \frac{5}{3} + 15y - 10 = 0 \Rightarrow y = -\frac{2}{3}$

But the y-coordinate of C is $-\frac{1}{3}$. This means C does not lie on l, i.e. A, B and C do not all lie on the same straight line.

[2 marks available — 1 mark for a correct method, 1 mark for the correct conclusion with explanation]

Q11 **a)** $3x + 4y = 18 \Rightarrow 3x + 4y - 18 = 0$

b)

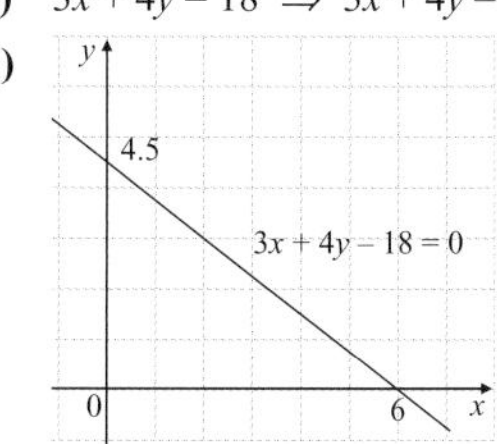

c) $x + 2y = 8 \Rightarrow x + 2y - 8 = 0$

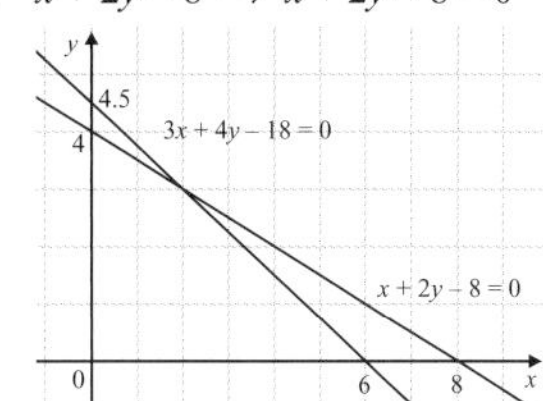

d) Read off the point of intersection from the graph:
$x = 2, y = 3$ — that is, the cost of a small cup is £2 and the cost of a large cup is £3.

Exercise 6.4 — Parallel Lines

Q1 a), c) and e) are parallel.

Rearrange each equation so it's in the form y = mx + c and then compare gradients. If a line is parallel to y = −3x + c, it'll have a gradient of −3.

Q2 **a)** $y = 4x + c$
Sub in $x = 3$ and $y = 2 \Rightarrow 2 = 4 \times 3 + c \Rightarrow -10 = c$
So $y = 4x - 10 \Rightarrow 4x - y - 10 = 0$

b) First rearrange the given equation:
$4x - 2y - 1 = 0 \Rightarrow -2y = -4x + 1 \Rightarrow y = 2x - \frac{1}{2}$
So the equation of the line you want is: $y = 2x + c$
Sub in $x = -4, y = -5 \Rightarrow -5 = 2(-4) + c \Rightarrow c = 3$
So $y = 2x + 3 \Rightarrow 2x - y + 3 = 0$

Q3 **a)** no **b)** yes **c)** yes **d)** no

Q4 **a)** Find the gradient of the other line first:
Rearrange $2x - 4y + 3 = 0$
$\Rightarrow 4y = 2x + 3 \Rightarrow y = \frac{1}{2}x + \frac{3}{4}$
So gradient, $m = \frac{1}{2}$
$y = \frac{1}{2}x + c$
Sub in $x = 4$ and $y = 3 \Rightarrow 3 = \frac{1}{2} \times 4 + c \Rightarrow c = 1$
So $y = \frac{1}{2}x + 1$

b) Rearrange $y = \frac{1}{2}x + 1$
$\Rightarrow \frac{1}{2}x - y + 1 = 0 \Rightarrow x - 2y + 2 = 0$

Q5 **a)** Gradient of the given line $m = 2$
$y = mx + c \Rightarrow y = 2x + c$
Sub in $x = 2, y = 1 \Rightarrow 1 = 2(2) + c \Rightarrow c = -3$
So $y = 2x - 3 \Rightarrow 2x - y - 3 = 0$

b) Rearrange the equation: $y = -5x + 11$, so $m = -5$
$y = mx + c \Rightarrow y = -5x + c$
Sub in $x = 3, y = -1 \Rightarrow -1 = -5(3) + c \Rightarrow c = 14$
So $y = -5x + 14 \Rightarrow 5x + y - 14 = 0$

c) Rearrange the equation: $y = \frac{1}{9}x + \frac{2}{3}$, so $m = \frac{1}{9}$
$y = mx + c \Rightarrow y = \frac{1}{9}x + c$
Sub in $x = -6, y = 2 \Rightarrow 2 = \frac{1}{9}(-6) + c \Rightarrow c = \frac{8}{3}$
So $y = \frac{1}{9}x + \frac{8}{3} \Rightarrow x - 9y + 24 = 0$

d) Rearrange the equation: $y = 4x + 4$, so $m = 4$
$y = mx + c \Rightarrow y = 4x + c$
Sub in $x = -6, y = -5 \Rightarrow -5 = 4(-6) + c \Rightarrow c = 19$
So $y = 4x + 19 \Rightarrow 4x - y + 19 = 0$

e) Rearrange the equation: $y = x - 13$, so $m = 1$
$y = mx + c \Rightarrow y = x + c$
Sub in $x = 0, y = 0 \Rightarrow 0 = 1(0) + c \Rightarrow c = 0$
So $y = x \Rightarrow x - y = 0$

f) Rearrange the equation: $y = 100 - \frac{1}{5}x$, so $m = -\frac{1}{5}$
$y = mx + c \Rightarrow y = -\frac{1}{5}x + c$
Sub in $x = 50, y = 50 \Rightarrow 50 = -\frac{1}{5}(50) + c \Rightarrow c = 60$
So $y = -\frac{1}{5}x + 60 \Rightarrow x + 5y - 300 = 0$

g) Rearrange the equation:
$y = \frac{60}{11} - \frac{5}{22}x$, so $m = -\frac{5}{22}$
$y = mx + c \Rightarrow y = -\frac{5}{22}x + c$
Sub in $x = 4, y = 8 \Rightarrow 8 = -\frac{5}{22}(4) + c \Rightarrow c = \frac{98}{11}$
So $y = -\frac{5}{22}x + \frac{98}{11} \Rightarrow 5x + 22y - 196 = 0$

h) Rearrange the equation:
$3x + 3 - 2y + 2 = 4 \Rightarrow y = \frac{3}{2}x + \frac{1}{2}$, so $m = \frac{3}{2}$
$\Rightarrow y = mx + c \Rightarrow y = \frac{3}{2}x + c$
Sub in $x = -2, y = 2 \Rightarrow 2 = \frac{3}{2}(-2) + c \Rightarrow c = 5$
So $y = \frac{3}{2}x + 5 \Rightarrow 3x - 2y + 10 = 0$

i) Rearrange the equation:
$3(y - 3x) = 2(4 + y) \Rightarrow 3y - 9x = 8 + 2y$
$\Rightarrow y = 9x + 8$, so $m = 9$
$\Rightarrow y = mx + c \Rightarrow y = 9x + c$
Sub in $x = 2, y = 3 \Rightarrow 3 = 9(2) + c \Rightarrow c = -15$
So $y = 9x - 15 \Rightarrow 9x - y - 15 = 0$

Q6 a) $m = \dfrac{7 - \frac{1}{2}}{5 - \frac{15}{4}} = \dfrac{\frac{13}{2}}{\frac{5}{4}} = \frac{13}{2} \times \frac{4}{5} = \frac{26}{5}$
$y - y_1 = m(x - x_1) \Rightarrow y - 7 = \frac{26}{5}(x - 5)$
$\Rightarrow 5y - 35 = 26x - 130 \Rightarrow 26x - 5y - 95 = 0$
[2 marks available — 1 mark for a correct method, 1 mark for a correct equation]

b) l_1 and l_2 are parallel if they have equal gradients.
The gradient of the line l_2 is $\dfrac{-15 - \left(-\frac{43}{5}\right)}{\frac{10}{13} - 2} = \frac{26}{5}$.
From part a), the gradient of l_1 is also $\frac{26}{5}$.
l_1 and l_2 have the same gradient, so they are parallel.
[2 marks available — 1 mark for calculating the gradient of l_2, 1 mark for the correct conclusion with explanation]

c) The gradient of l_3 is $\dfrac{6 - (-12)}{5 - \left(\frac{7}{5}\right)} = 5$.
l_1 and l_3 don't have the same gradient, so they are not parallel.
[2 marks available — 1 mark for calculating the gradient of l_3, 1 mark for the correct conclusion with explanation]

Q7 Write the equations of the lines l_1 and l_2 in the form $y = mx + c$:
l_1: $y = \frac{k}{7}x - \frac{3}{7}$ and l_2: $y = -\frac{(k-2)^2}{2}x + \frac{5}{2}$
If l_1 and l_2 are parallel, then their gradients are equal:
$\frac{k}{7} = -\frac{(k-2)^2}{2} \Rightarrow 7k^2 - 26k + 28 = 0$
The discriminant of this quadratic expression is:
$b^2 - 4ac = (-26)^2 - 4 \times 7 \times 28 = -108 < 0$
The discriminant is negative, so there are no real solutions to this quadratic equation. This means that the gradient of l_1 is never equal to the gradient of l_2, i.e. the lines l_1 and l_2 are not parallel for any value of k.
[5 marks available — 1 mark for finding the gradient of both equations, 1 mark for using the fact that parallel lines have equal gradients, 1 mark for obtaining a quadratic in k, 1 mark for showing that the quadratic has no real solutions, 1 mark for the correct conclusion]

Q8 a) The line through B and C is parallel to the line through A and D, which has equation $y = \frac{1}{2}x - 2$, so BC also has a gradient of $\frac{1}{2}$. The line passes through B(6, 7), so:
$y - y_1 = m(x - x_1) \Rightarrow y - 7 = \frac{1}{2}(x - 6)$
$\Rightarrow 2y - 14 = x - 6 \Rightarrow 2y = x + 8$
C is the point of intersection of the lines $2y = x + 8$ and $4y = 5x - 20$, so solve these equations simultaneously:
Multiply $2y = x + 8$ by 2, to get $4y = 2x + 16$.
Both equations have $4y$ on the left-hand side, so $2x + 16 = 5x - 20 \Rightarrow 36 = 3x \Rightarrow x = 12$
When $x = 12$, $2y = 12 + 8 = 20$, so $y = 10$.
So the coordinates of C are (12, 10).
[4 marks available — 1 mark for using the fact that BC is parallel to AD, 1 mark for correct equation of line through B and C, 1 mark for attempting to solve the equations simultaneously, 1 mark for the correct coordinates of C]

b) The line segment AB is parallel and equal in length to the line segment DC. To get from B(6, 7) to A(4, 0), you move 2 units to the left and 7 units down, so to get from C to D, you do the same movement.
So D has coordinates (12 – 2, 10 – 7) = (10, 3)
[2 marks available — 1 mark for a correct method, 1 mark for the correct coordinates of D]

Exercise 6.5 — Perpendicular Lines

Q1 a) $m = -1 \div 2 = -\frac{1}{2} \Rightarrow y = -\frac{1}{2}x + c$
Sub in $(-2, 5) \Rightarrow 5 = \left(-\frac{1}{2}\right) \times (-2) + c \Rightarrow c = 5 - 1 = 4$
So $y = -\frac{1}{2}x + 4$

b) Rearrange $x - 5y - 30 = 0 \Rightarrow y = \frac{1}{5}x - 6$
$m = -1 \div \frac{1}{5} = -5 \Rightarrow y = -5x + c$
Sub in $(5, 2) \Rightarrow 2 = -5 \times 5 + c \Rightarrow c = 2 + 25 = 27$
So $y = -5x + 27$

Q2 a) $m = -1 \div \frac{1}{4} = -4 \Rightarrow y = -4x + c$
Sub in $(-1, 2) \Rightarrow 2 = (-4) \times (-1) + c \Rightarrow c = 2 - 4 = -2$
So $y = -4x - 2 \Rightarrow 4x + y + 2 = 0$

b) Rearrange to get $y = -\frac{2}{3}x + \frac{1}{3}$
$m = -1 \div -\frac{2}{3} = \frac{3}{2} \Rightarrow y = \frac{3}{2}x + c$
Sub in $(-3, -1) \Rightarrow -1 = \frac{3}{2} \times (-3) + c \Rightarrow c = -1 + \frac{9}{2} = \frac{7}{2}$
So $y = \frac{3}{2}x + \frac{7}{2} \Rightarrow 2y = 3x + 7 \Rightarrow 3x - 2y + 7 = 0$

c) Rearrange to get $y = \frac{1}{2}x + \frac{1}{10}$
$m = -1 \div \frac{1}{2} = -2 \Rightarrow y = -2x + c$
Sub in $(6, -5) \Rightarrow -5 = -2 \times 6 + c \Rightarrow c = -5 + 12 = 7$
So $y = -2x + 7 \Rightarrow 2x + y - 7 = 0$

d) $m = -1 \div \frac{3}{2} = -\frac{2}{3} \Rightarrow y = -\frac{2}{3}x + c$
Sub in $(2, 1) \Rightarrow 1 = -\frac{2}{3} \times 2 + c \Rightarrow c = 1 + \frac{4}{3} = \frac{7}{3}$
So $y = -\frac{2}{3}x + \frac{7}{3} \Rightarrow 3y = -2x + 7 \Rightarrow 2x + 3y - 7 = 0$

e) Rearrange to get $y = \frac{4}{21}x + \frac{2}{21}$
$m = -1 \div \frac{4}{21} = -\frac{21}{4} \Rightarrow y = -\frac{21}{4}x + c$
Sub in $(0.5, 7) \Rightarrow 7 = -\frac{21}{4} \times 0.5 + c$
$\Rightarrow c = 7 + \frac{21}{8} = \frac{77}{8}$
So $y = -\frac{21}{4}x + \frac{77}{8} \Rightarrow 42x + 8y - 77 = 0$

f) Rearrange to get $10 - 5x + 15y = 2 \Rightarrow y = \frac{1}{3}x - \frac{8}{15}$
$m = -1 \div \frac{1}{3} = -3 \Rightarrow y = -3x + c$
Sub in $(-5, -1) \Rightarrow -1 = -3 \times -5 + c \Rightarrow c = -1 - 15 = -16$
So $y = -3x - 16 \Rightarrow 3x + y + 16 = 0$

g) Rearrange to get $56y + 8 = 2x - 3 \Rightarrow y = \frac{1}{28}x - \frac{11}{56}$
$m = -1 \div \frac{1}{28} = -28 \Rightarrow y = -28x + c$
Sub in $(7, 8) \Rightarrow 8 = -28 \times 7 + c \Rightarrow c = 8 + 196 = 204$
So $y = -28x + 204 \Rightarrow 28x + y - 204 = 0$

h) Rearrange to get $y = 4x + 0.2y + 1 \Rightarrow 0.8y = 4x + 1$
$\Rightarrow y = 5x + \frac{5}{4}$
$m = -1 \div 5 = -\frac{1}{5} \Rightarrow y = -\frac{1}{5}x + c$
Sub in $(3, 4.4) \Rightarrow 4.4 = -\frac{1}{5} \times 3 + c \Rightarrow c = 4.4 + \frac{3}{5} = 5$
So $y = -\frac{1}{5}x + 5 \Rightarrow x + 5y - 25 = 0$

Q3 **a)** Rearrange $3x + 4y - 1 = 0 \Rightarrow y = -\frac{3}{4}x + \frac{1}{4}$

Multiply the gradients of the lines: $\frac{4}{3} \times -\frac{3}{4} = -1$
So the lines are perpendicular.
Remember, if you multiply the gradients of two perpendicular lines you get −1.

b) Rearrange $3x + 2y - 3 = 0 \Rightarrow y = -\frac{3}{2}x + \frac{3}{2}$

Multiply the gradients of the lines: $\frac{3}{2} \times -\frac{3}{2} = -\frac{9}{4}$

So the lines are not perpendicular.

c) Rearrange $4x - y + 3 = 0 \Rightarrow y = 4x + 3$

Rearrange $2x + 8y + 1 = 0 \Rightarrow y = -\frac{1}{4}x - \frac{1}{8}$

Multiply the gradients of the lines: $4 \times -\frac{1}{4} = -1$

So the lines are perpendicular.

d) Rearrange $3x - 5y + 10 = 0 \Rightarrow y = \frac{3}{5}x + 2$

Rearrange $15x + 6y - 4 = 0 \Rightarrow y = \frac{2}{3} - \frac{5}{2}x$

Multiply the gradients of the lines: $\frac{3}{5} \times -\frac{5}{2} = -\frac{3}{2}$

So the lines are not perpendicular.

Q4 PQ: $m = \frac{7-(-2)}{-1-4} = -\frac{9}{5}$

So the gradient of the line perpendicular to PQ is $\frac{5}{9}$

$y = mx + c \Rightarrow y = \frac{5}{9}x + c$

Sub in (2, 5) $\Rightarrow 5 = \frac{5}{9} \times 2 + c \Rightarrow c = 5 - \frac{10}{9} = \frac{35}{9}$

So $y = \frac{5}{9}x + \frac{35}{9} \Rightarrow 5x - 9y + 35 = 0$

Q5 **a)** AB: $m = \frac{3-2}{4-0} = \frac{1}{4} \Rightarrow y = \frac{1}{4}x + c$

Sub in (0, 2) $\Rightarrow 2 = 0 + c \Rightarrow c = 2$

So $y = \frac{1}{4}x + 2$

BC: $m = \frac{-1-3}{5-4} = -4 \Rightarrow y = -4x + c$

Sub in (4, 3) $\Rightarrow 3 = -4 \times 4 + c \Rightarrow c = 19$

So $y = -4x + 19$

AC: $m = \frac{-1-2}{5-0} = -\frac{3}{5} \Rightarrow y = -\frac{3}{5}x + c$

Sub in (0, 2) $\Rightarrow 2 = 0 + c \Rightarrow c = 2$

So $y = -\frac{3}{5}x + 2$

b) The triangle is right-angled, as AB is perpendicular to BC:

$m_{AB} \times m_{BC} = \frac{1}{4} \times -4 = -1$

Q6 **a)** PR: $m_{PR} = \frac{3-(-1)}{3-1} = \frac{4}{2} = 2 \Rightarrow y = 2x + c$

Sub in (1, −1) $\Rightarrow -1 = 2(1) + c \Rightarrow c = -3$

So $y = 2x - 3$

QS: $m_{QS} = \frac{0-2}{4-0} = \frac{-2}{4} = -\frac{1}{2} \Rightarrow y = -\frac{1}{2}x + c$

Sub in (0, 2) $\Rightarrow 2 = -\frac{1}{2}(0) + c \Rightarrow c = 2$

So $y = -\frac{1}{2}x + 2$

b) From a), the product of the diagonals is $2 \times -\frac{1}{2} = -1$, so they are perpendicular i.e. PQRS could be a square, a rhombus or a kite.
If PQRS is a square, the diagonals will be the same length.
$PR = \sqrt{(3-1)^2 + (3-(-1))^2} = \sqrt{20} = 2\sqrt{5}$ and
$QS = \sqrt{(4-0)^2 + (0-2)^2} = \sqrt{20} = 2\sqrt{5}$, so PQRS is a square.

Q7 Rearrange the equation into $y = mx + c$:

$-2y = -3x + 6 \Rightarrow y = \frac{3}{2}x - 3$, so the line we want will have gradient $m = -1 \div \frac{3}{2} = -\frac{2}{3}$

Now sub in (a, b) to find c: $y = -\frac{2}{3}x + c$

$$b = -\frac{2}{3}a + c$$

$$c = b + \frac{2}{3}a$$

So the equation of line A is $y = -\frac{2}{3}x + \frac{2}{3}a + b$

You could also have given the line in the form 2x + 3y − 2a − 3b = 0 as the question didn't tell you which form to use.

Q8 The gradient of the line AB is $\frac{2-4}{5-1} = -\frac{1}{2}$.

So the gradient of the perpendicular bisector is:

$m = -1 \div -\frac{1}{2} = 2$

The bisector will pass through the midpoint of the line — this will be at $\left(\frac{1+5}{2}, \frac{4+2}{2}\right) = (3, 3)$.

So $y = 2x + c \Rightarrow 3 = 2(3) + c \Rightarrow c = 3 - 6 = -3$

So the equation of the perpendicular bisector is: $y = 2x - 3$.

Q9 **a)** l_2 is parallel to l_1, so it has a gradient of $-\frac{1}{2}$.

$y - y_1 = m(x - x_1) \Rightarrow y - (-1) = -\frac{1}{2}(x - 10)$

$\Rightarrow y = -\frac{1}{2}x + 4$

[2 marks available — 1 mark for a correct method, 1 mark for a correct equation]

b) Any line perpendicular (normal) to l_1 has a gradient of $-1 \div -\frac{1}{2} = 2$. So the equation of the normal to l_1 through $\left(-\frac{8}{5}, \frac{4}{5}\right)$ is:

$y - y_1 = m(x - x_1) \Rightarrow y - \frac{4}{5} = 2\left(x - \left(-\frac{8}{5}\right)\right) \Rightarrow y = 2x + 4$

[2 marks available — 1 mark for the correct gradient of the normal line, 1 mark for a correct equation]

c) The shortest distance is the distance along the line $y = 2x + 4$ from where it crosses l_1 to where it crosses l_2.

$y = 2x + 4$ crosses l_1 at $\left(-\frac{8}{5}, \frac{4}{5}\right)$, as given in the question.

To find where $y = 2x + 4$ crosses l_2, solve the equations $y = 2x + 4$ and $y = -\frac{1}{2}x + 4$ simultaneously:

$2x + 4 = -\frac{1}{2}x + 4 \Rightarrow \frac{5}{2}x = 0 \Rightarrow x = 0$

$y = 2(0) + 4 \Rightarrow y = 4$

So $y = 2x + 4$ crosses l_2 at (0, 4).

Therefore the shortest distance between l_1 and l_2 is the distance between the points $\left(-\frac{8}{5}, \frac{4}{5}\right)$ and (0, 4):

Shortest distance $= \sqrt{\left(0 - \left(-\frac{8}{5}\right)\right)^2 + \left(4 - \frac{4}{5}\right)^2} = \frac{8}{\sqrt{5}} = \frac{8\sqrt{5}}{5}$

[3 marks available — 1 mark for a correct method to find the shortest distance between the lines, 1 mark for using the formula for distance between two points, 1 mark for the correct answer]

Q10 **a)** Gradient $= \frac{10-0}{4-0} = \frac{5}{2}$, y-intercept = 0 (at point A).

So the equation of the line, l_1, through A and B is $y = \frac{5}{2}x$

[1 mark for correct equation of the line]

b) The gradient of l_1 is $\frac{5}{2}$, so the gradient of l_2 is $-1 \div \frac{5}{2} = -\frac{2}{5}$

$y - y_1 = m(x - x_1) \Rightarrow y - 0 = -\frac{2}{5}(x - 10)$

$\Rightarrow y = -\frac{2}{5}x + 4$

[3 marks available — 1 mark for calculation of gradient of perpendicular, 1 mark for a correct method to find the equation of the line, 1 mark for a correct equation]

c) Solving the simultaneous equations $y = \frac{5}{2}x$ and $y = -\frac{2}{5}x + 4$ gives the coordinates of the point of intersection of the lines l_1 and l_2:

$\frac{5}{2}x = -\frac{2}{5}x + 4 \Rightarrow 25x = -4x + 40 \Rightarrow x = \frac{40}{29}$

$y = \frac{5}{2} \times \frac{40}{29} = \frac{100}{29}$

So G has coordinates $\left(\frac{40}{29}, \frac{100}{29}\right)$.

[2 marks available — 1 mark for attempting to solve the equations simultaneously, 1 mark for the correct coordinates]

d) The coordinates of D, E and F are (2, 5), (7, 5) and (5, 0) respectively. The length of DE is $7 - 2 = 5$.

The length of FG is $\sqrt{\left(5 - \frac{40}{29}\right)^2 + \left(0 - \frac{100}{29}\right)^2}$

$= \sqrt{\left(\frac{105}{29}\right)^2 + \left(-\frac{100}{29}\right)^2} = \sqrt{\frac{11\,025}{841} + \frac{10\,000}{841}} = \sqrt{25} = 5$

Therefore the length of FG is equal to the length of DE.

[2 marks available — 1 mark for use of formula for distance FG, 1 mark for showing that the lengths are equal]

Q11 The shortest distance from a point to a line is the distance perpendicular to the line. So if the perpendicular to $2y + x = 38$ through the point (–2, 5) intersects the line at the point A, then the shortest distance from the point to the line is the distance between the points (–2, 5) and A.

$2y + x = 38 \Rightarrow y = -\frac{1}{2}x + 19$, so the gradient of the line is $-\frac{1}{2}$.

The gradient of any line perpendicular to $2y + x = 38$ is $-1 \div -\frac{1}{2} = 2$

So the equation of the perpendicular line through (–2, 5) is:

$y - y_1 = m(x - x_1) \Rightarrow y - 5 = 2(x - (-2)) \Rightarrow y = 2x + 9$

Find the point of intersection of $2y + x = 38$ and $y = 2x + 9$:

$2y + x = 38 \Rightarrow y = -\frac{1}{2}x + 19$,

then $-\frac{1}{2}x + 19 = 2x + 9 \Rightarrow 10 = \frac{5}{2}x \Rightarrow x = 4$

$y = 2(4) + 9 = 17$, so the point of intersection is (4, 17).

The distance from (–2, 5) to (4, 17) is:

$\sqrt{(4-(-2))^2 + (17-5)^2} = \sqrt{180} = 6\sqrt{5}$

So the shortest distance from the point to the line is $6\sqrt{5}$.

[6 marks available — 1 mark for correct gradient of perpendicular, 1 mark for a correct method to find the equation of the perpendicular, 1 mark for correct equation of perpendicular line, 1 mark for solving the equations simultaneously, 1 mark for the coordinates of the point of intersection, 1 mark for the correct answer]

Q12 a) Substitute $x = 8$ into the equation of l: $2y + 40 = 50 \Rightarrow y = 5$

Therefore P (8, 5) lies on the line l. *[1 mark]*

b) l crosses the x-axis when $y = 0$, so $2(0) + 5x = 50 \Rightarrow x = 10$

So the coordinates of Q are (10, 0). *[1 mark]*

c) $2y + 5x = 50 \Rightarrow y = -\frac{5}{2}x + 25$, so the gradient of l is $-\frac{5}{2}$.

Any line perpendicular to l has a gradient of $-1 \div -\frac{5}{2} = \frac{2}{5}$.

So the equation of l_1 is $y - 5 = \frac{2}{5}(x - 8) \Rightarrow y = \frac{2}{5}x + \frac{9}{5}$,

and the equation of l_2 is $y - 0 = \frac{2}{5}(x - 10) \Rightarrow y = \frac{2}{5}x - 4$.

[3 marks available — 1 mark for the correct perpendicular gradient, 1 mark for each correct equation]

d) The points of intersection of l with l_1 and l_2 are the points P (8, 5) and Q (10, 0) respectively.

So the quadrilateral looks like this:

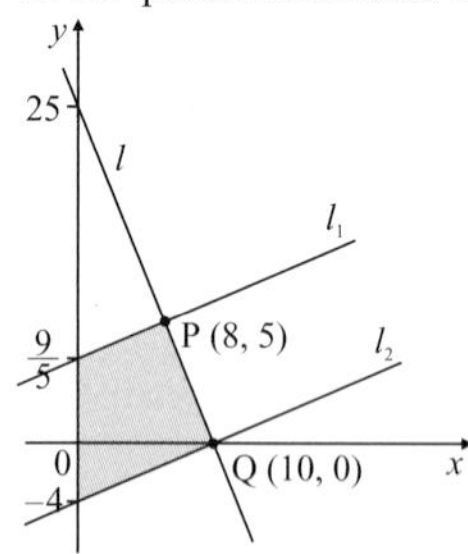

To find the area of the required quadrilateral, subtract the area of the triangle bounded by l, l_1 and the y-axis from the area of the triangle bounded by l, l_2 and the y-axis.

Area $= \frac{1}{2}(25 - (-4)) \times 10 - \frac{1}{2}\left(25 - \frac{9}{5}\right) \times 8 = \frac{261}{5}$

[3 marks available — 1 mark for a correct method, 1 mark for any correct area calculated, 1 mark for the correct area of the required quadrilateral]

Exercise 6.6 — Direct Proportion

Q1 a) $y \propto x \Rightarrow y = kx$

When $x = 8$, $24 = 8k \Rightarrow k = \frac{24}{8} = 3 \Rightarrow y = 3x$

So when $x = 5$, $a = 3 \times 5 = 15$

b) $y \propto x \Rightarrow y = kx$

When $x = 7$, $28 = 7k \Rightarrow k = \frac{28}{7} = 4 \Rightarrow y = 4x$

So when $y = 96$, $96 = 4a \Rightarrow a = \frac{96}{4} = 24$

Q2 a) $y \propto \frac{1}{x} \Rightarrow xy = k$

When $x = 6$, $y = 3 \Rightarrow k = 6 \times 3 = 18$

So $y = \frac{18}{x} = \frac{18}{9} = 2$

b) $y \propto \frac{1}{x} \Rightarrow xy = k$

When $x = 12$, $y = 12 \Rightarrow k = 12 \times 12 = 144$

So $x = \frac{144}{y} = \frac{144}{36} = 4$

Q3 a) The +2 means that the equation cannot be written in the form $y = kx$ (the graph also does not pass through the origin), so y is not directly proportional to x.

b) The equation can be written as $y = (a - b)x$, where the constant of proportionality is equal to $(a - b)$, so y is directly proportional to x.

c) Simplifying the equation gives $y = x - 2$, which cannot be written as $y = kx$, so y is not directly proportional to x.

d) Expanding the brackets gives:

$y = x^2 + 6x + 9 - (x^2 - 6x + 9)$

$\Rightarrow y = x^2 + 6x + 9 - x^2 + 6x - 9$

$\Rightarrow y = 12x$, so they are in direct proportion.

Q4 $y \propto x^2 \Rightarrow y = kx^2$

When $x = 4$, $40 = k \times 4^2 = 16k \Rightarrow k = \frac{5}{2}$

a) $y = \frac{5}{2}x^2 \Rightarrow y = \frac{5}{2} \times 2^2 = 10$

b) $y = \frac{5}{2}x^2 \Rightarrow 45 = \frac{5}{2}x^2 \Rightarrow x^2 = 18 \Rightarrow x = 3\sqrt{2}$

($x > 0$, so ignore the negative root)

Q5 If $y \propto x$ and $y \propto z$, then we can write $y = k_1x$ and $y = k_2z$, where k_1 and k_2 are constants. Equating y's: $k_1x = k_2z \Rightarrow x = \frac{k_2}{k_1}z$

$\frac{k_2}{k_1}$ must be a constant since k_1 and k_2 are constants.

So $x \propto z$ with constant of proportionality $\frac{k_2}{k_1}$.

Q6 $y \propto x \Rightarrow y = kx$

When $x = 3$, $y = 15 \Rightarrow 15 = 3k \Rightarrow k = 5$, so $y = 5x$.

[3 marks available — 1 mark for correct algebraic relationship between x and y, 1 mark for a straight-line graph with axes clearly labelled, 1 mark for the correct graph for $0 \leq x \leq 6$]

Q7 $F \propto m$ and $F = 15$ when $m = 12$.

So $F = km \Rightarrow 15 = 12k \Rightarrow k = \frac{15}{12} = 1.25$

So when $m = 18$, $F = 1.25 \times 18 = 22.5$ N

Q8 a) $x \propto \frac{1}{y} \Rightarrow x = \frac{k_1}{y}$ for some constant k_1.

$x \propto \sqrt{z} \Rightarrow x = k_2\sqrt{z}$ for some constant k_2.

So $\frac{k_1}{y} = k_2\sqrt{z} \Rightarrow y = \frac{k_1}{k_2} \times \frac{1}{\sqrt{z}} \Rightarrow y = \frac{K}{\sqrt{z}}$

for some constant $K = \frac{k_1}{k_2}$, i.e. $y \propto \frac{1}{\sqrt{z}}$.

[4 marks available — 1 mark for derivation of expression relating x and y, 1 mark for derivation of expression relating x and z, 1 mark for attempting to combine these expressions, 1 mark for correct derivation of result]

b) When $z = 225$, $y = 8$, so:

$y = \frac{K}{\sqrt{z}} \Rightarrow 8 = \frac{K}{\sqrt{225}} \Rightarrow 8 = \frac{K}{15} \Rightarrow K = 120$

So $y = \frac{120}{\sqrt{z}}$. When $z = 72$, $y = \frac{120}{\sqrt{72}} = 10\sqrt{2}$

[2 marks available — 1 mark for correct value of the constant of proportionality, 1 mark for the correct answer]

c) When $y = 105$:

$105 = \frac{120}{\sqrt{z}} \Rightarrow z = \left(\frac{120}{105}\right)^2 \Rightarrow z = \left(\frac{8}{7}\right)^2 \Rightarrow z = \frac{64}{49}$

[2 marks available — 1 mark for a correct method, 1 mark for the correct answer]

Q9 a) $P \propto T \Rightarrow P = kT$

When $P = 150\,000$, $T = 400 \Rightarrow 150\,000 = 400k \Rightarrow k = 375$

So $P = 375T$

[2 marks available — 1 mark for calculating the value of the constant of proportionality, 1 mark for the correct equation]

b) When $P = 216\,000$, $P = 375T \Rightarrow 216\,000 = 375T$

$\Rightarrow T = 576$ kelvins *[1 mark]*

c) The value of k is the increase in pressure for each increase in temperature of 1 kelvin. *[1 mark for a correct interpretation]*

d) If the temperature increases by 112 kelvins then the pressure increases by $375 \times 112 = 42\,000$ pascals. *[1 mark]*

Q10 a) $I \propto V \Rightarrow I = k_1V$

The graph of I against V passes through the point (4, 14), so:

$I = k_1V \Rightarrow 14 = 4k_1 \Rightarrow k_1 = \frac{7}{2}$. So $I = \frac{7}{2}V$

[2 marks available — 1 mark for attempting to use the information from the graph, 1 mark for the correct expression for I in terms of V]

b) When $I = 12$: $I = \frac{7}{2}V \Rightarrow 12 = \frac{7}{2}V$

$\Rightarrow V = \frac{24}{7} = 3.4$ volts (2 s.f.) *[1 mark]*

c) $I \propto \frac{1}{R} \Rightarrow I = \frac{k_2}{R}$

The graph of I against R passes through the point (200, 0.4),

so: $I = \frac{k_2}{R} \Rightarrow 0.4 = \frac{k_2}{200} \Rightarrow k_2 = 80$. So $I = \frac{80}{R}$

[2 marks available — 1 mark for attempting to use the information from the graph, 1 mark for the correct expression for I in terms of R]

d) When $R = 500$, $I = \frac{80}{500} = 0.16$ ohms *[1 mark]*

Exercise 6.7 — Sketching Cubic and Quartic Graphs

Q1 a) $y = -1.5x^4$ will be n-shaped and below the x-axis since the power is even and the coefficient is negative, so it must be graph D.

b) $y = 0.5x^3$ has an odd power and a positive coefficient so it will have a bottom-left to top-right curve. It must be graph B.

c) $y = 2x^6$ has an even power and a positive coefficient so it'll be u-shaped and above the x-axis. It must be graph A.

d) $y = -3x^3$ has an odd power of x and a negative coefficient so it must have a top-left to bottom-right curve. It must be graph C.

Q2 a)

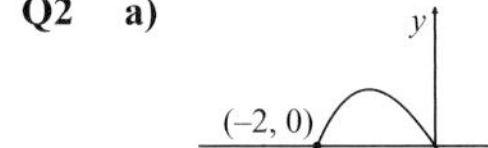

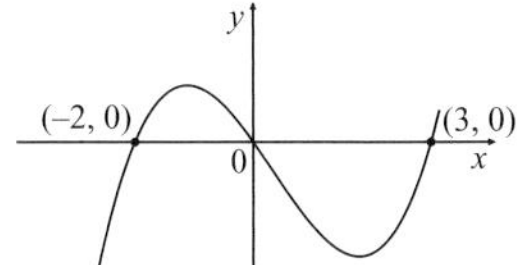

b)

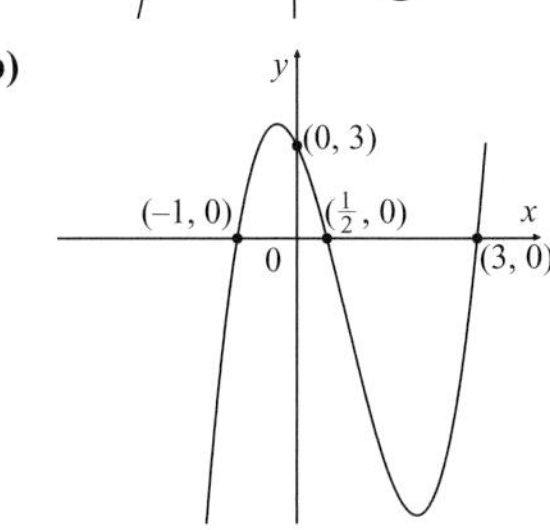

c)

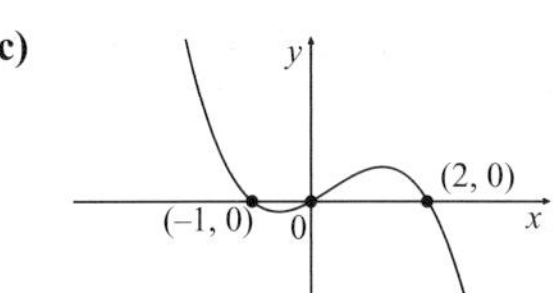

Your graphs don't need to look exactly like these — you don't need to get the size of the 'dips' right, as long as you've got the rough shape and the intercepts with the x-axis.

Q3 a)

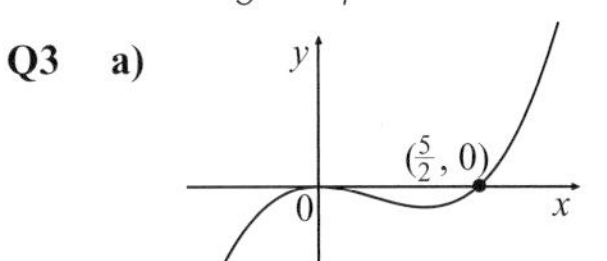

There's a repeated root at x = 0 because of the x^2 factor.

b)

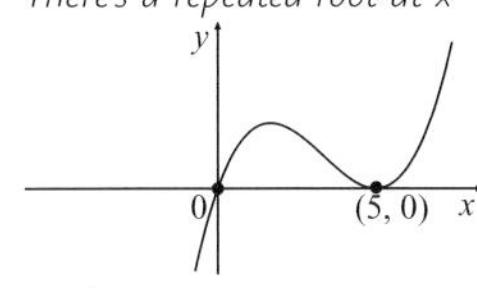

c)

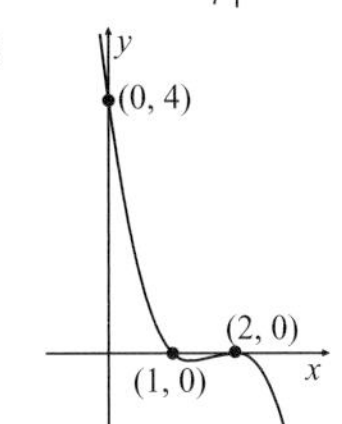

Remember — putting in values for x near the key points can really help you understand the shape of the graphs. E.g. for part c), pop in x = 1.5 and 2.5 to check that both give negative values for y.

Q4 a)

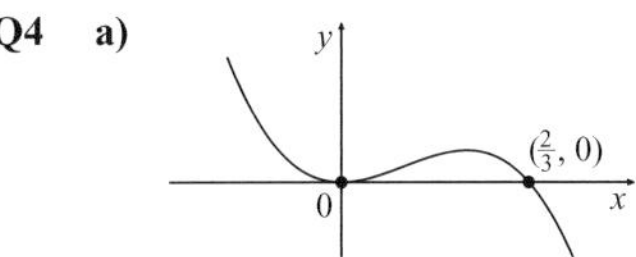

b)

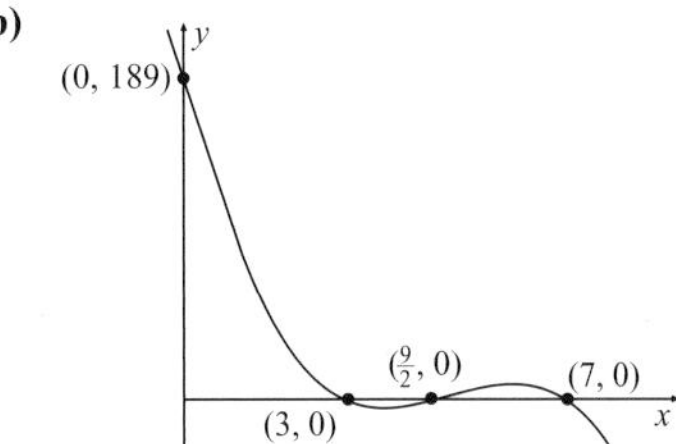

c)

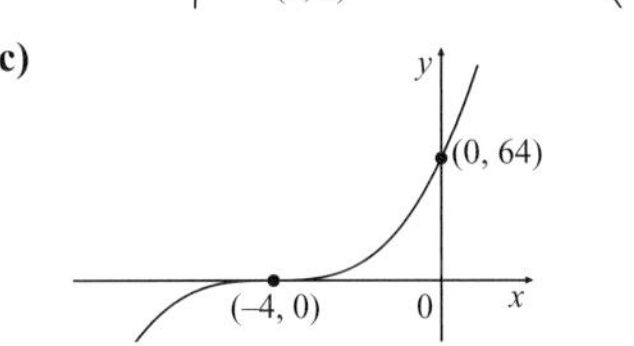

Q5 a) A **b)** D

c) C **d)** B

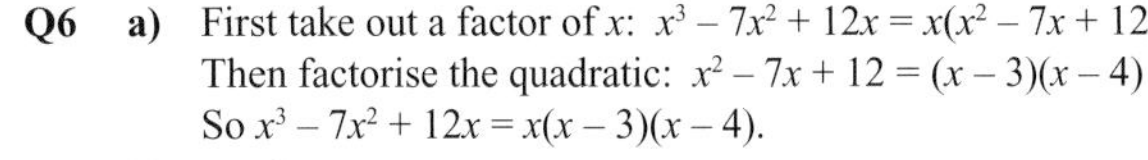

Q6 a) First take out a factor of x: $x^3 - 7x^2 + 12x = x(x^2 - 7x + 12)$

Then factorise the quadratic: $x^2 - 7x + 12 = (x - 3)(x - 4)$

So $x^3 - 7x^2 + 12x = x(x - 3)(x - 4)$.

b)

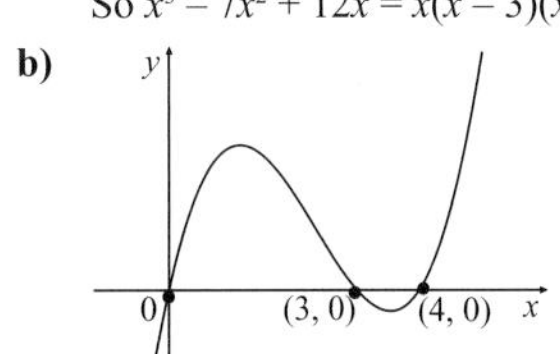

Q7 a) $x^3 - 16x = x(x^2 - 16) = x(x + 4)(x - 4)$
Using this information we can sketch the graph:

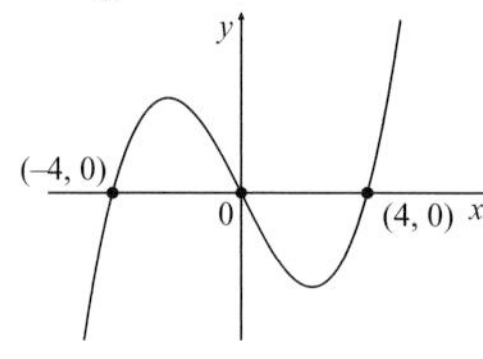

b) $2x^3 - 12x^2 + 18x = 2x(x^2 - 6x + 9) = 2x(x - 3)^2$
Using this information we can sketch the graph:

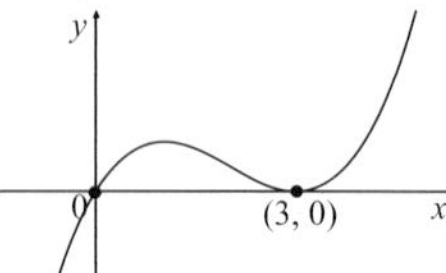

c) $-3x^2 - x^3 = -x^2(3 + x)$
Using this information we can sketch the graph:

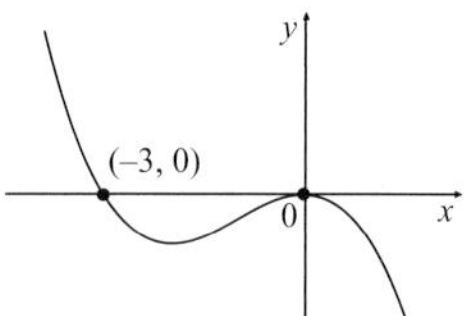

Q8 a)

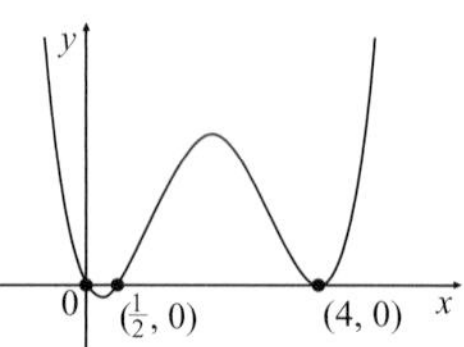

Watch out for the repeated root — the (x – 4) bracket is squared so it only touches the axis at x = 4.

b)

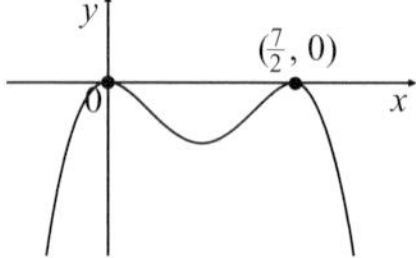

Here there are two double roots, so the graph never crosses the x-axis. Since the coefficient of x^4 is negative, the graph is below the x-axis.

c)

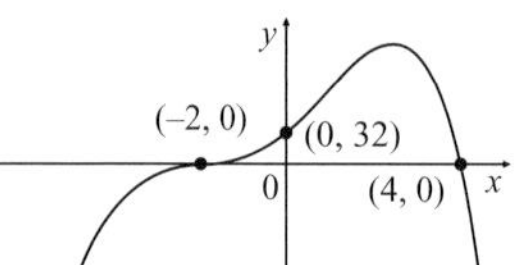

x = –2 is a triple root — the graph at this point looks like the graph of x^3.

Q9 $y = (9 - x^2)(x^2 - 40) = -(x + 3)(x - 3)(x + \sqrt{40})(x - \sqrt{40})$

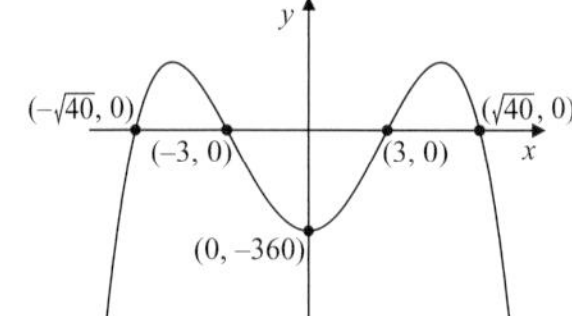

coefficient of x^4 is negative, y-intercept is at (0, –360), roots at $x = -\sqrt{40}, -3, 3, \sqrt{40}$

[4 marks available — 1 mark for a correct factorisation, 1 mark for a graph with the correct shape, 1 mark for the correct y-intercept, 1 mark for the correct x-axis intercepts]

Q10 a) $y = x^2(x^2 - 9x + 14) = x^2(x - 2)(x - 7)$

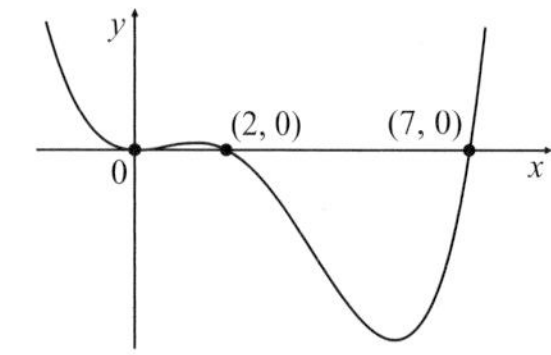

coefficient of x^4 is positive, double root at $x = 0$, roots at $x = 2$ and $x = 7$

b) $y = (x + 1)(2 - 3x)(4x^2 - 9) = (x + 1)(2 - 3x)(2x + 3)(2x - 3)$

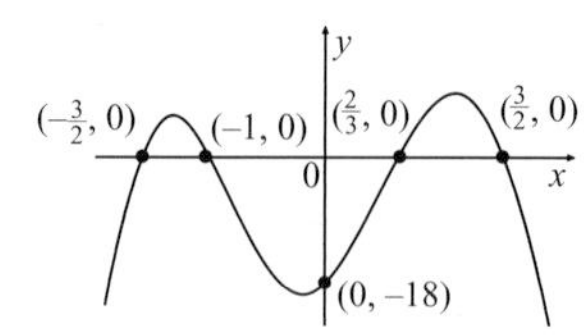

coefficient of x^4 is negative, y-intercept is at (0, –18), roots at $x = -\frac{3}{2}, -1, \frac{2}{3}, \frac{3}{2}$

c) $y = (x - 5)(2x^3 + 5x^2 - 3x)$
$= (x - 5)[x(2x^2 + 5x - 3)] = x(x - 5)(2x - 1)(x + 3)$

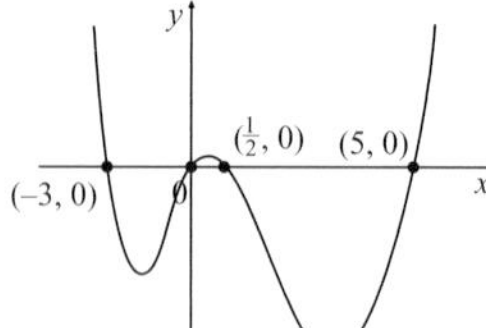

coefficient of x^4 is positive, roots at –3, 0, $\frac{1}{2}$, 5

Q11 The coefficients add up to zero, so $(x - 1)$ must be a factor.
Then use e.g. algebraic division to factorise:
$4x^3 + 4x^2 - 5x - 3 = (x - 1)(4x^2 + 8x + 3) = (x - 1)(2x + 3)(2x + 1)$
Using this information, sketch the graph:

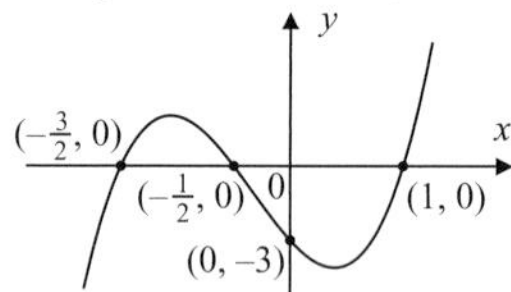

See Chapter 4 for more on factorising cubic and quadratic equations.

Q12 a) $x = 1$ is a root so $(x - 1)$ is a factor.
Using e.g. algebraic division:
$f(x) = (x + 1)(x - 1)(2x^2 - 3x - 2)$
$= (x + 1)(x - 1)(x - 2)(2x + 1)$

b) Using this information, sketch the graph:

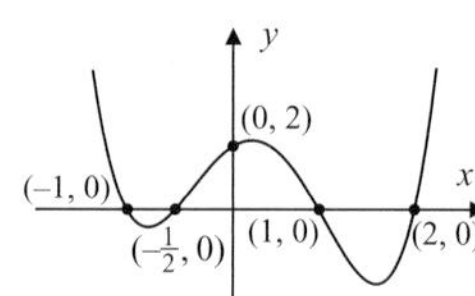

Q13 Fully factorise the quartic — the coefficients in the cubic part add up to zero, so $(x - 1)$ must be a factor.
Using e.g. algebraic division:
$y = (x - 3)(x^3 - 7x^2 + 14x - 8) = (x - 3)(x - 1)(x^2 - 6x + 8)$
$= (x - 3)(x - 1)(x - 2)(x - 4)$
Using this information, you can sketch the graph:

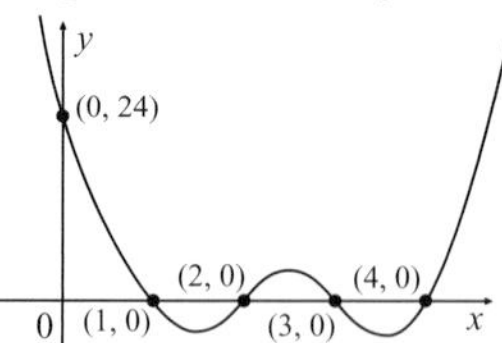

Q14 a) $(x - 2) = 0$ when $x = 2$ and
$(2x^2 + 5x - 1) = 0$ when $x = \frac{-5 + \sqrt{33}}{4} = 0.186...$
or $x = \frac{-5 - \sqrt{33}}{4} = -2.686...$ (from the quadratic formula).
f(x) is a positive cubic with y-intercept at $-2 \times -1 = 2$:

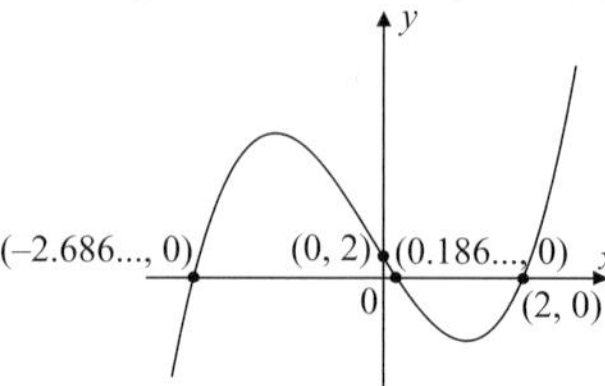

[4 marks available — 1 mark for obtaining the roots of the quadratic factor, 1 mark for a graph with the correct shape, 1 mark for the correct y-intercept, 1 mark for the correct x-axis intercepts]

b) $y = xf(x)$ is a positive quartic which crosses the x-axis at the same points as $y = f(x)$, and also passes through the origin.

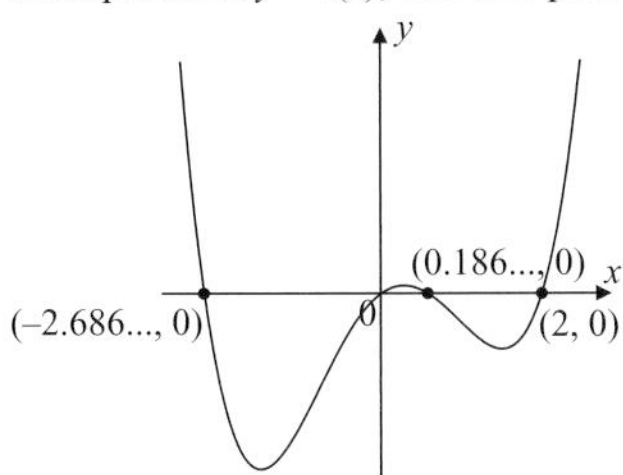

[2 marks available — 1 mark for a graph with the correct shape, 1 mark for all intercepts with the coordinate axes correct]

Exercise 6.8 — Graphs of Reciprocal Functions and Negative Powers

Q1 a) $y = x^{-2} = \frac{1}{x^2}$.

$n = 2$ is even so you'll get a graph with two bits next to each other. $k = 1$ is positive so the graph will all be above the axis so it must be graph D.

b) $y = -3x^{-3} = -\frac{3}{x^3}$.

$n = 3$ is odd so you'll get a graph with two bits opposite each other. $k = -3$ is negative so the graph will be in the top-left and bottom-right quadrants so it must be graph A.

c) $y = -\frac{3}{x^4}$.

$n = 4$ is even so you'll get a graph with two bits next to each other. $k = -3$ so the graph will all be below the x-axis so it must be graph B.

d) $y = 2x^{-5} = \frac{2}{x^5}$.

$n = 5$ is odd so you'll get a graph with two bits opposite each other. $k = 2$ is positive so the graph will be in the bottom-left and top-right quadrants so it must be graph C.

Q2 a)

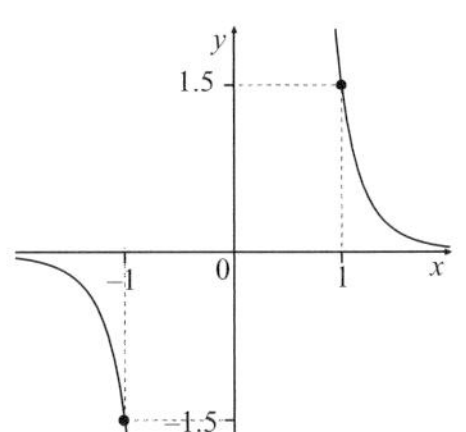

b)

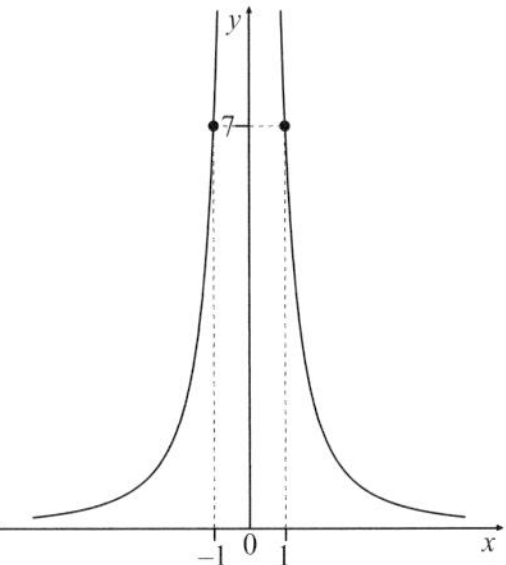

c)

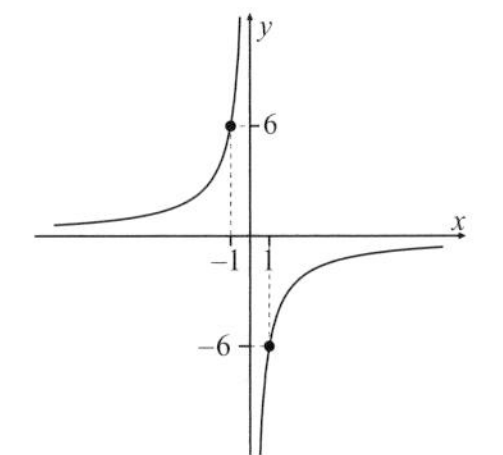

d)

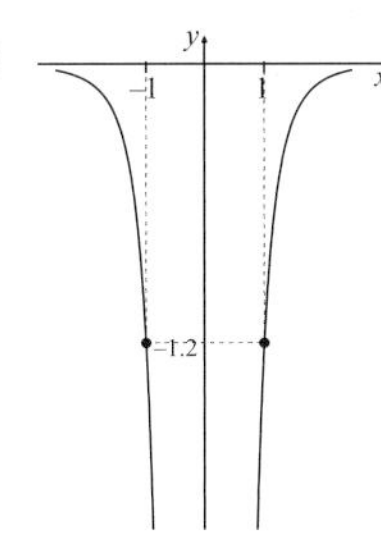

e)

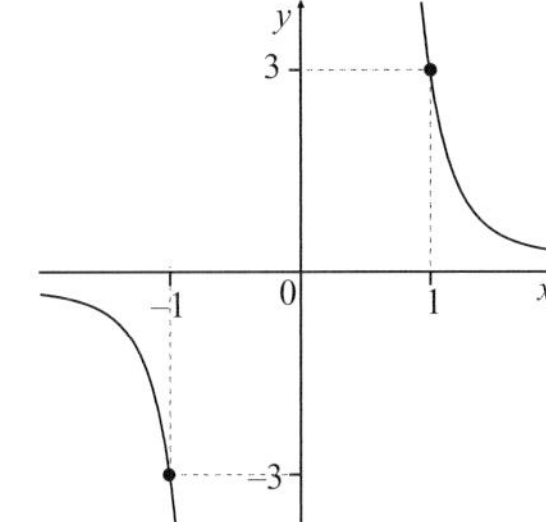

f)

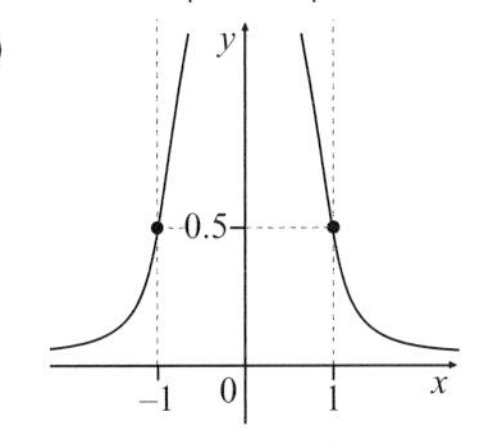

g)

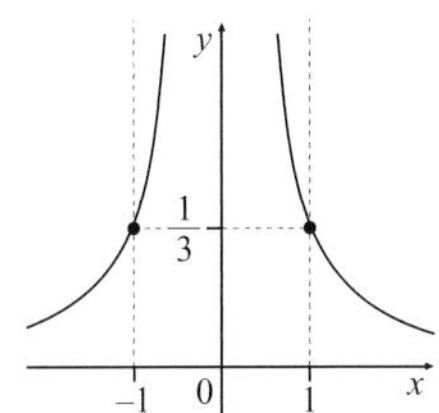

h)

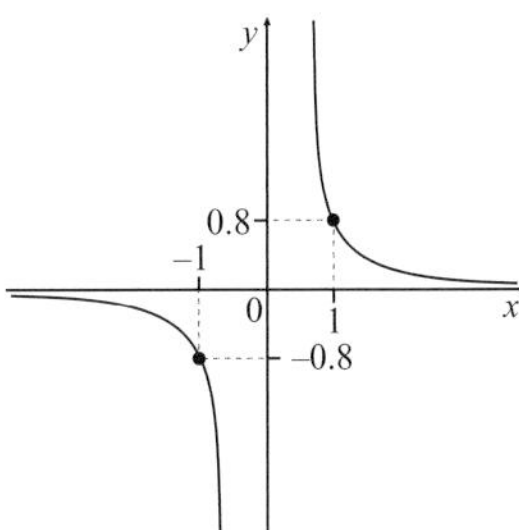

Q3 a) $y = -x^3 - 2x^2 = -x^2(x + 2)$

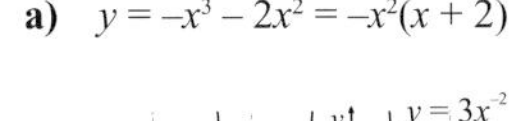

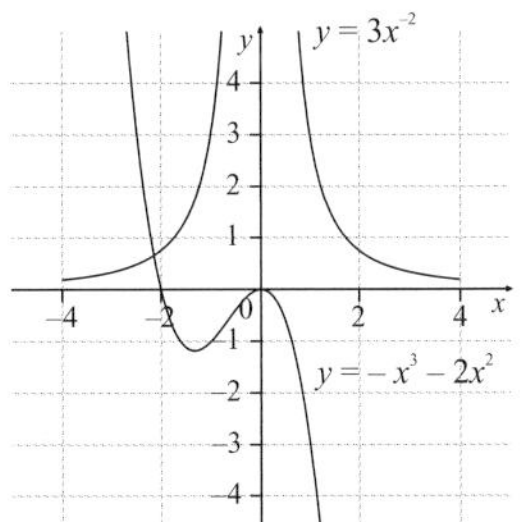

b) The number of real roots of the equation $3x^{-2} = -x^3 - 2x^2$ is the number of times the two graphs cross — this equation has 1 real root.

Q4 a) $\frac{1}{x} = \frac{1}{x^3} \Rightarrow x^3 = x \Rightarrow x^3 - x = 0 \Rightarrow x(x + 1)(x - 1) = 0$

So $x = -1$, $x = 0$ or $x = 1$. $x \neq 0$ as stated in the question, so the solutions are $x = -1$ and $x = 1$.

[2 marks available — 1 mark for a correct method, 1 mark for both correct x values only]

b) When $x = -1$, $y = \frac{1}{-1} = -1$

When $x = 1$, $y = \frac{1}{1} = 1$

So the points of intersection of the graphs are at $(-1, -1)$ and $(1, 1)$.

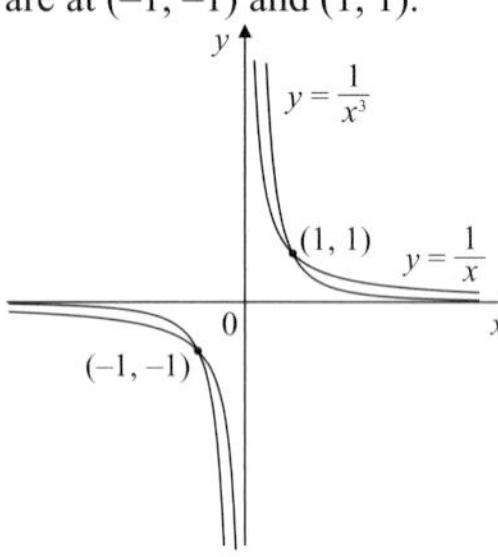

[3 marks available — 1 mark for correct shape of $y = \frac{1}{x}$, 1 mark for correct shape of $y = \frac{1}{x^3}$, 1 mark for both points of intersection labelled]

Q5 $y = \frac{1}{x^a}$ passes through (0.5, 8), so:

$8 = \frac{1}{0.5^a} \Rightarrow \left(\frac{1}{2}\right)^a = \frac{1}{8} \Rightarrow a = 3$

$y = bx^{-2}$ passes through (3, 2), so:

$2 = b \times 3^{-2} \Rightarrow 2 = b \times \frac{1}{9} \Rightarrow b = 18$

$y = \frac{c}{x^d}$ passes through (–1, 5) and (5, –0.0016), so:

$5 = \frac{c}{(-1)^d} \Rightarrow$ either $c = 5$ if d is even, or $c = -5$ if d is odd.

From the shape of the graph, you can tell that d is odd and $c = -5$.

$-0.0016 = \frac{-5}{5^d} \Rightarrow 5^d = 5 \div 0.0016 = 3125 \Rightarrow d = 5$

Q6 a)

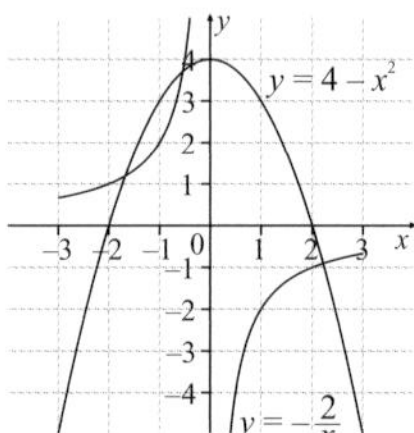

b) The solutions are at the points of intersection on the graph in part a). The actual solutions are $x = -0.54$, -1.68 and 2.21 (to 2 d.p.). Acceptable solutions are: between –0.4 and –0.7, between –1.6 and –1.8 and between 2.1 and 2.3.

Exercise 6.9 — Translations

Q1 a)

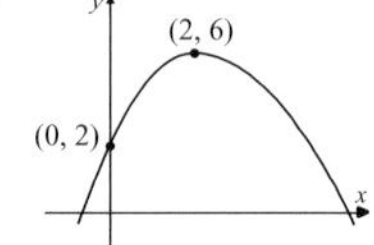

b)

(0, 4)
(–2, 0)
(3, 0)

Q2 a) The asymptotes are at $x = 0$ and $y = 0$.

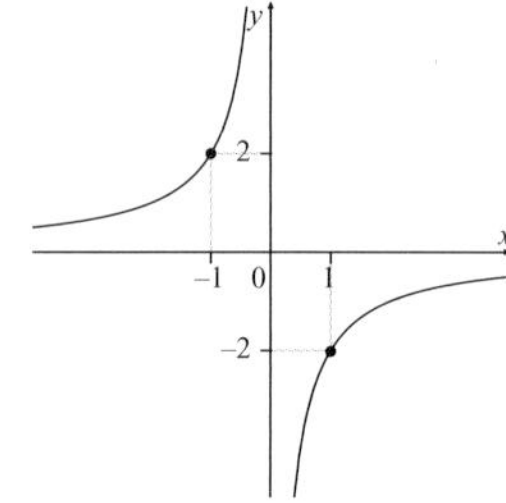

b) The asymptotes are at $x = -3$ and $y = 0$.

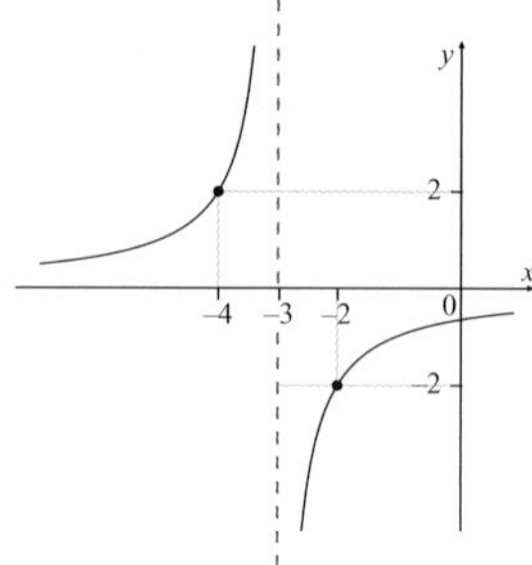

c) The asymptotes are at $x = 0$ and $y = 3$.

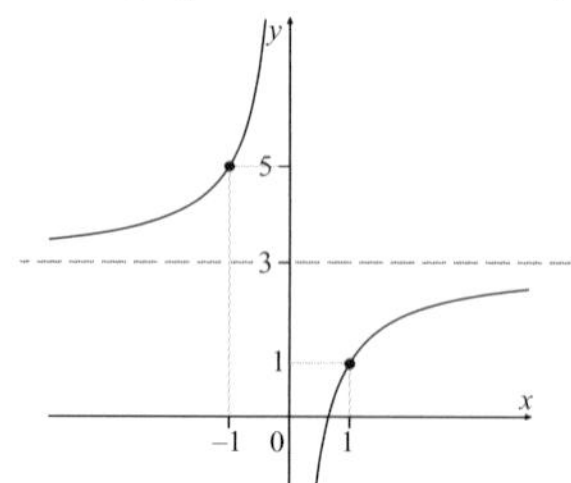

Q3 a) If $x^2(x - 4) = f(x)$, then $x^2(x - 4) + 1 = f(x) + 1$. The translation is 1 unit up, i.e. the graph is translated by the vector $\begin{pmatrix} 0 \\ 1 \end{pmatrix}$.

b) If $x^2(x - 4) = f(x)$, then $(x - 2)^2(x - 6) = f(x - 2)$. The translation is 2 units right, i.e. the graph is translated by the vector $\begin{pmatrix} 2 \\ 0 \end{pmatrix}$.

c) If $x^2(x - 4) = f(x)$, then $x(x + 4)^2 = f(x + 4)$. The translation is 4 units left, i.e. the graph is translated by the vector $\begin{pmatrix} -4 \\ 0 \end{pmatrix}$.

Q4 a) The graph is translated by the vector $\begin{pmatrix} \frac{3}{2} \\ -\frac{17}{3} \end{pmatrix}$.

[2 marks available — 1 mark for each correct component]

b) $\left(-2 + \frac{3}{2}, \frac{5}{7} - \frac{17}{3}\right) = \left(-\frac{1}{2}, -\frac{104}{21}\right)$ *[1 mark]*

Q5 If $x^3 + 3x + 7 = f(x)$, then $x^3 + 3x + 2 = f(x) - 5$. So the translation is 5 units down, i.e. the graph is translated by the vector $\begin{pmatrix} 0 \\ -5 \end{pmatrix}$.

Q6 If $f(x) = x^2 - 3x + 7$, then the translation is

$f(x + 1) = (x + 1)^2 - 3(x + 1) + 7 = x^2 + 2x + 1 - 3x - 3 + 7 = x^2 - x + 5$

Q7 a) and b)

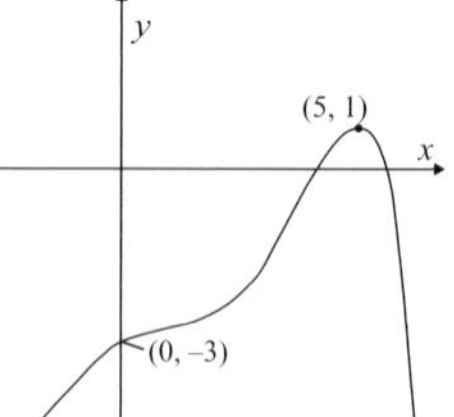

Q8 a) $f(x) = x^2 + 5$, so the translation is:

$g(x) = f(x + 3) = (x + 3)^2 + 5 = x^2 + 6x + 9 + 5 = x^2 + 6x + 14$

b) $g(x) = x^2 + 6x + 14$, so the translation is:

$h(x) = g(x) - 4 = x^2 + 6x + 14 - 4 = x^2 + 6x + 10$

Q9 Completing the square: $x^2 - \frac{5}{2}x + 8 = \left(x - \frac{5}{4}\right)^2 + \frac{103}{16}$

So the graph of $y = x^2$ is translated by the vector $\begin{pmatrix} \frac{5}{4} \\ \frac{103}{16} \end{pmatrix}$.

[2 marks available — 1 mark for correctly completing the square on the quadratic, 1 mark for the correct translation]

Q10 a) Completing the square: $2x^2 - 11x + 24 = 2\left(x - \frac{11}{4}\right)^2 + \frac{71}{8}$
The coordinates of the minimum point of $y = f(x)$ are $\left(\frac{11}{4}, \frac{71}{8}\right)$, so the coordinates of the minimum point of $y = f(x) + a$ are $\left(\frac{11}{4}, \frac{71}{8} + a\right)$
So $y = f(x) + a$ will not intersect the x-axis if:
$\frac{71}{8} + a > 0 \Rightarrow a > -\frac{71}{8}$
[3 marks available — 1 mark for correct y-coordinate of the minimum point, 1 mark for derivation of an appropriate inequality, 1 mark for the correct range of values for a]

b) The line of symmetry of $y = f(x - b)$ is $x = \frac{11}{4} + b$, so the line of symmetry of $y = f(x - b)$ will be between the lines $x = -2$ and $x = 2$ if:
$-2 < \frac{11}{4} + b < 2 \Rightarrow -2 - \frac{11}{4} < b < 2 - \frac{11}{4}$
$\Rightarrow -\frac{19}{4} < b < -\frac{3}{4}$
[2 marks available — 1 mark for derivation of appropriate inequalities, 1 mark for the correct range of values for b]

Q11 $y = \frac{1}{x}$ has asymptotes at $x = 0$ and $y = 0$. If $f(x) = \frac{1}{x}$:

a) $\frac{1}{x} - 4 = f(x) - 4$, i.e. $f(x)$ has been translated down by 4 units, so the translated asymptotes are $x = 0$ and $y = -4$.

b) $\frac{1}{x+3} = f(x+3)$, i.e. $f(x)$ has been translated left by 3 units, so the translated asymptotes are $x = -3$ and $y = 0$.

c) $\frac{1}{x-1} + 7 = f(x-1) + 7$, i.e. $f(x)$ has been translated right by 1 unit and up by 7 units, so the translated asymptotes are $x = 1$ and $y = 7$.

Q12 a) The asymptotes are at $x = 3$ and $y = 4$.
[2 marks available — 1 mark for each correct asymptote]

b) When $x = 0$, $y = 4 - \frac{5}{3} = \frac{7}{3}$, so the graph intersects the y-axis at $\left(0, \frac{7}{3}\right)$.
When $y = 0$, $4(3 - x) - 5 = 0 \Rightarrow x = \frac{7}{4}$, so the graph intersects the x-axis at $\left(\frac{7}{4}, 0\right)$.
[2 marks available — 1 mark for each correct axis intercept]

c)
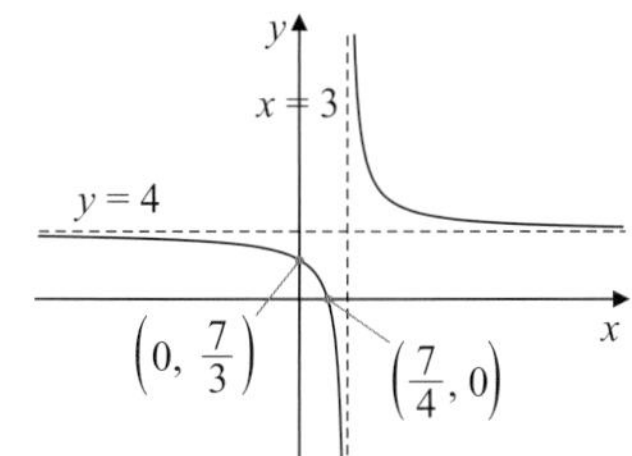

[2 marks available — 1 mark for the correct shape, 1 mark for the correct asymptotes and coordinate axes intercepts]

Q13 a)
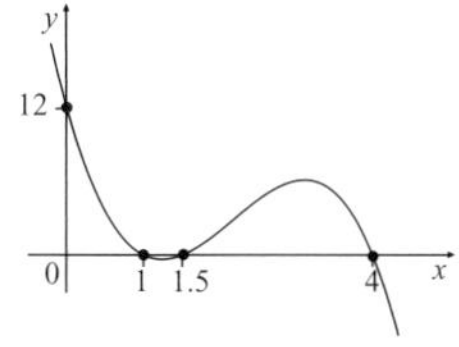

b) $f(x) = (x - 1)(2x - 3)(4 - x)$, so the translation is:
$f(x - 2) = ((x - 2) - 1)(2(x - 2) - 3)(4 - (x - 2))$
$= (x - 3)(2x - 4 - 3)(4 - x + 2)$
$= (x - 3)(2x - 7)(6 - x)$

c)

Q14 a) If the horizontal distance that the point A moves is k, then the vertical distance is $\frac{4}{3}k$. So this forms a right-angled triangle with hypotenuse of length 10, base of length k and perpendicular height $\frac{4}{3}k$. Using Pythagoras' theorem:
$k^2 + \frac{16k^2}{9} = 100 \Rightarrow 25k^2 = 900 \Rightarrow k^2 = 36$
$\Rightarrow k = 6$ or $k = -6$
The translation is in the direction of increasing x, so $k = 6$.
So the translation is described by the vector $\begin{pmatrix} 6 \\ 8 \end{pmatrix}$.
and the coordinates of A after translation are (8, 13).
[5 marks available — 1 mark for attempt to use Pythagoras' theorem, 1 mark for derivation of an appropriate quadratic to solve, 1 mark for correct value of k, 1 mark for correct translation described, 1 mark for correct coordinates]
You could also notice that the right-angled triangle will be a scaled version of the 3-4-5 triangle, which is indicated by the gradient of the line $y = \frac{4}{3}x$. If the hypotenuse is 10 (= 5 × 2) then the other two sides will be 3 × 2 = 6 and 4 × 2 = 8.

b) $g(x) = f(x - 6) + 8 = (x - 6)^2 + 9$ *[1 mark]*

Exercise 6.10 — Stretches and Reflections

Q1 a)
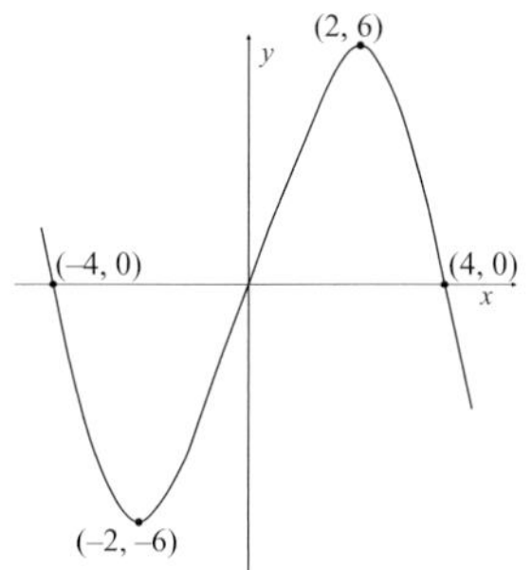

b)
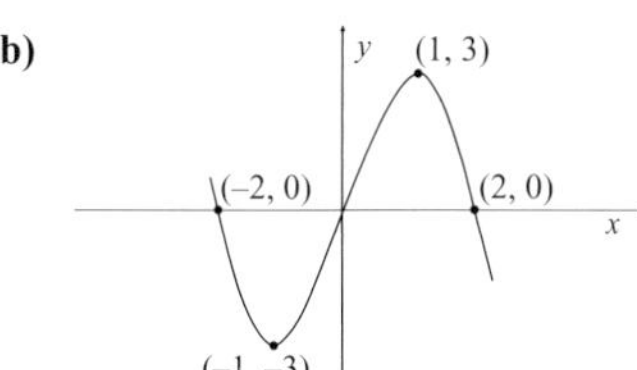

c)
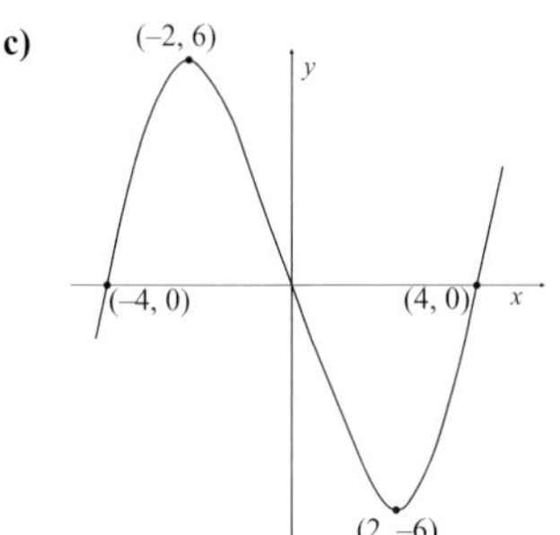

d)
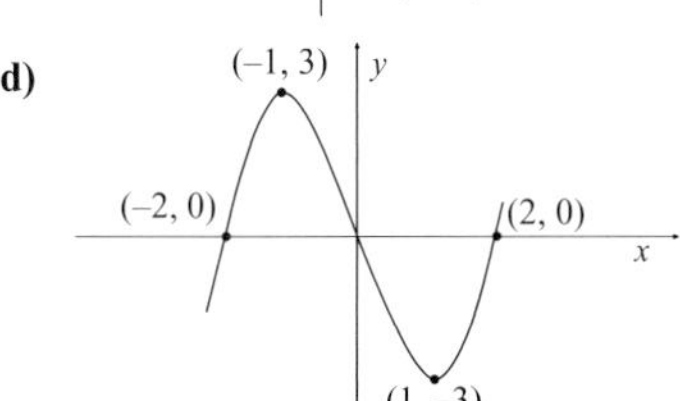

Q2 The graph has been squashed to half its width, so it's a horizontal stretch of scale factor $\frac{1}{2}$, so it must be b).

Q3 The graph has been reflected in the x-axis and stretched vertically by a factor of 3 so it must be b).

Q4 **a)** $f(x) = x^3 - x = x(x^2 - 1) = x(x + 1)(x - 1)$

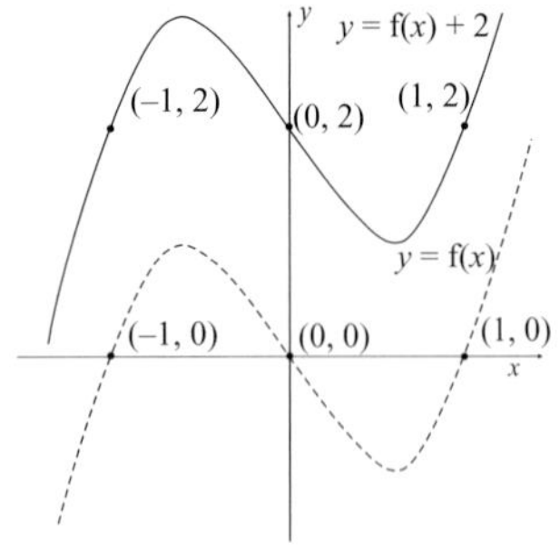

b)

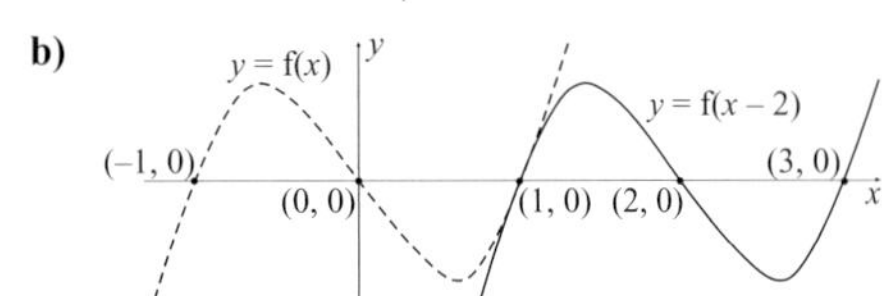

c)

y = f(–2x), (–0.5, 0), (0.5, 0), (–1, 0), (0, 0), (1, 0), y = f(x)

d)

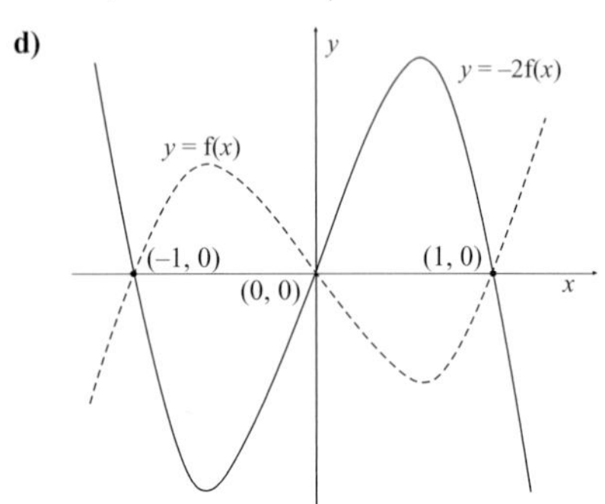

e)

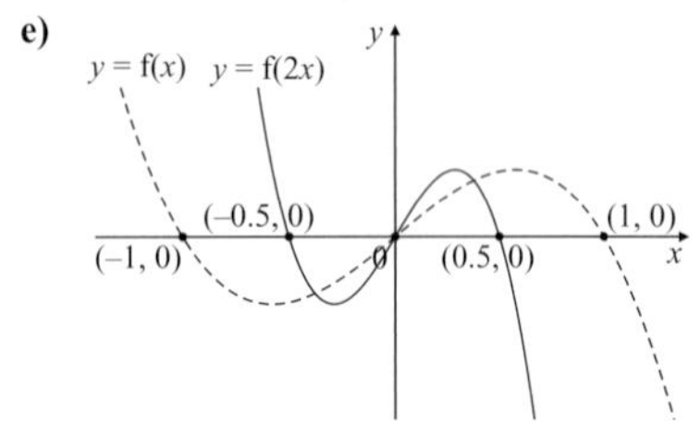

f)

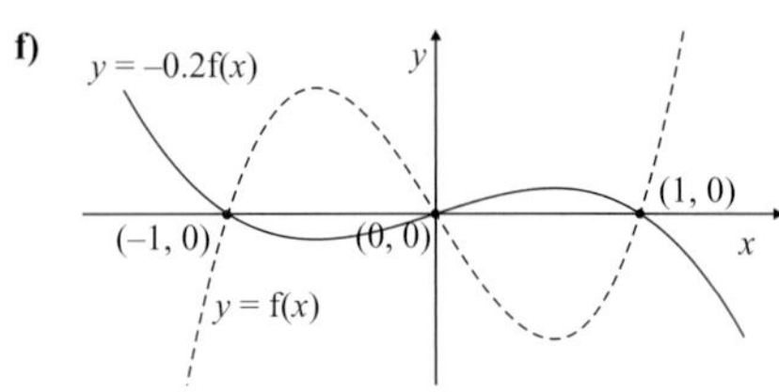

g)

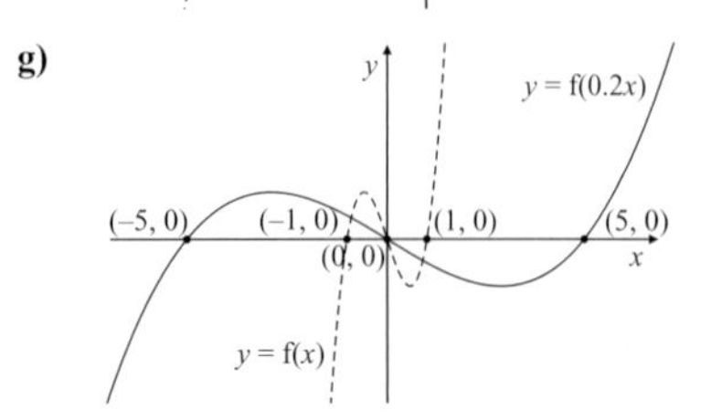

h)

y, y = 0.2f(x), (–1, 0), (1, 0), (0, 0), x, y = f(x)

Q5 $3x^3 + 6x + 12 = 3(x^3 + 2x + 4)$ so the whole function has been multiplied by 3. This means the transformation is a stretch vertically by a scale factor of 3.

Q6 $4x^2 - 2x + 4 = (-2x)^2 + (-2x) + 4$ so x has been replaced with $-2x$. The transformation is therefore a reflection in the y-axis followed by a horizontal stretch by a scale factor of $\frac{1}{2}$ (i.e. a squash).

Q7 Let $f(x) = e^x$. Then:

a)

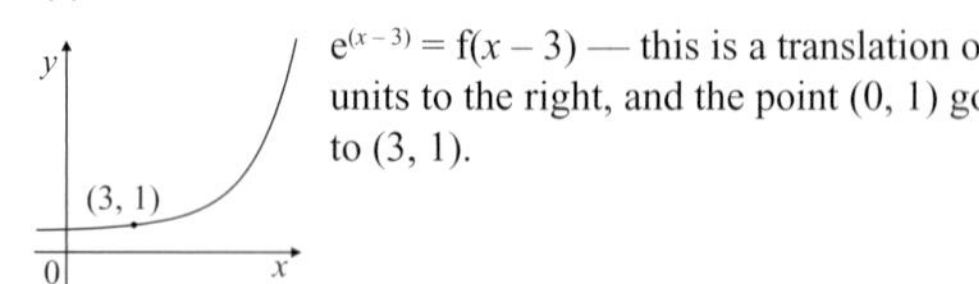

$e^{(x-3)} = f(x - 3)$ — this is a translation of 3 units to the right, and the point (0, 1) goes to (3, 1).

b)

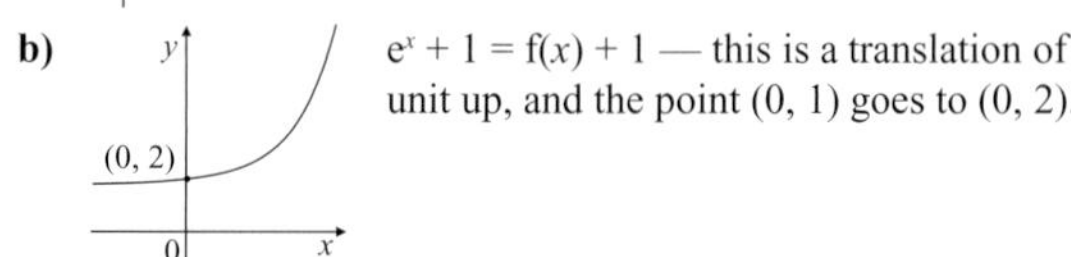

$e^x + 1 = f(x) + 1$ — this is a translation of 1 unit up, and the point (0, 1) goes to (0, 2).

c)

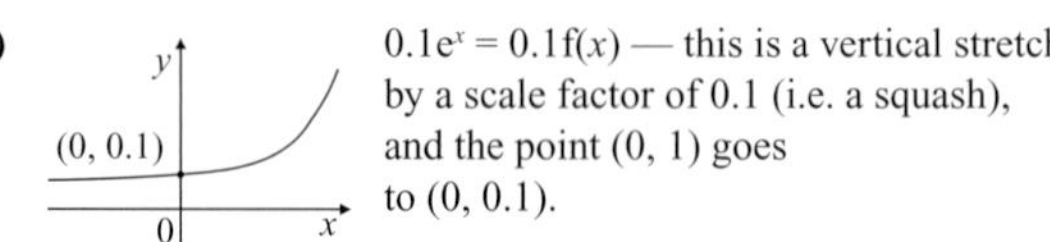

$0.1e^x = 0.1f(x)$ — this is a vertical stretch by a scale factor of 0.1 (i.e. a squash), and the point (0, 1) goes to (0, 0.1).

d)

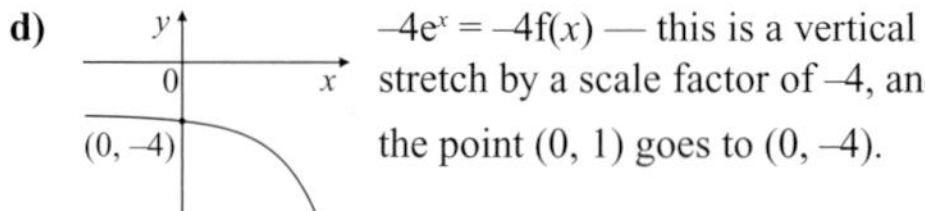

$-4e^x = -4f(x)$ — this is a vertical stretch by a scale factor of –4, and the point (0, 1) goes to (0, –4).

e)

$-\frac{1}{2}e^x = -\frac{1}{2}f(x)$ — this is a vertical stretch by a scale factor of $-\frac{1}{2}$ (i.e. a squash) and the point (0, 1) goes to $\left(0, -\frac{1}{2}\right)$.

f)

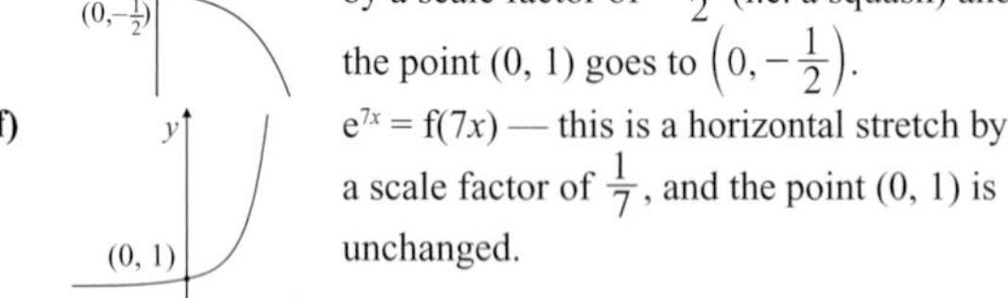

$e^{7x} = f(7x)$ — this is a horizontal stretch by a scale factor of $\frac{1}{7}$, and the point (0, 1) is unchanged.

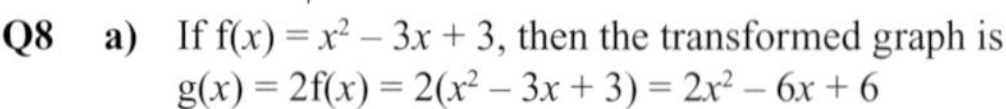

Q8 **a)** If $f(x) = x^2 - 3x + 3$, then the transformed graph is:
$g(x) = 2f(x) = 2(x^2 - 3x + 3) = 2x^2 - 6x + 6$

b) $g(x) = f(x + 3) = (x + 3)^2 - 3(x + 3) + 3$
$= x^2 + 6x + 9 - 3x - 9 + 3 = x^2 + 3x + 3$

c) $g(x) = f(4x) = (4x)^2 - 3(4x) + 3 = 16x^2 - 12x + 3$

Q9 **a)** $f(x) = x^2 - 6x - 7 = (x - 3)^2 - 16$, so the minimum point is at (3, –16). Solving $(x - 3)^2 - 16 = 0$ gives $x = -1$ or 7.
So the graph is:

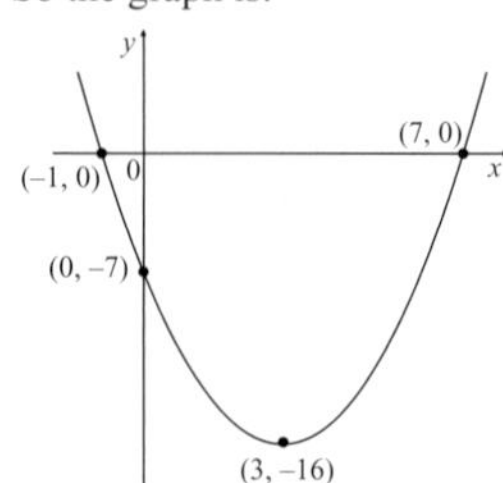

b) $y = -2f(x) = -2(x^2 - 6x - 7) = -2x^2 + 12x + 14$

c)

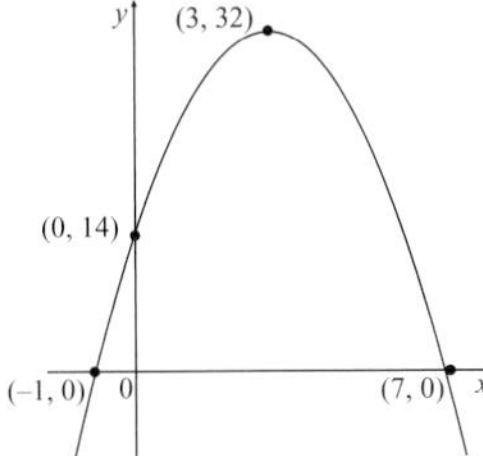

Q10 a) The asymptotes are $x = -3$ and $y = 2$ *[1 mark]*

b) (i) The transformation is a stretch of scale factor $\frac{1}{3}$ in the x-direction, so the equations of the asymptotes of $y = f(3x)$ are $x = -1$ and $y = 2$
[2 marks available — 1 mark for correct description of transformation, 1 mark for both correct asymptotes]

(ii) The transformation is a stretch of scale-factor $\frac{5}{3}$ in the y-direction and a reflection in the x-axis, so the equations of the asymptotes of $y = -\frac{5}{3}f(x)$ are $x = -3$ and $y = -\frac{10}{3}$.
[2 marks available — 1 mark for correct description of transformation, 1 mark for both correct asymptotes]

Q11 a) $f(5-x) = f\left(2\left(\frac{5}{2}\right)-x\right) \Rightarrow a = \frac{5}{2}$ *[1 mark]*

b) The points A, B, C and D will be reflected to the points with coordinates (5, 4), (3, 6), (–1, 2) and (–3, 4) respectively:

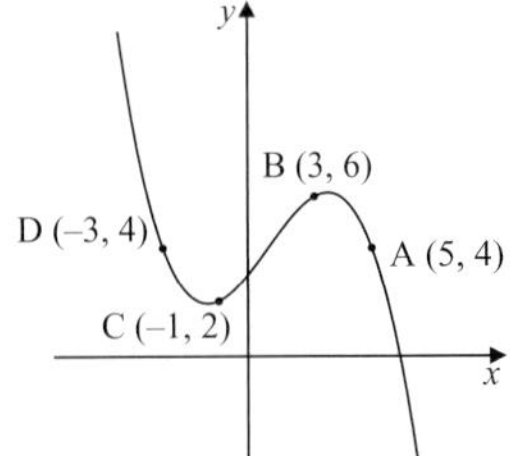

[3 marks available — 1 mark for correct shape, 1 mark for at least two points correctly labelled, 1 mark for all four points correctly labelled]

Exercise 6.11 — The Equation of a Circle

Q1 a) $x^2 + y^2 = 25$

b) $x^2 + y^2 = 49$

c) $x^2 + y^2 = 23$

d) $x^2 + y^2 = 18$

Q2 a) $a = 2, b = 5, r = 3 \Rightarrow (x-2)^2 + (y-5)^2 = 9$

b) $a = -3, b = 2, r = 5 \Rightarrow (x+3)^2 + (y-2)^2 = 25$

c) $a = -2, b = -3, r = 7 \Rightarrow (x+2)^2 + (y+3)^2 = 49$

d) $a = 3, b = 0, r = 4 \Rightarrow (x-3)^2 + y^2 = 16$

e) $a = -1, b = 3, r = 7 \Rightarrow (x+1)^2 + (y-3)^2 = 49$

f) $a = 5, b = 4, r = \sqrt{11} \Rightarrow (x-5)^2 + (y-4)^2 = 11$

g) $a = -7, b = 5, r = \sqrt{27} \Rightarrow (x+7)^2 + (y-5)^2 = 27$

h) $a = -10, b = 7, r = 11 \Rightarrow (x+10)^2 + (y-7)^2 = 121$

i) $a = 8, b = 0, r = \sqrt{17} \Rightarrow (x-8)^2 + y^2 = 17$

Q3 a) $a = 3, b = 2, r = 2 \Rightarrow (x-3)^2 + (y-2)^2 = 4$

b) $a = 1, b = -2, r = 3 \Rightarrow (x-1)^2 + (y+2)^2 = 9$

Q4 a) $a = 1, b = 5, r = \sqrt{4}$
So the centre is (1, 5) and the radius is 2.

b) $a = 3, b = 5, r = \sqrt{64}$
So the centre is (3, 5) and the radius is 8.

c) $a = 3, b = -2, r = \sqrt{25}$
So the centre is (3, –2) and the radius is 5.

d) $a = 6, b = 4, r = \sqrt{20}$
So the centre is (6, 4) and the radius is $2\sqrt{5}$.

e) $a = -8, b = -1, r = \sqrt{27}$
So the centre is (–8, –1) and the radius is $3\sqrt{3}$.

f) $a = 0, b = 12, r = \sqrt{147}$
So the centre is (0, 12) and the radius is $7\sqrt{3}$.

Q5 $a = 5, b = 3, r = 8 \Rightarrow (x-5)^2 + (y-3)^2 = 64$

Q6 $a = 3, b = 1, r = \sqrt{31} \Rightarrow (x-3)^2 + (y-1)^2 = 31$

Q7 $a = 0, b = -3, r = \sqrt{18}$
So the centre is (0, –3) and the radius is $3\sqrt{2}$.

Q8 $a = -3, b = -2, r = \sqrt{5} \Rightarrow (x+3)^2 + (y+2)^2 = 5$

Q9 a) $a = -9, b = 3$, so the centre is (–9, 3)

b) Radius $= \sqrt{45} = \sqrt{9 \times 5} = 3\sqrt{5}$

Q10 $a = 6, b = 3, r = 4\sqrt{5}$
So the equation of the circle is $(x-6)^2 + (y-3)^2 = 80$

a) $(-2-6)^2 + (7-3)^2 = 64 + 16 = 80$
So (–2, 7) is on the circle.

b) $(10-6)^2 + (-3-3)^2 = 16 + 36 = 52$
So (10, –3) is not on the circle.

c) $(14-6)^2 + (-1-3)^2 = 64 + 16 = 80$
So (14, –1) is on the circle.

d) $(2-6)^2 + (5-3)^2 = 16 + 4 = 20$
So (2, 5) is not on the circle.

Q11 The radius is the distance from the centre of a circle to a point on its circumference, so find the distance from (3, 5) to (10, 4) using Pythagoras:
Radius $= \sqrt{(5-4)^2 + (3-10)^2} = \sqrt{1+49} = \sqrt{50}$
So the equation of C is: $(x-3)^2 + (y-5)^2 = 50$.

Q12 Radius $= \sqrt{(9-7)^2 + (-2-(-11))^2} = \sqrt{4+81} = \sqrt{85}$
So the equation is $(x+2)^2 + (y-9)^2 = 85$.

Q13 a) Find the distance from A to the origin:
radius $= \sqrt{(1-0)^2 + (1-0)^2} = \sqrt{2}$
So the equation is $(x-1)^2 + (y-1)^2 = 2$

b) Radius $= \sqrt{(-7)^2 + 13^2} = \sqrt{218}$
So the equation is $(x+7)^2 + (y-13)^2 = 218$

c) Radius $= \sqrt{8^2 + (-6)^2} = 10$
So the equation is $(x-8)^2 + (y+6)^2 = 100$

d) Radius $= \sqrt{14^2 + 22^2} = \sqrt{680}$
So the equation is $(x-14)^2 + (y-22)^2 = 680$

Q14 a) (i) Length AB $= \sqrt{(-2-(-10))^2 + (7-(-3))^2}$
$= \sqrt{8^2 + 10^2} = \sqrt{164} = 2\sqrt{41}$

(ii) Midpoint AB $= \left(\frac{-3+7}{2}, \frac{-10+(-2)}{2}\right)$
$= \left(\frac{4}{2}, \frac{-12}{2}\right) = (2, -6)$

b) The radius is half of the length of the diameter AB so radius $= \sqrt{41}$, and the centre of the circle is the midpoint of the diameter (2, –6).
So the equation is $(x-2)^2 + (y+6)^2 = 41$.

Q15 a) Centre of C = (2, –3), radius $= \sqrt{17}$

(i) Distance from (–1, –6) to the centre of C
$= \sqrt{3^2 + 3^2} = \sqrt{18} > \sqrt{17}$, so (–1, –6) is outside C.

(ii) Distance from (2, 1) to the centre of C
$= \sqrt{0^2 + 4^2} = \sqrt{16} < \sqrt{17}$, so (2, 1) is inside C.

(iii) Distance from (–2, –2) to the centre of C
$= \sqrt{4^2 + 1^2} = \sqrt{17}$, so (–2, –2) is on the circumference of C.

b) (i) Centre of circle = (4, 8)
Distance from the centre of the circle to the centre of C
$= \sqrt{2^2 + 11^2} = \sqrt{125}$
$\sqrt{17} + \sqrt{17} = 2\sqrt{17} = \sqrt{68}$
$\sqrt{125} > \sqrt{68}$, so the circles do not intersect.

(ii) Centre of circle = (7, –1)
Distance from the centre of the circle to the centre of C
$= \sqrt{5^2 + 2^2} = \sqrt{29}$
$\sqrt{29} < \sqrt{68}$, so the circles intersect at two points.

(iii) Centre of circle = (4, –11)
Distance from the centre of the circle to the centre of C
$= \sqrt{2^2 + 8^2} = \sqrt{68} = 2\sqrt{17}$. This is the sum of the radii of the two circles, so the circles must just touch without overlapping. So the circles only intersect once.

Exercise 6.12 — Rearranging Circle Equations

Q1 **a)** Complete the square for the x's and y's:
$x^2 + y^2 + 2x - 4y - 3 = 0 \Rightarrow x^2 + 2x + y^2 - 4y - 3 = 0$
$\Rightarrow (x + 1)^2 - 1 + (y - 2)^2 - 4 - 3 = 0$
$\Rightarrow (x + 1)^2 + (y - 2)^2 = 8$
Centre is (–1, 2).

b) Radius $= \sqrt{8} = \sqrt{2 \times 4} = 2\sqrt{2}$

Q2 **a)** Complete the square for the x's and y's:
$x^2 + y^2 - 3x + 1 = 0 \Rightarrow x^2 - 3x + y^2 + 1 = 0$
$\Rightarrow \left(x - \frac{3}{2}\right)^2 - \frac{9}{4} + y^2 + 1 = 0 \Rightarrow \left(x - \frac{3}{2}\right)^2 + y^2 = \frac{5}{4}$
Centre is $\left(\frac{3}{2}, 0\right)$

b) Radius $= \sqrt{\frac{5}{4}} = \frac{\sqrt{5}}{2}$

Q3 **a)** Complete the square for the x's and y's:
$x^2 + y^2 + 2x - 6y - 6 = 0 \Rightarrow x^2 + 2x + y^2 - 6y - 6 = 0$
$\Rightarrow (x + 1)^2 - 1 + (y - 3)^2 - 9 - 6 = 0$
$\Rightarrow (x + 1)^2 + (y - 3)^2 = 16$
Radius = 4, centre is (–1, 3).

b) Complete the square for the x's and y's:
$x^2 + y^2 - 2y - 4 = 0 \Rightarrow x^2 + (y - 1)^2 - 1 - 4 = 0$
$\Rightarrow x^2 + (y - 1)^2 = 5$
Radius $= \sqrt{5}$, centre is (0, 1)

c) Complete the square for the x's and y's:
$x^2 + y^2 - 6x - 4y = 12 \Rightarrow x^2 - 6x + y^2 - 4y = 12$
$\Rightarrow (x - 3)^2 - 9 + (y - 2)^2 - 4 = 12 \Rightarrow (x - 3)^2 + (y - 2)^2 = 25$
Radius = 5, centre is (3, 2)

d) Complete the square for the x's and y's:
$x^2 + y^2 - 10x + 6y + 13 = 0 \Rightarrow x^2 - 10x + y^2 + 6y + 13 = 0$
$\Rightarrow (x - 5)^2 - 25 + (y + 3)^2 - 9 + 13 = 0$
$\Rightarrow (x - 5)^2 + (y + 3)^2 = 21$
Radius $= \sqrt{21}$, centre is (5, –3)

e) Complete the square for the x's and y's:
$x^2 + y^2 + 14x - 8y - 1 = 0 \Rightarrow x^2 + 14x + y^2 - 8y - 1 = 0$
$\Rightarrow (x + 7)^2 - 49 + (y - 4)^2 - 16 - 1 = 0$
$\Rightarrow (x + 7)^2 + (y - 4)^2 = 66$
Radius $= \sqrt{66}$, centre is (–7, 4)

f) Complete the square for the x's and y's:
$x^2 + y^2 - 4x + y = 3.75 \Rightarrow x^2 - 4x + y^2 + y = 3.75$
$\Rightarrow (x - 2)^2 - 4 + (y + 0.5)^2 - 0.25 = 3.75$
$\Rightarrow (x - 2)^2 + (y + 0.5)^2 = 8$
Radius $= 2\sqrt{2}$, centre is (2, –0.5)

g) Complete the square for the x's and y's:
$x^2 + y^2 + 2x + 3y - 1.25 = 0 \Rightarrow x^2 + 2x + y^2 + 3y - 1.25 = 0$
$\Rightarrow (x + 1)^2 - 1 + (y + 1.5)^2 - 2.25 - 1.25 = 0$
$\Rightarrow (x + 1)^2 + (y + 1.5)^2 = 4.5$
Radius $= \frac{3\sqrt{2}}{2}$, centre is (–1, –1.5)

h) Expand the brackets and simplify:
$x^2 - 4x + 4 + y^2 + 2x + 4y - 12 = 0$
$\Rightarrow x^2 - 2x + y^2 + 4y - 8 = 0$
Complete the square for the x's and y's:
$(x - 1)^2 - 1 + (y + 2)^2 - 4 - 8 = 0 \Rightarrow (x - 1)^2 + (y + 2)^2 = 13$
Radius $= \sqrt{13}$, centre is (1, –2)

Q4 The circle has equation $x^2 + (y + 3)^2 = 10$
Expand the brackets: $x^2 + y^2 + 6y + 9 = 10 \Rightarrow x^2 + y^2 + 6y - 1 = 0$
So $f = 0$, $g = 3$ and $c = -1$.

Q5 Find the radius of the circle:
Radius $= \sqrt{(-4)^2 + 2^2} = \sqrt{20} = 2\sqrt{5}$
So the circle has equation $(x + 4)^2 + (y - 2)^2 = 20$
Expand the brackets: $x^2 + 8x + 16 + y^2 - 4y + 4 = 20$
$\Rightarrow x^2 + y^2 + 8x - 4y = 0$
So $f = 4$, $g = -2$ and $c = 0$.

Q6 **a)** The circle has centre (–3, 1) and radius 4, so the equation is $(x + 3)^2 + (y - 1)^2 = 16$
Expand the brackets: $x^2 + 6x + 9 + y^2 - 2y + 1 = 16$
$\Rightarrow x^2 + y^2 + 6x - 2y - 6 = 0$
So $f = 3$, $g = -1$ and $c = -6$.

b) The circle has centre (3, –3) and goes through (0, 0) so the radius $= \sqrt{3^2 + (-3)^2} = \sqrt{18} = 3\sqrt{2}$
So the equation is $(x - 3)^2 + (y + 3)^2 = 18$
Expand the brackets:
$x^2 - 6x + 9 + y^2 + 6y + 9 = 18 \Rightarrow x^2 + y^2 - 6x + 6y = 0$
So $f = -3$, $g = 3$ and $c = 0$.

Q7 Divide by 2 to simplify: $x^2 + y^2 + 8x - 4y = 1$
Complete the square for the x's and y's:
$x^2 + 8x + y^2 - 4y - 1 = 0 \Rightarrow (x + 4)^2 - 16 + (y - 2)^2 - 4 - 1 = 0$
$\Rightarrow (x + 4)^2 + (y - 2)^2 = 21$
Radius $= \sqrt{21}$, centre is (–4, 2)

Q8 **a)** Completing the square for the x's and y's:
$(x - 3)^2 - 9 + (y - 5)^2 - 25 + 18 = 0$
$\Rightarrow (x - 3)^2 + (y - 5)^2 = 16$
So it has centre (3, 5), radius $= \sqrt{16} = 4$.

b) Following the method from a), it has centre (3, 5), radius = 6.

c) Following the method from a), it has centre (3, 5), radius = 2.

d) Following the method from a), it has centre (5, 3), radius = 4.

Comparing these, b) has the biggest radius so b) is A. d) has a different centre, so d) is C. a) has a bigger radius than c), so a) is B and c) is D.

Q9 **a)** Complete the square for the x's and y's:
$x^2 + y^2 + 6ax - 7y - \frac{3}{4} = 0 \Rightarrow x^2 + 6ax + y^2 - 7y - \frac{3}{4} = 0$
$\Rightarrow (x + 3a)^2 - 9a^2 + (y - \frac{7}{2})^2 - \frac{49}{4} - \frac{3}{4} = 0$
$\Rightarrow (x + 3a)^2 + (y - \frac{7}{2})^2 = 13 + 9a^2$
Radius $= \sqrt{13 + 9a^2}$, centre is $(-3a, \frac{7}{2})$

b) The point $\left(3, -\frac{1}{2}\right)$ is on the circle,
so $(3 + 3a)^2 + \left(-\frac{1}{2} - \frac{7}{2}\right)^2 = 13 + 9a^2$
$\Rightarrow 9 + 18a + 9a^2 + 16 = 13 + 9a^2$
$\Rightarrow 18a = -12 \Rightarrow a = -\frac{2}{3}$

Q10 **a)** Complete the square:
$x^2 - 18x + y^2 - 6y + 78 = 0$
$\Rightarrow (x - 9)^2 - 81 + (y - 3)^2 - 9 + 78 = 0$
$\Rightarrow (x - 9)^2 + (y - 3)^2 = 12$
C has centre with coordinates (9, 3) and radius $\sqrt{12} = 2\sqrt{3}$
[2 marks available — 1 mark for completing the square, 1 mark for stating the centre and radius]

b) The distance from the centre of the circle to the x-axis is 3.
The radius of the circle is $2\sqrt{3} = 3.46...$
$3.46... > 3$, so the circle intersects the x-axis.
The distance from the centre of the circle to the y-axis is 9.
The radius $2\sqrt{3} < 9$, so the circle doesn't intersect the y-axis.
[1 mark]

c) C intersects the x-axis when $y = 0$:
$(x - 9)^2 + (y - 3)^2 = 12 \Rightarrow (x - 9)^2 + (0 - 3)^2 = 12$
$\Rightarrow (x - 9)^2 = 3 \Rightarrow x - 9 = \pm\sqrt{3}$
$\Rightarrow x = 9 + \sqrt{3}$ or $x = 9 - \sqrt{3}$

So the coordinates of the points of intersection of the circle with the x-axis are $(9+\sqrt{3},0)$ and $(9-\sqrt{3},0)$.
[2 marks available — 1 mark for a method to solve the quadratic, 1 mark for both correct pairs of coordinates]
You could also solve the quadratic using the quadratic formula.

Q11 a) The centre of the circle has coordinates $(-4, 1)$.
Substitute $x = -4$ into the equation for l_1: $y = 2 \times -4 + 9 = 1$
So l_1 passes through the centre of the circle. *[1 mark]*

b) Solve the equations $y = 2x + 9$ and $y = kx - 5$ simultaneously:
$2x + 9 = kx - 5 \Rightarrow 14 = (k-2)x \Rightarrow x = \frac{14}{k-2}$
$y = 2\left(\frac{14}{k-2}\right) + 9 = \frac{28 + 9(k-2)}{k-2} = \frac{9k+10}{k-2}$
So the point of intersection has coordinates $\left(\frac{14}{k-2}, \frac{9k+10}{k-2}\right)$
[2 marks available — 1 mark for a correct method, 1 mark for the correct coordinates]

c) $D^2 = \left(\frac{14}{k-2} - (-4)\right)^2 + \left(\frac{9k+10}{k-2} - 1\right)^2$
$= \left(\frac{4k+6}{k-2}\right)^2 + \left(\frac{8k+12}{k-2}\right)^2 = \frac{4(2k+3)^2 + 16(2k+3)^2}{(k-2)^2}$
$= \frac{20(2k+3)^2}{(k-2)^2}$
[3 marks available — 1 mark for use of formula for the distance between two points, 1 mark for finding a common denominator, 1 mark for correctly simplifying to the required expression]

d) The lines intersect inside the circle if $D^2 < 20$:
$\frac{20(2k+3)^2}{(k-2)^2} < 20 \Rightarrow (2k+3)^2 < (k-2)^2$
$\Rightarrow 3k^2 + 16k + 5 < 0 \Rightarrow (3k+1)(k+5) < 0$
Solving this quadratic inequality gives $-5 < k < -\frac{1}{3}$
[3 marks available — 1 mark for setting up an inequality, 1 mark for attempting to solve, 1 mark for the correct range of values of k]

Exercise 6.13 — Using Circle Properties

Q1 a) Centre is $(3, 1)$

b) Gradient of radius $= \frac{1-4}{3-4} = \frac{-3}{-1} = 3$

c) Gradient of the tangent is $-\frac{1}{3}$,
use $y - y_1 = m(x - x_1)$ to find equation of tangent:
$y - 4 = -\frac{1}{3}(x-4) \Rightarrow 3y - 12 = -x + 4 \Rightarrow x + 3y = 16$
You're asked for the equation in a particular form, so don't forget to rearrange it.

Q2 a) Centre of the circle is $(3, -4)$
Gradient of radius $= \frac{-4-(-10)}{3-2} = 6$
Gradient of the tangent $= -\frac{1}{6}$
Use $y - y_1 = m(x - x_1)$ to find equation of tangent:
$y - (-10) = -\frac{1}{6}(x-2) \Rightarrow 6y + 60 = -x + 2$
$\Rightarrow x + 6y + 58 = 0$

b) Rearrange $x^2 + y^2 + 8x - 9 = 0$ and complete the square for the x terms to get: $(x+4)^2 + y^2 = 25$
Centre of the circle is $(-4, 0)$
Gradient of radius $= \frac{0-4}{-4-(-7)} = \frac{-4}{3}$
Gradient of the tangent $= \frac{3}{4}$
Use $y - y_1 = m(x - x_1)$ to find equation of tangent:
$y - 4 = \frac{3}{4}(x - (-7)) \Rightarrow y - 4 = \frac{3}{4}x + \frac{21}{4}$
$\Rightarrow 4y - 16 = 3x + 21 \Rightarrow 3x - 4y + 37 = 0$

c) Rearrange $x^2 + y^2 - 6x + 10y = 7$ and complete the square for the x terms: $(x-3)^2 + (y+5)^2 = 41$
Centre of the circle is $(3, -5)$
Gradient of radius $= \frac{-1-(-5)}{8-3} = \frac{4}{5}$
Gradient of the tangent $= -\frac{5}{4}$
Use $y - y_1 = m(x - x_1)$ to find equation of tangent:
$y - (-1) = -\frac{5}{4}(x-8) \Rightarrow y + 1 = -\frac{5}{4}(x-8)$
$\Rightarrow 4y + 4 = -5x + 40 \Rightarrow 5x + 4y - 36 = 0$

d) Centre of the circle is $(8, -2)$
Gradient of radius $= \frac{-2-(-5)}{8-6} = \frac{3}{2}$
Gradient of the tangent $= -\frac{2}{3}$
Use $y - y_1 = m(x - x_1)$ to find equation of tangent:
$y - (-5) = -\frac{2}{3}(x-6) \Rightarrow 3y + 15 = -2x + 12$
$\Rightarrow 2x + 3y + 3 = 0$

e) Centre of the circle is $(4, -2)$
Gradient of radius $= \frac{-2-(-3)}{4-9} = -\frac{1}{5}$
Gradient of the tangent $= 5$
Use $y - y_1 = m(x - x_1)$ to find equation of tangent:
$y - (-3) = 5(x-9) \Rightarrow y + 3 = 5x - 45 \Rightarrow 5x - y - 48 = 0$

f) Rearrange $x^2 + y^2 + 16x - 6y + 28 = 0$ and complete the square for the x terms:
$(x+8)^2 + (y-3)^2 = 45$
Centre of the circle is $(-8, 3)$
Gradient of radius $= \frac{9-3}{-11-(-8)} = \frac{6}{-3} = -2$
Gradient of the tangent $= \frac{1}{2}$
Use $y - y_1 = m(x - x_1)$ to find equation of tangent:
$y - 9 = \frac{1}{2}(x - (-11)) \Rightarrow 2y - 18 = x + 11 \Rightarrow x - 2y + 29 = 0$

g) Centre of the circle is $(-3, -1)$
Gradient of radius $= \frac{-4-(-1)}{-5-(-3)} = \frac{-3}{-2} = \frac{3}{2}$
Gradient of the tangent $= -\frac{2}{3}$
Use $y - y_1 = m(x - x_1)$ to find equation of tangent:
$y - (-4) = -\frac{2}{3}(x - (-5)) \Rightarrow 3y + 12 = -2x - 10$
$\Rightarrow 2x + 3y + 22 = 0$

h) Rearrange $x^2 + y^2 - 14x - 12y = 61$ and complete the square for the x terms: $(x-7)^2 + (y-6)^2 = 146$
Centre of the circle is $(7, 6)$
Gradient of radius $= \frac{6-1}{7-(-4)} = \frac{5}{11}$
Gradient of the tangent $= -\frac{11}{5}$
Use $y - y_1 = m(x - x_1)$ to find equation of tangent:
$y - 1 = -\frac{11}{5}(x - (-4)) \Rightarrow 5y - 5 = -11x - 44$
$\Rightarrow 11x + 5y + 39 = 0$

Q3 Centre of the circle is $(-1, 2)$
Gradient of radius $= \frac{2-(-1)}{-1-(-3)} = \frac{3}{2}$
Gradient of the tangent $= -\frac{2}{3}$
Use $y - y_1 = m(x - x_1)$ to find equation of tangent:
$y - (-1) = -\frac{2}{3}(x - (-3)) \Rightarrow 3y + 3 = -2(x+3)$
$\Rightarrow 3y + 3 = -2x - 6 \Rightarrow 2x + 3y + 9 = 0$

Q4 Rearrange $x^2 + y^2 + 2x - 7 = 0$ and complete the square for the x terms to get: $(x+1)^2 + y^2 = 8$
Centre of the circle is $(-1, 0)$
Gradient of radius $= \frac{0-2}{-1-(-3)} = \frac{-2}{2} = -1$
Gradient of the tangent $= 1$
Use $y - y_1 = m(x - x_1)$ to find equation of tangent:
$y - 2 = 1(x - (-3)) \Rightarrow y - 2 = x + 3 \Rightarrow y = x + 5$
You can give the equation in any form because it's not specified in the question.

Q5 Rearrange $x^2 + y^2 + 2x + 4y = 5$ and complete the square for the x and y terms to get: $(x + 1)^2 + (y + 2)^2 = 10$

Centre of the circle is $(-1, -2)$

Gradient of the radius $= \frac{-2-(-5)}{-1-0} = \frac{3}{-1} = -3$

Gradient of the tangent $= \frac{1}{3}$

Use $y - y_1 = m(x - x_1)$ to find equation of tangent:

$y - (-5) = \frac{1}{3}(x - 0) \Rightarrow 3y + 15 = x \Rightarrow x - 3y = 15$

Q6 Centre of the circle is $(2, 1)$

Gradient of radius $= \frac{7-1}{10-2} = \frac{6}{8} = \frac{3}{4}$

Gradient of the tangent $= -\frac{4}{3}$

Use $y - y_1 = m(x - x_1)$ to find equation of tangent:

$y - 7 = -\frac{4}{3}(x - 10) \Rightarrow 3y - 21 = -4x + 40 \Rightarrow 4x + 3y - 61 = 0$

Q7 The line from the centre of the circle to A has gradient: $\frac{1-4}{n-(-2)} = -\frac{3}{n+2}$

Since the tangent at A is perpendicular to this line,

$m_1 \times m_2 = -1 \Rightarrow -\frac{3}{n+2} \times \frac{5}{3} = -1 \Rightarrow -\frac{5}{n+2} = -1$

$\Rightarrow -5 = -1(n + 2) \Rightarrow n + 2 = 5 \Rightarrow n = 3$

You could also find the equation of this radius in the form y = mx + c, then substitute in the point (n, 1) to find n.

Q8 a) The line l is perpendicular to the chord AB. So find the gradient of AB:

Gradient of AB $= \frac{1-7}{-1-(-3)} = -\frac{6}{2} = -3$

So the gradient of l is $\frac{1}{3}$.

Then sub the gradient of l and point M $(-1, 1)$ into $y - y_1 = m(x - x_1)$ to find the equation:

$y - 1 = \frac{1}{3}(x - (-1)) \Rightarrow 3y - 3 = x + 1 \Rightarrow x - 3y + 4 = 0$

b) The centre is $(2, 2)$, so $a = 2$ and $b = 2$ in the equation $(x - a)^2 + (y - b)^2 = r^2$.

The radius is the length CA, which can be found using Pythagoras:

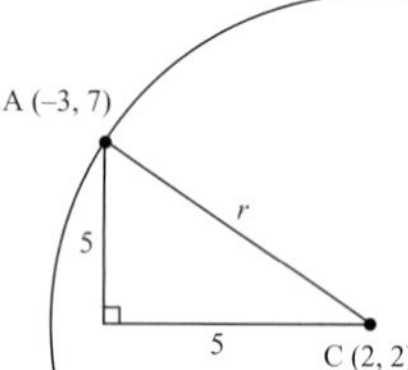

$r^2 = CA^2 = (-3 - 2)^2 + (7 - 2)^2 = (-5)^2 + 5^2 = 50$

So the equation of the circle is: $(x - 2)^2 + (y - 2)^2 = 50$

Q9 a) The equation of the circle is $(x - 2)^2 + (y - 4)^2 = 25$

Substitute $x = 15 - 2y$ into the circle equation to find the y-coordinates of the intersections:

$((15 - 2y) - 2)^2 + (y - 4)^2 = 25 \Rightarrow (13 - 2y)^2 + (y - 4)^2 = 25$

$\Rightarrow 169 - 52y + 4y^2 + y^2 - 8y + 16 = 25$

$\Rightarrow 5y^2 - 60y + 160 = 0 \Rightarrow y^2 - 12y + 32 = 0$

$\Rightarrow (y - 4)(y - 8) = 0$

So A and B have y-coordinates $y = 4$ and $y = 8$.

Substitute the y-values back into one of the original equations to find the x-coordinates:

When $y = 4$, $x = 15 - (2 \times 4) = 7$

When $y = 8$, $x = 15 - (2 \times 8) = -1$

So A $(7, 4)$ and B $(-1, 8)$.

Midpoint of AB, M $= \left(\frac{7-1}{2}, \frac{4+8}{2}\right) = (3, 6)$

So the length CM $= \sqrt{(3-2)^2 + (6-4)^2}$

$= \sqrt{1^2 + 2^2} = \sqrt{5}$ as required.

[7 marks available — 1 mark for finding the circle equation, 1 mark for forming a quadratic equation in x or y by substitution of the line equation, 1 mark for attempting to solve the quadratic, 1 mark for both correct y-values, 1 mark for both correct x-values, 1 mark for finding the coordinates of M, 1 mark for the correct length CM]

You could formulate the quadratic in x instead, then substitute to find the y-values.

b) Since M $(3, 6)$ is the midpoint of the chord AB, CM is perpendicular to AB. So ABC is a triangle with base AB and perpendicular height CM.

Length AB $= \sqrt{(7-(-1))^2 + (4-8)^2}$

$= \sqrt{8^2 + (-4)^2} = \sqrt{80} = 4\sqrt{5}$

So area ABC $= \frac{1}{2} \times \sqrt{5} \times 4\sqrt{5} = 10$ units^2

[3 marks available — 1 mark for using the fact that CM is perpendicular to AB, 1 mark for finding the length AB, 1 mark for calculating the final area]

Q10 a) If AC is the diameter, the angle ABC will be 90°. So find out if AB and BC are perpendicular.

Gradient of AB $= \frac{14-12}{4-(-2)} = \frac{2}{6} = \frac{1}{3}$

Gradient of BC $= \frac{2-14}{8-4} = \frac{-12}{4} = -3$

For perpendicular lines: $m_1 \times m_2 = -1$

$\frac{1}{3} \times -3 = -1$

As AB and BC are perpendicular, the angle ABC must be 90° and so AC must be the diameter of the circle.

b) Since AC is a diameter, the centre of the circle must be the midpoint of A and C.

$\left(\frac{(-2)+8}{2}, \frac{12+2}{2}\right) = \left(\frac{6}{2}, \frac{14}{2}\right) = (3, 7)$

The radius is the distance from the centre to a point on the circle, so choose a point and use Pythagoras' theorem (here using C: $(8 - 3)^2 + (2 - 7)^2 = r^2 \Rightarrow r^2 = 5^2 + 5^2 = 50$

So the equation of the circle is: $(x - 3)^2 + (y - 7)^2 = 50$

Q11 PQ is a chord of the circle, so the line through M and C is the perpendicular bisector of PQ.

Midpoint of PQ $= \left(\frac{-8-3}{2}, \frac{6+7}{2}\right) = \left(\frac{-11}{2}, \frac{13}{2}\right)$

Gradient of PQ $= \frac{7-6}{-3-(-8)} = \frac{1}{5}$

So the gradient of the perpendicular bisector is -5, and it passes through $\left(\frac{-11}{2}, \frac{13}{2}\right)$.

$y - y_1 = m(x - x_1) \Rightarrow y - \frac{13}{2} = -5(x + \frac{11}{2})$

$\Rightarrow y - \frac{13}{2} = -5x - \frac{55}{2} \Rightarrow 5x + y + 21 = 0$

Q12 a) Midpoint of XY $= \left(\frac{7-1}{2}, \frac{6-10}{2}\right) = (3, -2)$

Gradient of XY $= \frac{-10-6}{-1-7} = \frac{-16}{-8} = 2$ *[1 mark]*

So the perpendicular bisector passes through $(3, -2)$ and has a gradient of $-\frac{1}{2}$.

$y - y_1 = m(x - x_1) \Rightarrow y - (-2) = -\frac{1}{2}(x - 3)$

$\Rightarrow y = -\frac{1}{2}x - \frac{1}{2}$ *[1 mark]*

[2 marks available in total — as above]

b) Find the equation of the perpendicular bisector of e.g. YZ:

Midpoint of YZ $= \left(\frac{-1+13}{2}, \frac{-10-12}{2}\right) = (6, -11)$

Gradient of YZ $= \frac{-12-(-10)}{13-(-1)} = \frac{-2}{14} = -\frac{1}{7}$

So the perpendicular bisector passes through $(6, -11)$ and has a gradient of 7.

$y - y_1 = m(x - x_1) \Rightarrow y - (-11) = 7(x - 6)$

$\Rightarrow y + 11 = 7x - 42 \Rightarrow y = 7x - 53$

Now find the centre of the circle, which is the point where these lines intersect:

$-\frac{1}{2}x - \frac{1}{2} = 7x - 53 \Rightarrow -x - 1 = 14x - 106$
$\Rightarrow 15x = 105 \Rightarrow x = 7$

Substitute $x = 7$ into $y = 7x - 53$: $y - 49 - 53 = -4$
so the circle has its centre at (7, –4).

Radius $= \sqrt{(7-7)^2 + (6-(-4))^2} = \sqrt{10^2} = 10$

So the equation of the circle is: $(x - 7)^2 + (y + 4)^2 = 100$
[6 marks available — 1 mark for finding the gradient of either YZ or XZ, 1 mark for equation of its perpendicular bisector, 1 mark for solving the two line equations simultaneously for x, 1 mark for substituting for y, 1 mark for using Pythagoras' theorem to calculate the radius, 1 mark for the correct final equation for the circumcircle]

Q13 a) Find the perpendicular bisectors of two of the line segments XY, YZ and ZX.

XY: midpoint $= \left(\frac{8-4}{2}, \frac{2-4}{2}\right) = (2, -1)$

gradient $= \frac{-4-2}{-4-8} = \frac{-6}{-12} = \frac{1}{2}$

So the perpendicular bisector passes through (2, –1) and has a gradient of –2.

$y - y_1 = m(x - x_1) \Rightarrow y + 1 = -2(x - 2) \Rightarrow y = -2x + 3$

YZ: midpoint $= \left(\frac{-4+2}{2}, \frac{-4+8}{2}\right) = (-1, 2)$

gradient $= \frac{8-(-4)}{2-(-4)} = \frac{12}{6} = 2$

So the perpendicular bisector passes through (–1, 2) and has a gradient of $-\frac{1}{2}$.

$y - y_1 = m(x - x_1) \Rightarrow y - 2 = -\frac{1}{2}(x + 1) \Rightarrow y = -\frac{1}{2}x + \frac{3}{2}$

Now find the centre of the circle, which is the point where these lines intersect:

$-\frac{1}{2}x + \frac{3}{2} = -2x + 3 \Rightarrow -x + 3 = -4x + 6$
$\Rightarrow 3x = 3 \Rightarrow x = 1$

Substitute $x = 1$ into $y = -2x + 3$: $y = -2(1) + 3 = 1$
so the circle has its centre at (1, 1).

Radius $= \sqrt{(8-1)^2 + (2-1)^2} = \sqrt{49+1} = \sqrt{50}$

So the equation of the circle is: $(x - 1)^2 + (y - 1)^2 = 50$.

b) Find the perpendicular bisectors of two of the line segments XY, YZ and ZX.

XY: midpoint $= \left(\frac{2+5}{2}, \frac{6+9}{2}\right) = \left(\frac{7}{2}, \frac{15}{2}\right)$

gradient $= \frac{9-6}{5-2} = \frac{3}{3} = 1$

So the perpendicular bisector passes through $\left(\frac{7}{2}, \frac{15}{2}\right)$ and has a gradient of –1.

$y - y_1 = m(x - x_1) \Rightarrow y - \frac{15}{2} = -1(x - \frac{7}{2}) \Rightarrow y = -x + 11$

YZ: midpoint $= \left(\frac{5-5}{2}, \frac{9+9}{2}\right) = (0, 9)$

gradient $= \frac{9-9}{-5-5} = 0$

YZ is a horizontal line, so the perpendicular bisector is vertical and passes through (0, 9) — i.e. $x = 0$.

Now find the centre of the circle, which is the point where these lines intersect.
Substitute $x = 0$ into $y = -x + 11 \Rightarrow y = 11$.
So the circle has its centre at (0, 11).

Radius $= \sqrt{(2-0)^2 + (6-11)^2} = \sqrt{2^2 + (-5)^2} = \sqrt{29}$

So the equation of the circle is: $x^2 + (y - 11)^2 = 29$.

c) Find the perpendicular bisectors of two of the line segments XY, YZ and ZX.

XY: midpoint $= \left(\frac{14+22}{2}, \frac{14+6}{2}\right) = (18, 10)$

gradient $= \frac{14-6}{14-22} = \frac{8}{-8} = -1$

So the perpendicular bisector passes through (18, 10) and has a gradient of 1.

$y - y_1 = m(x - x_1) \Rightarrow y - 10 = x - 18 \Rightarrow y = x - 8$

YZ: midpoint $= \left(\frac{22+22}{2}, \frac{6+10}{2}\right) = (22, 8)$

The x-coordinates of Y and Z are the same, so YZ is a vertical line.

So the perpendicular bisector is horizontal and passes through (22, 8) — i.e. $y = 8$.

Now find the centre of the circle, which is the point where these lines intersect.
Substitute $y = 8$ into $y = x - 8 \Rightarrow x = 16$.
So the circle has its centre at (16, 8).

Radius $= \sqrt{(16-22)^2 + (8-6)^2} = \sqrt{(-6)^2 + 2^2} = \sqrt{40}$

So the equation of the circle is: $(x - 16)^2 + (y - 8)^2 = 40$.

d) Find the perpendicular bisectors of two of the line segments XY, YZ and ZX.

XY: midpoint $= \left(\frac{17-7}{2}, \frac{-14+10}{2}\right) = (5, -2)$

gradient $= \frac{-14-10}{17-(-7)} = \frac{-24}{24} = -1$

So the perpendicular bisector passes through (5, –2) and has a gradient of 1.

$y - y_1 = m(x - x_1) \Rightarrow y + 2 = x - 5 \Rightarrow y = x - 7$

YZ: midpoint $= \left(\frac{-7-11}{2}, \frac{10-2}{2}\right) = (-9, 4)$

gradient $= \frac{10-(-2)}{-7-(-11)} = \frac{12}{4} = 3$

So the perpendicular bisector passes through (–9, 4) and has a gradient of $-\frac{1}{3}$.

$y - y_1 = m(x - x_1) \Rightarrow y - 4 = -\frac{1}{3}(x + 9) \Rightarrow y = -\frac{1}{3}x + 1$

Now find the centre of the circle, which is the point where these lines intersect:

$-\frac{1}{3}x + 1 = x - 7 \Rightarrow -x + 3 = 3x - 21$
$\Rightarrow 4x = 24 \Rightarrow x = 6$

Substitute $x = 6$ into $y = x - 7$: $y = 6 - 7 = -1$
so the circle has its centre at (6, –1).

Radius $= \sqrt{(6-(-7))^2 + (-1-10)^2}$
$= \sqrt{13^2 + 11^2} = \sqrt{290}$

So the equation of the circle is: $(x - 6)^2 + (y + 1)^2 = 290$.

Q14 a) Radius $= \sqrt{(4-3)^2 + (3-(-1))^2} = \sqrt{1^2 + 4^2} = \sqrt{17}$
So the equation is $(x - 3)^2 + (y + 1)^2 = 17$.

b) Gradient of radius at (4, 3) $= \frac{3-(-1)}{4-3} = 4$

Gradient of the tangent $= -\frac{1}{4}$

Use $y - y_1 = m(x - x_1)$ to find equation of tangent:
$y - 3 = -\frac{1}{4}(x - 4) \Rightarrow y - 3 = -\frac{1}{4}x + 1 \Rightarrow y = -\frac{1}{4}x + 4$

The tangent crosses the x-axis at $x = 16$ and crosses the y-axis at $y = 4$.

Area of triangle $= \frac{1}{2} \times$ base $\times$ height
$= \frac{1}{2} \times 16 \times 4 = 32$ units^2

Q15 a) Find the perpendicular bisectors of two of the line segments AB, BC and CA.

AB: midpoint $= \left(\frac{2+11}{2}, \frac{-2+1}{2}\right) = \left(\frac{13}{2}, -\frac{1}{2}\right)$

gradient $= \frac{1-(-2)}{11-2} = \frac{3}{9} = \frac{1}{3}$

So the perpendicular bisector passes through $\left(\frac{13}{2}, -\frac{1}{2}\right)$ and has a gradient of –3.

$y - y_1 = m(x - x_1) \Rightarrow y + \frac{1}{2} = -3(x - \frac{13}{2}) \Rightarrow y = -3x + 19$

BC: midpoint = $\left(\frac{11+10}{2}, \frac{1-6}{2}\right) = \left(\frac{21}{2}, -\frac{5}{2}\right)$

gradient = $\frac{1-(-6)}{11-10} = 7$

So the perpendicular bisector passes through $\left(\frac{21}{2}, -\frac{5}{2}\right)$ and has a gradient of $-\frac{1}{7}$.

$y - y_1 = m(x - x_1) \Rightarrow y + \frac{5}{2} = -\frac{1}{7}(x - \frac{21}{2})$

$\Rightarrow y = -\frac{1}{7}x - 1$

Now find the centre of the circle, which is the point where these lines intersect:

$-\frac{1}{7}x - 1 = -3x + 19 \Rightarrow -x - 7 = -21x + 133$
$\Rightarrow 20x = 140 \Rightarrow x = 7$

Substitute $x = 7$ into $y = -3x + 19$: $y = -3(7) + 19 = -2$ so the circle has its centre at (7, –2).

Radius = $\sqrt{(7-2)^2 + (-2-(-2))^2} = \sqrt{5^2} = 5$

So the equation of the circle is: $(x - 7)^2 + (y + 2)^2 = 25$.

b) If BD is a diameter, BA and AD are perpendicular. Find the gradients of BA and AD:

$m_{BA} = \frac{1}{3}$ from part a).

$m_{AD} = \frac{-2-(-5)}{2-3} = \frac{3}{-1} = -3$

$-3 \times \frac{1}{3} = -1$, so BA and AD are perpendicular.

Therefore BD is a diameter.

You could have used BC and CD instead, or for centre X, you could have shown that $m_{BX} = m_{XD}$.

Chapter 6 Review Exercise

Q1 a) (i) gradient = $\frac{-1-(-19)}{2-(-4)} = \frac{18}{6} = 3$

$y - y_1 = m(x - x_1) \Rightarrow y - (-1) = 3(x - 2)$
$\Rightarrow y + 1 = 3(x - 2)$

You could have used (–4, –19) instead — this gives the equation y + 19 = 3(x + 4).

(ii) $y + 1 = 3(x - 2) \Rightarrow y = 3x - 6 - 1 \Rightarrow y = 3x - 7$

(iii) $3x - y - 7 = 0$

b) (i) gradient = $\frac{\frac{2}{3} - \left(-\frac{1}{3}\right)}{5-0} = \frac{1}{5}$

$y - y_1 = m(x - x_1) \Rightarrow y - \left(-\frac{1}{3}\right) = \frac{1}{5}x \Rightarrow y + \frac{1}{3} = \frac{1}{5}x$

(Or $y - \frac{2}{3} = \frac{1}{5}(x - 5)$ using the other point.)

(ii) $y + \frac{1}{3} = \frac{1}{5}x \Rightarrow y = \frac{1}{5}x - \frac{1}{3}$

(iii) $y = \frac{1}{5}x - \frac{1}{3} \Rightarrow 15y = 3x - 5 \Rightarrow 3x - 15y - 5 = 0$

c) (i) gradient = $\frac{-2-7}{-7-8} = \frac{-9}{-15} = \frac{3}{5}$

$y - y_1 = m(x - x_1) \Rightarrow y - 7 = \frac{3}{5}(x - 8)$

(Or $y + 2 = \frac{3}{5}(x + 7)$ using the other point.)

(ii) $y - 7 = \frac{3}{5}(x - 8) \Rightarrow y = \frac{3}{5}x - \frac{24}{5} + 7$
$\Rightarrow y = \frac{3}{5}x + \frac{11}{5}$

(iii) $y = \frac{3}{5}x + \frac{11}{5} \Rightarrow 5y = 3x + 11 \Rightarrow 3x - 5y + 11 = 0$

d) (i) gradient = $\frac{\frac{5}{2} - 5}{2-5} = \frac{-\frac{5}{2}}{-3} = \frac{5}{6}$

$y - y_1 = m(x - x_1) \Rightarrow y - 5 = \frac{5}{6}(x - 5)$

(Or $y - \frac{5}{2} = \frac{5}{6}(x - 2)$ using the other point.)

(ii) $y - 5 = \frac{5}{6}(x - 5) \Rightarrow y = \frac{5}{6}x - \frac{25}{6} + 5$
$\Rightarrow y = \frac{5}{6}x + \frac{5}{6}$

(iii) $y = \frac{5}{6}x + \frac{5}{6} \Rightarrow 6y = 5x + 5 \Rightarrow 5x - 6y + 5 = 0$

e) (i) gradient = $\frac{2-0}{1.3-1.8} = \frac{2}{-0.5} = -4$

$y - y_1 = m(x - x_1) \Rightarrow y = -4(x - 1.8)$

(Or $y - 2 = 4(x - 1.3)$ using the other point.)

(ii) $y = -4(x - 1.8) \Rightarrow y = -4x + 7.2$

(iii) $y = -4x + 7.2 \Rightarrow y = -4x + \frac{36}{5}$
$\Rightarrow 5y = -20x + 36 \Rightarrow 20x + 5y - 36 = 0$

f) (i) gradient = $\frac{-2.3-(-0.3)}{4.6-(-5.4)} = \frac{-2}{10} = -0.2$

$y - y_1 = m(x - x_1) \Rightarrow y - (-0.3) = -0.2(x - (-5.4))$
$\Rightarrow y + 0.3 = -0.2(x + 5.4)$

(Or $y + 2.3 = -0.2(x - 4.6)$ using other point.)

(ii) $y + 0.3 = -0.2(x + 5.4) \Rightarrow y + 0.3 = -0.2x - 1.08$
$\Rightarrow y = -0.2x - 1.38$

(iii) $y = -0.2x - 1.38 \Rightarrow y = -\frac{1}{5}x - \frac{69}{50}$
$\Rightarrow 50y = -10x - 69 \Rightarrow 10x + 50y + 69 = 0$

Q2 a) Length AB = $\sqrt{(4-(-2))^2 + (-10-4)^2}$
$= \sqrt{6^2 + (-14)^2}$
$= \sqrt{232} = 2\sqrt{58}$

[2 marks available — 1 mark for attempting to use Pythagoras' theorem on the x- and y-coordinates, 1 mark for the correct answer in surd form]

b) Gradient $m = \frac{-10-4}{4-(-2)} = \frac{-14}{6} = -\frac{7}{3}$

[2 marks available — 1 mark for change in y over change in x as a fraction, 1 mark for correct answer (or equivalent fraction)]

c) $y - y_1 = m(x - x_1) \Rightarrow y - 4 = -\frac{7}{3}(x - (-2))$
$\Rightarrow y - 4 = -\frac{7}{3}x - \frac{14}{3} \Rightarrow y = -\frac{7}{3}x - \frac{2}{3}$
$\Rightarrow 3y = -7x - 2 \Rightarrow 7x + 3y + 2 = 0$

[3 marks available — 1 mark for substituting a coordinate into an accepted method for the equation of a straight line, 1 mark for a correct line equation in any form, 1 mark for correct final answer as shown with integer coefficients]

Q3 a) Substituting $x = 2$ into the equation for l gives:
$y - 2(2) + 5 = 0 \Rightarrow y - 4 + 5 = 0 \Rightarrow y = -1$
So A lies on the line l. *[1 mark]*

b) $x = k \Rightarrow y - 2k + 5 = 0 \Rightarrow y = 2k - 5$ *[1 mark]*

c) The base of the triangle has length 10 – 2 = 8.
The height of the triangle is (2k – 5) – (–1) = 2k – 4
The area of the triangle = $\frac{1}{2} \times 8 \times (2k - 4) = 32 \Rightarrow k = 6$
So C has coordinates (6, 2(6) – 5) = (6, 7)
So the line through B and C has gradient:
$m = \frac{7-(-1)}{6-10} = \frac{8}{-4} = -2$
$y - y_1 = m(x - x_1) \Rightarrow y - 7 = -2(x - 6) \Rightarrow y = -2x + 19$

[3 marks available — 1 mark for the correct value of k, 1 mark for the correct gradient, 1 mark for correct equation of the line]

Q4 $4x - 6y = 7 \Rightarrow y = \frac{2}{3}x - \frac{7}{6}$, so the gradient of the line is $\frac{2}{3}$.

a) $8x + 12y = 15 \Rightarrow y = -\frac{2}{3}x + \frac{5}{4}$
The gradient is $-\frac{2}{3}$ so the line is not parallel to $4x - 6y = 7$.

[2 marks available — 1 mark for calculating the gradient, 1 mark for the correct conclusion]

b) $3y - 2x = 7 \Rightarrow y = \frac{2}{3}x + \frac{7}{3}$
The gradient is $\frac{2}{3}$ so the line is parallel to $4x - 6y = 7$.

[2 marks available — 1 mark for calculating the gradient, 1 mark for the correct conclusion]

c) $y = \frac{4x+3}{6} \Rightarrow y = \frac{2}{3}x + \frac{1}{2}$
The gradient is $\frac{2}{3}$ so the line is parallel to $4x - 6y = 7$.
[2 marks available — 1 mark for calculating the gradient, 1 mark for the correct conclusion]

Q5 **a)** D is the midpoint of AC, i.e. $D = (8, 2) = \left(\frac{1+p}{2}, \frac{7+q}{2}\right)$

So $8 = \frac{1+p}{2} \Rightarrow p = 8 \times 2 - 1 = 15$

and $2 = \frac{7+q}{2} \Rightarrow q = 2 \times 2 - 7 = -3$
[2 marks available — 1 mark for correct value of p, 1 mark for correct value of q]

b) Find the gradient of the line AD: $m_{AD} = \frac{2-7}{8-1} = -\frac{5}{7}$

So the gradient of l is $-1 \div -\frac{5}{7} = \frac{7}{5}$

$y - y_1 = m(x - x_1) \Rightarrow y - 2 = \frac{7}{5}(x - 8) \Rightarrow y - 2 = \frac{7}{5}x - \frac{56}{5}$

$\Rightarrow y = \frac{7}{5}x - \frac{46}{5} \Rightarrow 5y = 7x - 46 \Rightarrow 7x - 5y - 46 = 0$

[4 marks available — 1 mark for finding the gradient of AC, 1 mark for finding the perpendicular gradient, 1 mark for the correct line equation in any form, 1 mark for correct final answer with integer coefficients]

c) The equation of AB is $y = 7$, so substitute this into the equation from b):

$7x - 5(7) - 46 = 0 \Rightarrow 7x = 81 \Rightarrow x = \frac{81}{7}$
[2 marks available — 1 mark for using y = 7, 1 mark for correct answer]

Q6 **a)** l_1 is parallel so its gradient is also $\frac{3}{2}$:

$y = mx + c \Rightarrow y = \frac{3}{2}x + c \Rightarrow 2 = \frac{3}{2}(4) + c$

$\Rightarrow c = -4 \Rightarrow y = \frac{3}{2}x - 4$

b) Rearrange the equation to get $y = 2x - 7$.
l_2 is perpendicular so the gradient is $-1 \div 2 = -\frac{1}{2}$

$y = mx + c \Rightarrow y = -\frac{1}{2}x + c \Rightarrow 1 = -\frac{1}{2}(6) + c$

$\Rightarrow c = 4 \Rightarrow y = -\frac{1}{2}x + 4$

Q7 Gradient of RS $= \frac{9-3}{1-10} = \frac{6}{-9} = -\frac{2}{3}$,
so the gradient of the perpendicular is $\frac{3}{2}$.

$y = mx + c \Rightarrow y = \frac{3}{2}x + c \Rightarrow 9 = \frac{3}{2}(1) + c$

$\Rightarrow c = \frac{15}{2} \Rightarrow y = \frac{3}{2}x + \frac{15}{2}$

Q8 **a)** The gradient of the line segment AB is $\frac{13-9}{11-5} = \frac{4}{6} = \frac{2}{3}$
So the gradient of a line perpendicular to AB is $-1 \div \frac{2}{3} = -\frac{3}{2}$
The midpoint of the line segment has coordinates
$\left(\frac{5+11}{2}, \frac{9+13}{2}\right) = (8, 11)$
So the equation of the perpendicular bisector of AB is:

$y - y_1 = m(x - x_1) \Rightarrow y - 11 = -\frac{3}{2}(x - 8) \Rightarrow y = -\frac{3}{2}x + 23$

[3 marks available — 1 mark for calculation of gradient of perpendicular, 1 mark for coordinates of midpoint, 1 mark for correct equation of line]

b) The increase in x-coordinate from A to B is 6 and the increase in y-coordinate from A to B is 4. Since P is twice as far from A as from B, the increase in x-coordinate from A to P is 12 and the increase in y-coordinate from A to P is 8. So the coordinates of P are (17, 17). Then the equation of the line perpendicular to the line through A and B and passing through P is:

$y - 17 = -\frac{3}{2}(x - 17) \Rightarrow y = -\frac{3}{2}x + \frac{85}{2}$

[2 marks available — 1 mark for correct coordinates of P, 1 mark for correct equation of line]

Q9 y is directly proportional to x, so $y = kx$.
When $y = 3$, $x = 4.5$, so $3 = 4.5k \Rightarrow k = \frac{2}{3}$.

a) When $x = 21$, $y = \frac{2}{3} \times 21 = 14$

b) When $x = -3$, $y = \frac{2}{3} \times -3 = -2$

c) $x = \frac{y}{k}$, so when $y = 58$, $x = 58 \div \frac{2}{3} = 87$

Q10 **a)** $N \propto r \Rightarrow N = kr$
When $r = 48$, $N = 1536$:
$1536 = 48k \Rightarrow k = 32 \Rightarrow N = 32r$
[2 marks available — 1 mark for a correct method, 1 mark for the correct expression for N in terms of r]

b) The constant of proportionality is the number of seeds that the farmer plants in each row. *[1 mark]*

c) $N = 32r \Rightarrow 2720 = 32r \Rightarrow r = 85$ rows *[1 mark]*

Q11 $s = \frac{k}{t^3} \Rightarrow k = st^3$. When $s = 18$, $t = 6$, so $k = 3888$.

a) When $t = 3$, $s = \frac{3888}{3^3} = 144$

b) When $t = 0.5$, $s = \frac{3888}{0.5^3} = 31\,104$

c) $t = \sqrt[3]{\frac{3888}{s}}$. When $s = 486$, $t = \sqrt[3]{\frac{3888}{486}} = \sqrt[3]{8} = 2$

Q12 **a)** $F \propto \frac{1}{r^2} \Rightarrow F = \frac{k}{r^2}$
When $r = 3$, $F = 3.56 \times 10^{-6}$:
$3.56 \times 10^{-6} = \frac{k}{3^2} \Rightarrow k = 3.204 \times 10^{-5}$
So $F = \frac{3.204 \times 10^{-5}}{r^2}$
[3 marks available — 1 mark for a correct method, 1 mark for calculation of correct value of k, 1 mark for correct expression for F in terms of r]

b) When $r = 15$, $F = \frac{3.204 \times 10^{-5}}{15^2}$
$\Rightarrow F = 1.424 \times 10^{-7}$ newtons
[2 marks available — 1 mark for a correct method, 1 mark for the correct value of F]

c) For spheres A and C, $r = x$, so $F = \frac{5 \times 3.204 \times 10^{-5}}{x^2}$

$7.11 \times 10^{-9} = \frac{1.602 \times 10^{-4}}{x^2} \Rightarrow x = \sqrt{\frac{1.602 \times 10^{-4}}{7.11 \times 10^{-9}}}$

$\Rightarrow x = 150.105... \Rightarrow x = 150$ metres (to the nearest metre)
[2 marks available — 1 mark for a correct method, 1 mark for the correct value of x to the nearest metre]

Q13 **a)**

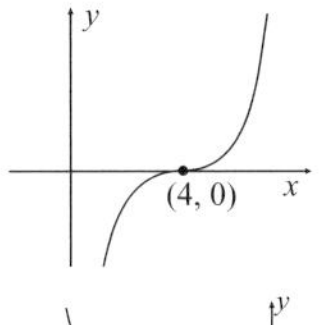

b)

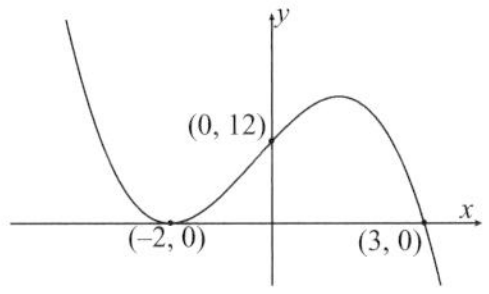

c) Factorise y fully: $y = (1 - x)(x - 2)(x - 4)$

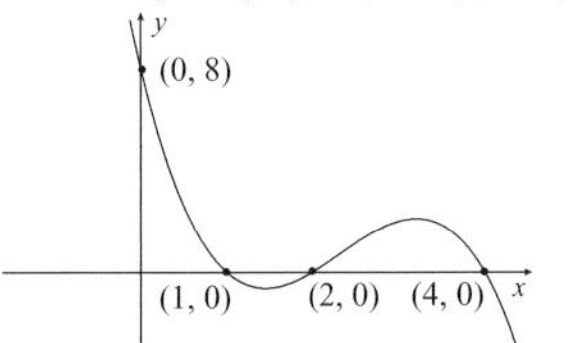

d)

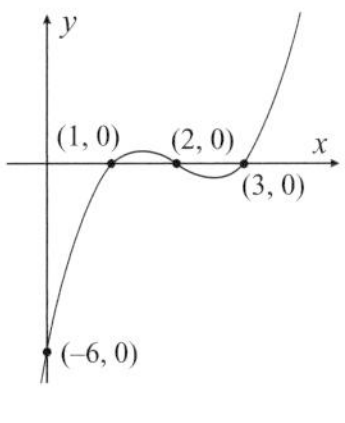

e) Factorise y fully: $y = 3x^2(x - 2)$

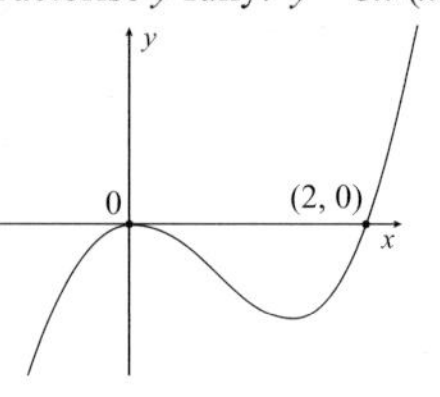

f) Factorise y fully: $y = x(x^2 - x - 12) = x(x - 4)(x + 3)$

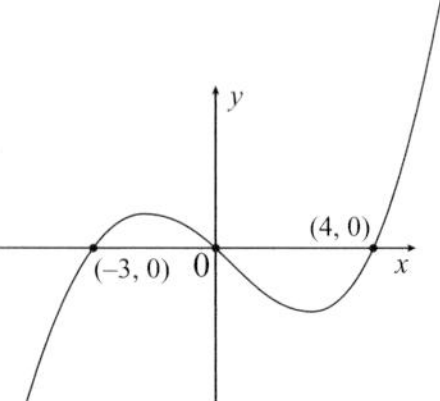

Q14 a)

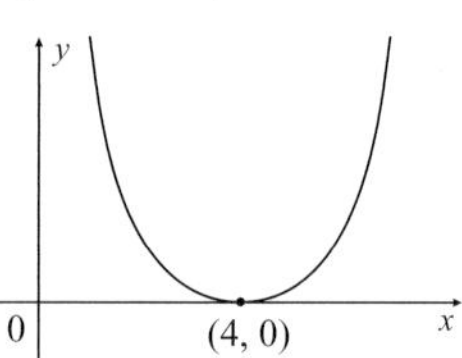

b)

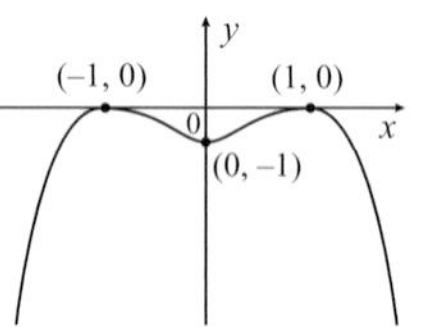

c) Factorise y fully: $y = x^2(x - 4)(x + 4)$

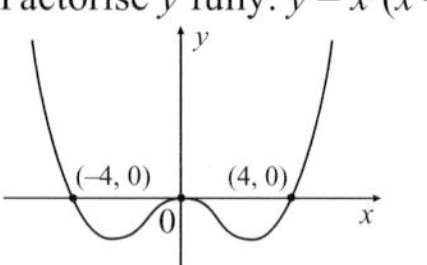

Q15 a)

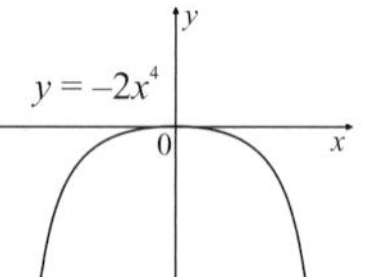

b)

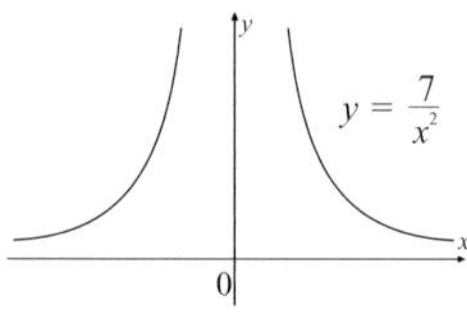

c)

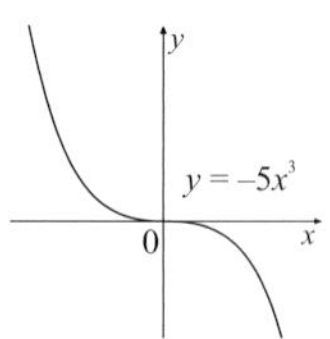

d)

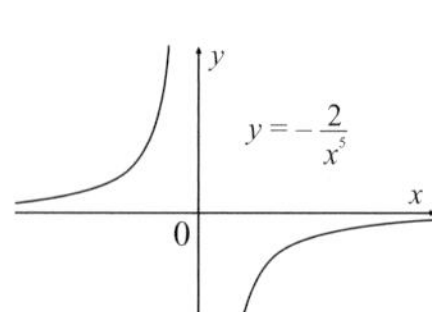

e)

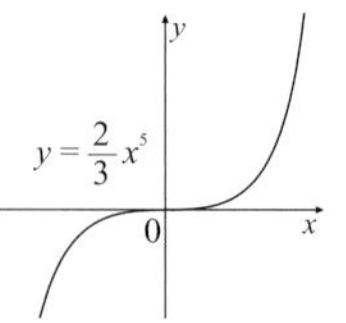

f)

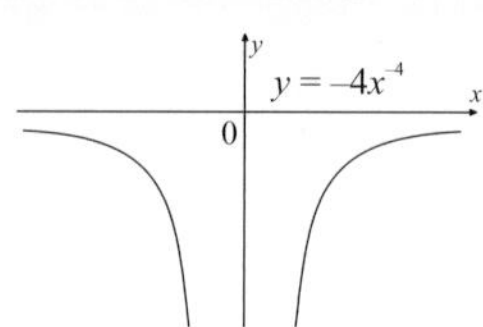

g)

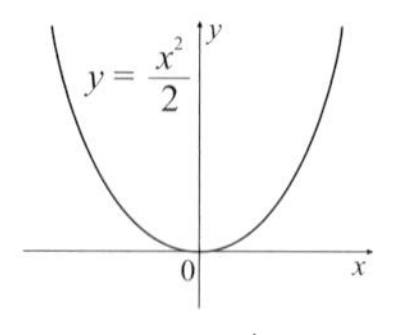

h)

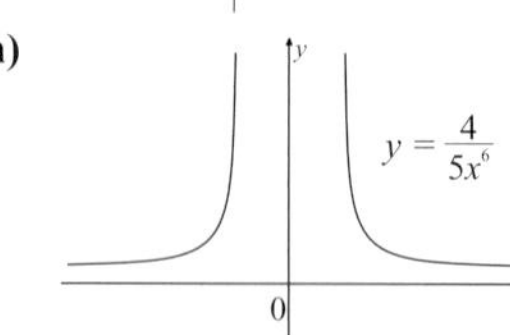

Q16

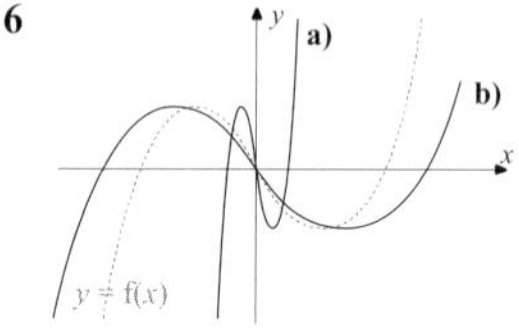

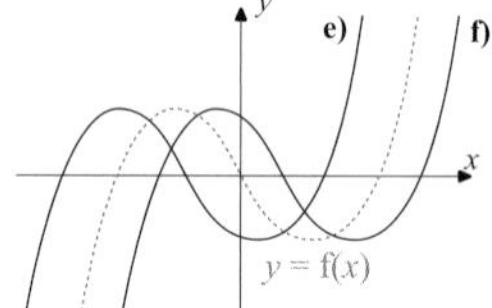

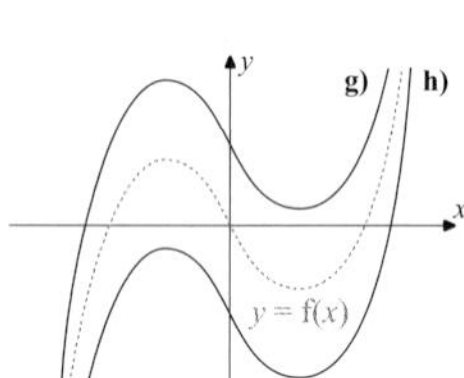

Q17 a) $g(x) = -\frac{1}{3}f(x)$ — vertical stretch, scale factor $-\frac{1}{3}$

b) $g(x) = f(\frac{1}{2}x)$ — horizontal stretch, scale factor 2

c) $f(x) = x^2 - 5x + 4$ and $g(x) = x^2 - 5x + 6$
$g(x) = f(x) + 2$ — vertical translation by 2 upwards

Q18 a) If $f(x) = (x + 1)(x + 3)(x + 7)$ then
$(1 - 2x)(3 - 2x)(7 - 2x) = f(-2x)$
So the transformation is a stretch of scale factor $\frac{1}{2}$ in the x-direction and a reflection in the y-axis.
[2 marks available — 1 mark for a correct method, 1 mark for the correct description]

b) If $f(x) = (x + 1)(x + 3)(x + 7)$ then
$(3x + 3)(2x + 6)(x + 7) = 3(x + 1) \times 2(x + 3) \times (x + 7)$
$= 6(x + 1)(x + 3)(x + 7) = 6f(x)$
So the transformation is a stretch of scale factor 6 in the y-direction.
[2 marks available — 1 mark for a correct method, 1 mark for the correct description]

Q19 a) Since $x = 2$ is a root, $(x - 2)$ is a factor by the Factor Theorem, so use algebraic division (or another suitable method) to factorise $(x - 2)$ out:
$f(x) = x(x^3 - 3x^2 + 4) = x(x - 2)(x^2 - x - 2)$
$= x(x - 2)(x - 2)(x + 1)$

Using this factorisation, sketch the graph:

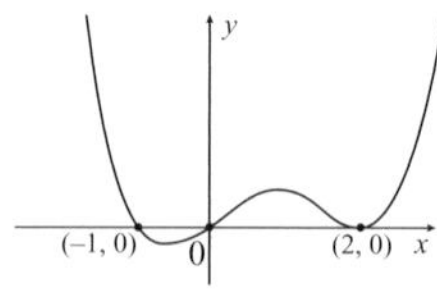

b)

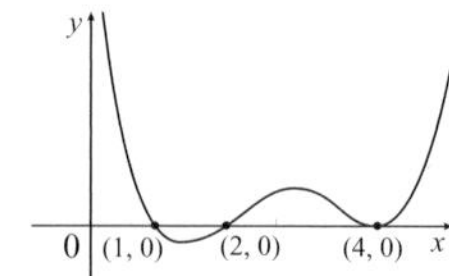

c) $g(x) = (x-2)^4 - 3(x-2)^3 + 4(x-2)$ or
$g(x) = (x-1)(x-2)(x-4)^2$
Substitute (x − 2) in place of x in f(x), or write down g(x) in its factorised form using the roots you know from the graph (or from part a)).

Q20 a)

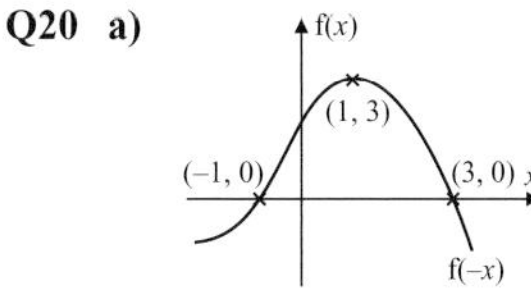

b)

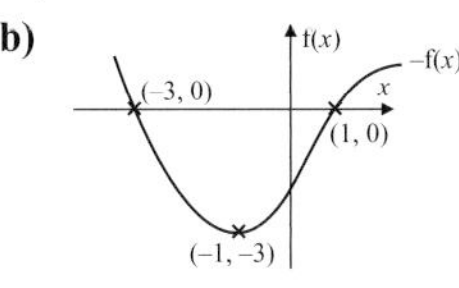

c)

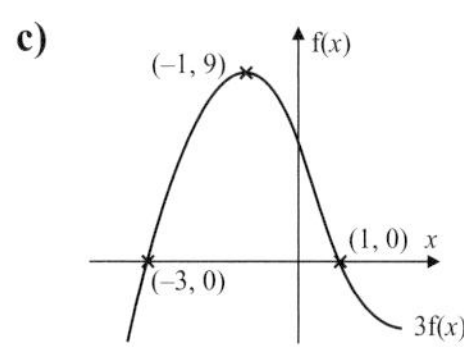

d)

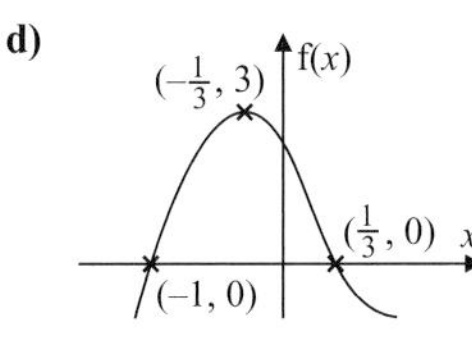

Q21 The horizontal asymptote has equation $y = -\frac{4}{5} \Rightarrow a = -\frac{4}{5}$
The vertical asymptote has equation $x = -6 \Rightarrow c = 6$
$\Rightarrow y = -\frac{4}{5} + \frac{b}{x+6}$
When $x = 4$, $y = -\frac{1}{2} \Rightarrow -\frac{1}{2} = -\frac{4}{5} + \frac{b}{10} \Rightarrow b = 3$
[3 marks available — 1 mark for the correct value of a, 1 mark for the correct value of b, 1 mark for the correct value of c]

Q22 a) $r = 3$, centre (0, 0)

b) $r = 2$, centre (2, −4)

c) Rearrange to get into $(x-a)^2 + (y-b)^2 = r^2$ form:
$x(x+6) = y(8-y) \Rightarrow x^2 + 6x + y^2 - 8y = 0$
$\Rightarrow (x+3)^2 - 9 + (y-4)^2 - 16 = 0 \Rightarrow (x+3)^2 + (y-4)^2 = 25$
So $r = 5$, centre (−3, 4)

Q23 $x^2 + (y+3)^2 = 14$

Q24 $x^2 + y^2 - 4x + 6y - 68 = 0 \Rightarrow x^2 - 4x + y^2 + 6y - 68 = 0$
$\Rightarrow (x-2)^2 - 4 + (y+3)^2 - 9 - 68 = 0 \Rightarrow (x-2)^2 + (y+3)^2 = 81$
So the centre is (2, −3) and the radius is 9.

Q25 Rearrange to find the coordinates of the centre:
$x^2 + y^2 - 12x + 2y + 11 = 0 \Rightarrow x^2 - 12x + y^2 + 2y + 11 = 0$
$\Rightarrow (x-6)^2 - 36 + (y+1)^2 - 1 + 11 = 0$
$\Rightarrow (x-6)^2 + (y+1)^2 = 26$
So the centre of the circle is (6, −1).
Gradient of the radius: $\frac{-1-(-2)}{6-1} = \frac{1}{5}$
So the gradient of the tangent is −5.
Use $y - y_1 = m(x - x_1)$ to find equation of tangent:
$y - (-2) = -5(x-1) \Rightarrow y + 2 = -5x + 5 \Rightarrow y = -5x + 3$

Q26 Use the centre of the circle to write the equation in the form $(x-2)^2 + (y+3)^2 = r^2$.
Then expand the brackets: $x^2 - 4x + 4 + y^2 + 6y + 9 = r^2$
$\Rightarrow x^2 + y^2 - 4x + 6y + 13 - r^2 = 0$
Comparing this with original equation gives:
$a = -4$, $b = 6$ and $-4 = 13 - r^2 \Rightarrow r^2 = 17 \Rightarrow r = \sqrt{17}$
[4 marks available — 1 mark for correctly substituting into the circle equation, 1 mark for correct value of a, 1 mark for the correct value of b, 1 mark for the correct value of r]

Q27 Find the point of intersection by solving the equations $3x + 2y - 12 = 0$ and $y = -5x - 1$ simultaneously:
$3x + 2(-5x-1) - 12 = 0 \Rightarrow 3x - 10x - 2 - 12 = 0$
$\Rightarrow -7x = 14 \Rightarrow x = -2$
When $x = -2$, $y = -5(-2) - 1 = 9$
So the coordinates of the point of intersection are (−2, 9).
Complete the square on the equation of the circle:
$x^2 - 12x + y^2 - 26y + 124 = 0$
$\Rightarrow (x-6)^2 - 36 + (y-13)^2 - 169 + 124 = 0$
$\Rightarrow (x-6)^2 + (y-13)^2 = 81$
So the circle has centre (6, 13) and radius $\sqrt{81} = 9$.
The distance from the centre of the circle to (−2, 9) is:
$\sqrt{((-2)-6)^2 + (9-13)^2} = \sqrt{80} < \sqrt{81}$
So the lines intersect inside the circle.
[4 marks available — 1 mark for attempting to solve the equations simultaneously, 1 mark for coordinates of point of intersection, 1 mark for finding the centre of the circle, 1 mark for explaining why the lines intersect inside the circle]

Q28 Complete the square of the equation of circle C_2:
$x^2 - 10x + y^2 + 6y + 21 = 0$
$\Rightarrow (x-5)^2 - 25 + (y+3)^2 - 9 + 21 = 0$
$\Rightarrow (x-5)^2 + (y+3)^2 = 13$
So C_2 has centre (5, −3) and radius $\sqrt{13}$.
The distance between the centres of the circles is
$\sqrt{(5-(-1))^2 + (-3-6)^2} = \sqrt{117} = 3\sqrt{13}$
The sum of the radii of the circles is $\sqrt{13} + \sqrt{13} = 2\sqrt{13} < 3\sqrt{13}$
So the circles do not intersect.
[4 marks available — 1 mark for finding the centre of C_2, 1 mark for calculating the distance between the centres of the circles, 1 mark for calculating the sum of the radii of the circles, 1 mark for showing that the circles do not intersect]

Q29

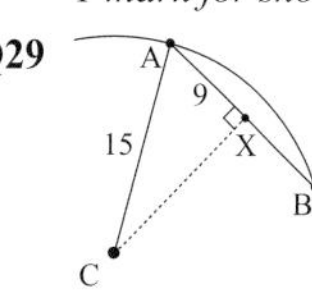

X is the midpoint of AB, so the length of AX is 9.
AC is a radius, so the length of AC is 15.

Since CX bisects the chord AB, the angle AXC is 90°, so triangle ACX is a right-angled triangle with hypotenuse AC.
Use Pythagoras' theorem to find CX:
$CX^2 = 15^2 - 9^2 = 144$, so $CX = \sqrt{144} = 12$.

Q30 a) Complete the square of the circle equation:
$x^2 + y^2 - 4x + 12y + 15 = 0 \Rightarrow x^2 - 4x + y^2 + 12y + 15 = 0$
$\Rightarrow (x-2)^2 - 4 + (y+6)^2 - 36 + 15 = 0$
$\Rightarrow (x-2)^2 + (y+6)^2 = 25$
So the centre is (2, −6) and the radius is 5.
[4 marks available — 1 mark for attempting to complete the square on the circle equation, 1 mark for the correct form of the equation as shown, 1 mark for finding the coordinates of the centre, 1 mark for finding the radius]

b) E.g. The y-value of the centre point is −6. Since the radius is 5 and 5 < 6, the entire circle must lie below the x-axis.
[2 marks available —2 marks for a fully supported argument, otherwise 1 mark for a partially supported argument]
An alternative proof is to show that there are no intersections between the circle and the x-axis — i.e. when y = 0, $(x-2)^2 = -11$, so there are no real roots. The centre of the circle is below the x-axis, so the entire circle must lie below the x-axis.

c) Substitute (−1, k) into the circle equation:
$(-1-2)^2 + (k+6)^2 = 25 \Rightarrow (k+6)^2 = 16$
$\Rightarrow (k+6) = \pm 4 \Rightarrow k = -2$ or $k = -10$
[3 marks available — 1 mark for substituting in −1 for x into the original equation and attempting to solve a quadratic equation to find k, 1 mark for finding k = −2, 1 mark for k = −10]

Q31 a) AB is a diameter so the chords BC and CA must be perpendicular (i.e. $m_{CA} \times m_{BC} = -1$):
$m_{BC} = \frac{-1-1}{4-0} = \frac{-2}{4} = -\frac{1}{2}$
$m_{CA} = \frac{1-a}{0-2} = \frac{a-1}{2}$
$m_{CA} \times m_{BC} = -1 \Rightarrow \frac{a-1}{2} \times -\frac{1}{2} = -1 \Rightarrow -\frac{a-1}{4} = -1$
$\Rightarrow a - 1 = 4 \Rightarrow a = 5$

b) The centre of the circle is the midpoint of the diameter AB, and the radius is half the length AB.
Centre $= \left(\frac{2+4}{2}, \frac{5-1}{2}\right) = (3, 2)$
Radius $= \frac{1}{2}\sqrt{(4-2)^2 + (-1-5)^2}$
$= \frac{1}{2}\sqrt{2^2 + (-6)^2} = \frac{1}{2}\sqrt{40} = \sqrt{10}$
So the equation of the circle is:
$(x-3)^2 + (y-2)^2 = 10$

Q32 a) The equation of the circle C is $(x-25)^2+(y-15)^2=125$
$x=20$ and $y=25$
$\Rightarrow (20-25)^2+(25-15)^2=25+100=125$
So P lies on the circumference of the circle C. *[1 mark]*

b) The gradient of the radius joining the centre of the circle and P is $\frac{15-25}{25-20}=\frac{-10}{5}=-2$
So the gradient of the tangent to the circle at P is $-1\div-2=\frac{1}{2}$
So the equation of the tangent line, l_1, through P is:
$y-25=\frac{1}{2}(x-20) \Rightarrow y=\frac{1}{2}x+15$
[2 marks available — 1 mark for the correct gradient of the tangent, 1 mark for the correct equation]

c) The line l_1 passes through the point (0, 15), i.e. the line l_1 intersects the y-axis at a point with the same y-coordinate as the centre of the circle. So, by symmetry, the other tangent to the circle through B is a vertical reflection of the line l_1 (i.e. a reflection in the line $y=15$).
So the equation of l_2 is $y=-\frac{1}{2}x+15$.
Similarly, by symmetry, the point Q is a reflection of the point P in the line $y=15$, so has coordinates (20, 5).
[2 marks available — 1 mark for the correct equation of l_2, 1 mark for the correct coordinates of Q]

d) The quadrilateral APBQ is a kite, so the area of APBQ
$=\frac{1}{2}\times$ length AB $\times$ length PQ $=\frac{1}{2}\times 25\times 20=250$ units²
[1 mark]
You could also split the quadrilateral APBQ into two congruent triangles, e.g. APB and AQB.

Q33 Find the perpendicular bisectors of two of the line segments AB, BC and CA.
AB: midpoint $=\left(\frac{4.5+2}{2},\frac{7.5+5}{2}\right)=(3.25, 6.25)$
gradient $=\frac{7.5-5}{4.5-2}=\frac{2.5}{2.5}=1$
So the perpendicular bisector passes through (3.25, 6.25) and has a gradient of -1.
$y-y_1=m(x-x_1) \Rightarrow y-6.25=-1(x-3.25) \Rightarrow y=-x+9.5$
BC: midpoint $=\left(\frac{2+4}{2},\frac{5+5}{2}\right)=(3, 5)$
gradient $=\frac{5-5}{4-2}=0$
BC is horizontal so the perpendicular bisector is vertical and passes through (3, 5) — i.e. $x=3$.
Now find the centre of the circle, which is the point where these lines intersect:
Substitute $x=3$ into $y=-x+9.5$: $y=-(3)+9.5=6.5$
so the circle has its centre at (3, 6.5).
Radius $=\sqrt{(3-2)^2+(6.5-5)^2}=\sqrt{1^2+1.5^2}=\sqrt{3.25}$
So the equation of the circle is: $(x-3)^2+(y-6.5)^2=3.25$

Q34 Find the perpendicular bisectors of two of the line segments PQ, QR and RS.
PQ: midpoint $=\left(\frac{2+6}{2},\frac{11+5}{2}\right)=\left(\frac{8}{2},\frac{16}{2}\right)=(4, 8)$
gradient $=\frac{5-11}{6-2}=\frac{-6}{4}=-\frac{3}{2}$
So the perpendicular bisector passes through (4, 8) and has a gradient of $\left(-1\div-\frac{3}{2}\right)=\frac{2}{3}$.
$y-y_1=m(x-x_1) \Rightarrow y-8=\frac{2}{3}(x-4)$
$\Rightarrow y=\frac{2}{3}x-\frac{8}{3}+8 \Rightarrow y=\frac{2}{3}x+\frac{16}{3}$
QR: midpoint $=\left(\frac{6+(-9)}{2},\frac{5+0}{2}\right)=\left(-\frac{3}{2},\frac{5}{2}\right)$
gradient $=\frac{0-5}{(-9)-6}=\frac{-5}{-15}=\frac{1}{3}$
So the perpendicular bisector passes through $\left(-\frac{3}{2},\frac{5}{2}\right)$ and has a gradient of $\left(-1\div\frac{1}{3}\right)=-3$.
$y-y_1=m(x-x_1) \Rightarrow y-\frac{5}{2}=(-3)\left(x-\left(-\frac{3}{2}\right)\right)$
$\Rightarrow y=-3x-\frac{9}{2}+\frac{5}{2} \Rightarrow y=-3x-2$
Now find the centre of the circle, which is the point where these lines intersect:
$\frac{2}{3}x+\frac{16}{3}=-3x-2 \Rightarrow 2x+16=-9x-6$
$\Rightarrow 11x=-22 \Rightarrow x=-2$
Substitute $x=-2$ into $y=-3x-2$:
$y=-3(-2)-2=6-2=4$
So the circle has its centre at (−2, 4).
You could have used the perpendicular bisector of RS here to find the centre of the circle — it has equation $y=2-x$.
The radius is the distance from the centre to one of the points — here we use Q:

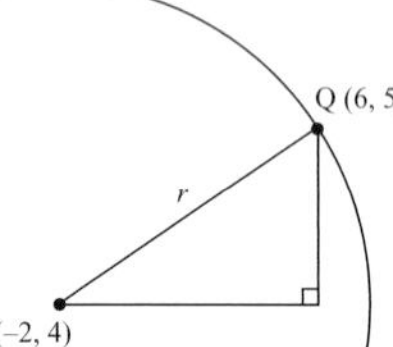

Use Pythagoras' theorem to find r^2:
$(6-(-2))^2+(5-4)^2=r^2 \Rightarrow 8^2+1^2=r^2 \Rightarrow r^2=65$
So the equation of the circle is: $(x+2)^2+(y-4)^2=65$.

Q35 a) Substitute the values $x=-4$ and $y=7$ into the equation of the line:
$\Rightarrow 7(k-2)=-4(3-k)+k^2-6$
$\Rightarrow 7k-14=-12+4k+k^2-6$
$\Rightarrow k^2-3k-4=0 \Rightarrow (k-4)(k+1)=0$
$\Rightarrow k=4$ or $k=-1$
[2 marks available — 1 mark for obtaining a quadratic in k, 1 mark for both correct values of k]

b) When $k=4$, $2y=-x+10 \Rightarrow y=-\frac{1}{2}x+5$
When $k=-1$, $-3y=4x-5 \Rightarrow y=-\frac{4}{3}x+\frac{5}{3}$
[3 marks available — 1 mark for attempting to substitute into the original equation, 1 mark for each correct equation]

c) Substituting $x=6$ and $y=-2$ into the equation of the line gives $-2(k-2)=6(3-k)+k^2-6$
$\Rightarrow -2k+4=18-6k+k^2-6$
$\Rightarrow k^2-4k+8=0$
The discriminant of this quadratic is
$b^2-4ac=(-4)^2-(4\times 1\times 8)=-16<0$
Therefore there are no real solutions to the quadratic equation $k^2-4k+8=0$, meaning l does not pass through the point (6, −2) for any real value of k.
[2 marks available — 1 mark for obtaining a quadratic in k, 1 mark for a correct explanation]

Q36 a) $m_{CD}=\frac{6-2}{6-(-4)}=\frac{4}{10}=\frac{2}{5}$
$y-y_1=m(x-x_1) \Rightarrow y-6=\frac{2}{5}(x-6)$
$\Rightarrow y-6=\frac{2}{5}x-\frac{12}{5} \Rightarrow y=\frac{2}{5}x+\frac{18}{5}$
$\Rightarrow 5y=2x+18 \Rightarrow 2x-5y+18=0$
[3 marks available — 1 mark for finding gradient of CD, 1 mark for any correct form of line equation with fractional coefficients, 1 mark for correct final answer with integer coefficients]

b) $y-y_1=m(x-x_1) \Rightarrow y-6=-1(x-6) \Rightarrow y=-x+12$
[2 marks available — 1 mark for substituting the gradient and point into a line equation, 1 mark for correct equation of BC in any form]

c) B is the point of intersection between BC and AB.
Find an equation for AB:
AB is parallel to CD, so the gradient is $\frac{2}{5}$.
$y - y_1 = m(x - x_1) \Rightarrow y - 7 = \frac{2}{5}(x - (-2))$
$\Rightarrow y - 7 = \frac{2}{5}x + \frac{4}{5} \Rightarrow y = \frac{2}{5}x + \frac{39}{5}$
When AB meets BC:
$-x + 12 = \frac{2}{5}x + \frac{39}{5} \Rightarrow -5x + 60 = 2x + 39$
$\Rightarrow 7x = 21 \Rightarrow x = 3$
Substitute x into an equation to find y:
$y = -(3) + 12 = 9$, so B has coordinates (3, 9).
[4 marks available — 1 mark for finding the equation of AB, 1 mark for attempting to solve the equations simultaneously, 1 mark for correct x-coordinate, 1 mark for correct y-coordinate]

d) Find gradient of DB: $m_{DB} = \frac{9-2}{3-(-4)} = 1$
The product of the gradients of perpendicular lines is –1.
$m_{BC} \times m_{DB} = -1 \times 1 = -1$, so BC and DB are perpendicular — i.e. –DBC = 90°.
[2 marks available — 1 mark for finding the gradient of DB, 1 mark for using the gradients of DB and BC to show they are perpendicular]

Q37 a) $4x + 3y = 24 \Rightarrow y = -\frac{4}{3}x + 8$, so the line has gradient $-\frac{4}{3}$
l_1 is perpendicular to $4x + 3y = 24$ so it has a gradient of
$-1 \div -\frac{4}{3} = \frac{3}{4}$
So the equation of l_1 is $y - 4 = \frac{3}{4}(x - 8) \Rightarrow y = \frac{3}{4}x - 2$
[3 marks available — 1 mark for correct gradient of l_1, 1 mark for use of a correct method to find its equation, 1 mark for a correct equation]

b) Solve the equations $4x + 3y = 24$ and $y = \frac{3}{4}x - 2$ simultaneously to find the coordinates of the point A:
$4x + 3(\frac{3}{4}x - 2) = 24 \Rightarrow \frac{25}{4}x - 6 = 24$
$\Rightarrow \frac{25}{4}x = 30 \Rightarrow x = \frac{24}{5}$
When $x = \frac{24}{5}$, $y = \frac{3}{4} \times \frac{24}{5} - 2 = \frac{18}{5} - 2 = \frac{8}{5}$
So the coordinates of A are $\left(\frac{24}{5}, \frac{8}{5}\right)$
[2 marks available — 1 mark for attempting to solve the equations simultaneously, 1 mark for the correct coordinates]

c) The coordinates of B and C are (8, 0) and (0, 4) respectively. If A, B and C lie on the same straight line, then A must lie on the line through B and C.
Gradient of BC $= \frac{-4}{8} = -\frac{1}{2}$, and the y-intercept = 4,
so the line through B and C has equation $y = -\frac{1}{2}x + 4$
When $x = \frac{24}{5}$, $y = -\frac{1}{2} \times \frac{24}{5} + 4 = \frac{8}{5}$
So A, B and C all lie on the same straight line.
[3 marks available — 1 mark for correct coordinates of B and C, 1 mark for equation of an appropriate line, 1 mark for showing that all three points lie on this line]

Q38 a) $y \propto x^2 \Rightarrow y = kx^2$
Expand and simplify $af(x) + (3x + b)g(x)$:
$ax^3 + 4ax^2 + 7ax + 2a + (3x^3 + 9x^2 + 18x + bx^2 + 3bx + 6b)$
$= (a + 3)x^3 + (4a + b + 9)x^2 + (7a + 3b + 18)x + (2a + 6b)$
Comparing coefficients: $a + 3 = 0$, $7a + 3b + 18 = 0$ and $2a + 6b = 0$
$a + 3 = 0 \Rightarrow a = -3$
$2(-3) + 6b = 0 \Rightarrow 6b = 6 \Rightarrow b = 1$
(Check: $7(-3) + 3(1) + 18 = -21 + 3 + 18 = 0$)
[4 marks available — 1 mark for expanding and simplifying, 1 mark for comparing coefficients to obtain equations in a and b, 1 mark for attempting to solve these equations simultaneously, 1 mark for the correct values of a and b]

b) Complete the square to find the value of x for which g(x) is at its minimum value:
$g(x) = x^2 + 3x + 6 = \left(x + \frac{3}{2}\right)^2 - \frac{9}{4} + 6 = \left(x + \frac{3}{2}\right)^2 + \frac{15}{4}$
So g(x) is at its minimum when $x = -\frac{3}{2}$.
Substituting the values from a), ignoring the x^3, x and constant terms because y only has an x^2 term:
$y = (4a + b + 9)x^2 = (-12 + 1 + 9)x^2 = -2x^2$
Substituting the values from a) into the other terms would give coefficients of 0 for those terms.
$y = -2\left(-\frac{3}{2}\right)^2 \Rightarrow y = -\frac{9}{2}$
[3 marks available — 1 mark for use of a correct method to find the value of x for which g(x) is minimal, 1 mark for correct value of x, 1 mark for correct value of y]

Q39 a) $\frac{3x-1}{x-2} \equiv \frac{3x-6+5}{x-2} \equiv \frac{3(x-2)}{x-2} + \frac{5}{x-2} \equiv 3 + \frac{5}{x-2}$
[2 marks available — 1 mark for attempting to rearrange, 1 mark for a correct solution]

b) The graph of $y = 3 + \frac{5}{x-2}$ takes the graph of $y = \frac{1}{x}$, stretches it vertically with a scale factor of 5, then translates it by 3 units up and 2 units right.
So the equations of the asymptotes are $y = 3$ and $x = 2$.
[2 marks available — 1 mark for each correct asymptote]

c) $f(0) = 3 + \frac{5}{-2} = \frac{1}{2}$, so $y = f(x)$ crosses the y-axis at $\left(0, \frac{1}{2}\right)$
$f(x) = 0 \Rightarrow 3(x - 2) + 5 = 0 \Rightarrow x = \frac{1}{3}$,
so $y = f(x)$ intersects the x-axis at $\left(\frac{1}{3}, 0\right)$

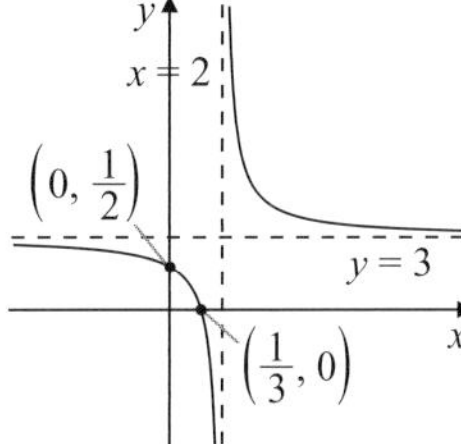

[3 marks available — 1 mark for the correct shape, 1 mark for the correct asymptotes, 1 mark for the correct intercepts with the coordinate axes]

Q40 a) Length $= \sqrt{(-2-3)^2 + (4-9)^2}$
$= \sqrt{(-5)^2 + (-5)^2} = 5\sqrt{2}$
Midpoint $= \left(\frac{-2+3}{2}, \frac{4+9}{2}\right) = (0.5, 6.5)$

b) Find the perpendicular bisectors of two of the line segments XY, YZ and ZX.
XY: from part a), midpoint = (0.5, 6.5)
gradient $= \frac{9-4}{3-(-2)} = \frac{5}{5} = 1$
So the perpendicular bisector passes through (0.5, 6.5) and has a gradient of –1.
$y - y_1 = m(x - x_1) \Rightarrow y - 6.5 = -(x - 0.5) \Rightarrow y = -x + 7$
YZ: midpoint $= \left(\frac{3+7}{2}, \frac{9+1}{2}\right) = (5, 5)$
gradient $= \frac{9-1}{3-7} = \frac{8}{-4} = -2$
So the perpendicular bisector passes through (5, 5) and has a gradient of $\frac{1}{2}$.
$y - y_1 = m(x - x_1) \Rightarrow y - 5 = \frac{1}{2}(x - 5) \Rightarrow y = \frac{1}{2}x + \frac{5}{2}$
Now find the centre of the circle, which is the point where these lines intersect:
$\frac{1}{2}x + \frac{5}{2} = -x + 7 \Rightarrow x + 5 = -2x + 14$
$\Rightarrow 3x = 9 \Rightarrow x = 3$
Substitute $x = 3$ into $y = -x + 7$: $y = -(3) + 7 = 4$
so the circle has its centre at (3, 4).
Radius $= \sqrt{(3-3)^2 + (9-4)^2} = \sqrt{5^2} = 5$
So the equation of the circle is: $(x - 3)^2 + (y - 4)^2 = 25$

c) CM bisects XY, so it is perpendicular. So CXY has base XY and perpendicular height CM.

Length CM = $\sqrt{(3-0.5)^2+(4-6.5)^2}$
$= \sqrt{2.5^2+(-2.5)^2} = \frac{5\sqrt{2}}{2}$

From part a), the length XY = $5\sqrt{2}$.

So the area of CXY = $\frac{1}{2} \times 5\sqrt{2} \times \frac{5\sqrt{2}}{2}$ = 12.5 units^2

Alternatively, you might notice that CX and CY are perpendicular, so you can also work out the area of CXY using CX and CY as the base and perpendicular height, both of which have length 5.

Q41 a) Substitute (9, p) into the circle equation:
$9^2 + p^2 - 10(9) - 7 = 0 \Rightarrow p^2 = 16 \Rightarrow p = 4$
($p > 0$ so ignore the negative root)
[2 marks available — 1 mark for substituting x = 9 into the circle equation, 1 mark for solving the equation for p and taking the positive root]

b) Complete the square to find the centre:
$(x-5)^2 - 25 + y^2 - 7 = 0$
$\Rightarrow (x-5)^2 + y^2 = 32$, so the centre is (5, 0).
Gradient of radius: $m = \frac{4-0}{9-5} = 1$
so the gradient of the tangent at A is –1.
$y - y_1 = m(x - x_1) \Rightarrow y - 4 = -1(x-9)$
$\Rightarrow y = -x + 13 \Rightarrow x + y = 13$
[5 marks available — 1 mark for completing the square on circle equation, 1 mark for finding centre point, 1 mark for finding the gradient of the radius, 1 mark for finding the gradient of the tangent, 1 mark for correct equation of tangent]

c) $x + y = 13$ meets the x-axis at Q (0, 13), so the distance OQ is 13. A is at (9, 4) so the perpendicular height of OAQ is 4.
Area of the triangle = $\frac{1}{2} \times$ base $\times$ height
$= \frac{1}{2} \times 13 \times 4 = 26$ units^2
[3 marks available — 1 mark for finding coordinates of Q, 1 mark for attempting to use coordinates to find base and height of triangle OAQ, 1 mark for correct area]

Q42 l_2: $5x + 7y = 80 \Rightarrow y = -\frac{5}{7}x + \frac{80}{7}$.
l_1 and l_2 both have a gradient of $-\frac{5}{7}$, so they are parallel.
This means that the points of intersection of l_1 and l_2 with the circle are the endpoints of a diameter of the circle.
Since l_1 and l_2 are tangents, they are perpendicular to this diameter, so find the equation of the line perpendicular to l_2 that passes through (9, 5):
Perpendicular gradient $= -1 \div -\frac{5}{7} = \frac{7}{5}$
$y - y_1 = m(x - x_1) \Rightarrow y - 5 = \frac{7}{5}(x - 9) \Rightarrow y = \frac{7}{5}x - \frac{38}{5}$
Find where this line crosses l_1:
$\frac{7}{5}x - \frac{38}{5} = -\frac{5}{7}x + 22 \Rightarrow 49x - 266 = -25x + 770$
$\Rightarrow 74x = 1036 \Rightarrow x = 14$
$y = -\frac{5}{7}(14) + 22 = -10 + 22 = 12$
So the coordinates of the point where l_1 touches the circle are (14, 12). The centre of the circle is the midpoint of the diameter joining (9, 5) and (14, 12), so:
Centre of C has coordinates $\left(\frac{9+14}{2}, \frac{5+12}{2}\right) = \left(\frac{23}{2}, \frac{17}{2}\right)$
The length of the diameter is $\sqrt{5^2+7^2} = \sqrt{74}$,
so the radius of C is $\frac{1}{2}\sqrt{74} = \sqrt{\frac{37}{2}}$
So the equation of C is $\left(x - \frac{23}{2}\right)^2 + \left(y - \frac{17}{2}\right)^2 = \frac{37}{2}$
[7 marks available — 1 mark for determining that the lines are parallel, 1 mark for using the fact that the points of contact of the lines with the circle form a diameter, 1 mark for calculating the equation of the line perpendicular to l_2, 1 mark for finding the coordinates of the point of intersection of l_1 with the circle, 1 mark for correct centre of the circle, 1 mark for correct radius, 1 mark for correct equation]

Q43 a) Consider the tangent to C_1 at point A. Because the circles only touch at one point, this line is also a tangent to C_2. The tangent is perpendicular to the radius of each circle at point A, meaning both radii must be parallel.
So, because both radii are parallel and pass through point A, they must form a straight line through the centre of each circle and A.
[2 marks available — 1 mark for attempting to use circle properties, 1 mark for a correct explanation]

b) The equation of the line through the centre of C_1 and A has a gradient of $\frac{6-(-2)}{7-5} = \frac{8}{2} = 4$
$y - y_1 = m(x - x_1) \Rightarrow y - 6 = 4(x - 7) \Rightarrow y = 4x - 22$
From part a), this line must pass through the centre of C_2.
Since l is a tangent to C_2 at (22, 21), the line perpendicular to l through (22, 21) will also pass through the centre of C_2.
Gradient of perpendicular $= -1 \div -4 = \frac{1}{4}$
Equation of perpendicular: $y - y_1 = m(x - x_1)$
$\Rightarrow y - 21 = \frac{1}{4}(x - 22) \Rightarrow y = \frac{1}{4}x + \frac{31}{2}$
So the centre of C_2 is the point of intersection between $y = 4x - 22$ and $y = \frac{1}{4}x + \frac{31}{2}$:
$4x - 22 = \frac{1}{4}x + \frac{31}{2} \Rightarrow 16x - 88 = x + 62$
$\Rightarrow 15x = 150 \Rightarrow x = 10$
When $x = 10$, $y = 4(10) - 22 = 18$
So the centre of C_2 has coordinates (10, 18).
The radius of C_2 is $\sqrt{(10-7)^2+(18-6)^2} = \sqrt{153}$,
so the equation of C_2 is $(x - 10)^2 + (y - 18)^2 = 153$.
[6 marks available — 1 mark for equation of line through the centres of both circles, 1 mark for the equation of line perpendicular to l through (22, 21), 1 mark for attempting to solve these equations simultaneously, 1 mark for the coordinates of the centre, 1 mark for the correct radius, 1 mark for the correct equation of the circle]

Chapter 7: The Binomial Expansion

Prior Knowledge Check

Q1 **a)** $25x^2$ **b)** 1 **c)** $-8z^3$ **d)** $z - 2$

Q2 **a)** $x^3 - 3x^2$ **b)** $10z^2 - 7z - 12$ **c)** $64 - 32w + 4w^2$
d) $(p - q)(p^2 - 2pq + q^2) = p^3 - 3p^2q + 3pq^2 - q^3$

Q3 **a)** $(12x^2 + x - 1)(5x + 4) = 60x^3 + 53x^2 - x - 4$
b) $(2x^5 - 8x^4 - 12x^3 + 24x^2) + (3x^4 - 12x^3 - 18x^2 + 36x) + (-x^3 + 4x^2 + 6x - 12)$
$= 2x^5 - 5x^4 - 25x^3 + 10x^2 + 42x - 12$

Q4 **a)** $\frac{x^2}{16}$ **b)** $\frac{-x^3}{8}$ **c)** $\frac{625x^4}{81}$

Exercise 7.1 — Binomial Expansions — $(1 + x)^n$

Q1 Pascal's triangle is

1
1 1
1 2 1
1 3 3 1

The expansion of $(1 + x)^3$ takes its coefficients of each term, in ascending powers of x, from the 4th row:
$(1 + x)^3 = 1 + 3x + 3x^2 + x^3$

Q2 **a)** $\binom{n}{n-r} = \frac{n!}{(n-r)!(n-(n-r))!} = \frac{n!}{(n-r)!r!}$
$= \frac{n!}{r!(n-r)!} = \binom{n}{r}$

b) Use $\binom{n}{r} = {}^nC_r$ to find the answers to part b).
(i) $(1 + x)^{10}$ = 1, 10, 45, 120, 210, 252, 210, 120, 45, 10, 1
(ii) $(1 + x)^{13}$ = 1, 13, 78, 286, 715, 1287, 1716, 1716, 1287, 715, 286, 78, 13, 1

Q3 **a)** ${}^6C_2 = 15$ **b)** $\binom{12}{5} = {}^{12}C_5 = 792$

c) $\frac{30!}{4!26!} = {}^{30}C_4 = 27\,405$ **d)** ${}^8C_8 = 1$

Q4 **a)** $\frac{9!}{4!5!} = \frac{9\times8\times7\times6\times5\times4\times3\times2\times1}{(4\times3\times2\times1)(5\times4\times3\times2\times1)}$
$= \frac{9\times8\times7\times6}{4\times3\times2\times1} = 3\times7\times6 = 126$

b) ${}^{10}C_3 = \frac{10!}{3!(10-3)!} = \frac{10\times9\times8}{3\times2\times1}$
$= 10\times3\times4 = 120$

c) $\frac{15!}{11!4!} = \frac{15\times14\times13\times12}{4\times3\times2\times1} = 15\times7\times13 = 1365$

d) $\binom{8}{6} = \frac{8!}{6!(8-6)!} = \frac{8\times7}{2\times1} = 4\times7 = 28$

Q5 $(1 + x)^{10} = 1 + {}^{10}C_1x + {}^{10}C_2x^2 + {}^{10}C_3x^3 + ...$
You can work out the coefficients ${}^nC_r$ using a calculator, or using the method below. Using the notation $\binom{n}{r}$ instead of ${}^nC_r$ for the coefficients is fine too.

${}^nC_r = \frac{n!}{r!(n-r)!}$,

${}^{10}C_1 = \frac{10!}{1!(10-1)!} = \frac{10\times9\times8\times...1}{1\times9\times8\times...1} = 10$

${}^{10}C_2 = \frac{10!}{2!(10-2)!} = \frac{10\times9\times8\times...1}{2\times1\times8\times7\times...1}$
$= \frac{10\times9}{2} = 45$

${}^{10}C_3 = \frac{10!}{3!(10-3)!} = \frac{10\times9\times8\times7\times...1}{3\times2\times1\times7\times...1}$
$= \frac{10\times9\times8}{3\times2}$
$= 10\times3\times4 = 120$

$(1 + x)^{10} = 1 + 10x + 45x^2 + 120x^3 + ...$
For the rest of this exercise you can use one of the methods shown in question 1 or 4 to find the coefficients ${}^nC_r$, or you can use a calculator.

Q6 $(1 + x)^7 = 1 + {}^7C_1x + {}^7C_2x^2 + {}^7C_3x^3 + ... = 1 + 7x + 21x^2 + 35x^3 + ...$

Q7 **a)** $(1 + x)^{11} = 1 + {}^{11}C_1x + {}^{11}C_2x^2 + ... = 1 + 11x + 55x^2 + ...$

b) $(1 + x)^{12} = 1 + {}^{12}C_1x + {}^{12}C_2x^2 + ... = 1 + 12x + 66x^2 + ...$

c) $(1 + x)^{15} = 1 + {}^{15}C_1x + {}^{15}C_2x^2 + ... = 1 + 15x + 105x^2 + ...$

d) $(1 + x)^{30} = 1 + {}^{30}C_1x + {}^{30}C_2x^2 + ... = 1 + 30x + 435x^2 + ...$

Q8 **a)** $(1 + x)^5 = 1 + {}^5C_1x + {}^5C_2x^2 + {}^5C_3x^3 + {}^5C_4x^4 + {}^5C_5x^5$
$= 1 + 5x + 10x^2 + 10x^3 + 5x^4 + x^5$
[2 marks available — 2 marks for the fully correct expansion, otherwise 1 mark for finding at least three correct terms]

b) $(1 + x)^6 = (1 + x)(1 + x)^5$ so you could multiply out the brackets by substituting in the $(1 + x)^5$ expansion.
[1 mark for a correct explanation]
Alternatively, you could use Pascal's triangle to add together consecutive pairs of coefficients from the expansion of $(1 + x)^5$ to give the coefficients of the terms in the expansion of $(1 + x)^6$. The exceptions to this are the x^6 term which will have a coefficient of 1 and the constant term which will be equal to 1.

c) $(1 + x)^6 = (1 + x)(1 + 5x + 10x^2 + 10x^3 + 5x^4 + x^5)$
$= 1 + 6x + 15x^2 + 20x^3 + 15x^4 + 6x^5 + x^6$ *[1 mark]*

Q9 The coefficient of x^{12} is ${}^{17}C_{12} = 6188$, so $a = 6188$.

Q10 **a)** First find the term in x in the expansion of $(1 + x)^5$:
$(1 + x)^5 = 1 + {}^5C_1x + ...$, so the term in x is $5x$. Now add the x-term in the second bracket: $5x + (-3x) = 2x$

b) The coefficient of x^4 is ${}^5C_4 = 5$.
The second bracket doesn't affect the term in x^4.

Q11 **a)** $(1 + x)^3 = {}^3C_0 + {}^3C_1x + {}^3C_2x^2 + {}^3C_3x^3$
$(1 + x)^4 = {}^4C_0 + {}^4C_1x + {}^4C_2x^2 + {}^4C_3x^3 + {}^4C_4x^4$

b) **(i)** Substitute $x = 1$ into $(1 + x)^3 = {}^3C_0 + {}^3C_1x + {}^3C_2x^2 + {}^3C_3x^3$ to give $2^3 = {}^3C_0 + {}^3C_1 + {}^3C_2 + {}^3C_3$
$\Rightarrow \binom{3}{0} + \binom{3}{1} + \binom{3}{2} + \binom{3}{3} = 2^3$

(ii) Substitute $x = 1$ into
$(1 + x)^4 = {}^4C_0 + {}^4C_1x + {}^4C_2x^2 + {}^4C_3x^3 + {}^4C_4x^4$
to give $2^4 = {}^4C_0 + {}^4C_1 + {}^4C_2 + {}^4C_3 + {}^4C_4$

c) $(1 + x)^n = \binom{n}{0} + \binom{n}{1}x + \binom{n}{2}x^2 + ... + \binom{n}{n-1}x^{n-1} + \binom{n}{n}x^n$
Substituting $x = 1$ gives:
$2^n = \binom{n}{0} + \binom{n}{1} + \binom{n}{2} + ... + \binom{n}{n-1} + \binom{n}{n}$

d) The row of Pascal's triangle is the row containing the numbers which correspond to the binomial coefficients of the form $\binom{12}{r}$. Using the result from c),
$\binom{12}{0} + \binom{12}{1} + \binom{12}{2} + ... + \binom{12}{11} + \binom{12}{12} = 2^{12} = 4096$

Q12 **a)** $(1 + x)^3 = 1 + {}^3C_1x + {}^3C_2x^2 + {}^3C_3x^3 = 1 + 3x + 3x^2 + x^3$
[2 marks available — 2 marks for the fully correct expansion, otherwise 1 mark for finding at least two correct terms]

b) $6 + 3x + 3x^2 + x^3 = 5 + (1 + 3x + 3x^2 + x^3) = 5 + (1 + x)^3$.
So the transformation needed is the translation $\begin{pmatrix}-1\\5\end{pmatrix}$.
[2 marks available — 1 mark for attempting to use the result from part a), 1 mark for the correct transformation]
Don't forget that there is a translation in the x-direction, too.

Q13 **a)** $(1 + x)^4 = 1 + {}^4C_1x + {}^4C_2x^2 + {}^4C_3x^3 + {}^4C_4x^4$
$= 1 + 4x + 6x^2 + 4x^3 + x^4$
[2 marks available — 2 marks for the fully correct expansion, otherwise 1 mark for finding at least two correct terms]

b) Substitute $\sqrt{5}$ for x in $(1 + x)^4$ to give
$(1 + \sqrt{5})^4 = 1 + 4\sqrt{5} + 6(\sqrt{5})^2 + 4(\sqrt{5})^3 + (\sqrt{5})^4$
$= 1 + 4\sqrt{5} + 30 + 20\sqrt{5} + 25 = 56 + 24\sqrt{5}$
[2 marks available — 1 mark for substituting $\sqrt{5}$ in the expansion of $(1 + x)^4$, 1 mark for the correct answer]

c) $\sqrt{\frac{56}{25} + \frac{24\sqrt{5}}{25}} = \frac{1}{5}\sqrt{(56 + 24\sqrt{5})} = \frac{1}{5}\sqrt{(1 + \sqrt{5})^4}$
$= \frac{1}{5}(1 + \sqrt{5})^2 = \frac{1}{5}(1 + 2\sqrt{5} + 5) = \frac{6}{5} + \frac{2\sqrt{5}}{5}$
[3 marks available — 1 mark for attempting to use the result from b), 1 mark for attempting to manipulate surds and indices, 1 mark for the correct answer]

Q14 **a)** ${}^nC_2 = \frac{n!}{2!(n-2)!} = \frac{n(n-1)}{2!} = \frac{n(n-1)}{2} = 28$
$\Rightarrow n(n-1) = 56 \Rightarrow n^2 - n - 56 = 0 \Rightarrow (n + 7)(n - 8)$
n is a positive integer, so $n = 8$.
Instead of factorising, you could find two consecutive positive integers which multiply to give 56. 8 × 7 = 56, so n = 8.

b) $\binom{m+2}{3} = \frac{(m+2)!}{3!((m+2)-3)!} = \frac{(m+2)(m+1)m}{6}$
$\Rightarrow (m + 2)(m + 1)m = 720$
You need to find three consecutive positive integers, m, $m + 1$ and $m + 2$, which multiply to give 720. Using trial and error you get $m = 8$.

Exercise 7.2 — Binomial Expansions — $(1 + ax)^n$

Q1 **a)** $(1 + 3x)^4 = 1 + {}^4C_1(3x) + {}^4C_2(3x)^2 + {}^4C_3(3x)^3 + {}^4C_4(3x)^4$
$= 1 + 4(3x) + 6(9x^2) + 4(27x^3) + 1(81x^4)$
$= 1 + 12x + 54x^2 + 108x^3 + 81x^4$

b) $(1 - x)^4 = 1 + {}^4C_1(-x) + {}^4C_2(-x)^2 + {}^4C_3(-x)^3 + {}^4C_4(-x)^4$
$= 1 - 4x + 6x^2 - 4x^3 + x^4$

c) $(1 - x)^6 = 1 + {}^6C_1(-x) + {}^6C_2(-x)^2 + {}^6C_3(-x)^3 + {}^6C_4(-x)^4 + {}^6C_5(-x)^5 + {}^6C_6(-x)^6$
$= 1 - 6x + 15x^2 - 20x^3 + 15x^4 - 6x^5 + x^6$
For parts b) and c) you could use the formula for the expansion of $(1 - x)^n$: $(1 - x)^n = 1 - {}^nC_1x + {}^nC_2x^2 - {}^nC_3x^3 + ...$

d) $(1-2x)^5 = 1 + {}^5C_1(-2x) + {}^5C_2(-2x)^2 + {}^5C_3(-2x)^3 + {}^5C_4(-2x)^4 + {}^5C_5(-2x)^5$
$= 1 + 5(-2x) + 10(4x^2) + 10(-8x^3) + 5(16x^4) + 1(-32x^5)$
$= 1 - 10x + 40x^2 - 80x^3 + 80x^4 - 32x^5$

e) $(1-4x)^3 = 1 + {}^3C_1(-4x) + {}^3C_2(-4x)^2 + {}^3C_3(-4x)^3$
$= 1 + 3(-4x) + 3(16x^2) + 1(-64x^3)$
$= 1 - 12x + 48x^2 - 64x^3$

f) $(1-5x)^5 = 1 + {}^5C_1(-5x) + {}^5C_2(-5x)^2 + {}^5C_3(-5x)^3 + {}^5C_4(-5x)^4 + {}^5C_5(-5x)^5$
$= 1 + 5(-5x) + 10(25x^2) + 10(-125x^3) + 5(625x^4) + 1(-3125x^5)$
$= 1 - 25x + 250x^2 - 1250x^3 + 3125x^4 - 3125x^5$

g) $(1+2x)^6 = 1 + {}^6C_1(2x) + {}^6C_2(2x)^2 + {}^6C_3(2x)^3 + {}^6C_4(2x)^4 + {}^6C_5(2x)^5 + {}^6C_6(2x)^6$
$= 1 + 6(2x) + 15(4x^2) + 20(8x^3) + 15(16x^4) + 6(32x^5) + 1(64x^6)$
$= 1 + 12x + 60x^2 + 160x^3 + 240x^4 + 192x^5 + 64x^6$

h) $(1+x)^9 = 1 + {}^9C_1x + {}^9C_2x^2 + {}^9C_3x^3 + {}^9C_4x^4 + {}^9C_5x^5 + \ldots$
$(1-x)^9 = 1 - {}^9C_1x + {}^9C_2x^2 - {}^9C_3x^3 + {}^9C_4x^4 - {}^9C_5x^5 + \ldots$
So: $(1+x)^9 - (1-x)^9 = 2({}^9C_1x + {}^9C_3x^3 + {}^9C_5x^5 + \ldots)$
The even powers cancel out, so only the terms with odd powers appear (and they're doubled because one term comes from each expansion).
$= 2(9x + 84x^3 + 126x^5 + 36x^7 + x^9)$
$= 18x + 168x^3 + 252x^5 + 72x^7 + 2x^9$

Q2 The term in x^4 is: ${}^{16}C_4(-2x)^4 = 1820(16x^4) = 29\,120x^4$

Q3 The first 3 terms will include 1 and the terms in x and x^2 so expand each bracket up to and including the term in x^2:
$(1+x)^3(1-x)^4 = (1 + 3x + 3x^2 + \ldots)(1 - 4x + 6x^2 - \ldots)$
$= 1 - 4x + 6x^2 + \ldots + 3x - 12x^2 + \ldots + 3x^2 + (\textit{higher power terms})$
$= 1 - x - 3x^2 + \ldots$

Q4 The expansion of $(1+x)^5(1+y)^7$ is the expansions of $(1+x)^5$ and $(1+y)^7$ multiplied together. We need the x^3 term from $(1+x)^5$ and the y^2 term from $(1+y)^7$. Multiplying the coefficients gives the x^3y^2 coefficient: x^3 coefficient: $\frac{5!}{3!(5-3)!} = \frac{5\times4}{2\times1} = 10$
y^2 coefficient: $\frac{7!}{2!(7-2)!} = \frac{7\times6}{2\times1} = 21$
x^3y^2 coefficient: $10 \times 21 = 210$

Q5 Find all the terms up to x^3 in both expansions:
$(1+4x)^4 = 1 + {}^4C_1(4x) + {}^4C_2(4x)^2 + {}^4C_3(4x)^3 + \ldots$
$= 1 + 4(4x) + 6(16x^2) + 4(64x^3) + \ldots$
$= 1 + 16x + 96x^2 + 256x^3 + \ldots$

$(1-6x)^3 = 1 + {}^3C_1(-6x) + {}^3C_2(-6x)^2 + {}^3C_3(-6x)^3$
$= 1 + 3(-6x) + 3(36x^2) + 1(-216x^3)$
$= 1 - 18x + 108x^2 - 216x^3$
So $(1+4x)^4(1-6x)^3 = (1 + 16x + 96x^2 + 256x^3 + \ldots) \times (1 - 18x + 108x^2 - 216x^3)$
You're only interested in the term in x^3, so just multiply out the terms which will give you x^3:
Term in $x^3 = (1 \times -216x^3) + (16x \times 108x^2) + (96x^2 \times -18x) + (256x^3 \times 1)$
$= -216x^3 + 1728x^3 - 1728x^3 + 256x^3 = 40x^3$
So the coefficient of x^3 is 40.

Q6 **a)** $(1+kx)^8 = 1 + {}^8C_1kx + {}^8C_2(kx)^2 + {}^8C_3(kx)^3 + \ldots$
$= 1 + 8kx + 28k^2x^2 + 56k^3x^3 + \ldots$

b) The fourth term is $56k^3x^3$, so $56k^3x^3 = 448x^3 \Rightarrow 56k^3 = 448$
$\Rightarrow k^3 = 8 \Rightarrow k = 2$

Q7 We need the coefficient of x^2 to equal 135:
${}^6C_2(-kx)^2 = 15k^2x^2$
So $15k^2 = 135 \Rightarrow k^2 = 9 \Rightarrow k = 3$
The question says k is positive so ignore the negative root.

Q8 $(1-3x)^6 = 1 + {}^6C_1(-3x) + {}^6C_2(-3x)^2 + {}^6C_3(-3x)^3 + \ldots$
$= 1 - 18x + 135x^2 - 540x^3 + \ldots$
$(1+x)(1-3x)^6 = (1+x)(1 - 18x + \ldots)$
$= 1 - 18x + \ldots + x - 18x^2 + \ldots \approx 1 - 17x$
You're told you can ignore x^2 and higher terms.

Q9 **a)** $\left(1+\frac{x}{2}\right)^{12} = 1 + {}^{12}C_1\left(\frac{x}{2}\right) + {}^{12}C_2\left(\frac{x}{2}\right)^2 + {}^{12}C_3\left(\frac{x}{2}\right)^3 + {}^{12}C_4\left(\frac{x}{2}\right)^4 + \ldots$
$= 1 + 6x + \frac{33}{2}x^2 + \frac{55}{2}x^3 + \frac{495}{16}x^4 + \ldots$
[3 marks available — 1 mark for attempting to use the binomial expansion, 1 mark for at least two correct terms, 1 mark for all five terms in the expansion correct]

b) $1 + \left(\frac{x}{2}\right) = 1.005$ when $x = 0.01$.
Substitute this value into the expansion:
$1.005^{12} \approx 1 + 6(0.01) + \frac{33}{2}(0.01)^2 + \frac{55}{2}(0.01)^3 + \frac{495}{16}(0.01)^4$
$1.005^{12} \approx 1.061677809 = 1.0616778$ to 7 d.p.
[2 marks available — 1 mark for using the correct value of x, 1 mark for the correct approximation]

Q10 **a)** $\left(1+\frac{3}{2}x\right)^{14} = 1 + {}^{14}C_1\left(\frac{3}{2}x\right) + {}^{14}C_2\left(\frac{3}{2}x\right)^2 + \ldots$
$= 1 + 14\left(\frac{3}{2}x\right) + 91\left(\frac{3}{2}x\right)^2 + \ldots = 1 + 21x + \frac{819}{4}x^2 + \ldots$
[3 marks available — 1 mark for attempting to use the binomial expansion, 1 mark for a partially correct expansion, 1 mark for the fully correct simplified expansion]

b) $1 + \frac{3}{2}x = 1.015$ when $x = 0.01$
Substituting $x = 0.01$ into the expansion from a) gives
$1.015^{14} = 1 + 21(0.01) + \frac{819}{4}(0.01)^2 + \ldots \approx 1.230475$
$= 1.2305$ to 5 s.f.
[2 marks available — 1 mark for using the correct value of x, 1 mark for the correct approximation]

Q11 Because $x > 1$, higher powers of x will not be small enough to ignore, so only taking the terms up to x^3 will not provide an accurate estimate.

Q12 **a)** Expansion of $(1+7x)^n = 1 + {}^nC_1(7x) + {}^nC_2(7x)^2 + \ldots$
So term in $x^2 = {}^nC_2 \times 49x^2$
${}^nC_2 = \frac{n!}{2!(n-2)!} = \frac{n(n-1)(n-2)!}{2(n-2)!} = \frac{n(n-1)}{2}$
So term in $x^2 = \frac{49n(n-1)}{2}x^2$
The coefficient of the term in x^2 is 490, so:
$\frac{49n(n-1)}{2} = 490 \Rightarrow \frac{n(n-1)}{2} = 10$
$\Rightarrow n(n-1) = 20 \Rightarrow n^2 - n - 20 = 0 \Rightarrow (n+4)(n-5) = 0$
So $n = -4$ or $n = 5$. Since n is positive, $n = 5$.

b) Term in $x^3 = {}^5C_3(7x)^3 = 10(343x^3) = 3430x^3$

Q13 **a)** $(1-4x)^6 = 1 + {}^6C_1(-4x) + {}^6C_2(-4x)^2 + \ldots$
$\approx 1 + 6(-4x) + 15(-4x)^2 = 1 - 24x + 240x^2$
[3 marks available — 1 mark for attempting to use the binomial expansion, 1 mark for a partially correct expansion, 1 mark for the fully correct simplified expansion]

b) The solutions can be approximated using the equation
$\frac{1}{100}(1 - 24x + 240x^2) = 3x \Rightarrow 1 - 24x + 240x^2 = 300x$
$\Rightarrow 240x^2 - 324x + 1 = 0$
$\Rightarrow x = \frac{324 \pm \sqrt{(-324)^2 - 4\times240\times1}}{2\times240} \Rightarrow x = 0.003093\ldots$
or $x = 1.3469\ldots \Rightarrow a \approx 0.0031$ and $b \approx 1.3$ to 2 s.f.
[3 marks available — 1 mark for substituting it into the equation correctly, 1 mark for attempting to solve the resulting equation, 1 mark for the correct approximate values of a and b to 2 s.f.]

c) The partial expansion of $(1-4x)^6$ found in a) is a good approximation for small values of x. As the true value of a is small, the approximation of a is good. However, the true value of b is relatively large, so the approximation of b is not as good.
[2 marks available — 1 mark for a correct explanation relating to a, 1 mark for a correct explanation relating to b]

Exercise 7.3 — Binomial Expansions — $(a + b)^n$

Q1 Using the formula for the expansion of $(a+b)^n$:

$$(a+b)^n = a^n + \binom{n}{1}a^{n-1}b + \binom{n}{2}a^{n-2}b^2 + \ldots + b^n$$

In this case $a = 3$ and $b = x$:

$$(3+x)^6 = 3^6 + {}^6C_1 3^5x + {}^6C_2 3^4x^2 + {}^6C_3 3^3x^3 + \ldots$$
$$= 729 + 6(243x) + 15(81x^2) + 20(27x^3) + \ldots$$
$$= 729 + 1458x + 1215x^2 + 540x^3 + \ldots$$

Q2 **a)** In this case $a = 2$ and $b = x$:

$$(2+x)^4 = 2^4 + {}^4C_1 2^3x + {}^4C_2 2^2x^2 + {}^4C_3 2x^3 + {}^4C_4 x^4$$
$$= 16 + 4(8x) + 6(4x^2) + 4(2x^3) + x^4$$
$$= 16 + 32x + 24x^2 + 8x^3 + x^4$$

b) In this case $a = 2$ and $b = 2x$:

$$(2+2x)^4 = 2^4 + {}^4C_1 2^3(2x) + {}^4C_2 2^2(2x)^2 + {}^4C_3 2(2x)^3 + {}^4C_4(2x)^4$$
$$= 16 + (4 \times 8 \times 2x) + (6 \times 4 \times 4x^2) + (4 \times 2 \times 8x^3) + 16x^4$$
$$= 16 + 64x + 96x^2 + 64x^3 + 16x^4$$

c) In this case $a = 2$ and $b = -2x$:

$$(2-2x)^4 = 2^4 + {}^4C_1 2^3(-2x) + {}^4C_2 2^2(-2x)^2 + {}^4C_3 2(-2x)^3 + {}^4C_4(-2x)^4$$
$$= 16 + (4 \times 8 \times -2x) + (6 \times 4 \times 4x^2) + (4 \times 2 \times -8x^3) + 16x^4$$
$$= 16 - 64x + 96x^2 - 64x^3 + 16x^4$$

Notice here that you could just use the result from part b) and change the sign of the odd-power terms.

d) In this case $a = \frac{1}{2}$ and $b = \frac{1}{2}x$:

$$\left(\frac{1}{2}+\frac{1}{2}x\right)^4 = \left(\frac{1}{2}\right)^4 + {}^4C_1\left(\frac{1}{2}\right)^3\left(\frac{1}{2}x\right) + {}^4C_2\left(\frac{1}{2}\right)^2\left(\frac{1}{2}x\right)^2 + {}^4C_3\left(\frac{1}{2}\right)\left(\frac{1}{2}x\right)^3 + {}^4C_4\left(\frac{1}{2}x\right)^4$$
$$= \frac{1}{16} + \left(4 \times \frac{1}{8} \times \frac{1}{2}x\right) + \left(6 \times \frac{1}{4} \times \frac{1}{4}x^2\right) + \left(4 \times \frac{1}{2} \times \frac{1}{8}x^3\right) + \frac{1}{16}x^4$$
$$= \frac{1}{16} + \frac{1}{4}x + \frac{3}{8}x^2 + \frac{1}{4}x^3 + \frac{1}{16}x^4$$

Q3 **a)** The term in x^5 is ${}^8C_5(\lambda x)^5 = 56\lambda^5x^5$
Therefore $56\lambda^5 = 57\,344 \Rightarrow \lambda^5 = 1024 \Rightarrow \lambda = \sqrt[5]{1024} = 4$

b) $(1+4x)^8 = 1 + {}^8C_1(4x) + {}^8C_2(4x)^2 + \ldots = 1 + 32x + 448x^2 + \ldots$

Q4 **a)** $(2+x)^8 = 2^8 + {}^8C_1 2^7x + {}^8C_2 2^6x^2 + {}^8C_3 2^5x^3 + {}^8C_4 2^4x^4 + \ldots$
$= 256 + 1024x + 1792x^2 + 1792x^3 + 1120x^4 + \ldots$
[3 marks available — 1 mark for attempting to use the binomial expansion, 1 mark for a partially correct expansion, 1 mark for the fully correct simplified expansion]

b) $2 + x = 2.01$ when $x = 0.01$
Hence: $2.01^8 = 256 + 1024(0.01) + 1792(0.01)^2 + 1792(0.01)^3 + 1120(0.01)^4 + \ldots$
≈ 266.4210032
An approximation to 2.01^8 is: 266.42100 (to 5 d.p.)
[2 marks available – 1 mark for letting x = 0.01 in the expansion from part a), 1 mark for the correct answer (allow answer correctly calculated from an incorrect expansion in part a)]

Q5 $(3+5x)^7 = 3^7 + {}^7C_1 3^6(5x) + {}^7C_2 3^5(5x)^2 + {}^7C_3 3^4(5x)^3 + \ldots$
$= 2187 + 25\,515x + 127\,575x^2 + 354\,375x^3 + \ldots$

Q6 **a)** $(2+2x)^5 = 2^5 + {}^5C_1 2^4(2x) + {}^5C_2 2^3(2x)^2 + {}^5C_3 2^2(2x)^3 + \ldots$
$= 2^5 + 5 \times 2^4 \times 2x + 10 \times 2^3 \times (2x)^2 + 10 \times 2^2 \times (2x)^3 + \ldots$
$= 32 + 160x + 320x^2 + 320x^3 + \ldots$
[4 marks available — 1 mark for substituting into the binomial formula correctly, 1 mark for one correct simplified term, 1 mark for a second correct simplified term, 1 mark for a fully correct expansion]

b) $2 + 2x = 2.04$ when $x = 0.02$
Hence:
$2.04^5 = 32 + 160(0.02) + 320(0.02)^2 + 320(0.02)^3 + \ldots$
$\approx 35.3305\ldots = 35.331$ (3 d.p.)
[2 marks available – 1 mark for letting x = 0.02 in the expansion from part a), 1 mark for the correct answer (allow answer correctly calculated from an incorrect expansion in part a)]

Q7 **a)**

$$\left(3+\frac{x}{4}\right)^{11} = 3^{11} + {}^{11}C_1 3^{10}\left(\frac{x}{4}\right) + {}^{11}C_2 3^9\left(\frac{x}{4}\right)^2 + {}^{11}C_3 3^8\left(\frac{x}{4}\right)^3 + {}^{11}C_4 3^7\left(\frac{x}{4}\right)^4 + \ldots$$
$$= 177\,147 + \frac{649\,539}{4}x + \frac{1\,082\,565}{16}x^2 + \frac{1\,082\,565}{64}x^3 + \frac{360855}{128}x^4 + \ldots$$

[3 marks available — 1 mark for attempting to use the binomial expansion, 1 mark for at least two terms in the expansion correct, 1 mark for all five terms correct]

b) $3 + \frac{x}{4} = 3.002$ when $x = 0.008$
Hence:

$$3.002^{11} = 177\,147 + \frac{649\,539}{4}(0.008) + \frac{1\,082\,565}{16}(0.008)^2 + \frac{1\,082\,565}{64}(0.008)^3 + \frac{360855}{128}(0.008)^4 + \ldots$$
$$\approx 178\,450.4169 = 178\,450.417 \text{ (3 d.p.)}$$

[2 marks available — 1 mark for using the correct value of x, 1 mark for the correct approximation]

Q8 Expand the first five terms of $(3+2x)^6$ and multiply by $(1+x)$:
$(3+2x)^6 = 3^6 + {}^6C_1 3^5(2x) + {}^6C_2 3^4(2x)^2 + {}^6C_3 3^3(2x)^3 + {}^6C_4 3^2(2x)^4 + \ldots$
$= 729 + 2916x + 4860x^2 + 4320x^3 + 2160x^4 + \ldots$

$(1+x)(3+2x)^6 = (3+2x)^6 + x(3+2x)^6$
$= (729 + 2916x + 4860x^2 + 4320x^3 + 2160x^4 + \ldots) + (729x + 2916x^2 + 4860x^3 + 4320x^4 + 2160x^5 + \ldots)$
$= 729 + 3645x + 7776x^2 + 9180x^3 + 6480x^4 + \ldots$
(The term in x^5 is the 6th term.)

Q9 Start by expanding $(2+3x)^7$. Only terms that will give the x^5-term in the expansion of $(2-x+x^2)(2+3x)^7$ are needed:
$(2+3x)^7 = (2)^7 + {}^7C_1(2)^6(3x) + {}^7C_2(2)^5(3x)^2 + {}^7C_3(2)^4(3x)^3 + {}^7C_4(2)^3(3x)^4 + {}^7C_5(2)^2(3x)^5 + \ldots$

The x^5-term in the expansion of $(2-x+x^2)(2+3x)^7$ will involve the x^3, x^4 and x^5 terms of $(2+3x)^7$, so work out these three terms:
x^3-term $= {}^7C_3(2)^4(3x)^3 = (35 \times 16 \times 27)x^3 = 15\,120x^3$
x^4-term $= {}^7C_4(2)^3(3x)^4 = (35 \times 8 \times 81)x^4 = 22\,680x^4$
x^5-term $= {}^7C_5(2)^2(3x)^5 = (21 \times 4 \times 243)x^5 = 20\,412x^5$
So the x^5-term of $(2-x+x^2)(2+3x)^7$
$= (2 \times 20\,412x^5) - (x \times 22\,680x^4) + (x^2 \times 15\,120x^3)$
$= 40\,824x^5 - 22\,680x^5 + 15\,120x^5 = 33\,264x^5$

So the coefficient of $x^5 = 33\,264$
[5 marks available — 1 mark for attempting to use the binomial expansion, 1 mark for finding at least one of the terms for x^3, x^4 and x^5 from the expansion of $(2+3x)^7$, 1 mark for finding all three correct terms, 1 mark for multiplying the coefficients by the correct values from $(2-x+x^2)$, 1 mark for the correct value of the coefficient]

Q10 a) Expand $(2-x)^5$ and multiply by $(1+3x)$:
$(2-x)^5 = 2^5 + {}^5C_1 2^4(-x) + {}^5C_2 2^3(-x)^2 + {}^5C_3 2^2(-x)^3 + {}^5C_4 2(-x)^4 + {}^5C_5(-x)^5$
$= 32 - 80x + 80x^2 - 40x^3 + 10x^4 - x^5$
$(1+3x)(2-x)^5 = (2-x)^5 + 3x(2-x)^5$
$= (32 - 80x + 80x^2 - 40x^3 + 10x^4 - x^5) + (96x - 240x^2 + 240x^3 - 120x^4 + 30x^5 - 3x^6)$
$= 32 + 16x - 160x^2 + 200x^3 - 110x^4 + 29x^5 - 3x^6$

b) Expand $(1+3x)^5$ and multiply by $(2-x)$:
$(1+3x)^5 = 1 + {}^5C_1(3x) + {}^5C_2(3x)^2 + {}^5C_3(3x)^3 + {}^5C_4(3x)^4 + {}^5C_5(3x)^5$
$= 1 + 15x + 90x^2 + 270x^3 + 405x^4 + 243x^5$
$(1+3x)^5(2-x) = 2(1+3x)^5 - x(1+3x)^5$
$= (2 + 30x + 180x^2 + 540x^3 + 810x^4 + 486x^5) - (x + 15x^2 + 90x^3 + 270x^4 + 405x^5 + 243x^6)$
$= 2 + 29x + 165x^2 + 450x^3 + 540x^4 + 81x^5 - 243x^6$

c) Expand $(1+3x)^2$ and $(2-x)^4$ and multiply together:
$(1+3x)^2 = 1 + {}^2C_1(3x) + {}^2C_2(3x)^2 = 1 + 6x + 9x^2$
$(2-x)^4 = 2^4 + {}^4C_1 2^3(-x) + {}^4C_2 2^2(-x)^2 + {}^4C_3 2(-x)^3 + {}^4C_4(-x)^4$
$= 16 - 32x + 24x^2 - 8x^3 + x^4$
$(1+3x)^2(2-x)^4 = (1 + 6x + 9x^2) \times (16 - 32x + 24x^2 - 8x^3 + x^4)$
$= (16 - 32x + 24x^2 - 8x^3 + x^4) + 6x(16 - 32x + 24x^2 - 8x^3 + x^4) + 9x^2(16 - 32x + 24x^2 - 8x^3 + x^4)$
$= 16 + 64x - 24x^2 - 152x^3 + 169x^4 - 66x^5 + 9x^6$

d) Expand $(1+3x)^3$ and $(2-x)^3$ and multiply together:
$(1+3x)^3 = 1 + {}^3C_1(3x) + {}^3C_2(3x)^2 + {}^3C_3(3x)^3$
$= 1 + 9x + 27x^2 + 27x^3$
$(2-x)^3 = 2^3 + {}^3C_1 2^2(-x) + {}^3C_2 2(-x)^2 + {}^3C_3(-x)^3$
$= 8 - 12x + 6x^2 - x^3$
$(1+3x)^3(2-x)^3 = (1 + 9x + 27x^2 + 27x^3) \times (8 - 12x + 6x^2 - x^3)$
$= (8 - 12x + 6x^2 - x^3) + 9x(8 - 12x + 6x^2 - x^3) + 27x^2(8 - 12x + 6x^2 - x^3) + 27x^3(8 - 12x + 6x^2 - x^3)$
$= 8 + 60x + 114x^2 - 55x^3 - 171x^4 + 135x^5 - 27x^6$

Q11 a) Expansion of $(1-5x)^n = 1 + {}^nC_1(-5x) + {}^nC_2(-5x)^2 + \ldots$
So term in $x^2 = {}^nC_2 \times 25x^2$

$${}^nC_2 = \frac{n!}{2!(n-2)!} = \frac{n(n-1)(n-2)!}{2(n-2)!} = \frac{n(n-1)}{2}$$

So term in $x^2 = \frac{25n(n-1)}{2}x^2$

The coefficient of the term in x^2 is 150, so:
$\frac{25n(n-1)}{2} = 150$
$\Rightarrow n(n-1) = 12 \Rightarrow n^2 - n - 12 = 0 \Rightarrow (n+4)(n-3) = 0$
So $n = -4$ or $n = 3$. Since n is positive, $n = 3$.

b) Term in $x^3 = {}^3C_3(-5x)^3 = 1 \times -125x^3 = -125x^3$

Q12 Expand each bracket up to the term in x^3:
$(1+2x)^5 = 1 + 5(2x) + 10(2x)^2 + 10(2x)^3 + \ldots$
$= 1 + 10x + 40x^2 + 80x^3 + \ldots$
$(3-x)^4 = 3^4 + 4(3)^3(-x) + 6(3)^2(-x)^2 + 4(3)(-x)^3 + \ldots$
$= 81 - 108x + 54x^2 - 12x^3 + \ldots$
Multiply the terms that will give a result in x^3:
$(1 \times -12x^3) + (10x \times 54x^2) + (40x^2 \times -108x) + (80x^3 \times 81) = 2688x^3$
So the coefficient of x^3 is 2688.

Q13 a) The coefficient of x^3 is: $\frac{n!}{3!(n-3)!} = \frac{n(n-1)(n-2)}{3 \times 2 \times 1}$

The coefficient of x^2 is: $\frac{n!}{2!(n-2)!} = \frac{n(n-1)}{2}$

The coefficient of x^3 is three times the coefficient of x^2, so:
$\frac{n(n-1)(n-2)}{3 \times 2 \times 1} = 3 \times \frac{n(n-1)}{2} \Rightarrow \frac{n-2}{3} = 3$
$\Rightarrow n = 11$

b) $(1+x)^{11} = 1 + 11x + 55x^2 + \ldots$
The coefficient of x^2 is $a \times$ (coefficient of x),
so $55 = 11a \Rightarrow a = 5$.

Q14 $(2 + \mu x)^8 = 2^8 + {}^8C_1 2^7(\mu x) + {}^8C_2 2^6(\mu x)^2 + \ldots$
$= 256 + (8 \times 128)(\mu x) + (28 \times 64)(\mu x)^2 + \ldots$
$= 256 + 1024\mu x + 1792\mu^2x^2 + \ldots$
The coefficient of x^2 is:
$87\,808 = 1792\mu^2 \Rightarrow \mu^2 = 49 \Rightarrow \mu = 7$ or -7.

Q15 Start by expanding the outer brackets:
$[(x+2)^3(x+3)^2]^2 = (x+2)^6(x+3)^4$
Now expand both brackets and multiply the expressions together as usual — you can ignore any powers of x greater than 2:
$(x+2)^6 = x^6 + {}^6C_1x^5(2) + \ldots + {}^6C_4x^2(2)^4 + {}^6C_5x(2)^5 + {}^6C_6(2)^6$
$= \ldots + 240x^2 + 192x + 64$
$(x+3)^4 = x^4 + {}^4C_1x^3(3) + {}^4C_2x^2(3)^2 + {}^4C_3x(3)^3 + {}^4C_4(3)^4$
$= \ldots + 54x^2 + 108x + 81$
$(x+2)^6(x+3)^4 = (\ldots + 240x^2 + 192x + 64) \times (\ldots + 54x^2 + 108x + 81)$
You're only interested in the term in x^2, so just multiply out the terms which will give you x^2:
Term in $x^2 = (240x^2 \times 81) + (192x \times 108x) + (64 \times 54x^2)$
$= 19\,440x^2 + 20\,736x^2 + 3456x^2$
$= 43\,632x^2$
So the coefficient of x^2 is 43 632.
[6 marks available — 1 mark for expanding the outer brackets, 1 mark for attempting to use the binomial expansion, 1 mark for expanding both sets of brackets correctly, 1 mark for attempting to multiply the expansions together, 1 mark for finding at least one correct x^2 term, 1 mark for the correct final answer]

Chapter 7 Review Exercise

Q1 $(n-4)! = 33! \times 34 \times 35 = 35!$
$n - 4 = 35$, so $n = 39$
[2 marks available — 1 mark for identifying that $(n-4)! = 35!$, 1 mark for the correct value of n]

Q2 a) $\binom{37}{33} = \frac{37!}{33!(37-33)!}$, so $\frac{37!}{33!k!} = \frac{37!}{33!(37-33)!}$
Therefore $k = (37 - 33) = 4$ *[1 mark]*

b) $p = \binom{37}{33}(-1)^{33} = -66\,045$
[2 marks available — 1 mark for a correct method to find p, 1 mark for the correct value of p]

Q3 a) $(1+x)^{40} = 1 + {}^{40}C_1x + {}^{40}C_2x^2 + \ldots = 1 + 40x + 780x^2 + \ldots$

b) $(1-x)^{20} = 1 + {}^{20}C_1(-x) + {}^{20}C_2(-x)^2 + \ldots = 1 - 20x + 190x^2 + \ldots$

c) $(1+3x)^{20} = 1 + {}^{20}C_1(3x) + {}^{20}C_2(3x)^2 + \ldots$
$= 1 + 60x + 1710x^2 + \ldots$

d) $(2+3x)^{10} = 2^{10} + {}^{10}C_1 2^9(3x) + {}^{10}C_2 2^8(3x)^2 + \ldots$
$= 1024 + 15\,360x + 103\,680x^2 + \ldots$

Q4 a) $(1+ax)^8 = 1 + {}^8C_1ax + {}^8C_2(ax)^2 + {}^8C_3(ax)^3 + {}^8C_4(ax)^4 + \ldots$
$= 1 + 8ax + 28a^2x^2 + 56a^3x^3 + 70a^4x^4 + \ldots$

b) Coefficient of $x^2 = 28a^2$ and coefficient of $x^3 = 56a^3$, so:
$28a^2 = 2(56a^3) \Rightarrow 28a^2 = 112a^3$
$\Rightarrow 1 = 4a$
$\Rightarrow a = \frac{1}{4}$
Coefficient of $x = 8a = 8 \times \frac{1}{4} = 2$

Q5 The x^2 term is given by $\binom{n}{2}(-3x)^2 = \frac{n(n-1)}{2} \times 9x^2$.
Therefore $\frac{9n(n-1)}{2} = 495$
$\Rightarrow 9n(n-1) = 990 \Rightarrow n(n-1) = 110 \Rightarrow n^2 - n - 110 = 0$
$\Rightarrow (n+10)(n-11) = 0$
So $n = -10$ or $n = 11$. Since n is positive, $n = 11$.
[4 marks available — 1 mark for the correct x^2 term in terms of n, 1 mark for a correct method leading to a quadratic equation, 1 mark for the correct quadratic equation, 1 mark for the correct answer]

Q6 **a)** $\left(1+\frac{x}{3}\right)^9 = 1 + {}^9C_1\left(\frac{x}{3}\right) + {}^9C_2\left(\frac{x}{3}\right)^2 + {}^9C_3\left(\frac{x}{3}\right)^3 + ...$

$= 1 + \frac{9}{3}x + \frac{36}{9}x^2 + \frac{84}{27}x^3 + ...$

$= 1 + 3x + 4x^2 + \frac{28}{9}x^3 + ...$

b) $1 + \frac{x}{3} = 1.003$ when $x = 0.009$

Hence:

$1.003^9 = 1 + 3(0.009) + 4(0.009)^2 + \frac{28}{9}(0.009)^3 + ...$

$\approx 1.0273262... = 1.027326$ (6 d.p.)

Q7 **a)** $(1+x)^{12} = 1 + {}^{12}C_1x + {}^{12}C_2x^2 + ...$
$= 1 + 12x + 66x^2 + ...$ *[1 mark]*

b) $x = 0.02 \Rightarrow 1 + 12x + 66x^2 = 1 + 12(0.02) + 66(0.02)^2$
$= 1.2664$

[2 marks available — 1 mark for substituting x = 0.02 into the expansion from part a), 1 mark for the correct answer]

c) The true value of 1.02^{12} is 1.2682...

So $\frac{1.2682... - 1.2664}{1.2682...} \times 100 = 0.1452...\%$

$\Rightarrow$ The percentage error is approximately 0.15% *[1 mark]*

Q8 $(1-3x)^8 = 1 + {}^8C_1(-3x) + {}^8C_2(-3x)^2 + {}^8C_3(-3x)^3 + ...$
$= 1 - 24x + 252x^2 - 1512x^3 + ...$

$1 - 3x = 0.97$ when $x = 0.01$

Hence:

$0.97^8 = 1 - 24(0.01) + 252(0.01)^2 - 1512(0.01)^3 + ...$
$\approx 0.7836... = 0.784$ (3 d.p.)

Q9 **a)** $(1+x)^{15} = 1 + {}^{15}C_1x + {}^{15}C_2x^2 + {}^{15}C_3x^3 + {}^{15}C_4x^4 + ...$
$= 1 + 15x + 105x^2 + 455x^3 + 1365x^4 + ...$

b) To find 2.01^{15}, you would need to substitute $x = 1.01$. Since $x > 1$, x^n is not small enough to ignore for large n, so the estimate would be inaccurate.

Q10 The coefficient of x^4 in the expansion of $(1 + ax)^5$ is ${}^5C_4a^4$
The coefficient of x^2 in the expansion of $(1 + ax)^9$ is ${}^9C_2a^2$
Therefore: $5a^4 = 36a^2$

$\Rightarrow 5a^4 - 36a^2 = 0$

$\Rightarrow a^2(5a^2 - 36) = 0$

$\Rightarrow a = 0,\ a = \frac{6\sqrt{5}}{5}$ or $a = -\frac{6\sqrt{5}}{5}$

But $a \neq 0$, so $a = \frac{6\sqrt{5}}{5}$ or $a = -\frac{6\sqrt{5}}{5}$

[3 marks available — 1 mark for a correct method leading to an equation in a, 1 mark for the correct equation, 1 mark for both correct possible values of a and the invalid solution clearly discarded]

Q11 $(1+4x)^2 = 1 + {}^2C_1(4x) + {}^2C_2(4x)^2 = 1 + 8x + 16x^2$
$(1-3x)^4 = 1 + {}^4C_1(-3x) + {}^4C_2(-3x)^2 + {}^4C_3(-3x)^3 + {}^4C_4(-3x)^4$
$= 1 + 4(-3x) + 6(-3x)^2 + 4(-3x)^3 + (-3x)^4$
$= 1 - 12x + 54x^2 - 108x^3 + 81x^4$
$\Rightarrow (1+4x)^2 + (1-3x)^4$
$= (1 + 8x + 16x^2) + (1 - 12x + 54x^2 - 108x^3 + 81x^4)$
$= 2 - 4x + 70x^2 - 108x^3 + 81x^4$

[3 marks available — 1 mark for attempting to use the binomial formula, 1 mark for correctly expanding (1 – 3x)⁴, 1 mark for the correct answer]

Q12 **a)** $\left(1+\frac{3}{4}x\right)^{17} = 1 + {}^{17}C_1\left(\frac{3}{4}x\right) + {}^{17}C_2\left(\frac{3}{4}x\right)^2 + {}^{17}C_3\left(\frac{3}{4}x\right)^3 + ...$

$= 1 + 17\left(\frac{3}{4}x\right) + 136\left(\frac{3}{4}x\right)^2 + 680\left(\frac{3}{4}x\right)^3 + ...$

$= 1 + \frac{51}{4}x + \frac{153}{2}x^2 + \frac{2295}{8}x^3 + ...$

[3 marks available — 1 mark for substituting into the formula, 1 mark for at least one correct term, 1 mark for a fully correct expression]

b) $1 + \frac{3}{4}x = 1.075$ when $x = 0.1$

Hence $1.075^{17} = 1 + \frac{51}{4}(0.1) + \frac{153}{2}(0.1)^2 + \frac{2295}{8}(0.1)^3 + ...$

≈ 3.326875

[2 marks available — 1 mark for letting x = 0.1 in the expansion from part a), 1 mark for the correct answer]

If you correctly calculated the answer from an incorrect expansion in part a), you can still get both marks for part b).

c) All of the terms of the expansion of $\left(1+\frac{3}{4}x\right)^{17}$ have positive coefficients, so when $x = 0.1$, all terms of the expansion will be positive. Adding further terms will increase the value of the approximation, so the approximation is an underestimate.

[1 mark for a correct explanation]

Q13 The coefficient of x^3 in $(1 + kx)^8$ has the form ${}^8C_3k^3 \Rightarrow a = 56k^3$

$\Rightarrow 7 < 56k^3 < 189 \Rightarrow \frac{1}{8} < k^3 < \frac{27}{8} \Rightarrow \frac{1}{2} < k < \frac{3}{2}$

[3 marks available — 1 mark for the correct expression for a in terms of k, 1 mark for forming inequalities in k, 1 mark for the correct solution set]

Q14 **a)** $n = 0 \Rightarrow V = 5$ m³ *[1 mark]*

b) 12 minutes after the leak appears $\Rightarrow n = 12$, so

$V \approx 5\left(1 + 12\left(-\frac{P}{100}\right) + 66\left(-\frac{P}{100}\right)^2\right) = 5 - \frac{3}{5}P + \frac{33}{1000}P^2$

[2 marks available — 1 mark for using n = 12, 1 mark for the correct expression]

c) Water leaks out at a rate of 1% per minute, so $P = 1$.

$V \approx 5 - \frac{3}{5} + \frac{33}{1000} = 4.433 \Rightarrow$ after 12 minutes there is approximately 4.433 m³ of water in the tank.

[2 marks available — 1 mark for using P = 1, 1 mark for the correct volume with units]

Q15 **a)** Term in $x^2 = {}^5C_24^3(2x)^2 = (10 \times 64 \times 4)x^2$
So coefficient of $x^2 = 2560$

b) Term in $x^2 = {}^8C_22^6(-5x)^2 = (28 \times 64 \times 25)x^2$
So coefficient of $x^2 = 44\ 800$

c) Find the term in x in the expansion of $\left(1+\frac{1}{2}x\right)^7$, then multiply by $2x$ to get the term in x^2.

Term in $x = {}^7C_11^6\left(\frac{1}{2}x\right) = \left(7 \times 1 \times \frac{1}{2}\right)x = \frac{7}{2}x$

Multiply by $2x$ to get: $\frac{7}{2}x \times 2x = 7x^2$

So coefficient of $x^2 = 7$

d) Start by expanding $(3x - 1)^9$. You don't need to write out the whole thing, since you're only interested in the terms which will give you the x^2-term in the expansion of $(5 + x)(3x - 1)^9$:

$(3x-1)^9 = (3x)^9 + {}^9C_1(3x)^8(-1) + {}^9C_2(3x)^7(-1)^2 + ...$
$+ ... + {}^9C_7(3x)^2(-1)^7 + {}^9C_8(3x)(-1)^8 + (-1)^9$

The x^2-term in the expansion of $(5 + x)(3x - 1)^9$ will involve the x^2 and x terms of $(3x - 1)^9$, so work out these two terms:

x^2-term: ${}^9C_7(3x)^2(-1)^7 = (36 \times 9 \times -1)x^2 = -324x^2$
x-term: ${}^9C_8(3x)(-1)^8 = (9 \times 3 \times 1)x = 27x$
So the x^2-term of $(5 + x)(3x - 1)^9$
$= (5 \times -324x^2) + (x \times 27x) = -1620x^2 + 27x^2 = -1593x^2$

So coefficient of $x^2 = -1593$

Q16 $(4 - 5x)^7 = 4^7 + {}^7C_14^6(-5x) + {}^7C_24^5(-5x)^2 + ...$
$= 16\ 384 - 143\ 360x + 537\ 600x^2 + ...$

Q17 $(x - x^{-1})^3 = x^3 + {}^3C_1x^2(-x^{-1}) + {}^3C_2x(-x^{-1})^2 + (-x^{-1})^3$
$= x^3 + 3x^2(-x^{-1}) + 3x(-x^{-1})^2 + (-x^{-1})^3$
$= x^3 - 3x + 3x^{-1} - x^{-3}$

[4 marks available — 1 mark for substituting into the binomial formula correctly, 1 mark for one correct simplified term, 1 mark for a second correct simplified term, 1 mark for a fully correct expansion]

Q18 a) $(3-2x)^7 = 3^7 + {}^7C_1 3^6(-2x) + {}^7C_2 3^5(-2x)^2 + {}^7C_3 3^4(-2x)^3 + \dots$
$= 2187 - 10\,206x + 20\,412x^2 - 22\,680x^3 + \dots$
$3 - 2x = 2.998$ when $x = 0.001$
Hence: $2.998^7 = 2187 - 10\,206(0.001) + 20\,412(0.001)^2 - 22\,680(0.001)^3 + \dots$
$\approx 2176.814\dots = 2176.81$ (2 d.p.)
For parts b)-d), use the expansion of $(3-2x)^7$ above.

b) $3 - 2x = 2.8$ when $x = 0.1$
Hence: $2.8^7 = 2187 - 10\,206(0.1) + 20\,412(0.1)^2 - 22\,680(0.1)^3 + \dots$
≈ 1347.84

c) $3 - 2x = 2.94$ when $x = 0.03$
Hence: $2.94^7 = 2187 - 10\,206(0.03) + 20\,412(0.03)^2$
w $- 22\,680(0.03)^3 + \dots$
$\approx 1898.578\dots = 1898.58$ (2 d.p.)

d) $3 - 2x = 3.002$ when $x = -0.001$
Hence: $3.002^7 = 2187 - 10\,206(-0.001) + 20\,412(-0.001)^2 - 22\,680(-0.001)^3 + \dots$
$\approx 2197.226\dots = 2197.23$ (2 d.p.)

Q19 a) (i) $(2+x)^6 = 2^6 + {}^6C_1 2^5x + {}^6C_2 2^4x^2 + {}^6C_3 2^3x^3 + \dots$
$= 64 + 192x + 240x^2 + 160x^3 + \dots$
$2 + x = 2.5$ when $x = 0.5$
Hence:
$2.5^6 = 64 + 192(0.5) + 240(0.5)^2 + 160(0.5)^3 + \dots \approx 240$

(ii) $(3-x)^6 = 3^6 + {}^6C_1 3^5(-x) + {}^6C_2 3^4(-x)^2 + {}^6C_3 3^3(-x)^3 + \dots$
$= 729 - 1458x + 1215x^2 - 540x^3 + \dots$
$3 - x = 2.5$ when $x = 0.5$
Hence:
$2.5^6 = 729 - 1458(0.5) + 1215(0.5)^2 - 540(0.5)^3 + \dots$
≈ 236.25

b) Since 244.14 is closer to 240 than to 236.25, $(2+x)^6$ provides the better approximation.

Q20 The coefficient of x^2 is ${}^8C_2 a^6 3^2$
The coefficient of x^5 is ${}^8C_5 a^3 3^5$
Therefore: $28 \times a^6 \times 3^2 = \frac{32}{27} \times 56 \times a^3 \times 3^5$
$\Rightarrow 28a^3 = \frac{32}{27} \times 56 \times 3^3$
$\Rightarrow a^3 = \frac{32 \times 56 \times 27}{27 \times 28} = 64$
$\Rightarrow a = \sqrt[3]{64} = 4.$

Q21 a) $(3x+4)^3 = (3x)^3 + {}^3C_1(3x)^2(4) + {}^3C_2(3x)(4^2) + {}^3C_3 4^3$
$= (3x)^3 + 3(3x)^2(4) + 3(3x)(4^2) + 4^3$
$= 27x^3 + 108x^2 + 144x + 64$
[4 marks available — 1 mark for substituting into the binomial formula correctly, 1 mark for one correct simplified term, 1 mark for a second correct simplified term, 1 mark for a fully correct expansion]

b) $27x^3 + 108x^2 + 144x + 56 = 0$
$\Rightarrow (27x^3 + 108x^2 + 144x + 64) - 8 = 0 \Rightarrow (3x+4)^3 - 8 = 0$
$\Rightarrow (3x+4)^3 = 8 \Rightarrow 3x + 4 = 2 \Rightarrow x = -\frac{2}{3}$
[3 marks available — 1 mark for using result from a), 1 mark for solving the correct equation in x, 1 mark for the correct answer]

Q22 a) $(2+x)^9 = 2^9 + {}^9C_1 2^8x + {}^9C_2 2^7x^2 + \dots$
$= 512 + 2304x + 4608x^2 + \dots$
[3 marks available — 1 mark for attempting to use the binomial expansion, 1 mark for a partially correct expansion, 1 mark for the fully correct simplified expansion]

b) Use the result from a) with $x = 0.01$ to give
$2.01^9 = 512 + 2304(0.01) + 4608(0.01)^2 + \dots \approx 535.5008$
[2 marks available — 1 mark for using x = 0.01, 1 mark for the correct answer]
If you correctly calculated the answer from an incorrect expansion in part a), you can still get both marks for part b).

c) A better approximation could be found by increasing the number of terms of the expansion of $(2+x)^9$ used.
[1 mark for a correct explanation]

Q23 a) $(x^2+2)^6 = (x^2)^6 + {}^6C_1(x^2)^5(2) + {}^6C_2(x^2)^4(2^2) + {}^6C_3(x^2)^3(2^3) + {}^6C_4(x^2)^2(2^4) + {}^6C_5(x^2)(2^5) + {}^6C_6 2^6$
$= (x^2)^6 + 6(x^2)^5(2) + 15(x^2)^4(2^2) + 20(x^2)^3(2^3) + 15(x^2)^2(2^4) + 6(x^2)(2^5) + 2^6$
$= x^{12} + 12x^{10} + 60x^8 + 160x^6 + 240x^4 + 192x^2 + 64$
[4 marks available — 1 mark for substituting into the binomial formula correctly, 1 mark for one correct simplified term, 1 mark for a second correct simplified term, 1 mark for a fully correct expansion]

b) $\left(1 + \frac{2}{x^2}\right)^6 = \left(\frac{x^2+2}{x^2}\right)^6 = \frac{1}{(x^2)^6}(x^2+2)^6 = \frac{1}{x^{12}}(x^2+2)^6$
$= \frac{1}{x^{12}}(x^{12} + 12x^{10} + 60x^8 + 160x^6 + 240x^4 + 192x^2 + 64)$
$= 1 + \frac{12}{x^2} + \frac{60}{x^4} + \frac{160}{x^6} + \frac{240}{x^8} + \frac{192}{x^{10}} + \frac{64}{x^{12}}$
[2 marks available — 1 mark for a correct method using the result from a), 1 mark for the correct answer]

Q24 a) $(2-5x)^7 = 2^7 + {}^7C_1(2^6)(-5x) + {}^7C_2(2^5)(-5x)^2 + \dots$
$= 2^7 + 7(2^6)(-5x) + 21(2^5)(-5x)^2 + \dots$
$= 128 - 2240x + 16\,800x^2 + \dots$
[4 marks available — 1 mark for substituting into the binomial formula correctly, 1 mark for one correct simplified term, 1 mark for a second correct simplified term, 1 mark for a fully correct expansion]

b) $x = 0.01 \Rightarrow (2-5x)^7 = 1.95^7$
$\Rightarrow 1.95^7 = 128 - 2240(0.01) + 16\,800(0.01)^2 + \dots \approx 107.28$
$0.195^7 = \left(\frac{1.95}{10}\right)^7 = 1.95^7 \times 10^{-7}$
$\Rightarrow 0.195^7 \approx 107.28 \times 10^{-7} = 0.000010728$
[2 marks available — 1 mark for finding an approximation for 1.95^7, 1 mark for using the approximation for 1.95^7 to find the correct approximation for 0.195^7]

Q25 a) $\left(\frac{x}{3} - 2\right)^6 = \dots + {}^6C_3\left(\frac{x}{3}\right)^3(-2)^3 + {}^6C_4\left(\frac{x}{3}\right)^2(-2)^4 + {}^6C_5\left(\frac{x}{3}\right)(-2)^5 + {}^6C_6(-2)^6$
You only need the terms up to x^3.
In ascending powers of x, that's:
$64 - 64x + \frac{80}{3}x^2 - \frac{160}{27}x^3 + \dots$

b) (i) $4x\left(\frac{x}{3} - 2\right)^6 = 4x(64 - 64x + \dots) = 256x - 256x^2 + \dots$
$\approx 256x - 256x^2$

(ii) $(3-x)\left(\frac{x}{3} - 2\right)^6 = (3-x)(64 - 64x + \frac{80}{3}x^2 - \dots)$
$= 192 - 192x + 80x^2 - \dots$
$- 64x + 64x^2 - \dots$
$\approx 192 - 256x + 144x^2$

(iii) Expand $(x+1)^{16}$ — you only need the terms up to the term in x^2:
$(x+1)^{16} = \dots + {}^{16}C_{14}x^2(1)^{14} + {}^{16}C_{15}x(1)^{15} + {}^{16}C_{16}(1)^{16}$
$= \dots + 120x^2 + 16x + 1$
$\left(\frac{x}{3} - 2\right)^6(x+1)^{16} = (64 - 64x + \frac{80}{3}x^2 - \dots) \times (\dots + 120x^2 + 16x + 1)$
$= \dots + 7680x^2 + 1024x + 64 - \dots - 1024x^2 - 64x + \dots + \frac{80}{3}x^2$
$\approx 64 + 960x + (6656 + \frac{80}{3})x^2$
$= 64 + 960x + \frac{20\,048}{3}x^2$

Q26 a) $(1-2x)^{11} = 1 + {}^{11}C_1(-2x) + {}^{11}C_2(-2x)^2 + \dots$
$= 1 + 11(-2x) + 55(-2x)^2 + \dots \approx 1 - 22x + 220x^2$
[3 marks available — 1 mark for attempting to use the binomial expansion, 1 mark for a partially correct expansion, 1 mark for the fully correct simplified expansion]

b) $(1-2x)^{11}(2+x)^{10}$
$= (1-22x+220x^2-...)(1024+5120x+11\,520x^2+...)$
$= 1024+5120x+11\,520x^2-22\,528x$
$-112\,640x^2+225\,280x^2+...$
$= 1024-17\,408x+124\,160x^2+...$
[3 marks available — 1 mark for multiplying the two expansions, 1 mark for correctly expanding the brackets to find the required terms, 1 mark for correctly simplifying to the correct answer]

c) Let $x = 0.001 \Rightarrow 2.001^{10} \times 0.998^{11}$
$\approx 1024 - 17\,408(0.001) + 124\,160(0.001)^2 = 1006.71616$
$= 1006.7162$ to 4 d.p.
[2 marks available — 1 mark for letting x = 0.001 in the expression from part b), 1 mark for the correct answer (allow answer correctly calculated from an incorrect expression in part b)]

Q27 a) $(2+7x)^7 = 2^7 + {}^7C_1(2^6)(7x) + {}^7C_2(2^5)(7x)^2 + ...$
$= 2^7 + 7(2^6)(7x) + 21(2^5)(7x)^2 + ... \approx 128 + 3136x + 32\,928x^2$
[3 marks available — 1 mark for attempting to use the binomial expansion, 1 mark for a partially correct expansion, 1 mark for the fully correct simplified expansion]

b) $2 + 7x = 2.035$ when $x = 0.005$
Hence $2.035^7 = 128 + 3136(0.005) + 32\,928(0.005)^2 + ...$
≈ 144.5032
[2 marks available — 1 mark for letting x = 0.005 in the expansion from part a), 1 mark for the correct answer (allow answer correctly calculated from an incorrect expansion in part a)]

c) $2 + 7x = 10.4$ when $x = 1.2$
Since $1.2 > 1$, x^n is not small enough to ignore for large values of n, so the approximation would be inaccurate.
[1 mark for a correct explanation]

Q28 a) $\frac{(7!)^8}{(8!)^7} = \frac{7^8\times6^8\times5^8\times4^8\times3^8\times2^8\times1^8}{8^7\times7^7\times6^7\times5^7\times4^7\times3^7\times2^7\times1^7}$
$= \frac{7\times6\times5\times4\times3\times2\times1}{8^7}$
$= \frac{7}{8}\times\frac{6}{8}\times\frac{5}{8}\times\frac{4}{8}\times\frac{3}{8}\times\frac{2}{8}\times\frac{1}{8} < 1 \Rightarrow (7!)^8 < (8!)^7$

b) ${}^{15}C_5 \times {}^{10}C_4 \times {}^6C_3 \times {}^3C_2 \times {}^1C_1$
$= \frac{15!}{5!10!}\times\frac{10!}{4!6!}\times\frac{6!}{3!3!}\times\frac{3!}{2!1!}\times\frac{1!}{1!0!}$
$= \frac{15!}{5!}\cdot\frac{1}{4!}\cdot\frac{1}{3!}\cdot\frac{1}{2!}\cdot\frac{1}{1!} = \frac{15!}{5!\times4!\times3!\times2!\times1!}$
Remember that 0! = 1.

c) $\binom{n}{2}+\binom{n-1}{2} = \frac{n(n-1)}{2!}+\frac{(n-1)(n-2)}{2!}$
$= \frac{n(n-1)}{2}+\frac{(n-1)(n-2)}{2} = \frac{1}{2}(n-1)(n+n-2)$
$= \frac{1}{2}(n-1)(2n-2) = \frac{1}{2}(n-1)\times2(n-1) = (n-1)^2$
which is a square number whenever $n \geq 2$ and n is an integer.

Q29 a) (i) $\binom{10}{7} = \frac{10!}{7!3!} = \frac{10\times9\times8}{3\times2\times1} = 10\times3\times4 = 120$

(ii) ${}^{12}C_3 = \frac{12!}{3!9!} = \frac{12\times11\times10}{3\times2\times1} = 2\times11\times10 = 220$

(iii) $\frac{8!}{5!3!} = \frac{8\times7\times6}{3\times2\times1} = 8\times7 = 56$

b) $\frac{13!}{9!4!}+\frac{13!}{10!3!} = \frac{10\times13!}{10\times9!4!}+\frac{4\times13!}{10!4\times3!}$
$= \frac{10\times13!+4\times13!}{10!4!} = \frac{14\times13!}{10!4!} = \frac{14!}{10!4!} = \binom{14}{10}$
Repeat this method for $\frac{14!}{10!4!}+\frac{14!}{11!3!}$
to get $\frac{15!}{11!4!} = \binom{15}{11}$ or $\binom{15}{4}$.

Q30 a) $\left(1-\frac{x}{2}\right)^8 = 1 + {}^8C_1\left(-\frac{x}{2}\right) + {}^8C_2\left(-\frac{x}{2}\right)^2 + ... = 1 - 4x + 7x^2 + ...$
[3 marks available — 1 mark for substituting into the binomial formula correctly, 1 mark for one correct simplified term, 1 mark for a fully correct expansion]

b) $f(x) = \left(1-\frac{x}{2}\right)^8(p+qx) = (1-4x+7x^2+...)(p+qx)$
x term: $(1\times qx) + (-4x\times p) = qx - 4px = (q-4p)x$
x^2 term: $(-4x\times qx) + (7x^2\times p) = -4qx^2 + 7px^2 = (-4q+7p)x^2$
So coefficient of the x term is $q - 4p$ and coefficient of the x^2 term is $-4q + 7p$, and you can form the following simultaneous equations:
$q - 4p = -26$ (1)
$-4q + 7p = 50$ (2)
(1) × 4:
$4q - 16p = -104$ (3)
Add (2) and (3) to solve for p and q:
$-9p = -54 \Rightarrow p = 6$
$q = -26 + 4\times6 = -2$
[6 marks available — 1 mark for a correct method to find either the coefficient of x or x² in the expansion of f(x), 1 mark each for the correct coefficients of x and x² in terms of p and q, 1 mark for the correct simultaneous equations, 1 mark for the correct value of p or for a correct method to solve the simultaneous equations, 1 mark for the correct values of both p and q]

Q31 a) $(2+kx)^{13} = 2^{13} + {}^{13}C_1 2^{12}kx + {}^{13}C_2 2^{11}(kx)^2 + ...$
$= 8192 + 53\,248kx + 159\,744k^2x^2 + ...$

b) Coefficient of $x = 53\,248k$ and coefficient of $x^2 = 159\,744k^2$, so:
$6(53\,248k) = 159\,744k^2 \Rightarrow 319\,488k = 159\,744k^2$
$\Rightarrow 159\,744k = 319\,488 \Rightarrow k = 2$

Q32 a) The expansion of $a(bx+c)^3$ is $ab^3x^3 + 3ab^2cx^2 + 3abc^2x + ac^3$
$\Rightarrow ab^3 = 108$ and $ac^3 = -32$
Since a and b are integers, then b^3 must be a cube number. And since a is positive, b^3 must also be positive.
The only positive cube numbers which divide 108 are 1 and 27. $b^3 = 1$ gives a non-integer value of c, so $b^3 = 27 \Rightarrow b = 3 \Rightarrow a = 4 \Rightarrow c^3 = -8 \Rightarrow c = -2$.
So $108x^3 - 216x^2 + 144x - 32 \equiv 4(3x-2)^3$

b) $108x^3 - 216x^2 + 117x - 14$
$= (108x^3 - 216x^2 + 144x - 32) + (-27x + 18)$
$= 4(3x-2)^3 - 9(3x-2)$
$= (3x-2)(4(3x-2)^2 - 9)$
$= (3x-2)(2(3x-2)+3)(2(3x-2)-3)$
$= (3x-2)(6x-1)(6x-7)$

Q33 a) $(5+2x)^4 = 5^4 + {}^4C_1 5^3(2x) + {}^4C_2 5^2(2x)^2 + {}^4C_3 5(2x)^3 + (2x)^4$
$= 5^4 + 4\times5^3\times2x + 6\times5^2\times(2x)^2$
$+ 4\times5\times(2x)^3 + (2x)^4$
$= 625 + 1000x + 600x^2 + 160x^3 + 16x^4$
[4 marks available — 1 mark for substituting into the binomial formula correctly, 1 mark for one correct simplified term, 1 mark for a further two correct simplified terms, 1 mark for a fully correct expansion]

b) $(5-2x)^4 = 625 - 1000x + 600x^2 - 160x^3 + 16x^4$
[2 marks available — 1 mark for negating terms involving odd powers of x in the expansion from a), or for a correct method to expand, 1 mark for the correct expansion]

c) $(5+2x)^4 + (5-2x)^4 = 1250 + 1200x^2 + 32x^4$
Hence:
$(5+2\sqrt{3})^4 + (5-2\sqrt{3})^4 = 1250 + 1200(\sqrt{3})^2 + 32(\sqrt{3})^4$
$= 5138$
[3 marks available — 1 mark for adding together the two expansions from a) and b), 1 mark for substituting $x = \sqrt{3}$, 1 mark for the correct answer]

Q34 a) $\left(2+\frac{1}{2}x\right)^5 = 2^5 + {}^5C_1(2^4)\left(\frac{1}{2}x\right) + {}^5C_2(2^3)\left(\frac{1}{2}x\right)^2 + {}^5C_3(2^2)\left(\frac{1}{2}x\right)^3 + {}^5C_4(2)\left(\frac{1}{2}x\right)^4 + {}^5C_5\left(\frac{1}{2}x\right)^5$

$= 2^5 + 5(2^4)\left(\frac{1}{2}x\right) + 10(2^3)\left(\frac{1}{2}x\right)^2 + 10(2^2)\left(\frac{1}{2}x\right)^3 + 5(2)\left(\frac{1}{2}x\right)^4 + \left(\frac{1}{2}x\right)^5$

$= 32 + 40x + 20x^2 + 5x^3 + \frac{5}{8}x^4 + \frac{1}{32}x^5$

[4 marks available — 1 mark for substituting into the binomial formula correctly, 1 mark for one correct simplified term, 1 mark for a further two correct simplified terms, 1 mark for a fully correct expansion]

b) $\frac{1}{32}x(1280 + 640x + 160x^2 + 20x^3 + x^4)$

$= 40x + 20x^2 + 5x^3 + \frac{5}{8}x^4 + \frac{1}{32}x^5$

$= \left(32 + 40x + 20x^2 + 5x^3 + \frac{5}{8}x^4 + \frac{1}{32}x^5\right) - 32$

$= \left(2+\frac{1}{2}x\right)^5 - 32$

$\Rightarrow$ the transformation is the translation $\begin{pmatrix}0\\-32\end{pmatrix}$.

[2 marks available — 1 mark for using the result from a), 1 mark for the correct transformation described]

Q35 a) $(2-3x)^4 = 2^4 + {}^4C_1(2^3)(-3x) + {}^4C_2(2^2)(-3x)^2 + {}^4C_3(2)(-3x)^3 + {}^4C_4(-3x)^4$

$= 2^4 + 4(2^3)(-3x) + 6(2^2)(-3x)^2 + 4(2)(-3x)^3 + (-3x)^4$

$= 16 - 96x + 216x^2 - 216x^3 + 81x^4$

[4 marks available — 1 mark for substituting into the binomial formula correctly, 1 mark for one correct simplified term, 1 mark for a further two correct simplified terms, 1 mark for a fully correct expansion]

b) $(2+3x)^4 = 16 + 96x + 216x^2 + 216x^3 + 81x^4$ *[1 mark]*

c) Using the results from a) and b) with $x = \sqrt{2}$ gives $(2+3\sqrt{2})^4 + (2-3\sqrt{2})^4$

$= (16 + 96\sqrt{2} + 216(\sqrt{2})^2 + 216(\sqrt{2})^3 + 81(\sqrt{2})^4) + (16 - 96\sqrt{2} + 216(\sqrt{2})^2 - 216(\sqrt{2})^3 + 81(\sqrt{2})^4)$

$= 32 + 432(\sqrt{2})^2 + 162(\sqrt{2})^4 = 32 + 864 + 648 = 1544$

$\Rightarrow \sqrt{(2+3\sqrt{2})^4 + (2-3\sqrt{2})^4 + 56} = \sqrt{1600} = 40$

[3 marks available — 1 mark for adding the results from a) and b) using the correct value of x, 1 mark for showing that $(2+3\sqrt{2})^4 + (2-3\sqrt{2})^4 = 1544$, *1 mark for the correct answer]*

Q36 a) $(2+x)^3 = 2^3 + {}^3C_1(2^2)(x) + {}^3C_2 3(2)(x)^2 + {}^3C_3 x^3$

$= 2^3 + 3(2^2)(x) + 3(2)(x)^2 + x^3$

$= 8 + 12x + 6x^2 + x^3$

b) Using the result from a) with $x = \sqrt{3}$ gives

$(2+\sqrt{3})^3 = 8 + 12\sqrt{3} + 6(\sqrt{3})^2 + (\sqrt{3})^3$

$= 8 + 12\sqrt{3} + 18 + 3\sqrt{3} = 26 + 15\sqrt{3}$

c) $\frac{702 + 405\sqrt{3}}{125} = \frac{27(26 + 15\sqrt{3})}{125} = \frac{27}{125}(26 + 15\sqrt{3})$

$= \frac{27}{125}(2+\sqrt{3})^3 \Rightarrow \left(\frac{702 + 405\sqrt{3}}{125}\right)^{\frac{2}{3}} = \left(\frac{27}{125}(2+\sqrt{3})^3\right)^{\frac{2}{3}}$

$= \left(\frac{3}{5}(2+\sqrt{3})\right)^2 = \frac{9}{25}(2+\sqrt{3})^2 = \frac{9}{25}(7 + 4\sqrt{3})$

$= \frac{63}{25} + \frac{36}{25}\sqrt{3}$

Chapter 8 — Trigonometry

Prior Knowledge Check

Q1 a) $\cos 35° = \frac{3}{a} \Rightarrow a = \frac{3}{\cos 35°} = 3.662... = 3.66$ cm (3 s.f.)

b) $\tan 28° = \frac{b}{6} \Rightarrow b = 6\tan 28° = 3.190... = 3.19$ cm (3 s.f.)

c) $\cos c° = \frac{5}{7} \Rightarrow c° = \cos^{-1}\left(\frac{5}{7}\right) = 44.415... = 44.4°$ (3 s.f.)

Q2 a) True **b)** False **c)** True

Remember that something is an identity when it's true for any value of the variable or variables.

Q3 The roots are where the graph crosses the x-axis. The graph crosses the y-axis at (0, –30), so the graph looks like this:

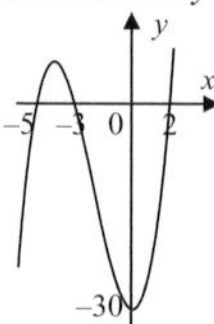

Exercise 8.1-8.3 — Trig Values and The Sine Rule

Q1 The angle at P measured anticlockwise from the positive x-axis is $41° + 90° = 131°$.
P is on the unit circle, so the coordinates are (cos 131°, sin 131°) = (–0.656, 0.755) (3 s.f.)
The angle at Q measured anticlockwise from the positive x-axis is $180° + 52° = 232°$.
Q is on the unit circle, so the coordinates are (cos 232°, sin 232°) = (–0.616, –0.788) (3 s.f.)
The angle at R measured anticlockwise from the positive x-axis is $360° - 23° = 337°$.
R is on the unit circle, so the coordinates are (cos 337°, sin 337°) = (0.921, –0.391) (3 s.f.)

Q2 a) The coordinates of S are $(\cos\theta, \sin\theta)$ since it's on the unit circle.
$\cos\theta = 0.899 \Rightarrow \theta = \cos^{-1}(0.899) = 26.0°$ (3 s.f.)
You can check the answer using the y-coordinate:
$\sin\theta = 0.438 \Rightarrow \theta = \sin^{-1}(0.438) = 26.0°$ (3 s.f.)

b) $\cos\theta = 0.669 \Rightarrow \theta = \cos^{-1}(0.669) = 48.0°$ (3 s.f.)

c) $\cos\theta = 0.089 \Rightarrow \theta = \cos^{-1}(0.089) = 84.9°$ (3 s.f.)

Q3 $OB = AC$, so using Pythagoras' theorem: $OB^2 = 12^2 + 15^2 = 369$

$\Rightarrow OB = \sqrt{369} = 3\sqrt{41} \Rightarrow \tan\angle OPB = \frac{3\sqrt{41}}{5}$

$\Rightarrow \angle OPB = \tan^{-1}\left(\frac{3\sqrt{41}}{5}\right) = 75.4102...° = 75.4°$ (3 s.f.)

[3 marks available — 1 mark for finding the length OB, 1 mark for a correct use of trigonometric functions to find ∠OPB, 1 mark for the correct answer]

Q4 a) x is the angle shown in the right-angled triangle. The adjacent length is $\sqrt{9^2 - 5^2} = 2\sqrt{14}$, so $\cos x = \frac{2\sqrt{14}}{9}$.

[2 marks available — 1 mark for $2\sqrt{14}$ *(or equivalent), 1 mark for correct value of cos x]*

b) Using the right-angled triangle in a) gives:

$\tan x = \frac{5}{2\sqrt{14}} \Rightarrow \tan x = \frac{5\sqrt{14}}{28}$ *[1 mark]*

When asked for an exact value, a rounded decimal answer is not acceptable — it won't get you the mark.

Q5 a) Drawing a line from the O to the midpoint (M) of the chord creates a right-angled triangle OAM with hypotenuse OA.

$\Rightarrow \cos\angle OAB = \frac{4.25}{6} = \frac{17}{24}$

$\Rightarrow \angle OAB = \cos^{-1}\left(\frac{17}{24}\right)$
$= 44.900...°$
$= 44.9°$ (3 s.f.)

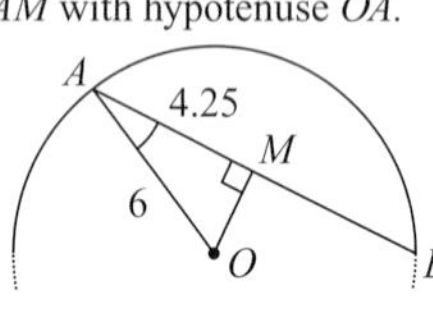

[1 mark for a correct method using trigonometry, 1 mark for the correct answer]

b) The shortest distance from O to the chord is the length of OM (i.e. the perpendicular distance from O to the chord).
Using Pythagoras' theorem: $OM = \sqrt{6^2 - 4.25^2}$
$= \sqrt{17.9375} = 4.2352... = 4.2$ (1 d.p.) *[1 mark]*

Q6 Using the sine rule: $\frac{a}{\sin A} = \frac{b}{\sin B}$

$\Rightarrow TW = \frac{FW \times \sin F}{\sin T} = \frac{15 \times \sin 39°}{\sin 82°} = 9.53$ cm (3 s.f.)

Q7 Angle $Q = 180° - 38° - 43° = 99°$

Using the sine rule: $\frac{a}{\sin A} = \frac{b}{\sin B}$

$\frac{PQ}{\sin 43°} = \frac{48}{\sin 99°} \Rightarrow PQ = \frac{48 \sin 43°}{\sin 99°} = 33.1 \text{ m (3 s.f.)}$

Q8 Using the sine rule: $\frac{a}{\sin A} = \frac{b}{\sin B}$

$\frac{\sin B}{14} = \frac{\sin 67°}{17} \Rightarrow \sin B = \frac{14 \times \sin 67°}{17} \Rightarrow B = 49.293...°$

So $A = 180° - 67° - 49.293...° = 63.7°$ (3 s.f.)

Q9 **a)** Using the sine rule: $\frac{a}{\sin A} = \frac{b}{\sin B}$

$\frac{\sin x}{17} = \frac{\sin 78°}{19} \Rightarrow \sin x = \frac{17 \times \sin 78°}{19}$

$\Rightarrow x = 61.1°$ (3 s.f.)

b) Using the sine rule: $\frac{a}{\sin A} = \frac{b}{\sin B}$

$\frac{x}{\sin 37°} = \frac{14}{\sin 102°} \Rightarrow x = \frac{14 \times \sin 37°}{\sin 102°} = 8.61 \text{ cm (3 s.f.)}$

c) Using the sine rule: $\frac{a}{\sin A} = \frac{b}{\sin B}$

$\frac{\sin x}{27} = \frac{\sin 24°}{13} \Rightarrow \sin x = \frac{27 \times \sin 24°}{13}$

$\Rightarrow x = 57.6°$ (3 s.f.)

d) The unlabelled angle is $180° - 22° - 29° = 129°$.

Using the sine rule: $\frac{a}{\sin A} = \frac{b}{\sin B}$

$\frac{x}{\sin 29°} = \frac{38}{\sin 129°} \Rightarrow x = \frac{38 \times \sin 29°}{\sin 129°} = 23.7 \text{ m (3 s.f.)}$

e) You can't find x directly from these values, so find the unlabelled angle instead (call it y) and then use angles in a triangle to find x.

Using the sine rule: $\frac{a}{\sin A} = \frac{b}{\sin B}$

$\frac{\sin y}{6} = \frac{\sin 71°}{11} \Rightarrow \sin y = \frac{6 \times \sin 71°}{11} \Rightarrow y = 31.046...°$

So $x = 180° - 71° - 31.046...° = 78.0°$ (3 s.f.)

f) The unlabelled angle is $180° - 52° - 63° = 65°$

Using the sine rule, $\frac{x}{\sin 52°} = \frac{57}{\sin 65°}$

$\Rightarrow x = \frac{57 \times \sin 52°}{\sin 65°} = 49.6 \text{ mm (3 s.f.)}$

Q10 Form a right-angled triangle CDX, with hypotenuse CD, by drawing a line DX parallel to AB and intersecting BC at the point X, then:

$\tan 42° = \frac{DX}{CX} = \frac{DX}{11.2 - 6.3}$

$\Rightarrow DX = 4.9 \tan 42° = 4.411...$

$\Rightarrow AB = 4.411... \Rightarrow \tan \angle ACB = \frac{4.411...}{11.2}$

$\Rightarrow \angle ACB = 21.500...°$

$\Rightarrow \angle ACD = 42° - 21.500...° = 20.499...° = 20.5°$ (3 s.f.)

[4 marks available — 1 mark for a correct method using trigonometry, 1 mark for calculating the length of DX (or AB), 1 mark for calculating the angle ∠ACB, 1 mark for the correct answer]

Q11 The diagram below models the information given, which is then simplified. You want to find W:

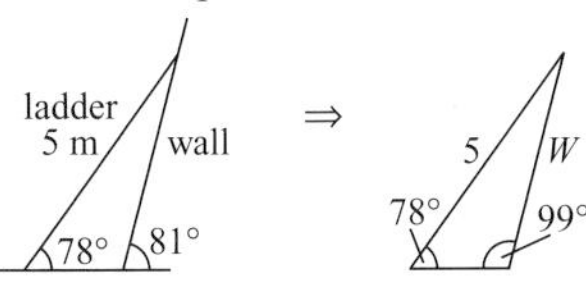

Using the sine rule: $\frac{a}{\sin A} = \frac{b}{\sin B}$

$\frac{W}{\sin 78°} = \frac{5}{\sin 99°} \Rightarrow W = \frac{5 \sin 78°}{\sin 99°} = 4.95 \text{ m (3 s.f.)}$

Q12 Start by sketching the triangle:

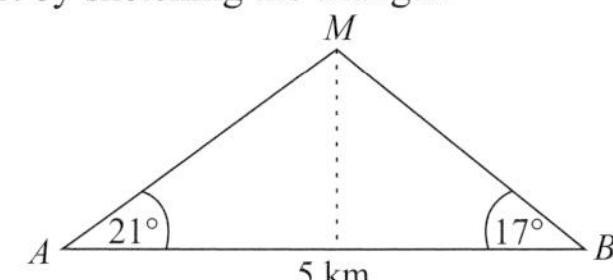

a) Angle $M = 180° - 21° - 17° = 142°$.

Using the sine rule: $\frac{a}{\sin A} = \frac{m}{\sin M}$

$\Rightarrow a = \frac{5 \times \sin 21°}{\sin 142°} = 2.91043... = 2.91 \text{ km (3 s.f.)}$

Here a is the distance BM and m is the distance AB.

b) To find the height, draw a line through the triangle from M at a right angle to AB (the dotted line shown in the diagram above).

Height $= \sin 17° \times 2.91043... = 0.85092...$ km
$= 851$ m (to the nearest m)

The final step just uses SOHCAHTOA — height is the opposite side and 2.91043... is the hypotenuse.

Q13 $2x\cos 30° + y\tan 45° = 2\sqrt{6} \Rightarrow x\sqrt{3} + y = 2\sqrt{6}$ ①

$2x\sin 45° - 4y\sin 60° = 2 - 6\sqrt{2} \Rightarrow x\sqrt{2} - 2y\sqrt{3} = 2 - 6\sqrt{2}$ ②

Rearrange ① $\quad y = 2\sqrt{6} - x\sqrt{3}$ ③

Sub ③ in ② $\quad (6 + \sqrt{2})x = 2 + 6\sqrt{2}$ ④

Rearrange ④ $\quad x = \frac{2 + 6\sqrt{2}}{6 + \sqrt{2}} = \frac{(2 + 6\sqrt{2})(6 - \sqrt{2})}{(6 + \sqrt{2})(6 - \sqrt{2})}$

$= \frac{34\sqrt{2}}{34} = \sqrt{2}$

$x = \sqrt{2}$ in ③ $\quad y = 2\sqrt{6} - \sqrt{2}\sqrt{3} = \sqrt{6}$

So the solution is $x = \sqrt{2}$ and $y = \sqrt{6}$.

[4 marks available — 1 mark for replacing trigonometric expressions with exact values, 1 mark for a correct method of solving simultaneous equations, 1 mark for correct x value, 1 mark for correct y value]

Q14 **a)** $\angle ABC = \angle BCA = (180° - 36°) \div 2 = 72°$

$\Rightarrow \angle BCD$ and $\angle CDB$ are also both equal to 72°

$\Rightarrow$ triangle BCD is isosceles with unequal side CD

$\Rightarrow$ the length of BD is r

$\angle ABD = \angle ABC - \angle DBC = 72° - 36° = 36°$

$\Rightarrow$ triangle ABD is isosceles with unequal side AB

$\Rightarrow$ the length of AD is equal to the length of BD

$\Rightarrow$ the length of AD is r

[2 marks available — 1 mark for correctly showing BD = r, 1 mark for correctly showing AD = r]

b) **(i)** Form a right-angled triangle by drawing a line through A and perpendicular to BC, meeting BC at point P.

$\Rightarrow \angle CAP = 18°$

$\Rightarrow \sin 18° = \frac{CP}{AC} = \frac{CP}{AD + DC} = \frac{\left(\frac{r}{2}\right)}{r + 1} = \frac{r}{2(r + 1)}$

[2 marks available — 2 marks for correctly deriving the expression, otherwise 1 mark for evidence of using the triangle APC (or ABP)]

(ii) Form a right-angled triangle by drawing a line through B and perpendicular to CD, meeting CD at point Q.

$\Rightarrow \angle CBQ = 18°$

$\Rightarrow \sin 18° = \frac{CQ}{BC} = \frac{\left(\frac{1}{2}\right)}{r} = \frac{1}{2r}$

[2 marks available — 2 marks for correctly deriving the expression, otherwise 1 mark for evidence of using the triangle BCQ (or BQD)]

c) Using the results from b) gives $\frac{r}{2(r + 1)} = \frac{1}{2r}$

$\Rightarrow r^2 = r + 1 \Rightarrow r^2 - r - 1 = 0$

[2 marks available — 1 mark for equating the expressions from b), 1 mark for correctly deriving the quadratic]

d) The solutions to the quadratic equation found in part c) are $r = \frac{1 + \sqrt{5}}{2}$ or $r = \frac{1 - \sqrt{5}}{2}$. But $r > 0$ since it is the length of the side of a triangle, so $r = \frac{1 + \sqrt{5}}{2}$.

$\Rightarrow \sin 18° = \frac{1}{2\left(\frac{1 + \sqrt{5}}{2}\right)} \Rightarrow \sin 18° = \frac{1}{1 + \sqrt{5}} = \frac{\sqrt{5} - 1}{4}$

[3 marks available — 1 mark for solving the quadratic equation, 1 mark for identifying the correct value of r, 1 mark for the correct and simplified value of sin 18°]

Q15 a) Using allied angles the missing angle at P is $180° - 135° = 45°$, so $\angle OPQ = 45° + 20° = 65°$.

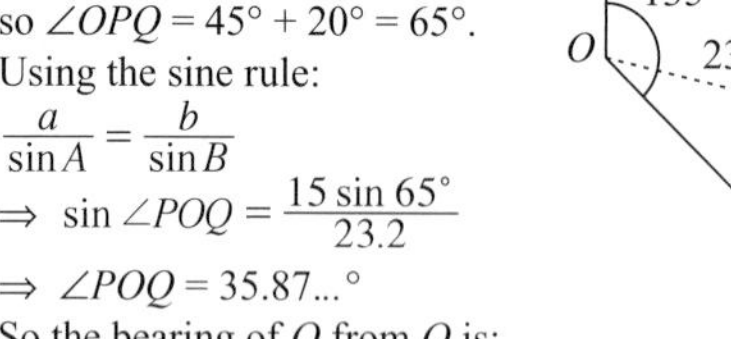

Using the sine rule:

$$\frac{a}{\sin A} = \frac{b}{\sin B}$$

$$\Rightarrow \sin \angle POQ = \frac{15 \sin 65°}{23.2}$$

$$\Rightarrow \angle POQ = 35.87...°$$

So the bearing of Q from O is:
$135° - 35.87...° = 099.128...°$, and the bearing of O from $Q = 180° + 099.128...° = 279.1°$ (1 d.p.)

[4 marks available — 1 mark for finding $\angle OPQ$, 1 mark for a correct use of the sine rule, 1 mark for finding $\angle POQ$, 1 mark for the correct answer]

b) $\angle OQP = 180° - 65° - 35.87...° = 79.128...°$

Using the sine rule: $\frac{OP}{\sin 79.128...°} = \frac{23.2}{\sin 65°}$

$$\Rightarrow OP = \frac{23.2 \sin 79.128...°}{\sin 65°} = 25.138... = 25.1 \text{ km (3 s.f.)}$$

[2 marks available — 1 mark for use of the sine rule, 1 mark for the correct answer]

Exercise 8.4 — The Cosine Rule

Q1 Using the cosine rule: $a^2 = b^2 + c^2 - 2bc \cos A$
$QR^2 = 9^2 + 10^2 - (2 \times 9 \times 10 \times \cos 42°) = 47.2...$
$QR = 6.87$ cm (3 s.f.)

Q2 Using the cosine rule: $a^2 = b^2 + c^2 - 2bc \cos A$

$$\Rightarrow \cos A = \frac{b^2 + c^2 - a^2}{2bc}$$

$$\Rightarrow D = \cos^{-1}\left(\frac{6^2 + 9^2 - 8^2}{2 \times 6 \times 9}\right) = 60.6° \text{ (3 s.f.)}$$

$$\Rightarrow E = \cos^{-1}\left(\frac{6^2 + 8^2 - 9^2}{2 \times 6 \times 8}\right) = 78.6° \text{ (3 s.f.)}$$

$$\Rightarrow F = \cos^{-1}\left(\frac{8^2 + 9^2 - 6^2}{2 \times 8 \times 9}\right) = 40.8° \text{ (3 s.f.)}$$

You could find the third angle by subtracting the other two from 180°.

Q3 a) Using the cosine rule: $a^2 = b^2 + c^2 - 2bc \cos A$

$$\cos x = \frac{15^2 + 12^2 - 9^2}{2 \times 15 \times 12}$$

$$\Rightarrow x = \cos^{-1}\left(\frac{15^2 + 12^2 - 9^2}{2 \times 15 \times 12}\right) = 36.9° \text{ (3 s.f.)}$$

b) Using the cosine rule: $a^2 = b^2 + c^2 - 2bc \cos A$

$$\cos x = \frac{14^2 + 12^2 - 21^2}{2 \times 14 \times 12}$$

$$\Rightarrow x = \cos^{-1}\left(\frac{14^2 + 12^2 - 21^2}{2 \times 14 \times 12}\right) = 107° \text{ (3 s.f.)}$$

c) Using the cosine rule: $a^2 = b^2 + c^2 - 2bc \cos A$

$$\cos x = \frac{10^2 + 7^2 - 4^2}{2 \times 10 \times 7}$$

$$\Rightarrow x = \cos^{-1}\left(\frac{10^2 + 7^2 - 4^2}{2 \times 10 \times 7}\right) = 18.2° \text{ (3 s.f.)}$$

d) Using the cosine rule: $a^2 = b^2 + c^2 - 2bc \cos A$
$x^2 = 43^2 + 17^2 - (2 \times 43 \times 17 \times \cos 42°)$
$x = \sqrt{1051.5...} = 32.4$ cm (3 s.f.)

e) Using the cosine rule: $a^2 = b^2 + c^2 - 2bc \cos A$
$x^2 = 56^2 + 32^2 - (2 \times 56 \times 32 \times \cos 27°)$
$x = \sqrt{966.63...} = 31.1$ mm (3 s.f.)

f) Using the cosine rule: $a^2 = b^2 + c^2 - 2bc \cos A$
$x^2 = 7^2 + 13^2 - (2 \times 7 \times 13 \times \cos 54°)$
$x = \sqrt{111.02...} = 10.5$ cm (3 s.f.)

Q4 Using the cosine rule: $a^2 = b^2 + c^2 - 2bc \cos A$
$\Rightarrow (JK)^2 = 24^2 + 29^2 - (2 \times 24 \times 29 \times \cos 62°)$
$\Rightarrow JK = \sqrt{763.4...} = 27.6$ cm (3 s.f.)

Q5 Using the cosine rule: $a^2 = b^2 + c^2 - 2bc \cos A$
$\Rightarrow (BC)^2 = 32^2 + 28^2 - (2 \times 32 \times 28 \times \cos 48°)$
$\Rightarrow BC = \sqrt{608.9...} = 24.7$ cm (3 s.f.)

Q6 The smallest angle is opposite the shortest side, so angle F is the smallest angle.
To be safe you could just work out all 3 angles and then see which is smallest.

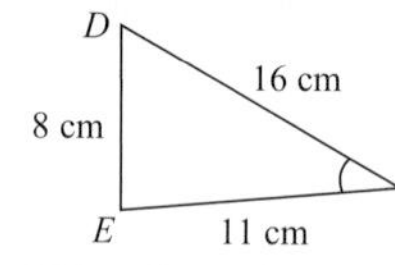

Using the cosine rule: $a^2 = b^2 + c^2 - 2bc \cos A$

$$\Rightarrow \cos F = \frac{11^2 + 16^2 - 8^2}{2 \times 11 \times 16}$$

$$\Rightarrow F = \cos^{-1}\left(\frac{11^2 + 16^2 - 8^2}{2 \times 11 \times 16}\right) = 27.2° \text{ (3 s.f.)}$$

Q7 The largest angle is opposite the longest side, so angle R is the largest angle.

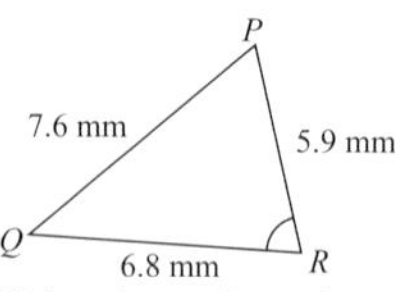

Using the cosine rule: $a^2 = b^2 + c^2 - 2bc \cos A$

$$\Rightarrow \cos R = \frac{6.8^2 + 5.9^2 - 7.6^2}{2 \times 6.8 \times 5.9}$$

$$\Rightarrow R = \cos^{-1}\left(\frac{6.8^2 + 5.9^2 - 7.6^2}{2 \times 6.8 \times 5.9}\right) = 73.1° \text{ (3 s.f.)}$$

Q8 $AP = 5.2$ cm (as AP is a radius of C_1) and similarly $BP = 4.3$ cm. The points A, P and B are the vertices of a triangle.

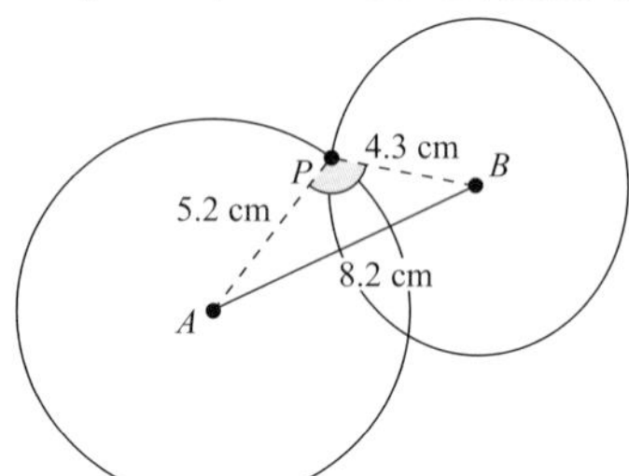

Using the cosine rule: $a^2 = b^2 + c^2 - 2bc \cos A$

$$\Rightarrow \cos \angle APB = \frac{5.2^2 + 4.3^2 - 8.2^2}{2 \times 5.2 \times 4.3}$$

$\Rightarrow \angle APB = \cos^{-1}(-0.485...) = 119.042... = 119.0°$ (1 d.p.)

[3 marks available — 1 mark for evidence of using the triangle APB, 1 mark for use of the cosine rule, 1 mark for correct answer]

Q9 Find the lengths XY, YZ and ZX.
$XY = \sqrt{(5 - -2)^2 + (8 - 2)^2} = \sqrt{85}$
$YZ = \sqrt{(5 - 3)^2 + (8 - -2)^2} = \sqrt{104}$
$ZX = \sqrt{(-2 - 3)^2 + (2 - -2)^2} = \sqrt{41}$

Using the cosine rule: $\cos A = \frac{b^2 + c^2 - a^2}{2bc}$.

So angle $XYZ = \cos^{-1}\left(\frac{104 + 85 - 41}{2 \times \sqrt{104} \times \sqrt{85}}\right) = 38.1°$ (3 s.f.)

It might help to draw a sketch here to make sure you're using the sides in the correct place in the cosine rule.

Q10 Using the cosine rule: $a^2 = b^2 + c^2 - 2bc \cos A$

$$\Rightarrow (BC)^2 = (2 + \sqrt{3})^2 + (2 - \sqrt{3})^2 - 2(2 + \sqrt{3})(2 - \sqrt{3})\cos 60°$$
$$= 4 + 4\sqrt{3} + 3 + 4 - 4\sqrt{3} + 3 - 1 = 13$$

$\Rightarrow BC = \sqrt{13}$ m

[3 marks available — 1 mark for use of the cosine rule, 1 mark for simplifying, 1 mark for correct answer]

Q11

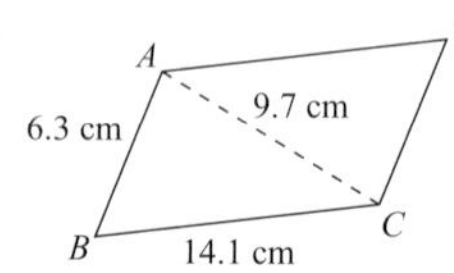

Using the cosine rule: $a^2 = b^2 + c^2 - 2bc \cos A$

$$\Rightarrow \cos \angle ABC = \frac{6.3^2 + 14.1^2 - 9.7^2}{2 \times 6.3 \times 14.1}$$

$\Rightarrow \angle ABC = 35.625...°$
$\Rightarrow \angle BAD = 180° - 35.625...° = 144.37...°$

Using the cosine rule again for triangle BCD:
$(BD)^2 = 6.3^2 + 14.1^2 - 2 \times 6.3 \times 14.1 \times \cos 144.37...°$
$\Rightarrow BD = 19.568... = 19.6$ cm (1 d.p.)
[4 marks available — 1 mark for use of the cosine rule, 1 mark for finding ∠ABC, 1 mark for finding ∠BAD, 1 mark for the correct answer]

Q12 a)

Using the cosine rule: $a^2 = b^2 + c^2 - 2bc \cos A$

$\Rightarrow \cos \angle AMB = \dfrac{1.2^2 + 1.45^2 - 2^2}{2 \times 1.2 \times 1.45}$

$\Rightarrow \angle AMB = \cos^{-1}(-0.131...) = 97.554... = 97.6°$ (3 s.f.)
[2 marks available — 1 mark for use of the cosine rule, 1 mark for the correct answer]

b) Using the cosine rule: $a^2 = b^2 + c^2 - 2bc \cos A$
$\Rightarrow (BM)^2 = 1.2^2 + 2^2 - 2 \times 1.2 \times 2 \times \cos 50° \Rightarrow BM = 1.53...$
So the change of length in $q = 1.53... - 1.45 = 0.08447...$ m
$= 8.45$ cm (3 s.f.)
[2 marks available — 1 mark for use of the cosine rule, 1 mark for the correct answer]

Q13 a)

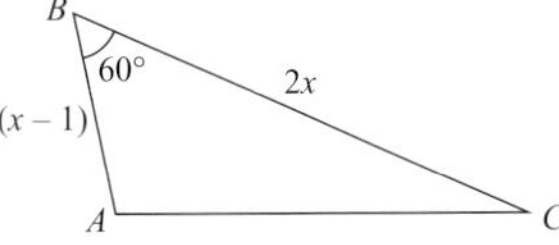

Using the cosine rule: $a^2 = b^2 + c^2 - 2bc \cos A$
$(AC)^2 = (x-1)^2 + (2x)^2 - 2(x-1)(2x)\cos 60°$
$= x^2 - 2x + 1 + 4x^2 - 2(x-1)(2x) \times \frac{1}{2}$
$= 5x^2 - 2x + 1 - 2x^2 + 2x$
$= 3x^2 + 1$
So $(\sqrt{13})^2 = 13 = 3x^2 + 1 \Rightarrow x^2 = 4 \Rightarrow x = 2$
You can ignore the negative value of x because it is a length.

b) The smallest angle is opposite the shortest side.
$AB = 2 - 1 = 1$, $BC = 2 \times 2 = 4$ and $AC = \sqrt{13}$.
AB is the shortest side, so C is the smallest angle.
Using the cosine rule: $a^2 = b^2 + c^2 - 2bc \cos A$

$\cos C = \dfrac{4^2 + \sqrt{13}^2 - 1^2}{2 \times 4 \times \sqrt{13}}$

$\Rightarrow C = \cos^{-1}\left(\dfrac{4^2 + \sqrt{13}^2 - 1^2}{2 \times 4 \times \sqrt{13}}\right) = 13.9°$ (3 s.f.)

Q14 Using the cosine rule on triangle OBC: $a^2 = b^2 + c^2 - 2bc \cos A$
$\Rightarrow (BC)^2 = 3^2 + 4^2 - 2 \times 3 \times 4 \times \cos 140° \Rightarrow BC = 6.586...$ m

Using the sine rule: $\dfrac{\sin \angle OBA}{5} = \dfrac{\sin 22°}{3}$

$\Rightarrow \angle OBA = \sin^{-1}\left(\dfrac{5 \sin 22°}{3}\right) = 38.63...°$

$\angle AOB = 180° - 22° - 38.63...° = 119.36...°$
$\angle AOC = 360° - 119.36° - 140° = 100.63...°$
Using the cosine rule on triangles OAB and OAC:
$(AB)^2 = 5^2 + 3^2 - 2 \times 5 \times 3 \times \cos 119.36...° \Rightarrow AB = 6.979...$ m
$(AC)^2 = 5^2 + 4^2 - 2 \times 5 \times 4 \times \cos 100.63...° \Rightarrow AC = 6.955...$ m
So the perimeter of ABC is:
$6.586... + 6.979... + 6.955... = 20.521... = 20.5$ m (3 s.f.)
[5 marks available — 1 mark for use of the cosine rule, 1 mark for the length of BC, 1 mark for use of the sine rule, 1 mark for the length of either AB or AC, 1 mark for the correct perimeter]

Exercise 8.5 — More Trig Rules

Q1 a) Area $= \frac{1}{2}ab \sin C = \frac{1}{2} \times 12 \times 10.5 \times \sin 53°$
$= 50.3$ cm² (3 s.f.)

b) Area $= \frac{1}{2}ab \sin C = \frac{1}{2} \times 9 \times 5 \times \sin 41° = 14.8$ mm² (3 s.f.)

c) Start by finding an angle (any angle is fine).
Using the cosine rule: $a^2 = b^2 + c^2 - 2bc \cos A$

$\Rightarrow \cos A = \dfrac{5^2 + 7^2 - 4.2^2}{2 \times 5 \times 7}$

$\Rightarrow A = \cos^{-1}\left(\dfrac{5^2 + 7^2 - 4.2^2}{2 \times 5 \times 7}\right) = 36.3...°$

Now you can find the area:
Area $= \frac{1}{2}ab \sin C = \frac{1}{2} \times 5 \times 7 \times \sin 36.3...°$
$= 10.4$ cm² (3 s.f.)
You could have found any angle to start off, then used the corresponding sides.

d) Find the length of another side (either side is fine):
Using the sine rule: $\dfrac{a}{\sin A} = \dfrac{b}{\sin B}$

$\dfrac{x}{\sin 94} = \dfrac{24}{\sin 32} \Rightarrow x = \dfrac{24 \times \sin 94}{\sin 32} = 45.17...$ m

The unlabelled angle is $180° - 94° - 32° = 54°$.
Now you can find the area:
Area $= \frac{1}{2}ab \sin C = \frac{1}{2} \times 24 \times 45.17... \times \sin 54°$
$= 439$ cm² (3 s.f.)

Q2 Area $= \frac{1}{2}ab \sin C = \frac{1}{2} \times 4 \times 7 \times \sin 49°$
$= 10.565... = 10.6$ cm² (3 s.f.)

Q3 Using the cosine rule $a^2 = b^2 + c^2 - 2bc \cos A$

$A = \cos^{-1}\left(\dfrac{1.9^2 + 2.7^2 - 2.9^2}{2 \times 1.9 \times 2.7}\right) = 75.954...°$

Then use the area formula:
Area $= \frac{1}{2} \times 1.9 \times 2.7 \times \sin 75.954...°$
$= 2.488... = 2.49$ m² (3 s.f.)

Q4 Area $= 30 = \frac{1}{2}ab \sin C = \frac{1}{2} \times 12 \times 8 \times \sin C$

$\Rightarrow \sin C = \dfrac{30}{48} \Rightarrow C = \sin^{-1}\left(\dfrac{30}{48}\right) = 38.7°$ (1 d.p.)

Q5 Find another side using the sine rule: $\dfrac{a}{\sin A} = \dfrac{b}{\sin B}$

$\dfrac{x}{\sin 35°} = \dfrac{14}{\sin 52°} \Rightarrow x = \dfrac{14 \times \sin 35°}{\sin 52°} = 10.19...$ cm

The unlabelled angle is $180° - 35° - 52° = 93°$.
Now you can find the area:
Area $= \frac{1}{2}ab \sin C = \frac{1}{2} \times 14 \times 10.19... \times \sin 93°$
$= 71.2$ cm² (3 s.f.)

Q6 Find an angle in the triangle using the cosine rule:
$a^2 = b^2 + c^2 - 2bc \cos A$

$\cos A = \dfrac{7^2 + 13^2 - 16^2}{2 \times 7 \times 13}$

$\Rightarrow A = \cos^{-1}\left(\dfrac{7^2 + 13^2 - 16^2}{2 \times 7 \times 13}\right) = 102.05...°$

So the area $= \frac{1}{2}ab \sin C = \frac{1}{2} \times 7 \times 13 \times \sin 102.05...°$
$= 44.5$ mm² (3 s.f.)

Q7 a)

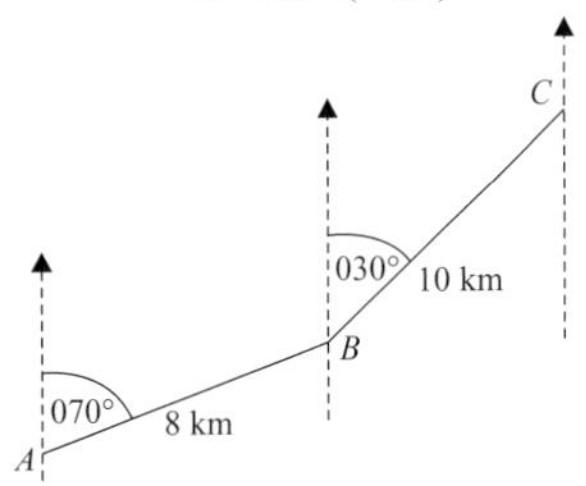

b) The angle anticlockwise from the vertical at B to A is $180° - 70° = 110°$ (parallel lines), so the angle ABC is $110° + 30° = 140°$. Now you can use the cosine rule to find the distance AC:
$a^2 = b^2 + c^2 - 2bc \cos A$
$\Rightarrow AC = \sqrt{(BC)^2 + (AB)^2 - 2(BC)(AB)\cos B}$
$\Rightarrow AC = \sqrt{100 + 64 - 160 \cos 140°}$
$= 16.928... = 16.9$ km (3 s.f.)

c) Find the angle ACB using the cosine rule:
$a^2 = b^2 + c^2 - 2bc \cos A$
$\Rightarrow \cos ACB = \frac{10^2 + 16.928...^2 - 8^2}{2 \times 10 \times 16.928...}$
$\Rightarrow ACB = \cos^{-1}\left(\frac{10^2 + 16.928...^2 - 8^2}{2 \times 10 \times 16.928...}\right) = 17.68°$ (2 d.p.)
The bearing required is therefore
$180° + 17.68° + 30°$ (parallel lines) $= 228°$ (3 s.f.).

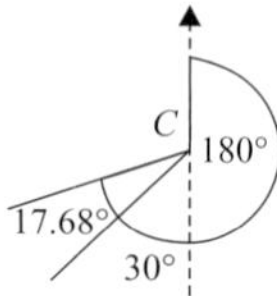

You could also have found angle ACB using the sine rule.

Q8 Using the cosine rule: $a^2 = b^2 + c^2 - 2bc \cos A$
$\Rightarrow AC = \sqrt{9^2 + 11^2 - (2 \times 9 \times 11 \times \cos 148)}$
$= 19.233... = 19.2$ m (3 s.f.)
Find the area of each triangle individually.
For the top triangle:
Area $= \frac{1}{2}ab \sin C = \frac{1}{2} \times 9 \times 11 \times \sin 148° = 26.231...\text{m}^2$
For the bottom triangle:
Area $= \frac{1}{2} \times 8 \times 19.233... \times \sin 79° = 75.519...\text{ m}^2$
So the area of the quadrilateral is
$26.231... + 75.519... = 101.750... = 102\text{ m}^2$ (3 s.f.).

Q9 a) Find QS using the cosine rule:
$a^2 = b^2 + c^2 - 2bc \cos A$
$(QS)^2 = 3^2 + 4^2 - (2 \times 3 \times 4 \times \cos 35°)$
$QS = \sqrt{5.3403...} = 2.310... = 2.31$ cm (3 s.f.)

b) Split the shape into two triangles as shown below.

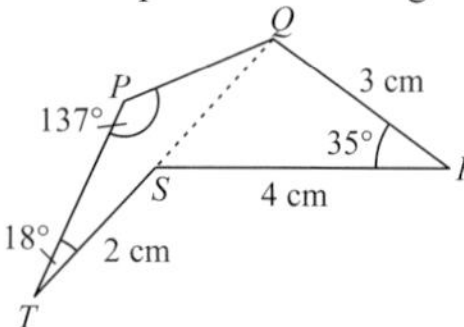

Find the area of each triangle individually. For QRS:
Area $= \frac{1}{2}ab \sin C = \frac{1}{2} \times 3 \times 4 \times \sin 35° = 3.441...\text{ cm}^2$
For PQT:
Side $QT = 2 + 2.310... = 4.310...$ cm
Find another side using the sine rule: $\frac{a}{\sin A} = \frac{b}{\sin B}$
Here, we find PQ: $\frac{PQ}{\sin 18°} = \frac{4.310...}{\sin 137°}$
$\Rightarrow PQ = \frac{4.310... \times \sin 18°}{\sin 137°} = 1.953...$ m
The missing angle is $180° - 18° - 137° = 25°$.
Now you can find the area:
Area $= \frac{1}{2}ab \sin C = \frac{1}{2} \times 4.310... \times 1.952... \times \sin 25°$
$= 1.779...\text{ cm}^2$ (3 s.f.)
So the total area of the shape is:
$3.441... + 1.779... = 5.220... = 5.22\text{ cm}^2$ (3 s.f.)

Q10 a) Find the area of each triangle individually:
In the top triangle:
Area $= \frac{1}{2}ab \sin C = \frac{1}{2} \times 11 \times 7 \times \sin 47° = 28.157...\text{ cm}^2$
In the bottom triangle, find the length of the dotted line using the cosine rule: $a^2 = b^2 + c^2 - 2bc \cos A$
$a^2 = 11^2 + 7^2 - 2 \times 11 \times 7 \times \cos 47°$
$a = \sqrt{64.972...} = 8.0605...$ cm
Area $= \frac{1}{2}ab \sin C = \frac{1}{2} \times 13 \times 8.0605... \times \sin 19°$
$= 17.057...\text{ cm}^2$
So the total area is:
$28.157... + 17.057... = 45.214... = 45.2\text{ cm}^2$ (3 s.f.)

b) Find the area of each triangle individually.
In the right-hand triangle:
Area $= \frac{1}{2}ab \sin C = \frac{1}{2} \times 27 \times 34 \times \sin 39° = 288.85...\text{ mm}^2$
In the left-hand triangle, find the length of the dotted line using the cosine rule:
$a^2 = b^2 + c^2 - 2bc \cos A$
$a^2 = 27^2 + 34^2 - 2 \times 27 \times 34 \times \cos 39°$
$a = \sqrt{458.16...} = 21.404...$ mm
Then use the cosine rule again to find an angle:
$\cos A = \frac{12^2 + 14^2 - 458.16...}{2 \times 12 \times 14}$
$\Rightarrow A = \cos^{-1}\left(\frac{12^2 + 14^2 - 458.16...}{2 \times 12 \times 14}\right) = 110.58...°$
Now you can find the area:
Area $= \frac{1}{2}ab \sin C = \frac{1}{2} \times 12 \times 14 \times \sin 110.58...°$
$= 78.634...\text{ mm}^2$
Total area $= 288.85... + 78.634...$
$= 367.49... = 367\text{ mm}^2$ (3 s.f.)

Q11 a)

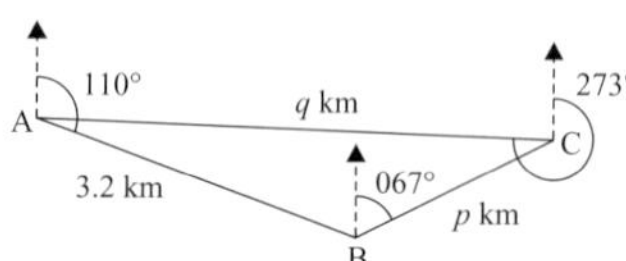

[3 marks available — 1 mark for at least two bearings labelled correctly, 1 mark for all bearings labelled correctly, 1 mark for all distances labelled correctly]

b) Using rules for angles around parallel lines:

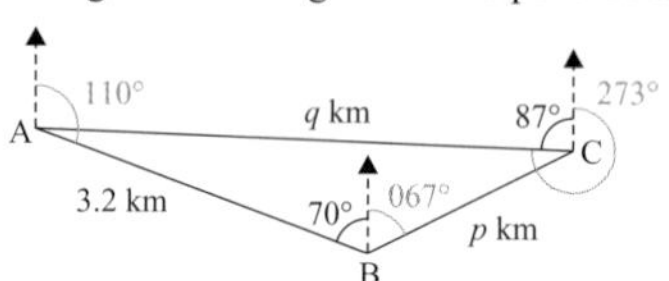

The angle anticlockwise from the bearing B to A is $180° - 110° = 70°$ so $\angle ABC = 70° + 67° = 137°$
The angle anticlockwise from the bearing C to B is $180° - 67° = 113°$ so $\angle ACB = 113° - 87° = 26°$
Then $\angle BAC = 180° - 26° - 137° = 17°$
[3 marks available — 1 mark for each correct angle]
You could also determine ∠BAC from 110° + 87° – 180° = 17°.

c) Using the sine rule: $\frac{a}{\sin A} = \frac{b}{\sin B}$
$\frac{3.2}{\sin 26°} = \frac{p}{\sin 17°} = \frac{q}{\sin 137°}$,
so $p = \frac{3.2 \times \sin 17°}{\sin 26°} = 2.134...$ km
$q = \frac{3.2 \times \sin 137°}{\sin 26°} = 4.978...$ km
So the total length of the walk is
$3.2 + 2.134... + 4.978... = 10.3$ km (3 s.f.)
[4 marks available — 1 mark for use of the sine rule, 1 mark for the correct value of p, 1 mark for the correct value of q, 1 mark for the correct answer]

Q12 Area $= \frac{1}{2}ab \sin C = \frac{1}{2} \times 24 \times b \times \sin 41° = 220$
$\Rightarrow b = \frac{2 \times 220}{24 \times \sin 41°} = 27.944...$ cm
Now you have two sides and an angle, find the third side using the cosine rule: $a^2 = b^2 + c^2 - 2bc \cos A$
$a^2 = (27.944...)^2 + 24^2 - (2 \times 24 \times 27.944... \times \cos 41°)$
$a = \sqrt{344.56...} = 18.562...$ cm
So the total perimeter $= 24 + 27.944... + 18.562...$
$= 70.5$ cm (3 s.f.)

Q13 a)

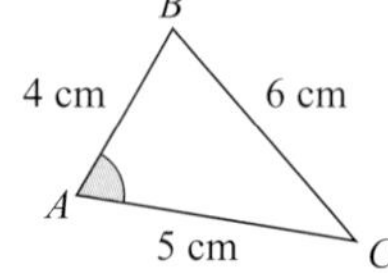

Using the cosine rule: $a^2 = b^2 + c^2 - 2bc\cos A$

$\Rightarrow \cos\angle CAB = \dfrac{4^2 + 5^2 - 6^2}{2\times 4\times 5} = \dfrac{1}{8}$.

[2 marks available — 1 mark for use of cosine rule, 1 mark for correct answer]

b) The answer from part a) gives the right-angled triangle shown in the diagram, where $\theta = \angle CAB$.

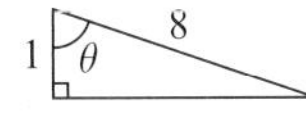

Using Pythagoras' theorem:
Missing length $= \sqrt{8^2 - 1^2} = 3\sqrt{7}$

So $\sin\theta = \dfrac{3\sqrt{7}}{8}$

$\Rightarrow$ Area of $\Delta ABC = \dfrac{1}{2}\times 4\times 5\times\dfrac{3\sqrt{7}}{8} = \dfrac{15\sqrt{7}}{4}$ cm^2

[3 marks available — 1 mark for the correct value of sin θ, 1 mark for using the formula for the area of a triangle, 1 mark for the correct answer]

Q14 ΔABC is divided into three isosceles triangles — ΔOAB, ΔOBC and ΔOAC.

Using $\angle AOB = 118°$ gives:
$\angle OAB = \angle OBA = (180° - 118°) \div 2 = 31°$
Using $\angle ABC = 68°$ gives:
$\angle OBC = \angle OCB = 68° - 31° = 37°$
Therefore:
$\angle BOC = 180° - 37° - 37° = 106°$ (angles in a triangle)
$\angle AOC = 360° - 118° - 106° = 136°$ (angles around a point)
The lengths $OA = OB = OC = 6$ cm (radius of the circle)
The area of ΔABC is equal to the sum of the areas of ΔOAB, ΔOBC and ΔOAC, so the area is:

$$\left(\frac{1}{2}\times 6^2\times\sin 118°\right) + \left(\frac{1}{2}\times 6^2\times\sin 106°\right) + \left(\frac{1}{2}\times 6^2\times\sin 136°\right)$$

$= 45.699... = 45.7$ cm^2 (3 s.f.)

[4 marks available — 1 mark for finding ∠AOC, 1 mark for finding ∠BOC, 1 mark for a correct use of the formula for the area of a triangle, 1 mark for the correct answer]

Exercise 8.6 — Trig Identities

Q1 Use $\tan\theta \equiv \dfrac{\sin\theta}{\cos\theta}$:

$$\frac{\sin\theta}{\tan\theta} - \cos\theta \equiv \frac{\sin\theta}{\left(\frac{\sin\theta}{\cos\theta}\right)} - \cos\theta \equiv \cos\theta - \cos\theta \equiv 0$$

Q2 Use $\sin^2\theta + \cos^2\theta \equiv 1$:
$\cos^2\theta \equiv 1 - \sin^2\theta \equiv (1 - \sin\theta)(1 + \sin\theta)$

Q3 Use $\sin^2 x + \cos^2 x \equiv 1$:
$\cos^2 x \equiv 1 - \sin^2 x$

$$\Rightarrow \cos x = \sqrt{1 - \sin^2 x} = \sqrt{1 - \left(\frac{1}{2}\right)^2} = \sqrt{\frac{3}{4}} = \frac{\sqrt{3}}{2}$$

You could have used your knowledge of common angles for this.

Q4 $\cos^2 x \equiv 1 - \sin^2 x$, $\tan x \equiv \dfrac{\sin x}{\cos x}$

$$\Rightarrow \tan x \equiv \frac{\sqrt{\sin^2 x}}{\sqrt{1 - \sin^2 x}} \equiv \frac{\left(\frac{\sqrt{3}}{2}\right)}{\left(\frac{1}{2}\right)} = \sqrt{3}$$

Q5 Use $\sin^2 x + \cos^2 x \equiv 1$:

$$\begin{aligned} 4\sin^2 x - 3\cos x + 1 &\equiv 4(1 - \cos^2 x) - 3\cos x + 1 \\ &\equiv 4 - 4\cos^2 x - 3\cos x + 1 \\ &\equiv 5 - 3\cos x - 4\cos^2 x \end{aligned}$$

Q6 Use $\tan x \equiv \dfrac{\sin x}{\cos x}$ and $\sin^2 x + \cos^2 x \equiv 1$:

$$(\tan x + 1)(\tan x - 1) \equiv \tan^2 x - 1 \equiv \frac{\sin^2 x}{\cos^2 x} - 1$$

$$\equiv \frac{1 - \cos^2 x}{\cos^2 x} - 1 \equiv \frac{1}{\cos^2 x} - \frac{\cos^2 x}{\cos^2 x} - 1 \equiv \frac{1}{\cos^2 x} - 2$$

Q7 a)

B, θ°, 11 cm, 60°, A, 12 cm, C

Using the sine rule: $\dfrac{\sin 60°}{11} = \dfrac{\sin\theta}{12} \Rightarrow \sin\theta = \dfrac{6\sqrt{3}}{11}$

[2 marks available — 1 mark for a correct use of the sine rule, 1 mark for the correct answer]

b) (i) $\cos^2\theta \equiv 1 - \sin^2\theta \Rightarrow \cos^2\theta = 1 - \left(\dfrac{6\sqrt{3}}{11}\right)^2 = \dfrac{13}{121}$

[2 marks available — 1 mark for use of an appropriate trigonometric identity, 1 mark for the correct answer]

(ii) $\tan^2\theta \equiv \dfrac{\sin^2\theta}{\cos^2\theta} = \dfrac{\left(\frac{6\sqrt{3}}{11}\right)^2}{\left(\frac{13}{121}\right)} = \dfrac{108}{13}$

[2 marks available — 1 mark for use of an appropriate trigonometric identity, 1 mark for the correct answer]

Q8 Here the student has divided both sides by $\sin\theta$. But $\sin\theta$ could equal 0, so you shouldn't divide by it. Instead the student should have rearranged:

$\cos\theta\sin\theta = \dfrac{1}{2}\sin\theta \Rightarrow \cos\theta\sin\theta - \dfrac{1}{2}\sin\theta = 0$

$\Rightarrow \sin\theta(\cos\theta - \dfrac{1}{2}) = 0$.

So there's a solution when $\cos\theta = \dfrac{1}{2} \Rightarrow \theta = 60°$, as the student found. But there's also a solution when $\sin\theta = 0 \Rightarrow \theta = 0°$. This was not found because the student had cancelled the $\sin\theta$ terms.

Q9 Use $\sin^2 x + \cos^2 x \equiv 1$ and $\tan x \equiv \dfrac{\sin x}{\cos x}$:

$$\tan x + \frac{1}{\tan x} \equiv \frac{\sin x}{\cos x} + \frac{\cos x}{\sin x} \equiv \frac{\sin^2 x + \cos^2 x}{\sin x\cos x} \equiv \frac{1}{\sin x\cos x}$$

Q10 Use $\sin^2\theta + \cos^2\theta \equiv 1$:

$$\begin{aligned} 2\cos^2 x + 5\sin x + 1 &\equiv 2(1 - \sin^2 x) + 5\sin x + 1 \\ &\equiv 2 - 2\sin^2 x + 5\sin x + 1 \\ &\equiv 3 + 5\sin x - 2\sin^2 x \\ &\equiv (3 - \sin x)(2\sin x + 1) \end{aligned}$$

If you're struggling to factorise, let y = sin x, then the expression becomes 3 + 5y − 2y².

Q11 Use $\sin^2 x + \cos^2 x \equiv 1$:

$$\begin{aligned} 4 + \sin x - 6\cos^2 x &\equiv 4 + \sin x - 6(1 - \sin^2 x) \\ &\equiv -2 + \sin x + 6\sin^2 x \\ &\equiv (2\sin x - 1)(3\sin x + 2) \end{aligned}$$

Q12 Use $\sin^2 x + \cos^2 x \equiv 1$:

$$\begin{aligned} &\sin^2 x\cos^2 y - \cos^2 x\sin^2 y \\ &\equiv (1 - \cos^2 x)\cos^2 y - \cos^2 x(1 - \cos^2 y) \\ &\equiv \cos^2 y - \cos^2 x\cos^2 y - \cos^2 x + \cos^2 x\cos^2 y \\ &\equiv \cos^2 y - \cos^2 x \end{aligned}$$

Q13

$$\frac{1}{2}\left(\frac{\sin x\cos x}{1 - \sin^2 x} + \frac{1 - \cos^2 x}{\sin x\cos x}\right) \equiv \frac{1}{2}\left(\frac{\sin x\cos x}{\cos^2 x} + \frac{\sin^2 x}{\sin x\cos x}\right)$$

$$\equiv \frac{1}{2}\left(\frac{\sin x}{\cos x} + \frac{\sin x}{\cos x}\right) \equiv \frac{1}{2}\times 2\tan x \equiv \tan x$$

[3 marks available — 1 mark for using cos²x ≡ 1 − sin²x, 1 mark for using tan x ≡ $\frac{\sin x}{\cos x}$, 1 mark for correct answer]

Q14 Use $\tan x \equiv \dfrac{\sin x}{\cos x}$ and $\sin^2 x + \cos^2 x \equiv 1$:

$$\frac{\tan^2 x + 1}{\tan^2 x} \equiv \frac{\left(\frac{\sin^2 x}{\cos^2 x}\right) + 1}{\left(\frac{\sin^2 x}{\cos^2 x}\right)} \equiv \frac{\cos^2 x\left(\frac{\sin^2 x}{\cos^2 x}\right) + \cos^2 x}{\cos^2 x\left(\frac{\sin^2 x}{\cos^2 x}\right)}$$

$$\equiv \frac{\sin^2 x + \cos^2 x}{\sin^2 x} \equiv \frac{1}{\sin^2 x}$$

Q15 Use $\sin^2 x + \cos^2 x \equiv 1$:

$$\begin{aligned} \frac{\sin^4 x - \cos^4 x}{\sin^2 x - \cos^2 x} &\equiv \frac{(\sin^2 x)^2 - (\cos^2 x)^2}{\sin^2 x - \cos^2 x} \\ &\equiv \frac{(\sin^2 x - \cos^2 x)(\sin^2 x + \cos^2 x)}{(\sin^2 x - \cos^2 x)} \\ &\equiv \sin^2 x + \cos^2 x \equiv 1 \end{aligned}$$

sin⁴ x − cos⁴ x can be written as a difference of two squares.

Q16 a) Using the cosine rule: $a^2 = b^2 + c^2 - 2bc\cos A$

$\Rightarrow \cos\theta = \dfrac{7^2 + 5^2 - 3^2}{2\times 7\times 5} = \dfrac{13}{14}$

[2 marks available — 1 mark for use of the cosine rule, 1 mark for the correct answer]

b) Using the trigonometric identity $\cos^2\theta + \sin^2\theta \equiv 1$ and using the fact that θ is an acute angle gives:

$$\sin\theta = \sqrt{1-\cos^2\theta} = \sqrt{1-\left(\frac{13}{14}\right)^2} = \frac{3\sqrt{3}}{14}$$

Using the identity $\tan\theta \equiv \frac{\sin\theta}{\cos\theta}$ gives:

$$\tan\theta = \frac{\left(\frac{3\sqrt{3}}{14}\right)}{\left(\frac{13}{14}\right)} = \frac{3\sqrt{3}}{13}$$

[3 marks available — 1 mark for using $\sin^2 x \equiv 1 - \cos^2 x$, 1 mark for finding $\sin\theta$, 1 mark for finding $\tan\theta$]

Q17 a) (i) Using the right-angled triangle with hypotenuse BP gives $\cos\theta = \frac{2x}{1.8} = \frac{10x}{9}$. *[1 mark]*

(ii) Using the right-angled triangle with hypotenuse AP gives $\sin\theta = \frac{3x}{1.2} = \frac{5x}{2}$. *[1 mark]*

b) Using the identity $\tan x \equiv \frac{\sin x}{\cos x}$ gives:

$$\tan\theta = \frac{\left(\frac{5x}{2}\right)}{\left(\frac{10x}{9}\right)} = \frac{9}{4} \Rightarrow \theta = 66.037...°$$

Therefore $\theta < 70°$ and so the ladder is not safe to use.

[3 marks available — 1 mark for substituting the values of $\sin\theta$ and $\cos\theta$ into the correct identity, 1 mark for correct value of $\tan\theta$, 1 mark for a correct written conclusion]

Q18 Look at the right-angled triangle below:

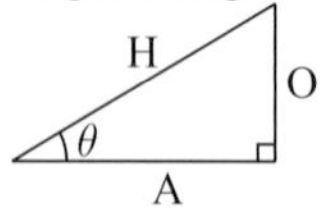

Here, $\sin\theta = \frac{O}{H}$ and $\cos\theta = \frac{A}{H}$.

Substitute these fractions into $\sin^2\theta + \cos^2\theta \equiv 1$:

$$\left(\frac{O}{H}\right)^2 + \left(\frac{A}{H}\right)^2 \equiv 1 \Rightarrow \frac{O^2}{H^2} + \frac{A^2}{H^2} \equiv 1$$

$\Rightarrow O^2 + A^2 \equiv H^2$ — this is Pythagoras' theorem.

Q19 a) B has coordinates (x, y) where $\cos\theta = \frac{x}{c}$ and $\sin\theta = \frac{y}{c}$.

Hence the coordinates of B are $(c\cos\theta, c\sin\theta)$.

[2 marks available — 1 mark for each correct coordinate]

b) The length of BC is the distance between the points $(c\cos\theta, c\sin\theta)$ and $(b, 0)$, so:

$$\begin{aligned} BC^2 &= (b - c\cos\theta)^2 + (c\sin\theta - 0)^2 \\ &= b^2 - 2bc\cos\theta + c^2\cos^2\theta + c^2\sin^2\theta \\ &= b^2 - 2bc\cos\theta + c^2(\cos^2\theta + \sin^2\theta) \\ &= b^2 + c^2 - 2bc\cos\theta \end{aligned}$$

The length of BC is also equal to a, hence $a^2 = b^2 + c^2 - 2bc\cos\theta$, which is the cosine rule.

[3 marks available — 1 mark for working to find the distance between two points, 1 mark for using $\sin^2 x + \cos^2 x \equiv 1$, 1 mark for obtaining the required result]

Exercise 8.7 — Graphs of Trig Functions

Q1

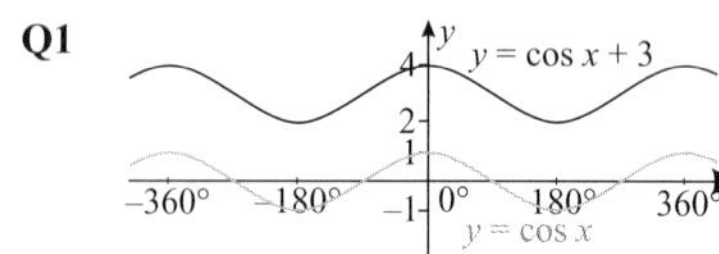

Q2

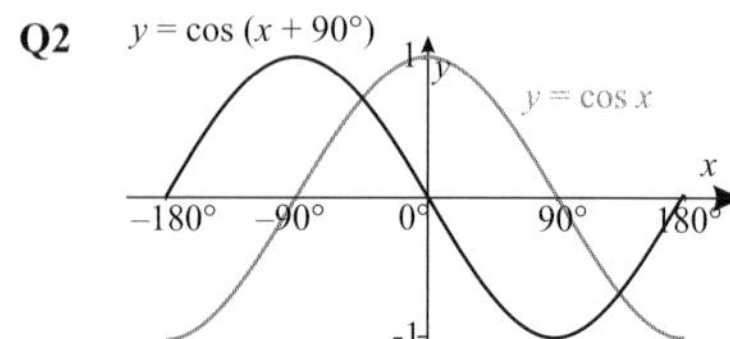

Q3

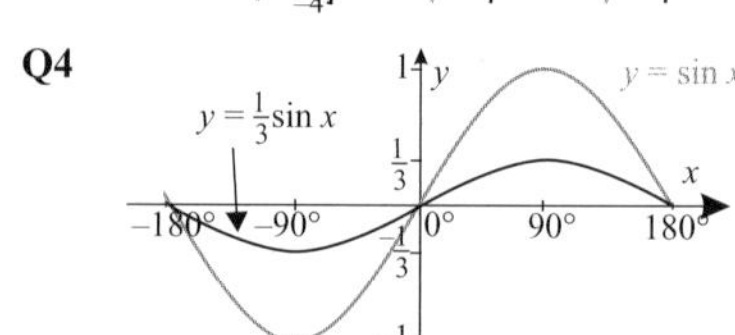

Q4

Q5

Q6

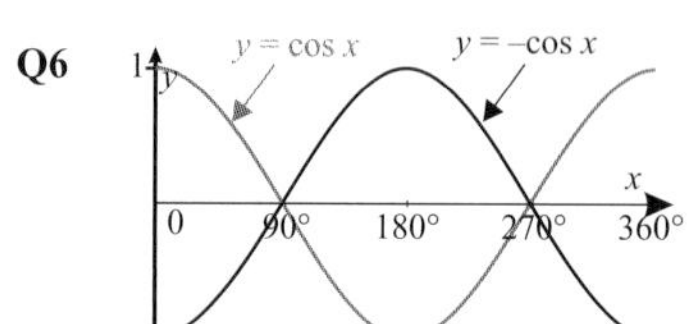

Q7

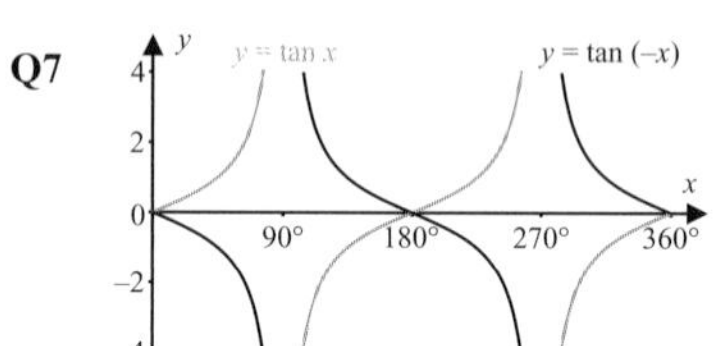

Q8 $y = \sin(x) + 4$

Q9 $y = \cos\frac{x}{5}$

Q10 a) The graph of $y = \tan x$ crosses the x-axis at $x = -180°$, $0°$ and $180°$ in the given interval.

The transformed graph has been stretched by a scale factor of $\frac{1}{2}$ parallel to the x-axis, so it will intersect the x-axis at $x = -90°$, $0°$ and $90°$. The transformed graph will also intersect the x-axis at $x = -180°$ and $180°$ because $\tan 2x$ will repeat every $90°$ rather than $180°$.

[2 marks available — 1 mark for at least three correct points of intersection, 1 mark for all five correct points of intersection and no incorrect answers included]

b) In the given interval, the equations of the asymptotes of $y = \tan x$ are $x = -90°$ and $x = 90°$, so the asymptotes of the transformed graph $y = \tan 2x$ are at $x = -45°$ and $x = 45°$. The transformed graph also has asymptotes of $x = -135°$ and $x = 135°$ because $\tan 2x$ repeats every $90°$.

[2 marks available — 1 mark for at least two correct asymptotes, 1 mark for all four correct asymptotes and no incorrect answers included]

Q11 a)

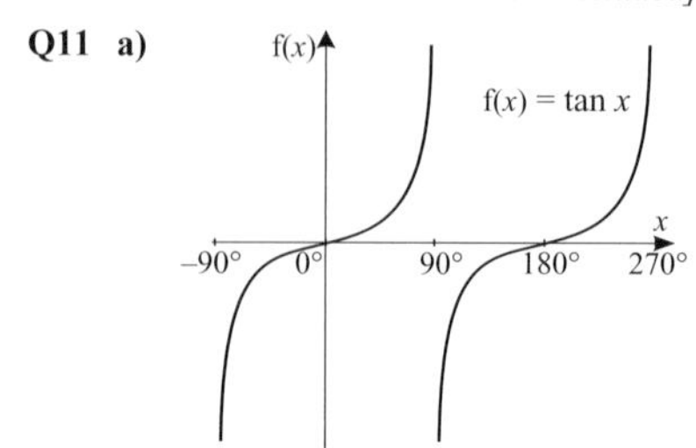

b) 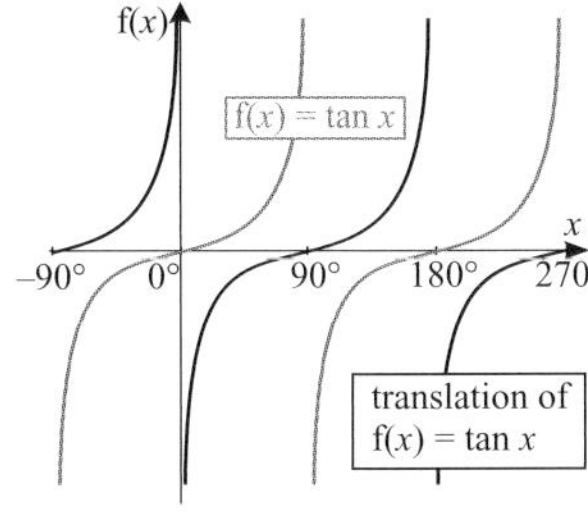

c) $f(x) = \tan (x + 90°)$
Because the graph of tan x repeats every 180°, the transformation could also be f(x) = tan (x – 90°).

Q12 a) 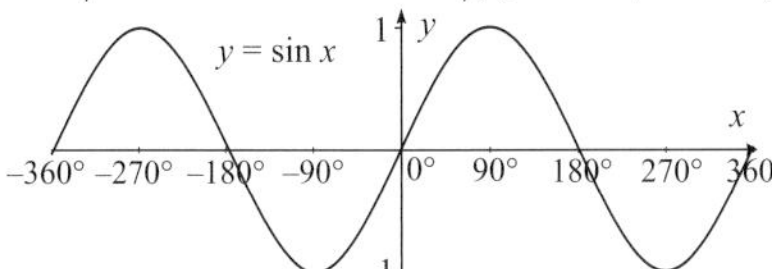

b) 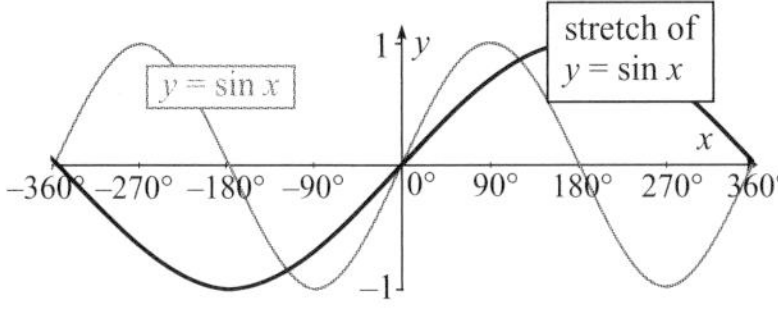

c) $y = \sin \frac{1}{2}x$

Q13 a) The graph has been translated to the left by 90°.

b) $y = \sin (x + 90°)$.

You might have noticed that this graph is exactly the same as the graph of y = cos x.

Q14 a) The graph is stretched vertically by a factor of 2.

b) $y = 2\cos x$

Q15 a) The graph is stretched horizontally by a factor of $\frac{1}{4}$.

b) $y = \tan 4x$

Q16 The graph of $y = \cos x$ crosses the x-axis at $x = 90°$. The transformed graph has the equation $y = \cos px$ (i.e. it's a horizontal stretch), so the graph must have been stretched by a factor of 2. So the equation of the transformed graph is $y = \cos \frac{x}{2}$, i.e. $p = \frac{1}{2}$.
p could be n + $\frac{1}{2}$ for any integer n, but you are asked for the smallest positive value of p.

Q17 a) A maximum of $y = \sin x$ occurs at (90°, 1).
Since (60°, 1) is a maximum of the transformed graph, the graph of sin x may have translated 30° to the left.
An equation for this transformed graph is
$y = \sin (x + 30°)$, i.e. $q = 30°$.

b) $y = \sin x$ is periodic — it repeats itself every 360°.
So q could also be 30° + 360° = 390°,
30° – 360° = –330°,
30° + 720° = 750° etc.

Q18 a) 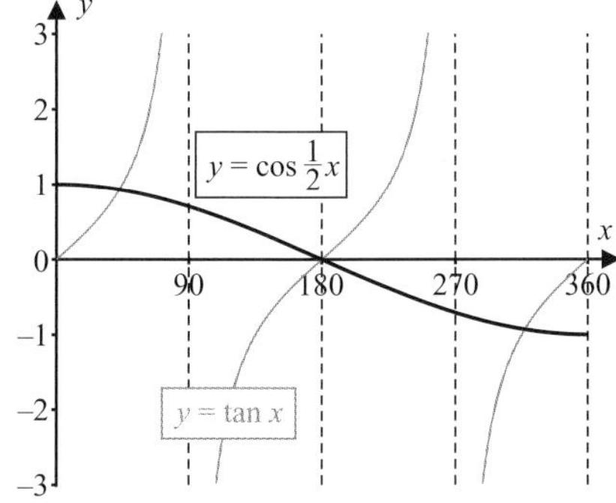

[3 marks available — 1 mark for the correct shape of each graph, 1 mark for indicating axis intercepts and maximum and minimum values of cos $\frac{1}{2}x$]

b) The number of solutions is equal to the number of intersections of the graphs of $y = \tan x$ and $y = \cos\left(\frac{1}{2}x\right)$.
There are a total of three intersections in the given range, so there are three solutions to the equation in the range.
[1 mark for the correct number of solutions]

Q19 a) (i) $a = -5$

(ii) Since $a < 0$ the minimum points of $y = a \sin bx$ correspond to maximum points of $y = \sin x$.
Considering increasing positive values of x, the point with coordinates (150°, –5) is the second minimum point of $y = a \sin bx$ and so it corresponds to the second maximum point of $y = \sin x$. The second maximum point of $y = \sin x$ occurs at $x = 450°$, so $150b = 450$, giving $b = 3$.

b) The transformations are a stretch of scale factor 5 in the y-direction followed by a reflection in the x-axis (or just a stretch of scale factor –5), and a stretch of scale factor $\frac{1}{3}$ in the x-direction.

c) 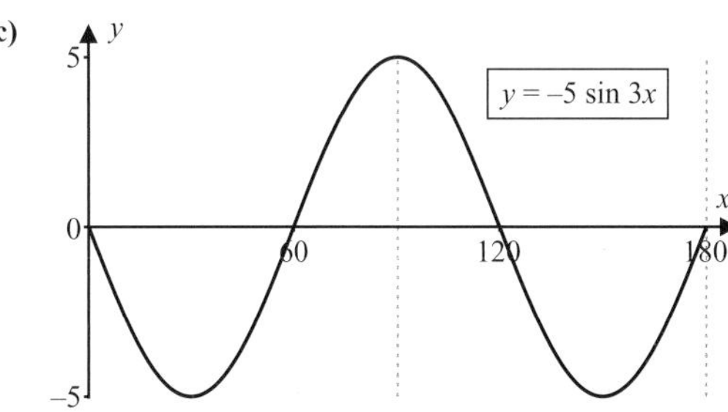

Exercise 8.8 — Solving Trig Equations by Sketching a Graph

Q1 a) 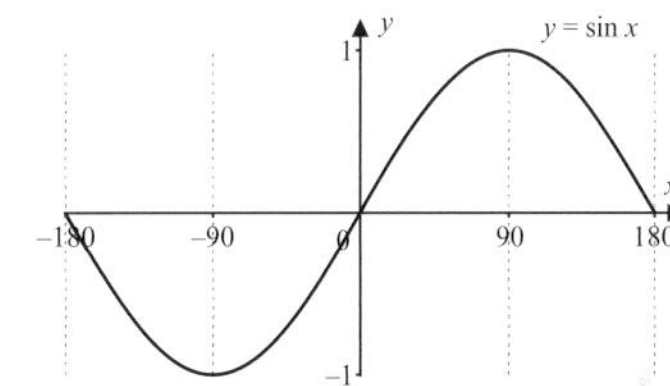

b) $\sin 45° = \frac{1}{\sqrt{2}}$ and $\sin 60° = \frac{\sqrt{3}}{2}$.

c) (i) 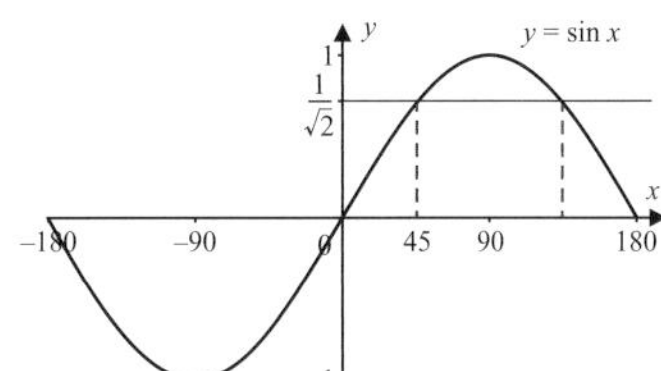

From part b), $x = 45°$ is one solution.
Using the symmetry of the graph, there is a second solution at $x = 180° – 45° = 135°$.

(ii) 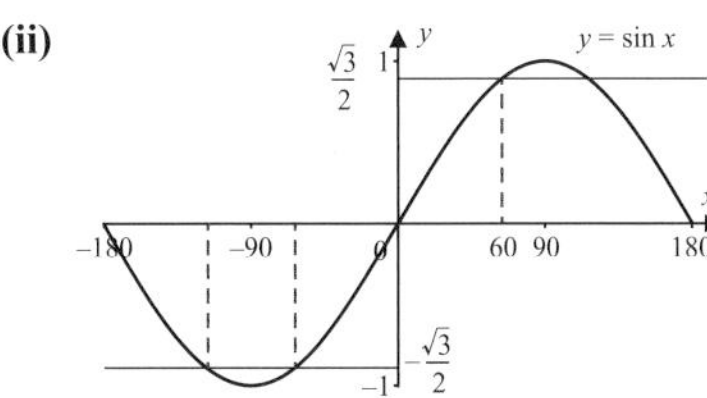

Using part b) and the symmetry of the graph, there are two solutions: $x = -60°$ and $x = -180° + 60° = -120°$.

Q2 a) Find the first solution using a calculator:
$\sin x = 0.75 \Rightarrow x = 48.6°$ (1 d.p.).
Then sketch a graph:

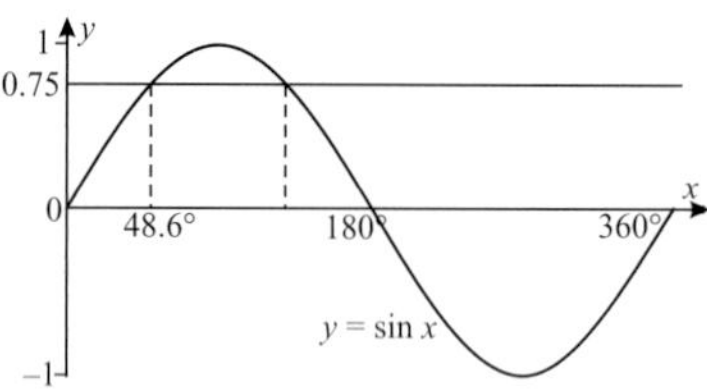

You can see from the graph that there are 2 solutions in the given interval. Using the symmetry of the graph, if one solution is at 48.6°, the other will be at $180° - 48.6° = 131.4°$ (1 d.p.).

b) Find the first solution: $\cos x = 0.31 \Rightarrow x = 71.9°$ (1 d.p.).
Then sketch a graph:

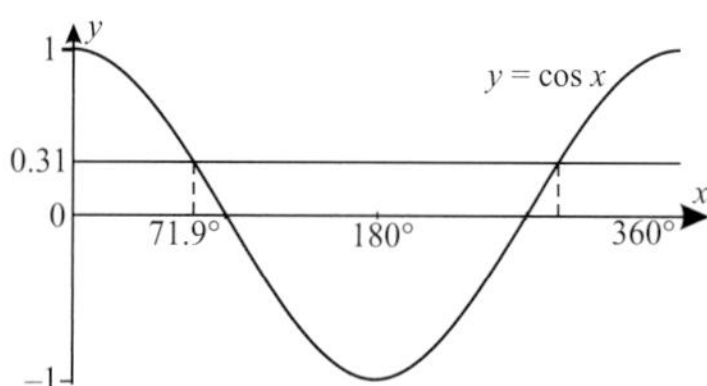

Using the symmetry of the graph to find the second solution: if one solution is at 71.9°, the other will be at $360° - 71.9° = 288.1°$ (1 d.p.).

c) Find the first solution: $\tan x = -1.5 \Rightarrow x = -56.3°$ (1 d.p.).
This is outside the given interval, so add on 180° to find the first solution: $-56.3° + 180° = 123.7°$ (1 d.p.).
Then sketch a graph:

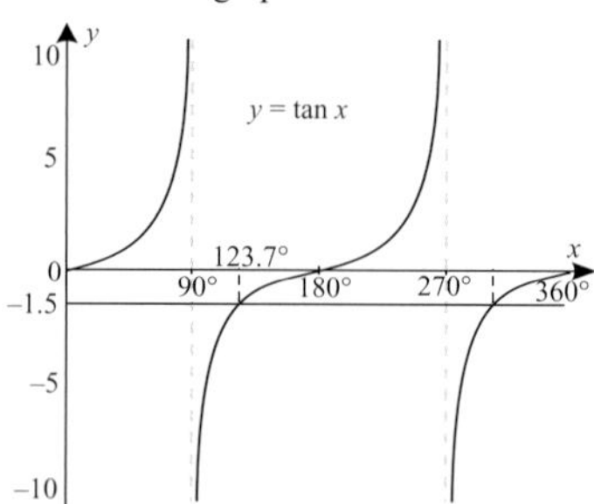

You can see from the graph that the next solution will be at $180° + 123.7° = 303.7°$ (1 d.p.) as $\tan x$ repeats every 180°.

d) Find the first solution: $\sin x = -0.42 \Rightarrow x = -24.8°$ (1 d.p.). This is outside the given interval, so add on 360° to find one solution: $-24.8° + 360°$ $= 335.2°$ (1 d.p.). Then sketch a graph:

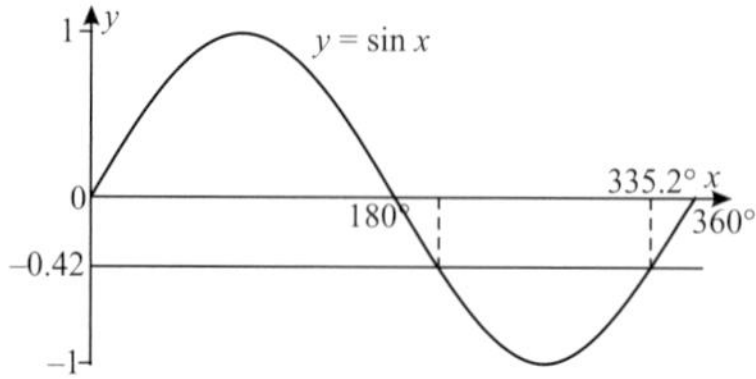

Using the symmetry of the graph, the solution you know is $360° - 335.2° = 24.8°$ away from 360°, so the other solution will be 24.8° away from 180°, i.e. at $180° + 24.8° = 204.8°$ (1 d.p.).

e) Find the first solution: $\cos x = -0.56 \Rightarrow x = 124.1°$ (1 d.p.).
Then sketch a graph:

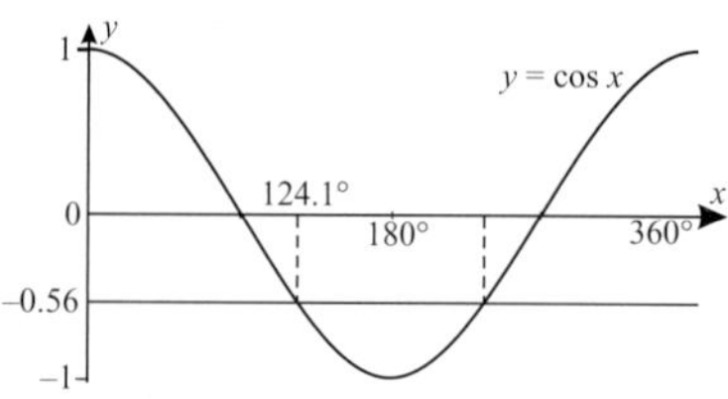

Using the symmetry of the graph to find the second solution: if one solution is at 124.1°, the other will be at $360° - 124.1° = 235.9°$ (1 d.p.).

f) Find the first solution: $\tan x = -0.67 \Rightarrow x = -33.8°$ (1 d.p.). This is outside the interval, so add 180° to find the first solution: $-33.8° + 180° = 146.2°$ (1 d.p.). Then sketch a graph:

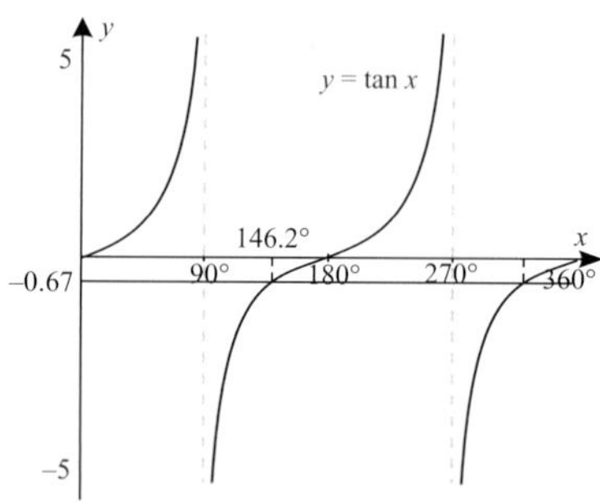

The next solution is at $180° + 146.2° = 326.2°$ (1 d.p.) as $\tan x$ repeats every 180°.

g) Find the first solution: $\sin x = 0.32 \Rightarrow x = 18.7°$ (1 d.p.).
Then sketch a graph:

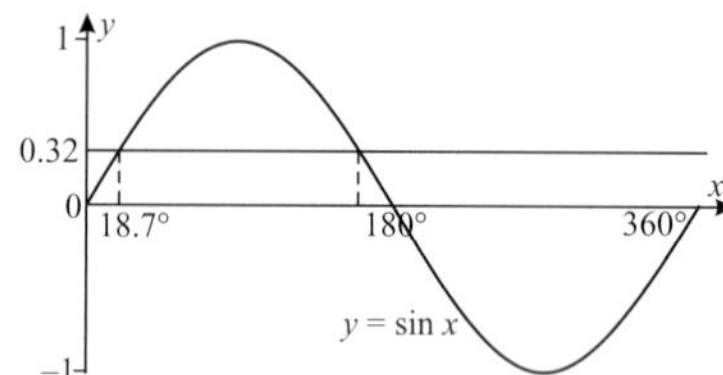

Using the symmetry of the graph, the other solution is $180° - 18.7° = 161.3°$ (1 d.p.).

h) Find the first solution: $\cos x = -0.89 \Rightarrow x = 152.9°$ (1 d.p.).
Then sketch a graph:

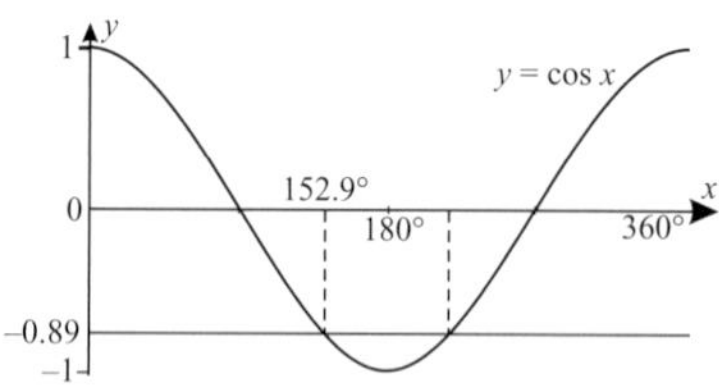

Using the symmetry of the graph, the other solution is $360° - 152.9° = 207.1°$ (1 d.p.).

i) Find the first solution: $\tan x = 2.3 \Rightarrow x = 66.5°$ (1 d.p.).
Then sketch a graph:

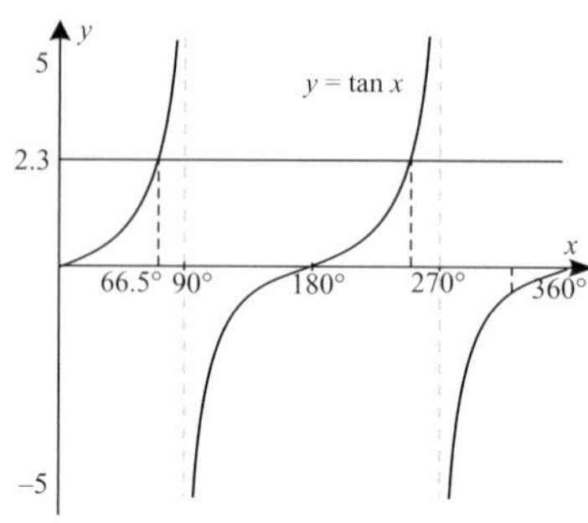

The next solution is at $180° + 66.5° = 246.5°$ (1 d.p.) as $\tan x$ repeats every 180°.

Q3 **a)** Using your knowledge of common angles, the first solution is at $x = 45°$. Then sketch a graph:

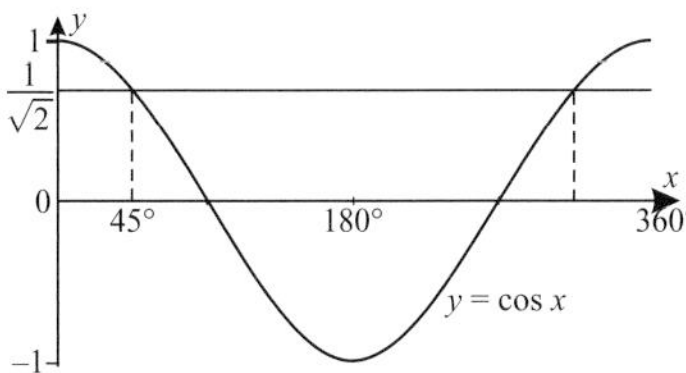

Using the symmetry of the graph, the second solution is at $360° – 45° = 315°$.

b) Using common angles, the first solution is at $x = 60°$. Then sketch a graph:

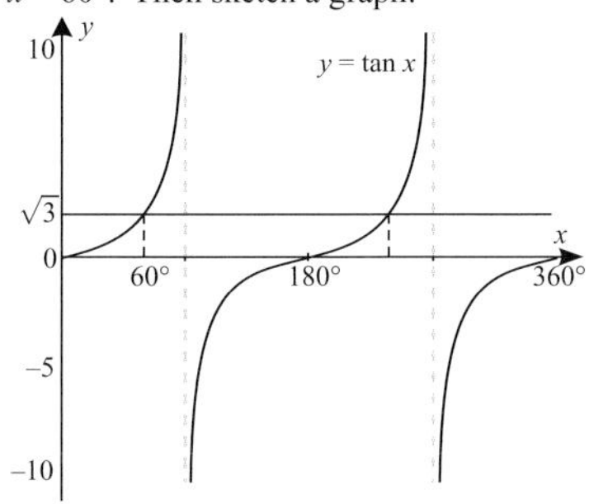

By the symmetry of the graph, the second solution is at $180° + 60° = 240°$.

c) Using common angles, the first solution is at $x = 30°$. Then sketch a graph:

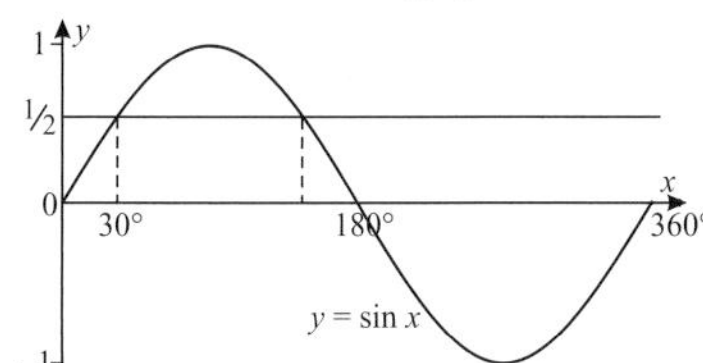

By the symmetry of the graph, the second solution is at $180° – 30° = 150°$.

d) Using common angles, the first solution is at $x = 30°$. Then sketch a graph:

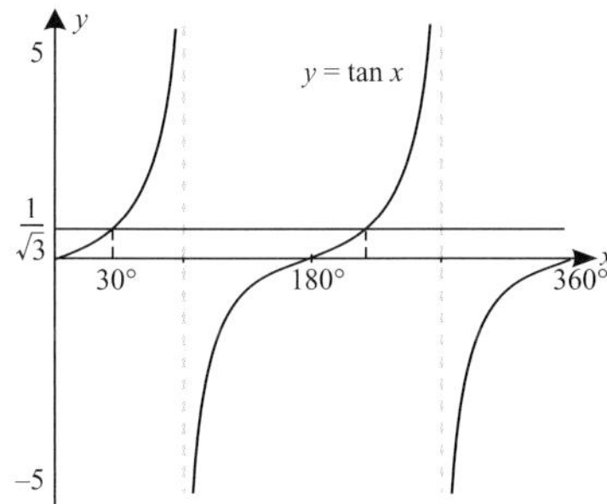

By the symmetry of the graph, the second solution is at $180° + 30° = 210°$.

e) Using common angles, the first solution is at $x = 45°$. Then sketch a graph:

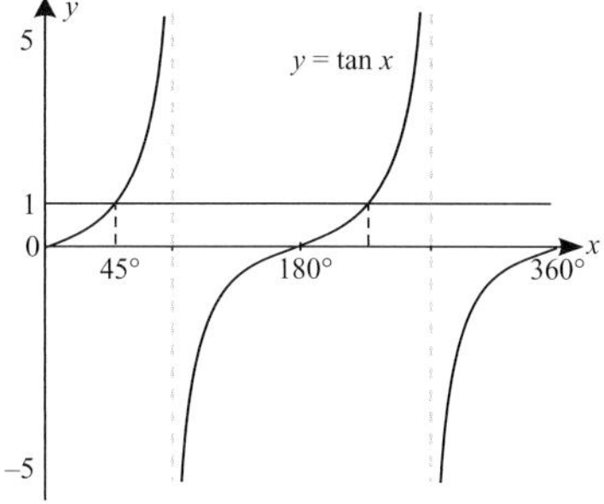

By the symmetry of the graph, the second solution is at $180° + 45° = 225°$.

f) Using your knowledge of common angles, the first solution is at $x = 30°$. Then sketch a graph:

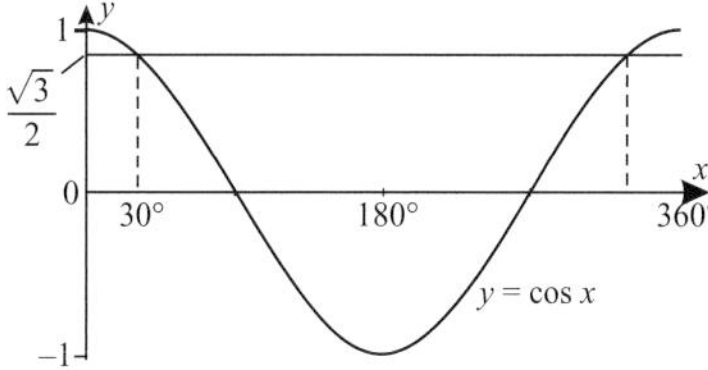

Using the symmetry of the graph, the second solution is at $360° – 30° = 330°$.

Q4 You're told that there is a solution at 44.43°. From the graph you can see that there is another solution in the given interval at $180° – 44.43° = 135.57°$ (2 d.p.).

Q5 You're told that there is a solution at 143.1°, and from the graph you can see that there is another solution in the given interval. The first solution is $180° – 143.1° = 36.9°$ away from 180°, so the other solution will be at $180° + 36.9° = 216.9°$ (1 d.p.).
You could have worked this one out by doing 360° – 143.1°.

Q6 You're told that there is a solution at 62.2° (3 s.f.). From the graph you can see that there are two other solutions in the given interval. The solutions are:
$180° + 62.2° = 242°$ (3 s.f.)
$360° + 62.2° = 422°$ (3 s.f.)

Q7 Find the first solution: $\tan x = 2.5 \Rightarrow x = 68.2°$ (1 d.p.). Then sketch a graph — this time the interval is bigger, so you'll need more repetitions of the tan shape:

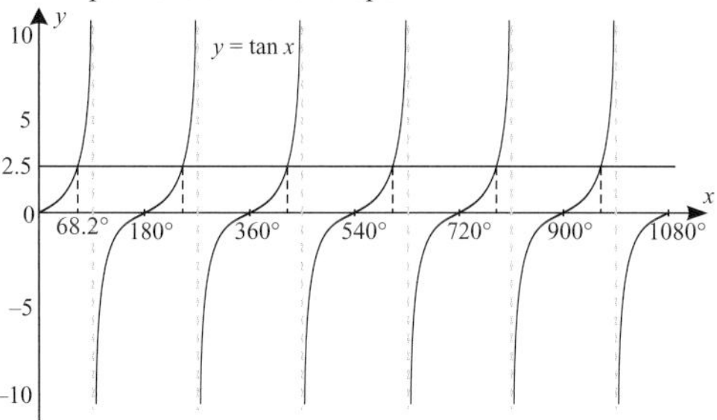

You can see from the graph that there are 6 solutions in the given interval — so just keep adding lots of 180° onto the first solution: $x = 68.2°, 248.2°, 428.2°, 608.2°, 788.2°, 968.2°$ (all to 1 d.p.).
You don't have to draw out the whole graph — sketch the first part to find the first solution, then keep adding on lots of 180° until the solutions are bigger than 1080°.

Q8 Find the first solution: $\sin x = 0.81 \Rightarrow x = 54.1°$ (3 s.f.).
Then sketch a graph for the interval $-360° \leq x \leq 360°$:

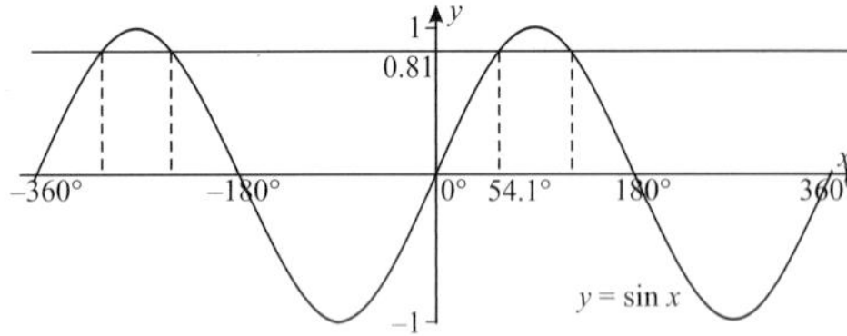

You can see from the graph that there are 4 solutions.
Using the symmetry of the graph, there's another solution at $180° - 54.1° = 126°$ (3 s.f.). To find the other 2 solutions, subtract 360° from the values you've just found:
$54.1° - 360° = -306°$ (3 s.f.) and $126° - 360° = -234°$ (3 s.f.).

Q9 Find the first solution: $\sin x = 0.23 \Rightarrow x = 13.3°$ (1 d.p.).
Then sketch a graph for the interval $-360° \leq x \leq 540°$:

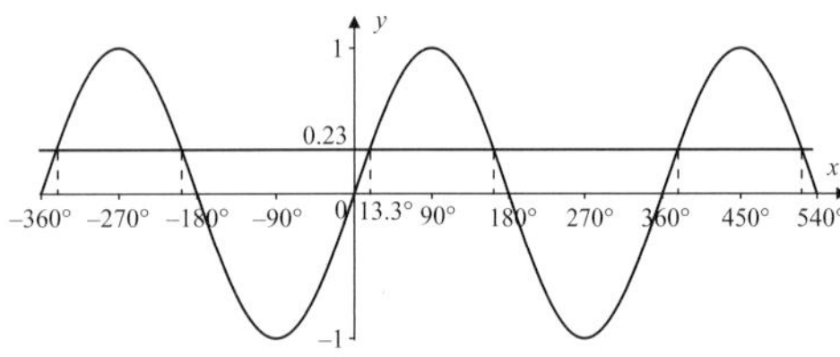

From the graph, there are 6 solutions in the interval.
Using the symmetry of the graph, there's another solution at $180° - 13.3° = 166.7°$ (1 d.p.). To find the other solutions, add or subtract 360° to the values you've just found:
$13.3° + 360° = 373.3°$ (1 d.p.)
$166.7° + 360° = 526.7°$ (1 d.p.)
$13.3° - 360° = -346.7°$ (1 d.p.)
$166.7° - 360° = -193.3°$ (1 d.p.)
So the solutions are:
$x = -346.7°, -193.3°, 13.3°, 166.7°, 373.3°$ and $526.7°$

Q10 The first solution: $\cos x = -0.96 \Rightarrow x = 164°$ (3 s.f.).
Then sketch a graph for the interval $-360° \leq x \leq 720°$:

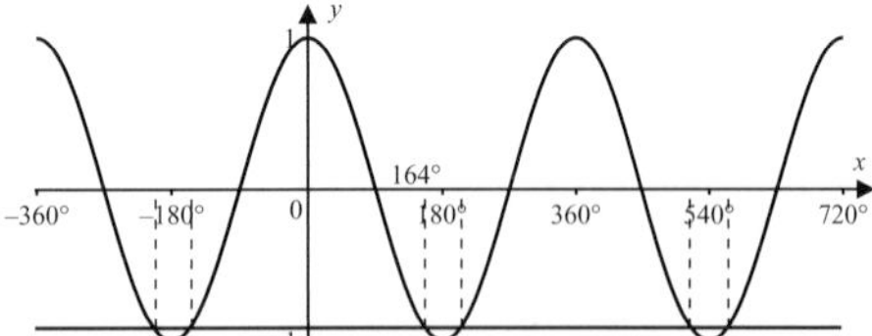

You can see from the graph that there are 6 solutions.
Using the symmetry of the graph, the other five are:
$-360° + 164° = -196°$ (3 s.f.)
$0° - 164° = -164°$ (3 s.f.)
$360° - 164° = 196°$ (3 s.f.)
$360° + 164° = 524°$ (3 s.f.)
$720° - 164° = 556°$ (3 s.f.)
So the solutions are:
$x = -196°, -164°, 164°, 196°, 524°, 556°$ (3 s.f.)

Q11 Find the first solution: $\tan x = -1.75 \Rightarrow x = -60.3°$ (1 d.p.).
Then sketch a graph for the interval $-360° \leq x \leq 720°$:

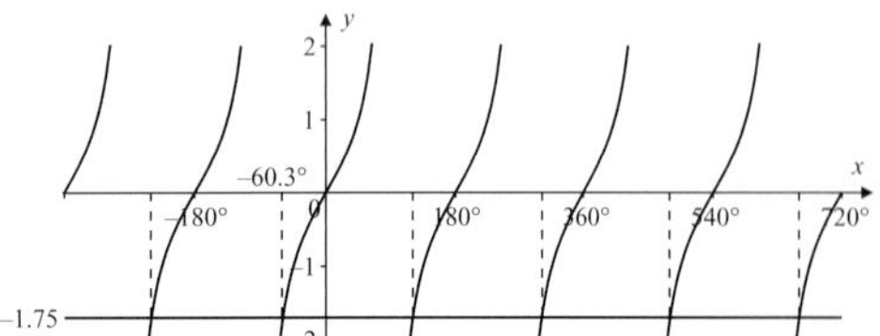

You can see from the graph that there are 6 solutions.
Using the symmetry of the graph, the other five can be found by adding or subtracting 180°.
$-60.3° - 180° = -240.3°$ (1 d.p.)
$-60.3° + 180° = 119.7°$ (1 d.p.)
$119.7° + 180° = 299.7°$ (1 d.p.)
$299.7° + 180° = 479.7°$ (1 d.p.)
$479.7° + 180° = 659.7°$ (1 d.p.)
So the solutions are:
$x = -240.3°, -60.3°, 119.7°, 299.7°, 479.7°$ and $659.7°$ (1 d.p.)

Q12 Rearrange the equation:
$5 \sin x = 3 \cos x \Rightarrow \frac{\sin x}{\cos x} = \frac{3}{5} \Rightarrow \tan x = \frac{3}{5}$,
then find the first solution: $x = 30.96...° = 31.0°$ (3 s.f.)
Then sketch a graph for the interval $0° \leq x \leq 360°$:

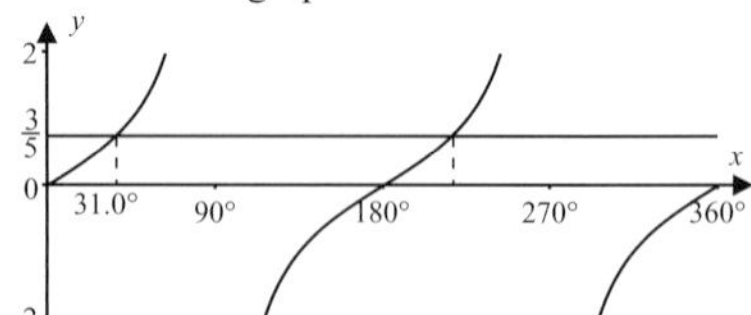

You can see from the graph that there are 2 solutions.
Using the symmetry of the graph, the other solution is:
$180° + 30.96...° = 210.96...° = 211°$ (3 s.f.)

Q13 Rearrange the equation:
$3 \cos x = -8 \sin x \Rightarrow \frac{\sin x}{\cos x} = -\frac{3}{8} \Rightarrow \tan x = -\frac{3}{8}$,
then find the first solution: $x = -20.556...° = -20.56°$ (2 d.p.).
This is outside the interval so add 180° to get $x = 159.44°$ (2 d.p.).
Then sketch a graph for the interval $0° \leq x \leq 360°$:

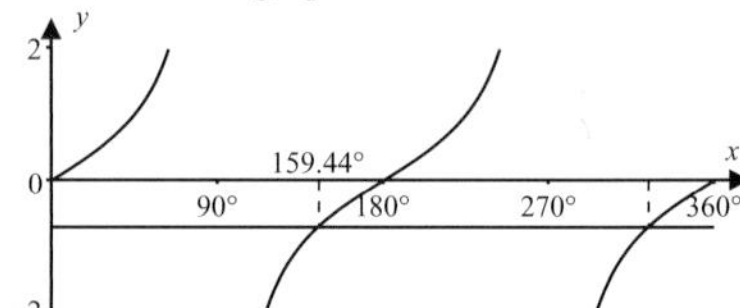

You can see from the graph that there are 2 solutions.
Using the symmetry of the graph, the other solution is:
$180° + 159.44° = 339.44°$ (2 d.p.)

Q14 a)

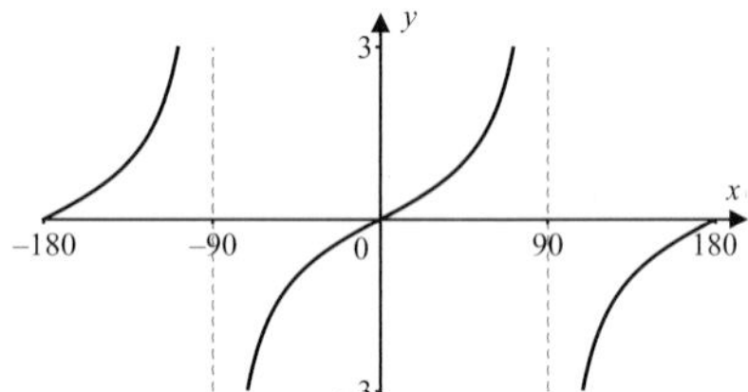

[2 marks available — 1 mark for the correct shape in the correct range, 1 mark for axis intercepts and asymptotes indicated]

b) Rearrange the equation:
$4 \cos x = 7 \sin x \Rightarrow \tan x = \frac{4}{7}$,
then find the first solution: $x = 29.7°$ (1 d.p.)
Mark this on the graph from part a):

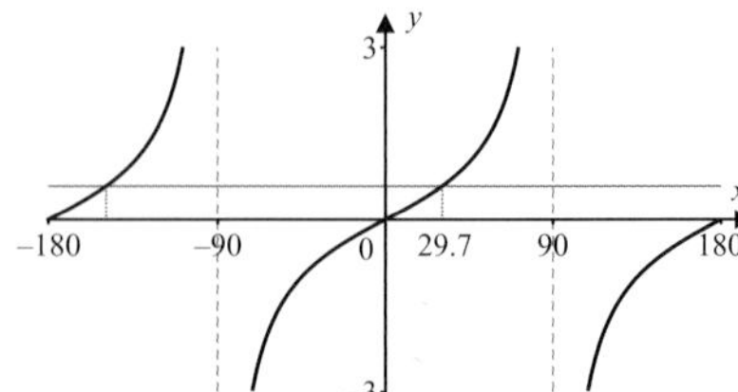

You can see from the graph that there are two solutions.
Using the symmetry of the graph, the other solution is:
$x = 29.7° - 180° = -150.3°$ (1 d.p.).
[3 marks available — 1 mark for forming an equation involving tan x, 1 mark for both correct solutions, 1 mark for indicating both solutions on the diagram]

Q15 a)

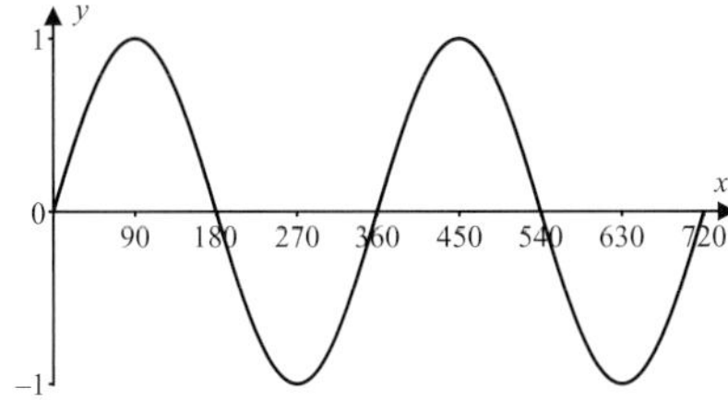

[2 marks available — 1 mark for the correct shape in the correct range, 1 mark for the axis intercepts, and maximum and minimum values indicated]

b) Rearrange the equation:
$5 \sin x - 3 = 0 \Rightarrow \sin x = \frac{3}{5}$,
then find the first solution: $x = 36.869... = 36.9°$ (1 d.p.)
Mark this on the graph from part a):

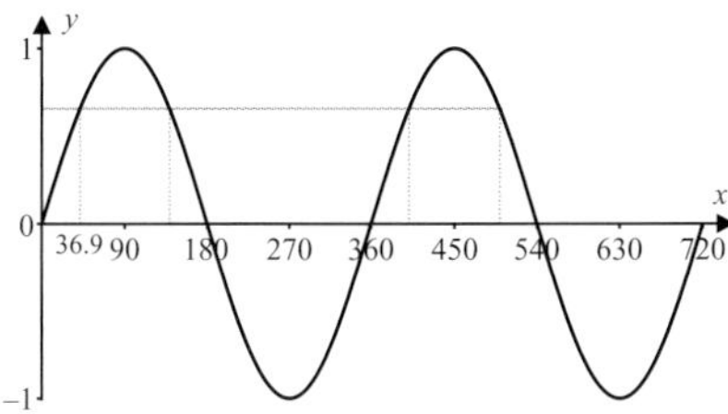

You can see from the graph that there are four solutions.
Using the symmetry of the graph, the other solutions are:
$x = 180° - 36.869...° = 143.1°$ (1 d.p.)
$x = 360° + 36.869...° = 396.9°$ (1 d.p.)
$x = 540° - 36.869...° = 503.1°$ (1 d.p.)
[3 marks available — 1 mark for rearranging the equation, 1 mark for any one correct solution, 1 mark for all four correct solutions]

c) Rearrange the equation: $15 \sin x = k \Rightarrow \sin x = \frac{k}{15}$
Equate the constant terms: $\frac{k}{15} = \frac{3}{5} \Rightarrow k = 9$
[1 mark for the correct answer]

Q16 a)

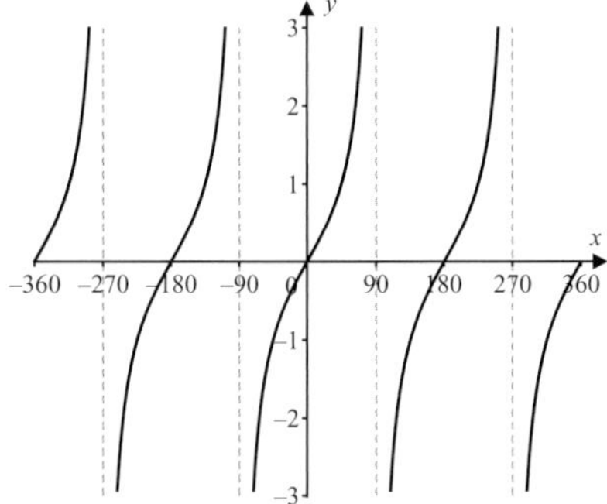

[2 marks available — 1 mark for correct shape in correct range, 1 mark for axis intercepts and asymptotes indicated]

b) Rearrange the equation: $2(\tan x - \sqrt{3}) = 3 - \sqrt{3} \tan x$
$\Rightarrow \tan x = \frac{3 + 2\sqrt{3}}{2 + \sqrt{3}} = \frac{\sqrt{3}(\sqrt{3} + 2)}{\sqrt{3} + 2} \Rightarrow \tan x = \sqrt{3}$,
then find the first solution: $x = \tan^{-1}(\sqrt{3}) = 60°$
Mark this on the graph from part a):

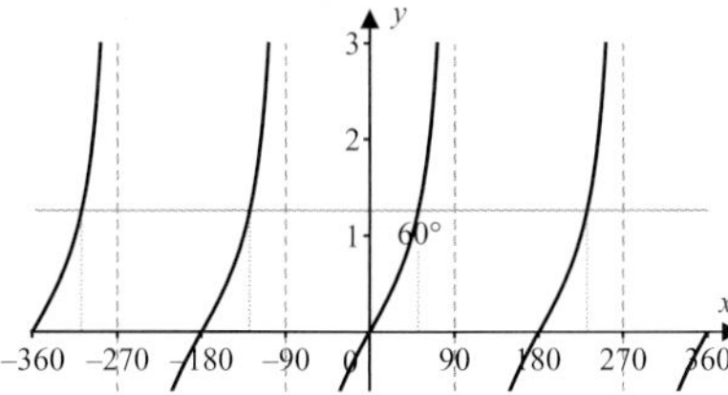

You can see from the graph that there are four solutions.

Using the symmetry of the graph, the other solutions are:
$x = 60° - 360° = -300°$
$x = 60° - 180° = -120°$
$x = 60° + 180° = 240°$
[4 marks available — 1 mark for using $\tan x = \sqrt{3}$ *, 1 mark for any one correct solution, 1 mark for all four correct solutions, 1 mark for solutions clearly indicated on diagram]*

Q17 a) $2 \sin x - 5 \cos y = \frac{1}{4}$ ①
$\sin x - \cos y = -\frac{1}{4}$ ②
$2 \times$ ② $-$ ① $\quad 3 \cos y = -\frac{3}{4} \Rightarrow \cos y = -\frac{1}{4}$ ③
Sub ③ in ② $\quad \sin x + \frac{1}{4} = -\frac{1}{4} \Rightarrow \sin x = -\frac{1}{2}$
[3 marks available — 1 mark for a correct method of solving simultaneous equations, 1 mark for showing the correct value of cos y, 1 mark for showing the correct value of sin y]

b) First solution of $\cos y = -\frac{1}{4}$ is $y = 104.5°$ (1 d.p.).
Then sketch a graph:

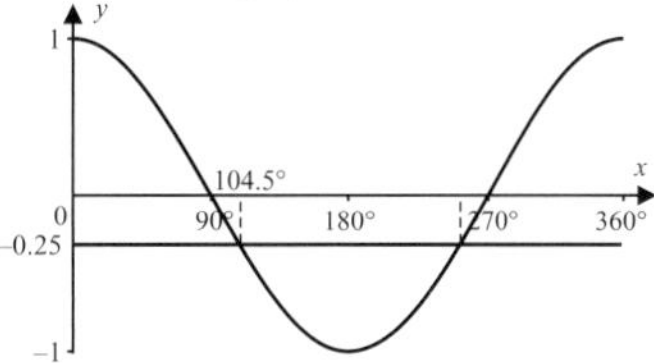

You can see from the graph that there are two solutions.
Using the symmetry of the graph, the other solution is
$y = 360° - 104.5° = 255.5°$
First solution of $\sin x = -\frac{1}{2}$ is $x = -30°$.
Then sketch a graph:

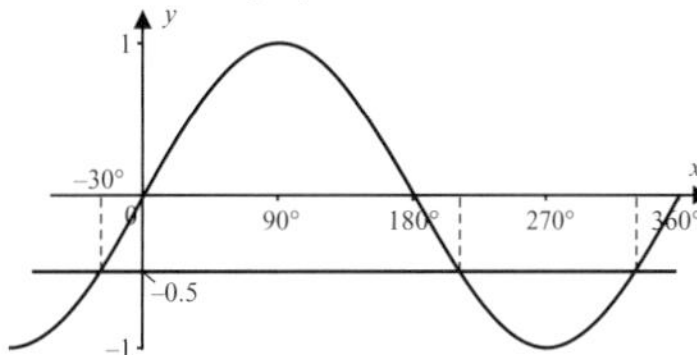

You can see from the graph that there are two solutions.
Using the symmetry of the graph, the solutions are
$x = 180° + 30° = 210°$, and
$x = 360° - 30° = 330°$
Therefore, the solution pairs are (210°, 104.5°), (210°, 255.5°), (330°, 104.5°) and (330°, 255.5°).
[3 marks available — 1 mark for both correct solutions to $\cos y = -\frac{1}{4}$*, 1 mark for both correct solutions to* $\sin x = -\frac{1}{2}$*, 1 mark for all four correct pairs of solutions]*

Exercise 8.9 — Solving Trig Equations Using a CAST Diagram

Q1 0.45 is positive, so look at the quadrants where sin x is positive:

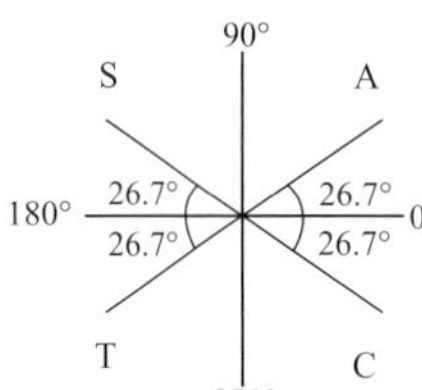

The second quadrant is the other one, so the only other solution is $180° - 26.7° = 153.3°$.

Q2 0.68 is positive, so look at the quadrants where cos x is positive:

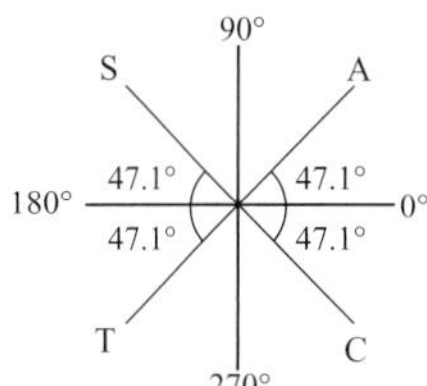

Cos is also positive in the fourth quadrant, so the other solution is $360° - 47.2° = 312.8°$.

Q3 **a)** Use a calculator to find the first solution:
$\cos x = 0.8 \Rightarrow x = 36.9°$ (1 d.p.). 0.8 is positive, so look at the quadrants where cos is positive:

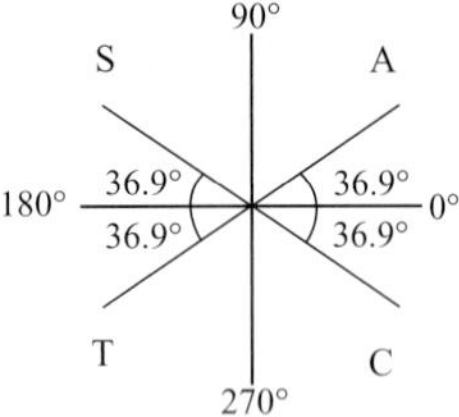

Cos is positive in the 4th quadrant, so the other solution is at 360° – 36.9° = 323.1° (1 d.p.).

b) Use a calculator to find the first solution:
$\tan x = 2.7 \Rightarrow x = 69.7°$ (1 d.p.). 2.7 is positive, so look at the other quadrants where tan is positive:

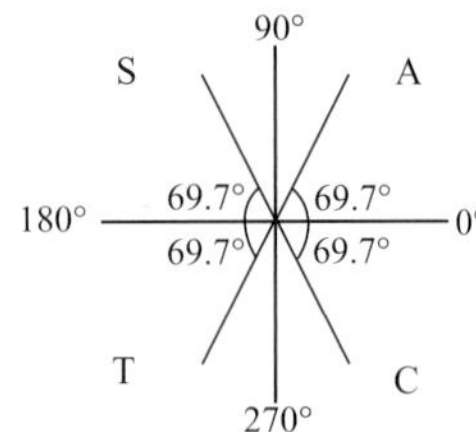

Tan is positive in the 3rd quadrant, so the other solution is at 180° + 69.7° = 249.7° (1 d.p.).

c) Use a calculator to find the first solution:
$\sin x = -0.15 \Rightarrow x = -8.6°$ (1 d.p.). –0.15 is negative, so look at the quadrants where sin is negative:

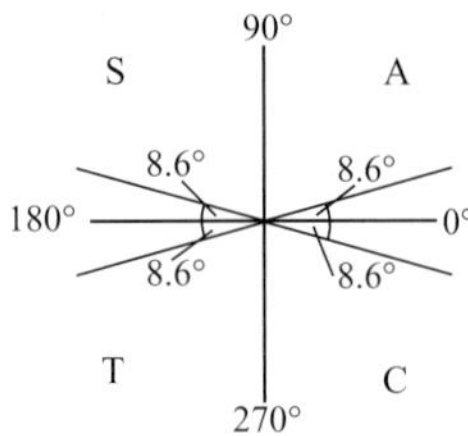

Sin is negative in the 3rd and 4th quadrants, so the solutions are at 180° + 8.6° = 188.6° and 360° – 8.6° = 351.4° (both to 1 d.p.).

d) Use a calculator to find the first solution:
$\tan x = 0.3 \Rightarrow x = 16.7°$ (1 d.p.). 0.3 is positive, so look at the other quadrants where tan is positive:

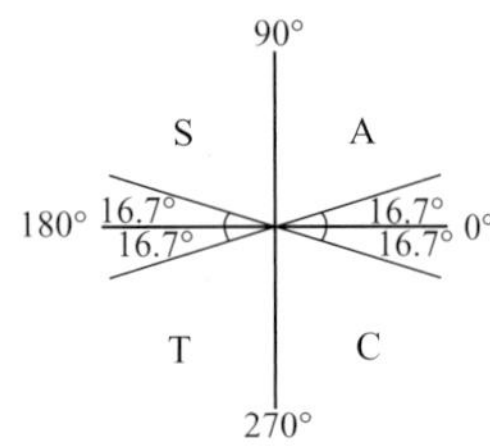

Tan is positive in the 3rd quadrant, so the other solution is at 180° + 16.7° = 196.7° (1 d.p.).

e) Use a calculator to find the first solution:
$\tan x = -0.6 \Rightarrow x = -31.0°$ (1 d.p.). –0.6 is negative, so look at the quadrants where tan is negative:

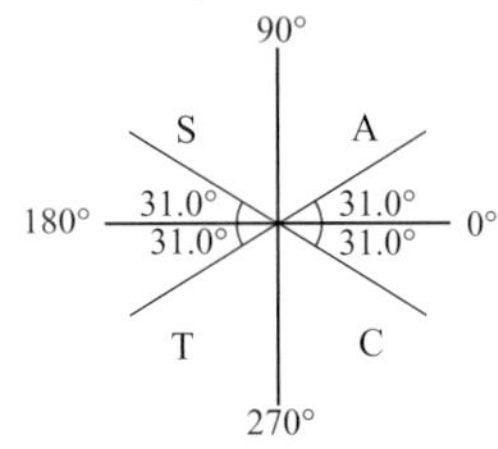

Tan is negative in the 2nd and 4th quadrants. So the solutions are at 180° – 31.0° = 149.0° and 360° – 31.0° = 329.0° (both to 1 d.p.).

f) Use a calculator to find the first solution:
$\sin x = -0.29 \Rightarrow x = -16.9°$ (1 d.p.).
–0.29 is negative, so look at the quadrants where sin is negative:

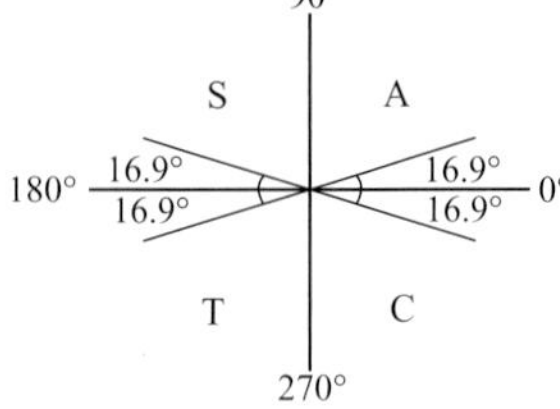

Sin is negative in the 3rd and 4th quadrants, so the solutions are at 180° + 16.9° = 196.9° and 360° – 16.9° = 343.1° (both to 1 d.p.).

Q4 –0.87 is negative, so look at the quadrants where sin x is negative:

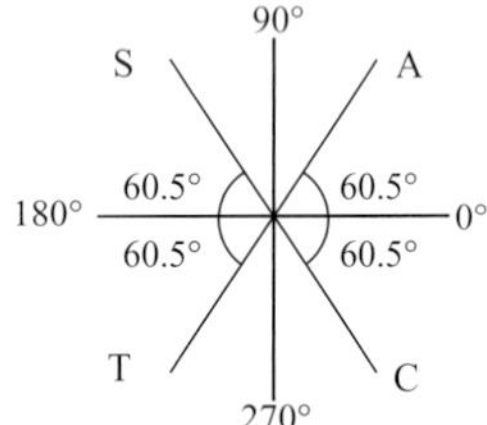

Sin is negative in the third and fourth quadrants, so the first two solutions are 180° + 60.5° = 240.5° (1 d.p.), and 360° – 60.5° = 299.5° (1 d.p.). To find the other solutions in the interval, subtract 360° from the solutions already found:
240.5° – 360° = –119.5° (1 d.p.) and
299.5° – 360° = –60.5° (1 d.p.)
So the solutions are: x = –119.5°, –60.5°, 240.5°, 299.5° (1 d.p.)
You could have found the negative solutions more directly by reading the CAST diagram in the negative (i.e. clockwise) direction. Reading clockwise from 0°, the angle in the 3rd quadrant is –119.5°.

Q5 **a)** The first solution is $x = -83.2°$ (3 s.f.).

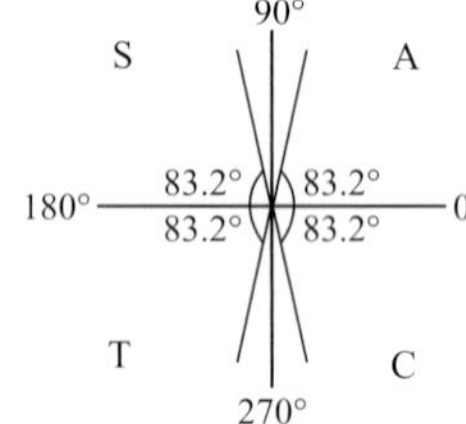

Tan is negative in the 2nd and 4th quadrants, so the solutions are at 180° – 83.2° = 96.8° and 360° – 83.2° = 277° (both to 3 s.f.).

b) The first solution is $x = 55.1°$ (3 s.f.).

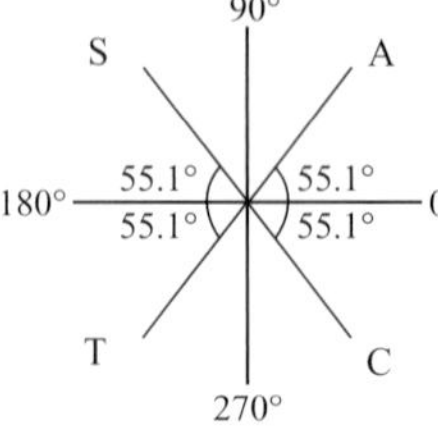

Sin is positive in the second quadrant, so the next solution is 180° – 55.1° = 125° (3 s.f.). To find the other solutions in the given interval, add on 360° to the solutions already found:
55.1° + 360° = 415° (3 s.f.) and 125° + 360° = 485° (3 s.f.).

c) The first solution is $x = 43.9°$ (3 s.f.).

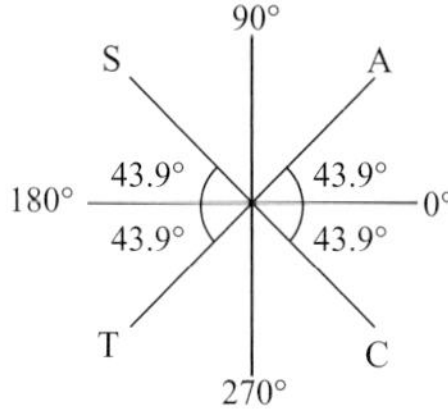

Cos is positive in the fourth quadrant, so the next solution is $360° - 43.9° = 316°$ (3 s.f.). To find the other solution in the interval, add on 360° to the solutions already found: $43.9° + 360° = 404°$ (3 s.f.).

d) The first solution is $x = 74.4°$ (3 s.f.).

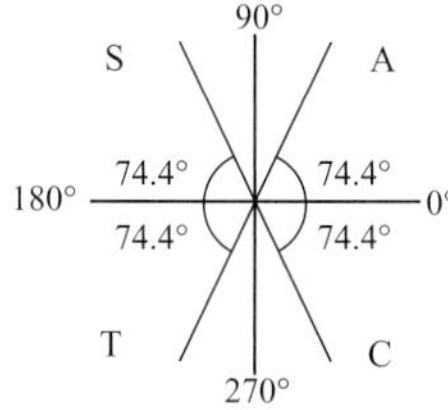

Tan is positive in the third quadrant, so the next solution is $180° + 74.4° = 254°$ (3 s.f.). This is outside the interval, so subtract 360°: $x = -106°$ (3 s.f.).

Q6 The first solution is $x = -3.4°$ (1 d.p.) — note that this is outside the given interval.

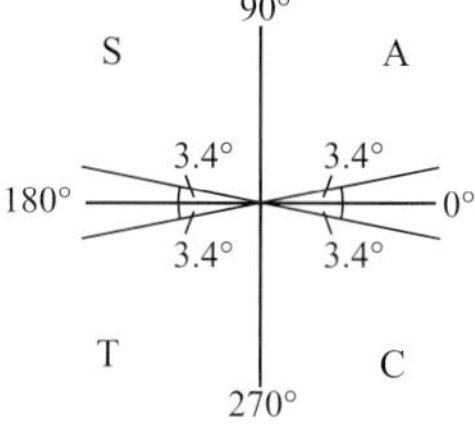

Using a CAST diagram, the solutions of $\sin x$ are negative in the third and fourth quadrants. So the first two solutions are $180° + 3.4° = 183.4°$ (1 d.p.) and $360° - 3.4° = 356.6°$ (1 d.p.). To find the other solutions in the given interval, keep adding 360° to the solutions already found:
$183.4° + 360° = 543.4°$ (1 d.p.)
$356.6° + 360° = 716.6°$ (1 d.p.)
$543.4° + 360° = 903.4°$ (1 d.p.)
$716.6° + 360° = 1076.6°$ (1 d.p.)
So the solutions are:
$x = 183.4°, 356.6°, 543.4°, 716.6°, 903.4°, 1076.6°$ (1 d.p.)

Q7 The first solution is $x = 85.2°$ (1 d.p.).

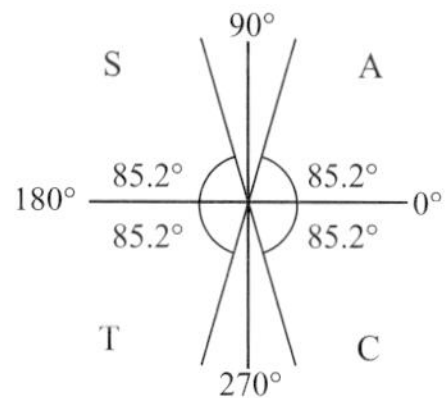

Using a CAST diagram, the solutions of $\tan x$ are also positive in the 3rd quadrant. So the next solution is $180° + 85.2 = 265.2°$. To find the other solutions in the given interval, subtract 360° from the solutions already found: $85.2° - 360° = -274.8°$ (1 d.p.) and $288.1° - 360° = -94.8°$ (1 d.p.)

Q8 Rearrange the equation:
$5 \cos x - 2 = 0 \Rightarrow 5 \cos x = 2$
$\Rightarrow \cos x = \frac{2}{5}$
So the first solution is:
$x = \cos^{-1}\left(\frac{2}{5}\right) = 66.4°$ (1 d.p.)

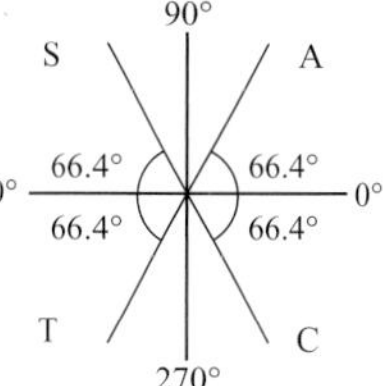

Cos is positive in the fourth quadrant, so the other solution is $360° - 66.4° = 293.6°$ (1 d.p.).

Q9 Rearrange the equation:
$\frac{1}{4} \tan x = 1.4 \Rightarrow \tan x = 5.6$
So the first solution is:
$x = \tan^{-1}(5.6) = 79.9°$ (3 s.f.).

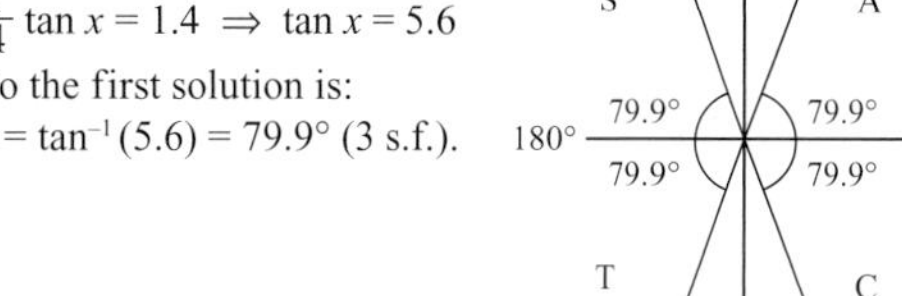

Tan is positive in the third quadrant, so the next solution is $180° + 79.9° = 260°$ (3 s.f.).

Q10 a) Rearrange the equation:
$4 \sin x - 3 = 0 \Rightarrow 4 \sin x = 3 \Rightarrow \sin x = \frac{3}{4}$
The first solution is:
$x = \sin^{-1}\left(\frac{3}{4}\right) = 48.6°$ (1 d.p.)

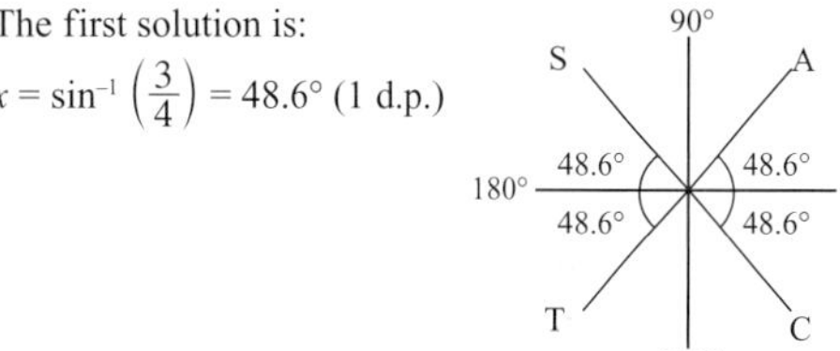

Sin is positive in the second quadrant, so the next solution is $180° - 48.6° = 131.4°$ (1 d.p.). To find the other solutions in the interval, add 360° to the solutions you've already found.
$48.6° + 360° = 408.6°$ (1 d.p.) and
$131.4° + 360° = 491.4°$ (1 d.p.)

b) Rearrange the equation:
$2 - 3 \cos x = 0 \Rightarrow 3 \cos x = 2 \Rightarrow \cos x = \frac{2}{3}$
The first solution is:
$x = \cos^{-1}\left(\frac{2}{3}\right) = 48.2°$ (1 d.p.)

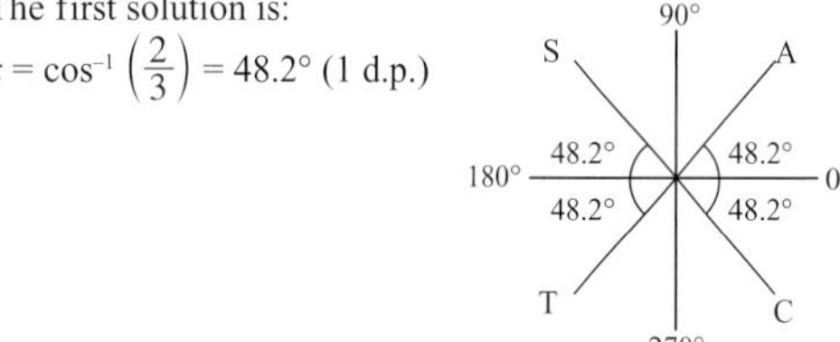

Cos is positive in the fourth quadrant, so the other solution is $0° - 48.2° = -48.2°$ (1 d.p.)

c) Rearrange the equation:
$6 \tan x = -11 \Rightarrow \tan x = -\frac{11}{6}$
The first solution is

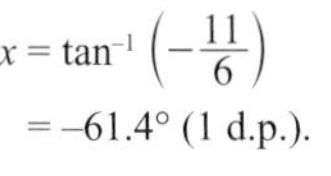

$x = \tan^{-1}\left(-\frac{11}{6}\right)$
$= -61.4°$ (1 d.p.).

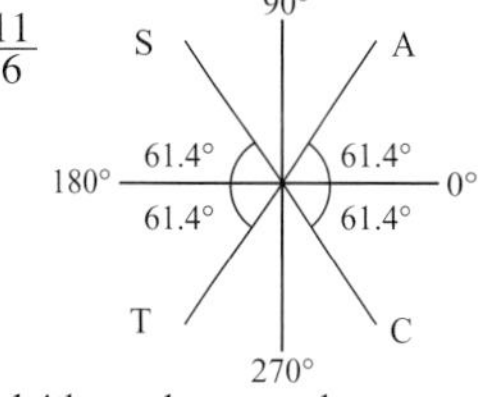

Tan is negative in the 2nd and 4th quadrants so the next solution is $180° - 61.4° = 118.6°$ (1 d.p.).
To find the other solutions in the interval, keep adding 180° to the solutions already found:
$118.6° + 180° = 298.6°$ (1 d.p.) and
$298.6° + 180° = 478.6°$ (1 d.p.)

d) Rearrange the equation:
$8 \sin x = -5 \Rightarrow \sin x = -\frac{5}{8}$
The first solution is
$x = \sin^{-1}\left(-\frac{5}{8}\right)$
$= -38.7°$ (1 d.p.).

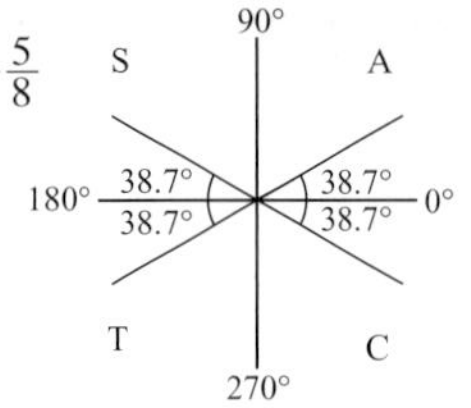

Sin is negative in the third and fourth quadrant, so the next solution is $180° + 38.7° = 218.7°$ (1 d.p.).
To find other solutions in the interval, add or subtract 360° from the solutions already found:
$218.7° - 360° = -141.3°$ (1 d.p.)
$-38.7° + 360° = 321.3°$ (1 d.p.)
$218.7° + 360° = 578.7°$ (1 d.p.)
$321.3° + 360° = 681.3°$ (1 d.p.)
So the solutions are:
$x = -141.3°, -38.7°, 218.7°, 321.3°, 578.7°, 681.3°$ (1 d.p.)

Q11 Rearrange the equation:
$\tan^2 x = \tan x \Rightarrow \tan^2 x - \tan x = 0$
$\Rightarrow \tan x (\tan x - 1) = 0$
$\Rightarrow \tan x = 0$ or $\tan x = 1$
So two solutions are:
$x = \tan^{-1}(0) = 0°$ and $x = \tan^{-1}(1) = 45°$
Tan is positive in the first and third quadrant, so two more solutions are:
$x = 0° + 180° = 180°$ and $x = 45° + 180° = 225°$
The solutions are $x = 0°, 45°, 180°, 225°$. 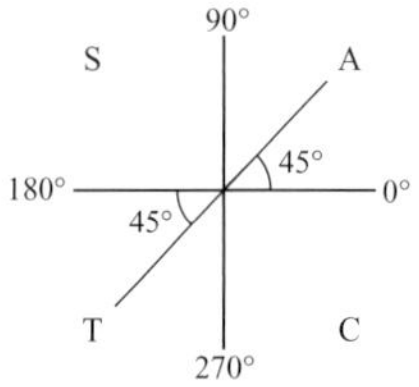
[4 marks available — 1 mark for rearranging, 1 mark for deducing tan x = 0 or tan x = 1, 1 mark for both solutions x = 0° and x = 180°, 1 mark for both solutions x = 45° and x = 225°]

Q12 a) If the angle YZX is acute:
$\angle YZX = 180° - (a + 26°)$
$\Rightarrow \sin(180° - (a + 26°)) = \frac{7.5}{10} = \frac{3}{4}$
$\Rightarrow \sin(a + 26°) = \frac{3}{4}$ 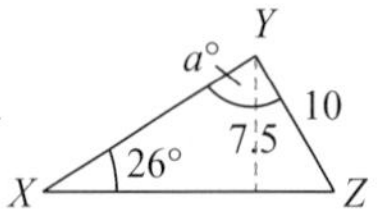
If the angle YZX is obtuse:
Using the right-angled triangle YZW shown in the diagram,
$\angle YZW = 180° - \angle YZX$
$= 180° - (180° - a - 26°)$
$= a + 26°$
$\Rightarrow \sin(a + 26°) = \frac{7.5}{10} = \frac{3}{4}$ 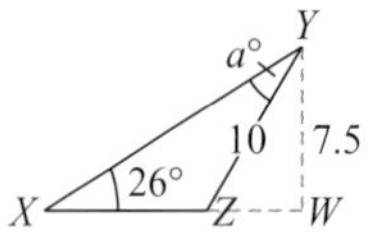
[4 marks available — 1 mark for considering both cases, 1 mark for at least one correct use of trigonometry, 1 mark for showing equality holds when ∠YZX is acute, 1 mark for showing equality holds when ∠YZX is obtuse]

b) $\sin(a + 26°) = \frac{3}{4}$
$\Rightarrow a + 26° = \sin^{-1}\left(\frac{3}{4}\right)$
$\Rightarrow a + 26° = 48.59...°$ is a solution
Sin is positive in the second quadrant, so the next solution is:
$a + 26° = 180° - 48.59...° = 131.40...°$
So possible values of a are:
$a = 48.59...° - 26° = 22.59...° = 22.6°$ (1 d.p.)
$a = 131.40...° - 26° = 105.40..° = 105.4°$ (1 d.p.) 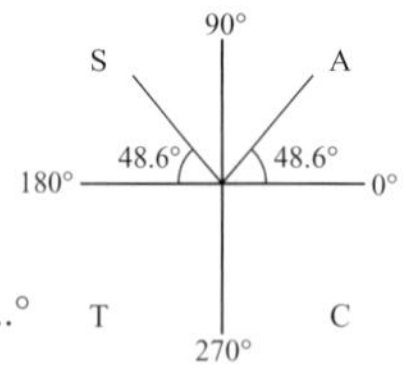
[2 marks available — 1 mark for each correct value of a]

Q13 a) $p\left(\frac{1}{2}\right) = 6\left(\frac{1}{2}\right)^3 + 11\left(\frac{1}{2}\right)^2 - 3\left(\frac{1}{2}\right) - 2 = 0$
So, by the factor theorem, $(2x - 1)$ is a factor of p(x).
Using long division:
p(x) = $(2x - 1)(3x^2 + 7x + 2)$
$= (x + 2)(3x + 1)(2x - 1)$

$$\begin{array}{r} 3x^2 + 7x + 2 \\ 2x - 1 \overline{)\, 6x^3 + 11x^2 - 3x - 2} \\ \underline{6x^3 - 3x^2} \\ 14x^2 - 3x \\ \underline{14x^2 - 7x} \\ 4x - 2 \\ 4x - 2 \end{array}$$

[3 marks available — 1 mark for showing that (2x – 1) is a factor with justification, 1 mark for obtaining a correct partial factorisation, 1 mark for correct full factorisation]

b) $6 \sin^3 \theta + 11 \sin^2 x - 3 \sin x - 2 = 0$
$\Rightarrow (\sin \theta + 2)(3 \sin \theta + 1)(2 \sin \theta - 1) = 0$
$\Rightarrow \sin \theta = -2, -\frac{1}{3}$ or $\frac{1}{2}$
$\sin \theta = -2$ has no real solutions
$\sin \theta = -\frac{1}{3} \Rightarrow \theta = -19.47...$
So $\theta = -19.5°$ (1 d.p.) is one solution.
Sin is negative in the third and fourth quadrant, so another solution is:
$\theta = -(180° - 19.47...) = -160.5°$ (1 d.p.) 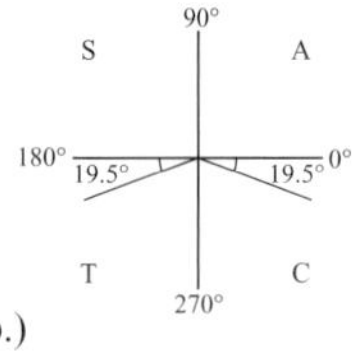
$\sin \theta = \frac{1}{2} \Rightarrow \theta = 30°$ is one solution.
Sin is positive in the first and second quadrant, so another solution is:
$\theta = 180° - 30° = 150°$ 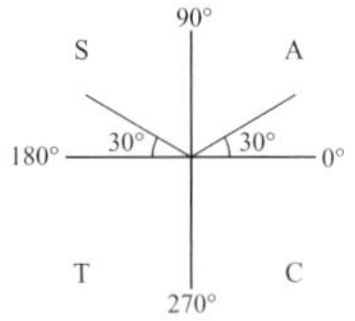
Therefore there are four solutions:
$\theta = -160.5°, -19.5°, 30°$ and $150°$
[4 marks available — 1 mark for using factorisation from a), 1 mark for considering the three values of sin θ, 1 mark for both θ = –19.5° and θ = –160.5°, 1 mark for both θ = 30° and θ = 150°]

Exercise 8.10 — Solving Trig Equations by Changing the Interval

For all the questions in this exercise, you can either sketch a graph or use a CAST diagram.

Q1 a) $\sin 2x = 0.6$, so look for solutions in the interval $0° \le 2x \le 720°$. The first solution is $2x = 36.87°$ (2 d.p.). Using a CAST diagram, sin is also positive in the 2nd quadrant, so there's another solution at $2x = 180° - 36.87° = 143.13°$ (2 d.p.).
The sin graph repeats every 360°, so add 360° onto the answers already found: $2x = 396.87°, 503.13°$ (2 d.p.).
These are solutions for $2x$, so divide them all by 2:
$x = 18.4°, 71.6°, 198.4°, 251.6°$ (1 d.p.).

b) $\tan 4x = 4.6$, so look for solutions in the interval $0° \le 4x \le 1440°$. The first solution is $4x = 77.74°$ (2 d.p.). From the graph, there will be another solution at $4x = 77.74° + 180° = 257.74°$ (2 d.p.). Then just keep adding on 180° to find the rest of the solutions within the interval:
$4x = 437.74°, 617.74°, 797.74°, 977.74°, 1157.74°, 1337.74°$ (2 d.p.)
These are solutions for $4x$, so divide them all by 4:
$x = 19.4°, 64.4°, 109.4°, 154.4°, 199.4°, 244.4°, 289.4°, 334.4°$ (1 d.p.).

c) $\cos 3x = -0.24$, so look for solutions in the interval $0° \le 3x \le 1080°$. The first solution is $3x = 103.89°$ (2 d.p.). Using the symmetry of the graph, there's another solution at $3x = 360° - 103.89° = 256.11°$ (2 d.p.). To find the other solutions within the interval, add on multiples of 360°:
$3x = 463.89°, 616.11°, 823.89°, 976.11°$ (2 d.p.). These are solutions for $3x$, so divide them all by 3: $x = 34.6°, 85.4°, 154.6°, 205.4°, 274.6°, 325.4°$ (1 d.p.).

d) $\sin 3x = 0.94$, so look for solutions in the interval $0° \le 3x \le 1080°$. The first solution is $3x = 70.05°$ (2 d.p.). Using a CAST diagram, sin is also positive in the 2nd quadrant, so there's another solution at $3x = 180° - 70.05° = 109.95°$ (2 d.p.). The sin graph repeats every 360°, so continue adding 360° onto the answers already found:
$3x = 430.05°, 469.95°, 790.05°, 829.95°$ (2 d.p.)
These are solutions for $3x$, so divide them all by 3:
$x = 23.4°, 36.7°, 143.4°, 156.7°, 263.4°, 276.7°$ (1 d.p.).

e) $\cos 5x = 0.5$, so look for solutions in the interval $0° \leq 5x \leq 1800°$. The first solution is $5x = 60°$. Using the symmetry of the graph, there's another solution at $5x = 360° - 60° = 300°$. To find the other solutions within the interval, add on multiples of 360°:
$5x = 420°, 660°, 780°, 1020°, 1140°, 1380°, 1500°, 1740°$
These are solutions for $5x$, so divide them all by 5:
$x = 12°, 60°, 84°, 132°, 156°, 204°, 228°, 276°, 300°, 348°$

f) $\tan 2x = -6.7$, so look for solutions in the interval $0° \leq 2x \leq 720°$. The first solution is $2x = -81.51°$ (2 d.p.) — this is outside the given interval, so add 180°: $2x = 98.49°$. From the graph, there will be another solution at $2x = 98.49° + 180° = 278.49°$ (2 d.p.). Then keep adding 180° to find the rest of the solutions within the interval:
$2x = 458.49°, 638.49°$ (2 d.p.)
These are solutions for $2x$, so divide them all by 2:
$x = 49.2°, 139.2°, 229.2°, 319.2°$ (1 d.p.).

Q2 $\tan \frac{x}{2} = 2.1$, so look for solutions in the interval $0° \leq \frac{x}{2} \leq 180°$. The first solution is $\frac{x}{2} = 64.54°$ (2 d.p.). This is the only solution in the interval, as tan doesn't repeat any values between 0° and 180° (looking at its graph). Multiply by 2 to get the value of x: $x = 129.1°$ (1 d.p.).

Q3 $\sin \frac{2x}{3} = 0.52$, so look for solutions in the interval $0° \leq \frac{2x}{3} \leq 180°$. The first solution is $\frac{2x}{3} = 31.33°$ (2 d.p.).
Using a CAST diagram, sin is also positive in the 2nd quadrant, so there's another solution at
$\frac{2x}{3} = 180° - 31.33° = 148.67°$ (2 d.p.).
These are solutions for $\frac{2x}{3}$, so divide them by $\frac{2}{3}$:
$x = 47.0°, 223.0°$ (1 d.p.)

Q4 $\cos \frac{x}{3} = \frac{\sqrt{3}}{2}$, so look for solutions in the interval $-60° \leq \frac{x}{3} \leq 60°$. The first solution is $\frac{x}{3} = 30°$ — using the symmetry of the graph, there's another solution at $0 - 30° = -30°$.
Multiply by 3 to get the values of x: $x = -90°, 90°$.

Q5 $\cos (x - 27°) = 0.64$, so look for solutions in the interval $-27° \leq x - 27° \leq 333°$. The first solution is $x - 27° = 50.2°$ (1 d.p.). Using the symmetry of the graph, there's another solution at $x - 27° = 360° - 50.2° = 309.8°$ (1 d.p.).
So the solutions are $x = 77.2°$ and $336.8°$ (1 d.p.).

Q6 $\tan (x - 140°) = -0.76$, so look for solutions in the interval $-140° \leq x - 140° \leq 220°$. The first solution is $x - 140° = -37.2°$ (1 d.p.). The tan graph repeats every 180°, so there's another solution at $x - 140° = -37.2° + 180° = 142.8°$ (1 d.p.)
(if you add on another 180°, the answer is outside the interval).
So the solutions are $x = 102.8°$ and $282.8°$ (1 d.p.).

Q7 $\tan (x + 73°) = 1.84$, so look for solutions in the interval $73° \leq x + 73° \leq 433°$. The first solution is $x + 73° = 61.5°$ (1 d.p.). This is out of the interval, but use this and the pattern of the graph of $\tan x$ to find the other solutions.
$\tan x$ repeats every 180°, so the next two solutions are $x + 73° = 241.5°$ and $x + 73° = 421.5°$ (1 d.p.).
So the two solutions are $x = 168.5°$ and $348.5°$ (1 d.p.).
[3 marks available — 1 mark for changing the interval, 1 mark for any solution to the initial equation, 1 mark for both correct solutions in the required interval]

Q8 $\sin (x - 45°) = -0.25$, so look for solutions in the interval $-225° \leq x - 45° \leq 315°$.
The first solution is $x - 45° = -14.5°$ (1 d.p.).
Using a CAST diagram, the other solutions are at $x - 45° = 180° + 14.5° = 194.5°$ and $x - 45° = -180° + 14.5° = -165.5°$.
So adding 45° to each solution gives
$x = -120.5°, 30.5°$ and $239.5°$ (1 d.p.).
[3 marks available — 1 mark for changing the interval, 1 mark for any solution to the initial equation, 1 mark for all three correct solutions in the required interval]
There's no solution at 360° − 14.5° because it's outside the interval.

Q9 $\cos (x + 22.5°) = 0.13$, so look for solutions in the interval $22.5° \leq x + 22.5° \leq 382.5°$.
The first solution is $x + 22.5° = 82.53°$ (2 d.p.).
Using the symmetry of the graph, there's another solution at $x + 22.5° = 360° - 82.53° = 277.47°$.
So subtracting 22.5° from each solution gives
$x = 60.0°$ and $255.0°$ (1 d.p.).

Q10 Rearrange to get $\tan (x - 32°) = 7.5$, so look for solutions in the interval $-212° \leq x - 32° \leq 148°$. The first solution is $x - 32° = 82.4°$ (1 d.p.). The graph of tan repeats every 180°, so there's another solution at $x - 32° = 82.4° - 180° = -97.6°$ (1 d.p.)
So the solutions are $x = -97.6° + 32° = -65.6°$ (1 d.p)
and $x = 82.4° + 32° = 114.4°$ (1 d.p.)

Q11 Rearrange to get $\cos 3x = 0.7$, so look for solutions in the interval $0° \leq 3x \leq 1080°$. The first solution is $3x = 45.57°$ (2 d.p.).
Using the symmetry of the graph, there's another solution at $3x = 360° - 45.57° = 314.43°$ (2 d.p.).
Add on 360° to find the other solutions in the interval:
$3x = 405.57°, 674.43°, 765.57°, 1034.43°$ (2 d.p.)
These are solutions for $3x$, so divide them all by 3:
$x = 15.2°, 104.8°, 135.2°, 224.8°, 255.2°, 344.8°$ (1 d.p.)
[4 marks available — 1 mark for changing the interval, 1 mark for any solution to the initial equation, 1 mark for any solution in the required interval, 1 mark for all remaining solutions in the required interval]

Q12 First, rearrange: $\frac{1}{2}\sin 3x - 0.61 = -0.75$
$\Rightarrow \frac{1}{2}\sin 3x = -0.14 \Rightarrow \sin 3x = -0.28$,
so look for solutions in the interval $0° \leq 3x \leq 1080°$.
The first solution is $3x = -16.26°$ (2 d.p.). This is outside the interval, but putting 16.26° into a CAST diagram and looking at the quadrants where sin is negative gives
$3x = 180° + 16.26° = 196.26°$
and $3x = 360° - 16.26° = 343.74°$ (2 d.p.).
Add multiples of 360° to find the other solutions in the interval:
$3x = 556.26°, 703.74°, 916.26°, 1063.74°$ (2 d.p.).
These are solutions for $3x$, so divide them all by 3:
$x = 65.4°, 114.6°, 185.4°, 234.6°, 305.4°, 354.6°$ (1 d.p.)

Q13 Rearrange to get $\cos (x - 67°) = 0.69$, so look for solutions in the interval $-67° \leq x - 67° \leq 473°$.
The first solution is $x - 67° = 46.4°$ (1 d.p.).
Using the symmetry of the graph, there's another solution at $x - 67° = 360° - 46.4° = 313.6°$ (1 d.p.). Add on 360° to find the other solution in the interval:
$x - 67° = 46.4° + 360° = 406.4°$.
So $x = 113.4°, 380.6°, 473.4°$ (1 d.p.)

Q14 Rearrange to get $\sin (x + 19°) = -\frac{\sqrt{2}}{2}$, so look for solutions in the interval $19° \leq x + 19° \leq 379°$.
The first solution is $x + 19° = -45°$.
This is outside the interval, so add 360°: $x + 19° = 315°$.
Using a CAST diagram, sin is also negative in the third quadrant, so there's another solution at $x + 19° = 180° + 45° = 225°$.
So $x = 206°, 296°$

Exercise 8.11 — Using Trig Identities to Solve Equations

For all the questions in this exercise, you can either sketch a graph or use a CAST diagram.

Q1 a) This equation has already been factorised.
Either $\tan x - 5 = 0$ or $3 \sin x - 1 = 0$.
$\tan x - 5 = 0 \Rightarrow \tan x = 5 \Rightarrow x = 78.7°$ (1 d.p.)
This is the first solution. tan repeats itself every 180°, so the other solution is 258.7° (1 d.p.).
$3 \sin x = 1 \Rightarrow \sin x = \frac{1}{3} \Rightarrow x = 19.5°$ (1 d.p.)
Using the symmetry of the graph, the other solution is $180° - 19.5° = 160.5°$ (1 d.p.).

b) $5 \sin x \tan x - 4 \tan x = 0 \Rightarrow \tan x(5 \sin x - 4) = 0$
So $\tan x = 0$ or $5 \sin x - 4 = 0$.
$\tan x = 0 \Rightarrow x = 0°, 180°$ and $360°$ (from the graph of $\tan x$).
$5 \sin x - 4 = 0 \Rightarrow \sin x = \frac{4}{5} \Rightarrow x = 53.1°$ (1 d.p.)
Using the symmetry of the graph, the other solution is $180° - 53.1° = 126.9°$ (1 d.p.).

c) $\tan^2 x = 9 \Rightarrow \tan x = 3$ or -3.
$\tan x = 3 \Rightarrow x = 71.6°$ (1 d.p.)
Using the repetition of the tan graph, the other solution is $180° + 71.6° = 251.6°$ (1 d.p.).
$\tan x = -3 \Rightarrow x = -71.6°$ (1 d.p.)
This is outside the interval. Add on 180° until you've found all the solutions within the interval:
$-71.6° + 180° = 108.4°$ (1 d.p.) and
$108.4° + 180° = 288.4°$ (1 d.p.).

d) $4 \cos^2 x = 3 \cos x \Rightarrow 4 \cos^2 x - 3 \cos x = 0$
$\Rightarrow \cos x(4 \cos x - 3) = 0$

So $\cos x = 0$ or $4 \cos x - 3 = 0$
$\cos x = 0 \Rightarrow x = 90°$
Using the cos graph, the other solution is 270°.
$4\cos x - 3 = 0 \Rightarrow \cos x = \frac{3}{4} \Rightarrow x = 41.4°$ (1 d.p.)
Using the symmetry of the graph, the other solution is $360° - 41.4° = 318.6°$ (1 d.p.).

e) $3 \sin x = 5 \cos x \Rightarrow \tan x = \frac{5}{3}$. The first solution is $x = 59.0°$ (1 d.p.). $\tan x$ repeats every 180°, so the other solution is 239.0° (1 d.p.).

f) $5 \tan^2 x - 2 \tan x = 0 \Rightarrow \tan x(5 \tan x - 2) = 0$.
So either $\tan x = 0$ or $\tan x = 0.4$. If $\tan x = 0$, then the solutions are $x = 0°, 180°$ and $360°$.
If $\tan x = 0.4$, the first solution is 21.8° (1 d.p.).
The graph of $\tan x$ repeats every 180°, so another solution is $x = 201.8°$ (1 d.p.).

g) $6\cos^2 x - \cos x - 2 = 0$
$\Rightarrow (3\cos x - 2)(2\cos x + 1) = 0$
So either $\cos x = \frac{2}{3}$ or $\cos x = -0.5$. If $\cos x = \frac{2}{3}$, the first solution is 48.2° (1 d.p.). Looking at the symmetry of the graph of $\cos x$, the other solution is $x = 360° - 48.2° = 311.8°$ (1 d.p.).
If $\cos x = -0.5$, the first solution is 120°.
Looking at the symmetry of the graph of $\cos x$, the other solution is $360° - 120° = 240°$.

h) $7 \sin x + 3 \cos x = 0 \Rightarrow 7 \sin x = -3 \cos x$
$\Rightarrow \tan x = -\frac{3}{7} \Rightarrow x = -23.2°$ (1 d.p.)
This is outside the required interval. Using a CAST diagram, tan is negative in the 2nd and 4th quadrants, so the solutions are $x = 180° - 23.2° = 156.8°$ (1 d.p.) and $x = 360° - 23.2° = 336.8°$ (1 d.p.).

Q2 a) $\tan x = \sin x \cos x \Rightarrow \frac{\sin x}{\cos x} - \sin x \cos x = 0$
$\Rightarrow \sin x - \sin x \cos^2 x = 0$
$\Rightarrow \sin x (1 - \cos^2 x) = 0$
$\Rightarrow \sin x (\sin^2 x) = 0$
$\Rightarrow \sin^3 x = 0$
So $\sin x = 0$.
The solutions are $x = 0°, 180°$ and $360°$.

b) $5 \cos^2 x - 9 \sin x = 3 \Rightarrow 5(1 - \sin^2 x) - 9 \sin x = 3$
$\Rightarrow 5 \sin^2 x + 9 \sin x - 2 = 0$
$\Rightarrow (5 \sin x - 1)(\sin x + 2) = 0$
So either $\sin x = 0.2$ or $\sin x = -2$. $\sin x$ can't be -2, so only $\sin x = 0.2$ will give solutions.
The first solution is $x = 11.54°$ (2 d.p.).
The interval covers three intervals of 360°, so there will be 6 solutions.

Looking at the symmetry of the sin graph and adding or subtracting 360°, the other solutions are
$x = -348.5°, -191.5°, 11.5°, 168.5°, 371.5°$ and $528.5°$ (1 d.p.).
If you'd used a CAST diagram here, you'd find 11.5° and 168.5° first, then add or subtract 360°.

c) $2 \sin^2 x + \sin x - 1 = 0$
$\Rightarrow (2 \sin x - 1)(\sin x + 1) = 0$
So $2 \sin x - 1 = 0$ or $\sin x + 1 = 0$.
$2 \sin x - 1 = 0 \Rightarrow \sin x = \frac{1}{2} \Rightarrow x = 30°$.
Using the symmetry of the graph, another solution is $180° - 30° = 150°$.
To find the other solutions in the required interval, subtract 360° from each of these:
$30° - 360° = -330°$, and $150° - 360° = -210°$.
$\sin x + 1 = 0 \Rightarrow \sin x = -1$
From the graph, the solutions to this are $x = -90°$ and $x = 270°$.

d) $2 \sin x \tan x = -3 \Rightarrow \frac{2 \sin^2 x}{\cos x} = -3$
$\Rightarrow 2 - 2 \cos^2 x = -3 \cos x$
$\Rightarrow 2 \cos^2 x - 3 \cos x - 2 = 0$
$\Rightarrow (\cos x - 2)(2 \cos x + 1) = 0$
$\cos x = 2$ has no solutions.
$\cos x = -\frac{1}{2} \Rightarrow x = 120°$
Using the symmetry of the graph, there is another solution at $360° - 120° = 240°$. Find the other solutions in the interval by subtracting 360°:
$x = -240°, -120°, 120°, 240°$.

e) $4 - \tan^2 x = 0 \Rightarrow (2 - \tan x)(2 + \tan x) = 0$
so either $\tan x = 2$ or $\tan x = -2$.
First, solve $\tan x = 2$: $x = 63.43°$ (2 d.p.)
The graph of tan repeats every 180°, so subtract 180° to find the other solution in the interval:
$x = 63.43° - 180° = -116.57°$.
Now, solve $\tan x = -2$: $x = -63.43°$
Add 180° to find the other solution in the interval:
$x = -63.43° + 180° = 116.57°$
So the solutions to $4 - \tan^2 x = 0$ are:
$x = -116.6°, -63.4°, 63.4°, 116.6°$ (1 d.p.)

Q3 a) $4 \sin^2 x = 3 - 3 \cos x \Rightarrow 4(1 - \cos^2 x) = 3 - 3 \cos x$
$\Rightarrow 4 - 4 \cos^2 x = 3 - 3 \cos x$
$\Rightarrow 4 \cos^2 x - 3 \cos x - 1 = 0$
(as required)

b) Solve the equation from a).
$4 \cos^2 x - 3 \cos x - 1 = 0$
$(4 \cos x + 1)(\cos x - 1) = 0$
So $4 \cos x + 1 = 0$ or $\cos x - 1 = 0$
$4 \cos x + 1 = 0 \Rightarrow \cos x = -\frac{1}{4} \Rightarrow x = 104.5°$ (1 d.p.)
Using the symmetry of the graph, the other solution is $360° - 104.5° = 255.5°$ (1 d.p.)
$\cos x - 1 = 0 \Rightarrow \cos x = 1$
Using the cos graph, the solutions are $x = 0°$ and $x = 360°$.

Q4 $3 \cos x - 2 \sin^2 x = 0 \Rightarrow 3 \cos x - 2(1 - \cos^2 x) = 0$
$\Rightarrow 2 \cos^2 x + 3 \cos x - 2 = 0$
$\Rightarrow (2 \cos x - 1)(\cos x + 2) = 0$
$\cos x = -2$ has no solutions and $\cos x = \frac{1}{2}$ has a first solution $x = 60°$. Using the symmetry of cos, there is another solution at $x = 360° - 60° = 300°$.
So the solutions of $3 \cos x - 2 \sin^2 x = 0$ are: $x = 60°, 300°$

Q5 $2 \sin^2 x + 5 \cos^2 x - 7 \cos x = 0$
$\Rightarrow 2(1 - \cos^2 x) + 5 \cos^2 x - 7 \cos x = 0$
$\Rightarrow 2 + 3\cos^2 x - 7 \cos x = 0$
$\Rightarrow (3 \cos x - 1)(\cos x - 2) = 0$

$\cos x = 2$ has no solutions, so you only need to solve $\cos x = \frac{1}{3}$.
The first solution is $x = 70.53°$, and by the symmetry of the cos graph, the other solution in the given interval is $x = 360° - 70.53° = 289.47°$.

So the solutions of $2\sin^2 x + 5\cos^2 x - 7\cos x = 0$ are:
$x = 70.5°, 289.5°$ (1 d.p.)

Q6 $9\sin^2 2x + 3\cos 2x = 7$
$\Rightarrow 9(1 - \cos^2 2x) + 3\cos 2x = 7$
$\Rightarrow 2 - 9\cos^2 2x + 3\cos 2x = 0$
$\Rightarrow 9\cos^2 2x - 3\cos 2x - 2 = 0$
$\Rightarrow (3\cos 2x + 1)(3\cos 2x - 2) = 0$

So either $\cos 2x = -\frac{1}{3}$ or $\cos 2x = \frac{2}{3}$.
For $\cos 2x = -\frac{1}{3}$, look for solutions in the interval $0° \le 2x \le 720°$.
The first solution is $2x = 109.47°$ (2 d.p.). Looking at the symmetry of the graph of $\cos x$, the other solutions are:
$2x = 250.53°, 469.47°$ and $610.53°$ (2 d.p.).
Dividing by 2 gives the solutions:
$x = 54.7°, 125.3°, 234.7°$ and $305.3°$ (1 d.p.).
For $\cos 2x = \frac{2}{3}$, again look for solutions in the interval $0° \le 2x \le 720°$. The first solution is $2x = 48.19°$ (2 d.p.). Looking at the symmetry of the graph of $\cos x$, the other solutions are $2x = 311.81°, 408.19°, 671.81°$ (2 d.p.).
Dividing by 2 gives the solutions:
$x = 24.1°, 155.9°, 204.1°$ and $335.9°$ (1 d.p.).

Q7 **a)** $\sin x - \sin x\cos^2 x \equiv \sin x(1 - \cos^2 x)$
Using $\sin^2 x + \cos^2 x \equiv 1$ gives:
$\sin x(1 - \cos^2 x) \equiv \sin x(\sin^2 x)$
$\equiv \sin^3 x$
[2 marks available — 1 mark for using the correct identity, 1 mark for simplifying and showing the correct result]

b) $3\sin x - 3\sin x\cos^2 x - 1 = 0$
$\Rightarrow 3(\sin x - \sin x\cos^2 x) - 1 = 0$
Then using the identity from part a),
$\Rightarrow 3\sin^3 x - 1 = 0$
$\Rightarrow \sin^3 x = \frac{1}{3} \Rightarrow \sin x = \frac{1}{\sqrt[3]{3}}$
Look for solutions in the interval $-180° \le x \le 180°$.
The first solution is $x = 43.9°$ (1 d.p.).
Using the symmetry of the graph of $\sin x$, there is another solution at $x = 180° - 43.9° = 136.1°$ (1 d.p.).
So the solutions are $x = 43.9°$ and $136.1°$ (1 d.p.).
[3 marks available — 1 mark for using result from part a), 1 mark for $x = 43.9°$, 1 mark for $x = 136.1°$]

Q8 $4\cos\frac{x}{2} - 3\sin^2\frac{x}{2} - 1 = 0 \Rightarrow 4\cos\frac{x}{2} - 3(1 - \cos^2\frac{x}{2}) - 1 = 0$
$\Rightarrow 3\cos^2\frac{x}{2} + 4\cos\frac{x}{2} - 4 = 0$
$\Rightarrow (3\cos\frac{x}{2} - 2)(\cos\frac{x}{2} + 2) = 0$

$\cos\frac{x}{2} = -2$ has no solutions, so you only need to solve $\cos\frac{x}{2} = \frac{2}{3}$ in the interval $0° \le \frac{x}{2} \le 360°$. The first solution is $\frac{x}{2} = 48.19°$ (2 d.p.). Using the symmetry of the graph, there's another solution at $\frac{x}{2} = 360° - 48.19° = 311.81°$ (2 d.p.).
These are solutions for $\frac{x}{2}$, so multiply them all by 2:
$x = 96.4°, 623.6°$ (1 d.p.)

Q9 Using the identity $\tan x = \frac{\sin x}{\cos x}$ gives:
$\frac{\cos x}{\tan x} + \sin x = 3 \Rightarrow \frac{\cos x}{\left(\frac{\sin x}{\cos x}\right)} + \sin x = 3$
$\Rightarrow \frac{\cos^2 x}{\sin x} + \sin x = 3 \Rightarrow \cos^2 x + \sin^2 x = 3\sin x$
$\Rightarrow 1 = 3\sin x \Rightarrow \sin x = \frac{1}{3}$
The first solution is $x = 19.5°$ (1 d.p.).
Looking at the symmetry of the graph of $\sin x$, the other solutions are $x = -340.5°, -199.5°$ and $160.5°$ (1 d.p.).
[4 marks available — 1 mark for using the correct identity, 1 mark for simplifying, 1 mark for one correct solution, 1 mark for the remaining three correct solutions]

Q10 $\cos x\sin^2 x - \cos x \equiv \cos x(\sin^2 x - 1)$
$\equiv -\cos x(1 - \sin^2 x)$
$\equiv -\cos x(\cos^2 x)$
$\equiv -\cos^3 x$

So solve $\cos^3 x = -0.86 \Rightarrow \cos x = \sqrt[3]{-0.86}$
The first solution is $x = \cos^{-1}(\sqrt[3]{-0.86}) = 162.0°$ (3 s.f.)
Using the symmetry of the graph, the other solution in the given interval is $x = 0° - 162.0° = -162.0°$ (3 s.f.)

Q11 $4\cos^2 x\tan x + \sin x = 0 \Rightarrow 4\cos^2 x\frac{\sin x}{\cos x} + \sin x = 0$
$\Rightarrow 4\sin x\cos x + \sin x = 0$
$\Rightarrow \sin x(4\cos x + 1) = 0$

Either $\sin x = 0$ or $\cos x = -\frac{1}{4}$, so solve separately:
First solve $\sin x = 0$: $x = 0, 180°, 360°$
Then solve $\cos x = -\frac{1}{4}$:
The first solution is $x = 104.5°$ (1 d.p).
Using the symmetry of cos, there is a solution at $x = 360° - 104.5° = 255.5°$. So the solutions are:
$x = 0, 104.5°, 180°, 255.5°, 360°$ (1 d.p.)

Q12 $\frac{\cos^2 x}{\sin x - 1} \equiv \frac{1 - \sin^2 x}{\sin x - 1} \equiv \frac{(1 - \sin x)(1 + \sin x)}{\sin x - 1}$
$\equiv \frac{-(\sin x - 1)(1 + \sin x)}{\sin x - 1} \equiv -(1 + \sin x)$

So $\frac{\cos^2 x}{\sin x - 1} = -0.25 \Rightarrow 1 + \sin x = 0.25 \Rightarrow \sin x = -0.75$
The first solution is $x = -48.6$ (1 d.p.). Using the symmetry of the graph, there is another solution at $-180° + 48.6° = -131.4°$.
Find the other solutions in the interval by adding 360° to the solutions already found:
$x = -131.4°, -48.6°, 228.6°, 311.4°$ (1 d.p.)

Q13 Points of intersection occur when $f(x) = g(x)$:
$2 + 3\cos^2 x = 7\sin x - 1 \Rightarrow 3\cos^2 x - 7\sin x + 3 = 0$
$\Rightarrow 3(1 - \sin^2 x) - 7\sin x + 3 = 0$
$\Rightarrow 3\sin^2 x + 7\sin x - 6 = 0$
$\Rightarrow (\sin x + 3)(3\sin x - 2) = 0$

$\sin x = -3$ has no solutions, so just solve $\sin x = \frac{2}{3}$:
The first solution is $x = 41.8°$ (3 s.f.).
Using the symmetry of the graph of $\sin x$, the other solution is at $x = 180° - 41.8° = 138.2°$ (3 s.f.)
$\sin x = \frac{2}{3}$ for these x-values, so find the y-coordinates:
$g(41.8°) = g(138.2°) = (7 \times \frac{2}{3}) - 1 = 3.67$ (3 s.f.)
So the points are $(41.8°, 3.67)$ and $(139.2°, 3.67)$.

Q14 **a)** Use the identity $\tan x = \frac{\sin x}{\cos x}$ and rearrange:
$5\sin x - 2\tan x = 2\cos x\sin x$
$\Rightarrow 5\sin x - 2\frac{\sin x}{\cos x} = 2\cos x\sin x$
$\Rightarrow 5 - 2\frac{1}{\cos x} = 2\cos x \Rightarrow 5\cos x - 2 = 2\cos^2 x$
You can divide by sin x because you're told that sin x ≠ 0.
$\Rightarrow 2\cos^2 x - 5\cos x + 2 = 0$
[3 marks available — 1 mark for using the identity $\tan x \equiv \frac{\sin x}{\cos x}$, 1 mark for cancelling sin x from both sides, 1 mark for simplifying to derive the correct result]

b) When $\sin x \ne 0$, using the result from part a):
$2\cos^2 x - 5\cos x + 2 = 0 \Rightarrow (2\cos x - 1)(\cos x - 2) = 0$
$\Rightarrow \cos x = \frac{1}{2}$ or $\cos x = 2$
So $x = \cos^{-1}(\frac{1}{2}) = 60°$ is a solution. Using the symmetry of the graph of $\cos x$, another solution is $-60°$.
There are no solutions to $\cos x = 2$.
$\sin x = 0$ when $x = 0$. Substituting $x = 0$ into the original equation shows that $x = 0$ is another solution.
So the solutions are: $x = 0°, 60°, -60°$.
[4 marks available — 1 mark for factorising the result from part a), 1 mark for each correct solution, $x = 0°, 60°, -60°$]

Q15 **a)** $4\sin^4 x + 7\sin^2 x\cos^2 x - 3\cos^4 x$
$\equiv 4(1 - \cos^2 x)^2 + 7(1 - \cos^2 x)\cos^2 x - 3\cos^4 x$
$\equiv 4 - 8\cos^2 x + 4\cos^4 x + 7\cos^2 x - 7\cos^4 x - 3\cos^4 x$
$\equiv 4 - \cos^2 x - 6\cos^4 x$
[3 marks available — 1 mark for using the identity $\sin^2 x = 1 - \cos^2 x$, 1 mark for expanding brackets, 1 mark for simplifying to derive the correct identity]

b) $4 \sin^4 x + 7 \sin^2 x \cos^2 x - 3 \cos^4 x = 6 - 14 \cos^2 x$
$\Rightarrow 4 - \cos^2 x - 6 \cos^4 x = 6 - 14 \cos^2 x$
$\Rightarrow 6 \cos^4 x - 13 \cos^2 x + 2 = 0$
$\Rightarrow (6 \cos^2 x - 1)(\cos^2 x - 2) = 0$
$\Rightarrow \cos^2 x = \frac{1}{6}$ or $\cos^2 x = 2$
But $\cos^2 x = 2$ has no real solutions.
So $\cos x = \frac{1}{\sqrt{6}}$ or $\cos x = -\frac{1}{\sqrt{6}}$, giving solutions $x = 65.905...° = 65.9°$ (1 d.p.) and $x = 114.094...° = 114.1°$ (1 d.p.) respectively.
Using the symmetry of $\cos x$, there are also solutions at $x = -65.9°$ (1 d.p.) and $x = -114.1°$ (1 d.p.).
[4 marks available — 1 mark for using result from a), 1 mark for obtaining both equations in $\cos^2 x$, 1 mark for both solutions $x = 65.9°$ and $x = -65.9°$, 1 mark for both solutions $x = 114.1°$ and $x = -114.1°$]

Q16 $3 \sin^2 x + (k^2 + 6) \cos x = 3 + 2k^2$
$\Rightarrow 3 - 3 \cos^2 x + (k^2 + 6) \cos x = 3 + 2k^2$
$\Rightarrow 3\cos^2 x - (k^2 + 6) \cos x + 2k^2 = 0$
$\Rightarrow (3 \cos x - k^2)(\cos x - 2) = 0 \Rightarrow \cos x = \frac{k^2}{3}$ or $\cos x = 2$
But $\cos x = 2$ has no real solutions.
If $\cos x = \frac{k^2}{3}$ has no solutions then $\frac{k^2}{3} > 1$ (since $\frac{k^2}{3}$ cannot be less than -1), so $k > \sqrt{3}$ or $k < -\sqrt{3}$.
[4 marks available — 1 mark for using $\sin^2 x = 1 - \cos^2 x$, 1 mark for factorising, 1 mark for deriving the inequality $\frac{k^2}{3} > 1$, 1 mark for correct set of possible values of k]

Q17 $f(x) = g(x) \Rightarrow 3 \cos^2 x = 1 - \sin x$
$\Rightarrow 3(1 - \sin^2 x) = 1 - \sin x$
$\Rightarrow 3 \sin^2 x - \sin x - 2 = 0$
$\Rightarrow (3 \sin x + 2)(\sin x - 1) = 0$

So either $\sin x = -\frac{2}{3}$ or $\sin x = 1$.
For $\sin x = -\frac{2}{3}$, the first solution is $x = -41.81...°$
This is outside the interval, so add 360° to get a value for x in the interval: $x = 318.18...°$.
By the symmetry of the sin graph, there is another solution at $180° - (-41.81...°) = 221.81...°$
For $\sin x = 1$, the first solution is $x = 90°$, and there are no other solutions in the given interval.
So the solutions are $x = 90°, 221.8°, 318.2°$ (1 d.p.)
[6 marks available — 1 mark for using the identity $\sin^2 x + \cos^2 x = 1$, 1 mark for constructing a quadratic equation in sin x, 1 mark for factorising to get two values for sin x, 1 mark for using the inverse sin function, 1 mark for at least two correct solutions, 1 mark for all three correct]

Chapter 8 Review Exercise

Q1 $\cos 30° = \frac{\sqrt{3}}{2}$, $\sin 30° = \frac{1}{2}$, $\tan 30° = \frac{1}{\sqrt{3}}$
$\cos 45° = \frac{1}{\sqrt{2}}$, $\sin 45° = \frac{1}{\sqrt{2}}$, $\tan 45° = 1$
$\cos 60° = \frac{1}{2}$, $\sin 60° = \frac{\sqrt{3}}{2}$, $\tan 60° = \sqrt{3}$

Q2 a) $\cos\theta = \frac{1}{2} \Rightarrow \theta = \cos^{-1}\left(\frac{1}{2}\right) = 60°$
b) $\cos\theta = \frac{\sqrt{3}}{2} \Rightarrow \theta = \cos^{-1}\left(\frac{\sqrt{3}}{2}\right) = 30°$
c) $\cos\theta = -1 \Rightarrow \theta = \cos^{-1}(-1) = 180°$

Q3 a) $\angle ABC = 180° - 37° - 58° = 85°$
Using the sine rule: $\frac{AB}{\angle ACB} = \frac{AC}{\angle ABC}$
$\frac{15}{\sin 58°} = \frac{AC}{\sin 85°}$ so $AC = \frac{15 \sin 85°}{\sin 58°} = 17.620...$
$= 17.6$ m (1 d.p.)
[2 marks available — 1 mark for a correct method using trigonometry, 1 mark for the correct answer]

b) $EB = ED - BD$
$BD = 15 \sin 37° = 9.027...$
$\tan 58° = \frac{BD}{DC} \Rightarrow DC = \frac{9.027...}{\tan 58°} = 5.640...$
$\Rightarrow ED = 5.640... \times \tan 70° = 15.498...$
$\Rightarrow EB = 15.498... - 9.027... = 6.470... = 6.5$ m (1 d.p.)
[2 marks available — 1 mark for a correct method using trigonometry, 1 mark for correct answer]

c) $AD = 15 \cos 37° = 11.979...$
$\tan \angle EAD = \frac{ED}{AD} = \frac{15.498...}{11.979...} = 1.2937...$
$\Rightarrow \angle EAD = \tan^{-1} 1.2937... = 52.297...°$
$\Rightarrow \angle EAB = 52.297...° - 37° = 15.297...° = 15.3°$ (1 d.p.)
[2 marks available — 1 mark for $\angle EAD = 52.297...°$, 1 mark for correct answer]

Q4 a) Angle $B = 180° - 30° - 25° = 125°$.
Using the sine rule: $\frac{a}{\sin A} = \frac{b}{\sin B}$
$\frac{6}{\sin 125°} = \frac{a}{\sin 30°} = \frac{c}{\sin 25°}$ so:
side $c = \frac{6 \sin 25°}{\sin 125°} = 3.095...$ m
side $a = \frac{6 \sin 30°}{\sin 125°} = 3.662...$ m
b) Area $= \frac{1}{2} ab \sin C = \frac{1}{2} \times 3.662 \times 6 \times \sin 25°$
$= 4.643... = 4.64$ m^2 (3 s.f.)

Q5 a) Using the right-angled triangle with hypotenuse AB gives $\sin B = \frac{h}{c} \Rightarrow h = c \sin B$
Using the right-angled triangle with hypotenuse AC gives $\sin C = \frac{h}{b} \Rightarrow h = b \sin C$
So $c \sin B = b \sin C \Rightarrow \frac{\sin B}{b} = \frac{\sin C}{c}$
[2 marks available — 1 mark for deriving at least one correct expression for h, 1 mark for deriving the correct equality]
b) $\frac{\sin 71°}{6.4} = \frac{\sin C}{4.3} \Rightarrow \sin C = \frac{4.3 \sin 71°}{6.4}$
$\Rightarrow C = \sin^{-1}(0.635...) = 39.440... = 39.4°$ (3 s.f.)
[2 marks available — 1 mark for using the result from a) with the correct values, 1 mark for the correct answer]

Q6 a) Using the cosine rule: $a^2 = b^2 + c^2 - 2bc \cos A$
$r^2 = 13^2 + 23^2 - (2 \times 13 \times 23 \times \cos 20°)$
so $r = \sqrt{136.06...} = 11.7$ km (3 s.f.)
$P = \cos^{-1}\left(\frac{23^2 + 136.06... - 13^2}{2 \times 23 \times \sqrt{136.06...}}\right) = 22.4°$ (3 s.f.),
$Q = \cos^{-1}\left(\frac{13^2 + 136.06... - 23^2}{2 \times 13 \times \sqrt{136.06...}}\right) = 138°$ (3 s.f.)
b) Area $= \frac{1}{2} ab \sin C = \frac{1}{2} \times 13 \times 23 \times \sin 20°$
$= 51.1$ km^2 (3 s.f.)

Q7 Using the cosine rule: $\cos A = \frac{b^2 + c^2 - a^2}{2bc}$
$A = \cos^{-1}\left(\frac{10^2 + 20^2 - 25^2}{2 \times 10 \times 20}\right) = 108.2°$ (1 d.p.)
$B = \cos^{-1}\left(\frac{10^2 + 25^2 - 20^2}{2 \times 10 \times 25}\right) = 49.5°$ (1 d.p.)
$C = \cos^{-1}\left(\frac{20^2 + 25^2 - 10^2}{2 \times 20 \times 25}\right) = 22.3°$ (1 d.p.)

Q8 a) Using the cosine rule: $a^2 = b^2 + c^2 - 2bc \cos A$
$\Rightarrow (\sqrt{10})^2 = (3\sqrt{2})^2 + x^2 - 2 \times 3\sqrt{2} \times x \times \cos 45°$
$\Rightarrow 10 = 18 + x^2 - 6x \Rightarrow x^2 - 6x + 8 = 0$
[2 marks available — 1 mark for correctly using the cosine rule, 1 mark for a correct derivation]
b) Solving the quadratic equation derived in a) gives $x = 4$ or $x = 2$ *[1 mark for both correct values of x]*

Q9 Using the sine rule: $\frac{\sin A}{a} = \frac{\sin B}{b}$

$\frac{\sin 35^\circ}{3} = \frac{\sin B}{5}$ so $B = \sin^{-1}\left(\frac{5\sin 35^\circ}{3}\right) = 72.93...^\circ$

By the symmetry of the sine graph, another solution is $B = 180° - 72.93...° = 107.06...°$

When $B = 72.93...°$:
$C = 180° - 35° - 72.93...° = 72.06...°$

Using the sine rule, $\frac{3}{\sin 35^\circ} = \frac{c}{\sin 72.06...^\circ}$

$\Rightarrow c = \frac{3\sin 72.06...^\circ}{\sin 35^\circ} = 4.976... = 4.98$ (3 s.f.)

When $B = 107.06...°$:
$C = 180° - 35° - 107.06...° = 37.93...°$

$\Rightarrow c = \frac{3\sin 37.93...^\circ}{\sin 35^\circ} = 3.215... = 3.22$ (3 s.f.)

Q10 The largest angle, A, is opposite the longest side and the smallest angle, B, is opposite the shortest side. Using the cosine rule:

$\cos A = \frac{b^2 + c^2 - a^2}{2bc} = \frac{4.9^2 + 11.6^2 - 13.2^2}{2 \times 4.9 \times 11.6} \Rightarrow A = 97.923...^\circ$

$\cos B = \frac{a^2 + c^2 - b^2}{2ac} = \frac{11.6^2 + 13.2^2 - 4.9^2}{2 \times 11.6 \times 13.2} \Rightarrow B = 21.571...^\circ$

So the difference is $97.923...° - 21.571...° = 76.4°$ (3 s.f.)

[4 marks available — 1 mark for correct use of cosine rule, 1 mark for correct largest angle, 1 mark for correct smallest angle, 1 mark for correct answer]

Q11 Using the sine rule: $\frac{\sin A}{a} = \frac{\sin B}{b}$

$\frac{\sin 37^\circ}{12} = \frac{\sin \angle PRQ}{16}$ so $\angle PRQ = \sin^{-1}\left(\frac{16\sin 37^\circ}{12}\right) = 53.36...^\circ$

By the symmetry of $\sin x$, there is another solution $\angle PRQ = 180° - 53.36...° = 126.63...°$

So the possible values of $\angle PQR$ are:
$\angle PQR = 180° - 37° - 53.36° = 89.63...°$ or
$\angle PQR = 180° - 37° - 126.63° = 16.36...°$

So the possible areas of ΔPQR are:

$A_1 = \frac{1}{2} \times 16 \times 12 \times \sin 89.63...° = 95.99... = 96.0$ m² (3 s.f.)

$A_2 = \frac{1}{2} \times 16 \times 12 \times \sin 16.36...° = 27.04... = 27.0$ m² (3 s.f.)

[6 marks available — 1 mark for using the sine rule, 1 mark for finding the acute angle PRQ, 1 mark for finding one of the possible values of angle PQR, 1 mark for finding the obtuse angle PRQ, 1 mark for using the area formula, 1 mark for both areas correct to 3 s.f.]

Q12 The triangle AOB and the shaded region form a sector with an area of $\frac{60}{360} = \frac{1}{6}$ of the total area of the circle.

Area of sector $= \frac{1}{6} \times \pi \times 8^2 = \frac{32\pi}{3}$ m²

Area of $\Delta AOB = \frac{1}{2} \times 8^2 \times \sin 60° = 16\sqrt{3}$ m²

$\Rightarrow$ Area of shaded region $= \frac{32\pi}{3} - 16\sqrt{3}$ m²

[4 marks available — 1 mark for a correct method of calculating the area of a triangle, 1 mark for the correct area of triangle AOB, 1 mark for the correct area of the sector, 1 mark for correct answer]

Q13 a) Let the side-length of the square base be x, then the area of the square base is x^2.
Using the cosine rule, $a^2 = b^2 + c^2 - 2bc\cos A$, on one of the triangular faces gives:
$x^2 = (\sqrt{2})^2 + (\sqrt{2})^2 - 2 \times \sqrt{2} \times \sqrt{2} \times \cos 30° = 4 - 2\sqrt{3}$
Therefore, the area of the square base is $4 - 2\sqrt{3}$ m².
[2 marks available — 1 mark for using the cosine rule, 1 mark for correct area of square base]

b) The area of one of the triangular faces is
$\frac{1}{2} \times \sqrt{2} \times \sqrt{2} \times \sin 30° = \frac{1}{2}$ m²
Therefore, the area of all four triangular faces is equal to 2 m².
So, the total surface area of the pyramid is $6 - 2\sqrt{3}$ m².
[2 marks available — 1 mark for finding the area of a triangular face, 1 mark for the correct answer]

Q14 $\tan x - \sin x\cos x \equiv \frac{\sin x}{\cos x} - \sin x\cos x$

$\equiv \frac{\sin x - \sin x\cos^2 x}{\cos x}$

$\equiv \frac{\sin x(1 - \cos^2 x)}{\cos x}$

$\equiv \frac{\sin x(\sin^2 x)}{\cos x}$

$\equiv \sin^2 x\tan x$

Q15 $\tan^2 x - \cos^2 x + 1 \equiv \frac{\sin^2 x}{\cos^2 x} - (1 - \sin^2 x) + 1$

$\equiv \frac{\sin^2 x}{\cos^2 x} + \sin^2 x$

$\equiv \frac{\sin^2 x + \sin^2 x\cos^2 x}{\cos^2 x}$

$\equiv \frac{\sin^2 x(1 + \cos^2 x)}{\cos^2 x}$

$\equiv \tan^2 x(1 + \cos^2 x)$

Q16 $(\sin y + \cos y)^2 + (\cos y - \sin y)^2$
$\equiv (\sin^2 y + 2\sin y\cos y + \cos^2 y) + (\cos^2 y - 2\sin y\cos y + \sin^2 y)$
$\equiv 2\sin^2 y + 2\sin y\cos y - 2\sin y\cos y + 2\cos^2 y$
$\equiv 2(\sin^2 y + \cos^2 y)$
$\equiv 2$

Q17 $\frac{\sin^4 x + \sin^2 x\cos^2 x}{\cos^2 x - 1} \equiv \frac{\sin^4 x + \sin^2 x(1 - \sin^2 x)}{1 - \sin^2 x - 1}$

$\equiv \frac{\sin^4 x + \sin^2 x - \sin^4 x}{-\sin^2 x}$

$\equiv \frac{\sin^2 x}{-\sin^2 x} \equiv -1$

Q18 $\frac{\cos x}{\tan x} + \sin x \equiv \cos x\frac{\cos x}{\sin x} + \sin x$

$\equiv \frac{\cos^2 x}{\sin x} + \frac{\sin^2 x}{\sin x}$

$\equiv \frac{\sin^2 x + \cos^2 x}{\sin x}$

$\equiv \frac{1}{\sin x}$

[3 marks available — 1 mark for using $\tan x \equiv \frac{\sin x}{\cos x}$, 1 mark for making a common denominator, 1 mark for using $\sin^2 x + \cos^2 x = 1$]

Q19 a)

b)

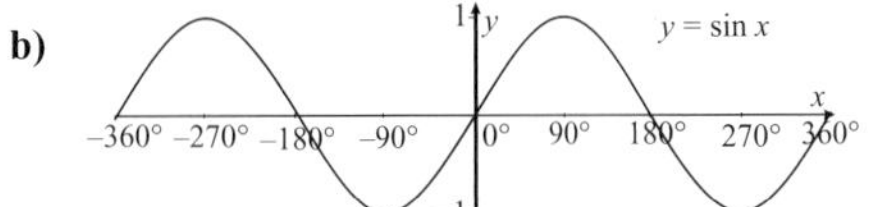

c)

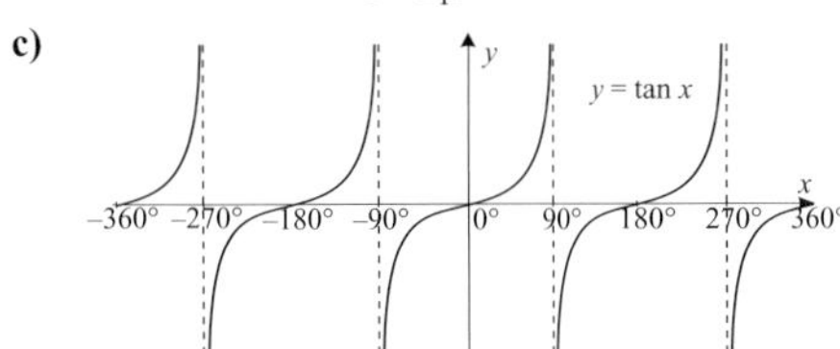

Q20 The graph has been reflected in the y-axis, and stretched vertically by a factor of $\frac{1}{2}$, so the equation is $y = -\frac{1}{2}\cos x$.

Q21 The graph has been stretched horizontally by a factor of $\frac{1}{2}$, so the equation is $y = \sin 2x$.

Q22 a)

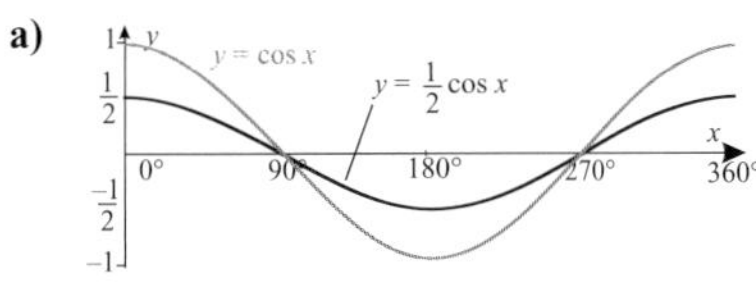

b) 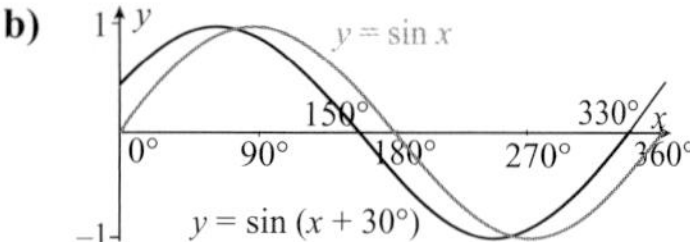

c) 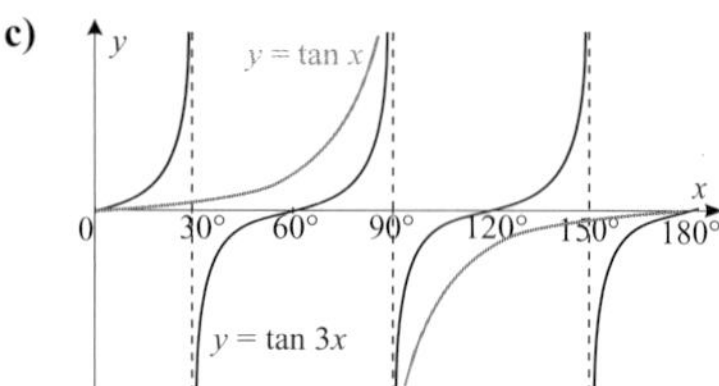

Q23 a) 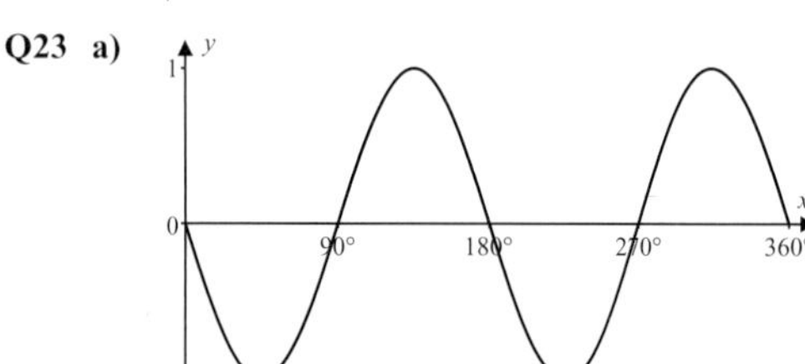

[2 marks available — 1 mark for the correct shape in the correct range, 1 mark for the axis intercepts and maximum and minimum values indicated]

b) 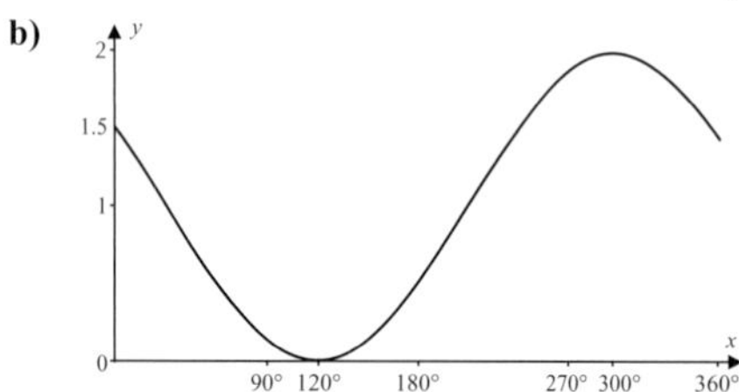

[2 marks available — 1 mark for the correct shape in the correct range, 1 mark for the axis intercepts and maximum and minimum values indicated]

Q24 Compare this graph with the graph of $y = \sin x$:
$y = \sin x$ has a maximum at 1, and this graph has an maximum at 3, so it has been stretched vertically by a factor of 3, i.e. $p = 3$.
$y = \sin x$ intersects the x-axis at $x = 180°$, and this graph intersects the x-axis at $x = 90°$, so it has been stretched horizontally by a factor of $\frac{1}{2}$, i.e. $q = 2$.
[3 marks available — 1 mark for identifying vertical stretch, 1 mark for identifying horizontal stretch, 1 mark for both correct values of p and q]

Q25 a) (i) g(x) intersects the x–axis at:
(–330°, 0), (–150°, 0), (30°, 0), (210°, 0)
[2 marks available — 2 marks for all four coordinates correct, otherwise 1 mark for two coordinates correct]

(ii) The equations of the asymptotes of g(x) are:
$x = -240°$, $x = -60°$, $x = 120°$, $x = 300°$
[2 marks available — 2 marks for all 4 equations correct, otherwise 1 mark for 2 equations correct]

b) As $f(x) = \tan x \equiv \frac{\sin x}{\cos x}$, asymptotes exist for any value of x such that $\cos x = 0$. *[1 mark]*

c) The graph of tan x has rotational symmetry around the origin, so tan (–30°) = –tan 30°.
So $\tan 30° = \frac{\sqrt{3}}{3}$.
[2 marks available — 1 mark for correct answer, 1 mark for a valid comment referring to rotational symmetry or odd functions]

Q26 a) (i) The first solution is $\theta = \sin^{-1}\left(\frac{\sqrt{3}}{2}\right) = 60°$.
By symmetry of the graph, another solution in the given interval is $\theta = 180° - 60° = 120°$.

(ii) The first solution is $\theta = \tan^{-1}(-1) = -45°$.
This is outside the interval, but the graph of tan repeats every 180°, so find the solutions by adding multiples of 180°:
$\theta = -45° + 180° = 135°$ and
$\theta = 135° + 180° = 315°$

(iii) The first solution is $\theta = \cos^{-1}\left(-\frac{1}{\sqrt{2}}\right) = 135°$.
By the symmetry of the cos graph, there is another solution at $360° - 135° = 225°$.

b) (i) Look for solutions in the interval $-720° \leq 4\theta \leq 720°$.
The first solution is $4\theta = \cos^{-1}\left(-\frac{2}{3}\right) = 131.81...°$.
By the symmetry of the graph, there's another solution at $4\theta = 360° - 131.81...° = 228.18...°$. Add or subtract 360° to find other solutions in the interval:
$4\theta = -588.18...°, -491.81...°, -228.2°, -131.81...°,$
$131.81...°, 228.18...°, 491.81...°, 588.18...°$
These are solutions for 4θ so divide each by 4:
$\theta = -147.0°, -123.0°, -57.0°, -33.0°,$
$33.0°, 57.0°, 123.0°. 147.0°$ (1 d.p.)

(ii) Look for solutions in the interval
$-145° \leq \theta + 35° \leq 215°$.
The first solution is $\theta + 35° = \sin^{-1}(0.3) = 17.45..°$
By the symmetry of the graph, there's another solution at $\theta + 35° = 180° - 17.45...° = 162.54...°$
So the solutions are $\theta = -17.5°$, $127.5°$ (1 d.p.)

(iii) Look for solutions in the interval $-90° \leq \frac{\theta}{2} \leq 90°$.
The first solution is $\frac{\theta}{2} = \tan^{-1}(500) = 89.89...°$
All other solutions are outside the interval.
This is a solution for $\frac{\theta}{2}$, so multiply by 2:
$\theta = 179.8°$ (1 d.p.)

Q27 $2\sin(x + 30°) = \frac{1}{4} \Rightarrow \sin(x + 30°) = \frac{1}{8}$
Look for solutions in the interval:
$-330° \leq x + 30° \leq 390°$.
The first solution is $(x + 30°) = 7.18...°$.
By the symmetry of sin, there is another solution
$x + 30° = 180° - 7.18...° = 172.82...°$
To find other solutions in the interval, add or subtract 360° from the solutions already found:
$x + 30° = -187.18...°, 7.18...°, 172.82...°, 367.18...°$
So $x = -217.2°, -22.8°, 142.8°, 337.2°$ (1 d.p.)
[5 marks available — 1 mark for using the inverse sin function, 1 mark for adapting the interval given the transformation of sin x to sin (x + 30°), 1 mark for finding the other solutions in the interval, 1 mark for a method to convert the solutions of (x + 30°) to the solutions of x, 1 mark for all four correct values of x]
You could also use a CAST diagram to find the other solutions to the equation.

Q28 a) 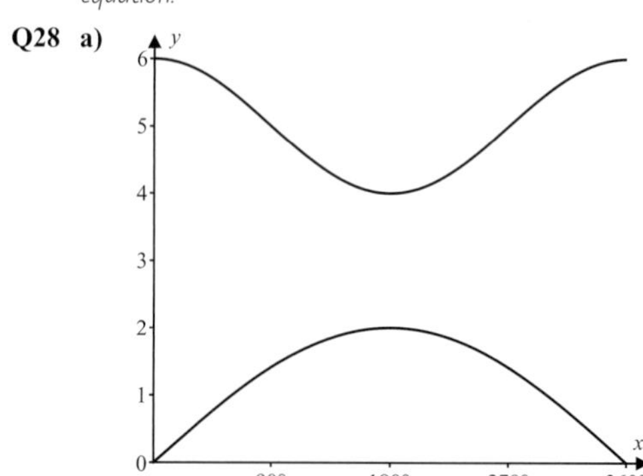

b) There are no points of intersection of the graphs of the two functions sketched in a) and so there are no solutions to the given equation in the range $0° \leq x \leq 360°$.

c) In this interval, the minimum value of $y = k + \cos x$ is $y = k - 1$ when $x = 180°$, and the maximum value is $y = k + 1$ when $x = 0°$ (or $x = 360°$).
The maximum of $y = 2\sin\left(\frac{1}{2}x\right)$ is $y = 2$ (when $x = 180°$) and the minimum is $y = 0$ (when $x = 0°$ or $x = 360°$).
So there are no points of intersection with the graphs when $k - 1 > 2$, i.e. $k > 3$, or when $k + 1 < 0$, i.e. $k < -1$.
The points of intersection occur when $k \geq -1$ and $k \leq 3$. Therefore, the equation will only have at least one solution for values of k in the interval $-1 \leq k \leq 3$.

Q29 a)

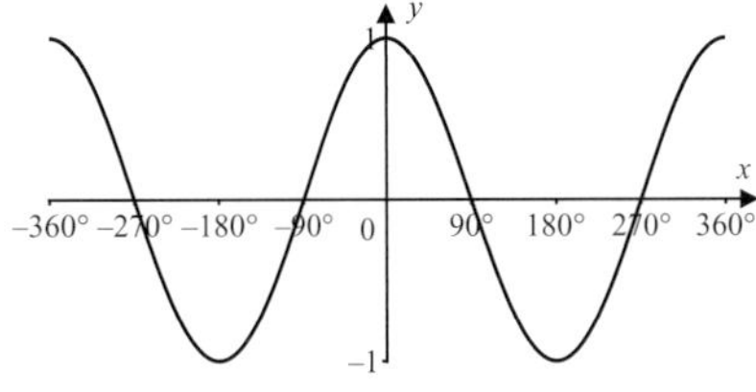

[2 marks available — 1 mark for the correct shape in the correct range, 1 mark for the axis intercepts and maximum and minimum values indicated]

b) Let $x = 2\theta$, then the equation $k\cos 2\theta + 1 = 0$ (for $-180° \leq \theta \leq 180°$) is equivalent to the equation $k\cos x + 1 = 0$ (for $-360° \leq x \leq 360°$) $\Rightarrow \cos x = -\frac{1}{k}$
k is a positive integer, so there are four solutions. Given that $x = a$ is the smallest positive solution, using the graph sketched in a), the four solutions are:
$x = a - 360°,\ -a,\ a,\ 360° - a$
$\Rightarrow 2\theta = a - 360°,\ -a,\ a,\ 360° - a$
$\Rightarrow \theta = \frac{1}{2}(a - 360°),\ -\frac{1}{2}a,\ \frac{1}{2}a,\ \frac{1}{2}(360° - a)$
[3 marks available — 1 mark for rearranging the equation, 2 marks for all four solutions, otherwise 1 mark for at least two correct solutions]

Q30 a)

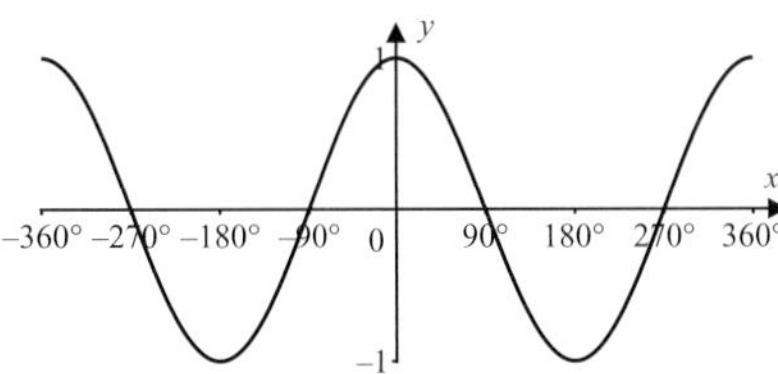

[2 marks available — 1 mark for the correct shape in the correct range, 1 mark for the axis intercepts and maximum and minimum values indicated]

b) $f(x) = \frac{3}{4} \Rightarrow \frac{2}{3 + 2\cos x} = \frac{3}{4}$
$\Rightarrow 8 = 9 + 6\cos x \Rightarrow \cos x = -\frac{1}{6}$
$\Rightarrow x = 99.594...° = 99.6°$ (1 d.p.)
Using the symmetry of the graph from a) to find the other solutions gives $x = -260.4°, -99.6°, 99.6°, 260.4°$.
[3 marks available — 1 mark for rearranging, 1 mark for at least one correct solution, 1 mark for all correct solutions]

c) The maximum of f(x) occurs whenever the denominator is at its smallest, which happens for minimum values of $\cos x$. Therefore, the maximum of f(x) is whenever $\cos x = -1$.
So the maximum value of f(x) is 2 and the first positive value of x at which it will occur is $x = 180°$.
[2 marks available — 1 mark for correct maximum value, 1 mark for correct value of x at which it occurs]

Q31 a) $3\sin x - 4\cos x = 0 \Rightarrow 3\sin x = 4\cos x$
$\Rightarrow \frac{\sin x}{\cos x} = \frac{4}{3} \Rightarrow \tan x = \frac{4}{3}$
[2 marks available — 1 mark for rearranging the equation to form $\frac{\sin x}{\cos x}$, 1 mark for using the identity $\tan x \equiv \frac{\sin x}{\cos x}$]

b) The first solution is $x = \tan^{-1}\left(\frac{4}{3}\right) = 53.13...° = 53.1°$ (1 d.p.).
The graph of tan repeats every 180°, so the other solution in the interval is: $53.13...° + 180° = 233.13...° = 233.1°$ (1 d.p.)
[3 marks available — 1 mark for using the inverse tan function, 1 mark for finding the solution x = 53.1°, 1 mark for both solutions of x correct to 1 d.p.]

Q32 $6\sin^2 x - \cos x - 5 = 0 \Rightarrow 6(1 - \cos^2 x) - \cos x - 5 = 0$
$\Rightarrow -6\cos^2 x - \cos x + 1 = 0$
$\Rightarrow 6\cos^2 x + \cos x - 1 = 0$
$\Rightarrow (3\cos x - 1)(2\cos x + 1) = 0$

Either $\cos x = \frac{1}{3}$ or $\cos x = -\frac{1}{2}$:
For $\cos x = \frac{1}{3}$, the first solution is $x = 70.52...°$.
By the symmetry of cos, there is another solution at $360° - 70.52...° = 289.47...°$
For $\cos x = -\frac{1}{2}$, the first solution is $x = 120°$. By the symmetry of cos, there is another solution at $360° - 120° = 240°$.
So the solutions to the equation are:
$x = 70.5°$ (1 d.p.), 120°, 240°, 289.5° (1 d.p.)

Q33 $3\tan x + 2\cos x = 0 \Rightarrow 3\frac{\sin x}{\cos x} + 2\cos x = 0$
$\Rightarrow 3\sin x + 2\cos^2 x = 0$
$\Rightarrow 3\sin x + 2(1 - \sin^2 x) = 0$
$\Rightarrow -2\sin^2 x + 3\sin x + 2 = 0$
$\Rightarrow 2\sin^2 x - 3\sin x - 2 = 0$
$\Rightarrow (\sin x - 2)(2\sin x + 1) = 0$

Either $\sin x = -2$ (this has no solutions) or $\sin x = -\frac{1}{2}$.
The first solution to $\sin x = -\frac{1}{2}$ is $x = -30°$. This is the only solution to the equation in the given interval.

Q34 $\tan x - 3\sin x = 0 \Rightarrow \frac{\sin x}{\cos x} - 3\sin x = 0$
$\Rightarrow \sin x - 3\sin x\cos x = 0$
$\Rightarrow \sin x\,(1 - 3\cos x) = 0$

Either $\sin x = 0$ or $\cos x = \frac{1}{3}$. For $\sin x = 0$:
The solutions are $x = 0°, 180°, 360°, 540°, 720°$.
For $\cos x = \frac{1}{3}$, the first solution is $x = 70.52...°$
By the symmetry of cos, there is another solution at $360° - 70.52...° = 289.47...°$. To find further solutions, add 360° to the solutions found already:
So the solutions are:
$x = 0°$, 70.5° (1 d.p.), 180°, 289.5° (1 d.p.), 360°, 430.5° (1 d.p.), 540°, 649.5° (1 d.p.), 720°

Q35 $8\sin^2 x + 2\sin x - 1 = 0 \Rightarrow (2\sin x + 1)(4\sin x - 1) = 0$
So either $\sin x = -\frac{1}{2}$ or $\sin x = \frac{1}{4}$.
For $\sin x = -\frac{1}{2}$, $x = -30°$. This is outside the interval, so add 360° to get the first solution: $-30° + 360° = 330°$
By the symmetry of $\sin x$, the other solution in the interval is $180° + 30° = 210°$.
For $\sin x = \frac{1}{4}$, the first solution is $x = 14.47...°$
By the symmetry of $\sin x$, the other solution in the interval is $180° - 14.47...° = 165.52...°$
So the solutions are: $x = 14.5°$ (1 d.p.), 165.5° (1 d.p.), 210°, 330°

Q36 Using the identity $\tan x \equiv \frac{\sin x}{\cos x}$ gives:
$2\cos(\theta - 80°) = 3\tan(\theta - 80°)$
$\Rightarrow 2\cos(\theta - 80°) = 3\frac{\sin(\theta - 80°)}{\cos(\theta - 80°)}$
$\Rightarrow 2\cos^2(\theta - 80°) = 3\sin(\theta - 80°)$
Now using the identity $\cos^2 x = 1 - \sin^2 x$:
$\Rightarrow 2 - 2\sin^2(\theta - 80°) = 3\sin(\theta - 80°)$
$\Rightarrow (2\sin(\theta - 80°) - 1)(\sin(\theta - 80°) + 2)$
$\Rightarrow \sin(\theta - 80°) = \frac{1}{2}$ or $\sin(\theta - 80°) = -2$

Look for solutions in the interval $-80° \leq \theta - 80° \leq 280°$.
There are no solutions to $\sin(\theta - 80°) = -2$. The first solution to $\sin(\theta - 80°) = \frac{1}{2}$ is $\theta - 80° = \sin^{-1}(\frac{1}{2}) = 30°$.
Using the symmetry of sin, subtract from 180° to find another solution: $\theta - 80° = 180° - 30° = 150°$.
So the values of θ which satisfy the original equation are $\theta = 30° + 80° = 110°$ and $\theta = 150° + 80° = 230°$.
[6 marks available — 1 mark for changing the interval, 1 mark for use of identity $\tan x \equiv \frac{\sin x}{\cos x}$, 1 mark for use of trig identity $\sin^2 x + \cos^2 x \equiv 1$, 1 mark for derivation of both equations in sin to solve, 1 mark for one correct value of $\theta - 80°$, 1 mark for second correct value of θ]

Q37 a) Factorising then using the identity $\cos^2 x \equiv 1 - \sin^2 x$ gives:
$$\cos^4 x - \cos^2 x \equiv \cos^2 x(\cos^2 x - 1) \equiv (1 - \sin^2 x)(-\sin^2 x) \equiv \sin^4 x - \sin^2 x$$
[2 marks available — 1 mark for using an appropriate trigonometric identity, 1 mark for a correct derivation]

b) Rearranging the identity in a) gives
$\sin^4 x - \cos^4 x \equiv \sin^2 x - \cos^2 x$
So $2\sin^4 x - 2\cos^4 x = \cos x - 1$
$\Rightarrow 2\sin^2 x - 2\cos^2 x = \cos x - 1$
$\Rightarrow 2(1 - \cos^2 x) - 2\cos^2 x = \cos x - 1$
$\Rightarrow 4\cos^2 x + \cos x - 3 = 0$
$\Rightarrow (4\cos x - 3)(\cos x + 1) = 0$
$\Rightarrow \cos x = \frac{3}{4}$ or $\cos x = -1$
$\Rightarrow x = 41.4°$ (1 d.p.), 180°, 318.6° (1 d.p.)
[4 marks available — 1 mark for use of result from a), 1 mark for derivation of both equations in cos x, 1 mark for two correct solutions, 1 mark for all three correct solutions]

Q38 a) Evaluate the function when $t = 3$:
$T(3) = 15 + 8\sin(45 \times 3) = 20.7$ (1 d.p.)
So after 3 hours, the temperature of the room is 20.7 °C.
[2 marks available — 1 mark for substituting t = 3 into the function, 1 mark for the correct answer rounded to an appropriate degree of accuracy]

b) The maximum value that $\sin\theta$ can take is 1 and the minimum value it can take is –1.
So the maximum value is $T(t) = 15 + 8(1) = 23$ °C and the minimum value is $T(t) = 15 + 8(-1) = 7$ °C.
[2 marks available — 1 mark for the correct maximum and 1 mark for the correct minimum]

c) $T(t) = 15 + 8\sin(45t) = 20$
$\Rightarrow \sin(45t) = \frac{5}{8} \Rightarrow 45t = \sin^{-1}\left(\frac{5}{8}\right) = 38.682...$
Using the symmetry of sin, there is another solution at $45t = 180 - 38.682... = 141.317...$
Divide the solutions by 45 to find the values of t:
$t = 0.896..., 3.140....$
The next solution is when $45t = 38.682... + 360$, i.e. $t = 398.682... \div 45 = 8.85$ which is outside the interval — the temperature reaches 20 °C twice during the first 8 hours.
[6 marks available — 1 mark for substituting 20 into the function, 1 mark for finding one correct value of 45t, 1 mark for one correct value of t, 1 mark for finding the second value of t, 1 mark for showing there are only two solutions in the interval 0 < t < 8, 1 mark for stating the temperature reaches 20 °C twice]

Q39 a) Using the identity $\cos^2 x + \sin^2 x \equiv 1$ gives:
$$\frac{1 - 2\sin\theta\cos\theta}{1 + 2\sin\theta\cos\theta} \equiv \frac{\cos^2\theta + \sin^2\theta - 2\sin\theta\cos\theta}{\cos^2\theta + \sin^2\theta + 2\sin\theta\cos\theta} \equiv \frac{(\sin\theta - \cos\theta)^2}{(\sin\theta + \cos\theta)^2} \equiv \left(\frac{\sin\theta - \cos\theta}{\sin\theta + \cos\theta}\right)^2$$
[2 marks available — 1 mark for using $\sin^2\theta + \cos^2\theta \equiv 1$, 1 mark for deriving the correct identity]

b)
$$\frac{\sin x - \sin^2 x}{\cos x + \cos^2 x} \equiv \frac{\sin x(1 - \sin x)}{\cos x(1 + \cos x)} \equiv \frac{\sin x(1 - \sin x)}{\cos x(1 + \cos x)} \times \frac{1 - \cos x}{1 - \cos x} \equiv \frac{\sin x(1 - \sin x)(1 - \cos x)}{\cos x(1 + \cos x)(1 - \cos x)} \equiv \frac{\sin x(1 - \sin x)(1 - \cos x)}{\cos x(1 - \cos^2 x)}$$
Using the identity $\cos^2 x + \sin^2 x \equiv 1$ gives:
$$\frac{\sin x - \sin^2 x}{\cos x + \cos^2 x} \equiv \frac{\sin x(1 - \sin x)(1 - \cos x)}{\sin^2 x \cos x} \equiv \frac{(1 - \sin x)(1 - \cos x)}{\sin x \cos x}$$
[3 marks available — 1 mark for correct working, 1 mark for using an appropriate correct trigonometric identity, 1 mark for deriving the correct identity]

Q40 a) Using trigonometry on the triangle AOD gives
$AO = AD \sin \angle ADO = 1.75 \sin 30° = 0.875$,
so the height of A above the ground is 0.875 m.
$\angle OAD = 180° - 90° - 30° = 60°$ (angles in a triangle), so
$\angle BAQ = 180° - 90° - 60° = 30°$ (angles on a line).
So the height of B above A is:
$AB \cos \angle BAQ = 1 \times \cos 30° = \frac{\sqrt{3}}{2} = 0.866...$ m
Therefore the height of B above the ground is:
$0.875 + 0.866... = 1.741...$ m $= 1.74$ m (2 d.p.)
[3 marks available — 1 mark for calculating the height of B above A, 1 mark for calculating the height of A above the ground (AO), 1 mark for the correct answer]

b) $\angle BYX = \angle ADO = 30°$ since BC and AD are parallel and XY is horizontal, hence:
$BX = BY \times \tan 30° \Rightarrow BX = \frac{1}{\sqrt{3}} BY$
Calculate the area of triangle XBY in two different ways, then set them equal to each other and solve the equation to find the length of BY:
Area of $\Delta XBY = \frac{1}{2} BX \times BY = \frac{1}{2\sqrt{3}} BY^2$
Area of $\Delta XBY = (1.75 \times 1) - 1.3 = 0.45$ m²
$\Rightarrow \frac{1}{2\sqrt{3}} BY^2 = 0.45 \Rightarrow BY = 1.248... = 1.25$ m (2 d.p.)
[2 marks available — 1 mark for a correct relationship between BX and BY, 1 mark for the correct answer]

c) The height of the waterline XY below B is
$BY \sin \angle BYX = 1.248... \times \sin 30° = 0.624...$ m
So the height of the surface of the water above the ground is $1.741... - 0.624... = 1.116...$m $= 1.12$ m (2 d.p.)
[2 marks available — 1 mark for the height of B above the line XY, 1 mark for the correct answer]

Q41 a)

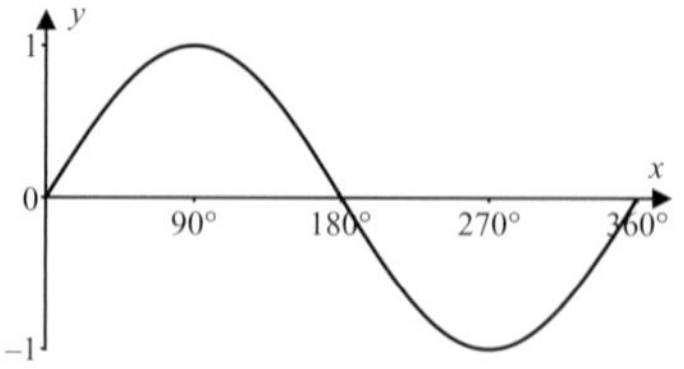

y
1
0
–1
x
90°
180°
270°
360°

[2 marks available — 1 mark for the correct shape in the correct range, 1 mark for the axis intercepts and maximum and minimum values indicated]

b) $-1 \leq \sin x \leq 1 \Rightarrow 0 \leq \sin^2 x \leq 1$
The maximum value of f(x) is 1 and will occur at any point where $\sin x$ is equal to ±1, which is $x = 90°$ and $x = 270°$.
The minimum value of f(x) is 0 and will occur at any point where $\sin x = 0$, which is $x = 0°$, 180° and 360°.
[2 marks available — 1 mark for correct maximum value and corresponding x-values, 1 mark for correct minimum value and corresponding x-values]

c) $f(x) = \frac{1}{4}$ whenever $\sin x = \sqrt{\frac{1}{4}} = \pm\frac{1}{2}$

The first solution is $x = \sin^{-1}(\frac{1}{2}) = 30°$. Using the symmetry of the sin graph, the other solutions are: $x = 180° - 30° = 150°$, $x = 30° + 180° = 210°$ and $x = 360° - 30° = 330°$.

[2 marks available — 1 mark for finding one solution, 1 mark for finding the remaining three solutions]

d)

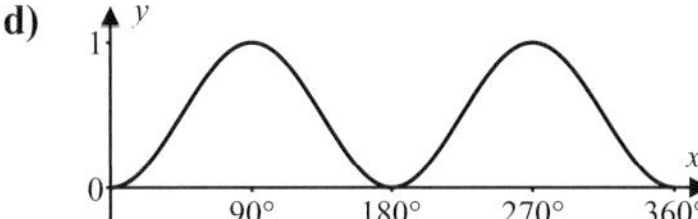

[2 marks available — 1 mark for the correct shape in the correct range, 1 mark for the axis intercepts and maximum and minimum values indicated]

Q42 a) The maximum value cos $30t$ can take is 1 and the minimum value it can take is –1. So the highest water level is $5.5 + 1 = 6.5$ ft, and the lowest water level is $5.5 - 1 = 4.5$ ft.

[1 mark for both correct answers]

b) Let $\theta = 30t$, then graph of $5.5 - \cos(30t)$ on the interval $0 \le t \le 24$ has the same shape as the graph of $5.5 - \cos(\theta)$ on the interval $0° \le \theta \le 720°$.

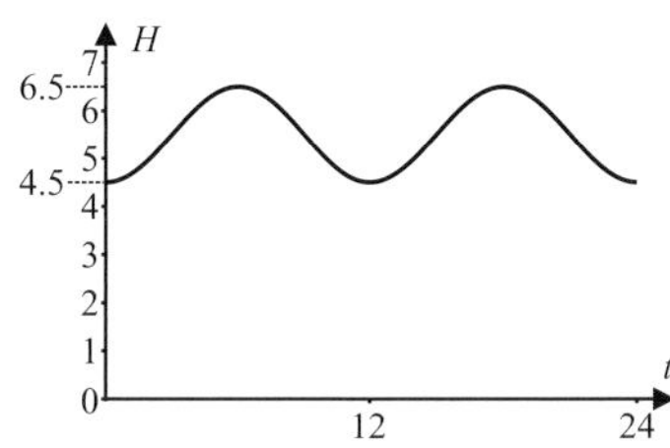

[2 marks available — 1 mark for the correct shape in the correct range, 1 mark for the axis intercepts and maximum and minimum values indicated]

The graph of 5.5 – cos(θ) is a reflection of cos(θ) in the x-axis, followed by a translation of 5.5 units in the y-direction.

c) $5.5 - \cos(30t) = 5 \Rightarrow \cos(30t) = 0.5$

One solution is $30t = \cos^{-1}(0.5) = 60° \Rightarrow t = 60 \div 30 = 2$

The graph from part b) shows there are three more solutions.

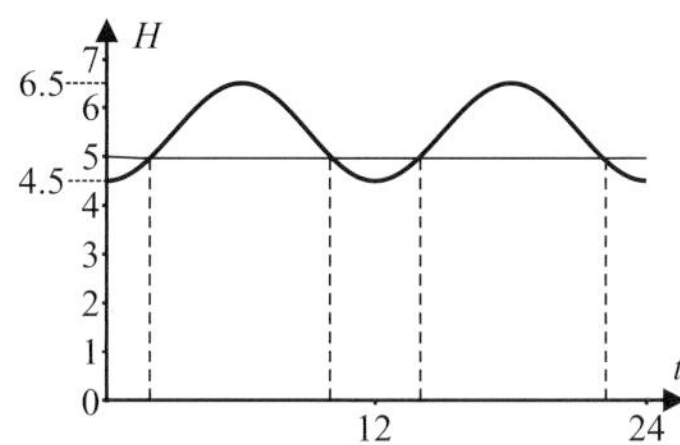

Using the symmetry of the graph, the other solutions are: $t = 12 - 2 = 10$, $t = 12 + 2 = 14$ and $t = 24 - 2 = 22$.

$t = 2$ corresponds to 2 a.m, $t = 22$ corresponds to 10 p.m.

The earliest time that Anna can leave the dock is 2 a.m.

The latest time that Anna can return to the dock is 10 p.m.

[4 marks available — 1 mark for using the correct equation, 1 mark for finding values of t in the interval $0 \le t \le 24$, 1 mark for the earliest time, 1 mark for the latest time]

Q43 a) Using identities $\tan x \equiv \frac{\sin x}{\cos x}$ and $\cos^2 x \equiv 1 - \sin^2 x$ gives:

$3 \cos x \tan x = 10 \cos^2 x - 6$

$\Rightarrow 3 \cos x \frac{\sin x}{\cos x} = 10(1 - \sin^2 x) - 6$

$\Rightarrow 3 \sin x = 10 - 10 \sin^2 x - 6$

$\Rightarrow 10 \sin^2 x + 3 \sin x - 4 = 0$

[4 marks available — 1 mark for using the identity $\tan x \equiv \frac{\sin x}{\cos x}$, 1 mark for using the identity $\cos^2 x \equiv 1 - \sin^2 x$, 1 mark for simplifying, 1 mark for rearranging and deriving the correct identity]

b) Look for solutions in the interval $-90° \le 2x \le 90°$. Using the result from a),

$3 \cos 2x \tan 2x = 10 \cos^2 2x - 6$

$\Rightarrow 10 \sin^2 2x + 3 \sin 2x - 4 = 0$

$\Rightarrow (2 \sin 2x - 1)(5 \sin 2x + 4) = 0$

$\Rightarrow \sin 2x = \frac{1}{2}$ or $\sin 2x = -\frac{4}{5}$

$\Rightarrow 2x = \sin^{-1}(\frac{1}{2}) = 30°$ or $2x = \sin^{-1}(-\frac{4}{5}) = -53.13...°$

From the symmetry of the graph of sin, there are no more solutions in the interval $-90° \le 2x \le 90°$. So there are two solutions: $x = 15°$ or $x = -26.56...° = -26.6°$ (3 s.f.).

[4 marks available — 1 mark for using the result from part a), 1 mark for factorising correctly, 1 mark for x = 15°, 1 mark for x = –26.6°]

Chapter 9: Exponentials and Logarithms

Prior Knowledge Check

Q1 Interest over 1 year: £1600 × 0.05 = £80

Total interest over 4 years: £80 × 4 = £320

Q2 Gradient = –7, y-intercept = (0, 8)

Q3

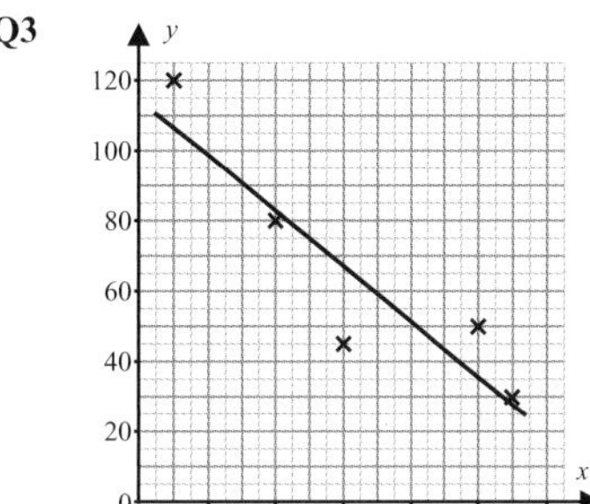

Q4 a) $\sqrt[3]{27} = 3$ **b)** 1

c) $\frac{1}{9^2} = \frac{1}{81}$ **d)** $(\sqrt{16})^3 = 4^3 = 64$

Q5 a) Let $u = x^{\frac{1}{2}}$, so $x - 7x^{\frac{1}{2}} + 6 = 0 \Rightarrow u^2 - 7u + 6 = 0$

b) $u^2 - 7u + 6 = 0 \Rightarrow (u - 1)(u - 6) \Rightarrow u = 1$ or $u = 6$

$\Rightarrow x^{\frac{1}{2}} = 1$ or $x^{\frac{1}{2}} = 6 \Rightarrow x = 1^2 = 1$ or $x = 6^2 = 36$

Q6 The graph of $y = f(-x)$ is the graph of $y = f(x)$ reflected in the y-axis, so the graph of $f(-x)$ has a minimum point at (–4, –6) and a maximum point at (2, 8).

Exercise 9.1 — Exponentials

Q1 a)

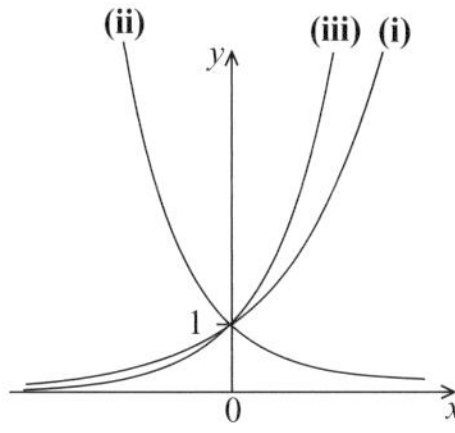

b)

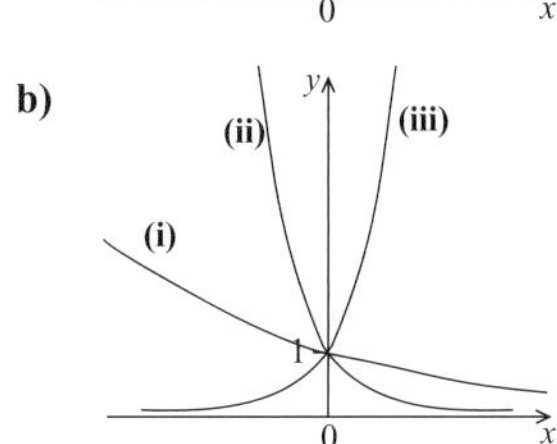

Q2 The graph cuts the y-axis at $y = \left(\frac{2}{3}\right)^{0+1} = \frac{2}{3}$ and doesn't cross the x-axis.

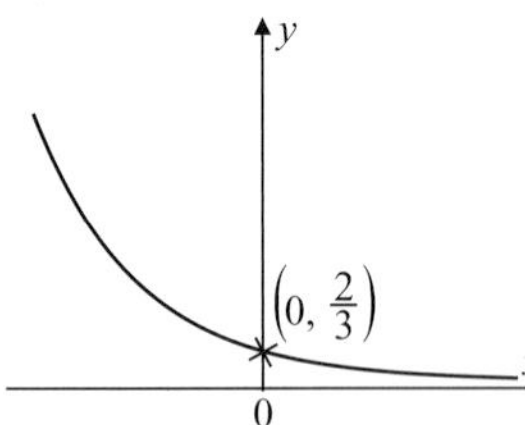

[2 marks available — 1 mark for a correct exponential shape with negative gradient, 1 mark for the correct y-intercept]

Q3 **a)** $y = 3e^{3x} = h(x)$ — a positive exponential graph passing through (0, 3) (when $x = 0$, $3e^0 = 3$).

b) $y = 3^x = f(x)$ — a positive exponential graph passing through (0, 1).

c) $y = 3e^{-x} = g(x)$ — a reflection of $y = 3e^x$ in the y-axis.

Q4 The graph cuts the y-axis at $y = e^{0+3} = e^3$ and doesn't cross the x-axis.

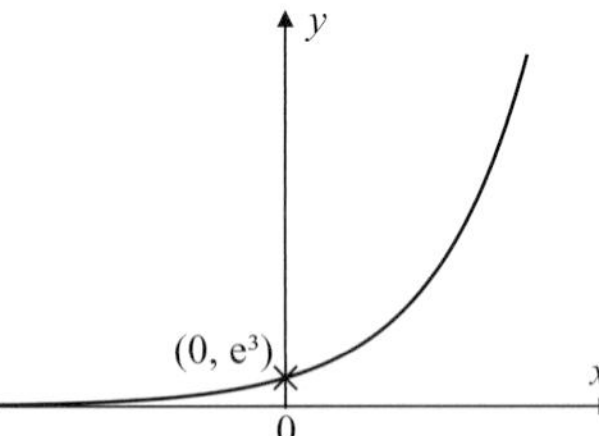

[2 marks available — 1 mark for a correct exponential shape with positive gradient, 1 mark for the correct y-intercept]

Q5 **a)** $f(-x) = e^{2(-x)} = e^{-2x} = (e^x)^{-2} = (g(x))^{-2}$ or $\frac{1}{(g(x))^2}$.
[2 marks available — 1 mark for an attempt to rewrite in terms of e^x, 1 mark for the correct answer]

b) $f(x-1) = e^{2(x-1)} = e^{2x-2} = \frac{e^{2x}}{e^2} = \frac{1}{e^2}(e^x)^2 = \frac{1}{e^2}g(x)^2$
[2 marks available — 1 mark for an attempt to rewrite in terms of e^x, 1 mark for the correct answer]

Q6 **a)** $y = f(x)$ is graph B — a positive exponential graph passing through (0, 1).

b) $y = f(x) + 2$ is graph C — a vertical translation of $f(x)$ by +2.

c) $y = f(-x)$ is graph A — a reflection of $f(x)$ in the y-axis.

Q7 **a)** $y = f(x+1) = e^{x+1}$ cuts the y-axis at $x = 0$, $y = e^{0+1} = e$.

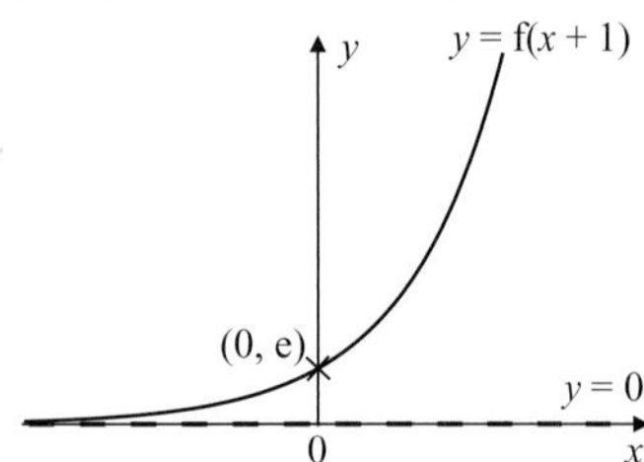

[3 marks available — 1 mark for a correct exponential shape with positive gradient, 1 mark for the correct y-intercept, 1 mark for the asymptote at y = 0 labelled]

b) $y = f(x) + 1 = e^x + 1$ cuts the y-axis at $x = 0$, $y = e^0 + 1 = 2$. As $y = e^x$ has an asymptote at $y = 0$, $y = e^x + 1$ has an asymptote at $y = 1$.

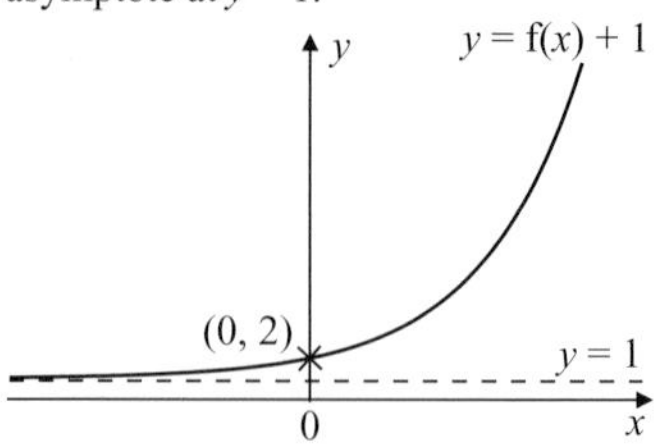

[3 marks available — 1 mark for a correct exponential shape with positive gradient, 1 mark for the correct y-intercept, 1 mark for the asymptote at y = 1 labelled]

Q8 **a)** $y = e^{3x}$, so the gradient at any value of x is $3e^{3x}$.
At $x = 0$, gradient $= 3e^{3\times0} = 3e^0 = 3 \times 1 = 3$
At $x = 1$, gradient $= 3e^{3\times1} = 3e^3$
The question asks for exact answers, so leave them in terms of e.

b) $y = 5e^{0.5x}$, so the gradient at any value of x is $2.5e^{0.5x}$.
At $x = -2$, gradient $= 2.5e^{0.5\times-2} = 2.5e^{-1} = \frac{2.5}{e}$
At $x = 2$, gradient $= 2.5e^{0.5\times2} = 2.5e^1 = 2.5e$

c) $x = 2.5e^{6t}$, so the gradient at any value of t is $15e^{6t}$.
At $t = \frac{1}{3}$, gradient $= 15e^{6\times\frac{1}{3}} = 15e^2$
At $t = 5$, gradient $= 15e^{6\times5} = 15e^{30}$

d) $y = 4e^{-2x}$, so the gradient at any value of x is $-8e^{-2x}$.
At $x = -5$, gradient $= -8e^{-2\times-5} = -8e^{10}$
At $x = 0.5$, gradient $= -8e^{-2\times0.5} = -8e^{-1}$

Q9 $y = Ae^{kx}$, so the gradient at any value of x is kAe^{kx}.
At $x = 2$, gradient $= kAe^{2k} = 12e^3 \Rightarrow 2k = 3 \Rightarrow k = 1.5$,
and $kA = 12 \Rightarrow 1.5A = 12 \Rightarrow A = 8$.
So $y = 8e^{1.5x}$. At $x = 4$, $y = 8e^{1.5\times4} = 8e^6$
and at $x = 12$, $y = 8e^{1.5\times12} = 8e^{18}$.

Q10 **a)** When $x = 0$, $y = Ae^{b(0)} = Ae^0 = A$, so y-intercept is at $(0, A)$.
[1 mark for the correct answer]

b) $y = Ae^{bx}$, so the gradient at any value of x is bAe^{bx}.
At $x = 4$, gradient $= bAe^{4b} = 2e^2 \Rightarrow 4b = 2 \Rightarrow b = 0.5$,
and $bA = 2 \Rightarrow A = 4$.
[3 marks available — 1 mark for knowing the gradient function, 1 mark for b, 1 mark for A]

Q11 **a)** $N = 500e^{kt}$, so the gradient at any value of x is $500ke^{kt}$.
Gradient $= 200e^{kt} \Rightarrow 500k = 200 \Rightarrow k = 0.4$
[2 marks available — 1 mark for knowing the gradient function, 1 mark for k]

b) 1 year = 12 months, so $t = 12$.
$N = 500e^{0.4\times12} = 60\,755$ (to the nearest whole number)
[1 mark for the correct answer]

Q12 "The gradient of the curve of $f(t)$ is always 0.4 times the value of $f(t)$" — this tells you that the gradient is directly proportional to the curve, i.e. it's the exponential function where $f(t) = Ae^{kt}$ for constants A and k.
You also know that the gradient of an exponential is kAe^{kt} — so $k = 0.4 \Rightarrow f(t) = Ae^{0.4t}$.
"When first counted, there were 7 rabbits" — this tells you that at $t = 0$, $f(t) = 7$
$\Rightarrow 7 = Ae^{0.4\times0} = Ae^0 = A$. So $f(t) = 7e^{0.4t}$.
An estimate for the number of rabbits after 5 years is:
$f(5) = 7 \times e^{0.4\times5} = 7 \times e^2 \approx 52$ rabbits.

Q13 $y = 4^x$ intercepts the y-axis at $x = 0$, $y = 4^0 = 1$.
$y = 2^{1-x}$ intercepts the y-axis at $x = 0$, $y = 2^{1-0} = 2$.
The graphs cross at $4^x = 2^{1-x} \Rightarrow (2^2)^x = 2^{1-x} \Rightarrow 2^{2x} = 2^{1-x}$
$\Rightarrow 2x = 1 - x \Rightarrow 3x = 1 \Rightarrow x = \frac{1}{3}$ and $y = 4^{\frac{1}{3}} = \sqrt[3]{4}$

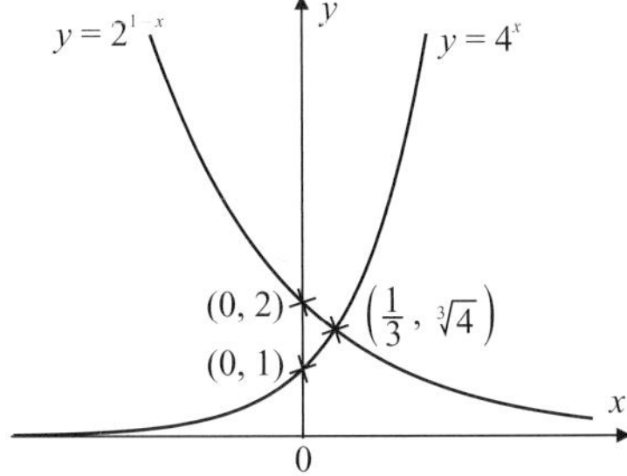

Exercise 9.2 — Logarithms

Q1 a) $\log_2 8 = 3$ b) $\log_5 625 = 4$
c) $\log_{49} 7 = \frac{1}{2}$ d) $\log_8 4 = \frac{2}{3}$
e) $\log_{10} \frac{1}{100} = -2$ f) $\log_2 0.125 = -3$
g) $\log_4 9 = x$ h) $\log_x 40 = 3$
i) $\log_8 x = 11$ j) $\log_{64} 512 = \frac{3}{2}$
k) $\log_{25} \frac{1}{5} = -\frac{1}{2}$ l) $\log_x 4096 = 2y$

Q2 a) $a = e^6$ b) $t = 5^{0.2}$
c) $m = 4^1 = 4$ d) $p = e^{13}$
e) $k = 10^5 = 100\,000$ f) $a = x^m$
g) $k = e^z$ h) $q = 10^r$

Q3 a) 3 b) –2
c) 0.477 (3 d.p.) d) 2.097 (3 d.p.)
e) 0.693 (3 d.p.) f) 0
g) 1.792 (3 d.p.) h) 2.996 (3 d.p.)
Use the 'log' or 'ln' button on your calculator for these.

Q4 a) $a = \log_2 4 \Rightarrow 2^a = 4 = 2^2 \Rightarrow a = 2$
b) $b = \log_3 27 \Rightarrow 3^b = 27 = 3^3 \Rightarrow b = 3$
c) $c = \log_5 0.2 \Rightarrow 5^c = 0.2 = \frac{1}{5} = 5^{-1} \Rightarrow c = -1$
d) $d = \log_{0.5} 0.25 \Rightarrow 0.5^d = 0.25 = 0.5^2 \Rightarrow d = 2$

Q5 a) $x^2 = 49 \Rightarrow x = 7$
b) $x^3 = 8 \Rightarrow x = 2$
c) $x^5 = 100\,000 \Rightarrow x = 10$
d) $x^5 = 3125 \Rightarrow x = 5$
e) $x^{\frac{1}{2}} = 3 \Rightarrow x = 3^2 \Rightarrow x = 9$
f) $x^{\frac{1}{3}} = 7 \Rightarrow x = 7^3 \Rightarrow x = 343$
g) $x^{\frac{1}{5}} = 2 \Rightarrow x = 2^5 \Rightarrow x = 32$
h) $x^{\frac{1}{4}} = 9 \Rightarrow x = 9^4 \Rightarrow x = 6561$
i) $x^{0.8} = 0.5 \Rightarrow x = 0.5^{\frac{1}{0.8}} \Rightarrow x = 0.420$ (3 s.f.)

Q6 a) (i) $e^x = 5 \Rightarrow \ln e^x = \ln 5 \Rightarrow x = \ln 5$
(ii) $\ln 5 = 1.61$ (3 s.f.)
b) (i) $\ln x = 8 \Rightarrow e^{\ln x} = e^8 \Rightarrow x = e^8$
(ii) $e^8 = 2980$ (3 s.f.)
c) (i) $e^{3t} = 11 \Rightarrow \ln e^{3t} = \ln 11 \Rightarrow 3t = \ln 11$
$\Rightarrow t = \frac{\ln 11}{3}$
(ii) $\frac{\ln 11}{3} = 0.799$ (3 s.f.)
d) (i) $\ln 10x = 4 \Rightarrow e^{\ln 10x} = e^4 \Rightarrow 10x = e^4 \Rightarrow x = \frac{e^4}{10}$
(ii) $\frac{e^4}{10} = 5.46$ (3 s.f.)

Q7 a) $2\log_a a = 2 \times 1 = 2$
[1 mark for the correct answer]
b) $\frac{1}{3}\log_b 1 = \frac{1}{3} \times 0 = 0$
[1 mark for the correct answer]

Q8 a) $a^2 = x$ and $a^4 = y$, so $y = x^2$
b) $a^3 = x$ and $(2a)^3 = y \Rightarrow 8a^3 = y$, so $y = 8x$
c) $e^5 = x$ and $e^{20} = y$, $(e^5)^4 = y$, so $y = x^4$

Q9 a) $0.001 = 10^{-3}$ and $4\sqrt{2} = \sqrt{2}^5 = 2^{2.5}$
So $\log_{10} 0.001 \times \log_2 4\sqrt{2} = \log_{10} 10^{-3} \times \log_2 2^{2.5}$
$= -3 \times 2.5 = -7.5$
[2 marks available — 1 mark for simplifying either log, 1 mark for the correct answer]
b) $\frac{\log_4 16^e}{e \ln e^7} = \frac{\log_4 (4^2)^e}{e \ln e^7} = \frac{\log_4 4^{2e}}{e \ln e^7} = \frac{2e}{e \times 7} = \frac{2}{7}$
[2 marks available — 1 mark for simplifying either log, 1 mark for the correct answer]

Q10 a) $\log_x \frac{81}{16} = 4 \Rightarrow x^4 = \frac{81}{16} \Rightarrow x = \sqrt[4]{\frac{81}{16}} = \frac{3}{2}$
[1 mark for the correct answer]
b) $\log_x \frac{3}{4} = \frac{1}{2} \Rightarrow x^{\frac{1}{2}} = \frac{3}{4} \Rightarrow x = \left(\frac{3}{4}\right)^2 = \frac{9}{16}$
[1 mark for the correct answer]

Q11 a) $\log_x 2 = \frac{1}{4} \Rightarrow x^{\frac{1}{4}} = 2 \Rightarrow x = 2^4 = 16$
[1 mark for the correct answer]
b) $\log_x 4e^2 = 2 \Rightarrow x^2 = 4e^2 \Rightarrow x = \sqrt{4e^2} = 2e$
[1 mark for the correct answer]

Q12 a) $y = \frac{1}{2}\log_{10} x \Rightarrow 2y = \log_{10} x \Rightarrow x = 10^{2y}$
[1 mark for the correct answer]
b) $y = e^{3x} \Rightarrow \ln y = 3x \Rightarrow x = \frac{1}{3}\ln y$
[1 mark for the correct answer]
c) $y = \ln x^2 \Rightarrow e^y = x^2 \Rightarrow x = \sqrt{e^y}$ or $e^{\frac{1}{2}y}$
[1 mark for the correct answer]

Q13 a) $\log_{10} b = 2(-2) + 3 \Rightarrow \log_{10} b = -1 \Rightarrow b = 10^{-1} \Rightarrow b = 0.1$
[1 mark for the correct answer]
b) $\log_{10} b = 2a + 3 \Rightarrow b = 10^{2a+3} \Rightarrow b = 10^3 \times 10^{2a}$
$\Rightarrow b = 1000 \times (10^2)^a \Rightarrow b = 1000 \times 100^a$
[2 marks available — 1 mark for rearranging into the form 'b = ...', 1 mark for the correct answer]

Q14 a) $y = \log_b x + 1 \Rightarrow b^y = b^{\log_b x + 1} \Rightarrow b^y = b^{\log_b x} \times b^1 \Rightarrow b^y = bx$
If $b = 1$, then $1^y = x$, but $1^y = 1$ for all real numbers y and $x > 1$, which means $1^y \neq x$ and so $b \neq 1$.
b) E.g. $y = \log_b x + 1 \Rightarrow b^y = bx$ (as above).
If b is negative then bx is also always negative.
But b^y is positive for some real values of y, e.g. when $y = 2$.
So when $y = 2$ and b is negative $b^y = bx$ has no real solutions.

Exercise 9.3 — Laws of Logs

Q1 a) $\log_a 2 + \log_a 5 = \log_a (2 \times 5) = \log_a 10$
b) $\ln 8 + \ln 7 = \ln (8 \times 7) = \ln 56$
c) $\log_b 8 - \log_b 4 = \log_b (8 \div 4) = \log_b 2$
d) $\log_m 15 - \log_m 5 = \log_m (15 \div 5) = \log_m 3$
e) $3 \log_a 4 = \log_a (4^3) = \log_a 64$
f) $2 \ln 7 = \ln (7^2) = \ln 49$
g) $\frac{1}{2}\log_b 16 = \log_b (16^{\frac{1}{2}}) = \log_b 4$
h) $\frac{2}{3}\log_a 125 = \log_a (125^{\frac{2}{3}}) = \log_a 25$
i) $\frac{1}{5}\ln 4^5 = \ln ((4^5)^{\frac{1}{5}}) = \ln (4^{5 \times \frac{1}{5}}) = \ln 4^1 = \ln 4$

Q2 a) $\log 0.5 = \log \frac{1}{2} = \log (2^{-1}) = -\log 2$
b) $\log\sqrt{3} = \log 3^{\frac{1}{2}} = \frac{1}{2}\log 3$
c) $\log 0.25 = \log \frac{1}{4} = \log (2^{-2}) = -2\log 2$
d) $\log\sqrt[3]{5} = \log 5^{\frac{1}{3}} = \frac{1}{3}\log 5$

Q3 **a)** $8\log_x \sqrt[4]{x} = 8\log_x x^{\frac{1}{4}} = 8 \times \frac{1}{4}\log_x x = 2$

b) $\log_x (x^2)^3 = \log_x x^6 = 6\log_x x = 6$

Q4 **a)** $\log_{10}x^2 + 2\log_{10}x = 2\log_{10}x + 2\log_{10}x = 4\log_{10}x$ or $\log_{10}x^4$

b) $2\log_a x - 5\log_a y = \log_a x^2 - \log_a y^5 = \log_a\left(\frac{x^2}{y^5}\right)$

Q5 **a)** $2\log_a 5 + \log_a 4 = \log_a (5^2) + \log_a 4$
$= \log_a (25 \times 4) = \log_a 100$

b) $3\log_m 2 - \log_m 4 = \log_m (2^3) - \log_m 4$
$= \log_m (8 \div 4) = \log_m 2$

c) $3\ln 4 - 2\ln 8 = \ln (4^3) - \ln (8^2) = \ln (64 \div 64) = \ln 1 = 0$

d) $\frac{2}{3}\ln 216 - 2\ln 3 = \ln (216^{\frac{2}{3}}) - \ln (3^2) = \ln (36 \div 9) = \ln 4$

e) $1 + \log_a 6 = \log_a a + \log_a 6 = \log_a 6a$

f) $2 - \log_b 5 = 2\log_b b - \log_b 5 = \log_b b^2 - \log_b 5 = \log_b\left(\frac{b^2}{5}\right)$

Q6 **a)** $\log_a 6 = \log_a (2 \times 3) = \log_a 2 + \log_a 3 = x + y$

b) $\log_a 16 = \log_a 2^4 = 4\log_a 2 = 4x$

c) $\log_a 60 = \log_a (2 \times 2 \times 3 \times 5)$
$= \log_a 2^2 + \log_a 3 + \log_a 5 = 2x + y + z$

Q7 $\log_3 5 - \log_3 \frac{1}{5} = \log_3\left(\frac{5}{\frac{1}{5}}\right) = \log_3 (5 \times 5) = \log_3 25$

[2 marks available — 1 mark for a correct method to write as a single log, 1 mark for the correct answer]

Q8 **a)** $\log_b b^3 = 3\log_b b = 3$

b) $\log_a \sqrt{a} = \log_a a^{\frac{1}{2}} = \frac{1}{2}\log_a a = \frac{1}{2}$

c) $\ln 4e - 2\ln 2 = \ln 4 + \ln e - \ln 2^2 = \ln 4 + 1 - \ln 4 = 1$

d) $\ln 9 + \ln \frac{e}{3} - \ln 3 = \ln 3^2 + \ln e - \ln 3 - \ln 3$
$= 2\ln 3 + \ln e - 2\ln 3 = \ln e = 1$

Q9 $\ln\sqrt{e} + 2\ln e^3 = \ln e^{0.5} + 2\ln e^3$
$= 0.5\ln e + (2 \times 3\ln e) = 0.5 + (2 \times 3) = 6.5$

[2 marks available — 1 mark for simplifying either ln in the expression, 1 mark for the correct answer]

Q10 **a)** $2\log_x b + \log_x a^3 = 2\log_x b + 3\log_x a = 2m + 3n$

b) $2\log_x\left(\frac{b}{a}\right) = 2(\log_x b - \log_x a) = 2(m - n) = 2m - 2n$

Q11 $10 + 2\log_a 3 = 10\log_a a + \log_a 3^2 = \log_a a^{10} + \log_a 3^2$
$= \log_a(a^{10} \times 3^2) = \log_a 9a^{10}$. So $n = 9a^{10}$.

[2 marks available — 1 mark for a correct method to write as a single log, 1 mark for the correct answer]

Q12 **a)** $\log_2 4^x = x\log_2 4 = x\log_2 2^2 = 2x\log_2 2 = 2x$

b) $\frac{\ln 54 - \ln 6}{\ln 3} = \frac{\ln (54 \div 6)}{\ln 3} = \frac{\ln 9}{\ln 3} = \frac{\ln 3^2}{\ln 3} = \frac{2\ln 3}{\ln 3} = 2$

Q13 $4 + \log_c \frac{1}{c^2} + \log_c \sqrt{c} = 4 + \log_c c^{-2} + \log_c c^{\frac{1}{2}}$
$= 4 - 2\log_c c + \frac{1}{2}\log_c c = 4 - 2 + \frac{1}{2} = 2\frac{1}{2}$

Q14 $2\log_a 6a^2 = 2\log_a 6 + 2\log_a a^2 = \log_a 6^2 + (2 \times 2) = \log_a 36 + 4$
So $p = 36$ and $q = 4 \Rightarrow \log_3\left(\frac{p}{q}\right) = \log_3\left(\frac{36}{4}\right) = \log_3 9 = 2$.

[3 marks available — 1 mark for a correct method to write in the form $\log_a p + q$, 1 mark for finding p and q, 1 mark for the correct answer]

Q15 $y = nx^{\frac{1}{m}} \Rightarrow \log_{10}y = \log_{10}(nx^{\frac{1}{m}}) \Rightarrow \log_{10}y = \log_{10}n + \log_{10}x^{\frac{1}{m}}$
$\Rightarrow \log_{10}y = \log_{10}n + \frac{1}{m}\log_{10}x \Rightarrow \frac{1}{m}\log_{10}x = \log_{10}y - \log_{10}n$
$\Rightarrow \log_{10}x = m(\log_{10}y - \log_{10}n) = \log_{10}y^m - \log_{10}n^m$

[3 marks available — 1 mark for a correct method to rearrange for either log x or x, 1 mark for expressing log x in the required form and 1 mark for the correct values of p and q.]

Alternatively you could do the rearranging before taking logs.

Exercise 9.4 — Changing the Base of a Log

Q1 **a)** $\frac{\log_{10} 2}{\log_{10} 9}$ **b)** $\frac{\log_{10} 8}{\log_{10} 4}$

c) $\frac{\log_{10} 16}{\log_{10} 17}$ **d)** $\frac{\log_{10} 14}{\log_{10} 21}$

Q2 **a)** 0.613 (3 s.f.) **b)** 0.315 (3 s.f.)

c) 2.33 (3 s.f.) **d)** 0.861 (3 s.f.)

If your calculator can't do logs of any base, you'll need to use the change of base formula.

Q3 $\log_9 5 = \frac{\log_3 5}{\log_3 9} = \frac{\log_3 5}{2} = \frac{1}{2}\log_3 5 = \log_3 5^{\frac{1}{2}} = \log_3 \sqrt{5}$

[2 marks available — 1 mark for a correct method to change the base, 1 mark for the correct answer]

Q4 **a)** $\log_{11} 19$

b) $\log_7 2$

c) $\log_3 4 \times \log_4 5 = \frac{\log_{10} 4}{\log_{10} 3} \times \frac{\log_{10} 5}{\log_{10} 4} = \frac{\log_{10} 5}{\log_{10} 3} = \log_3 5$

d) $\ln 2 \times \log_2 10 = \log_e 2 \times \log_2 10$
$= \frac{\log_{10} 2}{\log_{10} e} \times \frac{\log_{10} 10}{\log_{10} 2} = \frac{\log_{10} 10}{\log_{10} e} = \log_e 10 = \ln 10$

This question uses the 'change of base' formula in reverse.

Q5 $\log_{10} 3x = \frac{\ln 2}{\ln 10} = \log_{10} 2 \Rightarrow 3x = 2 \Rightarrow x = \frac{2}{3}$

Q6 **a)** $\log_4 10 - \log_4 \frac{1}{10} = \log_4 \frac{10}{\frac{1}{10}} = \log_4 100$

$\log_4 100 = \frac{\log_2 100}{\log_2 4} = \frac{\log_2 100}{2} = \log_2 100^{\frac{1}{2}} = \log_2 10$

[3 marks available — 1 mark for writing as a single log, 1 mark for a correct method to change the base, 1 mark for the correct answer]

b) $\log_8 x = \frac{\log_2 x}{\log_2 8} = \frac{\log_2 x}{3} \Rightarrow \frac{\log_2 x}{3} = \log_2 10$
$\Rightarrow \log_2 x = 3\log_2 10 = \log_2 10^3 \Rightarrow x = 10^3 = 1000$

[3 marks available — 1 mark for a correct method to change the base, 1 mark for a correct method to remove logs, 1 mark for the correct answer]

Q7 **a)** $\log_a 5 = \frac{\log_5 5}{\log_5 a} = \frac{1}{\log_5 a}$

So $\log_a 5 \times 3\log_5 a = \frac{1}{\log_5 a} \times 3\log_5 a = 3$

b) $\frac{1}{2}\log_a 9 = \frac{1}{2}\frac{\log_3 9}{\log_3 a} = \frac{1}{2}\frac{2}{\log_3 a} = \frac{2}{\log_3 a^2}$

$\frac{1}{2}\log_a 9 \times \log_3 a^2 = \frac{2}{\log_3 a^2} \times \log_3 a^2 = 2$

Q8 $\left(\frac{\log_3 2}{\log_3 e} + \log_e 3\right) - \left(\log_e 6 + \frac{\log_2 9}{\log_2 e}\right)$
$= (\log_e 2 + \log_e 3) - (\log_e 6 + \log_e 9)$
$= \ln (2 \times 3) - \ln (6 \times 9)$
$= \ln\frac{6}{54} = \ln\frac{1}{9} = \ln (3^{-2}) = -2\ln 3$

[4 marks available — 1 mark for a correct change of base, 1 mark for at least one correct method for writing as a single log, 1 mark for ln(6/54) or equivalent, 1 mark for the correct answer]

Exercise 9.5 — Solving Equations with Exponentials and Logs

Q1 **a)** Take logs of both sides: $\log 2^x = \log 3 \Rightarrow x\log 2 = \log 3$
$\Rightarrow x = \frac{\log 3}{\log 2} = 1.584... = 1.58$ (3 s.f.)

b) $7^x = 2 \Rightarrow \log 7^x = \log 2 \Rightarrow x\log 7 = \log 2$
$\Rightarrow x = \frac{\log 2}{\log 7} = 0.3562... = 0.356$ (3 s.f.)

c) $1.8^x = 0.4 \Rightarrow \log 1.8^x = \log 0.4 \Rightarrow x\log 1.8 = \log 0.4$
$\Rightarrow x = \frac{\log 0.4}{\log 1.8} = -1.558... = -1.56$ (3 s.f.)

Notice this solution is negative, because log 0.4 is negative.

d) $0.7^x = 3 \Rightarrow \log 0.7^x = \log 3 \Rightarrow x \log 0.7 = \log 3$
$\Rightarrow x = \frac{\log 3}{\log 0.7} = -3.080... = -3.08$ (3 s.f.)

e) $3^{5x} = 890 \Rightarrow \log 3^{5x} = \log 890$
$\Rightarrow 5x \log 3 = \log 890$
$\Rightarrow x = \frac{\log 890}{5 \log 3} = 1.24$ (3 s.f.)

f) $0.2^{4x} = 0.016 \Rightarrow \log 0.2^{4x} = \log 0.016$
$\Rightarrow 4x \log 0.2 = \log 0.016$
$\Rightarrow x = \frac{\log 0.016}{4 \log 0.2} = 0.642$ (3 s.f.)

g) $2^{3x-1} = 5 \Rightarrow \log 2^{3x-1} = \log 5 \Rightarrow (3x - 1)\log 2 = \log 5$
$\Rightarrow 3x \log 2 = \log 5 + \log 2 = \log (5 \times 2)$
$\Rightarrow x = \frac{\log 10}{3 \log 2} = 1.11$ (3 s.f.)

h) $0.4^{5x-4} = 2 \Rightarrow \log 0.4^{5x-4} = \log 2$
$\Rightarrow (5x - 4)\log 0.4 = \log 2$
$\Rightarrow 5x \log 0.4 = \log 2 + 4 \log 0.4$
$\Rightarrow x = \frac{\log 2 + 4 \log 0.4}{5 \log 0.4} = 0.649$ (3 s.f.)

Q2 $125 \times 5^x = 879 \Rightarrow 5^x = \frac{879}{125}$
$\Rightarrow x \log 5 = \log\left(\frac{879}{125}\right) \Rightarrow x = \log\left(\frac{879}{125}\right) \div \log 5 = 1.21$ (3 s.f.)
[2 marks available — 1 mark for taking logs, 1 mark for the correct answer]

Q3 **a)** $2^{4x} = 3^{100} \Rightarrow \log_2 2^{4x} = \log_2 3^{100}$
$\Rightarrow 4x \log_2 2 = 100 \log_2 3 \Rightarrow 4x = 100 \log_2 3$
$\Rightarrow x = 25 \log_2 3$

b) $11^{6x} = 10^{90} \Rightarrow \log_{11} 11^{6x} = \log_{11} 10^{90}$
$\Rightarrow 6x \log_{11} 11 = 90 \log_{11} 10 \Rightarrow 6x = 90 \log_{11} 10$
$\Rightarrow x = 15 \log_{11} 10$

c) $6^{50-x} = 2^{50} \Rightarrow \log_6 6^{50-x} = \log_6 2^{50}$
$\Rightarrow (50 - x) \log_6 6 = 50 \log_6 2 \Rightarrow 50 - x = 50 \log_6 2$
$\Rightarrow x = 50 - 50 \log_6 2 = 50(1 - \log_6 2)$
$= 50(\log_6 6 - \log_6 2) = 50 \log_6 3$

d) $4^{5+x} = 20^5 \Rightarrow \log_4 4^{5+x} = \log_4 20^5$
$\Rightarrow (5 + x) \log_4 4 = 5 \log_4 20 \Rightarrow 5 + x = 5 \log_4 20$
$\Rightarrow x = 5 \log_4 20 - 5 = 5(\log_4 20 - 1)$
$= 5(\log_4 20 - \log_4 4) = 5 \log_4 5$

Q4 Take logs of both sides of the inequality:
$\log 1.5^P > \log 1\,000\,000$
$\Rightarrow P \log 1.5 > \log 1\,000\,000$
$\Rightarrow P > \frac{\log 1\,000\,000}{\log 1.5} \Rightarrow P > 34.0732...$
So the smallest integer $P = 35$.

Q5 **a)** Take exponentials of both sides using base 10 (since the logarithm is base 10):
$10^{\log 5x} = 10^3 \Rightarrow 5x = 1000 \Rightarrow x = 200$

b) Take exponentials of both sides (using base 2):
$\Rightarrow 2^{\log_2 (x+3)} = 2^4 \Rightarrow x + 3 = 16 \Rightarrow x = 13$

c) Take exponentials of both sides (using base 3):
$\Rightarrow 3^{\log_3 (5-2x)} = 3^{2.5} \Rightarrow 5 - 2x = 3^{2.5}$
$\Rightarrow x = \frac{5 - 3^{2.5}}{2} = -5.294... = -5.29$ (3 s.f.)

Q6 **a)** $4^{x+1} = 3^{2x} \Rightarrow \log 4^{x+1} = \log 3^{2x} \Rightarrow (x + 1) \log 4 = 2x \log 3$
Multiply out the brackets: $x \log 4 + \log 4 = 2x \log 3$
Collect x-terms on one side:
$\log 4 = 2x \log 3 - x \log 4 = x (2 \log 3 - \log 4)$
$\Rightarrow x = \frac{\log 4}{2 \log 3 - \log 4} = 1.709... = 1.71$ (3 s.f.)

b) $2^{5-x} = 4^{x+3} \Rightarrow \log 2^{5-x} = \log 4^{x+3}$
$\Rightarrow (5 - x) \log 2 = (x + 3) \log 4$
But $\log 4 = \log 2^2 = 2 \log 2$
$\Rightarrow (5 - x) \log 2 = 2(x + 3) \log 2$
$\Rightarrow 5 - x = 2(x + 3)$
$\Rightarrow -1 = 3x \Rightarrow x = -\frac{1}{3}$

c) $3^{2x-1} = 6^{3-x} \Rightarrow \log 3^{2x-1} = \log 6^{3-x}$
$\Rightarrow (2x - 1) \log 3 = (3 - x) \log 6$
$\Rightarrow 2x \log 3 - \log 3 = 3 \log 6 - x \log 6$
$\Rightarrow 2x \log 3 + x \log 6 = 3 \log 6 + \log 3$
$\Rightarrow x (2 \log 3 + \log 6) = 3 \log 6 + \log 3$
$\Rightarrow x = \frac{3 \log 6 + \log 3}{2 \log 3 + \log 6} = 1.622... = 1.62$ (3 s.f.)

Q7 **a)** **(i)** $3^{x+1} = 3 \times 3^x = 3y$
[1 mark for the correct answer]

(ii) $3^{2x-1} = 3^{-1} \times 3^{2x} = \frac{(3^x)^2}{3} = \frac{y^2}{3}$
[1 mark for the correct answer]

b) $3^{x+1} - 6 = 3^{2x-1} \Rightarrow 3y - 6 = \frac{y^2}{3}$ where $y = 3^x$.
$y^2 - 9y + 18 = 0 \Rightarrow (y - 6)(y - 3) = 0 \Rightarrow y = 6$ or $y = 3$
When $y = 3$, $3^x = 3 \Rightarrow x = 1$
When $y = 6$, $3^x = 6$
$\Rightarrow x \log 3 = \log 6 \Rightarrow x = \frac{\log 6}{\log 3} = 1.63$ (3 s.f.)
[5 marks available — 1 mark for forming a quadratic in terms of y, 1 mark for a correct method to solve the quadratic, 1 mark for the correct solutions, 1 mark for x = 1, 1 mark for x = 1.63]

Q8 **a)** The graph cuts the y-axis at $y = 7^0 = 1$ and doesn't cross the x-axis.

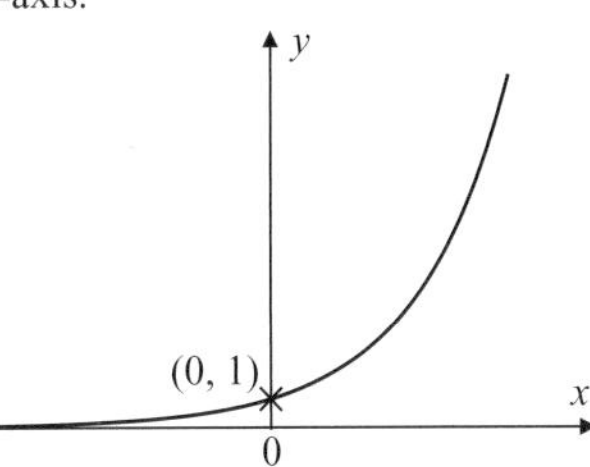

[2 marks available — 1 mark for a correct exponential shape with positive gradient, 1 mark for the correct y-intercept]

b) Let $y = 7^x$, then $7^{2x} - 3(7^x) + 2 = 0 \Rightarrow y^2 - 3y + 2 = 0$
$\Rightarrow (y - 2)(y - 1) = 0 \Rightarrow y = 1$ or $y = 2$.
$y = 1 \Rightarrow 7^x = 1 \Rightarrow x = 0$
$y = 2 \Rightarrow 7^x = 2 \Rightarrow x \log 7 = \log 2 \Rightarrow x = 0.356$ (3 s.f.)
[4 marks available — 1 mark for forming a quadratic, 1 mark for a correct method to solve the quadratic, 1 mark for both values of y, 1 mark for both values of x]

Q9 $4^{2x} = 3(2^{x-1}) \Rightarrow \log_2 4^{2x} = \log_2(3(2^{x-1}))$
$\Rightarrow 2x\log_2 4 = \log_2 3 + \log_2 2^{x-1} \Rightarrow 2x \times 2 = \log_2 3 + (x - 1)$
$\Rightarrow 4x = \log_2 3 + x - 1 \Rightarrow 3x = \log_2 3 - 1 \Rightarrow x = \frac{1}{3}(\log_2 3 - 1)$
[5 marks available — 1 mark for taking $\log_2$ of both sides, 1 mark for $\log_2 4^{2x} = 4x$, 1 mark for $\log_2 3 + \log_2 2^{x-1}$, 1 mark for $\log_2 2^{x-1} = x - 1$, 1 mark for working leading to the required result]

Q10 **a)** $\log_6 x = 1 - \log_6 (x + 1)$
$\Rightarrow \log_6 x + \log_6 (x + 1) = 1 \Rightarrow \log_6 x(x + 1) = 1$
Take exponentials of base 6 of both sides to get:
$\Rightarrow x(x + 1) = 6^1 \Rightarrow x^2 + x - 6 = 0$
$\Rightarrow (x + 3)(x - 2) = 0 \Rightarrow x = 2$
$x = -3$ is not a solution because logarithms of negative numbers don't exist.

b) $\log_2(2x+1) = 3 + 2\log_2 x$
$\Rightarrow \log_2(2x+1) = 3 + \log_2 x^2$
$\Rightarrow \log_2(2x+1) - \log_2 x^2 = 3 \Rightarrow \log_2 \frac{2x+1}{x^2} = 3$
Take exponentials of base 2 of both sides to get:
$\Rightarrow \frac{2x+1}{x^2} = 2^3 \Rightarrow 2x + 1 = 8x^2$
$\Rightarrow 8x^2 - 2x - 1 = 0 \Rightarrow (4x+1)(2x-1) = 0$
So $x = \frac{1}{2}$

Q11 $\log_3(x-1) = 2 - \log_3(2x+1) \Rightarrow \log_3(x-1) + \log_3(2x+1) = 2$
$\Rightarrow \log_3((x-1)(2x+1)) = 2 \Rightarrow (x-1)(2x+1) = 3^2$
$\Rightarrow 2x^2 - x - 1 = 9 \Rightarrow 2x^2 - x - 10 = 0$
$\Rightarrow (2x-5)(x+2) = 0 \Rightarrow x = 2.5$ or $x = -2$
But $x \neq -2$ as $\log_3(x-1)$ is undefined, so $x = 2.5$.
[5 marks available — 1 mark for writing as a single log, 1 mark for removing logs using exponentials, 1 mark for forming a quadratic, 1 mark for a correct method to solve the quadratic, 1 mark for the correct answer, including rejecting the negative solution]

Q12 $\log_2(11-6x) = 2\log_2(x-1) + 3$
$\Rightarrow \log_2(11-6x) - 2\log_2(x-1) = 3$
$\Rightarrow \log_2(11-6x) - \log_2((x-1)^2) = 3$
$\Rightarrow \log_2\left(\frac{11-6x}{(x-1)^2}\right) = 3 \Rightarrow \frac{11-6x}{(x-1)^2} = 2^3$
$\Rightarrow 11 - 6x = 8(x-1)^2 \Rightarrow 11 - 6x = 8x^2 - 16x + 8$
$\Rightarrow 8x^2 - 10x - 3 = 0 \Rightarrow (4x+1)(2x-3) = 0$
$\Rightarrow x = -0.25$ or $x = 1.5$
But $x \neq -0.25$ as $\log_2(x-1)$ is undefined, so $x = 1.5$.
[5 marks available — 1 mark for writing as a single log, 1 mark for removing logs using exponentials, 1 mark for forming a quadratic, 1 mark for a correct method to solve the quadratic, 1 mark for the correct answer, including rejecting the negative solution]

Q13 a) $e^{3x} = 27 \Rightarrow \ln(e^{3x}) = \ln 27 \Rightarrow 3x = \ln 27 = \ln(3^3)$
$\Rightarrow 3x = 3\ln 3 \Rightarrow x = \ln 3$
If you're asked to give your answer in the form ln a where a is a number, try and write the number inside the logarithm as a power of a and use the third log law to get it in the form you want.

b) $e^{(6x-1)} = \frac{1}{3} \Rightarrow \ln e^{(6x-1)} = \ln\left(\frac{1}{3}\right)$
$\Rightarrow 6x - 1 = \ln(3^{-1}) \Rightarrow 6x = 1 - \ln 3 \Rightarrow x = \frac{1}{6}(1 - \ln 3)$

c) $\frac{1}{3}e^{(1-x)} - 3 = 0 \Rightarrow e^{(1-x)} = 9 \Rightarrow \ln e^{(1-x)} = \ln 9$
$\Rightarrow 1 - x = \ln 9 \Rightarrow x = 1 - \ln(3^2) \Rightarrow x = 1 - 2\ln 3$

Q14 a) $5e^{3t} = 11 \Rightarrow e^{3t} = \frac{11}{5} \Rightarrow \ln e^{3t} = \ln\left(\frac{11}{5}\right)$
$\Rightarrow 3t = \ln\left(\frac{11}{5}\right) \Rightarrow t = \frac{1}{3}\ln\left(\frac{11}{5}\right)$

b) $e^{(0.5x+3)} = 9 \Rightarrow \ln e^{(0.5x+3)} = \ln 9 \Rightarrow 0.5x + 3 = \ln 9$
$\Rightarrow 0.5x = \ln 9 - 3 \Rightarrow x = 2(\ln 9 - 3)$

c) $10 - 3e^{(1-2x)} = 8 \Rightarrow 3e^{(1-2x)} = 2 \Rightarrow e^{(1-2x)} = \frac{2}{3}$
$\Rightarrow \ln e^{(1-2x)} = \ln\frac{2}{3} \Rightarrow 1 - 2x = \ln\frac{2}{3}$
$\Rightarrow 2x = 1 - \ln\frac{2}{3} \Rightarrow x = \frac{1}{2}(1 - \ln\frac{2}{3})$

d) $3\ln(2x) = 7 \Rightarrow \ln(2x) = \frac{7}{3}$
$\Rightarrow e^{\ln(2x)} = e^{\frac{7}{3}} \Rightarrow 2x = e^{\frac{7}{3}} \Rightarrow x = \frac{1}{2}e^{\frac{7}{3}}$

e) $\ln(5t-3) = 4 \Rightarrow e^{\ln(5t-3)} = e^4 \Rightarrow 5t - 3 = e^4$
$\Rightarrow t = \frac{1}{5}(e^4 + 3)$

f) $6 - \ln(0.5x) = 3 \Rightarrow \ln(0.5x) = 3 \Rightarrow e^{\ln(0.5x)} = e^3$
$\Rightarrow 0.5x = e^3 \Rightarrow x = 2e^3$

Q15 $e^{3x+1} = 10 \Rightarrow 3x + 1 = \ln 10 \Rightarrow x = \frac{\ln 10 - 1}{3} = 0.434$ (3 s.f.)
[2 marks available — 1 mark for taking ln of both sides, 1 mark for the correct answer]

Q16 a) $\ln 5 + \ln x = 7 \Rightarrow \ln(5x) = 7 \Rightarrow e^{\ln(5x)} = e^7$
$\Rightarrow 5x = e^7 \Rightarrow x = \frac{e^7}{5}$

b) $\ln(2x) + \ln(3x) = 15 \Rightarrow \ln(2x \times 3x) = 15$
$\Rightarrow \ln(6x^2) = 15 \Rightarrow e^{\ln 6x^2} = e^{15} \Rightarrow 6x^2 = e^{15}$
$\Rightarrow x = \sqrt{\frac{1}{6}e^{15}} = \frac{1}{\sqrt{6}}e^{\frac{15}{2}}$

c) $2\ln x - \ln 2x = 2 \Rightarrow \ln\left(\frac{x^2}{2x}\right) = 2$
$\Rightarrow \frac{x^2}{2x} = e^2 \Rightarrow x^2 = 2xe^2 \Rightarrow x(x - 2e^2) = 0$
$x \neq 0$ as $\ln x$ is not defined at 0, so $x = 2e^2$
You could also have cancelled the x's from the fraction before using the exponent.

d) $\ln(2x-7) + \ln 4 = -3 \Rightarrow \ln[4(2x-7)] = -3$
$\Rightarrow 8x - 28 = e^{-3} \Rightarrow x = \frac{e^{-3} + 28}{8}$ or $\frac{1}{8e^3} + \frac{7}{2}$

e) $\ln(x^2 - 4) - \ln(2x) = 0 \Rightarrow \ln\left(\frac{x^2-4}{2x}\right) = 0$
$\Rightarrow \frac{x^2-4}{2x} = e^0 = 1 \Rightarrow x^2 - 4 = 2x$
$\Rightarrow x^2 - 2x - 4 = 0 \Rightarrow x = \frac{2 \pm \sqrt{20}}{2} = 1 \pm \sqrt{5}$
But $x > 0$ otherwise $\ln 2x$ would be undefined, so $x = 1 + \sqrt{5}$
You might have spotted that $\ln(x^2 - 4) - \ln(2x) = 0$ $\Rightarrow \ln(x^2 - 4) = \ln(2x) \Rightarrow x^2 - 4 = 2x$, then solved the resulting quadratic to find the answer.

f) $3\ln(x^2) + 5\ln x = 2 \Rightarrow 6\ln x + 5\ln x = 2$
$\Rightarrow 11\ln x = 2 \Rightarrow \ln x = \frac{2}{11} \Rightarrow x = e^{\frac{2}{11}}$

g) Let $y = e^x$, then $2e^{2x} + e^x - 3 = 0$ is equivalent to the quadratic equation $2y^2 + y - 3 = 0$
$\Rightarrow (2y+3)(y-1) = 0$, so $y = 1$ or $y = -\frac{3}{2}$.
So $e^x = 1$ or $e^x = -\frac{3}{2}$. Negative values of e^x are not possible, so $e^x = 1 \Rightarrow x = \ln 1 = 0$.

h) Let $y = e^{4x}$, then $e^{8x} - e^{4x} - 6 = 0$ is equivalent to the quadratic equation $y^2 - y - 6 = 0$
$\Rightarrow (y-3)(y+2) = 0$, so $y = 3$ or $y = -2$.
So $e^{4x} = 3$ or $e^{4x} = -2$. Negative values of e^x are not possible, so $e^{4x} = 3 \Rightarrow x = \frac{1}{4}\ln 3$.

Q17 $\log_3 x + \log_3 y = 2 \Rightarrow \log_3(xy) = 2 \Rightarrow xy = 3^2 \Rightarrow xy = 9$
Substituting in $x = 3y$ gives $3y(y) = 9 \Rightarrow y^2 = 3 \Rightarrow y = \pm\sqrt{3}$.
Reject $y = -\sqrt{3}$ as y is positive.
When $y = \sqrt{3}$, $x = 3\sqrt{3}$.
[5 marks available — 1 mark for using log laws correctly, 1 mark for xy = 9, 1 mark for a correct method to solve simultaneous equations, 1 mark for a correct y-value, 1 mark for the correct x-value]
Negative values of x and y must be rejected to get full marks.

Q18 $9^{x-2} = 3^y \Rightarrow (3^2)^{x-2} = 3^y \Rightarrow 3^{(2(x-2))} = 3^y$ so $2(x-2) = y$
$\log_3 2x = 1 + \log_3 y \Rightarrow \log_3 2x - \log_3 y = 1$
$\Rightarrow \log_3 \frac{2x}{y} = 1 \Rightarrow \frac{2x}{y} = 3^1 \Rightarrow 2x = 3y$
Solve $2(x-2) = y$ and $2x = 3y$ simultaneously:
$2x = 3y$ so put this into $2(x-2) = y$
$\Rightarrow 3y - 4 = y \Rightarrow 2y = 4 \Rightarrow y = 2$ and $x = 3$

Q19 Substitute $y = 10^x \Rightarrow 2y^2 - 7y + 5 = 0$
$\Rightarrow (2y-5)(y-1) = 0 \Rightarrow 10^x = \frac{5}{2} = 2.5$ or $10^x = 1$
$\Rightarrow x = \log 2.5$ or $x = 0$

Q20 a) Let $y = 2^x$, then $2^{2x} - 5(2^x) + 4 = 0$ is equivalent to the quadratic equation $y^2 - 5y + 4 = 0$
$\Rightarrow (y-1)(y-4) = 0$, so $y = 1$ or $y = 4$
So $2^x = 4$ or $2^x = 1 \Rightarrow x = 2$ or $x = 0$.
The y^2 in the quadratic equation comes from $2^{2x} = (2^x)^2$.

b) Let $y = 4^x$, then $4^{2x} - 17(4^x) + 16 = 0$ is equivalent to the quadratic equation $y^2 - 17y + 16 = 0$
$\Rightarrow (y-1)(y-16) = 0$, so $y = 1$ or $y = 16$
So $4^x = 1$ or $4^x = 16 \Rightarrow x = 0$ or $x = 2$.

c) Let $y = 3^x$, then $3^{2x+2} = 3^{2x} \times 3^2 = y^2 \times 9 = 9y^2$.
So $3^{2x+2} - 82(3^x) + 9 = 0$ is equivalent to the quadratic equation $9y^2 - 82y + 9 = 0$.
$\Rightarrow (9y-1)(y-9) = 0$, so $y = \frac{1}{9}$ or $y = 9$.
So $3^x = \frac{1}{9}$ or $3^x = 9 \Rightarrow x = -2$ or $x = 2$.

d) Let $y = 2^x$, then $2^{2x+3} = 2^{2x} \times 2^3 = y^2 \times 8 = 8y^2$.
So $2^{2x+3} - 9(2^x) + 1 = 0$ is equivalent to the quadratic equation $8y^2 - 9y + 1 = 0$.
$\Rightarrow (8y - 1)(y - 1) = 0$, so $y = \frac{1}{8}$ or $y = 1$.
So $2^x = \frac{1}{8}$ or $2^x = 1 \Rightarrow x = -3$ or $x = 0$.

e) Substitute $y = e^{2x} \Rightarrow y^2 + 4y + 5 = 0$.
Using the quadratic formula:
$$x = \frac{-4 \pm \sqrt{4^2 - (4 \times 5 \times 1)}}{2} = \frac{-4 \pm \sqrt{16 - 20}}{2} = \frac{-4 \pm \sqrt{-4}}{2}$$
There are no real solutions since there is a negative square root.
The question says "where possible", which implies that there might not be any real solutions.

f) Substitute $y = e^x \Rightarrow 3y^2 + 10y + 3 = 0$
$\Rightarrow (3y + 1)(y + 3) = 0 \Rightarrow e^x = -\frac{1}{3}$ or $e^x = -3$,
both of which are impossible since $e^x > 0$.
There are no solutions.

Q21 a) $y = 2x^3 \Rightarrow \log_2 y = \log_2(2x^3) \Rightarrow \log_2 y = \log_2 2 + \log_2 x^3$
$\Rightarrow \log_2 y = 1 + 3\log_2 x$
[2 marks available — 1 mark for taking $\log_2$ of both sides, 1 mark for using log laws to give the required result]

b) $1 + 3\log_2 x = 1 + \log_2(7x^2 - 10x)$
$\Rightarrow \log_2 y = 1 + \log_2(7x^2 - 10x) \Rightarrow y = 2^1 \times (7x^2 - 10x)$
$\Rightarrow 2x^3 = 2(7x^2 - 10x) \Rightarrow x^3 = 7x^2 - 10x$
$\Rightarrow x^3 - 7x^2 + 10x = 0 \Rightarrow x(x^2 - 7x + 10) = 0$
$\Rightarrow x(x - 2)(x - 5) = 0 \Rightarrow x = 0, x = 2, x = 5$
But $x \neq 0$ as $\log_2 x$ is undefined, so $x = 2$ or $x = 5$.
[4 marks available — 1 mark for a correct method to remove logs, 1 mark for removing logs to form a cubic, 1 mark for a correct method to factorise the cubic, 1 mark for the correct answer]

Q22 a) (i) $\log_3 x^2 = 2\log_3 x = 2y$
[1 mark for the correct answer]

(ii) $\log_9 x = \frac{\log_3 x}{\log_3 9} = \frac{y}{2}$
[2 marks available — 1 mark for a correct method to change the base, 1 mark for the correct answer]

b) $\log_3 x^2 - 4 = \log_9 x \Rightarrow 2y - 4 = \frac{y}{2}$
$\Rightarrow 4y - 8 = y \Rightarrow 3y = 8 \Rightarrow y = \frac{8}{3}$
When $y = \frac{8}{3}$, $\frac{8}{3} = \log_3 x \Rightarrow x = 3^{\frac{8}{3}} = 18.7$ (3 s.f.)
[3 marks available — 1 mark for forming an equation in y, 1 mark for the correct value of y, 1 mark for the correct value of x]
You would still get all 3 marks if you correctly used a different method to solve the equation.

Q23 $\log_3(4 + 11x) - 2\log_3 x - 1 = 6\ln(\log_3 3)$
$\Rightarrow \log_3(4 + 11x) - 2\log_3 x - 1 = 6\ln(1)$
$\Rightarrow \log_3(4 + 11x) - 2\log_3 x - 1 = 0$
$\Rightarrow \log_3\left(\frac{4 + 11x}{x^2}\right) = 1 \Rightarrow \frac{4 + 11x}{x^2} = 3^1$
$\Rightarrow 4 + 11x = 3x^2 \Rightarrow 3x^2 - 11x - 4 = 0$
$\Rightarrow (3x + 1)(x - 4) = 0 \Rightarrow x = -\frac{1}{3}$ or $x = 4$
Reject negative solution as $x > 0$, so $x = 4$.
[6 marks available — 1 mark for showing 6 ln (log₃ 3) is equal to 0, 1 mark for writing logs on the left-hand side as a single log, 1 mark for removing logs from expression, 1 mark for rearranging to give a quadratic, 1 mark for a correct method to solve the quadratic, 1 mark for the correct answer]

Q24 $\log_2 \frac{x}{2} = \log_2 x - \log_2 2 = y - 1$
$$\log_4 \sqrt{x} = \frac{\log_2 \sqrt{x}}{\log_2 4} = \frac{\log_2 x^{\frac{1}{2}}}{2} = \frac{\frac{1}{2}\log_2 x}{2} = \frac{1}{4}y$$
$2\log_2 \frac{x}{2} + \log_4 \sqrt{x} - 8 = 0$
$\Rightarrow 2(y - 1) + \frac{1}{4}y - 8 = 0$
$\Rightarrow 2y - 2 + \frac{1}{4}y - 8 = 0 \Rightarrow \frac{9}{4}y = 10 \Rightarrow y = \frac{40}{9}$
When $y = \frac{40}{9}$, $\frac{40}{9} = \log_2 x \Rightarrow x = 2^{\frac{40}{9}} = 21.8$ (3 s.f.)
[6 marks available — 1 mark for rewriting $\log_2 \frac{x}{2}$ in terms of y, 1 mark for a correct method to change the base of $\log_4 \sqrt{x}$, 1 mark for rewriting $\log_4 \sqrt{x}$ in terms of y, 1 mark for forming an equation in y, 1 mark for the correct value of y, 1 mark for the correct value of x]

Exercise 9.6 — Modelling Exponential Growth and Decay

Q1 When $t = 10$, $A = \frac{A_0}{2}$ so $\frac{A_0}{2} = A_0 e^{-10k} \Rightarrow \frac{1}{2} = e^{-10k}$
$\Rightarrow k = -\frac{1}{10}\ln\left(\frac{1}{2}\right) = 0.0693... = 0.0693$ (3 s.f.)

a) You want to find t when $A = \frac{A_0}{4}$,
so $\frac{A_0}{4} = A_0 e^{(-0.0693... \times t)} \Rightarrow \frac{1}{4} = e^{(-0.0693... \times t)}$
$\Rightarrow t = -\frac{1}{0.0693...}\ln\left(\frac{1}{4}\right) = 20.0$ years (3 s.f.)
So after 20 years the substance will be reduced to a quarter of its original activity.
Note that a much easier way to do this would be to think of it as 'half and half again'. The substance will be a quarter of its activity after two half lives which is 2 × 10 = 20 years.

b) When $t = 5$, $A = 200$, so $200 = A_0 e^{(-0.0693... \times 5)}$,
so $A_0 = 200e^{(0.0693... \times 5)} = 283$ Bq (3 s.f.)

c) If $t = 15$, then $A = 283 \times e^{(-0.0693... \times 15)} = 100$ Bq (3 s.f.)

Q2 a) If $t = 0$, $T = 225 - 207e^0 = 18$ °C.

b) Let $t = 5$, then $T = 225 - 207e^{-\frac{5}{8}} = 114$ °C. (3 s.f.).

c) Let $T = 190$ °C. Then $190 = 225 - 207e^{-\frac{t}{8}}$
$\Rightarrow e^{-\frac{t}{8}} = \frac{190 - 225}{-207} = \frac{35}{207} \Rightarrow -\frac{t}{8} = \ln\left(\frac{35}{207}\right)$
$\Rightarrow t = -8\ln\left(\frac{35}{207}\right) = 14.2$ min (to 3 s.f.)
So the oven reaches 190 °C just after 12:14.

d)
T
T = 225
$T = 225 - 207e^{\left(-\frac{t}{8}\right)}$
18
0
t

e) As $t \to \infty$, $e^{-\frac{t}{8}} \to 0$, so $T \to 225 - 0 = 225$.
So in the model, the asymptote at $T = 225$ acts as a "cap" — even if left on forever, the oven temperature would never rise above 225 °C.

Q3 a) When $t = 10$, $V = 7500e^{-0.2 \times 10} = 7500e^{-2}$
$= 1015.0146... = £1015$ to the nearest £

b) Let $V = 500$, then $500 = 7500e^{-0.2t}$
$\Rightarrow e^{-0.2t} = \frac{500}{7500} = \frac{1}{15}$
$\Rightarrow -0.2t = \ln\left(\frac{1}{15}\right) \Rightarrow t = -5\ln\left(\frac{1}{15}\right) = 13.5$ (3 s.f.)
So the value will have fallen below £500 after 14 years.

c)
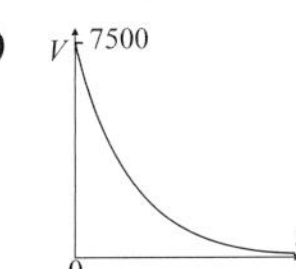

Q4 a) When $t = 0$, $T = 95 - 70e^{-0.1(0)} = 95 - 70 = 25$ °C
[1 mark for the correct answer]

b) $T = 95 - 70e^{-0.1(6)} = 56.6$ °C (3 s.f.)
[1 mark for the correct answer]

c) $70 = 95 - 70e^{-0.1t} \Rightarrow e^{-0.1t} = \frac{25}{70}$
$t = \frac{1}{-0.1}\ln\frac{25}{70} = 10.3$ minutes (3 s.f.)
[3 marks available — 1 mark for forming a suitable equation, 1 mark for a correct method to solve, 1 mark for the correct answer]

d) As $t \to \infty$, $e^{-0.1t} \to 0$ so $T \to 95 - 70(0) = 95$ °C.
[1 mark for the correct answer]

Q5 a) When $t = 0$, $F = 4$, so $F_0 = 4$.
When $t = 6$, $F = 10$ so $10 = 4e^{6g}$ so
$g = \frac{1}{6}\ln\left(\frac{10}{4}\right) = 0.1527... = 0.153$ (3 s.f.)
[4 marks available — 1 mark for the correct value of F_0, 1 mark for forming a suitable equation in g, 1 mark for a correct method to solve, 1 mark for the correct value of g]

b) Let $t = 12$, then $F = 4e^{(12 \times 0.1527...)} = 25$
So after 12 hours the fungus will be 25 mm^2.
[1 mark for the correct answer]

c) Let $F = 15$. Then $15 = 4e^{(0.1527... \times t)}$
$\Rightarrow e^{(0.1527... \times t)} = \frac{15}{4} \Rightarrow t = \frac{1}{0.1527...}\ln\left(\frac{15}{4}\right) = 8.66$ (3 s.f.).
The fungus will take 8.66 hours (or 8 hours 39 minutes) to grow to 15 mm^2.
[3 marks available — 1 mark for forming a suitable equation, 1 mark for a correct method to solve, 1 mark for the correct answer]

d) E.g. there's no restriction, so according to the model the fungus could grow infinitely large.
[1 mark for any valid limitation]

Q6 a) $C = C_0e^{-kt}$ and $C_0 = 2.5$
A half-life of 2 days means that the concentration halves every 2 days $\Rightarrow 0.5 = e^{-k(2)} \Rightarrow k = \frac{\ln 0.5}{-2} = 0.3465...$
When $t = 5$, $C = 2.5e^{-(0.3465...)(5)} = 0.442$ (3 s.f.)
[4 marks available — 1 mark for using the half-life to form an equation, 1 mark for finding the value of k, 1 mark for a correct method to find C when t = 5, 1 mark for the correct answer]

b) $0.2 = 2.5e^{(-0.3465...)t} \Rightarrow \ln(0.2) = \ln(2.5e^{(-0.3465...)t})$
$\Rightarrow \ln(0.2) = \ln(2.5) + -0.3465...t$
$\Rightarrow 0.3465...t = \ln(2.5) - \ln(0.2) \Rightarrow t = 7.28...$, so after 7 days the drug should be clear from the bloodstream.
[3 marks available — 1 mark for forming a suitable equation, 1 mark for a correct method to solve, 1 mark for the correct answer to a suitable degree of accuracy]

Q7 a) $1800 = 1500e^{2b} \Rightarrow \frac{6}{5} = e^{2b} \Rightarrow \ln\frac{6}{5} = \ln e^{2b} = 2b \ln e$
$\Rightarrow b = \frac{1}{2}\ln\frac{6}{5} = 0.09116...$
When $t = 5$, $P = 1500e^{5(0.09116...)} = 2366$ (to the nearest whole number)
[4 marks available — 1 mark for using t = 2 to form an equation, 1 mark for finding the value of b, 1 mark for a correct method to find P when t = 5, 1 mark for the correct answer]

b) Set $P = 3000$, then $3000 = 1500e^{0.09116...t} \Rightarrow 2 = e^{0.09116...t}$
$\Rightarrow t = \frac{1}{0.09116...}\ln 2 = 7.60356...$ years, so the population will exceed 3000 rats 8 years after 2015, which is 2023.
[3 marks available — 1 mark for forming a suitable equation, 1 mark for a correct method to solve, 1 mark for the correct answer]

Q8 a) 1200 trees means $N_0 = 1.2$
When $t = 4$, $N = 1.8$ so,
$1.8 = 1.2e^{k(4)} \Rightarrow e^{4k} = \frac{1.8}{1.2} \Rightarrow k = \frac{1}{4}\ln\frac{1.8}{1.2} = 0.1013...$
When $t = 12$, $N = 1.2e^{12(0.1013...)} = 4.05$, so 4050 trees.
[4 marks available — 1 mark for using t = 4 to form an equation, 1 mark for finding the value of k, 1 mark for a correct method to find N when t = 12, 1 mark for the correct answer]

b) Set $N = 5$, then $5 = 1.2e^{(0.1013...)t} \Rightarrow e^{(0.1013...)t} = \frac{5}{1.2}$
$\Rightarrow t = \frac{1}{0.1013...}\ln\frac{5}{1.2} \Rightarrow t = 14.0788...$ so the number of trees exceeds 5000 in the 15th month, which is August 2021.
[3 marks available — 1 mark for forming a suitable equation, 1 mark for a correct method to solve, 1 mark for the correct answer]

Q9 When $t = 0$, $N = 3$. So $3 = Ae^0 \Rightarrow A = 3$.

a) Let $t = 0.5$ (hours).
Then $N = 3e^{-t} = 3e^{-0.5} = 1.82$ mg/l.

b) Let $N = 0.1$. Then $0.1 = 3e^{-t}$ so
$t = -\ln\left(\frac{0.1}{3}\right) = 3.40$ hours (3 s.f.).

c)
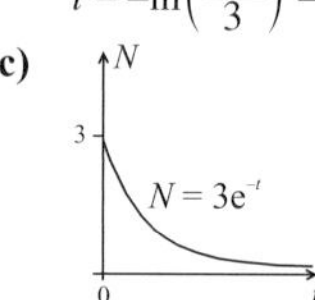

d) The gradient is $-3e^{-t}$.
The gradient of the curve Ae^{kt} is kAe^{kt}. Here, $k = -1$ and $A = 3$.

Q10 a) After 35 years the new percentage is 87.
Using $P_0 = 100$, set $P = 87$ and $t = 35$, then
$87 = 100e^{-35k} \Rightarrow e^{-35k} = 0.87 \Rightarrow \ln(e^{-35k}) = \ln(0.87)$
$\Rightarrow -35k = \ln(0.87) \Rightarrow k = \frac{\ln 0.87}{-35} = 0.003978...$
Set $t = 45$, then $P = 100e^{-(0.003978...)(45)} = 83.6\%$ (3 s.f.)
[4 marks available — 1 mark for using t = 35 to form an equation, 1 mark for finding the value of k, 1 mark for a correct method to find P when t = 45, 1 mark for the correct answer]

b) Set $P = 75$, $75 = 100e^{-0.003978...t} \Rightarrow e^{-0.003978...t} = 0.75$
$\Rightarrow t = \frac{1}{-0.003978...}\ln 0.75 \Rightarrow t = 72.3016...$ years, so one quarter of the forest will have been lost 73 years after 1985, which is the year 2058.
[3 marks available — 1 mark for forming a suitable equation, 1 mark for a correct method to solve, 1 mark for the correct answer]

Q11 a) The negative coefficient means that as t gets larger, V gets smaller — this is exponential decay.
The car will lose value over time.

b) When $t = 0$, $V = 1500 + 9000e^0 = £10\,500$.

c) Let $t = 5$, then $V = 1500 + 9000e^{-\frac{5}{3}} = £3200$ (3 s.f.).

d) Let $V = 2500$, then $2500 = 1500 + 9000e^{-\frac{t}{3}}$
$\Rightarrow 1000 = 9000e^{-\frac{t}{3}} \Rightarrow \frac{1}{9} = e^{-\frac{t}{3}}$
$\Rightarrow t = -3\ln\left(\frac{1}{9}\right) = 6.59$ (3 s.f.). The car will have a value less than £2500 after 7 whole years.
Note: After 6 years the car will still have a value above £2500 so the answer is 7 and not 6.

e)
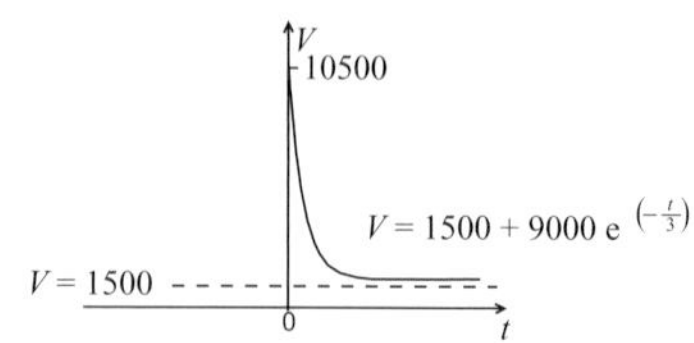

Q12 a) When $t = 0$, $H = 20e^{b \times 0} = 20$. So 20 represents the initial burnt area of forest, in hectares.

b) $b = \ln 1.8 = 0.5877... = 0.588$ (3 s.f.)

c) Let $t = 3$ then $H = 20e^{(0.5877... \times 3)}$
$= 117$ hectares (3 s.f.).

d) If $H = 500$, $500 = 20e^{(0.5877... \times t)} \Rightarrow 25 = e^{(0.5877... \times t)}$
$\Rightarrow \ln 25 = 0.5877... \times t$
$\Rightarrow t = \frac{1}{0.5877...}\ln 25 = 5.48$ hours (3 s.f.)

e) At $t = k$, $H = H_k = 20e^{(\ln 1.8)k}$
At $t = k + 1$, $H = H_{k+1} = 20e^{(\ln 1.8)(k+1)}$
$= 20e^{(\ln 1.8)k + \ln 1.8} = 20e^{(\ln 1.8)k}e^{\ln 1.8} = H_k \times 1.8$
Every hour the burnt area is multiplied by 1.8.
This represents a percentage increase of 80%.

f) E.g. if the fire burnt unchecked, then according to the model $H \to \infty$ as $t \to \infty$, i.e. the area of burnt forest would be infinitely large. This is clearly unrealistic, as the forest will have a finite area.

g) E.g. The model predicts that the first blog will continue to grow exponentially for years. In reality, it's likely that the growth will begin to slow over time, e.g. due to competition from other blogs, a decline in their popularity or due to the blog reaching a natural upper limit. The model predicts that the second blog will end up with less than one subscriber — it is unlikely that the blog would continue with so few subscribers, and the blogger would probably try and increase their number of subscribers rather than just watch them disappear.

Exercise 9.7 — Logarithmic Graphs in Linear Form

Q1 l is a straight line of the form $y = mx + c$, where $y = \log V$, $x = t$, gradient $m = -\frac{1}{40}$ and intercept $c = 4$, so:

$\log V = 4 - \frac{1}{40}t$. When the machine is 20 years old, $t = 20$,
so $\log V = 4 - \frac{1}{40} \times 20 = 4 - \frac{1}{2} = \frac{7}{2}$.
So $V = 10^{\frac{7}{2}} = £3162.2776... = £3200$ (to the nearest £100)

Q2 a) Using points (0, 4) and (3, 5) gives
gradient $= \frac{5-4}{3-0} = \frac{1}{3}$ and y-intercept = 4.
$\log_{10} y = \frac{1}{3}x + 4$
[2 marks available — 1 mark for the correct gradient, 1 mark for the correct equation]

b) $\log_{10} y = \frac{1}{3}x + 4 \Rightarrow y = 10^{\frac{1}{3}x+4} \Rightarrow y = 10^{\frac{1}{3}x} \times 10^4$
$\Rightarrow y = 10\,000 \times 10^{\frac{1}{3}x} \Rightarrow y = 10\,000 \times (10^x)^{\frac{1}{3}}$
[2 marks available — 1 mark for taking exponentials to get rid of the log, 1 mark for rearranging into the required form]

Q3 a) & e)
$y = at^b \Rightarrow \log y = \log a + b\log t$.
To plot the straight-line you need to find logs of both t and y (each to 3 d.p.):

$\log t$	0.845	1.146	1.322	1.447
$\log y$	2.350	3	3.200	3.600

You can now plot $\log y$ against $\log t$:

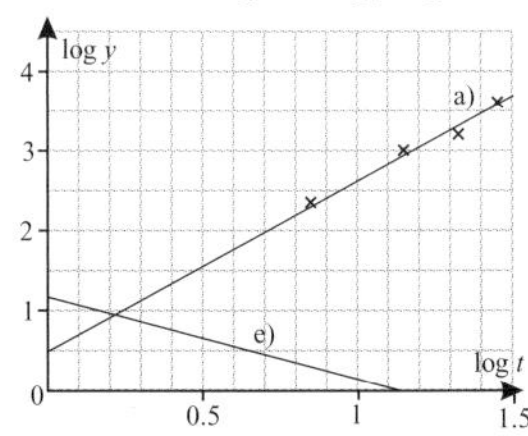

b) From the graph, when $\log t = 0$, $\log a = 0.5$
$\Rightarrow a = 3.16$ (3 s.f.)
b is the gradient of the graph, so take 2 points from the line of best fit — e.g. (0, 0.5) and (1.4, 3.5).
The gradient is: $b = \frac{3.5 - 0.5}{1.4 - 0} = 2.14$ (3 s.f.)
(so $y = 3.16t^{2.14}$)
You might have got slightly different values for a and b depending on your graph — as long as your values are close to the ones given here, that's fine. This will affect your answer to part c) too.

c) $y = 3.16 \times 10^{2.14} = 436.20... = 436$ subscribers

d) $y = 15t^{-1} \Rightarrow \log y = \log (t^{-1} \times 15) = -\log t + \log 15$

e) See part a) for graph.
When $\log t = 0$, $\log y = \log 15 = 1.176$ (3 d.p.).
When $\log y = 0$, $\log t = \log 15 = 1.176$ (3 d.p.).
So plot (0, 1.176) and (1.176, 0) and draw a straight line between them.

f) The graphs intersect at $\log t \approx 0.22$, so $t \approx 1.7$, which is approximately Day 2.

Q4 a) (i)

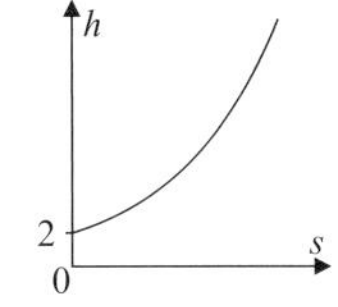

(ii)

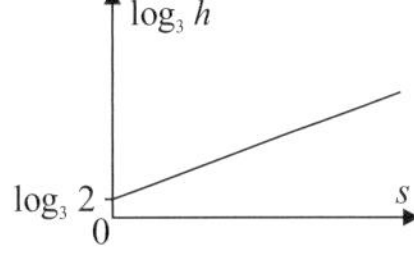

(iii) E.g. the second graph is more useful for calculations — it's easier to calculate the gradient of a straight line than it is a curve.

b) E.g. as $s \to \infty$, $h \to \infty$. This implies that the tank is capable of holding an infinite amount of water, which is obviously unrealistic.
A tank reaches its maximum capacity, H, at time S.
So adjust the model to say that for $s \geq S$, $h = H$.

Q5 The graph is of the form $p = at^b$
$\Rightarrow \log p = \log a + b\log t$. To find the straight-line form you need to find logs of both t and p (each to 3 d.p.):

$\log t$	0	0.477	0.602	0.778	0.954
$\log p$	0.301	1.146	1.342	1.643	1.944

You can now plot $\log p$ against $\log t$:

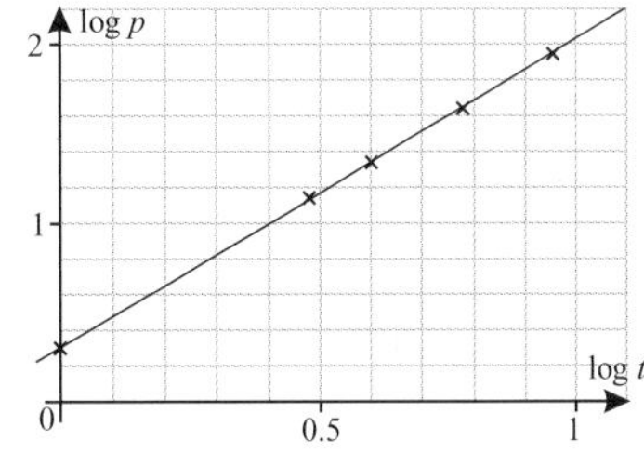

When $\log t = 0$, $\log a = 0.301 = \log 2 \Rightarrow a = 2$
b is the gradient of the graph, so take 2 points — e.g. (0, 0.301) and (0.602, 1.342). The gradient is
$\frac{1.342 - 0.301}{0.602 - 0} = \frac{1.041}{0.602} = 1.72... = 1.7$ (1 d.p.)
So the graph can be approximated using the equation $p = 2t^{1.7}$.

Q6 a) $16 = 5 \times 2^t \Rightarrow 3.2 = 2^t$
$\Rightarrow t = \log_2 3.2 = 1.6780... = 1.68$ seconds (3 s.f.)
[2 marks available — 1 mark for a correct method, 1 mark for the correct answer]

b) (i)

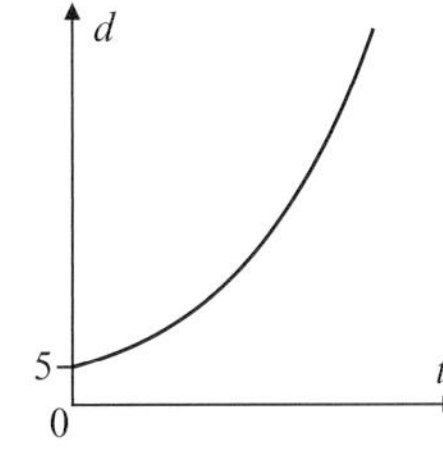

[2 marks available — 1 mark for an exponential shape with positive gradient, 1 mark for the correct intercept with the vertical axis]

(ii) E.g. The depth increases exponentially, which suggests that the silo is wider at the bottom and narrower at the top (a pyramid or cone shape).
[1 mark for a sensible suggestion]

c) (i) $d = 5 \times 2^t \Rightarrow \log_2 d = \log_2(5 \times 2^t)$
$\Rightarrow \log_2 d = \log_2(5) + \log_2(2^t)$
$\Rightarrow \log_2 d = \log_2(5) + t$

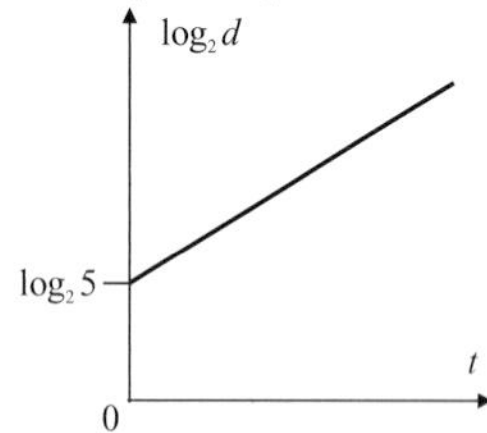

[2 marks available — 1 mark for a straight-line graph, 1 mark for going through $\log_2 5$ on the vertical axis]

(ii) The depth will just continue to increase but the silo can't fill up forever, so the model must only be valid for small values of t.
[1 mark for any valid limitation]

Q7 $x = kb^t$, so $\log x = \log k + t \log b$.
So to make a linear graph, you need to find $\log x$ (3 d.p.) for each value of x:

t	5	50	100	200	300
x	80.449	32.411	11.803	1.565	0.207
$\log x$	1.906	1.511	1.072	0.195	–0.684

You can now plot $\log x$ against t:

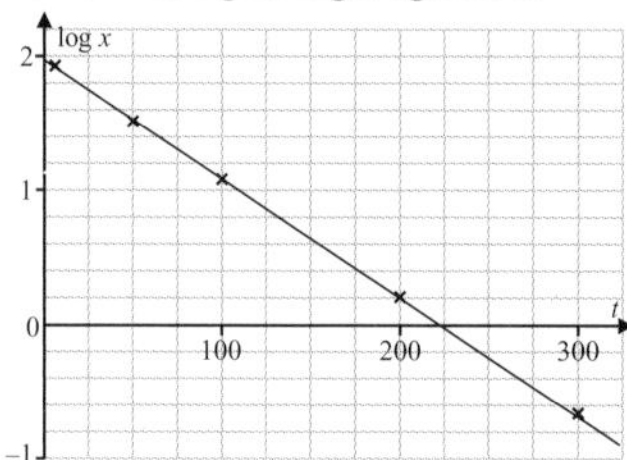

The line of best fit meets the vertical axis at around 1.95 — i.e. when $t = 0$, $\log x = 1.95 \Rightarrow x = 89.12... \approx 89$ Bq.
The line of best fit may vary slightly, so your reading might be a bit different. It should be between 1.92 and 2, so accept any answer between 83 Bq and 100 Bq.

Q8 a) $D = D_0 10^{-kt} \Rightarrow \log_{10} D = \log_{10}(D_0 10^{-kt})$
$\Rightarrow \log_{10} D = \log_{10} D_0 + \log_{10} 10^{-kt}$
$\Rightarrow \log_{10} D = \log_{10} D_0 - kt$
$\Rightarrow \log_{10} D = -kt + \log_{10} D_0$
[2 marks available — 1 mark for taking logs of both sides, 1 mark for rearranging to give the required result]

b)

t	10	15	20	25	30
D	50	42	32	26	22
$\log_{10} D$	1.698...	1.623...	1.505...	1.414...	1.342...

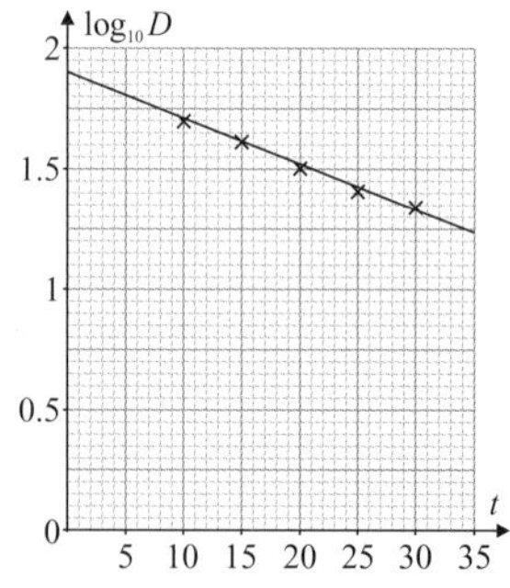

[4 marks available — 1 mark for a correct method to find the values in the table, 1 mark for the correct values in the table, 1 mark for plotting the points accurately, 1 mark for a suitable line of best fit]

c) Reading from the graph, $\log_{10} D_0 = 1.9$ (2 s.f.)
Gradient $= \frac{1.5 - 1.9}{21 - 0} = -0.01904... = -0.019$ (2 s.f.)
So $k = 0.019$ and $D_0 = 10^{1.9} = 79.43... = 79$ °C (2 s.f.)
At $t = 40$, $D = 79.43... \times 10^{-0.01904...(40)} = 13.74...$ °C
So the temperature is $20 + 13.74... = 33.74... = 34$ °C (2 s.f.).
[4 marks available — 1 mark for k, 1 mark for D_0, 1 mark for a correct method to find the temperature at t = 40, 1 mark for the correct answer]
Your answers may differ from the values given due to the accuracy of your line of best fit and rounding accuracy. Award the marks based on reading values correctly from your graph in part b).

Q9 Area = length × width. The area is always 120 m², so $lw = 120$. Take logs: $\log lw = \log 120$
$\Rightarrow \log l + \log w = \log 120 \Rightarrow \log l = \log 120 - \log w$
This can be plotted on a graph of $\log w$ against $\log l$:

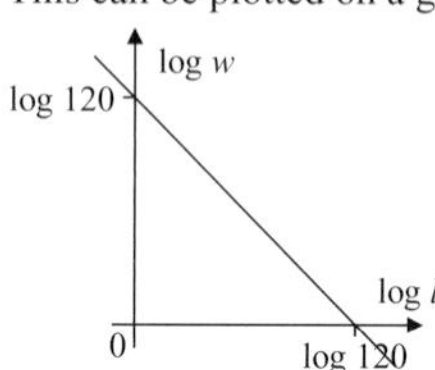

Q10 a) Using points (1, 6.6) and (2, 5.9) gives
gradient $= \frac{5.9 - 6.6}{2 - 1} = -0.7$
So $\log_{10} V = -0.7 \log_{10} t + c$
$\Rightarrow 6.6 = -0.7(1) + c \Rightarrow c = 7.3$
$\log_{10} V = -0.7 \log_{10} t + 7.3$
[3 marks available — 1 mark for gradient, 1 mark for intercept with the vertical axis, 1 mark for the correct equation]

b) $\log_{10} V = -0.7 \log_{10} t + 7.3 \Rightarrow V = 10^{7.3} t^{-0.7}$
So $a = 10^{7.3}$ and $k = 0.7$.
After 1 year it is worth $10^{7.3}(1^{-0.7}) = £19\,952\,623...$
After 2 years it is worth $10^{7.3}(2^{-0.7}) = £12\,282\,280...$
£19 952 623... – £12 282 280... = £7 670 342.88...
= £7 700 000 (2 s.f.)
[5 marks available — 1 mark for a correct method to remove logs, 1 mark for a, 1 mark for k, 1 mark for a correct method to calculate drop in value, 1 mark for the correct answer]

c) E.g. $V = 10^{7.3} t^{-0.7}$ is undefined when t = 0, and as $t \to 0$, $V \to \infty$.
[1 mark for any valid limitation]

Chapter 9 Review Exercise

Q1 a) $y = 4e^{-3x}$

b) Gradient $= -3 \times 4e^{-3x} = -12e^{-3x}$
(i) When $x = -1$, gradient $= -12e^{(-3 \times -1)} = -12e^3$
(ii) When $x = 0$, gradient $= -12e^{(-3 \times 0)} = -12$
(iii) When $x = 4$, gradient $= -12e^{(-3 \times 4)} = -12e^{-12}$

Q2 The graph cuts the y-axis at $y = 4 \times 5^{-0} = 4$ and doesn't cross the x-axis.

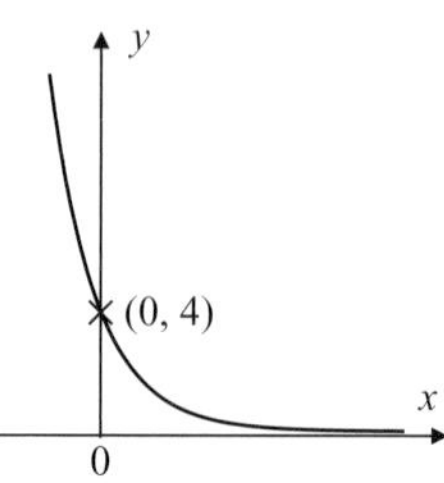

[2 marks available — 1 mark for a correct exponential shape with negative gradient, 1 mark for the correct y-intercept]

Q3 The gradient function of $y = 2e^{\frac{3}{2}x}$ is $\frac{3}{2} \times 2e^{\frac{3}{2}x} = 3e^{\frac{3}{2}x}$.
So the gradient at $x = \frac{1}{3}$ is $3e^{\frac{3}{2} \times \frac{1}{3}} = 3e^{\frac{1}{2}}$.
[2 marks available — 1 mark for knowing the gradient function, 1 mark for the correct answer]

Q4 Gradient of $y = e^{2x}$ at $x = \frac{1}{2}$ is $2 \times e^{2 \times \frac{1}{2}} = 2e$.
So the gradient of the tangent to $y = e^{2x}$ at $x = \frac{1}{2}$ is 2e *[1 mark]*.
Equation of tangent at $\left(\frac{1}{2}, e\right)$ is:
$y - e = 2e\left(x - \frac{1}{2}\right) \Rightarrow y = 2ex$ *[1 mark]*
In this equation, when $x = 0$, $y = 0$, so the tangent passes through the origin *[1 mark]*.

Q5 **a)** $\log_4 16 = 2$
b) $\log_{216} 6 = \frac{1}{3}$
c) $\log_3 \frac{1}{81} = -4$

Q6 **a)** 3 **b)** -3 **c)** $\log_3 9 = 2$

Q7 **a)** $\ln x = 3 \Rightarrow x = e^3$
b) $e^x = 4 \Rightarrow x = \ln 4$

Q8 **a)** $\log_{10} a = 3 \Rightarrow a = 10^3 = 1000$
$\log_{10} b = 1 \Rightarrow b = 10^1 = 10 \Rightarrow b^3 = 10^3 = 1000 = a$
So the statement $a = b^3$ is true.
[2 marks available — 1 mark for the correct answer, 1 mark for a suitable explanation]
b) $\ln a^2 = 8 \Rightarrow a^2 = e^8$
$\ln b = 2 \Rightarrow b = e^2 \Rightarrow b^3 = (e^2)^3 = e^6$
So the statement $a^2 = b^3$ is false.
[2 marks available — 1 mark for the correct answer, 1 mark for a suitable explanation]

Q9 **a)** $\log 3 + \log 5^2 = \log (3 \times 5^2) = \log 75$
b) $\log 36^{\frac{1}{2}} - \log 3 = \log\left(\frac{\sqrt{36}}{3}\right) = \log 2$
c) $\log 2 - \log 16^{\frac{1}{4}} = \log\left(\frac{2}{\sqrt[4]{16}}\right) = \log 1 = 0$

Q10 **a)** $6 \log_a \sqrt{x} = 6 \log_a x^{\frac{1}{2}} = 6 \times \frac{1}{2} \log_a x = 3 \log_a x$
b) $\log_a x^{\frac{3}{2}} + 2 \log_a x = \frac{3}{2} \log_a x + 2 \log_a x = \frac{7}{2} \log_a x$

Q11 $3 - \log_x \frac{1}{x^2} + 2 \log_x \sqrt{x} = 3 - \log_x x^{-2} + 2 \log_x x^{\frac{1}{2}}$
$= 3 + 2 \log_x x + \frac{1}{2} \times 2 \log_x x = 3 + 2 + \frac{1}{2} \times 2 = 6$
[3 marks available — 1 mark for evaluating $\log_x \frac{1}{x^2}$, 1 mark for evaluating $2 \log_x \sqrt{x}$, 1 mark for the correct answer]

Q12 $\log_b (x^2 - 1) - \log_b (x - 1) = \log_b\left(\frac{x^2 - 1}{x - 1}\right)$
$= \log_b\left(\frac{(x + 1)(x - 1)}{x - 1}\right) = \log_b (x + 1)$
Once you've combined the logs, you have to spot that the numerator is a difference of two squares, and use that to simplify the fraction.

Q13 E.g. $\frac{2 + \log_a 4}{\log_a 2a} = \frac{2 + 2\log_a 2}{\log_a 2 + \log_a a} = \frac{2(1 + \log_a 2)}{\log_a 2 + 1} = 2$

Q14 E.g. using the change of base formula:
a) $\log_7 12 = \frac{\log_{10} 12}{\log_{10} 7} = 1.28$ (3 s.f.)
b) $\log_5 8 = \frac{\log_{10} 8}{\log_{10} 5} = 1.29$ (3 s.f.)
c) $\log_{16} 125 = \frac{\log_{10} 125}{\log_{10} 16} = 1.74$ (3 s.f.)

Q15 **a)** $\log_2 3 \times 3 \log_3 5 = \log_2 3 \times 3 \frac{\log_2 5}{\log_2 3} = 3\log_2 5$ or $\log_2 125$
b) $\ln 4 \times 2 \log_2 5 = \ln 4 \times 2 \frac{\ln 5}{\ln 2} = \ln 2^2 \times 2 \frac{\ln 5}{\ln 2}$
$= 2 \ln 2 \times 2 \frac{\ln 5}{\ln 2} = 4 \ln 5$ or $\ln 625$

Q16 **a)**

x	-3	-2	-1	0	1	2	3
y	0.0156	0.0625	0.25	1	4	16	64

b)

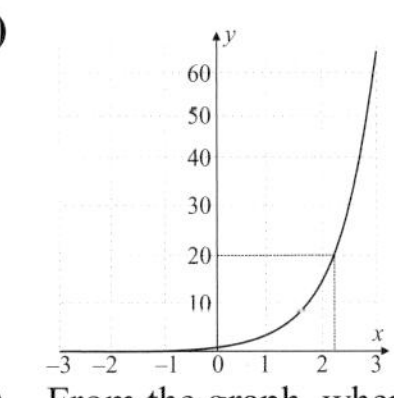

c) From the graph, when $y = 20$, $x = 2.2$
You may get a slightly different answer depending on your graph.
d) $4^x = 20 \Rightarrow \log 4^x = \log 20 \Rightarrow x \log 4 = \log 20$
$\Rightarrow x = \frac{\log 20}{\log 4} = 2.16$ (3 s.f.)

Q17 **a)** $10^x = 240 \Rightarrow \log 10^x = \log 240 \Rightarrow x \log 10 = \log 240$
$\Rightarrow x = \frac{\log 240}{\log 10} = \log_{10} 240 = 2.38$ (3 s.f.)
Recall that $\log_{10} 10 = 1$.
b) $\log_{10} x = 5.3 \Rightarrow x = 10^{5.3} = 200\,000$ (3 s.f.)
c) $10^{2x+1} = 1500 \Rightarrow \log 10^{2x+1} = \log 1500$
$\Rightarrow (2x + 1) \log 10 = \log 1500$
$\Rightarrow 2x + 1 = \log 1500 \Rightarrow x = \frac{\log 1500 - 1}{2} = 1.09$ (3 s.f.)
d) $4^{x-1} = 200 \Rightarrow \log 4^{x-1} = \log 200 \Rightarrow (x - 1) \log 4 = \log 200$
$\Rightarrow x = \frac{\log 200}{\log 4} + 1 = 4.82$ (3 s.f.)

Q18 **a)** $e^{2x} = 6 \Rightarrow \ln e^{2x} = \ln 6 \Rightarrow 2x \ln e = \ln 6$
$\Rightarrow x = \frac{\ln 6}{2} = 0.8959$ (4 d.p.)
b) $3e^{-4x+1} = 5 \Rightarrow \ln e^{-4x+1} = \ln \frac{5}{3} \Rightarrow -4x + 1 = \ln \frac{5}{3}$
$\Rightarrow x = \frac{\ln \frac{5}{3} - 1}{-4} = 0.1223$ (4 d.p.)
c) $\ln (x + 3) = 0.75 \Rightarrow e^{\ln (x+3)} = e^{0.75}$
$\Rightarrow x + 3 = e^{0.75} \Rightarrow x = e^{0.75} - 3 = -0.8830$ (4 d.p.)
d) $\ln x + \ln 5 = \ln 4 \Rightarrow \ln 5x = \ln 4 \Rightarrow 5x = 4$
$\Rightarrow x = 0.8000$ (4 d.p.)

Q19 **a)** $\log_a x^3 + \log_a \frac{1}{x} = \log_a\left(x^3 \times \frac{1}{x}\right) = \log_a x^2 = 2 \log_a x$
[2 marks available — 1 mark for writing as a single log, 1 mark for the correct answer]
b) $\log_{10} B + \log_{10} C = 5 \Rightarrow \log_{10} BC = 5$
Take exponentials of both sides of the equation:
$BC = 10^5 \Rightarrow B = \frac{10^5}{C}$
[2 marks available — 1 mark for a correct method to remove logs, 1 mark for the correct answer]

Q20 $e^x - \frac{40}{e^x} = 3 \Rightarrow (e^x)^2 - 40 = 3e^x$
Let $y = e^x$: $y^2 - 3y - 40 = 0$ *[1 mark]*
$\Rightarrow (y - 8)(y + 5) = 0 \Rightarrow y = 8, y = -5$, so $e^x = 8$ or $e^x = -5$.
Negative values of e^x are not possible, so $e^x = 8$ *[1 mark]*
$\Rightarrow x = \ln 8 = \ln (2^3) = 3 \ln 2$ *[1 mark]*

Q21 **a)** $\log_{10} y = 1 + \log_{10} (x + 2)$
$\Rightarrow \log_{10} y = \log_{10} 10 + \log_{10} (x + 2)$ *[1 mark]*
$\Rightarrow \log_{10} y = \log_{10} (10x + 20)$ *[1 mark]*
$\Rightarrow y = 10x + 20$
b) $10^{15x - y} = 10\,000 = 10^4$
$\Rightarrow (15x - y) \log 10 = 4 \log 10 \Rightarrow 15x - y = 4$
So the simultaneous equations are:
$y = 10x + 20$ ①
$15x - y = 4$ ②
E.g. substituting ① into ② gives:
$15x - 10x - 20 = 4 \Rightarrow 5x = 24 \Rightarrow x = 4.8$
Substituting $x = 4.8$ in ①: $y = 10 \times 4.8 + 20 = 68$
[3 marks available — 1 mark for taking logs to form a correct second linear equation, 1 mark for a correct method for solving the simultaneous equations, 1 mark for both answers correct]

Q22 a) $a^x = b^y \Rightarrow x = \log_a b^y$ *[1 mark]* $\Rightarrow x = y \log_a b$

b) From part a), if $2^{k-2} = 3^{2k-5}$, then $a = 2$, $b = 3$, $x = k - 2$ and $y = 2k - 5$, so: $k - 2 = (2k - 5)\log_2 3$ *[1 mark]*

$\Rightarrow k - 2 = 2k\log_2 3 - 5\log_2 3$ *[1 mark]*

$\Rightarrow k(1 - 2\log_2 3) = 2 - 5\log_2 3$

$\Rightarrow k = \dfrac{2 - 5\log_2 3}{1 - 2\log_2 3}$ *[1 mark]*

Q23 The population, P spiders, is linked to the time, t years, by the equation $P = 2000 \times 0.75^t$, so solve:
$2000 \times 0.75^t < 200$

$\Rightarrow 0.75^t < \dfrac{200}{2000} \Rightarrow \log 0.75^t < \log 0.1$

$\Rightarrow t\log 0.75 < \log 0.1 \Rightarrow t > \dfrac{\log 0.1}{\log 0.75}$

Watch out — dividing by log 0.75 means dividing by a negative, so you need to flip the inequality sign.

$\Rightarrow t > 8.0039...$ years. So the spiders are in danger of extinction in the 9th year.

Q24 a) Using $L_0 = 20$ and $t = 10$, $L = 20 \times e^{\frac{10}{12}} = 46.01...$
$= 46$ leopards *[1 mark]*

b) Find t when $L = 20 \times e^{\frac{t}{12}} = 60$

$\Rightarrow e^{\frac{t}{12}} = 3 \Rightarrow t = 12\ln 3 = 13.18...$

So it will be 13 years until the reserve runs out of space.

[3 marks available — 1 mark for forming a suitable equation, 1 mark for a correct method to solve, 1 mark for the correct answer]

c) Using $W_0 = 15$ and $t = 5$, $W = 15 \times e^{-\frac{5}{3}} = 2.833...$
So the model predicts that only 2 leopards will be left in the wild after 5 years.

[2 marks available — 1 mark for the correct value of W, 1 mark for the correct answer]

Q25 a) $V = 1000 + 8050e^{-0} = 1000 + 8050 = £9050$
[1 mark for the correct answer]

b) When $t = 5$, $V = 0.7 \times 9050 = £6335$.
$6335 = 1000 + 8050e^{-5k} \Rightarrow 5335 = 8050e^{-5k}$

$\Rightarrow e^{-5k} = \dfrac{5335}{8050} \Rightarrow \ln(e^{-5k}) = \ln\left(\dfrac{5335}{8050}\right)$

$\Rightarrow -5k = \ln\left(\dfrac{5335}{8050}\right) \Rightarrow k = 0.0822...$

At $t = 6$,
$V = 1000 + 8050e^{-(0.0822...)(6)} = 5913.62...$
$= £5914$ (to the nearest whole number)

[4 marks available — 1 mark for £6335, 1 mark for a correct method to find k, 1 mark for the correct value of k, 1 mark for the correct answer]

c) $£9050 \div 2 = £4525$
$4525 = 1000 + 8050e^{-(0.0822...)t} \Rightarrow 3525 = 8050e^{-(0.0822...)t}$

$\Rightarrow e^{-(0.0822...)t} = \dfrac{3525}{8050} \Rightarrow \ln(e^{-(0.0822...)t}) = \ln\left(\dfrac{3525}{8050}\right)$

$\Rightarrow -(0.0822...)t = \ln\left(\dfrac{3525}{8050}\right) \Rightarrow t = 10.036...$

So it will take 11 years for the value of the car to be half the sale price.

[3 marks available — 1 mark for £4525, 1 mark for a correct method to find t, 1 mark for the correct answer]

10.036... = 10.0 (3 s.f.), so accept 10 years as an answer too.

Q26 a) When $t = 0$, $Z = 10 + 20e^0 = 30$ zombies

b) When $t = 2$, $Z = 10 + 20e^2 = 157.78... = 157$ zombies

You could argue that if you're 0.78... transformed into a zombie, you're probably a zombie, so accept 158 as an answer too.

c) $Z = 60\,000\,000 = 10 + 20e^t$

$\Rightarrow e^t = \dfrac{60\,000\,000 - 10}{20} = 2\,999\,999.5$

$\Rightarrow t = \ln 2\,999\,999.5 = 14.91... = 15$ weeks

Q27 a) A = initial mass of ice = 100 kg *[1 mark]*.
$M = Ab^t \Rightarrow \log_{10} M = \log_{10} A + t\log_{10} b$ *[1 mark]*
So the gradient of the line $= \log_{10} b$

$\Rightarrow \log_{10} b = \dfrac{1.903 - 2}{10 - 0}$ *[1 mark]*

$= -0.0097$

$\Rightarrow b = 10^{-0.0097} = 0.9779... = 0.978$ (3 s.f.) *[1 mark]*

b) At the point where 60% of the ice has melted, the remaining mass is 40 kg $\Rightarrow M = 40$.

$\Rightarrow 40 = 100 \times 0.978^t \Rightarrow 0.978^t = 0.4$

$\Rightarrow t\log_{10} 0.978 = \log_{10} 0.4$

$\Rightarrow t = \dfrac{\log 0.4}{\log 0.978} = 41.1897...$
$= 41$ minutes to the nearest minute.

[2 marks available — 1 mark for a correct method, 1 mark for a correctly rounded final answer]

c) For large values of t the model predicts that some ice will always remain — the mass predicted by the model is always positive. However, in reality, the ice will completely melt and the mass will reduce to zero *[1 mark]*.

Q28 a) Find an equation in the form $\ln y = mt + c$.
The vertical intercept (c) is 7.5 and the gradient (m) is $-7.5 \div 15 = -0.5$. So $\ln y = -0.5t + 7.5$.
Then take exponentials of both sides to get the exponential equation $y = e^{7.5 - 0.5t}$ (or $y = e^{7.5}e^{-0.5t}$).

b) For this line, the vertical intercept (c) is 3.5 and the gradient (m) is 0.25. So $\ln y = 0.25t + 3.5$.
So the exponential equation is $y = e^{3.5 + 0.25t}$ (or $y = e^{3.5}e^{0.25t}$).

c) When $y = 20$, $\ln y = \ln 20 = 2.9957... \approx 3$.
From the graph, when $\ln y = 3$, $t = 9$, so it will reach a critical level in the 10th month.

You could also solve this algebraically — when y = 20, ln 20 = 7.5 − 0.5t ⇒ 0.5 t = 7.5 − ln 20 ⇒ t = 9.008...

d) E.g. the model predicts that the population of grey squirrels will continue to grow exponentially with time. However, in reality, factors such as the availability of resources will begin to slow their growth after a certain time.

Q29 a) $y = Ax^{-b} \Rightarrow \log_{10} y = \log_{10} Ax^{-b}$

$\Rightarrow \log_{10} y = \log_{10} x^{-b} + \log_{10} A$

$\Rightarrow \log_{10} y = -b\log_{10} x + \log_{10} A$

b) (i)

$\log_{10} x$	0	0.176...	0.301...	0.397...	0.477...	0.544...
$\log_{10} y$	0.880...	0.799...	0.732...	0.690...	0.653...	0.623...

(ii)

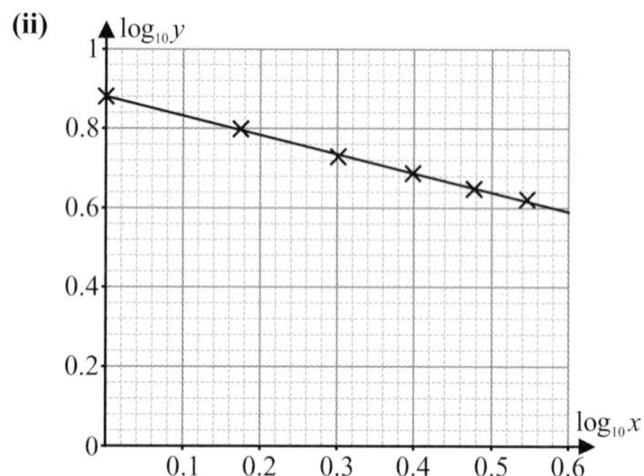

(iii) The line cuts the vertical axis at 0.88.
So $A = 10^{0.88} = 7.585... = 7.6$ (2 s.f.)

$b = -\text{gradient of the line} = -\dfrac{0.88 - 0.64}{0 - 0.5} = 0.48$.

(iv) $y = 7.6 \times 8^{-0.48} = 2.8011... = 2.8$ g/l (1 d.p.)

(v) E.g. As you get closer to the mouth of the river the salt concentration would grow exponentially, which is unrealistic.

Q30 a) Sea snail line gradient $= \dfrac{6 - 2}{4 - 0} = 1$.
So the line for sea snails has equation $\ln y = x + 2$.

Starfish line gradient $= \dfrac{5.5 - 2}{0 - 4} = -0.875$.

So the line for starfish has equation $\ln y = -0.875x + 5.5$.
The graphs cross when $x + 2 = -0.875x + 5.5$
$\Rightarrow x = 1.866...$ and $\ln y = 2 + 1.866... = 3.866...$
$y = 47.78...$

So the combined population would be
$47.78 \times 2 = 96$ (to the nearest whole number).
[5 marks available — 1 mark for the correct method to calculate gradients, 1 mark for the equation for sea snails, 1 mark for the equation for starfish, 1 mark for working out where they cross, 1 mark for the correct answer]

b) $\ln y = x + 2 \Rightarrow y = e^{x+2} \Rightarrow y = e^2e^x$
[2 marks available — 1 mark for using a correct method to remove ln, 1 mark for the correct answer]

c) The population of sea snails will grow exponentially, which is unrealistic.
[1 mark for any suitable observation]

Q31 a) Let $t = 0$ be the start of January 2020 when 100% of the tree is healthy. $P = Ae^{-kt} \Rightarrow 100 = Ae^{-k(0)} \Rightarrow A = 100$.
$t = 5$ will be the start of June 2020 when 93% of the tree is healthy. $P = 100e^{-kt} \Rightarrow 93 = 100e^{-5k}$
$\Rightarrow k = \frac{\ln 0.93}{-5} = 0.0145...$
When $P = 80$, $80 = 100e^{-(0.0145...)t}$
$\Rightarrow t = \frac{\ln 0.8}{-0.0145...} = 15.374...$
So the tree surgeon has $15.374... - 5 = 10.374 \approx 10$ months before she needs to cut the tree down.
[5 marks available — 1 mark for a correct method to find A and k, 1 mark for A, 1 mark for k, 1 mark for a correct method to find t when P = 80, 1 mark for the correct final answer]

b) At the start of 2020, $t = 0$, $P = 100\%$
At the start of 2021, $t = 12$, $P = 100e^{-(0.0145...)(12)} = 84.015...\%$
At the start of 2022, $t = 24$, $P = 100e^{-(0.0145...)(24)} = 70.585...\%$
At the start of 2023, $t = 36$, $P = 100e^{-(0.0145...)(36)} = 59.303...\%$
At the start of 2024, $t = 48$, $P = 100e^{-(0.0145...)(48)} = 49.823...\%$
So in 2023 the tree will rot less than 10%.
[3 marks available — 1 mark for using the formula where t is a multiple of 12, 1 mark for working out the value each year, 1 mark for the correct answer]

c) E.g. The tree will never completely rot away because P will never reach 0, which is unrealistic.
[1 mark for any suitable limitation]

Q32 a) The gradient function is $e^{0.2t}$ so the population is
$\frac{1}{0.2}e^{0.2t} = 5e^{0.2t}$.
[2 marks available — 1 mark for a correct method to use the gradient function, 1 mark for the correct answer]

b) $5e^{0.2t} = 30 \Rightarrow e^{0.2t} = 6 \Rightarrow t = \frac{\ln 6}{0.2} = 8.958...$
So in 8.958... years the population will hit 30 and begin to decline.
The gradient function for the decline is $-3e^{-0.1t}$, so the population can be modelled by $\frac{-3}{-0.1}e^{-0.1t} = 30e^{-0.1t}$.
The population in 2020 is $5e^{0.2(0)} = 5$.
So $30e^{-0.1t} = 5 \Rightarrow e^{-0.1t} = \frac{5}{30}$
$\Rightarrow t = \frac{1}{-0.1}\ln\left(\frac{5}{30}\right) = 17.917...$ years.
$17.917... + 8.958... = 26.876...$
So the population will be back at the levels of 2020 in 2046.
[6 marks available — 1 mark for a correct method to find when the population will be 30, 1 mark for 8.958... years, 1 mark for using the gradient function of the decline, 1 mark for a correct function for the population during the decline, 1 mark for a correct method to find when the population will be back to 5, 1 mark for a correct answer of 2046]

Chapter 10: Differentiation

Prior Knowledge Check

Q1 a) Gradient $= \frac{6-(-8)}{(-2)-5} = \frac{14}{-7} = -2$

b) Gradient $= \frac{(-1)-5}{(-3)-1} = \frac{-6}{-4} = \frac{3}{2}$

Q2 a) $x^2 + 5x - 6 = 0 \Rightarrow (x-1)(x+6) = 0 \Rightarrow x = 1$ or $x = -6$

b) $x^3 - 8x^2 + 12x = 0 \Rightarrow x(x^2 - 8x + 12) = 0$
$\Rightarrow x(x-2)(x-6) = 0 \Rightarrow x = 0, x = 2$ or $x = 6$

Q3 a) $4x - 1 < 0 \Rightarrow 4x < 1 \Rightarrow x < \frac{1}{4}$

b) $4x \geq 12x^2 \Rightarrow 4x - 12x^2 \geq 0 \Rightarrow x - 3x^2 \geq 0$
$\Rightarrow x(1-3x) \geq 0 \Rightarrow 0 \leq x \leq \frac{1}{3}$

Q4 a) $5^{-2} = \frac{1}{5^2} = \frac{1}{25}$

b) $64^{\frac{1}{2}} = \sqrt{64} = 8$

Q5 a) $y = x^3 - 9x = x(x^2 - 9) = x(x+3)(x-3)$
So the curve crosses the x-axis at $x = -3$, $x = 0$ and $x = 3$.
The coefficient of x^3 is positive, so the curve goes from the bottom left to the top right.

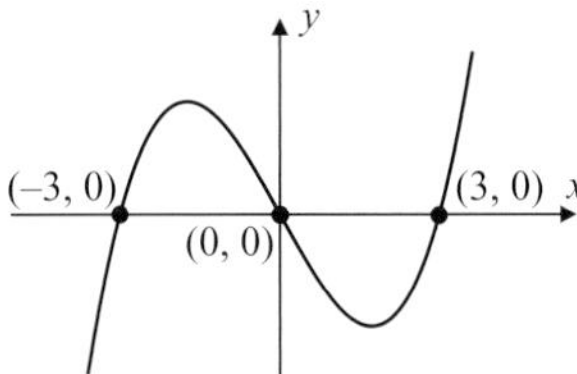

b) $y = (x-3)(x+1)(x+2)$, so the curve crosses the x-axis at $x = 3$, $x = -1$ and $x = -2$. The y-intercept is $-3 \times 1 \times 2 = -6$.
The coefficient of x^3 is positive, so the curve goes from the bottom left to the top right.

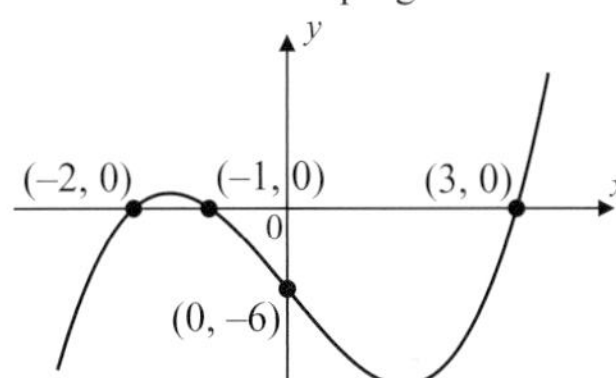

Exercise 10.1-10.2 — Finding the Gradient of a Curve and Differentiating from First Principles

Q1 *The gradient of the straight line joining points (x_1, y_1) and (x_2, y_2) is given by $\frac{y_2 - y_1}{x_2 - x_1}$.*

a) (i) When $x = 1$, $y = 1$ and when $x = 2$, $y = 8$
so the gradient is $\frac{8-1}{2-1} = \frac{7}{1} = 7$.

(ii) When $x = 1$, $y = 1$ and when $x = 1.5$, $y = 3.375$ so the gradient is $\frac{3.375-1}{1.5-1} = \frac{2.375}{0.5} = 4.75$.

(iii) When $x = 1$, $y = 1$ and when $x = 1.1$, $y = 1.331$ so the gradient is $\frac{1.331-1}{1.1-1} = \frac{0.331}{0.1} = 3.31$.

b) The gradients of the straight lines in part a) move closer to 3 as the value of x moves closer to 1.

Q2 a) $\frac{dy}{dx} = \lim_{h \to 0}\left[\frac{(x+h)-x}{(x+h)-x}\right] = \lim_{h \to 0}[1] = 1$

b) $f'(x) = \lim_{h \to 0}\left[\frac{(x+h)^3 - x^3}{(x+h)-x}\right]$
$= \lim_{h \to 0}\left[\frac{x^3 + 3x^2h + 3xh^2 + h^3 - x^3}{(x+h)-x}\right]$
$= \lim_{h \to 0}\left[\frac{3x^2h + 3xh^2 + h^3}{h}\right]$
$= \lim_{h \to 0}[3x^2 + 3xh + h^2] = 3x^2$

c) $f'(x) = \lim_{h\to 0}\left[\frac{2(x+h)-2x}{(x+h)-x}\right] = \lim_{h\to 0}\left[\frac{2x+2h-2x}{h}\right]$

$= \lim_{h\to 0}\left[\frac{2h}{h}\right] = \lim_{h\to 0}[2] = 2$

d) $f'(x) = \lim_{h\to 0}\left[\frac{2(x+h)^2-2x^2}{(x+h)-x}\right]$

$= \lim_{h\to 0}\left[\frac{2(x^2+2xh+h^2)-2x^2}{(x+h)-x}\right]$

$= \lim_{h\to 0}\left[\frac{2x^2+4xh+2h^2-2x^2}{(x+h)-x}\right]$

$= \lim_{h\to 0}\left[\frac{4xh+2h^2}{h}\right] = \lim_{h\to 0}[4x+2h] = 4x$

e) $f'(x) = \lim_{h\to 0}\left[\frac{(x+h)-7-(x-7)}{(x+h)-x}\right]$

$= \lim_{h\to 0}\left[\frac{x+h-7-x+7}{(x+h)-x}\right]$

$= \lim_{h\to 0}\left[\frac{h}{h}\right] = \lim_{h\to 0}[1] = 1$

f) $f'(x) = \lim_{h\to 0}\left[\frac{-(x+h)^3-(-x^3)}{(x+h)-x}\right]$

$= \lim_{h\to 0}\left[\frac{-x^3-3x^2h-3xh^2-h^3+x^3}{(x+h)-x}\right]$

$= \lim_{h\to 0}\left[\frac{-3x^2h-3xh^2-h^3}{h}\right]$

$= \lim_{h\to 0}[-3x^2-3xh-h^2] = -3x^2$

Q3 a) $\frac{dy}{dx} = \lim_{h\to 0}\left[\frac{5(x+h)^2+1-(5x^2+1)}{(x+h)-x}\right]$

$= \lim_{h\to 0}\left[\frac{5(x^2+2xh+h^2)+1-(5x^2+1)}{(x+h)-x}\right]$

$= \lim_{h\to 0}\left[\frac{5x^2+10xh+5h^2+1-5x^2-1}{(x+h)-x}\right]$

$= \lim_{h\to 0}\left[\frac{10xh+5h^2}{h}\right] = \lim_{h\to 0}[10x+5h] = 10x$

b) $\frac{dy}{dx} = \lim_{h\to 0}\left[\frac{(x+h)-(x+h)^2-(x-x^2)}{(x+h)-x}\right]$

$= \lim_{h\to 0}\left[\frac{(x+h)-(x^2+2xh+h^2)-(x-x^2)}{(x+h)-x}\right]$

$= \lim_{h\to 0}\left[\frac{x+h-x^2-2xh-h^2-x+x^2}{(x+h)-x}\right]$

$= \lim_{h\to 0}\left[\frac{h-2xh-h^2}{h}\right] = \lim_{h\to 0}[1-2x-h] = 1-2x$

c) $\frac{dy}{dx} = \lim_{h\to 0}\left[\frac{3(x+h)^3-3x^3}{(x+h)-x}\right]$

$= \lim_{h\to 0}\left[\frac{3(x^3+3x^2h+3xh^2+h^3)-3x^3}{(x+h)-x}\right]$

$= \lim_{h\to 0}\left[\frac{3x^3+9x^2h+9xh^2+3h^3-3x^3}{(x+h)-x}\right]$

$= \lim_{h\to 0}\left[\frac{9x^2h+9xh^2+3h^3}{h}\right]$

$= \lim_{h\to 0}[9x^2+9xh+3h^2] = 9x^2$

d) $\frac{dy}{dx} = \lim_{h\to 0}\left[\frac{2(x+h)^3+3(x+h)-(2x^3+3x)}{(x+h)-x}\right]$

$= \lim_{h\to 0}\left[\frac{2(x^3+3x^2h+3xh^2+h^3)+3(x+h)-(2x^3+3x)}{(x+h)-x}\right]$

$= \lim_{h\to 0}\left[\frac{2x^3+6x^2h+6xh^2+2h^3+3x+3h-2x^3-3x}{(x+h)-x}\right]$

$= \lim_{h\to 0}\left[\frac{6x^2h+6xh^2+2h^3+3h}{h}\right]$

$= \lim_{h\to 0}[6x^2+6xh+2h^2+3] = 6x^2+3$

e) $\frac{dy}{dx} = \lim_{h\to 0}\left[\frac{(x+h)^3+(x+h)-(x^3+x)}{(x+h)-x}\right]$

$= \lim_{h\to 0}\left[\frac{x^3+3x^2h+3xh^2+h^3+x+h-x^3-x}{(x+h)-x}\right]$

$= \lim_{h\to 0}\left[\frac{3x^2h+3xh^2+h^3+h}{h}\right]$

$= \lim_{h\to 0}[3x^2+3xh+h^2+1] = 3x^2+1$

f) $f'(x) = \lim_{h\to 0}\left[\frac{(2-(x+h))^2-(2-x)^2}{(x+h)-x}\right]$

$= \lim_{h\to 0}\left[\frac{4-4(x+h)+(x+h)^2-(4-4x+x^2)}{(x+h)-x}\right]$

$= \lim_{h\to 0}\left[\frac{4-4x-4h+x^2+2xh+h^2-4+4x-x^2}{(x+h)-x}\right]$

$= \lim_{h\to 0}\left[\frac{-4h+2xh+h^2}{h}\right]$

$= \lim_{h\to 0}[-4+2x+h] = -4+2x$

Q4 a) When $x = p$, $y = 2x^2 = 2p^2$, so $(p, 2p^2)$ lies on the curve for all real values of p. *[1 mark]*

b) When $x = p$,

$\frac{dy}{dx} = \lim_{h\to 0}\left[\frac{2(p+h)^2-2p^2}{h}\right] = \lim_{h\to 0}\left[\frac{2p^2+4ph+2h^2-2p^2}{h}\right]$

$= \lim_{h\to 0}\left[\frac{4ph+2h^2}{h}\right] = \lim_{h\to 0}[4p+2h] = 4p$

[4 marks available — 1 mark for correctly substituting into the formula, 1 mark for expanding the brackets, 1 mark for simplifying and cancelling h, 1 mark for taking the limit as h tends to zero to give the correct answer]

c) $4p = -8$, so $p = -2$ *[1 mark]*

Q5 a) $\frac{dy}{dx} = \lim_{h\to 0}\left[\frac{(x+h)^3+2(x+h)^2+3(x+h)-(x^3+2x^2+3x)}{(x+h)-x}\right]$

$= \lim_{h\to 0}\left[\frac{\left(x^3+3x^2h+3xh^2+h^3+2x^2+4xh+2h^2+3x+3h-x^3-2x^2-3x\right)}{(x+h)-x}\right]$

$= \lim_{h\to 0}\left[\frac{3x^2h+3xh^2+h^3+4xh+2h^2+3h}{h}\right]$

$= \lim_{h\to 0}[3x^2+3xh+h^2+4x+2h+3]$

$= 3x^2+4x+3$

b) (i) $x = -1$, so $\frac{dy}{dx} = 3(-1)^2+4(-1)+3 = 2$

(ii) $x = 2$, so $\frac{dy}{dx} = 3(2)^2+4(2)+3 = 23$

(iii) $x = 0$, so $\frac{dy}{dx} = 3(0)^2+4(0)+3 = 3$

Q6 a) Gradient $= \dfrac{\frac{1}{-1+h}-(-1)}{-1+h-(-1)} = \dfrac{\frac{1}{-1+h}+1}{h}$

$= \frac{1-1+h}{h(h-1)} = \frac{h}{h(h-1)} = \frac{1}{h-1}$

[3 marks available — 1 mark for a correct method to find the gradient, 2 marks for the correct fully simplified answer, otherwise 1 mark for a correct answer not fully simplified]

b) Taking the limit as h tends to zero, you get $\frac{1}{0-1} = -1$, so the gradient at A is -1.
[2 marks available — 1 mark for taking the limit as h → 0, 1 mark for showing the result]

Q7 a) $f(x) = 2x^2 + x$ so

$f'(x) = \lim_{h\to 0}\left[\frac{f(x+h)-f(x)}{h}\right]$

$= \lim_{h\to 0}\left[\frac{2(x+h)^2+(x+h)-2x^2-x}{h}\right]$

$= \lim_{h\to 0}\left[\frac{2x^2+4xh+2h^2+x+h-2x^2-x}{h}\right]$

$= \lim_{h\to 0}\left[\frac{4xh+2h^2+h}{h}\right] = \lim_{h\to 0}[4x+2h+1] = 4x+1$

[4 marks available — 1 mark for correctly substituting into the formula, 1 mark for correctly expanding the brackets, 1 mark for simplifying and dividing by h, 1 mark for taking the limit as h tends to zero to get the correct answer]

b) $x(2x + 1) = 15 \Rightarrow 2x^2 + x - 15 = 0 \Rightarrow (2x - 5)(x + 3) = 0$
$\Rightarrow x = \frac{5}{2}$ or -3, so the coordinates are $(\frac{5}{2}, 15)$ and $(-3, 15)$.
[2 marks available — 1 mark for a correct method to solve the quadratic, 1 mark for both correct pairs of coordinates]

c) The expression for the gradient is $4x + 1$.
So when $x = \frac{5}{2}$, the gradient $= 4\left(\frac{5}{2}\right) + 1 = 11$
and when $x = -3$, the gradient $= 4(-3) + 1 = -11$.
[2 marks available — 1 mark for each correct gradient]

Q8 a) $\frac{d}{dx}(af(x)) = \lim_{h\to 0}\left[\frac{af(x+h) - af(x)}{h}\right]$
$= a\lim_{h\to 0}\left[\frac{f(x+h) - f(x)}{h}\right] = af'(x)$

b) $\frac{d}{dx}(af(x) + bg(x))$
$= \lim_{h\to 0}\left[\frac{af(x+h) + bg(x+h) - af(x) - bg(x)}{h}\right]$
$= a\lim_{h\to 0}\left[\frac{f(x+h) - f(x)}{h}\right] + b\lim_{h\to 0}\left[\frac{g(x+h) - g(x)}{h}\right]$
$= af'(x) + bg'(x)$

Q9 $\frac{dy}{dx} = \lim_{h\to 0}\left[\frac{f(x+h) - f(x)}{h}\right]$
$= \lim_{h\to 0}\left[\frac{3(x+h)^2 + 2(x+h) - 3x^2 - 2x}{h}\right]$
$= \lim_{h\to 0}\left[\frac{3x^2 + 6xh + 3h^2 + 2x + 2h - 3x^2 - 2x}{h}\right]$
$= \lim_{h\to 0}\left[\frac{6xh + 3h^2 + 2h}{h}\right] = \lim_{h\to 0}[6x + 3h + 2] = 6x + 2,$
so when $x = 1$, $\frac{dy}{dx} = 6(1) + 2 = 8$.
[5 marks available — 1 mark for correctly substituting into the formula, 1 mark for correctly expanding the brackets, 1 mark for simplifying and dividing by h, 1 mark for taking the limit as h tends to zero, 1 mark for correct gradient]

Q10 a) 5 *[1 mark]*

b) $f'(x) = \lim_{h\to 0}\left[\frac{f(x+h) - f(x)}{h}\right] = \lim_{h\to 0}\left[\frac{k(x+h)^2 - kx^2}{h}\right]$
$= \lim_{h\to 0}\left[\frac{kx^2 + 2kxh + kh^2 - kx^2}{h}\right]$
$= \lim_{h\to 0}\left[\frac{2kxh + kh^2}{h}\right] = \lim_{h\to 0}[2kx + kh] = 2kx$
When $x = 1$, the gradient is 5, so $2k(1) = 5 \Rightarrow k = \frac{5}{2}$.
[6 marks available — 1 mark for correctly substituting into the formula, 1 mark for correctly expanding the brackets, 1 mark for simplifying and dividing by h, 1 mark for taking the limit as h tends to zero, 1 mark for the correct gradient in terms of k, 1 mark for the correct value of k]

Q11 a) They suggest that the gradient of the curve at P is roughly 5.

b) $\frac{dy}{dx} = \lim_{h\to 0}\left[\frac{(x+h)^2 + a(x+h) + b - x^2 - ax - b}{h}\right]$
$= \lim_{h\to 0}\left[\frac{2xh + h^2 + ah}{h}\right] = \lim_{h\to 0}[2x + h + a] = 2x + a$
So when $x = 1$, $2(1) + a \approx 5$, so $a \approx 3$.

Q12 a) $\frac{a-b}{\sqrt{a}+\sqrt{b}} = \frac{a-b}{\sqrt{a}+\sqrt{b}} \times \frac{\sqrt{a}-\sqrt{b}}{\sqrt{a}-\sqrt{b}}$
$= \frac{(a-b)(\sqrt{a}-\sqrt{b})}{(\sqrt{a}+\sqrt{b})(\sqrt{a}-\sqrt{b})} = \frac{(a-b)(\sqrt{a}-\sqrt{b})}{a-b} = \sqrt{a} - \sqrt{b}$
[2 marks available — 1 mark for a correct method to rationalise the denominator (or the numerator if starting with the LHS), 1 mark for a correct proof]

b) $f'(x) = \lim_{h\to 0}\left[\frac{f(x+h) - f(x)}{h}\right] = \lim_{h\to 0}\left[\frac{\sqrt{x+h} - \sqrt{x}}{h}\right]$
$= \lim_{h\to 0}\left[\frac{1}{h} \times \frac{(x+h) - x}{\sqrt{x+h}+\sqrt{x}}\right] = \lim_{h\to 0}\left[\frac{1}{h} \times \frac{h}{\sqrt{x+h}+\sqrt{x}}\right]$
$= \lim_{h\to 0}\left[\frac{1}{\sqrt{x+h}+\sqrt{x}}\right] = \frac{1}{2\sqrt{x}}$
[4 marks available — 1 mark for correctly substituting into the formula, 1 mark for using part a) to rewrite the numerator, 1 mark for cancelling and simplifying the expression inside the limit, 1 mark for taking the limit as h tends to zero to get the correct answer]

Exercise 10.3 — Differentiating x^n

Q1 a) $\frac{dy}{dx} = 1$
b) $\frac{dy}{dx} = 6x^5$
c) $\frac{dy}{dx} = 3x^2$
d) $\frac{dy}{dx} = 30x$
e) $\frac{dy}{dx} = -2x^{-3} = -\frac{2}{x^3}$
f) $\frac{dy}{dx} = 6x$
g) $\frac{dy}{dx} = 7$
h) $\frac{dy}{dx} = 2x^3$
i) $\frac{dy}{dx} = 0$
j) $\frac{dy}{dx} = \frac{3}{2}x^{-\frac{1}{2}} = \frac{3}{2\sqrt{x}}$
k) $\frac{dy}{dx} = -2x^{-2} = -\frac{2}{x^2}$
l) $\frac{dy}{dx} = -3x^{-4} = -\frac{3}{x^4}$

Q2 a) $f'(x) = 5x^4$
b) $f'(x) = 7x^6$
c) $f'(x) = -4x^{-5} = -\frac{4}{x^5}$
d) $f'(x) = 12x^2$
e) $f'(x) = -6x^{-4} = -\frac{6}{x^4}$
f) $f'(x) = 4x^{-\frac{1}{2}} = \frac{4}{\sqrt{x}}$
g) $f'(x) = x^{-\frac{2}{3}} = \frac{1}{\sqrt[3]{x^2}}$
h) $f'(x) = 0$
i) $f'(x) = -8x^{-3} = -\frac{8}{x^3}$
j) $f'(x) = -9x^2$
k) $f'(x) = 20x^{-5} = \frac{20}{x^5}$
l) $f'(x) = -12x^{-4} = -\frac{12}{x^4}$

Q3 a) $\frac{dy}{dx} = 4x \Rightarrow$ At $x = 4$, $\frac{dy}{dx} = 16$.
b) $\frac{dy}{dx} = -x^{-2} = -\frac{1}{x^2} \Rightarrow$ At $x = 2$, $\frac{dy}{dx} = -\frac{1}{4}$.
c) $\frac{dy}{dx} = -20x^4 \Rightarrow$ At $x = 1$, $\frac{dy}{dx} = -20$.
d) $y = 2x^{-1} \Rightarrow \frac{dy}{dx} = -2x^{-2} = -\frac{2}{x^2}$
$\Rightarrow$ At $x = 10$, $\frac{dy}{dx} = -\frac{1}{50}$.
e) $f'(x) = x^{-\frac{1}{2}} = \frac{1}{\sqrt{x}} \Rightarrow f'(9) = \frac{1}{3}$
f) $f'(x) = 4x^3 \Rightarrow f'(-2) = -32$
g) $f(x) = -250 \Rightarrow -250 = -2x^3 \Rightarrow 125 = x^3 \Rightarrow x = 5$
$f'(x) = -6x^2 \Rightarrow f'(5) = -150$
h) $f(x) = -\frac{3}{4} \Rightarrow -\frac{3}{4} = -3x^{-2} \Rightarrow \frac{1}{4} = \frac{1}{x^2}$
$\Rightarrow x = -2$ or $x = 2$
$f'(x) = 6x^{-3} = \frac{6}{x^3} \Rightarrow f'(2) = \frac{3}{4}$ and $f'(-2) = -\frac{3}{4}$

Q4 $y = 5x \Rightarrow \frac{dy}{dx} = 5$
$y = 5x^2 \Rightarrow \frac{dy}{dx} = 10x$. When $x = 1$, $\frac{dy}{dx} = 10$.
$y = 5x^3 \Rightarrow \frac{dy}{dx} = 15x^2$. When $x = 1$, $\frac{dy}{dx} = 15$.
So $y = 5x^3$ has the steepest gradient at point P.

Exercise 10.4 — Differentiating Functions

Q1 a) $\frac{dy}{dx} = 12x^2 - 2x$

b) $\frac{dy}{dx} = 1 + (-x^{-2}) = 1 - \frac{1}{x^2}$

c) $\frac{dy}{dx} = 6x + \frac{1}{2}x^{-\frac{1}{2}} = 6x + \frac{1}{2\sqrt{x}}$

d) $f'(x) = -10x^4 + 4 - (-2x^{-3}) = -10x^4 + 4 + \frac{2}{x^3}$

e) $f'(x) = \frac{3}{2}x^{\frac{1}{2}} - 1 = \frac{3}{2}\sqrt{x} - 1$

f) $f'(x) = 5 - 2(-3x^{-4}) + \frac{1}{3}x^{-\frac{2}{3}} = 5 + \frac{6}{x^4} + \frac{1}{3\sqrt[3]{x^2}}$

Q2 a) $\frac{d}{dx}(x(x^6 - 1)) = \frac{d}{dx}(x^7 - x) = 7x^6 - 1$

b) $\frac{d}{dx}((x-3)(x+4)) = \frac{d}{dx}(x^2 - 3x + 4x - 12)$

$= \frac{d}{dx}(x^2 + x - 12) = 2x + 1$

c) $\frac{d}{dx}(x(x-1)(x-2)) = \frac{d}{dx}(x(x^2 - x - 2x + 2))$

$= \frac{d}{dx}(x(x^2 - 3x + 2))$

$= \frac{d}{dx}(x^3 - 3x^2 + 2x)$

$= 3x^2 - 3(2x) + 2 = 3x^2 - 6x + 2$

d) $\frac{d}{dx}((x-3)(x+4)(x-1)) = \frac{d}{dx}((x-3)(x^2 + 3x - 4))$

$= \frac{d}{dx}(x^3 + 3x^2 - 4x - 3x^2 - 9x + 12)$

$= \frac{d}{dx}(x^3 - 13x + 12) = 3x^2 - 13$

e) $\frac{d}{dx}(x^2(x-4)(3-x^3)) = \frac{d}{dx}(x^2(3x - x^4 - 12 + 4x^3))$

$= \frac{d}{dx}(3x^3 - x^6 - 12x^2 + 4x^5)$

$= 9x^2 - 6x^5 - 24x + 20x^4$

f) $\frac{d}{dx}((x-3)^2(x^2-2)) = \frac{d}{dx}((x^2 - 3x - 3x + 9)(x^2 - 2))$

$= \frac{d}{dx}((x^2 - 6x + 9)(x^2 - 2))$

$= \frac{d}{dx}((x^4 - 6x^3 + 9x^2) + (-2x^2 + 12x - 18))$

$= \frac{d}{dx}(x^4 - 6x^3 + 7x^2 + 12x - 18)$

$= 4x^3 - 18x^2 + 14x + 12$

Q3 a) $\frac{dy}{dx} = 4x^3 - 2x$. At $x = 3$, $\frac{dy}{dx} = 102$.

b) $\frac{dy}{dx} = 10x^4 + (-x^{-2}) = 10x^4 - \frac{1}{x^2}$

At $x = -2$, $\frac{dy}{dx} = 159.75$.

c) $y = x(x-1)(x-2) = x(x^2 - 3x + 2) = x^3 - 3x^2 + 2x$

$\frac{dy}{dx} = 3x^2 - 6x + 2$. At $x = -3$, $\frac{dy}{dx} = 47$.

d) $y = 5(x^2 - 1)(3 - x) = 5(-x^3 + 3x^2 + x - 3)$

$= -5x^3 + 15x^2 + 5x - 15$

$\frac{dy}{dx} = -15x^2 + 30x + 5$. At $x = 0$, $\frac{dy}{dx} = 5$.

e) $y = \sqrt{x}(x-1) = x^{\frac{1}{2}}(x-1) = x^{\frac{3}{2}} - x^{\frac{1}{2}}$

$\frac{dy}{dx} = \frac{3}{2}x^{\frac{1}{2}} - \frac{1}{2}x^{-\frac{1}{2}} = \frac{3}{2}\sqrt{x} - \frac{1}{2\sqrt{x}}$

At $x = 4$, $\frac{dy}{dx} = 2.75$.

f) $f(x) = x^3(x^2 - 5) = x^5 - 5x^3$

$f'(x) = 5x^4 - 15x^2$, $f'(-1) = -10$

g) $f(x) = \frac{1}{x^2}(x^3 - x) = x - x^{-1}$

$f'(x) = 1 + x^{-2} = 1 + \frac{1}{x^2}$, $f'(5) = \frac{26}{25}$

h) $f(x) = \frac{3x^3 + 18x^2 + 24x}{x+4}$

$= \frac{3x(x+4)(x+2)}{x+4} = 3x(x+2) = 3x^2 + 6x$

$f'(x) = 6x + 6$, $f'(-2) = -6$

Q4 a) $y = 3x^{-1} - 4$, so $\frac{dy}{dx} = -3x^{-2} = -\frac{3}{x^2}$ *[1 mark]*

b) When the gradient is -2, $-\frac{3}{x^2} = -2 \Rightarrow x^2 = \frac{3}{2}$

$\Rightarrow x = \pm\sqrt{\frac{3}{2}} = \pm\frac{\sqrt{6}}{2}$ and $y = 3\left(\pm\frac{2}{\sqrt{6}}\right) - 4 = \pm\sqrt{6} - 4$.

So the points have coordinates

$\left(\frac{\sqrt{6}}{2}, \sqrt{6} - 4\right)$ and $\left(-\frac{\sqrt{6}}{2}, -\sqrt{6} - 4\right)$.

[3 marks available — 1 mark for the correct x-values, 1 mark for a correct method to find the y-values, 1 mark for both sets of coordinates correct]

Q5 a)

y
2
1
0
2
6
10
x
y = f′(x)

Work out the gradient for each bit of the line.
f′(x) = 2 for 0 ≤ x ≤ 2 and f′(x) = 1 for 6 ≤ x ≤ 10.

b)

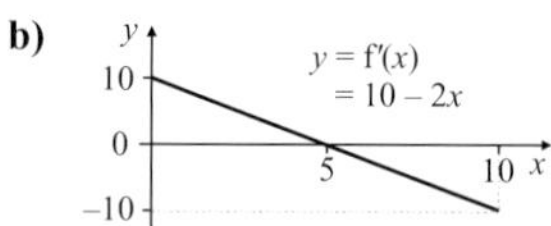

Differentiate and sketch the graph of the gradient function.

c)

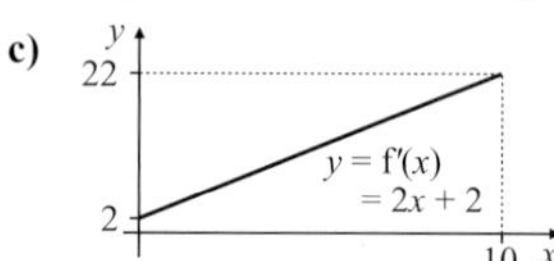

d)

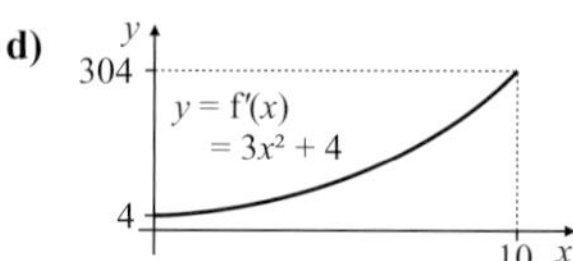

Q6 a) $f(x) = (x+3)(x+4) = x^2 + 7x + 12$

$f'(x) = 2x + 7$

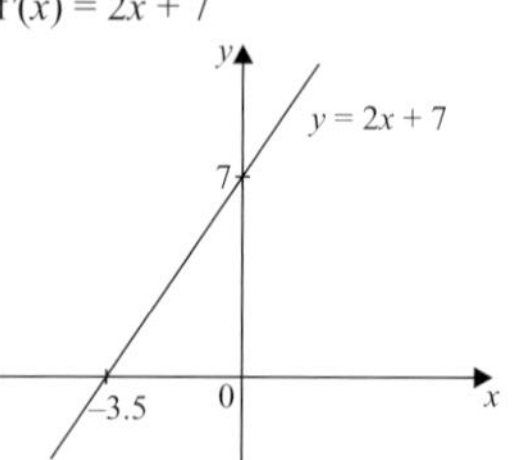

b) $f(x) = \frac{x^3 - 3x^2 + 2x}{x-1} = \frac{x(x-1)(x-2)}{x-1} = x^2 - 2x$

$f'(x) = 2x - 2$

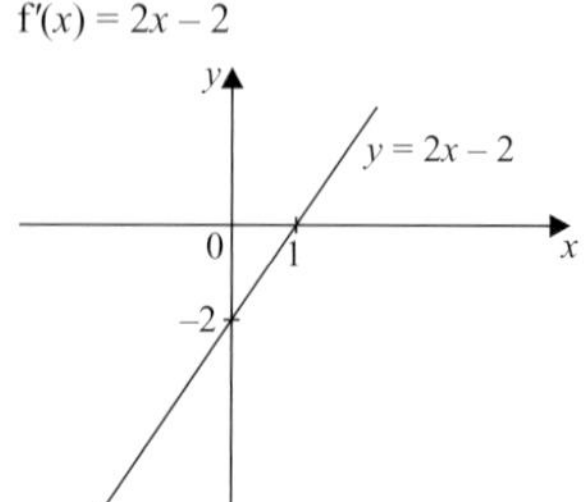

c) $f'(x) = 4x^3 - 12x^2 + 8x = 4x(x^2 - 3x + 2)$
$= 4x(x - 1)(x - 2)$

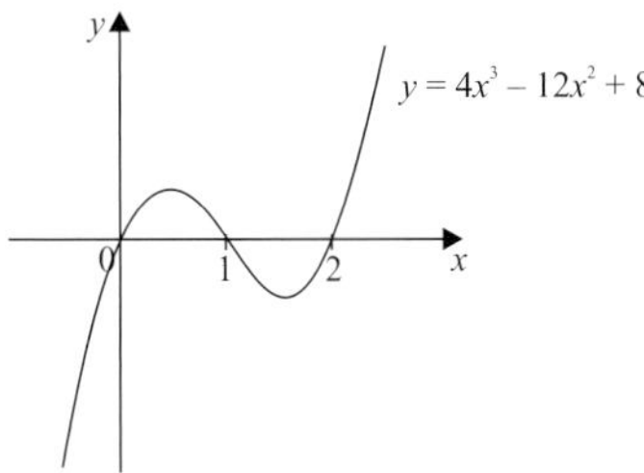

d) $f(x) = (x - 1)^2(x + 5) = (x^2 - 2x + 1)(x + 5)$
$= x^3 + 5x^2 - 2x^2 - 10x + x + 5 = x^3 + 3x^2 - 9x + 5$
$f'(x) = 3x^2 + 6x - 9 = 3(x^2 + 2x - 3) = 3(x - 1)(x + 3)$

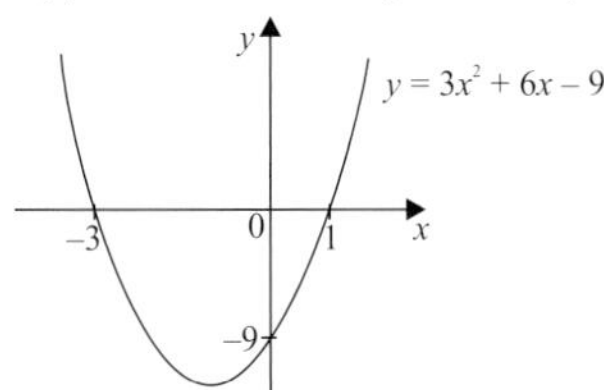

Q7 a) $\frac{dy}{dx} = 2x - 2$. If $2x - 2 = 0 \Rightarrow 2x = 2 \Rightarrow x = 1$
So $y = (1)^2 - 2(1) = -1$. Coordinates are $(1, -1)$.

b) $\frac{dy}{dx} = 6x + 4$. If $6x + 4 = 0 \Rightarrow 6x = -4 \Rightarrow x = -\frac{4}{6} = -\frac{2}{3}$
So $y = 3(-\frac{2}{3})^2 + 4(-\frac{2}{3}) = -\frac{4}{3}$.
Coordinates are $(-\frac{2}{3}, -\frac{4}{3})$.

c) $\frac{dy}{dx} = 10x - 3$. If $10x - 3 = 0 \Rightarrow 10x = 3$
$\Rightarrow x = \frac{3}{10} \Rightarrow y = 5(\frac{3}{10})^2 - 3(\frac{3}{10}) = -\frac{9}{20}$
Coordinates are $(\frac{3}{10}, -\frac{9}{20})$.

d) $\frac{dy}{dx} = 9 - 9x^2$. If $9 - 9x^2 = 0 \Rightarrow 9 = 9x^2 \Rightarrow 1 = x^2$
$\Rightarrow x = 1$ or -1
$\Rightarrow y = 9(1) - 3(1)^3 = 6$ or $y = 9(-1) - 3(-1)^3 = -6$
Coordinates are $(1, 6)$ and $(-1, -6)$.

e) $\frac{dy}{dx} = 6x^2 - 2x$. If $6x^2 - 2x = 0 \Rightarrow 2x(3x - 1) = 0$
$\Rightarrow 2x = 0$ or $3x - 1 = 0 \Rightarrow x = 0$ or $x = \frac{1}{3}$
$\Rightarrow y = 2(0)^3 - (0)^2 = 0$ or $y = 2(\frac{1}{3})^3 - (\frac{1}{3})^2 = -\frac{1}{27}$.
Coordinates are $(0, 0)$ and $(\frac{1}{3}, -\frac{1}{27})$.

f) $\frac{dy}{dx} = 6x^2 + 6x - 12$. If $6x^2 + 6x - 12 = 0$
$\Rightarrow 6(x^2 + x - 2) = 0 \Rightarrow x^2 + x - 2 = 0$
$\Rightarrow (x + 2)(x - 1) = 0 \Rightarrow x = -2$ or $x = 1$
$\Rightarrow y = 2(-2)^3 + 3(-2)^2 - 12(-2) = 20$ or
$y = 2(1)^3 + 3(1)^2 - 12(1) = -7$.
Coordinates are $(-2, 20)$ and $(1, -7)$.

Q8 a) $y = \frac{x^2 - 3x - 4}{x + 1} = \frac{(x - 4)(x + 1)}{x + 1} = x - 4 \Rightarrow \frac{dy}{dx} = 1$

b) $f(x) = \frac{x^4 - 9}{x^2 + 3} = \frac{(x^2 + 3)(x^2 - 3)}{x^2 + 3} = x^2 - 3 \Rightarrow f'(x) = 2x$

c) $f(x) = \frac{x^5 - 16x^3}{x + 4} = \frac{x^3(x + 4)(x - 4)}{x + 4} = x^3(x - 4) = x^4 - 4x^3$
$\Rightarrow f'(x) = 4x^3 - 12x^2$

d) $y = \frac{1}{x}(x - 3)(x - 4) = \frac{1}{x}(x^2 - 3x - 4x + 12)$
$= \frac{1}{x}(x^2 - 7x + 12) = x - 7 + \frac{12}{x} = x - 7 + 12x^{-1}$
$\Rightarrow \frac{dy}{dx} = 1 - 12x^{-2} = 1 - \frac{12}{x^2}$

e) $y = \sqrt{x}(x^3 - \sqrt{x}) = x^{\frac{1}{2}}(x^3 - x^{\frac{1}{2}}) = x^{\frac{7}{2}} - x$
$\Rightarrow \frac{dy}{dx} = \frac{7}{2}x^{\frac{5}{2}} - 1 = \frac{7}{2}\sqrt{x^5} - 1$

f) $f(x) = \frac{3 - \sqrt{x}}{\sqrt{x}} = \frac{3 - x^{\frac{1}{2}}}{x^{\frac{1}{2}}} = x^{-\frac{1}{2}}(3 - x^{\frac{1}{2}})$
$= 3x^{-\frac{1}{2}} - x^0 = 3x^{-\frac{1}{2}} - 1$
$f'(x) = 3(-\frac{1}{2}x^{-\frac{3}{2}}) = -\frac{3}{2}x^{-\frac{3}{2}} = -\frac{3}{2\sqrt{x^3}}$

g) $f(x) = \frac{x + 5\sqrt{x}}{\sqrt{x}} = \frac{x + 5x^{\frac{1}{2}}}{x^{\frac{1}{2}}} = x^{-\frac{1}{2}}(x + 5x^{\frac{1}{2}})$
$= x^{\frac{1}{2}} + 5x^0 = x^{\frac{1}{2}} + 5$
$f'(x) = \frac{1}{2}x^{-\frac{1}{2}} = \frac{1}{2\sqrt{x}}$

h) Factorising the numerator:
$f(x) = \frac{x - 3\sqrt{x} + 2}{\sqrt{x} - 1} = \frac{(\sqrt{x} - 2)(\sqrt{x} - 1)}{\sqrt{x} - 1} = \sqrt{x} - 2 = x^{\frac{1}{2}} - 2$
$f'(x) = \frac{1}{2}x^{-\frac{1}{2}} = \frac{1}{2\sqrt{x}}$

i) Factorising the numerator:
$f(x) = \frac{4 - x}{2 + \sqrt{x}} = \frac{(2 + \sqrt{x})(2 - \sqrt{x})}{2 + \sqrt{x}} = 2 - \sqrt{x} = 2 - x^{\frac{1}{2}}$
$f'(x) = -\frac{1}{2}x^{-\frac{1}{2}} = -\frac{1}{2\sqrt{x}}$

Q9 a) $(2 + x)^4 = 2^4 + 4(2^3 \times x) + 6(2^2 \times x^2) + 4(2 \times x^3) + x^4$
$= 16 + 32x + 24x^2 + 8x^3 + x^4$
[4 marks available — 1 mark for a correct method, 3 marks for the correct expansion, otherwise 2 marks for at least two terms correct, or 1 mark for one term correct]

b) $\frac{dy}{dx} = 32 + 48x + 24x^2 + 4x^3$
[3 marks available — 3 marks for the correct answer, otherwise 2 marks for at least two terms correct, or 1 mark for an attempt at differentiating]

c) When $x = 1$, $\frac{dy}{dx} = 32 + 48 + 24 + 4 = 108$.
[2 marks available — 1 mark for substituting in the correct x-value, 1 mark for the correct answer]

Q10 a) $f(2x) = (2x)^3 - 3(2x)^2 + 2 = 8x^3 - 12x^2 + 2$ *[1 mark]*

b) $f'(2x) = 24x^2 - 24x$
[2 marks available — 1 mark for at least one term correct, 1 mark for the correct answer]

Q11 $f(x) = (3kx)^{\frac{1}{2}} + k^{\frac{1}{2}} + 2x$,
so $f'(x) = \frac{1}{2}(3k)^{\frac{1}{2}}x^{-\frac{1}{2}} + 2 = \frac{\sqrt{3k}}{2\sqrt{x}} + 2$.
$f'(3) = 3$, so $\frac{\sqrt{3k}}{2\sqrt{3}} + 2 = \frac{\sqrt{k}}{2} + 2 = 3$
$\Rightarrow \frac{\sqrt{k}}{2} = 1 \Rightarrow \sqrt{k} = 2 \Rightarrow k = 4$.
[4 marks available — 1 mark for correct derivative, 1 mark for substituting in x = 3, 1 mark for a correct method to find k, 1 mark for the correct value of k]

Exercise 10.5 — Finding Tangents and Normals

Q1 a) $\frac{dy}{dx} = 9 - 4x$. At $(1, 7)$, $\frac{dy}{dx} = 5$
$\Rightarrow$ tangent has a gradient of 5 and has an equation of the form $y = 5x + c$.
Using the point $(1, 7)$, $7 = 5 + c$
$\Rightarrow c = 2$. So the tangent's equation is $y = 5x + 2$.

b) $\frac{dy}{dx} = 3x^2 - 2$. At $(2, 7)$, $\frac{dy}{dx} = 10$
$\Rightarrow$ tangent has a gradient of 10 and has an equation of the form $y = 10x + c$.
Using the point $(2, 7)$, $7 = 20 + c \Rightarrow c = -13$.
So the tangent's equation is $y = 10x - 13$.

c) $y = (x + 2)(2x - 3) = 2x^2 + x - 6$
$\frac{dy}{dx} = 4x + 1$. At $(2, 4)$, $\frac{dy}{dx} = 9$
$\Rightarrow$ tangent has a gradient of 9 and has an equation of the form $y = 9x + c$.

Using the point (2, 4), $4 = 18 + c \Rightarrow c = -14$.
So the tangent's equation is $y = 9x - 14$.

d) $y = x(x-1)^2 = x(x^2 - 2x + 1) = x^3 - 2x^2 + x$

$\frac{dy}{dx} = 3x^2 - 4x + 1$. At $(-1, -4)$, $\frac{dy}{dx} = 8$

$\Rightarrow$ tangent has a gradient of 8 and has an equation of the form $y = 8x + c$.
Using the point $(-1, -4)$, $-4 = -8 + c \Rightarrow c = 4$.
So the tangent's equation is $y = 8x + 4$.

e) $y = x^2(x+3) - 10 = x^3 + 3x^2 - 10$

$\frac{dy}{dx} = 3x^2 + 6x$. At (2, 10), $\frac{dy}{dx} = 24$

$\Rightarrow$ tangent has a gradient of 24 and has an equation of the form $y = 24x + c$.
Using the point (2, 10), $10 = 48 + c \Rightarrow c = -38$.
So the tangent's equation is $y = 24x - 38$.

f) $y = x(2x^2 - 2x - 12) = 2x^3 - 2x^2 - 12x$

$\frac{dy}{dx} = 6x^2 - 4x - 12$. At $(-1, 8)$, $\frac{dy}{dx} = -2$

$\Rightarrow$ tangent has a gradient of -2 and has an equation of the form $y = -2x + c$.
Using the point $(-1, 8)$, $8 = 2 + c \Rightarrow c = 6$.
So the tangent's equation is $y = -2x + 6$.

Q2 a) $y = x^{-1} + x + 3$

$\frac{dy}{dx} = -x^{-2} + 1$. At $(2, 5\frac{1}{2})$, $\frac{dy}{dx} = \frac{3}{4}$

$\Rightarrow$ tangent has a gradient of $\frac{3}{4}$ and has an equation of the form $y = \frac{3}{4}x + c$.

Using the point $(2, 5\frac{1}{2})$, $5\frac{1}{2} = 1\frac{1}{2} + c \Rightarrow c = 4$.

So the tangent's equation is $y = \frac{3}{4}x + 4$

$\Rightarrow 4y = 3x + 16 \Rightarrow 3x - 4y + 16 = 0$

b) $y = 4x^2 - 3x^{\frac{1}{2}}$

$\frac{dy}{dx} = 8x - 3(\frac{1}{2}x^{-\frac{1}{2}}) = 8x - \frac{3}{2}x^{-\frac{1}{2}}$.

At (1, 1), $\frac{dy}{dx} = 6\frac{1}{2}$

$\Rightarrow$ tangent has a gradient of $6\frac{1}{2}$ and has an equation of the form $y = 6\frac{1}{2}x + c$.

Using the point (1, 1), $1 = 6\frac{1}{2} + c \Rightarrow c = -5\frac{1}{2}$.

So the tangent's equation is $y = 6\frac{1}{2}x - 5\frac{1}{2}$

$\Rightarrow 2y = 13x - 11 \Rightarrow 13x - 2y - 11 = 0$.

c) $y = 3x^{-1} + 2x^{\frac{1}{2}}$

$\frac{dy}{dx} = 3(-x^{-2}) + 2(\frac{1}{2}x^{-\frac{1}{2}}) = -3x^{-2} + x^{-\frac{1}{2}}$

At $(4, 4\frac{3}{4})$, $\frac{dy}{dx} = \frac{5}{16}$

$\Rightarrow$ tangent has a gradient of $\frac{5}{16}$ and has an equation of the form $y = \frac{5}{16}x + c$.

Using the point $(4, 4\frac{3}{4})$, $4\frac{3}{4} = \frac{5}{4} + c \Rightarrow c = 3\frac{1}{2}$.

So the tangent's equation is $y = \frac{5}{16}x + 3\frac{1}{2}$

$\Rightarrow 16y = 5x + 56 \Rightarrow 5x - 16y + 56 = 0$.

d) $y = x^{-1} + 4x^{-2}$

$\frac{dy}{dx} = -x^{-2} + 4(-2x^{-3}) = -x^{-2} - 8x^{-3}$

At $(2, 1\frac{1}{2})$, $\frac{dy}{dx} = -\frac{5}{4}$

$\Rightarrow$ tangent has a gradient of $-\frac{5}{4}$ and has an equation of the form $y = -\frac{5}{4}x + c$.

Using the point $(2, 1\frac{1}{2})$, $1\frac{1}{2} = -\frac{5}{2} + c \Rightarrow c = 4$.

So the tangent's equation is $y = -\frac{5}{4}x + 4$

$\Rightarrow 4y = -5x + 16 \Rightarrow 5x + 4y - 16 = 0$.

e) $y = \frac{1}{3}x^2 - 4x^{\frac{1}{2}} - \frac{1}{3}$

$\frac{dy}{dx} = \frac{1}{3}(2x) - 4(\frac{1}{2}x^{-\frac{1}{2}}) = \frac{2}{3}x - 2x^{-\frac{1}{2}}$.

At $(4, -3)$, $\frac{dy}{dx} = \frac{5}{3}$

$\Rightarrow$ tangent has a gradient of $\frac{5}{3}$ and has an equation of the form $y = \frac{5}{3}x + c$.

Using the point $(4, -3)$, $-3 = \frac{20}{3} + c \Rightarrow c = -\frac{29}{3}$.

So the tangent's equation is $y = \frac{5}{3}x - \frac{29}{3}$

$\Rightarrow 3y = 5x - 29 \Rightarrow 5x - 3y - 29 = 0$.

f) $y = x - 2x^{-1} + 3x^{-2}$

$\frac{dy}{dx} = 1 + 2x^{-2} - 6x^{-3}$. At $(-3, -2)$, $\frac{dy}{dx} = \frac{13}{9}$

$\Rightarrow$ tangent has a gradient of $\frac{13}{9}$ and has an equation of the form $y = \frac{13}{9}x + c$.

Using the point $(-3, -2)$, $-2 = -\frac{13}{3} + c \Rightarrow c = \frac{7}{3}$.

So the tangent's equation is $y = \frac{13}{9}x + \frac{7}{3}$

$\Rightarrow 9y = 13x + 21 \Rightarrow 13x - 9y + 21 = 0$.

Q3 $xy + 2y - x^3 - 2x^2 = 0 \Rightarrow y(x+2) = x^3 + 2x^2$

$\Rightarrow y = \frac{x^3 + 2x^2}{x+2} = \frac{x^2(x+2)}{x+2} = x^2$

$\frac{dy}{dx} = 2x$, so the gradient at (2, 4) is $2 \times 2 = 4$.

So the equation of the tangent is:

$y - y_1 = m(x - x_1) \Rightarrow y - 4 = 4(x - 2) \Rightarrow y = 4x - 4$

[5 marks available — 1 mark for attempting to rearrange the given equation, 1 mark for a correct expression for y in terms of x, 1 mark for the correct gradient at (2, 4), 1 mark for a correct method to find the equation of the tangent, 1 mark for a correct equation of the tangent]

You can cancel $(x + 2)$ as it can't equal 0 because $x > 0$.

Q4 a) $\frac{dy}{dx} = 6x - 4$. At (2, 6), $\frac{dy}{dx} = 8$.

So the normal has a gradient of $-\frac{1}{8}$ and an equation of the form $y = -\frac{1}{8}x + c$.

Don't forget — the gradient of the normal to a curve at a point is $\frac{-1}{\text{Gradient of the curve}}$.

Using the point (2, 6), $6 = -\frac{1}{4} + c \Rightarrow c = 6\frac{1}{4}$

So the normal's equation is $y = -\frac{1}{8}x + 6\frac{1}{4}$

$\Rightarrow 8y = -x + 50 \Rightarrow x + 8y - 50 = 0$.

b) $y = x^3 + 4x^2 - 5x$

$\frac{dy}{dx} = 3x^2 + 8x - 5$. At $(-1, 8)$, $\frac{dy}{dx} = -10$.

So the normal has a gradient of $\frac{1}{10}$ and an equation of the form $y = \frac{1}{10}x + c$.

Using the point $(-1, 8)$, $8 = -\frac{1}{10} + c \Rightarrow c = \frac{81}{10}$

So the normal's equation is $y = \frac{1}{10}x + \frac{81}{10}$

$\Rightarrow 10y = x + 81 \Rightarrow x - 10y + 81 = 0$.

c) $y = x(x^2 - 3x + 2) = x^3 - 3x^2 + 2x$

$\frac{dy}{dx} = 3x^2 - 6x + 2$. At (3, 6), $\frac{dy}{dx} = 11$.

So the normal has a gradient of $-\frac{1}{11}$ and an equation of the form $y = -\frac{1}{11}x + c$.

Using the point (3, 6), $6 = -\frac{3}{11} + c \Rightarrow c = \frac{69}{11}$.

So the normal's equation is $y = -\frac{1}{11}x + \frac{69}{11}$

$\Rightarrow 11y = -x + 69 \Rightarrow x + 11y - 69 = 0$.

d) $y = x(x^2 + x - 12) - 10 = x^3 + x^2 - 12x - 10$

$\frac{dy}{dx} = 3x^2 + 2x - 12$. At $(-2, 10)$, $\frac{dy}{dx} = -4$.

So the normal has a gradient of $\frac{1}{4}$ and an equation of the form $y = \frac{1}{4}x + c$.

Using the point $(-2, 10)$, $10 = -\frac{1}{2} + c \Rightarrow c = \frac{21}{2}$.

So the normal's equation is $y = \frac{1}{4}x + \frac{21}{2}$

$\Rightarrow 4y = x + 42 \Rightarrow x - 4y + 42 = 0$.

e) $y = \frac{(x+2)(x^2-7x)}{x+2} = x^2 - 7x$

$\frac{dy}{dx} = 2x - 7$. At $(5, -10)$, $\frac{dy}{dx} = 3$.

So the normal has a gradient of $-\frac{1}{3}$ and an equation of the form $y = -\frac{1}{3}x + c$.

Using the point $(5, -10)$, $-10 = -\frac{5}{3} + c \Rightarrow c = -\frac{25}{3}$

So the normal's equation is $y = -\frac{1}{3}x - \frac{25}{3}$

$\Rightarrow 3y = -x - 25 \Rightarrow x + 3y + 25 = 0$.

f) $y = \frac{2x(x^2-16)}{x+4} = \frac{2x(x-4)(x+4)}{x+4} = 2x^2 - 8x$

$\frac{dy}{dx} = 4x - 8$. At $(3, -6)$, $\frac{dy}{dx} = 4$.

So the normal has a gradient of $-\frac{1}{4}$ and an equation of the form $y = -\frac{1}{4}x + c$.

Using the point $(3, -6)$, $-6 = -\frac{3}{4} + c \Rightarrow c = -\frac{21}{4}$

So the normal's equation is $y = -\frac{1}{4}x - \frac{21}{4}$

$\Rightarrow 4y = -x - 21 \Rightarrow x + 4y + 21 = 0$.

Q5 a) $y = \frac{2x^5 - 2x^4}{3x^3} = \frac{2}{3}x^2 - \frac{2}{3}x$

Remember — if the denominator is a single term, split the equation up into separate terms.

$\frac{dy}{dx} = \frac{2}{3}(2x) - \frac{2}{3} = \frac{4}{3}x - \frac{2}{3}$

At $(-2, 4)$, $\frac{dy}{dx} = -\frac{10}{3}$.

So the normal has a gradient of $\frac{3}{10}$ and an equation of the form $y = \frac{3}{10}x + c$.

Using the point $(-2, 4)$, $4 = -\frac{6}{10} + c \Rightarrow c = \frac{23}{5}$.

So the normal's equation is $y = \frac{3}{10}x + \frac{23}{5}$

$\Rightarrow 10y = 3x + 46 \Rightarrow 3x - 10y + 46 = 0$.

This question doesn't tell you which form to use to write the equations, so you can choose whichever is easiest for each part.

b) $y = \frac{5x^2 - 2x + 3}{x^2} = 5 - \frac{2}{x} + \frac{3}{x^2}$

$\frac{dy}{dx} = -2(-x^{-2}) + 3(-2x^{-3}) = \frac{2}{x^2} - \frac{6}{x^3}$

At $(2, 4\frac{3}{4})$, $\frac{dy}{dx} = -\frac{1}{4}$.

So the normal has a gradient of 4 and an equation of the form $y = 4x + c$.

Using the point $(2, 4\frac{3}{4})$, $4\frac{3}{4} = 8 + c \Rightarrow c = -\frac{13}{4}$.

So the normal's equation is $y = 4x - \frac{13}{4}$

$\Rightarrow 4y = 16x - 13 \Rightarrow 16x - 4y - 13 - 0$.

c) $y = 3xx^{-\frac{1}{2}} - x^2x^{-\frac{1}{2}} = 3x^{\frac{1}{2}} - x^{\frac{3}{2}}$

$\frac{dy}{dx} = 3(\frac{1}{2}x^{-\frac{1}{2}}) - \frac{3}{2}x^{\frac{1}{2}} = \frac{3}{2\sqrt{x}} - \frac{3}{2}\sqrt{x}$

At $(4, -2)$, $\frac{dy}{dx} = -\frac{9}{4}$.

So the normal has a gradient of $\frac{4}{9}$ and an equation of the form $y = \frac{4}{9}x + c$.

Using the point $(4, -2)$, $-2 = \frac{16}{9} + c \Rightarrow c = -\frac{34}{9}$.

So the normal's equation is

$y = \frac{4}{9}x - \frac{34}{9} \Rightarrow 9y = 4x - 34 \Rightarrow 4x - 9y - 34 = 0$.

d) $y = \frac{1}{x} - \frac{3}{x^2} - \frac{4}{x^3} + \frac{7}{4} = x^{-1} - 3x^{-2} - 4x^{-3} + \frac{7}{4}$

$\frac{dy}{dx} = -x^{-2} - 3(-2x^{-3}) - 4(-3x^{-4}) = -x^{-2} + 6x^{-3} + 12x^{-4}$

At $(-2, 1)$, $\frac{dy}{dx} = -\frac{1}{4}$.

So the normal has a gradient of 4 and an equation of the form $y = 4x + c$.

Using the point $(-2, 1)$, $1 = -8 + c \Rightarrow c = 9$.

So the normal's equation is $y - 4x + 9$.

e) $y = \frac{x^3 - 5x^2 - 4x}{x^{\frac{3}{2}}} = x^{\frac{3}{2}} - 5x^{\frac{1}{2}} - 4x^{-\frac{1}{2}}$

$\frac{dy}{dx} = \frac{3}{2}x^{\frac{1}{2}} - 5(\frac{1}{2}x^{-\frac{1}{2}}) - 4(-\frac{1}{2}x^{-\frac{3}{2}})$

$= \frac{3}{2}\sqrt{x} - \frac{5}{2\sqrt{x}} + \frac{2}{x\sqrt{x}}$

At $(4, -4)$, $\frac{dy}{dx} = 2$.

So the normal has a gradient of $-\frac{1}{2}$ and an equation of the form $y = -\frac{1}{2}x + c$.

Using the point $(4, -4)$, $-4 = -2 + c \Rightarrow c = -2$.

So the equation of the normal is $y = -\frac{1}{2}x - 2$

$\Rightarrow 2y = -x - 4 \Rightarrow x + 2y + 4 = 0$.

f) $y = \frac{4x^4 - 2x^2 + 3\sqrt{x}}{x^{\frac{5}{2}}} = 4x^{\frac{3}{2}} - 2x^{-\frac{1}{2}} + 3x^{-2}$

$\frac{dy}{dx} = 4(\frac{3}{2}x^{\frac{1}{2}}) - 2(-\frac{1}{2}x^{-\frac{3}{2}}) + 3(-2x^{-3}) = 6x^{\frac{1}{2}} + x^{-\frac{3}{2}} - 6x^{-3}$

At $(1, 5)$, $\frac{dy}{dx} = 1$.

So the normal has a gradient of -1 and an equation of the form $y = -x + c$.

Using the point $(1, 5)$, $5 = -1 + c \Rightarrow c = 6$.

So the equation of the normal is $y = 6 - x$.

Q6 a) $f'(x) = 3x^2 - 6x$. If $f'(x) = 9$, $3x^2 - 6x = 9 \Rightarrow 3x^2 - 6x - 9 = 0$

$\Rightarrow x^2 - 2x - 3 = 0$

$\Rightarrow (x-3)(x+1) = 0 \Rightarrow x = 3$ or $x = -1$.

So $x = 3$ since $x > 0$.

So $y = f(3) = 3^3 - 3(3)^2 + 3 = 3$.

The coordinates are $(3, 3)$.

b) The gradient of the tangent at $(3, 3)$ is 9 from part a). So the equation is of the form $y = 9x + c$. You know the tangent goes through $(3, 3)$ so use this point: $3 = 27 + c \Rightarrow c = -24$. So the equation is $y = 9x - 24$.

c) The gradient of the normal is $-\frac{1}{9}$ so the equation has the form $y = -\frac{1}{9}x + c$. Again, use the point $(3, 3)$, so $3 = -\frac{1}{3} + c \Rightarrow c = \frac{10}{3}$.

So the equation is $y = -\frac{1}{9}x + \frac{10}{3}$

$\Rightarrow 9y = -x + 30 \Rightarrow x + 9y - 30 = 0$.

Q7 a) Putting $x = -2$ into the equation gives:

$y = \frac{x^3 + x^2 + x + 5}{x^2}$

$= \frac{(-2)^3 + (-2)^2 + (-2) + 5}{(-2)^2}$

$= \frac{-8 + 4 - 2 + 5}{4} = -\frac{1}{4}$

so $(2, -\frac{1}{4})$ is a point on the curve.

b) $y = \frac{x^3 + x^2 + x + 5}{x^2} = x + 1 + \frac{1}{x} + \frac{5}{x^2}$

$\frac{dy}{dx} = 1 + 0 + (-x^{-2}) + 5(-2x^{-3}) = 1 - \frac{1}{x^2} - \frac{10}{x^3}$

At $(-2, -\frac{1}{4})$, $\frac{dy}{dx} = 2$.

So the gradient of the tangent at this point is 2 and it has equation $y = 2x + c$.

Using the point $(-2, -\frac{1}{4})$, $-\frac{1}{4} = -4 + c \Rightarrow c = \frac{15}{4}$.

So the equation of the tangent is $y = 2x + \frac{15}{4}$
$\Rightarrow 4y = 8x + 15 \Rightarrow 8x - 4y + 15 = 0$.

c) The gradient of the normal at $(-2, -\frac{1}{4})$ is $-\frac{1}{2}$ and so it has equation $y = -\frac{1}{2}x + c$.

Using the point $(-2, -\frac{1}{4})$, $-\frac{1}{4} = 1 + c \Rightarrow c = -\frac{5}{4}$.

So the equation of the normal is $y = -\frac{1}{2}x - \frac{5}{4}$

$\Rightarrow 4y = -2x - 5 \Rightarrow 2x + 4y + 5 = 0$.

Q8 a) $f(x) = \frac{(\sqrt{x}+1)(\sqrt{x}-2)}{1+\sqrt{x}} = \sqrt{x} - 2$

so $f'(x) = \frac{1}{2}x^{-\frac{1}{2}}$ or $\frac{1}{2\sqrt{x}}$

[3 marks available — 1 mark for attempting to factorise the numerator, 1 mark for a correct simplified expression for f(x), 1 mark for the correct derivative]

b) When $x = 1$, gradient of the curve $= \frac{1}{2}(1)^{-\frac{1}{2}} = \frac{1}{2}$

So the gradient of the normal is $-1 \div \frac{1}{2} = -2$.
When $x = 1$, $y = \sqrt{1} - 2 = -1$.
So the equation of the normal is:
$y - y_1 = m(x - x_1) \Rightarrow y - (-1) = -2(x - 1) \Rightarrow y = -2x + 1$
[4 marks available — 1 mark for the gradient of the curve, 1 mark for the correct gradient of the normal, 1 mark for finding y-coordinate of the point, 1 mark for the correct equation of the normal]

c) B has coordinates $(0, 1)$ and A has coordinates $\left(\frac{1}{2}, 0\right)$.

So OAB is a triangle with base width of $\frac{1}{2}$ and a vertical height of 1, so the area is $\frac{1}{2} \times \frac{1}{2} \times 1 = \frac{1}{4}$.

[3 marks available — 1 mark for the correct coordinates of point A, 1 mark for the correct coordinates of point B, 1 mark for the correct answer]

Q9 a) $(1 - x)^3 = 1 - 3x + 3x^2 - x^3$
[2 marks available — 2 marks for the correct answer, otherwise 1 mark for at least one term correct]

b) $\frac{dy}{dx} = -3 + 6x - 3x^2$
[2 marks available — 2 marks for the correct answer, otherwise 1 mark for at least one term correct]

c) When $x = 0$, $\frac{dy}{dx} = -3$ and $y = 1$,
so the equation is $y = -3x + 1$.
[2 marks available — 1 mark for the correct gradient, 1 mark for the correct answer]

Exercise 10.6 — Finding Second Order Derivatives

Q1 a) $\frac{dy}{dx} = 3x^2$ and $\frac{d^2y}{dx^2} = 6x$.

b) $\frac{dy}{dx} = 5x^4$ and $\frac{d^2y}{dx^2} = 20x^3$.

c) $\frac{dy}{dx} = 4x^3$ and $\frac{d^2y}{dx^2} = 12x^2$.

d) $\frac{dy}{dx} = 1$ and $\frac{d^2y}{dx^2} = 0$.

e) $\frac{dy}{dx} = 4x$ and $\frac{d^2y}{dx^2} = 4$.

f) $\frac{dy}{dx} = 12x^2$ and $\frac{d^2y}{dx^2} = 24x$.

g) $\frac{dy}{dx} = 2x^3$ and $\frac{d^2y}{dx^2} = 6x^2$.

h) $\frac{dy}{dx} = -6x^{-3} = -\frac{6}{x^3}$ and $\frac{d^2y}{dx^2} = 18x^{-4} = \frac{18}{x^4}$.

i) $y = x^{-1}$, so $\frac{dy}{dx} = -x^{-2} = -\frac{1}{x^2}$ and $\frac{d^2y}{dx^2} = 2x^{-3} = \frac{2}{x^3}$.

j) $y = x^{\frac{1}{2}}$, so $\frac{dy}{dx} = \frac{1}{2}x^{-\frac{1}{2}} = \frac{1}{2\sqrt{x}}$

and $\frac{d^2y}{dx^2} = -\frac{1}{4}x^{-\frac{3}{2}} = -\frac{1}{4(\sqrt{x})^3}$.

k) $y = x^{-2}$, so $\frac{dy}{dx} = -2x^{-3} = -\frac{2}{x^3}$ and $\frac{d^2y}{dx^2} = 6x^{-4} = \frac{6}{x^4}$.

l) $y = x\sqrt{x} = x^1x^{\frac{1}{2}} = x^{1+\frac{1}{2}} = x^{\frac{3}{2}}$,

so $\frac{dy}{dx} = \frac{3}{2}x^{\frac{1}{2}} = \frac{3}{2}\sqrt{x}$ and $\frac{d^2y}{dx^2} = \frac{3}{4}x^{-\frac{1}{2}} = \frac{3}{4\sqrt{x}}$.

Q2 a) $\frac{dy}{dx} = 2x + 4x^3 \Rightarrow \frac{d^2y}{dx^2} = 2 + 12x^2$.

b) $f'(x) = 3x^2 - 1 \Rightarrow f''(x) = 6x$.

c) $\frac{dy}{dx} = 12x^5 + 6x \Rightarrow \frac{d^2y}{dx^2} = 60x^4 + 6$.

d) $f'(x) = 4x^{-3} + 5 \Rightarrow f''(x) = -12x^{-4} = -\frac{12}{x^4}$.

e) $y = 4x^4 + x^{\frac{1}{2}}$, $\frac{dy}{dx} = 16x^3 + \frac{1}{2}x^{-\frac{1}{2}}$,

$\Rightarrow \frac{d^2y}{dx^2} = 48x^2 - \frac{1}{4}x^{-\frac{3}{2}} = 48x^2 - \frac{1}{4\sqrt{x^3}}$.

f) $f(x) = -x^5 - 4x^{\frac{1}{2}}$, $f'(x) = -5x^4 - 2x^{-\frac{1}{2}}$,

$\Rightarrow f''(x) = -20x^3 + x^{-\frac{3}{2}} = -20x^3 + \frac{1}{\sqrt{x^3}}$.

Q3 a) $f(x) = x(4x^2 - x) = 4x^3 - x^2$
$f'(x) = 12x^2 - 2x$, $f''(x) = 24x - 2$

b) $f(x) = (x^2 - 3)(x - 4) = x^3 - 4x^2 - 3x + 12$
$f'(x) = 3x^2 - 8x - 3$, $f''(x) = 6x - 8$

c) $f(x) = x^2(3x - x^2) = 3x^3 - x^4$
$f'(x) = 9x^2 - 4x^3$, $f''(x) = 18x - 12x^2$

d) $f(x) = (x^{-1} + 5)(x^{-1} - 5) = x^{-2} - 25$
$f'(x) = -2x^{-3} = -\frac{2}{x^3}$, $f''(x) = 6x^{-4} = \frac{6}{x^4}$

e) $f(x) = \frac{x^3 + 8}{x} = x^2 + 8x^{-1}$, $f'(x) = 2x - 8x^{-2} = 2x - \frac{8}{x^2}$,
$f''(x) = 2 + 16x^{-3} = 2 + \frac{16}{x^3}$

f) $f(x) = 3x^{\frac{1}{2}} + xx^{\frac{1}{2}} = 3x^{\frac{1}{2}} + x^{\frac{3}{2}}$

$f'(x) = \frac{3}{2}x^{-\frac{1}{2}} + \frac{3}{2}x^{\frac{1}{2}} = \frac{3}{2\sqrt{x}} + \frac{3}{2}\sqrt{x}$

$f''(x) = \frac{3}{2}(-\frac{1}{2}x^{-\frac{3}{2}}) + \frac{3}{2}(\frac{1}{2}x^{-\frac{1}{2}}) = -\frac{3}{4}x^{-\frac{3}{2}} + \frac{3}{4}x^{-\frac{1}{2}}$

$= -\frac{3}{4(\sqrt{x})^3} + \frac{3}{4\sqrt{x}} \left(= -\frac{3}{4x\sqrt{x}} + \frac{3}{4\sqrt{x}}\right)$

g) $f(x) = \frac{4x^5 + 12x^3 - 40x}{4(x^2 + 5)} = \frac{4x(x^4 + 3x^2 - 10)}{4(x^2 + 5)}$

$= \frac{4x(x^2 + 5)(x^2 - 2)}{4(x^2 + 5)} = x(x^2 - 2) = x^3 - 2x$

$f'(x) = 3x^2 - 2$, $f''(x) = 6x$

h) $f(x) = \frac{1}{x}(3x^4 - 2x^3) = 3x^3 - 2x^2$
$f'(x) = 9x^2 - 4x$, $f''(x) = 18x - 4$

i) $f(x) = \frac{x^2 - xx^{\frac{1}{2}} + 7x}{x^{\frac{1}{2}}} = x^2x^{-\frac{1}{2}} - xx^{\frac{1}{2}}x^{-\frac{1}{2}} + 7xx^{-\frac{1}{2}}$

$= x^{\frac{3}{2}} - x + 7x^{\frac{1}{2}}$

$f'(x) = \frac{3}{2}x^{\frac{1}{2}} - 1 + 7(\frac{1}{2}x^{-\frac{1}{2}}) = \frac{3}{2}\sqrt{x} - 1 + \frac{7}{2\sqrt{x}}$

$f''(x) = \frac{3}{2}(\frac{1}{2}x^{-\frac{1}{2}}) + \frac{7}{2}(-\frac{1}{2}x^{-\frac{3}{2}}) = \frac{3}{4\sqrt{x}} - \frac{7}{4(\sqrt{x})^3}$

Q4 a) $f'(x) = 45x^2$, so $f''(x) = 90x$ and $f''\left(\frac{1}{3}\right) = 30$.

b) $y = \frac{x^4}{12} - \frac{x^3}{6}$, so $\frac{dy}{dx} = \frac{x^3}{3} - \frac{x^2}{2}$, so $\frac{d^2y}{dx^2} = x^2 - x$

so at $x = 4$, $\frac{d^2y}{dx^2} = 12$.

c) $f'(x) = 3x^2 - 2x$, so $f''(x) = 6x - 2$ and $f''(3) = 16$.

d) $y = xx^{\frac{1}{2}} - x^{-1} = x^{\frac{3}{2}} - x^{-1}$ so $\frac{dy}{dx} = \frac{3}{2}x^{\frac{1}{2}} + x^{-2}$

so $\frac{d^2y}{dx^2} = \frac{3}{2}(\frac{1}{2}x^{-\frac{1}{2}}) - 2x^{-3} = \frac{3}{4\sqrt{x}} - \frac{2}{x^3}$

so at $x = 4$, $\frac{d^2y}{dx^2} = \frac{11}{32}$.

e) $f(x) = x^2(x^3 - 4x^2 - 5x) = x^5 - 4x^4 - 5x^3$
so $f'(x) = 5x^4 - 16x^3 - 15x^2$
and $f''(x) = 20x^3 - 48x^2 - 30x$.
$f''(-1) = -38$.

f) $y = \frac{x^3(x+6)(x-2)}{(x+6)} = x^3(x-2) = x^4 - 2x^3$
so $\frac{dy}{dx} = 4x^3 - 6x^2$, $\frac{d^2y}{dx^2} = 12x^2 - 12x$.
At $x = 5$, $\frac{d^2y}{dx^2} = 240$.

g) $f(x) = \frac{9x^2 + 3x}{3\sqrt{x}} = 3x^{\frac{3}{2}} + x^{\frac{1}{2}}$ so
$f'(x) = 3(\frac{3}{2}x^{\frac{1}{2}}) + \frac{1}{2}x^{-\frac{1}{2}} = \frac{9}{2}\sqrt{x} + \frac{1}{2\sqrt{x}}$ and so
$f''(x) = \frac{9}{2}(\frac{1}{2}x^{-\frac{1}{2}}) + \frac{1}{2}(-\frac{1}{2}x^{-\frac{3}{2}}) = \frac{9}{4\sqrt{x}} - \frac{1}{4(\sqrt{x})^3}$
$f''(1) = 2$.

h) $y = (x^{-2} + x^{-1})(5 - x) = 5x^{-2} - x^{-2}x + 5x^{-1} - xx^{-1}$
$= 5x^{-2} - x^{-1} + 5x^{-1} - 1 = 5x^{-2} + 4x^{-1} - 1$
$\frac{dy}{dx} = 5(-2x^{-3}) + 4(-x^{-2}) = -10x^{-3} - 4x^{-2}$
so $\frac{d^2y}{dx^2} = 30x^{-4} + 8x^{-3} = \frac{30}{x^4} + \frac{8}{x^3}$.
At $x = -3$, $\frac{d^2y}{dx^2} = \frac{2}{27}$.

Q5 a) $y = x^3 + 3x^2 \Rightarrow \frac{dy}{dx} = 3x^2 + 6x \Rightarrow \frac{d^2y}{dx^2} = 6x + 6$
$\frac{d^2y}{dx^2} = 18 \Rightarrow 6x + 6 = 18 \Rightarrow x = 2$
$\Rightarrow y = 2^3 + 3(2)^2 = 20$
So the coordinates of the point are (2, 20).

b) $f(x) = \frac{4}{15}x^{\frac{5}{2}} \Rightarrow f'(x) = \frac{2}{3}x^{\frac{3}{2}} \Rightarrow f''(x) = x^{\frac{1}{2}} = \sqrt{x}$
$f''(x) = 2 \Rightarrow \sqrt{x} = 2 \Rightarrow x = 4 \Rightarrow y = \frac{4}{15}(4)^{\frac{5}{2}} = \frac{128}{15}$
So the coordinates of the point are $(4, \frac{128}{15})$.

c) $y = (2x^2 + 4)(2x^2 - 4) = 4x^4 - 16 \Rightarrow \frac{dy}{dx} = 16x^3$
$\Rightarrow \frac{d^2y}{dx^2} = 48x^2$
$\frac{d^2y}{dx^2} = 768 \Rightarrow 48x^2 = 768 \Rightarrow x = -4$ or $x = 4$
$y = 4(\pm 4)^4 - 16 = 1008$
So the coordinates of the points are (–4, 1008) and (4, 1008).

d) $y = \frac{1}{4}x^4 - \frac{5}{3}x^3 + 2x^2 - 20x \Rightarrow \frac{dy}{dx} = x^3 - 5x^2 + 4x - 20$
$\Rightarrow \frac{d^2y}{dx^2} = 3x^2 - 10x + 4$
$\frac{d^2y}{dx^2} = 12 \Rightarrow 3x^2 - 10x + 4 = 12$
$\Rightarrow 3x^2 - 10x - 8 = 0$
$\Rightarrow (3x + 2)(x - 4) = 0$
$\Rightarrow x = -\frac{2}{3}$ or $x = 4$
When $x = -\frac{2}{3}$,
$y = \frac{1}{4}\left(-\frac{2}{3}\right)^4 - \frac{5}{3}\left(-\frac{2}{3}\right)^3 + 2\left(-\frac{2}{3}\right)^2 - 20\left(-\frac{2}{3}\right) = \frac{1196}{81}$
When $x = 4$,
$y = \frac{1}{4}(4)^4 - \frac{5}{3}(4)^3 + 2(4)^2 - 20(4) = -\frac{272}{3}$
So the coordinates of the points are:
$\left(-\frac{2}{3}, \frac{1196}{81}\right)$ and $(4, -\frac{272}{3})$.

Q6 a) $f(x) = (x-3)^3 = x^3 + 3x^2(-3) + 3x(-3)^2 + (-3)^3$
$= x^3 - 9x^2 + 27x - 27$
$f'(x) = 3x^2 - 18x + 27 = 3(x^2 - 6x + 9) = 3(x-3)^2$

b) $f''(x) = 6x - 18 = 6(x - 3)$

Q7 $f(x) = x - \frac{1}{\sqrt{x}} + \frac{1}{x}$ so $f'(x) = 1 + \frac{1}{2x^{\frac{3}{2}}} - \frac{1}{x^2} = \frac{2x^2 + \sqrt{x} - 2}{2x^2}$
and $f''(x) = -\frac{3}{4x^{\frac{5}{2}}} + \frac{2}{x^3} = \frac{8 - 3\sqrt{x}}{4x^3}$.

Hence: $4x^2f''(x) + 2xf'(x) - 2f(x)$
$= \frac{8 - 3\sqrt{x}}{x} + \frac{2x^2 + \sqrt{x} - 2}{x} - \frac{2x^2 - 2\sqrt{x} + 2}{x} = \frac{4}{x}$

[6 marks available — 1 mark for rewriting f(x) in a suitable form, 1 mark for attempting to differentiate, 1 mark for the correct derivative, 1 mark for the correct second derivative, 1 mark for attempting to write as a single fraction, 1 mark for the correct numerator]

Exercise 10.7 — Stationary Points

Q1 a) The graph has 2 stationary points — a minimum and a point of inflection.

b) The graph has 3 stationary points — a maximum, a minimum and a point of inflection.

Q2 a) $\frac{dy}{dx} = 2x + 3$. When $\frac{dy}{dx} = 0$, $2x + 3 = 0 \Rightarrow x = -\frac{3}{2}$

b) $y = (3 - x)(4 + 2x) = 12 + 2x - 2x^2$
$\frac{dy}{dx} = 2 - 4x$. When $\frac{dy}{dx} = 0$, $2 - 4x = 0 \Rightarrow x = \frac{1}{2}$

c) $\frac{dy}{dx} = 3x^2 + 8x - 3$. When $\frac{dy}{dx} = 0$, $3x^2 + 8x - 3 = 0$
$\Rightarrow (3x - 1)(x + 3) \Rightarrow x = \frac{1}{3}$ and $x = -3$

d) $\frac{dy}{dx} = 4x^3 - 36x^2$. When $\frac{dy}{dx} = 0$, $4x^3 - 36x^2 = 0$
$\Rightarrow 4x^2(x - 9) \Rightarrow x = 0$ and $x = 9$

Q3 a) $\frac{dy}{dx} = 4x - 5$. When $\frac{dy}{dx} = 0$, $4x - 5 = 0 \Rightarrow x = \frac{5}{4}$
When $x = \frac{5}{4}$, $y = 2\left(\frac{5}{4}\right)^2 - 5\left(\frac{5}{4}\right) + 2 = -\frac{9}{8}$
So the coordinates are $\left(\frac{5}{4}, -\frac{9}{8}\right)$.

b) $\frac{dy}{dx} = -2x + 3$. When $\frac{dy}{dx} = 0$, $-2x + 3 = 0 \Rightarrow x = \frac{3}{2}$
When $x = \frac{3}{2}$, $y = -\left(\frac{3}{2}\right)2 + 3\left(\frac{3}{2}\right) - 4 = -\frac{7}{4}$.
So the coordinates are $(\frac{3}{2}, -\frac{7}{4})$.

c) $\frac{dy}{dx} = -6 - 6x$.
When $\frac{dy}{dx} = 0$, $-6 - 6x = 0 \Rightarrow x = -1$
When $x = -1$, $y = 7 - 6(-1) - 3(-1)^2 = 10$.
So the coordinates are (–1, 10).

d) $y = (x - 1)(2x + 3) = 2x^2 + x - 3$
$\frac{dy}{dx} = 4x + 1$. When $\frac{dy}{dx} = 0$, $4x + 1 = 0 \Rightarrow x = -\frac{1}{4}$
When $x = -\frac{1}{4}$, $y = (-\frac{1}{4} - 1)(2(-\frac{1}{4}) + 3) = -\frac{25}{8}$.
So the coordinates are $(-\frac{1}{4}, -\frac{25}{8})$.

Q4 a) $\frac{dy}{dx} = 3x^2 - 3$.
When $\frac{dy}{dx} = 0$, $3x^2 - 3 = 0 \Rightarrow x = \pm 1$.
When $x = 1$, $y = 1^3 - 3(1) + 2 = 0$.
When $x = -1$, $y = (-1)^3 - 3(-1) + 2 = 4$.
So the coordinates are (1, 0) and (–1, 4).

b) $\frac{dy}{dx} = 12x^2$. When $\frac{dy}{dx} = 0$, $12x^2 = 0 \Rightarrow x = 0$
When $x = 0$, $y = 4(0)^3 + 5 = 5$.
So the coordinates are (0, 5).

c) $\frac{dy}{dx} = 9x^2 + 12x$.
When $\frac{dy}{dx} = 0$, $9x^2 + 12x = 0 \Rightarrow 3x(3x + 4) = 0$
$\Rightarrow x = 0$ and $x = -\frac{4}{3}$
When $x = 0$, $y = 3(0)^3 + 6(0)^2 = 0$.
When $x = -\frac{4}{3}$, $= 3\left(-\frac{4}{3}\right)^3 + 6\left(-\frac{4}{3}\right)^2 = \frac{32}{9}$.
So the coordinates are (0, 0) and $\left(-\frac{4}{3}, \frac{32}{9}\right)$.

d) $\frac{dy}{dx} = 12x^2 + 24x$.
When $\frac{dy}{dx} = 0$, $12x^2 + 24x = 0 \Rightarrow 12x(x + 2)$
$\Rightarrow x = 0$ and $x = -2$

When $x = 0$, $y = 4(0)^3 + 12(0)^2 + 8 = 8$.
When $x = -2$, $y = 4(-2)^3 + 12(-2)^2 + 8 = 24$.
So the coordinates are (0, 8) and (–2, 24).

Q5 $\frac{dy}{dx} = 3x^2 - 12x - 63$.
When $\frac{dy}{dx} = 0$, $3x^2 - 12x - 63 = 0 \Rightarrow x^2 - 4x - 21$
$\Rightarrow (x + 3)(x - 7) = 0$
$\Rightarrow x = -3$ and $x = 7$

When $x = -3$, $y = (-3)^3 - 6(-3)^2 - 63(-3) + 21 = 129$

When $x = 7$, $y = 7^3 - 6(7)^2 - 63(7) + 21 = -371$

So the coordinates are (–3, 129) and (7, –371).

Q6 $f'(x) = 5x^4 + 3$. When $f'(x) = 0$, $5x^4 + 3 = 0 \Rightarrow x^4 = -\frac{3}{5}$.
Finding a solution would involve finding the fourth root of a negative number. But $x^4 = (x^2)^2$, so x^4 is always positive and so there are no stationary points.

Q7 a) $\frac{dy}{dx} = 3x^2 - 14x - 5$

b) When $\frac{dy}{dx} = 0$, $3x^2 - 14x - 5 = 0$
$\Rightarrow (3x + 1)(x - 5) = 0$, so $x = -\frac{1}{3}$ and $x = 5$.
When $x = -\frac{1}{3}$, $y = \left(-\frac{1}{3}\right)^3 - 7\left(-\frac{1}{3}\right)^2 - 5\left(-\frac{1}{3}\right) + 2$
$= \frac{77}{27}$.
When $x = 5$, $y = 5^3 - 7(5)^2 - 5(5) + 2 = -73$.
So the coordinates are $(-\frac{1}{3}, \frac{77}{27})$ and (5, –73).

Q8 For stationary points to occur, $f'(x)$ must equal zero, so
$f'(x) = 3x^2 + k = 0 \Rightarrow -\frac{k}{3} = x^2$.
For this equation to have a solution, k can't be positive (or it would be taking the square root of a negative number), so $k \leq 0$.
Therefore, if the graph has no stationary points, $k > 0$.

Q9 a) $\frac{dy}{dx} = 1 + \frac{1}{2}kx^{-\frac{1}{2}}$
[2 marks available — 1 mark for differentiating $x^{\frac{1}{2}}$ correctly, 1 mark for the correct answer]

b) (i) When $x = \frac{9}{4}$, $\frac{dy}{dx} = 0$, so:
$1 + \frac{1}{2}k\left(\frac{9}{4}\right)^{-\frac{1}{2}} = 0 \Rightarrow 1 + \frac{1}{2}k\left(\frac{2}{3}\right) = 0$
$\Rightarrow 1 + \frac{1}{3}k = 0 \Rightarrow \frac{1}{3}k = -1 \Rightarrow k = -3$
[2 marks available — 1 mark for a correct method to find k, 1 mark for the correct answer]

(ii) $y = \frac{9}{4} - 3\sqrt{\frac{9}{4}} = -\frac{9}{4}$ *[1 mark]*

Exercise 10.8 — Maximum and Minimum Points

Q1 a) negative b) positive c) negative
d) negative e) positive

Q2 a) $\frac{dy}{dx} = 2x + 14$ $\frac{d^2y}{dx^2} = 2$

At (–7, –52), $\frac{d^2y}{dx^2} = 2 > 0$, so (–7, –52) is a minimum.
The curve is a quadratic so has only one stationary point and you know it'll be a minimum because it's a positive u-shaped quadratic.

b) $\frac{dy}{dx} = 3x^2 - 12$ $\frac{d^2y}{dx^2} = 6x$
At (2, –12), $\frac{d^2y}{dx^2} = 6 \times 2 = 12 > 0$, so (2, –12) is a minimum.

c) $\frac{dy}{dx} = 6x^2 - 2x$ $\frac{d^2y}{dx^2} = 12x - 2$
At $\left(\frac{1}{3}, -\frac{1}{27}\right)$, $\frac{d^2y}{dx^2} = 12\left(\frac{1}{3}\right) - 2 = 2 > 0$,
so $\left(\frac{1}{3}, -\frac{1}{27}\right)$ is a minimum.

d) $\frac{dy}{dx} = 8x^3 - 48x^2$ $\frac{d^2y}{dx^2} = 24x^2 - 96x$
At (6, 36), $\frac{d^2y}{dx^2} = 24 \times 6^2 - 96 \times 6 = 288 > 0$,
so (6, 36) is a minimum.

e) $\frac{dy}{dx} = 20x^4 + 60x^3$ $\frac{d^2y}{dx^2} = 80x^3 + 180x^2$
At (–3, –7), $\frac{d^2y}{dx^2} = 80 \times (-3)^3 + 180 \times (-3)^2$
$= -540 < 0$, so (–3, –7) is a maximum.

f) $\frac{dy}{dx} = 5x^4 - 20x^3 + 10x - 40$ $\frac{d^2y}{dx^2} = 20x^3 - 60x^2 + 10$
At (4, 64), $\frac{d^2y}{dx^2} = 20 \times 4^3 - 60 \times 4^2 + 10 = 330 > 0$, so (4, 64) is a minimum.

Q3 a) (1, 3)
All the clues are in the question — the derivative when x = 1 is zero so you know it's a stationary point, and the y-value when x = 1 is 3.

b) The second derivative at $x = 1$ is positive, so it's a minimum.

Q4 a) $\frac{dy}{dx} = -2x$. When $\frac{dy}{dx} = 0$, $x = 0$. When $x = 0$,
$y = 5 - 0 = 5$. So the coordinates are (0, 5).
$\frac{d^2y}{dx^2} = -2$, so it's a maximum turning point.

b) $\frac{dy}{dx} = x + 21$.
When $\frac{dy}{dx} = 0$, $x + 21 = 0 \Rightarrow x = -21$
When $x = -21$, $y = \frac{441}{2} - 441 + 12 = -\frac{417}{2}$
So the coordinates are $(-21, -\frac{417}{2})$.
$\frac{d^2y}{dx^2} = 1$, so it's a minimum turning point.

c) $\frac{dy}{dx} = 6x^2 - 6$. When $\frac{dy}{dx} = 0$, $6x^2 = 6 \Rightarrow x = \pm 1$
When $x = 1$, $y = 2 - 6 + 2 = -2$.
When $x = -1$, $y = -2 + 6 + 2 = 6$. So the coordinates are (1, –2) and (–1, 6). $\frac{d^2y}{dx^2} = 12x$.
At (1, –2), $\frac{d^2y}{dx^2} = 12$, so it's a minimum.
At (–1, 6), $\frac{d^2y}{dx^2} = -12$ so it's a maximum.

d) $\frac{dy}{dx} = 3x^2 - 6x - 24$. When $\frac{dy}{dx} = 0$, $x^2 - 2x - 8 = 0$
$\Rightarrow (x - 4)(x + 2) = 0 \Rightarrow x = 4$ and -2.
When $x = 4$, $y = 64 - 48 - 96 + 15 = -65$.
When $x = -2$, $y = -8 - 12 + 48 + 15 = 43$.
So the coordinates are (4, –65) and (–2, 43).
$\frac{d^2y}{dx^2} = 6x - 6$. At (4, –65), $\frac{d^2y}{dx^2} = 24 - 6 = 18$,
so it's a minimum.
At (–2, 43), $\frac{d^2y}{dx^2} = -12 - 6 = -18$, so it's a maximum.

e) $\frac{dy}{dx} = \frac{1}{3}x^3 + \frac{2}{3}x^2$. When $\frac{dy}{dx} = 0$, $\frac{1}{3}x^3 + \frac{2}{3}x^2 = 0$
$\Rightarrow \frac{1}{3}x^2(x + 2)$, so $x = 0$ and $x = -2$.
When $x = 0$, $y = 0 + 0 = 0$.
When $x = -2$, $y = \frac{4}{3} - \frac{16}{9} = -\frac{4}{9}$.
So the stationary points are (0, 0) and $(-2, -\frac{4}{9})$.
$\frac{d^2y}{dx^2} = x^2 + \frac{4}{3}x$. At (0, 0), $\frac{d^2y}{dx^2} = 0 + 0 = 0$, so you can't tell whether it's a maximum or minimum.
At $(-2, -\frac{4}{9})$, $\frac{d^2y}{dx^2} = 4 - \frac{8}{3} = \frac{4}{3}$, so it's a minimum.

f) $\frac{dy}{dx} = 4x^3 + 12x^2 + 8x$.
When $\frac{dy}{dx} = 0$, $x^3 + 3x^2 + 2x = 0$
$\Rightarrow x(x+2)(x+1) = 0$, so $x = 0$, -1 and -2.
When $x = 0$, $y = 0 + 0 + 0 - 10 = -10$.
When $x = -1$, $y = 1 - 4 + 4 - 10 = -9$.
When $x = -2$, $y = 16 - 32 + 16 - 10 = -10$.
So the stationary points are $(0, -10)$, $(-1, -9)$ and $(-2, -10)$.
$\frac{d^2y}{dx^2} = 12x^2 + 24x + 8$.
At $(0, -10)$, $\frac{d^2y}{dx^2} = 0 + 0 + 8 = 8$, so it's a minimum.
At $(-1, -9)$, $\frac{d^2y}{dx^2} = 12 - 24 + 8 = -4$, so it's a maximum.
At $(-2, -10)$, $\frac{d^2y}{dx^2} = 48 - 48 + 8 = 8$, so it's a minimum.

Q5 a) $f'(x) = 24x^2 + 32x + 8$. When $f'(x) = 0$, $3x^2 + 4x + 1 = 0$
$\Rightarrow (3x+1)(x+1) = 0$, so $x = -1$ and $-\frac{1}{3}$.
When $x = -1$, $f(x) = -8 + 16 - 8 + 1 = 1$.
When $x = -\frac{1}{3}$, $f(x) = -\frac{8}{27} + \frac{16}{9} - \frac{8}{3} + 1 = -\frac{5}{27}$.
So the coordinates are $(-1, 1)$ and $(-\frac{1}{3}, -\frac{5}{27})$.
$f''(x) = 48x + 32$. At $(-1, 1)$ $f''(x) = -48 + 32 = -16$, so it's a maximum.
At $(-\frac{1}{3}, -\frac{5}{27})$, $f''(x) = -\frac{48}{3} + 32 = 16$, so it's a minimum.

b) $f'(x) = x^2 - 12x - 45$. When $f'(x) = 0$, $x^2 - 12x - 45 = 0$
$\Rightarrow (x+3)(x-15) = 0 \Rightarrow x = -3$ and 15.
When $x = -3$, $y = -9 - 54 + 135 = 72$.
When $x = 15$, $y = 1125 - 1350 - 675 = -900$.
So the coordinates are $(-3, 72)$ and $(15, -900)$.
$f''(x) = 2x - 12$.
At $(-3, 72)$, $f''(x) = -6 - 12 = -18$, so it's a maximum.
At $(15, -900)$, $f''(x) = 30 - 12 = 18$, so it's a minimum.

c) $f'(x) = x^3 + 6x^2 - 16x$. When $f'(x) = 0$, $x^3 + 6x^2 - 16x = 0$
$\Rightarrow x(x^2 + 6x - 16) = 0 \Rightarrow x(x+8)(x-2)$, so $x = -8$, 0 and 2.
When $x = -8$, $f(x) = 1024 - 1024 - 512 + 1 = -511$.
When $x = 0$, $f(x) = 0 + 0 + 0 + 1 = 1$.
When $x = 2$, $f(x) = 4 + 16 - 32 + 1 = -11$.
So the coordinates are $(-8, -511)$, $(0, 1)$ and $(2, -11)$.
$f''(x) = 3x^2 + 12x - 16$.
At $(-8, -511)$, $f''(x) = 192 - 96 - 16 = 80$, so it's a minimum.
At $(0, 1)$, $f''(x) = -16$, so it's a maximum.
At $(2, -11)$, $f''(x) = 12 + 24 - 16 = 20$, so it's a minimum.

d) $f(x) = \frac{27}{x^3} + x = 27x^{-3} + x \Rightarrow f'(x) = -81x^{-4} + 1$.
When $f'(x) = 0$, $x^4 = 81 \Rightarrow x = \pm 3$.
When $x = 3$, $f(x) = \frac{27}{27} + 3 = 4$.
When $x = -3$, $f(x) = -\frac{27}{27} - 3 = -4$.
So the coordinates are $(3, 4)$ and $(-3, -4)$.
$f''(x) = 324x^{-5}$. At $(3, 4)$ $f''(x) = \frac{4}{3}$, so it's a minimum.
At $(-3, -4)$ $f''(x) = -\frac{4}{3}$, so it's a maximum.

Q6 a) $f'(x) = 3x^2 - 6x$. $f''(x) = 6x - 6$.

b) When $f'(x) = 0$, $3x^2 - 6x = 0 \Rightarrow x(x-2) = 0$, so $x = 0$ and $x = 2$.
When $x = 0$, $f(x) = 0 - 0 + 4 = 4$.
When $x = 2$, $f(x) = 8 - 12 + 4 = 0$.
So the coordinates are $(0, 4)$ and $(2, 0)$.
At $(0, 4)$ $f''(x) = 0 - 6 = -6$, so it's a maximum.
At $(2, 0)$ $f''(x) = 12 - 6 = 6$, so it's a minimum.

Q7 a) $y = x^2 + \frac{2000}{x} = x^2 + 2000x^{-1} \Rightarrow \frac{dy}{dx} = 2x - \frac{2000}{x^2}$
When $\frac{dy}{dx} = 0$, $2x = \frac{2000}{x^2} \Rightarrow x^3 = 1000 \Rightarrow x = 10$

b) $\frac{d^2y}{dx^2} = 2 + \frac{4000}{x^3}$. When $x = 10$,
$\frac{d^2y}{dx^2} = 2 + 4 = 6$, so it's a minimum.

Q8 c is an integer so differentiates to 0.
$f(x) = 2x^3 + 4x^2 + c \Rightarrow f'(x) = 6x^2 + 8x \Rightarrow f''(x) = 12x + 8$
At stationary points $f'(x) = 0$, $6x^2 + 8x = 0 \Rightarrow 2x(3x+4) = 0$
$\Rightarrow x = 0$ and $x = -\frac{4}{3}$
When $x = 0$, $f''(x) = 12(0) + 8 = 8 > 0$, so the point is a minimum.
When $x = -\frac{4}{3}$, $f''(x) = 12\left(-\frac{4}{3}\right) + 8 = -8 < 0$, so the point is a maximum.
When $x = -\frac{4}{3}$, $y = -\frac{260}{27}$, so $-\frac{260}{27} = 2\left(-\frac{4}{3}\right)^3 + 4\left(-\frac{4}{3}\right)^2 + c$
$\Rightarrow c = -\frac{260}{27} - 2\left(-\frac{4}{3}\right)^3 - 4\left(-\frac{4}{3}\right)^2 = -12$

Q9 $y = 5x - 1 + 2x^{-1}$, so stationary points occur when
$\frac{dy}{dx} = 5 - 2x^{-2} = 0 \Rightarrow 2 = 5x^2 \Rightarrow x^2 = \frac{2}{5}$
$\Rightarrow x = \pm\sqrt{\frac{2}{5}} \Rightarrow x = \pm\frac{\sqrt{10}}{5}$
Find the second derivative: $\frac{dy}{dx} = 5 - 2x^{-2}$, so $\frac{d^2y}{dx^2} = 4x^{-3}$.
When $x = \frac{\sqrt{10}}{5}$, $\frac{d^2y}{dx^2} = 4\left(\frac{\sqrt{10}}{5}\right)^{-3} = 5\sqrt{10}$, so it's a minimum.
When $x = -\frac{\sqrt{10}}{5}$, $\frac{d^2y}{dx^2} = 4\left(-\frac{\sqrt{10}}{5}\right)^{-3} = -5\sqrt{10}$, so it's a maximum.
When $x = \frac{\sqrt{10}}{5}$, $y = -1 + 2\sqrt{10}$,
so A has coordinates $\left(\frac{\sqrt{10}}{5}, -1 + 2\sqrt{10}\right)$.
When $x = -\frac{\sqrt{10}}{5}$, $y = -1 - 2\sqrt{10}$,
so B has coordinates $\left(-\frac{\sqrt{10}}{5}, -1 - 2\sqrt{10}\right)$.
[7 marks available — 1 mark for the correct derivative, 1 mark for setting the derivative equal to zero, 1 mark for a correct method to solve this equation, 1 mark for the correct values of x, 1 mark for the correct second derivative, 1 mark for the correct nature of each point, 1 mark for the correct values of y]

Q10 $f(x) = x^3 + ax^2 + bx + c \Rightarrow f'(x) = 3x^2 + 2ax + b$.
$\Rightarrow f''(x) = 6x + 2a$. At the point $(3, 10)$:
$10 = 3^3 + a(3^2) + b(3) + c \Rightarrow 10 = 27 + 9a + 3b + c$
As $(3, 10)$ is a stationary point, $0 = 3(3^2) + 2a(3) + b$
$\Rightarrow 0 = 27 + 6a + b$. We know that $f''(3) = 0$,
so $0 = 6(3) + 2a \Rightarrow 0 = 18 + 2a \Rightarrow a = -9$.
Then $0 = 27 + 6a + b = 27 + 6(-9) + b \Rightarrow b = 27$
And $10 = 27 + 9a + 3b + c = 27 + 9(-9) + 3(27) + c$
$\Rightarrow c = -17$. So $f(x) = x^3 - 9x^2 + 27x - 17$.

Q11 a) (i) $f'(x) = 3x^2 - 4x + 1$
$f'(x) = 0 \Rightarrow (3x-1)(x-1) = 0 \Rightarrow x = \frac{1}{3}$ or $x = 1$
[4 marks available — 1 mark for the correct derivative, 1 mark for setting f'(x) = 0, 1 mark for a correct method to solve the quadratic, 1 mark for the correct x-values]

(ii) $f''(x) = 6x - 4$
When $x = \frac{1}{3}$, $f''\left(\frac{1}{3}\right) = -2 < 0$, so it's a maximum.
When $x = 1$, $f''(1) = 2 > 0$, so it's a minimum.
[3 marks available — 1 mark for the correct second derivative, 1 mark for the correct nature of each stationary point]

b) $g(x) = \frac{1}{f(x)}$, so the maximum point of $f(x)$ corresponds to a minimum point of $g(x)$, and the minimum point of $f(x)$ corresponds to a maximum point of $g(x)$. So the stationary points of both functions have the same x-coordinates.
When $x = \frac{1}{3}$, $g\left(\frac{1}{3}\right) = \frac{27}{58}$, so $\left(\frac{1}{3}, \frac{27}{58}\right)$ is a stationary point.
$x = \frac{1}{3}$ is a maximum of $f(x)$, so it is a minimum of $g(x)$.
When $x = 1$, $g(1) = \frac{1}{2}$, so $\left(1, \frac{1}{2}\right)$ is a stationary point.
$x = 1$ is a minimum of $f(x)$, so it is a maximum of $g(x)$.
[4 marks available — 1 mark for each set of coordinates, 1 mark for the correct nature of each set of coordinates]

Q12 a) $\frac{dy}{dx} = \frac{3}{5} \times \frac{5}{3}x^{\frac{2}{3}} + \frac{3}{4} \times \frac{4}{3}x^{\frac{1}{3}} - 2 = x^{\frac{2}{3}} + x^{\frac{1}{3}} - 2$

[2 marks available — 1 mark for an attempt at differentiating, 1 mark for correctly simplifying to the required result]

b) At the stationary points, $x^{\frac{2}{3}} + x^{\frac{1}{3}} - 2 = 0$

$\Rightarrow (x^{\frac{1}{3}})^2 + x^{\frac{1}{3}} - 2 = 0 \Rightarrow (x^{\frac{1}{3}} - 1)(x^{\frac{1}{3}} + 2) = 0$

$\Rightarrow x^{\frac{1}{3}} = 1$ or $x^{\frac{1}{3}} = -2 \Rightarrow x = 1$ or -8

When $x = 1$, $y = -\frac{33}{20}$, and when $x = -8$, $y = \frac{39}{5}$.

So the coordinates of the stationary points are: $\left(1, -\frac{33}{20}\right)$ and $\left(-8, \frac{39}{5}\right)$.

[4 marks available — 1 mark for a correct method to find the stationary points, 1 mark for the correct values of $x^{\frac{1}{3}}$, 1 mark for the correct x-values, 1 mark for the correct coordinates]

c) $\frac{d^2y}{dx^2} = \frac{2}{3}x^{-\frac{1}{3}} + \frac{1}{3}x^{-\frac{2}{3}}$

When $x = 1$, $\frac{d^2y}{dx^2} = 1 > 0$, so it's a minimum,

When $x = -8$, $\frac{d^2y}{dx^2} = -\frac{1}{4} < 0$, so it's a maximum.

[3 marks available — 1 mark for the correct second derivative, 1 mark for the correct nature of each stationary point]

Q13 a) $\frac{dy}{dx} = 4x^3 + 3kx^2 + 2x$.

Stationary points occur when $\frac{dy}{dx} = 0$,

so $4x^3 + 3kx^2 + 2x = 0 \Rightarrow x(4x^2 + 3kx + 2) = 0$

so $x = 0$ or $4x^2 + 3kx + 2 = 0$.

As you know the only stationary point occurs at $x = 0$, the part in brackets can't have any solutions. This gives you information about the discriminant of the quadratic equation:

$b^2 - 4ac < 0 \Rightarrow 9k^2 < 32 \Rightarrow k^2 < \frac{32}{9}$.

b) When $x = 0$, $y = 0 + 0 + 0 + 17 = 17$, so the coordinates are (0, 17).

$\frac{d^2y}{dx^2} = 12x^2 + 6kx + 2$.

When $x = 0$, $\frac{d^2y}{dx^2} = 2$, so it's a minimum.

Q14 a) P has coordinates $\left(x, \frac{1}{x^2}\right)$, so by Pythagoras' theorem:

$OP^2 = x^2 + \left(\frac{1}{x^2}\right)^2 = x^2 + \frac{1}{x^4}$

[3 marks available — 1 mark for writing the coordinates of P in terms of x, 1 mark for a correct method, 1 mark for the correct answer]

b) $f(x) = x^2 + x^{-4} \Rightarrow f'(x) = 2x - \frac{4}{x^5}$

[2 marks available — 1 mark for an attempt at differentiating, 1 mark for correct result]

c) $f'(x) = 0 \Rightarrow 2x - \frac{4}{x^5} = 0 \Rightarrow 2x^6 - 4 = 0$

$\Rightarrow x^6 = 2 \Rightarrow x = \pm 2^{\frac{1}{6}}$

[2 marks available — 1 mark for attempting to solve for x, 1 mark for both correct answers]

d) $f''(x) = 2 + \frac{20}{x^6}$, so $f''(2^{\frac{1}{6}}) = 2 + \frac{20}{2} = 12 > 0$

and $f''(-2^{\frac{1}{6}}) = 2 + \frac{20}{2} = 12 > 0$.

So both x-values correspond to minimum points of f(x).

[3 marks available — 1 mark for correct second derivative, 1 mark for substituting in values, 1 mark for correct answers]

e) When $x = 2^{\frac{1}{6}}$, $OP^2 = (2^{\frac{1}{6}})^2 + \frac{1}{(2^{\frac{1}{6}})^4} = 2^{\frac{1}{3}} + \frac{1}{2^{\frac{2}{3}}}$

and when $x = -2^{\frac{1}{6}}$, $OP^2 = (-2^{\frac{1}{6}})^2 + \frac{1}{(-2^{\frac{1}{6}})^4} = 2^{\frac{1}{3}} + \frac{1}{2^{\frac{2}{3}}}$

These are both the same, so both points give the same minimum distance: $OP = \sqrt{2^{\frac{1}{3}} + 2^{-\frac{2}{3}}} = 1.37$ to 3 s.f.

[2 marks available — 1 mark for a correct method to find the minimum distance, 1 mark for the correct answer]

You can tell that both values of x will give the same distance from the origin as the graph is symmetrical about the y-axis.

Exercise 10.9 — Increasing and Decreasing Functions

Q1 a) $\frac{dy}{dx} = 2x + 7$. If the function is increasing, $\frac{dy}{dx} > 0$

$\Rightarrow 2x > -7 \Rightarrow x > -\frac{7}{2}$.

b) $\frac{dy}{dx} = 10x + 3$. If the function is increasing,

$\frac{dy}{dx} > 0 \Rightarrow 10x > -3 \Rightarrow x > -\frac{3}{10}$.

c) $\frac{dy}{dx} = \frac{1}{2}x - 6$. If the function is increasing, $\frac{dy}{dx} > 0$

$\Rightarrow \frac{1}{2}x - 6 > 0 \Rightarrow \frac{1}{2}x > 6 \Rightarrow x > 12$.

d) $\frac{dy}{dx} = -18x$. If the function is increasing, $\frac{dy}{dx} > 0$

$\Rightarrow -18x > 0 \Rightarrow x < 0$.

Be careful with the direction of the inequality sign if you're dividing by a negative number.

e) $\frac{dy}{dx} = -6x - 4$. If the function is increasing, $\frac{dy}{dx} > 0$

$\Rightarrow -6x - 4 > 0 \Rightarrow -6x > 4 \Rightarrow x < -\frac{2}{3}$.

f) $y = -\frac{3}{5}x^2 + \frac{8}{5}x - 2 \Rightarrow \frac{dy}{dx} = -\frac{6}{5}x + \frac{8}{5}$.

If the function is increasing, $\frac{dy}{dx} > 0$

$\Rightarrow -\frac{6}{5}x + \frac{8}{5} > 0 \Rightarrow -\frac{6}{5}x > -\frac{8}{5} \Rightarrow x < \frac{4}{3}$

Q2 a) $f'(x) = -3 - 4x$. If the function is decreasing,

$f'(x) < 0 \Rightarrow -4x < 3 \Rightarrow x > -\frac{3}{4}$.

b) $f(x) = (x + 3)(x - 2) = x^2 + x - 6 \Rightarrow f'(x) = 2x + 1$.

If the function is decreasing, $f'(x) < 0$

$\Rightarrow 2x + 1 < 0 \Rightarrow 2x < -1 \Rightarrow x < -\frac{1}{2}$.

c) $f(x) = (2x - 1)(x - 7) = 2x^2 - 15x + 7$

$\Rightarrow f'(x) = 4x - 15$. If the function is decreasing,

$f'(x) < 0 \Rightarrow 4x - 15 < 0 \Rightarrow x < \frac{15}{4}$.

d) $f(x) = (6 - 3x)(6 + 3x) = 36 - 9x^2 \Rightarrow f'(x) = -18x$.

If the function is decreasing, $f'(x) < 0$

$\Rightarrow -18x < 0 \Rightarrow x > 0$.

e) $f(x) = (1 - 2x)(7 - 3x) = 7 - 17x + 6x^2$

$f'(x) = -17 + 12x$. If the function is decreasing,

$f'(x) < 0 \Rightarrow 12x < 17 \Rightarrow x < \frac{17}{12}$.

f) $f(x) = (5x - 2)(2 - 5x) = -25x^2 + 20x - 4$

$\Rightarrow f'(x) = -50x + 20$. If the function is decreasing, $f'(x) < 0$

$\Rightarrow -50x + 20 < 0 \Rightarrow -50x < -20 \Rightarrow x > \frac{2}{5}$.

Q3 a) $\frac{dy}{dx} = 3x^2 - 12x - 15$. If the function is increasing,

$\frac{dy}{dx} > 0 \Rightarrow 3x^2 - 12x - 15 > 0$

$\Rightarrow x^2 - 4x - 5 > 0 \Rightarrow (x - 5)(x + 1) > 0$

For this expression to be > 0, both brackets must be positive or both brackets must be negative.

So either $x > 5$ and $x > -1$ or $x < 5$ and $x < -1$.

So the function is increasing when $x < -1$ and when $x > 5$.

Remember that you can use a different method, e.g. sketching the quadratic, to solve the inequality if you prefer.

b) $\frac{dy}{dx} = 3x^2 + 12x + 12$.

If the function is increasing, $\frac{dy}{dx} > 0$

$\Rightarrow 3x^2 + 12x + 12 > 0 \Rightarrow x^2 + 4x + 4 > 0$

$\Rightarrow (x + 2)(x + 2) > 0 \Rightarrow (x + 2)^2 > 0$

So x can be any real value except $x = -2$, which means that the function is increasing for all values of x except $x = -2$.

c) $y = x(x^2 - 4x - 16) = x^3 - 4x^2 - 16x$

$\frac{dy}{dx} = 3x^2 - 8x - 16$.

If the function is increasing, $\frac{dy}{dx} > 0$

$\Rightarrow 3x^2 - 8x - 16 > 0 \Rightarrow (3x + 4)(x - 4) > 0$

For this expression to be > 0, both brackets must be positive or both brackets must be negative.

So either $x > -\frac{4}{3}$ and $x > 4$ or $x < -\frac{4}{3}$ and $x < 4$.
So the function is increasing when $x < -\frac{4}{3}$ and when $x > 4$.

d) $y = \frac{x^3 + 3x^2 - 9x - 1}{9} = \frac{x^3}{9} - \frac{x^2}{3} - x - \frac{1}{9}$
$\frac{dy}{dx} = \frac{x^2}{3} - \frac{2x}{3} - 1$
If the function is increasing, $\frac{dy}{dx} > 0$
$\Rightarrow \frac{x^2}{3} - \frac{2x}{3} - 1 > 0 \Rightarrow x^2 - 2x - 3 > 0 \Rightarrow (x + 1)(x - 3) > 0$
For this expression to be > 0, both brackets must be positive or both brackets must be negative.
So either $x > -1$ and $x > 3$ or $x < -1$ and $x < 3$.
So the function is increasing when $x < -1$ and $x > 3$.

Q4 a) $f'(x) = 3x^2 - 6x - 9$. If the function is decreasing, $f'(x) < 0 \Rightarrow 3x^2 - 6x - 9 < 0 \Rightarrow x^2 - 2x - 3 < 0$
$\Rightarrow (x - 3)(x + 1) < 0$. For the expression to be < 0, one bracket must be positive and one negative.
So either $x < 3$ and $x > -1$ or $x > 3$ and $x < -1$.
The second situation is impossible, so $-1 < x < 3$.

b) $f'(x) = 3x^2 - 8x + 4$. If the function is decreasing, $f'(x) < 0 \Rightarrow 3x^2 - 8x + 4 < 0 \Rightarrow (3x - 2)(x - 2) < 0$.
For the expression to be < 0, either $x < \frac{2}{3}$ and $x > 2$ or $x > \frac{2}{3}$ and $x < 2$. The first situation is impossible, so $\frac{2}{3} < x < 2$.

c) $f'(x) = 9x^2 + 3x - 72$. If the function is decreasing, $f'(x) < 0$
$\Rightarrow 9x^2 + 3x - 72 < 0 \Rightarrow 3x^2 + x - 24 < 0$
$\Rightarrow (x + 3)(3x - 8) < 0$.
For the expression to be < 0, one bracket must be positive and one negative. So either $x > -3$ and $x < \frac{8}{3}$ or $x < -3$ and $x > \frac{8}{3}$. The second situation is impossible, so $-3 < x < \frac{8}{3}$.

d) $f(x) = \frac{2x^3 - x^2 - 8x + 3}{4} = \frac{1}{2}x^3 - \frac{1}{4}x^2 - 2x + \frac{3}{4}$
$f'(x) = \frac{3}{2}x^2 - \frac{1}{2}x - 2$. If the function is decreasing
$f'(x) < 0 \Rightarrow \frac{3}{2}x^2 - \frac{1}{2}x - 2 < 0 \Rightarrow 3x^2 - x - 4 < 0$
$\Rightarrow (3x - 4)(x + 1) < 0$. For the expression to be < 0, one bracket must be positive and one negative.
So either $x < \frac{4}{3}$ and $x > -1$ or $x > \frac{4}{3}$ and $x < -1$.
The second situation is impossible, so $-1 < x < \frac{4}{3}$.

Q5 $f'(x) = 3x^2 + 1$. x^2 can't be negative ($x^2 \geq 0$), so $f'(x)$ must always be positive and so $f(x)$ is an increasing function for all real values of x.

Q6 $f'(x) = -3 - 3x^2$. x^2 can't be negative ($x^2 \geq 0$), so $f'(x)$ is always ≤ -3 (so negative), so $f(x)$ is a decreasing function.

Q7 a) $\frac{dy}{dx} = 8x^3 + 1$. If the function is decreasing,
$\frac{dy}{dx} < 0 \Rightarrow 8x^3 + 1 < 0 \Rightarrow x^3 < -\frac{1}{8} \Rightarrow x < -\frac{1}{2}$

b) $\frac{dy}{dx} = 4x^3 - 36x$. If the function is decreasing,
$\frac{dy}{dx} < 0 \Rightarrow 4x^3 - 36x < 0 \Rightarrow 4x(x + 3)(x - 3) < 0$
For this to be true, there are 4 possibilities — all are less than zero, or one is less than zero and the other two are not:
Either $x < 0$ and $x < -3$ and $x < 3$, so $x < -3$
Remember, if x must be smaller than 0, −3 and 3, you can dismiss the two higher numbers and simplify it to x being smaller than −3.
Or $x < 0$ and $x > -3$ and $x > 3$ (impossible)
Or $x > 0$ and $x < -3$ and $x > 3$ (impossible)
Or $x > 0$ and $x > -3$ and $x < 3$
This gives ranges $x < -3$ and $0 < x < 3$.
You could also consider the graph of 4x(x + 3)(x − 3) and see where this takes negative values.

c) $\frac{dy}{dx} = 4x^3 - 6x^2 - 10x$. If the function is decreasing, $\frac{dy}{dx} < 0 \Rightarrow 4x^3 - 6x^2 - 10x < 0$
$\Rightarrow x(2x - 5)(x + 1) < 0$. For this to be true, there are 4 possibilities — all are less than zero, or one is less than zero and the other two are not:
Either $x < 0$ and $x < \frac{5}{2}$ and $x < -1$, so $x < -1$
Or $x < 0$ and $x > \frac{5}{2}$ and $x > -1$ (impossible)
Or $x > 0$ and $x < \frac{5}{2}$ and $x > -1$, so $0 < x < \frac{5}{2}$
Or $x > 0$ and $x > \frac{5}{2}$ and $x < -1$ (impossible)
This gives the ranges $x < -1$ and $0 < x < \frac{5}{2}$.

d) $\frac{dy}{dx} = 8x^3 + 4x^2 - 4x$. If the function is decreasing,
$\frac{dy}{dx} < 0 \Rightarrow 8x^3 + 4x^2 - 4x < 0 \Rightarrow 2x^3 + x^2 - x < 0$
$\Rightarrow x(2x - 1)(x + 1) < 0$
For this to be true, there are 4 possibilities — all are less than zero, or one is less than zero and the other two are not:
Either $x < 0$ and $x < \frac{1}{2}$ and $x < -1$, so $x < -1$
Or $x < 0$ and $x > \frac{1}{2}$ and $x > -1$ (impossible)
Or $x > 0$ and $x < \frac{1}{2}$ and $x > -1$
Or $x > 0$ and $x > \frac{1}{2}$ and $x < -1$ (impossible)
This gives the ranges $x < -1$ and $0 < x < \frac{1}{2}$.

Q8 a) $y = x^2 + \sqrt{x} = x^2 + x^{\frac{1}{2}} \Rightarrow \frac{dy}{dx} = 2x + \frac{1}{2\sqrt{x}}$
$\frac{dy}{dx} > 0$ for all $x > 0$, so the function is increasing for all $x > 0$.

b) $\frac{dy}{dx} = -x^{-2} + 16 = -\frac{1}{x^2} + 16$.
The function is increasing when $\frac{dy}{dx} > 0$
$\Rightarrow -\frac{1}{x^2} + 16 > 0 \Rightarrow x^2 > \frac{1}{16} \Rightarrow x > \frac{1}{4}$ and $x < -\frac{1}{4}$

c) $y = 4x^2 + \frac{1}{x} = 4x^2 + x^{-1} \Rightarrow \frac{dy}{dx} = 8x - \frac{1}{x^2}$
The function is increasing when $\frac{dy}{dx} > 0$
$\Rightarrow 8x - \frac{1}{x^2} > 0 \Rightarrow x^3 > \frac{1}{8} \Rightarrow x > \frac{1}{2}$

d) $y = -\frac{3x^{-2} + 18x}{2} = -\frac{3}{2}x^{-2} - 9x \Rightarrow \frac{dy}{dx} = \frac{3}{x^3} - 9$
The function is increasing when $\frac{dy}{dx} > 0$
$\Rightarrow \frac{3}{x^3} - 9 > 0 \Rightarrow \frac{1}{x^3} > 3$
When multiplying an inequality by a negative number, you need to flip the inequality sign — but here you don't know if x^3 is positive or negative. So consider the two cases:
If $x > 0$, then $x^3 > 0$, so $\frac{1}{x^3} > 3 \Rightarrow \frac{1}{3} > x^3 \Rightarrow x < \frac{1}{\sqrt[3]{3}}$
If $x < 0$, then $x^3 < 0$, so $\frac{1}{x^3} > 3 \Rightarrow \frac{1}{3} < x^3$
— but this is impossible since $x^3 < 0$ in this case.
So the function is only increasing when x is positive, i.e. for x in the interval $0 < x < \frac{1}{\sqrt[3]{3}}$.

Q9 If the function is decreasing, $\frac{dy}{dx} < 0$ for all x.
$\frac{dy}{dx} = -3 - 5ax^4 \Rightarrow -3 - 5ax^4 < 0 \Rightarrow ax^4 > -\frac{3}{5}$.
The right-hand side is negative, so as $x^4 \geq 0$, a must also be positive to make the LHS > RHS for all x. So $a > 0$.

Q10 If the function is increasing, $\frac{dy}{dx}$ will always be greater than 0.
$\frac{dy}{dx} = kx^{k-1} + 1 \Rightarrow kx^{k-1} + 1 > 0$.
When $k = 1$, $x^0 + 1 > 0$ — true for all x
When $k = 2$, $2x^1 + 1 > 0$ — not true for all x
When $k = 3$, $3x^2 + 1 > 0$ — true for all x
When $k = 4$, $4x^3 + 1 > 0$ — not true for all x, etc.
So k must be an odd number greater than zero.

Q11 a) Let $f(x) = x^3 + kx$. Then $f'(x) = 3x^2 + k$.
If $f(x)$ is increasing at $x = 3$, then $f'(3) > 0$
$\Rightarrow 27 + k > 0 \Rightarrow k > -27$
[3 marks available — 1 mark for the correct derivative, 1 mark for setting $f'(3) > 0$, 1 mark for the correct range of values for k]

b) Let $g(x) = 3 + mx - x^2$. Then $g'(x) = m - 2x$.
If $g(x)$ is decreasing at $x = 1$, then $g'(1) < 0$
$\Rightarrow m - 2 < 0 \Rightarrow m < 2$
[3 marks available — 1 mark for the correct derivative, 1 mark for setting $g'(1) < 0$, 1 mark for the correct range of values for m]

Q12 a) $\frac{dy}{dx} = 4x^3 + 12x^2 + 12x + 4$
[2 marks available — 1 mark for at least one correct term, 1 mark for the correct answer]

b) $\frac{d^2y}{dx^2} = 12x^2 + 24x + 12 = 12(x^2 + 2x + 1) = 12(x + 1)^2 > 0$
for all real values of x, except $x = -1$, when $\frac{d^2y}{dx^2} = 0$.
So $\frac{dy}{dx}$ is increasing everywhere apart from at $x = -1$.
[2 marks available — 1 mark for the correct derivative, 1 mark for a correct proof]

c) Since $\frac{dy}{dx}$ is increasing, no two different x-values can give the same gradient. *[1 mark]*

Q13 a) $y = x^{\frac{1}{2}} + 3x^{-\frac{3}{2}}$, so $\frac{dy}{dx} = \frac{1}{2}x^{-\frac{1}{2}} - \frac{9}{2}x^{-\frac{5}{2}}$
[3 marks available — 1 mark for rewriting y in terms of powers of x, 1 mark for each term correctly differentiated]

b) y is decreasing when $\frac{1}{2}x^{-\frac{1}{2}} - \frac{9}{2}x^{-\frac{5}{2}} < 0 \Rightarrow \frac{1}{2}x^2 - \frac{9}{2} < 0$
You can only multiply by $x^{\frac{5}{2}}$ because you know that $x < 0$.
$\Rightarrow x^2 - 9 < 0 \Rightarrow (x + 3)(x - 3) < 0 \Rightarrow -3 < x < 3$.
But $x > 0$, so y is decreasing for $0 < x < 3$.
[3 marks available — 1 mark for setting $\frac{dy}{dx} < 0$, 1 mark for a correct method to solve the quadratic inequality, 1 mark for the correct answer]

Exercise 10.10 — Curve Sketching

Q1 a) When $x = 0$, $y = 0^3 - 2(0)^2 = 0$, so the curve crosses the axes at (0, 0). When $y = 0$, $x^3 - 2x^2 = 0$
$\Rightarrow x^2(x - 2) = 0 \Rightarrow x = 0$ and $x = 2$.
So the curve also crosses the axes at (2, 0).
You already knew it crossed the x-axis at x = 0, so you can ignore that one.

b) $\frac{dy}{dx} = 3x^2 - 4x$. When $\frac{dy}{dx} = 0$, $3x^2 - 4x = 0$
$\Rightarrow x(3x - 4) = 0 \Rightarrow x = 0$ and $x = \frac{4}{3}$.
When $x = \frac{4}{3}$, $y = (\frac{4}{3})^3 - 2(\frac{4}{3})^2 = -\frac{32}{27}$.
So the coordinates are (0, 0) and $(\frac{4}{3}, -\frac{32}{27})$.

c) $\frac{d^2y}{dx^2} = 6x - 4$.
At $x = 0$, $\frac{d^2y}{dx^2} = -4$, so it's a maximum.
At $x = \frac{4}{3}$, $\frac{d^2y}{dx^2} = 4$, so it's a minimum.

d) A positive cubic goes from bottom left to top right:

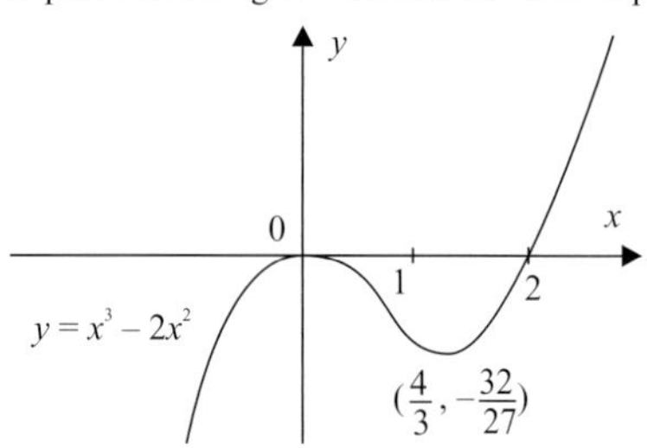

Q2 a) $x^3 + x^2 = 0 \Rightarrow x^2(x + 1) = 0 \Rightarrow x = 0$ or $x = -1$.

b) $f'(x) = 3x^2 + 2x$. When $f'(x) = 0$, $3x^2 + 2x = 0$
$\Rightarrow x(3x + 2) = 0 \Rightarrow x = 0$ and $x = -\frac{2}{3}$.
When $x = 0$, $y = 0$. When $x = -\frac{2}{3}$, $y = \frac{4}{27}$,
so the stationary points are at (0, 0) and $\left(-\frac{2}{3}, \frac{4}{27}\right)$.
$f''(x) = 6x + 2$. At (0, 0), $f''(x) = 2$, so it's a minimum.
At $(-\frac{2}{3}, \frac{4}{27})$, $f''(x) = -2$, so it's a maximum.

c)

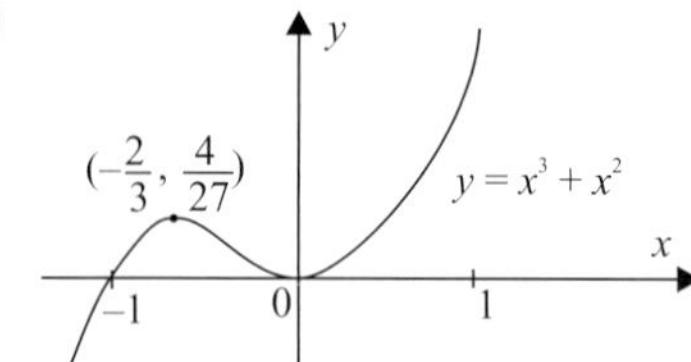

It's a positive cubic, so it goes from bottom left to top right.

Q3 a) $f'(x) = 4x^3 - 3x^2$, $f''(x) = 12x^2 - 6x$.

b) $f(x)$ is increasing for $f'(x) > 0 \Rightarrow 4x^3 - 3x^2 > 0$
$\Rightarrow x^2(4x - 3) > 0$, so either:
$x^2 > 0$ and $x > \frac{3}{4}$ ($\Rightarrow x > \frac{3}{4}$), or
$x^2 < 0$ and $x < \frac{3}{4}$ (x^2 can't be less than 0, so this situation is impossible)
So it's increasing when $x > \frac{3}{4}$.
$f(x)$ is decreasing for $f'(x) < 0 \Rightarrow 4x^3 - 3x^2 < 0$
$\Rightarrow x^2(4x - 3) < 0$, so either:
$x^2 < 0$ and $x > \frac{3}{4}$ (x^2 can't be less than 0, so this situation is impossible), or
$x^2 > 0$ and $x < \frac{3}{4}$
So it's decreasing when $x < \frac{3}{4}$, $x \neq 0$.

c) When $x = 0$, $f(x) = 0$. When $f(x) = 0$, $x^4 - x^3 = 0$
$\Rightarrow x^3(x - 1) = 0$, so $x = 0$ or $x = 1$.
So the curve crosses the axes at (0, 0) and (1, 0).
Stationary points occur when $f'(x) = 0$.
$f'(x) = 4x^3 - 3x^2 = 0 \Rightarrow x^2(4x - 3) = 0$, so $x = 0$ or $x = \frac{3}{4}$. When $x = 0$, $y = 0$ and when $x = \frac{3}{4}$, $y = -\frac{27}{256} = -0.11$ (2 d.p.).

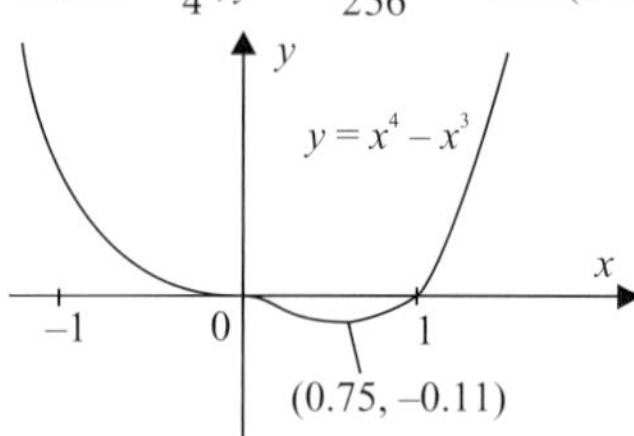

f'(0) = 0 so we cannot say whether the point (0, 0) is a maximum or a minimum — but the function is decreasing for x < 0.75 so (0, 0) must be a point of inflection.

Q4 a) When $x = 0$, $y = 0$. When $y = 0$, $3x^3 + 3x^2 = 0$
$\Rightarrow 3x^2(x + 1) = 0$, so $x = 0$ and -1.
When $\frac{dy}{dx} = 0$, $9x^2 + 6x = 0 \Rightarrow 3x(3x + 2) = 0$
so $x = 0$ and $x = -\frac{2}{3}$. When $x = -\frac{2}{3}$, $y = \frac{4}{9}$.
$\frac{d^2y}{dx^2} = 18x + 6$.
When $x = 0$, $\frac{d^2y}{dx^2} = 6$, so it's a minimum.
When $x = -\frac{2}{3}$, $\frac{d^2y}{dx^2} = -6$, so it's a maximum.

It's a positive cubic, so it'll go from bottom left to top right.

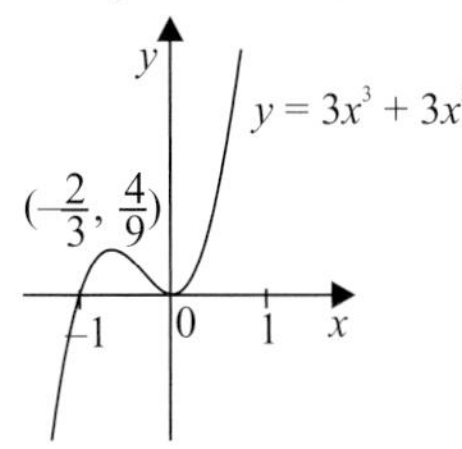

b) When $x = 0$, $y = 0$. When $y = 0$, $-x^3 + 9x = 0$
$\Rightarrow x(9 - x^2) = 0$, so $x = 0$ and $x = \pm 3$.
When $\frac{dy}{dx} = 0$, $-3x^2 + 9 = 0 \Rightarrow x = \pm\sqrt{3}$.
When $x = \sqrt{3}$, $y = 6\sqrt{3}$
and when $x = -\sqrt{3}$, $y = -6\sqrt{3}$, $\frac{d^2y}{dx^2} = -6x$.
When $x = \sqrt{3}$, $\frac{d^2y}{dx^2} = -6\sqrt{3}$, so it's a maximum.
When $x = -\sqrt{3}$, $\frac{d^2y}{dx^2} = 6\sqrt{3}$, so it's a minimum.
It's a negative cubic, so it'll go from top left to bottom right.

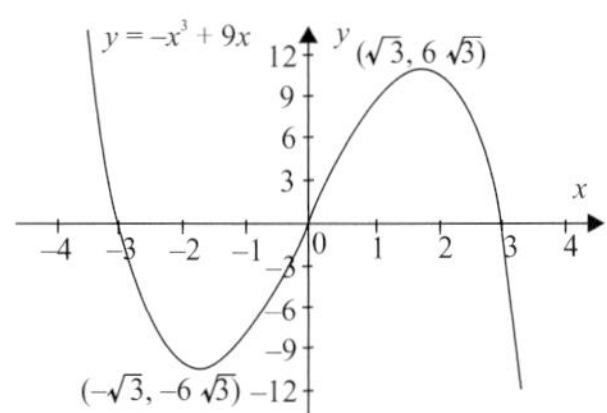

c) When $x = 0$, $y = 0$. When $y = 0$, $x^4 - x^2 = 0$
$\Rightarrow x^2(x^2 - 1) = 0$, so $x = 0$ and ± 1.
When $\frac{dy}{dx} = 0$, $4x^3 - 2x = 0 \Rightarrow x(2x^2 - 1) = 0$.
So $x = 0$ and $\pm\frac{1}{\sqrt{2}}$.
When $x = \frac{1}{\sqrt{2}}$, $y = -\frac{1}{4}$ and
when $x = -\frac{1}{\sqrt{2}}$, $y = -\frac{1}{4}$, $\frac{d^2y}{dx^2} = 12x^2 - 2$.
When $x = 0$, $\frac{d^2y}{dx^2} = -2$, so it's a maximum.
When $x = \frac{1}{\sqrt{2}}$, $\frac{d^2y}{dx^2} = 4$, so it's a minimum.
When $x = -\frac{1}{\sqrt{2}}$, $\frac{d^2y}{dx^2} = 4$, so it's a minimum.

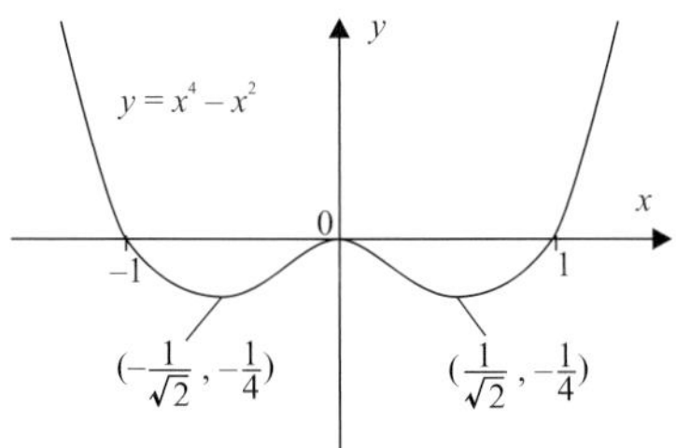

d) When $x = 0$, $y = 0$. When $y = 0$, $x^4 + x^2 = 0$
$\Rightarrow x^2(x^2 + 1) = 0$, so $x = 0$ ($x^2 = -1$ has no solutions).
When $\frac{dy}{dx} = 0$, $4x^3 + 2x = 0$
$\Rightarrow x(2x^2 + 1) = 0$, so $x = 0$.
$\frac{d^2y}{dx^2} = 12x^2 + 2$.
When $x = 0$, $\frac{d^2y}{dx^2} = 2$, so it's a minimum.

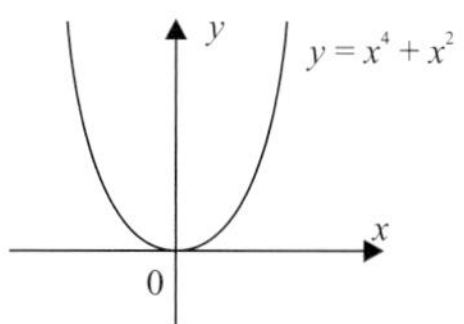

Q5 When $x = 0$, $y = 1$.
When $y = 0$, $(x + 1)(x - 1)^2 = 0$, so $x = 1$ and -1.
When $\frac{dy}{dx} = 0$, $3x^2 - 2x - 1 = 0 \Rightarrow (3x + 1)(x - 1) = 0$
so $x = 1$ and $-\frac{1}{3}$.
When $x = 1$, $y = 0$ and when $x = -\frac{1}{3}$, $y = \frac{32}{27}$.
$\frac{d^2y}{dx^2} = 6x - 2$.
When $x = 1$, $\frac{d^2y}{dx^2} = 4$, so it's a minimum.
When $x = -\frac{1}{3}$, $\frac{d^2y}{dx^2} = -4$, so it's a maximum.
It's a positive cubic, so it'll go from bottom left to top right.

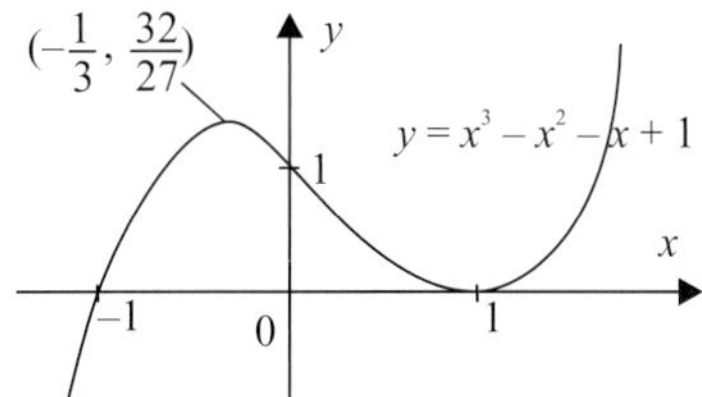

Q6 a) When $x = 2$, $x^3 - 4x = 8 - 8 = 0$.
When $x = -2$, $x^3 - 4x = -8 - (-8) = 0$
When $x = 0$, $x^3 - 4x = 0 - 0 = 0$.

b) $\frac{dy}{dx} = 3x^2 - 4$, $\frac{d^2y}{dx^2} = 6x$.
When $\frac{dy}{dx} = 0$, $3x^2 - 4 = 0 \Rightarrow x = \pm\frac{2\sqrt{3}}{3}$
$= \pm 1.2$ (to 1 d.p.)
When $x = \frac{2\sqrt{3}}{3}$, $y = -3.1$ (1 d.p.)
and when $x = -\frac{2\sqrt{3}}{3}$, $y = 3.1$ (1 d.p.).
So the coordinates of the stationary points to 1 d.p. are (1.2, –3.1) and (–1.2, 3.1).
At $(\frac{2\sqrt{3}}{3}, -3.1)$, $\frac{d^2y}{dx^2} = 6 \times \frac{2\sqrt{3}}{3} = 4\sqrt{3}$,
so it's a minimum.
At $(-\frac{2\sqrt{3}}{3}, 3.1)$, $\frac{d^2y}{dx^2} = 6 \times -\frac{2\sqrt{3}}{3} = -4\sqrt{3}$,
so it's a maximum.

c)

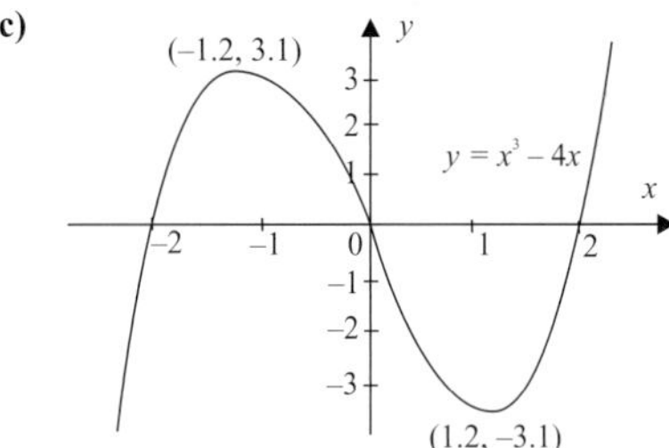

Q7 a) $f'(x) = 1 - \frac{1}{x^2}$. When $f'(x) = 0$, $1 - \frac{1}{x^2} = 0$
$\Rightarrow x^2 = 1 \Rightarrow x = \pm 1$. So the graph of $f(x) = x + \frac{1}{x}$ has stationary points at $x = 1$ and $x = -1$.

b) When $x = 1$, $y = 1 + 1 = 2$, and when $x = -1$,
$y = -1 - 1 = -2$. So the coordinates are (1, 2) and (–1, –2).
$f''(x) = \frac{2}{x^3}$. At (1, 2), $f''(x) = 2$, so it's a minimum.
At (–1, –2), $f''(x) = -2$, so it's a maximum.

c) $f(x) = x + \frac{1}{x}$.
As x tends to 0 from below (x is negative), $f(x)$ tends to $-\infty$.
As $x \to 0$ from above (x is positive), $f(x) \to \infty$.

d) As x tends to ∞, $f(x)$ tends to x
i.e. the graph tends towards the line $y = x$.
As x tends to $-\infty$, $f(x)$ tends to x
i.e. the graph tends towards the line $y = x$.

e)

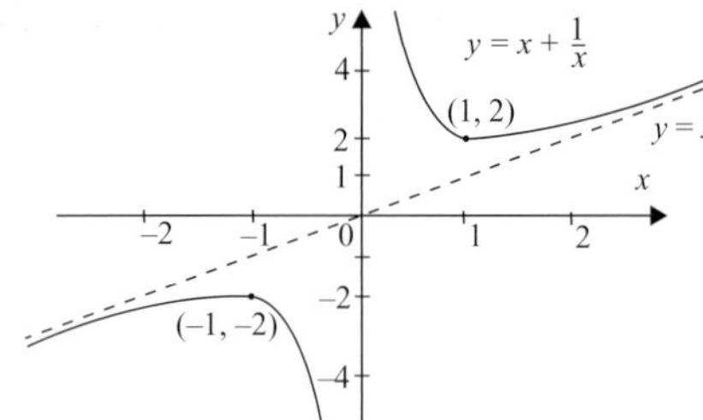

Q8 **a)** $\frac{dy}{dx} = 4x^3 - \frac{4}{\sqrt{x^3}}$. When $x = 1$, $\frac{dy}{dx} = 4 - 4 = 0$.

b) When $x = 1$, $y = 9$
As $x \to 0$, $y \to \infty$ and as $x \to \infty$, $y \to x^4$.
When $y = 0$, $x^4 + \frac{8}{\sqrt{x}} = 0 \Rightarrow \sqrt{x^9} = -8$. This has no solutions, so the curve doesn't cross the x-axis.
$\frac{d^2y}{dx^2} = 12x^2 + \frac{6}{\sqrt{x^5}}$. When $x = 1$, $\frac{d^2y}{dx^2} = 18$, so it's a minimum.

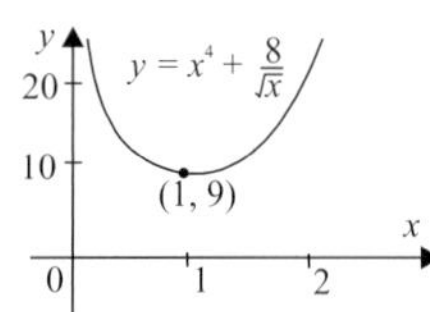

Q9 **a)** $\frac{dy}{dx} = 3x^2 + 4x$
$\frac{dy}{dx} = 0 \Rightarrow x(3x + 4) = 0 \Rightarrow x = 0$ or $x = -\frac{4}{3}$
When $x = 0$, $y = 1$. When $x = -\frac{4}{3}$, $y = \frac{59}{27}$.
So the stationary points are at (0, 1) and $\left(-\frac{4}{3}, \frac{59}{27}\right)$.
$\frac{d^2y}{dx^2} = 6x + 4$
When $x = 0$, $\frac{d^2y}{dx^2} = 4 > 0$ so (0, 1) is a minimum.
When $x = -\frac{4}{3}$, $\frac{d^2y}{dx^2} = -4 < 0$ so $\left(-\frac{4}{3}, \frac{59}{27}\right)$ is a maximum.

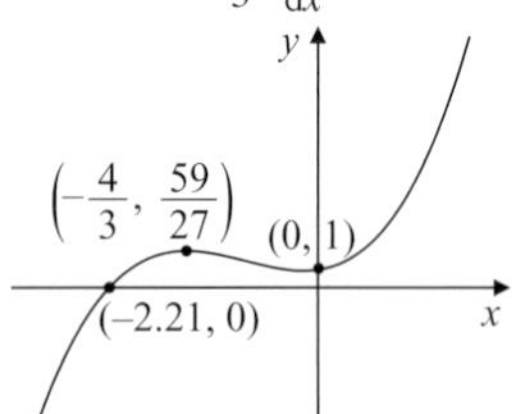

[8 marks available — 1 mark for the correct derivative, 1 mark for a correct method to find the stationary points, 1 mark for the correct coordinates of the stationary points, 1 mark for a correct method to determine the nature of the stationary points, 1 mark for the correct nature of each stationary point, 1 mark for the correct shape with only one x-intercept, 1 mark for a completely correct sketch]

b) $y = f'(x) = x(3x + 4)$, so it crosses the x-axis at $x = 0$ and $-\frac{4}{3}$, and the y-axis at $y = 0$. The minimum point occurs when $\frac{d^2y}{dx^2} = 6x + 4 = 0 \Rightarrow x = -\frac{2}{3}$, $y = -\frac{4}{3}$.

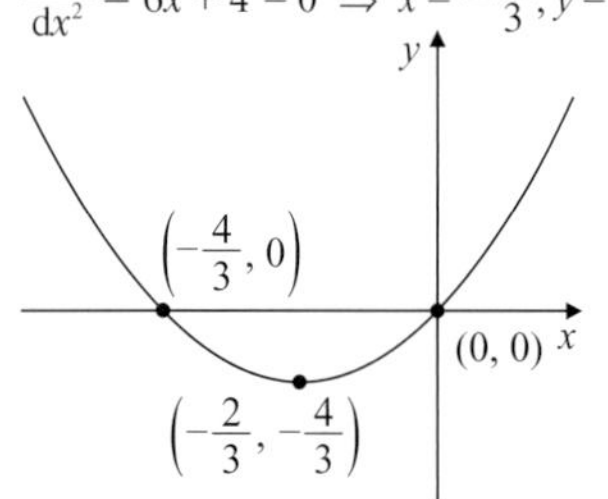

[4 marks available — 1 mark for correct intercepts, 1 mark for a correct method to find the minimum point, 1 mark for the correct coordinates of the minimum point, 1 mark for a fully correct sketch]

Q10 **a)** $y = (x - 1)(x - 2)(x + 3) = (x^2 - 3x + 2)(x + 3)$
$= x^3 - 3x^2 + 2x + 3x^2 - 9x + 6 = x^3 - 7x + 6$
So $\frac{dy}{dx} = 3x^2 - 7$. At the stationary points, $\frac{dy}{dx} = 0$
$\Rightarrow 3x^2 = 7 \Rightarrow x^2 = \frac{7}{3} \Rightarrow x = \pm\sqrt{\frac{7}{3}} \Rightarrow x = \pm 1.527...$
When $x = \sqrt{\frac{7}{3}}$, $y = \left(\sqrt{\frac{7}{3}} - 1\right)\left(\sqrt{\frac{7}{3}} - 2\right)\left(\sqrt{\frac{7}{3}} + 3\right)$
$= -1.128...$
When $x = -\sqrt{\frac{7}{3}}$, $y = \left(-\sqrt{\frac{7}{3}} - 1\right)\left(-\sqrt{\frac{7}{3}} - 2\right)\left(-\sqrt{\frac{7}{3}} + 3\right)$
$= 13.128...$
So the coordinates of the stationary points are (–1.53, 13.1) and (1.53, –1.13) to 3 s.f.
[4 marks available — 1 mark for expanding and simplifying the equation, 1 mark for the correct derivative, 1 mark for the correct x-values at the stationary points, 1 mark for the correct coordinates]

b)

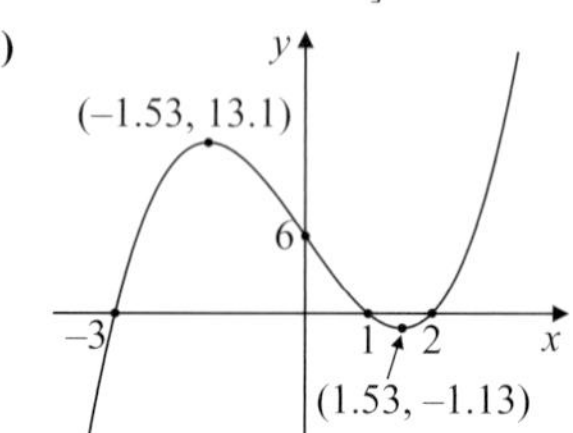

[3 marks available — 1 mark for the correct shape including the stationary points in the correct locations, 1 mark for the correct x-intercepts, 1 mark for the correct y-intercept]

c) When $x = -3$, $\frac{dy}{dx} = 3(-3)^2 - 7 = 20$,
so find the other x-value where $\frac{dy}{dx} = 20$:
$3x^2 - 7 = 20 \Rightarrow 3x^2 = 27 \Rightarrow x^2 = 9 \Rightarrow x = \pm 3$.
When $x = 3$, $y = 2 \times 1 \times 6 = 12$, so the equation is:
$y - y_1 = m(x - x_1) \Rightarrow y - 12 = 20(x - 3) \Rightarrow y = 20x - 48$
[5 marks available — 1 mark for the correct gradient at (–3, 0), 1 mark for a correct method to find the other x-value with the same gradient, 1 mark for the correct x-value, 1 mark for the corresponding y-value, 1 mark for the correct equation]

Exercise 10.11 — Speed and Acceleration Problems

Q1 **a)** $\frac{dx}{dt} = 6t - 7$

b) **(i)** $t = 2 \Rightarrow \frac{dx}{dt} = 12 - 7 = 5$ ms^{-1}

(ii) $t = 5 \Rightarrow \frac{dx}{dt} = 30 - 7 = 23$ ms^{-1}

c) If $\frac{dx}{dt} = 17 \Rightarrow 6t - 7 = 17 \Rightarrow 6t = 24 \Rightarrow t = 4$ s.

d) $\frac{d^2x}{dt^2} = 6$ ms^{-2}
Although you were asked for $\frac{d^2x}{dt^2}$ as a function of t, it happens to be constant in this example.

Q2 **a)** $\frac{dx}{dt} = 6t^2 - 8t$

b) If $\frac{dx}{dt} = 30$ then $6t^2 - 8t = 30 \Rightarrow 6t^2 - 8t - 30 = 0$
$\Rightarrow 3t^2 - 4t - 15 = 0 \Rightarrow (3t + 5)(t - 3) = 0$
$\Rightarrow t = 3$ or $t = -\frac{5}{3}$. But $t > 0$ so $t = 3$.
If $t = 3$, $x = 2t^3 - 4t^2 = 18$.
So $t = 3$ s and $x = 18$ m.

c) $\frac{d^2x}{dt^2} = 12t - 8$.

d) $t = 5 \Rightarrow \frac{d^2x}{dt^2} = 52$ ms^{-2}

e) If $\frac{d^2x}{dt^2} = 16 \Rightarrow 12t - 8 = 16 \Rightarrow 12t = 24 \Rightarrow t = 2$.
$\frac{dx}{dt} = 6t^2 - 8t = 8$ ms^{-1}.

Q3 **a)** $\frac{dx}{dt} = \frac{t}{2}$ ms^{-1}

b) $\frac{d^2x}{dt^2} = \frac{1}{2}$ ms^{-2}

c) $t = 45 \Rightarrow \frac{dx}{dt} = \frac{45}{2} = 22.5$ ms^{-1}

d) $\frac{dx}{dt} = 25$ ms^{-1} $\Rightarrow \frac{t}{2} = 25 \Rightarrow t = 50$ seconds

$\Rightarrow x = \frac{50^2}{4} = 625$ m

Q4 **a) & b)**

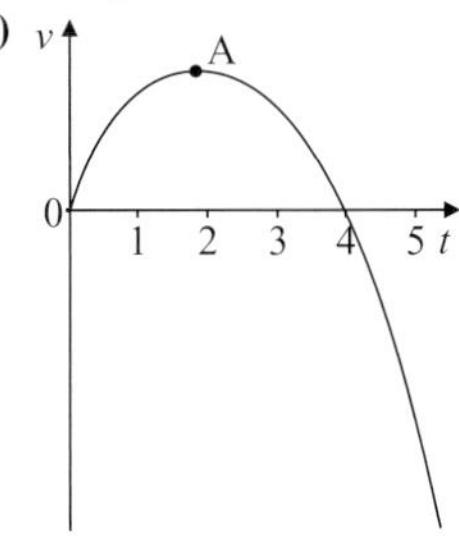

[4 marks available in total — 1 mark for the correct shape, 1 mark for the correct t-intercept, 1 mark for negative v at t = 5, 1 mark for A in the correct position]

The acceleration is zero when the gradient of the velocity-time graph is zero.

Q5 **a)** When $t = 1$, $v = 5t + 2 \Rightarrow \frac{dv}{dt} = 5$ ms^{-2} *[1 mark]*

b) When $t = 3$, $v = \frac{5}{4}t^2 + 7 \Rightarrow \frac{dv}{dt} = \frac{5}{2}t = \frac{5}{2} \times 3 = 7.5$ ms^{-2}

[2 marks available — 1 mark for the correct derivative, 1 mark for the correct answer]

Q6 **a)** $x = \frac{1}{4}t^3(t^2 - 8t + 16) = \frac{1}{4}t^5 - 2t^4 + 4t^3$

$\Rightarrow v = \frac{dx}{dt} = \frac{5}{4}t^4 - 8t^3 + 12t^2$

[4 marks available — 1 mark for the correct expansion of $(t-4)^2$, 1 mark for the correct expanded expression for x, 1 mark for an attempt at differentiating, 1 mark for the correct answer]

b) $a = \frac{d^2x}{dt^2} = 5t^3 - 24t^2 + 24t$

[2 marks available — 1 mark for an attempt at differentiating, 1 mark for the correct answer]

c) Find x when $\frac{dx}{dt} = 0$: $\frac{dx}{dt} = \frac{5}{4}t^4 - 8t^3 + 12t^2$

$\Rightarrow \frac{5}{4}t^4 - 8t^3 + 12t^2 = \frac{1}{4}t^2(5t^2 - 32t + 48)$

$= \frac{1}{4}t^2(5t - 12)(t - 4) = 0$

$\Rightarrow t = 0, t = \frac{12}{5}$ or $t = 4$

When $t = 0$ and $t = 4$, $x = 0$.

When $t = \frac{12}{5}$, $x = \frac{1}{4}\left(\frac{12}{5}\right)^3\left(\frac{12}{5} - 4\right)^2 = 8.847...$

So the greatest distance the car reaches from its starting position is 8.85 m (3 s.f.)

[4 marks available — 1 mark for setting the derivative equal to zero, 1 mark for attempting to solve this equation, 1 mark for finding t, 1 mark for the correct answer]

Exercise 10.12 — Length, Area and Volume Problems

Q1 Total length of fence for a rectangular area of length x m and width y m $= 2x + 2y$.

Total area $= 100 = xy \Rightarrow y = \frac{100}{x}$

Sub this into equation for length: $f(x) = 2x + \frac{200}{x}$

You want to minimise the length, so find $f'(x)$:

$f'(x) = 2 - \frac{200}{x^2}$. When $f'(x) = 0$, $2 - \frac{200}{x^2} = 0$

$\Rightarrow x^2 = 100 \Rightarrow x = 10$ (length can't be negative).

Check to see if this gives a minimum value by differentiating again:

$f''(x) = \frac{400}{x^3} \Rightarrow f''(10) = 0.4$, so it's a minimum.

Now find the value of y when $x = 10$:

$100 = xy \Rightarrow y = 10$.

Finally, length $= 2x + 2y = 20 + 20 = 40$ m.

Q2 Let the length of fence parallel to the wall be x and the lengths perpendicular to the wall be y.

We want to maximise area, i.e. $A = xy$.

Total length of fence $= 66 = x + 2y \Rightarrow y = \frac{66 - x}{2}$

So we want to maximise $A = x\left(\frac{66 - x}{2}\right) = 33x - \frac{x^2}{2}$.

$\frac{dA}{dx} = 33 - x$, so when $\frac{dA}{dx} = 0$, $x = 33$.

Check that this gives a maximum value by differentiating again:

$\frac{d^2A}{dx^2} = -1$, so it's a maximum.

When $x = 33$, $y = \frac{66 - 33}{2} = 16.5$.

Area $= 33 \times 16.5 = 544.5$ m^2.

If you'd labelled the sides the other way round, your working would be different but you'd still get the same answer.

Q3 **a)** Surface area = area of top and bottom plus area of curved face $= \pi r^2 + \pi r^2 + (2\pi r \times h) = 2\pi r^2 + 2\pi rh$.

To match the question, find an expression for h by thinking about the volume of the tin:

Volume = area of base × height $= \pi r^2 h = 500$

$\Rightarrow h = \frac{500}{\pi r^2}$. So surface area $= 2\pi r^2 + 2\pi r\frac{500}{\pi r^2}$

$= 2\pi r^2 + \frac{1000}{r}$.

b) $\frac{dA}{dr} = 4\pi r - \frac{1000}{r^2}$. When $\frac{dA}{dr} = 0$,

$4\pi r - \frac{1000}{r^2} = 0 \Rightarrow r = \sqrt[3]{\frac{250}{\pi}} = 4.30$ cm (3 s.f.).

Check that this gives a minimum value:

$\frac{d^2A}{dr^2} = 4\pi + \frac{2000}{r^3}$.

When $r = 4.30$, $\frac{d^2A}{dr^2} = 37.7$, so it's a minimum.

You don't really need to work out $\frac{d^2A}{dr^2}$ when $r = 4.30$ — you can tell it's positive straight away.

c) Surface area $= 2\pi r^2 + \frac{1000}{r} = 349$ cm^2 (3 s.f.).

Q4 **a)** Volume of the box = length × width × height

$= (40 - 2x) \times (40 - 2x) \times x = 4x^3 - 160x^2 + 1600x$

b) $\frac{dV}{dx} = 12x^2 - 320x + 1600$. When $\frac{dV}{dx} = 0$,

$12x^2 - 320x + 1600 = 0 \Rightarrow 3x^2 - 80x + 400 = 0$

$\Rightarrow (3x - 20)(x - 20) = 0 \Rightarrow x = 20$ or $x = \frac{20}{3}$.

Differentiate again to find which of these is a maximum:

$\frac{d^2V}{dx^2} = 24x - 320$. When $x = 20$,

$\frac{d^2V}{dx^2} = 160$, and when $x = \frac{20}{3}$, $\frac{d^2V}{dx^2} = -160$,

so V is a maximum when $x = \frac{20}{3}$.

Note that if x = 20, the volume of the box V = 0, so this can't be the maximum of V — it's always worth checking that answers are sensible in the context of the question.

So the maximum volume is:

$4\left(\frac{20}{3}\right)^3 - 160\left(\frac{20}{3}\right)^2 + 1600\left(\frac{20}{3}\right) = 4740$ cm^3 (3 s.f.)

Q5 **a)** The prism is made up of 5 shapes:

2 triangles with base x and height x (area $= \frac{1}{2}x^2$),

2 rectangles with width x and length l (area $= xl$) and 1 rectangle with width h and length l (area $= hl$).

So the total surface area is given by:

$A = x^2 + 2xl + hl$. To get rid of the l, find an expression for l by looking at the volume:

$300 = \frac{1}{2}x^2 l \Rightarrow l = \frac{600}{x^2}$

To get rid of the h, form an expression for it in terms of x. It's the hypotenuse of a right-angled triangle, so $h^2 = x^2 + x^2$

$\Rightarrow h = \sqrt{2x^2} = \sqrt{2}x$.

Now put these into the original formula for A:

$A = x^2 + 2x(\frac{600}{x^2}) + \sqrt{2}x(\frac{600}{x^2}) = x^2 + \frac{600(2 + \sqrt{2})}{x}$

b) $\frac{dA}{dx} = 2x - \frac{600(2+\sqrt{2})}{x^2}$. When $\frac{dA}{dx} = 0$,

$2x - \frac{600(2+\sqrt{2})}{x^2} = 0 \Rightarrow x^3 = 300(2+\sqrt{2})$

$\Rightarrow x = \sqrt[3]{600+300\sqrt{2}}$

Check that this gives a minimum value:

$\frac{d^2A}{dx^2} = 2 + \frac{1200(2+\sqrt{2})}{x^3}$.

When $x = \sqrt[3]{600+300\sqrt{2}}$, $\frac{d^2A}{dx^2} = 6$, so it's a minimum.

You don't really need to work out $\frac{d^2A}{dr^2}$ when $x = \sqrt[3]{600+300\sqrt{2}}$ — you can see it's positive.

Q6 a) There are 6 rectangular sides of the box which make up 3 identical pairs of sides. These sides have areas of xy, $2x^2$ and $2xy$, so the total surface area is:

$A = 2(xy + 2x^2 + 2xy) = 4x^2 + 6xy$

To get rid of y, rearrange the formula for the volume of the box: $V = x \times y \times 2x = 2x^2y$

$\Rightarrow 200 = 2x^2y \Rightarrow y = \frac{100}{x^2}$

so $A = 4x^2 + 6x\left(\frac{100}{x^2}\right) = 4x^2 + \frac{600}{x}$

b) $A = 4x^2 + 600x^{-1} \Rightarrow \frac{dA}{dx} = 8x - 600x^{-2} = 8x - \frac{600}{x^2}$

When $\frac{dA}{dx} = 0$, $8x - \frac{600}{x^2} = 0 \Rightarrow x^3 = 75$

$\Rightarrow x = 4.217...$

$= 4.22$ cm (3 s.f.)

Check that this gives a minimum value:

$\frac{d^2A}{dx^2} = 8 + 1200x^{-3}$.

When $x = 4.217...$, $\frac{d^2A}{dx^2} = 24$, so it's a minimum.

c) $x = 4.21...$ cm $\Rightarrow A = 4(4.217...)^2 + 600(4.217...)^{-1}$

$= 213.4... = 213$ cm^2 (3 s.f.)

Q7 a) The area of the vertical cross-section is $\frac{x}{2}(y + 3y) = 2xy$.

Area $= 20 \Rightarrow 2xy = 20 \Rightarrow y = \frac{10}{x}$.

So the volume is $20\left(x + \frac{10}{x}\right) = 20x + \frac{200}{x}$.

[4 marks available — 1 mark for a correct expression for the cross-sectional area, 1 mark for writing y in terms of x, 1 mark for an attempt to find the volume, 1 mark for showing the correct result]

b) $V = 20x + 200x^{-1} \Rightarrow \frac{dV}{dx} = 20 - 200x^{-2} = 20 - \frac{200}{x^2}$

The volume is minimised when $\frac{dV}{dx} = 0$

$\Rightarrow 20 - \frac{200}{x^2} = 0 \Rightarrow 20 = \frac{200}{x^2}$

$\Rightarrow 20x^2 = 200 \Rightarrow x^2 = 10 \Rightarrow x = \sqrt{10}$ (as $x > 0$).

$\frac{dV}{dx} = 20 - 200x^{-2} \Rightarrow \frac{d^2V}{dx^2} = 400x^{-3} = \frac{400}{x^3}$,

so when $x = \sqrt{10}$, $\frac{d^2V}{dx^2} = \frac{400}{(\sqrt{10})^3} = 4\sqrt{10} > 0$,

so the volume is minimised when $x = \sqrt{10}$.

[7 marks available — 1 mark for the correct derivative, 1 mark for setting the derivative equal to zero, 1 mark for attempting to solve this equation, 1 mark for the correct x-value, 1 mark for the correct second derivative, 1 mark for substituting in the calculated x-value, 1 mark for the correct conclusion]

c) Substituting in $x = \sqrt{10}$:

$V = 20\sqrt{10} + \frac{200}{\sqrt{10}} = 40\sqrt{10} = 126$ cm^3 (3 s.f.) *[1 mark]*

Q8 a) $A = 2(3x^2 + x(40 - 2x) + 3x(40 - 2x))$

$= 6x^2 + 80x - 4x^2 + 240x - 12x^2$

$= 320x - 10x^2$

[3 marks available — 1 mark for a correct method to find the surface area, 1 mark for correctly expanding the brackets, 1 mark for the correct simplified answer]

b) $\frac{dA}{dx} = 320 - 20x = 0 \Rightarrow 20x = 320 \Rightarrow x = \frac{320}{20} = 16$ cm

So the maximum surface area is:

$A = 320(16) - 10(16)^2 = 2560$ cm^2

[3 marks available — 1 mark for the correct derivative, 1 mark for the correct x-value, 1 mark for the correct area]

c) (i) The different parts of the box have different costs, e.g. a value of x that increases the size of the top and base could make the box more expensive. *[1 mark]*

(ii) The cost of the box, C, in pounds is:

$C = 0.75(6x^2) + 0.5(2x(40 - 2x) + 6x(40 - 2x))$

$= \frac{9}{2}x^2 + 4x(40 - 2x) = \frac{9}{2}x^2 + 160x - 8x^2$

$= 160x - \frac{7}{2}x^2$

So $\frac{dC}{dx} = 160 - 7x$. C is maximised when $\frac{dC}{dx} = 0 \Rightarrow 160 - 7x = 0 \Rightarrow x = \frac{160}{7}$.

So the maximum cost is:

$160\left(\frac{160}{7}\right) - \frac{7}{2}\left(\frac{160}{7}\right)^2 = £1829$ to the nearest £1.

[5 marks available — 1 mark for a correct method to find an expression for the cost, 1 mark for the correct simplified expression for the cost, 1 mark for the correct derivative, 1 mark for the correct x-value, 1 mark for the correct answer]

d) E.g. the model doesn't take into account the thickness of the material, which is likely to affect the cost / the surface area might be different due to imperfections in the material / there might be labour costs, which the model doesn't take into account / etc. *[1 mark for a suitable suggestion]*

Chapter 10 Review Exercise

Q1 a) $\frac{dy}{dx} = \lim_{h\to 0}\left[\frac{(x+h)+1-(x+1)}{(x+h)-x}\right]$

$= \lim_{h\to 0}\left[\frac{h}{h}\right] = 1$

b) $\frac{dy}{dx} = \lim_{h\to 0}\left[\frac{4(x+h)^2 - 4x^2}{(x+h)-x}\right]$

$= \lim_{h\to 0}\left[\frac{4x^2 + 8xh + 4h^2 - 4x^2}{(x+h)-x}\right]$

$= \lim_{h\to 0}\left[\frac{8xh + 4h^2}{h}\right] = \lim_{h\to 0}[8x + 4h] = 8x$

c) $\frac{dy}{dx} = \lim_{h\to 0}\left[\frac{3-(x+h)^3-(3-x^3)}{(x+h)-x}\right]$

$= \lim_{h\to 0}\left[\frac{3 - x^3 - 3x^2h - 3xh^2 - h^3 - 3 + x^3}{(x+h)-x}\right]$

$= \lim_{h\to 0}\left[\frac{-3x^2h - 3xh^2 - h^3}{h}\right]$

$= \lim_{h\to 0}[-3x^2 - 3xh - h^2] = -3x^2$

Q2 Using $\frac{dy}{dx} = \lim_{h\to 0}\left[\frac{f(x+h)-f(x)}{(x+h)-x}\right]$:

$\frac{dy}{dx} = \lim_{h\to 0}\left[\frac{(x+h)^3 + 4(x+h) - (x^3 + 4x)}{(x+h)-x}\right]$

$= \lim_{h\to 0}\left[\frac{x^3 + 3x^2h + 3xh^2 + h^3 + 4x + 4h - x^3 - 4x}{h}\right]$

$= \lim_{h\to 0}\left[\frac{3x^2h + 3xh^2 + h^3 + 4h}{h}\right]$

$= \lim_{h\to 0}[3x^2 + 3xh + h^2 + 4] = 3x^2 + 4$

[5 marks available — 1 mark for using and substituting into the formula, 2 marks for correctly expanding brackets (otherwise 1 mark for one mistake), 1 mark for simplifying and cancelling h, 1 mark for h tending toward zero to give correct answer]

Q3 a) $\frac{dy}{dx} = 2x$

b) $y = x^4 + x^{\frac{1}{2}} \Rightarrow \frac{dy}{dx} = 4x^3 + \frac{1}{2}x^{-\frac{1}{2}} = 4x^3 + \frac{1}{2\sqrt{x}}$

c) $y = 7x^{-2} - 3x^{-\frac{1}{2}} + 12x^3$

$\Rightarrow \frac{dy}{dx} = -14x^{-3} + \frac{3}{2}x^{-\frac{3}{2}} + 36x^2 = -\frac{14}{x^3} + \frac{3}{2\sqrt{x^3}} + 36x^2$

Q4 a) $\frac{dy}{dx} = 4x,\ x = 2 \Rightarrow \frac{dy}{dx} = 8$

b) $\frac{dy}{dx} = 8x - 1,\ x = 2 \Rightarrow \frac{dy}{dx} = 15$

c) $\frac{dy}{dx} = 3x^2 - 14x,\ x = 2 \Rightarrow \frac{dy}{dx} = -16$

Q5 a) Initially $t = 0$, so $v = 3(0)^2 + 4 = 4$ ml.

b) $\frac{dv}{dt} = 6t,\ t = 4 \Rightarrow \frac{dv}{dt} = 24$ ml/s

Q6 $f(x) = 4\sqrt{x} + \frac{a}{x^2} - 6x + b = 4x^{\frac{1}{2}} + ax^{-2} - 6x + b$

$f'(x) = 2x^{-\frac{1}{2}} - 2ax^{-3} - 6$

$f'(1) = -64 \Rightarrow 2 - 2a - 6 = -64 \Rightarrow 2a = 60 \Rightarrow a = 30$

$f(4) = -\frac{97}{8} \Rightarrow 8 + \frac{a}{16} - 24 + b = -\frac{97}{8}$

$\Rightarrow \frac{a}{16} + b = \frac{31}{8} \Rightarrow a + 16b = 62$

$a = 30$, so $30 + 16b = 62 \Rightarrow b = 2$

[4 marks available — 1 mark for correct f′(x), 1 mark for substituting x = 1 into f′(x) to get a = 30, 1 mark for substituting x = 4 into f(x) to get an equation in a and b, 1 mark for substituting a = 30 into the equation to get b = 2]

Q7 $y = x^{\frac{3}{2}} - 3x - 10 \Rightarrow \frac{dy}{dx} = \frac{3x^{\frac{1}{2}}}{2} - 3$

$x = 16 \Rightarrow y = 64 - 48 - 10 = 6$ and $\frac{dy}{dx} = 6 - 3 = 3$

Gradient of the tangent = 3,

so $y = 3x + c \Rightarrow 6 = 3(16) + c \Rightarrow c = -42$

So the equation of the tangent is $y = 3x - 42$,

which can be rearranged to $3x - y - 42 = 0$.

Gradient of the normal $= -\frac{1}{3}$,

so $y = -\frac{1}{3} + c \Rightarrow 6 = -\frac{1}{3}(16) + c \Rightarrow c = \frac{34}{3}$

So the equation of the normal is $y = -\frac{x}{3} + \frac{34}{3}$,

which can be rearranged to $x + 3y - 34 = 0$.

Q8 On the first curve, when $x = 4$

$\Rightarrow y = \frac{(4)^3}{3} - 2(4)^2 - 4(4) + \frac{86}{3} = \frac{64}{3} - 32 - 16 + \frac{86}{3}$

$= \frac{150}{3} - 48 = 2$

On the second curve, when $x = 4$, $y = \sqrt{4} = \pm 2$.

Both curves go through (4, 2) so they meet at this point.

Differentiating the first curve gives:

$\frac{dy}{dx} = x^2 - 4x - 4,\ x = 4 \Rightarrow \frac{dy}{dx} = 4^2 - 4(4) - 4 = -4$

Differentiating the second curve $y = x^{\frac{1}{2}}$ gives:

$\frac{dy}{dx} = \frac{1}{2}x^{-\frac{1}{2}} = \frac{1}{2\sqrt{x}},\ x = 4 \Rightarrow \frac{dy}{dx} = \frac{1}{2\sqrt{4}} = \frac{1}{4}$

Multiplying the gradients of the curves at (4, 2) gives $-4 \times \frac{1}{4} = -1$, so the two curves are perpendicular at this point.

Q9 a) $y = x^2 - 6$ and $y = 3 \Rightarrow x^2 - 6 = 3 \Rightarrow x^2 = 9 \Rightarrow x = -3$ or 3

So C and L intersect at $A(3, 3)$ and $B(-3, 3)$.

A and B could be the other way round.

b) $\frac{dy}{dx} = 2x$. At A, when $x = 3$, $\frac{dy}{dx} = 6$,

and at B, when $x = -3$, $\frac{dy}{dx} = -6$.

c) The normal at A has a gradient of $-1 \div 6 = -\frac{1}{6}$

and an equation in the form $y = -\frac{1}{6}x + c$.

At $A(3, 3)$, $3 = -\frac{3}{6} + c \Rightarrow c = 3 + \frac{1}{2} = \frac{7}{2}$

So the equation of the normal is $y = -\frac{1}{6}x + \frac{7}{2}$,

which can be rearranged as $x + 6y - 21 = 0$.

The normal at B has a gradient of $-1 \div -6 = \frac{1}{6}$

and an equation in the form $y = \frac{1}{6}x + c$.

At $B(-3, 3)$, $3 = -\frac{3}{6} + c \Rightarrow c = 3 + \frac{1}{2} = \frac{7}{2}$

So the equation of the normal is $y = \frac{1}{6}x + \frac{7}{2}$,

which can be rearranged as $x - 6y + 21 = 0$.

d) Both lines have the same y-intercept, so will intersect each other at $(0, \frac{7}{2})$.

Q10 a) $y = x^2 + 4x - 2 \Rightarrow \frac{dy}{dx} = 2x + 4$

When $x = 2$, $y = 10$ and $\frac{dy}{dx} = 8$.

The tangent has a gradient of 8 and an equation of the form $y = 8x + c$. Using the point (2, 10):

$10 = 16 + c \Rightarrow c = -6$

So the tangent has the equation $y = 8x - 6$,

which can be rearranged as $8x - y - 6 = 0$.

[3 marks available — 1 mark for finding $\frac{dy}{dx}$, 1 mark for substituting x = 2 and finding gradient of 8, 1 mark for correct equation of tangent in any appropriate form]

b) When $x = -1$, $y = -5$ and $\frac{dy}{dx} = 2$.

So the normal has a gradient of $-1 \div 2 = -\frac{1}{2}$ and an equation of the form $y = -\frac{1}{2}x + c$.

Using the point $(-1, -5)$:

$-5 = \frac{1}{2} + c \Rightarrow c = -\frac{11}{2}$

So the normal has the equation $y = -\frac{1}{2}x - \frac{11}{2}$, which can be rearranged as $2y = -x - 11$

$\Rightarrow x + 2y + 11 = 0$

[3 marks available — 1 mark for substituting x = –1 and finding gradient of 2, 1 mark for correct gradient of normal, 1 mark for correct equation of normal in any appropriate form]

c) ① $8x - y = 6$

② $x + 2y = -11$

① × 2 $16x - 2y = 12$ ③

② + ③ $17x = 1 \Rightarrow x = \frac{1}{17}$

$x = \frac{1}{17}$ in ① $\frac{8}{17} - y = 6 \Rightarrow y = \frac{8}{17} - 6 = -\frac{94}{17}$

So the tangent at $x = 2$ and normal at $x = -1$ intersect at point $V\left(\frac{1}{17}, -\frac{94}{17}\right)$.

[2 marks available — 1 mark for attempt to solve using simultaneous equations to find V, 1 mark for correct coordinates for V]

Q11 a) $y = 1$, $\frac{dy}{dx} = 0$

b) $y = x^3 - 2x^2 + 1$, $\frac{dy}{dx} = 3x^2 - 4x$

$\frac{dy}{dx} = 0 \Rightarrow 3x^2 - 4x = 0 \Rightarrow x(3x - 4) = 0$

$\Rightarrow x = 0$ or $x = \frac{4}{3}$

$x > 0$, so the solution for x must be $\frac{4}{3}$.

$y = x^3 - 2x^2 + 1 = \left(\frac{4}{3}\right)^3 - 2\left(\frac{4}{3}\right)^2 + 1$

$= \frac{64}{27} - \frac{32}{9} + 1 = -\frac{5}{27}$

So the coordinates of the point are $\left(\frac{4}{3}, -\frac{5}{27}\right)$.

c) The tangent at this point has a gradient of 0 and an equation in the form $y = (0)x + c$, so $c = -\frac{5}{27}$ and the equation is $y = -\frac{5}{27}$.

Q12 $y = x^3 + 4x^{-1} + 2x^{\frac{1}{2}} \Rightarrow \frac{dy}{dx} = 3x^2 - 4x^{-2} + x^{-\frac{1}{2}}$

When $x = 1$, $y = (1)^3 + 4(1)^{-1} + 2(1)^{-\frac{1}{2}} = 7$,

and $\frac{dy}{dx} = 3(1)^2 - 4(1)^{-2} + (1)^{-\frac{1}{2}} = 0$

The tangent to the curve at $x = 1$, has an equation in the form $y = (0)x + c$, so $c = 7$ and the equation is $y = 7$.

Q13 $y = 1 + x^{\frac{3}{2}} \Rightarrow \frac{dy}{dx} = \frac{3}{2}x^{\frac{1}{2}} = \frac{3\sqrt{x}}{2}$

When $x = 16$, $y = 1 + (16)^{\frac{3}{2}} = 65$, and $\frac{dy}{dx} = \frac{3\sqrt{16}}{2} = 6$

The tangent to the curve at $x = 16$ has an equation in the form $y = 6x + c$. Using the point (16, 65):

$65 = 6(16) + c \Rightarrow c = 65 - 96 = -31$

So the tangent has the equation $y = 6x - 31$, which can be rearranged as $6x - y - 31 = 0$.

The normal has a gradient of $-1 \div 6 = -\frac{1}{6}$ and an equation in the form $y = -\frac{1}{6}x + c$.

Using the point (16, 65): $65 = -\frac{16}{6} + c \Rightarrow c = 65 + \frac{16}{6} = \frac{203}{3}$

So the normal has the equation $y = -\frac{1}{6}x + \frac{203}{3}$,

which can be rearranged as $6y = -x + 406 \Rightarrow x + 6y - 406 = 0$

Q14 a) When $x = 0$, $y = 0 - 0^3 = 0$ so (0, 0) lies on C. *[1 mark]*

b) $y = x - x^3 \Rightarrow \frac{dy}{dx} = 1 - 3x^2$

At P, $x = 0$, so the gradient at P is $1 - 3(0)^2 = 1$, so the gradient of the normal at P is $-1 \div 1 = -1$.

When $x = 0$, $y = 0$, so the equation of the normal is $y = -x$.

[4 marks available — 1 mark for the correct derivative, 1 mark for the correct gradient at P, 1 mark for the correct gradient of the normal, 1 mark for the correct equation of the line]

c) The normal at P meets the curve C when $-x = x - x^3$

$\Rightarrow x^3 - 2x = 0 \Rightarrow x(x^2 - 2) = 0 \Rightarrow x = 0$ or $x = \pm\sqrt{2}$

When $x = \sqrt{2}$, $y = -\sqrt{2}$

When $x = -\sqrt{2}$, $y = -(-\sqrt{2}) = \sqrt{2}$

So A and B have coordinates $(\sqrt{2}, -\sqrt{2})$ and $(-\sqrt{2}, \sqrt{2})$.

[3 marks available — 1 mark for a correct method to find the x-values, 1 mark for the correct x-values, 1 mark for the correct coordinates]

Q15 a) $y = x^2 - 1 \Rightarrow \frac{dy}{dx} = 2x$

At P: $2x = -8 \Rightarrow x = -4$. So $y = (-4)^2 - 1 = 15$.

At Q: $2x = 4 \Rightarrow x = 2$. So $y = (2)^2 - 1 = 3$.

So P has coordinates (–4, 15) and Q has coordinates (2, 3).

[3 marks available — 1 mark for the correct derivative, 1 mark for a correct method to find the x-values, 1 mark for the correct coordinates]

b) Equation of the tangent at P(–4, 15):

$y - y_1 = m(x - x_1) \Rightarrow y - 15 = -8(x + 4) \Rightarrow y = -8x - 17$

Equation of the tangent at Q(2, 3):

$y - y_1 = m(x - x_1) \Rightarrow y - 3 = 4(x - 2) \Rightarrow y = 4x - 5$

[3 marks available — 1 mark for correct method to find equation of one tangent, 1 mark for each correct answer]

c) Solving the equations simultaneously:

$-8x - 17 = 4x - 5 \Rightarrow 12x = -12 \Rightarrow x = -1$

At $x = -1$, $y = 4(-1) - 5 = -9$

So the coordinates of R are (–1, –9).

[2 marks available — 1 mark for a correct method to find the x-coordinate of R, 1 mark for the correct answer]

Q16 a) $f(x) = x^3 - 3x \Rightarrow f'(x) = 3x^2 - 3$

$x = -1 \Rightarrow f'(x) = 3(-1)^2 - 3 = 0$

b) $f''(x) = 6x$

$$\begin{aligned} 2f''(x) - 3f'(x) + f(x) &= 2(6x) - 3(3x^2 - 3) + (x^3 - 3x) \\ &= 12x - 9x^2 + 9 + x^3 - 3x \\ &= x^3 - 9x^2 + 9x + 9 \\ &= x^3 + 9(1 + x - x^2) \end{aligned}$$

Q17 $f(x) = x^4 \Rightarrow f'(x) = 4x^3 \Rightarrow f''(x) = 12x^2$

$$\begin{aligned} f''(x) + 2f'(x) - 4f(x) &= 12x^2 + 2(4x^3) - 4(x^4) \\ &= 12x^2 + 8x^3 - 4x^4 \\ &= -4x^2(x + 1)(x - 3) \end{aligned}$$

Q18 $y = \frac{x - 1}{x^2} = \frac{x}{x^2} - \frac{1}{x^2} = x^{-1} - x^{-2}$

$\frac{dy}{dx} = -x^{-2} + 2x^{-3} = \frac{-x + 2}{x^3}$

$\frac{d^2y}{dx^2} = 2x^{-3} - 6x^{-4} = \frac{2x - 6}{x^4}$

Substitute in these expressions:

$\frac{d^2y}{dx^2} + \frac{4}{x}\left(\frac{dy}{dx}\right) + \frac{2}{x^2}y = \frac{2x - 6}{x^4} + \frac{4}{x}\left(\frac{-x + 2}{x^3}\right) + \frac{2}{x^2}\left(\frac{x - 1}{x^2}\right)$

Expand the brackets to get separate terms with a common denominator of x^4:

$\frac{2x - 6}{x^4} + \frac{-4x + 8}{x^4} + \frac{2x - 2}{x^4}$

Simplify the numerator:

$\frac{2x - 6 - 4x + 8 + 2x - 2}{x^4} = \frac{0}{x^4} = 0$

[5 marks available — 1 mark for rewriting y as two separate terms to be differentiated, 1 mark for correctly differentiating to get $\frac{dy}{dx}$, 1 mark for correctly differentiating to get $\frac{d^2y}{dx^2}$, 1 mark for correct substitution into left side of equation, 1 mark for expanding and simplifying to show that it equals zero]

Q19 a) $y = x^3 + 3x^{-1} \Rightarrow \frac{dy}{dx} = 3x^2 - 3x^{-2} = 3x^2 - \frac{3}{x^2}$

When $\frac{dy}{dx} = 0$, $3x^2 - \frac{3}{x^2} = 0 \Rightarrow 3x^4 = 3$

$\Rightarrow x^4 = 1$

$\Rightarrow x = -1$ or $x = 1$

When $x = -1$, $y = -1 - 3 = -4$, and when $x = 1$, $y = 1 + 3 = 4$.

So the stationary points are (–1, –4) and (1, 4).

b) $\frac{d^2y}{dx^2} = 6x + 6x^{-3}$

When $x = -1$, $\frac{d^2y}{dx^2} = -6 - 6 = -12 < 0$, so (–1, –4) is a maximum.

When $x = 1$, $\frac{d^2y}{dx^2} = 6 + 6 = 12 > 0$, so (1, 4) is a minimum.

Q20 $y = 2x^4 - x^2 + 4 \Rightarrow \frac{dy}{dx} = 8x^3 - 2x$

When $\frac{dy}{dx} = 0$, $8x^3 - 2x = 0 \Rightarrow 2x(4x^2 - 1) = 0$

$\Rightarrow 2x(2x - 1)(2x + 1) = 0$

$\Rightarrow x = 0$ and $-\frac{1}{2}$ and $\frac{1}{2}$

When $x = 0$, $y = 0 - 0 + 4 = 4$,

when $x = -\frac{1}{2}$, $y = \frac{1}{8} - \frac{1}{4} + 4 = \frac{31}{8}$, and

when $x = \frac{1}{2}$, $y = \frac{1}{8} - \frac{1}{4} + 4 = \frac{31}{8}$.

So the stationary points are (0, 4), $\left(-\frac{1}{2}, \frac{31}{8}\right)$, $\left(\frac{1}{2}, \frac{31}{8}\right)$.

$\frac{d^2y}{dx^2} = 24x^2 - 2$.

At (0, 4), $\frac{d^2y}{dx^2} = -2 < 0$, so the point is a maximum.

At $\left(-\frac{1}{2}, \frac{31}{8}\right)$ and $\left(\frac{1}{2}, \frac{31}{8}\right)$, $\frac{d^2y}{dx^2} = 6 - 2 = 4$,

so the points are minimums.

Q21 a) $y = x^2(x - 3)^2 = x^2(x^2 - 6x + 9) = x^4 - 6x^3 + 9x^2$

$\frac{dy}{dx} = 4x^3 - 18x^2 + 18x$

When $\frac{dy}{dx} = 0$, $4x^3 - 18x^2 + 18x = 0$

$\Rightarrow 2x(2x^2 - 9x + 9) = 0 \Rightarrow 2x(2x - 3)(x - 3) = 0$

$\Rightarrow x = 0$ and $x = \frac{3}{2}$ and $x = 3$

When $x = 0$, $y = 0$. When $x = \frac{3}{2}$, $y = \frac{81}{16}$, and when $x = 3$, $y = 0$.

The coordinates of the stationary points are (0, 0), $\left(\frac{3}{2}, \frac{81}{16}\right)$ (allow (1.5, 5.1)) and (3, 0).

[4 marks available — 1 mark for correct $\frac{dy}{dx}$, 1 mark for setting $\frac{dy}{dx}$ equal to zero, 1 mark for one correct pair of coordinates, 1 mark for the other two correct pairs of coordinates]

b) $\frac{d^2y}{dx^2} = 12x^2 - 36x + 18$.

When $x = 0$, $\frac{d^2y}{dx^2} = 0 - 0 + 18 = 18 > 0$,

so the point (0, 0) is a minimum.

When $x = \frac{3}{2}$, $\frac{d^2y}{dx^2} = 27 - 54 + 18 = -9 < 0$,

so the point $\left(\frac{3}{2}, \frac{81}{16}\right)$ is a maximum.

When $x = 3$, $\frac{d^2y}{dx^2} = 108 - 108 + 18 = 18 > 0$,

so the point (3, 0) is a minimum.

[3 marks available — 1 mark for $\frac{d^2y}{dx^2}$, 1 mark for correctly substituting one x-value from part a) to determine the nature of one point, 1 mark for correctly substituting the other two x-values to determine the nature of the other two points]

c)

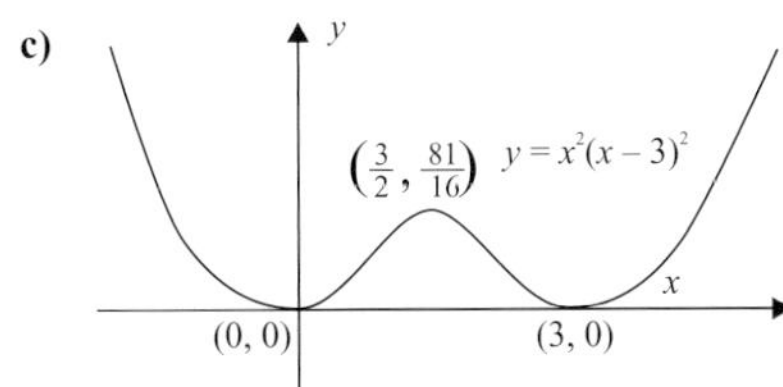

[3 marks available — 1 mark for correct shape, 1 mark for one stationary point correct and labelled, 1 mark for the other two stationary points correct and labelled]

Q22 a) $f'(x) = \frac{5x^4}{100} - \frac{39x^2}{60} + \frac{9}{5} = \frac{x^4}{20} - \frac{13}{20}x^2 + \frac{9}{5}$

[2 marks available — 1 mark for an attempt at differentiating, 1 mark for the correct answer]

b) Stationary points occur when $f'(x) = 0$

$\Rightarrow \frac{x^4}{20} - \frac{13}{20}x^2 + \frac{9}{5} = 0 \Rightarrow x^4 - 13x^2 + 36 = 0$

$\Rightarrow (x^2 - 9)(x^2 - 4) = 0 \Rightarrow (x + 3)(x - 3)(x + 2)(x - 2) = 0$

$\Rightarrow x = -3, x = 3, x = -2$ or $x = 2$.

So $y = f(x)$ has four stationary points.

[4 marks available — 1 mark for setting f'(x) = 0, 1 mark for attempting to factorise, 1 mark for the correct factorisation, 1 mark for a correct conclusion]

c) $f''(x) = \frac{x^3}{5} - \frac{13x}{10}$, so:

$f''(-3) = -1.5 < 0$, so it's a maximum.

$f''(3) = 1.5 > 0$, so it's a minimum.

$f''(-2) = 1 > 0$, so it's a minimum.

$f''(2) = -1 < 0$, so it's a maximum.

So there are maximum points at $x = 2$ and $x = -3$ and minimum points at $x = -2$ and $x = 3$.

[3 marks available — 1 mark for the correct second derivative, 1 mark for substituting the values from part b), 1 mark for all four values correct and the correct conclusion]

Q23 a) $\frac{dy}{dx} = 3ax^2 + 2bx + c$

For there to be two stationary points, $\frac{dy}{dx} = 0$ must have two real roots, so its discriminant must be positive:

$(2b)^2 - 4(3a)(c) > 0 \Rightarrow 4b^2 - 12ac > 0 \Rightarrow b^2 > 3ac$

[5 marks available — 1 mark for attempting to differentiate, 1 mark for the correct derivative, 1 mark for considering the discriminant, 1 mark for forming a correct inequality, 1 mark for a complete proof]

b) $b^2 < 3ac \Rightarrow b^2 - 3ac < 0$. The discriminant is negative, so the curve will have no stationary points. *[1 mark]*

c) (i) $b^2 = 16$ and $3ac = -6$, so $b^2 > 3ac$.

So the curve has two stationary points. *[1 mark]*

(ii) $b^2 = 4$ and $3ac = 15$, so $b^2 < 3ac$.

So the curve has no stationary points. *[1 mark]*

Q24 a) $y = 6(x^2 - x - 6) = 6x^2 - 6x - 36$

$\frac{dy}{dx} = 12x - 6$. If the function is increasing,

$\frac{dy}{dx} > 0 \Rightarrow 12x - 6 > 0 \Rightarrow 12x > 6 \Rightarrow x > \frac{1}{2}$.

If the function is decreasing, $\frac{dy}{dx} < 0 \Rightarrow x < \frac{1}{2}$.

b) $y = x^{-2} \Rightarrow \frac{dy}{dx} = -2x^{-3} = -\frac{2}{x^3} \Rightarrow x \neq 0$

If $x < 0$, $x^3 < 0$, so $-\frac{2}{x^3} > 0$, and if $x > 0$, $x^3 > 0$ so $-\frac{2}{x^3} < 0$.

x cannot equal 0, so the function is increasing when $x < 0$ and decreasing when $x > 0$.

Q25 $f(x) = x^4 - 14x^2 + 24x \Rightarrow f'(x) = 4x^3 - 28x + 24$

When $f'(x) = 0$, $4x^3 - 28x + 24 = 0 \Rightarrow x^3 - 7x + 6 = 0$

The coefficients add up to $1 + (-7) + 6 = 0$, so $(x - 1)$ must be a factor. Use algebra or division to find the quadratic factor:

$(x - 1)(x^2 + x - 6) \Rightarrow (x - 1)(x + 3)(x - 2) = 0$

$\Rightarrow x = 1$ or $x = -3$ or $x = 2$

If the function is increasing $f'(x) > 0$

$\Rightarrow 4x^3 - 28x + 24 > 0 \Rightarrow (x - 1)(x + 3)(x - 2) > 0$

For this to be true, there are 4 possibilities — all brackets are more than zero, or one is more than zero and two are less than zero.

Either $x > 1$ and $x > -3$ and $x > 2$, so $x > 2$

Or $x > 1$ and $x < -3$ and $x < 2$ (impossible)

Or $x < 1$ and $x > -3$ and $x < 2$

Or $x < 1$ and $x < -3$ and $x > 2$ (impossible)

So the function is increasing when $-3 < x < 1$ and $x > 2$, and is decreasing when $x < -3$ and $1 < x < 2$.

[7 marks available — 1 mark for finding f'(x), 1 mark for f(x) = 0, f(x) > 0 or f(x) < 0, 1 mark for at least one factor and hence root, 1 mark for other factors and hence roots, 1 mark for a correct method to find increasing and decreasing ranges (e.g. solving inequalities, determining nature of stationary points, sketching curve), 1 mark for partially correct ranges, 1 mark for fully correct ranges]

Q26 a) $f'(x) = 0 \Rightarrow (x + 1)(x^2 - 4) = 0$

$\Rightarrow (x + 1)(x + 2)(x - 2) = 0 \Rightarrow x = -1, x = -2$ or $x = 2$

[1 mark for all x-values correct]

b) $f(x)$ is increasing when $f'(x) > 0 \Rightarrow (x + 1)(x + 2)(x - 2) > 0$.

For this to be positive, either all brackets must be positive, or two brackets must be negative and one positive.

So either $x > 2$ (all brackets are positive), or $-2 < x < -1$ (two brackets are negative and one positive).

[3 marks available — 1 mark for setting f'(x) > 0, 1 mark for each correct region]

Q27 $g(x) = x + 3 - 4x^{-1}$, so $g'(x) = 1 + \frac{4}{x^2}$.

$x^2 > 0$ for all non-zero real values of x, so $1 + \frac{4}{x^2} > 0$ for all real values of x, $x \neq 0$, so $g(x)$ is an increasing function.

[3 marks available — 1 mark for correct method to differentiate at least one term, 1 mark for correct derivative, 1 mark for explanation of why g(x) is increasing]

Q28 $y = 3x^3 - 16x \Rightarrow \frac{dy}{dx} = 9x^2 - 16$

When $\frac{dy}{dx} = 0$, $9x^2 - 16 = 0 \Rightarrow (3x + 4)(3x - 4) = 0$

$\Rightarrow x = -\frac{4}{3}$ and $x = \frac{4}{3}$

When $x = -\frac{4}{3}$, $y = -\frac{64}{9} + \frac{64}{3} = \frac{128}{9}$, and

when $x = \frac{4}{3}$, $y = \frac{64}{9} - \frac{64}{3} = -\frac{128}{9}$.

When $y = 0$, $3x^3 - 16x = 0 \Rightarrow x(3x^2 - 16) = 0$

$\Rightarrow x = 0$ and $\pm\frac{4\sqrt{3}}{3}$

So the curve crosses the x-axis at $x = -\frac{4\sqrt{3}}{3}$, $x = 0$ and $x = \frac{4\sqrt{3}}{3}$.

The x^2 coefficient is positive, so sketch a bottom-left to top-right curve passing through all these points.

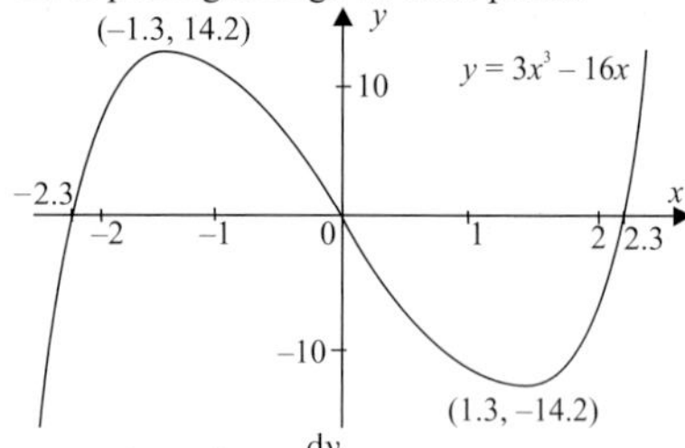

Q29 $y = -3x^3 + 6x^2 \Rightarrow \frac{dy}{dx} = -9x^2 + 12x$

When $\frac{dy}{dx} = 0$, $-9x^2 + 12x = 0 \Rightarrow 3x(-3x + 4) = 0$

$\Rightarrow x = 0$ and $x = \frac{4}{3}$

When $x = 0$, $y = 0$, and when $x = \frac{4}{3}$, $y = -\frac{64}{9} + \frac{32}{3} = \frac{32}{9}$.

When $y = 0$, $-3x^3 + 6x^2 = 0 \Rightarrow -3x^2(x - 2) = 0 \Rightarrow x = 0$ and 2

So the curve meets the x-axis at $x = 0$ and $x = 2$.

The x^2 coefficient is negative, so sketch a top-left to bottom-right curve passing through all these points.

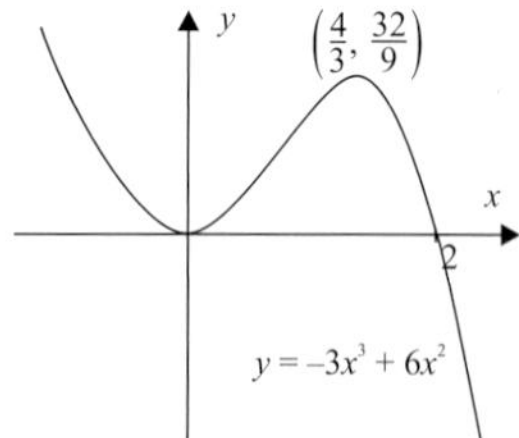

Q30 a) $y = 0 \Rightarrow 8x^2 - \frac{1}{x} = 0 \Rightarrow 8x^3 - 1 = 0$

$\Rightarrow x^3 = \frac{1}{8} \Rightarrow x = \frac{1}{2}$

So the curve crosses the x-axis at $\left(\frac{1}{2}, 0\right)$.

[2 marks available — 1 mark for a correct method, 1 mark for the correct answer]

b) $y = 8x^2 - x^{-1} \Rightarrow \frac{dy}{dx} = 16x + \frac{1}{x^2}$

Stationary points occur when $\frac{dy}{dx} = 0 \Rightarrow 16x + \frac{1}{x^2} = 0$

$\Rightarrow 16x^3 + 1 = 0 \Rightarrow x^3 = -\frac{1}{16}$

$\Rightarrow x = \sqrt[3]{-\frac{1}{16}} = -0.3968...$

Then $y = 8(0.3968...)^2 - \frac{1}{(0.3968...)} = 3.779...$

So the stationary point has coordinates (–0.397, 3.78) to 3 s.f.

[4 marks available — 1 mark for the correct derivative, 1 mark for attempting to solve derivative = 0, 1 mark for the correct x-value, 1 mark for the correct y-value]

c) When $x > 0$, $16x > 0$ and $\frac{1}{x^2} > 0$ for all real x,

so $\frac{dy}{dx} = 16x + \frac{1}{x^2} > 0$ for $x > 0$, therefore y is increasing.

[2 marks available — 1 mark for attempting to show that $\frac{dy}{dx} > 0$, 1 mark for a correct explanation]

d) $\frac{d^2y}{dx^2} = 16 - \frac{2}{x^3}$. When $x = -0.3968...$, $\frac{d^2y}{dx^2} = 48 > 0$, so the stationary point is a minimum.

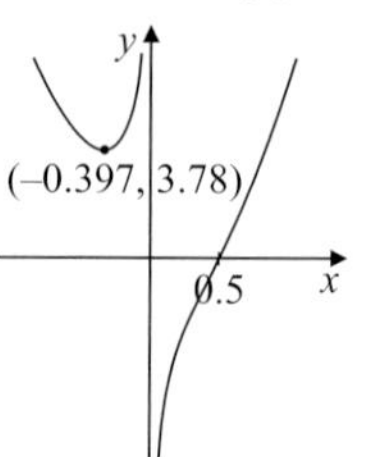

[5 marks available — 1 mark for a correct method to determine the nature of the turning point, 1 mark for correctly determining the nature of the turning point, 1 mark for the correct x-intercept, 1 mark for the correct shape for x > 0, 1 mark for the correct shape for x < 0]

Q31 $xy = 20 \Rightarrow y = \frac{20}{x} \Rightarrow x^2 + y^2 = x^2 + \left(\frac{20}{x}\right)^2 = x^2 + \frac{400}{x^2}$

$f(x) = x^2 + \frac{400}{x^2} = x^2 + 400x^{-2}$,

$f'(x) = 2x - 800x^{-3} = 2x - \frac{800}{x^3}$

If $f'(x) = 0$, $2x - \frac{800}{x^3} = 0 \Rightarrow 2x = \frac{800}{x^3}$

$\Rightarrow 2x^4 = 800$

$\Rightarrow x^4 = 400 \Rightarrow x = \sqrt{20}$

The question says x and y are positive so you can ignore the negative square root of 20.

$f''(x) = 2 + 2400x^{-4}$, $x = \sqrt{20}$

$\Rightarrow f''(x) = 2 + 6 = 8 > 0$, so $x = \sqrt{20}$ is a minimum.

$y = \frac{20}{x} = \frac{20}{\sqrt{20}} = \sqrt{20}$,

so the minimum value of $x^2 + y^2 = 20 + 20 = 40$.

Q32 a) Using Pythagoras' theorem:

$r^2 + (5h)^2 = 15^2 \Rightarrow r^2 + 25h^2 = 225$

$\Rightarrow r^2 = 225 - 25h^2$

$\Rightarrow r = \sqrt{225 - 25h^2}$

[2 marks available — 1 mark for use of Pythagoras' theorem and correct substitution, 1 mark for correct r in terms of h]

b) $V = \pi r^2 h = 10\pi h(225 - 25h^2) = 2250\pi h - 250\pi h^3$

[2 marks available — 1 mark for substituting part a) into the volume of a cylinder formula, 1 mark for correct formula for V in terms of h]

c) $\frac{dV}{dh} = 2250\pi - 750\pi h^2$

When $\frac{dV}{dh} = 0$, $2250\pi - 750\pi h^2 = 0$

$\Rightarrow 750\pi(3 - h^2) = 0 \Rightarrow h^2 = 3 \Rightarrow h = \pm\sqrt{3}$

h is a length, so you can ignore the negative solution.

$\frac{d^2V}{dh^2} = -1500\pi h$.

At $h = \sqrt{3}$, $\frac{d^2V}{dh^2} = -8162 < 0$, so it's a maximum.

When $h = \sqrt{3}$, $V = 2250\pi\sqrt{3} - 250\pi(\sqrt{3})^3$

$= 8162.09...\text{ cm}^3$

$= 8162\text{ cm}^3$ (to nearest cm³)

[5 marks available — 1 mark for correct $\frac{dV}{dh}$, 1 mark for making $\frac{dV}{dh} = 0$, 1 mark for correctly solving for h, 1 mark for substituting h value into part b), 1 mark for correct answer rounded to the nearest cm³]

Q33 a) $x = t^3 - 8t \Rightarrow \frac{dx}{dt} = 3t^2 - 8$

b) When $\frac{dx}{dt} = 19$, $3t^2 - 8 = 19 \Rightarrow 3t^2 = 27$

$\Rightarrow t^2 = 9 \Rightarrow t = 3$

When $t = 3$ seconds, $x = 27 - 24 = 3$ metres.

t is a time and cannot be negative, so ignore the negative square root of 9.

c) $\frac{d^2x}{dt^2} = 6t$

d) $t = 2$, $\frac{d^2x}{dt^2} = 12\text{ ms}^{-2}$

e) $\frac{d^2x}{dt^2} = 18,\ 6t = 18 \Rightarrow t = 3$

$\Rightarrow \frac{dx}{dt} = 27 - 8 = 19 \text{ ms}^{-1}$

Q34 $s = 4 + 12t^2 - t^3 \Rightarrow \frac{ds}{dt} = 24t - 3t^2 \Rightarrow \frac{d^2s}{dt^2} = 24 - 6t$

At $t = 4.5$ seconds, $\frac{d^2s}{dt^2} = 24 - 27 = -3 \text{ ms}^{-2}$

[4 marks available — 1 mark for finding $\frac{ds}{dt}$, 1 mark for finding $\frac{d^2s}{dt^2}$, 1 mark for substituting $t = 4.5$ into $\frac{d^2s}{dt^2}$, 1 mark for correct answer]

Q35 $h = \frac{1}{10}m^2 - \frac{1}{800}m^3 \Rightarrow \frac{dh}{dm} = \frac{1}{5}m - \frac{3}{800}m^2$

When $\frac{dh}{dm} = 0,\ \frac{1}{5}m - \frac{3}{800}m^2 = 0 \Rightarrow \frac{1}{5}m(1 - \frac{3}{160}m)$

$\Rightarrow m = 0 \text{ or } m = \frac{160}{3}$

$\frac{d^2h}{dm^2} = \frac{1}{5} - \frac{3}{400}m.$

When $m = 0$, $\frac{d^2h}{dm^2} = \frac{1}{5} > 0$, so the point is a minimum — there is no fuel when $m = 0$, so this cannot be the mass of fuel needed to reach the maximum height.

When $m = \frac{160}{3}$, $\frac{d^2h}{dm^2} = \frac{1}{5} - \frac{2}{5} = -\frac{1}{5} < 0$, so the point is a maximum.

So the mass of fuel needed to reach maximum height is $\frac{160}{3}$ g, which is 53.3 g (3 s.f.).

$h = \frac{(53.3...)^2}{10} - \frac{(53.3...)^3}{800} = 94.81... \approx 94.8 \text{ m (3 s.f.)}$

Q36 a) Since F is constant, $\frac{dW}{dt} = F\frac{dx}{dt} = Fv = P$ *[1 mark]*

b) $P = \frac{dW}{dt} = -3t + 8$

So when $t = 2$, $P = -3(2) + 8 = 2$

[3 marks available — 1 mark for each correct term in the derivative, 1 mark for the correct answer]

c) The maximum value occurs when $\frac{dW}{dt} = 0$

$\Rightarrow -3t + 8 = 0 \Rightarrow t = \frac{8}{3}.$

When $t = \frac{8}{3}$, $W = -\frac{3}{2}\left(\frac{8}{3}\right)^2 + 8\left(\frac{8}{3}\right) = \frac{32}{3}$

[3 marks available — 1 mark for setting the derivative equal to zero, 1 mark for the correct value of t, 1 mark for the correct answer]

d) $\frac{dP}{dt} = \frac{d^2W}{dt^2} = -3 < 0$ for all t, so it's a maximum.

[2 marks available — 1 mark for the correct derivative, 1 mark for the correct conclusion]

Q37 a) $v = \frac{dx}{dt} = 6 + 12t - 4t^3$

$\Rightarrow a = \frac{dv}{dt} = \frac{d^2x}{dt^2} = 12 - 12t^2$

[3 marks available — 1 mark for an attempt at differentiating, 1 mark for the correct first derivative, 1 mark for the correct second derivative]

b) Deceleration is negative acceleration, so the particle decelerates when $12 - 12t^2 < 0 \Rightarrow 12(1 - t^2) < 0$

$\Rightarrow t^2 > 1 \Rightarrow t > 1$ since $t > 0$, so $k = 1$.

[3 marks available — 1 mark for the correct inequality, 1 mark for a correct method to solve this inequality, 1 mark for the correct answer]

c) The maximum speed occurs either when $t = 0$, $t = 2$ or $12 - 12t^2 = 0$.

When $t = 0$, $v = 6 \text{ ms}^{-1}$.

When $t = 2$, $v = 6 + 24 - 32 = -2 \text{ ms}^{-1}$, so the speed is 2 ms^{-1}.

From part b), $12 - 12t^2 = 0$ when $t = 1$, so $v = 6 + 12 - 4 = 14 \text{ ms}^{-1}$. So the maximum speed is 14 ms^{-1}.

[2 marks available — 1 mark for using t = 1, 1 mark for the correct answer]

Q38 a) Using the perimeter, the length of the paper is $\frac{1}{2}(60 - 2x) = (30 - x)$ cm. This becomes the circumference of the circle when the paper is rolled up, so the radius is $r = \frac{30 - x}{2\pi}$.

[2 marks available — 1 mark for the correct length, 1 mark for the correct radius]

b) The height of the cylinder is x cm, so the volume is:

$V = \pi r^2 h = \pi\left(\frac{30 - x}{2\pi}\right)^2 x = \frac{1}{4\pi}x(30 - x)^2$

[2 marks available — 1 mark for a correct formula for the volume, 1 mark for substituting and rearranging correctly]

c) $V = \frac{1}{4\pi}x(30 - x)^2 = \frac{1}{4\pi}x(900 - 60x + x^2)$

$= \frac{1}{4\pi}(900x - 60x^2 + x^3)$

So $\frac{dV}{dx} = \frac{1}{4\pi}(900 - 120x + 3x^2)$

At the maximum, $\frac{dV}{dx} = 0$:

$\Rightarrow 900 - 120x + 3x^2 = 0 \Rightarrow x^2 - 40x + 300 = 0$

$\Rightarrow (x - 30)(x - 10) = 0 \Rightarrow x = 10 \text{ or } x = 30$

When $x = 30$, $V = 0$.

When $x = 10$, $V = \frac{1}{4\pi} \times 10(30 - 10)^2 = 318.30...$

So the maximum volume is 318 cm^3 (to 3 s.f.)

[5 marks available — 1 mark for correctly expanding the brackets, 1 mark for the correct derivative, 1 mark for solving $\frac{dV}{dx} = 0$, 1 mark for the correct x-value, 1 mark for the correct volume]

d) $\frac{d^2V}{dx^2} = \frac{1}{4\pi}(6x - 120) = \frac{3}{2\pi}(x - 20)$

When $x = 10$, $\frac{d^2V}{dx^2} = \frac{3}{2\pi}(10 - 20) = -\frac{15}{\pi} < 0$

so the volume is at a maximum.

[3 marks available — 1 mark for a correct method, 1 mark for using the x-value from c), 1 mark for the correct conclusion]

e) The curved surface area is the area of the piece of paper.

$A = x(30 - x) = 30x - x^2 \Rightarrow \frac{dA}{dx} = 30 - 2x.$

$\frac{dA}{dx} = 0 \Rightarrow 30 - 2x = 0 \Rightarrow x = 15.$

$\frac{d^2A}{dx^2} = -2 < 0$, so the area is at a maximum when $x = 15$.

The maximum area is $15 \times (30 - 15) = 225 \text{ cm}^2 = 0.0225 \text{ m}^2$.

So the smallest amount of paint required is $0.0225 \div 1.2 = 0.01875$ litres = 18.75 ml.

[5 marks available — 1 mark for a correct expression for the surface area, 1 mark for a correct method to find the x-value at the maximum, 1 mark for showing it is a maximum area, 1 mark for the correct maximum area, 1 mark for the correct answer]

Q39 a) $y = kx^{\frac{1}{2}} - \frac{1}{k}x^{-\frac{1}{2}}$, so

$\frac{dy}{dx} = \frac{1}{2}kx^{-\frac{1}{2}} + \frac{1}{2k}x^{-\frac{3}{2}} = \frac{k}{2\sqrt{x}} + \frac{1}{2kx\sqrt{x}} = \frac{k^2x + 1}{2kx\sqrt{x}}$

[4 marks available — 1 mark for rewriting y in terms of powers of x, 1 mark for an attempt at differentiating, 1 mark for the correct derivative, 1 mark for rearranging to give the correct result]

b) (i) When $x = 4$, $\frac{dy}{dx} = \frac{4k^2 + 1}{16k} = \frac{1}{4} \Rightarrow 4(4k^2 + 1) = 16k$

$\Rightarrow 4k^2 + 1 = 4k \Rightarrow 4k^2 - 4k + 1 = 0$

[2 marks available — 1 mark for correctly substituting x = 4, 1 mark for rearranging to give the correct result]

(ii) $4k^2 - 4k + 1 = 0 \Rightarrow (2k - 1)^2 = 0$

$\Rightarrow 2k - 1 = 0 \Rightarrow k = \frac{1}{2}$

[2 marks available — 1 mark for a correct method to solve the quadratic, 1 mark for the correct answer]

Q40 a) $y = \sqrt{\frac{x}{a}} = \frac{1}{\sqrt{a}}x^{\frac{1}{2}}$ so $\frac{dy}{dx} = \frac{1}{2\sqrt{a}}x^{-\frac{1}{2}} = \frac{1}{2\sqrt{ax}}$

[3 marks available — 1 mark for correctly writing y in terms of x, 1 mark for correctly differentiating $\sqrt{x}$, 1 mark for the correct answer]

b) At $x = \frac{1}{a}$, gradient $= \frac{1}{2\sqrt{1}} = \frac{1}{2}$
So the equation of the tangent is:
$y - y_1 = m(x - x_1) \Rightarrow y - \frac{1}{a} = \frac{1}{2}\left(x - \frac{1}{a}\right)$
$\Rightarrow y = \frac{1}{2}x - \frac{1}{2a} + \frac{1}{a} \Rightarrow y = \frac{1}{2}x + \frac{1}{2a}$
[3 marks available — 1 mark for the correct gradient, 1 mark for a correct method to find the equation of the line, 1 mark for the correct answer]

Q41 $y = x^3 \Rightarrow \frac{dy}{dx} = 3x^2$
The gradient is 3 when $3x^2 = 3 \Rightarrow x^2 = 1 \Rightarrow x = \pm 1$
When $x = 1$, $y = 1$, and when $x = -1$, $y = -1$.
So P has coordinates (1, 1) and Q has coordinates (–1, –1).
So the equation of the tangent at P is:
$y - y_1 = m(x - x_1) \Rightarrow y - 1 = 3(x - 1) \Rightarrow y = 3x - 2$
And the equation of the tangent at Q is:
$y + 1 = 3(x + 1) \Rightarrow y = 3x + 2$
The normals have a gradient of $-1 \div 3 = -\frac{1}{3}$,
so the equation of the normal at P is:
$y - 1 = -\frac{1}{3}(x - 1) \Rightarrow y = -\frac{1}{3}x + \frac{4}{3}$
And the equation of the normal at Q is:
$y + 1 = -\frac{1}{3}(x + 1) \Rightarrow y = -\frac{1}{3}x - \frac{4}{3}$
Point R is where $y = 3x - 2$ and $y = -\frac{1}{3}x - \frac{4}{3}$ intersect:
$3x - 2 = -\frac{1}{3}x - \frac{4}{3} \Rightarrow 9x - 6 = -x - 4 \Rightarrow 10x = 2 \Rightarrow x = 0.2$
$y = 3x - 2 = 0.6 - 2 = -1.4$, so R has coordinates (0.2, –1.4).
Distance $PR = \sqrt{0.8^2 + 2.4^2} = \frac{4}{5}\sqrt{10}$
Distance $QR = \sqrt{1.2^2 + 0.4^2} = \frac{2}{5}\sqrt{10}$
So area of $PRQS = \frac{4}{5}\sqrt{10} \times \frac{2}{5}\sqrt{10} = \frac{8}{25} \times 10 = 3.2$

Q42 a) $f(x) = x^2 - 2x^{-1} \Rightarrow f'(x) = 2x + 2x^{-2} = 2x + \frac{2}{x^2}$
$\Rightarrow f''(x) = 2 - 4x^{-3} = 2 - \frac{4}{x^3}$
[3 marks available — 1 mark for an attempt at differentiating, 1 mark for the correct first derivative, 1 mark for the correct second derivative]

b) When $x < 0$, $-\frac{4}{x^3} > 0$, so $f''(x) = 2 - \frac{4}{x^3} > 2 > 0$,
so $f'(x)$ is increasing.
[2 marks available — 1 mark for attempting to form an inequality in x, 1 mark for a correct proof]

c) $f'(x) > 0 \Rightarrow 2x + \frac{2}{x^2} > 0 \Rightarrow 2x^3 + 2 > 0$
$\Rightarrow x^3 > -1 \Rightarrow x > -1$
So $f(x)$ is increasing for $x > -1$.
[3 marks available — 1 mark for setting $f'(x) > 0$, 1 mark for rearranging to $x^3 > -1$, 1 mark for the correct answer]

Q43 Let the height of the equilateral triangle face be h.
Then splitting the face vertically down the middle forms a right-angled triangle with sides of lengths $\frac{1}{2}x$, h, and x.
Using Pythagoras' theorem:
$\left(\frac{1}{2}x\right)^2 + h^2 = x^2 \Rightarrow h^2 = x^2 - \frac{1}{4}x^2 = \frac{3}{4}x^2 \Rightarrow h = \frac{\sqrt{3}}{2}x$
Volume $= \frac{1}{2} \times x \times \frac{\sqrt{3}}{2}x \times y = \frac{\sqrt{3}}{4}x^2y = 50 \Rightarrow y = \frac{200}{\sqrt{3}x^2}$
Surface area $= 2\left(\frac{1}{2} \times x \times \frac{\sqrt{3}}{2}x\right) + 3xy = \frac{\sqrt{3}}{2}x^2 + 3xy$
$= \frac{\sqrt{3}}{2}x^2 + 3x\frac{200}{\sqrt{3}x^2} = \frac{\sqrt{3}}{2}x^2 + 200\sqrt{3}x^{-1}$
$\frac{dA}{dx} = \sqrt{3}x - 200\sqrt{3}x^{-2}$
$\frac{dA}{dx} = 0 \Rightarrow \sqrt{3}x - 200\sqrt{3}x^{-2} = 0 \Rightarrow \sqrt{3}x = 200\sqrt{3}x^{-2}$
$\Rightarrow x^3 = 200 \Rightarrow x = 5.8480... = 5.85$ (3 s.f.)
$y = \frac{200}{\sqrt{3}(5.8480...)^2} = 3.3763... = 3.38$ (3 s.f.)

Chapter 11: Integration

Prior Knowledge Check

Q1 a) $x^2 \times x^5 = x^{2+5} = x^7$

b) $\frac{x^9}{x^{-3}} = x^{9-(-3)} = x^{12}$

c) $(x^6)^3 = x^{6 \times 3} = x^{18}$

Q2 a) $x^2 - 4x + 4 = (x - 2)^2$

b) $5x^2 + 31x + 6 = (5x + 1)(x + 6)$

Q3 E.g. using algebraic division,
$x^3 + 5x^2 + 2x - 8 \div (x + 2) = x^2 + 3x - 4$
So $x^3 + 5x^2 + 2x - 8 = (x + 2)(x^2 + 3x - 4) = (x + 2)(x - 1)(x + 4)$
So the graph crosses the x-axis at $x = -4$, $x = -2$ and $x = 1$.
The coefficient of x^3 is positive, so the graph goes from the bottom left to the top right:

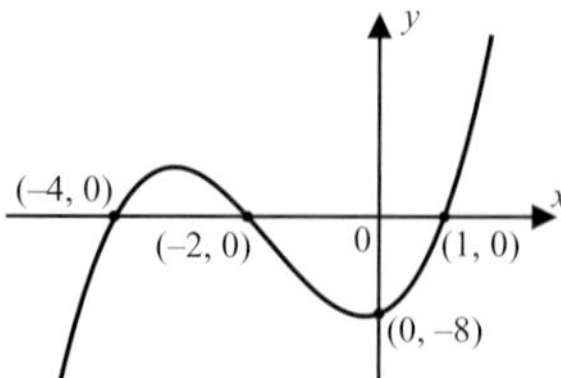

Q4 a) $\frac{dy}{dx} = 5(3x^4) = 15x^4$

b) $\frac{dy}{dx} = 2(2x^1) + -2(3x^{-3}) = 4x - 6x^{-3}$

c) Expanding the brackets gives $y = 2x^5 - 4x^{-3} - 2x^2 + 4x^{-6}$
Then $\frac{dy}{dx} = 5(2x^4) - -3(4x^{-4}) - 2(2x^1) + -6(4x^{-7})$
$= 10x^4 + 12x^{-4} - 4x - 24x^{-7}$

Exercise 11.1-11.2 — Integrating x^n

Q1 a) $y = \int \frac{dy}{dx}\,dx = \int x^7\,dx = \frac{x^8}{8} + C$

b) $y = \int \frac{dy}{dx}\,dx = \int 2x^3\,dx = 2\int x^3\,dx$
$= 2\left(\frac{x^4}{4}\right) + C = \frac{x^4}{2} + C$

c) $y = \int \frac{dy}{dx}\,dx = \int 8x\,dx = 8\int x\,dx$
$= 8\left(\frac{x^2}{2}\right) + C = 4x^2 + C$

d) $y = \int \frac{dy}{dx}\,dx = \int -5x^4\,dx = -5\int x^4\,dx$
$= -5\left(\frac{x^5}{5}\right) + C = -x^5 + C$

e) $y = \int \frac{dy}{dx}\,dx = \int 200x^{99}\,dx = 200\left(\frac{x^{100}}{100}\right) + C = 2x^{100} + C$

f) $y = \int \frac{dy}{dx}\,dx = \int x^{-3}\,dx = \frac{x^{-2}}{-2} + C = -\frac{1}{2x^2} + C$

g) $y = \int \frac{dy}{dx}\,dx = \int 4x^{-4}\,dx = 4\int x^{-4}\,dx$
$= 4\left(\frac{x^{-3}}{-3}\right) + C = \frac{4x^{-3}}{-3} + C = -\frac{4}{3x^3} + C$

h) $y = \int \frac{dy}{dx}\,dx = \int -6x^{-5}\,dx = -6\int x^{-5}\,dx$
$= -6\left(\frac{x^{-4}}{-4}\right) + C = \frac{3x^{-4}}{2} + C = \frac{3}{2x^4} + C$

i) $y = \int \frac{dy}{dx}\,dx = \int -12\,dx = \frac{-12x}{1} + C = -12x + C$

j) $y = \int \frac{dy}{dx}\,dx = \int x^{\frac{1}{2}}\,dx = \frac{x^{\frac{3}{2}}}{\left(\frac{3}{2}\right)} + C = \frac{2x^{\frac{3}{2}}}{3} + C$
Don't forget that dividing by a fraction is the same as multiplying by the flipped fraction.

k) $y = \int \frac{dy}{dx}\,dx = \int x^{\frac{1}{3}}\,dx = \frac{x^{\frac{4}{3}}}{\left(\frac{4}{3}\right)} + C = \frac{3x^{\frac{4}{3}}}{4} + C$

l) $y = \int \frac{dy}{dx}\,dx = \int 12x^{\frac{3}{2}}\,dx = \frac{12x^{\frac{5}{2}}}{\left(\frac{5}{2}\right)} + C = \frac{24x^{\frac{5}{2}}}{5} + C$

Q2 a) $f(x) = \int f'(x)\,dx = \int x^5\,dx = \frac{x^6}{6} + C$

b) $f(x) = \int f'(x)\,dx = \int -6x\,dx = -6\int x\,dx$
$= (-6)\left(\frac{x^2}{2}\right) + C = -3x^2 + C$

c) $f(x) = \int f'(x)\,dx = \int \frac{4}{3}\,dx = \left(\frac{4}{3}\right)\left(\frac{x^1}{1}\right) + C = \frac{4x}{3} + C$

d) $f(x) = \int f'(x)\,dx = \int 2x^{-2}\,dx = 2\int x^{-2}\,dx$
$= 2\left(\frac{x^{-1}}{-1}\right) + C = -2x^{-1} + C$

e) $f(x) = \int f'(x)\,dx = \int -9x^{-19}\,dx = -9\int x^{-19}\,dx$
$= (-9)\left(\frac{x^{-18}}{-18}\right) + C = \frac{x^{-18}}{2} + C$

f) $f(x) = \int f'(x)\,dx = \int \frac{x}{5}\,dx = \frac{1}{5}\int x\,dx$
$= \left(\frac{1}{5}\right)\left(\frac{x^2}{2}\right) + C = \frac{x^2}{10} + C$

g) $f(x) = \int f'(x)\,dx = \int -x^{-6}\,dx = -\int x^{-6}\,dx$
$= -\left(\frac{x^{-5}}{-5}\right) + C = \frac{x^{-5}}{5} + C$

h) $f(x) = \int f'(x)\,dx = \int \frac{5}{\sqrt{x}}\,dx = 5\int x^{-\frac{1}{2}}\,dx$
$= 5\left(\frac{x^{\frac{1}{2}}}{\left(\frac{1}{2}\right)}\right) + C = 10\sqrt{x} + C$

i) $f(x) = \int f'(x)\,dx = \int x^{-\frac{4}{3}}\,dx = \frac{x^{-\frac{1}{3}}}{\left(-\frac{1}{3}\right)} + C$
$= -3x^{-\frac{1}{3}} + C = -\frac{3}{\sqrt[3]{x}} + C$

j) $f(x) = \int f'(x)\,dx = \int 30x^{-0.8}\,dx = 30\int x^{-0.8}\,dx$
$= 30\left(\frac{x^{0.2}}{(0.2)}\right) + C = 150x^{0.2} + C$

k) $f(x) = \int f'(x)\,dx = \int -\frac{2}{3}x^{\frac{7}{3}}\,dx = -\frac{2}{3}\int x^{\frac{7}{3}}\,dx$
$= -\frac{2}{3}\left(\frac{x^{\frac{10}{3}}}{\left(\frac{10}{3}\right)}\right) + C = -\frac{1}{5}x^{\frac{10}{3}} + C$

l) $f(x) = \int f'(x)\,dx = \int -\frac{3}{4}x^{-\frac{5}{2}}\,dx = -\frac{3}{4}\int x^{-\frac{5}{2}}\,dx$
$= -\frac{3}{4}\left(\frac{x^{-\frac{3}{2}}}{\left(-\frac{3}{2}\right)}\right) + C = \frac{1}{2}x^{-\frac{3}{2}} + C$

Q3 a) $\int 12x^2\,dx = 12\int x^2\,dx = 12\left(\frac{x^3}{3}\right) + C = 4x^3 + C = ax^3 + C$
$\Rightarrow a = 4$

b) $\int 20x^{-9}\,dx = 20\int x^{-9}\,dx = 20\left(\frac{x^{-8}}{(-8)}\right) + C = -\frac{5}{2}x^{-8} + C$
$= \frac{a}{2}x^{-8} + C \;\Rightarrow\; a = -5$

c) $\int \frac{4}{5}x^a\,dx = \frac{4}{5}\int x^a\,dx = \frac{4}{5}\left(\frac{x^{a+1}}{a+1}\right) + C = \frac{8}{15}x^{\frac{3}{2}} + C$
$\Rightarrow a + 1 = \frac{3}{2} \;\Rightarrow\; a = \frac{1}{2}$

d) $\int \frac{(\sqrt[3]{x})}{6}\,dx = \frac{1}{6}\int x^{\frac{1}{3}}\,dx = \frac{1}{6}\left(\frac{x^{\frac{4}{3}}}{\left(\frac{4}{3}\right)}\right) + C = \frac{1}{8}x^{\frac{4}{3}} + C = \frac{x^a}{8} + C$
$\Rightarrow a = \frac{4}{3}$

e) $\int -9x^{-4}\,dx = -9\int x^{-4}\,dx = -9\left(\frac{x^{-3}}{(-3)}\right) + C = 3x^{-3} + C$
$= \frac{3}{x^3} + C = \frac{a}{x^a} + C \;\Rightarrow\; a = 3$

f) $\int \left(-\frac{1}{3}\right)^3\,dx = \left(-\frac{1}{3}\right)^3\int x^0\,dx = -\frac{1}{27}x^1 + C = -\frac{1}{27}x^a + C$
$\Rightarrow a = 1$

Q4 a) $\int x^{\frac{2}{3}}\,dx = \frac{x^{\frac{5}{3}}}{\left(\frac{5}{3}\right)} + C = \frac{3x^{\frac{5}{3}}}{5} + C$

b) $\int 7x^{\frac{4}{3}}\,dx = 7\int x^{\frac{4}{3}}\,dx = 7\left(\frac{x^{\frac{7}{3}}}{\left(\frac{7}{3}\right)}\right) + C = 3x^{\frac{7}{3}} + C$

c) $\int x^{-\frac{1}{2}}\,dx = \frac{x^{\frac{1}{2}}}{\left(\frac{1}{2}\right)} + C = 2x^{\frac{1}{2}} + C$

d) $\int 2x^{-\frac{1}{3}}\,dx = 2\int x^{-\frac{1}{3}}\,dx = 2\frac{x^{\frac{2}{3}}}{\left(\frac{2}{3}\right)} + C = 3x^{\frac{2}{3}} + C$

e) $\int 14x^{0.4}\,dx = 14\int x^{0.4}\,dx = 14\left(\frac{x^{1.4}}{1.4}\right) + C = 10x^{1.4} + C$

f) $\int -1.2x^{-0.6}\,dx = -1.2\int x^{-0.6}\,dx = -1.2\left(\frac{x^{0.4}}{0.4}\right) + C = -3x^{0.4} + C$

g) $\int -2x^{-\frac{5}{4}}\,dx = -2\int x^{-\frac{5}{4}}\,dx = -2\frac{x^{-\frac{1}{4}}}{\left(-\frac{1}{4}\right)} + C = 8x^{-\frac{1}{4}} + C$

h) $\int -\frac{3}{2}x^{-\frac{1}{2}}\,dx = -\frac{3}{2}\int x^{-\frac{1}{2}}\,dx = -\frac{3}{2}\left(\frac{x^{\frac{1}{2}}}{\left(\frac{1}{2}\right)}\right) + C = -3x^{\frac{1}{2}} + C$

i) $\int -\frac{4}{3}x^{-\frac{4}{3}}\,dx = -\frac{4}{3}\int x^{-\frac{4}{3}}\,dx = -\frac{4}{3}\left(\frac{x^{-\frac{1}{3}}}{\left(-\frac{1}{3}\right)}\right) + C = 4x^{-\frac{1}{3}} + C$

j) $\int \frac{1}{2}x^{\frac{5}{2}}\,dx = \frac{1}{2}\int x^{\frac{5}{2}}\,dx = \frac{1}{2}\left(\frac{x^{\frac{7}{2}}}{\left(\frac{7}{2}\right)}\right) + C = \frac{1}{7}x^{\frac{7}{2}} + C$

k) $\int \frac{2}{3}x^{\frac{7}{5}}\,dx = \frac{2}{3}\int x^{\frac{7}{5}}\,dx = \frac{2}{3}\left(\frac{x^{\frac{12}{5}}}{\left(\frac{12}{5}\right)}\right) + C = \frac{5}{18}x^{\frac{12}{5}} + C$

l) $\int 50.5x^{0.01}\,dx = 50.5\int x^{0.01}\,dx = 50.5\left(\frac{x^{1.01}}{(1.01)}\right) + C$
$= 50x^{1.01} + C$

Q5 a) $\int kx^9\,dx = k\int x^9\,dx = k\left(\frac{x^{10}}{10}\right) + C = \frac{k}{10}x^{10} + C$

b) $\int \frac{k}{2}x^{-3}\,dx = \frac{k}{2}\int x^{-3}\,dx = \frac{k}{2}\left(\frac{x^{-2}}{(-2)}\right) + C = -\frac{k}{4}x^{-2} + C$

c) $\int \frac{1}{5}x^{2k}\,dx = \frac{1}{5}\int x^{2k}\,dx = \frac{1}{5}\left(\frac{x^{2k+1}}{2k+1}\right) + C = \frac{x^{2k+1}}{5(2k+1)} + C$

d) $\int (k-1)x^{-\frac{1}{2}}\,dx = (k-1)\int x^{-\frac{1}{2}}\,dx = (k-1)\left(\frac{x^{\frac{1}{2}}}{\left(\frac{1}{2}\right)}\right) + C$
$= 2(k-1)x^{\frac{1}{2}} + C$

e) $\int -x^{-(k+1)}\,dx = -\int x^{-k-1}\,dx = -\left(\frac{x^{-k}}{(-k)}\right) + C$
$= \frac{1}{k}x^{-k} + C = \frac{1}{kx^k} + C$

f) $\int (kx)^{-\frac{3}{2}}\,dx = k^{-\frac{3}{2}}\int x^{-\frac{3}{2}}\,dx = k^{-\frac{3}{2}}\left(\frac{x^{-\frac{1}{2}}}{\left(-\frac{1}{2}\right)}\right) + C$
$= -2k^{-\frac{3}{2}}x^{-\frac{1}{2}} + C = -\frac{2}{\sqrt{k^3x}} + C$

Q6 a) $\int \frac{7y^b}{y}\,dy = 7\int \frac{y^b}{y}\,dy = 7\int y^{b-1}\,dy = 7\left(\frac{y^b}{b}\right) + C = \frac{7}{b}y^b + C$

b) $\int \frac{y^b}{(b-1)}\,dy = \frac{1}{b-1}\int y^b\,dy = \frac{1}{b-1}\left(\frac{y^{b+1}}{b+1}\right) + C$
$= \frac{y^{b+1}}{(b+1)(b-1)} + C = \frac{y^{b+1}}{b^2-1} + C$

c) $\int (b^2+b-2)y^{b-2}\,dy = (b^2+b-2)\int y^{b-2}\,dy$
$= (b^2+b-2)\left(\frac{y^{b-1}}{b-1}\right) + C = (b-1)(b+2)\left(\frac{y^{b-1}}{b-1}\right) + C$
$= (b+2)y^{b-1} + C$

Q7 $\int 4ax^{a-1}\,dx = 4a\int x^{a-1}\,dx = 4a\left(\frac{x^a}{a}\right) + C = 4x^a + C$
$\int (a+1)x^a\,dx = (a+1)\int x^a\,dx = (a+1)\left(\frac{x^{a+1}}{a+1}\right) + C = x^{a+1} + C$
When $\int 4ax^{a-1}\,dx = \int (a+1)x^a\,dx$ and C = 0 for both,
$4x^a = x^{a+1} \;\Rightarrow\; 4 = \frac{x^{a+1}}{x^a} \;\Rightarrow\; x = 4$

Exercise 11.3 — Integrating Functions

Q1 a) $f(x) = \int f'(x)\,dx = \int (5x + 3x^{-4})\,dx$
$= 5\int x\,dx + 3\int x^{-4}\,dx$
$= 5\left(\frac{x^2}{2}\right) + 3\left(\frac{x^{-3}}{-3}\right) + C = \frac{5x^2}{2} - x^{-3} + C$

b) $f(x) = \int f'(x)\,dx = \int 4x(x^2 - 1)\,dx$
$= \int (4x^3 - 4x)\,dx = 4\int x^3\,dx - 4\int x\,dx$
$= 4\left(\frac{x^4}{4}\right) - 4\left(\frac{x^2}{2}\right) + C = x^4 - 2x^2 + C$

c) $f(x) = \int f'(x)\,dx = \int (x-3)^2\,dx$
$= \int (x^2 - 6x + 9)\,dx$
$= \int x^2\,dx - 6\int x\,dx + 9\int 1\,dx$
$= \frac{x^3}{3} - 6\left(\frac{x^2}{2}\right) + 9\left(\frac{x^1}{1}\right) + C = \frac{x^3}{3} - 3x^2 + 9x + C$

d) $f(x) = \int f'(x)\,dx = \int x\left(6x + \frac{4}{x^4}\right)dx$
$= \int \left(6x^2 + \frac{4}{x^3}\right)dx = \int (6x^2 + 4x^{-3})\,dx$
$= 6\int x^2\,dx + 4\int x^{-3}\,dx$
$= 6\left(\frac{x^3}{3}\right) + 4\left(\frac{x^{-2}}{-2}\right) + C$
$= 2x^3 - 2x^{-2} + C = 2x^3 - \frac{2}{x^2} + C$

e) $f(x) = \int f'(x)\,dx = \int \left(x + \frac{2}{x}\right)^2 dx$
$= \int \left(x^2 + 4 + \frac{4}{x^2}\right)dx = \int (x^2 + 4 + 4x^{-2})\,dx$
$= \int x^2\,dx + 4\int 1\,dx + 4\int x^{-2}\,dx$
$= \frac{x^3}{3} + 4\left(\frac{x^1}{1}\right) + 4\left(\frac{x^{-1}}{-1}\right) + C = \frac{x^3}{3} + 4x - \frac{4}{x} + C$

f) $f(x) = \int f'(x)\,dx = \int x\left(3x^{\frac{1}{2}} - \frac{2}{x^{\frac{4}{3}}}\right)dx$
$= \int \left(3x^{\frac{3}{2}} - \frac{2}{x^{\frac{1}{3}}}\right)dx = \int (3x^{\frac{3}{2}} - 2x^{-\frac{1}{3}})\,dx$
$= 3\int x^{\frac{3}{2}}\,dx - 2\int x^{-\frac{1}{3}}\,dx$
$= 3\left(\frac{x^{\frac{5}{2}}}{\left(\frac{5}{2}\right)}\right) - 2\frac{x^{\frac{2}{3}}}{\left(\frac{2}{3}\right)} + C = \frac{6}{5}x^{\frac{5}{2}} - 3x^{\frac{2}{3}} + C$

g) $f(x) = \int f'(x)\,dx = \int \left(6\sqrt{x} - \frac{1}{x^2}\right)dx$
$= 6\int x^{\frac{1}{2}}\,dx - \int x^{-2}\,dx$
$= 6\left(\frac{x^{\frac{3}{2}}}{\left(\frac{3}{2}\right)}\right) - \frac{x^{-1}}{-1} + C$
$= \frac{12}{3}x^{\frac{3}{2}} + \frac{1}{x} + C = 4x^{\frac{3}{2}} + \frac{1}{x} + C$
$= 4x\sqrt{x} + \frac{1}{x} + C$

h) $f(x) = \int f'(x)\,dx = \int \left(\frac{2}{\sqrt{x}} - 7x^2\sqrt{x}\right)dx$
$= \int (2x^{-\frac{1}{2}} - 7x^2x^{\frac{1}{2}})\,dx = \int (2x^{-\frac{1}{2}} - 7x^{\frac{5}{2}})\,dx$
$= 2\int x^{-\frac{1}{2}}\,dx - 7\int x^{\frac{5}{2}}\,dx$
$= 2\left(\frac{x^{\frac{1}{2}}}{\left(\frac{1}{2}\right)}\right) - 7\frac{x^{\frac{7}{2}}}{\left(\frac{7}{2}\right)} + C$
$= 4x^{\frac{1}{2}} - 2x^{\frac{7}{2}} + C = 4\sqrt{x} - 2(\sqrt{x})^7 + C$

i) $f(x) = \int f'(x)\,dx = \int \left(5(\sqrt{x})^3 - \frac{3x}{\sqrt{x}}\right)dx$
$= \int (5(x^{\frac{1}{2}})^3 - 3xx^{-\frac{1}{2}})\,dx$
$= 5\int x^{\frac{3}{2}}\,dx - 3\int x^{\frac{1}{2}}\,dx$
$= 5\left(\frac{x^{\frac{5}{2}}}{\left(\frac{5}{2}\right)}\right) - 3\left(\frac{x^{\frac{3}{2}}}{\left(\frac{3}{2}\right)}\right) + C$
$= 2x^{\frac{5}{2}} - 2x^{\frac{3}{2}} + C = 2(\sqrt{x})^5 - 2(\sqrt{x})^3 + C$

j) $f(x) = \int f'(x)\,dx = \int (\sqrt{x}(1-x))\,dx$
$= \int (x^{\frac{1}{2}} - xx^{\frac{1}{2}})\,dx = \int x^{\frac{1}{2}}\,dx - \int x^{\frac{3}{2}}\,dx$
$= \frac{x^{\frac{3}{2}}}{\left(\frac{3}{2}\right)} - \frac{x^{\frac{5}{2}}}{\left(\frac{5}{2}\right)} + C$
$= \frac{2x^{\frac{3}{2}}}{3} - \frac{2x^{\frac{5}{2}}}{5} + C = \frac{2\sqrt{x^3}}{3} - \frac{2\sqrt{x^5}}{5} + C$

k) $f(x) = \int f'(x)\,dx = \int \left(3\sqrt[6]{x} - \frac{\sqrt{x}}{\sqrt[3]{x}}\right)dx$
$= \int (3x^{\frac{1}{6}} - x^{\frac{1}{2}}x^{-\frac{1}{3}})\,dx = \int (3x^{\frac{1}{6}} - x^{\frac{1}{6}})\,dx$
$= \int (2x^{\frac{1}{6}})\,dx = 2\int x^{\frac{1}{6}}\,dx$
$= 2\left(\frac{x^{\frac{7}{6}}}{\left(\frac{7}{6}\right)}\right) + C = \frac{12x^{\frac{7}{6}}}{7} + C$

l) $f(x) = \int f'(x)\,dx = \int \left(\frac{x^3 - 2x^2}{\sqrt{x}}\right)dx$
$= \int (x^{\frac{5}{2}} - 2x^{\frac{3}{2}})\,dx = \int x^{\frac{5}{2}}\,dx - 2\int x^{\frac{3}{2}}\,dx$
$= \frac{x^{\frac{7}{2}}}{\left(\frac{7}{2}\right)} - \frac{2x^{\frac{5}{2}}}{\left(\frac{5}{2}\right)} + C = \frac{2x^{\frac{7}{2}}}{7} - \frac{4x^{\frac{5}{2}}}{5} + C$

Q2 a) $\int \left(\frac{5}{7}x^4 + \frac{2}{3}x + \frac{1}{4}\right)dx$
$= \frac{5}{7}\int x^4\,dx + \frac{2}{3}\int x^1\,dx + \frac{1}{4}\int x^0\,dx$
$= \frac{5}{7}\left(\frac{x^5}{5}\right) + \frac{2}{3}\left(\frac{x^2}{2}\right) + \frac{1}{4}\left(\frac{x^1}{1}\right) + C$
$= \frac{x^5}{7} + \frac{x^2}{3} + \frac{x}{4} + C$

b) $\int (x^{-\frac{1}{2}} + x^{\frac{1}{2}})\,dx = \int x^{-\frac{1}{2}}\,dx + \int x^{\frac{1}{2}}\,dx$
$= \frac{x^{\frac{1}{2}}}{\left(\frac{1}{2}\right)} + \frac{x^{\frac{3}{2}}}{\left(\frac{3}{2}\right)} + C = 2\sqrt{x} + \frac{2\sqrt{x^3}}{3} + C$

c) $\int (3x^{-2} + 3x^{-\frac{1}{3}})\,dx = 3\int x^{-2}\,dx + 3\int x^{-\frac{1}{3}}\,dx$
$= 3\left(\frac{x^{-1}}{(-1)}\right) + 3\left(\frac{x^{\frac{2}{3}}}{\frac{2}{3}}\right) + C = -\frac{3}{x} + \frac{9\sqrt[3]{x^2}}{2} + C$

d) $\int (x^{\frac{5}{4}} + x^{\frac{4}{5}})\,dx = \int x^{\frac{5}{4}}\,dx + \int x^{\frac{4}{5}}\,dx$
$= \left(\frac{x^{\frac{9}{4}}}{\frac{9}{4}}\right) + \left(\frac{x^{\frac{9}{5}}}{\frac{9}{5}}\right) + C = \frac{4x^{\frac{9}{4}}}{9} + \frac{5x^{\frac{9}{5}}}{9} + C$

e) $\int \left(\frac{1}{2}x^{-\frac{1}{2}} + 3x^{-\frac{2}{3}} + 4x^{-\frac{3}{4}}\right)dx$
$= \frac{1}{2}\int x^{-\frac{1}{2}}\,dx + 3\int x^{-\frac{2}{3}}\,dx + 4\int x^{-\frac{3}{4}}\,dx$
$= \frac{1}{2}\left(\frac{x^{\frac{1}{2}}}{\frac{1}{2}}\right) + 3\left(\frac{x^{\frac{1}{3}}}{\frac{1}{3}}\right) + 4\left(\frac{x^{\frac{1}{4}}}{\frac{1}{4}}\right) + C$
$= x^{\frac{1}{2}} + 9x^{\frac{1}{3}} + 16x^{\frac{1}{4}} + C = \sqrt{x} + 9\sqrt[3]{x} + 16\sqrt[4]{x} + C$

f) $\int \left(-\frac{4}{x^3} + \frac{1}{\sqrt{x^3}}\right)dx = -4\int x^{-3}\,dx + \int x^{-\frac{3}{2}}\,dx$
$= -4\left(\frac{x^{-2}}{(-2)}\right) + \left(\frac{x^{-\frac{1}{2}}}{-\frac{1}{2}}\right) + C = 2x^{-2} - 2x^{-\frac{1}{2}} + C$
$= \frac{2}{x^2} - \frac{2}{\sqrt{x}} + C$

Q3 a) $\int \left(\frac{2}{\sqrt{x}} - \frac{\sqrt{x}}{\sqrt{x}}\right)dx = \int (2x^{-\frac{1}{2}} - 1)\,dx = 2\int x^{-\frac{1}{2}}\,dx - \int 1\,dx$
$= 2(2x^{\frac{1}{2}}) - x + C = 4x^{\frac{1}{2}} - x + C = 4\sqrt{x} - x + C$
[3 marks available — 1 mark for rewriting as $2x^{-\frac{1}{2}} - 1$, 1 mark for correct integration, 1 mark for + C]

b) $\int (3\sqrt{x} - 2x\sqrt{x})\,dx = \int (3x^{\frac{1}{2}} - 2x^{\frac{3}{2}})\,dx$
$= 3\int x^{\frac{1}{2}}\,dx - 2\int x^{\frac{3}{2}}\,dx$
$= 3\left(\frac{2}{3}x^{\frac{3}{2}}\right) - 2\left(\frac{2}{5}x^{\frac{5}{2}}\right) + C = 2x^{\frac{3}{2}} - \frac{4}{5}x^{\frac{5}{2}} + C$
[3 marks available — 1 mark for rewriting as $3x^{\frac{1}{2}} - 2x^{\frac{3}{2}}$, 1 mark for correct integration, 1 mark for + C]

Q4 a)
$$\int (0.55x^{0.1} - 3x^{-1.5}x)\,dx = \int (0.55x^{0.1} - 3x^{-0.5})\,dx$$
$$= 0.55\int x^{0.1}\,dx - 3\int x^{-0.5}\,dx$$
$$= 0.55\left(\frac{x^{1.1}}{1.1}\right) - 3\left(\frac{x^{0.5}}{0.5}\right) + C$$
$$= 0.5x^{1.1} - 6x^{0.5} + C$$

b)
$$\int \left(8x^3 - \frac{2}{\sqrt{x}} + \frac{5}{x^2}\right) dx = \int (8x^3 - 2x^{-\frac{1}{2}} + 5x^{-2})\,dx$$
$$= 8\int x^3\,dx - 2\int x^{-\frac{1}{2}}\,dx + 5\int x^{-2}\,dx$$
$$= 8\left(\frac{x^4}{4}\right) - 2\left(\frac{x^{\frac{1}{2}}}{\left(\frac{1}{2}\right)}\right) + 5\left(\frac{x^{-1}}{-1}\right) + C$$
$$= 2x^4 - 4x^{\frac{1}{2}} - 5x^{-1} + C = 2x^4 - 4\sqrt{x} - \frac{5}{x} + C$$

c)
$$\int \left((\sqrt{x})^5 + \frac{1}{2\sqrt{x}}\right) dx = \int \left((x^{\frac{1}{2}})^5 + \frac{1}{2}x^{-\frac{1}{2}}\right) dx$$
$$= \int x^{\frac{5}{2}}\,dx + \frac{1}{2}\int x^{-\frac{1}{2}}\,dx$$
$$= \left(\frac{x^{\frac{7}{2}}}{\left(\frac{7}{2}\right)}\right) + \frac{1}{2}\left(\frac{x^{\frac{1}{2}}}{\left(\frac{1}{2}\right)}\right) + C$$
$$= \frac{2x^{\frac{7}{2}}}{7} + x^{\frac{1}{2}} + C = \frac{2}{7}(\sqrt{x})^7 + \sqrt{x} + C$$

d)
$$\int \left(\sqrt{x}\left(7x^2 - 1 - \frac{2}{x}\right)\right) dx$$
$$= \int (x^{\frac{1}{2}}(7x^2 - 1 - 2x^{-1}))\,dx$$
$$= \int (7x^{\frac{5}{2}} - x^{\frac{1}{2}} - 2x^{-\frac{1}{2}})\,dx$$
$$= 7\int x^{\frac{5}{2}}\,dx - \int x^{\frac{1}{2}}\,dx - 2\int x^{-\frac{1}{2}}\,dx$$
$$= 7\left(\frac{x^{\frac{7}{2}}}{\left(\frac{7}{2}\right)}\right) - \left(\frac{x^{\frac{3}{2}}}{\left(\frac{3}{2}\right)}\right) - 2\left(\frac{x^{\frac{1}{2}}}{\left(\frac{1}{2}\right)}\right) + C$$
$$= 2x^{\frac{7}{2}} - \frac{2}{3}x^{\frac{3}{2}} - 4x^{\frac{1}{2}} + C$$
$$= 2(\sqrt{x})^7 - \frac{2}{3}(\sqrt{x})^3 - 4\sqrt{x} + C$$

e)
$$\int (3x - 5\sqrt{x})^2\,dx = \int (9x^2 - 30x\sqrt{x} + 25x)\,dx$$
$$= \int (9x^2 - 30x^{\frac{3}{2}} + 25x)\,dx$$
$$= 9\int x^2\,dx - 30\int x^{\frac{3}{2}}\,dx + 25\int x\,dx$$
$$= 9\left(\frac{x^3}{3}\right) - 30\left(\frac{2}{5}x^{\frac{5}{2}}\right) + 25\left(\frac{1}{2}x^2\right) + C$$
$$= 3x^3 - 12(\sqrt{x})^5 + \frac{25}{2}x^2 + C$$

f)
$$\int \left(\frac{2x^3 - \sqrt{x}}{x}\right) dx = \int \left(\frac{2x^3}{x} - \frac{\sqrt{x}}{x}\right) dx$$
$$= \int (2x^2 - x^{-\frac{1}{2}})\,dx$$
$$= 2\int x^2\,dx - \int x^{-\frac{1}{2}}\,dx$$
$$= 2\left(\frac{x^3}{3}\right) - \left(\frac{x^{\frac{1}{2}}}{\left(\frac{1}{2}\right)}\right) + C = \frac{2}{3}x^3 - 2\sqrt{x} + C$$

g)
$$\int \left(\frac{(5x-3)^2}{\sqrt{x}}\right) dx = \int \left(\frac{(25x^2 - 30x + 9)}{\sqrt{x}}\right) dx$$
$$= \int \left(\frac{25x^2}{\sqrt{x}} - \frac{30x}{\sqrt{x}} + \frac{9}{\sqrt{x}}\right) dx$$
$$= \int (25x^{\frac{3}{2}} - 30x^{\frac{1}{2}} + 9x^{-\frac{1}{2}})\,dx$$
$$= 25\int x^{\frac{3}{2}}\,dx - 30\int x^{\frac{1}{2}}\,dx + 9\int x^{-\frac{1}{2}}\,dx$$
$$= 25\left(\frac{x^{\frac{5}{2}}}{\left(\frac{5}{2}\right)}\right) - 30\left(\frac{x^{\frac{3}{2}}}{\left(\frac{3}{2}\right)}\right) + 9\left(\frac{x^{\frac{1}{2}}}{\left(\frac{1}{2}\right)}\right) + C$$
$$= 10x^{\frac{5}{2}} - 20x^{\frac{3}{2}} + 18x^{\frac{1}{2}} + C$$
$$= 10(\sqrt{x})^5 - 20(\sqrt{x})^3 + 18\sqrt{x} + C$$

h)
$$\int (x^{\frac{1}{2}} + 1)(x^{-\frac{1}{2}} - 3)\,dx = \int (1 - 3x^{\frac{1}{2}} + x^{-\frac{1}{2}} - 3)\,dx$$
$$= \int (x^{-\frac{1}{2}} - 3x^{\frac{1}{2}} - 2)\,dx$$
$$= \int x^{-\frac{1}{2}}\,dx - 3\int x^{\frac{1}{2}}\,dx - 2\int 1\,dx$$
$$= \left(\frac{x^{\frac{1}{2}}}{\left(\frac{1}{2}\right)}\right) - 3\left(\frac{x^{\frac{3}{2}}}{\left(\frac{3}{2}\right)}\right) - 2\left(\frac{x^1}{1}\right) + C$$
$$= 2x^{\frac{1}{2}} - 2x^{\frac{3}{2}} - 2x + C$$

i)
$$\int (x(2x + \sqrt{x})^2)\,dx = \int (x(4x^2 + 4x^{\frac{3}{2}} + x))\,dx$$
$$= \int (4x^3 + 4x^{\frac{5}{2}} + x^2)\,dx$$
$$= 4\int x^3\,dx + 4\int x^{\frac{5}{2}}\,dx + \int x^2\,dx$$
$$= 4\left(\frac{x^4}{4}\right) + 4\left(\frac{x^{\frac{7}{2}}}{\left(\frac{7}{2}\right)}\right) + \frac{x^3}{3} + C$$
$$= x^4 + \frac{8x^{\frac{7}{2}}}{7} + \frac{x^3}{3} + C$$

j)
$$\int (\sqrt{x} + 2\sqrt[3]{x})^2\,dx = \int (x^{\frac{1}{2}} + 2x^{\frac{1}{3}})^2\,dx$$
$$= \int (x + 4x^{\frac{5}{6}} + 4x^{\frac{2}{3}})\,dx$$
$$= \int x\,dx + 4\int x^{\frac{5}{6}}\,dx + 4\int x^{\frac{2}{3}}\,dx$$
$$= \frac{x^2}{2} + 4\left(\frac{x^{\frac{11}{6}}}{\left(\frac{11}{6}\right)}\right) + 4\left(\frac{x^{\frac{5}{3}}}{\left(\frac{5}{3}\right)}\right) + C$$
$$= \frac{x^2}{2} + \frac{24x^{\frac{11}{6}}}{11} + \frac{12x^{\frac{5}{3}}}{5} + C$$

Q5
$$\int y\,dx = \int (2x - 1 + 5x^{-\frac{1}{2}})\,dx = 2\int x\,dx - \int 1\,dx + 5\int x^{-\frac{1}{2}}\,dx$$
$$2\left(\frac{1}{2}x^2\right) - x + 5(2x^{\frac{1}{2}}) + C = x^2 - x - 10\sqrt{x} + C$$

[3 marks available — 1 mark for rewriting third term as $5x^{-\frac{1}{2}}$, 1 mark for correctly integrating, 1 mark for + C]

Q6
$$y = \int \frac{dy}{dx}\,dx = \int \left(1.5x^2 - \frac{4}{x^3}\right) dx$$
$$= \int (1.5x^2 - 4x^{-3})\,dx = 1.5\int x^2\,dx - 4\int x^{-3}\,dx$$
$$= 1.5\left(\frac{x^3}{3}\right) - 4\left(\frac{x^{-2}}{-2}\right) + C = \frac{x^3}{2} + \frac{2}{x^2} + C$$

Q7
$$f(x) = \int f'(x)\,dx = \int \left(\frac{4}{3(x^{\frac{1}{3}})^4} + 5x^{\frac{3}{2}}\right) dx$$
$$= \int \left(\frac{4}{3x^{\frac{4}{3}}} + 5x^{\frac{3}{2}}\right) dx = \int \left(\frac{4}{3}x^{-\frac{4}{3}} + 5x^{\frac{3}{2}}\right) dx$$
$$= \frac{4}{3}\int x^{-\frac{4}{3}}\,dx + 5\int x^{\frac{3}{2}}\,dx = \frac{4}{3}\left(\frac{x^{-\frac{1}{3}}}{\left(-\frac{1}{3}\right)}\right) + 5\frac{x^{\frac{5}{2}}}{\left(\frac{5}{2}\right)} + C$$
$$= -4x^{-\frac{1}{3}} + 2x^{\frac{5}{2}} + C\left(= -\frac{4}{\sqrt[3]{x}} + 2(\sqrt{x})^5 + C\right)$$

Q8 a)
$$\int \left(4x^2 + \frac{3}{\sqrt{x}} - 2\right) dx$$
$$= \int (4x^2 + 3x^{-\frac{1}{2}} - 2)\,dx$$
$$= 4\int x^2\,dx + 3\int x^{-\frac{1}{2}}\,dx - 2\int x^0\,dx$$
$$= 4\left(\frac{x^3}{3}\right) + 3\left(\frac{x^{\frac{1}{2}}}{\frac{1}{2}}\right) - 2\left(\frac{x^1}{1}\right) + C$$
$$= \frac{4x^3}{3} + 6x^{\frac{1}{2}} - 2x + C = \frac{4x^3}{3} + 6\sqrt{x} - 2x + C$$

b)
$$\int (3\sqrt{x} + 3)^2\,dx$$
$$= \int (9x + 18\sqrt{x} + 9)\,dx$$
$$= 9\int x\,dx + 18\int x^{\frac{1}{2}}\,dx + 9\int x^0\,dx$$
$$= 9\left(\frac{x^2}{2}\right) + 18\left(\frac{x^{\frac{3}{2}}}{\frac{3}{2}}\right) + 9\left(\frac{x^1}{1}\right) + C$$
$$= \frac{9x^2}{2} + 12x^{\frac{3}{2}} + 9x + C = \frac{9x^2}{2} + 12\sqrt{x^3} + 9x + C$$

c) $\int\left(\frac{(\sqrt{x}+3)(\sqrt{x}-1)}{\sqrt{x}}\right)dx = \int\left(\frac{x+2\sqrt{x}-3}{\sqrt{x}}\right)dx$

$= \int\left(\frac{x}{\sqrt{x}}+\frac{2\sqrt{x}}{\sqrt{x}}-\frac{3}{\sqrt{x}}\right)dx$

$= \int(x^{\frac{1}{2}}+2-3x^{-\frac{1}{2}})\,dx$

$= \int x^{\frac{1}{2}}\,dx + 2\int 1\,dx - 3\int x^{-\frac{1}{2}}\,dx$

$= \left(\frac{x^{\frac{3}{2}}}{\left(\frac{3}{2}\right)}\right)+2\left(\frac{x^1}{1}\right)-3\left(\frac{x^{\frac{1}{2}}}{\left(\frac{1}{2}\right)}\right)+C$

$= \frac{2}{3}x^{\frac{3}{2}}+2x-6x^{\frac{1}{2}}+C$

$= \frac{2}{3}(\sqrt{x})^3+2x-6\sqrt{x}+C$

d) $\int\left(\sqrt{x}\left(\sqrt{x}-\frac{1}{\sqrt{x}}\right)^2\right)dx = \int\left(\sqrt{x}\left(x-2+\frac{1}{x}\right)\right)dx$

$= \int\left(x\sqrt{x}-2\sqrt{x}+\frac{\sqrt{x}}{x}\right)dx$

$= \int(x^{\frac{3}{2}}-2x^{\frac{1}{2}}+x^{-\frac{1}{2}})\,dx$

$= \int x^{\frac{3}{2}}\,dx - 2\int x^{\frac{1}{2}}\,dx + \int x^{-\frac{1}{2}}\,dx$

$= \left(\frac{x^{\frac{5}{2}}}{\left(\frac{5}{2}\right)}\right)-2\left(\frac{x^{\frac{3}{2}}}{\left(\frac{3}{2}\right)}\right)+\left(\frac{x^{\frac{1}{2}}}{\left(\frac{1}{2}\right)}\right)+C$

$= \frac{2}{5}x^{\frac{5}{2}}-\frac{4}{3}x^{\frac{3}{2}}+2x^{\frac{1}{2}}+C$

$= \frac{2}{5}(\sqrt{x})^5-\frac{4}{3}(\sqrt{x})^3+2\sqrt{x}+C$

e) $\int\left(\frac{(\sqrt{x^3}+6)(\sqrt{x^3}-6)}{\sqrt{x^3}}\right)dx = \int\left(\frac{x^3-36}{x^{\frac{3}{2}}}\right)dx$

$= \int(x^{\frac{3}{2}}-36x^{-\frac{3}{2}})\,dx$

$= \int x^{\frac{3}{2}}\,dx - 36\int x^{-\frac{3}{2}}\,dx$

$= \left(\frac{x^{\frac{5}{2}}}{\frac{5}{2}}\right)-36\left(\frac{x^{-\frac{1}{2}}}{\left(-\frac{1}{2}\right)}\right)+C$

$= \frac{2x^{\frac{5}{2}}}{5}+72x^{-\frac{1}{2}}+C$

$= \frac{2\sqrt{x^5}}{5}+\frac{72}{\sqrt{x}}+C$

f) $\int\left(\frac{3x-\sqrt{x}-2}{\sqrt{x}-1}\right)dx = \int\left(\frac{(3\sqrt{x}+2)(\sqrt{x}-1)}{\sqrt{x}-1}\right)dx$

$= \int(3x^{\frac{1}{2}}+2)\,dx$

$= 3\int x^{\frac{1}{2}}\,dx + 2\int x^0\,dx$

$= 3\left(\frac{x^{\frac{3}{2}}}{\frac{3}{2}}\right)+2\left(\frac{x^1}{1}\right)+C$

$= 2x^{\frac{3}{2}}+2x+C$

$= 2\sqrt{x^3}+2x+C$

Q9 a) $f(x)=0 \Rightarrow (2-\sqrt{x})^2=0 \Rightarrow 2-\sqrt{x}=0$

$\Rightarrow \sqrt{x}=2 \Rightarrow x=4$

[2 marks available — 2 marks for the correct answer, otherwise 1 mark for correct working]

b) $f(2)=(2-\sqrt{2})^2=4-4\sqrt{2}+2=6-4\sqrt{2}$

[2 marks available — 2 marks for the correct answer, otherwise 1 mark for correct working]

c) $\int f(x)\,dx = \int(4-4x^{\frac{1}{2}}+x)\,dx$

$= 4\int 1\,dx - 4\int x^{\frac{1}{2}}\,dx + \int x\,dx$

$= 4x-4\left(\frac{2}{3}x^{\frac{3}{2}}\right)+\frac{1}{2}x^2+C = \frac{1}{2}x^2-\frac{8}{3}x^{\frac{3}{2}}+4x+C$

[3 marks available — 1 mark for rewriting in powers of x, 1 mark for correctly integrating, 1 mark for + C]

Q10 $\int\left(\frac{2n^2x^2+3x^3}{nx}\right)dx = \int\left(\frac{2n^2x^2}{nx}+\frac{3x^3}{nx}\right)dx$

$= \int\left(2nx+\frac{3x^2}{n}\right)dx$

$= 2n\int x\,dx + \frac{3}{n}\int x^2\,dx$

$= 2n\left(\frac{x^2}{2}\right)+\frac{3}{n}\left(\frac{x^3}{3}\right)+C$

$= nx^2+\frac{x^3}{n}+C$

Exercise 11.4 — Integrating to Find Equations of Curves

Q1 a) $f(x) = \int f'(x)\,dx = \int 4x^3\,dx = 4\int x^3\,dx$

$= 4\left(\frac{x^4}{4}\right)+C = x^4+C$

At the point (0, 5), $x = 0$ and $f(x) = y = 5$, so $5 = 0^4 + C$. So $C = 5$ and $f(x) = x^4 + 5$.

b) $f(x) = \int f'(x)\,dx = \int(3x^2-4x+3)\,dx$

$= 3\int x^2\,dx - 4\int x\,dx + 3\int 1\,dx$

$= 3\left(\frac{x^3}{3}\right)-4\left(\frac{x^2}{2}\right)+3\left(\frac{x^1}{1}\right)+C = x^3-2x^2+3x+C$

At the point (1, –3) $x = 1$ and $f(x) = y = -3$, so $-3 = 1^3 - 2(1^2) + 3(1) + C = 2 + C$. So $C = -5$ and $f(x) = x^3 - 2x^2 + 3x - 5$.

c) $f(x) = \int f'(x)\,dx = \int 6x(x+2)\,dx$

$= \int(6x^2+12x)\,dx = 6\int x^2\,dx + 12\int x\,dx$

$= 6\left(\frac{x^3}{3}\right)+12\left(\frac{x^2}{2}\right)+C = 2x^3+6x^2+C$

At the point (–1, 1) $x = -1$ and $f(x) = y = 1$, so $1 = 2(-1)^3 + 6(-1)^2 + C = 4 + C$. So $C = -3$ and $f(x) = 2x^3 + 6x^2 - 3$.

d) $f(x) = \int f'(x)\,dx = \int\left(\frac{5}{x^2}+2x\right)dx$

$= \int(5x^{-2}+2x)\,dx$

$= 5\int x^{-2}\,dx + 2\int x\,dx$

$= 5\left(\frac{x^{-1}}{-1}\right)+2\left(\frac{x^2}{2}\right)+C = -\frac{5}{x}+x^2+C$

At the point (5, 4) $x = 5$ and $f(x) = y = 4$, so $4 = -\frac{5}{5}+5^2+C = 24+C$. So $C = -20$ and $f(x) = -\frac{5}{x}+x^2-20$.

e) $f(x) = \int f'(x)\,dx = \int 3x^2(x-4)\,dx$

$= \int(3x^3-12x^2)\,dx$

$= 3\int x^3\,dx - 12\int x^2\,dx$

$= 3\left(\frac{x^4}{4}\right)-12\left(\frac{x^3}{3}\right)+C = \frac{3}{4}x^4-4x^3+C$

At the point (2, –10) $x = 2$ and $f(x) = y = -10$, so $-10 = \frac{3}{4}(2^4)-4(2^3)+C = -20+C$. So $C = 10$ and $f(x) = \frac{3}{4}x^4-4x^3+10$.

f) $f(x) = \int f'(x)\,dx = \int(3x+1)(x-1)\,dx$

$= \int(3x^2-2x-1)\,dx$

$= 3\int x^2\,dx - 2\int x\,dx - \int 1\,dx$

$= 3\left(\frac{x^3}{3}\right)-2\left(\frac{x^2}{2}\right)-\left(\frac{x^1}{1}\right)+C = x^3-x^2-x+C$

At the point (3, –3) $x = 3$ and $f(x) = y = -3$, so $-3 = 3^3 - 3^2 - 3 + C = 15 + C$.

So $C = -18$ and $f(x) = x^3 - x^2 - x - 18$.

g) $f(x) = \int f'(x)\,dx = \int x\left(x + \frac{3}{x^3}\right)dx$

$= \int \left(x^2 + \frac{3}{x^2}\right)dx = \int x^2\,dx + 3\int x^{-2}\,dx$

$= \frac{x^3}{3} + 3\left(\frac{x^{-1}}{-1}\right) + C = \frac{x^3}{3} - \frac{3}{x} + C$

At the point (–3, 5) $x = -3$ and $f(x) = y = 5$,

so $5 = \frac{(-3)^3}{3} - \frac{3}{-3} + C = -8 + C$.

So C = 13 and $f(x) = \frac{x^3}{3} - \frac{3}{x} + 13$.

h) $f(x) = \int f'(x)\,dx = \int \frac{9x^3 + 2x^{-2}}{x}\,dx$

$= \int \left(\frac{9x^3}{x} + \frac{2x^{-2}}{x}\right)dx = \int (9x^2 + 2x^{-3})\,dx$

$= 9\int x^2\,dx + 2\int x^{-3}\,dx$

$= 9\left(\frac{x^3}{3}\right) + 2\left(\frac{x^{-2}}{-2}\right) + C = 3x^3 - \frac{1}{x^2} + C$

At the point (–1, 2) $x = -1$ and $f(x) = y = 2$,

so $2 = 3(-1)^3 - \frac{1}{(-1)^2} + C = -4 + C$.

So C = 6 and $f(x) = 3x^3 - \frac{1}{x^2} + 6$.

i) $f(x) = \int f'(x)\,dx = \int \sqrt{x}(3 + x)\,dx$

$= \int (3\sqrt{x} + x\sqrt{x})\,dx = \int (3x^{\frac{1}{2}} + x^{\frac{3}{2}})\,dx$

$= 3\int x^{\frac{1}{2}}\,dx + \int x^{\frac{3}{2}}\,dx$

$= 3\left(\frac{x^{\frac{3}{2}}}{\frac{3}{2}}\right) + \frac{x^{\frac{5}{2}}}{\frac{5}{2}} + C = 2x^{\frac{3}{2}} + \frac{2x^{\frac{5}{2}}}{5} + C$

At the point (1, 4), $x = 1$ and $f(x) = y = 4$,

so $4 = 2(1)^{\frac{3}{2}} + \frac{2(1)^{\frac{5}{2}}}{5} + C = \frac{12}{5} + C$

So $C = \frac{8}{5}$ and $f(x) = 2x^{\frac{3}{2}} + \frac{2x^{\frac{5}{2}}}{5} + \frac{8}{5}$

j) $f(x) = \int f'(x)\,dx = \int \frac{2 - 3\sqrt[6]{x}}{\sqrt{x}}\,dx$

$= \int \left(\frac{2}{\sqrt{x}} - \frac{3x^{\frac{1}{6}}}{\sqrt{x}}\right)dx = \int (2x^{-\frac{1}{2}} - 3x^{-\frac{1}{3}})\,dx$

$= 2\int x^{-\frac{1}{2}}\,dx - 3\int x^{-\frac{1}{3}}\,dx$

$= 2\left(\frac{x^{\frac{1}{2}}}{\frac{1}{2}}\right) - 3\left(\frac{x^{\frac{2}{3}}}{\frac{2}{3}}\right) + C = 4x^{\frac{1}{2}} - \frac{9x^{\frac{2}{3}}}{2} + C$

At the point (64, –33), $x = 64$ and $f(x) = y = -33$, so

$-33 = 4(64)^{\frac{1}{2}} - \frac{9(64)^{\frac{2}{3}}}{2} + C = -40 + C$

So C = 7 and $f(x) = 4x^{\frac{1}{2}} - \frac{9x^{\frac{2}{3}}}{2} + 7$

Q2 a) $y = f(x) = \int f'(x)\,dx = \int (6x^2 + 6x - 5)\,dx$

$= 6\int x^2\,dx + 6\int x\,dx - 5\int 1\,dx$

$= 6\left(\frac{x^3}{3}\right) + 6\left(\frac{x^2}{2}\right) - 5\left(\frac{x^1}{1}\right) + C$

$= 2x^3 + 3x^2 - 5x + C$

At the origin, $x = 0$ and $y = 0$,
so $0 = 2(0)^3 + 3(0)^2 - 5(0) + C = 0 + C$.
So C = 0 and $y = 2x^3 + 3x^2 - 5x$.

b) $y = 2x^3 + 3x^2 - 5x = x(2x^2 + 3x - 5) = x(2x + 5)(x - 1)$

So when $y = 0$, $x = 0$ or $x = -\frac{5}{2}$ or $x = 1$.

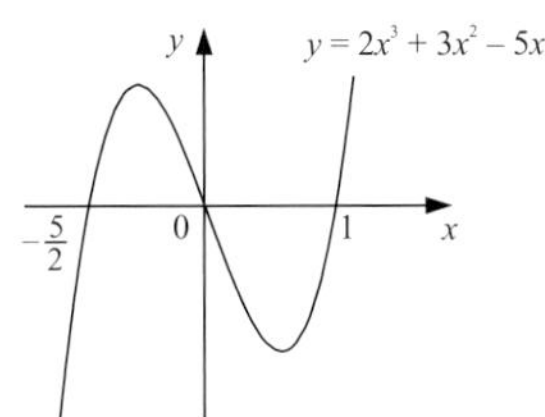

Q3 $f(x) = \int \frac{3x - x^2}{x}\,dx = \int (3 - x)\,dx = 3\int 1\,dx - \int x\,dx$

$= 3x - \frac{1}{2}x^2 + C$

At (4, 5), $x = 4$ and $y = 5$ $\Rightarrow$ $5 = 3 \times 4 - \frac{1}{2} \times 4^2 + C = 4 + C$

$\Rightarrow C = 1$

So $f(x) = 3x - \frac{1}{2}x^2 + 1$.

[4 marks available — 1 mark for simplifying to 3 – x, 1 mark for integrating all terms correctly, 1 mark for using the point (4, 5) to find C, 1 mark for correct final answer including C = 1]

Q4 $y = f(x) = \int f'(x)\,dx = \int \left(\frac{3}{\sqrt{x}} + 2x\right)dx$

$= \int (3x^{-\frac{1}{2}} + 2x)\,dx = 3\int x^{-\frac{1}{2}}\,dx + 2\int x\,dx$

$= 3\left(\frac{x^{\frac{1}{2}}}{\left(\frac{1}{2}\right)}\right) + 2\left(\frac{x^2}{2}\right) + C = 6x^{\frac{1}{2}} + x^2 + C = 6\sqrt{x} + x^2 + C$

At the point (4, 9) $x = 4$ and $y = 9$, so $9 = 6\sqrt{4} + 4^2 + C = 28 + C$

So $C = -19$ and $y = 6\sqrt{x} + x^2 - 19$.

Q5 $y = \int \frac{dy}{dx}\,dx = \int \left(3\sqrt{x} + \frac{1}{x^2}\right)dx = \int (3x^{\frac{1}{2}} + x^{-2})\,dx$

$= 3\int x^{\frac{1}{2}}\,dx + \int x^{-2}\,dx = 3\left(\frac{x^{\frac{3}{2}}}{\left(\frac{3}{2}\right)}\right) + \left(\frac{x^{-1}}{-1}\right) + C$

$= 2x^{\frac{3}{2}} - \frac{1}{x} + C = 2(\sqrt{x})^3 - \frac{1}{x} + C$

At the point (1, 7), $x = 1$ and $y = 7$, so

$7 = 2((\sqrt{1})^3) - \frac{1}{1} + C = 1 + C$.

So C = 6 and $y = 2(\sqrt{x})^3 - \frac{1}{x} + 6$.

Q6 $y = \int \frac{dy}{dt}\,dt = \int (\sqrt{t} - 3)^2\,dt = \int (t - 6\sqrt{t} + 9)\,dt$

$= \int t\,dt - 6\int t^{\frac{1}{2}}\,dt + 9\int 1\,dt$

$= \frac{t^2}{2} - 6\left(\frac{t^{\frac{3}{2}}}{\left(\frac{3}{2}\right)}\right) + 9\left(\frac{t^1}{1}\right) + C$

$= \frac{t^2}{2} - 4t^{\frac{3}{2}} + 9t + C = \frac{t^2}{2} - 4(\sqrt{t})^3 + 9t + C$

When $t = 4$, $y = 9$ so $9 = \frac{4^2}{2} - 4(\sqrt{4})^3 + 9(4) + C = 12 + C$.

So $C = -3$ and $y = \frac{t^2}{2} - 4(\sqrt{t})^3 + 9t - 3$.

Q7 $f(x) = \int f'(x)\,dx = \int (\sqrt{x}(5x - 1))\,dx$

$= \int (5x\sqrt{x} - \sqrt{x})\,dx = \int (5x^{\frac{3}{2}} - x^{\frac{1}{2}})\,dx$

$= 5\int x^{\frac{3}{2}}\,dx - \int x^{\frac{1}{2}}\,dx = 5\left(\frac{x^{\frac{5}{2}}}{\left(\frac{5}{2}\right)}\right) - \left(\frac{x^{\frac{3}{2}}}{\left(\frac{3}{2}\right)}\right) + C$

$= 2x^{\frac{5}{2}} - \frac{2}{3}x^{\frac{3}{2}} + C = 2(\sqrt{x})^5 - \frac{2}{3}(\sqrt{x})^3 + C$

When $x = 1$, $f(x) = y = \frac{1}{3}$ so $\frac{1}{3} = 2(\sqrt{1})^5 - \frac{2}{3}(\sqrt{1})^3 + C = \frac{4}{3} + C$

So $C = -1$ and $f(x) = 2(\sqrt{x})^5 - \frac{2}{3}(\sqrt{x})^3 - 1$

Q8 $y = f(x) = \int f'(x)\,dx = \int \left(x^2 + \frac{2}{x^{\frac{3}{2}}}\right)dx$

$= \int (x^2 + 2x^{-\frac{3}{2}})\,dx = \int x^2\,dx + 2\int x^{-\frac{3}{2}}\,dx$

$= \frac{x^3}{3} + 2\left(\frac{x^{-\frac{1}{2}}}{\left(-\frac{1}{2}\right)}\right) + C = \frac{x^3}{3} - \frac{4}{\sqrt{x}} + C$

When $x = 1$, $y = -\frac{5}{3}$ so $-\frac{5}{3} = \frac{1^3}{3} - \frac{4}{\sqrt{1}} + C = -\frac{11}{3} + C$

So C = 2 and $y = \frac{x^3}{3} - \frac{4}{\sqrt{x}} + 2$

Q9 $y = \int \frac{dy}{dx}\,dx = \int \left(\frac{x-6}{x^3} + 2\right) dx$

$= \int \left(\frac{x}{x^3} - \frac{6}{x^3} + 2\right) dx = \int (x^{-2} - 6x^{-3} + 2)\,dx$

$= \int x^{-2}\,dx - 6\int x^{-3}\,dx + 2\int 1\,dx$

$= \left(\frac{x^{-1}}{-1}\right) - 6\left(\frac{x^{-2}}{-2}\right) + 2\left(\frac{x^1}{1}\right) + C = -\frac{1}{x} + \frac{3}{x^2} + 2x + C$

When $x = 3$, $y = -1$ so $-1 = -\frac{1}{3} + \frac{3}{3^2} + 2(3) + C = 6 + C$.

So $C = -7$ and $y = -\frac{1}{x} + \frac{3}{x^2} + 2x - 7$.

Q10 a) $\frac{dy}{dx} = \frac{(x+2)(x-2)}{\sqrt{x}} = \frac{x^2-4}{\sqrt{x}} = \frac{x^2}{x^{\frac{1}{2}}} - \frac{4}{x^{\frac{1}{2}}} = x^{\frac{3}{2}} - 4x^{-\frac{1}{2}}$

b) $y = \int \frac{dy}{dx}\,dx = \int (x^{\frac{3}{2}} - 4x^{-\frac{1}{2}})\,dx$

$= \int x^{\frac{3}{2}}\,dx - 4\int x^{-\frac{1}{2}}\,dx = \left(\frac{x^{\frac{5}{2}}}{\frac{5}{2}}\right) - 4\left(\frac{x^{\frac{1}{2}}}{\frac{1}{2}}\right) + C$

$= \frac{2x^{\frac{5}{2}}}{5} - 8x^{\frac{1}{2}} + C = \frac{2\sqrt{x^5}}{5} - 8\sqrt{x} + C$

At point $\left(1, \frac{7}{5}\right)$, $\frac{7}{5} = \frac{2\sqrt{(1)^5}}{5} - 8\sqrt{1} + C = -\frac{38}{5} + C$

So $C = 9$ and $y = \frac{2\sqrt{x^5}}{5} - 8\sqrt{x} + 9$

Q11 a) Gradient of curve at P = gradient of tangent at P = 3 *[1 mark]*

b) $f'(x) = 3 = 2 + \frac{3}{\sqrt{x}} \Rightarrow \frac{3}{\sqrt{x}} = 1 \Rightarrow \sqrt{x} = 3 \Rightarrow x = 9$

$y - 3x = 1 \Rightarrow y - 3 \times 9 = 1 \Rightarrow y = 28 \Rightarrow P = (9, 28)$

[3 marks available — 1 mark for setting f'(x) = 3, 1 mark for correct value of x, 1 mark for correct final answer]

c) $y = \int (2 + 3x^{-\frac{1}{2}})\,dx = 2\int 1\,dx + 3\int x^{-\frac{1}{2}}\,dx$

$= 2x + 3(2x^{\frac{1}{2}}) = 2x + 6\sqrt{x} + C$

At P, $x = 9$ and $y = 28 \Rightarrow 28 = 2 \times 9 + 6 \times \sqrt{9} + C = 36 + C$

$\Rightarrow C = -8$

So the equation of the curve is $y = 2x + 6\sqrt{x} - 8$

[5 marks available — 1 mark for each term correctly integrated, 1 mark for using given coordinates to find C, 1 mark for correct value of C = –8, 1 mark for final answer]

Q12 a) $f(x) = \int -2x^{-2}\,dx = -2\int x^{-2}\,dx = -2(-x^{-1}) + C = \frac{2}{x} + C$

At $(-1, 4)$, $x = -1$ and $y = 4 \Rightarrow 4 = -\frac{2}{1} + C \Rightarrow C = 6$

So the equation of the curve is $f(x) = \frac{2}{x} + 6$

[4 marks available — 1 mark for rewriting as $-2x^{-2}$, 1 mark for correct integration, 1 mark for using given coordinates to find C, 1 mark for correct final answer]

b)

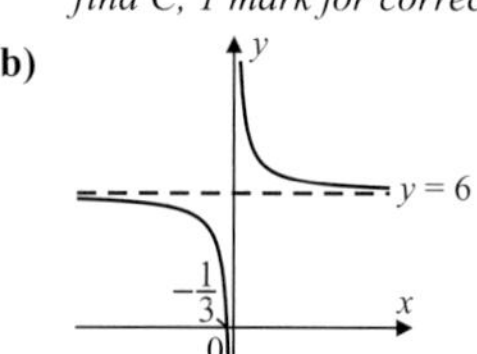

[3 marks available — 1 mark for correct shape of curve, 1 mark for asymptote at y = 6, 1 mark for x-intercept at $-\frac{1}{3}$]

Q13 a) $f(x) = \int (3x^{\frac{1}{2}} - 2x^{-\frac{1}{2}})\,dx = 3\int x^{\frac{1}{2}}\,dx - 2\int x^{-\frac{1}{2}}\,dx$

$= 3\left(\frac{2}{3}x^{\frac{3}{2}}\right) - 2(2x^{\frac{1}{2}}) + C = 2x^{\frac{3}{2}} - 4\sqrt{x} + C$

At $(0, 0)$, $x = 0$ and $y = 0 \Rightarrow 0 = 2 \times 0 - 4 \times 0 + C \Rightarrow C = 0$

So the equation of the curve is $f(x) = 2x^{\frac{3}{2}} - 4\sqrt{x}$.

[5 marks available — 1 mark for rewriting as $3x^{\frac{1}{2}} - 2x^{-\frac{1}{2}}$, 1 mark for correct integration of each term, 1 mark for finding C = 0, 1 mark for correct final answer]

b) Point P is at $y = 0$ so set $2x^{\frac{3}{2}} - 4\sqrt{x} = 2\sqrt{x}(x-2) = 0$

$\Rightarrow 2\sqrt{x} = 0$ or $(x - 2) = 0 \Rightarrow x = 0$ or $x = 2 \Rightarrow P = (2, 0)$

[2 marks available — 1 mark for attempting to solve f(x) = 0, 1 mark for correct final answer]

Q14 $v = \int \frac{dv}{dt}\,dt = \int (6t - t^2)\,dt = 6\int t\,dt - \int t^2\,dt$

$= 6\left(\frac{t^2}{2}\right) - \frac{t^3}{3} + C = 3t^2 - \frac{t^3}{3} + C$

When $v = 0$, $t = 10$, so $0 = 3(10)^2 - \frac{10^3}{3} + C = -\frac{100}{3} + C$,

$\Rightarrow C = \frac{100}{3} \Rightarrow v = 3t^2 - \frac{t^3}{3} + \frac{100}{3}$

So when $t = 0$, $v = \frac{100}{3} = 33.3\ \text{ms}^{-1}$ (3 s.f.).

Q15 When $x = 2$, $f'(x) = 18$, so $3(2)^2 + 2k - k = 18$

$\Rightarrow 12 + k = 18 \Rightarrow k = 6$, so $f'(x) = 3x^2 + 6x - 6$.

$f(x) = \int f'(x)\,dx = \int (3x^2 + 6x - 6)\,dx$

$= 3\int x^2\,dx + 6\int x\,dx - 6\int 1\,dx$

$= 3\left(\frac{x^3}{3}\right) + 6\left(\frac{x^2}{2}\right) - 6x + C$

$= x^3 + 3x^2 - 6x + C$

When $x = 2$, $y = 7$, so $7 = 2^3 + 3(2)^2 - 6(2) + C$

$\Rightarrow 7 = 8 + C \Rightarrow C = -1$

So $f(x) = x^3 + 3x^2 - 6x - 1$.

Exercise 11.5 — Evaluating Definite Integrals

Q1 a) $\int_{-2}^{0} (4x^3 + 2x)\,dx = [x^4 + x^2]_{-2}^{0}$

$= (0^4 + 0^2) - ((-2)^4 + (-2)^2)$

$= -(16 + 4) = -20$

b) $\int_{-2}^{5} (x^3 + x)\,dx = \left[\frac{x^4}{4} + \frac{x^2}{2}\right]_{-2}^{5}$

$= \left(\frac{5^4}{4} + \frac{5^2}{2}\right) - \left(\frac{(-2)^4}{4} + \frac{(-2)^2}{2}\right)$

$= \frac{625}{4} + \frac{25}{2} - \frac{16}{4} - \frac{4}{2} = \frac{651}{4}$

c) $\int_{-5}^{-2} (x+1)^2\,dx = \int_{-5}^{-2} (x^2 + 2x + 1)\,dx$

$= \left[\frac{x^3}{3} + x^2 + x\right]_{-5}^{-2}$

$= \left(\frac{(-2)^3}{3} + (-2)^2 + (-2)\right) - \left(\frac{(-5)^3}{3} + (-5)^2 + (-5)\right)$

$= \left(\frac{-8}{3} + 4 - 2\right) - \left(\frac{-125}{3} + 25 - 5\right) = 21$

d) $\int_{3}^{4} (6x^{-4} + x^{-2})\,dx = \left[\frac{6x^{-3}}{-3} + \frac{x^{-1}}{-1}\right]_{3}^{4}$

$= \left[-\frac{2}{x^3} - \frac{1}{x}\right]_{3}^{4} = \left(-\frac{2}{4^3} - \frac{1}{4}\right) - \left(-\frac{2}{3^3} - \frac{1}{3}\right)$

$= -\frac{2}{64} - \frac{1}{4} + \frac{2}{27} + \frac{1}{3} = \frac{109}{864}$

e) $\int_{1}^{2} \left(x^2 + \frac{1}{x^2}\right) dx = \int_{1}^{2} (x^2 + x^{-2})\,dx = \left[\frac{x^3}{3} + \frac{x^{-1}}{-1}\right]_{1}^{2}$

$= \left[\frac{x^3}{3} - \frac{1}{x}\right]_{1}^{2} = \left(\frac{2^3}{3} - \frac{1}{2}\right) - \left(\frac{1^3}{3} - \frac{1}{1}\right)$

$= \frac{8}{3} - \frac{1}{2} - \frac{1}{3} + 1 = \frac{17}{6}$

f) $\int_{1}^{4} (3x^{-4} + \sqrt{x})\,dx = \int_{1}^{4} (3x^{-4} + x^{\frac{1}{2}})\,dx$

$= \left[\frac{3x^{-3}}{-3} + \frac{x^{\frac{3}{2}}}{\left(\frac{3}{2}\right)}\right]_{1}^{4} = \left[-\frac{1}{x^3} + \frac{2}{3}(\sqrt{x})^3\right]_{1}^{4}$

$= \left(-\frac{1}{4^3} + \frac{2}{3}(\sqrt{4})^3\right) - \left(-\frac{1}{1^3} + \frac{2}{3}(\sqrt{1})^3\right)$

$= \left(-\frac{1}{64} + \frac{2}{3} \times 2^3\right) - \left(-1 + \frac{2}{3}\right) = \frac{1085}{192}$

g) $\int_{0}^{1} (2x+3)(x+2)\,dx = \int_{0}^{1} (2x^2 + 7x + 6)\,dx$

$= \left[\frac{2x^3}{3} + \frac{7x^2}{2} + 6x\right]_{0}^{1}$

$= \left(\frac{2 \times 1^3}{3} + \frac{7 \times 1^2}{2} + (6 \times 1)\right) - \left(\frac{2 \times 0^3}{3} + \frac{7 \times 0^2}{2} + (6 \times 0)\right)$

$= \left(\frac{2}{3} + \frac{7}{2} + 6\right) - 0 = \frac{61}{6}$

h) $\int_1^4 \frac{x^2+2}{\sqrt{x}}\,dx = \int_1^4 (x^{\frac{3}{2}} + 2x^{-\frac{1}{2}})\,dx$

$= \left[\frac{x^{\frac{5}{2}}}{\left(\frac{5}{2}\right)} + 2\frac{x^{\frac{1}{2}}}{\left(\frac{1}{2}\right)}\right]_1^4 = \left[\frac{2}{5}(\sqrt{x})^5 + 4\sqrt{x}\right]_1^4$

$= \left(\frac{2}{5}(\sqrt{4})^5 + 4\sqrt{4}\right) - \left(\frac{2}{5}(\sqrt{1})^5 + 4\sqrt{1}\right)$

$= \left(\frac{2}{5}\times 2^5 + 8\right) - \left(\frac{2}{5} + 4\right)$

$= \frac{64}{5} + 8 - \frac{2}{5} - 4 = \frac{82}{5}$

i) $\int_4^9 \left(\frac{1}{x} + \sqrt{x}\right)^2 dx = \int_4^9 \left(\frac{1}{x^2} + 2\frac{\sqrt{x}}{x} + x\right) dx$

$= \int_4^9 (x^{-2} + 2x^{-\frac{1}{2}} + x)\,dx$

$= \left[\frac{x^{-1}}{-1} + \frac{2x^{\frac{1}{2}}}{\left(\frac{1}{2}\right)} + \frac{x^2}{2}\right]_4^9$

$= \left[-\frac{1}{x} + 4\sqrt{x} + \frac{x^2}{2}\right]_4^9$

$= \left(-\frac{1}{9} + 4\sqrt{9} + \frac{9^2}{2}\right) - \left(-\frac{1}{4} + 4\sqrt{4} + \frac{4^2}{2}\right)$

$= -\frac{1}{9} + 12 + \frac{81}{2} + \frac{1}{4} - 8 - 8 = \frac{1319}{36}$

j) $\int_4^{16} \left(\frac{\sqrt{x}-1}{x^2}\right) dx = \int_4^{16} (x^{-\frac{3}{2}} - x^{-2})\,dx$

$= \left[\frac{x^{-\frac{1}{2}}}{\left(-\frac{1}{2}\right)} - \frac{x^{-1}}{(-1)}\right]_4^{16} = [-2x^{-\frac{1}{2}} + x^{-1}]_4^{16} = \left[-\frac{2}{\sqrt{x}} + \frac{1}{x}\right]_4^{16}$

$= \left(-\frac{2}{\sqrt{16}} + \frac{1}{16}\right) - \left(-\frac{2}{\sqrt{4}} + \frac{1}{4}\right)$

$= -\frac{1}{2} + \frac{1}{16} + 1 - \frac{1}{4} = \frac{5}{16}$

k) $\int_1^9 x^{\frac{1}{2}}(5x - x^{-\frac{1}{2}})\,dx = \int_1^9 (5x^{\frac{3}{2}} - 1)\,dx$

$= \left[\frac{5x^{\frac{5}{2}}}{\frac{5}{2}} - \frac{x^1}{1}\right]_1^9 = [2x^{\frac{5}{2}} - x]_1^9$

$= (2(9)^{\frac{5}{2}} - 9) - (2(1)^{\frac{5}{2}} - 1)$

$= 486 - 9 - 2 + 1 = 476$

l) $\int_1^4 (1+x^2)(1+\sqrt{x})\,dx = \int_1^4 (1 + x^{\frac{5}{2}} + x^2 + x^{\frac{1}{2}})\,dx$

$= \left[\frac{x^1}{1} + \frac{x^{\frac{7}{2}}}{\frac{7}{2}} + \frac{x^3}{3} + \frac{x^{\frac{3}{2}}}{\frac{3}{2}}\right]_1^4 = \left[x + \frac{2x^{\frac{7}{2}}}{7} + \frac{x^3}{3} + \frac{2x^{\frac{3}{2}}}{3}\right]_1^4$

$= \left(4 + \frac{2(4)^{\frac{7}{2}}}{7} + \frac{4^3}{3} + \frac{2(4)^{\frac{3}{2}}}{3}\right)$

$- \left(1 + \frac{2(1)^{\frac{7}{2}}}{7} + \frac{1^3}{3} + \frac{2(1)^{\frac{3}{2}}}{3}\right)$

$= 4 + \frac{256}{7} + \frac{64}{3} + \frac{16}{3} - 1 - \frac{2}{7} - \frac{1}{3} - \frac{2}{3} = \frac{1364}{21}$

Q2 a) $\int_1^3 (2x^2 + 3x - 2)\,dx = \left[2\left(\frac{x^3}{3}\right) + 3\left(\frac{x^2}{2}\right) - 2x\right]_1^3$

$= \left(\frac{2\times 3^3}{3} + \frac{3\times 3^2}{2} - 2\times 3\right) - \left(\frac{2\times 1^3}{3} + \frac{3\times 1^2}{2} - 2\times 1\right)$

$= 18 + \frac{27}{2} - 6 - \frac{2}{3} - \frac{3}{2} + 2 = \frac{76}{3}$

[5 marks available — 1 mark for expanding to $2x^2 + 3x - 2$, 1 mark for any two terms correctly integrated, 1 mark for the third term correctly integrated, 1 mark for subbing in the limits, 1 mark for the correct final answer]

b) $\int_1^4 \frac{1}{2}x^{\frac{1}{2}}\,dx = \left[\frac{1}{2}\left(\frac{2}{3}x^{\frac{3}{2}}\right)\right]_1^4 = \frac{1}{3}(\sqrt{4})^3 - \frac{1}{3}(\sqrt{1})^3 = \frac{8}{3} - \frac{1}{3} = \frac{7}{3}$

[4 marks available — 1 mark for rewriting as $\frac{1}{2}x^{\frac{1}{2}}$, 1 mark for correctly integrating, 1 mark for subbing in the limits, 1 mark for the correct final answer]

Q3 $\int_{-1}^3 (4x - 5x^3 + 7)\,dx = \left[4\left(\frac{x^2}{2}\right) - 5\left(\frac{x^4}{4}\right) + 7\left(\frac{x^1}{1}\right)\right]_{-1}^3$

$= \left[2x^2 - \frac{5x^4}{4} + 7x\right]_{-1}^3 = \left(18 - \frac{405}{4} + 21\right) - \left(2 - \frac{5}{4} - 7\right)$

$= -56$

Q4 $\int_0^1 (3 - 4\sqrt{x} + \frac{1}{2}x^2)\,dx = \left[3\left(\frac{x^1}{1}\right) - 4\left(\frac{x^{\frac{3}{2}}}{\frac{3}{2}}\right) + \frac{1}{2}\left(\frac{x^3}{3}\right)\right]_0^1$

$= \left[3x - \frac{8x^{\frac{3}{2}}}{3} + \frac{x^3}{6}\right]_0^1 = \left(3 - \frac{8}{3} + \frac{1}{6}\right) - (0 - 0 + 0) = \frac{1}{2}$

Q5 $\int_1^3 (x^2 - 2x + k)\,dx = \left[\frac{x^3}{3} - x^2 + kx\right]_1^3$

$= \left(\frac{3^3}{3} - 3^2 + 3k\right) - \left(\frac{1^3}{3} - 1^2 + k\right)$

$= 9 - 9 + 3k - \frac{1}{3} + 1 - k = \frac{2}{3} + 2k = \frac{26}{3} \Rightarrow 2k = \frac{24}{3} = 8$

$\Rightarrow k = 4$

[6 marks available — 1 mark for each term correctly integrated, 1 mark for subbing in the limits, 1 mark for setting equal to $\frac{26}{3}$ and attempting to solve for k, 1 mark for the correct answer]

Q6 a) $\int_0^a x^3\,dx = \left[\frac{x^4}{4}\right]_0^a = \left(\frac{a^4}{4}\right) - \left(\frac{0^4}{4}\right) = \frac{a^4}{4}$

So $\frac{a^4}{4} = 64 \Rightarrow a^4 = 64\times 4 = 256 \Rightarrow a = 4$

a can't be −4 since the question tells you that a > 0.

b) $\int_0^a 2x^4\,dx = \left[\frac{2x^5}{5}\right]_0^a = \left(\frac{2a^5}{5}\right) - \left(\frac{2(0)^5}{5}\right) = \frac{2a^5}{5}$

So $\frac{2a^5}{5} = 4a^4 \Rightarrow a^5 = 10a^4 \Rightarrow a = 10$

Q7 a) The area is all above the x-axis so just integrate:

$\int_0^4 (x + \sqrt{x})\,dx = \int_0^4 (x + x^{\frac{1}{2}})\,dx$

$= \left[\frac{x^2}{2} + \frac{x^{\frac{3}{2}}}{\left(\frac{3}{2}\right)}\right]_0^4 = \left[\frac{1}{2}x^2 + \frac{2}{3}(\sqrt{x})^3\right]_0^4$

$= \left(\frac{1}{2}(4)^2 + \frac{2}{3}(\sqrt{4})^3\right) - \left(\frac{1}{2}(0)^2 + \frac{2}{3}(\sqrt{0})^3\right)$

$= \left(\frac{16}{2} + \frac{2}{3}\times 2^3\right) - 0 = \frac{40}{3}$

b) The limits aren't shown on the graph, but they are just the roots of the equation $0 = 4 - x^2$.

Set $y = 0$: $4 - x^2 = 0 \Rightarrow x^2 = 4 \Rightarrow x = 2$ or -2.

So the limits of integration are –2 and 2:

$\int_{-2}^2 (4 - x^2)\,dx = \left[4x - \frac{x^3}{3}\right]_{-2}^2$

$= \left((4\times 2) - \frac{2^3}{3}\right) - \left((4\times(-2)) - \frac{(-2)^3}{3}\right)$

$= \left(8 - \frac{8}{3}\right) - \left(-8 - \frac{-8}{3}\right)$

$= 8 - \frac{8}{3} + 8 - \frac{8}{3} = \frac{32}{3}$

c) This area lies above and below the x-axis so you'll have to integrate the bits above and below the axis separately.

First you need to find the points where the curve crosses the axis: $y = x(x-1)(x-3)$ is already factorised, so it's easy.

If $x(x-1)(x-3) = 0$ then either $x = 0$, $x = 1$ or $x = 3$. So these are the three points where the curve crosses the axis.

The area above the x-axis is between 0 and 1 so integrate:

$\int_0^1 x(x-1)(x-3)\,dx = \int_0^1 (x^3 - 4x^2 + 3x)\,dx$

$= \left[\frac{x^4}{4} - \frac{4x^3}{3} + \frac{3x^2}{2}\right]_0^1$

$= \left(\frac{1^4}{4} - \frac{4\times 1^3}{3} + \frac{3\times 1^2}{2}\right) - \left(\frac{0^4}{4} - \frac{4\times 0^3}{3} + \frac{3\times 0^2}{2}\right)$

$= \frac{1}{4} - \frac{4}{3} + \frac{3}{2} - 0 = \frac{5}{12}$

The area below the x-axis is between 1 and 3, so integrate:

$\int_1^3 x(x-1)(x-3)\,dx = \int_1^3 (x^3 - 4x^2 + 3x)\,dx$

$= \left[\frac{x^4}{4} - \frac{4x^3}{3} + \frac{3x^2}{2}\right]_1^3$

$= \left(\frac{3^4}{4} - \frac{4\times 3^3}{3} + \frac{3\times 3^2}{2}\right) - \left(\frac{1}{4} - \frac{4}{3} + \frac{3}{2}\right)$

$= \left(\frac{81}{4} - \frac{108}{3} + \frac{27}{2}\right) - \frac{5}{12} = -\frac{8}{3}$

Areas cannot be negative so the area of the bit below the x-axis is $\frac{8}{3}$. So the total area is $\frac{5}{12} + \frac{8}{3} = \frac{37}{12}$.

d) This area lies above and below the x-axis so you'll have to integrate the bits above and below the axis separately.
$y = x^2 + x - 6 = (x + 3)(x - 2)$, so the curve crosses the x-axis at $x = -3$ and $x = 2$. The area below the x-axis is between $x = -3$ and $x = 2$, so integrate:

$\int_{-3}^2 (x^2 + x - 6)\,dx = \left[\frac{x^3}{3} + \frac{x^2}{2} - 6x\right]_{-3}^2$

$= \left(\frac{2^3}{3} + \frac{2^2}{2} - 6\times 2\right) - \left(\frac{(-3)^3}{3} + \frac{(-3)^2}{2} - 6\times(-3)\right)$

$= \left(\frac{8}{3} + 2 - 12\right) - \left(-9 + \frac{9}{2} + 18\right) = -\frac{125}{6}$

Areas cannot be negative so the area below the x-axis is $\frac{125}{6}$.

The area above the x-axis is between $x = 2$ and $x = 3$, so integrate:

$\int_2^3 (x^2 + x - 6)\,dx = \left[\frac{x^3}{3} + \frac{x^2}{2} - 6x\right]_2^3$

$= \left(\frac{3^3}{3} + \frac{3^2}{2} - 6\times 3\right) - \left(\frac{2^3}{3} + \frac{2^2}{2} - 6\times 2\right)$

$= \left(9 + \frac{9}{2} - 18\right) - \left(\frac{8}{3} + 2 - 12\right) = \frac{17}{6}$

So the total area is $\frac{125}{6} + \frac{17}{6} = \frac{71}{3}$.

Q8 a) At P, $x = p$ and $y = 0 \Rightarrow 0 = 3\sqrt{p} - 2p = \sqrt{p}(3 - 2\sqrt{p})$

$\Rightarrow \sqrt{p} = 0$ or $3 - 2\sqrt{p} = 0$

$\Rightarrow p = 0$ or $3 = 2\sqrt{p}$

$\Rightarrow \sqrt{p} = \frac{3}{2} \Rightarrow p = \frac{9}{4}$

[3 marks available — 1 mark for setting y = 0, 1 mark for attempting to factorise $3\sqrt{p} - 2p$, 1 mark for showing the correct result]

b) $\int_0^{\frac{9}{4}} \left(3x^{\frac{1}{2}} - 2x\right)dx = \left[3\left(\frac{2}{3}x^{\frac{3}{2}}\right) - x^2\right]_0^{\frac{9}{4}} = \left[2x^{\frac{3}{2}} - x^2\right]_0^{\frac{9}{4}}$

$= \left(2\times\left(\sqrt{\frac{9}{4}}\right)^3 - \left(\frac{9}{4}\right)^2\right) - 0 = \frac{27}{4} - \frac{81}{16} = \frac{27}{16}$

[5 marks available — 1 mark for showing integral of function with limits 0 and $\frac{9}{4}$, 1 mark for each term correctly integrated, 1 mark for subbing in limits, 1 mark for the correct answer]

Q9 The graph of $y = (x - 1)(3x + 9)$ crosses the x-axis at $x = 1$ and $x = -3$.

a)

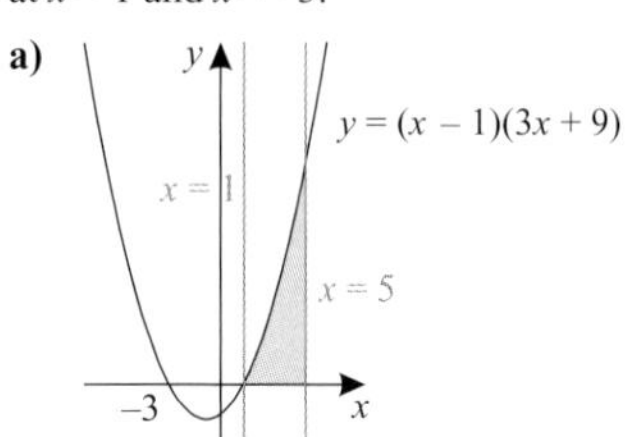

Work out the area above the x-axis between $x = 1$ and $x = 5$:

$\int_1^5 (x-1)(3x+9)\,dx = \int_1^5 (3x^2 + 6x - 9)\,dx$

$= [x^3 + 3x^2 - 9x]_1^5$

$= (5^3 + 3(5)^2 - 9(5)) - (1^3 + 3(1)^2 - 9(1)) = 155 + 5 = 160$

b)

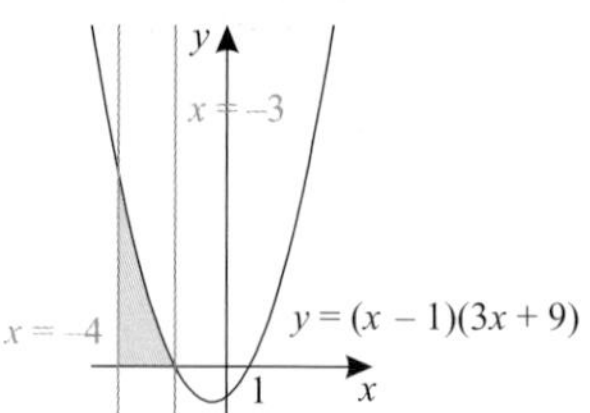

Use the integration from part a) to work out the area above the x-axis between $x = -3$ and $x = -4$:

$\int_{-4}^{-3} (x-1)(3x+9)\,dx = [x^3 + 3x^2 - 9x]_{-4}^{-3}$

$= ((-3)^3 + 3(-3)^2 - 9(-3)) - ((-4)^3 + 3(-4)^2 - 9(-4))$

$= 27 - 20 = 7$

c)

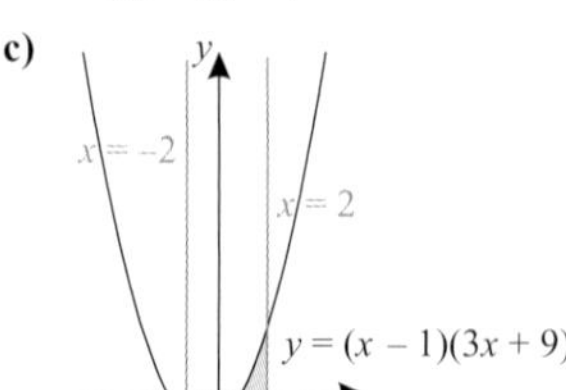

Between $x = -2$ and $x = 2$ the graph crosses the x-axis at $x = 1$, which means the area lies both above and below the x-axis.
Work out the area between $x = -2$ and $x = 1$:

$\int_{-2}^1 (x-1)(3x+9)\,dx = [x^3 + 3x^2 - 9x]_{-2}^1$

$= (1^3 + 3(1)^2 - 9(1)) - ((-2)^3 + 3(-2)^2 - 9(-2))$

$= -5 - 22 = -27$

So the area below the x-axis is 27.
Now work out the area between $x = 1$ and $x = 2$:

$\int_1^2 (x-1)(3x+9)\,dx = [x^3 + 3x^2 - 9x]_1^2$

$= (2^3 + 3(2)^2 - 9(2)) - (1^3 + 3(1)^2 - 9(1)) = 2 - (-5) = 7$

So the area above the x-axis is 7.
Therefore the total area is $27 + 7 = 34$.

d)

Between $x = -6$ and $x = 0$, the graph crosses the x-axis at $x = -3$ which means the area lies both above and below the x-axis.
Work out the area between $x = -6$ and $x = -3$:

$\int_{-6}^{-3} (x-1)(3x+9)\,dx = [x^3 + 3x^2 - 9x]_{-6}^{-3}$

$= ((-3)^3 + 3(-3)^2 - 9(-3)) - ((-6)^3 + 3(-6)^2 - 9(-6))$

$= 27 - (-54) = 81$

So the area above the x-axis is 81.
Now work out the area between $x = -3$ and $x = 0$:

$\int_{-3}^0 (x-1)(3x+9)\,dx = [x^3 + 3x^2 - 9x]_{-3}^0$

$= ((0)^3 + 3(0)^2 - 9(0)) - ((-3)^3 + 3(-3)^2 - 9(-3))$

$= 0 - 27 = -27$

Area cannot be negative, so the area below the x-axis is 27.
So the total area is $81 + 27 = 108$.

Q10 $y = \frac{20}{x^5}$ is positive between $x = 1$ and $x = 2$, so:

$\int_1^2 \frac{20}{x^5}\,dx = \int_1^2 20x^{-5}\,dx = \left[\frac{20x^{-4}}{-4}\right]_1^2 = \left[-\frac{5}{x^4}\right]_1^2$

$= \left(-\frac{5}{2^4}\right) - \left(-\frac{5}{1^4}\right) = -\frac{5}{16} + 5 = \frac{75}{16}$

So the area is $\frac{75}{16}$.

Q11 In order to find this area, you need to split it into two sections and find the area of each section separately:

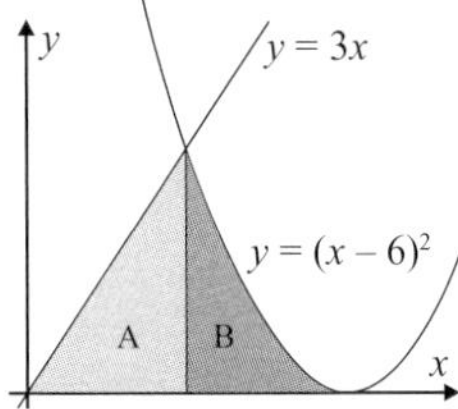

First, find the places where the graphs meet the x-axis.
$y = 3x$ crosses the x-axis at $x = 0$
$y = (x - 6)^2$ touches the x-axis at $x = 6$
The point of intersection is where the two lines meet, i.e. where $3x = (x - 6)^2$. So solve this to find x:
$3x = (x - 6)^2 = x^2 - 12x + 36$
$x^2 - 15x + 36 = 0$
$(x - 12)(x - 3) = 0$
So $x = 3$ or $x = 12$, and since you're looking for the intersection between $x = 0$ and $x = 6$, you want the solution $x = 3$.
Now the graph looks like this:

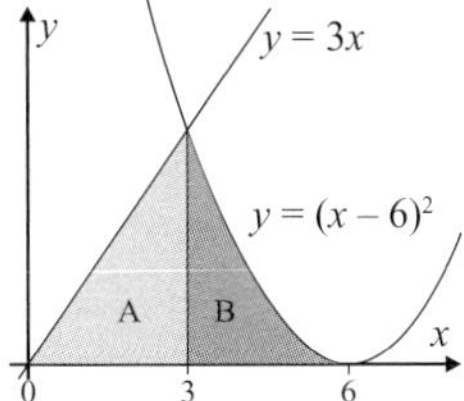

Now find the areas of the two sections.
Area A is a triangle with base length 3.
For the height, substitute $x = 3$ into the equation of the line: $y = 3 \times 3 = 9$
So the area of the triangle is $\frac{1}{2} \times 3 \times 9 = \frac{27}{2}$

Area B $= \int_3^6 (x-6)^2\,dx = \int_3^6 (x^2 - 12x + 36)\,dx$
$= \left[\frac{1}{3}x^3 - 6x^2 + 36x\right]_3^6$
$= (72 - 216 + 216) - (9 - 54 + 108) = 72 - 63 = 9$

So the total area is $\frac{27}{2} + 9 = \frac{45}{2}$.

Q12 $y = x^3 + 4x^2 + 3x = x(x^2 + 4x + 3) = x(x + 3)(x + 1)$

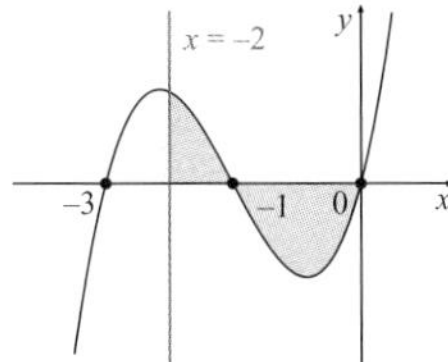

The graph of $y = x^3 + 4x^2 + 3x$ crosses the x-axis at $x = -3$, $x = -1$ and $x = 0$, so between $x = -2$ and $x = 0$ (the y-axis) the graph crosses the x-axis at $x = -1$ which means the area lies above and below the x-axis.
Work out the area between $x = -2$ and $x = -1$:

$\int_{-2}^{-1} (x^3 + 4x^2 + 3x)\,dx = \left[\frac{x^4}{4} + \frac{4x^3}{3} + \frac{3x^2}{2}\right]_{-2}^{-1}$
$= \left(\frac{(-1)^4}{4} + \frac{4(-1)^3}{3} + \frac{3(-1)^2}{2}\right) - \left(\frac{(-2)^4}{4} + \frac{4(-2)^3}{3} + \frac{3(-2)^2}{2}\right)$
$= \frac{5}{12} - \left(-\frac{2}{3}\right) = \frac{13}{12}$

So the area above the x-axis is $\frac{13}{12}$.
Work out the area between $x = -1$ and $x = 0$:

$\int_{-1}^{0} (x^3 + 4x^2 + 3x)\,dx = \left[\frac{x^4}{4} + \frac{4x^3}{3} + \frac{3x^2}{2}\right]_{-1}^{0}$
$= \left(\frac{(0)^4}{4} + \frac{4(0)^3}{3} + \frac{3(0)^2}{2}\right) - \left(\frac{(-1)^4}{4} + \frac{4(-1)^3}{3} + \frac{3(-1)^2}{2}\right)$
$= 0 - \frac{5}{12} = -\frac{5}{12}$

So the area below the x-axis is $\frac{5}{12}$.
Therefore the total area is $\frac{13}{12} + \frac{5}{12} = \frac{18}{12} = \frac{3}{2}$.

Q13 a) First, evaluate the integral, treating A as a constant.
$\int_2^3 (1 - 2Ax)\,dx = [x - Ax^2]_2^3 = (3 - 9A) - (2 - 4A) = 1 - 5A$
From the question, you know that this is equal to $6A^2$, so set up and solve the quadratic.
$1 - 5A = 6A^2 \Rightarrow 6A^2 + 5A - 1 = 0$
$(6A - 1)(A + 1) = 0$, so $A = \frac{1}{6}$ or $A = -1$

b) Again, integrate the function with constant A:
$\int_{-2}^{2} \left(\frac{21}{8}x^2 + \frac{A}{x^2}\right) dx = \int_{-2}^{2} \left(\frac{21}{8}x^2 + Ax^{-2}\right) dx$
$= \left[\frac{21}{8} \times \frac{1}{3}x^3 - Ax^{-1}\right]_{-2}^{2}$
$= \left[\frac{7}{8}x^3 - \frac{A}{x}\right]_{-2}^{2}$
$= \left(\frac{7}{8}(8) - \frac{A}{2}\right) - \left(\frac{7}{8}(-8) - \frac{A}{-2}\right)$
$= \left(7 - \frac{A}{2}\right) - \left((-7) + \frac{A}{2}\right) = 14 - A$
Set this equal to $3A^2$ from the question to form a quadratic in A.
$14 - A = 3A^2 \Rightarrow 3A^2 + A - 14 = 0$
$(3A + 7)(A - 2) = 0$, so $A = -\frac{7}{3}$ or $A = 2$

c) Evaluate the integral, treating A as a constant.
$\int_4^5 (2A^2 - 6x^2)\,dx = [2A^2x - 2x^3]_4^5 = (10A^2 - 250) - (8A^2 - 128)$
$= 2A^2 - 122$
From the question, you know that this is equal to $120A$, so set up and solve the quadratic.
$2A^2 - 122 = 120A \Rightarrow 2A^2 - 120A - 122 = 0$
$\Rightarrow 2(A + 1)(A - 61) = 0$
So $A = -1$ or $A = 61$.

d) Evaluate the integral, treating A as a constant.
$\int_1^4 (A - 2\sqrt{x})^2\,dx = \int_1^4 (A^2 - 4Ax^{\frac{1}{2}} + 4x)\,dx$
$= \left[A^2x - \frac{8Ax^{\frac{3}{2}}}{3} + 2x^2\right]_1^4$
$= (4A^2 - \frac{64A}{3} + 32) - (A^2 - \frac{8A}{3} + 2) = 3A^2 - \frac{56A}{3} + 30$
From the question, you know that this is equal to $10 - A^2$, so set up and solve the quadratic.
$3A^2 - \frac{56A}{3} + 30 = 10 - A^2$
$4A^2 - \frac{56A}{3} + 20 = 0 \Rightarrow 12A^2 - 56A + 60 = 0$
$\Rightarrow 3A^2 - 14A + 15 = 0 \Rightarrow (3A - 5)(A - 3) = 0$,
so $A = \frac{5}{3}$ or $A = 3$

Q14 a) $\int_1^3 (10t - t^2)\,dt = \left[5t^2 - \frac{1}{3}t^3\right]_1^3$
$= (45 - 9) - \left(5 - \frac{1}{3}\right) = \frac{94}{3}$ m (or $31\frac{1}{3}$ m)

b) First work out at what times the object's velocity is 0:
$10t - t^2 = 0 \Rightarrow t(10 - t) = 0$
So $t = 0$ or $t = 10$
This means the object starts at time $t = 0$ and comes to rest at $t = 10$. To find the total distance travelled, integrate between these limits:
$\int_0^{10} (10t - t^2)\,dt = \left[5t^2 - \frac{1}{3}t^3\right]_0^{10}$
$= \left(500 - \frac{1000}{3}\right) - 0$
$= \frac{500}{3}$ m (or $166\frac{2}{3}$ m)

Q15 $\int_1^3 (x + x^{-\frac{3}{2}})\,dx = \left[\frac{x^2}{2} - 2x^{-\frac{1}{2}}\right]_1^3 = \left(\frac{3^2}{2} - 2\left(\frac{1}{\sqrt{3}}\right)\right) - \left(\frac{1^2}{2} - 2\left(\frac{1}{\sqrt{1}}\right)\right)$

$= \frac{9}{2} - \frac{2}{\sqrt{3}} - \frac{1}{2} + 2 = 6 - \frac{2}{\sqrt{3}} = 6 - \frac{2\sqrt{3}}{3}$

[5 marks available — 1 mark for rewriting as $x + x^{-\frac{3}{2}}$, 1 mark for each term correctly integrated, 1 mark for subbing in the limits, 1 mark for the correct final answer in surd form]

Q16 a) At the intersections: $y = 12 + 4x - x^2 = 3x$
$\Rightarrow x^2 - x - 12 = 0 = (x - 4)(x + 3) \Rightarrow x = -3$ and $x = 4$
At P, $x = -3 \Rightarrow y = 3(-3) = -9 \Rightarrow P = (-3, -9)$
At Q, $x = 4 \Rightarrow y = 3(4) = 12 \Rightarrow Q = (4, 12)$
[4 marks available — 1 mark for attempting to solve simultaneous equations, 1 mark for the quadratic $x^2 - x - 12 = 0$, 1 mark for both correct values of x, 1 mark for both P and Q correct]

b) Find the roots of $y = 12 + 4x - x^2$:
$12 + 4x - x^2 = 0 \Rightarrow x^2 - 4x - 12 = 0$
$\Rightarrow (x + 2)(x - 6) = 0 \Rightarrow x = -2$ or $x = 6$
Use the negative root and the x-coordinate of Q as the limits to find the area under the curve and above the x-axis:

$\int_{-2}^{4} (12 + 4x - x^2)\,dx = \left[12x + 2x^2 - \frac{x^3}{3}\right]_{-2}^{4}$

$= \left(12(4) + 2(4)^2 - \frac{(4)^3}{3}\right) - \left(12(-2) + 2(-2)^2 - \frac{(-2)^3}{3}\right)$

$= \frac{176}{3} - \left(-\frac{40}{3}\right) = 72$

The origin, Q (4, 12) and (4, 0) form a triangle with the area:
$\frac{1}{2} \times 4 \times 12 = 24$
So the total shaded region has an area of:
$72 - 24 + \frac{55}{6} = \frac{343}{6}$

[5 marks available — 1 mark for finding the negative root of $y = 12 + 4x - x^2$, 1 mark for attempting to integrate the curve with correct limits, 1 mark for integrating correctly, 1 mark for finding the area of the triangle below $y = 3x$, 1 mark for correct final answer]

Alternatively, you could have integrated the combined function $y = 12 + x - x^2$ with the upper limit 4 and lower limit −3.

Q17 a) Set $y = x^2 = x^2 - 6x + 9$, so $-6x + 9 = 0 \Rightarrow 6x = 9 \Rightarrow x = \frac{3}{2}$
Then $y = \left(\frac{3}{2}\right)^2 = \frac{9}{4}$, so coordinates of A $= \left(\frac{3}{2}, \frac{9}{4}\right)$.
[2 marks available — 2 marks for the correct answer, otherwise 1 mark for correct working]

b) Factorise $y = x^2 - 6x + 9$ to find where the graph touches the x-axis: $x^2 - 6x + 9 = 0 \Rightarrow (x - 3)^2 = 0 \Rightarrow x = 3$.

$R = \int_0^{\frac{3}{2}} x^2\,dx + \int_{\frac{3}{2}}^{3} (x^2 - 6x + 9)\,dx = \left[\frac{x^3}{3}\right]_0^{\frac{3}{2}} + \left[\frac{x^3}{3} - 3x^2 + 9x\right]_{\frac{3}{2}}^{3}$

$= \left(\frac{1}{3}\left(\frac{3}{2}\right)^3 - \frac{0^3}{3}\right) + \left[\frac{x^3}{3} - 3x^2 + 9x\right]_{\frac{3}{2}}^{3}$

$= \frac{9}{8} + \left(\left(\frac{3^3}{3} - 3(3^2) + 9(3)\right) - \left(\frac{1}{3}\left(\frac{3}{2}\right)^3 - 3\left(\frac{3}{2}\right)^2 + 9\left(\frac{3}{2}\right)\right)\right)$

$= \frac{9}{8} + 9 - 27 + 27 - \frac{9}{8} + \frac{27}{4} - \frac{27}{2} = 9 + \frac{27}{4} - \frac{27}{2} = \frac{9}{4}$

[5 marks available — 1 mark for integration of $y = x^2$ with correct limits, 1 mark for integration of $y = x^2 - 6x + 9$ with correct limits, 1 mark for the correct value of each integral, 1 mark for the correct answer]

Chapter 11 Review Exercise

Q1 a) $\int 18x\,dx = 18\int x\,dx = 18\left(\frac{x^2}{2}\right) + C = 9x^2 + C$

b) $\int -x^4\,dx = -\int x^4\,dx = -\left(\frac{x^5}{5}\right) + C = -\frac{1}{5}x^5 + C$

c) $\int \frac{1}{\sqrt{2}}\,dx = \frac{1}{\sqrt{2}}\int x^0\,dx = \frac{1}{\sqrt{2}}\left(\frac{x^1}{1}\right) + C = \frac{1}{\sqrt{2}}x + C$

d) $\int 6\sqrt{x}\,dx = 6\int x^{\frac{1}{2}}\,dx = 6\left(\frac{x^{\frac{3}{2}}}{\left(\frac{3}{2}\right)}\right) + C = 4x^{\frac{3}{2}} + C$

e) $\int \frac{1}{2}x^{-2}\,dx = \frac{1}{2}\int x^{-2}\,dx = \frac{1}{2}\left(\frac{x^{-1}}{(-1)}\right) + C = -\frac{1}{2}x^{-1} + C$

f) $\int 15x^{\frac{3}{2}}\,dx = 15\int x^{\frac{3}{2}}\,dx = 15\left(\frac{x^{\frac{5}{2}}}{\left(\frac{5}{2}\right)}\right) + C = 6x^{\frac{5}{2}} + C$

g) $\int -\frac{2}{x^3}\,dx = -2\int x^{-3}\,dx = -2\left(\frac{x^{-2}}{(-2)}\right) + C = x^{-2} + C$

h) $\int -27x^{-10}\,dx = -27\int x^{-10}\,dx = -27\left(\frac{x^{-9}}{(-9)}\right) + C = 3x^{-9} + C$

i) $\int -9x^{-\frac{1}{2}}\,dx = -9\int x^{-\frac{1}{2}}\,dx = -9\left(\frac{x^{\frac{1}{2}}}{\left(\frac{1}{2}\right)}\right) + C = -18x^{\frac{1}{2}} + C$

j) $\int (3x)^{-4}\,dx = 3^{-4}\int x^{-4}\,dx = \frac{1}{81}\left(\frac{x^{-3}}{(-3)}\right) + C = -\frac{1}{243}x^{-3} + C$

k) $\int -\frac{3}{5}x^{-0.9}\,dx = -\frac{3}{5}\int x^{-0.9}\,dx = -\frac{3}{5}\left(\frac{x^{0.1}}{0.1}\right) + C = -6x^{0.1} + C$

l) $\int -\frac{11}{6(\sqrt[3]{x^2})}\,dx = -\frac{11}{6}\int x^{-\frac{2}{3}}\,dx = -\frac{11}{6}\left(\frac{x^{\frac{1}{3}}}{\left(\frac{1}{3}\right)}\right) + C$

$= -\frac{11}{2}x^{\frac{1}{3}} + C$

Q2 a) $\int 10x^{-6}\,dx = 10\int x^{-6}\,dx = 10\left(\frac{x^{-5}}{(-5)}\right) + C = -2x^{-5} + C$
$= ax^{-5} + C \Rightarrow a = -2$

b) $\int 4x^{15}\,dx = 4\int x^{15}\,dx = 4\left(\frac{x^{16}}{16}\right) + C = \frac{4}{16}x^{16} + C = \frac{1}{4}x^{16} + C$
$= \frac{1}{a}x^{16} + C \Rightarrow a = 4$

c) $\int -\frac{a^2}{x^3}\,dx = -a^2\int x^{-3}\,dx = -a^2\left(\frac{x^{-2}}{(-2)}\right) + C = \frac{a^2}{2}x^{-2} + C$
$= \frac{a}{x^2} + C \Rightarrow \frac{a^2}{2} = a \Rightarrow a^2 - 2a = 0 = a(a - 2)$
$\Rightarrow a = 0$ or $a = 2$, but $a \neq 0 \Rightarrow a = 2$

d) $\int \frac{1}{2\sqrt{x}}\,dx = \frac{1}{2}\int x^{-\frac{1}{2}}\,dx = \frac{1}{2}\left(\frac{x^{\frac{1}{2}}}{\left(\frac{1}{2}\right)}\right) + C = x^{\frac{1}{2}} + C = x^a + C$
$\Rightarrow a = \frac{1}{2}$

e) $\int 14x^a\,dx = 14\int x^a\,dx = 14\left(\frac{x^{a+1}}{a+1}\right) + C = \frac{14}{a+1}x^{a+1} + C$
$= 6(\sqrt[3]{x^7}) + C = 6x^{\frac{7}{3}} + C \Rightarrow a + 1 = \frac{7}{3} \Rightarrow a = \frac{4}{3}$

f) $\int \frac{24}{5}x^a\,dx = \frac{24}{5}\int x^a\,dx = \frac{24}{5}\left(\frac{x^{a+1}}{a+1}\right) + C$
$= \frac{24}{5(a+1)}x^{a+1} + C = \frac{8}{15}x^{a+1} + C \Rightarrow \frac{24}{5(a+1)} = \frac{8}{15}$
$\Rightarrow \frac{24}{5(a+1)} = \frac{24}{45} \Rightarrow 5(a+1) = 45 \Rightarrow a + 1 = 9 \Rightarrow a = 8$

Q3 a) $\int (x^{-\frac{1}{2}} + 4 - 5x^3)\,dx$
$= \int x^{-\frac{1}{2}}\,dx + 4\int x^0\,dx - 5\int x^3\,dx$
$= \frac{x^{\frac{1}{2}}}{\left(\frac{1}{2}\right)} + 4\left(\frac{x^1}{1}\right) - 5\left(\frac{x^4}{4}\right) + C$
$= 2\sqrt{x} + 4x - \frac{5x^4}{4} + C$

b) $\int (2x + 3x^{-2})\,dx = 2\int x\,dx + 3\int x^{-2}\,dx$
$= 2\left(\frac{x^2}{2}\right) + 3\left(\frac{x^{-1}}{-1}\right) + C = x^2 - \frac{3}{x} + C$

c) $\int \left(6x^2 - \frac{1}{3}x^{-\frac{1}{2}}\right)dx = 6\int x^2\,dx - \frac{1}{3}\int x^{-\frac{1}{2}}\,dx$
$= 6\left(\frac{x^3}{3}\right) - \frac{1}{3}\left(\frac{x^{\frac{1}{2}}}{\frac{1}{2}}\right) + C = 2x^3 - \frac{2\sqrt{x}}{3} + C$

Q4 $\int (3x^2 - x^{-2})\,dx = 3\int x^2\,dx - \int x^{-2}\,dx$
$= 3\left(\frac{1}{3}x^3\right) - \frac{x^{-1}}{(-1)} + C = x^3 + \frac{1}{x} + C$
[3 marks available — 1 mark for rewriting second term as x^{-2}, 1 mark for any one term correctly integrated, 1 mark for correct answer (including + C)]

Q5 $\int\left(\frac{5}{3}x^{\frac{2}{3}}-\frac{4}{\sqrt{x}}+(2x)^3-\frac{3}{2x^2}\right)dx$

$=\int\left(\frac{5}{3}x^{\frac{2}{3}}-4x^{-\frac{1}{2}}+8x^3-\frac{3}{2}x^{-2}\right)dx$

$=\frac{5}{3}\int x^{\frac{2}{3}}\,dx-4\int x^{-\frac{1}{2}}\,dx+8\int x^3\,dx-\frac{3}{2}\int x^{-2}\,dx$

$=\frac{5}{3}\left(\frac{x^{\frac{5}{3}}}{\frac{5}{3}}\right)-4\left(\frac{x^{\frac{1}{2}}}{\frac{1}{2}}\right)+8\left(\frac{x^4}{4}\right)-\frac{3}{2}\left(\frac{x^{-1}}{-1}\right)+C$

$=x^{\frac{5}{3}}-8x^{\frac{1}{2}}+2x^4+\frac{3}{2}x^{-1}+C=\sqrt[3]{x^5}-8\sqrt{x}+2x^4+\frac{3}{2x}+C$

[5 marks available — 1 mark for writing the original function as powers of x, 1 mark for attempting to raise powers of each term by one and dividing by result, 1 mark for two correct terms, 1 mark for other two correct terms, 1 mark for C with at least two terms correct]

Q6 $\int\frac{(1-\sqrt{x})(1+\sqrt{x})}{x^3}\,dx=\int\frac{1-x}{x^3}\,dx=\int(x^{-3}-x^{-2})\,dx$

$=-\frac{1}{2}x^{-2}+x^{-1}+C=-\frac{1}{2x^2}+\frac{1}{x}+C$

[5 marks available — 1 mark for simplifying numerator to $1-x$, 1 mark for rewriting as $x^{-3}-x^{-2}$, 1 mark for each term correctly integrated, 1 mark for + C]

Q7 a) $y=\int(x+3)(x-3)\,dx=\int(x^2-9)\,dx=\int x^2\,dx-9\int 1\,dx$

$=\frac{1}{3}x^3-9x+C$

At (3, 4), $x=3$ and $y=4 \Rightarrow 4=\frac{1}{3}3^3-9\times3+C=-18+C$

$\Rightarrow C=22$

So the equation of the curve is $y=\frac{1}{3}x^3-9x+22$.

[4 marks available — 1 mark for expanding to x^2-9, 1 mark for correct integration of each term, 1 mark for C = 22]

b) $y=\int\frac{2}{3}x^{-2}\,dx=\frac{2}{3}\int x^{-2}\,dx=\frac{2}{3}(-x^{-1})+C=-\frac{2}{3x}+C$

At (1, 1), $x=1$ and $y=1 \Rightarrow 1=-\frac{2}{3}+C \Rightarrow C=\frac{5}{3}$

So the equation of the curve is $y=-\frac{2}{3x}+\frac{5}{3}$.

[3 marks available — 1 mark for rewriting to $\frac{2}{3}x^{-2}$, 1 mark for correct integration, 1 mark for C = $\frac{5}{3}$]

Q8 $y=\int\left(3x^2-\frac{7}{\sqrt{x}}\right)dx=3\int x^2\,dx-7\int x^{-\frac{1}{2}}\,dx$

$=3\left(\frac{x^3}{3}\right)-7\left(\frac{x^{\frac{1}{2}}}{\frac{1}{2}}\right)+C=x^3-14x^{\frac{1}{2}}+C=x^3-14\sqrt{x}+C$

At (1, 0), $x=1$ and $y=0 \Rightarrow 0=(1)^3-14\sqrt{1}+C \Rightarrow C=13$

So the equation of the curve is $y=x^3-14\sqrt{x}+13$.

Q9 $y=\int(3x^2+2x-1)\,dx=3\int x^2\,dx+2\int x\,dx-\int 1\,dx$

$=3\left(\frac{1}{3}x^3\right)+2\left(\frac{1}{2}x^2\right)-x+C=x^3+x^2-x+C$

At (–1, 4), $x=-1$ and $y=4 \Rightarrow 4=(-1)^3+(-1)^2-(-1)+C$

$=1+C$

$\Rightarrow C=3$

So the equation of the curve is $y=x^3+x^2-x+3$.

[4 marks available — 1 mark for any two terms correctly integrated, 1 mark for the third term correctly integrated, 1 mark for C = 3, 1 mark for the correct final answer]

Q10 a) $y=\int 2(3x-6.5)\,dx=\int(6x-13)\,dx$

$=6\int x\,dx-13\int x^0\,dx$

$=6\left(\frac{x^2}{2}\right)-13\left(\frac{x^1}{1}\right)+C=3x^2-13x+C$

At (1, 2), $x=1$ and $y=2 \Rightarrow 2=3(1)^2-13(1)+C$

$\Rightarrow C=12$

So the equation of the curve is $y=3x^2-13x+12$.

b) $y=3x^2-13x+12=(3x-4)(x-3)$

When $y=0$, $x=\frac{4}{3}$ or $x=3$.

When $x=0$, $y=12$.

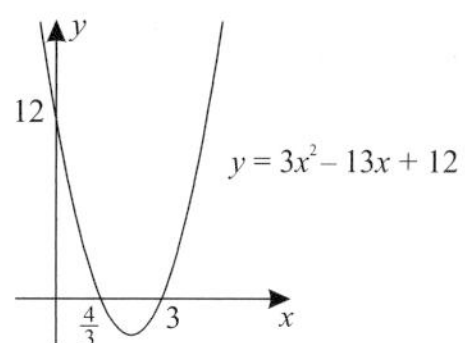

Q11 a) $y=\int(-2x+5)\,dx=-2\int x\,dx+5\int 1\,dx$

$=-2\left(\frac{x^2}{2}\right)+5x+C=-x^2+5x+C$

$x=1$ when $y=0 \Rightarrow -(1)^2+5(1)+C=0 \Rightarrow C=-4$

$\Rightarrow y=-x^2+5x-4$

[3 marks available — 1 mark for any one term correctly integrated, 1 mark for second term correctly integrated, 1 mark for the correct answer]

b) At the x-intercepts: $y=-x^2+5x-4=-(x-1)(x-4)=0$

$\Rightarrow x=1$ and $x=4$

At the y-intercept: $x=0 \Rightarrow y=-0^2+5(0)-4=-4$

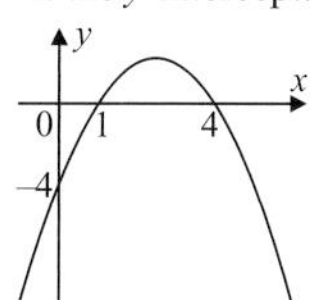

[3 marks available — 1 mark for the correct curve shape, 1 mark for both x-intercepts correctly labelled, 1 mark for the y-intercept correctly labelled]

Q12 $y=\int\left(6x^2-12-\frac{8}{x^2}\right)dx=6\int x^2\,dx-12\int x^0\,dx-8\int x^{-2}\,dx$

$=6\left(\frac{x^3}{3}\right)-12\left(\frac{x^1}{1}\right)-8\left(\frac{x^{-1}}{-1}\right)+C=2x^3-12x+\frac{8}{x}+C$

At (–2, 5), $x=-2$ and $y=5$, so

$5=2(-2)^3-12(-2)+\frac{8}{(-2)}+C=4+C \Rightarrow C=1$

So the curve has the equation $y=2x^3-12x+\frac{8}{x}+1$.

Q13 $f'(x)=\frac{5x^2+1}{x^{\frac{1}{2}}}-10=\frac{5x^2}{x^{\frac{1}{2}}}+\frac{1}{x^{\frac{1}{2}}}-10=5x^{\frac{3}{2}}+x^{-\frac{1}{2}}-10$

$f(x)=\int(5x^{\frac{3}{2}}+x^{-\frac{1}{2}}-10)\,dx=5\left(\frac{x^{\frac{5}{2}}}{\frac{5}{2}}\right)+\left(\frac{x^{\frac{1}{2}}}{\frac{1}{2}}\right)-10\left(\frac{x^1}{1}\right)+C$

$=2x^{\frac{5}{2}}+2x^{\frac{1}{2}}-10x+C$

$=2\sqrt{x^5}+2\sqrt{x}-10x+C$

At (1, –9), $x=1$ and $y=-9$,

so $-9=2\sqrt{1^5}+2\sqrt{1}-10(1)+C=-6+C \Rightarrow C=-3$

So the curve has the equation $y=2\sqrt{x^5}+2\sqrt{x}-10x-3$.

Q14 $\frac{d^2y}{dx^2}=12x$, $\frac{dy}{dx}=\int 12x\,dx=12\int x\,dx$

$=12\left(\frac{x^2}{2}\right)+C_1=6x^2+C_1$

When $x=-2$, $\frac{dy}{dx}=-8$,

so $6(-2)^2+C_1=-8 \Rightarrow C_1=-32 \Rightarrow \frac{dy}{dx}=6x^2-32$

So $y=\int(6x^2-32)\,dx=6\int x^2\,dx-32\int x^0\,dx$

$=6\left(\frac{x^3}{3}\right)-32\left(\frac{x^1}{1}\right)+C_2$

$=2x^3-32x+C_2$

When $x=-2$ and $y=-13$, $-13=2(-2)^3-32(-2)+C_2$

$\Rightarrow -13=-16+64+C_2 \Rightarrow C_2=-61$

So the equation of the curve $y=f(x)$ is $y=2x^3-32x-61$.

[7 marks available — 1 mark for correctly integrating $\frac{d^2y}{dx^2}$, 1 mark for setting $\frac{dy}{dx}$ equal to –8 and attempting to substitute in x = –2, 1 mark for correct C_1 value, 1 mark for equation for $\frac{dy}{dx}$ using C_1 or calculated value as coefficient of x, 1 mark for substituting x = –2, y = –13 and C_1 = –32 into equation for y, 1 mark for correct C_2 value, 1 mark for writing equation for y using values found]

Q15 a) $\int_0^1 (4x^3 + 3x^2 + 2x + 1)\,dx = [x^4 + x^3 + x^2 + x]_0^1$
$= (1^4 + 1^3 + 1^2 + 1) - (0^4 + 0^3 + 0^2 + 0) = 4$

b) $\int_1^6 \frac{3}{x^2}\,dx = \int_1^6 3x^{-2}\,dx = \left[3\left(\frac{x^{-1}}{-1}\right)\right]_1^6 = \left[-\frac{3}{x}\right]_1^6$
$= \left(-\frac{3}{6}\right) - \left(-\frac{3}{1}\right) = -\frac{1}{2} - (-3) = \frac{5}{2}$

c) $\int_1^2 \left(\frac{8}{x^5} + \frac{3}{\sqrt{x}}\right) dx = \int_1^2 (8x^{-5} + 3x^{-\frac{1}{2}})\,dx$
$= \left[8\left(\frac{x^{-4}}{-4}\right) + 3\left(\frac{x^{\frac{1}{2}}}{\frac{1}{2}}\right)\right]_1^2 = [-2x^{-4} + 6x^{\frac{1}{2}}]_1^2$
$= \left[-\frac{2}{x^4} + 6\sqrt{x}\right]_1^2 = \left(-\frac{2}{2^4} + 6\sqrt{2}\right) - \left(-\frac{2}{1^4} + 6\sqrt{1}\right)$
$= -\frac{33}{8} + 6\sqrt{2}$

d) $\int_4^9 \sqrt{x}(1 - 2\sqrt{x})\,dx = \int_4^9 (x^{\frac{1}{2}} - 2x)\,dx$
$= \left[\left(\frac{x^{\frac{3}{2}}}{\frac{3}{2}}\right) - 2\left(\frac{x^2}{2}\right)\right]_4^9 = \left[\frac{2x^{\frac{3}{2}}}{3} - x^2\right]_4^9$
$= \left(\frac{2(9)^{\frac{3}{2}}}{3} - 9^2\right) - \left(\frac{2(4)^{\frac{3}{2}}}{3} - 4^2\right)$
$= 18 - 81 - \frac{16}{3} + 16 = -\frac{157}{3}$

e) $\int_1^4 \frac{3\sqrt{x} + 2x^4}{x^2}\,dx = \int_1^4 \left(\frac{3\sqrt{x}}{x^2} + \frac{2x^4}{x^2}\right) dx$
$= \int_1^4 3x^{-\frac{3}{2}} + 2x^2\,dx = \left[3\left(\frac{x^{-\frac{1}{2}}}{-\frac{1}{2}}\right) + 2\left(\frac{x^3}{3}\right)\right]_1^4$
$= \left[-6x^{-\frac{1}{2}} + \frac{2x^3}{3}\right]_1^4 = \left[-\frac{6}{\sqrt{x}} + \frac{2x^3}{3}\right]_1^4$
$= \left(-\frac{6}{\sqrt{4}} + \frac{2(4)^3}{3}\right) - \left(-\frac{6}{\sqrt{1}} + \frac{2(1)^3}{3}\right)$
$= -3 + \frac{128}{3} + 6 - \frac{2}{3} = 45$

f) $\int_{-1}^{0.5} \frac{2x^5 + 4x^4}{5x^3}\,dx = \int_{-1}^{0.5} \frac{2x^2}{5} + \frac{4x}{5}\,dx$
$= \left[\frac{2}{5}\left(\frac{x^3}{3}\right) + \frac{4}{5}\left(\frac{x^2}{2}\right)\right]_{-1}^{0.5} = \left[\frac{2x^3}{15} + \frac{2x^2}{5}\right]_{-1}^{0.5}$
$= \left(\frac{2(0.5)^3}{15} + \frac{2(0.5)^2}{5}\right) - \left(\frac{2(-1)^3}{15} + \frac{2(-1)^2}{5}\right)$
$= \frac{1}{60} + \frac{1}{10} + \frac{2}{15} - \frac{2}{5} = -\frac{3}{20}$

Q16 $\int_{-2}^0 (9x^2 - 12x + 4)\,dx = \left[9\left(\frac{x^3}{3}\right) - 12\left(\frac{x^2}{2}\right) + 4x\right]_{-2}^0$
$= [3x^3 - 6x^2 + 4x]_{-2}^0 = -(3(-2)^3 - 6(-2)^2 + 4(-2))$
$= 24 + 24 + 8 = 56$
[5 marks available — 1 mark for expanding to get $9x^2 - 12x + 4$, 1 mark for two terms correctly integrated, 1 mark for third term correctly integrated, 1 mark for subbing in the limits, 1 mark for the correct answer]

Q17 $I = \int_a^6 (4x - 5)\,dx = \left[4\left(\frac{x^2}{2}\right) - 5\left(\frac{x^1}{1}\right)\right]_a^6$
$= [2x^2 - 5x]_a^6 = (2(6)^2 - 5(6)) - (2a^2 - 5a)$
$= 42 - 2a^2 + 5a$
If $I = 24$, $42 - 2a^2 + 5a = 24 \Rightarrow 2a^2 - 5a - 18 = 0$
$\Rightarrow (2a - 9)(a + 2) = 0$
$\Rightarrow a = \frac{9}{2}$ or $a = -2$
[6 marks available — 1 mark for correct integration, 1 mark for correctly substituting in limits, 1 mark for making equation in terms of a equal to 24, 1 mark for simplifying quadratic function and making equal to zero, 1 mark for factorising quadratic, 1 mark for correct a-values]

Q18 a) $\int_1^k (2x^3 - x)\,dx = \left[2\left(\frac{x^4}{4}\right) - \frac{x^2}{2}\right]_1^k = \left[\frac{x^4}{2} - \frac{x^2}{2}\right]_1^k$
$= \left(\frac{k^4}{2} - \frac{k^2}{2}\right) - \left(\frac{1^4}{2} - \frac{1^2}{2}\right) = \frac{k^4 - k^2}{2} = 36$
So $k^4 - k^2 - 72 = 0$. Set $u = k^2$: $u^2 - u - 72 = (u - 9)(u + 8) = 0$
$\Rightarrow u = 9$ or $u = -8$, but $u = k^2 > 0 \Rightarrow k^2 = 9$.
So $k = \pm\sqrt{9}$, but $k > 0$, so $k = 3$.
[6 marks available — 1 mark for each term integrated correctly, 1 mark for subbing in limits and rearranging for quartic, 1 mark for factorising, 1 mark for rejecting $k^2 = -8$, 1 mark for the correct answer]

b) $\int_2^5 (x^2 + kx - 2)\,dx = \left[\frac{x^3}{3} + k\left(\frac{x^2}{2}\right) - 2x\right]_2^5$
$= \left(\frac{5^3}{3} + \frac{5^2k}{2} - 2(5)\right) - \left(\frac{2^3}{3} + \frac{2^2k}{2} - 2(2)\right)$
$= \frac{125}{3} + \frac{25k}{2} - 10 - \left(\frac{8}{3} + \frac{4k}{2} - 4\right) = 33 + \frac{21k}{2} = \frac{129}{2}$
$\Rightarrow \frac{21k}{2} = \frac{63}{2} \Rightarrow k = 3$
[4 marks available — 1 mark for any two terms correctly integrated, 1 mark for the third term correctly integrated, 1 mark for subbing in the limits and rearranging, 1 mark for the correct answer]

Q19 a) $\int_{-3}^3 (9 - x^2)\,dx = \left[9\left(\frac{x^1}{1}\right) - \frac{x^3}{3}\right]_{-3}^3$
$= \left[9x - \frac{x^3}{3}\right]_{-3}^3 = \left(9(3) - \frac{3^3}{3}\right) - \left(9(-3) - \frac{(-3)^3}{3}\right)$
$= 27 - 9 + 27 - 9 = 36$

b)

$y = 9 - x^2$

Q20 a) $A = \int_1^8 x^{-\frac{1}{3}}\,dx = \left[\frac{3x^{\frac{2}{3}}}{2}\right]_1^8 = \frac{3(8)^{\frac{2}{3}}}{2} - \frac{3(1)^{\frac{2}{3}}}{2} = 6 - \frac{3}{2} = \frac{9}{2}$

b) Factorise the equation to find where the graph crosses the x-axis:
$y = x^2 + 8x + 7 = (x + 7)(x + 1)$
$\Rightarrow$ where $y = 0$, $x = -7$ or $x = -1$
A is split into an area below the x-axis between $x = -7$ and $x = -1$ and an area above the x-axis between $x = -1$ and $x = 0$, so integrate separately for each area:
$\int_{-7}^{-1} (x^2 + 8x + 7)\,dx = \left[\frac{x^3}{3} + 8\left(\frac{x^2}{2}\right) + 7\left(\frac{x^1}{1}\right)\right]_{-7}^{-1}$
$= \left[\frac{x^3}{3} + 4x^2 + 7x\right]_{-7}^{-1}$
$= \left(\frac{(-1)^3}{3} + 4(-1)^2 + 7(-1)\right) - \left(\frac{(-7)^3}{3} + 4(-7)^2 + 7(-7)\right)$
$= -\frac{1}{3} + 4 - 7 + \frac{343}{3} - 196 + 49 = -36$
Area cannot be negative, so the area below the x-axis is 36.
$\int_{-1}^0 (x^2 + 8x + 7)\,dx = \left[\frac{x^3}{3} + 4x^2 + 7x\right]_{-1}^0$
$= \left(\frac{(0)^3}{3} + 4(0)^2 + 7(0)\right) - \left(\frac{(-1)^3}{3} + 4(-1)^2 + 7(-1)\right)$
$= 0 + \frac{1}{3} - 4 + 7 = \frac{10}{3}$
So the total area of A is $36 + \frac{10}{3} = \frac{118}{3}$

Q21 a) You want to find the area between the curve, the x-axis and the lines $x = 0$ and $x = 2$.
$A = \int_0^2 (x^3 - 5x^2 + 6x)\,dx = \left[\frac{x^4}{4} - 5\left(\frac{x^3}{3}\right) + 6\left(\frac{x^2}{2}\right)\right]_0^2$
$= \left[\frac{x^4}{4} - \frac{5x^3}{3} + 3x^2\right]_0^2$
$= \left(\frac{2^4}{4} - \frac{5(2)^3}{3} + 3(2)^2\right) - \left(\frac{(0)^4}{4} - \frac{5(0)^3}{3} + 3(0)^2\right)$
$= 4 - \frac{40}{3} + 12 - 0 = \frac{8}{3}$

b) $A = \int_1^4 2\sqrt{x}\,dx = \int_1^4 2x^{\frac{1}{2}}\,dx$

$= \left[2\left(\frac{x^{\frac{3}{2}}}{\frac{3}{2}}\right)\right]_1^4 = \left[\frac{4x^{\frac{3}{2}}}{3}\right]_1^4$

$= \left(\frac{4(4)^{\frac{3}{2}}}{3}\right) - \left(\frac{4(1)^{\frac{3}{2}}}{3}\right) = \frac{32}{3} - \frac{4}{3} = \frac{28}{3}$

c) Integrate $y = 2x^2$ between $x = 0$ and $x = 2$:

$\int_0^2 2x^2\,dx = \left[2\left(\frac{x^3}{3}\right)\right]_0^2 = \left[\frac{2x^3}{3}\right]_0^2$

$= \left(\frac{2(2)^3}{3}\right) - \left(\frac{2(0)^3}{3}\right) = \frac{16}{3}$

Integrate $y = 12 - 2x$ between $x = 2$ and $x = 6$:

$\int_2^6 (12 - 2x)\,dx = \left[12\left(\frac{x^1}{1}\right) - 2\left(\frac{x^2}{2}\right)\right]_2^6$

$= [12x - x^2]_2^6 = (12(6) - 6^2) - (12(2) - 2^2)$

$= 72 - 36 - 24 + 4 = 16$

So the total area of A is $\frac{16}{3} + 16 = \frac{64}{3}$.

You could have used the formula for the area of a triangle to work out the second area, taking 8 as the height and 6 – 2 = 4 as the base length.

d) Integrate $y = x + 3$ between $x = 1$ and $x = 4$:

$\int_1^4 (x + 3)\,dx = \left[\frac{x^2}{2} + 3\left(\frac{x^1}{1}\right)\right]_1^4$

$= \left[\frac{x^2}{2} + 3x\right]_1^4 = \left(\frac{4^2}{2} + 3(4)\right) - \left(\frac{1^2}{2} + 3(1)\right)$

$= 8 + 12 - \frac{1}{2} - 3 = \frac{33}{2}$

You could have found this area using the trapezium formula.

Integrate $y = x^2 - 4x + 7$ between $x = 1$ and $x = 4$:

$\int_1^4 (x^2 - 4x + 7)\,dx = \left[\frac{x^3}{3} - 4\left(\frac{x^2}{2}\right) + 7\left(\frac{x^1}{1}\right)\right]_1^4$

$= \left[\frac{x^3}{3} - 2x^2 + 7x\right]_1^4$

$= \left(\frac{4^3}{3} - 2(4)^2 + 7(4)\right) - \left(\frac{1^3}{3} - 2(1)^2 + 7(1)\right)$

$= \frac{64}{3} - 32 + 28 - \frac{1}{3} + 2 - 7 = 12$

Subtract the area below $y = x^2 - 4x + 7$ between $x = 1$ and $x = 4$ from the area below $y = x + 3$ between $x = 1$ and $x = 4$:

$A = \frac{33}{2} - 12 = \frac{9}{2}$

Alternatively, you could have subtracted $x^2 - 4x + 7$ from $x + 3$ first, and then integrated the result between $x = 1$ and $x = 4$.

Q22 a) $\frac{dy}{dx} = 3x^2 - 15x + 12 = (3x - 12)(x - 1) = 0$

So stationary points are at $x = 1$ and $3x = 12$

$\Rightarrow x = 1$ and $x = 4$

[4 marks available — 1 mark for correctly differentiating two terms, 1 mark for correctly differentiating the third term, 1 mark for setting $\frac{dy}{dx} = 0$, 1 mark for the correct answer]

b) You want to find the area between the curve, the x-axis and the lines $x = 1$ and $x = 4$.

$A = \int_1^4 \left(x^3 - \frac{15}{2}x^2 + 12x + 10\right)dx$

$= \left[\frac{x^4}{4} - \frac{15}{2}\left(\frac{x^3}{3}\right) + 12\left(\frac{x^2}{2}\right) + 10x\right]_1^4$

$= \left[\frac{x^4}{4} - \frac{5}{2}x^3 + 6x^2 + 10x\right]_1^4 = \left(\frac{4^4}{4} - \frac{5}{2}(4)^3 + 6(4)^2 + 10(4)\right) - \left(\frac{1^4}{4} - \frac{5}{2}(1)^3 + 6(1)^2 + 10(1)\right)$

$= 64 - 160 + 96 + 40 - \left(\frac{1}{4} - \frac{5}{2} + 6 + 10\right)$

$= 40 - \frac{55}{4} = \frac{105}{4}$

[6 marks available — 1 mark for attempting to integrate with the correct limits, 3 marks for correctly integrating all four terms, otherwise 2 marks for correctly integrating three terms or 1 mark for correctly integrating two terms, 1 mark for correctly subbing in the limits, 1 mark for the correct answer]

Q23 a) Factorise the equation to find where the graph crosses the x-axis:

$y = -x^3 + 7x^2 - 10x = -x(x - 2)(x - 5)$

$\Rightarrow$ where $y = 0$, $x = 0$ or $x = 2$ or $x = 5$

The shaded area is split into an area below the x-axis between $x = 0$ and $x = 2$ and an area above the x-axis between $x = 2$ and $x = 5$, so integrate separately for each area:

$\int_0^2 (-x^3 + 7x^2 - 10x)\,dx = \left[-\left(\frac{x^4}{4}\right) + 7\left(\frac{x^3}{3}\right) - 10\left(\frac{x^2}{2}\right)\right]_0^2$

$= \left[-\frac{x^4}{4} + \frac{7x^3}{3} - 5x^2\right]_0^2$

$= \left(-\frac{2^4}{4} + \frac{7(2)^3}{3} - 5(2)^2\right) - \left(-\frac{(0)^4}{4} + \frac{7(0)^3}{3} - 5(0)^2\right)$

$= -4 + \frac{56}{3} - 20 - 0 = -\frac{16}{3}$

Area cannot be negative, so the area below the x-axis is $\frac{16}{3}$.

$\int_2^5 (-x^3 + 7x^2 - 10x)\,dx = \left[-\frac{x^4}{4} + \frac{7x^3}{3} - 5x^2\right]_2^5$

$= \left(-\frac{5^4}{4} + \frac{7(5)^3}{3} - 5(5)^2\right) - \left(-\frac{2^4}{4} + \frac{7(2)^3}{3} - 5(2)^2\right)$

$= -\frac{625}{4} + \frac{875}{3} - 125 + 4 - \frac{56}{3} + 20 = \frac{63}{4}$

So the total area shaded is $\frac{16}{3} + \frac{63}{4} = \frac{253}{12}$

b) The shaded area is split into an area below the x-axis between $x = -1$ and $x = 0$, above the x-axis between $x = 0$ and $x = 2$ and below the x-axis between $x = 2$ and $x = 3$. Integrate for these three areas separately:

$\int_{-1}^0 (x^4 - 3x^3 - 4x^2 + 12x)\,dx$

$= \left[\left(\frac{x^5}{5}\right) - 3\left(\frac{x^4}{4}\right) - 4\left(\frac{x^3}{3}\right) + 12\left(\frac{x^2}{2}\right)\right]_{-1}^0$

$= \left[\frac{x^5}{5} - \frac{3x^4}{4} - \frac{4x^3}{3} + 6x^2\right]_{-1}^0$

$= \left(\frac{(0)^5}{5} - \frac{3(0)^4}{4} - \frac{4(0)^3}{3} + 6(0)^2\right) - \left(\frac{(-1)^5}{5} - \frac{3(-1)^4}{4} - \frac{4(-1)^3}{3} + 6(-1)^2\right)$

$= (0 - 0 - 0 + 0) - \left(-\frac{1}{5} - \frac{3}{4} + \frac{4}{3} + 6\right) = -\frac{383}{60}$

Area cannot be negative, so the area below the x-axis between $x = -1$ and $x = 0$ is $\frac{383}{60}$.

$\int_0^2 (x^4 - 3x^3 - 4x^2 + 12x)\,dx = \left[\frac{x^5}{5} - \frac{3x^4}{4} - \frac{4x^3}{3} + 6x^2\right]_0^2$

$= \left(\frac{2^5}{5} - \frac{3(2)^4}{4} - \frac{4(2)^3}{3} + 6(2)^2\right) - \left(\frac{(0)^5}{5} - \frac{3(0)^4}{4} - \frac{4(0)^3}{3} + 6(0)^2\right)$

$= \left(\frac{32}{5} - 12 - \frac{32}{3} + 24\right) - (0 - 0 - 0 + 0) = \frac{116}{15}$

$\int_2^3 (x^4 - 3x^3 - 4x^2 + 12x)\,dx = \left[\frac{x^5}{5} - \frac{3x^4}{4} - \frac{4x^3}{3} + 6x^2\right]_2^3$

$= \left(\frac{3^5}{5} - \frac{3(3)^4}{4} - \frac{4(3)^3}{3} + 6(3)^2\right) - \left(\frac{2^5}{5} - \frac{3(2)^4}{4} - \frac{4(2)^3}{3} + 6(2)^2\right)$

$= \left(\frac{243}{5} - \frac{243}{4} - 36 + 54\right) - \left(\frac{32}{5} - 12 - \frac{32}{3} + 24\right)$

$= \frac{117}{20} - \frac{116}{15} = -\frac{113}{60}$

Area cannot be negative, so the area below the x-axis between $x = 2$ and $x = 3$ is $\frac{113}{60}$.

So the total area shaded is $\frac{383}{60} + \frac{116}{15} + \frac{113}{60} = 16$

Q24 a) At roots $y = 0 \Rightarrow x^3 - 4x^2 + 3x = x(x^2 - 4x + 3)$

$= x(x - 3)(x - 1) = 0$

$\Rightarrow x = 0, x = 1$ and $x = 3$

So A has x-coordinate = 1 and B has x-coordinate = 3.

[3 marks available — 1 mark for correctly factorising, 1 mark for each correct x-coordinate for A and B]

b) The shaded area is split into an area above the x-axis between $x = 0$ and $x = 1$ and an area below the x-axis between $x = 1$ and $x = 3$, so integrate separately for each area:

$$\int_0^1 (x^3 - 4x^2 + 3x)\,dx = \left[\frac{x^4}{4} - \frac{4x^3}{3} + \frac{3x^2}{2}\right]_0^1$$
$$= \left(\frac{(1)^4}{4} - \frac{4(1)^3}{3} + \frac{3(1)^2}{2}\right) - \left(\frac{(0)^4}{4} - \frac{4(0)^3}{3} + \frac{3(0)^2}{2}\right)$$
$$= \frac{1}{4} - \frac{4}{3} + \frac{3}{2} = \frac{5}{12}$$

$$\int_1^3 (x^3 - 4x^2 + 3x)\,dx = \left[\frac{x^4}{4} - \frac{4x^3}{3} + \frac{3x^2}{2}\right]_1^3$$
$$= \left(\frac{(3)^4}{4} - \frac{4(3)^3}{3} + \frac{3(3)^2}{2}\right) - \left(\frac{(1)^4}{4} - \frac{4(1)^3}{3} + \frac{3(1)^2}{2}\right)$$
$$= \left(\frac{81}{4} - 36 + \frac{27}{2}\right) - \frac{5}{12} = -\frac{9}{4} - \frac{5}{12} = -\frac{8}{3}$$

Area cannot be negative, so the area below the x-axis between $x = 1$ and $x = 3$ is $\frac{8}{3}$.

So the total area shaded is $\frac{5}{12} + \frac{8}{3} = \frac{37}{12}$

[5 marks available — 1 mark for attempting to integrate with correct limits, 1 mark for two terms correctly integrated, 1 mark for third term correctly integrated, 1 mark for subbing in the limits, 1 mark for correct final answer]

Q25 a)

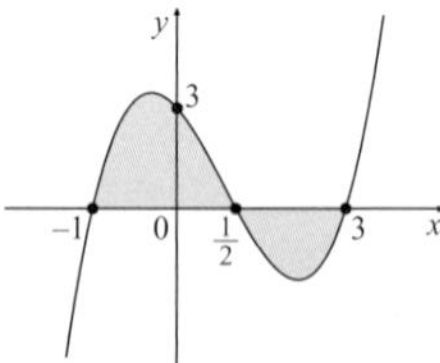

[3 marks available — 1 mark for correct curve shape, 1 mark for correct y-intercept, 1 mark for correct x-intercepts]

b) Between $x = -1$ and $x = 3$, the graph crosses the axes at $x = \frac{1}{2}$ which means the area lies both above and below the x-axis (as shown on the diagram for part a)).

$y = (x + 1)(2x - 1)(x - 3) = (x + 1)(2x^2 - 7x + 3)$
$= 2x^3 - 5x^2 - 4x + 3$

So integrate $y = 2x^3 - 5x^2 - 4x + 3$ between $x = -1$ and $x = \frac{1}{2}$ to find the area above the x-axis:

$$\int_{-1}^{\frac{1}{2}} (2x^3 - 5x^2 - 4x + 3)\,dx$$
$$= \left[2\left(\frac{x^4}{4}\right) - 5\left(\frac{x^3}{3}\right) - 4\left(\frac{x^2}{2}\right) + 3\left(\frac{x^1}{1}\right)\right]_{-1}^{\frac{1}{2}}$$
$$= \left[\frac{1}{2}x^4 - \frac{5}{3}x^3 - 2x^2 + 3x\right]_{-1}^{\frac{1}{2}}$$
$$= \left(\frac{1}{2}\left(\frac{1}{2}\right)^4 - \frac{5}{3}\left(\frac{1}{2}\right)^3 - 2\left(\frac{1}{2}\right)^2 + 3\left(\frac{1}{2}\right)\right)$$
$$- \left(\frac{1}{2}(-1)^4 - \frac{5}{3}(-1)^3 - 2(-1)^2 + 3(-1)\right)$$
$$= \left(\frac{1}{32} - \frac{5}{24} - \frac{1}{2} + \frac{3}{2}\right) - \left(\frac{1}{2} + \frac{5}{3} - 2 - 3\right)$$
$$= \frac{79}{96} - \left(-\frac{17}{6}\right) = \frac{117}{32}$$

[4 marks available — 1 mark for writing integral with limits of $x = -1$ and $x = \frac{1}{2}$, 1 mark for correctly integrating y, 1 mark for attempting to substitute the limits into integrated function, 1 mark for correct area above x-axis]

c) Integrate $y = 2x^3 - 5x^2 - 4x + 3$ between $x = \frac{1}{2}$ and $x = 3$ to find the area below the x-axis:

$$\int_{\frac{1}{2}}^{3} (2x^3 - 5x^2 - 4x + 3)\,dx = \left[\frac{1}{2}x^4 - \frac{5}{3}x^3 - 2x^2 + 3x\right]_{\frac{1}{2}}^{3}$$
$$= \left(\frac{1}{2}(3)^4 - \frac{5}{3}(3)^3 - 2(3)^2 + 3(3)\right)$$
$$- \left(\frac{1}{2}\left(\frac{1}{2}\right)^4 - \frac{5}{3}\left(\frac{1}{2}\right)^3 - 2\left(\frac{1}{2}\right)^2 + 3\left(\frac{1}{2}\right)\right)$$
$$= \left(\frac{81}{2} - 45 - 18 + 9\right) - \left(\frac{1}{32} - \frac{5}{24} - \frac{1}{2} + \frac{3}{2}\right)$$
$$= -\frac{27}{2} - \frac{79}{96} = -\frac{1375}{96}$$

Area cannot be negative so the area below the x-axis is $\frac{1375}{96}$.

So the total area enclosed is $\frac{117}{32} + \frac{1375}{96} = \frac{863}{48}$.

[4 marks available — 1 mark for writing integral with limits of $x = \frac{1}{2}$ and $x = 3$, 1 mark for correct area below x-axis, 1 mark for finding negative area below x-axis and omitting negative sign, 1 mark for correct total area]

Q26 a) $V = \int (2t - 3t^2)\,dt = 2\left(\frac{1}{2}t^2\right) - 3\left(\frac{1}{3}t^3\right) + C = t^2 - t^3 + C$

Particle was initially at rest, so $V = 0$ when $t = 0$

$\Rightarrow 0 = 0^2 - 0^3 + C \Rightarrow C = 0 \Rightarrow V = t^2 - t^3$

[4 marks available — 1 mark for each term integrated correctly, 1 mark for + C, 1 mark for correct final answer]

b) $t = 10 \Rightarrow V = 10^2 - 10^3 = 100 - 1000 = -900\ \text{ms}^{-1}$

[2 marks available — 2 marks for correct answer, otherwise 1 mark for correct working]

Q27 a) $\int 2x^3\,dx = 2\int x^3\,dx = 2\left(\frac{x^4}{4}\right) + C = \frac{1}{2}x^4 + 0$

$\int \frac{1}{4}x\,dx = \frac{1}{4}\int x^1\,dx = \frac{1}{4}\left(\frac{x^2}{2}\right) + C = \frac{1}{8}x^2 + 0$

So $\int 2x^3\,dx = \int \frac{1}{4}x\,dx \Rightarrow \frac{1}{2}x^4 = \frac{1}{8}x^2$

$\Rightarrow \frac{1}{2}x^4 - \frac{1}{8}x^2 = 0 \Rightarrow \frac{1}{2}x^2\left(x^2 - \frac{1}{4}\right) = 0$

$\Rightarrow \frac{1}{2}x^2\left(x - \frac{1}{2}\right)\left(x + \frac{1}{2}\right) = 0 \Rightarrow x = 0$ or $x = \frac{1}{2}$ or $x = -\frac{1}{2}$

b) $\int x^0\,dx = \frac{x^1}{1} + C = x - 3$

$\int \frac{3}{2x^{\frac{1}{2}}}\,dx = \frac{3}{2}\int x^{-\frac{1}{2}}\,dx = \frac{3}{2}\left(\frac{x^{\frac{1}{2}}}{\left(\frac{1}{2}\right)}\right) + C = 3x^{\frac{1}{2}} + 15$

So $\int x^0\,dx = \int \frac{3}{2x^{\frac{1}{2}}}\,dx \Rightarrow x - 3 = 3x^{\frac{1}{2}} + 15$

$\Rightarrow x - 3x^{\frac{1}{2}} - 18 = 0$. Set $u = x^{\frac{1}{2}}$, So $u^2 - 3u - 18 = 0$

$\Rightarrow (u - 6)(u + 3) = 0 \Rightarrow x^{\frac{1}{2}} = u = 6$ (as $x^{\frac{1}{2}} > 0$)

$\Rightarrow x = 6^2 = 36$

c) $\int 3x^2\,dx = 3\int x^2\,dx = 3\left(\frac{x^3}{3}\right) + C = x^3 - 4$

$\int 13\,dx = 13\int x^0\,dx = 13\left(\frac{x^1}{1}\right) + C = 13x + 8$

So $\int 3x^2\,dx = \int 13\,dx \Rightarrow x^3 - 4 = 13x + 8$

$\Rightarrow x^3 - 13x - 12 = 0.$

Using the Factor Theorem with $x = -1$,

$(-1)^3 - 13(-1) - 12 = 0 \Rightarrow (x + 1)$ is a factor

$\Rightarrow x^3 - 13x - 12 = (x + 1)(x^2 - x - 12) = (x + 1)(x + 3)(x - 4)$

$\Rightarrow x = -1$ or $x = -3$ or $x = 4$

Q28 $\int \frac{(k^2 + 2k - 15)x^k}{x^4}\,dx = (k^2 + 2k - 15)\int \frac{x^k}{x^4}\,dx$

$= (k^2 + 2k - 15)\int x^{k-4}\,dx = (k^2 + 2k - 15)\left(\frac{x^{k-3}}{(k-3)}\right) + C$

$= (k - 3)(k + 5)\left(\frac{x^{k-3}}{k-3}\right) + C = (k + 5)x^{k-3} + C = \frac{6}{x^2} + C$

$\Rightarrow (k + 5)x^{k-3} = 6x^{-2} \Rightarrow k + 5 = 6 \Rightarrow k = 1$

You also could have equated the powers: $k - 3 = -2 \Rightarrow k = 1$.

Q29 $y = \int (x^2 + 2\alpha x + \alpha^2)\,dx = \frac{x^3}{3} + \alpha x^2 + \alpha^2 x + C$

At (3, 18), $x = 3$ and $y = 18 \Rightarrow 18 = \frac{3^3}{3} + 3^2\alpha + 3\alpha^2 + C$

$\Rightarrow 9 = 9\alpha + 3\alpha^2 + C$ ①

At $\left(1, -\frac{2}{3}\right)$, $x = 1$ and $y = -\frac{2}{3} \Rightarrow -\frac{2}{3} = \frac{1^3}{3} + 1^2\alpha + 1\alpha^2 + C$

$\Rightarrow -1 = \alpha + \alpha^2 + C$

$\Rightarrow C = -\alpha^2 - \alpha - 1$ ②

Subbing (2) into (1): $9 = 9\alpha + 3\alpha^2 - \alpha^2 - \alpha - 1$

$\Rightarrow 2\alpha^2 + 8\alpha - 10 = 0 = (2\alpha + 10)(\alpha - 1)$

$\Rightarrow \alpha = 1$ or $\alpha = -5$

From the question, $\alpha > 0$, so $\alpha = 1$.

[7 marks available — 1 mark for expanding to $f'(x) = x^2 + 2\alpha x + \alpha^2$, 1 mark for two terms correctly integrated, 1 mark for third term correctly integrated, 1 mark for formulating each of equations (1) and (2), 1 mark for solving simultaneously to find α, 1 mark for correct α]

Q30 a) Gradient of tangent at $(1, 0) = 2 \times 1 - \frac{4}{1^3} = -2$

So gradient of normal at $(1, 0) = -1 \div -2 = \frac{1}{2}$

At P(1, 0), $x = 1$ and $y = 0 \Rightarrow 0 = \frac{1}{2}(1) + c \Rightarrow c = -\frac{1}{2}$

$\Rightarrow y = \frac{1}{2}x - \frac{1}{2} \Rightarrow x - 2y - 1 = 0$

[4 marks available — 1 mark for finding the gradient of the tangent, 1 mark for finding the gradient of the normal, 1 mark for a correct equation for the normal, 1 mark for correct answer in the correct form]

b) $y = \int (2x - 4x^{-3})\,dx = 2\left(\frac{x^2}{2}\right) - 4\left(\frac{x^{-2}}{-2}\right) + C = x^2 + \frac{2}{x^2} + C$

At P: $0 = 1^2 + \frac{2}{1^2} + C = 3 + C \Rightarrow C = -3$

So the equation of the curve is $y = x^2 + \frac{2}{x^2} - 3$.

[5 marks available — 1 mark for rewriting as $2x - 4x^{-3}$, 1 mark for each term correctly integrated, 1 mark for using the given coordinates to find $C = -3$, 1 mark for correct final answer]

c) Set $f(x) = 0 = x^2 + \frac{2}{x^2} - 3 \Rightarrow x^4 + 2 - 3x^2 = 0 = x^4 - 3x^2 + 2$

Set $u = x^2 \Rightarrow u^2 - 3u + 2 = 0 \Rightarrow (u - 1)(u - 2) = 0$

$\Rightarrow u = 1$ or $u = 2 \Rightarrow x = \pm 1$ or $x = \pm\sqrt{2}$

P has an x-coordinate of 1, so $x > 1$ and hence $x = \sqrt{2}$.

[5 marks available — 1 mark for attempting to solve $f(x) = 0$, 1 mark for multiplying through to form a quartic, 1 mark for attempting to solve using a valid method, 1 mark for finding $x = 1$ or $x = \sqrt{2}$, 1 mark for the correct final answer]

Q31 $y = \int_2^3 (3x^{\frac{1}{2}} - 2x^{-\frac{1}{2}})\,dx = \left[3\left(\frac{2}{3}x^{\frac{3}{2}}\right) - 2(2x^{\frac{1}{2}})\right]_2^3 = \left[2x^{\frac{3}{2}} - 4\sqrt{x}\right]_2^3$

$= (2(\sqrt{3})^3 - 4\sqrt{3}) - (2(\sqrt{2})^3 - 4\sqrt{2})$

$= 6\sqrt{3} - 4\sqrt{3} - 4\sqrt{2} + 4\sqrt{2} = 2\sqrt{3}$ so $k = 2$

[5 marks available — 1 mark for rewriting as $3x^{\frac{1}{2}} - 2x^{-\frac{1}{2}}$, 1 mark for each term correctly integrated, 1 mark for using the limits correctly, 1 mark for the correct answer]

Q32 Factorise $y = 2x^3 - 15x^2 + 36x - 28$ using the Factor Theorem:

If $x = 2$, $y = 2(2)^3 - 15(2)^2 + 36(2) - 28$

$= 16 - 60 + 72 - 28 = 0$

$\Rightarrow (x - 2)$ is a factor

Using e.g. algebraic division:

$y = 2x^3 - 15x^2 + 36x - 28 = (x - 2)(2x^2 - 11x + 14)$

$= (x - 2)^2(2x - 7)$

The double root is at $x = 2$, so $a = 2$.

Integrate the function between $x = 0$ and $x = 2$:

$\int_0^2 (2x^3 - 15x^2 + 36x - 28)\,dx$

$= \left[2\left(\frac{x^4}{4}\right) - 15\left(\frac{x^3}{3}\right) + 36\left(\frac{x^2}{2}\right) - 28\left(\frac{x^1}{1}\right)\right]_0^2$

$= \left[\frac{x^4}{2} - 5x^3 + 18x^2 - 28x\right]_0^2$

$= \left(\frac{2^4}{2} - 5(2)^3 + 18(2)^2 - 28(2)\right)$

$\quad - \left(\frac{(0)^4}{2} - 5(0)^3 + 18(0)^2 - 28(0)\right)$

$= 8 - 40 + 72 - 56 - 0 = -16$

Area cannot be negative so the area is 16.

Q33 a) Integrate $y = 9 - \frac{1}{3}\sqrt{x^3}$ between $x = 0$ and $x = 9$:

$\int_0^9 \left(9 - \frac{1}{3}x^{\frac{3}{2}}\right)dx$

$= \left[9\left(\frac{x^1}{1}\right) - \frac{1}{3}\left(\frac{x^{\frac{5}{2}}}{\frac{5}{2}}\right)\right]_0^9 = \left[9x - \frac{2}{15}x^{\frac{5}{2}}\right]_0^9$

$= \left(9(9) - \frac{2}{15}(9)^{\frac{5}{2}}\right) - \left(9(0) - \frac{2}{15}(0)^{\frac{5}{2}}\right)$

$= 81 - \frac{162}{5} - 0 = \frac{243}{5} = 48.6\text{ m}^2$

So the plan meets the requirement of at least 40 m² floor space.

b) Integrate $y = 2 - \frac{1}{2}x^2$ between $x = 0$ and $x = 2$:

$\int_0^2 \left(2 - \frac{1}{2}x^2\right)dx$

$= \left[2\left(\frac{x^1}{1}\right) - \frac{1}{2}\left(\frac{x^3}{3}\right)\right]_0^2 = \left[2x - \frac{1}{6}x^3\right]_0^2$

$= \left(2(2) - \frac{1}{6}(2)^3\right) - \left(2(0) - \frac{1}{6}(0)^3\right)$

$= 4 - \frac{4}{3} - 0 = \frac{8}{3}\text{ m}^2$

So there is $48.6\text{ m}^2 - \frac{8}{3}\text{ m}^2 = 45.9\text{ m}^2$ (3 s.f.) of floor space left.

Q34 a) Use the Factor Theorem to find a linear factor of $y = x^3 - 2x^2 - 9x + 18$:

When $x = 2$, $y = (2)^3 - 2(2)^2 - 9(2) + 18 = 0$, so $(x - 2)$ is a factor.

So $y = (x - 2)(x^2 + nx - 9) \Rightarrow -2x^2 = nx^2 - 2x^2$

$\Rightarrow n = 0 \Rightarrow y = (x - 2)(x^2 - 9)$

$= (x - 2)(x - 3)(x + 3)$

So the curve crosses the x-axis where $x = 2$, and $x = 3$ and $x = -3$.

[3 marks available — 1 mark for one correct linear factor, 1 mark for two other correct linear factors, 1 mark for all correct x-values]

b) Split the area into two sections and find the areas separately.

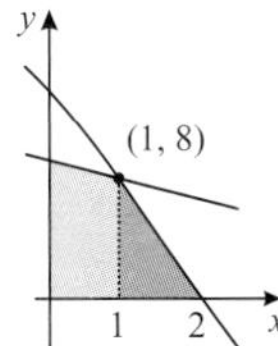

To find the area to the left, integrate $y = 12 - 4x$ between $x = 0$ and $x = 1$.

$\int_0^1 (12 - 4x)\,dx = \left[12\left(\frac{x^1}{1}\right) - 4\left(\frac{x^2}{2}\right)\right]_0^1 = [12x - 2x^2]_0^1$

$= (12(1) - 2(1)^2) - (12(0) - 2(0)^2) = 10$

To find the area to the right, integrate $y = x^3 - 2x^2 - 9x + 18$ between $x = 1$ and $x = 2$.

$\int_1^2 (x^3 - 2x^2 - 9x + 18)\,dx$

$= \left[\left(\frac{x^4}{4}\right) - 2\left(\frac{x^3}{3}\right) - 9\left(\frac{x^2}{2}\right) + 18\left(\frac{x^1}{1}\right)\right]_1^2$

$= \left[\frac{x^4}{4} - \frac{2x^3}{3} - \frac{9x^2}{2} + 18x\right]_1^2$

$= \left(\frac{(2)^4}{4} - \frac{2(2)^3}{3} - \frac{9(2)^2}{2} + 18(2)\right)$

$\quad - \left(\frac{(1)^4}{4} - \frac{2(1)^3}{3} - \frac{9(1)^2}{2} + 18(1)\right)$

$= \frac{50}{3} - \frac{157}{12} = \frac{43}{12}$

So the total area is $10 + \frac{43}{12} = \frac{163}{12}$.

[7 marks available — 1 mark for correctly splitting the area in two and attempting to integrate the two areas separately, 1 mark for each correctly integrated function, 1 mark each for correctly substituting the limits into the integrated functions, 1 mark for at least one correct positive area, 1 mark for correct total area]

Q35 a) $\frac{dy}{dx} = 2 - x^{-\frac{1}{2}} = 2 - \frac{1}{\sqrt{x}}$

So at $x = 4$, the gradient of the tangent $= 2 - \frac{1}{\sqrt{4}} = \frac{3}{2}$.

So the equation of the tangent is $y = \frac{3}{2}x + c$.

At $x = 4$: $y = 2(4) - 2(\sqrt{4}) + 1 = 5 \Rightarrow 5 = \frac{3}{2}(4) + c$

$\Rightarrow c = 5 - 6 = -1$

So $y = \frac{3}{2}x - 1 \Rightarrow 3x - 2y - 2 = 0$

[4 marks available — 1 mark for correct differentiation, 1 mark for finding the gradient at P, 1 mark for finding c = –1, 1 mark for rearranging to show the correct result]

b) First find the area under the curve:

$\int_0^4 (2x - 2x^{\frac{1}{2}} + 1)\,dx = \left[2\left(\frac{1}{2}x^2\right) - 2\left(\frac{2}{3}x^{\frac{3}{2}}\right) + x\right]_0^4$

$= \left[x^2 - \frac{4}{3}(\sqrt{x})^3 + x\right]_0^4 = \left((4)^2 - \frac{4}{3}(8) + 4\right) - (0) = \frac{28}{3}$

The tangent crosses the x-axis at $y = \frac{3}{2}x - 1 = 0 \Rightarrow x = \frac{2}{3}$

Area under the tangent is area of the triangle with base $= 4 - \frac{2}{3} = \frac{10}{3}$ and height $= 5$

$\Rightarrow$ Area $= \frac{1}{2} \times \frac{10}{3} \times 5 = \frac{50}{6} = \frac{25}{3}$

The shaded region is the area under the curve minus the area of the triangle under the tangent:

Area of R $= \frac{28}{3} - \frac{25}{3} = \frac{3}{3} = 1$

[7 marks available — 1 mark for correct integration, 1 mark for correctly substituting the limits, 1 mark for finding area under the curve, 1 mark for finding x-intercept of tangent, 1 mark for finding area under the tangent, 1 mark for subtracting area under tangent from area under curve, 1 mark for the correct answer]

Chapter 12: Vectors

Prior Knowledge Check

Q1 a) $\begin{pmatrix}3\\2\end{pmatrix} + \begin{pmatrix}4\\-3\end{pmatrix} = \begin{pmatrix}3+4\\2-3\end{pmatrix} = \begin{pmatrix}7\\-1\end{pmatrix}$

b) $\begin{pmatrix}5\\-2\end{pmatrix} - \begin{pmatrix}-1\\6\end{pmatrix} = \begin{pmatrix}5-(-1)\\(-2)-6\end{pmatrix} = \begin{pmatrix}6\\-8\end{pmatrix}$

c) $5\begin{pmatrix}4\\-3\end{pmatrix} = \begin{pmatrix}5\times4\\5\times(-3)\end{pmatrix} = \begin{pmatrix}20\\-15\end{pmatrix}$

Q2 $a^2 + b^2 = c^2$, so the missing length $= \sqrt{5^2 + 12^2} = \sqrt{169} = 13$ cm

Q3 a) $\tan x = \frac{5}{3} \Rightarrow x = \tan^{-1}\left(\frac{5}{3}\right) = 59.0°$ (3 s.f.)

b) $\sin 20° = \frac{x}{7} \Rightarrow x = 7 \sin 20° = 2.39$ cm (3 s.f.)

c) $\cos x = \frac{4}{11} \Rightarrow x = \cos^{-1}\left(\frac{4}{11}\right) = 68.7°$ (3 s.f.)

Q4 $\cos\theta = \frac{4^2 + 6^2 - 5^2}{2\times4\times6} = \frac{9}{16} \Rightarrow \theta = \cos^{-1}\left(\frac{9}{16}\right) = 55.8°$ (3 s.f.)

Exercise 12.1 — Introducing Vectors

Q1 a) vector **b)** scalar **c)** vector

Q2 a)

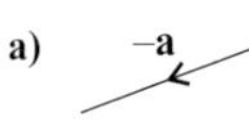

b)

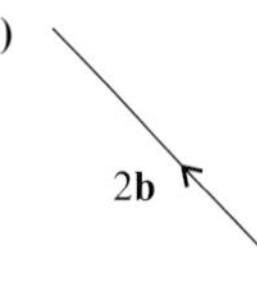

c)

a + b
b
a

d)

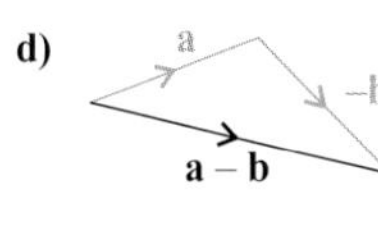

Q3 a) $\overrightarrow{AC}$ **b)** $\overrightarrow{BA}$ **c)** $\overrightarrow{DB}$

Q4 a) $\overrightarrow{XY} = -q$

b) $\overrightarrow{YZ} = \overrightarrow{YX} + \overrightarrow{XZ} = q + p$

c) $\overrightarrow{ZY} = \overrightarrow{ZX} + \overrightarrow{XY} = -p - q$
or $\overrightarrow{ZY} = -\overrightarrow{YZ} = -q - p$

Q5

A p B
q q
D p C

a) $\overrightarrow{AC} = \overrightarrow{AB} + \overrightarrow{BC} = \mathbf{p} + \mathbf{q}$, so $\overrightarrow{AB} + \overrightarrow{AC} = 2\mathbf{p} + \mathbf{q}$

[2 marks available — 1 mark for finding $\overrightarrow{AC}$, 1 mark for the correct answer]

b) $\overrightarrow{AD} + \overrightarrow{BA} = \mathbf{q} - \mathbf{p}$, so $2(\overrightarrow{AD} + \overrightarrow{BA}) = 2(\mathbf{q} - \mathbf{p}) = 2\mathbf{q} - 2\mathbf{p}$

[2 marks available — 1 mark for finding $\overrightarrow{AD} + \overrightarrow{BA}$, 1 mark for the correct answer]

Q6 $\overrightarrow{BC} = \overrightarrow{BD} + \overrightarrow{DC} = \overrightarrow{BD} - \overrightarrow{CD}$

$\overrightarrow{AB} = \overrightarrow{CD}$ as the two sides are parallel and the same length, so $\overrightarrow{BC} = \overrightarrow{BD} - \overrightarrow{CD} = \overrightarrow{BD} - \overrightarrow{AB} = \mathbf{m} - \mathbf{n}$.

Q7 a) $\overrightarrow{DF} = \frac{2}{3}\overrightarrow{DC}$. $\overrightarrow{DC}$ is parallel to $\overrightarrow{AB}$ and the same length because ABCD is a rectangle, so $\overrightarrow{DC} = \overrightarrow{AB} = \mathbf{b}$. So $\overrightarrow{DF} = \frac{2}{3}\mathrm{b}$.

b) $\overrightarrow{BE} = \overrightarrow{BA} + \overrightarrow{AE} = -\overrightarrow{AB} + \frac{1}{2}\overrightarrow{AD} = -\mathrm{b} + \frac{1}{2}\mathrm{d}$

c) $\overrightarrow{EF} = \overrightarrow{ED} + \overrightarrow{DF} = \frac{1}{2}\overrightarrow{AD} + \overrightarrow{DF} = \frac{1}{2}\mathrm{d} + \frac{2}{3}\mathrm{b}$

Q8 a) 2**e** **b)** –2**d**

c) **d** – **e** **d)** 2**e** – **d**

e) **e** – 2**d** **f)** –**d** – **e**

Q9 $\overrightarrow{JL} = \overrightarrow{JD} + \overrightarrow{DL}$

J is the midpoint of ED, so $\overrightarrow{JD} = \frac{1}{2}\overrightarrow{ED} = \frac{1}{2}\mathbf{d}$.

And L is the midpoint of DF, so $\overrightarrow{DL} = \frac{1}{2}\overrightarrow{DF}$.

$\overrightarrow{DF} = \overrightarrow{DE} + \overrightarrow{EF} = -\mathbf{d} + \mathbf{f} \Rightarrow \overrightarrow{DL} = \frac{1}{2}(\mathbf{f} - \mathbf{d})$

So, $\overrightarrow{JL} = \frac{1}{2}\mathbf{d} + \frac{1}{2}(\mathbf{f} - \mathbf{d}) = \frac{1}{2}\mathbf{f}$.

Q10 a) $\overrightarrow{AB} = \overrightarrow{AO} + \overrightarrow{OB} = -(\mathbf{p} + \mathbf{q}) + (\mathbf{p} + 2\mathbf{q}) = \mathbf{q}$ *[1 mark]*

b) $\overrightarrow{AC} = \overrightarrow{AB} + \overrightarrow{BC} = \mathbf{q} + 3\mathbf{q} = 4\mathbf{q}$

$\overrightarrow{OC} = \overrightarrow{OA} + \overrightarrow{AC} = \mathbf{p} + \mathbf{q} + 4\mathbf{q} = \mathbf{p} + 5\mathbf{q}$

[2 marks available — 1 mark for finding $\overrightarrow{AC}$, 1 mark for the correct answer]

Q11 a) $\overrightarrow{AD} = \overrightarrow{AB} + \overrightarrow{BC} + \overrightarrow{CD} = \mathbf{a} + \mathbf{b} - \frac{1}{2}\mathbf{a} = \frac{1}{2}\mathbf{a} + \mathbf{b}$, so

$\overrightarrow{AM} = \frac{1}{2}\overrightarrow{AD} = \frac{1}{2}\left(\frac{1}{2}\mathbf{a} + \mathbf{b}\right) = \frac{1}{4}\mathbf{a} + \frac{1}{2}\mathbf{b}$

[2 marks available — 1 mark for finding $\overrightarrow{AD}$, 1 mark for the correct answer]

b) $\overrightarrow{BD} = \overrightarrow{BC} + \overrightarrow{CD} = \mathbf{b} - \frac{1}{2}\mathbf{a}$

$\overrightarrow{BP} = \frac{3}{4}\overrightarrow{BD} = \frac{3}{4}\left(\mathbf{b} - \frac{1}{2}\mathbf{a}\right) = \frac{3}{4}\mathbf{b} - \frac{3}{8}\mathbf{a}$

[2 marks available — 1 mark for finding $\overrightarrow{BD}$, 1 mark for the correct answer]

c) $\overrightarrow{PM} = \overrightarrow{PB} + \overrightarrow{BA} + \overrightarrow{AM} = -\left(\frac{3}{4}\mathbf{b} - \frac{3}{8}\mathbf{a}\right) - \mathbf{a} + \frac{1}{4}\mathbf{a} + \frac{1}{2}\mathbf{b}$

$= \left(\frac{3}{8} + \frac{1}{4} - 1\right)\mathbf{a} + \left(\frac{1}{2} - \frac{3}{4}\right)\mathbf{b} = -\frac{3}{8}\mathbf{a} - \frac{1}{4}\mathbf{b}$

[2 marks available — 1 mark for a correct method, 1 mark for the correct answer]

Q12 Any vector that is a multiple of 3**t** – 2**u** is acceptable, e.g. 6**t** – 4**u**, 6**u** – 9**t**, $\frac{3}{2}\mathbf{t} - \mathbf{u}$, etc.

Q13 $\overrightarrow{YZ} = -\mathbf{a} + \mathbf{b}$, so $\overrightarrow{YP} = \frac{1}{2}\overrightarrow{YZ} = \frac{1}{2}(-\mathbf{a} + \mathbf{b})$.

This means, $\overrightarrow{PQ} = -\overrightarrow{YP} + \overrightarrow{YQ} = -\frac{1}{2}(-\mathbf{a} + \mathbf{b}) + -\frac{1}{2}(-\mathbf{a}) = -\frac{1}{2}\mathbf{b}$.

$\overrightarrow{PQ}$ is a scalar multiple of $\overrightarrow{XZ}$, so they're parallel.

Q14 $\overrightarrow{US} = \overrightarrow{UT} + \overrightarrow{TS} = -\overrightarrow{TU} - \overrightarrow{ST} = -(\mathbf{v} - \mathbf{w}) - (2\mathbf{v} + \mathbf{w}) = -3\mathbf{v}$.

This is a scalar multiple of **v**, so is parallel to **v**.

Q15 $\overrightarrow{YZ} = \overrightarrow{YX} + \overrightarrow{XZ} = -\overrightarrow{XY} + \overrightarrow{XZ}$
$= -(3\mathbf{a} - 4\mathbf{b} + 2\mathbf{c}) + \mathbf{a} - 2\mathbf{b} - 2\mathbf{c}$
$= -2\mathbf{a} + 2\mathbf{b} - 4\mathbf{c} = 2(\mathbf{a} - \mathbf{b} + 2\mathbf{c})$

This is a scalar multiple of $\mathbf{a} - \mathbf{b} + 2\mathbf{c}$, so they're parallel.

Q16 $\overrightarrow{YZ} = \overrightarrow{AZ} - \overrightarrow{AY} = \mathbf{u} - (-\mathbf{t}) = \mathbf{t} + \mathbf{u} = \overrightarrow{XY}$.
These are the same vector, so X, Y and Z are collinear.

Q17 $4\mathbf{b} + 8\mathbf{a} = 4(2\mathbf{a} + \mathbf{b}) = -4(-\mathbf{b} - 2\mathbf{a})$,
so $4\mathbf{b} + 8\mathbf{a}$, $2\mathbf{a} + \mathbf{b}$ and $-\mathbf{b} - 2\mathbf{a}$ are parallel.

$2\mathbf{p} + \mathbf{q} = 2\left(\frac{1}{2}\mathbf{q} + \mathbf{p}\right)$, so $2\mathbf{p} + \mathbf{q}$ and $\frac{1}{2}\mathbf{q} + \mathbf{p}$ are parallel.
$10\mathbf{a} - 5\mathbf{b} = 5(2\mathbf{a} - \mathbf{b})$, so $10\mathbf{a} - 5\mathbf{b}$ and $2\mathbf{a} - \mathbf{b}$ are parallel.

Q18 $\overrightarrow{AB} = \overrightarrow{OB} - \overrightarrow{OA} = \mathbf{b} - \mathbf{a}$
$\overrightarrow{BC} = \overrightarrow{OC} - \overrightarrow{OB} = (5\mathbf{a} - 4\mathbf{b}) - \mathbf{b} = 5(\mathbf{a} - \mathbf{b})$
So $\overrightarrow{BC} = -5\overrightarrow{AB}$, so A, B & C lie on the same straight line — i.e. they are collinear.

Q19 $\overrightarrow{QR} = 2\mathbf{m} + 3\mathbf{n}$ and $\overrightarrow{RS} = \mathbf{m} + \frac{3}{2}\mathbf{n} = \frac{1}{2}\overrightarrow{QR}$.
This shows they're scalar multiples, so they are parallel.
Therefore, Q, R and S are collinear.

Q20 $\overrightarrow{OA} = 4\mathbf{a} - 2\mathbf{b}$
$\overrightarrow{AC} = \overrightarrow{AB} + \overrightarrow{BD} + \overrightarrow{DC} = 2\mathbf{b} + 4\mathbf{a} - \mathbf{b} - \frac{5}{2}\mathbf{b} - \mathbf{a}$
$= 3\mathbf{a} - \frac{3}{2}\mathbf{b} = \frac{3}{4}\overrightarrow{OA}$

This shows that $\overrightarrow{OA}$ and $\overrightarrow{AC}$ are scalar multiples of one another, so they're parallel. Therefore, O, A and C are collinear and OAC is a straight line.

Q21 $\overrightarrow{BC} = \overrightarrow{AC} - \overrightarrow{AB} = \mathbf{p} - (\mathbf{q} - \frac{1}{2}\mathbf{p}) = \frac{3}{2}\mathbf{p} - \mathbf{q}$
$\overrightarrow{CD} = \overrightarrow{AD} - \overrightarrow{AC} = (-5\mathbf{p} + 4\mathbf{q}) - \mathbf{p} = -6\mathbf{p} + 4\mathbf{q}$
$-6\mathbf{p} + 4\mathbf{q} = -4(\frac{3}{2}\mathbf{p} - \mathbf{q}) = -4\overrightarrow{BC}$
$\overrightarrow{BC}$ and $\overrightarrow{CD}$ are scalar multiples of one another, so they're parallel. They also meet at point C, so B, C and D are collinear.

Q22 a) $\overrightarrow{PS} = \overrightarrow{PQ} + \overrightarrow{QR} + \overrightarrow{RS}$
$= (-\mathbf{a}) + (-\frac{1}{2}\mathbf{a} + \mathbf{b}) + (\frac{5}{2}\mathbf{a} - 3\mathbf{b}) = \mathbf{a} - 2\mathbf{b}$

b) $\mathbf{a} - 2\mathbf{b} = -2(-\frac{1}{2}\mathbf{a} + \mathbf{b}) = -2\overrightarrow{QR}$, so $\overrightarrow{PS}$ and $\overrightarrow{QR}$ are parallel. Since $\overrightarrow{PQ}$ and $\overrightarrow{RS}$ are not scalar multiples of each other, they are not parallel, so PQRS must be a trapezium.

Q23 X is the midpoint of AC, so $\overrightarrow{AX} = \overrightarrow{XC} = \mathbf{a}$.
So, $\overrightarrow{DX} = \mathbf{a} - \mathbf{b} + \mathbf{a} = 2\mathbf{a} - \mathbf{b}$ and $\overrightarrow{XB} = -\mathbf{a} + 3\mathbf{a} - 2\mathbf{b} = 2\mathbf{a} - 2\mathbf{b}$.
This shows $\overrightarrow{DX}$ and $\overrightarrow{XB}$ are not scalar multiples of one another, so are not parallel. Therefore, D, X and B are not collinear and DXB is not a straight line.

Q24 a) $\overrightarrow{CD} = \overrightarrow{CB} + \overrightarrow{BA} + \overrightarrow{AD} = \overrightarrow{AD} - \overrightarrow{BC} - \overrightarrow{AB}$
$= \frac{3}{2}\mathbf{a} - \mathbf{a} - (\mathbf{b} - \mathbf{a}) = \frac{3}{2}\mathbf{a} - \mathbf{b}$

$\overrightarrow{BE} = \overrightarrow{BA} + \overrightarrow{AE} = \overrightarrow{AE} - \overrightarrow{AB} = (2\mathbf{a} - \mathbf{b}) - (\mathbf{b} - \mathbf{a}) = 3\mathbf{a} - 2\mathbf{b}$
$\overrightarrow{BE} = 2\overrightarrow{CD}$, so they are parallel.

b) $\overrightarrow{AO} = \overrightarrow{AB} + \overrightarrow{BO} = \overrightarrow{AB} + \frac{1}{3}\overrightarrow{BE} = (\mathbf{b} - \mathbf{a}) + \frac{1}{3}(3\mathbf{a} - 2\mathbf{b}) = \frac{1}{3}\mathbf{b}$
$\overrightarrow{OC} = \overrightarrow{OB} + \overrightarrow{BC} = \overrightarrow{BC} - \frac{1}{3}\overrightarrow{BE} = \mathbf{a} - \frac{1}{3}(3\mathbf{a} - 2\mathbf{b}) = \frac{2}{3}\mathbf{b}$
$\overrightarrow{AO}$ and $\overrightarrow{OC}$ are scalar multiples of one another, so they are parallel and therefore A, O and C are collinear — they lie on the same straight line.

Q25 a) $\overrightarrow{AD} = \overrightarrow{AB} + \overrightarrow{BC} + \overrightarrow{CD} = \mathbf{p} + \mathbf{q} + \mathbf{r} = \overrightarrow{DP}$
$\overrightarrow{PC} = \overrightarrow{PD} + \overrightarrow{DC} = -(\mathbf{p} + \mathbf{q} + \mathbf{r}) - \mathbf{r} = -\mathbf{p} - \mathbf{q} - 2\mathbf{r}$
$\overrightarrow{CM} = \frac{3}{4}\overrightarrow{CF}$ and $\overrightarrow{CF} = \overrightarrow{CB} + \overrightarrow{BA} + \overrightarrow{AF} = -\mathbf{q} - \mathbf{p} + \mathbf{r}$
$\Rightarrow \overrightarrow{CM} = \frac{3}{4}(\mathbf{r} - \mathbf{p} - \mathbf{q})$
$\overrightarrow{PM} = \overrightarrow{PC} + \overrightarrow{CM} = (-\mathbf{p} - \mathbf{q} - 2\mathbf{r}) + \frac{3}{4}(\mathbf{r} - \mathbf{p} - \mathbf{q})$
$= -\frac{7}{4}\mathbf{p} - \frac{7}{4}\mathbf{q} - \frac{5}{4}\mathbf{r}$
[6 marks available — 1 mark for $\overrightarrow{DP}$, 1 mark for a correct method to find $\overrightarrow{PC}$, 1 mark for finding $\overrightarrow{PC}$ correctly, 1 mark for a correct method to find $\overrightarrow{CM}$, 1 mark for finding $\overrightarrow{CM}$, 1 mark for a correct method leading to the required result]
There are other ways to answer this question and you'd get the marks for showing the result with a correct method.

b) As ABCDEF is a regular hexagon, you can write $\mathbf{r}$ in terms of $\mathbf{p}$ and $\mathbf{q}$, $\mathbf{r} = \mathbf{q} - \mathbf{p}$. Substituting this into the answer in part a) gives, $\overrightarrow{PM} = -\frac{7}{4}\mathbf{p} - \frac{7}{4}\mathbf{q} - \frac{5}{4}\mathbf{r}$
$= -\frac{7}{4}\mathbf{p} - \frac{7}{4}\mathbf{q} - \frac{5}{4}(\mathbf{q} - \mathbf{p}) = -\frac{1}{2}\mathbf{p} - 3\mathbf{q}$
*[2 marks available — 1 mark for writing **r** in terms of **p** and **q**, 1 mark for the correct answer]*

Q26 $\overrightarrow{PR} = \overrightarrow{PQ} + \overrightarrow{QR} = (\mathbf{a} + 2\mathbf{b}) + (3\mathbf{a} + \mathbf{b}) = 4\mathbf{a} + 3\mathbf{b}$
So $\overrightarrow{PM} = \frac{1}{2}\overrightarrow{PR} = 2\mathbf{a} + \frac{3}{2}\mathbf{b}$
$\overrightarrow{PS} = \overrightarrow{PM} + \overrightarrow{MS} = 2\mathbf{a} + \frac{3}{2}\mathbf{b} + \frac{1}{2}(\mathbf{a} - \frac{1}{2}\mathbf{b}) = \frac{5}{2}\mathbf{a} + \frac{5}{4}\mathbf{b}$
Now, $\overrightarrow{PT} = m\overrightarrow{PS}$ and $\overrightarrow{PT} = \overrightarrow{PQ} + n\overrightarrow{QR}$ for some scalars m and n.
$\overrightarrow{PT} = m\overrightarrow{PS} = m(\frac{5}{2}\mathbf{a} + \frac{5}{4}\mathbf{b}) = \frac{5}{2}m\mathbf{a} + \frac{5}{4}m\mathbf{b}$
$\overrightarrow{PT} = \overrightarrow{PQ} + n\overrightarrow{QR} = (\mathbf{a} + 2\mathbf{b}) + n(3\mathbf{a} + \mathbf{b}) = (3n + 1)\mathbf{a} + (n + 2)\mathbf{b}$
Equating coefficients of $\mathbf{a}$ and $\mathbf{b}$ gives simultaneous equations:
$\frac{5}{2}m = 3n + 1$ and $\frac{5}{4}m = n + 2 \Rightarrow 2(3n + 1) = 5m = 4(n + 2)$
$\Rightarrow 3n + 1 = 2n + 4 \Rightarrow n = 3$
So $\overrightarrow{PT} = (3(3) + 1)\mathbf{a} + ((3) + 2)\mathbf{b} = 10\mathbf{a} + 5\mathbf{b}$
You might also have found $m = 4$.

Exercise 12.2 — Position Vectors

Q1 Position vector for Jack's house: $\begin{pmatrix} 2 \\ 3 \end{pmatrix}$

Position vector for Jack's school: $\begin{pmatrix} 4 \\ -5 \end{pmatrix}$

Q2 a) $2\mathbf{i} - 4\mathbf{j}$ **b)** $-\mathbf{i} - 2\mathbf{j}$
c) $5\mathbf{i} + 7\mathbf{j}$ **d)** $3\mathbf{i} - 7\mathbf{j}$

Q3 a) C (–1, 2), D (4, –3)

b) $\overrightarrow{CD} = \overrightarrow{OD} - \overrightarrow{OC} = (4\mathbf{i} - 3\mathbf{j}) - (-\mathbf{i} + 2\mathbf{j}) = 5\mathbf{i} - 5\mathbf{j}$
$\overrightarrow{DC} = -\overrightarrow{CD} = -(5\mathbf{i} - 5\mathbf{j}) = -5\mathbf{i} + 5\mathbf{j}$

Q4 a) $\mathbf{a} + \mathbf{b} + \mathbf{c} = \begin{pmatrix} -1 \\ -2 \end{pmatrix} + \begin{pmatrix} 3 \\ -2 \end{pmatrix} + \begin{pmatrix} 4 \\ 3 \end{pmatrix} = \begin{pmatrix} 6 \\ -1 \end{pmatrix}$

b) $\mathbf{c} - 2\mathbf{b} = \begin{pmatrix} 4 \\ 3 \end{pmatrix} - 2\begin{pmatrix} 3 \\ -2 \end{pmatrix} = \begin{pmatrix} -2 \\ 7 \end{pmatrix}$

c) $3\mathbf{a} - \mathbf{b} + 2\mathbf{c} = 3\begin{pmatrix} -1 \\ -2 \end{pmatrix} - \begin{pmatrix} 3 \\ -2 \end{pmatrix} + 2\begin{pmatrix} 4 \\ 3 \end{pmatrix} = \begin{pmatrix} 2 \\ 2 \end{pmatrix}$

d) $5\mathbf{a} - 5\mathbf{c} = 5\begin{pmatrix} -1 \\ -2 \end{pmatrix} - 5\begin{pmatrix} 4 \\ 3 \end{pmatrix} = \begin{pmatrix} -25 \\ -25 \end{pmatrix}$

Q5 a) $\mathbf{b} = \frac{1}{3}\left(\begin{pmatrix} 1 \\ 6 \end{pmatrix} - \begin{pmatrix} -2 \\ 3 \end{pmatrix}\right) = \frac{1}{3}\begin{pmatrix} 3 \\ 3 \end{pmatrix} = \begin{pmatrix} 1 \\ 1 \end{pmatrix}$
[2 marks available — 1 mark for a correct method, 1 mark for the correct answer]

b) $\mathbf{c} = \left(\begin{pmatrix} -2 \\ 3 \end{pmatrix} + \begin{pmatrix} 1 \\ 1 \end{pmatrix}\right) - \begin{pmatrix} -1 \\ -3 \end{pmatrix} = \begin{pmatrix} -1 \\ 4 \end{pmatrix} - \begin{pmatrix} -1 \\ -3 \end{pmatrix} = \begin{pmatrix} 0 \\ 7 \end{pmatrix}$
[2 marks available — 1 mark for a correct method, 1 mark for the correct answer]

Q6 $\mathbf{p} + 3\mathbf{q} + \mathbf{r} = \begin{pmatrix} -1 \\ -2 \end{pmatrix} + 3\begin{pmatrix} 3 \\ -2 \end{pmatrix} + \begin{pmatrix} -4 \\ 5 \end{pmatrix} = \begin{pmatrix} 4 \\ -3 \end{pmatrix} = 4\mathbf{i} - 3\mathbf{j}$
$12\mathbf{i} - 9\mathbf{j} = 3(4\mathbf{i} - 3\mathbf{j})$ — this is a scalar multiple of $\mathbf{p} + 3\mathbf{q} + \mathbf{r}$, so they are parallel.

Q7 $\overrightarrow{PR} = \overrightarrow{PO} + \overrightarrow{OR} = -\begin{pmatrix}2\\-3\end{pmatrix} + \begin{pmatrix}4\\-6\end{pmatrix} = \begin{pmatrix}2\\-3\end{pmatrix}$

$\overrightarrow{QR} = \overrightarrow{QO} + \overrightarrow{OR} = -\begin{pmatrix}-2\\3\end{pmatrix} + \begin{pmatrix}4\\-6\end{pmatrix} = \begin{pmatrix}6\\-9\end{pmatrix}$

$\overrightarrow{QR} = \begin{pmatrix}6\\-9\end{pmatrix} = 3\begin{pmatrix}2\\-3\end{pmatrix} = 3\overrightarrow{PR}$ so P, Q and R are collinear.

[3 marks available — 1 mark for finding $\overrightarrow{PR}$, 1 mark for finding $\overrightarrow{QR}$, 1 mark for correctly concluding that P, Q and R are collinear]

Q8 a) $\overrightarrow{AB} = \overrightarrow{OB} - \overrightarrow{OA} = 4\mathbf{i} - (3\mathbf{i} - 3\mathbf{j}) = \mathbf{i} + 3\mathbf{j}$

[2 marks available — 1 mark for a correct method, 1 mark for the correct answer]

b) $\overrightarrow{OC} = \begin{pmatrix}-4\\2\end{pmatrix} = -4\mathbf{i} + 2\mathbf{j}$

$3\overrightarrow{AB} = 3(\mathbf{i} + 3\mathbf{j}) = 3\mathbf{i} + 9\mathbf{j} = 2\overrightarrow{CD} \Rightarrow \overrightarrow{CD} = 1.5\mathbf{i} + 4.5\mathbf{j}$

So $\overrightarrow{OD} = \overrightarrow{OC} + \overrightarrow{CD} = (-4\mathbf{i} + 2\mathbf{j}) + (1.5\mathbf{i} + 4.5\mathbf{j}) = -2.5\mathbf{i} + 6.5\mathbf{j}$

[3 marks available — 1 mark for using $\overrightarrow{AB}$ correctly, 1 mark for finding $\overrightarrow{CD}$, 1 mark for the correct answer]

Q9 $\overrightarrow{OA} = \begin{pmatrix}2\\4\end{pmatrix}$, $\overrightarrow{OB} = \begin{pmatrix}0\\1\end{pmatrix}$, $\overrightarrow{OC} = \begin{pmatrix}-1\\3\end{pmatrix}$

You could use unit form instead of column vectors to answer this question if you prefer.

$\overrightarrow{AB} = \overrightarrow{OB} - \overrightarrow{OA} = \begin{pmatrix}0\\1\end{pmatrix} - \begin{pmatrix}2\\4\end{pmatrix} = \begin{pmatrix}-2\\-3\end{pmatrix}$

$\overrightarrow{BC} = \overrightarrow{OC} - \overrightarrow{OB} = \begin{pmatrix}-1\\3\end{pmatrix} - \begin{pmatrix}0\\1\end{pmatrix} = \begin{pmatrix}-1\\2\end{pmatrix}$

$\overrightarrow{CA} = \overrightarrow{OA} - \overrightarrow{OC} = \begin{pmatrix}2\\4\end{pmatrix} - \begin{pmatrix}-1\\3\end{pmatrix} = \begin{pmatrix}3\\1\end{pmatrix}$

Q10 Diagonal $\overrightarrow{AC} = \begin{pmatrix}3\\-1\end{pmatrix} - \begin{pmatrix}-4\\6\end{pmatrix} = \begin{pmatrix}7\\-7\end{pmatrix} = 7\mathbf{i} - 7\mathbf{j}$

i.e. the **i**- and **j**- components are equal length.
So the sides of the square ABCD have length 7.

E.g.

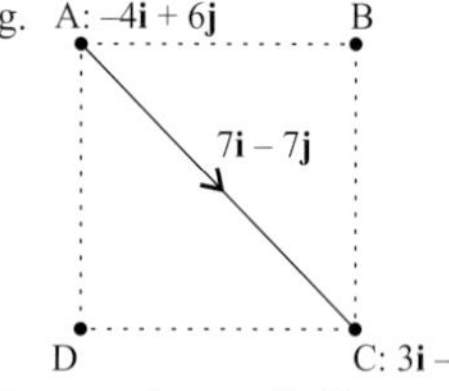

B has coordinates (3, 6) or position vector $3\mathbf{i} + 6\mathbf{j}$ and D has coordinates (–4, –1) or position vector $-4\mathbf{i} - \mathbf{j}$.

You might have B and D the other way around, depending on how you labelled the points.

Q11 $\overrightarrow{PM} = \overrightarrow{MQ}$ because M is the midpoint of PQ. This is because the lines are the same length and point in the same direction.

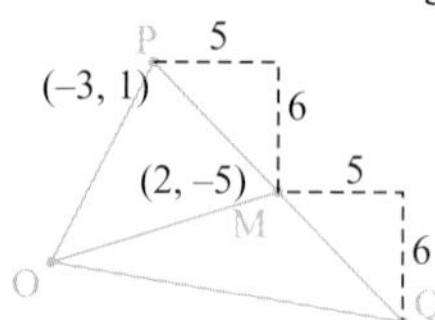

$\overrightarrow{MQ} = \overrightarrow{PM} = \overrightarrow{OM} - \overrightarrow{OP} = 2\mathbf{i} - 5\mathbf{j} - (-3\mathbf{i} + \mathbf{j}) = 5\mathbf{i} - 6\mathbf{j}$

So $\overrightarrow{OQ} = \overrightarrow{OM} + \overrightarrow{MQ} = 2\mathbf{i} - 5\mathbf{j} + (5\mathbf{i} - 6\mathbf{j}) = 7\mathbf{i} - 11\mathbf{j}$

Q12 a) $\overrightarrow{OP} = \overrightarrow{OA} + \overrightarrow{AP} = \overrightarrow{OA} + \frac{2}{3}\overrightarrow{AB} = \begin{pmatrix}-2\\4\end{pmatrix} + \frac{2}{3}\begin{pmatrix}4-(-2)\\-5-4\end{pmatrix}$

$= \begin{pmatrix}-2\\4\end{pmatrix} + \frac{2}{3}\begin{pmatrix}6\\-9\end{pmatrix} = \begin{pmatrix}-2\\4\end{pmatrix} + \begin{pmatrix}4\\-6\end{pmatrix} = \begin{pmatrix}2\\-2\end{pmatrix}$

b) $\overrightarrow{PB} = \overrightarrow{OB} - \overrightarrow{OP} = \begin{pmatrix}4\\-5\end{pmatrix} - \begin{pmatrix}2\\-2\end{pmatrix} = \begin{pmatrix}2\\-3\end{pmatrix}$

Q13 a) $\overrightarrow{BC} = \overrightarrow{BO} + \overrightarrow{OC} = \overrightarrow{OC} - \overrightarrow{OB} = \begin{pmatrix}5\\6\end{pmatrix} - \begin{pmatrix}2\\5\end{pmatrix} = \begin{pmatrix}3\\1\end{pmatrix}$

[2 marks available — 1 mark for a correct method, 1 mark for the correct answer]

b) As ABCD is a parallelogram, $\overrightarrow{AD} = \overrightarrow{BC}$,

so $\overrightarrow{OD} = \overrightarrow{OA} + \overrightarrow{AD} = \overrightarrow{OA} + \overrightarrow{BC} = \begin{pmatrix}1\\2\end{pmatrix} + \begin{pmatrix}3\\1\end{pmatrix} = \begin{pmatrix}4\\3\end{pmatrix}$,

$\Rightarrow$ D has coordinates (4, 3)

[2 marks available — 1 mark for a correct method, 1 mark for the correct answer]

c) Let the new parallelogram be A'B'C'D', then:

$\overrightarrow{OA'} - \overrightarrow{OA} = \begin{pmatrix}4\\1\end{pmatrix} - \begin{pmatrix}1\\2\end{pmatrix} = \begin{pmatrix}3\\-1\end{pmatrix} \Rightarrow \overrightarrow{OC'} = \begin{pmatrix}5\\6\end{pmatrix} + \begin{pmatrix}3\\-1\end{pmatrix} = \begin{pmatrix}8\\5\end{pmatrix}$

So new position vector of point C is $8\mathbf{i} + 5\mathbf{j}$

[2 marks available — 1 mark for a correct method, 1 mark for the correct answer]

You could also have found $\overrightarrow{AC}$ and used that to find $\overrightarrow{A'C'}$.

Q14 a) $\overrightarrow{PR} = \overrightarrow{PO} + \overrightarrow{OR} = \overrightarrow{OR} - \overrightarrow{OP} = (3\mathbf{i} - 2\mathbf{j}) - (\mathbf{i} + \mathbf{j}) = 2\mathbf{i} - 3\mathbf{j}$

[2 marks available — 1 mark for a correct method, 1 mark for the correct answer]

b) $\overrightarrow{SQ} = \overrightarrow{SO} + \overrightarrow{OQ} = \overrightarrow{OQ} - \overrightarrow{OS} = (2\mathbf{i} + 3\mathbf{j}) - (-\mathbf{i} - \mathbf{j}) = 3\mathbf{i} + 4\mathbf{j}$

[2 marks available — 1 mark for a correct method, 1 mark for the correct answer]

Q15 a) $\overrightarrow{AB} = \overrightarrow{AO} + \overrightarrow{OB} = \overrightarrow{OB} - \overrightarrow{OA} = (5\mathbf{i} - 2\mathbf{j}) - (-\mathbf{i} + \mathbf{j}) = 6\mathbf{i} - 3\mathbf{j}$

[2 marks available — 1 mark for a correct method, 1 mark for the correct answer]

b) (i) $\overrightarrow{AC} = \overrightarrow{AB} + \overrightarrow{BC} = \overrightarrow{AB} + \frac{1}{3}\overrightarrow{AB} = (6\mathbf{i} - 3\mathbf{j}) + \frac{1}{3}(6\mathbf{i} - 3\mathbf{j})$

$= (6\mathbf{i} - 3\mathbf{j}) + (2\mathbf{i} - \mathbf{j}) = 8\mathbf{i} - 4\mathbf{j}$

[3 marks available — 1 mark for writing $\overrightarrow{AC}$ in terms of $\overrightarrow{AB}$, 1 mark for correct working, 1 mark for the correct answer]

(ii) $\overrightarrow{OC} = \overrightarrow{OA} + \overrightarrow{AC}$ $(-\mathbf{i} + \mathbf{j}) + (8\mathbf{i} - 4\mathbf{j}) = 7\mathbf{i} - 3\mathbf{j}$

[2 marks available — 1 mark for a correct method, 1 mark for the correct answer]

Q16 a) $\overrightarrow{OD} = \begin{pmatrix}-7\\-2\end{pmatrix}$, $\overrightarrow{OE} = \begin{pmatrix}-3\\-1\end{pmatrix}$, $\overrightarrow{OF} = \begin{pmatrix}-1\\5\end{pmatrix}$, $\overrightarrow{OG} = \begin{pmatrix}-3\\10\end{pmatrix}$

$\overrightarrow{DE} = \overrightarrow{OE} - \overrightarrow{OD} = \begin{pmatrix}-3\\-1\end{pmatrix} - \begin{pmatrix}-7\\-2\end{pmatrix} = \begin{pmatrix}4\\1\end{pmatrix}$

$\overrightarrow{EF} = \overrightarrow{OF} - \overrightarrow{OE} = \begin{pmatrix}-1\\5\end{pmatrix} - \begin{pmatrix}-3\\-1\end{pmatrix} = \begin{pmatrix}2\\6\end{pmatrix}$

$\overrightarrow{FG} = \overrightarrow{OG} - \overrightarrow{OF} = \begin{pmatrix}-3\\10\end{pmatrix} - \begin{pmatrix}-1\\5\end{pmatrix} = \begin{pmatrix}-2\\5\end{pmatrix}$

$\overrightarrow{GD} = \overrightarrow{OD} - \overrightarrow{OG} = \begin{pmatrix}-7\\-2\end{pmatrix} - \begin{pmatrix}-3\\10\end{pmatrix} = \begin{pmatrix}-4\\-12\end{pmatrix}$

b) The vacuum cleaner could have travelled along vector $\overrightarrow{DE} + \overrightarrow{EF} = \overrightarrow{DF} = \begin{pmatrix}4\\1\end{pmatrix} + \begin{pmatrix}2\\6\end{pmatrix} = \begin{pmatrix}6\\7\end{pmatrix}$

Q17 E.g. $\overrightarrow{PR} = \overrightarrow{OR} - \overrightarrow{OP}$, so $\overrightarrow{OR} = \overrightarrow{PR} + \overrightarrow{OP} = \begin{pmatrix}4\\7\end{pmatrix} + \begin{pmatrix}3\\0\end{pmatrix} = \begin{pmatrix}7\\7\end{pmatrix}$

So the coordinates of R are (7, 7).

$\overrightarrow{QR} = \overrightarrow{OR} - \overrightarrow{OQ} = \begin{pmatrix}7\\7\end{pmatrix} - \begin{pmatrix}3\\3\end{pmatrix} = \begin{pmatrix}4\\4\end{pmatrix}$

Q18 $\overrightarrow{AC} = \overrightarrow{OC} - \overrightarrow{OA} = (4\mathbf{i} - 2\mathbf{j}) - (\mathbf{i} - \mathbf{j}) = 3\mathbf{i} - \mathbf{j}$

$\overrightarrow{BD} = \overrightarrow{OD} - \overrightarrow{OB} = (3\mathbf{i} + \mathbf{j}) - (-4\mathbf{j}) = 3\mathbf{i} + 5\mathbf{j}$

Q19 a) $\overrightarrow{AB} = \overrightarrow{AO} + \overrightarrow{OB} = \overrightarrow{OB} - \overrightarrow{OA} = (7\mathbf{i} + 3\mathbf{j}) - (\mathbf{i} - \mathbf{j}) = 6\mathbf{i} + 4\mathbf{j}$

$\overrightarrow{CD} = \overrightarrow{CO} + \overrightarrow{OD} = \overrightarrow{OD} - \overrightarrow{OC} = (5\mathbf{i} - 2\mathbf{j}) - 8\mathbf{i} = -3\mathbf{i} - 2\mathbf{j}$

$\Rightarrow \overrightarrow{AB} = -2(-3\mathbf{i} - 2\mathbf{j}) = -2\overrightarrow{CD} \Rightarrow \overrightarrow{AB}$ is parallel to $\overrightarrow{CD}$.

[4 marks available — 1 mark for a correct method to find $\overrightarrow{AB}$ or $\overrightarrow{CD}$, 1 mark for finding $\overrightarrow{AB}$, 1 mark for finding $\overrightarrow{CD}$, 1 mark for correctly showing that $\overrightarrow{AB}$ is a multiple of $\overrightarrow{CD}$]

b) $\overrightarrow{BD} = \overrightarrow{BC} + \overrightarrow{CD}$

$\overrightarrow{BC} = \overrightarrow{BO} + \overrightarrow{OC} = \overrightarrow{OC} - \overrightarrow{OB} = 8\mathbf{i} - (7\mathbf{i} + 3\mathbf{j}) = \mathbf{i} - 3\mathbf{j}$

$\Rightarrow \overrightarrow{BD} = (\mathbf{i} - 3\mathbf{j}) + (-3\mathbf{i} - 2\mathbf{j}) = -2\mathbf{i} - 5\mathbf{j}$

$\overrightarrow{OM} = \overrightarrow{OB} + \frac{1}{2}\overrightarrow{BD} = (7\mathbf{i} + 3\mathbf{j}) + \frac{1}{2}(-2\mathbf{i} - 5\mathbf{j}) = 6\mathbf{i} + \frac{1}{2}\mathbf{j}$

[3 marks available — 1 mark for a correct method to find $\overrightarrow{BD}$ or $\overrightarrow{DB}$, 1 mark for finding $\overrightarrow{BD}$ or $\overrightarrow{DB}$, 1 mark for the correct answer]

Q20 a)

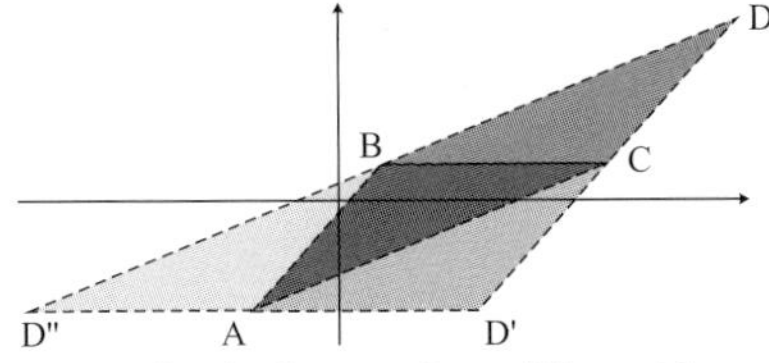

From a sketch, there are 3 possible positions of D:

D' = (–2 + (6 – 1))**i** – 3**j** = 3**i** – 3**j**

D'' = (–2 – (6 – 1))**i** – 3**j** = –7**i** – 3**j**

D''' = (1 + (6 – (–2)))**i** + (1 + (1 – (–3)))**j** = 9**i** + 5**j**

[4 marks available — 1 mark for identifying 3 potential positions of D, 1 mark for each correct answer]

b) If a < 0, then D must equal D'' = –7**i** – 3**j**. Diagonals $\overrightarrow{BA}$ and $\overrightarrow{CD}$ bisect each other so P is the midpoint of either vector.

$\overrightarrow{BA} = \overrightarrow{BO} + \overrightarrow{OA} = \overrightarrow{OA} - \overrightarrow{OB} = (-2\mathbf{i} - 3\mathbf{j}) - (\mathbf{i} + \mathbf{j}) = -3\mathbf{i} - 4\mathbf{j}$

$\overrightarrow{BP} = \frac{1}{2}\overrightarrow{BA} = -\frac{3}{2}\mathbf{i} - 2\mathbf{j}$

$\Rightarrow \overrightarrow{OP} = \overrightarrow{OB} + \overrightarrow{BP} = (\mathbf{i} + \mathbf{j}) + \left(-\frac{3}{2}\mathbf{i} - 2\mathbf{j}\right) = -\frac{1}{2}\mathbf{i} - \mathbf{j}$

*[4 marks available — 1 mark for deducing that D must be –7**i** – 3**j**, 1 mark for finding either diagonal, 1 mark for a correct method to find the position vector of P, 1 mark for the correct answer]*

Exercise 12.3 — Calculating with Vectors

Q1 a) (i) $\sqrt{6^2 + 8^2} = \sqrt{36 + 64} = \sqrt{100} = 10$

(ii) $\theta = \tan^{-1}\frac{8}{6} = 53.13°$

Both components are positive, so direction = 53.13°

b) (i) $\sqrt{12^2 + (-5)^2} = 13$

(ii) $\theta = \tan^{-1}\frac{-5}{12} = -22.62°$

The horizontal component is positive and the vertical component is negative, so direction = 360° – 22.62° = 337.38°

c) (i) $\sqrt{2^2 + 4^2} = \sqrt{20} = 2\sqrt{5}$

(ii) $\theta = \tan^{-1}\frac{4}{2} = 63.43°$

Both components are positive, so direction = 63.43°

d) (i) $\sqrt{(-3)^2 + (-1)^2} = \sqrt{10}$

(ii) $\theta = \tan^{-1}\frac{-1}{-3} = 18.43°$

Both components are negative, so direction = 180° + 18.43° = 198.43°

e) (i) $\sqrt{(24)^2 + (-7)^2} = 25$

(ii) $\theta = \tan^{-1}\frac{-7}{24} = -16.26°$

The horizontal component is positive and the vertical component is negative, so direction = 360° – 16.26° = 343.74°

f) (i) $\sqrt{(-\sqrt{13})^2 + 6^2} = \sqrt{13 + 36} = \sqrt{49} = 7$

(ii) $\theta = \tan^{-1}\frac{6}{-\sqrt{13}} = 59.00°$

The horizontal component is negative and the vertical component is positive, so direction = 180° – 59.00° = 121.00°

g) (i) $\sqrt{3^2 + (\sqrt{7})^2} = 4$

(ii) $\theta = \tan^{-1}\frac{\sqrt{7}}{3} = 41.41°$

Both components are positive so direction = 41.41°

h) (i) $\sqrt{0^2 + (-7)^2} = 7$

(ii) The horizontal component is 0 and the vertical component is negative, so direction = 270.00°

Q2 $|\overrightarrow{OS}| = \sqrt{10^2 + 5^2} = \sqrt{100 + 25} = \sqrt{125} = 5\sqrt{5}$

Q3 a) (0, 1) has the position vector **j**, and (2, 2) has the position vector 2**i** + 2**j**. Find the vector to get from one point to the other: (2 – 0)**i** + (2 – 1)**j** = 2**i** + **j**.
The distance between the points is the magnitude of the resultant vector: $\sqrt{2^2 + 1^2} = \sqrt{5}$.

b) (–3, 2) has position vector –3**i** + 2**j**, and (4, 3) has position vector 4**i** + 3**j**. Find the vector to get from one point to the other: (4 – (–3))**i** + (3 – 2)**j** = 7**i** + **j**.
The distance between the points is the magnitude of the resultant vector: $\sqrt{7^2 + 1^2} = \sqrt{50} = 5\sqrt{2}$

c) (–1, –1) has the position vector –**i** – **j**, and (0, 4) has the position vector 4**j**. Find the vector to get from one point to the other: (0 –(–1))**i** + (4 – (–1))**j** = **i** + 5**j**.
The distance between the points is the magnitude of the resultant vector: $\sqrt{1^2 + 5^2} = \sqrt{26}$

Q4 a) **a** + **b** = (2**i** + **j**) + (2**i** – 4**j**) = 4**i** – 3**j**
The magnitude of the resultant is $\sqrt{4^2 + (-3)^2} = 5$

b) **u** + **v** = 4**i** – 4**j**, $|4\mathbf{i} - 4\mathbf{j}| = \sqrt{4^2 + (-4)^2} = \sqrt{32} = 4\sqrt{2}$

c) $\mathbf{f} + \mathbf{g} = \begin{pmatrix} 24 \\ -10 \end{pmatrix}, \left|\begin{pmatrix} 24 \\ -10 \end{pmatrix}\right| = \sqrt{24^2 + (-10)^2} = 26$

d) $\mathbf{d} + \mathbf{e} = \begin{pmatrix} 3 \\ -6 \end{pmatrix}, \left|\begin{pmatrix} 3 \\ -6 \end{pmatrix}\right| = \sqrt{3^2 + (-6)^2} = \sqrt{45} = 3\sqrt{5}$

e) **s** + **t** = –5**j**, $|-5\mathbf{j}| = \sqrt{(-5)^2} = 5$

f) $\mathbf{w} + \mathbf{x} = \begin{pmatrix} -9 \\ 0 \end{pmatrix}, \left|\begin{pmatrix} -9 \\ 0 \end{pmatrix}\right| = \sqrt{(-9)^2} = 9$

Q5 a) $\frac{3\mathbf{i}}{|3\mathbf{i}|} = \frac{3\mathbf{i}}{\sqrt{3^2}} = \mathbf{i}$

b) $\begin{pmatrix} 1 \\ 2 \end{pmatrix} \times \frac{1}{\sqrt{1^2 + 2^2}} = \frac{1}{\sqrt{5}}\begin{pmatrix} 1 \\ 2 \end{pmatrix}$

c) $5\mathbf{i} - 4\mathbf{j} \times \frac{1}{\sqrt{5^2 + (-4)^2}} = \frac{5}{\sqrt{41}}\mathbf{i} - \frac{4}{\sqrt{41}}\mathbf{j}$

d) $\begin{pmatrix} -2 \\ -6 \end{pmatrix} \times \frac{1}{\sqrt{(-2)^2 + (-6)^2}} = \begin{pmatrix} -2 \\ -6 \end{pmatrix} \times \frac{1}{2\sqrt{10}} = \frac{1}{\sqrt{10}}\begin{pmatrix} -1 \\ -3 \end{pmatrix}$

Q6 a) $\overrightarrow{AB} = \overrightarrow{AO} + \overrightarrow{OB} = \overrightarrow{OB} - \overrightarrow{OA} = (3\mathbf{i} - 2\mathbf{j}) - (\mathbf{i} + \mathbf{j}) = 2\mathbf{i} - 3\mathbf{j}$

[2 marks available — 1 mark for a correct method, 1 mark for the correct answer]

b) (i) Magnitude = $|\overrightarrow{AB}| = \sqrt{2^2 + (-3)^2} = \sqrt{13}$

[2 marks available — 1 mark for a correct method, 1 mark for the correct answer]

(ii) Direction = $\tan^{-1}\left(-\frac{3}{2}\right) = -56.309...°$

= 360° – 56.309...° = 303.7° (1 d.p.)

[2 marks available — 1 mark for a correct method, 1 mark for the correct answer]

c) $\frac{1}{\sqrt{13}}(2\mathbf{i} - 3\mathbf{j}) = \frac{2}{\sqrt{13}}\mathbf{i} - \frac{3}{\sqrt{13}}\mathbf{j}$ *[1 mark]*

Q7 $\overrightarrow{AC} = \overrightarrow{AB} + \overrightarrow{BC} = 3\mathbf{i} - 2\mathbf{j} + \mathbf{i} + 5\mathbf{j} = 4\mathbf{i} + 3\mathbf{j}$

$|\overrightarrow{AC}| = \sqrt{4^2 + 3^2} = 5$

So unit vector = $\frac{4}{5}\mathbf{i} + \frac{3}{5}\mathbf{j}$

Q8 $\overrightarrow{BA} = (2\mathbf{i} - \mathbf{j}) - (7\mathbf{i} - 13\mathbf{j}) = -5\mathbf{i} + 12\mathbf{j}$,

$|\overrightarrow{BA}| = \sqrt{(-5)^2 + 12^2} = \sqrt{169} = 13$

So unit vector = $-\frac{5}{13}\mathbf{i} + \frac{12}{13}\mathbf{j}$

Q9 a) $\overrightarrow{AB} = \overrightarrow{AO} + \overrightarrow{OB} = \overrightarrow{OB} - \overrightarrow{OA} = (5\mathbf{i} - 2\mathbf{j}) - 7\mathbf{i} = -2\mathbf{i} - 2\mathbf{j}$

[2 marks available — 1 mark for a correct method, 1 mark for the correct answer]

b) (i) $\overrightarrow{OM} = \overrightarrow{OA} + \frac{1}{2}\overrightarrow{AB} = 7\mathbf{i} + \frac{1}{2}(-2\mathbf{i} - 2\mathbf{j}) = 6\mathbf{i} - \mathbf{j}$

[2 marks available — 1 mark for a correct method, 1 mark for the correct answer]

(ii) $|\overrightarrow{OM}| = \sqrt{6^2 + (-1)^2} = \sqrt{37}$, so the unit vector in the direction of $\overrightarrow{OM}$ is $\frac{1}{\sqrt{37}}(6\mathbf{i} - \mathbf{j}) = \frac{6}{\sqrt{37}}\mathbf{i} - \frac{1}{\sqrt{37}}\mathbf{j}$.

[3 marks available — 1 mark for using Pythagoras' theorem, 1 mark for finding $|\overrightarrow{OM}|$, 1 mark for the correct answer]

Q10 a) $\mathbf{a} = \sqrt{2}\cos 45\,\mathbf{i} + \sqrt{2}\sin 45\,\mathbf{j}$

$= \left(\sqrt{2} \times \frac{1}{\sqrt{2}}\right)\mathbf{i} + \left(\sqrt{2} \times \frac{1}{\sqrt{2}}\right)\mathbf{j} = \mathbf{i} + \mathbf{j}$

b) $\mathbf{b} = \sqrt{7}\cos 60\,\mathbf{i} + \sqrt{7}\sin 60\,\mathbf{j}$
$= \sqrt{7}\times\frac{1}{2}\,\mathbf{i} + \left(\sqrt{7}\times\frac{\sqrt{3}}{2}\right)\mathbf{j} = \frac{\sqrt{7}}{2}\mathbf{i} + \frac{\sqrt{21}}{2}\mathbf{j}$

c) $3\cos 33°\,\mathbf{i} + 3\sin 33°\,\mathbf{j}$

d) $5\cos 76°\,\mathbf{i} + 5\sin 76°\,\mathbf{j}$

c) and d) don't give exact values when evaluated, so leave them in terms of cos and sin.

Q11 $|\mathbf{d}| = \sqrt{8^2 + (-6)^2} = \sqrt{100} = 10$
The magnitude of **c** is seven times the magnitude of **d**, so $\mathbf{c} = 7\mathbf{d} = 7(8\mathbf{i} - 6\mathbf{j}) = 56\mathbf{i} - 42\mathbf{j}$

Q12

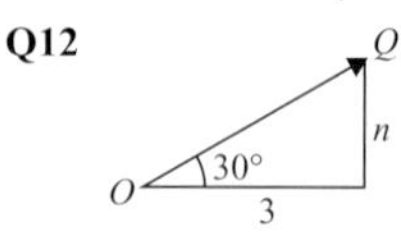

$\tan 30° = \frac{n}{3} \Rightarrow \frac{\sqrt{3}}{3} = \frac{n}{3} \Rightarrow n = \sqrt{3}$

[2 marks available — 1 mark for setting tan 30° = $\frac{n}{3}$, 1 mark for the correct answer]

Q13 **v** makes an angle $\tan^{-1}\left(\frac{4}{a}\right) = 51°$ below the x-axis,
so $\left(\frac{4}{a}\right) = \tan(51°) = 1.234... \Rightarrow a = \frac{4}{1.234...} = 3.239...$
So $|\mathbf{v}| = \sqrt{3.239...^2 + 4^2} = 5.147... = 5.15$ (2 d.p.)

Q14

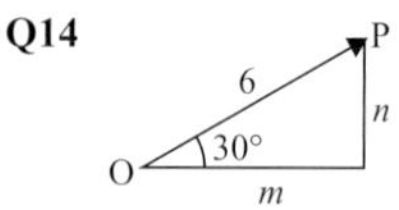

$\cos 30° = \frac{m}{6} \Rightarrow m = 6\cos 30° = 6\times\frac{\sqrt{3}}{2} = 3\sqrt{3}$
$\sin 30° = \frac{n}{6} \Rightarrow n = 6\sin 30° = 6\times 0.5 = 3$

[3 marks available — 1 mark for a correct method to find m or n, 1 mark for the correct value of m, 1 mark for the correct value of n]

Q15 $|\overrightarrow{AB}|$ and $|\overrightarrow{BC}|$ form two sides of a triangle.

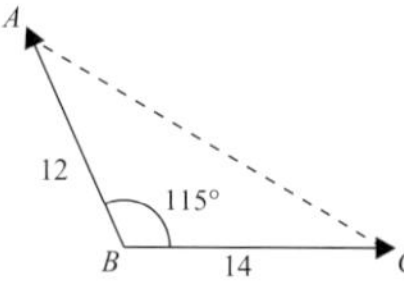

Use the cosine rule to find the remaining side:
$|\overrightarrow{CA}|^2 = 12^2 + 14^2 - (2\times 12\times 14\times\cos 115°)$
$|\overrightarrow{CA}| = \sqrt{481.99...} = 21.954... = 21.95$ (2 d.p.)

Q16 a) $\overrightarrow{PR} = \begin{pmatrix}1\\5\end{pmatrix} - \begin{pmatrix}-4\\-5\end{pmatrix} = \begin{pmatrix}5\\10\end{pmatrix}$ so
$|\overrightarrow{PR}| = \sqrt{5^2 + 10^2} = \sqrt{125} = 5\sqrt{5}$

$\overrightarrow{QS} = \begin{pmatrix}8\\3\end{pmatrix} - \begin{pmatrix}-5\\1\end{pmatrix} = \begin{pmatrix}13\\2\end{pmatrix}$ so $|\overrightarrow{QS}| = \sqrt{13^2 + 2^2} = \sqrt{173}$

[3 marks available — 1 mark for finding the vectors $\overrightarrow{PR}$ and $\overrightarrow{QS}$, 1 mark for attempting to use Pythagoras to find the length, 1 mark for both lengths correct]

b) $\overrightarrow{QR} = \begin{pmatrix}1\\5\end{pmatrix} - \begin{pmatrix}-5\\1\end{pmatrix} = \begin{pmatrix}6\\4\end{pmatrix}$

$\overrightarrow{PS} = \begin{pmatrix}8\\3\end{pmatrix} - \begin{pmatrix}-4\\-5\end{pmatrix} = \begin{pmatrix}12\\8\end{pmatrix}$

$\overrightarrow{PS} = 2\overrightarrow{QR}$, i.e. they are scalar multiples of each other, so the vectors are parallel.

$|\overrightarrow{PS}| = 2|\overrightarrow{QR}|$, i.e. $PQ = 2QR$, so the parallel sides are not equal in length. Therefore $PQRS$ must be a trapezium.

[4 marks available — 1 mark for finding $\overrightarrow{PS}$ and $\overrightarrow{QR}$, 1 mark for showing they are parallel, 1 mark for stating PQ = 2QR, 1 mark for using this to show that PQRS is a trapezium]

You could also find the vectors $\overrightarrow{PQ}$ and $\overrightarrow{RS}$ and show they are not parallel.

Q17 E.g. use the cosine rule with the triangle formed by **a** and **b**.
$|\mathbf{a}| = \sqrt{3^2 + 3^2} = \sqrt{18}$, $|\mathbf{b}| = \sqrt{(-2)^2 + 5^2} = \sqrt{29}$
To be able to use the cosine rule to find θ, you also need to know the magnitude of the resultant vector
$\mathbf{a} - \mathbf{b} = \begin{pmatrix}5\\-2\end{pmatrix}$. $|\mathbf{a} - \mathbf{b}| = \sqrt{5^2 + (-2)^2} = \sqrt{29}$

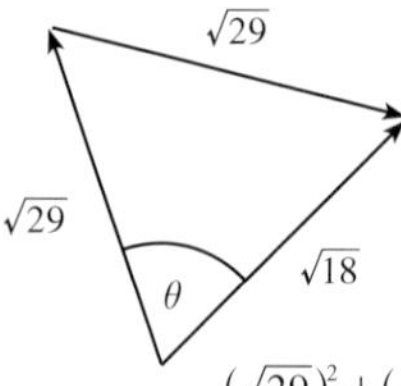

So, $\cos\theta = \frac{(\sqrt{29})^2 + (\sqrt{18})^2 - (\sqrt{29})^2}{2\times\sqrt{29}\times\sqrt{18}}$
$= \frac{18}{2\times\sqrt{29}\times 3\sqrt{2}} = \frac{3}{\sqrt{29}\times\sqrt{2}} = \frac{3}{\sqrt{58}}$

$\Rightarrow \theta = \cos^{-1}\left(\frac{3}{\sqrt{58}}\right) = 66.80°$ (2 d.p.).

Q18 $\overrightarrow{WZ}$ is horizontal, so you can make a right-angled triangle:

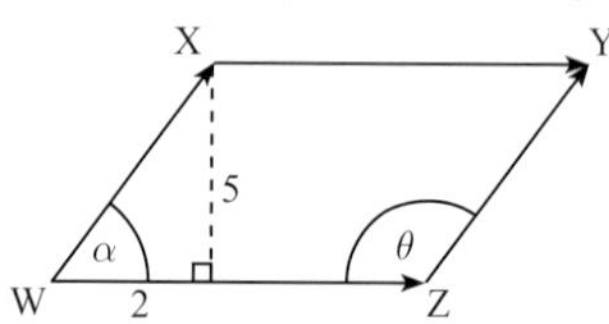

So, find the angle α between $\overrightarrow{WX}$ and $\overrightarrow{WZ}$,
$\tan\alpha = \frac{5}{2} \Rightarrow \alpha = \tan^{-1}\frac{5}{2}$
$\overrightarrow{WX}$ and $\overrightarrow{ZY}$ are parallel, so $\theta = 180° - \alpha$
$= 180° - \tan^{-1}\frac{5}{2}$
$= 111.8°$ (1 d.p.)

You could also find θ by using the cosine rule with the lengths of $\overrightarrow{WZ}$, $\overrightarrow{ZY}$ and $\overrightarrow{WY}$ — you should get the same answer.

Q19 $\overrightarrow{AB} = \overrightarrow{AO} + \overrightarrow{OB} = \overrightarrow{OB} - \overrightarrow{OA} = \begin{pmatrix}7\\\alpha\end{pmatrix} - \begin{pmatrix}5\\2\end{pmatrix} = \begin{pmatrix}2\\\alpha-2\end{pmatrix}$

$|\overrightarrow{AB}| = \sqrt{(\alpha-2)^2 + 2^2} = 2\sqrt{5} \Rightarrow (\alpha-2)^2 + 2^2 = (2\sqrt{5})^2$
$\Rightarrow (\alpha-2)^2 = 16 \Rightarrow (\alpha-2)^2 - 16 = 0 = (\alpha-2-4)(\alpha-2+4)$
$\Rightarrow (\alpha-6)(\alpha+2) = 0 \Rightarrow \alpha = 6$ or $\alpha = -2$

[6 marks available — 1 mark for a correct method to find $\overrightarrow{AB}$, 1 mark for $\overrightarrow{AB}$ correct, 1 mark for using Pythagoras' theorem, 1 mark for forming a quadratic in α, 1 mark for a correct method to solve the quadratic, 1 mark for both correct values of α]

Q20 $\overrightarrow{PQ} = \overrightarrow{PO} + \overrightarrow{OQ} = \overrightarrow{OQ} - \overrightarrow{OP} = \begin{pmatrix}5\\2\end{pmatrix} - \begin{pmatrix}2\\-1\end{pmatrix} = \begin{pmatrix}3\\3\end{pmatrix}$

$\overrightarrow{QR} = \overrightarrow{QO} + \overrightarrow{OR} = \overrightarrow{OR} - \overrightarrow{OQ} = \begin{pmatrix}6\\-3\end{pmatrix} - \begin{pmatrix}5\\2\end{pmatrix} = \begin{pmatrix}1\\-5\end{pmatrix}$

$\overrightarrow{RP} = \overrightarrow{RO} + \overrightarrow{OP} = \overrightarrow{OP} - \overrightarrow{OR} = \begin{pmatrix}2\\-1\end{pmatrix} - \begin{pmatrix}6\\-3\end{pmatrix} = \begin{pmatrix}-4\\2\end{pmatrix}$

So $|\overrightarrow{PQ}| = \sqrt{3^2 + 3^2} = \sqrt{18}$, $|\overrightarrow{QR}| = \sqrt{1^2 + (-5)^2} = \sqrt{26}$
and $|\overrightarrow{RP}| = \sqrt{(-4)^2 + 2^2} = \sqrt{20}$. Using the cosine rule:
$Q = \cos^{-1}\left(\frac{18 + 26 - 20}{2\sqrt{18\times 26}}\right) \Rightarrow Q = 56.3099...° = 56.3°$ (1 d.p.)

[6 marks available — 1 mark for a correct method to find the vectors, 1 mark for finding all 3 vectors, 1 mark for using Pythagoras to find the side lengths, 1 mark for all correct side lengths, 1 mark for using the cosine rule, 1 mark for the correct answer]

There are other ways to answer this question and you'd get the marks for giving the correct answer with any correct method.

Q21 a) $\overrightarrow{AB} = \overrightarrow{AO} + \overrightarrow{OB} = \overrightarrow{OB} - \overrightarrow{OA} = \begin{pmatrix}4\\-1\end{pmatrix} - \begin{pmatrix}1\\-2\end{pmatrix} = \begin{pmatrix}3\\1\end{pmatrix}$

$\overrightarrow{BC} = \overrightarrow{BO} + \overrightarrow{OC} = \overrightarrow{OC} - \overrightarrow{OB} = \begin{pmatrix}3\\-4\end{pmatrix} - \begin{pmatrix}4\\-1\end{pmatrix} = \begin{pmatrix}-1\\-3\end{pmatrix}$

$\overrightarrow{AC} = \overrightarrow{AO} + \overrightarrow{OC} = \overrightarrow{OC} - \overrightarrow{OA} = \begin{pmatrix} 3 \\ -4 \end{pmatrix} - \begin{pmatrix} 1 \\ -2 \end{pmatrix} = \begin{pmatrix} 2 \\ -2 \end{pmatrix}$

$\Rightarrow |\overrightarrow{AB}| = \sqrt{3^2+1^2} = \sqrt{10}$, $|\overrightarrow{BC}| = \sqrt{(-1)^2+(-3)^2} = \sqrt{10}$,

$|\overrightarrow{AC}| = \sqrt{2^2+(-2)^2} = \sqrt{8}$

$\Rightarrow |\overrightarrow{AB}| = |\overrightarrow{BC}| \neq |\overrightarrow{AC}|$, so ABC is an isosceles triangle.

b) Using the cosine rule,

Angle ABC $= \cos^{-1}\left(\frac{10+10-8}{2\sqrt{10\times10}}\right)$

$= \cos^{-1}\left(\frac{12}{20}\right) = 53.1301...° = 53.1°$ (1 d.p.)

c) Area of triangle $= \frac{1}{2}$ab sin C

$= \frac{1}{2}(\sqrt{10\times10})\sin 53.1301...° = 4$ units^2

Exercise 12.4 — Modelling with Vectors

Q1 **a)** $|\mathbf{a}| = \sqrt{1^2+2^2} = \sqrt{5}$ ms^{-2}

b) $|\mathbf{b}| = \sqrt{(-1)^2+(-1)^2} = \sqrt{2}$ ms^{-2}

c) $|\mathbf{c}| = \sqrt{3^2+2^2} = \sqrt{13}$ ms^{-2}

d) $|\mathbf{d}| = \sqrt{(-2)^2+3^2} = \sqrt{13}$ ms^{-2}

Q2 From the diagram you can see that

$\overrightarrow{AB} = \begin{pmatrix} 10 \\ 0 \end{pmatrix}$, $\overrightarrow{BC} = \begin{pmatrix} -3 \\ 6 \end{pmatrix}$, $\overrightarrow{CD} = \begin{pmatrix} -7 \\ 2 \end{pmatrix}$.

Now, calling the start point of the path S and the end point T:

$\mathbf{p} = \overrightarrow{ST} = \overrightarrow{SB} + \overrightarrow{BC} + \overrightarrow{CT} = \frac{3}{10}\overrightarrow{AB} + \overrightarrow{BC} + \frac{1}{2}\overrightarrow{CD}$

$= \frac{3}{10}\begin{pmatrix} 10 \\ 0 \end{pmatrix} + \begin{pmatrix} -3 \\ 6 \end{pmatrix} + \frac{1}{2}\begin{pmatrix} -7 \\ 2 \end{pmatrix} = \begin{pmatrix} 3 \\ 0 \end{pmatrix} + \begin{pmatrix} -3 \\ 6 \end{pmatrix} + \begin{pmatrix} -3.5 \\ 1 \end{pmatrix}$

$= \begin{pmatrix} -3.5 \\ 7 \end{pmatrix}$, so $x = -3.5$ and $y = 7$.

Q3 E.g. use the cosine rule with the triangle formed by $\mathbf{v}_1$ and $\mathbf{v}_2$.

$|\mathbf{v}_1| = \sqrt{3^2+(-2)^2} = \sqrt{13}$, $|\mathbf{v}_2| = \sqrt{1^2+3^2} = \sqrt{10}$.

To be able to use the cosine rule, you also need to know the length of the resultant of these two vectors,

$\mathbf{v}_1 + \mathbf{v}_2 = \begin{pmatrix} 4 \\ 1 \end{pmatrix}$, so $|\mathbf{v}_1 + \mathbf{v}_2| = \sqrt{4^2+1^2} = \sqrt{17}$

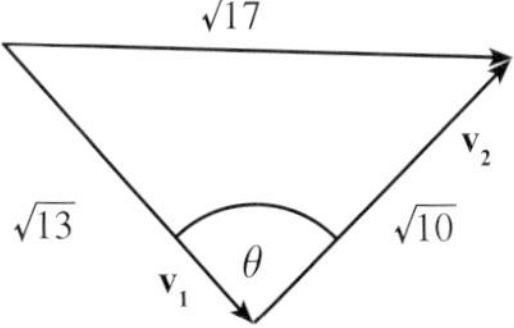

Using the cosine rule:

$\cos\theta = \frac{(\sqrt{13})^2+(\sqrt{10})^2-(\sqrt{17})^2}{2\times\sqrt{13}\times\sqrt{10}} = \frac{13+10-17}{2\sqrt{130}} = \frac{3}{\sqrt{130}}$

$\Rightarrow \theta = \cos^{-1}\left(\frac{3}{\sqrt{130}}\right) = 74.74°$ (2 d.p.)

Q4 **a)** When $t = 2$, $\mathbf{v} = 2 \times 2(2\mathbf{i} - \mathbf{j}) = (8\mathbf{i} - 4\mathbf{j})$ ms^{-1}

b) When $t = 3$, $\mathbf{v} = (12\mathbf{i} - 6\mathbf{j})$ ms^{-1}.

Speed $= |\mathbf{v}|$ at $t = 3$: $\sqrt{12^2+(-6)^2} = 6\sqrt{5}$ ms^{-1}.

c) $\theta = \tan^{-1}\left(\frac{1}{2}\right) = 26.56...°$ below the positive horizontal.

So the direction of **v** (anticlockwise from the positive horizontal) is $360° - 26.56...° = 333.43...° = 333.4°$ (1 d.p.)

Q5 **a)** When $t = 1.5$, $\mathbf{s} = 2 \times 1.5^2(-\mathbf{i} + 7\mathbf{j})$ m $= (-\frac{9}{2}\mathbf{i} + \frac{63}{2}\mathbf{j})$ m

b) $\theta = \tan^{-1}\left(\frac{7}{1}\right) = 81.86...°$ above the negative horizontal.

So the direction of **s** (anticlockwise from the positive horizontal) is $180° - 81.86...° = 98.13... = 98.1°$ (3 s.f.).

c) When $t = 2.5$, $\mathbf{s} = 2 \times 2.5^2(-\mathbf{i} + 7\mathbf{j})$ m $= (-12.5\mathbf{i} + 87.5\mathbf{j})$ m

You need the vertical component of the overall displacement (i.e. the **j** component), so the firework is 87.5 m from the ground.

Q6

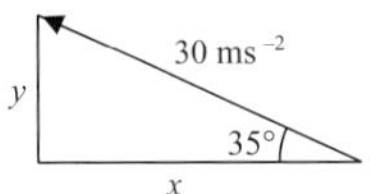

Use trigonometry to find x and y:

$\cos 35° = \frac{x}{30}$ and $\sin 35° = \frac{y}{30}$

$\Rightarrow x = 30\cos 35° = 24.574... = 24.57$ (2 d.p.)

$y = 30\sin 35° = 17.207... = 17.21$ (2 d.p.)

The x-component is negative, so $\mathbf{a} = -24.57\mathbf{i} + 17.21\mathbf{j}$ (2 d.p.)

Q7 $\overrightarrow{EF}$ is parallel to $\overrightarrow{GH}$, as $-2(-\mathbf{i} - \frac{3}{2}\mathbf{j}) = 2\mathbf{i} + 3\mathbf{j}$.

$\overrightarrow{HE}$ has two negative components, while $\overrightarrow{FG}$ has one positive and one negative, so they cannot be parallel. So this quadrilateral has one and only one pair of parallel sides. This means it must be a trapezium.

Q8 **a)** $\overrightarrow{PQ} = \overrightarrow{PO} + \overrightarrow{OQ} = \overrightarrow{OQ} - \overrightarrow{OP} = (3\mathbf{i} - 2\mathbf{j}) - (2\mathbf{i} + \mathbf{j}) = \mathbf{i} - 3\mathbf{j}$

$\overrightarrow{QR} = \overrightarrow{QO} + \overrightarrow{OR} = \overrightarrow{OR} - \overrightarrow{OQ} = (3\mathbf{i} - 4\mathbf{j}) - (3\mathbf{i} - 2\mathbf{j}) = -2\mathbf{j}$

$\overrightarrow{RP} = \overrightarrow{RO} + \overrightarrow{OP} = \overrightarrow{OP} - \overrightarrow{OR} = (2\mathbf{i} + \mathbf{j}) - (3\mathbf{i} - 4\mathbf{j}) = -\mathbf{i} + 5\mathbf{j}$

So $|\overrightarrow{PQ}| = \sqrt{1^2+(-3)^2} = \sqrt{10}$ m, $|\overrightarrow{QR}| = \sqrt{(-2)^2} = 2$ m

and $|\overrightarrow{RP}| = \sqrt{(-1)^2+5^2} = \sqrt{26}$ m.

$\sqrt{10} + \sqrt{26} + 2 = 10.3$ m (1 d.p.)

[5 marks available — 1 mark for a correct method to find the vectors, 1 mark for finding all 3 vectors, 1 mark for using Pythagoras to find the side lengths, 1 mark for all correct side lengths, 1 mark for the correct answer]

b) Largest angle is at Q, opposite the longest side RP, so using the cosine rule:

$Q = \cos^{-1}\left(\frac{10+2^2-26}{2\times\sqrt{10}\times2}\right) = 161.5650...° = 161.6°$ (1 d.p.)

[3 marks available — 1 mark for correctly identifying the largest angle, 1 mark for using the cosine rule or other correct method, 1 mark for the correct answer]

c) Using Area $= \frac{1}{2}$ ab sin C:

Area $= \frac{1}{2}(\sqrt{10})(2)\sin 161.5650...° = 1$ m^2

[2 marks available — 1 mark for a correct method, 1 mark for the correct answer]

Q9 **a)**

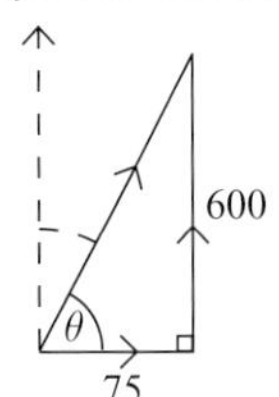

The two vectors form a right-angled triangle.

$\tan\theta = \frac{600}{75} = 8 \Rightarrow \theta = \tan^{-1} 8 = 82.87...°$.

So the aircraft's actual bearing is

$90° - 82.87...° = 7.12...° = 007.1°$ (1 d.p.)

b) Speed is the magnitude of the resultant vector. Using Pythagoras, speed $= \sqrt{600^2+75^2} = \sqrt{365\,625}$

$= 604.67$ km/hr (2 d.p.)

Q10 Drawing the vectors end to end:

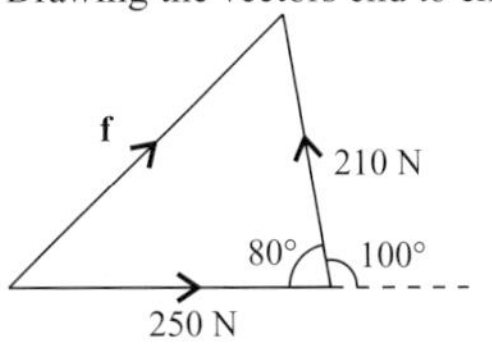

The triangle isn't a right-angled triangle, so you need to use the cosine rule:

$|\mathbf{f}|^2 = 210^2 + 250^2 - (2 \times 210 \times 250 \times \cos 80°)$

$|\mathbf{f}| = \sqrt{88366.94...} = 297.3$ N (1 d.p.)

Q11 a) $(-2\mathbf{i} - 4.8\mathbf{j})\ \text{ms}^{-1}$ *[1 mark]*

b) Angle between $\mathbf{j}$ and $\mathbf{v} = 90° + \alpha$

$\alpha = \tan^{-1}\left(\frac{4.8}{2}\right) = \tan^{-1}(2.4) = 67.3801...°$

$\Rightarrow 90° + 67.3801...° = 157.4°$ (1 d.p.)

[3 marks available — 1 mark for a correct method, 1 mark for the correct value of α, 1 mark for the correct answer]

Q12 $\overrightarrow{PR} = \overrightarrow{OR} - \overrightarrow{OP} = (6\mathbf{i} + 6\mathbf{j}) - (2\mathbf{i} + 3\mathbf{j}) = 4\mathbf{i} + 3\mathbf{j}$

$|\overrightarrow{PR}| = \sqrt{4^2 + 3^2} = 5$

$\overrightarrow{QS} = \overrightarrow{OS} - \overrightarrow{OQ} = (\mathbf{i} + 5\mathbf{j}) - (7\mathbf{i} + 4\mathbf{j}) = -6\mathbf{i} + \mathbf{j}$

$|\overrightarrow{QS}| = \sqrt{(-6)^2 + 1^2} = \sqrt{37}$

Q13 a)

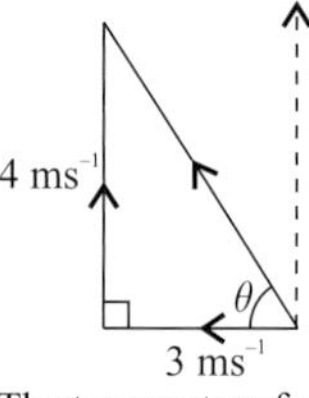

The two vectors form a right-angled triangle.

$\tan\theta = \frac{4}{3} \Rightarrow \theta = \tan^{-1}\frac{4}{3} = 53.13...°$.

Bearings are measured clockwise from North, so Ray travels on the bearing $270° + 53.13...° = 323°$ (3 s.f.)

b) Speed is the magnitude of the resultant vector, so Ray's speed is $\sqrt{3^2 + 4^2} = 5\ \text{ms}^{-1}$.

Q14 $\overrightarrow{PW} = \overrightarrow{PQ} + \overrightarrow{QW}$. Because W divides QR in the ratio $a:b$, we get that: $\overrightarrow{QW} = \frac{a}{a+b}\overrightarrow{QR}$

$\overrightarrow{QR} = \overrightarrow{QP} + \overrightarrow{PR} = (-\mathbf{s}) + \mathbf{t} = \mathbf{t} - \mathbf{s}, \Rightarrow \overrightarrow{QW} = \frac{a}{a+b}(\mathbf{t} - \mathbf{s})$

We also know that $\overrightarrow{PQ} = \mathbf{s}$, so if we substitute these back into the formula for $\overrightarrow{PW}$ we get:

$\overrightarrow{PW} = \mathbf{s} + \frac{a}{a+b}(\mathbf{t} - \mathbf{s}) = \left(1 - \frac{a}{a+b}\right)\mathbf{s} + \frac{a}{a+b}\mathbf{t}$.

The question tells us that $\overrightarrow{PW} = \frac{5}{9}\mathbf{s} + \frac{4}{9}\mathbf{t}$

$\Rightarrow \frac{5}{9}\mathbf{s} + \frac{4}{9}\mathbf{t} = \left(1 - \frac{a}{a+b}\right)\mathbf{s} + \frac{a}{a+b}\mathbf{t}$.

By equating the coefficients of $\mathbf{t}$ this gives you

$\frac{4}{9} = \frac{a}{a+b} \Rightarrow a = 4$ and $b = 5$

Equating the coefficients just means setting the numbers in front of the same variable equal to one another.

Q15 a)

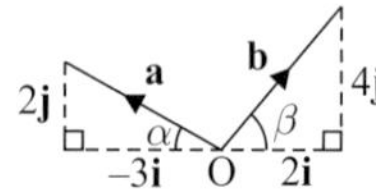

$\alpha = \tan^{-1}\frac{2}{3} = 33.6900...°$ and $\beta = \tan^{-1}\frac{4}{2} = 63.4349...°$.

Angle between $\mathbf{a}$ and $\mathbf{b}$ is

$180° - \alpha - \beta = 180° - 33.6900...° - 63.4349...°$

$= 82.8749...° = 82.9°$ (1 d.p.).

[3 marks available — 1 mark for a correct method to find α or β, 1 mark for finding both α and β, 1 mark for the correct answer]

Alternatively you could find the angle between each vector and the j direction, then add them together.

b) Distance = Speed × Time, so after 3 seconds, the position vectors are $3(-3\mathbf{i} + 2\mathbf{j}) = (-9\mathbf{i} + 6\mathbf{j})$ m and $3(2\mathbf{i} + 4\mathbf{j}) = (6\mathbf{i} + 12\mathbf{j})$ m. The vector between them is $(6\mathbf{i} + 12\mathbf{j}) - (-9\mathbf{i} + 6\mathbf{j}) = 15\mathbf{i} + 6\mathbf{j}$. So the distance between them is $\sqrt{15^2 + 6^2} = \sqrt{261} = 16.2$ m (1 d.p.)

[4 marks available — 1 mark for both position vectors after 3 seconds, 1 mark for finding the vector between them, 1 mark for using Pythagoras to find the magnitude, 1 mark for the correct answer]

Alternatively you could find the magnitude of the position vectors and use the cosine rule with your answer to part a).

Chapter 12 Review Exercise

Q1 a) –b **b)** 3a

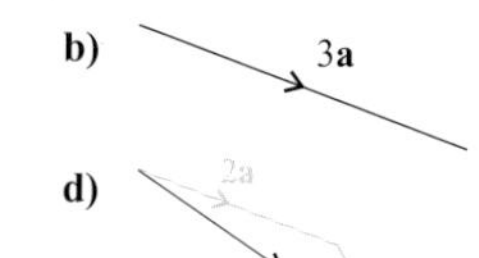

c) a + b **d)** 2a – b

e) b – a

Q2 a) $\overrightarrow{AB} = -\overrightarrow{OA} + \overrightarrow{OB} = \mathbf{b} - \mathbf{a}$

b) $\overrightarrow{BA} = -\overrightarrow{OB} + \overrightarrow{OA} = \mathbf{a} - \mathbf{b}$

c) $\overrightarrow{CB} = -\overrightarrow{OC} + \overrightarrow{OB} = \mathbf{b} - \mathbf{c}$

d) $\overrightarrow{AC} = -\overrightarrow{OA} + \overrightarrow{OC} = \mathbf{c} - \mathbf{a}$

Q3 a) $\overrightarrow{QR} = -\overrightarrow{RQ} = -\mathbf{b}$ *[1 mark]*

b) $\overrightarrow{RP} = \overrightarrow{RQ} + \overrightarrow{QP} = \overrightarrow{RQ} - \overrightarrow{PQ} = \mathbf{b} - \mathbf{a}$ *[1 mark]*

c) $\overrightarrow{PR} = -\overrightarrow{RP} = -(\mathbf{b} - \mathbf{a}) = \mathbf{a} - \mathbf{b}$ *[1 mark]*

Q4 a) E.g. $\mathbf{a}$ and $4\mathbf{a}$

b) E.g. $6\mathbf{i} + 8\mathbf{j}$ and $9\mathbf{i} + 12\mathbf{j}$

c) E.g. $6\mathbf{i} - 2\mathbf{j}$ and $9\mathbf{i} - 3$

d) E.g. $\begin{pmatrix}6\\10\end{pmatrix}$ and $\begin{pmatrix}9\\15\end{pmatrix}$

Q5 a) $\overrightarrow{AB} = \overrightarrow{AC} + \overrightarrow{CB} = \overrightarrow{CB} - \overrightarrow{CA} = 6\mathbf{p} - 4\mathbf{q}$

b) $\overrightarrow{AP} = \frac{1}{2}\overrightarrow{AC} = -\frac{1}{2}\overrightarrow{CA} = -\frac{1}{2}(4\mathbf{q}) = -2\mathbf{q}$

c) $\overrightarrow{AM} = \frac{1}{2}\overrightarrow{AB} = \frac{1}{2}(6\mathbf{p} - 4\mathbf{q}) = 3\mathbf{p} - 2\mathbf{q}$

d) $\overrightarrow{PM} = \overrightarrow{PA} + \overrightarrow{AM} = \overrightarrow{AM} - \overrightarrow{AP} = (3\mathbf{p} - 2\mathbf{q}) - (-2\mathbf{q}) = 3\mathbf{p}$

Q6 $\overrightarrow{PM} = \frac{3}{4}\overrightarrow{US} + \frac{1}{2}\overrightarrow{ST}$

$\overrightarrow{US} = \overrightarrow{UT} - \overrightarrow{ST} = (3\mathbf{b} - \mathbf{a}) - 4\mathbf{a} = 3\mathbf{b} - 5\mathbf{a}$

So $\overrightarrow{PM} = \frac{3}{4}(3\mathbf{b} - 5\mathbf{a}) + \frac{1}{2}(4\mathbf{a})$

$= \frac{9}{4}\mathbf{b} - \frac{15}{4}\mathbf{a} + 2\mathbf{a} = \frac{9}{4}\mathbf{b} - \frac{7}{4}\mathbf{a}$

Q7 $\overrightarrow{CD} = \overrightarrow{CA} + \overrightarrow{AD} = \overrightarrow{AD} - \overrightarrow{AC} = \mathbf{p} - \mathbf{q} = -(\mathbf{q} - \mathbf{p}) = -\overrightarrow{BC}$

So $\overrightarrow{BC}$ is parallel to $\overrightarrow{CD}$, and points B, C and D are collinear.

[3 marks available — 1 mark for a correct method, 1 mark for finding correct $\overrightarrow{CD}$, 1 mark for correctly concluding that B, C and D are collinear]

Q8 a) $\overrightarrow{BC} = \overrightarrow{BA} + \overrightarrow{AC} = \overrightarrow{AC} - \overrightarrow{AB} = \mathbf{q} - \mathbf{p}$

$\Rightarrow \overrightarrow{BM} = \frac{3}{5}\overrightarrow{BC} = \frac{3}{5}(\mathbf{q} - \mathbf{p})$ and $\overrightarrow{AN} = \frac{3}{5}\overrightarrow{AC} = \frac{3}{5}\mathbf{q}$

So $\overrightarrow{NM} = \overrightarrow{NA} + \overrightarrow{AB} + \overrightarrow{BM} = -\frac{3}{5}\mathbf{q} + \mathbf{p} + \frac{3}{5}(\mathbf{q} - \mathbf{p}) = \frac{2}{5}\mathbf{p}$

$\overrightarrow{AB}$ is a multiple of $\overrightarrow{NM}$, so the vectors are parallel.

[4 marks available — 1 mark for finding $\overrightarrow{BM}$, 1 mark for finding $\overrightarrow{AN}$, 1 mark for finding $\overrightarrow{NM}$, 1 mark for stating $\overrightarrow{NM}$ is a multiple of $\overrightarrow{AB}$]

b) $\overrightarrow{NM} = \frac{2}{5}\overrightarrow{AB}$ so the ratio $\overrightarrow{AB} : \overrightarrow{NM} = 1 : \frac{2}{5} = 5:2$. *[1 mark]*

Q9 a) $\overrightarrow{YZ} = 2(\mathbf{a} - \mathbf{b}) - 2\mathbf{b} = 2\mathbf{a} - 4\mathbf{b} = -2(2\mathbf{b} - \mathbf{a}) = -2\overrightarrow{XY}$.

This shows they're scalar multiples, so $\overrightarrow{YZ}$ is parallel to $\overrightarrow{XY}$. Therefore X, Y and Z are collinear.

b) $\overrightarrow{XY} = \mathbf{q} - 3\mathbf{p}$,

$\overrightarrow{YZ} = 4\mathbf{q} - 9\mathbf{p} - \mathbf{q} = 3\mathbf{q} - 9\mathbf{p} = 3(\mathbf{q} - 3\mathbf{p}) = 3\overrightarrow{XY}$.

This shows they're scalar multiples, so $\overrightarrow{YZ}$ is parallel to $\overrightarrow{XY}$. Therefore X, Y and Z are collinear.

Q10 a) $2\mathbf{d} - \mathbf{f} = 2\begin{pmatrix}3\\2\end{pmatrix} - \begin{pmatrix}3\\-1\end{pmatrix} = \begin{pmatrix}3\\5\end{pmatrix}$

b) $\mathbf{d} - \mathbf{e} - \mathbf{f} = \begin{pmatrix}3\\2\end{pmatrix} - \begin{pmatrix}-1\\-2\end{pmatrix} - \begin{pmatrix}3\\-1\end{pmatrix} = \begin{pmatrix}1\\5\end{pmatrix}$

c) $\mathbf{f} - 3\mathbf{d} + \mathbf{e} = \begin{pmatrix}3\\-1\end{pmatrix} - 3\begin{pmatrix}3\\2\end{pmatrix} + \begin{pmatrix}-1\\-2\end{pmatrix} = \begin{pmatrix}-7\\-9\end{pmatrix}$

d) $-2\mathbf{e} + \mathbf{d} - \mathbf{f} = -2\begin{pmatrix}-1\\-2\end{pmatrix} + \begin{pmatrix}3\\2\end{pmatrix} - \begin{pmatrix}3\\-1\end{pmatrix} = \begin{pmatrix}2\\7\end{pmatrix}$

Q11 $\overrightarrow{XO} = -6\mathrm{i} + \mathrm{j} = \begin{pmatrix}-6\\1\end{pmatrix}$ and $\overrightarrow{YO} = 4\mathrm{i} - 7\mathrm{j} = \begin{pmatrix}4\\-7\end{pmatrix}$

Q12 a) $\overrightarrow{PQ} = \overrightarrow{PO} + \overrightarrow{OQ} = \overrightarrow{OQ} - \overrightarrow{OP} = 3\mathbf{i} + 5\mathbf{j} - (\mathbf{i} - 2\mathbf{j}) = 2\mathbf{i} + 7\mathbf{j}$

[2 marks available — 1 mark for a correct method, 1 mark for the correct answer]

b) $|\overrightarrow{PQ}| = \sqrt{2^2 + 7^2} = \sqrt{53}$, so the unit vector in the direction of $\overrightarrow{PQ}$ is $\frac{1}{\sqrt{53}}(2\mathbf{i} + 7\mathbf{j}) = \frac{2}{\sqrt{53}}\mathbf{i} + \frac{7}{\sqrt{53}}\mathbf{j}$

[3 marks available — 1 mark for using Pythagoras' theorem, 1 mark for finding $|\overrightarrow{PQ}|$, 1 mark for the correct answer]

Q13 $\overrightarrow{RS} = \begin{pmatrix}-5\\-7\end{pmatrix} - \begin{pmatrix}3\\-1\end{pmatrix} = \begin{pmatrix}-8\\-6\end{pmatrix}$

So $|\overrightarrow{RS}| = \sqrt{(-8)^2 + (-6)^2} = \sqrt{100} = 10$

Q14 a) $\overrightarrow{MN} = \overrightarrow{ON} - \overrightarrow{OM} = (3\mathbf{i} + 3\mathbf{j}) - (-7\mathbf{i} + 6\mathbf{j}) = 10\mathbf{i} - 3\mathbf{j}$

[2 marks available — 1 mark for subtracting the position vectors, 1 mark for correct answer]

b) $|\overrightarrow{MN}| = \sqrt{10^2 + (-3)^2} = \sqrt{109} = 10.4$ (1 d.p.)

[2 marks available — 1 mark for correctly using Pythagoras, 1 mark for the correct answer]

Q15 $\overrightarrow{AC} = \overrightarrow{AB} + \overrightarrow{BC} = \overrightarrow{BC} - \overrightarrow{BA} = \begin{pmatrix}3\\-2\end{pmatrix} - \begin{pmatrix}1\\1\end{pmatrix}\begin{pmatrix}2\\-3\end{pmatrix}$

$\Rightarrow |\overrightarrow{AC}| = \sqrt{2^2 + (-3)^2} = \sqrt{13}$

[4 marks available — 1 mark for subtracting $\overrightarrow{BA}$ from $\overrightarrow{BC}$, 1 mark for finding $\overrightarrow{AC}$, 1 mark for correctly using Pythagoras, 1 mark for the correct final answer]

Q16 $\mathbf{q}$ is parallel to $\mathbf{p}$, so $\mathbf{q} = n(5\mathbf{i} - 12\mathbf{j}) = 5n\mathbf{i} - 12n\mathbf{j}$ for some scalar n.

$|\mathbf{q}| = 65$, so $65 = \sqrt{(5n)^2 + (-12n)^2}$
$= \sqrt{25n^2 + 144n^2} = \sqrt{169n^2} = 13n$

$13n = 65 \Rightarrow n = 5$, so $\mathbf{q} = 5(5\mathbf{i} - 12\mathbf{j}) = 25\mathbf{i} - 60\mathbf{j}$.

Q17 a) Area ABC $= \frac{1}{2}(10)(12)\sin 50°$
$= 60\sin 50° = 45.9626...$ units^2 $= 45.96$ units^2 (2 d.p.)

[2 marks available — 1 mark for a correct method, 1 mark for the correct answer]

b) Using the cosine rule:
$|\overrightarrow{CB}| = \sqrt{10^2 + 12^2 - 2 \times 10 \times 12\cos 50°}$
$= \sqrt{244 - 240\cos 50°} = 9.4726... = 9.47$ (2 d.p.)

[2 marks available — 1 mark for using the cosine rule, 1 mark for the correct answer]

Q18 $\mathbf{c}$ is parallel to $\mathbf{d}$, so $\mathbf{c} = n(6\mathbf{i} - 9\mathbf{j}) = 6n\mathbf{i} - 9n\mathbf{j}$ for some scalar n.

$|\mathbf{c}| = \sqrt{13}$, so $\sqrt{13} = \sqrt{(6n)^2 + (-9n)^2}$
$= \sqrt{36n^2 + 81n^2} = \sqrt{117n^2} = 3n\sqrt{13}$

$3n\sqrt{13} = \sqrt{13} \Rightarrow n = \frac{1}{3}$, so $\mathbf{c} = \frac{1}{3}(6\mathbf{i} - 9\mathbf{j}) = 2\mathbf{i} - 3\mathbf{j}$.

*[4 marks available — 1 mark for writing **c** as a scalar multiple of **d**, 1 mark for finding an expression for the length of c, 1 mark for finding the scalar multiple, 1 mark for the correct vector]*

Q19 a) $-5\mathbf{a} + 2\mathbf{b} = -5(-3\mathbf{i} + 4\mathbf{j}) + 2(\mathbf{i} + 2\mathbf{j}) = 15\mathbf{i} - 20\mathbf{j} + 2\mathbf{i} + 4\mathbf{j}$
$= 17\mathbf{i} - 16\mathbf{j}$

[2 marks available — 1 mark for correct substitution, 1 mark for correct answer]

b) Magnitude $= |\mathbf{a}| = \sqrt{(-3)^2 + 4^2} = 5$

Angle above the negative horizontal $\alpha = \tan^{-1}\left(\frac{4}{3}\right) = 53.13...°$

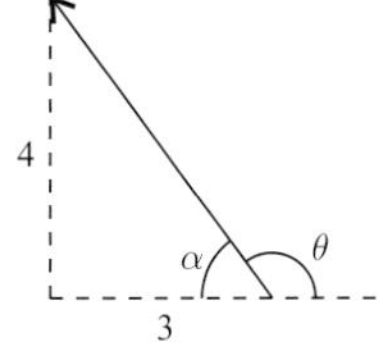

So the direction $\theta = 180 - \alpha = 126.9°$ (1 d.p.)

[4 marks available — 1 mark for using Pythagoras to find magnitude, 1 mark for correct magnitude, 1 mark for finding the angle α, 1 mark for the correct direction of the vector]

Q20 $\overrightarrow{AB} = \begin{pmatrix}x\\1\end{pmatrix} - \begin{pmatrix}2\\-3\end{pmatrix} = \begin{pmatrix}x-2\\4\end{pmatrix}$

$|\overrightarrow{AB}| = \sqrt{(x-2)^2 + 16} = 5 \Rightarrow (x-2)^2 + 16 = 25$
$\Rightarrow (x-2)^2 = 9$
$\Rightarrow (x-2) = \pm 3$
$\Rightarrow x = 5$ or $x = -1$

The direction of $\overrightarrow{OB}$ is less than 90°, so both the **i** and **j** component of B must be positive. This means you can disregard the negative solution — so $x = 5$.

Q21

$|\mathbf{v}| = \sqrt{4^2 + (-6)^2} = \sqrt{52}$
$|\mathbf{u}| = \sqrt{(-1)^2 + (-3)^2} = \sqrt{10}$
$|\mathbf{v} - \mathbf{u}| = |5\mathbf{i} - 3\mathbf{j}| = \sqrt{5^2 + (-3)^2} = \sqrt{34}$

Using the cosine rule: $\cos\theta = \frac{\sqrt{52}^2 + \sqrt{10}^2 - \sqrt{34}^2}{2 \times \sqrt{52} \times \sqrt{10}}$

$\Rightarrow \theta = \cos^{-1}\left(\frac{\sqrt{52}^2 + \sqrt{10}^2 - \sqrt{34}^2}{2 \times \sqrt{52} \times \sqrt{10}}\right)$
$= 52.1250...° = 52.13°$ (2 d.p)

Q22 a)

Angle between **u** and the horizontal $= \tan^{-1}\left(\frac{2}{6}\right)$
$= 18.4349...° = 18.4°$ (1 d.p.)

[2 marks available — 1 mark for a correct method, 1 mark for the correct answer]

b) Magnitude $= |\mathbf{v}| = \sqrt{3^2 + 1^2} = \sqrt{10}$ ms^{-1}

[2 marks available — 1 mark for a correct method, 1 mark for the correct answer]

c) Angle between **v** and the horizontal $= \tan^{-1}\left(\frac{1}{3}\right) = 18.4349...°$
So angle between vectors is
$180° - 2 \times 18.4349...° = 143.1301...° = 143.1°$ (1 d.p.)

[2 marks available — 1 mark for a correct method, 1 mark for the correct answer]

Q23 a) $\tan^{-1}\left(\frac{-2}{5}\right) = -21.8°$ (1 d.p.)
$\Rightarrow$ The angle is 21.8° clockwise from the positive **i** direction.

[2 marks available — 1 mark for a correct method, 1 mark for the correct answer]

b) $\mathbf{v} = \begin{pmatrix}5 \times 5\\-2 \times 5\end{pmatrix} = \begin{pmatrix}25\\-10\end{pmatrix}$

$\Rightarrow |\mathbf{v}| = \sqrt{25^2 + (-10)^2} = \sqrt{725} = 5\sqrt{29}$ ms^{-1}

*[3 marks available — 1 mark for finding **v** at t = 5, 1 mark for using Pythagoras, 1 mark for the correct answer]*

Q24 a) For $t = 3$, $\mathbf{v} = (6\mathbf{i} + \mathbf{j})$ ms^{-1} $\Rightarrow |\mathbf{v}| = \sqrt{6^2 + 1^2} = \sqrt{37}$ ms^{-1}

[2 marks available — 1 mark for a correct method, 1 mark for the correct answer]

b) Angle anticlockwise from **i**
$= \tan^{-1}\left(\frac{\frac{1}{3}t}{2t}\right) = \tan^{-1}\left(\frac{1}{6}\right) = 9.4623...°$
$\Rightarrow$ bearing $= 90° - 9.4623...° = 080.5°$ (1 d.p.)

[3 marks available — 1 mark for a correct method, 1 mark for finding angle 9.4623...°, 1 mark for the correct answer]

Q25 Bearings are measured from North, so the angle the velocity makes with **i** is $171° - 90° = 81°$.

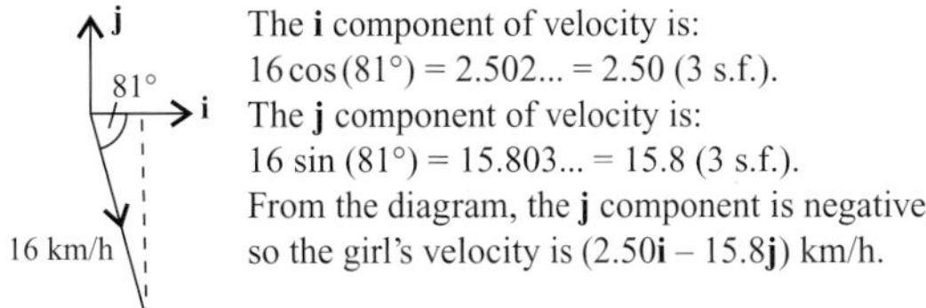

The **i** component of velocity is:
$16\cos(81°) = 2.502... = 2.50$ (3 s.f.).
The **j** component of velocity is:
$16\sin(81°) = 15.803... = 15.8$ (3 s.f.).
From the diagram, the **j** component is negative, so the girl's velocity is $(2.50\mathbf{i} - 15.8\mathbf{j})$ km/h.

Q26 a) $\mathbf{v} = \begin{pmatrix}1.5\\-1\end{pmatrix}$ ms^{-1} *[1 mark]*

b) Angle clockwise from **i** to **v** = $\tan^{-1}\left(\frac{1}{1.5}\right) = 33.6900...°$
Bearings are measured from North,
so the bearing is 90° + 33.6900...° = 123.7° (1 d.p.)
[3 marks available — 1 mark for a correct method, 1 mark for finding angle 33.6900...°, 1 mark for the correct answer]

c) Speed = $|\mathbf{v}| = \sqrt{1.5^2 + (-1)^2} = \sqrt{3.25}$
Distance = speed × time = $\sqrt{3.25} \times 10$
$= \sqrt{325} = 5\sqrt{13}$ m
[3 marks available — 1 mark for using Pythagoras, 1 mark for using distance formula, 1 mark for the correct answer]
Alternatively, you could find the displacement vector at 10 seconds, then use Pythagoras to calculate the distance.

Q27 a) $\mathbf{v} = (-4\mathbf{i} - 20\mathbf{j})$ ms^{-1} *[1 mark]*

b) $|\mathbf{v}| = \sqrt{(-4)^2 + (-20)^2} = \sqrt{416} = 20.4$ ms^{-1} (3 s.f.)
[2 marks available — 1 mark for using Pythagoras, 1 mark for the correct answer]

c) Distance = speed × time = $\sqrt{416} \times 8 = 163$ m (3 s.f.)
[2 marks available — 1 mark for a correct method, 1 mark for the correct answer]

Q28 a) $\overrightarrow{AB} = \overrightarrow{AO} + \overrightarrow{OB} = \overrightarrow{OB} - \overrightarrow{OA} = (2\mathbf{i} - 1.5\mathbf{j}) - (\mathbf{i} + \mathbf{j}) = \mathbf{i} - 2.5\mathbf{j}$
$\overrightarrow{BC} = \overrightarrow{BO} + \overrightarrow{OC} = \overrightarrow{OC} - \overrightarrow{OB}$
$= (1.5\mathbf{i} - 2.5\mathbf{j}) - (2\mathbf{i} - 1.5\mathbf{j}) = -0.5\mathbf{i} - \mathbf{j}$
$\overrightarrow{CA} = \overrightarrow{CO} + \overrightarrow{OA} = \overrightarrow{OA} - \overrightarrow{OC}$
$= (\mathbf{i} + \mathbf{j}) - (1.5\mathbf{i} - 2.5\mathbf{j}) = -0.5\mathbf{i} + 3.5\mathbf{j}$
$\Rightarrow |\overrightarrow{AB}| = \sqrt{1^2 + (-2.5)^2} = \sqrt{7.25}$,
$|\overrightarrow{BC}| = \sqrt{(-0.5)^2 + (-1)^2} = \sqrt{1.25}$ and
$|\overrightarrow{CA}| = \sqrt{(-0.5)^2 + (3.5)^2} = \sqrt{12.5}$
$\Rightarrow$ perimeter = $\sqrt{7.25} + \sqrt{1.25} + \sqrt{12.5}$
= 7.3461... = 7.35 m (3 s.f.)
[5 marks available — 1 mark for a correct method to find the vectors, 1 mark for finding all 3 vectors, 1 mark for using Pythagoras to find the side lengths, 1 mark for all correct side lengths, 1 mark for the correct answer]

b) The biggest angle is opposite the longest side, so is at B.
Using the cosine rule:
Angle ABC = $\cos^{-1}\left(\frac{7.25 + 1.25 - 12.5}{2\sqrt{7.25 \times 1.25}}\right)$
= 131.6335...° = 132° (to 3 s.f.)
[3 marks available — 1 mark for identifying angle at B, 1 mark for using cosine rule, 1 mark for correct answer]

c) Area = $\frac{1}{2} \times \sqrt{7.25} \times \sqrt{1.25} \times \sin 131.6335...° = 1.125$ m^2
[2 marks available — 1 mark for a correct method, 1 mark for the correct answer]

Q29 Draw the vectors end to end:
Then the angle opposite R is
180° – 80° – 65° = 35°.

Using the cosine rule:
$R^2 = 10^2 + 11^2 - 2 \times 10 \times 11 \times \cos 35°$
$R^2 = 40.786... \Rightarrow R = 6.386... = 6.39$ N (3 s.f.)
[3 marks available — 1 mark for finding the angle 35° between the vectors, 1 mark for attempting to use the cosine rule, 1 mark for the correct answer]

Q30 ① $3\mathbf{a} + 2\mathbf{b} = \begin{pmatrix} 4 \\ 9 \end{pmatrix}$

② $-\mathbf{a} + 4\mathbf{b} = \begin{pmatrix} -6 \\ 11 \end{pmatrix}$

① × 2 $\quad 6\mathbf{a} + 4\mathbf{b} = \begin{pmatrix} 8 \\ 18 \end{pmatrix}$ ③

③ – ② $\quad 7\mathbf{a} = \begin{pmatrix} 14 \\ 7 \end{pmatrix} \Rightarrow \mathbf{a} = \begin{pmatrix} 2 \\ 1 \end{pmatrix}$

a in ① $\quad 3\begin{pmatrix} 2 \\ 1 \end{pmatrix} + 2\mathbf{b} = \begin{pmatrix} 4 \\ 9 \end{pmatrix} \Rightarrow 2\mathbf{b} = \begin{pmatrix} -2 \\ 6 \end{pmatrix} \Rightarrow \mathbf{b} = \begin{pmatrix} -1 \\ 3 \end{pmatrix}$

$p\mathbf{a} + q\mathbf{b} = \begin{pmatrix} 1 \\ 32 \end{pmatrix} \Rightarrow \begin{pmatrix} 2p \\ p \end{pmatrix} + \begin{pmatrix} -q \\ 3q \end{pmatrix} = \begin{pmatrix} 1 \\ 32 \end{pmatrix}$

Giving simultaneous equations:
① $\quad 2p - q = 1$
② $\quad p + 3q = 32$
Rearrange ② $\quad p = 32 - 3q$ ③
Sub ③ in ① $\quad 2(32 - 3q) - q = 1 \Rightarrow 64 - 7q = 1 \Rightarrow q = 9$
$q = 9$ in ③ $\quad p = 32 - 3 \times 9 = 5$
So $p = 5$ and $q = 9$.

Q31 The speed of the current and the resultant speed are perpendicular, so use Pythagoras' theorem to find the required speed for the swimmer:

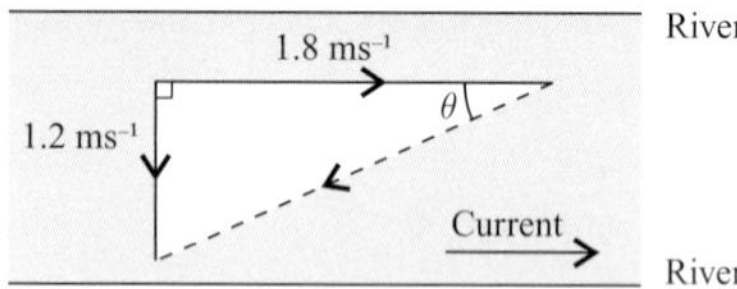

Speed = $\sqrt{1.8^2 + 1.2^2} = 2.163... = 2.16$ ms^{-1} (3 s.f.)
Then also using the right-angled triangle, he should swim at an upstream angle θ to the river bank, where
$\theta = \tan^{-1}\left(\frac{1.2}{1.8}\right) = 33.69... = 33.7°$ (3 s.f.).
[4 marks available — 1 mark for using Pythagoras, 1 mark for the correct speed, 1 mark for a correct method to find θ, 1 mark for the correct answer]

Practice Paper

Q1 $3\mathbf{p} - 2\mathbf{q} = 3\begin{pmatrix} -3 \\ 2 \end{pmatrix} - 2\begin{pmatrix} 6 \\ 10 \end{pmatrix} = \begin{pmatrix} -9 \\ 6 \end{pmatrix} - \begin{pmatrix} 12 \\ 20 \end{pmatrix} = \begin{pmatrix} -9 - 12 \\ 6 - 20 \end{pmatrix}$
$= \begin{pmatrix} -21 \\ -14 \end{pmatrix} = -7\begin{pmatrix} 3 \\ 2 \end{pmatrix} = -7\mathbf{r}$
Since $3\mathbf{p} - 2\mathbf{q}$ is a scalar multiple of **r**, $3\mathbf{p} - 2\mathbf{q}$ is parallel to **r**.
*[2 marks available — 1 mark for expressing 3**p** – 2**q** as a single vector, 1 mark for showing 3**p** – 2**q** = –7**r**]*

Q2 a) Any non-zero negative value of x proves the statement is incorrect, e.g.:
When $x = -4$, $x^2 = 16$ and $\sqrt{x^2} = \sqrt{16} = 4 \neq x$.
[1 mark for correct counter-example with demonstration that $\sqrt{x^2} \neq x$ for that value]

b) Let $n = 2k$ represent a positive even number.
Then $2n^2 + 2n + 6 = 2(2k)^2 + 2(2k) + 6 = 8k^2 + 4k + 6$
$= 4(2k^2 + k + 1) + 2$
So $2n^2 + 2n + 6$ is not exactly divisible by 4 for any positive number, as dividing by 4 leaves a remainder of 2.
[3 marks available — 1 mark for using n = 2k or equivalent, 1 mark for writing part of expression as multiple of 4, 1 mark for correct interpretation]

Q3 $f'(x) = \lim_{h \to 0}\left[\frac{f(x+h) - f(x)}{(x+h) - x}\right]$
$= \lim_{h \to 0}\left[\frac{4(x+h)^2 - 4(x+h) + 3 - (4x^2 - 4x + 3)}{(x+h) - x}\right]$
$= \lim_{h \to 0}\left[\frac{4x^2 + 8xh + 4h^2 - 4x - 4h + 3 - 4x^2 + 4x - 3}{(x+h) - x}\right]$
$= \lim_{h \to 0}\left[\frac{8xh + 4h^2 - 4h}{h}\right] = \lim_{h \to 0}[8x + 4h - 4] = 8x - 4$
[4 marks available — 1 mark for correct substitution into expression for f′(x), 1 mark for correct expansion of brackets, 1 mark for correct simplification of expression, 1 mark for correct answer]

Q4 $2\log_5(2x - 1) = 1 + \log_5(3 - x)$
$\Rightarrow \log_5(2x - 1)^2 = \log_5 5 + \log_5(3 - x)$
$\Rightarrow \log_5(2x - 1)^2 = \log_5(5(3 - x)) \Rightarrow (2x - 1)^2 = 5(3 - x)$
$\Rightarrow 4x^2 - 4x + 1 = 15 - 5x \Rightarrow 4x^2 + x - 14 = 0$
$\Rightarrow (4x - 7)(x + 2) = 0 \Rightarrow x = \frac{7}{4}$ or $x = -2$

But $x = -2$ is not a valid solution since $2x - 1 = -5 < 0$ and $\log_5 n$ isn't defined for $n \leq 0$, so $\frac{7}{4}$ is the only solution.

[4 marks available — 1 mark for suitable manipulation of logs, 1 mark for correct elimination of logs, 1 mark for both correct solutions resulting from quadratic, 1 mark for identifying correct valid solution]

Q5 a) Using the Factor Theorem, if $(x - 3)$ and $(x + 2)$ are factors of p(x), then p(3) = 0 and p(–2) = 0.

So $p(3) = 2(3)^3 + a(3)^2 + b(3) + 18 = 0$

$\Rightarrow 54 + 9a + 3b + 18 = 0$

$\Rightarrow 9a + 3b = -72 \Rightarrow 3a + b = -24$

And $p(-2) = 2(-2)^3 + a(-2)^2 + b(-2) + 18 = 0$

$\Rightarrow -16 + 4a - 2b + 18 = 0 \Rightarrow 4a - 2b = -2 \Rightarrow 2a - b = -1$

Solve these equations simultaneously:

(1) $3a + b = -24$

(2) $2a - b = -1$

(1) + (2) $5a = -25 \Rightarrow a = -5$

$a = -5$ in (1) $3(-5) + b = -24 \Rightarrow b = -9$

[3 marks available — 1 mark for use of p(3) and p(–2), 1 mark for correct equations derived from p(3) and p(–2), 1 mark for correct values of both a and b]

b) Using part a) substitute a and b, then factorise:

$p(x) = 2x^3 - 5x^2 - 9x + 18 = (x - 3)(x + 2)(cx - d)$

By comparing coefficients:

$2x^3 = x \times x \times cx \Rightarrow c = 2$

$18 = -3 \times 2 \times -d \Rightarrow d = 3$

So $p(x) = (x - 3)(x + 2)(2x - 3)$

[1 mark for correct factorisation]

Q6 a)

$$\int \frac{9x^2 - 3x^3}{\sqrt{x^3}}\,dx = \int \left(\frac{9x^2}{x^{\frac{3}{2}}} - \frac{3x^3}{x^{\frac{3}{2}}}\right) dx$$

$$= 9\int \frac{x^2}{x^{\frac{3}{2}}}\,dx - 3\int \frac{x^3}{x^{\frac{3}{2}}}\,dx$$

$$= 9\int x^{\frac{1}{2}}\,dx - 3\int x^{\frac{3}{2}}\,dx$$

$$= 9\left(\frac{x^{\frac{3}{2}}}{\frac{3}{2}}\right) - 3\left(\frac{x^{\frac{5}{2}}}{\frac{5}{2}}\right) + C$$

$$= 6x^{\frac{3}{2}} - \frac{6x^{\frac{5}{2}}}{5} + C$$

[3 marks available — 1 mark for writing each term in function as a power of x, 1 mark for correct powers in integral, 1 mark for fully correct expression]

b)

$$\text{Area} = \int_0^2 \frac{9x^2 - 3x^3}{\sqrt{x^3}}\,dx = \left[6x^{\frac{3}{2}} - \frac{6}{5}x^{\frac{5}{2}}\right]_0^2$$

$$= \left(6(2)^{\frac{3}{2}} - \frac{6}{5}(2)^{\frac{5}{2}}\right) - \left(6(0)^{\frac{3}{2}} - \frac{6}{5}(0)^{\frac{5}{2}}\right)$$

$$= 6(2\sqrt{2}) - \frac{6}{5}(4\sqrt{2}) - 0 = \frac{36}{5}\sqrt{2}$$

[3 marks available — 1 mark for correct limits on definite integral, 1 mark for attempting to evaluate at limits of integration, 1 mark for answer in correct form (accept $\frac{36\sqrt{2}}{5}$)]

Q7 a) $\overrightarrow{AB} = \begin{pmatrix}3\\7\end{pmatrix} - \begin{pmatrix}1\\1\end{pmatrix} = \begin{pmatrix}2\\6\end{pmatrix}$

$|\overrightarrow{AB}| = \sqrt{2^2 + 6^2} = \sqrt{40} = 2\sqrt{10}$

[3 marks available — 1 mark for correct $\overrightarrow{AB}$, 1 mark for correct magnitude in any form, 1 mark for fully simplified magnitude]

b) Let the angle at vertex A be θ:

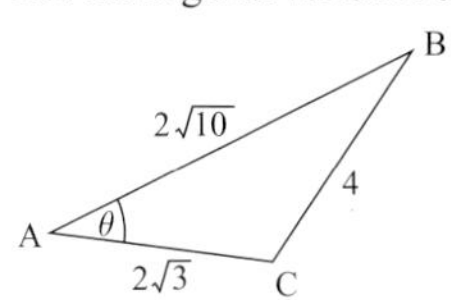

Then using the cosine rule:

$$\cos\theta = \frac{(2\sqrt{10})^2 + (2\sqrt{3})^2 - 4^2}{2 \times 2\sqrt{10} \times 2\sqrt{3}}$$

$$\Rightarrow \theta = \cos^{-1}\left(\frac{(2\sqrt{10})^2 + (2\sqrt{3})^2 - 4^2}{2 \times 2\sqrt{10} \times 2\sqrt{3}}\right) = 34.75... = 34.8° \text{ (1 d.p.)}$$

[2 marks available — 1 mark for attempting to use cosine rule, 1 mark for correct answer to one decimal place]

c) Area $= \frac{1}{2} \times 2\sqrt{10} \times 2\sqrt{3} \times \sin 34.75...°$

$= 6.244... = 6.2$ (1 d.p.)

[2 marks available — 1 mark for using formula for area of triangle, 1 mark for correct answer to one decimal place]

Q8 a) $f(x) = 2 - 6x + 8x^2 - 2x^3$

$f'(x) = -6 + 8(2x) - 2(3x^2) = -6 + 16x - 6x^2$

When $x = 1$, $f'(x) = -6 + 16(1) - 6(1)^2 = 4$

The gradient of the curve at P is 4, so the tangent has a gradient of 4 and an equation in the form $y = 4x + c$.

At P, $x = 1$ and $y = 2$, so $2 = 4(1) + c \Rightarrow c = -2$

So the equation of the line is $y = 4x - 2$.

[4 marks available — 1 mark for one correct term of f′(x), 1 mark for other correct terms of f′(x), 1 mark for correct gradient of f(x) at x = 1, 1 mark for correct equation of line]

b) At Q, $2 - 6x + 8x^2 - 2x^3 = 4x - 2$

$\Rightarrow 0 = 2x^3 - 8x^2 + 10x - 4 \Rightarrow 0 = x^3 - 4x^2 + 5x - 2 = g(x)$

Since the coefficients of g(x) add up to 0, $(x - 1)$ is a factor of g(x). Divide g(x) by $(x - 1)$ to factorise the function:

$$\begin{array}{r} x^2 - 3x + 2 \\ x - 1\,\overline{)\,x^3 - 4x^2 + 5x - 2} \\ -(x^3 - x^2) \\ \hline -3x^2 + 5x \\ -(-3x^2 + 3x) \\ \hline 2x - 2 \\ -(2x - 2) \\ \hline 0 \end{array}$$

So $g(x) = (x - 1)(x^2 - 3x + 2) = (x - 1)(x - 1)(x - 2)$

This means l intersects the curve again at $x = 2$.

When $x = 2$, $y = 4(2) - 2 = 6$, so Q has the coordinates (2, 6).

[3 marks available — 1 mark for setting equations to each other and rearranging to equal zero, 1 mark for correct factorisation of g(x), 1 mark for correct coordinates of Q]

Q9 a)

$$(2x + 3) = \binom{5}{0}(2x)^5(3)^0 + \binom{5}{1}(2x)^4(3)^1 + \binom{5}{2}(2x)^3(3)^2 + \binom{5}{3}(2x)^2(3)^3 + \binom{5}{4}(2x)^1(3)^4 + \binom{5}{5}(2x)^0(3)^5$$

$$= (1 \times 32x^5 \times 1) + (5 \times 16x^4 \times 3) + (10 \times 8x^3 \times 9) + (10 \times 4x^2 \times 27) + (5 \times 2x \times 81) + (1 \times 1 \times 243)$$

$$= 32x^5 + 240x^4 + 720x^3 + 1080x^2 + 810x + 243$$

[4 marks available — 1 mark for substituting into the binomial formula correctly, 1 mark for one correct simplified term, 1 mark for a further three correct simplified terms, 1 mark for a fully correct expansion]

b) $(2x - 3)^5 = 32x^5 - 240x^4 + 720x^3 - 1080x^2 + 810x - 243$

[1 mark for correct answer]

c)

$$(2x + 3)^5 - (2x - 3)^5 = 32x^5 + 240x^4 + 720x^3 + 1080x^2 + 810x + 243 - (32x^5 - 240x^4 + 720x^3 - 1080x^2 + 810x - 243)$$

$$= 480x^4 + 2160x^2 + 486$$

So $480x^4 + 2160x^2 + 486 = 475x^4 + 2138x^2 + 501$

$\Rightarrow 5x^4 + 22x^2 - 15 = 0$

Let $u = x^2 \Rightarrow 5u^2 + 22u - 15 = 0 \Rightarrow (5u - 3)(u + 5) = 0$

$\Rightarrow u = \frac{3}{5}$ or $u = -5$

$u = x^2 > 0$, so $\frac{3}{5}$ is the only solution

$\Rightarrow x = \sqrt{\frac{3}{5}} = \frac{\sqrt{15}}{5}$

[3 marks available — 1 mark for correct substitution of binomial expansions and rearranging to get an equation equal to zero, 1 mark for correct values of x², 1 mark for correct x-value]

Q10 a) $f(x) = \frac{2x-4}{4-x} = \frac{2x-8+4}{4-x} = \frac{2(x-4)+4}{4-x}$

$= \frac{2(x-4)}{4-x} + \frac{4}{4-x} = -2 + \frac{4}{4-x}$

[2 marks available — 1 mark for each of a and b]

You could also use algebraic division to find the answer.

b) When $x = 0$, $y = \frac{2(0)-4}{4-0} = -1$,

so the curve intersects the y-axis at $(0, -1)$.

When $y = 0$, $0 = \frac{2x-4}{4-x} \Rightarrow 0 = -2 + \frac{4}{4-x}$

$\Rightarrow 2 = \frac{4}{4-x}$

$\Rightarrow 2(4-x) = 4$

$\Rightarrow 4 - x = 2 \Rightarrow x = 2$

So the curve intersects the x-axis at $(2, 0)$.

$y = \frac{1}{x}$ has asymptotes at $x = 0$ and $y = 0$.

If $g(x) = \frac{1}{x}$, then:

$\frac{1}{4-x} = g(4-x)$, i.e. $g(x)$ has been translated 4 units left and reflected in the y-axis, so the asymptotes have been translated 4 units left and reflected — the horizontal asymptote isn't changed by the translation, and neither asymptote is changed by the reflection, so the asymptotes are $x = 4$ and $y = 0$.

$\frac{4}{4-x} = 4g(4-x)$, i.e. $g(4-x)$ has been stretched vertically by a scale factor of 4, so the asymptotes aren't changed — they are still $x = 4$ and $y = 0$.

$-2 + \frac{4}{4-x} = 4g(4-x) - 2$, i.e. $4g(4-x)$ has been translated down 2 units, so the asymptotes are translated down 2 units. The vertical asymptote doesn't change, so the asymptotes are $x = 4$ and $y = -2$.

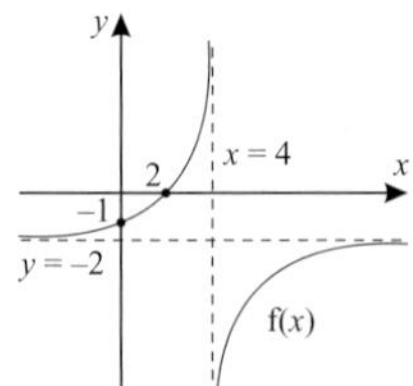

[3 marks available — 1 mark for correct curve shape, 1 mark for both correct axis intercepts labelled, 1 mark for both correct asymptotes labelled]

Q11 a) $q(0) = a + b(0) = 90 \Rightarrow a = 90$

$q(7) = a + b(7) = 34 \Rightarrow 90 + 7b = 34$

$\Rightarrow 7b = -56 \Rightarrow b = -8$

[2 marks available — 1 mark for each correct value]

b) Pressure in tank $P \geq$ pressure in tank Q

$\Rightarrow p(t) \geq q(t) \Rightarrow 72 + 10t - 2t^2 \geq 90 - 8t$

$\Rightarrow 0 \geq 2t^2 - 18t + 18 \Rightarrow 0 \geq t^2 - 9t + 9$

Use the quadratic formula to find t where the above quadratic is equal to 0:

$t = \frac{-(-9) \pm \sqrt{(-9)^2 - 4 \times 1 \times 9}}{2 \times 1} = \frac{9 \pm 3\sqrt{5}}{2}$

$t^2 - 9t + 9 < 0$ between these two points,

so $\frac{9 - 3\sqrt{5}}{2} \leq t \leq \frac{9 + 3\sqrt{5}}{2}$. So the time the pressure in $P \geq$ pressure in Q is:

(Sketch: y against x, parabola through $\frac{9-3\sqrt{5}}{2}$ and $\frac{9+3\sqrt{5}}{2}$, region below axis shaded, origin 0.)

$\frac{9 + 3\sqrt{5}}{2} - \frac{9 - 3\sqrt{5}}{2} = 6.708...$ minutes

$= 6$ minutes 42 seconds

[4 marks available — 1 mark for recognising p(t) ≥ q(t), 1 mark for rearranging to get correct quadratic inequality with 0 on one side, 1 mark for correctly solving quadratic inequality, 1 mark for time period given to nearest second]

c) E.g. The models predict that the pressure in both tank P and Q will eventually become negative, which is impossible.

[1 mark for any correct reason]

Q12 a) $\frac{\sin^4 x - \cos^4 x}{\cos^2 x} + \tan^2 x$

$= \frac{(\sin^2 x + \cos^2 x)(\sin^2 x - \cos^2 x)}{\cos^2 x} + \tan^2 x$

$= \frac{\sin^2 x - \cos^2 x}{\cos^2 x} + \tan^2 x = \frac{\sin^2 x}{\cos^2 x} - \frac{\cos^2 x}{\cos^2 x} + \tan^2 x$

$= \tan^2 x - 1 + \tan^2 x = 2\tan^2 x - 1$

[3 marks available — 1 mark for use of trig identity $\sin^2 x + \cos^2 x = 1$, 1 mark for use of trig identity $\tan x = \frac{\sin x}{\cos x}$, 1 mark for correct algebraic manipulation]

You may have used different steps to prove the identity, but as long as they're correct you'll get the marks.

b) $\frac{\sin^4 x - \cos^4 x}{\cos^2 x} + \tan^2 x = 3\tan x - 1$

$\Rightarrow 2\tan^2 x - 1 = 3\tan x - 1 \Rightarrow 2\tan^2 x - 3\tan x = 0$

$\Rightarrow \tan x(2\tan x - 3) = 0 \Rightarrow \tan x = 0$ or $\tan x = \frac{3}{2}$

$\tan x = 0 \Rightarrow x = -180°, 0°, 180°$

$\tan x = \frac{3}{2} \Rightarrow x = -123.690...°, 56.309...°$

So the solutions to the equation are $x = -180°, -123.7°, 0°, 56.3°, 180°$.

[4 marks available — 1 mark for substituting result from part a) and rearranging equation equal to zero, 1 mark for solving quadratic to give correct values of tan x, 1 mark for using $\tan^{-1}$ to get correct values of x, 1 mark for all answers in given domain]

Q13 a) $M = \left(\frac{0 + (-2)}{2}, \frac{0 + 4}{2}\right) = (-1, 2)$

Gradient of $l_1 = \frac{4-2}{4-(-1)} = \frac{2}{5}$

So l_1 has an equation in the form $y = \frac{2}{5}x + c$.

At M, $x = -1$, $y = 2$, so $2 = \frac{2}{5}(-1) + c \Rightarrow c = \frac{12}{5}$

So the equation of l_1 is $y = \frac{2}{5}x + \frac{12}{5}$.

l_2 is perpendicular to l_1, so has a gradient of $-1 \div \frac{2}{5} = -\frac{5}{2}$.

So l_2 has an equation in the form $y = -\frac{5}{2}x + d$.

At D, $x = 6$, $y = 0$, so $0 = -\frac{5}{2}(6) + d \Rightarrow d = 15$

so the equation of l_2 is $y = -\frac{5}{2}x + 15$.

At T, $y = \frac{2}{5}x + \frac{12}{5}$ and $y = -\frac{5}{2}x + 15$,

so $\frac{2}{5}x + \frac{12}{5} = -\frac{5}{2}x + 15 \Rightarrow \frac{29}{10}x = \frac{63}{5} \Rightarrow x = \frac{126}{29}$

When $x = \frac{126}{29}$, $y = \frac{2}{5}\left(\frac{126}{29}\right) + \frac{12}{5} = \frac{120}{29}$

So the coordinates of T are $\left(\frac{126}{29}, \frac{120}{29}\right)$.

[6 marks available — 1 mark for correct coordinates of M, 1 mark for correctly calculating gradient of l_1, 1 mark for correct equation of l_1, 1 mark for use of negative reciprocal to find gradient of l_2, 1 mark for setting equations equal to each other to find coordinates of T, 1 mark for coordinates of T]

b) Length of $AD = 6$

Length of $AT = \sqrt{\left(\frac{126}{29} - 0\right)^2 + \left(\frac{120}{29} - 0\right)^2} = 6$

Length of $DT = \sqrt{\left(\frac{126}{29} - 6\right)^2 + \left(\frac{120}{29} - 0\right)^2} = 4.46$ (3 s.f.)

AD and AT have equal lengths, and DT has a different length, so ADT is isosceles.

[2 marks available — 1 mark for finding AT and DT, 1 mark for correct justification that ADT is isosceles]

Q14 a) Volume of cylinder $= \pi r^2 h \Rightarrow \pi r^2 h = 128\pi \Rightarrow h = \frac{128}{r^2}$

Surface area of cylinder $(S) = 2\pi r^2 + 2\pi rh$

$$= 2\pi r^2 + 2\pi r\left(\frac{128}{r^2}\right)$$

$$= 2\pi r^2 + \frac{256\pi}{r}\text{ cm}^2$$

[2 marks available — 1 mark for rearranging formula for volume to find h, 1 mark for correct surface area expression]

b) $S = 2\pi r^2 + \frac{256\pi}{r} = 2\pi r^2 + 256\pi r^{-1}$

$\Rightarrow \frac{dS}{dr} = 2(2\pi r) + (-1)(256\pi r^{-2}) = 4\pi r - 256\pi r^{-2}$

$\Rightarrow \frac{d^2S}{dr^2} = 4\pi - (-2)(256\pi r^{-3}) = 4\pi + 512\pi r^{-3}$

When $\frac{dS}{dr} = 0$, $4\pi r - 256\pi r^{-2} = 0$

$\Rightarrow 4\pi r = 256\pi r^{-2} \Rightarrow r^3 = 64 \Rightarrow r = 4$

When $r = 4$, $\frac{d^2S}{dr^2} = 4\pi + 512\pi(4)^{-3} = 12\pi > 0$,

so $r = 4$ is minimum point.

When $r = 4$, $S = 2\pi(4)^2 + \frac{256\pi}{4} = 32\pi + 64\pi = 96\pi\text{ cm}^2$

[5 marks available — 1 mark for correct expression for $\frac{dS}{dr}$, 1 mark for correct expression for $\frac{d^2S}{dr^2}$, 1 mark for correct solution for r using $\frac{dS}{dr} = 0$, 1 mark for using $\frac{d^2S}{dr^2}$ to determine r = 4 is a minimum, 1 mark for correct exact value of S with correct units]

Q15 a) $\log_{10}P = \log_{10}a + t\log_{10}b$,

which has the form of a straight line.

Gradient $= \frac{5.012 - 4.762}{20} = 0.0125$

At $t = 0$, $y = 4.762$, so the line has the equation

$\log_{10}P = 0.0125t + 4.762$

[3 marks available — 1 mark for forming linear equation for $\log_{10}P$ in terms of t, 1 mark for correct gradient, 1 mark for correct equation]

b) $\log_{10}a = 4.762 \Rightarrow a = 10^{4.762} = 57\,809.60...$

$\log_{10}b = 0.0125 \Rightarrow b = 10^{0.0125} = 1.02920...$

In 2012, $t = 12$, so $P = 10^{4.762}(10^{0.0125})^{12} = 81\,658.23...$

$= 81\,700$ (to nearest hundred)

[3 marks available — 1 mark for correct value of a, 1 mark for correct value of b, 1 mark for correct predicted value to nearest hundred]

c) From part a) you know that $\log_{10}P = 0.0125t + 4.762$, so:

$\log_{10}100\,000 = 0.0125t + 4.762$

$\Rightarrow 5 = 0.0125t + 4.762 \Rightarrow 0.0125t = 0.238 \Rightarrow t = 19.04$

$t = 19.04$ corresponds to the year 2019,

so the population first reaches 100 000 in 2019

[2 marks available — 1 mark for substituting into equation from part a) and rearranging to get t, 1 mark for correct year]

Q16 a) E.g. A and B lie on the vertical line $x = 10$, and B and C lie on the horizontal line $y = 10$, so the sides AB and BC form a right angle and ABC is a right-angled triangle.

You could also use Pythagoras' theorem to show it's a right-angled triangle.

[1 mark for correct explanation]

b) The hypotenuse of the triangle AC must be the diameter of the circle D_1 since the angle in a semicircle is a right-angle.

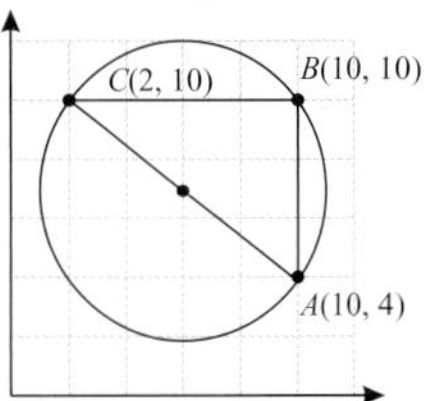

The midpoint of AC is the centre of D_1.

Midpoint of $AC = \left(\frac{10+2}{2}, \frac{4+10}{2}\right) = (6, 7)$

Length of $AC = \sqrt{(10-2)^2 + (4-10)^2} = 10$

Radius of $D_1 = \frac{1}{2} \times AC = 5$

So D_1 has equation $(x-6)^2 + (y-7)^2 = 25$.

[3 marks available — 1 mark for correct centre, 1 mark for correct radius, 1 mark for correct circle equation]

c) When $x = 9$ and $y = 11$,

$(x-6)^2 + (y-12)^2 = (9-6)^2 + (11-12)^2$
$= 3^2 + (-1)^2 = 9 + 1 = 10$

$(x-6)^2 + (y-7)^2 = (9-6)^2 + (11-7)^2$
$= 3^2 + 4^2 = 9 + 16 = 25$

So M lies on the circumference of D_1 and D_2 and is a point of intersection of the circles. The line $x = 6$ lies across the centres of both circles, so is a line of symmetry.

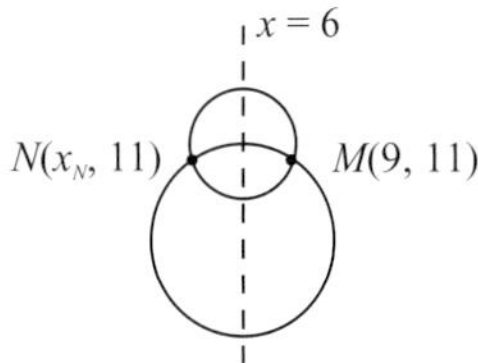

M is 3 right from $x = 6$, so N is 3 left from $x = 6$ and has coordinates (3,11).

[2 marks available — 1 mark for showing M is point of intersection of circles with correct explanation, 1 mark for correct coordinates of N]

d) Work out the gradient of the radius from centre of $D_2(6, 12)$ to $M(9,11)$:

Gradient of radius $(D_2M) = \frac{12-11}{6-9} = -\frac{1}{3}$

So the tangent to D_2 at M has the gradient

$-1 \div -\frac{1}{3} = 3$ and an equation in the form $y = 3x + c$.

At M, $x = 9$ and $y = 11$, so $11 = 3(9) + c \Rightarrow c = -16$

So the tangent to D_2 at M has the equation $y = 3x - 16$.

By symmetry, you know the tangent to D_2 at N has the gradient -3 and an equation in the form $y = -3x + c$.

At N, $x = 3$ and $y = 11$, so $11 = -3(3) + c \Rightarrow c = 20$

So the tangent to D_2 at N has the equation $y = -3x + 20$.

The tangents intersect where $3x - 16 = -3x + 20$

$\Rightarrow 6x = 36 \Rightarrow x = 6$ and $y = 3(6) - 16 = 2$

When $x = 6$, $y = 2$, $(x-6)^2 + (y-7)^2 = (6-6)^2 + (2-7)^2 = 25$

So the tangent lines to D_2 intersect on the circumference of D_1.

You could also have started by working out the gradient of the radius from the centre of D_2 to N.

[6 marks available — 1 mark for correct gradient of radius, 1 mark for use of negative reciprocal to find gradient of one tangent to D_2 from gradient radius, 1 mark each for correct equation of tangents to D_2, 1 mark for correct intersection point of tangents, 1 mark for clearly showing that intersection point lies on circumference of D_1]

A

Acceleration
The rate of change of an object's velocity with respect to time.

Algebraic division
Dividing one algebraic expression by another.

Algebraic expression
An expression which contains constants and / or variables.

Assumption
A simplification of a real-life situation used in a model.

Asymptote
A line that a curve gets infinitely closer to, but never touches.

B

Bearing
A direction, given as an angle measured clockwise from north.

Binomial
A polynomial with only two terms e.g. $a + bx$.

Binomial coefficient
The coefficients of the terms of a binomial expansion.
For the binomial expansion $(1 + x)^r$, the coefficient of x^r is: $\frac{n!}{r!(n-r)!}$

Binomial expansion
The result of expanding a binomial raised to a power — e.g. $(a + bx)^n$.

Binomial formula
A formula that describes the general terms of a binomial expansion.

C

Chord
A line joining two points that lie on the circumference of a circle.

Coefficient
The constant multiplying the variable(s) in an algebraic term e.g. 4 in the term $4x^2y$.

Collinear points
Three or more points are collinear if they all lie on the same straight line.

Common denominator
A denominator (i.e. bottom of a fraction) that is shared by all fractions in an expression.

Common factor
A factor that is shared by all the terms in an expression.

Completing the square
Rewriting a quadratic function as: $p(x + q)^2 + r$. Useful for solving equations or sketching curves.

Component
The effect of a vector in a given direction.

Constant
A fixed numerical value in an expression.

Constant of integration
A constant term coming from an indefinite integration representing any number.

Cosine rule
A rule for finding the missing sides or angles in a triangle when you know all of the sides, or two sides and the angle between them.

Cubic equation
An equation that can be written $ax^3 + bx^2 + cx + d = 0$ (where $a \neq 0$).

D

Decreasing function
A function for which the gradient is always less than zero.

Definite integral
An integral that is evaluated over an interval given by two limits, representing the area under the curve between those limits.

Derivative
The result you get when you differentiate something.

Differentiation
A method of finding the rate of change of a function with respect to a variable.
$\frac{dy}{dx}$ is 'derivative of y with respect to x'.

Direct proportion
A relationship between two variables where multiplying one of them by any constant has the same effect on the other one.

Discriminant
The discriminant of a quadratic function $ax^2 + bx + c$ is the value of $b^2 - 4ac$.

Displacement
A vector measurement of an object's distance from a particular point.

Disproof by counter-example
Finding one example of where a statement doesn't hold, hence showing that it is false.

Divisor
The number or expression you're dividing by in a division.

E

e
An irrational number for which the gradient of $y = e^x$ is equal to e^x.

Elimination
Method for solving linear simultaneous equations, by matching coefficients and then eliminating a variable.

Equation
A mathematical statement containing an '=' sign and at least one variable or constant.

Exponential decay
Exponential decay happens when the rate of decay gets slower and slower as the amount gets smaller (negative exponential growth).

Exponential function
A function of the form $y = a^x$.
$y = e^x$ is known as 'the' exponential function.

Exponential growth
Exponential growth happens when the rate of growth gets faster and faster as the amount gets bigger.

Expression
Any combination of numbers, variables, functions and operations (+, –, ×, ÷ etc.). Unlike an equation, it doesn't have an equals sign.

F

f'(x)
The derivative of f(x) with respect to x.

f''(x)
The second order derivative of f(x) with respect to x.

Factor
A factor of a term or expression is something that divides into it.

Factorial
n factorial, written $n!$, is the product of all integers from 1 to n.
So $n! = 1 \times 2 \times ... \times n$.

Factorising
The opposite of multiplying out brackets. Brackets are put in to write an expression as a product of its factors.

Factor Theorem
A theorem that helps you factorise a polynomial. If $f(a) = 0$, then $(x - a)$ is a factor of f(x).

Force
An influence that can change the motion of a body (i.e. cause an acceleration).

Formula
A standard equation used to calculate a quantity or measure, e.g. volume.

Function
A function gives different 'outputs' for different 'inputs'. They are usually defined by an algebraic expression — plugging in different input values for the variable produces different output values.

Function notation f(x)
Standard way of referring to functions. E.g. function g defined by $g(x) = x^2 + 5$.

Fundamental Theorem of Calculus
The fact that if differentiating takes you from one function to another, then integrating the second function will take you back to the first (with a constant of integration).
Written algebraically, this is:
$\int f(x)\,dx = F(x) + C \Leftrightarrow f(x) = \frac{d}{dx}(F(x))$

G

Gradient
A number representing the steepness of a straight line or of a curve at a given point.

Gradient function
A function that can be used to find the gradient at any point on a curve.

I

i unit vector
The standard horizontal unit vector (i.e. along the x-axis).

Identity
An equation that is true for all values of the variable, denoted by the '$\equiv$' sign.

Increasing function
A function for which the gradient is always greater than zero.

Indefinite integral
An integral that includes a constant of integration which comes from integrating without limits.

Index
For a^n, n is the index and is often referred to as a power.

Inequality
An expression that contains one of the following symbols: $>$, $<$, $\geq$, $\leq$. Like an equation, but produces a range of solutions.

Integer
A positive or negative whole number (including 0).

Integral
The result you get when you integrate something.

Integration
Process for finding a function, given its derivative — the opposite of differentiation.

Intercept
The coordinates at which the graph of a function crosses one of the axes.

Inverse function
An inverse function, e.g. $f^{-1}(x)$, reverses the effect of the function f(x).

Inverse proportion
A relationship between two variables where multiplying one of them by any constant causes the other to be divided by the same constant.

Irrational number
A number that can't be expressed as the quotient (division) of two integers. Examples include surds, e and π.

J

j unit vector
The standard vertical unit vector (i.e. along the y-axis).

L

Limits (integration)
The numbers between which you integrate to find a definite integral.

Linear factor
A factor of an algebraic expression of degree 1 — e.g. $ax + b$.

Linear inequality
An inequality that can be written as $ax + b > cx + d$.

Logarithm
The logarithm to the base a of a number x (written $\log_a x$) is the power to which a must be raised to give that number.

M

Magnitude
The size of a quantity. The magnitude of a vector is the distance between its start point and end point.

Maximum
The highest point on a graph, or on a section of a graph (this is a local maximum).

Minimum
The lowest point on a graph, or on a section of a graph (this is a local minimum).

Model
A mathematical description of a real-life situation, in which certain assumptions are made about the situation.

Modulus
The modulus of a vector is the same as its magnitude.

N

Natural logarithm
The inverse function of e^x, written as $\ln x$ or $\log_e x$.

^nC_r
The binomial coefficient of x^r in the binomial expansion of $(1 + x)^n$.
Also written $\binom{n}{r}$.

Normal
A straight line passing through a curve that is perpendicular (at right angles) to the curve at the point where it crosses the curve.

P

Pascal's triangle
A triangle of numbers showing the binomial coefficients. Each term is the sum of the two above it.

Point of inflection
A stationary point on a graph where the gradient doesn't change sign on either side of the point.

Polynomial
An algebraic expression made up of the sum of constant terms and variables raised to positive integer powers.

Position vector
The position of a point relative to a fixed origin, O, given in vector form.

Power
Another word for index.

Proof
Using mathematical arguments to show that a statement is true or false.

Proof by deduction
Using known facts to build up an argument to prove that a statement is true or false.

Proof by exhaustion
Splitting a situation into separate cases that cover all possible scenarios, then showing that the statement is true for each case, hence true overall.

Q

Quadratic equation
An equation that can be written $ax^2 + bx + c = 0$, where $a \neq 0$.

Quadratic formula
A formula for solving a quadratic equation $ax^2 + bx + c = 0$ given by $x = \frac{-b \pm \sqrt{b^2 - 4ac}}{2a}$.

Quadratic inequality
An inequality that can be written as $ax^2 + bx + c \geq 0$, where $a \neq 0$. It can be solved by looking at the shape of the quadratic graph.

R

Rationalising the denominator
The process of removing surds from the denominator of a fraction.

Rational number
A number that can be written as the quotient (division) of two integers, where the denominator is non-zero.

Reciprocal function
A function of the form $y = \frac{k}{x^n}$ $(n > 0)$, where k is a constant.

Repeated root
If a quadratic (or cubic or quartic) has the same factor twice (or three times) when factorised, this gives a repeated root.

Resultant
The single vector that has the same effect as two or more vectors added together.

Root
The roots of a function $f(x)$ are the values of x where $f(x) = 0$.

S

Scalar
A quantity that has a magnitude but not a direction.

Second order derivative
The result of differentiating a function twice — it tells you the rate of change of the gradient of a function.
$\frac{d^2y}{dx^2}$ means 'second order derivative of y with respect to x'.

Set
A collection of objects or numbers (called elements).

Simultaneous equations
A set of equations containing two or more unknown quantities, often x and y, for which the same set of values satisfy each equation.

Sine rule
A rule for finding missing sides or angles in a triangle. It can be used if you know any two angles and a side, and in some cases, if you know two sides and an angle that isn't between them.

Solution
The value or values (usually of a variable) that satisfy a problem, e.g. an equation or inequality.

Speed
The magnitude of an object's velocity.

Stationary point
A point on a curve where the gradient is zero.

Substitution
Method for solving simultaneous equations, where you replace each occurrence of one unknown with an expression in terms of the other unknown.

Surd
A number that can only be expressed precisely by using a square root sign.

T

Tangent
A straight line that just touches a curve at a point. Its gradient is the same as the curve's gradient at that point.

Term
A collection of numbers, variables and brackets all multiplied or divided together.

Turning point
A stationary point that is a (local) maximum or minimum point of a curve.

U

Unit vector
A vector of magnitude one unit.

V

Variable
A letter in an expression representing an unknown which, unlike a constant, can take on different values.

Vector
A quantity that has both a magnitude and a direction.

Velocity
The rate of change of an object's displacement with respect to time.

Vertex
Turning point of a graph — the maximum or minimum point for a quadratic graph.

acceleration 274, 325
algebra 16-30
algebraic fractions
  adding and subtracting 21, 22
  simplifying 23
algebraic long division 73, 74
approximations using binomial expansions 164
area of a triangle 183
area under a curve 298, 299
assumptions (modelling) 2
asymptotes 127

bases 220, 221
  changing bases 226, 227
binomial coefficients 161
binomial expansions 158-167
  $(1 + x)^n$ 158-161
  $(1 + ax)^n$ 163
  $(a + b)^n$ 166, 167
  approximations 164
  formula 159, 161, 163, 166
brackets
  expanding brackets 16, 17
  factorising 19, 20

CAST diagrams 198-206
changing the base of a logarithm 226, 227
changing the interval of a trig function 201-204
choose (^nC_r) 161
chords 144
circles 137-147
  properties of circles 144-147
  rearranging circle equations 141, 142
  with centre (0, 0) 137
  with centre (a, b) 137-139
circumcircles 146, 147
collinear points 312, 313
column vectors 317
  translations 129
completing the square 46-48
components of vectors 316, 317
constant of integration 289-295
coordinate geometry 108-147
cos x 175
  graph 189
  solving equations 195-206
  solving cos $kx = n$ 201, 202
  solving cos $(x + c) = n$ 203, 204
cosine rule 180, 183, 184, 322
counter-examples 9
cubics 65-74
  factorising (x is a factor) 65, 66
  factorising (x isn't a factor) 70-74
  graphs 123-125
curve sketching 58-62, 123-134, 270-272

decreasing functions 268
definite integration 297-300
derivatives 248-278
diameter 144
difference of two squares 20
differentiation 248-278
  curve sketching 270-272
  from first principles 249, 250
  increasing and decreasing functions 268
  maximum and minimum points 265, 270-272
  modelling 274-278
  of functions 254, 255
  of x^n 252, 253
  second order derivatives 261
  stationary points 262-265, 270-272
  tangents and normals 257-259
direct proportion 120, 121
direction (of a vector) 310, 321, 322
discriminant 54-56
disproof by counter-example 9

e^x 216-218
equation of a circle 137-142
  rearranging 141, 142
  with centre (0, 0) 137
  with centre (a, b) 137-139
equation of a straight line 108-118
  $ax + by + c = 0$ 111, 112
  parallel lines 114, 115
  perpendicular lines 116-118
  $y = mx + c$ 108, 109
  $y - y_1 = m(x - x_1)$ 108
equivalence notation 7
expanding brackets 16, 17
exponentials 216-218, 228, 229
  exponential growth and decay 232-234
  gradient of an exponential graph 217, 218
  graphs 216, 217
  solving equations 228, 229

factorials 160
factorising 19, 20
  algebraic long division 73, 74
  cubics 65-74
  difference of two squares 20
  quadratics 39-41
Factor Theorem 67-71
first principles (differentiation) 249, 250
function notation 7
Fundamental Theorem of Calculus 289, 297

gradient
  of a curve 248
  of a straight line 108-118
  of an exponential graph 217, 218
graph sketching
  cubics 123-125
  exponentials 216, 217
  inequalities 91, 92
  logarithms 221
  negative powers 127
  quadratics 58-62
  quartics 123-125
  reciprocals 127
  trig functions 189-192, 195
  using differentiation 270-272
graph transformations 129-134, 190-192
  stretches and reflections 132-134
  translations 129, 130
  trig functions 190-192

i, **j** vectors 316, 317
identities 7, 186, 187, 205, 206
increasing functions 268
indefinite integration 289-295
indices 25, 26
  negative 127
inequalities 83-92
  graphs 91, 92
  linear 83, 84
  quadratic 86-88
integration 289-300
  area under a curve 298, 299
  definite 297-300
  finding equations of curves 294, 295
  indefinite 289-295
  of functions 292
  of x^n 290
intersection 7
interval notation 83
irrational numbers 28, 216

laws of indices 25, 26
laws of logarithms 224, 225
limit (differentiation from first principles) 249
limit (integration) 297
limitations of modelling 3, 234
ln x 220-222
logarithms 220-238
  changing the base 226, 227
  laws of logs 224, 225
  logarithmic graphs 237, 238
  solving equations 228, 229
logical notation 7

magnitude 310, 320-322
maximum and minimum points 265, 270-272
maximum or minimum value problems 276-278
modelling 2, 3
  criticising and refining 3, 234
  exponential growth and decay 232-234
  using differentiation 274-278
  with vectors 325-327

natural logarithm 220-222
^nC_r notation 161
negative powers 127
normals 116-118, 257-259

parallel lines 114, 115
parallel vectors 312
parallelogram rule 310
Pascal's triangle 158
perpendicular bisector 144
perpendicular lines 116-118
  to a curve 257-259
polynomials 39-74
  differentiating 252-255
  graphs 58-62, 123-125
  integrating 290-292
position vectors 316, 317
problem solving 4, 5
proof 8, 9
  by deduction 8
  by exhaustion 9
  disproof by counter-example 9
proportion 120, 121
Pythagoras' theorem 137, 175, 320

quadratics 39-62
  completing the square 46-48
  discriminant 54-56
  factorising ($a = 1$) 39, 40
  factorising ($a \neq 1$) 40, 41
  functions 51-56
  graphs 58-62
  inequalities 86-88
  involving functions of x 49
  quadratic formula 43, 44
  roots 51-56
quartic graphs 123, 124

radius 137
rational numbers 8, 28
rationalising the denominator 30
reciprocal functions 127
reflections (of graphs) 132-134, 191
resultant vector 310
roots of functions 51-56, 67

scalars 310
  scalar multiplication 311, 312
second order derivatives 261
set notation 7, 83
simultaneous equations 95-100
  solving by elimination 95, 96
  solving by substitution 98-100
sin x 175
  graph 189
  solving equations 195-206
  solving sin $kx = n$ 201, 202
  solving sin $(x + c) = n$ 203, 204
sine rule 177, 183
SOHCAHTOA 175
solving equations
  cubic 65, 66, 70-74
  exponentials and logarithms 228, 229
  quadratic 39-49
  simultaneously 95-100
  trigonometric 195-206
speed 274
stationary points 262-265, 270-272
straight-line equations 108-118
stretches (of graphs) 132-134, 191
surds 28-30

tan x 175, 186, 205
  graph 190
  solving equations 195-206
  solving tan $kx = n$ 201, 202
  solving tan $(x + c) = n$ 203, 204
tangents
  to a circle 144, 145
  to a curve 248, 249, 257-259
transformations (of graphs) 129-134, 190-192
translations (of graphs) 129, 130, 191
trigonometry 175-206
  changing the interval 201-204
  graphs 189-192, 195
  identities 186, 187, 205, 206
  rules 177-184
  solving equations 195-206
  trig triangles 175
  values from the unit circle 176
turning points 265

union 7
unit circle 176
unit vectors 316, 321

vectors 310-327
  adding and subtracting 310, 311
  angle between two vectors 322
  collinear points 312, 313
  column vectors 129, 317
  direction 310, 321, 322
  i, **j** vectors 316, 317
  magnitude 310, 320-322
  modelling 325-327
  parallel 312
  position vectors 316, 317
  resultant 310
  scalar multiplication and division 311, 312
  translation vectors 129, 130
  unit vectors 316, 321
vertex points 58-62

These are the formulas you'll be given in the exam, but make sure you know exactly **when you need them** and **how to use them**.

Binomial Series

$$(a+b)^n = a^n + \binom{n}{1}a^{n-1}b + \binom{n}{2}a^{n-2}b^2 + \dots + \binom{n}{r}a^{n-r}b^r + \dots + b^n \quad (n \in \mathbb{N})$$

$$\text{where } \binom{n}{r} = {}^n\mathrm{C}_r = \frac{n!}{r!(n-r)!}$$

Exponentials and Logarithms

$$\log_a x = \frac{\log_b x}{\log_b a}$$

$$e^{x \ln a} = a^x$$

Mensuration

Surface area of sphere = $4\pi r^2$

Area of curved surface of cone = $\pi r \times$ slant height

Differentiation from First Principles

$$f'(x) = \lim_{h \to 0} \frac{f(x+h) - f(x)}{h}$$

MEPMT52